Behavioral
Decisions in
Organizations

All Problems Are Human Problems

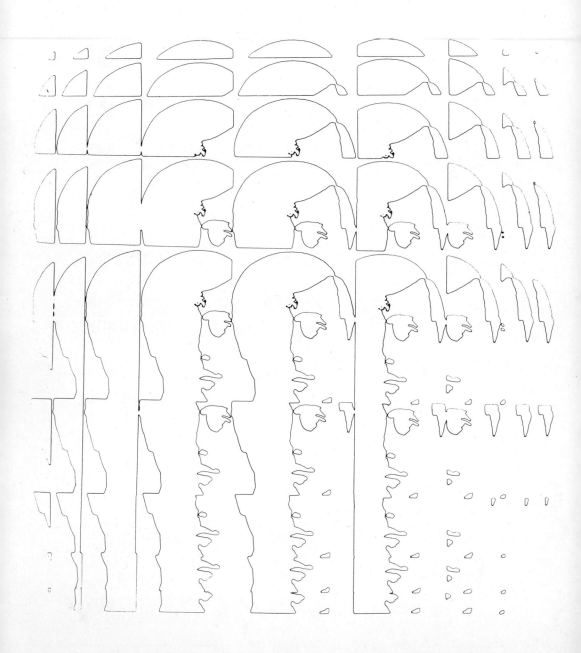

Behavioral Decisions in Organizations

Alvar O. Elbing

State University of New York
at Albany

Scott, Foresman and Company

Foreword

The study of behavior in organizations is a vastly complex field, with contributions from many disciplines and viewpoints, and often involving controversy among those who write and teach the subject. In part, this controversy arises because the authors of various viewpoints are looking at different variables or phenomena in an organization. However, organizations do not come packaged in neat compartments, such as "authority systems," or "human need systems," or "input-output systems." Each approach may contain truth, but it is limited or bounded truth, based on *ceteris paribus*—other things assumed away. But in an organization in real life, other things are never equal.

The controversy or confusion is compounded by a further division of viewpoints based on assumptions about the *purpose* of learning about organizations. Some models are excellent for the social scientist who wants to understand organizations in the aggregate, or perhaps to change the world by rational and impersonal application of science to the running of real-world organizations. Some of these same models might be complete failures if a practicing employee or executive tries to use them blindly in his daily behavior or decision making. The reverse is also true. Some models might be more useful to the practicing member of an organization than as contributions to the scientific description of organizations.

For the wise planner of business school curricula, or indeed for the wise student who hopes to become a successful member of a business organization, one answer is an eclectic approach, not for the sake of eclecticism itself, but because there is truth and usefulness in such a wide variety of approaches.

Alvar Elbing has developed an approach to learning about organizational behavior, and making effective decisions in human situations, which takes advantage of the eclectic approach, but which also goes beyond this approach in an important way. His overriding purpose is to have men who will live in business organizations, working in and managing them, understand the nature of organizations—and even more importantly to learn a decision or action process for solving human problems in the organization. He calls this process a *critical method.* It is distinguished from the scientific method in that there is no one, or even cluster of, decision-making models or methods that are applicable in general to the myriad human problems which arise in organizational life. The richness of such life, and the fact that   v no one theory can solve a concrete problem, mean that (1) the businessman must draw on a variety of knowledge, (2) he must have a combined intellectual-emotional grasp of problems and concepts, and (3) he must use his own mind systematically—critically—to cope with variables in a problem that are not covered by theory, or that are covered by contradictory theories. Science alone, as we are all so forcefully aware today, cannot even truly solve the engineering problems of the world, much less its human problems—particularly when the concept of scientific method is reduced to the connotations of mathematics and the physical sciences.

In a more detailed sense, this book is about two skills necessary for effective decision making by members of an organization, each of which can be learned. The first is a systematic decision process which can be conceptualized in five steps—the recognition of disequilibrium in the human system, the diagnosis of the problem, the conceptualization or statement of the problem, the choice among solutions, and the implementation of the decision with appropriate behavior. This process can be learned, by a combination of knowledge of the process (covered in various chapters and reinforced by the case practice), and emotional grasp of the process (which must be learned by practice).

The second skill of the effective decision maker in a human organization is not a decision *process*, but the ability to apply *substantive knowledge* of organizational phenomena—of individual human beings, of interpersonal relations, of group relations, of human systems and their environments, and of the way individual values influence assumptions about organizations. These substantive concepts are covered in the third section of the book.

For the education and learning of those who will live in and manage ongoing organizations in the world of action, I am in agreement that this approach should be part of the business school curriculum. For those who expect to become researchers, teachers, or scholars, the action-oriented approach is not as important as the scientific-research approach. Nevertheless, I sometimes feel that even the most distinguished men of science might live a more productive life in organizations if they, too, had been exposed at some point in their training to this particular approach to decision making about the human problems of organizations.

Seattle, Washington   Charles E. Summer
June 1970

Preface

This book is specifically designed for and organized around a step-by-step decision-making framework for those organizational problems which involve the human factor. In addition to this practical, managerial decision-making framework, the book presents selected cases and readings fundamental to an understanding of organizational behavior.

The book is divided into two major parts: the model of the decision process, and the collection of readings. The two have been carefully related to each other. In examining the decision making process step by step, reference is made to concepts from the behavioral sciences wherever they clarify that process. Conversely, readings from the behavioral sciences have been chosen and arranged with an eye to their direct applicability to the decision process, and the nature of this applicability is made clear in the text.

Since the focus of this book is on the manager of a system or subsystem in a human organization, the subject of the book could be labeled "organizational decision making." The book's purpose is more specialized, however. It is not primarily concerned with such matters as structure of the organization, personnel selection, division titles, or formal hierarchical patterns. Rather it is concerned with the dynamics of the interpersonal relationships involved in the functioning of the organization as a social system. The goal of the book is the development of that kind of skill in managing the interpersonal organization which builds a maximally productive social system so as to avoid the human crises which cripple productivity.

The book is organized around the decision framework for three reasons: First, the end managerial goal of the study of organizational behavior is results in terms of management action. Second, the problem of decision making which faces the manager is the starting point from which he necessarily approaches his organizational environment. Thus, the arrangement of this book keeps the manager focused on the responsible goals of his decision-making process—choice and action—rather than on mere passive learning of abstracted knowledge.

Third, experience in management development programs and in the college classroom shows that cognitive learning is improved when given a decision-problem orientation. By contrast, students who *begin* with cognitive knowledge, while they may quickly learn to recite memorized terminology, often abandon concepts learned by rote when faced with a practical management problem in an organization, or when faced in the classroom with a case exercise or with a concrete group experience in which they are directly involved. They have not been trained to see the relationship between memorized theories and the practical situations in which they actually participate. However, when practical decision-making questions are raised first, these questions motivate the students to seek and to find, from the cognitive material, *action-oriented concepts,* concepts which do make a difference in their actual behavior when approaching problems.

This book is organized into four sections. Section I considers the issue of a systematic approach to decision-making in the human realm. This section is particularly designed to orient three groups of students to the course: (1) those students who may have advanced technical backgrounds in some areas but who have little or no background in the human factors of management; (2) those students who are already experienced managers, but who have not approached the management of people as a systematic discipline; and (3) those students who have some technical knowledge in the behavioral sciences, but who have never approached human behavior from the standpoint of management.

Section II provides a step-by-step model for decision making. It takes the reader from the question of how he determines in the first place that a decision is called for, to the final process of implementation and feedback. The six chapters contain a careful in-depth inquiry into the basic problems of decision making which face the manager of any type of organization, and examine systematic guidelines for each of these decision problems. This decision framework has been used in years of graduate, undergraduate and management development classes, and has proven its workability as an organizing framework for a course in organizational behavior.

Integrated with the six decision chapters are 25 case studies which provide concrete situations the student can use to exercise his developing skill in rigorously applying systematic method in the decision process. Furthermore, the cases were chosen and integrated in such a way as to help clarify each systematic step in the decision process. The cases include some classics, some new cases, some short, and some long. The instructor is, of course, free to bring in his own cases to supplement this offering, but the book offers sufficient cases to provide an excellent beginning experience in the use of systematic decision making in organizational situations.

Section III supplies basic readings in the area of human behavior which serve as a foundation for the development of a reservoir of knowledge in this subject area. The readings are not intended to be exhaustive, but represent a sound starting point for the student who is attempting to understand the behavior he observes in organizations around him. These readings provide fundamental concepts for the study of the *individual, two-person interaction, small groups and intergroup behavior, and the environment of the total organization as a social system.* Again, the instructor is free to supplement these findings with his own favorites or with additional readings suggested in the Instructor's Guide. The purpose of grouping the readings together in one section, rather than at the end of chapters, is to avoid any suggestion that it is possible to solve a particular organizational problem simply by reading one particular article. The concept is stressed throughout that every human situation has complex variables and numerous causal factors.

Section IV takes up the value dimension inherent in all decision making. It provides a framework useful for examining social value issues and the social consequences of managing today's organizations. The readings here present some of the key value issues facing today's managers.

The design of this book, with emphasis on the decision process, is not arbitrary. The decision process is the heart of behavioral change in an organization. It is through the decision-making process, whether by design or default, that human organizations are developed and changed, for better or for worse.

In the preparation of this volume I am indebted to many. A deep debt goes to John W. Hennessey, Jr., now Dean of The Amos Tuck School of Business Administration at Dartmouth College, and to Robert H. Guest, Professor of Organizational Behavior at The Tuck School, who for five years were my colleagues in the area of organizational behavior. The numerous insights acquired while working with them must be recognized as underlying many of the points in this book. I am also indebted to Dean Hennessey for so freely granting permission for the use of cases.

I also wish to acknowledge the help and support of Professor Albert Mossin, Chairman of the Department of Management, State University of New York at Albany, and of my colleagues in that department. Together they created an environment in which it was possible to pursue such a project to its completion.

Two other people must be recognized for the influence they have had on this volume. Professor Theodore Barnowe of the University of Washington got me started in this area both as a student of his and as a teaching colleague. Earlier, Professor Frederick Seubert, now at the University of Oregon, was of considerable influence on my thinking while I studied under him at the University of California at Berkeley. I gratefully acknowledge the influence of these men.

Also for the use of cases, I wish to thank Professors Ben Lindberg, C. B. Richards, and H. F. Dobyns. I also wish to thank Andrew R. Towl, Director of Case Development, and John A. Seiler, Paul Lawrence, Harold Craig, John D. Glover, Frederick V. Fortmiller, and Richard L. Balch, now or previously associated with the Harvard University Graduate School of Business Administration, for their cooperation and permission to use copyrighted cases.

In addition, the thoughtful comments on the manuscript of Charles E. Summer, Fremont Shull, and Andre DelBecque deserve special thanks.

Many people have participated in the mechanics of this project. I wish to give special thanks to Mrs. Diana Watkins and Miss Debbie DeFlumer for being available when needed; and to Robert St. Clair and Robert Runck of Scott, Foresman for their masterful editorial assistance.

It is only fitting that the primary acknowledgment go to my "colleague" of the past 20 years, my wife Carol, who regards methods for solving human problems as the crucial issue of our children's generation. It is to her that this book is dedicated.

Although I benefited greatly from all this help, I of course absolve all these friends and colleagues of any responsibility for the final contents. That must be mine.

Delmar, New York   Alvar O. Elbing
June 1970

Contents

Part I

The Basic Issue of Method

Chapter 1   A Behavioral Approach to Human Problems   3

Standards of Method in the Study of Behavior and Its Management   *Connotations of the Scientific Method*   *The Concept of Critical Method as a Standard*   *The Specifications for Critical Method*   *Critical Method and Mathematical Terminology*   *Noncritical Method*   *Critical Method in the Behavioral Sciences and in Decision Making*   Definition of Terms   *Behavioral Science Decision Making*   Orientation to Decision Making as a Systematic Process   *Decision Making in New Situations*   *Human Decisions and Technical Decisions*   The Purpose of This Book   The Organization of The Book   Goals of The Reader

Readings on the Concept of Method and Organizational Behavior

George Lundberg   *Can Science Solve Social Problems?*   23
George F. F. Lombard   *Self-Awareness and the Scientific Method*   36
Gordon W. Allport   *Freedom*   45
C. West Churchman   *Rational Decision Making*   49
Kenneth D. Benne   *Case Methods in the Training of Administrators*   58
Herbert A. Shepard   *The T-Group as Training in Observant Participation*   65
Henry C. Smith   *Empathy*   73
Henry P. Knowles and Borje O. Saxberg   *Human Relations and the Nature of Man*   90
Craig C. Lundberg   *Toward Understanding Behavioral Science by Administrators*   109

Part II
A Framework for The Decision Process

Chapter 2   The Perception of Disequilibrium   127

Structured and Unstructured Stimuli   *Structured Stimuli   Unstructured Stimuli*   Self-Awareness and Unstructured Stimuli   *Identification and Acceptance of Feelings   Three Steps to Self-Awareness   Separation of Feelings from Situations   Examining Our Behavior*   Roadblocks in the Decision-Making Process   *The Tendency to Evaluate   The Tendency to Equate New and Old Experiences   The Tendency to Use Available Solutions   The Tendency to Deal with Problems at Face Value   The Tendency to Direct Decisions Toward a Single Goal   The Tendency to Confuse Symptoms and Problems   The Tendency to Overlook "Unsolvable" Problems   The Tendency to Look at the Referent*   Conclusion

Case Studies

Redmond Manufacturing Company Case   137
The Jim Baxter Case   138
Gray Drake Airlines Case   141
Thomas Motor Company Case   147

Chapter 3   The Diagnostic Process: Criteria   151

The Importance of Diagnosis   Criterion 1: Differentiating Between Language and Events   Criterion 2: Specifying the Degree of Precision of Available Information   *Distinguishing Fact and Opinion   Verifying the Judgment*   Criterion 3: Specifying Underlying Causes Rather Than Blame   Criterion 4: Specifying Multiple Causality   Criterion 5: Explicitly Formulating the Final Working Diagnosis   Summary of Criteria

Case Studies

Crescent Airlines Case   162
The National Insurance Company Case   166
Electronic Systems Company Case   177
The Foster Creek Post Office Case   183

Chapter 4   The Diagnostic Process: Behavioral Models   189

The Individual Behavior Model   The Interpersonal Behavior Model   The Group Behavior Model   The Usefulness of the Models   Time as a Factor in Diagnosis   The Cost of Search   Summary

Case Studies

The Oscar Larson Case   202
The Hern File Case   205
California Paper Company Case   223
Case of the Changing Cage   230

Chapter 5   The Problem Statement   235

The Significance of Problem Definition   The Criteria of Sound Problem Formulation   Criterion 1: Stating the Problem Explicitly   Criterion 2: Including a Working Diagnosis in the Problem Statement   Criterion 3: Specifying the Standard Violated   *The Hierarchy of Standards Governing Problem Identification   Conflicting Standards*   Criterion 4: Stating the Problem in Specific Behavioral Terms   Criterion 5: Avoiding Statement of the Problem as Merely an Implied Solution   Criterion 6: Specifying Whose Problem It Is   Criterion 7: Differentiating Long-Run and Short-Run Problems Requiring Solution   Criterion 8: The Problem Should Not Be Stated as a Dilemma   Summary

Case Studies

Electrical Manufacturing Company Case   248
A Shade of Gray   251
The Bellevue Candy Company Case   253
Merdon State College Athletic Authority Case   262

Chapter 6   Solution Choice   271

The Solution Criteria of Quality and Acceptability   Criterion 1: Determining That a Solution Is of a Quality Satisfactory to Meet Organizational Goals   Criterion 2: Determining That a Solution Is Acceptable   *Observers' Reactions to Decisions   Employee Participation in Decision Making*   Criterion 3: Evaluating a Solution in Terms of Anticipated Responses to It   Criterion 4: Focusing on Present Solutions and Not Past Possibilities   Criterion 5: Considering the Risks of Each Alternative Solution   Criterion 6: Arranging Multiple Solutions in Proper Sequence   Summary

Case Studies

The Case of Savemore Food Store 5116   284
Slade Company Case   288
Providence City Bank Case   299
Modern Decorators Case   304

Chapter 7   Implementation   314

> The Importance of Considering Implementation as a Separate
> Decision Step   Some Basic Considerations for Sound Imple-
> mentation   *Assessment of Workability   Motivating and Acti-*
> *vating Each Change in Behavior   Provision for Feedback   Plan-*
> *ning and Carrying Out Leadership Functions*   Preventive Deci-
> sion Making   Summary

Case Studies

> *West Yanga College of Engineering Case*   324
> *Crownbar Corporation Case*   329
> *Worthington Bank Case*   335
> *Northeastern Electric Light and Power Corporation Case*   338
> *A Dilemma for President Watkins*   345

Part III

Behavioral Science Foundations for Management

The Individual

> Alvar O. Elbing   *Perception, Motivation, and Business Behavior*
>   353
> Abraham Maslow   *A Theory of Human Motivation*   366
> Mason Haire   *The Problem of Learning and The Law of Effect*
>   383
> Kurt Lewin   *The Psychology of Success and Failure*   387
> Douglas M. McGregor   *The Human Side of Enterprise*   394
> Kingsley Davis   *Status and Related Concepts*   405
> Rollo May   *The Nature of Anxiety and Its Relation to Fear*   418
> Edward J. Shoben   *Toward a Concept of the Normal Personality*
>   429

Interpersonal Relations

> Chris Argyris   *Interpersonal Barriers to Decision Making*   441
> Abraham Zaleznik   *Managerial Behavior and Interpersonal*
>   *Competence*   464
> Warren G. Bennis   *Interpersonal Communication*   480
> Jack R. Gibb   *Defensive Communication*   484
> Carl Rogers and Fritz Roethlisberger   *Barriers and Gateways to*
>   *Communication*   491
> Alvar O. Elbing   *A Model for Viewing Decision Making in Inter-*
>   *action Situations from an Historical Perspec-*
>   *tive*   502

Group and Intergroup Behavior

Muzafer Sherif   *Group Formation*   515
Herbert Thelen and Watson Dickerman   *The Growth of Groups*   529
Dorwin Cartwright   *Achieving Change in People: Some Applications of Group Dynamics Theory*   537
Josephine Klein   *Changing Ideas in Theory and Practice*   550
Leland P. Bradford, Dorothy   *How to Diagnose Group Problems* Stock, and Murray Horwitz   561
Daniel Katz and Robert L. Kahn   *The Taking of Organizational Roles*   575
Edgar H. Schein   *Organizational Socialization and the Profession of Management*   604
Mort Stern   *Ex-Policeman Tells What Makes a "Bad Cop"*   622
Muzafer Sherif   *Intergroup Relations and Leadership*   627
Robert K. Merton   *The Self-Fulfilling Prophecy*   642

Organizations and Leadership

Chris Argyris   *Organizational Leadership*   658
Warren G. Bennis   *New Patterns of Leadership for Tomorrow's Organizations*   686
Jack R. Gibb   *Is Help Helpful?*   695
James V. Clark   *A Healthy Organization*   701
Mason Haire   *Organizations*   718
Robert H. Guest   *Technology and Change: The Meaning of Work*   745
Edgar H. Schein   *Organizational Effectiveness*   767

Part IV

Value Dimensions of The Decision Process

Chapter 8   The Value Issue of Business   781

Economics as a Value System   *Economics as "Moral"*   *Economics as "Amoral"*   The Shortcomings of Economics as a Value System   Business as a Social System   *Business and the Individual*   *Business and Other Groups*   *Business and Society in the United States*   *Business and Foreign Societies*   A New Social Value Theory for Business   Conclusions

Readings on the Value Issue

Erich Fromm   *Personality and the Marketplace*   791
Dorothy Lee   *Personal Significance and Group Structure*   800
Dero A. Saunders   *Executive Discontent*   811
Jacques Ellul   *A Look at the Future*   817
John W. Ward   *The Ideal of Individualism
        and the Reality of Organization*   825
Carl Rogers   *The Place of the Individual
        in the New World of the Behavioral Sciences*   839
Robert Hutchins and Joseph P. Lyford   *Living Without Guilt*
                        855

Index   871

Part I

The Basic Issue
of Method

Chapter One

A Behavioral Approach
to Human Problems

As man walks on the face of the moon, photographs Mars from a space vehicle, measures continental drift in inches per year, and contemplates farming the seas, it would seem that he already knows a great deal about decision making. The number of individual decisions necessary to make a moon shot, for example, can be estimated in the billions, most of which must necessarily have been correct decisions or the space craft would not have splashed down on target—mission accomplished. Measured by their intended results, however, not all decisions currently being made in our society are "correct" ones. The decision-making know-how which got us to the moon has not directly transferred to the human area of decision making.

Solving the problems of human beings is quite different from solving the problems of things. The nature of the difference between these two kinds of decision situations, and the basis of the problem of transferring guidelines from one to the other, is pointed up in the following analogy:

> If the foot of a walking man hits a pebble, energy is transferred from the foot to the stone; the latter will be displaced and will eventually come to rest again in a position which is fully determined by such factors as the amount of energy transferred, the shape and weight of the pebble, and the nature of the surface on

3

which it rolls. If, on the other hand, the man kicks a dog instead of the pebble, the dog may jump up and bite him. In this case the relation between the kick and the bite is of a very different order. It is obvious that the dog takes the energy for his reaction from his own metabolism and not from the kick. What is transferred, therefore, is no longer energy, but rather information (Watzlawick, *et al.*, 1967, p. 29).

The dynamics of animal-human action and reaction—cause and effect—is not the same as the dynamics of mass and density, speed and time. And when man "kicks" *man,* the variables become even more complex.

The purpose of this book is to pursue the peculiarities of decision making in the realm of human behavior, not merely in the one-to-one situation or the small group, but in the total social system of the large organization. It undertakes the systematic study of decision making on specifically human problems, from the vantage point of the manager who has a unique responsibility for the results of that behavior.

To those individuals coming from technical studies where problems of human behavior are not directly involved, the adjustment to human variables is a major one. In the real firm, which is inescapably a social system as well as a technical system, every technical plan, however sophisticated and rationally it may be worked out, is dependent on the human social system of the organization to carry it out. The specialist who tries to maneuver people in a social system the way he maneuvers "widgets" can indeed botch up productivity. He can even botch up the productivity of the widgets, which, after all, require human cooperation.

Yet, if a person's attention if focused on technical results—such as productivity and profits—and he has been allowed to ignore the human factors in the organization, he may come to the study of organizational behavior with the attitude that it is an obstacle put in the way of getting those technical results that interest him. But the purpose of the study of management of human behavior is to develop the skills that prevent the human crises which *thwart* production.

Standards of Method in The Study of Behavior and Its Management

Before going directly to a step-by-step analysis of the decision-making process, let us consider the basic question of method. This question needs clarification, particularly for those individuals coming from three orientations: (1) those who may have advanced technical backgrounds in some areas but who may have little or no background in the human factors of management; (2) those who are already experienced managers, but who have not approached the management of people as a systematic discipline; and (3) those who may have technical knowledge in the behavioral sciences but who have approached human behavior in terms of research and model building, rather than as a management action concept.

Connotations of The Scientific Method

To students coming from technical fields, and even to a majority of laymen, the concept of method is synonomous with the concept of "scientific method," and connotes mathematical terminology or the methods of the physical sciences, or both. It conjures up images of certain tools—laboratories, test tubes, computers, and so on. It conjures up images of things or activities which can be quantified, measured, counted, charted, graphed, or weighed. The person for whom "scientific method" carries such connotations usually reacts in one of two ways when faced with the question of method in relation to the human problems of an organization.

On the one hand he may wrench particular techniques or tools from mathematics or the physical sciences, and try to apply them to human problems—even where they do not fit. To get around this impasse, he may then change the statement of the problem to make it fit his borrowed tools and techniques. He may even choose to ignore certain aspects of the problem, because they do not fit his borrowed methods.

On the other hand, he may use the *criteria* of mathematics and the physical sciences to declare that human problems are not amenable to rigorous method, and conclude that everything in the human realm is hunch and guesswork. Depending on his temperament, he may even decide that human management requires a mystical talent —or he may dismiss it as an imprecise and inferior endeavor, in terms of his particular concept of "scientific method."

The above approaches to human management are built into a concept of systematic method where "scientific" method is viewed as encompassing primarily the techniques and tools of the physical sciences and mathematics. The difficulty is resolved, however, when we recognize that the essential criteria of rigorous method in the realm of human behavior do *not* necessarily involve procedures, techniques, and tools designed for the physical sciences or mathematics. Rather, the essential criterion of method—any method that will qualify as rigorous method—is that it constitute *that method most appropriate to the nature of the given problem which best withstands the tests of critical appraisal.*

The Concept of Critical Method as a Standard

In this book the term *critical method* is used for the study of human behavior rather than *scientific method.* Because the connotations of the term scientific method involve concepts of quantified data and the hardware of laboratories or computers, the term "critical method" may be a more useful concept as a standard for the analysis and management of human behavior. Whichever term the student chooses, however, his training in decision making in the management of human behavior will be meaningless unless he adheres to the most rigorous standard of method. The results of lax standards of method are no less dire in the field of analyzing and managing human behavior than they are in any other field. Therefore, the insistence on a standard of critical method, although it recognizes that not all human problems are amenable to the techniques of the physical sciences and mathematics, forestalls the conclusion that in the management of human behavior there are no objective criteria for method at all, and that any method is as good as any other. Some methods, and the solutions derived from them, hold up much better under objective critical inquiry than other methods, and it is insisted in this book that the most critical methods available be used, that is, those methods which hold up best under critical tests.

The Specifications for Critical Method

Throughout his training in the analysis and management of human behavior, the student should continuously measure his methods against the basic criteria of critical method, which include the following minimum specifications:

1. Critical method begins with a bona fide *question*. Its point of beginning is not a fixed answer or solution, but a proposition or hypothesis which carries with it a burden of proof. In the emotion-filled realm of human problems, there is a tendency to jump to conclusions and to start with solutions. Such a process, whether it is labeled "intuition," "common sense," "statement of authority," "tradition," "human nature," or whatever, is no part of critical or scientific method. No method is a "critical method" that does not start with a question open to inquiry and investigation.

2. The end point of critical method (or scientific method) is not a fixed, absolute answer. Nothing is handed down as final dogma or declared to be above criticism. Answers are always subject to restatement as hypotheses for further investigation. An answer is acceptable only so long as no alternative answer can be offered that is supported by a stronger case.

3. Critical method is that method which best stands up under the tests of evidence, reasoning, investigation, criticism, and assessment. This means that the method is specified in words (or some other explicit form) and presented so that the method itself is readily amenable to question, replication, testing, investigation, and final assessment.

4. In a field where critical method prevails, opposing opinions on the same questions are not considered a matter of tolerance.

Rather, disagreements are considered matters for investigation. The method itself provides a basis for critical choice among competing answers. To resolve a disagreement, that answer is considered preferable which, at the given time, best stands up under the severest tests of objective criticism.

5. Critical method distinguishes between symbols used for data and the data itself, and does not make generalizations or conclusions beyond those warranted by the data.

It may be noted that the above criteria fit the "scientific method" of the physical sciences, as well as any other critical method deserving the name. Critical methods, like scientific methods, are not methods which provide absolute or final answers, but merely those methods which at a given time and for a given problem best withstand the severest independent tests and severest rational criticism available (Elbing and Elbing, 1967, Ch. 12). The value—to the manager of a human system—of the concept of critical method, as contrasted to the traditional concept of scientific method, is that the term "critical" does not connote specific techniques inappropriate to the analysis or management of human behavior. It places its emphasis on the criteria most appropriate to the human problems of actual, dynamic organizations, whereas the commonplace use of the term "scientific" is appropriate primarily to controlled experimentation.

Critical Method and Mathematical Terminology

Let us be clear that the use of mathematical terminology is not to be equated with scientific or critical method *automatically*. A method may be fully stated in mathematical terminology throughout and not pass the above tests of critical method. A problem statement, a statement of method, or a statement of conclusion can be expressed in mathematical terminology and still be inadequate for the totality of the problem, or be incorrect, or be an inferior alternative among those available, or even be irrelevant to the problem. Consider, for example, a simple mathematical expression of a basic relationship:

$$2 + 2 = 4$$

This is probably the first quantitative relationship a child learns, and is seldom questioned. But what do we have when we add two cups of water and two cups of sugar? This question may also be relevant when we "add together" the behavior of two employees and two other employees. Of what do we have four? Obviously, the application of mathematical terminology is not the crucial test of critical method.

As stated earlier, one essential characteristic of critical method is its presentation in specific language so that it is amenable to criticism. In theory, of course, the most precise language is mathematical language. And in theory, it would be possible to reduce most decision situations to mathematical terminology. However, the ultimate issue of precision for the decision maker involves factors other than the precision of language alone. In fact, in the dynamics of organizational behavior, no method in whatever language is ultimately precise which is too inefficient to be workable in the problem situation for which it is designed. If the problem has changed by the time it can be symbolized in the chosen language, it can hardly be considered precise.

The superiority of mathematical terminology as ultimately more efficient, more precise, and more critical, in the area of human problems has yet to be demonstrated. This book begins with the arbitary judgment that reducing the discussion here to mathematical terminology would *not* increase the efficiency of the critical method. Obviously, there are many points in a given decision making process where information expressed in mathematical terms might be very useful to the decision maker in a human situation, and where mathematical procedures might be usefully brought in. However, in the present state of our understanding, attempting to reduce the total decision-making process to mathematical language might consume more time in converting problems to mathematical terms than dealing with urgent problems. In an action situation where time is a factor, the opportunity for effective management action may pass. There is also the danger, mentioned before, that in an attempt to reduce a problem to mathematical terms, those features least amenable to mathematical expression may be slighted.

Noncritical Method

Having presented the minimum specifications for critical method, it is vital that we distinguish when methods are "noncritical," and therefore *unacceptable*. Any method of decision making or of problem solving which is so vague and unspecified that it is not amenable to objective assessment is a "noncritical" method. Any method which starts with a conclusion, or immediately superimposes a solution or assumes an answer (instead of starting with a *bona fide* question, problem, or hypothesis) is a noncritical method. Similarly, any method, or solution growing out of it, which cannot stand up under objective reasoning, investigation, and assessment in comparison with alternative methods or solutions, is a "noncritical" method. Finally, any method which consists merely of the application of untested dogma, or tradition, or absolute principles which are not open to inquiry, is a "noncritical" method.

Although attempts are often made to justify various methods because they are based on common sense or intuition or are habitual or traditional methods that "come naturally," such "justifications" merely signify that a method is noncritical. Intuition and common sense can be valuable if they produce hypotheses that can be tested by a critical method, but they are not critical methods in themselves. The distinguishing mark of a critical method is that it is accessible to critical examination and best passes the tests of critical assessment.

As we have mentioned, there are those for whom the whole concept of method in the human realm is something alien. It can only be pointed out that one is bound to use *some* method. However inarticulate, however haphazard, however unexamined, each person's way of arriving at decisions is his "method." Even the choice of ignoring a particular human problem of management is a *de facto* choice of method with reference to the problem. Ultimately the manager chooses whether to use the most critical methods possible, or to settle for some nebulous lesser standard.

Critical Method in the Behavioral Sciences and in Decision Making

Specifically, this book urges the use of critical method in two areas important to the manager. First, it promotes the use of information and concepts about human behavior derived from the "behavioral sciences," which, being derived from the best critical methods available and having already passed the severest tests of critical assessment available, are preferable to mere personal hunches. Every choice and action with reference to other human beings is based on behavioral assumptions acquired from a lifetime of personal experience. Although there are those who attempt to avoid making assumptions about human behavior, such assumptions are unavoidable in any form of management. These assumptions may be fully recognized and clearly stated, or they may be unrecognized and implicit. In this sense, we are all "psychologists" and "sociologists," whether we draw from the accumulated research findings of professional psychologists and sociologists or restrict ourselves to our own "findings." (This very fact, that each person through his own set of experiences has developed his own findings, is the greatest deterrent to the use of critical method in the human realm.) It is one of the major purposes of this book to promote the most valid concepts of behavior available from the behavioral sciences, and to promote management which is in accordance with these concepts. Part III of this book consists of readings from the behavioral sciences specifically applicable to organizations.

Second, this book promotes the use of critical method in the management process of *decision making,* and specifically promotes the idea that each step of the decision process should be tested against the general criteria of critical method. Chapters 2 through 7 present a systematic, critical method for each step of the decision process.

Definition of Terms

Having advocated the systematic use of a critical method in the behavioral sciences and in decision making, let us now define the two basic terms *behavioral science* and *decision making*.

Behavioral Science

The term *behavioral science* is not restricted to investigations in a particular academic discipline; it refers, instead, to particular methods and purposes of investigation. In this book, the term *behavioral science* denotes any social science, such as psychology, sociology, and anthropology, insofar as it is a study of the *behavior* of human beings in their physical and social environment and utilizes experimental and observational methods. The behavioral sciences use critical method in that they start with *bona fide* questions, employ highly developed procedures that are self-critical, offer objective tests for distinguishing between opposing answers to a question, and contain no dogma regarded as above investigation.

Bradford, Gibb, and Benne (1964) have described the value to the decision maker of behavioral science methods:

> What is the morality of science? One element is an obligation to face all of the facts involved in a problem and its solution. Frequently, human facts are not faced by practical decision makers—facts about feelings, motivations, personal and collective potentialities for growth, contribution potentials of persons and subgroups—as they define and attempt to solve social problems. Not only do decision makers neglect to face the facts of other people's behavioral involvements, but they also frequently neglect to face and manage their own involvements as persons. Their difficulty arises partly from lack of knowledge and skill in making sense of behavioral facts, and also from resistances toward becoming aware of the human consequences of their actions. Ideally, behavioral scientists have faced both of these difficulties in their studies and can be of help to practical men in facing their own similar difficulties (p. 8).

Even though he may shun knowledge of the behavioral sciences, a manager cannot avoid "psychologizing." Indeed, his own behavior is necessarily based on some form of psychological and sociological assumptions about the nature of human beings and their behavior. Also, the manager must deal with employees who perceive behavior, remember past behavior, impute various motivations to behavior, have various needs, and whom the manager may label as bored, sick, unhappy, upset, lazy, and so on. The way a manager views and labels those reactions, and the way in which his underlying theory of human behavior allows him to interpret these reactions, denotes his own brand of "behavioral science." And his own brand of "behavioral science" will determine his methods for dealing with employees.

The issue is, therefore, not whether the manager uses behavioral assumptions or not. All action must reflect some such assumptions. The issue is how sound are his behavioral assumptions. The critical methods of the behavioral sciences can help the manager understand how feelings and behavior occur, how his own frame of reference enters into the decision-making process, how his own assumptions about human behavior stand up to the knowledge produced by the scientific study of human behavior, and how decisions about people can be more realistic, and therefore more workable.

Decision Making

Decision making is often considered to consist of problem solving, or planning, or organizing, and is sometimes extended to include all aspects of thinking and acting. However, the literature on decision making in business organizations stresses *choice making* as the key feature. Choice may be exercised in a simple situation, as in the selection of a pen from a well-stocked desk drawer, the choice of lunch from a menu, which route to walk from one office to another. Or it may require a complicated decision about a situation that involves conflicting goals and values, many minds, and much expenditure of time: a long-range plan for an entire organization, an appropriate offer to make in upcoming union negotiations, or the selection of a new company president. Although the consequences of these decisions are not all of the same magnitude, all the situations do involve selection of the best alternative among several choices. Whatever one may label the process (the label is not of crucial importance), the *process* is similar in all these cases. Thus selection among alternatives seems to be the key concept in the term *decision making*.

This concept of decision making is frequently expressed in the literature on the subject. The philosopher-sociologist Harald Ofstad (1961) states that "to make a decision [means] to make a judgment regarding what one *ought* to do in a certain situation after having deliberated on some alternative courses of action" (p. 15). Many writers agree on definitions similar to that of Ofstad. Irwin Bross (1953) states: "The process of selecting one action from a number of alternatives is what I shall mean by decision" (p. 1). Feldman and Kanter (1965) suggest that "the decision problem is that of selecting a path which will move the system—individual, computer program, or organization—from some initial state to some terminal state" (pp.

614–615). Claude George (1964) makes this point even more explicitly: " 'to decide' means to cut short, to cut off. However, we must frequently give it the connotation of reaching a conclusion, or of making up our minds. This, of course, implies deliberation and thought, making it a conscious act. In contrast, when a 'decision' is a natural reaction or an unconsicous act, it is not truly a decision but would be more properly labeled a habit or a reflex act" (p. 21). Ofstad makes a similar distinction; he calls the unconscious process "compulsion" rather than "decision." In summary, decision making is generally defined as being concerned with making conscious choices among alternatives.[1]

Many writers, however, do not limit their definition of decision making to a selection or choice among alternatives. Although they may agree that the "choice step" is the characteristic step in a decision-making process, they define decision making in a much broader sense. Don Taylor (1965) suggests that "decision making is that thinking which results in the choice among alternative courses of action" (p. 48), and therefore his definition includes the entire thinking process related to the problem prior to a decision choice. Herbert Simon (1960) considers decision making synonymous with managing: "In treating decision making as synonymous with managing, I shall be referring not merely to the final act of choice among alternatives, but rather to the whole process of decisions" (p. 1). Leonard Sayles (1964) also refers to a broader process when he says: "Decision making is an organizational process. It is shaped as much by the pattern of interaction of managers as it is by the contemplation and cognitive processes of the individual" (p. 207). In this view, the primary concern of decision making goes beyond the point of choice and includes the whole process of the manager functioning in his environment.

Because this book is concerned with decision making in the broader sense, the term will always be used to refer to the total problem-solving process, which includes, but is not limited to, the key act of choosing among alternatives. Specifically, it treats the following five steps as a model of the total management decision-making process (see Figure 1):

1. Identification of a disequilibrium: observing and becoming sensitive to potential problem situations.
2. Diagnosis of the problem situation: attempting to understand what is happening in a particular situation.
3. Definition of the problem to be solved: identifying and stating a problem in relation to organizational and personal goals.

---

1. In his chapter "Rational Decision Making," C. West Churchman (1968) raises some questions about this process.

4. Determination of alternative methods and solutions and choice of the best solution: selecting a course of action from a series of alternatives.
5. Implementation of the chosen solution: the entire process of actualizing the chosen solution.

Figure 1   The Decision-Making Process

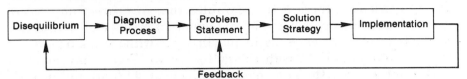

Feedback

These five steps are integral parts of the process and cannot be avoided in decision making. Whether followed consciously or unconsciously, explicitly or implicitly, they are inherent in the role of the manager in the following ways:

1. A manager inevitably experiences feelings of disequilibrium and regards some situations as problem situations, whether or not he has a clear, rational basis for his identification.
2. His response to the disequilibrium necessarily involves an assumption about the underlying cause, or a diagnosis of the situation, whether or not his diagnosis is rational, systematic, and explicit.
3. His response to the disequilibrium necessarily includes a definition of the problem to be solved, whether his definition of the problem is ambiguous or clear, sound or unsound, explicit or implicit.
4. His response constitutes a selection of method and solution, whether by conscious design or not.
5. Finally, his response also constitutes his implementation of his choice, whether or not it actually leads to the solution of the problem.

In other words, the decision-making steps examined in this book are *necessarily* taken by every decision maker, whether explicitly or implicitly, critically or noncritically. The goal of this book is to aid the decision maker in taking these steps effectively.

Orientation to Decision Making as a Systematic Discipline

There are unique problems in approaching decision making as a systematic discipline which should be faced at the outset. One problem is that decision making is a process in which everyone has already acquired a good deal of experience. Since early childhood we have all been developing our own personal decision method. Much of that experience has been reasonably successful, at least successful enough to have kept us alive and brought us to our present situations.

However, past experience in decision making is no guarantee that our experiences have taught us the best possible methods of analysis, the best possible hypotheses about motivation, or the best possible methods of decision making and problem solving. Learning from experience is usually random. Furthermore, although we all *learn experiences,* there is no guarantee that we *learn from experiences.* In fact, it is possible to learn downright errors and second-rate methods from experience, as in playing golf without taking lessons from a professional. As with the golfer, so with the manager: it is only training in systematic method which enables us to correctly analyze situations so that we can truly learn from experience in those situations.

A second shortcoming of learning only from experience is that it is necessarily circumscribed by the limits of the particular situations and events which happen to come our way. Thus, although all of us are "experienced" decision makers, our lifetime of decision making has been limited in scope. The management trainee has seldom been placed in an actual managerial position, and therefore has not been called upon to make managerial decisions. The marketing manager has seldom been called upon to make production decisions, nor the executive vice president to make presidential decisions. Thus, each individual's sphere of decision making is generally circumscribed by the limits of his own social or organizational role. Therefore, although we all have made decisions all our lives, the scope of our decision making has been definitely limited by the roles we have occupied.

There is a third problem in decision making based only on experience. Even if what we have learned in limited past roles is adequate as a decision method, we are all called upon from time to time to make decisions in new situations. A parent's decisions about his first child, the beginning investor's decisions in the stock market, the graduate's decisions about his first job, the vice president's decisions as acting president, the president's decisions in response to new legislation—all are new decision-making challenges for the individual. These challenges require insights and understanding not already developed from past experience. The individual today finds himself in a world of change, where he continually faces new situations. How does he react in new situations where decisions are called for?

Decision Making in New Situations

In new situations, individual reactions vary. One person may assume that a new situation is identical to an old one and base his decision on this assumption. A former vice president for marketing who has just been made president may view a marketing problem the same way he did when he was responsible only for marketing. Another person may seek the help of a colleague who he believes has had suitable, comparable experiences. The new mother may seek child-rearing advice from her own mother just as a young manager might query an experienced manager. Other individuals might hire a consulting expert, or seek spiritual guidance, or the advice and emotional support of a friend, or various combinations of these alternatives. Still others may decide to do nothing.

What one does at such a time—how he defines a unique situation and reacts to it—will reflect his personal frame of reference *vis-à-vis* the situation in which he finds himself. As Gordon Allport (1955) explains, "The way a man defines his situation constitutes for him its reality" (p. 84). Thus a decision maker who views all human behavior as arising from random chance will define reality differently, and therefore behave differently, than one who views all human behavior as motivated. A person who believes behavior is predestined will behave differently than one who views man as capable of making choices. It is in new situations that the decision maker's basic understanding of human behavior is, so to speak, put to the test.

What generally happens in new decision situations is that the individual defines his new situation in old terms. For example, the experienced manager of an organization who has developed set patterns of decision making may tend to see the human problems he encounters as of a few general "types," for which he has set solutions. Rather than attempting to objectively analyze problems, he is "solution oriented," and sees the decision situations which face him in terms of his habitual solutions. Thus, what long experience can mean is not always more and more objective analysis and more and more systematic methods of decision making; rather it can mean the reduction of new human-decision situations to the limited frame of reference of the manager's past perceptions.

Past decision-making experience in the realm of human problems is not the same thing as past experience in, say, solving mathematical problems. In many "technical" fields, such as mathematics, the same methods and even the same answers can be applied to the same problems. In the human realm, however, every decision situation is unique. A human situation is never exactly repeated. Its history of having occurred before makes it different from the first event. Similarly, a human act which is repeated has a different meaning the second time by virtue of its being a repetition. This means that in the human realm, there is no mathematical formula for decision making or problem solving which can be simply applied to "Problem A." "Problem A" never happens a second time. To a far greater extent than is true of "technical fields," then, each new experience encountered is a unique one. Any assumption that a particular experience is "the same as" a prior experience is, in reality, a judgment which can be made only *after* a careful diagnosis of both situations, not before it.

Thus, a further major problem in decision making as a systematic discipline is that of avoiding the temptation to classify a new situation simply as being like "that old familiar one" so that handy old decision-making formulas can be used. In the human realm, this tendency can be fatal to effective management.

The potential validity of assuming that two situations are even similar is not the same for all kinds of situations. The cause-and-effect relationship of some variables is more predictable than for other variables—that is, the behavior of some variables is more consistent over time. The more "technical" a situation, the more that nonhuman relationships are the primary variables, the greater the possibility that one situation may indeed be similar to another. Two mechanical problems on a production line may turn out to be virtually identical. By contrast, however, the more human nontechnical behavior is involved in the problem situations being compared, the less similarity one can automatically count on.

Human Decisions and Technical Decisions

Although the distinction between human decisions and technical decisions may appear to be a simple one, the implications of the distinction are very significant. The storehouse of knowledge and skill concerning technical phenomena has increased, and is increasing more rapidly than our knowledge and skill in human management. In part, this difference has resulted from the fact that it is much easier to transfer understanding of the physical sciences and technology from generation to generation than it is to transfer understanding of human behavior. Each new generation is able to build upon the science and technology of the previous generation simply through intellectual mastery of its content.

However, although factual "knowledge" *about* human behavior is similarly transferable, the kind of full understanding of human behavior that is required for management skill cannot be gained through any intellectual process alone. In fact, skill in the application of insights about human behavior is a variable partially independent of the intellectual knowledge itself. A certain degree of personal maturity is required in order for knowledge about human behavior to be realized in the action process of decision making about human problems. The development of such maturity of comprehension requires structured experiences, as well as intellectual concepts. And ordinarily the individual gains the appropriate structured experiences only through systematic training.

Even in an age of science such as our own, decision making in the human area is not a matter of knowing "right" solutions suggested by models and research in the behavioral sciences. (Although these theories may aid more and more in designing the structures of organizations.) In the many day-to-day decisions which must be made between worker and coworker, supervisor and employee, or executive and manager, effective decisions depend (equally, or many times more importantly) on the decision maker's having developed an emotional comprehension of the relationships among the behavioral science knowledge available, and his own unique organization, and his skill in applying his knowledge to the action process of managing in that organization. An engineer with "complete" knowledge about a set of technical relationships may approach a given situation with little concern for his "self-awareness" or for the impact he has on the reaction of all the variables involved. A manager with complete "knowledge" of human behavior, however, is still not free of his own norms, values, and attitudes. Further, his own behavior is an important variable in any human management situation.

Because "predigested" help is much more readily available in the technical realm than in the human realm, technical problems are being more easily and rapidly solved than are human problems. As a consequence of this fact, the decision maker is apt to try to find "technical" solutions for human problem situations. Indeed, he may reduce essentially human problems to their technical features, so that more easily managed technical solutions can be applied.

The disparity between our understanding of technological developments and the human problems that accompany them appears to many observers to be widening. Technological development has tended to breed progressively more technological development, but awareness of human problems has increased slowly. The widening gap has become one of the major problems of our society. For the manager of a sociotechnical organization, this phenomenon may present two problems: (1) technological advances may be thwarted by intrinsic human problems which have gone unsolved, even where the technical change could aid the persons who resist it (this is certainly a factor in automation); and (2) the technological changes initiated by an organization may have social repercussions in the organization or throughout the total community that create as many human problems as they attempt to solve (certainly a factor in organizations involved in mass communication media). Hence, greater understanding of human behavior and greater skill in its management are vital goals for the development of today's managers.

The Purpose of This Book

The purpose of this book is to help the manager develop effectiveness in making decisions in human systems. In pursuit of this purpose, the book involves two steps. First, it examines carefully that process of decision making which is effective in the human dimension of organizational management. Secondly, it identifies from the behavioral sciences selected concepts necessary to a fundamental understanding of organiaztional behavior.

Although distinct in some ways, the two purposes are not kept in mutual isolation. In taking up the decision-making process step by step, reference is made to concepts from the behavioral sciences wherever they clarify that process. Conversely, readings from the behavioral sciences are chosen and arranged with an eye to their direct applicability to the practical decision-making process.

The focus of the book is on the manager as decision makcr. We often speak as if an organization makes decisions or takes action. But, of course, organizations do not act. Groups do not act. Teams do not act. It is always the individuals who make up the organization, group, or team who decide and act. When a group acts, we are really observing the sum of coincidental individual decisions to act. Because the chief source of decision making in a given organizational system is the manager, this book is an approach to behavior from the manager's vantage point.

The role of the manager as the key figure in the behavior of organizations is stressed by many management writers. According to Churchman (1968), for example, the term *manager* refers not just to "someone having the authority and responsibility for making choices," since that can be applied to everyone, but to someone who has such authority and responsibility "within a 'system'" (p. 18).[2] French (1964) suggests that the task of the manager is not only to define enterprise goals, assemble resources, and design the organizational system, but also to "visualize the processes essential to the attainment of these goals" (p. 52). Newman, *et al.* (1967) define a manager as "a man who gets things done by working with people and other resources; in order to reach an objective, he coordinates the activities of others rather than perform operations himself" (p. 9).

Thus, the concept of a manager is an organizational or "systems" concept, the manager having primary control over the framework of his system or subsystem. However, it is important to remember that the manager does not have total control over the system for which he is accountable, since other systems and subsystems influence "his" system and its output. On the other hand, he has some influence on any system with which he comes in contact, even though he may not be organizationally accountable for it.

Although this book is concerned with the manager of a system or subsystem, it is not primarily concerned with the structure of organizations, personnel selection, division titles, formal hierarchical patterns, or the like. Rather, it is concerned with the dynamics of the interpersonal relationships involved in the functioning of the organi-

---

2. See Craig Lundberg (1963) for a discussion of the general concept of *systems* as applied to business organizations.

zation as a social system. It is concerned with how managers make decisions within organizations and how these *individual* decisions acquire the status of *organizational* decisions. Furthermore, it is necessarily concerned with the factors which influence individual and collective behavior in organizations. These factors include not only the enrivonmental, technical, and social variables operating in a given organization, but the internal psychological variables operating in the manager as well.

The Organization of The Book

This book is intended to be practical, and is organized so as to aid the manager in the achievement of practical managerial skills. It begins from the position of the manager and examines his decision processes, step-by-step, in problem situations involving human behavior. Part II examines the five stages of the decision-making process. Each chapter includes case studies designed to assist the reader in understanding and applying each step.[3] The goal is to provide a systematic and rational approach to human decision situations, an approach which will provide the manager the utmost flexibility in dealing with problems unique to his own organization, yet provide him with a general framework of systematic guidelines applicable to any decision situation involving human variables. The book is organized with the decision framework preceding the readings (Part III) in order to promote the development of a managerial action approach to the behavioral sciences rather than a theoretical or research approach.

Part III is organized around the second goal of the book: to provide a reservoir of knowledge and information about the behavioral sciences which is directly relevant to the decision-making process. Part III consists of readings and references on subjects in the behavioral sciences useful in human decision making. The organization of the material enables these readings to be studied in conjunction with the decision-making steps of Part II.

Part IV goes beyond the behavioral sciences to include material on the important value dimension inherent in all decision making.

Goals of The Reader

The material in this book will, of course, be tailored by each person to suit his own personal goals. The manager with long years of experience, having developed his own style or approach, may seek only to uncover new opportunities in human management which he had not before envisioned. Or he may be seeking primarily to broaden and sharpen his behavioral concepts. Or he may be seeking to remove certain weaknesses or bad habits developed in his own decision-making processes. He is all too aware that sometimes very small changes

---

3. See Benne for a discussion of the case method.

in his managerial approach may make a large difference in the operation of his firm.

A student inexperienced in management, on the other hand, may regard the entire book simply as a foundation for developing realistic attitudes toward human behavior, and plan to use the book as a reference, applying various specific points to human problems as they arise in his career. Although a number of cases are offered to allow the student to apply the concepts of this book, many students report that a comprehension of the relevance of some concepts and skills developed in this book grows with on-the-job experience.

To those who are accustomed to taking for granted the human factor in management, it may seem that to analyze the decision process in detail and to present a host of behavioral science findings applicable to organizations is to make complicated something which ought to be simple. A manager should beware, however, of easy formulas for human management. Many simplistic "common-sense" formulas for human management actually make the manager's job more difficult, because such formulas never face, much less solve, most of the problems which actually arise in organizations.

On the other hand, the end result of sound learning and training in organizational behavior is to make the decision maker's job of human management a simpler one. As in many areas of learning, the explanation of an advanced concept or a systematic step in the decision process may be more difficult and time consuming in the telling than it is in the doing. But a sound concept or method which may be difficult in the learning turns out to be far easier in the end, because it is effective. In short, learning about organizational behavior and decision making is, in the last analysis, like learning about differential calculus. Ultimately, it makes sound problem solving easier, not more difficult.

In summary, the primary focus of this book is on the individual decision maker in situations where the problems or contemplated solutions to problems involve human factors. The goal is to provide a useful way of approaching the decision-making process and to assist the organizational decision maker to better understand the human factor in decision making through increased knowledge of human behavior in general, through increased awareness of his own behavioral processes, and through a knowledge of what attitudes and specific skills are required in the step-by-step decision-making process.

References

Allport, Gordon. *Becoming.* Yale University Press, 1955. See selection in Part I.

Benne, Kenneth D. "Case Methods in the Training of Administrators." In *Research Papers and Technical Notes,* No. 28. Boston University Human Relations Center. Reprinted in Part I.

Bradford, Leland P., Jack R. Gibb, and Kenneth D. Benne. *T-Group Theory and Laboratory Method*. Wiley, 1964.

Bross, Irwin D. J. *Design for Decision*. Macmillan, 1953.

Churchman, C. West. *Challenge to Reason*. McGraw-Hill, 1968. See selection in Part I.

Elbing, Alvar O., Jr., and Carol J. Elbing. "Critical and Noncritical Methods." In *The Value Issue of Business*, Chap. 12. McGraw-Hill, 1967.

Feldman, Julian, and Herschel E. Kanter. "Organizational Decision Making." In *Handbook of Organizations*, ed. James G. March. Rand McNally, 1965.

French, Wendell. *The Personnel Management Process*. Houghton Mifflin, 1964.

George, Claude, Jr. *Management in Industry.* Prentice-Hall, 1964.

Lundberg, Craig. "Toward Understanding Behavioral Science by Administrators." *California Management Review*, Vol. 6, No. 1 (1963), 43–52. Reprinted in Part III.

Lundberg, George. *Can Science Save Us?* London: Longmans, Green, 1947. See selection in Part I.

Newman, William H., Charles E. Summer, and E. Kirby Warren. *The Process of Management*, 2nd ed. Prentice-Hall, 1967.

Ofstad, Harald. *An Inquiry into the Freedom of Decision*. Oslo: Norwegian Universities Press, 1961.

Sayles, Leonard. *Managerial Behavior*. McGraw-Hill, 1964.

Schlaifer, Robert. *Probability and Statistics for Business Decisions*. McGraw-Hill, 1959.

Simon, Herbert. *New Science of Management Decisions*. Harper & Row, 1960.

Taylor, Donald W. "Decision Making and Problem Solving." In *Handbook of Organizations*, ed. James G. March. Rand McNally, 1965.

Taylor, Frederick W. *The Principles of Scientific Management*. Harper & Row, 1911.

Watzlawick, Paul, Janet H. Beavin, and Don D. Jackson. *Pragmatics of Human Communication*. Norton, 1967.

Readings on the Concept of Method and Organizational Behavior

The purpose of the readings in this section is to raise several basic questions about approaching the process of decision making. What, for example, is the applicability of scientific processes in the solution of human problems? How important is "self-awareness" in the process of inquiring into decision-making situations? What is "freedom"? What is our point of view about the nature of human relationships in the world around us? What is the role of "rationality" in decision making? What assumptions do we make about the "nature of man" and how appropriate are these assumptions? Can the case method of instruction assist us in approaching these problems? Can the behavioral sciences play an important role in a manager's decision-making process?

These broad questions are basic to any discussion of decision making. They cannot be avoided: If they are not dealt with explicitly by the decision maker, they will, nonetheless, be dealt with implicitly, for the approach to each decision necessarily reflects assumptions about the answer to each question. The readings that follow do not purport to supply absolute answers to these questions, but they do provide a sound starting point for their critical examination. If there is a single theme that runs throughout this section, it is the importance of one's conscious awareness of the methods he uses in dealing with problems of human behavior. Methods of decision making, just as the methods of every other process and undertaking, should be appropriate to their purpose and should meet the rigorous criteria of the "critical method."

George Lundberg

Can Science Solve Social Problems?

Traditional thoughtways . . . are perhaps chiefly responsible for the failure thus far to take the social sciences seriously. It would be unfair to imply, however, that all skepticism regarding social science is of this character. Many thoughtful people, including scientists of distinction and unquestioned competence in their own fields, genuinely feel that there are certain differences between the subject matter of the physical and the social sciences which preclude the applicability of the same general methods to both. I do not refer here to the lapses of the great and near-great in physical science, literature, and art who frequently make childish pronouncements on the social order. I have in mind rather the serious student who has given some consideration to the matter.

For example, one distinguished scientist, Julian Huxley, has urged that a basic difference between the physical and the social sciences is that in the latter "the investigator is inside instead of outside his material" (1940). This is supposed to be so self-evident as to require no analysis. It turns out on examination to be little more than a figure of speech designed to call attention to the danger of biased observations and interpretation—a danger which is present in all science and which can, in any case, be circumvented or reduced only through the use of scientific instruments and methods of procedure which are part of scientific training in *any* field.

When an anthropologist goes to a remote savage tribe to study its social behavior, why is he any more inside his material than when he studies a colony of anthropoid apes, beavers, ants, the white rats in

From *Can Science Save Us?* Longmans, Green & Company, New York, 1947, pp. 16–34. Reprinted by permission of David McKay Company, Inc., New York City.

the laboratory, an ecological distribution of plants or, for that matter, the weather, the tides, or the solar system? When a biologist studies his own body or takes his own temperature he is presumably very much inside or part of the phenomena he studies. At what point exactly in this series does the mysterious transition from outside to inside of one's material take place? Nor is it necessary to go to a distant land and study savages in order to make the point. I can give as objective and verifiable a report on some of the social events that take place in the community where I now live as I can on the meteorological events that take place there. Both involve problems of observing and reporting accurately the events which I am studying.

In doing this, we need to use instruments as far as possible to sharpen our observation, to check it, and to report it accurately. These instruments and skills do not exist ready-made in any field. They have to be invented. They may be quite elementary as yet in much social investigation, consisting of little more than a pencil, a schedule, a standardized test, or the recording of an interview. But we also have at our command the movie camera with sound equipment with which social behavior can be observed in its cruder aspects with the same accuracy as any physical behavior is observed. When I use these instruments, I am no more "inside" my material than when I photograph an eclipse.

The invention of units and instruments with which to systematize observation is part of the scientific task in all fields. (Neither calories nor calorimeters came ready-made in the phenomena of physics.) They have to be invented to apply to the behavior in question, just as units of income or standards of living and scales for measuring them have to be invented. I am not making light of the difficulties involved in inventing either such units or appropriate instruments of scientific observation. Nor should we minimize the problems of interpreting the data which we observe. But here again we have at our disposal the same rules of logic, statistics, and scientific method that we apply to observations of physical events.

Most people's acquaintance with science has involved laboratories and controlled experiments. Indeed, the word science probably conjures up to most people the image of a man in a white coat looking critically at a test tube. Accordingly, another insuperable obstacle to social science is usually urged. How can a piece of society be put in a test tube?

The importance of laboratory experimentation in the advancement of certain sciences cannot be denied. But the matter of laboratory control varies greatly with different sciences. The solar system has never been brought into any laboratory. Astronomical laboratories do contain very ingenious symbolic and mechanical representations of the astronomical aspects of that system and remarkable instruments for observing it. These every science must unquestionably develop. Beyond this, the question of laboratory conditions becomes one of convenience and mechanical ingenuity. Statistical devices which permit the observation of two or more variables while the others are held constant, in the sense that their influence is measured and allowed for, are already in common use. In any event, actual experimentation in the social sciences is not impossible. The interested reader will find it worth his while to examine the literature on this subject.[1]

Another fatal obstacle to a full-fledged natural science of human social phenomena is alleged to be the presence in the latter of a unique and mysterious something called *motives*. When we start investigating human motives, the investigators' own motives become involved, we are told.

What is meant by motives? The word is used to designate those circumstances to which we find it "reasonable" to attribute an occurrence. The motive which we impute to an act is accordingly entirely relative to the frame of reference we adopt and accept as reasonable. The same event may be attributed to economic motives, the Oedipus complex, or the conjunction of the planets, according to whether one is an economic determinist, a Freudian, or an astrologer. To a scientist, the motives of a stone rolling downhill or of a boy murdering his father are simply the full set of circumstances resulting in either event. These conditions are equally subject to scientific investigation in both cases.

The circumstances, of course, will be of a very different type in the two cases. They will involve, in the case of the boy, "mental" and emotional factors of great subtlety ("complexity," "intangibility," "subjectivity"). But unless we are prepared to contend that for such phenomena other methods than those of science are more reliable, we have in fact no choice but to develop and improve scientific techniques appropriate to such investigation. Already our progress in this direction is not inconsiderable. Psychiatric and criminological techniques, including such devices as lie-detectors and brain-wave machines, strongly suggest that human motives are anything but immune to scientific investigation.

As for the scientist's own motives becoming involved, the only motive of a properly trained scientist in the face of a scientific problem is to solve the problem according to criteria specified by science. In short, the motive of the sociologist and physicist are exactly the same in the face of a scientific problem. *The motive is to find an answer that meets the requirements of a scientific answer.* The fact

1. For a summary and a critical discussion, see Greenwood (1945).

that the social scientist has always been a part of a social structure is no more a handicap to his objective study than is the fact that he is also part of the physical universe which he studies. Error, corruption, and bias, conscious and unconscious, are constant dangers inherent in *all* observation, both physical and social. Proper scientific training teaches the ethics of science as well as technical skill and the use of corrective instruments to reduce to a minimum the errors that beset our unchecked senses in every field.

Those who are oppressed with the feeling that the methods of science are inadequate in the determination of motives would do well to consider the methods by which motives are, in fact, determined today. One common method is to assemble twelve good men and true, farmers, bookkeepers, salesmen—anybody that comes to hand—subject them to a mass of evidence regarding the circumstances of a certain event, after which the judge charges them to determine whether or not "the motive" of one of the principals in the affair was fraudulent, felonious, malicious, etc. And how do these worthy citizens proceed with the assignment? They draw on their own lives and experience, on what their randon and unsystematic observation of human behavior in the past has taught them, plus what they may have learned from folklore, the Bible, and perhaps books on history and psychoanalysis. Against this background they lay the testimony, and on this basis they decide "the" motive. The procedure is far from perfect, as we know, and it is not claiming too much to assert that scientists properly trained for this kind of work would make fewer mistakes. But we think highly enough of even the ability of the lay jury to determine human motivation to make their decision the basis of life or death for free citizens. The very crudeness of present methods of determining human motives is a good reason for turning to science in this important problem.

In view of the prevalence of the hopelessly biased social and political proposals that are currently offered in the name of science, it is not surprising that many people should conclude that the preference of the researcher influences all conclusions in social research. Have any of the corrective instruments mentioned above actually been produced?

There are scores of instruments in use today in the social sciences that detect, reduce, or measure the bias of our senses and the prejudice of different observers. Have we any examples of sociological conclusions uninfluenced by the author's likes, dislikes, and group affiliations? Let each one answer for himself. Does a *scientific* public opinion poll predict the election results irrespective of the sentiments of the poll-taker? Does the prediction of the number of marriages, divorces, school enrollment, or success in college vary according to the marital or educational status or hopes of the predicter? These personal characteristics and wishes in no way influence the predictions of a properly trained social scientist. Or consider the Census Bureau's facts and generalizations regarding trends in our population, labor force, and income. Are these conclusions Communist, Capitalist, or Fascist? The question makes no more sense than to ask whether the law of gravity is Catholic, Protestant, or Pagan.

Any comprehensive review of the present status and achievements of the social sciences is obviously beyond the scope of the present discussion. Although I think it is unquestionably true that the social sciences have made, during the present century, more actual progress than in all preceeding history, it would be absurd to pretend that this progress is, as yet, reflected to any great extent in our management of social affairs. Scientific information of a more or less reliable character is more widely diffused than ever before, but the scientific mode of thought has obviously made very little headway. Practically no one approaches the major social problems of the day in a spirit of disinterested scientific study. The idea that these problems are to be solved, if at all, by the use of instruments of precision in hands that do not shake with fear, with anger, or even with love (see Duffus, 1934), does not seem to have occurred even to many people who pass for social scientists. They have joined the journalist and the soapbox crusader in the hue and cry of the mob. Their supposedly scholarly works bristle with assessments of praise and blame, personalities, and verbal exorcisms which have no place whatever in the scientific universe of discourse. Not only do these angry men pass in the public eye as great social scientists of the day, but they not infrequently presume to patronize honest scientists who stay with their proper tasks of building a science and the instruments by means of which any difficult problems are to be solved.

But behind this fog, this dust storm of books about the inside of various political movements, the private life and morals of its leaders, and the treatises on democracy, substantial work is going on. Men are patiently accumulating data about human behavior in a form which in the fullness of time will permit a type of generalization which has never before been possible. Some are engaged in the undramatic but fundamental work, basic to all science, of classifying the multitudes of human groups and behavior patterns as a first step toward the formulation of generalizations regarding them. Still others are pioneering in the construction of actuarial and other tables from which may be predicted not only the prevalence of births, deaths, marriages, and divorces, but also the probable relative degrees of happiness in marriage, the probable success or failure of probation and parole, and many other equally "human" eventualities. A wealth of valuable information and generalizations has already been developed about the social characteristics and behavior of populations, such as the distribution of wealth, occupations, mobility, intelligence, and the various conditions with which these characteristics vary. Important instruments have been invented in recent years for measuring opinion, status, social participation, and many phenomena of communication and interpersonal relations.

Indeed the invention and perfection of instruments for the more accurate and precise observation and recording of social phenomena must be regarded as among the most important developments in the social sciences. It is easy to point to the flaws in these instruments, as it was easy to point to the flaws in the early microscopes and telescopes. But, without these beginnings and the patient centuries of undramatic labor, sciences like bacteriology could not have appeared at all.

Finally, there are those, and they may be the most important of all, who are experimenting with and inventing new systems of symbolic representation of phenomena. New adaptations of mathematics by which otherwise hopeless complexities can be comprehended are quite fundamental but do not lend themselves to popular display. The work of Leibnitz, Faraday, and Hertz was not the popular science of their day. Yet it is by virtue of their strange calculations with strange symbols that men today fly and broadcast their speech around the earth. This should be remembered by "writers" and others who complain that social scientists are adopting "jargon" and "esoteric" symbols which go beyond the vocabulary of the current "best-seller."

If I deal primarily with these more obscure and undramatic labors of social scientists, it is because I regard them as more important in the long run than the conspicuous contemporary achievements which are common knowledge. I do not overlook or underestimate these more obvious and demonstrable achievements. The transition in our time to more humane treatment of children, the poor, and the unfortunate, by more enlightened education, social work, and penology, must in a large measure be attributed to the expanding sciences of psychology and sociology. I know, of course, that whenever a war or a depression occurs journalists and preachers point to the impotence of economists and political scientists either to predict or prevent these disasters. The fact is that the course of events following World War I, down to and including the present, was predicted with great accuracy by large numbers of social scientists. That nothing was done about it is not the special responsibility of social scientists. "Doing something about it" is the common responsibility of all members of a community, including scientists, and especially of those who specialize in mass education, mass leadership, and practical programs.

It is not my main purpose to review the past and present

achievements of the social sciences. . . . I am here concerned primarily with the probable future of the social sciences. Even if I should
admit that social scientists are today merely chipping flint in the
Stone Age of their science, I do not see that we have any choice but to
follow the rough road that other sciences have traveled. The attainment of comparable success may seem remote, and the labors involved may seem staggering. But is the prospect really unreasonably
remote? Suppose that someone four hundred years ago had delivered
an address on the future of the physical sciences and suppose that he
had envisioned only a small fraction of their present achievements.
What would have been the reaction of even a sophisticated audience
to predictions of men flying and speaking across oceans, seeing un-
dreamed-of worlds, both through microscopes and telescopes, and the
almost incredible feats of modern engineering and surgery? Nothing
I have suggested, I think, in the way of mature social science with
comparable practical application seems as improbable as would the
story of our prophetic physicist of four hundred or even one hundred
years ago.

The time is passing when the solid achievements of social science and its future prospects can be dismissed with a far-away look,
an ethereal smile, and the remark that unfortunately science neglects
"*the* human factor." *The* human factor is apparently something as
mysterious and inscrutable as the soul or other ectoplasmic manifestations. In any event, no one seems to be able to give any further light
on the nature of *the* human factor. The assumption that there is any
such single factor is itself gratuitous. What we do find on inquiry are
a lot of human factors—all the loves, hates, jealousies, prejudices,
fears, hopes, and aspirations of men. We know what we know about
these factors through observation of human behavior and what more
we need or want to know is to be learned in that way and in no other.
There is nothing more mysterious about human factors than about
other phenomena which have not yet become the subject of serious
scientific study. Of course, the trades and professions which have a
vested interest in obscurantism, mysteriousness, and ignorance will
oppose the advancement of science into this field as they have in
other domains. But I suspect their efforts will not avail. Science has
already so firm a hold on the imaginations of men that they will insist
on invoking this powerful tool also in the explanation of the mysterious human factor. *The* human factor will then be found to be no
factor at all, but merely a vague word designating a great variety of
behavior which social scientists have hitherto been too lazy or ignorant to approach by the same methods that have clarified the factors
in other phenomena of nature.

We have hitherto lacked boldness and an adequate vision of the
true task of social science. Research in this field is today for the most

part a quest for superficial remedies, for commercial guidance, and for historical and contemporary "human interest" stories. Everybody recognizes the importance of bookkeeping, census taking, studying the condition of the Negro population, and predicting the number of girdles that will be purchased in department stores a year from now. But there are types of research the immediate practical uses of which are not so obvious, yet which are essential to scientific development.

Shall we or shall we not assume that we can formulate laws of human behavior which are comparable to the laws of gravity, thermodynamics, and bacteriology? These latter laws do not of themselves create engineering wonders or cure disease. Nevertheless they constitute knowledge of a kind which is indispensable. The present argument is obviously handicapped in its most crucial respect, namely, its inability, in the space here available, to exhibit laws of social behavior comparable to the physical laws mentioned. Yet we have made considerable progress in this direction.

Finally, we come to what is regarded by many people, including scientists, as the most fundamental difference of all between the physical and the social sciences. "To understand and describe a system involving values," says Huxley, "is impossible without some judgment of values." "Values," he goes on to say, "are deliberately excluded from the purview of natural science."

It would be difficult to find a better example of confused thinking than that offered by current discussions of "values" and their supposed incompatibility with science. A principal cause of the confusion is a semantic error which is extremely common in the social sciences. In this case, it consists in converting the verb "valuating," meaning any discriminatory or selective behavior, into a noun called "values." We then go hunting for the *things* denoted by this noun. But there are no such things. There are only the valuating *activities* we started with. What was said above about motives applies with equal force to values. They are clearly inferences from behavior. That is, we say a thing *has* value or *is* a value when people behave toward it so as to retain or increase their possession of it. It may be economic goods and services, political office, a mate, graduation, prestige, a clear conscience, or anything you please. Since valuations or values are empirically observable patterns of behavior, they may be studied as such by the same general techniques we use to study other behavior.

As a matter of fact, everybody is more or less regularly engaged in such study of other people's values. It is quite essential to any kind of satisfactory living in any community. We try to find out as soon as possible what the values of our neighbors are. How do we find out? We observe their behavior, including their verbal behavior. We listen to what other people say about them, we notice what they spend their money for, how they vote, whether they go to church, and a hundred other things. On a more formal and scientific level, opinion polls on men and issues are taken to reflect the values of large groups. Economists, of course, have been studying for years certain kinds of evaluations of men through the medium of prices.

There appears to be no reason why values should not be studied as objectively as any other phenomena, for they are an inseparable part of behavior. The conditions under which certain values arise, i.e., the conditions under which certain kinds of valuating behavior takes place, and the effects of "the existence of certain values" (as we say) in given situations, are precisely what the social sciences must study and what they are studying. These values or valuating behaviors, like all other behavior, are to be observed, classified, interpreted, and generalized by the accepted techniques of scientific procedure.

Why, then, is the value problem considered unique and insurmountable in the social sciences?

The main reason seems to be that social scientists, like other people, often have strong feelings about religion, art, politics, and economics. That is, they have their likes and dislikes in these matters as they have in wine, women, and song. As a result of these preferences, both physical and social scientists frequently join other citizens to form pressure groups to advance the things they favor, including their own economic or professional advancement, Labor, Capital, Democracy, the True Church, or what not. To do so is the right of every citizen, and there is no canon of science or of civil law which requires scientists to abjure the rights which are enjoyed by all other members of a community.

The confusion about values seems to have arisen because both scientists and the public have frequently assumed that, when scientists engage in ordinary pressure-group activity, that activity somehow becomes science or scientific activity. This is a most mischievous fallacy. It is not surprising, perhaps, that the public should be confused on this point, because it may not always be clear when a scientist is expressing a scientific conclusion and when he is expressing a personal preference. But it is unpardonable for scientists themselves to be confused about what they know and say in their capacity as scientists and what they favor in religion, morals, and public policy. To pose as disinterested scientists announcing scientific conclusions when in fact they are merely expressing personal preferences is simple fraud, no matter how laudable or socially desirable may be the scientists' "motives" and objectives.

But is it possible for a person to play two or more distinct roles, such as scientist and citizen, without confusing the two? The answer is that it is being done every day. It is the most obvious commonplace that the actress who plays Juliet in the afternoon and Lady Macbeth at night does not allow her moral or other preference for one of these roles to influence her performance of the other. In any event, her competence is measured by her ability to play each role convincingly. During the same day she may also be expected to fulfill the roles of wife, mother, etc. Likewise, the chemist who vigorously campaigns against the use of certain gases in war obviously cannot allow that attitude to influence in the slightest degree the methods of producing or analyzing these gases. Science, as such, is nonmoral. There is nothing in scientific work, as such, which dictates to what ends the products of science shall be used.

In short, it is not true that "to understand and describe a system involving values is impossible without some judgment of values." I can certainly report and understand the bald fact that a certain tribe kills its aged and eats them without saying one word about the goodness or badness of that practice according to my own standards, or allowing these standards of mine to prevent me from giving an accurate report of the facts mentioned. The only value judgments which any properly trained scientist makes about his data are judgments regarding their relevance to his problem, the weight to be assigned to each aspect, and the general interpretation to be made of the observed events. These are problems which no scientist can escape, and they are not at all unique or insuperable in the social sciences.

Have scientists, then, no special function or obligation in determining the ends for which scientific knowledge is to be used? As scientists, *it is their business to determine reliably the immediate and remote costs and consequences of alternate possible courses of action,* and to make these known to the public. Scientists may then *in their capacity as citizens* join with others in advocating one alternative rather than another, as they prefer.

To the extent that their reputation and prestige is great, and to the extent that their tastes are shared by the masses of men, scientists will, of course, be influential in causing others to accept the goals the scientists recommend. In this sense, social science will doubtless become, as physical science already is, an important influence in determining the wants of men. That is, as a result of scientific knowledge, men will not want impossible or mutually exclusive things. They will not seek to increase foreign trade and at the same time establish more comprehensive and higher tariffs. They will not seek to reduce crime but at the same time maintain a crime-promoting penal system. They will not destroy the productive power of a nation and still expect it to be peaceful, prosperous, and democratic. They will not expect a world organization to be conjured into existence by semantically deranged "statesmen" before the necessary preceding integration of the constituent units has been achieved.

The development of the social sciences and the diffusion of scientific knowledge will doubtless greatly influence in the above ways the wants, wishes, and choices of men. But there is still an important difference between a statement of fact and the dictation of conduct. It is one thing for a physicial to tell a patient: "Unless you undergo this operation, which will cost so much in time, money, and pain, you will probably die in one month." It is another matter to say: "Science, for which I am an accredited spokesman, says you shall undergo this operation." Any scientist who pretends that science authorizes him to make the latter statement is a fraud and a menace. Dictation of this type has not accompanied the rise of physical science and it need not result from the full maturity of the social sciences. This needs to be kept in mind especially in these days of much worry about brain trusts and whether, with the development of atomic fission, scientists must become a priestly class dictating all public policy.

The misunderstanding regarding the relation of scientists to practical affairs is so widespread and mischievous as to warrant further emphasis. The *application* of scientific knowledge obviously involves value judgments of some sort. This problem is equally present in the other sciences. After we know how to produce dynamite and what it will do, there remains the question: Shall we drop it from airplanes to destroy cathedrals and cities, or shall we use it to build roads through the mountains? After we know the effects of certain drugs and gases, the question still remains: Shall we use them to alleviate pain and prevent disease, or shall we use them to destroy helpless and harmless populations? There is certainly nothing in the well-developed sciences of chemistry or physics which answers these questions. Neither is it the business of the social sciences to answer (except *conditionally*, as we have seen) the question of what form of government we should have, what our treatment of other races should be, whether we should tolerate or persecute certain religious groups, whether and to what degree civil liberties should be maintained, and a multitude of other questions which agitate us. What, then, are social scientists for and what should they be able to do?

Broadly speaking, it is the business of social scientists to be able to predict with high probability the social weather, just as meteorologists predict sunshine and storm. More specifically, social scientists should be able to say what is likely to happen socially under stated conditions. A competent economist or political scientist should be able to devise, for example, a tax program for a given country which will yield with high probability a certain revenue and which will fall in whatever desired degrees upon each of the income groups of the area concerned. Social scientists should be able to state also what will be the effect of the application of this program upon income, investments, consumption, production, and the outcome of the next election. Having devised such a tax program and clearly specified what it will do, it is not the business of the social scientists any more than it is the business of any other citizens to secure the adoption or defeat of such a program. In the same way, competent sociologists, educators, or psychologists should be able to advise a parent as to the most convenient way of converting a son into an Al Capone or into an approved citizen, according to what is desired.

My point is that no science tells us *what to do* with the knowledge that constitutes the science. Science only provides a car and a chauffeur for us. It does not directly, as science, tell us where to drive. The car and the chauffeur will take us into the ditch, over the precipice, against a stone wall, or into the highlands of age-long human aspirations with equal efficiency. If we agree as to where we want to go and tell the driver our goal, he should be able to take us there by any one of a number of possible routes, the costs and conditions of each of which the scientist should be able to explain to us. When these alternatives have been made clear, it is also a proper function of the scientist to devise the quickest and most reliable instrument for detecting the wishes of his passengers. But, except in his capacity as one of the passengers, the scientist who serves as navigator and chauffeur has no scientific privilege or duty to tell the rest of the passengers what they *should* want. There is nothing in either physical or social science which answers this question. Confusion on this point is, I think, the main reason for the common delusion that the social sciences, at least, must make value judgments of this kind.

But it does follow, as we have seen, that science, by virtue of its true function, as outlined above, may be of the utmost importance in helping people to decide intelligently what they want. . . . It may be noted that the broad general wants of people are perhaps everywhere highly uniform. They want, for example, a certain amount of physical and social security and some fun. It is disagreement over the means toward these ends, as represented by fantastic ideologies, that results in conflict and chaos. I have pointed out that, in proportion as a science is well developed, it can describe with accuracy *the consequences* of a variety of widely disparate programs of action. These consequences, if reliably predicted, are bound strongly to influence what people will want. But it remains a fact that science, in the sense of a predicter of consequences, is only *one* of the numerous influences that determine an individual's wants and his consequent behavior. Science and scientists are still the servants, not the masters, of mankind. Accordingly, those scientists who contend that they can scientifically determine not only the means but the ends of social policy should be exposed as scientific fakers as well as would-be dictators. Yet this is the very group which professes to be concerned about the democratic implications of the position I am here defending!

Finally, this view seems to some people to do away with what they call "the moral basis of society." Obviously, it does nothing of the sort. The question is not about the moral basis of society but about the social basis of morals. We merely advocate a scientific basis for morality. Presumably, all will agree that morals exist for man, not man for morals. Morals are those rules of conduct which man thinks have been to his advantage through the ages. Why should we then not all agree that we want the most authentic possible appraisal of that subject?

There appears, then, to be no reason why the methods of science cannot solve social problems. Neither should we expect more from social than from physical science. As *science*, both physical and social sciences have a common function, namely, to answer scientific questions. These answers will always be of an impersonal, conditional type: "*If* the temperature falls to 32°F., *then* water (H_2O) will freeze." "*If* a certain type of tax is adopted, *then* certain types of industrial activity will decrease." Neither of these statements carries any implications as to whether or how the knowledge should be used. Far from being a weakness, this characteristic of scientific knowledge is its greatest strength. The wants of men will change with changing conditions through the ages. The value of scientific knowledge lies precisely in this impersonal, neutral, general validity for whatever purposes man desires to use it.

For this reason, those scientists and others who try to identify science with some particular social program, sect, or party must be regarded as the most dangerous enemies of science. They are more dangerous than its avowed enemies, because the defenders of "democratic," "communist," "religious," or "moral" science pose as defenders of science and carry on their agitation in the name of lofty social sentiments. That this group is confused rather than malicious is evident from their proposal that scientists should take an oath not to engage in scientific activity which may be "destructive" or contrary to "toleration," "justice," etc. The absurdity of the proposal is readily apparent, if we consider any actual scientific work. No scientist can foresee all the uses to which his work may be put, and in any event it is a commonplace that the *same* drug may be used to cure or to kill people. It may be granted that preposterous proposals of this kind are a temporary hysterical phenomenon superinduced by such dramatic developments as the atomic bomb. It may be granted that the agitators are motivated by lofty social sentiments. Unfortunately, the same has been said for prominent proponents of the Inquisition.

The uses to which scientific or other knowledge is to be put have always been and will continue to be a legitimate concern of men. Science, as we have noted, can be valuable in helping men to decide that question. . . . Our warning here has been directed against attempts to corrupt scientific methods and results by allowing them to be influenced by the temporary, provincial, ethnocentric preferences of particular scientists or pressure groups.

References

Duffus, R. L. *Harper's,* December 1934.

Greenwood, E. *Experimental Sociology.* King's Crown Press, 1945.

Huxley, Julian. "Science Natural and Social." *Scientific Monthly,* January 1940.

George F. F. Lombard

Self-Awareness and the Scientific Method

The recent successes of the natural sciences have arisen from the use of controlled experiments. In teaching and research they receive primary attention. This is entirely appropriate to the needs and opportunities of those sciences: the whole history of controlled experiments in them has been that they are fruitful of new knowledge. Their history in the social sciences, with few exceptions, is that they have not. Since one man's meat is frequently another's poison, the techniques of the controlled experiment are not what I wish students of human behavior would learn from the natural sciences. My reasons for this reside in two familiar but neglected skills without which science has nowhere progressed.

Experiments may fail for many reasons: only those based on relevant observation of nature have any chance of fruitful results.

From *Science,* Vol. 112, September 15, 1950, pp. 289–293. Reprinted by permission of the American Association for the Advancement of Science and the author.

Since before Galileo's "fantastically artificial" neglect of friction in his experiments with motion, the experiments of natural scientists have, on the whole, been relevant to the nature of things; the results of the polls taken before the 1948 elections are evidence that many in the social sciences have not.

Claude Bernard (1927) said, "The experimental idea is by no means arbitrary or purely imaginative; it must always have support in observed reality; that is to say, in nature" (p. 38). This concept of experiment is quite different from one current in the social sciences today, namely, that the limit of experiment is the ingenuity of the experimenter. But how are scientists to know what is relevant to nature? The difficulties here are great, especially so because research itself may distort the natural happening of events. How can that be studied which study itself distorts?

Natural scientists have long been aware of the problem posed by the relationship of the researcher to his data. To be sure, in some of the natural sciences the presence of a researcher does not greatly affect the phenomena being studied. In others the phenomena must be shielded from, for example, the heat or electricity of an investigator's body. In biology and physiology the problems are quite different and often complex, even in simple experiments. Here also, thanks to the work of such investigators as Bernard, Cannon, and others, many of the obstacles have been overcome.

In the social sciences, the sensitiveness of the phenomena being studied to the presence of an investigator is especially great. This sensitiveness of human life to interaction with other human beings is familiar to all of us, and not only in research. It is demonstrated in every relationship. To clarify the point, let me take extreme examples.

Restrictive controls, short of the extinction of life itself, produce in those controlled diverse reactions, in all of which may be recognized attempts of the self to maintain its integrity. This seems to be true of parental, educational, administrative, military, and governmental controls. For example, this aspect of human behavior continually plagues the administrator who seeks to initiate change. In research, too, what we seek to control again and again resists the investigator and in often subtle ways upsets his plans. So, for many years, experiments in industry with rest pauses for workers were inconclusive: sometimes production increased following their introduction; sometimes it did not. Investigators cussed "human nature" until the researchers at Hawthorne began to understand the nature of their relationship to the workers in the test room (Roethlisberger and Dickson, 1939, Ch. 8).

Impressive though reactions to violation of integrity are in human life, the positive effects of a relationship with others can be even more startling. The capacities of human beings to respond to warmth and appreciation with adaptation and growth are tremendous, although these powers are often latent. An article by Vincent Sheean entitled "On Love," in the July, 1949, *Atlantic Monthly*, gives an instance in point. Philosophy, religion, medicine, several of the social sciences, practical men of affairs, and military leaders have all documented this phenomenon. Whether human beings welcome or resist a relationship, their active response to one is apparent. My point is that in the social sciences, as in all science, an investigator's skills in handling his relationship to his data are of great importance.

But, granted an investigator needs skills in relating himself to his data, he must still make relevant observations. Although some physical scientists have had truly exceptional capacity in this direction, they have seldom made explicit the processes by which they achieved their results. Often, I suspect, they are not aware that there have been processes. Often they don't have to be conscious of them: their work has progressed far enough so that frequently they can take for granted the observations of nature on which an experiment is based. "At some time and in some way not recorded," (Conant, 1947, p. 37) is a fairly typical description of the origin of an observation that led to fruitful experiment.

Not all records of observation are this incomplete. President Conant refers to Galileo and a pump that "was once called to his attention" (p. 33), and to Galvani, the frog's legs, and two people who are identified only as "one of the persons who were present" and "another one who was there." The fact that such careful observers as Galileo and Galvani failed to record the particulars of the situation in which their first observations occurred is indicative of the point I wish to make. Who was the person "who was present" who noticed the movement of the frog's legs? Who was "another one" who noticed that a spark seemed to excite the action? What was the background of their thinking that made them mention these observations to Galvani as possibly significant? Particularly, what in Galvani's thinking led him to seize at once on their remarks with "incredible zeal and eagerness," even though he "at the time had something else in mind and was deep in thought"? (Conant, 1947, p. 67).[1] Would that all of us when deep in thought could thus turn our minds into fruitful channels.

More detailed instances of how relevant observations have occurred can readily be found in Mach, Poincaré, Bernard, and others who have documented the progress of science. Cannon's *The Way of an Investigator* supplies us with valuable material. We also know

---

1. Cannon (1945, p. 69), without quoting sources, gives a slightly different account of these incidents, in which the same failure to record precisely the original observations is apparent.

something of the observations that led to the development of penicillin and radar. In all this material three phrases are used over and over again: "an accidental observation," "a hunch," and "chance." These words make me curious. Just what do they mean?

Two possibilities occur at once. The words hardly seem adequate as descriptive of a *process of thought*. On the other hand, they may reflect an *attitude of mind* that glories in the obviously brilliant results of the controlled experiment, to the neglect of the skilled observation. It is as if this attitude were saying, "What could be less worthy of attention than an accident, a hunch, or chance?" The choice of these words signifies how little the process is thought to deserve attention—and how little it receives. "It happened once; it was accidental; it will not happen again." "We made the most we could of it; why pay more attention to it?" A hunch: "A small thing; random; inexplicable. Now, when we can control the variables . . ."

Webster lists fourteen meanings for the word "chance." The fourteenth is: "The fortuitous . . . element in . . . existence; that which happens . . . in connection with events to which it bears no necessary relation." The first meaning is, simply, "The happening of events; the way in which things befall." I call to your attention the contrast of connotations in the fortuitous, the unrelated, and the inexplicable, on the one hand, and the happening of events, nature, on the other. Priestley redefines chance as "the observation of *events arising from unknown causes*" (Conant, 1949, p. 53). "Chance," with causes unknown, is surely distinct from chance without cause.

Please note, my claim is not that fortune plays no role in observation. Indeed it does; but when we have said that, have we said all there is to say? To me it seems not, though what else there is, is both difficult and complex to describe.

Certainly a skill of observation is something much more than what is involved when I say, "I see you." You are visible reality—at least, I find it fruitful for many purposes to assume that you are. What I mean by the process of observation is much more complex. To observe things in this other sense involves a way of thinking about things, as well as the data that are observed. Two psychologists, Snygg and Combs (1949) have recently stated the dual nature of the process as follows:

> The progress of science . . . is in two directions. The first is toward the discovery of new facts. This unceasing search is continually turning up new facts inexplicable in the old frames of reference. In turn, the scientist is forced to develop new frames of reference. Once a more adequate frame of reference has been achieved, its effectiveness is soon demonstrated by the discovery of a great number of new facts and relations (p. 5).

A skill of observation is, then, a capacity to *discriminate between reality as it actually is and reality as any one of us sees it,* determined as it is for us by the frames of reference, the conceptual schemes, which we habitually use. Some psychologists speak of this difference as the difference between "reality" and "perceived reality." To learn to step outside the conceptual schemes one habitually uses in search of new and more fruitful ones is no mean accomplishment. Science and philosophy have long pondered the problem.

President Conant's book *On Understanding Science* is helpful in giving us examples of the difficulties in the way of this learning process. Swammerdam, who experimented with frogs' legs but failed to push the work as Galvani did; Rey, whose work on calcination of tin should have exposed the phlogiston theory of combustion; the need of a new concept to "fit the times" if it is to be useful; and the "power of an old concept" to prevail against contradictory evidence are all to the point. President Conant says, "The history of science . . . fails to demonstrate any uniform way in which new experimental facts and observations generate the fruitful notions in the minds of great investigators" (p. 17).

Bernard has this to say: "Apropos of a given observation, no rules can be given for bringing to birth in the brain a correct and fruitful idea that may be a sort of intuitive anticipation of successful research" (p. 33).

These difficuties sound ominous for my purpose, but they give us a clue, for our question need not be the rules for getting from a *given* observation to an experimental idea. Our question can be, rather, "Are there any conditions of the mind which seem to assist the making of new observations?"

Bernard discusses at some length "a few general principles for the guidance of minds applying themselves to research (in experimental medicine)." Cannon, among others, speaks of "hard labor" (p. 67) and "the prepared mind" (p. 79). Both Conant and Cannon quote Pasteur, "Chance favors the prepared mind." Henderson's (1938) statement of the "conditions [necessary] for understanding" is well known: "first, intimate, habitual, intuitive familiarity with things; secondly, systematic knowledge of things; and thirdly, an effective way of thinking about things" (p. 6). His more precise description of "systematic knowledge" is by no means as familiar: "*Accurate observation of things and events*, selection, guided by judgment born of familiarity and experience, of the salient and recurrent phenomena, and their classification and methodical exploitation" (italics mine) (Henderson, 1941, p. 1).

Henderson's remarks describe usefully—at least, as he was wont to say, "to a first approximation"—the *outward* organization of training necessary to prepare a mind for fruitful observation. Since it is in the mind that an idea is generated, the process of creating one has an *inner* aspect as well. These outward conditions will not be productive unless they stimulate the growth of this inner capacity. A key to the reality as our existing conceptual schemes permit us to perceive it is awareness of our own frames of reference. If we know what they are, we are in a position to distinguish between them and reality. We can "see" that the world is round, not flat; that weights and feathers fall uniformly; that not all unions are "bad" and all managements "good," or vice versa.

In many of us, awareness of this sort remains low; in others it develops into an overriding—sometimes neurotic—conviction of sin that leads to crises of indecision and inaction. In still others, it achieves a balance that permits effective discrimination between reality and what we see as reality.

At this point I am faced with a difficult choice. The strict logic of my topic requires that I should describe as precisely as possible just what is the balance in the processes of the mind that leads to effective awareness. To do so would take me far into several theories of psychology, from which we would emerge convinced that the "gaps" in what is now known are more important than the "blocks" of what is known. Consequently, I propose to leap this hurdle by calling attention to two aspects of it: first, that the gap is there, and, second, that I am neglecting it.

Let me say only that a new idea worthy of attention seems always to spring from reflection. Consequently, balanced awareness involves an effective alternation between reflective thinking and concentrated attention. This fact is important in linking the general conditions of training of which I have been speaking with this inner process of mind; for it follows that training must supply adequate material—that is, experience—for reflection, as well as an opportunity for the two kinds of thinking to develop in effective alternation with each other. The conditions Henderson laid down meet these requirements; but it is precisely at this point that we need to know much more about what learning is, and what the conditions are that favor it.

Let me repeat, the difficulty of acquiring an awareness of one's own frames of reference is great. It is especially so in the social sciences, where the investigator's own frames of reference, from which he draws the meaningfulness of his whole life, are called into question. Difficult and even painful as this learning process may be, it is nonetheless inevitable in the accumulation of knowledge; else the researcher fails to separate what he brings to the situation from the data he is studying.

Skills in handling our relationship to the data we seek to study and skills in making relevant observations are related. Both require the inner quality of awareness of self of which I have been speaking. On the one hand, awareness of self increases our capacity for handling ourselves in relation to our data by forcing on us continuous and critical inner appraisal and reappraisal of what we are doing in relation to an external reality. On the other hand, it reinforces our capacity for accurate observation by making us conscious of the difference between that which we see (perceived reality) and reality. This awareness is as necessary in the training of social scientists as it is in general education for citizenship.

In the social sciences we often proceed as though we were unaware of the existence of the need. Our attempts to meet it have until recently been in one of two directions, both relatively sterile compared with progress in other sciences. On the one hand, we study situations far removed from what is familiar to us because we hope that the gross determinants of the behavior occurring in them will persist and be obvious to the investigator in spite of his presence. Studies of primitive tribes and cultures and of other groups at the fringe of our civilization have taken this direction. These studies are eminently worth while in their own right, and much of general value has been learned from them. Yet their methods leave us with a sense of something missing when we focus them on the problems of modern life. Too often, sensing "the shadow but not the substance" of our relationship to our data, we retreat into a pseudo-objectivity that defeats itself. By attempting to make our questionnaires, tests, and laboratory-type experiments completely objective, we arrive at a typical norm so far removed from the uniqueness of the particular instance that the knowledge gained is all but useless in application.

Why I believe the quality of awareness is necessary in the training of a social scientist will, I hope, be clear by now. That quality in him is the seed from which new understandings of the way things happen will grow.

I believe this quality is equally needed today in general education in training for citizenship. When a boy-girl relationship becomes that of husband and wife, a couple cannot assume that communication between them over mutually created problems of children, housekeeping, and career will be eased by the understanding that arises from a common background. Indeed, most of us sooner or later have to realize that no such community of background exists. Under these conditions understanding, if it is to be achieved, must be demonstrated in face-to-face interactions in the present. This means that each of us must be able to recognize and behave in terms of what is important in our relationships here and now. Distinguishing this present reality from the way in which our past experiences have taught us to see it is vital to securing, first, understanding; then, communication and active cooperation.

Difficulties of communication between people exist not only in family relationships. They are a common symptom of our times. In industry they exist at every level of organization, between worker and worker, between foreman and worker, between staff specialist and line executive. They are particularly important and difficult between representatives of different organizations—business and government, business and labor, labor and government, government and government.

Let me take brief examples from foreign affairs; the needs are only less dramatic, hardly less acute, in the domestic economy. An administrator of the Economic Cooperation Administration interested in improving the efficiency of manufacturing in Europe, or a nutrition expert of the United Nations Food and Agricultural Organization seeking to improve the diet of southeast Asia, must each be aware of the threat to existing customs that his methods present. Without this awareness, what he is doing will inevitably seem to be destroying established ways of doing things, rather than creating new freedoms. His relationship and the relationship of our country to those peoples then come to be hated and feared, instead of becoming relationships through which they can seek the help to help themselves.

Administrative skills in instances such as these go a long way toward making good intentions effective, but they are never wholly so without understanding and support in the wider community. Indeed, now that destruction for one may mean destruction for all, whole nations are called on for an awareness of self in relation to others such as has never before been required. At these levels the problems are of an entirely different order than any I have discussed up to this point. Yet, in peace and in war, citizen awareness of the effects of national policy is imperative. For example, however disastrous bombing may be to lives and property, it may also arouse to action a will to resist. The stubborn "happening of events" will then bring it about that this living resistance will replace both lives and property. If this should happen, bombing becomes a boomerang of a kind no primitive ever wished to possess. Even the *threat* of bombing may arouse such resistance.

And the threat is today a reality in the lives of all of us. Surely general education's responsibility to address the problems of communication between peoples cannot neglect these aspects of understanding: understanding of how what I myself do, of how what we as a nation do, affects and is affected by, the social realities of the divided world in which we live.

Many noted students of the social scene—Toynbee, Fromm, Rogers, Liebman, Whitehead—point to something closely akin to what I have been calling a conscious awareness of self in relation to the external world, as the chief need of civilization today. Our igno-

rance of what is required at these more complex levels is appalling;
yet conditions make it necessary to face the problems of research and
education that are involved.

At the simpler levels, useful leads for organizing training in
awareness are available, though neglected. One does not need to be a
skilled observer to recognize that education does an uneven job in
providing would-be researchers and citizens with foundations for the
development of these skills.

In both school and college the emphasis is on systems of knowledge, a quite different thing from "systematic knowledge." Our conceptual schemes are more often "theories of explanation" (Henderson, 1941, pp. 8–10) than fruitful ways of helping us to new
observations. We leave the acquisition of "intuitive familiarity" to
chance, or neglect it entirely, in spite of good examples set us in
engineering, and especially in medicine.

Beyond this, experience suggests that training organized under
the burden of responsibility in connection with the handling of actual
situations provides a favorable climate for self-awareness to mature
into active skill. Henderson makes much of this point and refers both
to medical training and to what I believe was once known as "Milner's
Kindergarten" as a case in point in a quite different field, that of
government administration (see also Buchan, 1940 ed., pp. 100 ff).
Yet, everywhere in education, especially in the training of ourselves,
the teachers, neglect and chance have captured the "burden of responsibility."

I could mention "self-directive" interviewing as a promising new
tool of research for some fields of the social sciences. The recent
suggestion of an "internal frame of reference" as an appropriate
conceptual scheme for psychology may be most fruitful. Role-playing
and several forms of group discussion, such as group therapy and
group dynamics, are having some success in developing effective
self-awareness. Semantics and psychoanalysis also have important
contributions, as may the psychodrama and sociodrama. I would be
overly self-aware indeed if I did not mention, too, our rather different
use of case method instruction in human relations in General Education at Harvard College and in the Graduate School of Business
Administration. We have plans for new, as yet untried, ways of
training in social skills under the burden of responsibility.

I have now tried—I am sure, inadequately—to clarify two aspects of scientific method, the importance of which I wish students of
human behavior could learn from the natural sciences. I have described them as skills of handling oneself in relation to one's data and
as skills of making relevant observations of nature. An inner quality
of the mind, which I have called self-awareness, seems to me a key to

their acquisition. At this stage of the growth of knowledge in the social sciences, I give techniques of experimentation secondary emphasis. As social scientists learn to handle their relations with their data and to make relevant observations, I am confident that experimentation will reappear in ways that do not distort the happening of events. Our start is to learn to make accurate observations of nature.

References

Bernard, Claude. *An Introduction to the Study of Experimental Medicine.* Schuman, 1927.

Buchan, John. *Pilgrim's Way.* Houghton Mifflin, 1940.

Cannon, Walter B. *The Way of an Investigator.* Norton, 1945.

Conant, James B. *The Growth of the Experimental Sciences.* Harvard University Press, 1949.

————. *On Understanding Science.* Yale University Press, 1947.

Henderson, L. J. "The Study of Man." *Science,* Vol. 94, 1941.

————. "Sociology 23: Introductory Lectures." Mimeographed. Harvard University, rev. October 1938.

Roethlisberger, F. J., and W. J. Dickson. *Management and the Worker.* Harvard University Press, 1939.

Snygg, Donald, and A. W. Combs. *Individual Behavior.* Harper, 1949.

Gordon W. Allport

Freedom

When we say that we select from the available elements of culture, or that we act in accordance with our conscience, or that we refer our decisions to our schemata of values, we are skirting the problem of freedom. No other issue causes such consternation for the scientific psychologist. One may look through a hundred successive American

From *Becoming* by Gordon W. Allport, 1955 Yale University Press, pp. 82–88. Copyright © 1955 by Yale University Press. Reprinted by permission.

books in psychology and find no mention of "will" or "freedom." It is customary for the psychologist, as for other scientists, to proceed within the framework of strict determinism, and to build barriers between himself and common sense lest common sense infect psychology with its belief in freedom. For the same reason barriers are erected against theology. But to our discomfort recent events have raised the issue all over again. Existentialism insists on freedom; much of the psychotherapy now in vogue presupposes it; psychology's new concern with values is at bottom a concern with choices, and therefore revives the problem of freedom. Up to now the tug of war between free will and determinism has been marked by naïveté. Just as we have learned with some success to transcend the monolithic oppositions between mind and body, nature and nurture, we should strive for better perspective in our view of freedom and determinism. The following considerations may help.

1. In the first place, it is essential that we distinguish the viewpoint of the scientist from that of the acting person. The superior wisdom of the scientist may unfortunately blind him to the process of growth that is actually taking place. The scientist's frame of reference is like the frame of an omniscient being: to him all things have time, place, and determined orbits. But this frame is definitely not the frame of the acting person. The situation is much like that of the watcher from the hilltop who sees a single oarsman on the river below. From his vantage point the watcher notes that around the bend of the river, unknown as yet to the oarsman, there are dangerous rapids. What is present to the watcher's eye still lies in the future for the oarsman. The superior being predicts that soon the boatman will be portaging his skiff—a fact now wholly unknown to the boatman who is unfamiliar with the river's course. He will confront the obstacle when it comes, decide on his course of action, and surmount the difficulty. In short, the actor is unable to view his deeds in a large space-time matrix as does an all-wise God, or the less wise demigods of science. From his point of view he is working within a frame of choice, not of destiny. As psychologists we ought to know, and do know, that the way a man defines his situation constitutes for him its reality. Choice for him is a paramount fact; how matters appear to the watcher on the hill is irrelevant. It is because existentialism takes always the acting person's point of view that it insists so strongly upon the attribute of freedom in man's nature.

2. Even when we take the view of the scientist we note that certain conditions make for *relatively* more or less freedom for the individual. One of the conditions we are most sure of is self-insight. A therapist of even the most deterministic persuasion assumes that a patient who achieves a high degree of self-objectification, who sees his personal equation clearly written out, is at last in a position to weigh his inclinations, comprehend his limitations, and follow with

some success a self-chosen course of action. If this were not so every system of therapy would operate on false pretense. Psychotherapy gives hope that a corrected self-image, a more rational assessment of one's behavior, will reduce compulsions, induce order, and free channels of development to accord with chosen aims. Hence even a scientific psychology concedes that self-knowledge may lead to a relative freedom.

3. Similarly, relative freedom, we know, depends upon the individual's possession of multiple possibilities for behavior. To state the point paradoxically, a person who harbors many determining tendencies in his neuropsychic system is freer than a person who harbors few. Thus a person having only one skill, knowing only one solution, has only one degree of freedom. On the other hand, a person widely experienced and knowing many courses of conduct has many more degrees of freedom. It is in this sense that the broadly educated man is freer than the man narrowly trained. Today we are witnessing the frightening things that political leaders with one-channeled minds can do. What alarms us is their simplicist view of social and political reality. They know only one solution; and this solution is totalitarian and spurious. Their lack of tolerance and fear of dissent reflect their own lack of freedom. One-channeled minds can never comprehend that truth may have many channels.

4. Finally, psychology knows that there is relatively greater freedom in certain modes of choosing than in others. Man's effort is not particularly effective when he tries to meet an impulse head on, by cracking his knuckles and gritting his teeth. Centering attention upon an impulse often brings with it a strong desire to perform the impulsive act. "The evil I would not, that I do." This law of "reversed effort" is familiar to us all (see Brown, 1929, pp. 150–52). And at this level freedom often seems to be a cruel illusion.

But when I stop cracking my knuckles and become momentarily reflective, asking myself whether "on the whole" this is the course of action I want to take, the picture is changed. The very act of asking "on the whole" brings with it a lessened strain and opens new pathways of decision. This moment of reflection serves to set into activity the larger systems of propriate striving, and their activation may blot out or absorb incompatible segmental systems and impulses, leaving the individual free to be himself.[1]

The psychologist knows that most of the specific acts we per-

<hr>

1. The point at issue here is of considerable theoretical importance. According to psychoanalytic conceptions the defeated impulse is thought to be repressed, and to continue to plague the individual from the limbo of the unconscious. I am suggesting that under certain circumstances—especially when the comprehensive propriate motive holds sway—the incompatible impulses are not normally repressed; they simply evaporate. Freud himself made a similar observation, though he did not follow through its theoretical implications. In a too seldom quoted passage he writes that he has become "mindful of the distinction between the mere *repression* and the true *disappearance* of an old desire or impulse" (my italics) (Freud, 1927, pp. 82 ff.).

form ordinarily proceed in accordance with superordinate systems of motivation. If the superordinate system involves, let us say, a loyalty, then the individual, by calling the system to mind, automatically gives it precedence. Under its dominance decisions follow. The weakness of the habit theory lies in assuming that all acts, by the principles of repetition and reward, are theoretically of equal importance in building the structure of personality. Habits appear and disappear not only in conformity with the principles of frequency and reward but also as subsidiary events in relation to a central or propriate structure. William James hastened to repair his doctrine of habits by affirming that the one ultimate act of freedom at man's disposal is his ability "to keep the selected idea uppermost," by which he meant that when we call upon our self-image we automatically reappraise, inhibit, steer, or activate subordinate courses of conduct. Higher-level systems determine the "go" of the lower, and it is for this reason that man is able to keep as closely as he does to his own major systems of value.

It sometimes happens that the very center of organization of a personality shifts suddenly and apparently without warning. Some impetus, coming perhaps from a bereavement, an illness, or a religious conversion, even from a teacher or book, may lead to a reorientation. In such cases of traumatic recentering it is undoubtedly true that the person had latent within him all of the capacities and sentiments that suddenly rise from a subordinate to a superordinate position in his being. What he had once learned mechanically or incidentally may suddenly acquire heat and liveliness and motor power. What once seemed to him cold, "out there," "not mine" may change places and become hot and vital, "in here," "mine."

I mention this phenomenon of saltatory becoming, not because it is frequent or typical but because it illustrates the complexity and lability of the organizational process. Becoming is not a mere matter of forging links to a chain. It sometimes involves the shifting of dominance from segmental systems to comprehensive systems, or from one comprehensive system to another. Just why or how such shifts occur we cannot say. When they are better understood we can align them with our discussions of determinism and freedom.

These considerations fall short of solving the problem of freedom. They urge us, however, to forego naïve solutions. That there are upper limits to the possibilities of growth in each life no one can deny. But it seems likely that these limits are movable by virtue of the capacities for reflection, for self-objectification, and to a degree by breadth of education, and by the effort an individual may put forth. From the ethical and theological points of view the stretching toward this limit, whatever it is, is as much of a triumph for a life of slight potential as for a life whose potentials are great.

References

Brown, William. *Science and Personality*. Yale University Press, 1929.

Freud, Sigmund. *The Problem of Anxiety*. Norton, 1927.

C. West Churchman

Rational Decision Making

The concept of reason will be forever elusive for mankind, because we can never hope to pin down so important a concept in terms that will be satisfactory forever. The many meanings of reason that we have inherited from our philosophical forebears are inadequate in our present age, and any definition of reason that we attempt to develop now will be unreasonable for the next generations.

Suppose we look at the meaning of these comments carefully, first by discussing some ideas about reason that we have inherited and, second, by considering a somewhat radical idea of what reason could come to mean in our present age.

Of the many meanings given to the concept of reason, perhaps the most predominant in the history of thought has been a definition of reason that has tied it closely to logic.

The general idea here is that reason consists of logical and consistent sets of steps that go from first principles to rigidly derived conclusions. The steps satisfy all the requirements that formal logic imposes on the so-called reasoning process.

This idea has manifested itself in the history of thought in many ways. One of the most fascinating is Spinoza's *Ethics,* which begins with certain axioms about existence and derives therefrom a whole plan of behavior of the human being. Philosophers from time to time have tried to use Spinoza's axiomatic method in developing more up to date and more satisfactory logics that would help man to decide how his life should be conducted. These are called *rational decision-making models*.

Now few would deny that logic forms a very important part of any definition of reason; nevertheless we should realize that logic in no way constitutes the sufficient condition for rationality. We have already seen that formal logic is at best a way of organizing our thinking process, and the organization itself depends on "managerial principles" that are not captured by formal logic. These managerial principles are to be construed as a part of the rational process and logic cannot be considered to provide the whole story. Furthermore, most of us are probably now convinced that formal logic can by no means provide the kind of "starting principles" that Spinoza found satisfactory in the writing of his *Ethics* several centuries ago.

So much for "formal logic." As I say, it cannot provide sufficient content for the meaning of reason.

On the other hand, philosophers have often extended the meaning of logic to cover many things that the formal logician does not consider. Hegel, for example, in his writings in the last century described logic as the whole process of developing an understanding of the world. This idea of logic was captured in his dialectical method. Similarly, scientists often use the term *logic* to refer to the methods by which they reach their conclusions in their empirical investigations, and they frankly confess that these methods go beyond the rigorous principles of formal logic. Indeed, Karl Popper calls one of his books *The Logic of Discovery,* thereby implying that there is an underlying process in the way in which the scientist comes upon new insights, and also implying that formal logic does not capture all there is to say about logic itself.

When logic is used in this more general sense, it becomes difficult to know whether we should identify logic and reason. But we can agree that the extensions of logic as they occur, for example, in Soviet writings, or the present discussions of the logic of discovery, encompass only a part of the process of rational decision making. . . .

On the basis of these remarks, we can also agree that reason is not equivalent to what might be called calculation; for example, the processes carried on by a computer do not express all there is to be said about the concept of reason.

No more is reason to be identified with "thinking" in the sense in which the concept of thinking is used in modern psychology. C. G. Jung in his *Psychological Types* developed the idea that the human mind could be thought of as displaying four functions: thinking, intuition, sensation, and feeling. Here he clearly recognized that reason or rationality is a broader concept than thinking, because he states that both thinking and feeling are "rational" functions. It seems from his book as though he regards thinking to be more closely allied to formal logic or to calculation than is feeling, which, as he describes it, is an evaluating function. Apparently Jung conceived of thinking as the ways in which the mind tries to organize its concepts, while feeling provides the ways in which the mind tries to evaluate the various situations in which it finds itself. On the other hand, Jung does say that sensation and intuition are "nonrational," and in this regard he has gone along with similar kinds of thinking that have occurred in existentialism, in oriental philosophy, and in many other expressions of philosophy in modern days. In all these cases, there has grown up a kind of pride in the antirational, as though the rational represents only a segment of the human life, and as though much is to be said for that part of life which is nonrational or even opposed to reason.

. . . I think such philosophies constitute an unsatisfactory narrowing of the concept of reason. Indeed, the meaning of reason goes beyond any of the so-called functions in Jungian terms; it characterizes the whole of life including the functions of intuition and sensation. Reason has to do with the way in which human beings understand what human life means.

Suppose, instead of discussing further how psychologists and philosophers define reason, we turn to the planners, to the economists, management scientists, and their like. The experiences of these people provide a rich insight into the meaning of reason; maybe the different opinions we will find about the meaning of reason among the planners will provide us with a basis for trying to develop an adequate definition.

In societies with powerful ruling classes it is easy to define rational planning. Reason is taken to be the set of principles that keep the ruling class in power, much as reason in any patriarchal household is the principle that "Father knows best." Reason comes to be the basis of planning as it is dictated by the power elite of a society.

It is this concept of reason, of course, that modern man has repeatedly tried to deny. Instead he has generated a concept of rational planning that arises not from the power elements of a society but from man's own inner convictions.

To develop this idea of rational planning, the management scientists have followed a long tradition in philosophy, economics, and other disciplines, of attempting to set down in a fairly precise way the "rational rules of behavior." The attempt is quite similar to the idea that the meaning of reason is to be found in logic, but now the axioms express rules of behavior rather than rules of dealing with ideas and symbols.

Some management scientists actually believe that certain of these rules of rational behavior are invariant, this is, they will never change no matter how human conditions themselves may change.

They are, in fact, something like the so-called invariant rules of logic which many philosophers in the past believed to be rules of thinking that must apply no matter what the context.

What does such a rational rule of behavior look like? Consider an individual capable of clearly expressing his preferences between certain states of nature. For example, he might be able to say that he prefers listening to a symphony concert to watching a grade-B western movie. He not only says he has this preference, but we will allow for the moment that there is sufficient evidence that this preference, as he has expressed it, is correct, so we know what things he prefers to other things. The rational rules of behavior describe how these preferences should be related one to another.

For example, suppose the individual does prefer symphony concerts to western movies, that is, that he prefers A to B. Next, suppose that he prefers western movies to sitting alone at home at night, so that, for example, if there are no symphony concerts and there is a western movie showing at the corner, he would prefer to go to the movie rather than be left alone to his own devices in his own living room. Let's call being left alone to his own devices in his own living room C. Now we know this much about our hero: he prefers A to B, and he prefers B to C. The rule of behavior in this case states that, if he behaves rationally, he *must* prefer A to C, that is, he must prefer going to a symphony concert over sitting at home alone in his own living room. By the rules of rational behavior, we expect him to voice this preference. But if now we discover that he expresses a preference of C to A, that is, that he prefers sitting alone to going to symphony concerts, then according to the management scientist, such an individual is irrational, or "inconsistent." He is irrational because, although he prefers A to B and B to C, he nonetheless prefers C to A.

Of course the management scientist recognizes that people do display irrational behavior, and indeed in many preference tests that are given, say, in consumer market surveys, customers often show such "irrationalities" when presented with paired comparisons of products. Thus the market surveyor may show product A and B and ask the customer which he prefers, and the consumer will check A. The surveyor later on shows B and C, and the customer checks B. Subsequently the surveyor shows C and A, and the customer "irrationally" checks C. An explantion for this behavior may be easy to find. The customer may have changed his earlier preferences, or he may have really preferred all three equally. The axiom of rational behavior we are considering is not concerned with lapses of memory on the part of the individual, nor is it concerned with inaccurate expressions of preference when the individual is not sure what he really wants. The axiom states that if someone truly prefers A to B and B to C, then it would be irrational of him *truly* to prefer C to A "in the same circumstances at the same time." The need to add specifications to the simple rational rule reminds us of the need to elaborate the "law of contradiction" to the point where the "law" began to lose its meaning.

Other axioms of rational behavior will readily occur to anyone who thinks about the matter. For example, if someone prefers A to B, he should not simultaneously prefer B to A.

Why should we regard such axioms to be rational? And why should we believe that these axioms must hold no matter where the individual may be, no matter what may happen to future generations of man?

In addition to reminding us of the struggles to find the laws of logic, the axioms also recall attempts to define moral precepts such as one finds in the Ten Commandments. "Thou shalt not lie" is a precept that was supposed to classify all behavior of a certain kind as immoral and therefore, presumably, irrational. The Ten Commandments are therefore ten necessary conditions for determining whether conduct is rational. Such moral precepts are with us today, but few management scientists would say that these older offerings constitute a reliable basis for defining rational decision making. We have come to suspect that each Commandment has its exceptions, and that unless these exceptions are carefully listed and founded on more fundamental concepts of reasoning, there is no justification for accepting any Commandment by itself as a partial definition of rational behavior. Thus most of us believe that it is perfectly all right to lie or kill on occasion, especially when lying or killing will increase the probability of our own survival or of our nation's survival.

Some philosophers have attempted to overcome the difficulties of rigorous rules of moral conduct by suggesting more "basic" principles, such as the principle that every man ought to preserve his own happiness, but now the rule is far too vague to apply. Furthermore, the rule does not even seem to be valid in cases where a person prefers to sacrifice his happiness for the sake of some more desirable goal, for example, the safety of his loved ones. For this reason the management scientists have tried to seek more basic principles of rational conduct.

One of the more fascinating developments of principles of rational conduct has occurred in *game theory*—a theory that tries to describe rational conduct in the context of conflict. It sets forth "rational" rules governing "fair play" and tries to discover optimal strategies that can be followed by an individual when he is facing his opponent in a situation governed by certain recognizable rules.

The reader will readily find two very serious objections to the management scientist's approach to rational decision making. On the one hand, he will come to feel that even though it may be true that these axioms define rational behavior, nevertheless they cover so little of practical importance that their contribution to the meaning of rationality is very small indeed.

For example, we would all like to know the rational way of solving some of the persistent international problems of our day. We would also like to be able to recognize rational urban and regional development plans. We would like to know how to allocate our water resources. We would like to know how rationally to design our educational systems, and so on. It doesn't seem to help us a great deal to know that if we prefer A to B and B to C, then A is preferred to C. Also, it does not seem to help us very much to follow the rules prescribed by game theory. These rules still leave so much open that they hardly seem sufficient to provide a basis for planning.

Nevertheless, this objection in some sense misses the point. What the management scientists are saying is that if we are able to collect reliable information concerning preferences, then by means of the axioms of rational behavior, we will be able to identify *the* set of optimal plans. In other words, the axioms of rational behavior provide the way of processing the basic information for rational plans, provided that information concerning preferences is available.

A more serious objection to the management scientist's notion of rational behavior is to question whether these axioms of rational behavior tell us anything at all. Indeed, they may simply follow from their own definition of preference. The question therefore is whether their definition of preference is a suitable basis for defining rationality. It is much as though the management scientist were telling us that this is how preference "ought rationally" to be defined, without his attempting at all to justify his own beliefs. And indeed in many of tion of the authors to use their own personal attitudes as a justifica- the writings of the management scientists one finds a strong inclina- tion of what they say about the rules of rational behavior. What they are saying is that if a man prefers A to B according to *their* concept of preference, and B to C according to their concept of preference, then he must prefer A to C according to their concept of preference. They are not telling us whether their concept of preference is a suitable one.

How could one object to the management scientists' concept of preference? Why, one could object to it because one might find it completely irrelevant with respect to the notions of rationality. We have been repeatedly hinting in this discourse that rationality has to do with goals as well as the means of the attainment of goals. But the concept of rationality as expressed in the rules of behavior mentioned above tells us nothing about whether the goals are rational or irrational. Indeed, these rules of behavior are as applicable to the policies of a criminal or a dictator as they are to the policies of an enlightened society. They would tell a criminal the best way to rob a house; they would tell a dictator the best way to eliminate a minority group; in each case the optimal way to evil is to act "in accordance with rational rules of behavior." Indeed, if preference is used in such a broad way as the so-called rules of rational behavior imply, it is doubtful whether preference so used has anything to do with rational planning.

For this reason, . . . it seems desirable to introduce into the concept of rationality other considerations than a mere preference ordering.

These considerations have to do with the meaning of Nature itself. The idea here is that Nature "expresses" a type of rationality and that we should seek to discover what is the rational in Nature so that each may adapt what he had found to his own behavior. Of all the places that men may seek to find clues concerning the rationality of Nature, perhaps the best is in the behavior of the members of the living species. The rationality of an insect, of a bacterium, of an animal, expresses some aspect of the total rationality of Nature itself.

Hence scientists have attempted to explore the nature of the living to gain thereby some clues concerning the way in which human lives can be rationally conducted. In some cases, they have also explored the nature of the nonliving—the physical universe—to search for clues concerning rationality. Thereby in recent years we have been exposed to cybernetics, in which the "well-adjusted" physical system becomes the prototype of all living rational behavior.

This theory of rationality made a lot of sense to the biologists of the nineteenth and the twentieth centuries. It also makes sense to today's evolutionary industrial theorists. Modern industry began with very crude machinery, crudely operated. After a while men learned how to build better machines, but they neglected the living standards of the worker. After a while they were forced to recognize the worker's claims, but they couldn't determine how to use him efficiently. Along came industrial engineering and efficiency went up. Along came automation, and it went up even more. Along came operations research and management science and even greater refinements were introduced. At each stage we redeveloped our notion of rational industrialization. Today we don't hesitate to say that the manager who ignores worker rights or uses old methods of manufacturing is "backward," that is, "irrational." We think he is backward or irrational because what he is doing comes earlier in the evolutionary process of industrialization than what is now done. Hence our use of terms like "underdeveloped nations." We all expect that the industrial leaders and scientists of a generation hence will consider us to be backward. How irrational our methods will appear to the inhabitants of the twenty-third century!

It's all very happy thinking, this evolutionary concept of rationality, but it also has much about it that seems naïve. At times the whole philosophy appears to be saying that any change is a good change, even if automation leads many citizens into economic disaster, even if technology destroys individual creativeness, even if science blows us all to our doom. Get on with the industrial evolution regardless of where it leads us, at all costs! Whatever change is proposed, do it!

Can we really expect that "Nature" will provide us with the clues of rationality? Isn't this way of putting the matter absurd? It assumes that Nature is a kind of Great Mother, who, if we listen to her carefully, will provide us with the lessons that we need to conduct our lives correctly. There is no question, of course, that in the popular discussions of science people do talk about Nature in exactly this way, and psychologists would probably have no difficulty in pointing out that the people who do talk this way are much influenced by some kind of mother complex. Game theorists, for example, often describe experimentations as a "game with Nature," as though Mother Nature sat across a board and made certain moves, which were then observed by the experimenter, who then tried to cope with Mother Nature's moves in some appropriate rational fashion. It may be that we learn from Nature a great deal, but the lesson of Immanuel Kant should never be forgotten, that whatever rationality we may "find" in Nature, we have put there ourselves, simply because Nature is our own creation. It is in fact our description of what the largest system is like.

I said at the outset I would try out a more radical approach to the meaning of reason. Naturally this is done with all the hesitations that go along with radical approaches. This approach at best can only be regarded as a kind of working hypothesis. It is a suggestion based on much . . . about the ethics of the whole system. When discussing management and science, I kept saying to myself over and over again that science could be looked at as a kind of management, or that management could be looked at as a kind of science. Saying that science can become a way of managing didn't imply automation or any other form of mechanical decision making, because none of this is science. Science is the creative discovery of knowledge. Management science is the process of trying to look at science as a management function. Similarly, management can be looked at as a scientific function, that is, as a way of finding out about the world.

. . . Reason is the process by which man is able to look at himself, but it should be added that the way anything can look at itself is through a series of frameworks. The conclusion is that a social institution becomes rational to the extent that it can be considered to function like some other institution. Thus management becomes rational to the extent that it can be viewed as science, and science becomes rational to the extent that it can be viewed as management. So, too, for the other important social institutions. Religion becomes rational to the extent that it can be viewed as a science, or as a management. And management becomes rational again in the way in which it can be viewed as a religion. The evolution of the rationality of politics will also include the development of politics as a science, as a management, as a religion, as an educational system. Hence what has been said on the well-informed public turns out to be a proposal to make politics more of an educational system, that is, to develop a political life of our society in which politics will create the well-informed public.

Much needs to be said to make this idea of rationality clearer and more convincing. It is an idea that borrows from the philosophy of reason in Nature, but tries to overcome the more passive aspects of evolutionary philosophy. It says that man becomes more rational to the extent that he becomes reflective. But reflection is not merely a "looking inward"; it is not a direct self-examination. Rather, the rationality of reflection comes from using as much of the world, or the "whole system," as one possibly can to understand oneself.

If we say that the manager should think of himself as a scientist, we do not mean that he should try to become a scientist according to today's standards. For today's science is not reflective: it has a very narrow view of what it is. Today's science is not very rational. But if management could be considered as a science, then management would change, and so would science. Both would become more rational. The way in which management can be viewed as science opens up our eyes to the deeper meanings of science.

It is impossible to determine the rationality of conduct in one framework alone, as those who try to develop basic axioms of rational behavior attempt to do. Nor is rational conduct simply a development along certain prescribed lines, as evolutionary theory suggests. The test of the rationality of an institution, or a company, or a person, is the determination of the manner in which X functions as Y, and the way in which Y functions as X. For something to be able to look at itself, it must look at itself as though it were something other. What is not explained is the meaning of "function as." What is entailed in "considering" management as science, or science as management? In the end, the answer will probably be "I'm not sure."

Kenneth D. Benne

Case Methods in the Training of Administrators

Some image of the social role of the administrator is required in order to assess the uses and limitations of case methods in the training of persons to perform the role. My delineation of the role must be brief.

The administrator in any organization with work to perform must simultaneously meet two sets of organizational requirements in any decision he is called upon to make. One set of requirements may be called system *task* requirements. The other set may be named system *building* and *maintenance* requirements (see Benne and Sheats, 1948, pp. 42–47). The *task* requirements look to the effective organization of interdependent effort in and around the system in order to meet its production goals and, in an industrial establishment, its sales and distribution goals as well. The *building* and *maintenance* requirements have to do with keeping the interpersonal, interdepartmental, and public relations of the social system in good repair and in improving these where they need improvement.

Task and building-maintenance requirements in an organization do not always jibe, though both are important. The technically soundest change in a method of production, fully justified from the point of view of task effectiveness, may, if introduced by an administrator without adequate attention to the maintenance requirements of the organization, result in deepened and irrational tensions within the internal and external relationships of the organization, and in increased suspicion and distrust among personnel that may disrupt both the communication and power-authority systems in the plant. On the other hand, an administrator, seeking only to create a "happy" crew within and a "happy" public outside the organization, may jeopardize the task effectiveness previously achieved by the organization and thwart further improvements in task effectiveness. Both sets of requirements must be served and reconciled simultaneously in adequate administrative judgments and actions.

Exerpted from "Case Methods in the Training of Administrators," Boston University Human Relations Center Research Reports and Technical Notes, Number 28. Reprinted by permission.

Actually, the human situation in which the role of the administrator is embedded is more complex than this analysis suggests. The requirements of the confronting situation upon the administrator in his role are communicated to him through the expectations of people —persons and groups—whom he perceives to be significant in his environment—"significant others" as the social philosopher George Mead called them. And his perceptions, both of which others are significantly to be taken into account in his judgments and of what their expectations with respect to his conduct are, are subject to all the distortions, conscious and unconscious, to which human perception generally is subject. The expectations, as he perceives these, stemming from his board, from his subordinate managers, from employees, from customers, from unions, from his own ideal image of an administrator, from other administrators in his professional group, these and others—varied, often conflicting—play upon him in the actual definition of his administrative role judgments and behaviors.

This view of the human situation of the administrator in its determination of his judgments and conduct raises a whole series of questions about the training he needs, in addition to the more familiar questions concerning the knowledges and skills required with respect to technical processes of production, sales, and distribution. How sensitive is the administrator to the complex of interrelated human forces and factors in his working situations? How accurate are his perceptions of the actual demands and expectations of the various reference groups and persons that he must take into account in making his practical judgments? How able is he to gather relevant and accurate information from observing, talking with, and listening to the people with and through whom he must work? How well can he set priorities in stepwise planning for conflict resolution, reconciling factors of urgency and importance in his judgments? How flexible is he in adapting his strategy of intervention in the processes of his organization to changing demands and conditions without impairing the integrity of his own value system and role image? How aware is he of his own motivations—which, if unknown to him, may cloud his judgments, often deluding himself more than others around him? How well can be translate his judgments of what he needs to do into actual behavior consistent with these judgments? Do his skills of timing and intervention square with his diagnostic judgments of the changing requirements of his situation? Can he hold multiple and conflicting factors, forces, and requirements in mind as he judges, acts, and evaluates the effects of his judgments and actions?

It is training questions such as these that have led many of those responsible for administrative training and development to turn to case methods of instruction to supplement or to supplant more traditional methods of educating administrative leaders. This shift has been due both to dissatisfactions of practicing administrators with the effectiveness of their traditional training in equipping them to answer affirmatively such questions as above, and to the fact that traditional methods were not designed primarily to answer the kinds of training questions indicated.

The questions fall logically into two general classes. The first class of questions has to do with the arts of *diagnosing* administrative situations (including the self of the administrator), arts involving observation, listening, analysis and assessment of forces and factors, and prediction of trends, potentialities, and valid directions. The second class has to do with the arts of *intervention* and *participation* in the situation as diagnosed, arts involving strategic planning, manipulation of forces and factors, behavior and action. In brief, administrators require training in the combined and interrelated arts of *observation* and *participation* in the setting of the organizational systems they administer.

Traditional methods of administrator training have erred in two principal ways. First, they have understressed the arts of diagnosing action situations in terms of their manageability and changeability. Second, they have tended to separate diagnostic training from prescriptive training on how to act in particular practical situations. Some of the important conceptual tools for use in diagnosis have been taught traditionally in departmentalized courses in the humanities, particularly history, and, more recently, in the behavioral sciences— psychology, sociology, economics (often not taught as a behavioral science), and anthropology. But the learning of these conceptual tools has not typically been hooked up in the educational process to concrete decision situations where historical, psychological, sociological, economic, and anthropological variables are complexly intertwined and need to be seen and weighed in their interrelations for purposes of adequate situational diagnosis. Nor, typically, have administrators been taught to see the operational meanings of these concepts in terms of directly observable clusters of symptomatic behaviors and patterns of immediate experience.

Training in strategies of action, participation, and intervention, where formalized, has tended to take the form of rules of conduct and principles of method, taught apart from the diagnosis of actual situations in and to which rules and methods must be adapted and applied. Some "average" situation is assumed in the prescriptions proffered by the trainer, though the administrator always must act in a unique, never in an "average," situation. This assumption of an "average" or "normal" situation has prevailed in much "practical" training in how to do this or that—how to delegate, how to discipline a subordinate, and so on. Prescriptive training has typically been undertaken apart from the diagnosis of concrete and unique situations, however necessary such diagnosis is for any intelligent determination of what rules of action or strategy are appropriate and applicable and of what adaptations of general rules needs to be made. Where action training has been undertaken exclusively through apprenticeship in actual work situations, it has been difficult for the trainee to get the degree of detachment and freedom necessary for achieving generalizable learnings through making "mistakes" and analyzing and evaluating these, in terms of both their "diagnostic" and their "action" adequacies and inadequacies. The actual work situation sets more or less drastic limits to "experimental" and potentially "mistaken" behavior, however necessary such behavior may be for adequate learning.

In its most general sense, what do "case methods" involve? Case methods involve the confrontation of people in training with concrete human situations, situations with some temporal and developmental span, in which a whole complex of determinants of behavior are at work. Trainees are asked to diagnose these situations, to analyze them in terms of why events happen as they do, why the people involved act as they do. If the trainees are asked to prescribe and test verbally alternative behaviors for managing the situation confronted, they are asked to do so in terms of the diagnosis made, of the evidence available as to the dynamics of the situation, including the dynamics of the "manager" in it. Diagnosis and prescription are thus tied together in any adequate case analysis.

What typical forms has "case method," in this general sense, taken in its American development? And what are the virtues and limitations of these various forms in relation to the requirements upon administrator training outlined above?

1. One form of case is a printed description of some actual organizational behavior in which an administrator takes part (see Andrews, 1951, and Roethlisberger, 1954). When a trainee analyzes such a case in a group setting—as it should always be analyzed for full training effect—he discovers the variety and complexity of factors that function in an actual situation to determine what happens in it. He discovers also the differences between his viewpoint, which assumes some implicit or explicit schema of human motivation and social determination, and the viewpoints of others in the group. He may thus discover gaps and inconsistencies in his own diagnostic apparatus, blindspots to certain kinds of factors and forces, overweightings of some kinds of variables as compared with others, projections of subjective interpretations which he finds it difficult to distinguish from the "objective" evidence presented, etc. And, if the case discussions are well conducted, he may, over time, broaden his

repertoire of diagnostic schemes and acquire some of the attitudes required for dependable and accurate diagnosis—suspension of judgment, acceptance of variety in people and situations, and humility before the complexities of organizational, group, and individual behavior. These are good in training for the administrative skills of participant-observation.

2. But cases studied in this way are still "out there" so far as the trainee is concerned—away from his own responsibility for moving from diagnostic judgments to action as part of a changing and developing situation. One adaptation of case method designed to open up a trainee's own processes of practical judgment to self-examination (and, hopefully, improvement) has been called the incident-process method (Pigors, 1954). This method was devised by Paul Pigors as a tool for training industrial managers. It involves the confrontation of trainees with a critical incident in the human relations of an organization—an incident requiring adjudication and decision. Originally, Pigors used actual arbitration cases as subject matter. The situation is briefly presented. The training group must decide what further information it needs in order to make a decision. Further information is available but the trainer who has it will furnish any part of it only if asked specifically by the group for that part. Individual decisions are written after the group has gathered information seen as needed and has discussed it. These decisions are presented publicly and debated with pressure toward a common decision. The group then hears the official decision and analyzes where and why its fact-finding and fact interpretation processes fell short.

This method moves the trainees closer to self-examination of actual decision-making processes and may, therefore, be used to diagnose and improve processes of practical administrative judgment. But again, the behavior, the action, of the trainee based upon such judgments is not brought to the point of behavioral testing and of subsequent analysis of behavioral consequences. The behavior analyzed is the behavior of someone else, the situation judged is a situation of which the trainee, strictly speaking, is not a part, though his own thinking about this situation is pressed toward closure, made public, and analyzed. Diagnosis and judgment are still separated, from the point of view of training, from the shape and testing of one's own actual behavior in a situation based on one's own accompanying diagnosis and judgment of that situation.

3. A case method designed for action-training by J. L. Moreno has sought to bridge this gap. This method, originally named sociodrama, has been elaborated by others under the different names of reality-practice, role-playing, and participative case method (Moreno, 1946; 1953). A problematic situation is presented to or invented by

the trainees, and some trainees are asked, not to talk about the situation, but to assume parts (roles) of people in it and to enact the developing situation toward some sort of resolution. Other trainees as well as the trainer observe the actual behavior as dramatically developed. Observations are made public along with inner feelings and thoughts of the actors. Faults in diagnosis, faults in action on diagnosis, discrepancies between diagnoses and actions are located and clarified through analysis and discussion. The same or analogous situations may be re-practiced to test the analysis and to retrain both the diagnoses and actions of the participants. This method brings processes of diagnosis and action into close relationship within the training process. It brings the trainee's own behavior and actions into the open for analysis and guided practice. It thus moves toward the ideal of training of the administrator as actor-judger or participant-observer. But the situation is still not completely "real"—the players are acting but they are enacting a character which is at least in part some one else in a situation which is in a measure projected beyond or outside the actual training situation. Many of their own personal projections into the role played are revealed in the action and analyzed in the analysis of the action. But the situation is still a make-believe one.

4. A further refinement of case method requires members of a group of trainees to analyze their own actual behavior in a group situation as a living example of an organization in process of development (Benne; Bennis; National Training Laboratories). The task of the group must be sufficiently undefined, its procedures sufficiently unprescribed and unroutinized, to permit and require members to reveal their own behavior as participant-observers and actor-judgers for public observation and analysis as they struggle to organize the life and production of the group. The case in this form is not "out there" as it happened or is happening to some one else. The self of the trainee is in it, a part of it, revealing its characteristic patterns of relating to and dealing with itself, with superiors, peers, and subordinates for analysis by the trainee, with the reactions of others to his own behavior and his reactions to the behavior of others as part of the data for testing and analysis. Such training has been shown to lead in many instances to effective transfer to a variety of practical administrative situations outside the protected environment of the "laboratory" group. What is transferred seems to be not alone the particular substantive skills of diagnosis-action actually practiced and learned in the training group. A method of learning through participant-observation is also transferred to the work situation so that on-the-job growth by the administrator can continue with some measure of commitment and discipline achieved to support this continuation of growth.

In summary, an analysis of the role of the administrator has emphasized his responsibility for helping the people in and around the social system of an enterprise to meet more adequately and collaboratively the task and building-maintenance requirements of that enterprise. This role image emphasizes the understandings, values, and skills of participant-observer, of judger-actor, as essential to its effective performance. But the skills of observation and of participation, of diagnostic judgment and of action must be learned in relation to each other if role behavior is to be effectively trained. Traditional methods of administrator training have understressed the development of diagnostic judgment and have tended to separate diagnostic from action training. Case methods that involve the confrontation of trainees with a concrete, complex behavioral situation for analysis (diagnosis, judgment, and prescription) have been developed to meet these faults in traditional training. A spectrum of case methods, all with demonstrated usefulness in administrator training, has been reviewed, with the degree of the trainee's own personal involvement and participation in the case to be analyzed as the chief dimension of difference.

References

Andrews, Kenneth. *Case Methods of Teaching Human Relations and Administration.* Harvard University Press, 1951.

Benne, Kenneth D. "Comments on Training Groups." Paper obtainable on request from Boston University Human Relations Center and to appear as part of a book to be published by the National Training Laboratories, National Education Association, Washington, D. C.

————, and Paul Sheats. "Functional Roles of Group Members." *Journal of Social Issues,* Vol. 4, 1948.

Bennis, Warren G. "Patterns and Vicissitudes in Training Groups." Paper obtainable on request from Boston University Human Relations Center and to appear as part of a book to be published by the National Training Laboratories, National Education Association, Washington, D. C.

Moreno, J. L. *Who Shall Survive?* Beacon House, 1953.

————. *Psychodrama,* Vol. 1. Beacon House, 1946.

National Training Laboratories. *Explorations in Human Relations Training: An Assessment of Experience, 1947–1953.* National Education Association, Washington, D. C.

Pigors, P. and F. "Case Methods on the Spot." *Adult Leadership,* Vol. 3, No. 6, 1954.

Roethlisberger, Fritz. "Training for Human Relations: An Interim Report of a Program for Advanced Training and Research in Human Relations." Harvard University Division of Research, Graduate School of Business Administration, 1954.

Herbert A. Shepard

The T-Group as Training in Observant Participation

Value Premises and Training Goals

The trainer's primary responsibilities are to facilitate the development of valid communication in the group and to help members make explicit the processes of that development. The purpose of the former is to provide to members the experience of working in a group with a high potential for member satisfaction and problem solving; the purpose of the latter is to ensure that members profit from the experience by gaining skill in observant participation so that they can improve the productive potential of other groups in which they participate.

Thus development of the group towards valid communication is not an end in itself: it is part of the training method for improving skills in observant participation. By skills in observant participation are meant the abilities not only to act but also to monitor the action and accurately assess its consequences for the actor in relation to the others, and for the group in relation to its goals. The skills are easier to describe than to learn. Barriers to learning are produced by the process of socialization. Maturation in any society entails learning to ignore certain matters just as it entails learning to notice certain things. Such analyses as Riesman's (1950) point to preoccupation with the consequences of action in terms of individual goals—popularity or power—and inattention to consequences in terms of collaborative achievement. Cultural emphasis on individualism, that is, on the dangers of risking one's reputation on another's judgment, reduces potential for cooperating and sharing responsibility. In a culture that makes personal isolation synonymous with personal autonomy, T-group training means the reawakening of painful processes which gave rise to present patterns of interpersonal adaptation.

The ultimate value premise underlying the T-group is one which also underlies scientific work, namely, that it is a good thing to know what you are doing. The trainee should come to have a better under-

From *Theory of Training*, Massachusetts Institute of Technology Series. Used by permission.

standing of what takes place between himself and others; he should be able better to assess the consequences for himself and others of actions that he is moved to take; and with this enhanced alertness a wider range of action alternatives should become available to him. In short, he should gain greater control over his external and internal communication.

Knowledge of what one is doing is never complete, but there are plateaus of understanding coordinate with degrees of self-acceptance. The T-group has a limited potency. More modestly, then, its purpose is to increase understanding, possibly at the risk of certain defenses of the self; while providing a richer basis for self-estccm coupled with apperceptive habits for understanding more fully. The T-group training should enable the member to see more, and to use what he sees constructively for himself and others.

Valid Communication as a Training Objective

The term "valid communication" can be understood by identifying two organic properties of individuals and groups: their components are living and in communication. If a person is to "know what he is doing," the "components" of the person must come to be in non-distorting communicative relations with one another and with the environment. A person's communication with self and others is often characterized by what Sullivan (1947) called "selective inattention," whereby he quite consistently overlooks certain aspects of what transpires. For example, he may by gesture or tonal quality, or modal behavior patterns, tell others more than he intends, or something more than or other than, he tells himself.

Groups are also capable of selective inattention. For example, member involvement in what is apparently a mutually enlightening discussion of leadership theory may be motivated by a need to influence the trainer, or may constitute a fight for dominance among some of the members. In other words, the activity of the group tells the observer something more than or other than, it tells the members. Like a person, the group has cause for such oversights. Recognition of these other aspects of group activity would destroy some operating assumptions about the character of mutual relations in the group, assumptions that are needed for the maintenance of a reasonable degree of comfort.

Valid communication in a group is associated with the absence of such phenomena as selective inattention. More positively, valid communication refers to such states as the following: the member's perception of his relation to the group and of the effects of his action on the group are in accord with other members' perceptions of these things; the announced purpose of an activity corresponds with the efforts being made by members. Conditions necessary for valid communication appear to be the existence of sufficient mutual acceptance and identification among members that feelings about any issue arising in the group can be expressed and accepted.

Characterization of valid communication by the statement that the announced purpose of an activity corresponds with the efforts being made by members matches Sullivan's (1947) description of mental health for the person, namely, that the self becomes co-extensive with the personality. In this sense, one might speak of T-group training as therapy of the group as a human entity, to be distinguished from "group therapy" for the individuals in the group.

The Trainer's Role

The trainer's major responsibility is to help the group identify and overcome obstacles to valid communication. For this task, his own skills of observant participation are his principal resource. Any set of rules for trainer behavior would have to be bound by many conditional statements. Moreover, experience has not progressed far enough to validate any system. Hence, adherence to a doctrine is likely to prove as unserviceable to trainer and group as does adherence by a trainee to the imperatives of social relations that he brings to the group.

However, certain features of the training situation should be borne in mind by the trainer as guides to action. The first is his role as a projective figure for the group. During the early meetings he appears to be the group's *raison d'être:* most members see no other cause for meeting and no other force restraining them from leaving. Members' conscious and unconscious fantasies about the trainer are the major determinants of group activity. Most members feel that the trainer is observing them keenly; they may describe themselves as guinea pigs. In fact, however, it is the behavior of the trainer that receives careful scrutiny. His face is studied for obscure messages, his place in the seating arrangement noted, his cigarette consumption watched. His remarks are carefully attended to and judged unintelligible. He is an object of love and hate, of oppression and protection, of desertion and impotence, and his importance to the group is vigorously denied and affirmed.

From this it follows that the trainer can be quite sure of being misunderstood in a variety of ways. But the knowledge that he will be misunderstood gives him no license: what he does and how he does it are important. Misunderstanding one's situation is a most reliable means of avoiding learning. Assuming that there are a number of things the trainees would have learned before now had it been safe to do so, some protective misunderstanding is to be expected. A large part of the trainee's task is to sort those of his reactions which are based on misunderstanding from those which are based on accurate perception. For that task, the trainer's behavior is of considerable importance. If the trainee tends to project certain kinds of unacceptable motivations and activities on a certain class of other persons, and if the trainer is in that class, it will simplify the trainee's task if the trainer's behavior does not provide objective confirmation of the trainee's misgivings. Projection of undesirable features on the trainer is one thing; production of undesirable features by the trainer is another. This does not mean that the trainer should be a paragon of virtue; only that he should be free to choose whether to act in accordance with his impulses, and that he make his choice with the group's welfare in mind.

In particular, the trainer should avoid exploiting or being victimized by the dependency and counterdependency needs of members. This rule places severe restrictions on the trainer's freedom of action. For example, even reflecting an individual's statement in a group setting may be an unfortunate act. It singles out the individual for response by the trainer, legitimizes his fantasy of uniqueness, and assures him that a special bond exists between himself and the trainer. Similarly, a supportive statement by the trainer may confirm the member's worst suspicions about himself—namely, that his survival depends on the support of more powerful persons.

The existence of dependency phenomena implies that, in general, the trainer should not treat the group members as "individuals." It implies that his contributions should be largely restricted to comments directed to the group about the group. How then can the trainer respond to individual appeals? He may ask whether the question is a matter of concern to the whole group. If he receives an affirmative response, it becomes a group appeal, and can be responded to. If he receives a negative response, other members will relieve him of the necessity for carrying the matter further. Or he may explicitly assume that the member's statement is representative of, or on behalf of, an effective segment of the group. These may not be the only, or the most appropriate alternatives. The point is that he should be aware of the disservice he can do the group member by responding inappropriately. It is difficult to avoid either the dependency seduction or the counterdependency trap, and the counterdependent's charge that the trainer "won't tell us anything" or "won't give a straight answer" often contains a grain of truth because of the trainer's difficulties in finding an appropriate way of responding to individual appeals and challenges.

Through the portion of group life when the trainer is the focus of dependency and counterdependency needs of members, he has a certain range of choice regarding the extent to which these needs are to be highlighted and made the subject of special experiential and theoretical consideration. The personality and training philosophy of the trainer, as well as the professional needs of the group members, determine his interest in introducing or avoiding explicit considera- tion of dependency, and this in turn has much to do with his method of opening a T-group. Trainers who do not wish dependency and authority problems to be given special emphasis provide the protec- tion usually given by authority figures without demanding the usual price of that protection, namely, control over member behavior. Trainers who would emphasize dependency neither provide protec- tion nor seek to control.

The trainer who provides protection without demanding control may arouse feelings of guilt so that the group tries to outguess him and carry out his desires, but as the group gains in cohesiveness, the trainer can drop any paternalistic elements in his role and reduce the guilt and concern with pleasing him.

The trainer who violates expectations of protection, however, arouses hostility which can be readily turned against himself. He gives the group no reward for efforts to please him. Moreover, he withholds protection when the group is confronted with a situation full of uncertainties, and thus is responsible for creating an anxious situation. Rather than being a permissive leader, he is a leader who fails. Needless to say, the authority-dependency-counterdependency problem comes into sharp focus.

Both of these training modes produce a power gap, so that a leadership struggle usually ensues among the group members. It is possible that members who seek to control the group receive more punishment from the other members if the trainer has been a permis- sive leader. Although hostility aroused by the leader who fails may be expressed in intermember combat, there is, so to speak, a natural tendency for it to be directed against the trainer himself, and he can, with the exercise of a little skill, assist nature.

Trainer dependency and power struggle die away together, since they are aspects of the same problem. The end of this phase is usually symbolized by some ritual of acceptance of the trainer as member. After this point, power considerations are less frequently sources of distortion in communication, and the central issues become those of intimacy, trust, and sharing responsibility.

The keynote of the T-group is interpersonal uncertainty, and training is learning to reduce uncertainty by consensual validation of experience. The ambiguity of the trainee's relationship to the trainer accounts for only part of the interpersonal uncertainty, and attention is focussed on this relationship only as long as the trainer is seen as the major source of reward or punishment. The logic appears to be that if a particular kind of relationship can be established with the trainer, the trainee need not be concerned about the rest of the group. When this possibility evaporates, the trainee is likely to become alarmed. The intensity with which dangers of being engulfed by the group, of losing his personal identity, of enforced conformity are felt by the trainee is in a way a measure of his self-acceptance, or lack of it. Thus, when the central issues are interdependence and responsibility sharing, members may feel their self-esteem and "integrity" threatened by the group.

Neither in his relations with the trainer nor in his relations with other members, however, is the trainee likely to consider consensual validation a feasible method of reducing interpersonal uncertainty. The reasons for this are twofold; first, the trainee may fear that his real feelings and view of the situation would not be shared by other members, especially if his real feelings are already threatening to his self-esteem. Hence, to communicate them might make his situation worse. Second, the group culture is both a consequence and cause of this reticence on the part of members. It is, typically, a denial of members' real feelings. Instead of consensual validation, a number of other methods for reducing uncertainty are adopted by the group, and the adoption of these methods by the group implies to each member that his feelings are not shared by the others. The alternative methods of reducing uncertainty are, broadly speaking, efforts to transform perceptions or efforts to transform the situation, or both. Perceptual transformations involve classifying the experience as something familiar and either irrelevant to or supportive of self-esteem: such descriptive terms as "boring," "unreal," "fascinating" or "bull session" represent efforts at reclassification. Attempts to transform the situation include adopting Robert's rules of order, efforts to make the trainer take an "instructor" role, inviting in experts, and undertaking to split or fragment the group (by adjournment, scapegoating of members, coffee breaks, fighting, voting, buzz-grouping, etc.)

Obviously the trainer will not be of service to the group by actively contributing to the construction of these transformations. But since they are necessary collaborative moves to avoid anxiety, he can only complicate the situation by confronting the group with a threatening interpretation. In other words, neither rewarding behavior nor punishing behavior is appropriate. All that the trainer seeks is that group members have a better understanding of why certain events took place, of what made the events necessary. Moreover, the trainer should avoid being caught up in individualistic delusions in his own understanding of the group movement; that is, he should avoid scapegoating any members, which is one of the group's favorite methods of avoiding responsibility.

Given these considerations, there are a number of constructive roles that the trainer may take. One of these is clarification of the group's problem. Another is an estimate of possible consequences of present activity. A third is summarizing what appear to be different orientations expressed by various segments of the group. A fourth is uncovering group-shared hidden agenda—but this requires the most painstaking examination of possible consequences, since it is the most powerful method available to the trainer.

It should be borne in mind that whatever the trainer does during the dependency phase is likely to be misapprehended—his statements will appear weak and ineffectual to dependent members, obstructive and confusing to counterdependent members. They are likely to be treated as incomprehensible, or apparently ignored. When this happens, it is tempting to think that they were just poorly timed, or poorly phrased, or that they were wrong, or "too far ahead" of the group. Quite often, however, they have considerable private significance to some group members, but the terms on which these members are integrated with one another at the moment preclude shared consideration of the trainer's statement—not necessarily in the sense that *any* statement of the trainer's must be ignored, but that consideration of this particular statement would alter the terms under which they are collaborating.

The problems of the trainer's role are only the problems of any group membership role, with certain added complications. One of these derives from the trainer's prior commitment to the group: he retains a strong sense of responsibility for what happens throughout all phases of the training. The fact that he has, realistically, relatively little control over some of the things that may happen, simply means that he is more like other group members than he or they sometimes think. The other special complications of the trainer's role are the expectations and projections of group members, which are strongly focussed on him during at least part of the group life. These expectations and projections are the major distinctive features of the trainer's role. In some ways they make the trainer exceptionally powerful; in other ways they greatly restrict his effectiveness.

These characteristics of the trainer role must also be taken into account in his contacts with group members outside the group meetings. As might be expected, one of the commonest out-of-meeting situations confronting the trainer is the dependent member seeking a private, exploitative relationship. However, forces other than dependency may cause a trainee to seek a private relationship with the trainer. The important principles for the trainer to bear in mind are that all private relationships involving segments of the group create communicative confusion in the group, and that the centrality of the trainer's role means that his concealed involvements are especially disconcerting. This consideration has led some trainers to establish a rule of no communication with members outside the meeting. In the usual laboratory environment, the objection to this rule is that it is impossible to obey. An amendment to the effect that the trainer will not discuss the T-group outside meetings is a false remedy, since the relationship rather than the subject matter—the process rather than the content—is what concerns the trainee.

A more workable rule is that significant trainer-member or member-member relationships outside the meetings be discussed in the group as soon as it becomes feasible to do so, since they are likely to be crucial elements of process and a basis for generalization about group relations. For example, if the process of communicating back-home status and presenting other credentials is not done at the meeting, it will inevitably be done outside the meeting as a way of discovering subgroups into which to escape, and it is important to make the existence of this process explicit at the group meeting.

The rule that significant outside relationships should be discussed in the meetings does not provide an answer to all questions that can be raised about trainer-member relations. The trainer's desire to examine such relationships in the meetings should be made explicit to members, but the initiative, as well as the timing, should rest with them. A member may have been unable to form any attachments in the group to relieve intense anxiety, and sought out the trainer as a last resort. The trainer would only increase the member's distress by exposing the relationship before the latter is ready. It is possible, but unlikely, that the member will be unable to bring up the matter in the group at any time. Similarly, the trainer may sometimes take the initiative in seeking out a member where the group's development or the member's integrity has been seriously threatened by events in the meeting. This is a matter of the trainer's judgment in predicting events that will probably occur if he does not intervene privately to prevent the immobilization of the group or member. In the sadder cases, where his judgment was not adequate to the situation, the trainer may have to seek out members privately to begin the process of restoring working relationships in the group after an unfortunate event.

References

Riesman, D. *The Lonely Crowd.* Yale University Press, 1950.

Sullivan, H. S. *Conceptions of Modern Psychiatry.* W. A. White Psychiatric Foundation, 1947.

Henry Clay Smith

Empathy

The question of the level of empathy has been of basic philosophic and psychological concern (Bakan, 1956). Hume and other philosophers in the tradition of "epistemological loneliness" have viewed man as being essentially alone. They see him as capable of understanding the behavior of other men but incapable of really understanding their experiences. Following this tradition, behaviorists have attempted to understand men through a study of their behavior alone.

By contrast, most clinicians assume that man can understand others by assuming that their experiences are similar to his own. It should be apparent from this that when we say that we are all pretty much alike it does not mean that we must all be psychotic, or that we must all have children, or that we must all have had the experience of our parents dying. In fact we need not have had these experiences. Rather, in the way in which all yearning is the same, all pain is the same, and all fantasy is the same, we can have these experiences. The method whereby we may become aware of the relationship between experience and behavior is through the use of systematic self-observation. Thus at the extreme, the behaviorist sees empathy as the source of all error; the clinician, the source of all truth.

Empathy, as we define it, is the tendency of a perceiver to assume that another person's feelings, thoughts, and behavior are similar to his own. Blackman (1958) defines empathy and distinguishes it from the related terms *projection, identification,* and *sympathy* in the following way:

> Empathy is the ability to step into another person's shoes and to step back just as easily into one's own shoes again. It is not projection, which implies that the wearer's shoes pinch him and that he wishes someone else in them; it is not identification, which involves stepping into another person's shoes and then being unable or unwilling to get out of them; and it is not sympathy, in which a person stands in his own shoes while

From *Empathy and Ideology, Aspects of Administrative Innovation,* ed. Charles Press and Alan Arian. Rand McNally, 1966. Reprinted by permission of Rand McNally & Co. and the author, H. C. Smith.

observing another person's behavior, and while reacting to him in terms of what he tells you about his shoes—if they pinch, one commiserates with him, if they are comfortable, one enjoys his comfort with him.

This definition implies that when we think we have stepped into another person's shoes we actually have; our definition implies that we can only be sure that we are being empathic and not being projective by comparing the similarities we assume between ourselves and another person with the actual similarities between ourselves and him.

Freudians, non-Freudians, sociologists, and psychologists stress that similarity to others forms the foundation for understanding them (Cf. Fenichel, 1945; Sullivan, 1956; Mead, 1934; Rogers, 1959). What they do not stress is that assumed similarities can be wrong as well as right, can lead to mistaken as well as correct judgments. The focus here is, therefore, not on empathy alone, but, rather, it is on empathic *accuracy*, the ability of an individual to perceive correctly the ways in which he is like another person and the ways in which he is different.

Here we shall discuss four topics: (1) the relationship between empathy and emphatic accuracy and how each is measured, (2) the social-psychological processes which are correlated with the process of empathy, (3) the personality of the empathizer, and (4) the implications for the administrator and administration.

The Measurement of Empathy and Empathic Accuracy

Although everyone assumes some similarity between himself and others, some are more empathic than others. There are three related measures which will aid us in dealing with empathy and empathic accuracy: (1) the empathy score, (2) the actual similarity score, and (3) the empathic accuracy score. The empathy score is a measure of *assumed* similarity. The common way of measuring empathy is to have people answer questions as they themselves would answer them and then answer the same questions as they think someone else would answer them. The number of questions that a man answers for others in the same way he answers them for himself is his empathy score. Table 1 illustrates this method of measuring empathy.[1]

The actual similarity score is obtained by comparing the response of an individual about his own feelings, thoughts, or behavior

1. The content of empathy measures have varied widely. Livensparger (1965) used items from the Strong Vocational Interest Bank; Chance and Meaders (1960) used items from the Edwards Inventory; Rogers (1959) employed the Gough Adjective Check List; Dymond (1954) used the MMPI. Strayer (1960), p. 244.

Table 1   Empathy Inventory

This inventory measures three things: (1) your knowledge of the interests of the majority of men; (2) your knowledge of the interests of the majority of women; and (3) your own interests. Follow the separate directions for each part.

(1) Knowledge of Men

A large and representative group of educated men checked whether they liked or disliked the various occupations, activities and school subjects below. Mark one (1) if you think the **majority of men** checked that they **"liked"** the interest. Mark two (2) if you think the **majority** checked that they **"disliked"** the interest. Note that the numbering skips lines on the answer sheet (1,2,3,4, ... 9,10,11,12, ... 17, etc.) **Mark your answers in agreement with the numbers.**

1. Manufacturer	2. Musical comedy	3. Auctioneer	4. Auto salesman
9. Art galleries	10. Symphony concerts	11. Auto racer	12. Auto repairman

Etc.

(2) Knowledge of Women

A large and representative group of women checked whether they liked or disliked the various occupations, activities and school subjects below. Mark one (1) if you think the majority of women checked they **liked** the interest. Mark two (2) if you think the majority checked that they **disliked** the interest. Note that the numbering skips lines as in part (1).

65. Costume designer	66. Proof reader	67. Companion to elderly person	68. Accountant
73. Bank teller	74. Magazine writer	75. Telephone operator	76. Buyer of merchandise

Etc.

(3) Personal Interests

The following is a list of occupations, activities and school subjects, etc. You are to indicate whether you like or dislike each of the items. If you like the item, mark one (1) on the answer sheet. If you dislike it, mark two (2). Note that the items are numbered so that you now return to the top of the answer sheets and use the numbers left blank.

5. Manufacturer	6. Musical comedy	7. Auctioneer	8. Auto salesman

Etc.

Source: Livensparger, 1965.

with the responses of another individual. The actual similarity score is the number of times in which two people have *independently* made the same response about themselves. We can, therefore, measure the actual similarity between them without either being aware of the other. We cannot, however, measure assumed similarity (empathy) without having a perceiver make a conscious attempt to predict the responses of another person. The empathic accuracy score is measured by dividing the assumed similarity score (empathy score) by the actual similarity score (see Figure 1). The actual similarity score is the number of similarities between myself and you regardless of whether I know about them or not. The assumed similarity score (empathy) is the number of similarities I assume between myself and you regardless of whether they are based on correct observations or mistaken projections of my own attitudes on to you. The empathic accuracy score is the assumed similarity score divided by the actual similarity score. If the ratio is less than one, I have assumed less

Figure 1   Measures Related to the Empathic Accuracy Score

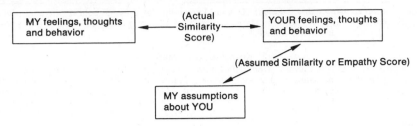

similarity between myself and you than actually exists; if more than one, I assumed more similarity than actually exists.

One might think that a perceiver who had a perfectly accurate *level* of empathy with a person would also have perfect empathic accuracy. That this is not necessarily correct is illustrated by Table 2, a hypothetical response to the first four items in the test in Table 1.

Table 2   Hypothetical Responses

	Manufacturer	Musical Comedy	Auctioneer	Auto Sales-man
Responses of the Perceiver	"dislike"	"dislike"	"like"	"like"
Responses that the perceiver assumes for the person	"like"	"dislike"	"like"	"dislike"
Response of the Person	"dislike"	"like"	"dislike"	"like"

In this example, the perceiver assumes he is similar to the person on two items (musical comedy and auctioneer) and is actually similar on two items (manufacturer and auto salesman), but he is wrong in all of his specific assumptions about similarity and dissimilarity. The reason for introducing this example is that it is fairly true of what happens in many life situations. For example, Bronfenbrenner (1958), who found a correlation of .86 between empathy (assumed similarity) and actual similarity, found only a correlation of .21 between empathy and the degree of empathic accuracy. That is, individuals were much more accurate in predicting their general level of similarity or dissimilarity to another person than in predicting the specific items on which they would make the same or a different response.

Individuals tend to underestimate their similarity to others. For example, Livensparger, using the test shown in Table 1, determined the three measures described above for fifty-seven college men and women. He multiplied the empathic accuracy score by 100. When the result was 100, it indicated that the student's empathy and actual similarity scores were identical. He found that the average student assumed too little similarity (94). The individual variations, however, were very wide, some students having scores of less than 50 and some having scores of more than 150.

The problem of empathic accuracy seems to be most acute at the extremes: Individuals tend to overestimate their similarities to those that are most like themselves and to overestimate their dissimilarities to those that are least like themselves. Clinical psychologists as well as laymen suffer from this difficulty. Giedt (1955) had 48 clinicians judge a series of patients of varying ages and backgrounds and with different problems. He concluded:

> Raters seemed particularly likely to misjudge patients whose socioeconomic and cultural status was either quite close to their own or quite distant from their own. . . . The patient whose socioeconomic and cultural position was most distant from that of the raters—a rather nomadic fellow who shared few of the high aspirations probably characteristic of most of the raters—seemed to be least well understood, and his behavior was often interpreted on the basis of an improper frame of reference. Thus reading pulp magazines and having been involved in fights as a boy—behavior which probably differed from that of the raters—was incorrectly related to impulsivity and lack of control. The patient who had a fairly high-level, managerial status had an outlook on life perhaps so close to that of the raters that they could hardly accept the possibility of serious psychopathology in him. This patient was rated far too high in adherence to reality, apparently on the assumption that no high-level person such as this could be very unrealistic.

The clinician has the greatest difficulty in judging those who are most or least like himself. He seems to have a similar difficulty in dealing with these extreme groups in a therapy situation. Carson and Heine (1962) had sixty clinical trainees give therapy once a week for sixteen weeks to sixty patients. Before therapy, clinicians and patients completed the *Minnesota Multiphasic Personality Inventory.* Patients were assigned to clinicians on the basis of their similarity or dissimilarity to them. The sixty clinician-patient pairs were divided into five groups, the first group being composed of those with the most similar profiles and the fifth group being composed of those with the least similar profiles. After the sixteen weeks, the success of therapy for each pair was independently determined. Patients in the groups that were most and least like their therapists were least benefited by the therapy; patients who were moderately like their therapists (the three middle groups) were most benefited by therapy.

Processes Leading to Empathy

Four interrelated social-psychological processses frequently associated with empathy are identification, attraction, generalization and familiarity.

Identification is the process by which a person acts like another person without being encouraged or taught to do so. Children identify with their parents: A daughter feeds and cares for her doll as her mother feeds and cares for her; a son walks, talks, and thinks like his father. In a similar manner, spectators at a sport identify with the athletes, and students identify with other students. The process is reciprocal: We feel, think, and act as we think others are feeling, thinking, and acting; we assume that others are feeling, thinking, and acting as we are. We empathize with those with whom we identify.

Attraction is related to empathy. The more we like a person, the more we assume that he is like us. But liking someone, while related to assumed similarity (empathy), need not rest on actual similarity. Convincing evidence comes from a study of seventeen students at the University of Michigan (Newcomb, 1956). They were all transfer students, all strangers to each other, and all residents of the same cooperative house. In return for spending five hours a week being interviewed and filling out questionnaires, they were given free room and board for the semester. The men were given no voice in the selection of roommates, but (within the limits of the university regulations) they were given complete freedom to conduct the house, including the cooking and eating arrangements, as they chose. Before their arrival, each of the seventeen men filled out a questionnaire covering attitudes toward a wide range of issues: classical music, immortality, sexual morality, house rules, university regulations about driving, etc. During the semester, the men completed a variety of personality inventories and rated themselves and each other on numerous rating scales. They also reported whom they liked and disliked. From these data, an index of each man's liking for each of the other men was calculated and also an index of his assumed similarity (empathy) to each of them. Result: the greater the attraction, the greater the empathy ($r = .69$).

It is not surprising that students assumed that those they liked were like them. It *is* surprising that there was no relationship between attraction and actual similarity. A quite different study reached the same conclusion. Silkiner (1962) correlated the favorableness of foreign student attitudes toward the United States and the degree of assumed similarity (empathy) between their interests and those of the typical American man. Result: the more favorable their attitude, the greater their empathy. He then correlated favorableness of attitude with actual similarity. Result: no realtionship.

Generalization is a key process in empathy: "When a person finds that he has some characteristics in common with another person, he tends to perceive himself as having other characteristics like that person" (Burnstein, *et al.,* 1962). If we are aware of a few dissimilarities, we assume many more.

Generalization works both ways: We ascribe our traits to the person we perceive as similar; we also ascribe *his* traits to ourselves. Burnstein and his associates brought more than a hundred junior high school boys together in the school gymnasium and asked them to complete a "describe yourself questionnaire." One part of the questionnaire asked them to rate their excellence in swimming, ability to hold breath under water, etc. Two weeks later, the boys were separated into groups of a dozen each and then addressed by a "deep-sea diver" who described his career and stressed his excellence in swimming, ability to hold his breath under water, etc. In some groups, the diver (a confederate) stressed that he was similar to the boys: He was born and raised in their rural neighborhood, went to the same school, had a father who worked in the same factory that employed most of the fathers of the boys, etc. In other groups, the diver stressed that he was *dissimilar:* He was born and raised in a big city, went to a large city school, had a father who was a fisherman, etc. At the end of each group meeting, the diver asked the boys to again rate themselves on their excellence in swimming, etc. The boys who had heard the "low similarity" speech rated themselves about as they had two weeks before; the boys who heard the "high similarity" speech changed their ratings of themselves so that their characteristics were more like those that the diver described himself as possessing.

Familiarity is correlated with empathy. The longer we know a person, the more we tend to assume we are like him. Students were brought into a room two at a time and seated at different desks so that they could not see each other (Bieri, 1953). Each then took a test which pictured twenty-four situations with three different kinds of responses. Each chose the response that he would make in each situation. The pair was then very briefly introduced to each other and asked, even though they did not know each other very well, to fill out the test as they thought their partner had filled it out. Assumed similarity was measured by determining the number of situations in which a student picked the same response for his partner as he had picked for himself. The pairs of students were then given two topics to discuss for twenty minutes. Afterward, each member of the pair was to answer the test as he thought his partner had. Higher assumed similarity after interaction was found.

The relationship between empathy and accuracy also increases with the length of acquaintanceship. In the conclusion to his intensive study of the members of a cooperative house, Newcomb (1956) states:

Early acquaintance is characterized by a continuing process of reciprocal scanning: What kinds of things does this person view as important? Whatever they are, how does he feel about them, and also about the things I regard as important (including myself)? If the discrepancies seem not too glaring, explorative communication continues, and with it comes the possibility of changes in the scale of importance, and in attitudes toward things of varying degrees of importance. In the long run (four months, in my own investigation), attraction and association came to be relatively concentrated upon those who are perceived, usually with a considerable accuracy as having notions similar to one's own of what is important and as having attitudes similar to one's own toward important things.

Interrelations among variables. The process of identification, attraction, generalization, and familiarity are intimately interwoven: We identify with those we like, we like those with whom we identify, etc. The relationship, for example, between familiarity and attraction has been formulated as the Law of Propinquity: "As the frequency of interaction between two persons increases, the degree of their liking for one another increases." The law is pervasive.

Beier and Stumpf (1959) reached the same conclusion. They started out to determine the influence of various kinds of cues on judgments of intelligence, sociability, and other personality characteristics. To do so, they presented four persons one at a time to over two hundred students under different conditions: (1) The students heard only the voices of the subjects from behind a screen; (2) the students then heard the subjects and saw them making gestures but did not see their faces; (3) the students heard their voices and saw their faces and observed them making gestures; and (4) the students had all of these cues and also heard the subject discuss a topic for three minutes. The students rated the subjects after each presentation. The more familiar students became with a subject, the more favorable their ratings became.

The ratios of empathy to actual similarity scores vary with the saliency of the processes of identification, attraction, generalization, and familiarity. People identify more with their own than the opposite sex. Consistently, Livensparger (1965) found erroneously high levels of empathy with the same sex (108) and erroneously low levels with the opposite sex (81). American students have more obvious similarities to and familiarity with American than foreign students. Silkiner (1962) using a test roughly similar to that shown in Table 1 measured the levels of empathy of American and foreign male and female students to American men. He reported the empathy scores as follows: for the American male students, 78; for the foreign male students, 60; for the American women, 70; and for the foreign women, 51. All groups were in reality more similar than they assumed. Foreign women, however, underestimated their similarity to American men by the greatest amount.

The Personality of the Empathizer

Chance and Meaders (1960) measured differences in personality between those people who assumed little and those who assumed a great deal of similarity to two individuals that they heard on tape recordings.

The authors concluded that those who assumed high similarity (empathy) had a "highly developed need for social interaction although strongly tinged with dependence upon and conformity to the constraints that others impose." Those who assumed low similarity were "nonconforming, impatient with custom and authority, disinclined to plan and to accept schedules, wanting to be in the limelight, not strongly motivated toward seeking contacts with others, seeking new experiences, and preferring aggressive modes of behavior." Table 3 summarizes these findings.

Table 3   Personality Characteristics of High and Low Empathizers

Low Empathizers	High Empathizers
Expressive	Inhibited
Dominating	Submissive
Independent	Dependent
Aloof	Gregarious
Cool	Warm
Aggressive	Unaggressive

Source: Chance and Meaders, 1960.

A similar result emerged from a study using a different approach (Fiedler, 1961). Leaders were first asked to describe themselves by rating their agreement with statements such as "I like good food" and by choosing from pairs of adjectives such as "calm-exciting." Each leader was then asked to use the same alternatives in describing the man he thought was his best and the man he thought was his poorest subordinate. The number of statements on which a leader assumed that the best and poorest subordinates were like himself were counted. Finally, the difference in assumed similarities to the best and to the poorest workers were determined. Those leaders who assumed about the same amount of similarity to these opposites were found to be more dependent on others, more concerned about the attitude of others toward them, and more unwilling to reject unsatisfactory workers. Those leaders who assumed much more similarity to the best worker than to the poorest worker were more independent, more indifferent to the attitudes of others, and readier to reject people they judged to be unsatisfactory. They were distant from people.

The aloofness of the nonempathizers may be related to childhood experiences. Stotland and Dunn (1963) measured the degree of identification of students who were watching another student in an anxious situation. They compared the anxiety levels of firstborn children with students who had at least one older brother or sister. Students with older siblings were more anxious. "The first and only born . . . react as if they only use the other person's performance level as a guide to self-evaluation and do not really 'feel with' him."

Stotland and Dunn also compared the empathic anxiety of students with low and high self-esteem. Those of high self-esteem identified more with the student in trouble. "These results are reminiscent of the clinician's belief that only those who really love themselves can love others."

Sources of Empathic Errors

While some people are more accurate in judging others, all make errors. Here we shall briefly consider six of the most common and influential of these errors: (1) the rigidity of levels, (2) the prevalence of simple thinking, (3) the dangers of psychological-mindedness, (4) the error of least effort, (5) faulty stereotypes, and (6) the cancerous hypothesis.

Even after the briefest exposure, we can gain a clear picture of what a person is like. Our pictures, however, vary widely from the darkest gray to the rosiest pink. Some people think that most people are "no damn good" while others think the best of everyone. The general level at which a perceiver operates reflects a stable and central personality quality. It also has a pervasive influence on all of his judgments of himself and others. The problem is not so much the level that a perceiver has as the rigidity and inflexibility of his level. More or less regardless of his own qualities, who he is judging, or what he is judging, a perceiver tends to stick to a constant level. Those who have the highest empathic accuracy are those who have learned to realistically adapt their level to changing persons and situations.

We perceive a person as a unified and simple whole. So strong is the tendency to think in simple terms that it is hard to avoid describing everyone as either "bad" or "good," "right" or "wrong," "strong" or "weak." One common way of achieving a simple picture of a person is to fail to observe or to forget facts that do not fit. The same result can be achieved in the opposite way. We can accumulate an excessive number of facts, many of which are ambiguous and some of which seem to conflict. Then it is possible to unconsciously pick facts that fit the picture we had before we began accumulating them.

The use of "psychology" and psychology-mindedness is a potent source of error, for preoccupation with the psychological underground leads one to overlook significant facts that lie on the surface. The preoccupation may also lead to the view that we are all moved by primitive and blind impulses when, in fact, we are largely reasonable players of social roles. Also, it is hard to see in the underground and thus easy to mistake our own projected feelings for the reality. Perhaps most relevant of all, the most enthusiastic proponents of psychological-mindedness are not those with deep involvement with others but those with a desire to protect and enhance their own self-esteem. Mastery of the "psychological point of view" may be comforting, but it may also be deceptive.

It is possible to surface after a brief dip in the literature of empathy with the idea that we are generally preoccupied with assessing the fundamental nature of the people we meet. In fact we are usually interacting with others in well-defined situations and are playing rather specific roles. The question before us is not: What is he like? It is: What do I do next? In such a situation, we naturally strive to *reduce* the information we need to sustain the interaction process. We seek to know the least amount about another person that is consistent with playing an immediate social role effectively. While this principle of least effort is helpful in playing our social role, it is not helpful in increasing our empathic accuracy.

A stereotype is our picture of the social role that the members of a particular group play; stereotype accuracy is the adequacy of our knowledge of these roles; and stereotyping is the process of applying our knowledge of these roles to making predictions about how individuals playing them will behave. Stereotyping is inevitable; it is, also, on the whole, very helpful. Still, stereotypes can be mistaken and misused. Stereotype accuracy depends, in part, upon the number of persons in the group we have known. Not infrequently, the number is one. We meet one Australian, form an impression of his personality, and use that impression in making predictions about all Australians. Even more serious, the number may be zero. Children and adults learn stereotypes from those about them without any firsthand experience with the groups: Koreans, Negroes, Jews, Texans, Catholics, etc. One of the most certain ways of reducing empathic errors is through training in stereotype accuracy.

One sort of error is so typical of judgments of personality, so persistent, and seemingly so unavoidable that it should be constantly borne in mind. It is the result of a hypothesis that, like cancer, grows in a wild and uncontrollable way. A Texas company, for example, needed a new head for their research and development section. The autocratic president announced his choice. The members of the section unanimously objected to his appointment saying that he was "unimpressive." His dwarf-like physique played a large part in the informal discussions of his unimpressiveness, strongly suggesting that the group was generalizing from this single physical quality to many psychological ones. Nonetheless, the man was appointed, was highly successful, and was eventually promoted to a higher position. The country was combed for his replacement. There was general agreement on the best available man although it was incidentally remarked by those who recommended him that "he tends to talk a great deal when he is nervous." He came, was interviewed, and was rejected because he seemed "arrogant, egotistical, and opinionated." Again, it seemed clear, there was a wild generalization from one obvious behavioral trait to many subtle ones.

The Improvement of Empathic Accuracy

To be effective, training designed to improve empathic accuracy should focus upon the unified person, should make it easy for the trainee to change his theories about people, and should provide realistic feedback. Like all principles, these are easier to state than to apply successfully. Sensitivity training laboratories, analyses of clinical interactions, and role-playing are three widely used efforts to apply them.

Sensitivity Training Laboratories

The procedures of sensitivity training involve a "laboratory" composed of 30 to 150 people, meeting in a conference setting for two or three weeks. A training group meets for thirty to forty hours, carrying on a study of its own processes. Most laboratories also involve a wide range of other activities: lectures and demonstrations reviewing material from the social sciences, consultation on back-home problems, and planned exercises. The exercises may range from replications of classic experiments in social psychology to full-scale organizational simulation designs that continue for a day or two.

To determine whether training achieves all or any of its goals is extraordinarily difficult. The persons appearing for human relations training are highly self-selected, and it is excessively difficult to get comparable pools of subjects to serve as members of control groups. Ordinarily the number of participants in any particular training laboratory is relatively small. Where training laboratories are composed of persons from widely spread geographical areas, getting accurate follow-up measures is difficult; where laboratories are held with members of an ongoing organization, it is almost impossible to separate the presumed outcomes of the laboratory. In an effort to solve these problems, Miles (1960) used thirty-four elementary school principals attending a two-week training laboratory at Bethel, Maine, in 1958.

Each principal was matched with another principal who did not attend the conference. In addition, each participating principal gave names of six to eight associates on the job who could describe his job behavior.

Miles determined that there was no change in either the experimental or control group in a leadership behavior scale given before and after training. There was a change in both the experimental and control groups in their participation habits as measured by a group participation scale. There were significant changes in the experimental but not in the control group in the way they perceived themselves: "listens more," "communicates better," "shares decisions more," "gives help to teachers," etc. However, there was no relation between the amount of this change and the initial expressed desire for improvement. "If anything the relationship was inverse . . . a high wish to change in this sample was a kind of defensive protestation."

A feedback technique is often utilized in sensitivity training. A rule is sometimes made by the trainees that before anyone can speak of his ideas he must first repeat what was said and felt by the person who had spoken before him. Comments after using the technique are, commonly, "For the first time in my life I find that I am really listening to what others say." The pattern has some obvious advantages over the client-to-therapist or supervisor-to-trainee type of feedback: (1) The relationships involved are not those of superior-inferior type; (2) the perceiver obtains feedback from the rest of the group as well as from the person perceived; and (3) each trainee has a chance to be the perceiver, the person being perceived, and the observer of perceiver-person interactions.

Analyses of Clinical Interactions

The training of clinicians is consciously directed at the goal of empathic accuracy: Does the therapist, for example, feel a "slight depression and mild anxiety" because he is realistically identifying with the client or because he is projecting some of his own irrelevant feelings into the situation? One way of answering the question is for the therapist to communicate back to the client what he assumes the client is feeling. The client can then correct or amplify the therapist's impressions. Another way is to have the expert supervisor listen to the taped interview and to correct what he judges to be empathic errors. While such knowledge of results is more adequate than in a formal course, it may not be adequate enough to increase accuracy. It may have its most significant effect in the tendency of the clinician to identify with his supervisor rather than his client, i.e., to attent to the inner feelings of the client in the way that he thinks his supervisor does.

Having trainees discuss responses they would make in specific situations may be helpful in developing some therapeutic skills. Such discussions, however, do not give the trainee any knowledge of how well he understands a particular person. If the format were changed it might. Suppose, for example, that trainees were first presented with an actual interaction sequence between therapist and client and were then given five alternative responses of the client to the last remark of the therapist, one of which the client actually made. If the trainee makes the correct choice in a series of such sequences, he would be given some objective knowledge of his understanding of the person. The first selection of such sequences and alternatives might result in all the trainees failing to choose the correct response. However, this problem would be readily solved by trying out the sequences and eliminating or revising those that were inadequate.

A more serious problem is that both trainer and trainee may resist the win-lose nature of such situations. Such resistance might be reduced by selecting and testing the interaction samples so that trainees could be exposed to them according to their difficulty. Trainees are often anxious and defensive in realistic social interactions. To meet this difficulty, the initial cases could be tape recorded and only the final ones would be actual interactions.

Role-Playing Session

Practice in playing the role of a person might be of considerable help in improving empathic accuracy. In role-playing the player pretends he is the person and acts out situations as he thinks the person would behave in them. Bronfenbrenner and Newcomb (1948) have given a helpful analysis of some of the aspects of the person which the role-player should be aware of and attempt to incorporate into his portrayal of the person:

> *Verbal content:* slips of the tongue, omissions and blocks, sudden shift in train of thought, frequent repetitions, etc.
> *Voice characteristics:* speed, rhythm, pitch, intensity, dropping or raising of voice, change in speed, etc.
> *Bodily movements and postural adjustments:* relaxed, jerky, abortive, controlled, immobilized, etc.

The comments of both the trainer and other trainees may be of help in developing the accuracy of the role-player's performance.

Role-playing has been used for many purposes. The critical differences between role-playing for developing empathic accuracy and for other purposes are: (1) The participants play the roles of actual persons with known responses instead of fictional persons with unknown responses; (2) the stress is upon the exact imitation of another person rather than upon a free interpretation that encourages the role-player to project his own personality into the situation; and (3) an exclusive concern with understanding the other person rather than with relating to the person in an affective way. The utility of role-playing for increasing empathic accuracy for a particular person could be determined by comparing the accuracy of predictions for the person before and after his role was played.

Implications for the Administrator

Can an administrator make mistakes by having too much empathy, i.e., by assuming too much similarity between himself and others? He can and does, for he often jumps to the conclusion that, because a person is like him in obvious ways, he will be like him in less obvious ways. He is, therefore, very likely to assume too easily that other administrators will think and act like himself. He is also likely to err by assuming too little similarity between himself and his subordinates, by assuming that his subordinates will think about a problem less like he does than they actually do.

Can an administrator have too much empathic accuracy, i.e., understand people too well for his own good or the good of the organization? The common-sense answer would be "no," for it is a centuries-old principle that "The good leader knows his men." The best empirical check of the principle was made in a military setting (Showel, 1960). In this study, infantry trainees in the process of completing their six-month tour of duty were asked for the following facts about themselves: (1) first name, (2) last name, (3) whether or not during the past week they had been on KP, (4) whether or not during the past week they had been on passes or leave, (5) their rifle qualification score, (6) the amount of schooling they had completed, (7) their main job or activity before entering the Army, (8) their principal hobby or interest, (9) their ambition for a future civilian career. Then the squad leaders were given the last names of the trainees under them and asked to provide the same information about each trainee (first name, rifle scores, etc.). A squad leader's answers were corrected against the answers given by the trainees themselves. Each correct answer was awarded one point. The average number of correct answers for his men was the squad leader's *interpersonal knowledge score*.

Was interpersonal knowledge related to leadership effectiveness? As a measure of effectiveness, each squad leader was separately rated by his sergeant, trainee guide, and platoon leader on a scale from 1 ("the very best type of squad leader") to 7 ("the worst kind of squad leader"). In addition, each squad leader took a battery of leader-reaction tests that required him to perform as a leader in three tactical situations, to take part in leadership group discussions, and to lead a squad through dismounted drill. When interpersonal knowledge scores were related to each of these measures of effectiveness, *all* the measures correlated significantly with interpersonal knowledge. Com-

mon sense is vindicated: People who know people are more successful in dealing with them.

What are the qualities of the administrator with high empathic
accuracy? Motivation is the first essential: Men learn what they want
to learn. The people of high empathic accuracy are those who find
their greatest satisfactions in human relations, who are considerate
and responsible in dealing with others, who want to give to others
rather than to get something from them, but who are not dependent
on them. Openness to new experiences is another essential. Those
who are most understanding of others are sympathetic to new ideas
about people and capable of looking at old facts in new ways. They
are curious, plastic, nondefensive, skeptical, tolerant, liberal, and
ready for change. Learning about people also requires boldness—a
willingness to approach people, to ask questions, and to express
feelings and get responses to them. Studies consistently indicate that
those of high empathic accuracy are active and forceful people to the
point that they are sometimes described (and describe themselves) as
egotistical and conceited. Finally, they are intelligent. They are capable of considering and making sense out of the fragments of facts
they gather about people by the use of complex concepts.

References

Bakan, D. "Clinical Psychology and Logic." *American Psychologist*, Vol. 11,
    1956.

Beier, E. G., and J. Stumpf. "Cues Influencing Judgments of Personality Charac-
    teristics." *Journal of Consulting Psychology*, Vol. 23, 1959.

Bieri, J. "Changes in Interpersonal Perception Following Social Interactions."
    Journal of Abnormal and Social Psychology, Vol. 48, 1953.

Blackman, N., K. Smith, R. Brokman, and J. Stern. "The Development of
    Empathy in Male Schizophrenics." *Psychiatric Quarterly*, Vol. 32, 1958.

Bronfenbrenner, U., and T. Newcomb. "Improvisations—An Application of
    Psycho-drama in Personality Diagnosis." *Sociatry*, Vol. 1, 1948.

————, J. Harding, and M. Gallway. "The Measurement of Skill in Social Per-
    ception." In *Talent and Society*, ed. D. C. McClelland. Van Nostrand, 1958.

Burnstein, E., E. Stotland, and A. Zander. "Similarity to a Model and Self-
    Evaluation." *Journal of Abnormal and Social Psychology*, Vol. 62, 1962.

Carson, R. C., and R. W. Heine. "Similarity and Success in Therapeutic Dyads."
    Journal of Consulting Psychology, Vol. 26, 1962.

Chance, J., and W. Meaders. "Needs and Interpersonal Perception." *Journal of
    Personality*, Vol. 28, 1960.

Dymond, R. F. "A Scale for Measurement of Empathic Ability." *Journal of Con-
    sulting Psychology*, Vol. 8, 1954.

Fenichel, O. *The Psychoanalytic Theory of Neurosis.* Norton, 1945.

Fiedler, F. E. "Leadership and Leadership Effectiveness Traits: A Reconceptuali-
zation of the Leadership Trait Problem." In *Leadership and Interpersonal
Behavior,* ed. L. Petrullo and B. M. Bass. Holt, Rinehart and Winston,
1961.

Giedt, F. H. "Comparison of Visual Content and Auditory Cues in Interviewing."
Journal of Consulting Psychology, Vol. 19, 1955.

Livensparger, D. "Empathy Inventory." Unpublished manuscript, 1965.

Mead, G. H. *Mind, Self and Society.* University of Chicago Press, 1934.

Miles, M. B. "Human Relations Training: Processes and Outcomes." *Journal of
Counseling Psychology,* Vol. 7, 1960.

Newcomb, T. M. "The Prediction of Interpersonal Attraction." *American Psychologist,* Vol. 11, 1956.

Rogers, C. R. "Relationship Between Real Similarity and Assumed Similarity
with Favorability Controlled." *Journal of Abnormal and Social Psychology,*
Vol. 59, 1959.

Showel, M. "Interpersonal Knowledge and Voted Leader Potential." *Journal of
Abnormal and Social Psychology,* Vol. 61, 1960.

Silkiner, D. S. "A Cross-cultural Study of the Measurement, Determinants and
Effects of Stereotype Accuracy." Unpublished M. A. thesis, Michigan State
University, East Lansing, 1962.

Stotland, E., and R. E. Dunn. "Empathy, Self-Esteem and Birth Order." *Journal
of Abnormal and Social Psychology,* Vol. 66, 1963.

Strayer, F. K. "Empathy and Social Perception." *Dissertation Abstracts,* Vol. 21,
1960.

Sullivan, H. S. *Conceptions of Modern Psychiatry.* Norton, 1956.

Henry P. Knowles
and Borje O. Saxberg

Human Relations
and the Nature of Man

We all know how little boys love fighting. They get their heads
punched. But they have the satisfaction of having punched the
other fellow's head (Bergson, 1935, p. 284).

The principle of co-operation is the most dominant and biologically the most important (Montague, 1962, p. 50).

The point is constantly made that traditional organizations work on
the assumption that people are essentially opposed to work and lack
the capacity for self-direction and personal responsibility. Modern
theories of organization take the opposite view; i.e., people do have
the capacity to become psychologically involved in cooperative activity and, under certain conditions, to be virtually self-motivated and
self-controlled.

Douglas McGregor, among others, has noted how these implicit
assumptions about the nature of man influence organization and
leadership in his now classic discussion of Theory X and Theory Y.
The former assumes that man is innately lazy and unreliable, and
leads to organization and control based on external or imposed authority. The latter assumes that man can be basically self-directed
and creative at work if properly motivated; this assumption is said to
lead toward an integrative organizational strategy.

However, neither McGregor nor other writers in this field have
undertaken to reveal how deeply the roots of these assumptions about
man penetrate our culture and thus how powerfully they influence
human relations in our society. Not only are these assumptions important in theories of human organization, but they are also crucial in
every system of thought involved with human and social control.
Whether concerned with organizational strategy, the ancient social

From *Harvard Business Review*, March–April 1967. © 1967 by the President and
Fellows of Harvard College; all rights reserved.

order of the Zuñi, or the political theories of a Machiavelli or a Locke, one cannot escape the underlying relatedness and importance of what is assumed about man himself.

Managers need to know more about the nature, sources, and effects of one assumption or the other in order (1) to sort out and understand their own ideas about the nature of humanity, and (2) to evaluate the fundamental influence of these ideas on managerial decisions. It may be asserted that no other variable weighs more heavily on the ultimate form and quality of organizational and inter-personal relations.

The question of the basic nature of man is, of course, as old as history and probably as old as society itself. The argument, in its many forms, stems from the ancient philosophical debate as to whether man is an end or a means. Reducing the argument to its simplest terms, and considering only the extremities of the spectrum, we treat a person as an *end* when we permit him to establish his own purposes and to choose and decide for himself. Contrariwise, we treat a person as a *means* when we limit his choices and utilize him primarily as an instrument for our own ends and purposes.

Implicit in these values are central assumptions concerning (*a*) whether man is "good" or "evil," (*b*) whether he has the ability to cooperate voluntarily or must be forced to cooperate, (*c*) whether he is a "pilot" capable of choosing or a "robot" imprisoned by circum-stances and incapable of choice.[1] Values such as these lie at the very core of philosophies of religion, politics, education, organization, and human relations.

It is our intention in this article to describe how the choice of one or the other of these sets of values has influenced a number of systems of thought concerned with questions of human regulation and control. We do not intend to emphasize the growing body of empirical evidence which indicates that the quality of individual and group performance varies from one kind of assumption and system to the other. This area is adequately covered in the writings of such men as Chris Argyris, Rensis Likert, and, of course, McGregor. Rather, we shall explore some of the cultural roots and branches of optimistic-pessimistic assumptions about human nature in order to show that an underlying unity exists along this dimension in a variety of human-social control systems.

Man: Pessimistic View

In their polar aspects, attitudes about human nature range from pessimism to optimism—from assumptions that evilness, predatory

---

1. The terms "pilot" and "robot" have been borrowed from Ford and Urban (1965), pp. 595 ff.

competition, and aggression on the one hand, to goodness, cooperation, and virtue on the other, constitute the central predispositions of
men and, therefore, of the social order. Let us begin our discussion by
examining how certain ideas about human-social control have been
affected by the pessimistic or "means" view of man. This is the
attitude that man is essentially evil and driven by aggressive and
uncooperative motives and drives.

Fear versus Love

As early giants in the history of Western idea makers, Niccolo
Machiavelli and Thomas Hobbes—a pair of political scientists—provide us with a suitable starting point. It will be recalled that Machiavelli in *The Prince* (1515) urged that, because of man's rebellious
and uncooperative behavior, he must be strictly and ruthlessly controlled by anyone who aspires to gain or maintain a position of power.
A ruler, in his view, must put aside any question of morality and must
achieve control at any price and by whatever means he can find: "It is
much safer to be feared than loved. . . . For it may be said of men in
general that they are ungrateful, voluble, dissemblers, anxious to
avoid dangers, and covetous of gain" (Machiavelli, 1950 ed., p. 61).

In all fairness, however, it must be made clear that he did not
advocate his "end justifies the means" philosophy to benefit the prince
or the ruler but to benefit the people. He assumed that only the ruler
is competent to judge what the necessary ends are and must be. In
furtherance of these ends, then, the ruler must resort to means which
appear ruthless and deceitful.

Hobbes in the *Leviathan* (1651) outlined a theory of social
relationships which makes him a direct intellectual descendant of
Machiavelli. According to Hobbes (1958 ed.), since men covet prestige, material goods, and power and expect to attain these at their
discretion, they live in perpetual fear of their neighbors: "And therefore if any two men desire the same thing, which nevertheless they
cannot both enjoy, they become enemies" (p. 105).

Law must therefore define what is honest and virtuous. But, in
order for law to be applicable, a common authority must exist to
enforce it. Man recognizes this need out of fear of loss of life and
property. As a consequence, he enters into a social contract in which
he gives up to a central authority whatever rights he has had in
nature. In this way, he brings about the creation of a commonwealth
ruled by a sovereign. Each man is individually bound to this authority, or Leviathan, and the latter's powers are irrevocable. The sovereign is a despot; whatever he wills becomes the people's will. As the
Leviathan, he represents the supremacy of law, absolute authority
and power, and the bureaucracy of the state.

Survival of the Fittest

Both Machiavelli and Hobbes viewed human nature primarily as a product of experience. They perceived in mankind a predominance of aggressive and selfish motives as a result of socialization rather than biological inheritance, and they designed political systems in order to constrain and control human behavior and thus create order in society.

Such orderliness in nature as a whole was also evident to Charles Darwin, who, through his research into the causes of variations in species and the contribution of these variations to the survival of species in nature, became convinced that survival was assured through a process of natural selection.

Darwin thought that survival was guaranteed only to those who were the best representatives of the species and best adapted to the conditions of the environment. The survivors were those who through physical prowess and mental agility were able to win in the competition for food and mate. The suggestion here is clear, that nature is a never-ending struggle—a competition—and that a permanent state of war exists among and between all species and the natural environment.

Darwin's interpreters suggested that as with animals so with man. Herbert Spencer, who was quick to find social implications in Darwin's biological theory, argued that among men the fittest survive; indeed, they are the only ones entitled to survive. In this, the process of natural selection in man's world favors the aggressive and the strong. Man, in this scheme, is a predatory creature. Spencer's interpretations of Darwinian theory underlie much of the creed of many nineteenth century U. S. industrialists and their philosophy of the "stewardship" of the rich and the "gospel of wealth."

(It is to be noted that Darwin himself was not willing to accept Spencer's theory that the law of natural selection applied to the human race. Actually, he turned the argument around. Man's weakness, Darwin thought, becomes his greatest strength; it forces man to establish cooperative relationships with others for protection and maintenance. In addition, Darwin attributed to man a moral feeling —one of sympathy and compassion—rather than indifference toward the weak and defective. Unhappily, it has been his fate to become associated with "survival of the fittest" as a scientific theory which is applied to man as well as other natural species.)

The Invisible Hand

Often associated with Darwin as a supporter of the idea of self-regulation in human society is Adam Smith. A century earlier, he placed his special emphasis on the automaticity of economic affairs.

Under his doctrine of the invisible hand, there is a just allocation of a nation's scarce resources through the price mechanism which reflects supply and demand conditions of the market. By pursuing his self-interest, each individual can further not only his own fortune but also that of society as a whole.

It is this idea of self-interest as prime mover which has led many to assume that Smith considered man to possess a basically selfish, rather than a virtuous, nature. The economic doctrine of laissez-faire which Smith originated has meant "permission to do or make what you choose"; hence, noninterference with personal indulgence. This, when combined with self-interest as motivator, would seem, ergo, to support the notion that man is by nature self-seeking, predatory, and interested only in his own good at the expense of his weaker and less fortunate fellows. For example:

> It is not from the benevolence of the butcher, the brewer, or the baker that we expect our dinner, but from their regard of their own interest. We address ourselves not to their humanity, but to their self-love, and never talk to them of our own necessities, but of their advantage (Smith, 1937 ed., p. 14).

Though there is ample evidence to indicate that Smith, like Darwin, recognized that morality and government must and do govern the actions of men, he has nevertheless become, with Darwin, a symbol of individualism.

(Smith, at one time, occupied a professorial chair in moral philosophy, and in *The Theory of Moral Sentiment* (1759) made it clear that he relied on natural law and, as a reflection of that, on a natural morality which prescribed three cardinal virtues: justice, prudence, and benevolence. Though he recognized some truth in the aphorism that private vices become public virtues, he clearly assumed that, as a reflection of a natural state of equality, men in pursuit of enlightened self-interest are characterized by adherence to justice— "a scrupulous refusal ever to hurt or injure anyone else, in the pursuit of one's own interest or advantage." Smith was not concerned with production and the accumulation of goods per se, but rather with the ends served thereby. In effect, the welfare of the ordinary man was on his mind to such an extent that he implicitly took the side of the underdog, which he perceived the ordinary laboring man to be.)

Sex and Aggression

Sigmund Freud, the father of psychoanalysis and the first to explore man's unconscious mind, took a clearer position on human nature than did Machiavelli, Hobbes, Darwin, or Smith. According to Freud, man is motivated by innate instincts and drives that he constantly struggles to pacify in ways which are antithetical to the norms of society. (These instincts and drives have been identified with sex and aggression but were really intended by Freud to refer to nature's and man's hankering to stay alive.) To the extent that society succeeds in curbing these animal forces, man becomes civilized and his energies can be turned toward socially acceptable goals. But, said Freud pessimistically:

> Psychoanalysis has concluded . . . that the primitive, savage, and evil impulses of mankind have not vanished in any individual, but continue their existence, although in repressed state . . . and . . . they wait for opportunities to display their activity." [2]

Freud further observed, in his *Civilization and Its Discontents* (1930), that society, itself, is perpetually threatened by the underlying hostilities which exist between human beings. Periodically, these feelings explode into open aggression which persists until the participants can once more be brought under control. However, society's attempts to neutralize destructive impulses through a "cultural superego," which defines for man what is "good" and what is "bad," create feelings of guilt. This, Freud said, is man's most urgent and important problem (1961, p. 81). The anxieties generated by this constant clash between man's basic nature and the demands and needs of society increase human unhappiness and lead to mental illness. Thus, Freud seems to suggest, man is essentially doomed:

> From his [Freud's] point of view society, by its very nature, forces man to repress his inborn aggression more and more. The outlook for the future is that the more civilized he becomes, the more potentially destructive he becomes (Thompson, 1957, p. 151).

Warrior and Weaponmaker

Recent evidence has been uncovered which seems to support the idea that man has been an aggressor and warrior since the beginning of his existence. Under the direction of L. S. B. Leakey, excavations conducted in South Africa—among what now appear to be the earliest remnants of man's ancestors—have uncovered man's earliest tools and have established that among them weapons occupied the most important place. The indications are that these were used not only for killing in the acquisition of food but also against man—for protection, in the defense of mate or of territory, and in the conduct

---

2. In a letter from Freud to Dr. van Eeden, quoted in Jones (1957), p. 368.

of war. While the evidence is mixed, it has led some to theorize that a warlike, aggressive nature is a part of every man's inheritance.

As a consequence, it can be argued that Darwin's law of nature, survival of the fittest, also applies to man. Such an emphasis on aggression over a span of hundreds of thousands of years, Robert Ardrey has argued, must have had a permanent effect on his hereditary structure: "Man is a predator with an instinct to kill and a genetic cultural affinity for the weapon" (1961, p. 166).

In this view the urge to aggression, the desire to dominate others, is an instinct or drive transmitted from generation to generation through the genes.

The predisposition of men toward aggression has also been noted by one of the most renowned philosophers of our own time, Henri Bergson, who wrote:

> But no matter the thing taken, the motive adduced: the origin of war is ownership, individual or collective, and since humanity is predestined to ownership by its structure, war is natural. So strong, indeed, is the war instinct, that it is the first to appear when we scratch below the surface of civilization in search of nature. We all know how little boys love fighting. They get their heads punched. But they have the satisfaction of having punched the other fellow's head (op. cit., p. 284).

Bergson clearly joins with those who take a pessimistic view of man. By assuming that innate, predatory, and selfish instincts are first causes, he cannot conceive of a human society—with its dependence on material possessions—as capable of avoiding conflict through the processes of reason and self-control.

Manager and Managed

The underlying ideas about human nature which have been previously outlined will also be found among some thinkers whose work focuses on the relationship between the manager and the managed in business and industry. These are the writers who are generally associated with the scientific management movement and who date from about 1900.

At this time, Frederick W. Taylor, who pioneered this movement in the United States, saw a need for management to exert close control over the indifferent behavior of workmen in order to ensure their adherence to the objectives and goals of business enterprise. In spite of all the human values which have been inputed to his writings, it seems clear that Taylor and his followers made these six basic assumptions about human nature:

1. The employee is a "constant" in the production equation. The implication here is that man has a fixed nature.
2. The employee is an inert adjunct of the machine, prone to inefficiency and waste unless properly programmed.
3. The employee is by nature lazy; only managers honor the "hard work" creed of the Protestant Ethic.
4. The employee's main concern is self-interest. At work, this is always expressed in economic values.
5. Given appropriate expression, these values will make man fiercely competitive among his peers as an accumulator of financial rewards.
6. Man (at least the working man) must therefore be tightly controlled and externally motivated in order to overcome his natural desire to avoid work unless the material gains available to him are worth his effort.

In accordance with these assumptions, Taylor thought that management must assume the responsibility for specifying in detail the method to be followed by the employee in order to gain an approximation of his full output potential. In addition, a piece-rate plan would have to be included as a financial incentive to ensure maximum performance.

At about the same time, a contemporary of Taylor was developing a similar pattern of thought in Europe regarding the relationship between manager and managed. While Taylor concerned himself mainly with the shop environment, Max Weber designed the features of his ideal bureaucracy, viewing the organization from the top downward.

Again, in the elements of Weber's bureaucracy—specialization of personnel, impersonality, a hierarchy of authority relationships, entry and advancement by competitive examination, written policies, rules and procedures, and others—we find the Weberian image of man as a reluctant cog in an organizational machine. Thus the great majority of employees are confined to tightly controlled and dependent relationships with their superiors.

The pervasiveness of the Taylor-Weber approach to organization and management is evident throughout industrial organization today. Management scholars such as Urwick, Mooney, and Brown, as well as important business executives like Cordiner of General Electric, Greenwalt of DuPont, and Kappel of AT&T, have generally adhered to this model of managerial control and the underlying values which emphasize the need to minimize employee resistance to work—to support the Protestant Ethic—and a consequent need for autocratic rule and the traditional bureaucratic hierarchy.

Man: Optimistic View

Now let us turn from the foregoing cynical view of the nature of man to the view which emphasizes man's strength as a potentially creative, social being. As in dealing with the opposite view discussed earlier, we shall examine how an assumption that human beings have worth and goodness influences a wide-ranging sample of systems of social control. The examples used are not intended to be other than illustrative, straddling such divergent systems of human thought as political government, psychoanalysis, sociology, and business organization.

Social Instinct and Reason

Although separated in time by sixteen centuries, Marcus Tullius Cicero and John Locke shared remarkably similar ideas about the governing of men. Cicero in *On the Commonwealth* (51 B.C.) argued that men by nature believe in goodness and well-doing, and abhor savagery and baseness. On the assumption of mutual advantage, they come together in obedience to a social instinct and, where enough individuals are involved, form a democratic association or commonwealth for the benefit of all. Out of this emerges a leader who governs voluntary subjects through a moral claim to their allegiance rather than through regulation based on force.

Locke, in *The Second Treatise of Government*, contended that men of reason are inherently disposed toward mutual support and cooperation:

> The state of nature has a law of nature to govern it, which obliges everyone; and reason, which is that law, teaches all mankind who will but consult it that, being all equal and independent, no one ought to harm another in his life, health, liberty, or possessions (1952 ed., p. 5).

In other words, Locke argued that man's fundamental potential is reason and *reason itself* establishes cooperation as the basis for human relationships.

Under Locke's concept of the social contract, agreement is reached between free men to entrust to the community the authority to protect the common welfare. This custodianship is continued through tacit consent and is subject to the rule of majority. For Locke, man is naturally disposed toward doing good, and government is essentially a convenience. The sovereign is assumed to will what the people will. Locke believed that man's mind at birth is a *tabula rasa*, a blank sheet of paper and, therefore, that man becomes a person through sense impressions, mediated by reason, which he derives from social experience.

Thus the human mind and character are shaped by interaction with the world; whatever man becomes is a function of reason and social interaction. The function of government, therefore, is not to create its own laws as a controlling force but to discover what natural forces bring man to a state of reason *in which he can control himself.*

Cooperation and Survival

Two men of science, W. C. Allee, a biologist, and Ashley Montagu, a cultural anthropologist, have advanced ideas from their own fields about human nature which correspond in important respects with those of Cicero and Locke. They have argued that nature, from a biological standpoint, supports the concept of survival through cooperation rather than competition.

Allee reported in his *Cooperation Among Animals* the results of a wealth of research which provides evidence that cooperative, social relationships increase the probability of survival for any single individual as well as for a species as a whole. One of his simple experiments showed that it takes proportionately less toxic colloidal silver to kill a single goldfish in an aquarium than if the aquarium holds a number of goldfish. He suggested that the ability of a group of goldfish to neutralize a poison appears to increase faster than that of a single goldfish. He concluded his discussion of complex animal life in this way:

> The conclusion seems inescapable that the more closely knit societies arose from some sort of simple aggregation . . . such an evolution could come about most readily with the existence of an underlying pervasive element of unconscious proto-cooperation, or automatic tendency toward mutual aid among animals (1951, p. 29).

As Allee explored further evidences of cooperation in higher animals, he came to this conclusion:

> All through the animal kingdom—from amoeba to insects, or to man—animals show automatic unconscious proto-cooperation or even true cooperation. There is much evidence that the drift toward natural cooperation is somewhat stronger than the opposing tendency toward disoperation [among crowded animals] (*ibid.*, p. 203).

However, in spite of his argument that a cooperative-social instinct is readily found in nature, Allee also recognized a counterprinciple. This principle was that threat or force will be employed on the part of individuals, animal or man, to dominate others in a group in order to establish a hierarchy or pecking order. And he felt impelled to add that "much can be said for an established order of dominance and subordination" (*ibid.*, p. 204).

Allee pointed to evidences from the animal world which seem to reveal that any single individual thrives better where the pecking order is firmly established than where constant reorganization is in progress. He also saw evidence for this on the world scene. However, in all cases, Allee believed there will finally appear a subordinate to challenge the existing order. Thus he concluded that a pecking order brings peace and stability for the *short* run, but that an integrated unit characterized by natural cooperation promises stability for the *long* run.

Montagu agreed in all essential respects with Allee. He argued that from a biological point of view men prefer to survive through cooperation rather than competition: "The principle of co-operation is the most dominant and biologically the most important" (*op. cit.*, p. 50).

Montagu, of course, was particularly concerned with man rather than with the animal world. He believed that man from infancy on must rely on others for the satisfaction of his needs, and therefore affinity for interdependence is a fundamental reflection of the social state:

All of man's natural inclinations are toward the development of goodness, toward the continuance of states of goodness and the discontinuance of unpleasant states (*ibid.*, p. 57).

Thus warfare is considered by Montagu, as it was by Allee, as a human invention derived from economic or materialistic, rather than biological, considerations.

'Blank Page' Concept

On the basis of their more sanguine views of man's nature, these men, from Cicero through Montagu, have set forth behavioral concepts which support the idea of cooperation over aggression in human relationships and the need for strengthening these relationships through a constructive process of learning. Much of modern thought in psychoanalysis and psychotherapy, in sociology and social psychology, and in the field of organizational studies is also based on an optimistic view of man's nature. It resists Descartes' assumption that men are born with innate ideas and a more or less given nature.

Thus many modern behavioral scientists tend, like Locke, to think of man as entering life with a mind like a blank page on which experience is then impressed, and out of which the form and content of his personality are molded. To this way of thought, man's behavior is acquired in life and changes with experience. It is not solely predetermined by the genes, nor is it fixed and irrevocable. Out of these views have emerged new ways of perceiving man as an individual and as a member of a group.

Earlier, we outlined the pessimistic view of man on which Freud based his psychoanalytic theory. Freud's assumption about man's innate nature affected his theories in the same way as Hobbes's assumptions about man influenced his theories of government and society—man, left to his own devices, will prey on other men to satisfy his desires and must, in the interests of all, be restrained by forces in society.

The psychoanalysts who followed Freud have made distinctive contributions to modern views of the nature of man. From among them has emerged a group which broke with Freud on the issue of the basic nature of man, the so-called neo-Freudians, represented in this discussion by Harry Stack Sullivan, Erich Fromm, and Karen Horney. The neo-Freudians base their theories of human behavior on the assumption that the development of personality is influenced primarily by external societal forces and events rather than by biogenetically determined, innate instincts or drives.

Freud, of course, assumed that man and society are basically divided—on the one hand, a set of drives in man (sex and aggression) which are at the root of man's evil and, on the other, a set of rules in the human culture which inhibit and control the individual. The neo-Freudians argue that there is no dichotomy between man and society. According to Fromm: "The most beautiful as well as the most ugly inclinations of man are not a part of a fixed and biologically given human nature but result from the social process" (1941, p. 12).

Necessarily then, if man is to be understood, major attention must be given to those forces in his environment which influence the molding of his personality.

J. A. C. Brown in *The Social Psychology of Industry* has described the difference between Freudian and neo-Freudian ideas about the nature of man as the difference between thinking of man as being "pushed from behind" or "drawn from in front." This, in a rough way, is the difference between psychological determinism or behaviorist psychology—with its focus on drives, instincts, or the conditioned reflex as a source of behavior—and subjectivist theories of psychology, which perceive psychic energy as being derived from personal goals and personal perceptions of reality. Sullivan's theory of personality development, like those of Fromm and Horney, belongs in this latter category.

According to Sullivan, the individual begins life with certain potentials and two basic goals: satisfaction and security. The extent to which he realizes his potential and achieves his goals depends on his experiences with other people. The pursuit of "satisfaction" has to do with satisfying physical needs like sleep, hunger, and sex.

However, the manner in which such needs are satisfied does not depend on the innate characteristics of an individual but reflects behavior patterns which are the product of interpersonal relations. It is in relation to other people that an individual seeks "security"—that is, in the avoidance of anxiety caused by feelings of disapproval or inadequacy in a social situation. Thus the matter of psychological security is culture-bound, and the form and content of the human personality is a product of specific cultural forces.

Sullivan defines the anxiety-free condition of "euphoria" as a tensionless state similar to that experienced by a new-born and sleeping child who has yet to discover that he has arrived in a threatening environment. Such an infant is at peace with the world or, in Rousseau's terms, in a state of oneness and harmony with nature. Only exposure to the anxieties which arise out of human relationships can change this profound sense of well-being into a state of tension. This state of tension then promotes education and learning through which the self-system of an individual finally emerges.

The self-system, as Sullivan defines it, represents that portion of an individual's potential which is realized, while the "true self" contains the maximum potentialities which could have, under ideal conditions of experience, been developed. Since it is an unfortunate fact of life in our culture that interpersonal experience is far from ideal, Sullivan felt that most people are "inferior caricatures of what they might have been" (Brown, 1961, p. 167).

Cultural Determination

Fromm does not accept the "blank page" concept of Locke but, nevertheless, strongly rejects the idea that instincts are the primary source of human behavior. Fromm concedes that man comes into existence with a set of drives and instincts. However, he argues that their particular patterns of development and their manifestation in the behavior of individuals are culturally determined: "Any given social order does not *create* these fundamental strivings but it determines which of the limited number of potential passions are to become manifest or dominant" (1955, p. 14).

From this, it is clear that Fromm considers that human potentialities depend to a very large extent on the *will to productiveness which society succeeds in bringing to man*. The individual is shaped by society. The environment in which the individual exists, therefore, becomes a primary factor in the way he responds to life and work.

Fromm emphasizes in his theory that man is faced with a desire to be part of nature. Animals, through their instinctual equipment, seem able to accommodate themselves to the external environment through what appears to be an automatic process and, therefore, to achieve close ties with nature. Man, in contrast, through self-awareness and reason is alienated from nature.

In fact, in industrial society he is often alienated from himself, from meaningful human relationships, and from his work. In this process man is caught in a tug-of-war between self-reliance, power, control over nature, independence, and escape from isolation, competition, hostility, and insecurity. He must find his path by relating to things and to people. Ideally, he should succeed in establishing a productive relationship in which he is able to feel and act in accordance with his potential for contributing to constructive human life.

Pilot or Robot?

As our final example of modern psychoanalytic thought, we consider Karen Horney. In her writings Horney agrees with Sullivan and Fromm in the view that Freud gave biological and genetic factors an excessive role in character formation. Taking the position that man's nature is not instinctive but learned, she was one of the first analysts to emphasize the importance of interpersonal relations in behavior development. What an individual learns—that is, how he reacts to life with others—is influenced most by the way he is treated by others.

It was Horney's view that all individuals in their natural development seek sentiments of liking and approval from others. Where interpersonal relationships do not have such support, anxiety develops and begins to interfere with the growth of a healthy personality. In such cases people respond to others in three basic ways: (1) by "moving toward people"—feeling inadequate, they become attached and dependent; (2) by "moving against people"—rejected, they become rebellious and aggressive; or (3) by "moving away from people" —they seek comfort for rejection in symbolic substitutes and fantasy. Neurotic behavior occurs when there is conflict over which response pattern to adopt in a given situation. Various defense mechanisms help solve such conflicts but at the expense of genuineness in human relationships and of needed problem-solving behavior.

Because of her emphasis on the importance of situational factors in personality development, Horney tended to look to a person's present interpersonal involvements for the causes and solutions to neurotic problems. She did not deny that a connection exists between an individual's current responses and his early life—a connection which was so important a part of Freud's thinking—but she argued that one must look to the present situation for clues as to what triggered these responses.

Man is not, therefore, doomed by a set of prenatally determined instincts, nor are his patterns of behavior eternally established by early life experience. Horney's concept of man is cheerful and optimistic, not gloomy and pessimistic. Man is born neither a devil nor a saint; he simply reflects in his behavior the nature of relationships developed since the time of his birth with people who were important to him.

The insights into human nature which have been outlined above and which summarize the thinking of an important school of modern psychotherapy are based on the confident viewpoint that man is not doomed by a fixed and evil nature from which he cannot escape. Rather, they would seem to suggest just the opposite: man has within himself the potential to grow and develop significantly in cooperation with others. Man is a pilot not a robot. What is needed is not a method of controlling innately selfish or even predatory drives toward war with other men, but a means of tapping man's potential for joining in productive relationships with others.

Individual or Environment?

One of the first social scientists to apply this concept of man to analysis of industrial organizations was Elton Mayo of Harvard University. Mayo's view of human nature was optimistic and anti-Freudian. To illustrate:

> The concealed assumption of the doctrine of original sin invalidates the psychoanalytic findings. The theory that life is a strenuous fight to subdue perversion, that the human mind is by nature "pathogenic" (i.e., predisposed to the pathological) is not a starting point for biological observation (1960, p. 152).

In other words, the concept that life on earth is an atonement for original transgressions of God's laws, and that man is cursed with a set of evil instincts which must be curbed by society, is inadequate as a base for observing and understanding man's behavior in daily life.

Mayo argued that too much attention was being given in industrial settings to *individuals* as the source of noncooperative and unproductive relationships between the leadership of the organization and those who are employed to accomplish the work. He pointed out that developments in sociology and in social anthropology had already opened to serious question whether a merely psychological study of individuals in an organization is a logical approach to a comprehension of their behavior as workers.

On the contrary, Mayo said, such individuals constitute a group which develops responses to the total organizational environment. On the basis of this, the research interview program at the Hawthorne Works, originally consisting of isolated interviews, was restructured so that interviewers were assigned to study individuals over extended periods in relation to their jobs, the informal social organization in which they worked, and company policy.

The original isolated interviewing method was based on the premise that personal behavior or misbehavior was a result of personal rationality or irrationality; the second method assumed that the individual was only one of a number of interdependent variables relating to behavior. These other variables were part of the working environment and included such factors as leadership, working conditions, and working group membership. Science, inspired by the work of early sociologists and anthropologists, was at last beginning to show, contrary to Hobbesian theory, that man was more victim than antagonist in his environment.

Behavioral Science Man

While the initial thrust toward change in managerial philosophy and practice can be traced back to the origin of the human relations movement in the 1930s, it has continued through the present time in two somewhat divergent directions: (1) toward the fusion of the scientific organizational behavior approach with a new, more humanistic management philosophy, and (2) toward organizational reeducation and change through sensitivity or laboratory training. In both cases the importance of the roles played by behavioral and other social scientists in defining the relationship between the manager and the managed is becoming more and more evident.

While Mayo's work resulted in increasing the emphasis on human relations mainly in normative terms, much of the subsequent direction of this work is based on the research and findings of the behavioral sciences of sociology, psychology, social psychology, and cultural anthropology. Research workers such as Argyris, McGregor, and Likert have identified themselves with A. H. Maslow's theory of the need hierarchy as an aspect of human nature. Given the assumption that a satisfied need does not motivate, man is seen as satisfying in ascending order the needs of hunger in an extended sense: safety, social affection, esteem, and finally self-actualization or self-fulfillment.

The challenge for management today is seen by these authors as one of providing man at work with the opportunity to grow and mature continually into a human being who, because of a favorable working climate, is able to realize his own goals best by working for the success of the organization of which he is a member. Implicit in their assumptions is the idea that man has an essential nature which is defined by the broad spectrum of his needs, capacities, and tendencies. These needs, as expressed by Maslow, "are on their face good or neutral rather than evil" (1954, p. 340).

In a continuing reflection of the neo-Freudian view of man, we find McGregor stating, "If employees are lazy, indifferent, unwilling to take responsibility, intransigent, uncreative, uncooperative" (1960, p. 48), this is due to the traditional bureaucratic assumptions and methods of organization and control. Argyris, in a similar vein suggests, "Mutual understanding, trust, self-esteem, openness, internal commitment, fully functioning human beings who aspire to excellence . . . these values can not only be protected, but indeed increased, in an industrial setting" (1962, p. 5).

In the world of work, therefore, man is seen by the behavioral scientists as responding to the influences of his organizational environment. Given the opportunity, he will participate creatively in furthering the objectives of the organization. If frustrated, his behavior will characteristically revert to the basic need level of hunger; he will turn apathetic, slovenly, and totally alienated from an orientation toward work as a central life interest.

Such a basic underlying belief in man as a creative human being oriented toward constructive rather than destructive activities is even more clearly represented in the sensitivity training movement. Through this process of reeducation and skill development, Warren G. Bennis and his collaborators see the way to democratization of management—a condition which they view as essential in the face of accelerating technological change, the increasing proportion of professionals in the work force, and the consequent necessity of the organization to accept the values of science and scientific inquiry in order to survive in the future.

("Democracy" is here defined not as permissiveness or laissez-faire but as a system of values by which people in organizations are assumed to feel "internally compelled" to live. These include free communication, the consensus principle, influence based on competence rather than position, acceptance of emotion as fact, and a "basically human bias" in dealing with conflict) (see Slater and Bennis, 1964, p. 51).

In Bennis's terms, the "organization man" becomes a signpost on the road pointing the way to the kinds of flexibility and adaptability which are essential if the democratic environment in which science and scientists can flourish is to be realized. Whether one agrees or not, it is well known among men of science that personalities are only of passing interest compared to the contribution they hope to make to the accumulation of new knowledge.

Where Do You Stand?

We have confined the discussion to the pessimistic-optimistic views for the sake of simplicity and clarity, although it is, of course, a matter of common observation that all of the possible social processes are located along a continuum whose polar extremities are mutual cooperation and predatory competition.

As opposite ends of a spectrum, cooperation and competition are closely related to love and hate, friendship and enmity, harmony and discord, collaboration and opposition. They may therefore be used to describe a person's *basic* or *characteristic* propensity toward his fellowman. In terms of his attitudes toward others, every man will find himself at some point on this spectrum, depending on the particular situation in which he is involved.

However, each man is drawn by the force of his own history and experience toward some primary tendency, some central quality of being, which determines the general pattern of his social behavior. Peripheral changes occur in this pattern to accommodate the demands of the various roles he plays, but there would seem to be a core pattern which represents his basic beliefs concerning the nature of man. Man is evil or man is good, depending on man's experience with mankind.

The examples from the history of human thought that we have cited illustrate this concept of the *primary tendency* in the kind of view one man takes of another. They also clearly indicate that cooperation and competition, or goodness and evilness, as human characteristics are not discrete activities or qualities but rather exist in various mixtures in human nature.

Hobbes's *primary tendency,* for example, was to view man as evil. Nevertheless, his idea of the "social contract" contains the implicit assumption of *cooperative* activity among men by which they give up their rights to a ruling Leviathan to gain protection from one another. Bergson said that war in a materialistic society is natural, but he noted that collective ownership leads to cooperation within groups to protect members from outsiders. Even Freud, who comes closest to a concept of innately evil men straining against societal constraints to satisfy their needs, conceded that man may become "good" because of his dependency on others; he will, in short, *cooperate* when he finds helping behavior in other men.

Among those whose primary tendency is to view man as good, we find similar ambivalences:

Locke argued that reason evoked cooperation among men. However, he implied that the "social contract" exists between ruler and ruled to control man's acquired *competitive*, aggressive nature.

The neo-Freudians believed that man's goodness or evilness was a product of experience—that is, competitive (hating) experiences lead to malfunctioning by societal standards, but cooperative (loving) experiences lead to satisfaction and to development.

The psychoanalytic assumptions and clinical findings of the neo-Freudians to the effect that man has basic worth and is capable of constructive psychic responses in an environment of understanding and encouragement have received scientific support among modern experimenters. Behavioral Science Man, whether the setting has been in the laboratory or in the field—in a business, education, or government organization—is a "good" man whose potential for productive growth and self-actualization has too often been stunted by his superiors' outmoded assumptions that he is "bad." Therefore, for their purposes, he must be manipulated like a puppet on a string.

Conclusion

The quality of human relations in any organization, from the political state to the business enterprise, reflects first of all its members', and particularly its leaders', views of the essential character of humanity itself. It makes a great deal of difference in systems of social control whether those involved tend to view man, in general, as good or evil. If we assume that man is good, we can believe that misbehavior is a reactive response rather than a manifestation of character. This will lead to a search for causes in his experience rather than in his nature. If we are to find a cause for behavioral failure, we are more apt to look outside the offender than inside and thus consider a whole new range of variables and contributory circumstances.

If, on the other hand, we assume that man himself is bad, a priori, then we are prone to assume that misbehavior is caused by something within him which we cannot alter directly. Accordingly, our attention will focus on limiting his freedom to choose and to act through external curbs or controls. In limiting the causes of behavior, we exclude ourselves from powerful internal sources of control.

Thus the underlying human value which predominates is readily perceived in (a) the way social relationships are structured, (b) the kinds of rewards and penalties that are used, (c) the character of the communication process which links people together, and (d) the other elements of social control that characterize a relationship or an organization.

References

Allee, W. C. *Cooperation among Animals.* Schuman, 1951.

Ardrey, Robert. *African Genesis.* Dell, 1961.

Argyris, Chris. *Interpersonal Competence and Organizational Effectiveness.* Irwin, 1962.

Bergson, Henri. *The Two Sources of Morality and Religion.* Doubleday, Anchor Book ed., 1935.

Brown, J. A. C. *Freud and the Post-Freudians.* Penguin, 1961.

Ford, Donald H., and Hugh B. Urban. *Systems of Psychotherapy.* Wiley, 1965.

Freud, Sigmund. *Civilization and Its Discontents,* trans. James Strachey. Norton, 1961.

Fromm, Eric. *The Sane Society.* Holt, Rinehart, & Winston, 1955.

————. *Escape from Freedom.* Farrar and Rinehart, 1941.

Hobbes, Thomas. *Leviathan.* Bobbs-Merrill, Library of Liberal Arts ed., 1958.

Jones, Ernest. *The Life and Work of Sigmund Freud,* Vol. 2. Basic Books, 1957.

Locke, *The Second Treatise of Government.* Liberal Arts Press, 1952.

McGregor, Douglas. *The Human Side of Enterprise.* McGraw-Hill, 1960.

Machiavelli, Niccolo. *The Prince and the Discourses.* Random House, 1950.

Maslow, A. H. *Motivation and Personality.* Harper, 1954.

Mayo, Elton. *The Human Problems of an Industrial Civilization.* Viking, 1960.

Montague, Ashley. *Men in Process.* Times Mirror, Mentor ed., 1962.

Slater, Philip E., and Warren G. Bennis. "Democracy Is Inevitable." *Harvard Business Review,* March–April 1954.

Smith, Adam. *An Inquiry into the Nature and Causes of the Wealth of Nations.* Random House, 1937.

Thompson, Clara. *Psychoanalysis: Its Evolution and Development.* Grove Press, Evergreen ed., 1957.

Craig C. Lundberg

Toward Understanding Behavioral Science by Administrators

For nearly a decade executives have been exhorted to make more extensive use of the behavioral and social sciences.[1] For approximately the same length of time they have also been advised to simultaneously develop their conceptual skills.[2] Many distinguished men both within and outside of the practice of administration have joined this chorus of urging. Most executives would nod in agreement with these admonitions, for the changes in contemporary society and the

© 1963 by the Regents of the University of California. Reprinted from *California Management Review,* Vol. 6, No. 1, pp. 43–52, by permission of The Regents and the author.

1. More recent urging with an authoritative ring appears in Gordon and Howell (1959). Also see Wadia (1961), pp. 7–10.
2. Much of this can, perhaps, be traced back to Katz (1955), pp. 33–42.

growing pressures on administrators make such agreement obvious to nearly all who participate in organizational leadership. Most executives, however, also feel somewhat unsure as to just what they should do or just how they should go about either using social science or conceptualizing on their own—especially about the social problems of human organizations. This article is directed to those executives who are responsible for the human-social problems in their organizations (in other words, nearly everyone), who are intrigued by behavioral science, and who are especially interested in developing a means with which to make sense out of the new knowledge now becoming available.

Bits and Pieces

In courses, periodicals, books, and in the advice of staff experts, the knowledge available in the social and behavioral sciences is usually offered up in bits and pieces. Now we learn something interesting about psychological stress, now about leadership, now about intergroup relations, now about conflict between organizations, and so on. The technical jargon which abounds leads to confusion and misunderstanding, sometimes to the point where contradictions seem to appear. Seldom is the executive offered the means for relating, accurately interpreting, and evaluating these disparate items and bewildering languages. Yet businessmen, government officials, and other institutional managers continuously express their need for some reasonably simple concept or scheme for interpreting and relating that which the social and behavioral sciences and their representatives have to offer. Even when executives are eager to develop one on their own, they find little assistance. When they query "How?" or "In what direction?" few answers appear. Although this is the state of affairs, we should not dismiss lightly the magnitude of the tasks of relating the expanding knowledge of the newer sciences and of giving direction for conceptual development.

Clearly, the problem of understanding and utilizing the available knowledge of human beings in modern organizational settings is receiving more and more attention. Perhaps this will become a major problem facing the administrator of the future, who, many have predicted, will have to be conceptually as well as interpersonally skilled. Just as the know-how of the shop foreman gave way to technical specialists, perhaps administration by means of a "feel for the situation" is giving way to more rigorous conceptual practices and their corresponding human skills.

No Infallible Rituals

The contribution of this article is admittedly small as far as conceptual development is concerned. We offer no principles or infallible rituals. In accordance with our belief that concept development is both a personal and an individual task, we restrict ourselves to some comments on conceptual trends and to an example of how an idea from the social sciences may be exploited by the pracitioner. For the task of integration, however, somewhat more is offered. We suggest a central and significant concept, discuss it, and then construct a scheme (albeit a simple one) to use in thinking about how the bits and pieces of behavioral science information may be conceptually related. In addition, the concept and scheme are discussed with an eye to their practical applications, proffered as enabling a more systematic and comprehensive, and hence more effective, diagnosis of human problems and selection of action by executives.

The following discussion is meant to be restricted to the human problems of organization life. We do this for two reasons. First, there is the obvious importance of human beings and their relationships with one another for organizational success. Conceptual effort devoted to the human aspects of enterprise, therefore, may be especially fruitful and significant. Second, there is our belief that the majority of the problems with which top executives have to deal are human and social problems, not economic, physical, or technical problems as many persons have a propensity to believe.[3] This propensity is natural, however, because of our experiences in solving problems and making spectacular achievements in the nonsocial fields. It is the old story of tending to see problems only in areas in which we feel we can solve them.

Shifts in Outlook

As science has progressed in the study of the social and the behavioral, there have been some shifts or trends in outlook and direction of major importance. We may label two such trends as reintegration and dynamic systems.

The *reintegration* trend refers to the fact that the half century of schisms among the social sciences is rapidly disappearing. A variety of reasons have been advanced to explain this trend. Some writers would believe it is only to gain mutual support in the face of their critics. Others believe it is because of the recent appreciation of the key place psychological postulates play in all social sciences, even those concerned with large events like strikes, wars, or inflations (see Simon, 1954, p. 389). Still others believe reintegration to be the mature response to the discovery of "new" problems, problems which demand a variety of research skills and which, hence, encourage interdisciplinary cooperation. Regardless of the reasons, reintegration is occurring and the new fields which are appearing confirm this opinion. Even a cursory knowledge of fields such as conflict resolution, values, cultural psychology, social psychology, social change,

---

3. An eloquent statement of this point can be found in Boulding (1962), pp. 162–67.

and decision making indicates the variety of scholars and scientists involved in each.

Dynamic Systems

The trend toward *dynamic systems* refers to the shift from mechanistic, relatively stable, simple cause and effect models of description and explanation to models more often patterned after the living organism—complex, changeable, active and dynamic, exhibiting feedback loops and distinguishable parts. This trend is easily recognized in theories of organization. Not so long ago we thought of people and organizations in mechanistic terms; in fact the prime model or prototype was the machine. As the knowledge in the behavioral sciences has accumulated, the assumptions which permitted a machine theory of organization have been shown to be false. In organizational theory and administrative science, however, we are really just beginning to derive analogies to an organic model.[4] The key here is our acknowledgment that every act or element must be considered in a complex way because its integration into its environment is complex. Where constant change is recognized, the true complexity we have to unravel in our analysis is nearly overwhelming.

As the first trend, reintegration, continues, we should progress much more rapidly than in the past. Both of these trends in behavioral science require renewed emphasis on research in its descriptive and predictive senses rather than in a prescriptive sense.[5]

While the above discussion seems to imply a growing unity or consistency in social science, most of us do not have the intimate knowledge which permits a qualified judgment on the matter. To most of us, and especially to the newcomer, the social and behavioral sciences may seem to be splintered or scattered into numerous, unrelated specialties. Upon reflection, however, we are able to differentiate more general fields. By examining the core phenomena under study in any of these fields, we discover that they are related to one another in at least one way. The phenomena central to the different fields of study are at different "levels"; that is, they deal with different levels of complexity dependng on the definition of the unit of analysis they focus upon.[6]

Since the behavioral sciences revolve around the study of behav-

---

4. This is echoed in a number of "modern classics," such as March and Simon (1958) and Haire (1959).

5. This is the age-old distinction between the "is" and the "ought." That everyone, including executives, has trouble in separating normative (value) propositions from descriptive statements (of fact) is well known. This confusion leads to the incalculable error of assuming that men, once they have been doing something for some time, know what they are doing. A recent article clearly discusses the differences between prescriptive, descriptive, and predictive research. See Shull (1962), pp. 124–38.

6. The concept of "levels" is utilized by many other writers. For a stimulating recent example, see Clark (1962), pp. 16–30.

ior, and the social sciences are concerned with the behavior of man, we may illustrate this notion of levels by referring directly to the sciences of man. Psychology focuses on man as an individual, sociology on collective man, anthropology on cultural man.[7] Other fields study parts of these major social sciences as, for example, the study of the personality, investigation of the small work group, social change in economic institutions, and so on. As we think about the phenomena of the behavioral sciences and this idea of "levels," the thought strikes that we would have the beginnings of a means for ordering our knowledge, and perhaps for understanding, if we could discover something common to the phenomena at the various "levels."

The two trends noted above and the suggested fruitfulness of finding a way of comprehending phenomena at different levels prompts a brief digression, one which asks how one goes about building general theoretical systems. Why these? Because the goal of science, and eventually applied sciences such as management, will be achieved by what is here termed general theoretical systems—wider and wider and better and better systems of knowledge enabling us to describe, explain, and predict with ever-increasing accuracy.[8]

Two Approaches

There seem to be two general approaches. One is to develop theories within each distinct field and then eventually to attempt to relate or synthesize these theories. As social science fields vary as to the complexity in their units of social analysis, this approach, while relatively easy in the short run, is in the long run difficult. The other approach is initially to focus on some phenomena which are found in many fields, or to use the same conceptual orientation in many fields, then to build explanatory models in each field, letting the increasing congruence of models that occur with continuing verification and refinement become the general theoretical system. Historically sciences have gone their separate ways; in other words, they have followed the first approach. The adherents of the second approach (associated with the efforts of reintegration, and the use of dynamic systems) are of more recent vintage. What is required, then, to meet our primary objective of developing a device to make sense out of our knowledge of the behavioral sciences is to make sure that the device is not inconsistent with the trends of reintegration, dynamic systems, and hence the second approach to achieving the goals of science. Let us now turn to this endeavor, taking our cue from a word that has appeared frequently in this article up to this point.

---

7. Note the naturally more complex sciences use simplifying assumptions or assume areas constant in order to study them in manageable pieces.

8. A similar description may be found in Boulding (1956), pp. 200–201.

Hardy Concept

Throughout the history of modern science and its technological and applied offspring, one of the hardiest concepts of all is that labeled "system." Certainly the literature in all fields (regardless of their stage of development) is replete with the term. More often than not it is not only a prevalent, but also a central, concept (often implicit, however).[9] We cannot think of astronomy without thinking of the solar system, or of physiology without thinking of the nervous system, the circulatory system, the digestive system, and so forth. Sociology has its social system; physics, its atomic systems; economics, its monetary system. The applied fields too have utilized the idea. We speak, and with some familiarity, of communications systems, early-warning systems, feedback systems, records systems—almost ad infinitum. The point to be emphasized goes beyond the mere frequency of the use of the term. Peculiarly enough, few people until now have noticed the wide use of the concept. At the present time, however, this fact is achieving some notice, perhaps even some notoriety.[10]

Those readers who have used the term "system" in some delimited technical sense may feel that the examples given herein stretch their credulity; that the concept has been made so broad that almost anything goes. Others may accuse the writer of fastening onto a terminological similarity when in fact different concepts are employed. While the examples of systems noted above may seem unrelated, before a priori rejecting the argument out of hand, perhaps we should ask ourselves if it is possible to note characteristics common to all "systems." The following seem to be exhibited minimally in all systems:

1. There are a number of parts.
2. These parts are related to one another in an interdependent fashion.
3. The interrelated parts exist in an environment which is more or less complex.

Because we are interested in the human-social aspects of organizations, we add a characteristic to this list to designate *behavioral systems.*

---

9. The reader will note the following assumption of phenomena ordered into systems is consistent with science's assumption of order in nature.
10. In fact, associations like The Society for General Semantics Research are stimulating a growing amount of such work. The writer would like to acknowledge that much of the stimulus for the present article is due to the provocative writings of Richard L. Meier, University of Michigan, specifically his "Explorations in the Realm of Organization Theory" (1958, 1959, 1960, and 1961).

4. The parts exhibit an ordered pattern of activity (not random) which is congruent with achieving certain system ends.[11]

From this list it is clear that behavioral systems act and that they are both physical entities as well as conceptual products.[12] Throughout this article the word "system" refers to real or empirical systems, those that exist in the world of space-time. Purely formal or conceptual systems (mathematical or logical in character), it should be noted, do not necessarily describe empirical systems. Our designation of a behavior system makes it obviously an empirical one that has a conceptual counterpart and that behaves in that it exhibits observable action.

Characteristics

Perhaps before discussing systems (read "behavioral" from now on) further, we should briefly examine an example of a system's characteristics. Let us turn to a complicated system, one that is man-made and important to all of us—the business firm. Businesses certainly have a number of parts, both people and things. These vary in size and kind as well as in other ways; some human, such as individual and work teams, others nonhuman, such as equipment, materials, or goods. That the parts of a business are related is obvious from inspection. The example of the automobile assembly line provides an almost exaggerated example. Literally thousands of different parts, people, and processes are coordinated so effectively that cars may be driven off the line. Business certainly has ends (goals or objectives), whether the end is conceived of as profit, growth, share of market, quality of service, employee satisfaction, community recognition, or something else. As for the environment of business, think of the many ways we refer to it—as the industry, the market, the economy, the community, etc. Let us continue using the business firm as an example as we return to a discussion of system characteristics. Systems may vary in several ways:

1. By size. Systems can have parts from two to any number (each part, of course, may in turn be a system). Size implies complexity. Businesses range from the corner newsboy to General Motors Corporation.

2. By form. Systems can vary in the number of relationships

---

11. Our everyday speech is filled with reference of system ends, e.g., goals, objectives, aims, missions, purposes, and so on.

12. The last line requires very careful reading. It may be helpful to indicate what is not a system. "In simple, naive, commonsense terms, then, a *real* system is all of a thing. Even though it is possible to construct a *conceptual* system which includes Grandpa's moustache, Chinese hokku poetry, and the Brooklyn Bridge, this would not correspond to a real system . . . because these things are not surrounded by a single boundary, are not continuous in space-time, and do not have recognizable functional interrelationships" (Miller, 1956, pp. 33–34).

between the parts up to the point where every part is related to every other part. Another term for form is structure. Again, the extreme examples are rather easy to suggest. Some businesses exist where individual employees know and deal with only one or a few others. At the other extreme are those firms where everyone has some sort of relationship to everyone else.

3. By tolerance for internal variation. Systems can vary as to their capacity for accommodating internal strain and stress before the action becomes disruptive or pathological, that is to say, dysfunctional in terms of goal achievement. In business, the boss who excessively demands attention to detail, the high turnover of a certain class of personnel, the disruption and chaos following a particularly bad accident are all examples of problems which usually impede organizational goal attainment but which do not necessarily result in ruin. The partnership dissolved because of the rigid habits of two strong-willed men, however, is an example of where the tolerance for internal variation was exceeded, resulting in the destruction of the system.

4. By the number and kind of transactions with their environments. Systems can, therefore, vary in the degree to which their boundaries are open or closed. The designation of a boundary for a system is open to much confusion if we rely on common-sense notions. To be sure, physical limits to systems often exist as in the case of the human skin, but expecting all systems to be bounded by such tangible means is not very fruitful. Since parts need not be tangible, neither need the boundaries be. In business, a firm that represents a relatively closed system (no perfectly closed system can exist) would have few suppliers and customers and deal with them infrequently. The firm that is comparatively open would receive and ship large numbers of a wide variety of products, would use and provide a variety of services, and so forth.

5. By number and kind of system ends. Systems can vary as to whether they have one goal or more than one. They can vary as to whether the goal(s) relate to internal relationships or with the relations of the system to its environment. Thus, for example, a business firm may be concerned only with the satisfaction of constituent groups (internal relationships), with its sources of supply, or its marketing strategy (relations with the environments). The number of business objectives may also vary. Some people would espouse the goal as putting profit in the ownership's pocket. Others see a variety of coexistent goals.

6. By adaptiveness of goal(s). Systems can vary as to their flexibility in modifying an existent goal or in acquiring new goals. This characteristic is related to the system's self-regulating mechanisms. We are reminded of the way some businesses have expanded their employee services or have diversified product lines or have gone

from family to public ownership, etc. The negative examples are no less poignant—the buggy whip firm stubbornly refusing to see any future in automobiles until it was too late, or the manufacturers who confined themselves to ice boxes, steam locomotives, coonskin coats, or any one of the thousands of other obsolete products.

Perhaps the heuristic value of the system concept has been sufficiently exhibited. Now let us reintroduce our main concern and ask how the concept might be made use of to order and integrate bodies of knowledge.

Starting Point

Our starting point is the idea introduced earlier: that one system can include other systems as parts. Extending this idea we visualize the system which is a part of a more inclusive system as also being composed of parts which are systems. Or the first system is a part of a larger system which in turn may be a part, etc. Thus "systems" occur at different "levels." Now we have the germ of a notion for relating various phenomena. Earlier we noted that the central phenomena of the behavioral sciences occur on different levels. If we conceive of behavioral science as various kinds of systems, then we have systems at various levels which represent different phenomena. This structure can be illustrated by arbitrarily selecting three system complexity levels of concern to the executive. They are the level of the individual, the group, and the organization or institution.[13] Translating these into terms consistent with our discourse we have the *personal system*, the *interpersonal* or *social system*, and the formalized *multi-group system* with nonhuman elements. Further systems could be added, such as the community and the society. Note the successive inclusiveness of the levels and that more and more physical as well as nonhuman aspects enter into each more inclusive level.

Behavioral science knowledge can now be viewed as reporting on *system parts, system structure* (form), *system goals*, or *system processes* (transactions, tolerances, and adaptiveness) at several system levels. Maintaining the three levels designated, we will use brief examples to demonstrate how the knowledge which exists in the jargons of various fields of study can be translated into the common language of the systems concept.

At the level of the personal system, psychologists, psychoanalysts, psychiatrists, and others refer to needs, motives, drives, and health (system goals); the self, ego, abilities, interests, characteristics, and physiological aspects (system parts); personality and character (system structure); learning, perceiving, and rationalizing (sys-

---

13. Organization is characterized quite similarly although not explicitly as a "system" by Chris Argyris in a paper attempting to integrate the individual and the organization. See Argyris (1962), pp. 57–98.

tem processes). We also recognize how some specialists focus exclusively on one or a few aspects at this level, treating these as a system. The neurologist studies the structure and processes of the brain and nervous system. The analyst works mainly with the development, structure, and processes of the id, ego, and superego as the parts of a psychic system. The examples can be multiplied easily.

At the level of the interpersonal or social system, social workers, sociologists, social psychologists, and others refer to integrativeness, specific tasks, maintenance of a dynamic equilibrium, and member satisfaction (system goals); leaders, roles, and interactions (system parts); sociometric configuration, communication nets, influence, and activity patterns (system structure); initiating, group locomotion, and problem solving (system processes). A concept often employed by writers about the social system is "cohesiveness," a concept which is defined as "the attractiveness of belonging to a group." This characteristic can be translated as either referring to the composite of a certain kind of personal system goal, or as an aspect of interpersonal system structure, and exhibits how one might relate the work done at different levels—synthesization that is rare at the present time.

At the level of the multi-group or organization system microeconomists, cultural anthropologists, sociologists, political scientists, organization consultants, and others refer to continuity, profit, balance of power, and efficiency (system goals); plant parties, teams, capital, staff, and agencies (system parts); authority, status, cost, and power (system structure); legislating, researching, planning, servicing, and producing (system processes). The examples at this level, as at other levels, can be multiplied until our knowledge is exhausted.

Combining the concepts of system and levels we can construct a scheme [14] which allows us to visualize the relationships that exist between and within the three system levels, thus providing a comprehensive view which permits us to note exactly where we are knowledgeable and where gaps exist in our social science knowledge. The scheme takes the form of a matrix. This form of scheme not only aids our visualization and emphasizes the three important levels, but what is more important, it emphasizes the system relations *within* and *between* systems on the same or different levels.

Before examining the relationships this scheme aids us in observing, we should note some features of the matrix:

1. Each system at the three levels represents the relationship possibility which is *within* that system. Thus for level A, the personal

14. A scheme may be clarified by comparison to other conceptual devices. A frame of reference is not always explicit, complete, or logical. Its purpose is simply to comprehend or understand. A scheme is explicit, abstract, and logical. Its purpose is to order and explore. A theory is logically rigorous and has clearly specified variables that have some validated relationship. Its purpose is to explain.

system, we might speak of *intra*personal system relations, for B the social system of *intra*social system relations, or for C the organizational system of *intra*organizational relations.

2. The three cells that fall along the diagonal, cells A-A', B-B', and C-C', represent the relationships *between* two systems of the same kind or level. Thus we are noting here the *possibility* of a relationship between two or more individuals, groups, or organizations.

3. The matrix also permits us to think of the relations between systems where a system at a lower level is related to a more inclusive level. Cells A-B', A-C', and B-C' represent these relationships.

4. The matrix permits the converse of the above just as easily, where a more inclusive system is related to one at a lower level. Cells B'-A, C'-A, and C'-B represent these relationships. Note that these are the same cells as above but are read in the reverse order.

Because of limitations in space, our examples of the scheme will be restricted to mentioning a few typical problems or conflicts for each cell. In keeping with our previous examples these will be problems familiar to those with business experience. We shall consider problems within each cell, that is, representative of intrasystem problems first. Following this discussion, problems associated with "between" system relations will be offered (intersystem conflicts).

Sick Organizations

When a personal system has a problem we commonly say it is unhealthy. Mental illness often provides for bizarre or exaggerated examples; the hypochondriac has pathological fears relating to his "goals" of system maintenance, or in plain language, he is afraid he is well. Just as an individual can be "sick," so can a group or an organization. How many of us have seen committees or even business firms cease to exist because of withering away or exploding to pieces? If we examine these cases, we find such things as the committee that is trying to persist without any real goals, or the firm which cannot function effectively because its structure is obscure or has gaps in it, etc. The last cell in the matrix embraces perhaps the most dramatic of all conflicts, for example, those associated with union-management relations. Of course, everyday competition between the firms in an industry to maintain or increase their share of the market also falls into this cell although it is far less dramatic.

Conflicts between systems are often as dramatic as the sample of "internal" system conflicts just mentioned. In cell A-A', for instance we find what is popularly called "personality clashes," or "incompatibility." Cell A-B' contains the often-studied case of the deviant worker, more familiarly called "rate-buster," who always produces to the limit of his ability no matter where "the boys" have pegged production output (see figure 1).

Rare Examples

The examples of conflicts in cell A-C′ are somewhat rare. When a man just doesn't fit into an organization, he usually doesn't last. In fact, one of the main jobs of the personnel department is to screen out the obvious misfits before employment. Once in a while, however, a "maverick" is noted, although nonconformity in any extreme sense is disrupting to most organization systems. The often experienced rivalry between the "oldtimers" and the "newcomers" illustrates the

Figure 1   Levels and Interrelation of Systems Used in Ordering Behavioral Science Knowledge Applicable to Administration (Note: As System Levels Increase in Size and Complexity, More Nonhuman Parts Appear)

System Levels*		Personal A′	Interpersonal B′	Multi-Group C′
Individual or Personal	A			
Group or Interpersonal	B			
Organization or Multi-Group	C			

sort of conflicts in cell B-B′. The "wars" between two fighting or "bopping" clubs of juvenile delinquents offers a nonindustrial example. Most organizations with any history have experienced the tensions and pressures created by the "young Turks." This sort of problem falls into cell B-C′, as do the attempts at engineering a change in management by a minority group through a secret collection of proxies. Perhaps these examples will provide the reader with the stimulus to think of examples that are more pertinent to his own experiences.

Relating Information

Now we have a means of relating the behavioral science information at our disposal. Let us consider how the executive might enhance his administrative practices by utilizing the systems scheme.

The practical uses of the scheme are broadly conceived to be two in number:

1. It may be used as an aid in diagnosing the real or potential human problems in organizations.

2. It may be used to check the appropriateness of a course of action prior to implementing it.

These two uses and their implications will be discussed in order.

When faced with a problem, especially a serious or difficult one, the administrator is often tempted to act quickly just to get the choice behind him. This sort of administrative behavior depends on the apparent problem being the real one and on the executive's being able to manipulate the situation as he sees fit. The attitude of "suspended diagnosis" is fostered by the system scheme, for it counsels the necessity of a look at levels other than the one of the apparent problem. How often the manifested problem, whether it be grievance, gripe, or rumor, is only symptomatic of the underlying and more basic problem(s). This points out the well-known fact that "a" problem can simultaneously occur at several levels, that human-social problems especially are complex and dynamic ones. Although we like our problems to come from one cause and hence to have simple solutions, we recognize that this is seldom the case.

The scheme of system levels with its multicellular form continually reminds the man responsible for action that the source of a problem can reside in more than one system level and in more than one system relationship. Multicausation is, therefore, brought to the forefront and the interrelatedness of all kinds of system parts as well as the systems themselves is stressed. The scheme permits, almost demands, a *systematic diagnosis*. Faced with a problem or a symptom, the administrator can use the scheme to examine several kinds of systems at several levels. This systematic diagnosis leads to more *objectivity* and to a more *comprehensive diagnosis*. No longer, if the scheme is applied, can our problems be compartmentalized. No longer can a problem be simply labeled and acted upon as if it were definitely isolated. When problem diagnosis is more thorough—and the scheme should foster this—then a very practical aspect of our conceptualization effort has appeared.

Related Use

A second and related practical use of the scheme of system levels is the aid it provides in selecting a course of action appropriate to the diagnosed problem. We recognize the existence of courses of action which appear to be popular with various executives. One man believes, or at least acts as if he believes, that an interview will fix almost anything. Another just as consistently calls a group meeting or names a committee. Another executive simply fires his problems, or so he thinks; the list of favorite techniques and pet solutions is a long one and the incidence of men who administer in this way is higher than we might wish to acknowledge.[15] Each assumes that a favorite action solves his problem, as if the problem were isolated in time and not related to other matters. The system scheme becomes a control device in this regard. We now ask of our intended course of action: Is it at the same level as the problem? A contrary example makes the *point:* Why create a new policy (level of organization system) when worker X definitely needs psychiatric treatment (level of individual systems)? Here the action proposed concerns the system's tolerance for internal variation while the problem in fact concerns a sick system part. It is hypothesized that action may be taken at a higher level of system than the problem when the problem is not serious and when the larger system has influence over the subsystem (part). This influence may be from power, economic or job threat, for example, or attractiveness; that is, when goal satisfaction for the subsystem coincides with that of the inclusive system.[16] We see, then, that application of the scheme has a second practical use in controlling spurious courses of action and in producing more realistic expectations on the extent of solution to complex problems.

This article has noted and discussed a key concept, conceptually elaborated it into a scheme, and hinted at some ways that the scheme might be practically applied. The usefulness of the preceding has not been established, only suggested. It should be pointed out here that concepts and schemes of and by themselves guarantee nothing. Since the ideas presented are rather simple ones, some readers will no doubt be suspicious of them. For some reason, in our society, if an idea is neither very large nor very complicated (preferably both), it is not felt to be worth considering. Yet complex ideas are difficult to remember and to apply in the rush of day-to-day administration. Executives cannot always take the time to apply the complex idea or afford an expert to do it for them. For ideas like those presented in this article, there is only one real test for the executive—the pragmatic test of application. This test is urged for the concept of "system" and the scheme of system levels.

Concepts and schemes in no way reduce the need for intelligent and responsible management. Ideas, in fact, are the very fuel of such management. Some ideas help and others hinder, some can be acquired fully formed and others have to be developed. The ideas available to executives from the social and behavioral sciences are rapidly becoming legion, and the executive's job more and more requires him to acquire these ideas, relate them one to another, build on them, and

---

15. A list of such habitual courses of action is provided by Fuller (1956), pp. 122–37. Some examples are: "Tell 'Em, Sell 'Em, Explain It to Them," "Exercise Line Authority," "Operate on the 'Paper' Organization."

16. This latter view is the basis of theory of administration having considerable impact today. Douglas McGregor of M.I.T. is one of the foremost writers in this vein. See his *The Human Side of Enterprise* (1960). Also see Likert (1961).

judiciously apply them to a concrete set of problems. This challenge is as exciting as it is heavy with responsibility. In lieu of a "how-to-do-it" solution, this article has been intended to provide a stimulus for the thoughtful administrator.

References

Argyris, Chris. "The Integration of the Individual and the Organization." In *Social Science Approaches to Business Behavior*, ed. G. B. Strother. Irwin, 1962.

Boulding, Kenneth E. "Where Are We Going if Anywhere?" *Human Organization*, Vol. 21, No. 2, 1962.

———. "General Systems Theory: The Skeleton of a Science." *Management Science*, Vol. 2, April 1956.

Clark, James V. "A Healthy Organization." *California Management Review*, Vol. 4, No. 4, 1962.

Fuller, Stephen H. "What Is an Unsatisfactory Examination Paper?" In *The Case Method of Teaching Human Relations and Administration*, ed. R. K. Andrews. Harvard University Press, 1956.

Gordon, R. A., and J. E. Howell. *Higher Education for Business*. Columbia University Press, 1959.

Haire, Mason, ed. *Modern Organization Theory*. Wiley, 1959.

Katz, Robert L. "Skills of an Effective Administrator." *Harvard Business Review*, Vol. 33, No. 1, 1955.

Likert, Rensis. *New Patterns of Management*. McGraw-Hill, 1961.

McGregor, Douglas. *The Human Side of Enterprise*. McGraw-Hill, 1960.

March, James, and Herbert Simon. *Organizations*. Wiley, 1958.

Meier, Richard L. "Explorations in the Realm of Organization Theory." *Behavioral Science*, Vol. 3, 1958; Vol. 4, 1959; Vol. 5, 1960; and Vol. 6, 1961.

Miller, James G. "Toward a General Theory for the Social Sciences." In *The State of the Social Sciences*, ed. Leonard D. White. University of Chicago Press, 1956.

Shull, Fremont A., Jr. "The Nature and Contribution of Administrative Models and Organizational Research." *Journal of the Academy of Management*, Vol. 5, No. 2, 1962.

Simon, Herbert A. "Some Strategic Considerations in the Construction of Social Science Models." In *Mathematical Thinking in the Social Sciences*, ed. Paul F. Lazarsfeld. Science Research Associates, 1954.

Wadia, Maneck S. "Management Education and the Behavioral Sciences." *Advanced Management*, Vol. 26, No. 9, September 1961.

Part II

A Framework
for the Decision Process

Chapter Two

The Perception
of Disequilibrium

The first step in decision making seems so obvious that it is commonly glossed over. This first step is the manager's perception that a situation or organizational process is in a state of *disequilibrium*— that it is not as it ought to be. He perceives the situation as requiring a solution. When a situation is perceived as being in disequilibrium —that is, perceived as requiring a solution—the decision-making process has begun.

This step of the decision process is likely to be taken for granted. Ordinarily, little attention is given to *why* certain situations are perceived as being in disequilibrium and others are not. It is, instead, the situation itself, already perceived as being in disequilibrium, which grips the manager's attention. It is the violated "ought" that motivates him. It is the solution process that begins to usurp his energies. Yet that first step, the perception that a problem situation in fact exists, is basic to the entire decision process of organizational management.

The crux of the matter is this: No solution can be effective if it solves the wrong problem. And no problem can even begin to be solved if the manager does not recognize its existence. Thus the only problems that can be dealt with by decision makers are those they *perceive* as problems and, furthermore, perceive as falling within their scope of responsibility or interest. Problems that are unperceived as such pass the manager by. His inadvertent decision is to do nothing.

Yet managers usually spend much more time solving problems, or attempting to solve them, than they spend considering the important questions involved in this step: On what basis do I decide what to solve? How am I alerted to those things I call problems? What signals give me clues to disequilibria in situations and processes?

Structured and Unstructured Stimuli

The environment of the decision maker contains an infinite amount of "data," that is, an infinite number of sensory clues he could possibly perceive. Obviously, however, he does not perceive all the data—some is irrelevant to his interests or role; some is outside the scope of his experience; some is misinterpreted; and some is not perceived as data. Nonetheless, whenever he makes a decision he is responding to selected bits of data. The data he regards as relevant to his job can be thought of, from his point of view, as information. *Information*, then, means that part of the available data that has meaning to the decision maker.

The sources of the clues or information that may initiate the decision-making process, that produce awareness of disequilibrium, are, of course, many and varied. They may be personal or organizational, historic or current, internal or external to the organization, chronic or acute. For the purposes of this analysis, it will be useful to group stimuli that arouse feelings of disequilibria in the decision maker into those that are *structured* and those that are *unstructured*. In terms of the decision-making process, the distinction is significant.

Structured Stimuli

Part of the manager's job is to give structure to the information that pertains to his organizational management. He organizes and routinizes much crucial information so that it comes to him through formal routes that have been set up to monitor the activities for which he is responsible. A personnel manager, for example, may set up an index to monitor turnover, accident rates, or grievances. A production manager may monitor scrap rates, down time, and inventory levels. A marketing manager may be watching the ratio of this year's sales to last year's. A financial manager may regularly scrutinize the level of accounts receivable. Out of potential chaos, selected information is rationally structured to meet a manager's functional needs.

The particular structure applied to the information may be created by the manager. For example, he may set up a procedure for the systematic reporting of organizational turnover rates, production figures, or tolerance levels on controlled processes. Or he may merely monitor a structure that was created elsewhere, outside the organization. For example, he may monitor gross national product figures, the delivery schedules of suppliers, official readings of the levels of water pollution, or daily stock market averages. These are all examples of structured stimuli in the manager's environment.

Structured stimuli, therefore, are signal systems set up in advance to warn the decision maker when certain important states of disequilibrium may warrant decision making. Thus, the disequilibrium point is identified by the signal system itself, so that in effect, the first step of the decision-making process is initiated by the signal system. Specified "crisis points" can often be rationally determined ahead of time. Even crisis points which are not constant, but change in relation to specific variables, can be a predetermined part of the system.

It might be said that the major task of a good manager is to structure as much of the necessary information in his environment as possible so as to free himself for other activities. However, the danger inherent in placing total reliance on structured clues is the possibility that monitoring will pick up only the information selected by the system, and overlook other meaningful information. Nevertheless, the structuring of information is an important part of management which, if handled well, can significantly increase managerial productivity.

Unstructured Stimuli

Regardless of how well a manager structures his environment, not all the clues that may alert him to the possible existence of a problem can be structured in advance. Unplanned-for stimuli often arouse a feeling of disequilibrium. An offhand comment by a superior or a subordinate, an unexpected piece of news, conflicting reports from different sources, or even an indefinable feeling of the decision maker that something in the organization is "not right," may be perceived as signaling problems even though they do not fall into a structured category.

The principal source of unstructured stimuli is the social system of the organization. It is primarily in the behavior of his organization's employees that the aware manager discovers clues to the existence of problems, and it is in his manner of responding to these unstructured stimuli that he most clearly demonstrates his skill and sensitivity.

Although the consequences of the collective behavior of employees can generally be structured and monitored in terms of output, turnover, absenteeism, wage levels, union membership figures, and so on, other factors, such as the satisfactions and dissatisfactions that result in high or low morale among workers, are less easily structured. In such instances it is his sensitivity to unstructured "messages" and his knowledge about behavior that enables the manager to diagnose these messages, and further, enables him to initiate a decision-making process at the appropriate time.

Thus a major concern of the manager must be the perception of unstructured stimuli in the area of human behavior—stimuli that may indicate potential problems. As indicated in the Introduction, the primary purpose of this book is to assist the manager in dealing with these unstructured stimuli.

Self-Awareness and Unstructured Stimuli

One of the most important factors in the perception of unstructured stimuli is perception itself. The psychological findings on the perception process indicate that man does not simply "mirror" reality; his perception of any situation is a complex behavioral process, influenced as significantly by internal psychological factors as by external stimuli. Thus, man's perceptions are a psychological "structuring" of the given stimuli. By such processes as the selection, addition, omission, and interpretation of data, which are based on numerous factors in his past experience, he shapes what he sees. Hence the organization and labeling of information is as much a function of the observer as of the data observed (Elbing, 1962).

Each person has his own *frame of reference,* his own "system of functional relations among factors operative at a given time which determine psychological structuring and hence behavior" (Sherif and Sherif, 1956, p. 80). That frame of reference includes all the internal factors that are important to the individual—for example, his attitudes, norms, values, beliefs, fears, goals, etc.—as well as all the external stimuli which supplement the original stimulus situation, such as other people, the location, the physical environment, the sequence of acts, and the like. All of these internal and external factors operate psychologically to structure the otherwise unstructured stimuli; and new information tends to be organized so as to maintain preexisting views. Table 1 illustrates the psychological structuring process.

In order for the individual to process data psychologically, it must have some form or structure. He cannot exist in a totally amorphous or ambiguous situation. The structure of the data may be external to the individual—that is, it may exist in the stimulus or the environment—or it may be imposed by him. The relationship between the amount of structure inherent in a stimulus (or assigned to it beforehand) and the amount of psychological structuring necessarily imposed by the decision maker is generally inverse. That is, the greater its external organization, the clearer it will seem to the manager, offering him less opportunity to structure it from his own frame

Table 1   Individual Frame of Reference in Decision Making

Stimulus Situation	Frame of Reference Through Which Stimulus Is Perceived	Behavior
Structured (few alternatives as to meaning) ↕ Unstructured (many alternatives as to meaning)	Internal factors (needs, sets, motives, values, etc.) ↓ Psychological structuring ──▶ Behavior ↑ External factors (other people, situations, etc.)	

Source: Sherif and Sherif (1956), p. 79 (adapted).

of reference. On the other hand, the less structured the stimulus, the greater the need for internal structuring to make it meaningful so that the decision maker can respond to it. In any case, a stimulus must have structure of one form or another before a decision maker can respond to it. And the less clear the stimulus, the greater the role the individual's own structuring will play in perception.

Thus the organization of the real world around him is to a large extent determined by the individual decision maker's frame of reference. For a manager to successfully understand that world—its infinite number of data—he must first have an accurate insight into his own frame of reference. Such self-awareness must rank high on the decision maker's priority list. How can he go about increasing it?

Identification and Acceptance of Feelings

A first step in gaining a better sense of self-awareness is developing the ability *to identify* and *to accept* one's own feelings, which is not so simple or easy as might be supposed. Feelings of discomfort, guilt, envy, joy, anger, fear, satisfaction, or whatever, are generally vague experiences unless we make a special effort to identify them in words. Furthermore, we cannot be clear about the nature of our feelings if we do not accept them—something that works in two ways. Unless we can accept our true feelings, we are very likely unwilling to identify them honestly. And unless we accept them after we have identified them, our emotional energy may be expended in guilt rather than in the all-important process of deciding what to do about them. Accepting the fact that we have certain feelings need not lead only to acts of self-justification. The point is that we must *know how we feel,* and only then can we begin to understand our own frame of reference.

But feelings are not always easy to define. How often do we feel uncomfortable for no apparent reason? How often are some feelings confused with other, conflicting feelings; or their *referent* (object toward which they are directed) not recognized? And because it is easy to transfer feelings from one situation to another, our resultant behavior may be highly inappropriate. (How many of us get nasty with a secretary or the switchboard operator after being criticized by our boss?)

It is understandable, then, that our feelings in a particular situation or our general emotional state at a particular time have a great deal to do with how we structure external stimuli. Unstable feelings in ourselves may cause us to view the behavior of others as constituting a problem. It is thus possible to label a particular stimulus as a symptom of disequilibrium solely because of our own psychological structuring, regardless of the true meaning of the stimulus situation. The greater the awareness we have of our own states of feeling, the greater is our ability to differentiate between the inherent structure of external stimuli and the structure our own feelings impose upon those stimuli.

Three Steps to Self-Awareness

To manage the behavior of others requires that we be able to manage our own behavior, which involves developing awareness of our own feelings. To develop this awareness, we should train ourselves to take the following steps habitually in response to our own emotions:

1. *Know what we are feeling.* It is necessary that we allow ourselves to fully experience our true feelings and to identify exactly how we are feeling at any given time, rather than to seal off our feelings as being inappropriate or wrong even before they are recognized. Feelings not faced may eventually express themselves in ways we would rather not have happen.

2. *Identify the probable cause and referent of our feelings.* Relating our feelings to their cause can assist us in accepting them as legitimate, and assist us in understanding whether or not the feeling is appropriate to the situation at issue, or only to some prior experience of our own. Understanding our own feelings can assist us in more clearly differentiating external stimuli from our subjective frame of reference, and can prepare us for doing something constructive about our feelings.

3. *Express feelings at the appropriate time.* Feelings should be expressed, not suppressed. Rather than letting feelings build up and influence our life in a general way, we should express them in their *appropriate* situations. If, for example, the behavior of a subordinate makes us angry, it is one thing to express that feeling by saying to ourselves—or even aloud—"I'm mad!" It is another to fire the subordi-

nate summarily. As managers, we must train ourselves to express our feelings in a nondestructive manner. The point is that *we* must decide the manner and place for expressing feelings, rather than letting the feelings manage us.

Separation of Feelings from Situations

The next stage in developing self-awareness and self-manage-ment is development of the ability to distinguish feelings from the situations that give rise to them. This means that we train ourselves to perceive, not vague, uncomfortable situations, but ourselves as uncomfortable and the situations as separate. Further, we learn to distinguish between our own feelings and those of others, rather than color others' behavior with feelings we impute to them. An objective and rational response to unstructured stimuli is impossible unless we understand the role or effect of our own perception of situations.

Examining Our Behavior

Finally, we can develop self-awareness and self-management through the habit of reflecting upon and questioning our own re-sponses. When confronted by a particular stimulus, why did we behave as we did? Did we perceive it as similar to some prior stimu-lus? Did we behave in a manner which suggests that we applied a ready-made structure to it? Perhaps the most important step in the decision-making process, and the most difficult step to understand, is discovering how or why we identify certain stimuli as reflecting a problem—an organization out of equilibrium—while we ignore other stimuli. This is an important matter for analytical reflection, for the only problems we can eventually solve, or even attempt to solve, are those we can identify.

In interpreting our behavior we will find it useful to compare it with the behavior of others in a common or similar situation. Did we react differently than others in the situation? Why? Why did others see it differently? This is not a question of whose behavior is "right" or "wrong," but an attempt to understand by reflecting on our re-sponses how we structured the stimuli in that situation. Discussing a situation with someone who behaved differently may furnish useful insights into how and why each person structured it differently. Indeed, a major purpose of case discussions in the classroom is that individuals can respond differently to a stimulus situation and exam-ine the reasons for their different responses.

Once we understand that our own perceptual processes tend to structure our experiences, we can watch for the ways by which we habitually structure situations that interfere with objective observa-tion. Lombard (1950) has usefully defined *observation* as "the capac-ity to discriminate between reality as it actually is and reality as any one of us sees it" (p. 291). Any roadblock to objective observation of organizational disequilibria impairs the entire decision-making process.

Roadblocks in the Decision-Making Process

Since the objective recognition of "disequilibrium" initiates the decision process, it is important to recognize those factors that hamper decision-making effectiveness. There are a number of potential roadblocks to this first step in decision making. The following are the most common.

The Tendency to Evaluate. When first confronted with decision-making situations, most people have a tendency to evaluate rather than to investigate. Clyde Kluckhohn (1951), the noted anthropologist, sees this tendency to evaluate as a basic human characteristic. A tardy worker is "bad"; someone else's way of doing something is "wrong"; our own way is "right." This tendency to respond with an immediate evaluation must be retrained. Evaluation precludes inquiry into a fuller understanding of the situation—why the worker was late, or why someone approached a situation differently from how we did. Always, the keynote to the decision-making process is to substitute inquiry for evaluation.

The Tendency to Equate New and Old Experiences. Because our own experiences seem so clear to us, they usually become the basis of our approach to future situations. As we have noted, however, relying on past experiences tends to make us search for similarities between a current and a prior experience and to reduce a new situation to the terms of an old one. Even in truly similar situations, the second will differ from the first—if only because the two occurred at different points in time. Experience can be useful, but in general people merely learn an *experience* rather than learning *from* that experience. A person who works in an authoritarian environment, for example, tends to learn behavior that is appropriate to such an environment; he is less likely to learn about the *effects* of authoritarianism as compared with other leadership styles. To learn *from* an experience, one must make a conscious inquiry, which begins by viewing each situation as basically unique, not simply a reflection of an old experience.

The Tendency to Use Available Solutions. The ready availability of an apparent solution may make an administrator more or less indifferent to the precise nature of a problem that confronts him. Thus overemphasis on solutions may block progress through the decision-making process. Having taken an advanced course in modern marketing methods, for example, a student may see all problems in terms of marketing solutions. Similarly, having acquired a new computer, a businessman may define all his problems in terms of computer solutions. This factor can even be built into a specific professional discipline. The professional views problems in terms of the solutions available in his specialty. When we focus on an available solution, we may also inadvertently define the disequilibrium to fit that preconceived solution.

The Tendency to Deal with Problems at Face Value. When we are presented with information about a problem, our reaction may be to deal with it in the terms in which it is presented. Then, once the situation has been defined, further inquiry may be blocked. The manager should take his cue from the physician, who begins with the symptoms his patient defines. But he does not stop there. He also makes firsthand investigations.

The Tendency to Direct Decisions Toward a Single Goal. Behavior is usually goal-oriented. Certainly organizational behavior is oriented toward organizational goals, but sometimes organizational goals are reduced to a single goal in the mind of a manager. Tending to view all situations in terms of this one goal, he may overlook other goals more relevant in a specific situation. For example, a sales manager attempting to increase sales volume in a territory may emphasize fast-moving products and neglect the company's policy of maintaining a diversified line. A clear picture of goals, both individual and organizational, and of the hierarchical relationships among goals, is essential for a clear understanding of decision-making situations.

The Tendency to Confuse Symptoms and Problems. Identifying stimuli which suggest that an organization may be out of equilibrium is only the first step in the decision-making process. Even if our goals, values, and standards are clear, and even if we are aware of our reasons for identifying certain stimuli for closer examination, we cannot always tell whether a particular stimulus is itself the problem, a symptom of the problem, or both. A stimulus that tells us something is wrong may indeed constitute the problem. On the other hand, a stimulus which is not itself a problem may be a symptom of another problem. Or a stimulus may constitute one problem and also be a symptom of other problems in the organization.

Consider the case of an employee who initiates a large number of grievances: the washroom is dirty, the cafeteria's lunches are cold, the stockroom workers are uncooperative. If we responded to these stimuli without further examination, we might accept the grievances as the only problems (and indeed the grievances, the disequilibria, may be the only problems). On the other hand, they may be evidence that the individual is having difficulty adjusting to his job and needs help. Or further investigation might reveal that his complaints are only a symptom of unrest in an entire unit of the organization. He may be the person who has the least tolerance for such unrest and, therefore, is the first to express grievances. Moreover, a better understanding of the situation may be required to determine whether these grievances result from the problems of one employee or from a problem situation, or both.

The Tendency to Overlook "Unsolvable" Problems. Situations that have been long endured as problem situations may eventually be labeled unsolvable. For example, a long-time employee who is difficult to get along with may come to be viewed as being "that way," and everyone adjusts to his behavior. After a time, his behavior is regarded as an "unsolvable" problem and taken for granted. Eventually, the tendency is to cease defining his behavior as a problem at all. Then, when a crisis occurs, the personality of the long-time employee may be overlooked in the tally of factors that caused the crisis. The manager should make a special effort not to overlook long-term "unsolvable" problems as part of the overall disequilibrium picture.

The Tendency to Look at the Referent. Value judgments may reveal more about the evaluator than about their object. If, for example, we are told that water is hot, we have been told very little about the temperature of the water. For this evaluation to be clear, we must understand its context—the evaluator's expectations, his experience with water under these circumstances, and so on. Hot water is a different thing to a person making tea than to a barber preparing lather, to a mother bathing an infant, to a summertime swimmer, or to an Artic explorer. Despite the fact that such an evaluation is relative, we nevertheless tend to inspect the referent, the water, to confirm its "hotness." Similarly, if in a human situation we are told that an employee is irresponsible, we are apt to look first for signs of his irresponsibility. A more appropriate first step in such a case is to consider the evaluator and attempt to understand why he made this evaluation, what evidence he had, and what the circumstances were, and in this context determine whether we agree with his evaluation.

The Tendency to Respond Automatically. All the foregoing tendencies add up to a tendency to preconceive the nature of a disequilibrium, and preconception has a strong effect on the structure of decision making. It leads to premature, automatic responses, rather than to the systematic inquiry which constitutes effective decision making.

Conclusion

It is vital to distinguish between a disequilibrium that calls our attention to the fact that something is wrong, and the problem itself. Although these phenomena may be identical, more often they will be different and distinct. In human management, the decision-making process is usually initiated by the perception that something is wrong, that there is a problem, that something is out of equilibrium, that a situation requires a decision. Generally, the manager tends to focus on the situation rather than on his perception of it, but both require analysis if the problem's definition is to be objective and lead to appropriate decision making.

The process of understanding what is really going on—what is really wrong—is called *diagnosis*, the second step in the decision-making process and the subject of Chapter 3.

References

Dearborn, D. C., and H. Simon. "Selective Perception: A Note on the Departmental Identification of Executives." *Sociometry,* June 1958.

Elbing, Alvar O., Jr. "Perception, Motivation and Business Behavior." In *Interdisciplinary Studies in Business Behavior,* ed. Joseph McGuire. South-Western, 1962. Reprinted in Part III.

Kluckhohn, Clyde, *et al.* "Values and Value-Orientation in the Theory of Action." In *Toward A General Theory of Action,* ed. Talcott Parsons and Edward Shils. Harvard University Press, 1951.

Lombard, George F. F. "Self-Awareness and the Scientific Method." *Science,* September 15, 1960. Reprinted in Part I.

Sherif, Muzafer, and Carolyn Sherif. *An Outline of Social Psychology,* rev. ed. Harper & Row, 1956.

Wittreich, W. J. "Visual Perception and Personality." *Scientific American,* April 1959.

Redmond Manufacturing Company Case

The Redmond Manufacturing Company produced machinery in the suburbs of a large Eastern city. In the inspection department were 60 men and women. A rush job of inspecting 2000 spindles with attach-

From Ben A. Lindberg, *Cases in Personnel Administration* © 1954. Reprinted by permission of Prentice-Hall, Inc., Englewood Cliffs, New Jersey.

ments assembled had been brought into the department. It was a two-day job and there were two inspections to be made. The woman who had been assigned to the job had finished the first inspection when she found that her children had scarlet fever, and she had to leave the job to nurse them.

Some of the other inspectors discovered that the children had been sick a week before the mother knew that they had scarlet fever. The foreman turned the job over to another woman to complete. She refused, stating that she was afraid of catching the disease. Her stand became known to the rest of the workers, and they all backed her up. Although the foreman tried to get someone else to do the job, the others were all ready to walk out if forced to touch the spindles. The boxes lay on the floor a full day after the woman left.

On the morning of the second day the foreman told the personnel director of the problem. The personnel director called in the production manager to see whether the spindles could be disinfected. The production manager said that before any disinfecting could be done each piece would have to be disassembled, a process which involved taking out three screws and two springs on each of the 2000 spindles. Otherwise, the disinfecting solution would rust the polished portions of the piece. Besides being expensive, this operation would cause a long delay on a rush job that was scheduled for shipment that very afternoon.

Both men wanted to meet the shipping promise.

The Jim Baxter Case

During the early 1930s, Jim Baxter pumped gas and worked as a mechanic's helper in order to support his wife and recently adopted son, Jon. The job was new to him, quite different from the plant job he had before the Depression. After a few years of experience in the garage, however, he found a real interest in it and exhibited considerable ability in repairing automobile and truck engines. By 1938 Jim

This case was written under the supervision of Alvar O. Elbing. Names of people and places have been disguised.

was in charge of all the engine repair work for the garage. The owner Gus, at age 60, was glad to have Jim take care of the heavy work and manage the two boy helpers.

In the spring of 1940, Gus suffered a stroke and was unable to continue working. At the insistence of Gus's wife, Jim, although reluctant to do so, took over total responsibility of the service station. However, the long hours and constant problems with Gus's nephew (hired by Gus's wife as assistant mechanic), led Jim to leave the garage and set up an engine machine shop on the other side of town.

Jim had saved enough to rent a small one-room shop in a building which housed two other businesses—a radiator shop and a general automobile repair and maintenance garage. Since little paperwork or customer contact was required in any of these businesses, the small office in the front of the building was shared by all.

Much of Jim's business came from service-station owners with whom he had made contact through Gus. Since most gas stations are not equipped to do overhaul work, they send the engine blocks out to shops such as Jim's for replacement or grinding of valves, reboring the head, replacing rings, etc. Delivery and pickup of the finished block is done by the customer—whether service station, car dealer, or industrial plant.

With the great increase in sales of automobiles after World War II, Jim was flooded with business. But rather than expand, he decided to accept just as much as he and a boy helper could do. Excess business was turned away.

In 1945 Jim's only son Jon entered junior high school. On the way home from school Jon passed his father's shop and often went in to help for a couple of hours before dinner. Jon enjoyed the work. By the time he was 16 he was able to completely overhaul an engine himself, with his father's instruction. Thereafter during summers and on Saturday mornings, Jim paid Jon mechanic's wages for his work. Although the Baxters wanted Jon to go to college, when he graduated from high school he immediately began working full time at the shop.

Both Jon and his father were meticulous workmen and highly regarded for their friendly service and craftsmanship. Jon was especially conscious of doing a good job. He usually rechecked micrometer readings several times, always cleaned burrs from ground or drilled materials, double-checked fittings—in general he was very cautious and clean. Jon felt that his work was an extension of himself. Poor craftsmanship would be a reflection on his integrity.

In many ways Jon was like his father. He was interested in working hard and earning a fair day's wage. He was seldom known to raise his voice and his social life was limited to his family and a weekly evening at the local rifleman's club for archery practice and a few beers. Both their lives centered around the shop.

About 1960, Jim began to seriously think of the future of the business after he passed away. An accountant friend suggested that heavy inheritance taxes could be avoided if he sold the business to Jon for a reasonable price. His son in turn would hire his father, while paying for the shop over a period of five years or more. Confronted with these ideas, which could only be of benefit to him, Jon graciously accepted the offer.

The plan was carried out during the early 1960s. Official ownership passed to Jon in 1967. Although Jim was nearly 70, he continued to work every day. Any suggestion that he slow down or retire was laughed off. If pressed, he took it as an insult and countered with a stern face and silence. Mrs. Baxter died in 1965 after a short illness, leaving the shop Jim's only source of pleasure and contact with the world.

For a man his age Jim was very healthy. In the two years after Mrs. Baxter's death, however, his thinking ability and sight definitely began to show signs of deterioration. Jon had suspected this for several years but largely ignored the occasional side remarks to this effect made by the mechanics in the radiator shop or garage. During the next year things were different, however. Early in the spring, several engines were returned because of poor workmanship. Rechecking the records Jon determined that in each case it was work his father had done. Although it was not an extreme burden, the additional cost and labor needed to fix the engines wiped out the original profit on the job. Unfortunately, two of the engines were from the same dealer, who began taking his work elsewhere.

After considerable pressure from his son, Jim agreed to take a short vacation early in June to visit his only surviving brother. In five days he was back on the job, claiming he couldn't stand the boredom. Two weeks later, a marine engine was returned that had been in the shop a week earlier for an overhaul. The local marine owner was furious. The engine was for one of his ferry boats, which was now inoperative during the height of the season.

Jon was very concerned about the loss of another good customer. His father had worked on the engine, grinding the valve seats unevenly. This caused one valve to crack and two others to be badly burned after the engine had been replaced in the ferry. Jim claimed that the probable cause of the mishap was defective valves, something Jon found impossible to believe.

Increasingly Jon spent time checking his father's work before it was sent out. He worried so much about losing customers that he wouldn't leave his father alone in the shop. Late in August another customer was lost due to Jim's work. Shortly thereafter a very frustrated Jon wondered what could be done about the situation.

Gray Drake Airlines Case

Tim Botz was a student at Eastern State University in Dover, New Hampshire. He was 21 years of age and a native of Kellte, Maine, a small town right across the New Hampshire state line.

Tim's major was business administration. During the fall quarter of his senior year at Eastern State, he signed up for a nine-credit transportation course, which was to continue over the remainder of his senior year. As a part of this course, he was assigned to do research for Gray Drake Airlines, a small independent company that operated scheduled flights linking the main cities of the New England States. Gray Drake had flights connecting New York; Boston; Portland, Maine; Dover and Portsmouth, New Hampshire; Derby and New Haven, Connecticut; Middlebury, Vermont; Lexington, Massachusetts; and Concord, New Hampshire. They had 20 planes in use. The crews consisted of flight attendants and pilots. There were 50 of the former working for the company and 30 pilots (see Figure 1). The company's home office was in Dover.

The directors of Gray Drake Airlines interviewed Tim at a board meeting and expressed pleasure at having a student from the University do research for them. Consequently, they created a nonsalaried position, director of research, for Tim. He was to be given full access to company files, office space, telephone, mimeograph work, etc. The board of directors recommended that Tim work on the problems of publicity and passenger comfort.

In September, when Tim started to work for the company, he was taken around by Mr. N. S. Roake, his immediate superior (see Figure 1), and introduced to the department heads. It was made clear at this time that anything that Tim suggested, if it had the approval of Mr. Roake, was to be followed. An interoffice memo was also sent around explaining Tim's position and asking that cooperation be accorded him. By October, Tim had decided that the best way to gain the information he needed would be to distribute questionnaires to the passengers. Tim felt that the speediest way to do this would entail having the chief flight attendant distribute the questionnaires on his

Figure 1   Gray Drake Airlines Organization Chart

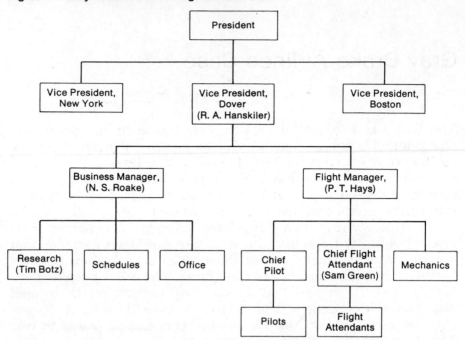

periodic rounds of checks on the flight attendants.[1] The flight attendants would distribute the questionnaires to the passengers as they embarked on their trip and collect them at the end of the flight. The flight attendant could then either mail the completed questionnaires to Dover or give them to the chief flight attendant on his next trip. This plan was approved of by Mr. Roake, as were the questionnaires. Tim then personally made a pretesting by going on several flights and administering the questionnaires. By the middle of November, he felt that he was actually ready to begin work.

Tim then went to the chief flight attendant to explain the procedure to him. He was surprised to find that he had had previous contact with the chief flight attendant, Sam Green. Tim had first met Mr. Green in the summer of 1953 when, in connection with a sociology class at Eastern State, he had done a project on personality research. Among those on his list to interview, a list of names of volunteers furnished by the instructor, Green's name occurred. Consequently, Tim had two personal interviews with Green during that summer. During the interviews, Sam was quite agreeable and furnished Tim with much helpful information about himself and his background.

---

1. On Gray Drake Airlines, because the flights were so short, there were no stewardesses. The flight attendant undertook the necessary duties concerning the passengers, baggage, mail, etc.

Sam Green was 26 years old. In 1945 when he graduated from a Maine high school, he entered the service for three years. Upon returning, he started at Eastern State University. He majored in architecture and also pledged a fraternity. After three years of college, during which he received many low grades, he went to work as a flight attendant for Gray Drake Airlines. Two years later, because of his leadership ability, he was offered the job of chief flight attendant. He had held this job about six months when Tim first started doing survey work for the company.

When Tim entered Green's office to discuss his current research for the airlines, Tim felt that Green was distant or cool compared with what Tim expected, and he decided that perhaps, for some reason, Green did not wish to remember their previous encounter. Hence Tim did not mention it but merely presented his plan concerning the distribution and collection of the questionnaires. Tim was aware of the interoffice letter sent out to all the men explaining his position with the airlines and the fact that all the personnel were to cooperate with him. He mentioned this to Green and received only a grunt of recognition. During the interview, Green talked very little and seemed to focus his attention elsewhere. Tim left the interview without a feeling of accomplishment but did feel that he had tried his best.

At the beginning of the first week in December, Tim left 1000 questionnaires [2] with the secretary in Green's office (Green was not in then). Tim attached a memo reminding Green of the procedure to be followed. Tim felt that this was a good time to start distribution, as the Christmas rush was nearing. He mentioned this in his note to Green. The following day Tim checked with the secretary and learned that she had personally given the materials to Green the previous afternoon. She commented that Green had read the memo and shrugged his shoulders. But she did see that when he left for his weekly trip he stuffed over half of the questionnaires into his brief case. This seemed like a good omen to Tim. During the two weeks that followed, Tim expected to receive some of the completed questionnaires either by mail or personally from Green; but none came in. As Green did not return to home base, Tim concluded that everything was tied up by the Christmas rush. As the end of the school quarter neared and he was busy with tests, Tim decided to let things rest until January.

The second week of January, Tim returned to his office at Gray Drake Airlines expecting to find many completed questionnaires. However, none were there; and, in checking with the secretary, he learned that Green had left no message for him. Tim then went to see

2. A copy of this qustionnaire appears at the end of this case.

Mr. Roake and explained what had happened. Roake was busy gathering material to take to an airlines convention the following day in New York. His only suggestion was that Tim see Green and get to the bottom of the situation. Tim returned to the office, picked up another batch of questionnaires, and went into Green's office. After an exchange of pleasantries, the following discussion took place:

Tim: Well, Sam, I've been waiting for a report on my questionnaires, but as yet have received no information, nor have I received any completed questionnaires. So, I concluded that you brought them back with you. Do you have them?

Sam: Yes, some were completed. I stuck them somewhere. Let's see now. [He rummaged through several desk drawers and finally pulled out about seventy-five and handed them to Tim.]

Tim: [Tim glanced over them for a moment and noted that they were correctly filled out.] But Sam, what about the rest? You know during the Christmas rush, both Mr. Roake and I agreed, was an ideal time to query our passengers. And you were fully indoctrinated with the policies of distribution and the importance of this survey. What happened?

Sam: Well, we were pretty busy. I did what I could. [Pause.] Excuse me, but I have a luncheon date and must be going.

Tim: Before you go, here are some more questionnaires. Please try to get them completed and back by your next trip. You'll be back in about two weeks, won't you?

Sam: Sure, sure, kid, I'll see you in a couple of weeks.

Tim felt discouraged, but he felt that a start could be made with the seventy-five completed ones he had. He could begin coding them at any rate.

During the next two weeks, no questionnaires were returned, and Tim began to worry. He personally contacted seven flight attendants who came into Dover during his hours at the office. From four of the seven he learned that they had not received any questionnaires to distribute from Green, and three said they had been handed a few by Green who mumbled something about "some college kid's scheme." As a result, Tim felt they were completely ignorant of the whole research project. Tim explained fully to each of them what the project was aimed at, his part in it, what their share of the job was, and also showed them a copy of the interoffice memo written by Roake authorizing utmost cooperation for the project. The men all seemed interested and Tim left fifty questionnaires with each of them to distribute that day. They promised to return them promptly.

Within the next week all but 100 of these were returned completed and with requests for more. However, as yet there was no word from Green. Tim felt that the project was definitely under way. He concluded that perhaps he had been wrong in giving the job to Green to take care of. But as Tim had only been able to contact ten flight attendants personally at Dover, he saw no other way to distribute the questionnaires except through the fieldman, Green. In repeated attempts to see Green during his next few days at the home office, Tim met with no success. Green was either too busy to be disturbed or he was out. As Tim felt that he had almost exhausted the supply of new passengers coming to and going from Dover (most of the planes flying from Dover carried the same passengers on business trips to and from New York, Boston, and Portland), he felt that in order to get a well-rounded and unbiased survey it was mandatory that he reach the opinion of passengers in the six other outlying cities where Gray Drake planes flew. Consequently, he wrote an interoffice memo (shown at the end of this case) to Green and also sent copies to Mr. Roake, Mr. Hays (Green's boss), and Mr. Hanskiler, the vice president in charge of the Dover port. Eight days passed and Tim received neither an answer from Green nor any completed questionnaires. He wondered what to do.

Gray Drake Airlines Survey Questionnaire

To improve Gray Drake Airlines' service to you, we would appreciate your completing the following questionnaire (sealing it if you wish) and returning it to your flight attendant. You may omit any question that you do not wish to answer.

At what town did you board? _____

At what town will you get off? _____

About how many times have you flown by commercial, scheduled airlines in the past year? _____

About how many times have you flown by Gray Drake Airlines in the past year? _____

Please rate the ground personnel that served you before this flight:

Below average   Average   Excellent

Courtesy _____

Appearance _____

Efficiency _____

Willingness to cooperate _____

Comments: _____

Please rate the flight attendant now on duty regarding:

Below average   Average   Excellent

Courtesy _____

Appearance _____

Efficiency _____

Willingness to cooperate _____

Comments: _____

What is the purpose of your trip today?

_____Business only _____Recreation only _____Business and recreation _____Vacation _____I live there _____Visit to my family Other_____

If the purpose of your trip is business, what type of business are you engaged in? _____

What has influenced you most in choosing to fly Gray Drake Airlines?
_____Newspaper advertising _____Radio advertising _____Friends _____Mail addressed to me _____News item Other_____

If Gray Drake Airlines' service had not been available, how would you have made this trip?
_____Automobile _____Train _____Bus _____Another airline _____Uncertain

If Gray Drake Airlines' service were discontinued:
Would you, as an individual, be inconvenienced? _____Yes _____No
Would it impair the efficiency of your business? _____Yes _____No
Would it place your organization at a disadvantage? _____Yes _____No

Do you have any comments regarding this aircraft?
_____

Is your annual income under $5000 _____ over $5000? _____
Would you mind giving us your name and home address?
Name: _____ Mr. _____ Mrs. _____ Miss _____
Address _____
Would you mind giving us your approximate age? _____
Additional remarks regarding service, schedules, personnel, etc.

Thank you very much,

TIMOTHY JONAS BOTZ, *Director*
Gray Drake Airlines Research
Eastern State University

Interoffice Memorandum

February 10, 1954

To: Sam Green
From: Tim Botz
Subject: Questionnaire distribution

I have found it extremely difficult to work out a method whereby the inflight questionnaires can be distributed to flight attendant personnel. My many attempts to discuss this project with you have met with disinterest and abruptness, which I am at a loss to comprehend. I do lack the necessary instructions from your office in order to execute this portion of the project.

As it is my understanding that you were to cooperate with me in this endeavor, I am therefore making this final attempt to solicit your help. I naturally desire to get this work under way as soon as possible, and my memorandum of the eleventh [3] sufficiently covered the implements necessary to the project.

Your response at the earliest possible date will be greatly appreciated.

Respectfully,

Timothy Jonas Botz

cc: N. S. Roake
P. T. Hays
R. A. Hanskiler

---

3. This refers to the first memo Tim sent to Green, accompanying the first group of questionnaires left in Green's office.

Thomas Motor Company Case

The Thomas Motor Company was a Plymouth-Dodge agency in Brownville, Michigan. The company was founded in 1927 by Mr. Edward P. Thomas. Until his unexpected death in September, 1954, Mr. Thomas had been an active, respected citizen of the community and a successful businessman. Mr. Thomas's eldest son, John, succeeded to the presidency of the company.

John Thomas graduated in engineering from Mid-State University in 1947 and went to work as a salesman for Industrial Chemical Company in a nearby region. It had always been understood that he would take over the reins of the Thomas Motor Company when his father retired. John and his family returned to Brownville immediately after the elder Thomas's fatal heart attack.

John Thomas learned much about the business in a short time.

In the first 13 months, he made very few administrative changes and he was guided chiefly by the recommendations of the experienced men who had worked for his father.

The Thomas Motor Company had two major divisions: sales and service. The service division had an auto-service center located downtown with the showrooms and main office. The truck-service center had its shop on the outskirts of town, about ten blocks from the main office.

The truck-repair shop regularly employed a service manager, four mechanics, a cashier-bookkeeper, and a parts man (although in late 1955 the latter was scheduled to be drafted into the service in six weeks and no replacement had yet been obtained).

The foreman and service manager of the truck center was Mr. Titus Nolan. He had been with the company since it was organized in 1927. His job included talking with customers regarding the cost and time of each job and assigning the work to the mechanics. Nolan also worked on the trucks himself when time allowed, although he had worked more closely with the men in the past than he now had time to. His ability as a foreman and a first-rate mechanic was widely respected; also Nolan was known as a quiet, unassuming man who, in the other mechanics' words, "takes things as they come and doesn't easily get excited."

The other truck mechanics were Bob, Jim, Ralph, and Dexter, an apprentice. (Their ages were 34, 32, 36, and 24, respectively.) In late 1955, Bob and Jim had been working in the shop about ten years. Ralph Turner had been employed by the Thomas Motor Company for the past 15 months. Dexter had been there for one year.

Ralph had previously worked in his father's trucking company, doing maintenance work on the trucks in their own shop. However, they did not have enough work to use their own shop profitably all of the time, as it developed, and so its use was discontinued. As a result, Mr. Turner and Ralph decided that Ralph would go to work for Mr. Thomas, and his father would send all of his truck repair and maintenance work there. This was quite a large account, and one the Thomas Company was happy to obtain.

When Ralph first came to work he asked to do the repairs on his father's trucks. Mr. Nolan said that Ralph could do this as much as was practicable. About two months later, Mr. Nolan had an opportunity to talk to the senior Turner about his agreement. Nolan explained that the usual method of working in the shop involved each man's becoming more or less of a specialist on certain kinds of jobs and being assigned to these kinds of repairs as much as possible. Nolan felt that this led to increased efficiency and better workmanship. Also, he explained that since Mr. Turner's trucks were serviced at uneven intervals—sometimes two or three trucks at a time, sometimes none—he felt that Mr. Turner could be better served if the repairs were handled in the usual way by different men. Mr. Turner accepted this proposal.

Mr. Nolan passed the word on to Ralph. Ralph said he could see the logic of this and would accept "anything you decide upon." Nolan said at a later time that he expected this reaction from Ralph, because Ralph seemed to be getting along so well with the job and with the other men in the shop. He was "a very cooperative employee," in Nolan's words.

The mechanics were paid the going union-scale wage for their craft, and the only pay differentials were based on seniority. Dexter, new to the trade, was paid considerably less than the others.

Mr. Nolan considered Bob, Jim, and Ralph about equal in overall skill as mechanics, but Bob was the fastest man in the shop, with Jim a close second. Ralph was somewhat slower, and of course Dexter was a good deal slower because of lack of experience.

When a job was taken into the truck shop, the customer was usually told what the labor cost would be when he left the truck. From past experience the mechanic could usually judge fairly well whether he was losing too much time in the job, or whether he was going to finish on schedule or ahead of time. He tried to get ahead of the job he was doing so he could go across the street for coffee about 10 a.m. and again at 2:30 p.m. It was also an unwritten law that if a mechanic was not ahead on his job, he would not be able to go for coffee. Bob and Jim were almost always able to go, and Ralph was rarely able to go.

Dexter was almost always assigned to help one of the other mechanics. He would go for coffee if the man he was working with was able to go. Mr. Nolan, the parts man, and the cashier almost always went. These coffee sessions were looked upon as pleasant social occasions.

About August, 1955, Ralph Turner began to make mistakes in his work, which Nolan attributed to haste on Ralph's part. Nolan checked the men's work carefully, and he was usually able to catch errors in the shop. However, several of Ralph's mistakes were not caught and proved to be quite serious. The first incident involved his not allowing enough clearance on a valve job. This customer returned about a week later very angry; and, although the garage did the work again free of charge, it lost a very good account.

At this time, Nolan talked to Ralph and told him to slow down and take his time even if he ran over the time that the job usually took. Ralph complained that the shop was too dirty and that this was the reason he made mistakes. He had been able to keep his own shop very clean and free from dirt when he worked for his father. Nolan replied that it wasn't possible to keep this shop as clean as Ralph's previous one because there wasn't sufficient spare time but that he felt the shop was as clean as most shops of this type. Ralph was a good deal more careful and worked at a slower rate for a couple of weeks. During this time he was never able to take a coffee break.

Nolan also noticed that Ralph had gradually shown, since he stopped working exclusively on his father's trucks, an increasing tendency to be interested in what other mechanics were doing on his father's vehicles when they were in the shop for repair. Several times Nolan had spoken to Ralph when the latter was found, during the lunch hour, tampering with a Turner truck on which one of the other mechanics was assigned to work. Nolan did not take this very seriously nor did he speak to Ralph, except mildly, because he felt it showed simply that Ralph was "eager and just solicitous about those old Dodge friends of his."

About two months later, in October, 1955, Ralph failed to replace the rubber retainer in a set of hydraulic brakes he was repairing. The mistake very nearly caused a serious accident, and another account was lost. Nolan again appealed to Ralph to slow down. Ralph said that he was finding it very difficult to work with Dexter. (Nolan had been assigning Dexter to help Ralph for the previous three weeks.) Ralph said that Dexter seemed only bent on getting out for coffee. He felt that Dexter was not skillful enough to be working as fast as he tried to. He stated, "Dexter only wants to push me, not to learn from me."

Nolan replied he would have Dexter work with Bob or Jim but that he had wanted him to learn from all the men. Ralph agreed to be as careful as possible and to work more slowly.

About this same time, Ralph told his father that he had come to feel that the other mechanics had a prejudice against him. He said he could hardly work with the roar of the radio they had going at all times, either baseball or music. He had asked Bob to turn it off when Bob went out for coffee. Bob had given him a blank look and a grunt and turned it off for a couple of days.

Ralph continued, "The radio seems to be on louder than ever now. They never even think about me enough to turn it down when they go out for coffee. Furthermore, I think they are the kind that would talk about me behind my back, especially Dexter."

Nolan kept a close watch on Ralph's work. He recounted the whole problem to John Thomas when he came by one day in December, 1955.

Nolan concluded by saying, "Ralph certainly is a changed man since we first hired him. In fact, if I weren't concerned about our losing the Turner account, I'd fire Ralph right now. We just can't afford his attitude and his errors. As it is, I'm afraid he's going to quit, and we'll lose the account anyway."

Chapter Three

The Diagnostic
Process: Criteria

The second step of the decision-making process is *diagnosis*. In this step the decision maker performs a careful inquiry into all the information relevant to the situation perceived to be in disequilibrium, in order to determine the exact problem that needs solution. The central purpose of this chapter is to demonstrate the importance of diagnosis in the decision process, to examine common difficulties in its execution, and to establish criteria for effective diagnosis.

The Importance of Diagnosis

In some kinds of situations it is obvious that an explicit diagnosis is required. If a machine breaks down, we do not attempt to fix it without determining precisely how the mechanism works and the source of the difficulty. However, when we are confronted by interpersonal problems, problems in the human rather than the technical realm, we tend to bypass systematic diagnosis and act on the basis of rather sketchy diagnostic assumptions.

For example, when we are confronted with the worker who submits numerous grievances, it is easy to apply value judgments about workers who file grievances, or about workers in general, or about this worker in particular. Thus we can forego a systematic diagnosis and summarize the problem in a handy prejudgment: "People who file grievances are troublemakers"; "All workers are lazy; that's the problem"; or "This guy is a malingerer." By so evaluating the stimuli presented to us, we merely categorize the problem in terms of preestablished stereotypes, which may or may not bear upon a particular situation. Thus we make an *implicit* diagnosis, based only on our first perceptions rather than on an investigation of the situation.

The consequences of weak or faulty diagnosis in some situations can be very serious: an innocent man may be convicted of a crime; a costly government program may fail to achieve its goal; a merger between two corporations may collapse; a valuable employee may be fired. Thus a poor diagnosis can lead to costly wrong decisions.

No solution is better than the quality of the diagnosis on which it is built. If, for example, we decide that a formerly productive worker, who is not now producing his quota, is slackening his effort with the purpose of cheating the company, we may have only one course of action: to fire him. But a sophisticated diagnosis would first inquire into other explanations for his behavior: Why has the worker's behavior changed? Why *now*? What needs does he feel he is satisfying by behaving this way at this time? How do other workers respond to the same stimuli? It may well be that, through sound diagnosis, the worker's misbehavior can be rectified in such a way that he will return to his former state of productivity.

Decision making should never be based on hasty, implicit diagnoses; it should be based on explicit, conscious, systematic, diagnostic investigation. In other words, a decision maker should use a critical rather than a noncritical method in the diagnostic process (see Chapter 1). Specifically, a sound diagnosis must meet the following criteria:

1. A sound diagnosis differentiates between events and the language used to describe events.
2. A sound diagnosis specifies the degree of precision of available information.
3. A sound diagnosis specifies underlying causes, not just fixes blame.
4. A sound diagnosis specifies multiple causality, rather than a single cause.
5. In its final working form, a sound diagnosis is explicitly formulated, not vague.

Criterion 1: Differentiating between Language and Events

The words people use to explain "what happened" are a manager's best source of clues to the nature of the problem. It is of primary importance that the manager, in weighing this information, be keenly aware of the effect language can have on it. The difficulty with language is that words do not automatically mirror facts. As S. I.

Hayakawa (1949) observes, "The map is not the territory" (p. 31). Just as a map is not the actual land mass of a state or country, the language people use to explain a situation is not the situation itself. Because words cannot be direct replicas of the realities they supposedly represent, the decision maker must always be keenly aware that language is only an abstraction of a real situation.

Most importantly, the decision maker must be aware that the language a person chooses for representing a particular event reflects the perceptions of that person. The observer's perception is necessarily imprecise, and his language is a further imprecise abstraction of his perception. In making his diagnoses, therefore, the decision maker must be wary of taking at face value the language in which information is presented to him. Language can alter and distort the perception of past situations. Furthermore, it may reflect more about the reporter than about the situation reported. Therefore if a union leader, for example, in a particular plant describes all problems in terms of management exploitation, and a manager in the same plant brands the same problems as union harassment, it is necessary to go beyond these stereotyped accusations to understand a given situation.

The importance of language in the definition of problems is dramatically demonstrated by Orvis Collins' (1946) study of ethnic relationships in a small New England factory. Because the workers regarded some jobs as properly assigned to the "Yankees" and some as properly assigned to the Irish, the latter threatened a walkout when a Yankee was hired as a janitor, a job perceived as "belonging" to the Irish. The dispute was ended, according to Collins, when the job title was changed to "sanitary engineer," a Yankee-sounding title. In this case, the differentiation of language from the real situation was the chief factor in solving the problem.

A similar problem involving the disparity of language and event can occur when a job description differs from the way the job is performed. A managerial incumbent, for example, may tend to concentrate on those aspects of his job that attract him, and ignore or delegate aspects he does not like. He may also be asked to take on temporary duties that become, in time, permanent. In effect, the job will become tailored, probably in an evolutionary way, to his particular skills, abilities, and temperament.

After a few years, what the incumbent does may come to vary substantially from the formal job description on file in the personnel office. If the manager is then promoted or leaves the company, the personnel officer charged with replacing him is well advised to verify the accuracy of the job description before he specifies the skills and experience required of applicants for that job. If he relies only on the job description, he may hire an ineffective replacement.

A sound diagnosis, therefore, differentiates between language and actual events, but the ambiguity of language is not the only problem; the decision maker must also know how accurate his information is.

Criterion 2: Specifying the Degree
of Precision of Available Information

Partly because language is imprecise, an important phase of diagnosis is the examination of information to determine its degree of precision. Just as we must differentiate between language and events, we must also differentiate between two *scales* of precision: first, whether a specific bit of information is a fact or only an opinion; second, the degree of *certainty* with which it has been verified as one or the other.

Distinguishing Fact and Opinion

Although it may be a *fact* that a person holds a particular *opinion,* the substance of the opinion itself is not necessarily factual. A manager who complains that every new subordinate is uncooperative (his opinion), may be failing to recognize that he has not made his expectations explicit to them (the fact). In discussing the Thomas Motor Company case following Chapter 2, we attempt to understand Ralph Turner's feelings or opinions about the other workers in the garage. We could say it is his opinion that they leave the radio playing when they go on their coffee break just to annoy him. One of our diagnostic tasks is to determine if in fact this is Turner's opinion. If it is, it is important to our understanding of his behavior. Opinions are always important factors in diagnosis, whether they are factual or not. A second task is to determine whether the content of the opinion is factual—if, indeed, the other workers' intent is to annoy Turner. This also is important to our reconstruction of the situation. The differentiation of factual from nonfactual opinion is a crucial step in the decision process, but a difficult one.

One difficulty in making the distinction between fact and opinion is that opinions are usually stated as though they were facts: "This job was well done"; "He is our best foreman"; "The competition uses illegal procedures." Such opinions include the speaker's judgment of the event. It is part of the diagnostician's job to sort out facts from opinions. A job might be judged well done by one manager because it met his tolerance standards; it might be only adequate to another manager. The "best" foreman may be the one who lets the men quit work early, or it may be the one who gets the greatest productivity from them; it all depends on the vantage point of the speaker. Opinions, then, are useful sources of information in the diagnostic process, but not until an implicit value standard has been identified and their degree of factual precision clarified.

Verifying the Judgment

Once we have judged whether or not an important opinion is in the realm of fact, we must determine the extent to which that judgment can be verified and therefore considered certain. For example, in the Thomas Motor case let us suppose the manager has formed a judgment: (1) Turner's opinion (the radio is left on to spite him) is important to the diagnosis, but (2) the fact is, it was *not* done for that reason. The manager's next step is to determine the degree of certainty he can ascribe to his judgment.

The process of verification involves differentiating facts, inferences, speculations, and assumptions. Using the information available to us in the case, we cannot verify, in an absolute sense, either Turner's motivation or that of the other workers. We do have some verifiable clues, however. We know that Turner was not bothered by the radio when the men were there, that the radio played all the time, and that no behavioral evidence exists to suggest that the other workers were antagonistic to Turner. Given these *facts,* we can say that the manager's judgment is probably correct: Turner's opinion does not conform to the facts. Such a judgment, made with a strong degree of supporting evidence, is called an *inference.*

The stronger the evidence (the facts) supporting a diagnostic judgment, the stronger the inference and the more reliable is the diagnosis. If supporting evidence is very strong, an inference can be as reliable and useful as a fact. If, however, the evidence for an inference is not strong, the inference is weak.

Judgments further down the scale of certainty, where lines of reasoning arise from clues in the situation but where verification is not possible, are labeled *speculation.* For example, when the inspectors in the Redmond Manufacturing case (following Chapter 2) refused to examine the spindles, they were judging the spindles to be contaminated with scarlet fever germs. The fact of the case is that a woman whose children had scarlet fever performed the first inspection of the spindles. However, because the inspectors' conviction that she had therefore contaminated the spindles is not verifiable, their judgment must be labeled a speculation, not an inference.

Further down the hierarchy of certainty are *assumptions,* lines of reasoning that arise entirely from a subjective frame of reference or from personal theories, and that are independent of verifiable clues in a real situation. Suppose that, in attempting to diagnose the reasons for the inspectors' behavior, we judged that their response was motivated by their membership in a union attempting to organize the company. This judgment is an assumption, rather than an inference or speculation, because there is no factual evidence in the real situation to support it. An important point about speculations and assumptions must be kept in mind, however; despite their lack of verification, they *may*, nonetheless, be facts. Moreover, speculations and assumptions may offer the best available explanation for a situation. However, they cannot be equated with facts; their degree of certainty is relatively much lower.

It is apparent that speculations and assumptions are considerably less reliable than facts and inferences, and therefore must be approached warily in the process of trying to determine what has actually occurred in a situation. A good diagnosis will rely most on facts and inferences, holding speculations and assumptions in reserve as tentative hypotheses, always open to question.

In making a diagnosis it is helpful explicitly to label units of information as facts, opinions, inferences, speculations, or assumptions, as the case may be, as an aid in the important process of clarifying the soundness of evidence. Making such distinctions among levels of certainty points up where information is only weakly supported by evidence, and keeps us searching for the strongest evidence available. Our diagnostic process does not stop with superficial speculation; we always attempt to improve the level of certainty of the evidence we are using.

As we have said, a diagnosis is an attempt to explain what happened in some period in the past. Something did indeed happen, but of course no exact record is available for our examination. An instant slow-motion replay, so effective for televised sports, is essentially what we attempt to replicate with a diagnosis. The continuum of certainty shown below is offered simply as an aid to conceptualizing the idea that some information has a higher probability than other information of reflecting what actually did happen.

Continuum of Certainty

100%	
Certainty	Facts
of	Inferences
our	Speculations
judgments	Assumptions
0%	

To sum up, verified *facts* are our surest form of information (so long as they are not deceiving or misleading). *Inferences* are strong or weak in direct relation to the strength or weakness of their supporting evidence. *Speculations* are only hypotheses, based on clues found in external situations; and *assumptions* are hypotheses we apply to a situation primarily from our personal frame of reference.

Criterion 3: Specifying Underlying Causes Rather than Blame

A good diagnostic process is guided by the attempt to understand rather than judge. Its purpose is to investigate the dynamics of a situation and to determine the causes of difficulty. The trained diagnostician withholds judgment, and asks, "What makes this situation tick? What are the sources of trouble?"

This criterion is vital because, when problems irritate us, our human tendency is to seek guilty culprits and fix blame. The tendency to evaluate is antithetical to the diagnostic process because it impedes objectivity; at the diagnostic stage of decision making, it is of no help to make value judgments. Instead, we must try to understand what is going on and put together a sound explanation of why particular events occurred. We are therefore trying to understand, not looking for "sins"; we are looking for causes, not culprits. Our goal is to maintain what Leighton (1949) described as the "functional point of view."

Looking for causal relationships is very different from attempting to fix blame on someone. The attempt to fix blame is based on the assumption of a deliberate attempt to disrupt an organization.

Such an assumption was implicit in the conflict between the marketing vice president and the manager of research and development in a large textile company; each blamed the other for the company's failure to develop new products. Marketing accused R & D of ignoring customer tastes in its new designs, and R & D accused marketing of not trying to sell its innovations. The real problem was that each group was only attempting to protect itself, and refused to fully consider new product ideas from the other group. Although they continued to blame each other, neither group attempted to discover the real cause of the conflict.

Attempting to fix blame may also rest on the assumption that another's contrary view is due to an unconscious psychological set. One manager, for example, may think that another disagrees with him merely because the latter is a negative sort of person, and that the real blame rests with the organizational superiors who tolerate such persons. Such a "chain of blame" can take us through the various levels of an organization—and all the way back to Adam and Eve, without ever providing a useful diagnosis.

Another difficulty with premature value judgment is that its primary function may be to serve the evaluator's immediate emotional needs. Rather than contributing to an understanding of the human needs that gave rise to a problem situation, such value judgments shift the decision maker's focus to himself, to his own needs and values. If, for example, an accident occurs in a plant that results in a slowdown of production, the plant manager no doubt will be upset, and might either deplore the "carelessness" of a worker (fix blame) or inquire into the conditions that caused the accident. His calling the worker careless (a value judgment) tells us more about the manager than about the cause of the accident. It is one thing to judge a situation *after* we understand its causes and are ready to make a decision; it is quite a different thing to do this before we have attempted to understand precisely why certain events occurred.

Although seeking to fix blame is not a useful diagnosis, it does give the illusion that the problem has been alleviated: "It's *his* fault!" But of course placing blame does nothing to remedy the conditions that have caused a problem. A person who has been blamed may well attempt to minimize his own involvement and counter with, "No it's not; it's *your* fault!" At that point, the decision maker has added nothing to his diagnosis.

It is by no means easy to suppress the tendency to prematurely evaluate. Clyde Kluckhohn (1951), the anthropologist, believes that the evaluating tendency is a strong force in human behavior: "Surely one of the broadest generalizations to be made by a natural historian observing the human species is that man is an evaluating animal" (p. 403).

One major difficulty in attempting to suppress premature evaluation is that problem situations are called to our attention by a value judgment—by the feeling that something is "not right." We consider a situation to be in a state of disequilibrium if it is beyond the tolerance limits of our values, goals, standards, policies, expectations, or some other value reference. Difficult though it may be, however, the value judgment involved in defining a state of disequilibrium must be followed by a conscious attempt to avoid the use of the value judgment that made us interested in the first place. The manager who opposes everything a union stands for must understand the union's rationale before he can resolve problems in the union-management relationship. It is only by suspending value judgments that we can develop an understanding of causes and make a sound diagnosis, the only basis for formulating a cure.

To avoid the use of value judgments in the diagnostic step, we must form the habit of explicitly asking the fundamental diagnostic question: *Why?* (Why did he behave as he did? Why did they respond as they did?) Then, to get at the interaction patterns involved, we must ask the second major diagnostic question: *How?* (How does this situation motivate X? How do X and Y motivate each other's behavior?).

Although this questioning process seems easy, consider some typical responses: "John is out of work today." "That's too bad!" "The turnover rate dropped two percent last month." "Good!" "Smith failed to meet the deadline for the annual report." "That's terrible." "I've been on the same job for thirteen years." "That's wonderful!" or ". . . terrible!"—depending on how the respondent feels about seniority benefits. "Management granted a four percent across-the-board salary increase." "That's not enough!" or "Great!" In short, as Kluckhohn (1951) has noted, we tend to express our feelings—our evaluations—before we inquire into meaning.

In addition to asking *why* and *how* as a basis for analysis and investigation, the decision maker should learn to draw out the views of the other persons involved in the situation being studied. Much information necessary to a sound diagnosis can be gained only through skill in eliciting full and accurate information from others. The difficulty of acquiring this skill should not be underestimated, however. Even though we might consciously attempt to avoid value judgments in our diagnoses, they are a subtle part of our reactions to other people.

If, for example, we attempt to obtain the point of view of an employee who seems threatened or anxious, we may wish to relieve his anxiety by being supportive. We would say to him, in effect: "What you are saying is all right; you are a good person." Such support, of course, is an evaluation we make from our own vantage point and it may color the story we are attempting to learn. Also, our attempt to explain or interpret another person's statements to him is essentially biased by our own point of view. Even when we ask questions to bring out more details, we choose questions which may reflect our values rather than the important features of a situation. To avoid the pitfalls of being evaluative as we attempt to draw out full and accurate information from another person is a skill that requires training and practice, but it is essential in understanding the causes of a problem situation.

Criterion 4: Specifying Multiple Causality

The tendency to evaluate is generally coupled with a tendency to search for a single cause in a problem situation. Certainly the search for a scapegoat assumes that one person is responsible for an event, but such an effort is usually fruitless. A human problem situation generally involves at least two persons and a variety of organizational events, and this is especially true in our modern-day, complicated organizations. Disequilibrium is less often the result of a single event than the product of a variety of events interacting in ways that may be physical or emotional, real or imagined, or internal or external to an organization.

In the Thomas Motor case, for example, the changed work environment and Ralph Turner's new workplace come into direct conflict with his foreman's rules on coffee breaks. Finding himself left out of this daily social get-together, he returns to finding satisfaction in tinkering with his father's trucks. But this solution is not satisfactory for his helper, Dexter, who complains about being left out of the coffee breaks when he works with Turner. Turner then begins to make serious mistakes in his work. The foreman makes the hasty assumptive diagnosis of a single cause for Turner's mistakes: that he is working too fast. As a consequence, the foreman's "solution" is to tell Turner to slow down.

A systematic diagnosis would reveal that Turner's behavior results, not from one cause, too much speed, but from a combination of factors: his expectations of the job, the pressures of the new environment, the new work procedures, the response of his helper, the leadership approach of his foreman, and the reactions of the other workers. This example points up the importance of our fourth criterion of a sound diagnostic process, that the decision maker should not assume a single cause for a problem but, instead, should search for multiple factors.

Criterion 5: Explicitly Formulating the Final Working Diagnosis

The end goal of the decision maker's diagnostic process is to formulate a working diagnosis on which to base his problem-solving procedures. To accomplish this, he must assess the available information, not all of which is of equal value. As discussed earlier, the decision maker's environment contains an infinite number of data, and he must determine which data are relevant information. Then he must weigh this information to determine the soundest explanation for what has occurred. Finally, he must settle on a stated working diagnosis as a basis for his problem-solving procedures.

It is important that this working diagnosis be explicitly stated, for two important reasons: (1) an explicit diagnostic statement facilitates checking the relevance of the diagnosis to the statement of the problem; and (2) an explicit diagnosis facilitates assessing the relevance and importance of any new information which may be discovered later.

The manager may check his statement of the working diagnosis against the following questions: (1) Does the diagnosis take into account all the available relevant information? (Or is it based on incomplete information?) (2) Does the diagnosis specify the degree of certainty of information and the relative importance of information? (Or is it merely a collection of unassessed data?) (3) Does the diagnosis *specify* problems, causes, events, persons, interactions, facts, evidence, and so on? (Or is it merely a vague generalization about human nature or psychological principles which provide little guidance for devising specific solutions for specific problems?) (4) Does the diagnosis include an examination of the relationships among points of view? (Or does it describe factors in the situation as if they were independent?) (5) Is the diagnosis organized in such a way that it facilitates identification of the central problem to be solved? (Or is it organized merely to facilitate such irrelevant goals as fixing blame, abstract theorizing, self-justification, etc.?)

Summary of Criteria

The entire diagnostic process, if it is to be soundly based and eventually helpful in the process of solving problems, should meet the following criteria:

1. It should differentiate between the actual events in the problem situation and the language used to describe these events.
2. It should specify the degree of precision of the available information by differentiating between facts and opinions, and by clearly labeling bits of information as facts, inferences, speculations or assumptions.
3. It should specify and explain the factors which have caused the given situation, rather than merely fixing blame.
4. It should examine the multiple causes and their relationships, rather than claim a single cause.
5. It should result in a clear and explicit statement of a final working diagnosis.

In Chapter 4 we will continue our discussion of the diagnostic process and develop several basic models useful for understanding human behavior. These models serve as fundamental reference points for conceptualizing the decision-making situation.

References

Allport, Gordon W. "What Units Shall We Employ?" In *Assessment of Human Motives,* ed. Gardner Lindzey. Holt, Rinehart and Winston, 1958.

Collings, Orvis. "Ethnic Behavior in Industry: Sponsorship and Rejection in a New England Factory." *American Journal of Sociology,* Vol. 51, January 1946.

Chase, Stuart. *Power of Words.* Harcourt, Brace, 1954.

Gragg, Charles I. "Whose Fault Is It?" *Harvard Business Review,* Vol. 42, No. 1, January–February 1964.

Hayakawa, S. I. *Language in Thought and Action.* Harcourt, Brace, 1949.

Kelly, George A. "Man's Construction of His Alternatives." In *Assessment of Human Motives,* ed. Gardner Lindzey. Holt, Rinehart and Winston, 1958.

Kluckhohn, Clyde, *et. al.* "Values and Value-Orientation in the Theory of Action." In *Toward a General Theory of Action,* ed. Talcott Parsons and Edward Shils. Harvard University Press, 1951.

Leighton, Alexander. *Human Relations in a Changing World*. Dutton, 1949.

Likert, Rensis. *The Human Organization*. McGraw-Hill, 1967.

Ready, R. K. *The Administrator's Job*. McGraw-Hill, 1967.

Crescent Airlines Case

Crescent Airlines, Inc., is one of the principal scheduled carriers serving the Mississippi Valley. It has expanded its operations steadily from 1938, when Captain George Wolfe first began carrying passengers between Minneapolis and Milwaukee. [In 1957] Crescent operated 25 daily flights connecting such cities as Minneapolis, Milwaukee, Chicago, Dubuque, Kansas City, Memphis, New Orleans, and Houston. The airplane used for most of Crescent's operations [was] the DC6B. This craft [was in 1957] in standard use in many of the nation's larger airlines.

In order to understand the problem which occurred at the Memphis airport on the evening of April 5, 1957, the reader must become familiar with some facts about Crescent's passenger policies. There are 66 seats on a DC6B airplane; however, one of these is always reserved for the second stewardess, and five others, which form a semicircle at the rear of the plane, are reserved as a lounge. There are tables in the lounge for card playing, along with racks of magazines and newspapers.

Crescent's *Operations Manual* states that the five lounge seats in a DC6B will not be sold in advance except under the following conditions:

1. On specifically designated short trips.
2. When there exists a bona fide oversale at flight departure time, that is, when a passenger has confirmed space or has been ticketed in error.
3. When the general office issues instructions lifting the 66-seat

limit. This is done regularly at crowded holiday travel times when the company thinks customer good will would merit sacrificing the lounge to carry more travelers. These orders are issued over the signature of the superintendent of passenger service.

These policies are based entirely on such considerations as passenger comfort and customer relations. There are no safety factors involved.

It is also important to explain the two classes of nonrevenue passengers who fly Crescent. There are (a) "positive" and (b) "space-available" passengers. Nonrevenue "positive" passengers have all the privileges of a fare-paying customer. They may make advance reservations, and these will be honored in the standard way. Company officials traveling for business reasons are "positive" passengers, for example. On the other hand, "space-available," nonrevenue passengers may not make reservations and often cannot be sure of their seat on a plane until takeoff time. Employees of Crescent and their families are allowed a certain number of "space-available" passes each year, depending on their length of service.

On the evening of April 5, Crescent Airlines' Flight 37 was preparing to depart from the Memphis airport at its scheduled time, 10 p.m. Flight 37 was a first-class, nonstop DC6B trip from Memphis to Chicago, due to arrive at 12:36 a.m. It was, as usual, officially limited to 60 passengers. On this particular night, Flight 37 was sold out by 9 p.m., and some people had to be turned down after that. About 9:30 a 61st passenger had to be added because he came from another line's connecting flight with confirmed space on Crescent's Flight 37.

Two of Crescent Airlines' executives were on Flight 37's passenger list on April 5. They were traveling on a "positive" basis, with reservations made several weeks previously. The men, both stationed in the Chicago general office, were Mr. William Warner, reservations manager, and Mr. Alva Borden, superintendent of passenger relations (see Figure 1). They were returning home after a week of business traveling.

Fifteen minutes before flight time, Warner and Borden walked up to Crescent's check-in booth in the terminal to get their gate passes. As they did, they recognized Mary Deaver, wife of August Deaver, Crescent's superintendent of passenger service. Mrs. Deaver had her three-year-old son Jimmy with her. The two were traveling on a "space-available" basis and were returning home to Chicago after attending Mrs. Deaver's father's funeral in Georgia. They had already traveled 500 miles that day, and Mrs. Deaver expressed concern to Warner and Borden about having to wait six hours because Flight 37 was filled.

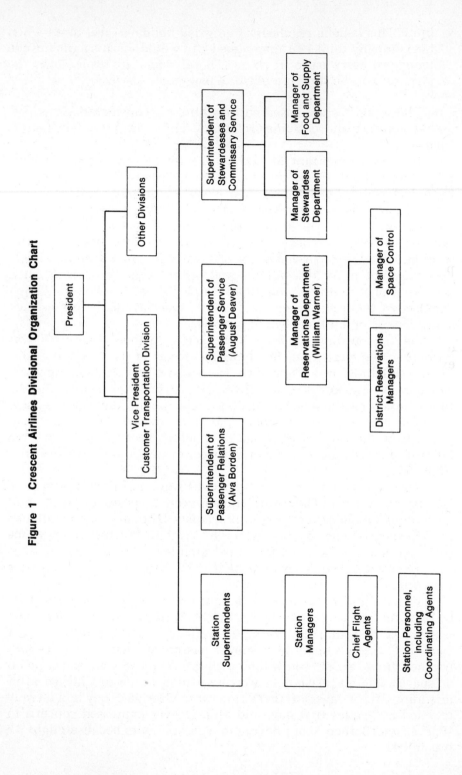

Figure 1   Crescent Airlines Divisional Organization Chart

President

Vice President Customer Transportation Division

Other Divisions

Superintendent of Passenger Relations (Alva Borden)

Superintendent of Passenger Service (August Deaver)

Superintendent of Stewardesses and Commissary Service

Manager of Stewardess Department

Manager of Food and Supply Department

Manager of Reservations Department (William Warner)

District Reservations Managers

Manager of Space Control

Station Superintendents

Station Managers

Chief Flight Agents

Station Personnel, including Coordinating Agents

Warner and Borden discussed Mrs. Deaver's situation and decided it would be possible for her to travel on this flight even though it was a violation of the 60-seat restriction. The two executives had agreed with one another (but did not tell Mrs. Deaver) that they would give up their own seats if this proved necessary to facilitate Mrs. Deaver's travel. Then they sought out John Washburn, chief flight agent of Crescent's operation at the Memphis station, with whom they were mutually acquainted. Mr. Washburn had been in his Memphis job only six months, but he had been a chief flight agent at other stations. When they found Mr. Washburn in his office, Mr. Borden advised him that they had decided to lift the 60-seat restriction for Mrs. Deaver and that he and Mr. Warner would assume all responsibility.

Mrs. Deaver had a good deal of hand baggage in addition to her child to handle, and the two executives and the chief flight agent assisted her at flight departure time. They were almost to the loading steps when they were approached by Joseph Hall, a coordinating agent who was Mr. Washburn's subordinate. Mr. Hall notified the chief flight agent that there would be 63 passengers on the airplane if the woman and child were permitted to board. Mr. Washburn advised him that he was aware of this and that it was all right, according to the two company officers. Thereupon the coordinating agent pointed out politely, but firmly, that this was nevertheless a violation of company rules.

"It will be all right," chief agent Washburn said.

"You know it's against our station and company rules," the coordinating agent repeated.

"Yes, I know," the chief agent said and again assured him it was all right.

"Well, I don't think they should be allowed to go. This is a violation," Mr. Hall insisted and continued to belabor the point for another several minutes. Mr. Washburn continued to explain his point.

Mr. Borden stated that he had heard enough and that they were all going on board. He advised Mrs. Deaver to board the plane with her son, and he and Mr. Warner followed them up the steps. The coordinating agent turned away, visibly disturbed with the affair.

As the party proceeded up the steps of the loading ramp, chief agent Washburn told the two Crescent executives, "I can't understand why Joe did that. He's never done anything like that before. He's been a good man."

Mr. Borden said with some vigor that it seemed to him to be a case of "gross insubordination."

Mr. Washburn nodded and then turned to go back down the ramp. When the group reached the door of the airplane, the two stewardesses greeted them hesitantly and one of them stated, "I'm sorry we are filled to our limit. We cannot receive these extra two passengers." Mr. Warner felt that an air of confusion and resentment was created as he and Mr. Borden attempted to assure the stewardesses that all was well.

The senior stewardess remarked, "Well, next time there are only 60 seats and *I'm* traveling, I wonder what the policy will be." At this moment the last of the 63 passengers boarded the plane, and as he did so the senior stewardess said rather drily, "Oh, are you going too!"

Mr. Warner became aware that some of the passengers were beginning to hear this discussion, and he was very uncomfortable. He had not said much himself since the opening remarks of the conversation with the stewardesses, but he agreed with the feelings Mr. Borden was expressing to the girls in a continuously stronger tone. At the same time, he felt nothing could be gained by further argument. He wondered what, if anything, he should do.

The National Insurance Company Case

In early May, 1966, Dick Hart, a junior administrative assistant in the field administration department of the East City branch office of the National Insurance Company and a recent graduate of the company's management training program, was filling in as head of the accounting section for Don Gallen, who was away for two weeks on a troubleshooting visit to another company office located in a Southern city.

One afternoon, while wondering how to handle a minor problem, Hart was notified that Robert Magee, the department manager, wished to see him in his office. When Hart arrived in the office, Magee told him to sit down as he wanted to discuss a very important problem that had arisen. Magee said that he was very concerned about a letter

---

This case was written under the supervision of Alvar O. Elbing. Names of people and places have been disguised.

he had recently received from the home office in regard to the premium collection (accounts receivable) situation in the East City office.

While not revealing the specific contents of the letter, Magee implied that he now had a serious problem on his hands, of which he had not been previously aware. Magee told Hart: "I always thought I had two good men working for me in this area in Bottomley and Gallen. They've been handling these things for years and now I find out that they've been letting me down. Why, I bet they've been covering things up so that I wouldn't find out. Bottomley is my assistant manager and I can't rely on him at all. And when Gallen gets back, I'm going to call him on the carpet about this. With all the other things he's involved in, I might have to do something drastic—I just don't know how to go about it."

Magee then went over with Hart a few things that he wanted done that day, and a few minutes later dismissed him. Magee left Hart with the following admonition: "I want you to concentrate on clearing up those old files and that other junk that Gallen has stuffed away in his desk. I'd like to have that all cleared out before he gets back."

The National Insurance Company was a large casualty and fire insurance operation spread out across the country. The company had a large home office in a Northeastern city, and 75 branch offices of varying size in most of the principal cities of the country. The company did not directly sell its product, but contracted with independent agencies, who were at the same time salesmen and customers of the company. The agencies were customers in the sense that they usually contracted with a number of companies and could place an individual piece of business with whichever company they chose.

The branch office structure of the company was headed by a management committee, composed of all the department managers. However, the leadership of the committee was nominal, since each department was integrated and reported to a home office territorial supervisor who was a corporate officer. Locally, each department manager was completely responsible for the operation of his own department.

The East City branch office was one of the larger branch offices of the company and was located in a medium-size Northeastern city. Robert Magee, a mild-mannered man, was the manager of the field administration department; he was 59 years old and had been employed by the company for 37 years. He had held the position of manager at East City for the past 13 years and prior to that had been the assistant manager for five years. Magee, although he had attended an Eastern university, was not a college graduate. In his middle-management capacity as a department manager, Magee's salary was $16,500 per year.

Magee's department carried out most of the clerical duties in connection with the various types of policies issued by the office, and also, as a major function, handled the collection and reporting of insurance premiums. The department employed about 100 female clerks who staffed the various operational sections. The sections were usually supervised by a female clerical supervisor. Administratively, Magee was aided by an assistant manager and one or more staff assistants, depending on the manpower available in the company. The staff assistants were usually assigned as administrators in charge of the various sections. In this capacity, they worked directly with the clerical supervisors.

The field administration department was charged with the annual accomplishment of four specific "management objectives": (1) service (to the independent agencies), (2) expense management, (3) employment (of college graduates for the management training program), and (4) premium collection. Magee, as manager, was evaluated on how well the department accomplished these objectives. The department performance was measured under a standard system used in all the offices throughout the country.

The accounting section, consisting of administrative assistant Don Gallen, a female clerical supervisor, and 14 clerks, had the job of premium collection and reporting. In the company accounting system, the independent agencies directly billed and collected payment from their clients. On a monthly basis, they submitted to the company their accounting, together with payment for the premiums that had become due and had been collected in the second month prior to the payment month. From their payment, the agencies deducted the commissions earned on the various policies.

Premiums that remained unpaid beyond the third month after they had become due were considered "delinquent" and were subject to a variety of company collection procedures, that could eventually culminate in legal action. In carrying out its collection function, the section's main tasks consisted of keeping abreast of the agencies' accounts and taking quick action on actual or potential delinquents.

The company, as a whole, had been experiencing trouble in attaining the standards set in the collection area. Periodically, the East City office received letters from the home office concerning the problem that faced the company and outlining actions that the offices should take to improve the situation. The East City office during this time had generally been attaining "unsatisfactory" ratings on its collection objective; however, its performance in this area was consistently superior to the performance of the company as a whole.

In addition to collecting the premiums, the accounting section had the responsibility of balancing the agency accounts as they were

received and periodically reporting these payments, plus miscellaneous monetary transactions, to the home office. In connection with
this function, an internal accounting device, called the "agency pending account," came into considerable use. This account was chiefly
used to maintain workflow when an agency reported a premium or
commission that differed from what was shown on company records.
By putting the amount of the difference in this account, the company
also was able to mark the premium "paid" on its records immediately,
resolving the "difference" with the agency at a later date. A continuing
function of the accounting section was the clearance of these "differences" by reaching agreement with the agency involved and then
either collecting the shortage or refunding the overage.

Although manager Magee had delegated responsibility for the
successful functioning of the accounting section to his assistant manager, Frank Bottomley (age 59), the key person in the accounting
section was Don Gallen, a junior administrative assistant. Gallen
(age 37) had been hired by the company as a clerk in 1948, at a
salary of $37.50 per week, following his graduation from a local high
school. During the subsequent time, he spent 15 years in the National
Guard, achieving the rank of warrant officer. In 1958, Gallen was
promoted and given the clerical supervisory title of collection supervisor. On September 1, 1965, upon the recommendation of Robert
Magee, Gallen was promoted and given the administrative title of
junior administrative assistant,[1] and his salary increased to $5300 per
year. After this promotion, he continued in his usual role in the
accounting section.

Don Gallen was generally acknowledged to be proficient in all
phases of company accounting procedure and to have by far the
greatest knowledge of this aspect of anyone in the East City office. In
addition, most of his associates considered Gallen intelligent, an
interesting conversationalist, and well versed on current events. Gallen seemed to be very well liked by everyone in the office. A tall,
reed-thin man, Don was thought to be a confirmed bachelor; however,
in June 1965 he surprised everyone by marrying a former company
employee. Don's best friend among National employees was Frank
Bottomley, the department assistant manager, who was soon to retire.
Don described Bottomley as "a real square shooter. He's not afraid to
tell you when you're wrong—I've been chewed out by him more than
once, but he'll tell you when you're right. He's forgotten more about
this work than Magee will ever know."

Although Gallen was experienced and well versed in company
procedures, some of his associates felt that he lacked real supervisory

---

1. An administrative title was under the jurisdiction of the territorial supervisor
in the home office. The title "junior administrative assistant" was usually given to
graduates of the management training program. A clerical title was under the jurisdiction of local management.

ability. He often admitted that he found giving orders to female employees quite difficult and preferred to think of himself as a "helper" to the employees in the section rather than a "leader." In his own words, "I never could chew out one of these girls. I'm just not cut out for it."

Many National employees held the opinion that Don Gallen had a real drinking problem, although there was no unanimity of opinion as to whether he was actually an alcoholic. As far as could be determined, the basis on which most of the opinion rested was the fact that there were many occasions when liquor was quite noticeable on his breath. Gallen's alleged drinking problem was often the subject of conversation and crude jokes, particularly with members of the marketing department, such as "Don never takes a coffee break, he takes booze breaks." This matter was of considerable concern to Robert Magee, and he had discussed the situation with Gallen on several occasions. Gallen, however, had never been observed to be less than alert and in full control of his capacities while in the office. A review of his personnel card showed a total of 15 absences in 19 years, the longest of which was 8 working days, and there had been no absences since 1964. The reasons shown on the personnel card for the absences were various minor illnesses.

In addition to his main function as head of the accounting section, Gallen performed a variety of formal and informal functions for the National Insurance Company:

1. He was often delegated specific responsibilities, such as administration of the mail and supply operation.
2. Many of the female employees asked his advice on work problems of varying nature, including female supervisors from other sections who informally sought his advice.
3. He trained the young men who were going through the management training program in company accounting procedures.
4. He furnished telephone assistance for agencies with accounting problems, and usually had the responsibility for explaining new company procedures to them. Eight to ten problem calls per day would be a good estimate of the average number of such calls.
5. He was the informal liaison between the field administration department and the marketing department on accounting matters.
6. He sometimes handled the local aspect of negotiations with attorneys, bankruptcy referees, etc., when the company was initiating legal action.[2]

---

2. The actual negotiations were handled by a specialized department in the home office. On a local level, it was more usual for the manager or assistant manager to be involved.

In addition to the above duties, Don Gallen had been periodically requested by the home office to make short visits to other offices that were encountering serious accounting problems and furnish technical assistance to these offices. These troubleshooting trips, one of which he was on when Magee had called Hart into his office, were usually of two to four weeks' duration and had occurred about four times in the past ten years. Once, when the field administration department manager of the office Gallen was visiting had requested that Don be allowed to stay for a few weeks longer than was originally scheduled, Magee wrote to the home office and requested Gallen's immediate return, as "allowing him to stay away longer would seriously undermine East City's accounting operation."

Gallen, after each of these troubleshooting visits, had returned with words of high praise from the manager of the other office. One such manager, one of the most respected in the company, had said in a letter to Magee that Gallen "was one of the most competent National employees with whom I have ever been associated." In addition to these complimentary words from the people in these offices, there were others associated with the company who held the accounting section administrator in high regard. The independent agencies, who were the actual company customers, almost universally had a fine word for him, and in March 1966 Magee received a letter from one such agent, which stated in part:

> It is with great pleasure and with some tardiness that we write this letter to compliment the excellent work and service of Don Gallen. We like a man who is efficient and solves problems without procrastination and Don Gallen is such a person. It is a pleasure to encounter the pleasant, business-like reception that Don always gives us. He is one more reason why it is nice to do business with the National Insurance Company.

Returning to his desk following the meeting with Magee, Dick Hart reflected on what he had been told. He was very curious, but supposed that he would have to wait until Don Gallen came back to the office later that week to see how things would turn out. Strangely enough, when Gallen did return, nothing startling occurred, and things seemed to go on as usual at the East City office—with Gallen and Bottomley serving in their usual capacities.

However, as the weeks passed, Magee apparently was becoming more and more dissatisfied with Bottomley's work as assistant manager. He wrote several letters to the home office regarding his problem with Bottomley, and in one of these letters included the request that Bottomley be transferred to some other office "for the good of all concerned" and that East City be sent a new assistant manager. He was also keeping a personal file on Bottomley's activities, and in this file he noted the specific complaints that "Bottomley doesn't do his share in the office, he regularly disappears for periods up to one hour in the afternoon without telling me where he is going, and he leaves the office 15 minutes early every afternoon." Magee did not note that Bottomley always came into the office 45 minutes early in the morning. Possibly he was not aware of this as he, Magee, did not usually come in until around 8:45 a.m. (the office began work at 8:15 a.m.).

The territorial supervisor for the East City office, with whom Magee was in contact regarding the Bottomley situation, apparently did not wish to recommend any drastic action. In a return communication, he noted that Frank Bottomley had indicated that he would probably retire in a few months, upon reaching age 60, and in addition he suggested the possibility that a medical problem contributed to Bottomley's seemingly lackadaisical attitude. He further suggested that Magee talk about the situation with Frank, and if there were no medical problem involved, Magee should insist on a full day's work from Frank until such time as he retired. In the territorial supervisor's words, "The company could not permit Frank to retire on the job six months early."

On February 28, 1967, after 40 years' service with the company, Frank Bottomley did retire, and in the following week he and his wife moved to a small Florida retirement community. At the testimonial dinner given to honor Frank for his long service to the company, Robert Magee spoke briefly on the subject of "what a strong right arm Frank has been to me since his transfer here ten years ago. I feel a deep sense of personal loss tonight." Earlier in the evening, after his second martini, Bottomley had told one of the staff assistants that one of his primary reasons for moving to Florida was "to put as many miles as possible between myself and that nitwit, Magee. The one amazing thing about the past ten years is that I've kept my sanity."

Bottomley was succeeded as assistant manager by Rob Clark, age 29, who had previously been a senior administrative assistant on Magee's staff. Clark had been transferred to East City in 1965 from an office in a Southern city, and by this time was quite familiar with the situation in East City. In fact, he had received an early briefing five minutes after he had stepped off the plane that had brought him to East City, when Magee, who had met Rob at the airport, informed him that there were two men in the department, Bottomley and Gallen, who "just were not doing their jobs." Robert Magee then asked the travel-weary young man to help him with his "Bottomley problem" by following the assistant manager and "finding out what he's up to." Clark somehow managed to avoid this sleuthing operation, but he was later to say of his first meeting with his new boss, "I was about ten seconds from jumping on the next plane out of East City that was going back where I came from. I think the only thing that kept me there was the fact that I didn't quite believe my ears."

As the time passed for Clark in his new office, he learned more and more of its unique characteristics. Often his thoughts went back to that first day at the airport, and eventually he made a discovery that, to him, seemed to bring the events of that day into better perspective. Through discussions with the other staff members in the department, Clark found that these men believed that Magee had a favorite tactic that he used whenever he thought that there was a man on his staff who was not doing a good job. According to Clark's new associates, Magee, through requests to the territorial supervisor, had tried to have at least two staff members (not counting either Bottomley or Gallen) deposed through one means or another. One of these men had recently resigned and the other had been transferred to another department in the company.

As assistant manager of the field administration department, Clark quickly became immersed in the duties of his new office. In early March 1967 he wrote what he thought was a routine memorandum to the territorial supervisor in the home office requesting a "waiver relief" from an entry that had been in the agency pending account for an excessive length of time. As later events were to show, this item was not so routine.[3]

Meanwhile, with the Bottomley situation resolved by Frank's retirement, Robert Magee turned his attention to his other "problem child," Don Gallen. He began to make regular additions to a personal file he had been keeping, and at this point drew up a "balance sheet" on Gallen, listing his assets and liabilities. In Magee's estimation, Gallen's assets were far outweighed by his liabilities. Chief among the deficiencies he noted were the following:

1. After a short lapse, he was again noticing liquor on Gallen's breath, which he identified as vodka.
2. Collection files seemed to be missing, which Magee attributed to Gallen's inefficiency.
3. Gallen "sat on" many files which needed current attention.
4. Gallen didn't write enough letters, as Magee's personal survey showed an average of only 2.7 per day.[4]
5. Gallen "sat on" company checks which had been issued, and which Magee thought should have been released.

---

3. When agreement regarding a "difference" in the agency pending account could not be reached with the agency involved, it was usual procedure for the home office to approve removal of this entry from the account.

4. Presumably, Magee was concerned that the East City office would not have documented file information to prove that effective collection action was being taken.

According to Magee's file, he had talked to Gallen several times about his deficiencies, but apparently, from Magee's standpoint, the results of these discussions had not been fruitful.

Around May 1, 1967, Magee discovered what he thought were some serious irregularities in the agency pending account. These were concerned with several entries, over a year old, that appeared quite questionable in nature. Although Magee didn't realize it at the time, these entries actually dated back several years and had arisen through "manipulation" of the account. For a certain agency, some large commercial policy premiums had been reported "paid" on the company record by putting the entire premium in the agency pending account as a "shortage difference." In order that these entries would not be questioned by the home office accounting department, they were periodically deleted and reentered to keep them in a somewhat "current" status. In the case of the reentries, there were occasions when false names on the entry captions had been used. The total shortage difference for these entries amounted to $4850. It was later definitely established that no embezzlement was involved.

Shortly after making this discovery, Magee directed his staff members, including Clark and Gallen, not to become further involved with these problems as he, apparently, had decided to handle the situation personally. He also told them at this time that he was aware of the facts that lay behind the problem. In connection with his decision, he retained what he thought were pertinent files under lock and key in his office. He also wrote to the home office and requested that a company auditor be sent to East City to examine the situation in order to get to the bottom of the problem. This request was not granted.

In early June 1967, assistant company secretary Michael Strong, the territorial supervisor for field administration, made a routine periodic visit to the East City office. The purpose of these visits was to get a firsthand look at office operation, to discuss problems with administrative personnel on a personal basis, and to furnish assistance on any relevant problem in which he could be of help.

Shortly after he arrived, and while talking with Clark, Strong brought up the subject of the "waiver relief" request about which Clark had written to him in March. Strong suggested that this entry looked a little "fishy." It was later brought out that this entry was quite similar to the group of entries Magee had discovered earlier—a premium had been "paid" by creating a "shortage difference" in the agency pending account. This case, however, involved a much smaller amount of money.

Magee and Strong then went into Magee's office to discuss the situation. Shortly, they summoned Don Gallen to tell them what he knew about it. As Gallen later described the meeting, "It was like the Gestapo. They treated me like a criminal. Magee didn't give me, one of his own men, any support; he told Strong that he didn't know anything about it and then went off and sat in the corner. Strong started to pace around the room, his hands behind his back, asking me all sorts of questions, just like the Gestapo. I never felt worse in my life." Rob Clark, who was later called in to "testify," confirmed the tone of the meeting, saying that Gallen looked like a "lamb led to a slaughter."

The interrogation of Don Gallen continued until about 20 minutes past the normal office closing time. At this point Gallen said, "Gentlemen, my wife has been waiting for me outside the building for over 20 minutes; you'll have to excuse me now." Strong answered, "Look, Don, I'm only going to be here for a day and a half, and I want to get to the bottom of this before I leave." Magee then said, "You'd better stay, Don, this is more important!" Don Gallen replied, "Not to me, it isn't. Good afternoon, Gentlemen." Gallen then left the office to meet his wife.

The next morning the meeting was resumed. Right at the start, Gallen told Strong that he was completely responsible for making the entries in the account, that he knew now that it was wrong, that he accepted complete responsibility, but that there was nothing he could do about it.[5] Shortly after this "confession," Strong dismissed the meeting. Later that day, Gallen was to tell Dick Hart that he was very upset over how he had been treated the day before, saying "If my wife hadn't talked me out of it, I'd have come in today and quit right on the spot!"

Shortly after the meeting was dismissed, Strong and Rob Clark went out to have coffee. Strong began to discuss what had transpired and asked Clark for his recommendation on handling the situation in regard to Don Gallen. Clark answered by saying, "If you mean do I recommend firing him, the answer is no! He is far too valuable around here, and, besides, I think that he might be covering up for Bottomley or someone else in this whole business—you know how he felt about Bottomley." To this, Strong replied that he was going to have to go back and "tell Dave Collins [vice president in charge of field administration] that I've done something about this. [Clark later discovered that Collins never knew anything about the situation.] Besides, you know that both Bob [Magee] and I are very concerned about Gallen's drinking; also, I am personally ashamed that we have a

5. Although it was never completely established exactly why the entries were initially made, it was presumed that someone in the accounting section had gotten a promise of payment from the agency and had tried to eliminate a large delinquency before payment was received.

man on our staff to whom we are paying such a low salary." (Gallen's annual salary was about $1500 less than that earned by a college-trained junior administrative assistant.)

Later that afternoon, Michael Strong left East City to return to the home office. A few days later, Robert Magee wrote a letter to Strong stating that nothing further could be resolved concerning the questionable entries, that Strong now knew the entire situation, and he requested that the East City office be granted a "waiver relief" of responsibility for the entries.

On July 15, 1967, Magee called Don Gallen into his office and closed the door behind them. He told Gallen that because of his part in connection with the agency pending account problem, the home office people would have to let him go. However, Gallen would be permitted to resign, and also would be allowed to stay until the end of September in order to find another job and accrue his vested rights in the company's pension plan.[6] Magee was very sorry, but "there was no alternative."

The following day Don Gallen wrote a one-paragraph letter of resignation, effective with the close of business, September 30, 1967. The letter gave no specific reason for the resignation. It was agreed between Magee and Gallen that the resignation would not be made public until after Gallen left the company. To accomplish this, it was agreed that Gallen would commence his regular vacation three weeks prior to the resignation date and just never come back. (Throughout the previous years, Gallen had accrued a substantial vacation backlog because it was felt that the office couldn't be without his services for too long a period at any one time.)

During the next few weeks, Gallen told a few men in the field administration department that he had quit and would be leaving in September, but asked that they not say anything about this. On August 15, Magee called Gallen into his office and inquired if he was having any luck in finding a job. When Gallen replied in the negative, Magee reminded him that "the home office definitely wants you out of here by the end of September."

On Friday, September 6, 1967, at 4:30 p.m., Don Gallen got up from his desk and very quietly ended twenty years of association with the National Insurance Company.

---

6. Accrued upon completion of twenty years' employment.

Electronic Systems Company Case

The Electronic Systems Company was a growing concern in 1966, having experienced continuous, comfortable growth in its first ten years of operation. Its founder and owner, Francis Walker, was a classical success-story entrepreneur. He conceived an idea for a new electronic component, invented and initially developed it in the basement of his home, and sold it on the basis of quality, price, and quick delivery service. It was an exciting company, created from scratch in Walker's image. It employed around 250 people and its sales approached $4 million. Although the company was molded by him in every significant detail, he had gathered around him associates who shared his passions and his enthusiasms and who expressed outstanding commitments to the goals of the organization.

One such enthusiastic employee was Barry Welch, who came to work at Electronic Systems after having completed his tour of duty with the Air Force in the latter part of the 1950s. Later, around 1962 or 1963, Barry expressed a desire for a college education. The company offered to finance part of the expense, so Barry enrolled in the evening division of a local college, majoring in physics and minoring in math. (When I arrived at the company in 1968, Welch was in the second semester of his junior year.)

It was not uncommon in this young organization to find that several employees wore various departmental "hats." For example, after several years as a process engineer in the research and development laboratory, Barry was the prime organizer and supervisor of the raw-material and finished-goods stockrooms and the production control department. These three areas were managed by Welch until 1967, when Mr. Walker, seeing a need for a new and improved information system and professing great faith in Welch's ability as an organizer and manager, decided to send Welch to one of IBM's data processing schools. Before leaving for school, Welch agreed that when he returned he would devote his full time to the management of the data processing department, relinquishing his responsibilities in

This case was written by Craig T. Galipeau, under the supervision of Alvar O. Elbing. Names of people and places have been disguised.

the other three areas. (It should be noted here that, in each of the three areas, Welch had developed capable managerial personnel prior to his departure.)

It was at this time that Mr. Walker sensed his business was growing too big for a one-man operation. Numerous new contracts from both government and commercial sources made the future look optimistic, but the workload for one man was difficult. Mr. Walter decided to seek outside help. Therefore, in response to various offers, he sold his company to a Wall Street investment firm that was very much impressed with Electronic Systems' great potential for sales growth. Mr. Walker was retained as a member of the board of directors, and also served in a consultive capacity as vice president for planning and development.

The investment firm hired Mr. Daniel Wilson as the new president of Electronic Systems. He, too, quickly saw the need for an improved information system as a tool for decision making. Therefore, Welch's initial project for the new president was to expedite plans for the proposed IBM equipment by training key punchers and machine operators and designing the initial systems. Organizationally, the new data processing department was to be managed by Welch, who would report directly to the controller, Thomas Haley. Haley had worked for a leading optical company before Wilson asked him to join Electronic Systems in the latter half of 1967.

Although Haley had little knowledge of data processing operations, the organization established by Electronic Systems reflected the organization used by the majority of new companies in the data processing field. Mr. Haley, however, was quite familiar with the application of a total accounting system, which could be generated by the hardware in Barry's department. Even so, the main objective and top priority of the new equipment was to be its use for logistic purposes—production control, production, and inventory control—with the marketing system given second priority and the accounting system given least priority.

In June of 1968 I was hired for the summer to assist Barry in the design and implementation of the management information system. During my second week of work with Barry, I discovered what I thought to be a redundant system in one of the early systems applications. Barry confirmed my finding and showed no particular surprise. He then related how he had argued this particular point with Mr. Haley early in its application.

Barry: I explained to Haley earlier that this type of a thing would happen. And now this proves me correct.

Author: Well, couldn't he see that eventually we would run into this problem?

Barry: No. He didn't buy my argument that this would happen in the first place. Besides, it appears to me that as long as we get a system going as fast as possible, he doesn't care if it is right or wrong.

The president, Mr. Wilson, would usually pay a visit to Barry's office several times a week, complimenting Barry on what a fine job he was doing. Since very little application was made of the machines at this time, Mr. Wilson always expressed interest in the proposed overall system that Barry and I were working on. He was very pleased to see some of the ideas we had arrived at already, commenting that we seemed to be in good shape to meet the target date for our oral presentation in August. (Mr. Wilson gave us the go-ahead for implementing logistics subsystems before our August target date, however.)

At the same time, Mr. Haley did not find Barry's work satisfactory. As mentioned previously, the top priority for machine and design time was given to the logistics systems. However, Mr. Haley was continually putting pressure on Barry to get the complete accounting system established on the machines. This irritated Barry, and our conversations at coffee breaks and lunch continually centered around Haley and his accounting system.

Pressured by Haley, Barry devoted many hours in the evenings and on Saturdays and even Sundays in attempting to please him. These overtime hours were always devoted to such things as the budgets, payroll, accounts receivables, etc. Yet no appreciable recognition came from Haley—just complaints about the "bugs" that are found in any new system.

The rest of the workers in the firm, of course, had knowledge of Barry's overtime duties and would good-naturedly kid him about his department. Coffee and lunch breaks were always filled with laughter, with Barry bearing the brunt of all the jokes and harassment. All the men at the table (production men, industrial engineers, accountants, salesmen) were well liked by each other, and the majority would spend much of their social time together outside the plant. Since they all knew the trouble Barry was having with Haley, they, too, began to criticize Barry's work.

Production man: Hey, "punch-card," those reports your girls passed out this morning were useless garbage.

Barry: Look, you give me garbage, my machines will give you garbage back. [Laughter.]

Salesman: Who are you kidding? I give you good, accurate data, and the reports I get, too, are completely useless. Are you sure you know what you are doing over there, Barry? Maybe Tom will help you get straightened out. [Laughter.]

Barry: Yeah, by the way "Little Haley" [referring to Jim, the head of the accounting department], did Tom see that memo I left on his desk this morning?

Jim: Oh yeah, he told me to take care of it as usual, and then went back to reading his *Wall Street Journal* so he could have some free time later on this afternoon to play golf with his kid.

Barry: Beautiful! That's par for the course.

Production man: Well Barry, you better get back over there and get those budgets out so Tom won't have so much work during the day. When are you guys going to relieve me of some paperwork?

All this kidding, however, developed into a hassle between the vice president for manufacturing and Mr. Haley. At one of our meetings, the vice president said he felt the data processing department was not living up to its expectations of relieving some of the paperwork from the foremen while at the same time yielding reliable information. He asserted that too much time was being spent on the accounting system and not enough time in the production area. Mr. Haley disagreed vehemently. The vice president then requested that a report be submitted showing the actual time Barry spent in each area. (Although the report showed less actual running time for accounting reports, the production people were not getting the various reports which were promised them in the beginning, nor was their system as completely "debugged" as Haley's system.)

One morning in late July, Mr. Haley called Barry into his office. It was the time of the annual review at Electronic Systems, and I knew of Barry's expectations for a raise in salary. After two hours or so, Barry was back in the data processing department, looking very unhappy.

Author: Well, how'd it go?

Barry: I'm sending out résumés starting tonight. I can't hack that bald jerk much longer.

Author: You mean he didn't give you a raise?

Barry: Oh sure. I got a raise all right. But even with the raise I'll be making less than I did this year. You see, the raise puts me into another salary bracket where you don't collect any overtime pay or anything less than sixteen hours in a month. Right now, he's got me working about fifteen hours or so, but I get compensated for it. I'm getting the hell out of this joint as soon as I can. By the way, he wants me to get that lousy payroll on the machines soon, and you know what a tough job that will be.

Author: Yeah, the men from IBM told me it would be a long time getting that baby to work.

Barry just sat in his office the rest of the day, staring at the walls. The next morning he came in with his résumé to get my opinion of it. It looked impressive; and I realized how serious he was about leaving Electronic Systems.

During the first week in August, Barry worked almost exclusively with card design and programming for the new payroll system. Mr. Haley asked Barry to work Saturday to try to iron out some of the problems with the payroll system. Since our presentation of the proposed system was due in a few weeks, I also received the go-ahead to work Saturdays. That Saturday Barry was preparing the cards for all salaried personnel at Electronic Systems from a classified file, and my work was interrupted several times that morning with either Barry's laughter or his cries of disbelief.

Barry: Boy! You wouldn't believe what this guy is making. You should see the raise he got—and for what? He sure has got the wool pulled over someone's eyes.

Back to work for a few minutes. Then laughter from Barry's corner.

Barry: Hey, Craig. Here's another guy with a lousy deal. Gee, the job he has done here has been fantastic. Do you know when he's on vacation, he still spends his time in here? Boy, this place doesn't appreciate him. And what a lousy salary.

It was from this time on that Barry felt he was not the only employee of Electronic Systems who was being shortchanged. Of course, this made him sulk even more, and he sat staring at the walls and pondering his future. During the following week and up until the time I left, a steady stream of people came to Barry's office to discuss their common predicament—their dislike of Haley, who handled the majority of reviews and salary allotments. The air was filled with talk of résumés and new employer contacts.

In the weeks before our proposed presentation was to be made, two men from IBM were brought in to consult with Barry and me on the system. They presented some helpful suggestions for our system and were of useful support in many of our departmental meetings. However, they showed great concern that Barry had not yet written any standard operating procedures which would be of use to the company in times of Barry's absence. Barry always countered by saying he would begin writing them and developing a manual that week. However, Barry and I knew better. Barry had always told me that this knowledge would be kept in his head until he thought it was appropriate to record it. It was, as Barry said, his "job security," for as long as he held that knowledge in his head, they needed him. Besides, he also felt it would be a good way to get back at Mr. Haley if and when Barry left.

It was at this time that Mr. Haley again came under attack from the vice president of manufacturing and the plant manager over the monthly work-in-process inventory. Earlier in 1968, Haley had promised that this would be taken out of the hands of the foremen and handled by the data processing machines. This, of course, would save many man-hours by the production-line workers, and the foremen were pleased to hear they would be spared the task. However, by August (although this sytem was running in June when I arrived), Electronic Systems was still running parallel systems. One was done monthly by the machines, the other was done monthly by the workers on the line. To top it all off, neither system ever came close to the other in reporting the work-in-process inventory.

This was a great thorn in Haley's side, as he was constantly kept aware of the speech he made promising elimination of the monthly physical inventory by production workers. Again, he was under attack for devoting too much time to the accounting system. Finally, Haley cornered Barry in his office and told him to solve the problem. Barry told Haley what the problem was from the data processing angle. However, this problem could easily have been solved by correcting just one of the daily reporting procedures incurred on the production line. Barry knew how to solve this problem quite simply. Haley did not, and neither would the foremen whom Haley went to question. It was Barry's secret, and he gave me a little smile as Haley left his office.

During the end of the week prior to our week-long proposal presentation, Mr. Haley called Barry into his office and told him he was not to attend the first few meetings but was to continue working on the payroll system. Electronic Systems was experiencing great difficulty with this system—so much that a team from IBM, which specialized in payroll installations, agreed to assist Barry later in the month of August.

Barry missed the first day of meetings, but pressure was put on Haley by the various people attending the meeting to allow Barry to be present at the rest of them. Since Barry was to run the operation, many were very much interested in his views. At the end of the week, we had won over the majority, and Mr. Wilson gave his O.K. to that part of the system that had not already been implemented.

When I was making my rounds of goodbys to the various personnel, the most common piece of advice given to me was not to come back to work at Electronic Systems full time. Most of the workers told me that if I came back next summer, there was a good chance they would be gone. They were starting to get responses from the résumés they, too, had sent out during the summer.

The Foster Creek
Post Office Case

The United States Post Office in Foster Creek, New York, is a small, first-class office serving a suburban community of 11,000. Normally, the post office employs eleven people—a postmaster, an assistant postmaster, six carriers (including one parcel-post truck driver), and three clerks.

Each postal employee's job requirements are minutely subdivided and explicitly prescribed by the *Post Office Manual*—a large, two-volume publication of the U.S. Post Office Department in Washington, D.C. There is a "suggested" rate per minute and/or day for sorting and delivering letters, of which every postal employee is well aware. The work is highly prescribed, routine, and repetitive, with little basis for the development of individual initiative. Although each man contrives a few little tricks (which he may or may not pass along to his fellow workers) for easing his *own* work load, there is little incentive for a postal employee to attempt to improve any part of the mail delivery system *as a whole*. Each man performs pretty much as he is expected to perform (nothing more or less). Roger, the assistant postmaster, clearly verbalized this attitude, "The inspectors can't get us if we go by the book [manual]."

The irregular, unannounced visits by the district postal inspectors arouse a strange fear in *all* the employees at the Foster Creek Post Office. Although each of the eleven employees is fairly well acquainted with the inspectors, there is something disturbing about the presence of a man whose recommendations may mean the loss of your job. The security of their position in the post office is highly valued by employees of Foster Creek, some of whom are no longer young and must provide for their families. It is customary, therefore, to see an entire post office staff snap to attention and work harder at the arrival, or possibility of arrival, of a postal inspector.

Larry, the Foster Creek postmaster, had a philosophy regarding the affairs of his office which was: "Keep the patrons and the inspectors happy." Outside of this requirement and an additional one which

This case was written under the supervision of Alvar O. Elbing. Names of people and places have been disguised.

made it imperative that each employee punch in and off the time clock at the exact appointed time (this requirement was primarily for the ease of bookkeeping), each man could do his job pretty much as he wished. The clerks reported at 6 a.m. to sort the day's mail into different stacks for the carriers who arrived at 7 a.m. The carriers then "cased" (further sorting according to street and number) their letters and usually were "on the road" by 9 a.m. They were required to be back in the office at 3:30 p.m., if possible, for further casing, and at 5 p.m. all the carriers went home.

In the summer months when the mail is relatively light and the weather is clear, each carrier easily finishes his route (including time allowed for a half-hour lunch break) by 1:30 p.m. It is standard procedure for the men to relax at home for two hours before reporting back in at 3:30 p.m. In the winter, on the other hand, with snow piled high in the yards, each carrier can no longer take the shorter route

Figure 1   Foster Creek Post Office Formal Organization

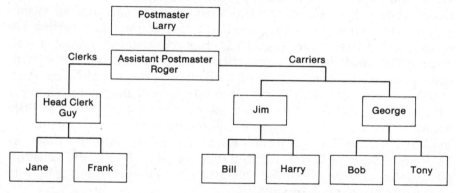

across the yards, and the men often finish long after 3:30 p.m. Larry is well aware of this procedure and says: "It all balances out, and in the hot summer they can use the extra hours to take it easy."

At 3:30 p.m. (or so) the day's big social event takes place at the post office. With the cry of "Flip for Cokes," all the employees except Jane, the one female clerk, match dimes to see who will be the day's loser and provide cokes for the others. This daily gaming is one of the many examples of the free and frequent sociability which exists among the ten male employees. Although the office's formal organization is detailed by postal regulations (see Figure 1), owing to the similar socioeconomic status and interests of the employees, the post office atmosphere is very relaxed and informal (see Figure 2). Many of the men bowl together; they go to the same church; and they often attend high school graduations and funerals affecting the families of their coworkers.

On payday (every Friday), each of the ten male employees

contributes 50 cents of his paycheck to "the fund." This fund is used for coffee and donuts, to provide sick employees with flowers and "get-well" cards, and to purchase a ham to be shared at work during Christmas time.

Other important parts of each day are the regular morning and afternoon conversations. In the morning, the talk invariably turns to news items in the morning's paper. In addition, the men often talk about "those politicians in Washington" and the possibility of a postal pay raise. In the afternoons, the men relate any interesting experiences from the day's rounds. These experiences range from dog bites to coffee with an attractive female patron.

In general the eleven employees of the Foster Creek Post Office enjoyed their work. They comprised a close-knit team doing similar

Figure 2   Foster Creek Post Office Informal Organization

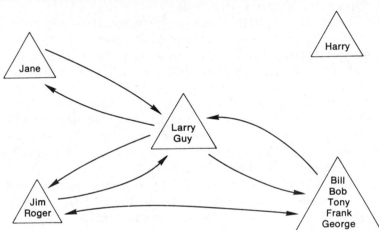

and somewhat distasteful work, but, as George, a senior carrier, put it, "We get good, steady pay; and it's a lot easier than digging ditches."

In mid-June, 1968, Larry filed a request for a carrier to replace a regular Foster Creek carrier who had died suddenly. At 7 a.m. on Monday, July 8th, Harry reported for work as a permanent replacement.

Harry was a tall, skinny man with thinning hair, long fingers, and wire-rimmed eye glasses. He appeared to be in his fifties. He seemed nervous and shy, and when Larry introduced him to the Foster Creek regulars, Harry stared at the floor and said only "Hi!" Initial opinions of this new carrier were mixed. Jim, another senior carrier, probably best expressed the employees' sentiments when he said: "He's not too friendly—yet—he's probably a little nervous here —but *man* can he case mail!"

Harry was an excellent caser. For 27 years he had been a clerk in the main post office. The attitudes and work environment in big city post offices differ markedly from those in smaller offices (as Larry was quick to point out when any of Foster Creek's employees complained). In the city post offices, where competition for the few available positions is extremely keen, a man must not only be very competent but must follow the postal regulations *to the letter*. As Harry said quietly to Roger upon his arrival at Foster Creek, "Things were just too pushy in the city. And besides, my wife and I wanted to move out here in the country to have a house and garden of our own to take care of."

Harry had a well-kept and attractive house and garden. It was apparent that Harry loved to take care of his lawn and garden, because he spent all day Sunday working on it. As a member of the Foster Creek Building and Loan Association, Larry knew that Harry had purchased the property with cash.

On Wednesday, Harry's third day at work, the opinions regarding Harry had become more concrete. As Jim said: "Harry's strange. He thinks he's better than all of us, coming from that city office. He never talks to us or says anything about himself. All he does is stand there and case mail, but *man* is he fast at that!"

The first real problem arose on the fourth day. Harry had learned his route well enough so that he, too, was able to finish by 1:30 p.m. His ability to case and "tie out" (gathering the mail in leather straps) his mail so quickly put him on the road by 8:30 in the morning—ahead of the other four carriers.

On this Thursday afternoon Harry reported back to the post office at 1:15, having finished his entire route. Upon seeing this, Roger's first reaction was to say, "Go home and have some lunch, Harry. Relax at home for a little while."

Harry replied, "I've had my lunch. There are letters on my case. I've got to do them now. I've got to do my job." Having said this, he began to case the several hundred letters which had piled up since the morning. He finished these quickly, and then went on and cased all the mail which was lying on the other four carriers' cases. When the four regular carriers returned at 3:30 p.m., they were, to say the least, surprised.

Bill, the youngest and least energetic of the carriers, thanked Harry. However, Jim and George in particular were very angry. They grumbled about having a "newcomer" interfere, with his "city tricks" and "fancy casing." They were especially angry that Harry had violated the 3:30 rule. They were determined that he would not be the one who would make them lose their precious privileges, and they complained to Larry about Harry. The postmaster told Harry to case only his own mail, and to take it easy when walking his route in the future.

The next day, Friday, was payday. Each man contributed his share to "the fund." Harry refused. "I don't drink coffee," was his only answer. No one pushed the matter further, although discontent over Harry had developed among all the employees.

As the next week passed by, Harry appeared to sink into an even deeper shell. He punched in at 7 a.m. and punched out at 5 p.m. In between, he neither looked at nor spoke to any of the other employees. He continued to report back into the office before 3:30, case all his own mail, and then sit on the stool in front of his case reading magazines. Larry was worried primarily about Harry's exposure to the public as he sat at his case reading, and so on Friday of Harry's second week, Harry's and Bill's cases were switched (see Figure 3).

Figure 3   Foster Creek Post Office Layout

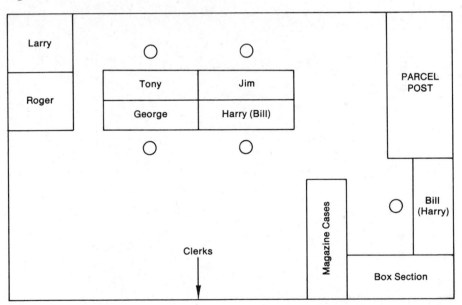

When each of the carriers reported in on Friday afternoon, Bill was told that his case was moved so as to give him more room to handle his quickly growing route (which, in part, was true). Harry said nothing about the switch, but went straight to work in his new location.

During Harry's third week at the post office, Larry began to worry even more about his behavior. Although the carrier was hidden from the public now, a postal inspector could catch Harry reading at his case very easily.

On Thursday, July 18th, Larry's worst fears were realized. An inspector came to the Foster Creek Post Office. As he walked in, Harry was sitting quietly at his case, reading as usual. The inspector looked at Harry, then at Larry.

Larry explained that Harry had an easier route than the other carriers. Because of this and his ability as a caser, Harry was able to finish his route more easily. Larry pointed out that he did not know what to say to the carrier, for he had finished all his *required* work. The inspector suggested that Larry readjust the routes to give Harry more houses to deliver and more mail to case. This was attempted, but Jim, George, and Tony reacted unfavorably.

Chapter Four

The Diagnostic
Process: Behavioral Models

We have seen that, in order to make a sound diagnosis, it is important to have verifiable evidence about the situation at issue, to arrange the evidence into a meaningful pattern. This arranging is to some extent determined by the perceptual framework we bring to the diagnostic process. That is, when faced with human problems, we necessarily approach them with basic assumptions about human behavior in general. Often these assumptions are so deeply rooted in our personal frame of reference that we consider them as universal truths about human nature. However, if these assumptions are not accurate, they will be useless when brought to bear on a particular problem. Therefore, it is important to have sound concepts of human behavior in mind when we pattern the evidence before us into a diagnosis.

This chapter will introduce frameworks, or models, that can serve as a sound basis for diagnosing human behavior. These frameworks or models are useful in three general ways. First, they serve as references to aid our understanding of particular patterns of behavior. Second, they serve as a basis for arranging data to help in visualizing the relationships among items of information. Third, they offer rudimentary blueprints for formulating a final working diagnosis.

Three basic models of human behavior will be examined in this chapter: the *individual* behavior model, an effective starting point for observing human behavior; the *interpersonal* behavior model, which   189 clarifies the reciprocal nature of interaction; and the *group* behavior model, which clarifies the role of group norms and values in behavior.

The Individual Behavior Model

Figure 1, the basic behavioral model, was discussed in Chapter 2. Although in.Chapter 2 we used this model to demonstrate the effect of the decision maker's frame of reference on his own perceptions of data, it is equally useful to his understanding the behavior of someone else, especially to clarify the effect of that person's frame of reference on his perceptions.

Figure 1   Individual Behavior

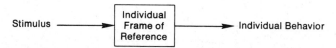

In using this model we must remind ourselves that we can never fully understand another's frame of reference; it is essentially a "black box" to us.[1] Thus we have only his behavior (output) as primary evidence as a basis for inferences about his motives, goals, values, and the like. In addition, we may have evidence of the stimulus to which he is responding (input): an incident or event that coincided with his change in behavior may have provided the stimulus for his reaction.

In attempting to relate stimulus to behavior, however, the decision maker must use caution, because he and the subject may not perceive the stimulus in the same way. Indeed, the subject may be responding to an entirely different stimulus not apparent to the decision maker. Pressures within the subject that relate to earlier events or even to situations outside the organization may be the actual stimuli.

Thus it is obvious that, as we make inferences in our attempts to explain the behavior of others, we come face to face again with our own frame of reference—another reason why it is essential to a good diagnosis that we have insight into our own frame of reference. How do *we* view people and behavior in general? Do we assume that workers are basically lazy or industrious, or responsible or irresponsible—or do we assume that workers attempt to satisfy specific needs in specific circumstances as they perceive them to be satisfiable? Understanding our own frame of reference is a first step to understanding others'.

---

1. This concept and term derives from World War II combat experience. When the enemy's communication boxes were captured, they could not be opened for fear of a booby trap; therefore, to understand the contents of the box, an intelligence investigator was restricted to the inferences he could draw from the box's inputs and outputs.

In addition to understanding the effect of our frame of reference on what we perceive, it is necessary that, as decision makers, we understand the various forces that operate within an individual whose behavior we are observing. Here it is helpful to attempt to *empathize;* that is, to put ourselves in the other person's place and view his world from within his psychological frame of reference, attempting to experience how *he* sees and feels a given situation. What forces determine how he psychologically processes the data presented to him? It is here that the manager's reservoir of knowledge about human behavior is put to direct use. A general awareness of basic psychological processes aids immeasurably in making logical inferences about the causes of behavior. It can aid inquiry, shift the decision maker's focus from his own frame of reference to that of the subject, and help him understand behavior that might otherwise appear irrational or illogical.

If we begin with the assumption that all his behavior is rational to the person behaving, we can ask ourselves *why* he believes his behavior is rational—how does he see it as satisfying his needs? Using Maslow's (1943) conceptualization of a need hierarchy as an analytical model, we can attempt to explain the basis of behavior that appears to us to be irrational. For example, a person who leaves a high-paying job for a lower-paying job must see the new situation as satisfying a need that was not satisfied formerly. To view such a move as irrational, and thereupon dismiss it, merely reflects a value judgment from the observer's point of view. Further inquiry may identify higher-order needs that were unsatisfied: needs for social relationships, ego satisfaction, or self-actualization, for example. Inferences can then be made as to why this person viewed the new situation as a greater source of satisfaction.

The individual model provides a starting point for systematic inquiry into the reasons why a person behaves as he does. Its application involves three vital diagnostic steps: (1) identifying the stimulus that provokes a pattern of behavior; (2) discovering how the individual may have structured that stimulus; (3) determining, in non-evaluative terms, the causes of the behavior. Although the model does not provide the *answer* to a behavioral problem, it does provide a systematic framework for sorting out the information necessary for the understanding required as a basis for solving such problems.

The Interpersonal Behavior Model

Up to this point we have focused on the internal variables that influence the behavior of individuals. As we have seen, these variables include all the psychological residue from an individual's past experiences that constitute his personality, his "psychological set," his way of structuring the world around him. These internal variables, however, are not the only factors that influence individual behavior; the individual is influenced by the world around him, by the situations in which he finds himself, and by the other people with whom he comes in contact. These *external variables* can strongly influence the form of an individual's psychological reactions. The social environment in a plant, for example—whether authoritarian or democratic, hostile or friendly—is one important variable in determining individual behavior; leadership style is another; and the attitude of one's peers is still another. In attempting to understand an individual's behavior, therefore, a manager should try to understand both that individual's internal psychological processes and the external environment in which he is operating at the time.

A special kind of *external* variable that is particularly important for the manager to understand is the influence of one person on another in a two-person interaction situation. To better understand this type of situation, let us consider a second model (actually an extension of the first). The purpose of this model (Figure 2) is to aid

Figure 2   Interpersonal Behavior

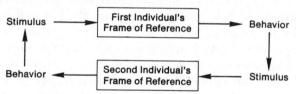

examination of a situation in which the behavior of one individual acts as a stimulus to another.

When one person addresses another, the response he receives will to some extent influence his future behavior. An emotional overture ordinarily elicits a different response than does a calm overture. Agreement usually generates a different response than does disagreement, and inquiry is differently received than evaluation. Indeed, if an individual's responses do not correspond to the approachs made to him, this is a clue to the manager that especially strong internal motivations are operating that may require investigation. If, for example, an individual is angry or anxious, even a polite overture from another person may be perceived as an attack and evoke a hostile response. Such a response is not independent of external variables, because some stimulus from the second person was required to activate it. However, in this case, the internal variables were dominant in shaping the response.

In the interpersonal behavior model we can see the relationship between an individual's internal variables and the external stimuli from another person, both of which influence his responses. Although this is an easily visualized interaction process, the explanation of a real-life interchange is not always simple.

The Thomas Motor case is an interesting example of two-person interaction over time. In each situation where Ralph Turner was having trouble, the foreman responded by telling him to slow down. He avoided giving hostile criticism and exerting external pressure, merely suggesting that Turner work more slowly so as to avoid making similar mistakes. If our diagnosis of Chapter 3 is correct, and part of Turner's problem stems from internal stimuli (his frustration at his inability to join in on the coffee breaks) the foreman's suggestions, in omitting consideration of internal variables, are external variables which further frustrate Turner. Each time Turner is told to slow down, he responds by attacking something in the shop. Thus we see how external and internal variables interact to set a pattern of apparently illogical behavior.

In this connection it is useful to note that an individual's own behavior can serve as a stimulus for his future behavior. A lie, for example, may stimulate continued lying. A choice of clothing may be the stimulus for an individual's demeanor and the *role* [2] he will play. Or a point of view, once expressed, may be perceived as requiring consistent expression of the same point of view. All of these stimuli may result principally from the behavior of the individual, without much influence from the outside world.

In viewing situations of human interaction, we must look beyond personalities and examine the interaction *situation*, if we want to understand fully the causes for the behavior we see. In most situations, man is not motivated by innate character traits. Ralph Turner, for example, does not behave badly because he is innately irritable, clumsy, lazy, or unskilled. Defining behavior in terms of "innate" traits is not an aid to understanding a problem, nor does it constitute diagnosis. Generally, a person's responses involve environmental stimuli that he believes have importance for him. Thus, Ralph Turner's behavior was related, not only to internal factors, but also to the foreman's acts. The interpersonal behavior model is useful for reminding the diagnostician that behavioral responses are determined by, among other factors, two-person interaction in a situation.

The Group Behavior Model

The two-person interaction model (discussed above) showed us how the behavior of one individual influences the behavior of another. In many situations this model can be expanded to explain the behavior of larger numbers of people. For example, behavior at a cocktail party may primarily consist of a number of two-person interactions.

In other situations, however, when a number of persons interact with one another, it is necessary to go beyond the interpersonal model

---

2. For a discussion of roles, see Katz and Kahn (1966).

to understand behavior. When individuals regularly work together and generate more or less constant relationships, they may form a group that takes on a certain character of its own and influences the individual behavior of its members. Thus the effect of group structure on the behavior of individual workers is an important external variable in diagnosis.

A *group* is characterized by a pattern of relationships that ordinarily is established gradually, over time. When individuals come into contact with each other under similar circumstances over a fairly long period of time, their behavior tends to become more and more predictable. If their interpersonal experiences have demonstrated that responding to one another can result in the satisfaction of individual needs, they begin to *identify* with each other, which means that the responses of others (formerly external stimuli) become internalized: the norms of behavior that have been established in the relationships among group members gradually become the individual, internalized norms of each member.

The term *group*, as it is used in behavioral science literature, is a special, technical term. Two social psychologists, Muzafer and Carolyn Sherif (1956), define it as follows:

A group is a social unit which consists of a number of individuals who stand in (more or less) definite status and role relationships to one another and which possesses a set of values and norms of its own regulating the behavior of individual members, at least in matters of consequence to the group (p. 144).

It is important that the concept of a group be differentiated from other types of social systems. According to the Sherifs, *social system* refers only to an aggregate of individuals having some relationship to one another. Thus a plant is a social system from the moment it opens. The Sherifs refer to social systems that are not yet groups simply as "togetherness situations," in which the qualities that formally constitute a group either are not present or are present only in rudimentary forms. It is therefore inappropriate to use group concepts to explain individual behavior in togetherness situations, inasmuch as internal psychological variables still dominate that behavior. A simple expansion of the interpersonal model may be adequate for analyzing interpersonal behavior in togetherness situations. However, if the relationships in a togetherness situation continue over time, a group may form (see Figure 3). "Group" is a longitudinal concept, at the opposite extreme from a togetherness situation on a continuum of social systems.

The Sherifs have identified four important factors that eventually lead to the development of groups: (1) common motivation; (2)

development of group norms and values; (3) emergence of reciprocal expectations by members of each other's behavior; (4) member acceptance of group norms and values and their application by members, even in situations where the others are not present.

It is important to stress here the point that "group" is a *psychological* concept; that is, group norms and values become the *personal* norms and values of all individuals who identify with the group. A group, it must be remembered, does not act; it is the individuals who act. Thus the usefulness of the group concept is that it helps us understand individual behavior based on group norms and values.

Figure 3   The Development of Social Systems over Time (Sherif and Sherif, 1956, p. 144, adapted)

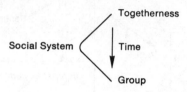

George Homans (1950) offers a useful conceptualization of the emergence of group norms and values in work situations. His definition of *group* is simpler than, but compatible with, the Sherifs:

> We mean by a group a number of persons who communicate with one another often over a span of time, and who are few enough so that each person is able to communicate with all the others . . . face-to-face (p. 1).

Homans analyzes the environment of a group and finds it is made up of physical, technical, and social factors. The environment of a work group, for example, includes physical objects (tables, walls, doors, lights), level of technical development (craft, manned assembly line, automated assembly line), and social relationships (interactions with superiors, peers, subordinates, and others). Furthermore, the environment of the group includes all the factors, both within the organization and in the broader community, which constitute the background for establishing the requirements of a particular job.

Conditioned by this environment, the organization identifies various tasks to be performed in order to accomplish the goals of the organization. These tasks are performed by men who have various relationships to one another and who hold various attitudes toward the tasks. Homans labels the elements of the work situation *activities*, *interactions*, and *sentiments*, and he calls their overall pattern the *external system*. These elements also become the starting point for the emergence of a group, Homans' *internal system*.

Thus, in the Homans model, three sets of systems provide the basis for analysis: the *internal* system (the emergent group), which exists within and alongside the *external* system (the requirements of the organization), which exists within a particular *environment.* These systems interrelate with one another and are mutually interdependent (see Figure 4). And just as the three systems are interde-

Figure 4   Group Behavior in the Organizational Environment (Homans, 1950, adapted)

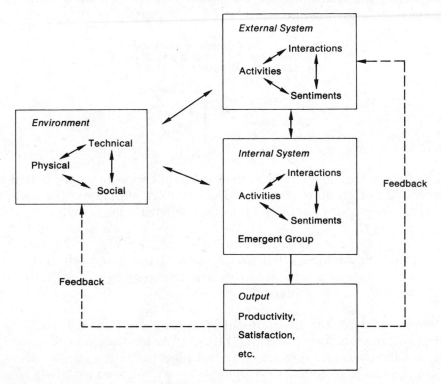

pendent, all the elements of each system are interdependent. They are not closed systems but dynamic, interacting systems, which strongly influence each other.

The Foster Creek Post Office case at the end of Chaper 3 may help clarify Homan's concepts. Within the environment of the village of Foster Creek and its post office, the post office workers developed certain ways of going about their jobs. Their basic *activities* consisted of sorting and delivering mail on various routes according to a schedule. To do this they had to *interact* with each other and with supervisors, inspectors, and community residents in a particular way. They were also expected to hold certain *sentiments* about their jobs ("Neither snow nor rain, . . ."), most of which were spelled out in the post office manual. These activities, interactions, and sentiments constituted the external system (the job requirements) within the physical, technical, and social environment of the post office.

Within the environment and paralleling the external system, an internal system or group evolved. Numerous group activities and interactions developed which were related to but not required by the external system: flipping for Cokes, contributing to the paycheck "fund," selecting topics of conversation, regulating delivery times, and so on. Group sentiments about the jobs, especially in relation to job security, are also observable. Although these group norms and values were not unrelated to the standards of the established system, the postal workers preserved their unique relationship to their group in the particular manner the members wanted it preserved. In short, the social system in the Foster Creek Post Office is an example of a strongly knit group in the sense we have been using the term.

The importance of understanding the interwoven fabric of activities, interactions, and sentiments is that, as has been discussed, when a group forms in a particular situation, its emerging norms and values tend to become the norms and values of the participating individuals, for whom the group is thus a *reference* group. Frequently, these norms and values affect the work output of the members—as it did, for example, in the post office case. This factor becomes crucial for the manager who wishes to improve output.

According to Homans' work-group model, there are three possible sources for the causes of a problem: the environment, the external system, or the internal system. Of these three causal sources, a manager is *least able to bring about change in the internal system*, the characteristic structure of the group. He cannot change group norms and values in the same way he can change aspects of the environment (lights, desks, etc.) and the external system (e.g., postal regulations). If norms and values have been internalized by workers, the effectiveness of an organizational plan for change will necessarily be in part determined by its compatibility with the group's norms. If group norms and values are not taken into consideration, even a very rational plan for change may be resisted. One problem that faces the manager, therefore, is determining how a group will react to changes in the environment or in the external system.

The output of the Foster Creek Post Office met everyone's expectations and equilibrium existed—until Harry began working there. Harry had worked in a different environment, with different organizational requirements, and his behavior reflected different norms and values. Much of Harry's behavior threatened the work group at Foster Creek since it violated the group's norms. His behavior was soon viewed as deviate by the Foster Creek work group and the group's attitudes toward him reflected that feeling.

Not only did Harry's behavior violate group norms, it differed from the expectations of the postmaster: Harry's work broke the speed standards that had been set at Foster Creek, and he completed all his work early in the afternoon. The postmaster attempted to preserve equilibrium by changing the men's work stations, moving Harry's sorting cage into a corner and out of sight so he could not be seen reading magazines in his spare time. Harry's isolation preserved the group's norms, but it only temporarily relieved a symptom. When the postal inspector discovered the problem, he considered it necessary to find a solution that would meet the standards of the external system, as described in the postal manual. In the inspector's presence, the postmaster of course had to fall in line. The resulting "solution" was not a real solution of the problem, however, because it did not allay the group's distress at having its norms and established prerogatives violated.

In diagnosing work-group behavior from the vantage point of management, it is important to consider both the norms of the group and the relationship between it and the management group—that is, the *intergroup* relationship.[3] When two individuals meet (for example, a manager and a factory worker), they create not only an interpersonal situation but also an intergroup situation. In order for a manager to understand and deal with a problem which involves groups, therefore, he must recognize and deal with norms and values that relate to him both as a person and as a member of the management group. From the following example, written by a manager, we can draw some fairly clear inferences about the relationship between a worker group and a management group. (Proper names and designations have been disguised.)

> I was transferred [to general manufacturing] from River Glen, South Carolina, where Modern Chemical has a new fiber plant. The River Glen plant was built in 1965. The entire plant, including the shop, is air conditioned, and incorporates the latest in "daylight" lighting. The grounds are beautifully landscaped. River Glen has no union, and in general the employees seem enthusiastic about making fiber. They are paid a straight day rate. Measured against standard motion-time study (MTS) data, the plant averages 85 to 90 percent productivity.
>
> The general manufacturing plant was a shock to me. Although the hourly workers are generally paid more than those in River Glen, their productivity is only 40 to 45 percent of MTS. The shop starts at 7:00 a.m. but there is seldom a machine operating at 8:00 a.m. when the office force arrives. The machines start around 8:30 and shut down at 11:00 to 11:30 a.m.

---

3. For a discussion of intergroup behavior, see Sherif (1962).

for an unofficial two-hour lunch. During this morning work period there is a 40-minute coffee break. The afternoon period of actual production work is from 1:00 to 3:00 p.m.

I work in manufacturing engineering and have developed some communication with the shop. One day I needed a small pad milled and a hole drilled and tapped in a brass fitting for my boat. It fit in my pocket, and since it was a five-minute job I took it to a machinist to be done.

He said he needed a shop order for two hours in order to do it and it would require a sketch by a union draftsman. When I told him it was for my boat, he said "o.k." and did the operations in less than five minutes. He said he would be glad to do any personal work I brought in, since he was bored at not being able to work very much during the day. I never had another occasion to use him for personal work, but I get engineering jobs done "free" by telling him they are for my boat.

This example shows that the machinist at first responded to the engineer as an out-group member (a member of management, not of the union). However, when the engineer presented himself as an individual with a personal problem, he was able to get around existing group norms and intergroup behavior patterns. The purpose of this example is not to suggest that the engineer's method was necessarily the best one for dealing with group norms, but it does point up the role of group norms in interaction. Problems involving group norms can scarcely be solved until they are first consciously understood.

The small group is thought by many to be the most fruitful level of analysis for understanding behavior in the workplace, and the literature of small group behavior is extensive.[4] However, the purpose here is limited to introducing some of the basic concepts which provide a framework for considering the effect of group norms and values on individual behavior.

The Usefulness of the Models

The usefulness of models of human behavior derives from the help they provide in systematically conceptualizing problem situations. Such models do not give "answers" to *specific* problems: rather, they help focus on potentially fruitful questions and lines of inquiry. They put the decision maker in a position where he may be able to examine not only the unit under consideration but, in addition, all the relevant relationships in the given system. The three models that

4. See Thelen and Dickerman (1949), pp. 309–316; Klein (1961), pp. 119–132; and M. Sherif (1956), pp. 54–58.

have been presented in this chapter are the models that are fundamental to understanding the situations most often faced by the diagnostician. Together, they provide a basic framework for performing
the diagnostic process and eventually formulating a workable diagnosis.

Numerous additional models for special situations are available
in the literature to assist the decision maker. From these and from the
basic models presented, the decision maker can construct his own
more specific behavioral models for his own particular organization,
based on his experience in the organization over time. As he develops
these models, he is in a better position not only to understand his
organization, but also to identify occasions when the organization is
in disequilibrium.

Time as a Factor in Diagnosis

A final word about the diagnostic process pertains to the concept
of time. A diagnosis is always related to time. When a student is
presented with a written case study of a problem situation, its time
parameters have already been drawn for him. The case writer has
begun the case at the point *he* considered its beginning and has ended
it at the point of crisis, or at the point when he considers that
sufficient information has been made available for the decision-making process.

In the dynamic situation of the workplace, however, it is up to
the *diagnostician* to decide how far back in time he must search for
causes and how extensively he must spread his inquiry. He must also
recognize that, as each day passes, conditions change, so that although he has completed his formal diagnosis, new information may
still become available. He must therefore retain *time flexibility,* since
it is possible that information may come to light tomorrow that can
completely alter his conclusion. Certainly, a diagnosis must always be
open to reinterpretation if more information becomes available. Indeed, one of the values of formulating a working diagnosis is that it
provides a specific framework into which additional information can
be readily and meaningfully incorporated.

As more and more time elapses after the original problem incident, the process of finding facts and separating them from opinions
becomes more and more difficult. To avoid the loss of information,
therefore, a decision maker must begin his diagnosis as soon as
possible. The more background and knowledge he has of human
behavior in general, the more skillfully and rapidly he will be able to
use information as it comes in, and eventually make a sound diagnosis of the behavior in a given situation. This, of course, points up the
importance for diagnosis of the study of organizational theories and
organizational behavior. The study of behavior provides the manager

with concepts that can greatly faciliate the entire diagnostic process in decision making.

The Cost of Search

In concluding our discussion of the diagnostic process it should be noted that the process is not cost-free. There is a cost connected with any search process, whether that process be efficient or inefficient, effective or ineffective, vague or specific. There are instances in which the time cost involved in accurate and complete diagnosis is not warranted by the severity of the problem or the importance of the solution. However, it should be kept in mind that if a problem is important enough to warrant a solution, it is important enough to warrant an *effective* solution. Good solutions rarely result from inadequate or faulty diagnoses. Thus, in the long run, cost is minimized through a systematic diagnosis which identifies the correct problem and its underlying causes. A "solution" which does not solve the problem may be more costly than investment in the accurate diagnosis which leads to a workable solution.

Summary

This chapter has examined the process of diagnosis, which is the foundation for decision making. A sound diagnosis—one that adheres to specific, rigorous criteria—can lead the way to a clear statement of a problem and the selection of an optimal solution. Reliance on hunches from a personal frame of reference can lead only to a weak diagnosis and an unsound solution. In approaching a problem situation, the decision maker will greatly benefit from the systematic application of a sound, orderly model to the data. Proceeding on the basis of such systematic analysis, the decision maker can better make a precise identification of the problems that face him.

The following chapter takes up the definition of the problem.

References

Hickman, C. A., and M. H. Kuhn. *Individuals, Groups and Economic Behavior.* Dryden, 1956.

Homans, George. *The Human Group.* Harcourt, Brace and World, 1950.

Katz, Daniel, and Robert L. Kahn. "The Taking of Organizational Roles." In *The Social Psychology of Organizations.* Wiley, 1966. Reprinted in Part III.

Klein, Josephine. *Working With Groups.* Hutchinson University Library, 1961. Selection in Part III.

March, James, and Herbert Simon. *Organizations.* Wiley, 1958.

Maslow, Abraham. "A Theory of Motivation." *Psychological Review,* Vol. 50 (1943), 370–96. Abridged in Part III.

Sherif, Muzafer. "Experiments in Group Conflict and Cooperation." *Scientific American,* Vol. 195 (1956), 54–58.

Sherif, Muzafer. "Inter-group Relations and Leadership." In *Intergroup Relations and Leadership,* ed. M. Sherif. Wiley (1962), 3–21. Abridged in Part III.

————, and Carolyn Sherif. *An Outline of Social Psychology.* Harper & Row, 1956.

Simon, Herbert. *Models of Man: Social and Rational.* Wiley, 1957.

Thelen, Herbert, and Watson Dickerman. "The Growth of Groups." *Educational Leadership,* Vol. 6, No. 5 (February 1949) 309–16. Reprinted in Part III.

Turner, Ralph H. "Role Taking, Role Standpoint and Reference Group Behavior." *American Journal of Sociology,* Vol. 61 (1956), 316–28. Abridged in *Role Theory,* ed. Biddle and Thomas. Wiley, 1966.

The Oscar Larson Case

Oscar Larson had recently accepted the position of time-study man at Svenska Malmfabriken (SMF) in Stockholm, Sweden. He had an excellent reputation in the time-study field. After graduating with honors from the Royal Institute of Technology with a degree in administrative engineering, he worked with several companies in Sweden. Later he had a position in the time-study field in the United States with a firm of consulting engineers. For about two years he was in charge of the installation of incentive systems. After five years in the United States, he returned to Sweden, where he worked for two well-known Swedish companies before he accepted his position with SMF.

Larson was well known in professional circles in Sweden. He had held several offices in the Swedish Society for Time Study. During the first few weeks after he reported for work, he remained in the time-study department offices, where he got acquainted with the time-study methods and techniques used at SMF. This indoctrination included becoming familiar with the standard data books, the job descriptions, the incentive calculations, the fatigue allowances, and the many other technical details that are involved in the practice of modern time study.

From Ben A. Lindberg, *Cases in Personnel Administration* © 1954. Reprinted by permission of Prentice-Hall, Inc., Englewood Cliffs, New Jersey.

The first job that Larson was given to time study at SMF was in a lathe department. It was a new operation, currently on a "temporary, estimated pay rate." Many of the elements of the operation had been time studied previously, and for these elements, synthetic data were available. As was customary, however, Larson time studied the entire operation from beginning to end. The final results of the time study indicated a rate revision from Kr. 1.69 to Kr. 1.42.[1] In accordance with the union agreement, the rate was posted on a bulletin board, and a copy of the job specifications was sent to the local union office.

The union had five days in which to protest the rate change. A formal protest was filed on the second day. Larson participated in the subsequent hearing. In the meeting with the local union officers he explained in great detail virtually every step that had led to the establishment of the new rate. He demonstrated how the operation had been analyzed into elements; how each element had been carefully described; how each element had been timed or "read" on a continuous clocking basis during several consecutive operations; how certain readings had been circled in red because of unusual or unnecessary motions occurring during the performance of these elements; how from the various readings the normal time for each element had been calculated; and how he had added certain agreed-upon allowances before arriving at the total time allowed for each piece.

Larson was very careful in answering questions that were raised by members of the union committee. He did his very best to give a thorough explanation of every point that was questioned. As he stated afterwards to his supervisor, "I really went into detail with them. I spent about two hours with them, and I'm sure that they understand. I know that I convinced them that there was no error in my time study." At the end of the session, the union spokesman had come to the time-study supervisor and said, "Mr. Larson has explained to us how this time study was made. There is certainly a lot to time study, and we don't understand all about it. We can't find anything wrong with his study, but we don't like the way the rate has been cut."

Nevertheless the new rate was put into effect, and the local union officers did not appeal this action.

Soon afterwards, Oscar Larson was given his second time-study job at SMF. This job was also on an operation in a lathe department. Again Oscar made a thorough study of the operation and, as a result, the rate was revised from Kr. 1.63 to Kr. 1.34. As previously had been the case, the local union officers protested this rate revision.

Again, Larson met with the union committee to explain in detail how the operation had been timed by showing them the original time-study data. He explained how the operation had been analyzed

---

1. One *krona* is equal to about 20 cents.

into elements; how each had been carefully described; how each element had been timed on a "continuous clocking" basis; how certain readings had been circled in red because of unusual or unnecessary motions occurring during the reading; how from the various readings the normal time for each element had been calculated; and how certain agreed-upon allowances had been added before the total time allowed for each piece was reached. The union spokesman again came to the time-study supervisor and said: "Mr. Larson has explained again to us how this time study was taken. We don't understand all of it, but we can't find anything wrong with it. Still we don't like the new rate."

The rate, however, was put into effect, and the union officers did not appeal this action.

About a week later, Larson was sent out on his third time-study job at SMF, which was on an operation on a milling machine. As was his habit, he first made a detailed study of the operation. The "standard method" had been agreed upon with the operator and the foreman. The operation had then been analyzed, that is, resolved into its component elements. Larson had carefully explained to the operator the meaning of each element and the reason why it was necessary to study each element separately. He had asked the operator if he had anything to add—or if there was anything in the explanation that needed further elaboration. The operator had shaken his head and Oscar Larson said, "All right, then, I shall start to time you when you put the next piece in the fixture." He walked over to assume the "timing position," that is, a position from which he could have a relatively unobstructed view of the worker, the work, and the milling machine.

Larson was casually observing the operation, waiting for the new cycle to begin, when he noticed the operator lift his arm and stop the machine. Then the operator picked up a wiping rag . . . wiped his hands . . . slowly and deliberately . . . and advanced by short . . . halting steps . . . towards Larson. Something seemed all of a sudden different to Larson . . . and he realized that all the other milling machines had been stopped. Only the steady hum of machinery in adjoining departments could be sensed. In the milling machine department the men had stopped their machines and picked up their wiping rags. They were wiping their hands . . . slowly and deliberately . . . and were advancing towards him . . . haltingly and silently . . . but steadily. Soon they were right in front of him . . . still wiping their hands . . . slowly and deliberately . . . while looking straight at him.

Suddenly the silence was broken by a quiet, unemotional voice: "Maybe the engineer had better leave the department" Larson looked around at this group of quiet men who were wiping their hands . . .

slowly and deliberately . . . and he . . . decided to leave. The men followed him. In the adjoining department the same quiet voice said: "Maybe the engineer had better leave the building." More workers shut down their machines, picked up a wiping rag, wiped their hands . . . slowly and deliberately . . . and joined the men from the milling machine department.

When the group came out to the factory yard, the quiet voice was heard again: "Maybe the engineer had better go to the gate." Larson followed his instruction. By this time some 200 workers were walking with him. It was a very quiet procession. Larson could hear only the sound of walking feet, the distant hum of operating machinery, and an occasional slight sigh and heavy breathing from the men who were walking with him.

As the group approached the gate, someone yelled to the gatekeeper: "Maybe the gatekeeper had better open the gate for the engineer." The gate was opened. Larson came to the gate, and the quiet, unemotional voice was heard again: "Maybe the engineer had better go outside the gate." As Larson walked out, he heard someone yell: "Maybe the gatekeeper had better close the gate." The gate was closed, and as Larson looked back, he saw the men returning to their jobs . . . wiping their hands with their wiping rags . . . slowly . . . deliberately . . . and . . . silently.

The Hern File Case

The memoranda and letters reproduced or summarized herein are from the file of Stanley Hern, a junior in the School of Commerce and Finance at Pennel City College.

1. *February 14, 1956.* Associate Professor Leeds wrote Hern reminding him of several previous oral requests that he return to Leeds a term paper he had submitted during the fall term in Leeds' course, Personnel 357. He asked Hern to bring or mail in this paper immediately.

2. *February 21, 1956.* Professor Leeds wrote Hern that since he had not returned the term paper as requested in the February 14 letter, he (Leeds) had referred the matter to the discipline committee of the School of Commerce and Finance.
3. *February 27, 1956.* Professor Worthington, chairman of the discipline committee, wrote Hern asking him to appear at 2 p.m., March 9, in connection with "reported irregularities in Personnel 357." He asked Hern to submit in writing, prior to the committee hearing, a statement presenting the facts as he understood them; and he told Hern: "If you do not comply, you expose yourself to drastic penalties."
4. *February 29, 1956.* Hern wrote Professor Worthington to the effect that he could not prepare a written statement until he was informed, in writing, what the charges against him were and who had filed them.
5. *March 2, 1956.* Professor Worthington sent Hern the following letter:

> Professor Leeds has written you twice, asking that you come to his office. You have ignored these, so Professor Leeds, in accordance with the regulations of Pennel City College, has referred the matter to our committee for action.
>
> I strongly urge you to turn in at once the written statement requested in my letter of February 27 and to try to make your peace with Professor Leeds prior to your required appearance before the discipline committee on March 9.

6. *March 6, 1956.* Hern wrote Professor Worthington that, in his opinion, the latter had evaded in his letter of March 2 Hern's February 29 request that he be informed as to the exact nature of the charges he was expected to reply to by written statement. He added: "My sin appears to be a failure to answer my mail. Is there a regulation which requires me to do so?"
7. *March 8, 1956.* Professor Leeds sent Professor Worthington the following memorandum:

> At your request I would like to submit in writing the facts of the Hern case. I will attempt to set down here the essence of my original presentation to you.
>
> Mr. Stanley Hern was a student in my section of Personnel 357 during the fall semester 1955–1956. There was nothing in his behavior or performance in this class until the incident in question that seems to me to have any bearing on understanding his case. He was an average student as measured by the exami-

nations which were a part of the course, and he attended class regularly although he did not take a very active part in the discussions. Later evidence leads me to hypothesize that his mental attitude toward this course and its rather unique teaching-learning process was relatively negative.

As a required part of the course, each student was asked at the beginning to write a personal experience as a term paper, to be submitted in the twelfth week of the semester. During the semester we discussed many times in class what this assignment involved and what would be acceptable as a personal experience. I invited the students to consult with me as they progressed on this assignment, and many students did come to see me. Mr. Hern talked with me briefly about a personal experience in the armed services that he thought might make a good term paper. My response was to encourage him to develop it.

The papers were submitted to me at the beginning of the twelfth week of the semester, and I spent the next week reading and evaluating them. When I came upon Mr. Hern's, I discovered that it was a rather thin disguise of some material we have used many times in the course, but did not use in the fall semester, 1955–56. This is copyrighted by Grayson University. I immediately got out a copy and compared Mr. Hern's work with it. In Mr. Hern's version all of the names had been altered along with a few numbers. There was no notation of any kind that would lead the reader to believe that this was anything but an original study prepared by student Hern. Although some paragraphs had been juxtaposed, Mr. Hern's paper was word-for-word extracted from the Grayson original. There was no reasonable doubt that Mr. Hern had copied the Grayson material with the intention of submitting it to me as his own.

I clipped Mr. Hern's paper to a mimeographed copy of the Grayson material, gave it no grade, and wrote in the upper right-hand corner that this was not an adequate fulfillment of the assignment and that I would like to see him personally to discuss this.

When I returned the papers in class, Hern approached me at the end of the period with a question about why I had given him a copy of the Grayson material. When I explained that his paper was in fact taken from it, Mr. Hern denied that this was so. I explained to him that I had established this fact beyond any doubt. After that, Mr. Hern's response was to the effect that a situation had developed at his wife's place of employment which was so similar to the Grayson case that it seemed to him unnecessary to attempt to write it up when the authors of the Grayson material had already performed this task so adequately. My response to Mr. Hern was that this was a very serious problem, which had to be settled between us, and that I would appreciate his visiting me at his earliest convenience in my office. Mr. Hern's demeanor during this conversation surprised me with its implicit and rather aggressive communication that any indiscretion in this matter was mine rather than his.

The following day Mr. Hern came to my office to keep an appointment we had made several days previously for the purpose of discussing the fact that he might not be able to attend our final examination because of an impending out-of-town trip. Our discussion of this problem was quite brief and routine. (As it turned out, Mr. Hern was in attendance at the examination.) When this matter had been discussed and Hern rose to leave, I again urged upon him the seriousness of his having submitted the Grayson material as his own and requested both that he come to talk about the matter and bring his paper. At this point, he put on my desk a copy of what he said was a changed version of his paper, which he said I could read or not read. I responded that I would put it in his file but that it was not in any way either a substitute for our conference or an influence upon my feeling about his original act.

Since that time, Mr. Hern has never come to see me nor has he responded in any way to my letters requesting that he see me and that he return the paper he had originally submitted. I should add that I have never submitted a grade for Mr. Hern for Personnel 357 but have retained his grade card in my possession.

8. *March 9, 1956.* The discipline committee met with Hern. The minutes of the meeting read:

The second case before the committee concerned Stanley Hern, a student in Professor Leeds' Personnel 357 class. Professor Leeds appeared before the committee and reported that Hern was involved in plagiarism in connection with a class assignment. Professor Leeds reported that he had written two letters to the student asking him to return the material in question and discuss the situation. The student had not responded to the letters. Professor Leeds finally informed the student by letter that the matter had been turned over to the school discipline committee. Professor Leeds outlined the circumstances for the committee as set forth in his written statement (attached). (See Leeds' memorandum of March 8.)

Following Professor Leeds' statement, the committee

called in Mr. Hern. He appeared in an Air Force Lieutenant's uniform. When Professor Worthington apologized for the few minutes' wait, Hern answered that he had until 4 p.m., when he was to report at Fort Eustis. Professor Worthington asked him about his military status and, in the following exchange, Mr. Hern replied in turn that he was (*a*) on active duty, (*b*) on active reserve duty, (*c*) on ready reserve subject to recall on two weeks' notice but not actually on active duty at present. The purpose of Professor Worthington's question was to put the student at ease, but in the course of questioning it appeared the student had no reason to be wearing the uniform. Mr. Hern was then asked to tell the committee about the problem before the committee. Mr. Hern asked to know what the charges were. Professor Connolly replied that the committee was not a trial board and was preferring no charges. It was aware that a problem had arisen between Mr. Hern and one of the school's faculty members and the committee's wish was to help solve this problem. Before attempting to go any further, the committee asked the student to give his version of the circumstances leading to the presentation of this problem to the committee. Mr. Hern replied that he had nothing to say and asked again for a statement of charges. When asked how he would account for the difficulty between him and the instructor he replied, "Personality conflict." In response to a request that he tell the committee what might have led to the personality conflict, he drew a memo from his briefcase in which Professor Leeds had commended him for his work on another assignment. Mr. Hern refused to elaborate on the matter of personality conflict.

There followed efforts by each member of the committee to persuade Mr. Hern to tell his story of what had occurred between Professor Leeds and himself. Mr. Hern's reply to each plea was that he had nothing to say. The committee recessed for a few moments, asking Mr. Hern to wait in the outer office.

It was decided to warn Mr. Hern that unless he would cooperate with the committee by furnishing information in connection with this problem he could expect that a severe penalty would be assessed. The purpose of this warning was not to penalize but to try to induce him to cooperate with the committee. He still refused to communicate his version of the situation to the committee. He was then dismissed with the statement that he would hear from the committee within a few days.

Professor Clark moved and Professor Connolly seconded a motion that the committee recommend to the dean that Mr. Hern be suspended from the school for one year, effective June 15, 1956.

9. *March 16, 1956.* Dean Potts wrote Hern:

> You are hereby suspended from school for one year, effective June 15, 1956. Reinstatement at the end of this period will be approved only if you are then able to persuade the discipline committee that your attitude is so improved as to justify their permitting you to proceed further toward a professional degree in business.
>
> If the term were not already well under way, I would suspend you as of today, causing you to lose credit for this semester's work.
>
> If you wish to appeal to the president, you must ask him for a review within twenty days.

10. *April 17, 1956.* An *ad hoc* committee appointed by the president met to consider Hern's appeal. The minutes of this meeting follow:

Committee members: Berry, Chairman, Jewett, Thornlee

The Chairman made an opening statement reviewing events leading up to the present meeting:

1. That Hern had been suspended for one year by the dean of the School of Commerce and Finance upon recommendation of the discipline committee of that school.
2. That Hern apparently felt this was an injustice and had appealed to the president.
3. That the president had requested this committee to review the case and report its findings to him.
4. That the committee was open-minded about the case, had every desire to be fair and had arranged this meeting with the student before arranging any meeting with Professor Leeds or with the discipline committee.

The Chairman then requested Hern to give his view of what had happened, step by step, leading up to the suspension.

Hern demonstrated considerable interest in the composition of the *ad hoc* committee, leaving the impression that he believed the matter was actually being referred back to the School of Commerce and Finance since two members of the committee were from its faculty.

Hern stated he felt two problems were involved, one being his relationship with Professor Leeds and the other his relationship with the discipline committee.

Problem 1. Hern indicated that there were several possible sources of friction between himself and Leeds and that the lack of specific charges made it impossible for him to know what or which activity was being questioned. He seemed more desirous of discussing other incidents than the term paper incident. The committee asked him specifically about the incident of the paper turned in to Professor Leeds. Hern stated that he had used the Grayson material as a guide to aid him in writing up a similar case which had occurred in his wife's place of employment. When questioned why he had bothered to change the names of the people if he planned merely to use this material as a guide, he said because he liked the new names better (paper one). He then wrote up his own paper (paper two) using paper one as a guide. He stated that he inadvertently turned paper one in to Professor Leeds instead of paper two.

When Professor Leeds returned paper one to him with a copy of the Grayson material, Hern submitted paper two. When questioned as to the present location of paper one, he said he had destroyed it. When questioned why he had destroyed it, he said he destroyed all his papers. He stated that there was no plagiarism involved at all. He stated he felt paper two satisfied Professor Leeds' requirement. He received Professor Leeds' letters of March 16 and March 23 after the end of the semester and made no reply, feeling that he was no longer a student of Professor Leeds and that his problem with Leeds had been solved when he turned in paper two.

The committee expressed to Hern its feeling that he used very poor judgment in making no response to Professor Leeds' letters and that, since he had received no grade for the course, he was still very much a student of Leeds, had to satisfy Leeds' requirements for the course, and was injudicious in not complying with Leeds' request for him to come in.

Problem 2. Speaking of his relationship with the discipline committee, Hern said that the discipline committee did not state the reason why he was called before it and that he did not know why he was there; that the discipline committee did not mention the question of the term paper but asked merely if he had anything to say about Professor Leeds. He said he had taken the term paper with him to the discipline committee meeting and was prepared to discuss it and would have done so, if a question concerning it had been asked.

The *ad hoc* committee expressed its feeling that Hern was extremely technical and legalistic in his relation with the discipline committee, that he undoubtedly knew why he was there, and that, if he had opened up to the discipline committee, the present penalty against him might not have been imposed.

The committee asked Hern if he would be willing to discuss this matter now with the discipline committee if given an opportunity. He made no definite answer to this question but left the impression that he would be willing to talk about any specific matters brought up to him.

Hern expressed concern over the penciled notation on his record to the effect that he would not be allowed to reregister and that a transcript of his record could not be issued. He stated if this meant he could not transfer to another school and finish his last year of college, the penalty was more severe than that imposed by the dean.

The committee felt Hern was not completely frank and cooperative but was somewhat reluctant to discuss the obvious problem freely. He was probably more cooperative with this committee than he had been with the discipline committee but only because the specific issue was presented to him directly.

11. *April 24, 1956.* The *ad hoc* committee held a second meeting. The chairman's notes on this read:

The *ad hoc* committee met April 24, 1956, to discuss the Hern case. One question which arose during the discussion was, "Had the discipline committee at any time specifically stated to Hern that they wished to discuss the term paper incident with him?" (The minutes of the meeting of the discipline committee with Hern had not mentioned this specific incident.) It appeared advisable to ask the discipline committee this question before proceeding further.

The chairman of the *ad hoc* committee then telephoned Professors Worthington, Connolly, and Clark and asked them if they would possibly be able to meet with the *ad hoc* committee, then in session. They were all willing to come, as was Mrs. Culver, ex-officio member and secretary of the committee.

It was established in the ensuing discussion that the discipline committee had made no specific mention of the term paper incident in their meeting with Hern.

The approach of the discipline committee, which has been successful in all other cases, is simply to state to the student that "certain irregularities appeared in such and such a course; the committee would like to understand what occurred and would like the student to recite his version." The committee has wished to be an aid to the student in getting any irregularities straightened out. It has not looked upon itself as a trial board supposed to prefer formal charges against the student, dig out fact, weigh evidence from student and faculty, and hand down a decision.

The *ad hoc* committee expressed the view that Hern had some basis for complaint, if he wished to be technical and legalistic, since the discipline committee had not specifically brought to his attention the term paper incident that started the chain of events leading to his appearance before the committee. Most members of the discipline committee agreed they would be willing to invite Hern to appear before it again and to make specific mention of the term paper incident, hoping that Hern then would open up as he had with the *ad hoc* committee.

One member of the discipline committee felt this would be making a trial board out of the discipline committee and would encourage students like Hern to feel they could force a faculty committee trying to be informal and friendly to fit a student's preconceived notions of what such a committee should be. This member of the committee was willing to give Hern another opportunity to meet with the committee but preferred to conduct such a meeting along the lines of the previous one, without making specific mention of the term paper incident. This member, however, did say he would yield on this point if there were a chance of Hern's bringing unfavorable publicity upon the college.

There was some discussion then of the title "discipline committee" and whether this should not be changed to something which does not sound punitive. There was also some discussion regarding the function of the committee and whether it should be a fact-finding board, prefer charges, etc.

Most members of the discipline committee felt that they would like to continue asking any student to tell his side of the story, and if this did not elicit any information, to then specifically mention the incident which had brought the student before the committee.

12. *May 10, 1956.* The *ad hoc* committee reported its findings to the president. These were:

1. The discipline committee of the School of Commerce and Finance has always tried to be informal and friendly; it does not believe it should operate as a trial board and prefer charges. It has always heretofore been successful in getting a student's cooperation simply by asking him to state his version of the difficulty he was in. Following this customary procedure in the Hern case, the discipline committee made no specific mention to Hern of the term paper incident which

precipitated the chain of events leading to his appearance before the committee.

2. Hern has viewed the situation as a legalistic one in which definite charges should be placed against a student, or at least the specific incident or incidents which bring the student before the committee should be stated by the committee. The fact that this was not done is, in our opinion, the crux of this case, because it is viewed by Hern as a loophole in his hearing.

3. There is a great deal of evidence that Hern's attitude has been poor and his judgment questionable. This committee certainly does not condone his behavior in many respects. Yet he has been suspended for a year for noncooperation with the discipline committee. We feel this penalty is so serious that the discipline committee should have another meeting with Hern, bring up specific matters it wishes to discuss, and try again to get him to state his version.

4. We believe Hern, if given another opportunity to meet with the discipline committee and if asked directly about the term paper incident, will tell the committee his version.

5. The discipline committee has expressed a willingness to give Hern another hearing and direct specific questions to him about the term paper incident.

6. Dean Potts had no intention of preventing Hern from attending another university by withholding a transcript. The dean has written the registrar a letter requesting that the penciled notation to that effect on Hern's record be deleted. A copy of this letter has been sent to Hern. (This finding is in connection with the next to the last paragraph in the minutes of the *ad hoc* committee meeting of April 17, 1956.)

13. *May 21, 1956.* Professor Worthington informed Hern that as a result of his appeal, the discipline committee had agreed to grant him another hearing. He asked Hern to present himself, for this purpose, at 2:30 p.m., May 28.

14. *June 7, 1956.* The president sent Hern a brief note:

> Professor Worthington informs me that you did not take advantage of the offer of his committee to grant you a rehearing. I therefore have no recourse other than to confirm the terms of your suspension as outlined in Dean Potts's letter of March 16.

15. *June 7, 1956.* The president instructed the dean of students to study existing regulations on student discipline with possible revision in mind, "in the light of the Hern case." Excerpts from

the new sections on student conduct and discipline, drafted by the dean of students under the presidential directive and adopted officially by the faculty of Pennel City College in June, 1957, follow:

SECTION I. STUDENT CONDUCT

Standards. Attendance at the college presupposes that students will observe the laws and deport themselves according to accepted standards of personal and group conduct. It presupposes further that they will abide by such rules, regulations, and procedures as are or may be established by the college for all students or by the various schools and departments for their own students. Failure to observe such laws, standards, rules, regulations, or procedures shall render students subject to penalties, which may include dismissal from the college.

SECTION II. DISCIPLINE

Schools. (*a*) The dean and faculty of each school are responsible for the administration of discipline for infractions of rules and regulations of the school or for unacceptable conduct by students in matters relating to their academic or professional progress. (*b*) The instructor is responsible for the maintenance of order and proper conduct in the classroom, and he is authorized to take such steps as are necessary to preserve order and to maintain the effective cooperation of the class in fulfilling the objectives of the course.

III. INTERPRETATIONS, PROCEDURES, AND RECORDS

A. *Interpretations.* The procedures set forth below shall be interpreted and administered in such a way as to assure the student charged with a breach of conduct of a fair hearing. Formalities are not required in initial disciplinary proceedings, but, in the case of reviews and rehearings, more formal procedures are desirable. Conduct disciplinary proceedings are not to be construed as adversary proceedings or judicial trials.

B. *Procedures and Records in Initial Disciplinary Proceedings.* The officer, committee, faculty members, or student organization responsible for maintaining discipline (hereinafter called "disciplinary authority") shall be guided by the following principles:

1. The student involved shall be informed by the disciplinary authority, orally or in writing, of the charge against him at the earliest reasonable time;
2. The student shall be given an opportunity to be heard by the

disciplinary authority and to present evidence, testimonial or documentary, in his own behalf;

3. Every effort shall be made by the disciplinary authority to bring the matter to a speedy conclusion;

4. (*a*) In all instances of disciplinary action by a faculty member, the report shall be filed with the executive officer of the department in which the course is offered. The executive officer shall notify his dean. The dean shall notify the dean of any other school in which the student may be enrolled. Either dean may initiate such additional disciplinary action as the circumstances warrant. (*b*) In all instances of disciplinary action by officers, faculty committees, or student organizations, the report shall be filed with the dean to whom they are responsible, or, if a presidential committee, with the president;

5. The officer with whom the report is filed, within five days thereafter, shall notify the student in writing, and, if possible, orally, of the action taken and of his right to request a review. The written notification shall point out that the request for review must be in writing and must be filed with the officer sending the notice not more than twenty days from the day upon which the oral notice was given or the written notice would be received in the normal course of events.

C. *Review.* (1) In all cases where disciplinary action is taken, the student involved shall be advised that he has the right to request one review of the case, such review to be accorded by the next immediate superior of the officer or agency taking the action, except as hereinafter provided (see paragraph C2 below). Such requests for review must be made in writing within the twenty-day period provided above. Action taken by faculty members or school disciplinary committees shall be subject to review by the dean of the school in which the case arose. Actions of the Dean of Men and/or the Dean of Women shall be subject to review by the Dean of Students. Actions taken by the dean of a school or the Dean of Students shall be subject to review by the president. (2) In cases involving expulsion or suspension, the record of the case shall be forwarded to the president for review before the decision is announced. In these cases, the president, after reviewing the record, should indicate (*a*) his approval of the action, or (*b*) his suggestions as to additional steps which should be taken on the matter. No further review will be provided in such cases.

SECTION IV. DELEGATION

Authority to Delegate. Responsibility for taking disciplinary action may in certain cases be delegated by the Dean of Students or by the dean of a school to a committee of the college faculty, to a committee of the faculty of the school concerned, to student organizations, or to a student-faculty committee, subject to such terms and conditions, not in conflict with this part, as may be necessary to assure a sound disciplinary program.

[Sections I, II(*b*), and IV above had been in effect since 1954. Section III, however, was new except for B4(*a*), which was also carried over from the 1954 action. Section III C replaced section III of the 1954 rules, which had said only:]

Review. Disciplinary decisions of the Dean of Students, or of the school, or of the instructor are final, subject to such review as the president may establish, except that any disciplinary action resulting in the permanent dismissal of a student from the college must have the approval of the president.

16. *July 16, 1956.* Hern wrote Dean Potts to inquire whether the registrar would honor requests from other universities for copies of his transcript.
17. *July 23, 1956.* Dean Potts replied that he had already instructed the registrar, as of June 25, to delete its "hold" notation on Hern's transcript and that it was now available to other universities. Dean Potts wrote: "Without such release, it would have been difficult or impossible for you to obtain admission to another university. This was not our intention."
18. *October 15, 1956.* Professor Leeds sent a memorandum to the registrar:

Mr. Stanley Hern has been the central party in a discipline case which grew out of his behavior in Personnel 357. This case involved protracted problems. It is now closed, and I am free to submit the enclosed grade card (E), withheld until now with the knowledge of your office.

19. *August 23, 1957.* The registrar's office wrote a routine letter to Hern suggesting that he make an attempt to clear his record of the still-in-force suspension before his transcript was requested by any other university to which he might wish to apply for admission.

20. *September 16, 1957.* The admissions committee of Darberry State University wrote to the registrar of Pennel City College:

> We have received a transcript from your office for Stanley Hern, who last attended Pennel City College in the spring semester, 1956. On this transcript there is a notation: "3/16/56, suspended from the School of Commerce and Finance for one year, effective 6/15/56. Reinstatement not automatic. Must be allowed by school's discipline committee."
>
> We would appreciate it if you would let us know the reason for this student's suspension and if he would be accepted again by your school.

This letter was referred to Dean Potts for disposition.

21. *September 20, 1957.* Dean Potts replied:

> This is in answer to your request to the registrar concerning Mr. Stanley Hern.
>
> Mr. Hern became subject to disciplinary action when one of his professors reported that he had turned in a term paper that was supposed to be original but was instead a direct copy from a standard text with the names of individuals changed. It is entirely probable that Mr. Hern would not have been suspended had he pleaded a misunderstanding as to the assignment or admitted that he had committed an improper action. Mr. Hern, however, preferred to take a legalistic attitude, refused to answer questions from the committee members, and regarded our whole investigation as a trial procedure subject to the laws of evidence, which it definitely was not.
>
> Mr. Hern was suspended more for his attitude than for his indiscretion as regards the term paper.

22. *January 8, 1958.* Hern wrote Dean Potts that he wished to appeal his "E" grade in Personnel 357.

23. *January 13, 1958.* Dean Potts wrote Hern that the grade in Personnel 357 was not subject to change and that he had no right to appeal.

24. *January 28, 1958.* Hern wrote Dean Potts again, asking why his "E" grade could not be appealed. Dean Potts made a notation on Hern's letter:

> Not to be answered. Useless to keep this matter going, in view of Hern's attitude.

25. *February 18, 1958.* Hern wrote Dean Potts a third letter along the lines of the previous two and asked for a citation of "the regula-

tion which prohibits appeal." He also requested an itemized listing of all his week-to-week grades in Personnel 357.

26. *July 8, 1958.* Hern wrote Dean Potts asking the latter to arrange
for him to appear before the discipline committee during the
week of July 21.

27. *July 10, 1958.* Dean Potts sent a memorandum to Professors
Lowery, Berry, Connolly, and Clark, and Mrs. Culver. This read:

> Mr. Stanley Hern, who was suspended for one year in 1956
> for plagiarism in Professor Leeds' class, has asked for a hearing
> before the discipline committee for the purpose of lifting his
> suspension. Are you free to meet with him on Monday, July 21,
> at 3:30 p.m.? If not, when during that week? When I have all
> your replies, I will write Mr. Hern as to the exact time.
>
> Professor Lowery is the only present member of the disci-
> pline committee on campus this summer, and I am therefore
> asking him to be chairman. Professors Berry, Connolly, and
> Clark, and Mrs. Culver were all involved in the Hern case at the
> time of suspension. The five of you would seem to be, with Mrs.
> Culver acting as secretary ex officio, a reasonable interim com-
> mittee to hear the case.

28. *July 21, 1958.* The minutes of the *ad hoc* discipline committee to
hear the Hern appeal, prepared by Mrs. Culver, were approved as
follows:

> Present: Professor Lowery, Chairman, Professors Berry,
> Connolly, Clark, and Mrs. Culver, secretary ex officio.
>
> The committee asked Mr. Hern to state his reasons for
> asking for a meeting at this time. It was pointed out that this
> could have been done a year earlier, and the committee was
> interested in what he had been doing since his suspension as
> well as his present purpose in asking for the lifting of the
> suspension.
>
> Mr. Hern replied that his letter of suspension had given him
> the right to a meeting with the committee at any time after one
> year and that he was exercising that right at this time. He said it
> was up to the committee to decide whether he would be allowed
> to finish his education since he is prevented from being admitted
> to other schools because of his suspension from this college.
>
> The committee asked him why he thought the suspension
> should be lifted, to which Mr. Hern replied that he had done no
> harm to the school, but the school had definitely damaged him
> by suspending him. He repeated that it was up to the committee
> to take action to clear his record and permit him to complete his

education. When asked where he planned to continue his education if the suspension were lifted, he replied he could not say at this time.

Mr. Hern replied to questions about his activities the past two years that he felt they had no bearing on the case. Through further questioning, the committee learned that Hern had taken some night school courses at Darberry State University but had been denied admission as a degree candidate because of his suspension. He said he had been told he could appeal to their admissions board, but he had not done so because he felt it was up to this school to clear his record.

The committee then excused Mr. Hern in order to discuss possible action with regard to this situation. It was generally agreed that Hern's attitude had not changed appreciably, but the committee was also in agreement that continuance of the suspension could accomplish nothing of benefit either to him or the school.

The committee's decision was to recommend to the dean that the suspension of Stanley Hern be lifted at this time.

29. *July 23, 1958.* Dean Potts wrote to Hern:

On the recommendation of the discipline committee which heard your appeal on July 21, I am lifting your suspension, effective immediately. You are therefore free to register for the fall or any subsequent semester, at your option.

30. *July 25, 1958.* At Dean Potts's request, Mrs. Culver wrote up from her notes an informal digest of the sequence of events at the July 21 hearing. This read:

The committee had asked Hern to wait in the foyer for a few minutes while they discussed the procedure to be followed. (This was where I came in, a little late because of a 3:30 appointment.) I gathered from the discussion that Professor Connolly had greeted Hern cordially as he entered the outer office and that his efforts to be pleasant had been repulsed by Hern.

The committee agreed upon a plan of action and called Hern in. After asking him if he knew all the members present, Professor Lowery asked him to tell the committee why he had decided to ask that his suspension be lifted now, almost a year after it could have been removed from his record. He replied, "You people have taken the authority upon yourselves to decide the future of my education." He said that he had a letter (here he consulted a sheet of paper he had brought with him which looked to me like a list of names and dates) from the Dean dated April 17, 1956, stating that he could call a meeting of the committee at any time after one year. "So now I am calling it," he said, "and it's up to you to decide." He added he had been told that the college would not deny him a release to enter another school, but that it had, and he felt he had been deceived since he had been refused admission to another school because of his suspension.

When asked for more details, he repeated that such information had nothing to do with the question before the committee. "I feel that I did the college no damage," he said, "but the college has caused me damage. I believe this could be proved in court."

Here Professor Connolly interposed a remark that he was reasonably certain no legal recourse would be possible in these circumstances. Hern replied that it might take a long time, but he had been told that compensation for damages was possible in his situation. (I felt there was implied a threat to sue if the committee did not lift the suspension.) I asked him if his purpose in calling the meeting was to build a case, but he did not answer the question.

Hern continued to refuse to give information on his activities since his suspension or to state his reasons for feeling the suspension should be lifted at this time. "It is up to you to decide," he repeated.

Intermittently, during the early part of the meeting, Professor Lowery attempted to explain at length and to no avail the committee's desire to reach a reasonable decision on the basis of information concerning Hern's activities since his suspension and his plans for the future. Little information was obtained as a result of these explanations and questions.

Eventually, Professor Connolly burst out with the statement, "Hern, I'm sorry for you. You're scared, and you are hurting yourself by your attitude that the college is a den of wolves out to get you. Why don't you try us and see if we are really so bad, after all. Come on, tell us about yourself, your experiences in the past two years, and your plans for the future. Give us a chance to show you that we can be fair and reasonable, that we are your friends."

To this, Hern replied, "Professor Connolly, I did not come here to get my knees dirty."

Whereupon Professor Connolly rose from his chair and said, "Hern, I will have no more to do with you since you apparently have no intention of cooperating in this discussion." Turning to Professor Lowery, he asked to be excused, and started for the door. But as he neared the door, he stopped and said, "Oh, hell, I'll stay," and returned to his seat. At this Hern laughed derisively, watching Professor Connolly as he resumed his place at the table.

Professor Berry then asked Hern if he remembered him from the appeal committee of two years ago. When Hern replied, "Yes," Professor Berry asked him if he was correct in his remembrance that Hern had said he would be willing to give information to the committee if he could have another hearing at that time. When Hern agreed this was correct, Professor Berry asked him why, then, he refused to answer the questions of this committee. Hern replied that what he had been doing or what he was going to do had no bearing on this committee's decision. "Besides," he said, "I can't 'prophesize' what I will be doing in the future."

In the following few minutes, the committee, by asking specific questions as to the school to which he had applied for admission and his understanding of the reason for its disapproval, was able to garner some facts about Hern's activities in this connection. Hern admitted he had been told he could appeal the denial of admission by appearing before the admissions board of the other school. He said he did not do so because he felt it was up to this college to release him.

Members of the committee then continued their pleading with Hern for cooperation and a change of attitude, to no avail.

(About this time, I scribbled a note to Professor Lowery asking if we could have a recess, because I felt this pleading was getting us nowhere.)

Professor Lowery then asked if the committee would agree to a recess for a few moments. Other members of the committee seemed rather taken aback but made no objection, so Professor Lowery asked Hern to step out into the outer office and wait.

I then told the committee I had asked for the recess because it seemed obvious to me that exhorting Hern to cooperate was getting us nowhere. I asked if they did not feel that we made better progress when we asked specific questions and pieced together the information.

The consensus was that we could not get much in any case, and perhaps we should decide what to do without further questions to Hern.

It was agreed that there seemed to be little change in Hern's attitude. Although the committee was aware of the dean's statement of the conditions under which the suspension would be lifted, i.e., that Hern's attitude change, all members seemed to feel that nothing could be gained by continuing the suspension.

The original offense in the class was not so serious that it should be punished further, they believed.

There was some concern as to whether the dean would agree to the recommendation, but the committee decided to recommend that the suspension be lifted.

The question of what to tell Hern was discussed, first with the idea of telling him that the committee deplored his continued resistant attitude but would reluctantly recommend lifting his suspension. Further discussion, however, led to the decision to tell him he would be informed by letter from the dean as to the result of this meeting.

Hern was then called back into the room and was asked if he had anything in particular he wanted the committee to know. He had nothing to add, so he was told he would be notified by letter of the decision.

Meeting then adjourned.

California Paper Company Case

The toughest immediate decision facing Wes Palmer, general manager of the hardboard division of the California Paper Company, when he returned from a three weeks' vacation was what to do about George Sherman, the general superintendent. Sherman, a few days after Wes left on vacation, had gotten the company into serious trouble with the state pollution commission. The manufacturing vice president had immediately reported this to Wes by long-distance telephone. He said: "I don't want to fire Sherman in your absence. You will have to decide what to do yourself when you get back. It's your problem. But if you keep him and he gets us into another jam, I'll fire you."

George Sherman had been associated with Wes Palmer and the

From *Organizational Behavior: Cases and Readings,* by Austin Grimshaw and John W. Hennessey. Copyright © 1960 by McGraw-Hill, Inc. Used with the permission of McGraw-Hill Book Company and John W. Hennessey.

California Paper Company for six years, in one capacity or another. He was currently about 50 years old, of less than medium height, thin and wiry. He was a mechanical engineer, with a bachelor's degree from the University of Illinois. During the four years preceding the entry of the United States into World War II, he had owned and managed a small plastics plant in the Midwest. When materials became hard to obtain because of wartime shortages and restrictions, he had sold this business, coming out pretty well financially on the sale. He then had headed for the Pacific Coast, where he spent the remaining war years as a shipyard superintendent. At war's end he had purchased a machine shop, obtained some profitable subcontracts, and done very well. When he sold this a couple of years later, he had accumulated a total capital in excess of $50,000. He had reinvested this in a lime quarry. This had failed, partly because it was unfavorably located from the standpoint of freight rates and partly because bad weather for two successive years had resulted in a poor agricultural market for fertilizers. The bank from which he had borrowed heavily had finally instituted foreclosure proceedings and he had ended up broke. For a short time thereafter he had worked as inspector on a power dam.

Wes Palmer first met George Sherman while he was employed at the dam. George read in a newspaper that the California Paper Company was building a highly mechanized hardboard mill and that Wes Palmer had been named to manage it. He went to see Wes and asked him for a job. Wes then was dividing his time about equally between his old job as head of California Paper Company's research laboratories and an interim post as company liaison man with the contractor building the new hardboard mill.[1] Wes told George that he might be able to fit him into the mechanical end of the mill operation when it started up but that for the time being, at least, nothing was available.

When the hardboard mill was about 50 percent finished, Wes hired George to check on the contractor's compliance with specifications and to calculate periodically, as a basis for payments to the contractor, the percent of contract currently completed. George also helped in the laboratory on problems involved in making hardboard from the waste wood, including bark, resulting from lumbering and sawmill operations. He proved to be a pretty good lab man and got along well personally with the small staff of technicians employed there.

When the mill was nearly ready for operation, Wes announced four major appointments to his staff:

---

1. Wes Palmer had a master's degree in chemistry, with a major in chemistry and a minor in chemical engineering. He had over a dozen years of research laboratory experience, during which he had worked on problems of synthetic rubber, turpentine, and hardboard development.

1. Jay Miller as general superintendent. Miller had many years of experience in Celotex and softboard manufacture but none in hardboard. The two processes were very different.
2. Paul Wilding as quality control manager.
3. George Sherman as plant engineer, in charge of plant maintenance. In this capacity George would have a foreman with a crew of 12 under him.
4. Lloyd Hayes as master mechanic, in charge of equipment maintenance.

During the first five years of operation, production of the hardboard mill increased tremendously, as know-how increased, manufacturing problems were solved one by one, and the selling organization developed new customers:

1st year	6 million square feet produced			
2nd "	12	"	"	"	"
3rd "	20	"	"	"	"
4th "	30	"	"	"	"
5th "	39	"	"	"	"

This more than sixfold increase was accomplished with the original equipment and with an expansion in work force from the original sixty to only eighty.

As with any new mill, there were many mechanical headaches, many process changes to make. Production secrets and know-how were carefully guarded by competing hardboard manufacturers and each newcomer to the field had to learn by trial and error. Wes Palmer and his staff had to feel their way along in spite of the fact that the mill and processes had been very well engineered in advance in California Paper Company's research laboratory, which had installed a small-scale pilot plant. The research and pilot plant production, unfortunately, had been done on one-quarter-inch board, whereas sales turned out to be 70 percent one-eighth-inch board.

At frequent intervals throughout the five years of operation, Wes wryly recalled, George Sherman had shown a positive talent for getting into trouble himself or causing trouble for others. As he looked back, Wes could remember at least one unpleasant incident each year in which George had been involved. He particularly remembered the following ones.

First Year: Jay Miller, the first general superintendent, proved to be very excitable. When anything went wrong he acted like a wild man. George made a point of recounting to Wes many of Jay's difficulties, slanted in a manner calculated to make Jay appear incompetent and slightly ridiculous. Wes realized that George was trying to undercut Jay and suspected that Jay knew this also.

Wes was acutely aware, from his own observations, that Jay was not working out as general superintendent. He had decided, however, to give Jay a six months' trial, in the hope that he would gradually get on top of the situation. The situation and Jay's morale deteriorated steadily, however, and at the end of six months Wes had to let him go. The hard facts, not George's snide remarks, led him to this decision.

When he heard about Jay's dismissal, Jack Ross, a shop committeeman, said to Wes: "You fired the wrong man. It should have been Sherman." Wes interpreted this remark at the time as an expression of loyalty toward Jay. When he finally made up his mind that Jay must go, Wes also decided to give George a shot at the general superintendent's job. Lloyd Hayes moved up to plant engineer, taking over responsibility for both plant maintenance and equipment maintenance. The position of master mechanic was abolished.

Within a few weeks, George started a campaign to undermine the shipping superintendent, one of his subordinates. Wes, tired of George's constant carping, removed the shipping superintendent from George's jurisdiction. Thereafter he reported directly to Wes, handling scheduling as well as shipping.

Second Year: During the first half of this year George did a good job of solving mechanical problems as they came along. On the human side he did not do nearly as well. He got into trouble several times with members of the work force and with the union. The situation, however, did not at any time get out of control.

Then came a six weeks' strike, called by the local and confined to the hardboard mill. Several customers cancelled their orders and sought new sources of supply during this period. As a result, when the mill started up again it operated on a four-day-a-week basis until markets were reestablished.

A month after the men came back, one of the workers made a serious mistake. George dressed him down on the spot, swearing at him several times. The worker started to take a punch at George, thought better of it in time, and took his grievance to the union instead.

This incident occurred on a Friday afternoon. On the following Monday morning the men gathered at the gate but didn't come into the mill. When Wes arrived, he asked what the trouble was. The men told him their side of the story, which varied somewhat from the sweetened-up version George had fed Wes over the weekend. Wes listened a few minutes, then said: "You've got a contract which says you work, pending settlement of grievances through the regular grievance procedure. You're violating it." He then called the union business agent, who persuaded the men to go back to work.

On Monday afternoon Wes and George met with the business

agent and the grievance committee. The union position was that, because of his actions on Friday, the crews would refuse in the future to take orders directly from George. They would have to be transmitted instead through the foremen. The crews would, however, continue as in the past to take orders direct from Wes. Wes said: "O.K. George will give his orders via the foreman. And so will I."

George blamed Jack Ross, the shop committeeman who had told Wes nearly two years earlier that he had fired the wrong man, for stirring up this trouble. He said: "I'll get that _____." Wes replied: "Leave him alone or he'll get you instead."

George was pretty subdued for a month or so. Then he gradually began chatting with the men again. He got along particularly well with the skilled mechanics, except for an occasional man he didn't like and managed to get rid of.

Third Year: For seven weeks, early in this year, the mill was shut down by an industry-wide strike. While the strike was on, George was upset because he had no work to do. He had no outside interests and therefore had developed a bad habit of working nine or ten hours a day. Idleness bored him.

During the startup period following the strike, George complained to Wes on several occasions about Paul Wilding, the quality-control manager. Finally the two men got into a big wrangle, which Wes had to settle himself. George said that Paul was too critical about quality and was interrupting production too often, without cause. Wes backed Paul, then said: "You two get along, or else; if you don't, one of you is going." Thereafter the two men ignored each other completely.

Later in the third year, headquarters executives of the California Paper Company instructed Wes to begin direct distribution of hardboard to industrial customers, on a nationwide basis. Prior to this change, the industrial market had been served through a single distributor. During the transition period Wes had to spend more time than usual on sales, less on production. He was at first away from the mill for three weeks at a time, every four months, traveling with his newly appointed sales manager. During his absences, George was in charge at the mill.

On one occasion, while Wes was away on a trip, George refused to alter the mill schedule to accommodate a wholesale customer. He had been asked to do so by Wallace Goodyear, the mill's sales liaison man with the distributor, who had continued on as the mill's exclusive outlet to the wholesale and retail trade. Wes, reviewing this dispute on his return, came to the following conclusions:

1. George was correct in deciding not to alter the schedule.
2. Wallace had been a little arrogant in demanding that the schedule be changed.

3. George, knowing he was in the right, had in refusing Wallace's demand gone out of his way to antagonize him, deliberately needled him.

George and Wallace did not engage in any further infighting. Instead they maintained a quiet truce and kept away from each other thereafter as much as possible.

Fourth Year: Upon his return from a sales trip, Wes found waiting on his desk a formal grievance from the union. This stated that George Sherman had, in violation of the seniority clause on promotion in the contract, ignored a man with a long and satisfactory service record and filled a vacancy at higher hourly pay by assigning it instead to a man with substantially less. seniority. The union demanded enforcement of the seniority provision in favor of the man passed over.

Wes did a little checking of the facts on his own, then called George and the union representatives in. He said to George: "Why didn't you make this promotion in accordance with the contract?"

George first claimed that the man with most seniority had not applied for the job. When the union representatives produced evidence that this was definitely not true, George shifted his ground, stating that the complainant did not have the necessary skills to hold down the job. During the ensuing conversation it became clear that George had passed the man by because he did not like him personally.

Wes reversed George's decision and awarded the complainant the disputed job on a trial basis.[2] Then, when the union representatives had left his office, he gave George a real going over. He told George that the manufacturing vice president had gotten wind of the incident through the union while he was away and had recommended to Wes that he fire George out of hand. This was by no means the first time, Wes told George, that the manufacturing vice president had discussed George with him in uncomplimentary terms.

Soon after this episode, Wes was informed from several sources that George was backbiting him. He called George in, quoted several of his more sarcastic remarks, and said to him: "Let's have no more of this behind-my-back stuff. When you've got something to criticize me about, tell me to my face."

Toward the end of this year, George got the company into really serious trouble with the state pollution commission, which had been uneasy for some time about pulp discharge from the hardboard mill. Their commission's engineers frequently set up test screens in the rivers below the mill to determine whether the pulp content was so high as to endanger fish life therein. The commission had served

---

2. The man worked out fine, easily qualifying for the job on a permanent basis.

notice on the company during the third year of mill operation that they would require it to put in a pulp impounding pond if the existing pollution level was exceeded in the future by any substantial amount.

One day while George was walking through the mill, he suddenly decided that he wanted a chest containing waste pulp cleaned. He immediately told a workman to dump the whole chest of waste pulp directly into the river, without putting it through the effluent screen as usual. This was in definite violation of explicit instructions which Wes had given him and which he in turn had passed on to his foremen and their crews.

The concentrated discharge of pulp from the emptied chest rammed into a test screen which the state fisheries department had recently set up to keep fish out of a series of irrigation ditches fed by the river. The screen broke, the fisheries department protested by telephone to the pollution commission, and the latter's resident engineer in turn invited Wes and the manufacturing vice president to inspect the damage. They narrowly averted issuance of a shut-down order by promising, on their word of honor, that pulp would never be dumped directly into the river again. A few weeks later, nevertheless, the commission instructed the company to start work immediately on a pulp impounding pond. This cost $200,000. While it probably would have been necessary to build this facility a year or so later anyhow, as hardboard output continued to increase, the investment of $200,000 was financially embarrassing at the moment.

When Wes got back from his inspection of the fish screen he was boiling mad. He said to George: "Why in __ did you do it?"

George first denied having anything to do with the dumping. It was news to him, he said. He had just heard about it himself. Wes then confronted him with the man who had actually performed the dumping operation, at George's specific order. George then said: "O.K. I told him to."

Wes was so angry that he didn't trust himself to speak. Instead he walked away, just to cool off.

Fifth Year: While Wes was on vacation, as described in the first paragraph of this case, a waste pulp chest was dumped directly into the river again, instead of being discharged through the screen into the new impounding pond. George was not directly responsible on this occasion, in the sense that he had specifically ordered this done. As general superintendent he could be held responsible, however, for not making certain that direct dumping never happened again.

The fish screen was smashed for the second time. The pollution commission's resident engineer immediately called on the manufacturing vice president and told him that his solemn promise had been broken. The vice president called in George, who said: "I just heard about the dumping myself a few minutes ago." The state engineer, the vice president, and George then went down to the fish screen to look at the damage.

When they returned to the mill, George told the vice president that he would get the facts from the shift foreman and report back immediately. In a few minutes he reported back, saying that the shift foreman had gone off duty and no one seemed to know anything about the incident.

The manufacturing vice president then conducted his own investigation. He found the employee who had dumped the chest. This man told him that he had washed out the chest's contents through the screen into the impounding pond. When he thought the chest was empty, he had pulled the plug. It was not completely empty, however, and the residue had gone directly into the river.

In response to further questioning by the vice president, the employee said that George had told him: "You needn't bother to keep the gate from the chests to the river locked when you're emptying chests into the impounding pond." The gate had been unlocked for the past several weeks.

The vice president confronted George with the facts he had just unearthed. George admitted telling the employee that he didn't have to make sure the gate was locked before beginning the chest-dumping operation. The vice president, as related in the first paragraph of the case, didn't want to fire George while Wes was away. Instead, he left this decision to Wes on his return.

Case of The Changing Cage

I

The voucher-check filing unit was a work unit in the home office of the Atlantic Insurance Company. The assigned task of the unit was to file checks and vouchers written by the company as they were cashed and returned. This filing was the necessary foundation for the main function of the unit: locating any particular check for examination

This case was taken from "Topography and Culture: The Case of the Changing Cage" (*Human Organization*, Vol. 16, No. 1) by C. B. Richards and H. F. Dobyns, with the permission of the authors and publishers, The Society of Applied Authropology.

upon demand. There were usually eight to ten requests for specific checks from as many different departments during the day. One of the most frequent reasons checks were requested from the unit was to determine whether checks in payment of claims against the company had been cashed. Thus efficiency in the unit directly affected customer satisfaction with the company. Complaints or inquiries about payments could not be answered with the accuracy and speed conducive to client satisfaction unless the unit could supply the necessary document immediately.

Toward the end of 1952, nine workers manned this unit. There was an assistant (a position equivalent to a foreman in a factory) named Miss Dunn, five other fulltime employees, and three parttime workers.

The work area of the unit was well defined. Walls bounded the unit on three sides. The one exterior wall was pierced by light-admitting north windows. The west interior partition was blank. A door opening into a corridor pierced the south interior partition. The east side of the work area was enclosed by a steel mesh reaching from wall to wall and floor to ceiling. This open metal barrier gave rise to the customary name of the unit—"the voucher cage." A sliding door through this mesh gave access from the unit's territory to the work area of the rest of the company's agency audit division, of which it was a part, located on the same floor.

The unit's territory was kept inviolate by locks on both doors, fastened at all times. No one not working within the cage was permitted inside unless his name appeared on a special list in the custody of Miss Dunn. The door through the steel mesh was used generally for departmental business. Messengers and runners from other departments usually came to the corridor door and pressed a buzzer for service.

The steel mesh front was reinforced by a rank of metal filing cases where checks were filed. Lined up just inside the barrier, they hid the unit's workers from the view of workers outside their territory, including the section head responsible for overall supervision of this unit according to the company's formal plan of operation.

II

On top of the cabinets which were backed against the steel mesh, one of the male employees in the unit neatly stacked pasteboard boxes in which checks were transported to the cage. They were later reused to hold older checks sent into storage. His intention was less getting these boxes out of the way than increasing the effective height of the sight barrier so the section head could not see into the cage "even when he stood up."

The girls stood at the door of the cage which led into the corridor and talked to the messenger boys. Out this door also the workers slipped unnoticed to bring in their customary afternoon snack. Inside the cage, the workers sometimes engaged in a good-natured game of rubber-band "sniping."

Workers in the cage possessed good capacity to work together consistently and workers outside the cage often expressed envy of those in it because of the "nice people" and friendly atmosphere there. The unit had no apparent difficulty keeping up with its work load.

III

For some time prior to 1952 the controller's department of the company had not been able to meet its own standards of efficient service to clients. Company officials felt the primary cause to be spatial. Various divisions of the controller's department were scattered over the entire 22-story company building. Communication between them required phone calls, messengers, or personal visits, all costing time. The spatial separation had not seemed very important when the company's business volume was smaller prior to World War II. But business had grown tremendously since then and spatial separation appeared increasingly inefficient.

Finally, in November of 1952, company officials began to consolidate the controller's department by relocating two divisions together on one floor. One was the agency audit division, which included the voucher-check filing unit. As soon as the decision to move was made, lower-level supervisors were called in to help with planning. Line workers were not consulted, but were kept informed by assistants of the planning progress. Company officials were concerned about the problem of transporting many tons of equipment and some 200 workers from two locations to another single location without disrupting work flow. So the move was planned to occur over a single weekend, by means of the most efficient resources available. Assistants were kept busy planning positions for files and desks in the new location.

Desks, files, chairs, and even wastebaskets were numbered prior to the move, and relocated according to a master chart checked on the spot by the assistant. Employees were briefed as to where the new location was, and which elevators they should take to reach it. The company successfully transported the paraphernalia of the voucher-check filing unit from one floor to another over one weekend. Workers in the cage quit Friday afternoon at the old stand, and reported back Monday at the new.

The exterior boundaries of the new cage were still three building walls and the steel mesh, but the new cage possessed only one door— the sliding door through the steel mesh into the work area of the rest of the agency-audit division. The territory of the cage had also been reduced in size. An entire bank of filing cabinets had to be left behind in the old location, to be taken over by the unit moving there. The new cage was arranged so that there was no longer a row of metal filing cabinets lined up inside the steel mesh and obstructing the view into the cage.

IV

When the workers in the cage inquired about the removal of the filing cabinets from along the steel-mesh fencing, they found that Mr. Burke had insisted that these cabinets be rearranged so his view into the cage would not be obstructed by them. Miss Dunn had tried to retain the cabinets in their prior position, but her efforts had been overridden.

Mr. Burke disapproved of conversation. Since he could see workers conversing in the new cage, he "requested" Miss Dunn to put a stop to all unnecessary talk. Attempts by female clerks to talk to messenger boys brought the wrath of her superior down on Miss Dunn, who was then forced to reprimand the girls.

Mr. Burke also disapproved of an untidy working area, and any boxes or papers which were in sight were a source of annoyance to him. He did not exert supervision directly, but would "request" Miss Dunn to "do something about those boxes." In the new cage, desks had to be completely cleared at the end of the day, in contrast to the work-in-progress piles left out in the old cage. Boxes could not accumulate on top of filing cases.

The custom of afternoon snacking also ran into trouble. Lacking a corridor door, the food bringers had to venture forth and pack their snack tray back through the work area of the rest of their section, bringing this hitherto unique custom to the attention of workers outside the cage. The latter promptly recognized the desirability of afternoon snacks and began agitation for the same privilege. This annoyed the section head, who forbade workers in the cage from continuing this custom.

V

Mr. Burke later made a rule which permitted one worker to leave the cage at a set time every afternoon to bring up food for the rest. This rigidity irked the cage personnel, accustomed to a snack when the mood struck, or none at all. Having made his concession to the cage force, Mr. Burke was unable to prevent workers outside the cage from doing the same thing. What had once been unique to the workers in the cage was now common practice in the section.

Although Miss Dunn never outwardly expressed anything but compliance to and approval of superiors' directives, she exhibited definite signs of anxiety. All cage workers reacted against Burke's increased domination. When he imposed his decisions upon the voucher-check filing unit, he became "Old Grandma" to its personnel. The cage workers sneered at him and ridiculed him behind his back. Workers who formerly had obeyed company policy as a matter of course began to find reasons for loafing and obstructing work in the new cage. One of the changes that took place in the behavior of the workers had to do with their game of rubber-band sniping. All knew Mr. Burke would disapprove of this game. It became highly clandestine and fraught with dangers. Yet shooting rubber bands *increased*.

Newly arrived checks were put out of sight as soon as possible, filed or not. Workers hid unfiled checks, generally stuffing them into desk drawers or unused file drawers. Since boxes were forbidden, there were fewer unused file drawers than there had been in the old cage. So the day's work was sometimes undone when several clerks hastily shoved vouchers and checks indiscriminately into the same file drawer at the end of the day.

Before a worker in the cage filed incoming checks, she measured with her ruler the thickness in inches of each bundle she filed. At the end of each day she totaled her input and reported it to Miss Dunn. All incoming checks were measured upon arrival. Thus Miss Dunn had a rough estimate of unit intake compared with file input. Theoretically, she was able to tell at any time how much unfiled material she had on hand and how well the unit was keeping up with its task. Despite this running check, when the annual inventory of unfiled checks on hand in the cage was taken at the beginning of the calendar year 1953, a seriously large backlog of unfiled checks was found. To the surprise and dismay of Miss Dunn, the inventory showed the unit to be far behind schedule, filing much more slowly than before the relocation of the cage.

Chapter Five

The Problem Statement

After diagnosis, the next step in sound decision making is selection and definition of the problem to be solved. This chapter will explain the significance of this step in the overall decision process, and further will present the criteria for defining the problem in a manner conducive to systematic solution. First, let us consider the significance of problem definition to the decision process.

The Significance of Problem Definition

Definition of the problem, like the diagnostic step, is generally glossed over when the human problems of organizational management are considered. Frequently, the definition of the problem is assumed to be obvious and is taken for granted. *Solving* the problem is assumed to present the real difficulty, and usually claims our best efforts. Psychologically, it is uncomfortable to focus attention on a problem. This discomfort is relieved when instead we consider solutions.

In the formal study of decision making, the learning process itself prolongs each step, so the discomfort of postponing solutions is aggravated. As a result, some analysts of the decision process *begin* with a consideration of alternative management solutions or courses of action. Case studies, for example, often end with the question "What would you do?," directing the reader first to a solution and only afterward to its justification. Quantitative approaches, such as deci-   235 sion theory, tend to emphasize the manipulation of the variables related to solutions rather than inquiry into the problem itself.

Any consideration of alternative solutions before the problem is well defined may sabotage the effectiveness of the entire decision process. Actual management experience indicates that inadequate definition of a problem is a far more common cause of failure in the decision process than an inadequate weighing of alternative solutions. This is true because the original formulation of a problem structures the kinds of solutions that appear for consideration in the first place. No proposed solution can be better than the formulation of the problem it is designed to solve. If a problem has been inadequately defined, the "solution" cannot be adequate. Therefore an important part of skillful management is skill in defining problems, which includes concomitant development of the emotional capacity to tolerate the impatience and discomfort involved in focusing on the problem long enough to define it adequately, before indulging in the relief of considering solutions.

The Criteria of Sound Problem Formulation

There are certain definite guidelines or criteria against which problem formulation should be assessed before an attempt is made to consider solutions. The following criteria, essential to sound problem formulation, are those which experience has shown to be most often neglected in the management decision process:
1. The problem should be stated explicitly.
2. The problem statement should include a working diagnosis.
3. The problem statement should specify the standard violated.
4. The problem should be stated in specific behavioral terms.
5. The problem statement should not be expressed merely as an implied solution.
6. The problem statement should specify whose problem it is.
7. The problem statement should differentiate the short run and the long run in a problem situation.
8. The problem should not be stated as a dilemma.

Criterion 1: Stating the Problem Explicitly

Unbelievable as it may seem, the application of decision making to human problems rarely includes an explicit statement of the problem to be solved. There is a tendency to assume that, because a disequilibrium has been felt and/or a problem situation has been diagnosed and understood, the specific problem is too obvious to require explicit statement. Nevertheless, all our thinking may not alter our preliminary view of a problem unless the various relationships have been spelled out. Vague, general complaints about communications problems or low morale, for example, are less easily solved than explicit statements of the particular actions that resulted in those conditions. The more explicitly the problem can be stated, the more explicit can be the consideration of solutions.

Training in the decision process should include training in the writing of explicit problem statements. An excellent decision-making habit, which is especially valuable in the face of complex human problems, is to thrash out a problem statement on paper before attempting to tackle the problem. This process forces the manager to clarify and sharpen his formulation of the problem in a way that "thinking through" alone does not. As a result, he is less apt to base his actions on shifting impressions and feelings about a vaguely defined "problem cloud." In a very real sense, a well-defined problem is already half solved.

Criterion 2: Including a Working Diagnosis in the Problem Statement

The formulation of a problem statement should include, as an integral part, the manager's final working diagnosis, which is an important key for considering alternative courses of action. As has been indicated, a working diagnosis is always subject to change on the basis of further information, but it nevertheless should be explicitly stated. An explicit working diagnosis helps the manager focus on causes rather than mere symptoms in choosing and defining the precise problem he wants to solve.

A problem statement should *not* be a mere description of a symptom or symptoms. In the Oscar Larson case at the end of Chapter 4, for example, it would not be helpful if the problem were merely defined as the workers' adverse reaction to Larson, because this reaction is really a symptom that something more fundamental is wrong in the relationship between management and the work force. As we have said, symptoms may constitute problems in themselves, but a problem statement that is confined to symptoms, and contains no diagnosis of causes, is inadequate. Most often the critical problem— the problem to be solved—will be related to underlying causes.

Criterion 3: Specifying the Standard Violated

Effective problem definition should specify the standard according to which a situation is considered to be a problem. The object of the diagnostic stage of the decision process is to understand what is happening in a particular situation. But understanding a situation is not the same as determining whether a problem exists that needs solution. Two factors must be present before we can identify a situation as a problem: (1) the situation must be relevant to an accepted standard or set of standards, and (2) the situation must involve behavior that violates such standards.

One of the most common failings in decision making is to omit conscious consideration of the standards by which one situation is judged as a problem and another as not a problem. This omission can be wasteful. Ambivalence or vagueness about standards on the part of the manager means ambivalence and vagueness about methods and goals in the later stages of decision making.

Further, the degree of importance assigned to various standards is often taken for granted rather than made explicit. However, when we consciously make explicit the standards by which we define problems, we sometimes become aware that a particular standard is more important or less important in the total picture than we had unconsciously assumed. Thus, a part of solving the problem may be actually altering the priority we give certain standards.

As the manager attempts to specify which standards are relevant to a given situation, what possible standards does he consider? What are the sources of the standards to be applied? Standards have their roots in different "levels" of the decision maker's frame of reference, ranging from rather specific individual habits or personality traits to high-level abstractions about the "rights of man." These levels are not mutually exclusive; several may be functioning as standards at the same time. A given situation may well violate different levels and therefore give rise to the identification of more than one problem to be solved. The following hierarchy of standards is offered as an aid to the manager in specifying which standards may be relevant to the assessment of a particular situation.

The Hierarchy of Standards Governing Problem Identification

Personality Factors. Our habits, tastes, preferences, style or way of life, and self-image together constitute a standard that we apply to the world around us. Conflicting personal standards present conflicts in problem definition.[1]

Group Norms. Our identification with the norms of a reference group—be it informal friendship group, formal club group, or assigned work group—and our perceptions of violations of these norms together constitute a second level of standards we apply to our environment. Conflicting norms among the reference groups of an individual may lead to inner conflicts about problem definition.[2]

Individual Values. Although some individual values change when an individual changes reference groups, others reflect deeper,

---

1. For a discussion of personality factors that can influence decision making, see Leavitt (1964), especially Chs. 1–7.
2. For a discussion of the effects of group norms on individual decision making, see Sherif and Sherif (1956).

longer lasting convictions that can withstand and supersede group norms. Many major individual values are set in childhood and resist rapid change. Such values originate in a reference group (the family, for example) and thus can determine which groups become new reference groups for the individual. Group norms which differ from deep-seated values may produce psychological conflict and hence difficulty in identifying problems. Conflicts also arise when values considered desirable differ from what is immediately desired in a particular situation.[3]

Rationalized Organizational Goals. Our role in an organization is associated with standards and goals that we perceive as applicable to situations that arise in that organization. In a business, for example, our views on such factors as profitability, reduced costs, general economic conditions, corporate goals, physical property, success, corporate image, the marketplace, responsibility to stockholders, and the assumptions of the economic model are standards against which we measure behavior.[4]

Rationalized National Goals. Judgments about the nation's position in the world are also standards of behavior. Views on world leadership, peace and war, poverty and wealth, and the proper international role of the nation are standards often applied in organizational situations.[5]

Concepts of Ultimate Human Values. Justice, equality, opportunity, freedom, the pursuit of happiness, and the nature and purpose of man are some of the broader concepts we incorporate in our standards of behavior. Abstract though they may be, they can be decisive standards when they are applied to specific situations.[6]

Conflicting Standards

It is easy to see that a particular event might cause some individuals to refer to one level of the hierarchy, and others to a different level. For example, a person who identifies work problems solely in terms of rationalizing organizational goals might perceive an increased number of grievances solely in terms of workers' unwillingness to do the jobs assigned them in the manner determined by

3. For a discussion of individual values and decision making, see Ofstad (1961), especially Ch. 7.

4. For a discussion of the rationalized goals of economics and decision making, see Elbing and Elbing (1967), especially Sec. 1.

5. For a discussion of the relationship between national goals and organizational decision making, see McClelland (1962).

6. For a discussion of ultimate values and decision making, see John Galbraith (1958 and 1964).

management. Another person might perceive the situation in broad terms of the "rights of man" and its effects on the personalities of the workers. *The decision maker must recognize that situations do not present themselves as prelabeled and predefined problems. A problem is in part defined by the standards each observer applies.*

Two types of problems can arise for a decision maker as a result of conflict of standards. On the one hand, he may find himself in a position where his own various standards conflict with each other. The sales manager of a medium-sized manufacturing company, for example, was charged with *de facto* racial discrimination by a higher executive because of the small number of black people in his division. His difficulty in resolving the situation was complicated by two factors: he had not developed the ability to handle his feelings of discomfort when black people applied for jobs, and furthermore, one of the norms of his peer group (other managers on the same level in the community) was to resist the pressures of black organizations. However, this manager did not see himself as a racist or as a person who discriminated against others, and he believed that the country's needs required everyone to help solve the racial problem. Moreover, on the highest level of abstraction, he believed that every individual has the right to equal job opportunities. But because this manager was able to verbalize his value conflicts, he was able to distinguish among them, place them in a hierarchy of personal importance, and make specific decisions as to which values took precedence in various situations.

Verbalizing and choosing among our own values may not seem to be a crucial managerial skill. However, unless we can verbalize internal value conflicts, we cannot separate their personal and their external aspects. Many problems therefore will remain enigmas to us, needlessly and perhaps unsolvably structured as dilemmas. Approaching problems as dilemmas because of unspecified internal conflicts always erodes a manager's skill in solving them.

The second type of conflict-of-standards problem which can arise for the decision maker is a conflict between his standards and those of others in his organization with whom he has direct contact. Let us suppose that the sales manager resolved his internal conflict about hiring blacks in terms of the national interest and the equal rights of men, but that his immediate superior resisted the idea. The sales manager (or any other subordinate) is then faced with the necessity of either "going along" with the boss or resisting him and endangering his own organizational position and economic security. The gravest temptation in such a value conflict is to take a "short cut," that is, to avoid confronting and articulating the problem and making a decision, and instead, merely to act in each situation upon the line of least resistance. This habit, however, is extremely corrosive of the managerial role and mitigates the development of a high level of managerial skill. The essence of improving managerial skill lies in perceiving disequilibria, diagnosing and defining problems (including value conflicts), specifying alternatives, and making decisions— rather than allowing events to develop by default.

Three managers, two in business and one in government, whose superiors held discriminatory policies, made three different decisions. One, after trying but failing to change his superior's policy and after consultation with his family, found another job. The second manager kept his job and became active in community programs outside the firm, hoping that a change in community norms would gradually alter his superior's policies. The third, who himself was a member of a racial minority and had been completely on his own since the age of fourteen, said in effect: "Let those people who feel discriminated against make it on their own the way I did." Although each solution is too complex for easy labeling as right or wrong, a notable factor in all three cases that was each manager actually made a value decision, rather than merely ignoring the issue.

It can be shown that, over time, as individuals live in a similar environment and become able to satisfy their needs, they tend to develop and to apply similar norms, values, and standards. Executives in the same office, mechanics in the same shop, or teachers in the same school tend to define a particular problem in the same way as a result of their close relationships over time. Under such circumstances a problem may appear to be absolute and clear-cut. In reality, it may not be that the problem is clear-cut but that the application of standards is consistent and unquestioned. Outsiders viewing the situation might define the problem quite differently.

The more explicit we can be about the hierarchy of standards being applied to a situation, the more explicit can be our definition of the problem, and therefore, the more appropriate our solutions. If conflicts over standards exist but go unrecognized, solutions may be blocked. In many hospitals, for example, where the problems associated with the shortage of nurses are frequently defined in organizational terms—work assignments, shifts, and supervisory relationships—the standards implicitly applied by the nurses often relate to the maintenance of their professional status. The result is that the hospitals' solutions often overlook the nurses' professional status and are therefore resisted by the nurses.

Criterion 4: Stating the Problem in Specific Behavioral Terms

It is important that the problem statement be couched in specific behavioral terms rather than vague, general terms. A common pitfall of problem identification, especially for students who are first learning about the behavioral sciences, is verbalizing a problem in broad generalizations about human behavior rather than in operational terms relevant to a specific situation. A problem merely labeled as a personality conflict, a lack of communication, a defense mechanism, a projection, a feeling of guilt, or in other general or categorical terms has not been identified adequately for solution. Although these statements can offer considerable insight into human behavior, as stated in general form they give few specific clues to the events or attitudes that have caused the problem, clues which the decision maker needs as guides to choice and action.

Another danger in using general labels as problem statements is that they suggest a fixed condition. For example, to say that a problem is a result of a personality conflict suggests that two personalities are in more or less constant conflict. Although it is conceivable that two individuals can be so generally antagonistic to one another that they are almost always in conflict, it is more often the case that two individuals tolerate one another generally but come into conflict under specific circumstances. It is much more fruitful for the decision maker to identify and understand these circumstances than to simply label the problem a conflict of personalities. The more specific and operational the problem statement, the more easily a solution can be devised that deals directly with the cause of the problem.

It is possible, of course, that a manager will encounter employees who have serious emotional problems and whose behavior might properly be defined as psychologically abnormal. These problems, however, are usually beyond the competence of the typical manager and should be fully diagnosed and dealt with by a psychologist or psychiatrist who has the appropriate skills. Our discussion is limited to the typical cases that confront the organizational administrator: job-related emotional problems that arise among individuals who normally function satisfactorily within the organization. In these cases, the manager will find it much more useful to state the problem in specific behavioral terms, rather than giving the problem some psychological label.

Not only should the problem be stated in specific behavioral terms, the standard by which something is judged to be a problem should also be stated in specific behavioral terms. Unless the standard is stated in this way, it is too vague to facilitate a clear definition of the problem. Furthermore, a standard for behavior constitutes part of the goal of the decision process. Unless the goal of the decision process is also stated in specific behavioral terms, it is too vague to provide a guideline for choice and action. Thus the manager should attempt to answer explicitly three closely related questions: What specific behavioral standards are being violated? What specific behavioral change is wanted? What behavior would constitute a solution to the problem? It can be seen that only when the implied goal for change is stated in specific behavioral terms is it useful in determining whether or not any contemplated course of action is relevant.

Criterion 5: Avoiding Statement of the Problem as Merely an Implied Solution

Because there is such a strong tendency to think in terms of solutions, problems are often framed in terms of solutions available or popular. A problem laid out in solution terms tends to block adequate analysis and adequate consideration of alternative choices. For example, when asked for a problem statement for the case of the employee who submitted an excessive number of grievances, a student offered: "The problem is how to arrange time for more social contact." Because this statement is a disguised solution, it tends to preclude consideration of such alternative solutions as rotating, transferring, promoting, or even discharging the employee. The built-in restriction of an implied solution allows a manager little flexibility. Although the tendency to be solution-oriented is a critical problem for businessmen, it is in no sense unique to them (a cartoon that appeared during an international crisis showed former President Charles de Gaulle of France sitting behind his desk and saying: "Find me some problems to fit my solutions").

Once committed to a particular course of action—whether it be the centralization of purchasing, the introduction of a new computer, the need to reduce the number of employees, the application of decision theory, or whatever—the decision maker may tend to define future problems in terms of preconceived and available solutions. Allowing solutions to shape problems can be costly. For example, during the early days of introducing electronic data processing to government, a large eastern state wished to fully utilize its new equipment and decided that the cost of preparing its payroll could be reduced by automating the process. However, because EDP was not appropriate to the particular payroll problems of that organization, automating the process more than tripled the cost. The problem had been defined in terms of the new "solution," and it was months before the problem was redefined.

A subtle variation of solution orientation arises from the tendency (discussed earlier) to learn experiences themselves rather than to learn *from* them. For example, an executive who progresses up the organizational hierarchy learns ways of solving problems that are related to his experiences in a particular organizational role. As he moves into organizational levels where new types of problems occur, he may define them in terms of the solutions he learned in the past. Focusing on formerly useful solutions, he may err in defining new problems.

Another difficulty in stating problems in terms of solutions is that it may lead to ignoring problems that have no obvious solutions. For example, problems arising from summer heat in the workplace, poor commuter train schedules, or the disruptive personality of a firm's owner-manager might be written off as unsolvable. Since these kinds of problems have no obvious solutions, they may never be explicitly identified as problems. They may then be ignored, even though they might be very real contributing factors which ought to be taken into account when solutions are considered.

Specifying a problem apart from a consideration of solutions can help us maintain awareness of the role of problem factors in the total picture, and help us more realistically and comprehensively evaluate situations in which they are involved. Furthermore, many an "unsolvable" problem, when clearly identified as a problem, has turned out to be solvable after all.

Criterion 6: Specifying Whose Problem It Is

It is extremely helpful in sorting out a particular problem situation to define *whose* problem it is—in several senses. First, the manager should answer the question, "*Who* is experiencing disequilibrium or discomfort?'" Part of a problem's solution may only be the reduction of personal discomfort.

Thus far our discussion of problem identification has rested on the assumption that there is such a thing as a single problem. But this of course is a fallacy: *there is no such thing as a problem by itself.* Furthermore, this assumption implies that a particular situation will be perceived by everyone in the same terms, or indeed even as a problem at all. Obviously, everyone will apply his own hierarchy of standards to identifying problems. (This is one reason why it is so difficult for groups to define problems quickly.) An individual who is aware of the history of a certain set of events may, for example, define a situation differently than one who does not have this historical awareness. Therefore it is vital that a problem statement specify how each of the key persons involved experiences a problem. The manager concerned that a subordinate did not respond to a situation the same way the manager responded might well ask himself whether the incident could be perceived as a problem by the subordinate.

It is important at this point to distinguish among (1) an organizational problem, (2) the discomfort of a manager, and (3) the discomfort of others involved in the situation. The discomfort of either the manager or other participants may be solved without the organizational problem necessarily being solved. Conversely, an organizational problem may be solved without resolving the human discomfort involved. By distinguishing who has what problem, we can differentiate between organizational problems and personal problems, and have a better basis for considering solutions.

Second, it is important to specify who has the responsibility for solving a problem. Wherever possible, the person who has responsibility in the organizational structure for dealing with a particular type of problem should be the one to solve it. If a problem is clearly the responsibility of a particular individual, it is vital not to let it be solved by a less appropriate person, or by inaction.

It is not only internal situations that cause problems for an organization. Rapid changes in technology, racial conflict, hard-core unemployment, activist political behavior, student unrest, labor demands, and community demands for "law and order" produce an environment, at least partly external to the organization, which may result in problems for which no one in the organization is assigned responsibility, and which past generations of managers did not even think of as problems. Failure to clearly identify responsibility within the organization for the identification of new problem areas impinging on the organization from the outside may result in the organization's failure to perceive a problem before it is too late for choice or action. A striking example occurred during the 1968/69 academic year, when many American universities found themselves facing problems with which they were totally unprepared to deal. The standards which governed problem definition by students (and other groups in society) changed quickly, without a coincident change of standards within university administrations, and without adequate recognition by the administrations of the forces building up to challenge them. In most cases no one had been thinking in terms of "new" problem areas external to the established framework of organizational operation, because no one had seen such problems as within his sphere of responsibility.

This kind of crisis points up the necessity for making explicit in any problem statement just whose responsibility it is to come to grips with the problem, particularly in cases where new problems fall outside the established organizational chart.

Criterion 7: Differentiating Long-Run and Short-Run Problems Requiring Solution

A situation that has fallen into disequilibrium may be a problem in both the short run and the long run. For example, when a worker quits in anger, the problem may have been caused by an immediate crisis in his situation. At the same time, it may be symptomatic of a basic or long-run problem situation in the work group or in the entire organization. In such a case, a short-run solution for the immediate problem alone would not be an adequate solution. Long-run plans need to be made for building, over time, the kind of social system in the organization that handles problems before they become crises. When faced with a problem in the short run, it is always necessary to consider the relationship of that problem and its solution to the long-run picture.

The opposite is also true, of course. When confronted with what might be considered long-run problems, it is important not to overlook the immediate short-run crises. In discussing the Crescent Airlines case, for example, students often dwell primarily on the philosophical issue of employee-employer relations and on general ways in which management can avoid the kind of situation that occurred in this case. In focusing on the problem entirely in long-run terms, however, they often overlook the fact that at the end of the case there is a heated argument going on between the Superintendent of Passenger Relations and the stewardess, which can be heard by the passengers on the aircraft. Although *we* are told that no safety issue exists, it is not clear that the *passengers* are aware of this. Any solution to this problem must include a solution for the immediate disruption of operations.

Criterion 8: The Problem Should Not Be Stated as a Dilemma

Some managers in effect circumvent the entire decision process by never seeing or stating problems, but only dilemmas. Every problem is somehow structured as an unsolvable predicament. Usually underlying such habitual structuring of dilemmas is a desire for some satisfaction other than solving the problem—possibly a desire for ego building, sympathy, or attention; or a desire to vent anger or gain vengeance; or a desire to avoid the effort, responsibility, or risk involved in problem solving. If the decision maker's primary desire is for something other than the solution of the problem, no amount of his going through the motions of the decision steps can keep him from sabotaging his own efforts.

In one large manufacturing firm, for example, the managers of two departments, although ostensibly engaged in mutual decision making on a corporate problem, were in reality engaged in competitive infighting to reduce the other's sphere of influence. Both came up with problem statements structured as dilemmas. Each man avoided defining the problem in solvable terms, lest the solution of the problem bring some success for the other manager.

On occasions when our own ego is deeply at stake, all of us may resort to structuring problems as dilemmas. However, for the manager who wishes effectively to manage his own feelings, explicit definition of the problem to be solved and the goal for change, both stated in behavioral terms, can help him gain awareness of the real problem, separate from his own personal motivations. If personal motivations are allowed to continue to structure problem statements and goals, however, problems may remain mere dilemmas, subverting a constructive decision process.

Summary

Definition of the problem is presented as a separate step in the decision-making process because it is a crucial act by which all following acts of the decision process are determined. There is a temptation to bypass an explicit problem statement, but this step requires explicit formulation through systematic critical method if subsequent steps of the decision process are to be sound. Indeed, the formulation of the problem structures the kinds of solutions subsequently considered. Therefore, the problem definition should meet eight important criteria:

1. The problem should be stated explicitly.
2. The problem statement should include a working diagnosis.
3. The problem statement should specify the standard violated.
4. The problem should be stated in specific behavioral terms.
5. The problem statement should not be expressed merely as an implied solution.
6. The problem statement should specify whom the problem affects (that is, who is suffering discomfort and who is responsible for a solution).
7. The problem statement should differentiate the short run and the long run in a problem situation.
8. The problem should be stated as a problem, not as a dilemma.

Once the problem facing the decision maker is clearly identified he is in a position to consider alternative solutions. Thus the fourth step of the decision process is the selection of the best solution from the available alternatives, a matter taken up in Chapter 6.

References

Elbing, Alvar O., Jr., and Carol J. Elbing. *The Value Issue of Business.* McGraw-Hill, 1967.

Galbraith, John K. "Economics and the Quality of Life." *Science*, Vol. 145, July 1964.

———. *The Affluent Society.* Houghton Mifflin, 1958.

Leavitt, Harold. *Managerial Psychology*, rev. ed. University of Chicago Press, 1964.

McClelland, David C. "Business Decisions and National Achievement." *Harvard Business Review*, July–August 1962.

Ofstad, Harald. *An Inquiry into the Freedom of Decision.* Norwegian Universities Press, 1961.

Sherif, Muzafer, and Carolyn Sherif. *An Outline of Social Psychology*, rev. ed. Harper & Row, 1956.

Electrical Manufacturing Company Case

Electrical Manufacturing Company is a large international company that manufactures many types of electrical machinery, appliances, and military hardware. The company was organized late in the 19th century to capitalize on anticipated rapid development in the electrical industry. There was, indeed, rapid development, especially during the period 1915 to 1930 and after World War II. During the years 1945 to 1950, the company had a period of accelerated growth. By that time the various divisions of the company overlapped and were only loosely coordinated. The company was organized primarily along geographical lines.

In 1950, under new management, the company was completely restructured into a large number of autonomous departments, collected into divisions appropriate to the market or industry served. Each department was responsible for its own business welfare, supposedly having direct control over all the inputs of financial and human resources needed for success. Each general manager, in theory at least, was made completely responsible for the welfare and success of his department. If the department did not meet the goals set by the corporate headquarters, the general manager was usually replaced.

While this decentralization had many useful aspects, it led to a short-range view of departmental success. Few general managers survived to savor long-range successes if immediate profit goals were not realized. This emphasis on short-run profits led to the use of high-cost "emergency" expedients in certain areas of manufacturing,

---

This case was written under the supervision of Alvar O. Elbing. Names of people and places have been disguised.

to reduced emphasis on quality control, to only marginal investment in new facilities, and occasionally to doubtful personnel policies.

At the same time, the sharp profit-and-loss perspective provided for many significant improvements in operating efficiency, including improved channels for communication and better cost control.

One large factory in the Midwest was totally engaged in the design and manufacture of heavy naval machinery. In 1965 this plant employed about 6,000 people, including a large number of technicians and engineers who worked in engineering, manufacturing, and sales. Many of these individuals had spent their entire careers, ranging up to 50 years, with the company.

One of the engineers, Mr. Frank Johnson, had very great influence on the character of the organization and its product between 1945 and 1950. He was an enthusiastic and persuasive leader, filled with imaginative ideas and the ability to sell them to management and to the consumer. He was also an innovator and possessed many patents. His technical decisions tended to be impulsive, and were frequently inaccurate, but he was equally quick to reverse his direction when this proved to be true. His decisiveness was a major asset. His vast experience more than offset his shortcomings and enabled him to make major contributions and receive significant recognition for them.

Jack Stover "grew up" under Johnson, and reported to him in various capacities for 25 years. Jack's personal characteristics complemented those of his boss; he was steady, conscientious, and reliable, and he served as legman, "interpreter," fact collector, and stabilizer. In this environment, Jack grew steadily in his level of contribution and influence. By 1960 he had acquired managerial responsibilities for a large number of other people and was widely recognized for his contributions to the business.

Jack was a small man physically, but this was generally unnoticed. He lived on a conservative scale, well within his income and status. He seemed relatively happy and cheerful and was regarded as a good superior by those who reported to him.

In 1955 the old section manager retired and a new one, from another organization, replaced him. The new manager, Mr. Ray Latimer, was Frank Johnson's direct superior and was an entirely different type of engineer. Technically brilliant, he possessed a cold, analytical mind which responded only to "the facts." His phenomenal ability to digest, qualify, and analyze data continually amazed his colleagues, but his cold, calculating mind seemed to be impervious to emotion. His instinctive behavior was to turn the entire organization into data gatherers, who collected facts for him to analyze, and to make the important decisions himself. Latimer's tendency to question subordinates in great detail generally affected morale, resulting in a loss of self-confidence for many of them.

Mr. Johnson found this atmosphere stifling. He frequently rebelled, with characteristic impatience. His impetuous though often sound decisions were difficult to justify to Latimer, and the relationship developed an ever-increasing strain. Finally, Johnson retired, becoming a consultant at age 58 and taking a pension at 60.

Latimer promptly replaced Johnson with an individual more like himself—cool, unemotional, and logical. This new manager assumed direct control over the activities of Jack Stover.

Stover began to age visibly after the departure of Johnson. It became apparent that his natural pessimism, as well as his ego, had been helped or bolstered by his association with the ebullient Johnson. He developed new outlooks, often predicting grim happenings at the hands of the Russians, the competitors, the unions, and the minorities. He continually prophesied a 1932-type depression, which he thought was sure to occur within three months.

His technical contributions became fewer as he tried to satisfy his new bosses, who demanded that he know more and more details about an ever increasing variety of problems. His natural tendency to depend on and develop his subordinates was continually questioned, and it became apparent that he could never please those who were over him.

When walking with him, his taller associates would often see him stride out and urge them to walk faster. He developed a taste for expensive things. He bought a new car every year and a second home on the lake. He joined numerous exclusive organizations. He often exaggerated or misquoted others in defense of his points. He began taking personal credit for the ideas of associates and subordinates. Throughout these years, however, he seemed to retain a warm personality. He was usually available for discussion, although he was frequently defensive and pessimistic.

Five years after Johnson retired, a general reorganization occurred and Stover lost his managerial position. He became a "consultant" with loosely defined responsibilities "befitting his broad experience." His trend toward pessimistic outlooks accelerated after this harsh experience. His contemporaries and former subordinates agreed that Stover had been reduced to a fraction of his old effectiveness.

A Shade of Gray

Calvin McGruder was the union shop steward at Tinytogland, a children's clothing manufacturing firm in a midwestern state.

The company-union contract between the Amalgamated Clothing Workers' Union and Tinytogland stipulated that the union steward had the right to work overtime if any of his union subordinates worked, and if he were qualified for the work being performed.

Due to heavy snow predictions and an accumulation of almost five inches by midnight, Tuesday, the plowing crew was scheduled to report for early overtime assignment to start at 4 a.m. Wednesday to plow out roads and the parking lot. This crew consisted of one driver and three shovel men. Plowing was done by a large plow attached to the front of a heavy truck. When McGruder was notified of the overtime, he exercised his right to the assignment and was scheduled in as a shovel man.

Upon arrival at the garage where the plowing operation would start, he found that the regular driver was late. Since there was no truck key, rather than reporting to the foreman McGruder obtained an emergency key from the plant protection man. He then returned to the garage and stated that he would do the plowing. Though he initially had trouble backing the truck out of the garage, he drove to the front parking lot and started to plow. However, during his first swipe he hit a manhole cover and bent one of the plow braces. He then backed up but lost control and ran into a parked car belonging to a fellow employee, causing considerable damage to the car (later determined to be $217). The truck was not damaged other than the plow brace.

At this point the regular driver appeared and took over the remainder of the job.

The following information was obtained by the labor relations supervisor after his arrival at 7 a.m. Wednesday morning.

1. McGruder had been told only to help out the plow crew as a shovel man. He was not then classified and had never held the company classification "truck driver," nor had he ever driven the truck

This case was written under the supervision of Alvar O. Elbing. Names of people and places have been disguised.

before. Truck driving required a chauffeur's license, and his act was strictly on his own.

2. McGruder had only within the past month regained his driving license for a pleasure car, which had been revoked for the prior year due to an accident in which he had been found at fault.

3. McGruder had already made arrangements with the owner of the car he struck to pay for repairs. He had asked the owner not to report the accident because, if it were reported, he could lose his license again. The owner had assured him he would not report the accident if his car was properly repaired.

4. McGruder readily admitted he had driven the truck and had hit the car. He was not questioned regarding the damage to the plow.

5. State law required that accidents involving damage over $150 be reported.

At 1 p.m. the labor relations supervisor reported to the industrial relations manager of the plant to ask for advice as to how to proceed. The two of them discussed the following items.

1. In trying to determine what prompted McGruder to drive the plow truck, they decided that probably the best explanation was that he was trying to become qualified on the plow so he could exercise overtime rights against the operator in future overtime assignments.

2. The facts would undoubtedly substantiate discipline of McGruder, either on a charge of "unauthorized operation of company equipment" or "careless use of company equipment." The maximum discipline that could probably be justified would be "one day off." If disciplinary action were taken, it should be in accordance with company policy that discipline be "corrective" rather than punitive.

3. McGruder had been a very troublesome committeeman and had filed many grievances almost on whim. If disciplinary action were taken, it was anticipated that he would probably file 10 to 20 additional grievances.

4. At the staff meeting that day, the plant manager remarked offhandedly that "we will probably have 30 to 40 grievances before the day is over." This indicated that he expected a disciplinary investigation to be held.

5. During the day many facetious inquiries had been made of both the industrial relations manager and the labor relations supervisor as to what would happen to "our new truck driver."

6. On the bottom of the state accident reporting form is the following notation: "An accident causing death, personal injury, or damage over $150 to the property of any one person must be reported

within 10 days. Failure to report within 10 days is a misdemeanor, and subjects license and/or registration to suspension until report is filed."

If disciplinary action were to be taken, it should be done as quickly as possible, and no later than the following day.

The Bellevue Candy Company Case

The Bellevue Candy Company was founded by John Warrington. With three employees and a small amount of capital, Mr. Warrington began making and selling bulk chocolates in 1890 in San Francisco, California. By 1954, the company had grown to a prominent competitive position among candy companies in the eleven Western states, and it employed 150 men and women in its plant.

John Warrington was born on a farm in Ohio in 1860. He left school at the age of 16 to work full time on the family farm, along with his two brothers. When he was 19, John left the farm for a job as telegrapher at a small local railroad depot. During the following seven years, he rose to the position of depot agent; and his two brothers joined him in this vocation. In 1886, John left Ohio to seek his fortune in the West. He settled in San Francisco and with his two brothers, who followed him, bought a small grocery store there. Four years later, John left his brothers to run the grocery business and bought the small candy store which has become the Bellevue Candy Company.

In the course of the development of the company, Mr. Warrington had at one time or another personally performed every function in the business in both the plant and office. In the early days he had actually made much of the candy, handled purchases, performed shipping functions (including traffic routing), and all office duties including credit work, cashiering, bookkeeping, payrolls, and sales management. Consequently he had an intimate knowledge of the details of every department from firsthand experience. In fact, most methods and procedures were of his personal design and invention.

Warrington was a man of strong opinion, and he ruled the company with an iron hand. Although he had no stated, well-defined policies as such, he was guided in all things by his own sense of right or wrong and would make no compromise with his own principles of fairness and justice. He was considered a strict disciplinarian, yet no one was discharged for anything short of extreme breaches of honesty or moral conduct. Because of his perfectionist ideals and his detailed knowledge of the business, he found it extremely difficult to delegate authority.

Mr. Warrington died in October 1945, and the presidency and management of the company passed to Ralph King, a nephew.

Ralph King had gone to work for Bellevue Candy Company upon graduation from the University of California in 1923. King had worked in various types of business during summer vacations from the time of his freshman year in high school to high-school graduation. His various jobs included work in a shipyard, battery factory, longshoring, service station, airplane factory, and a short term at sea as a quartermaster. At the end of his freshman year in college, he spent one and a half years in the purchasing department of the Beach Oil Company. From the time he returned to the University of California in his sophomore year, he earned most of his college expenses working part time in a clothing store.

Mr. King's first job with the Bellevue Candy Company was in the bookkeeping department. During his first two years, he worked in practically every department in the office. His final assignment in the office was to conduct a reorganization of the cost-accounting procedures, which at that time were extremely complicated and laborious. The information coming from the department was usually in such great detail and made available so late that it was of almost no practical value.

After completing the cost-accounting reorganization, King was assigned for six months as an assistant to the production manager in the plant. After that King was put in the sales department to develop statistical sales data and to work as a sales correspondent. In the course of this period, King gradually acquired experience traveling with the salesmen calling on the trade; for a short time he covered a territory himself. King completed his tour of duty in the sales department with about two years as sales manager of "boxed chocolates," one of the three divisions.

By that time Mr. Warrington concluded that King's background and experience with the company warranted his promotion to an executive position, and he was given the title of assistant treasurer. The only duty explicitly given him was that of signing checks. From then on Mr. King made his own place in the management of the business with very little direction or suggestion from Mr. Warrington. By picking up loose ends and assuming responsibility for things which were not otherwise assigned, more by tacit agreement than by definite assignment, Mr. King in a short time assumed general supervision over the functions of purchasing, cost accounting, payrolls, and personnel; and he acquired a certain amount of vague authority over certain phases of production.

Looking back on these years, Mr. King reports that he felt that this arrangement worked well, even though occasionally he found himself overruled either as a result of lack of communication or by direct disagreement on the part of Mr. Warrington.

When Mr. Warrington died in 1945, he bequeathed control of the company to Mr. King. The other stockholders, all of whom were close relatives of the former president, unanimously supported Mr. King in his new role. Over the years, Mr. King had become a stockholder himself; and, at the time of Mr. Warrington's death, King owned approximately 15 percent of the shares, acquired through gifts and purchases. None of the other stockholders had been active in the management of the company.

Mr. Warrington's death created a situation of uncertainty and doubt in the minds of the employees as to the future management and policies of the company. Sensing this, Mr. King immediately wrote a letter to each employee, including plant, office, and outside sales personnel, announcing that he was assuming the presidency and that as far as possible past management policies would be continued as before. He also stated that by building on its good reputation for quality products and fair dealing, the company should achieve even greater success in the future. Everyone was assured of continued security in his job as long as he continued to carry out his job satisfactorily. Mr. King appealed for full cooperation from everyone.

Mr. King also called a meeting of the department heads and foremen shortly thereafter, in December. His purpose was to ask for their cooperation in calming the natural speculation and fears involved in a change of management, especially in wartime. He felt that the supervisory personnel were in the strongest position to instill confidence in the workers. He also stated that, because of the change, a certain amount of reorganizing of company functions and lines of authority would have to be made. At the moment, the final reorganization plan was not fully developed. He requested patience, understanding, and forbearance for the next few days while such plans were being matured.

Several innovations in company procedure were soon put into effect. Each department was to become a more independent unit, handling its own affairs, such as discipline problems, pretty much by itself. A strategy board composed of the top six executives was formed to work jointly on company problems. Any member of this board could call a meeting at any time. An advertising and sales board was formed to work on common problems. Committee organization was put to work in various ways. In short, a general decentralization of authority came about.

In January 1946, about three weeks after the first meeting, a second meeting was called at which time a general policy of reorganization was laid out, indicating as nearly as possible the position of each person present in relation to the overall plan. This was followed by at least one conference and in many cases several conferences with each individual involved, from department-head status on up.

One of the most important of these conferences was held with Bill Adams, maintenance foreman. Mr. Adams had operated for many years quite independently of the plant superintendent, to whom he was formally responsible.

In 1923 Bill Adams, mechanic, came to work for the Bellevue Candy Company. He was responsible for mechanical maintenance, adjustment and repair of all mechanical equipment, and installation of new equipment. He was hired by Mr. Warrington and told he was to work under direct supervision of the plant superintendent, Bob Perkins. The machinery which was Adams' special concern was used in the manufacturing and packing lines, which operated under the supervision of three foremen. Packing lines were operated by crews of women, varying from three or four to fifteen in number.

Although the candymakers, dippers, wrappers, and packers were all unionized, Bill Adams was not a member of a union. His remuneration was on a monthly salary basis without regard to hours worked.

Mr. Warrington formed a strong liking for Bill Adams and over a period of time gradually encouraged him to report directly any lack of efficiency that he observed in the course of his rounds of the plant, regarding production, handling of personnel, and other phases of operation which came to his attention. Mr. Warrington checked frequently with Bill Adams, and the door of his office was always open to Adams for the purpose of reporting to him any happenings, incidents, or occurrences which Adams thought would be of interest to the president.

In speaking of this unusual employee-employer relationship, Mr. King said that it may have come about partly because of the president's socially isolated position in the company. He explained that after a certain level in the executive chain is reached, friends in the plant become more courteous and less close. King thought the presidency, an essentially lonely job, effectively cut Warrington off from the grapevine of the organization. This, he felt, was a possible explanation for Warrington's use of Adams.

Adams' relationships were at times strained because of his reports to the front office; but as a result Adams came to feel responsible solely to Mr. Warrington. Soon Mr. Perkins felt he had no control over Adams. If he attempted to give him directions, he frequently found himself thwarted by Adams' appealing to Mr. Warrington. In many cases Warrington overruled Perkins when differences of opinion arose between Adams and the superintendent.

Mr. Adams practically ignored any suggestions from Perkins, occasionally even interfering with production schedules by choosing his own order and methods of making repairs of disabled equipment. Mr. Perkins refrained from reporting these things to Mr. Warrington, because he felt that Mr. Warrington was more likely to side with Adams on any case at issue. He preferred not to cross Adams any more than necessary, because he realized that Adams was in a position to put him in a bad light with Warrington if he so chose. In brief, Bill Adams became a "privileged employee" and practically a law unto himself, immune from supervision.

When Mr. King took over the presidency, he explained both in a general meeting and in an individual conference with Bill Adams that Bill's status was changed to the extent that he would work under the supervision of and be responsible to the plant superintendent, Mr. Perkins. Bill accepted this explanation without comment or any apparent reaction.

In February, 1946, the situation with respect to Bill changed somewhat. Mr. Perkins left the company to seek other employment.

In explaining Mr. Perkins' leaving, Mr. King described that it was his policy, at the time of reorganization, to give first chance for positions of responsibility to employees already on the payroll, many of whom had been with the company twenty-five or more years. Under the new setup some of the former employees who were given additional responsibility found themselves unable to assume their new role. One young supervisor, for example, found that he had become very uneasy and fearful of making mistakes without the constant watchful eye of Mr. Warrington. He left the company rather than continue in the job that now gave him wider latitude and freedom but that also involved more decision making and less direct supervision.

Mr. Perkins, on the other hand, left for quite another reason. In a five-page letter to Mr. King, he outlined all of the policies and personalities of the company to which he had found objection. While Mr. Perkins indicated that he felt Mr. King was making some progress in resolving these problems, he felt that some of the problems were so ingrained in the company structure that Mr. Perkins preferred to find his future in another organization. One of the problems ranking high on Mr. Perkins' list was Bill Adams.

Mr. Perkins was replaced from outside the organization by Tod Johnson, a man with considerable experience in handling labor and personnel problems and some experience in production. Bill Adams did not apply for this job or show any interest in securing it.

It soon developed that Mr. Adams refused to accept the authority of Mr. Johnson, his new superintendent. After struggling with the problem for about six months, Johnson laid the matter in Mr. King's lap in July, 1946.

As he thought about this case, Mr. King reviewed the factors he thought were most important. Mr. King did not have as high an opinion of Mr. Adams' ability, either general or mechanical, as Mr. Warrington previously had had. Mr. King also was well aware from years of personal observation that Adams had created many animosities among the other employees, partly because of his special status over the years and also partly because of lack of tact in his contacts with other department heads and employees who worked on the machines for which he was mechanically responsible. King concluded that there was very little likelihood of Adams' conforming to the new organization.

However, he did rate him as having better-than-average mechanical skill, and he had long years of experience with the machines in the plant. Also, because of Adams' length of service and a feeling that Adams' position in the company and his attitude toward his position were to some extent a natural outgrowth of the way he had been handled over the years, Mr. King wished to give Bill every chance.

A week after Mr. Johnson had presented the case of Bill Adams, Mr. King decided on action which he felt was appropriate and fair. He called Adams into his office, discussed the matter at great length, and presented his plan of action. Mr. King proposed that Bill take a six-month vacation with pay beginning August 1, 1946. He was to stay entirely away from the plant until such time as he had either located another job or felt that he would be able to accept the authority of Mr. Johnson and approach his job in a spirit of cooperation with everyone concerned.

King explained to Bill that apparently the many brief conferences he had had with Bill had failed to convince him of the real necessity for respecting the new organization of the company. King continued by saying that he realized the change was sudden, and that Bill had been conditioned by many years to a different pattern, but that the change had to be, and he was therefore giving Bill this last opportunity to change.

King said at a later time that he had made this generous proposal because in his opinion Adams had, over a period of years, not been entirely adequately remunerated for the responsibility which he carried. Adams had willingly worked overtime, including occasional Saturdays and Sundays, without extra pay or remuneration in any form. Furthermore, from the time Adams started to work for the company the department had grown from Adams and one assistant to Adams and four assistants. In fact, King said, this group constituted a larger repair department than was actually needed under the conditions at that time. The four other mechanics could carry on the necessary work during Adams' absence. King felt justified in making this one last desperate attempt to salvage Bill for the company.

Bill admitted some blame on his part, but he was not fully convinced that he should shoulder all or a major part of the blame. He said he was not in sympathy with the program outlined, but he finally agreed to accept the offer on the terms laid down.

Adams returned at the end of six months, February 1, 1947, and stated that he was grateful for the opportunity to rehabilitate himself and that he was now ready to return to work. He promised full cooperation with everyone.

The situation was reasonably good for nearly two and a half years, until July, 1949. Then a perceptible, though gradual, deterioration took place. The work in the mechanical department began to get behind, and Bill's tendency to ignore Johnson's requests began to reappear. Although Adams was not as openly defiant as previously, he found subtler ways to circumvent Mr. Johnson's orders and requests. When confronted with some lack of performance, he would devise one excuse after another, such as some emergency arising which needed prior attention or a lack of adequate tools. These excuses were sometimes hard to refute without considerable investigation on Johnson's part, and Johnson felt that usually the excuses were manufactured to fit the event.

Eventually, in March, 1952, Mr. Johnson again laid the matter in Mr. King's lap. However, before any action could be taken, Adams contracted a disease that doctors pronounced incurable. While the number of months or years left to Adams could not be determined with accuracy, he was destined to live in the shadow of an ever-increasing possibility of succumbing to the disease. Adams was put under treatment on the job, which lasted about six months. Then Adams was unable to report for work, so he was given a leave of absence for an indefinite period.

The company had a health and welfare program which covered most of the treatment and compensation for time lost at $25 per week. The company made up the difference between the compensation and Adams' regular salary. King justified this action again because of Adams' length of service plus the fact that the company had no retirement plan but had an informal policy, extending over many years, of making partial payments to retired employees.

(Although this particular case was not of interest to the union, because neither the mechanics nor office employees were organized, the union was beginning to look on pensions as a bargaining point. The company had a very good relationship with the union and made an effort to keep the union advised of all changes and procedures in company employee policy.)

By May, 1953, after approximately eight months' leave of absence, Adams had made a remarkable degree of recovery, in view of the nature of the illness, and he was again able to return to work—at first on a part-time basis and eventually on a full-time basis. The situation with respect to relations with employees and production superintendent was far from satisfactory; but it was tolerated another 18 months.

In November, 1954, Mr. King and Mr. Johnson discussed the problem several times, but before they arrived at any decision, Adams became involved in an altercation with another foreman. Finally Adams suggested that both he and the other foreman should take the dispute to Mr. King for settlement. The other foreman stated that he did not feel that it merited the president's attention and suggested instead that they carry the matter to Mr. Johnson. Adams rejected this solution and turned on his heel and walked off. The other foreman reported the matter to Mr. Johnson, who in turn brought the matter to Mr. King's attention.

Mr. King called all three men, Adams, the foreman, and Mr. Johnson, to his office. King stated that he understood that the foreman and Adams had had difficulties and that Adams had wanted to take the matter up with the president. Mr. King asked Adams to state his case.

Adams immediately arose from his seat and made the statement, "Let's drop the whole affair."

Mr. King said, "I am not going to drop the whole affair. I want to get the facts."

Adams sat down briefly and said that he was "fed up," that things were "not the same any more," that the business was being run very loosely, that there were lots of things going on Mr. King did not know anything about, that there was no longer any incentive to do a good job, and that he got no satisfaction out of his work. He started to leave the office, turned, said "I quit," and left immediately.

The three other men looked at each other; Mr. King said "I guess that's it," and the meeting was ended.

One hour later Adams returned, turned in his keys to Mr. King, and reiterated his former position. He said that everything in the company was "going to pot."

Mr. King said, "Nothing is perfect in this imperfect world, but, since I took over as president, sales have doubled and profits have more than doubled. So the company can't be doing too badly even if it is making some mistakes."

Adams retorted, "That's because the company has no decent competition any more."

Mr. King smiled and said, "It looks like the whole world is going to pot. In any event, I am sorry to see things end this way between us, and I sincerely wish you all the luck in the world in making a better connection."

Mr. King immediately sat down and dictated a letter confirming acceptance of Adams' resignation and enclosed a check equal to three months' salary as a token of best wishes and to assist Adams until he found a new connection. This all happened on Friday.

The following day, Adams phoned Mr. King at his home and apologized for his actions of the day before, stating that when he got home his wife had pointed out what a terrible thing he had done and what a fool he had made of himself. He said he would like to forget the whole thing and return to work on Monday. Mr. King said that it looked to him as if the matter was beyond consideration. When Adams insisted on discussing the matter further, Mr. King refused to prolong the phone conversation and told Adams if he insisted on further conversation to come to the office on Monday.

Adams appeared on Monday. Placing his check for three months' salary on King's desk, Bill apologized and pointed out that at his age (61) and state of health it was very unlikely that he could find another job. As his wife had pointed out, Adams, by quitting, was losing the medical insurance and life insurance benefits furnished by the company. He stated that his home and car were paid for, but he had no other assets. It was imperative for him to get his old job back, Bill concluded, with some feeling.

Merdon State College Athletic Authority Case

In January, 1951, the Board of Athletic Authority of Merdon State College met for the first time to consider the desirability of increased emphasis on intercollegiate sports and on upgrading athletic competition.

Merdon State College was located in a large midwestern city and, under the leadership of its president, Philip Kirkman, had developed from a state teachers' college with an enrollment of 1000 students in 1945 to a state-supported liberal arts college of 3500 students in 1951. Kirkman had been one of the first midwestern advocates of general education, and the college had gained considerable academic status since he assumed the presidency. After the war, he had greatly increased the quality of teaching by bringing capable young men to Merdon State College, offering them higher faculty rank than they might have received elsewhere. Kirkman was very well thought of in academic circles and was the chairman of the state association of college presidents.

In the fall of 1950, Kirkman appointed Tilden Langston as dean of students at a salary of $8500 a year. Dean Langston was well known and highly regarded by other student personnel administrators and had recently received attractive job offers from three universities. Langston accepted the position at Merdon State College in part because of the challenge he saw there and in part because of his regard for Kirkman. He had approached his new job cautiously and had, according to Kirkman, built up an excellent relationship with his coworkers, the faculty, and many student leaders.

On coming to Merdon State College, Langston bought a house near the campus for his wife and three children, a boy of 18 and two girls, 14 and 10. Langston was sending his son, who had been a star basketball player in high school, to a small eastern college which had only an intramural athletic program.

This case, Merdon State College Athletic Authority, EA-A 134R, was prepared by Frederick V. Fortmiller under the direction of Richard L. Balch of the Harvard University Graduate School of Business Administration as a basis for classroom discussion rather than to illustrate either effective or ineffective handling of administrative situations. Copyright © 1954 by the President and Fellows of Harvard College. Used by specific permission.

At Merdon State College, Langston was immediately involved in several problems. The system of student government was being reorganized. As dean of students, he was one of 12 voting members of the student senate, the new student governing body, and the only faculty member. A new student advisory system needed to be developed because the rapid and extensive growth of the student body had made the previous advising practices inadequate. He believed all of the other functions of the dean of student's office also required reorganizing to meet the changed conditions. He also discovered that, athletically, the school was in a period of transition.

Merdon State College fielded teams in virtually every sport, with competition at about a class D level. The school had, for 15 years, been a member of the Middle States Conference, which was made up of seven small teachers' colleges in addition to Merdon State College. Football competition was limited to the conference membership and to other comparable small schools. The basketball and track teams scheduled stronger regional opponents, but the fundamental emphasis was on conference competition. In other sports, opponents were chosen largely on a local basis. Athletics had long been under the sole jurisdiction of the physical education department, and there had been little or no consultation with the college administration, general faculty, or student body. All the coaches were regular members of the physical education staff, holding faculty rank and having regular teaching responsibilities.

Athletic facilities and funds for major items of athletic equipment were provided by the college in the physical education budget. The student body, through its student activities board, provided funds for all direct items of expense attributable to the intercollegiate athletics program (game officials, traveling expenses, game uniforms, etc.) and received all gate receipts. The student activities board managed ticket sales, provided ushers, leased space to vendors, printed and sold game programs, paid guarantees for visiting teams, and administered all other similar activities. Game receipts were insufficient to cover even these direct items, and the deficit was supported by an allocation from student-activity dues.

A few months before Kirkman appointed Langston as dean, he had brought Cal Salvio to Merdon State College to be the new head football coach and had given him the rank of full professor. The president had selected Salvio without consulting the physical education department; consequently, Salvio felt responsible only to Kirkman. Salvio was a vigorous, dynamic man of small stature, who had turned out state championship football teams for ten years at Merdon High School. Later, he was head football coach at a small eastern college, which scheduled strong nationally rated opponents. Unsuccessful in the postwar years in building a winning team for the eastern school, and under heavy alumni pressure, he was pleased to resign and to accept the position at Merdon State College in his old home town.

Kirkman remarked to Salvio after the first rally of the season: "Cal, I hope the team does fairly well this year. Merdon has got to grow up to meet its new responsibilities. These include athletics. A college of our size ought to be known and supported in our area, both academically and on the athletic field. I don't want to see us in the 'big time,' but I would like to see us grow up a little."

The 1950 football season, Salvio's first as head football coach, was the most successful in the school's history. The team won the Middle States Conference championship and went on to a regional post-season bowl game. By the end of the season, in November, 1950, intense interest among the students, supported by the first athletic gate receipts of any consequence, led Kirkman to seek a stronger student and college administration voice in the conduct of athletics. He felt a need for greater central control and for formally established operating policies. Also, he wanted the students to have a voice in these policies because of their importance to the athletic program. Therefore, he appointed a joint student-faculty committee to study the intercollegiate athletic program. This committee was made up of two student leaders, Salvio, Langston, and two faculty members (including Mr. Morton, chairman of the physical education department).

The two student members of the committee, Charles Romano and Ken O'Shea, were both veterans, and each had great influence in the student body. Romano was student body president; while O'Shea, as treasurer of the student senate, was chairman of the student activities board, which administered the funds for the conduct of all student activities. O'Shea headed the fraternity faction, and Romano was the first nonfraternity man ever elected to a major student office.

The committee members decided to establish a permanent administrative body, the Board of Athletic Authority, and a charter was drawn up outlining its responsibilities. The charter specified that the board was to establish and approve all policies dealing with athletics and designated a director of intercollegiate athletics as the board's chief administrative officer.

The new board was to consist of six voting members: Dean Langston, representing President Kirkman; Mr. Hooper, the college business manager; Lang Gilman, the track coach, representing the physical education department; Ken O'Shea, the senate treasurer and chairman of the student activities board; Lee Downs, the president of the varsity letter society; and John Dickson, a student member at large, appointed by the student body president, Charles Romano, and approved by the student senate.

There were also to be ex officio members: Cal Salvio, the football coach; Bill Ives, the student body graduate manager; Professor Pierce, the college representative to the Middle States Conference; and Frank Cutler, vice president of the student body.

A simple majority of the voting members was required to approve a motion.

Immediately after the charter of the Board of Athletic Authority was drawn up, Kirkman appointed Salvio to the newly created post of director of intercollegiate athletics. As such, Salvio was to administer all functions of the intercollegiate program. This responsibility had formerly been vested in Morton, chairman of the physical education department. Morton had been at Merdon State College for over 20 years and was a strong advocate of the kind of "low-pressure" athletics the school had been conducting in the past. Some of the faculty saw Salvio's appointment as tacit approval by Kirkman of a more vigorous intercollegiate program.

After the winning football season, there was strong feeling on the campus that more emphasis should be placed on athletics. Many of the students and a few members of the faculty were clamoring for a higher level of competition, in the hope that this would gain more recognition for the school. Located in the downtown area of a large midwestern city, Merdon State College was not very well known to the people of the community, and was frequently confused with the more renowned Merdon University, which, although only a third the size of Merdon State College, consistently fielded a football team which competed successfully against the strongest teams in the nation.

All but a handful of students at Merdon State College were commuters. Many had made a considerable financial sacrifice to attend. Tuition was nominal, but most of the students came from low-income families, and little scholarship aid was available. Over two-thirds of the student body worked part time, averaging 16 hours per week. Some students worked 40 and even 60 hours per week in addition to going to classes.

The alumni had little influence in the affairs of the school. The total group was small, and most were teachers scattered over the country. However, as the successful football season progressed, a number of members of the larger postwar classes, which had seen Merdon State College change to a liberal arts school, became interested and vocal in its development.

The newly constituted Board of Athletic Authority met in January, 1951. The first item considered was a suggestion by Dickson that Merdon State College withdraw from the Middle States Conference and make exploratory contacts with the Upper West Athletic Association. The UWAA did not represent "big-time" athletics, but was a league of schools, of comparable size and academic standards to

Merdon State College, which fielded substantially stronger teams than were represented in the Middle States Conference.

Langston opposed this action from the beginning. At the first meeting of the board, he stated his view:

> This action is contrary to the aims of Merdon State, as I see them. This is an institution of learning with high standards. We should pride ourselves on this fact and not on the ability of our football team to beat XYZ University. Anyone can watch our team play on Saturdays and enjoy the game when the team plays as it did this fall.
>
> But is further emphasis on athletics the true end and purpose of Merdon State? Gentlemen, when President Kirkman led this school from a small teachers' college to an institution of liberal arts, the choice was made for us. Merdon is no longer primarily a place to train people to do a specific job like teaching. Neither should we become an institution primarily to train healthy males in athletic prowess and to provide a number of other young people to watch the athletics.
>
> You'll say this is old-fashioned, I know. But I am not saying we should cut out football or *any* sports; I *am* saying that an overemphasis on sports defeats the purposes of this college by inducing a false sense of values among the students which is incompatible with what we are trying to build here. [He grips the table, his knuckles white.]
>
> I feel very strongly about this. Merdon State today is a young institution. Most of us have been here but a few years. My own association has been even shorter. For Merdon's sake, we should move more slowly and avoid a hasty judgment. Let's not let one successful season go to our heads.

Heated debate followed, and the meeting was adjourned without a vote being taken, to allow the members to report back to their respective groups.

The day after this meeting, Langston went to see Kirkman. Toward the end of the conversation, in which Langston reiterated his views, Kirkman said:

> Tilden, I see your point, and it's a good one. But aren't you visualizing an extreme situation? Academically, our objectives are much more similar to the schools in the UWAA than to any one of the teachers' colleges in the Middle States Conference. This doesn't seem to me to be an overemphasis on athletics, but merely a readjustment to our new size and curriculum. Be realistic, Tilden, and don't let this take on an importance all out of

proportion to its significance. Let's show our confidence in the board and let them decide without any pressure from us.

The faculty was sharply split over the question of athletic emphasis, and many were wary of expressing an opinion. Student sentiment was more obvious. Following the first board meeting, the student newspaper carried articles under two headlines:

DEAN LANGSTON SAYS "GO SLOW" ON ENTRANCE INTO UWAA

SALVIO SAYS "TEAM CAN DO IT": STUDENT SENATE PASSES ATHLETIC RESOLUTION

The following editorial appeared under the headlines:

The Student Senate resolved today that O'Shea, Downs, and Dickson, members of the Board of Athletic Authority, should vote in favor of a stronger football schedule. Charles Romano, president of the senate, submitted the resolution, which stated that since the football team has shown itself capable, it is now feasible to enter the Upper West Athletic Association. Ken O'Shea stated that student-activity dues could be lowered if the football team had the type of competition which would attract spectators and increase gate receipts.

The whole policy of an increased pace in athletics is consistent with the growth of Merdon State. We are proud of our college, and a successful football team would bring more spirit to the whole student body. The editors of this paper, who have been critical of much that the senate has done in the past, feel that this is one of the most constructive moves it has made. A true student government should be active in forming policy and not just approving college administration policy.

Cal Salvio has brought confidence and a fighting spirit to the football team. The student senate has shown the way. We say: "Hats off to the senate."

On February 20, 1951, the board voted 4 to 2 (Langston and Gilman against) to approve a tentative football schedule for 1951, submitted by Salvio, which included most of the members of the UWAA, and which was substantially stronger than previous schedules had ever been. By the same margin (and with the same men voting against the issue), the board empowered Salvio to apply for formal admission to the UWAA as soon as possible.

The next meeting of the Board of Athletic Authority was held on March 19, 1951. The minutes of the last meeting were read, and

Professor Pierce reported on the completion of the 1951 football schedule.

The next speaker to be recognized was Cal Salvio, who said:

Men, I have a problem. I think I went over this with you, Bill [nodding to Ives across the table]. Anyway, I was talking with President Kirkman the other day, and he thought something could be worked out. As you know, we have strong opponents next season. This board has gone on record in favor of the schedule and entering the UWAA, and I think it's great that you're all behind us. The problem I have is twofold, and I'll try to explain the situation to you.

You may not know this, but last season the "M" Club, a recently organized alumni booster group, pledged to give books and part-time work to one of the sophomores on the squad and to pay the tuition of another boy. Well, this raised a stink on the squad, not only because two of the boys were getting help and others weren't, but because the "M" Club didn't fulfill all its pledges to the boys. We all know that the big guns of the alumni aren't too big and aren't well organized. They are mostly recent graduates of the college and not too well-heeled as far as money goes. But they wanted to do something, and they tried. Well, that's one part of the problem. The "M" Club wants to help the squad in some way. The club is bound to do something, even if it's not effective or supervised by the college.

The second part of my problem is this: Most of the boys on the football squad have to work part time to come to State, just like most of the other students who come here. They aren't privileged characters. Most of the boys have a tough time being on the football squad, working, and getting their studies done. I might add that the academic average of the squad was damn good. With the heavier schedule coming up, we have to have all the men in there pitching all the time. And we have to attract good men to carry out the policy which this board approved when it voted for a heavier schedule—as good as any of the teams we play attract. President Kirkman and I talked this over, and I talked with Bill Ives also. They agree with me when I say that we must have some form of subsidy for the boys on the squad who need it. Why penalize a man just because he wants to play football?

As I said before, the problem is twofold. The men on the squad should have some sort of help, and we should be able to attract the kind of fellow to Merdon who will enable us to compete successfully. If we don't, the "M" Club is going to try to do it, anyway. This will be worse than if the thing is well organized and run by the college. O.K., that's my speech. What do you say?

Considerable confusion and hubbub followed. Downs finally got the floor and said:

I talked with some members of the squad after the last varsity letter club meeting, and I agree with Mr. Salvio. If we don't take a hand in this, we'll be in the soup. As Mr. Salvio said, we have to have the men to compete, and we might as well not have a team at all if the men of the squad don't know where they stand with the college or the "M" Club. Besides, I understand that all the UWAA teams give help of one kind or another to their players. We're going to have to do the same thing to keep up with them.

After the other two student members had expressed similar opinions, Langston got up to speak. He reiterated what he had said at the previous meeting, and ended by saying:

Gentlemen, I was afraid this was going to happen. Are sports going to become a *part* of the educational process at Merdon State, or are we going to make football an end in itself? It has always been my belief that playing the game is more important than playing because one gets paid for it. I think subsidies are a very dangerous thing. In effect, we would be sponsoring a professional team and not just a group of boys who are interested in playing because they like the game. It seems to me that we should set up rules that would control the "M" Club or any other group that wants to pay our boys. I don't like this any more than our new schedule.

It was finally decided that each member of the board would talk with the people he represented and sound out their opinions before voting on the issue.

After the meeting, Langston left immediately for Kirkman's office, where he told the president what had taken place and continued: "This has gotten way out of hand. I didn't know that the 'M' Club had given help to two of the boys on the squad. We can't allow this subsidization to continue!"

Kirkman put down his papers and interrupted Langston:

Look, Tilden, I know how you feel. I don't like the subsidy idea, either. But as Salvio pointed out to me, all of the schools in the UWAA are doing it, and we've got to do something to get boys good enough to compete. I'm so convinced that we've got to upgrade our competition that I'm willing to go along—to a point. I think the board must clearly spell out, and put definite limits on, what it is going to do for the players. We can't allow a frenzied bidding and counterbidding to "break" the student body. Nor can we allow the "M" Club to handle this sub rosa. You know how I feel. Now, you do what you think best. I'll leave it in your hands.

For the next week, in various formal and informal gatherings, feelings ran high. The student newspaper printed interviews with the president of the "M" Club and members of the football squad. Having turned the issue over to Langston, Kirkman did not publicly express himself. The student senate did not consider the question; but some of its members, in newspaper interviews, appeared sympathetic to giving the boys on the football squad some kind of financial aid. They also indicated preference for a subsidy administered by the student body or the college, rather than by the alumni. Several other student leaders and a few of the more outspoken faculty members took forthright stands, in interviews, against "letting athletics get out of hand."

On March 30, 1951, the Board of Athletic Authority was to reconvene to consider the subsidy question. Langston, feeling himself to be in a very difficult position, was considering what he should do.

Chapter Six

Solution Choice

The early stages of the decision-making process—identifying a disequilibrium, diagnosing the situation, and stating the problem—lead to the fourth step: selection of a particular course of action designed either to return the organization to a previous state of equilibrium or to bring it to a new state of equilibrium. The manager's skill in creating an operational solution to a stated problem is the test of all the preceding steps in the decision-making process and is therefore the test of his decision-making ability. It is therefore essential that this stage of the process be approached just as systematically and just as critically as the earlier stages.

Fortunately, a considerable body of literature is available on solution choice. Most of the literature on decision making, in fact, centers on this particular step, ranging from generalized normative models of behavior to proposed solutions for the most specific problems.[1] This chapter presents a framework for the development of knowledge and skill in choosing a solution.

Although the literature on decision making stresses the choice of a solution as the key step of the decision process, experience with both managers and students shows that they have a tendency to overemphasize this step in the total process. In most cases, if the diagnosis has been accurate and thorough and the problem has been accurately and clearly defined, alternative solutions often stand out

---

1. For a bibliography of this material, see Taylor (1965), pp. 82–86.

with corresponding clarity, and the choice of a course of action is not difficult. The choice step more often fails because of errors in diagnosis and problem definition than from any other cause.

The process of choosing a solution begins when the decision maker, alone or in discussion with others, compiles as many ideas for alternative solutions as possible. The process of creating ideas for alternative solutions is one more process in decision making where evaluation must be postponed if the process is to be effective. Studies have shown that ideas are more prolific and come more rapidly in a nonevaluative atmosphere. At this early stage, therefore, the decision maker should minimize analysis and evaluation of the solutions that occur to him or to others. If the problem has been clearly stated, "brainstorming" is much more productive than immediately scrutinizing each tentative offering.[2] However, once a list of solutions has been compiled, they should be assessed in terms of the following essential criteria:

1. A solution should be of a quality satisfactory to meet organizational goals.
2. A solution must be acceptable to those affected by it and to those who must implement it.
3. A solution should be evaluated in terms of the anticipated responses to it.
4. The choice of a solution should focus on present alternatives, not past possibilities.
5. The risks of each alternative solution should be considered.
6. Multiple solutions should be arranged in a proper sequence.

The Solution Criteria of Quality and Acceptability

Every proposed solution may be assessed from two standpoints, often confused, but quite distinct from each other. The first is *quality*, in the sense that, if implemented, the solution actually solves the problem and meets organizational goals. The second is its *acceptability* to those who must live with it and implement it, and hence its potential capacity to be implemented in the social system. These two criteria are quite different from one another. Neither one can be omitted in the assessment of solutions for human problems in organizations.

In some technical decision situations which have only a minimal

---

2. In general, there is controversy over the effectiveness of brainstorming. See Osborn (1963) for an affirmative treatment; see Taylor, Berry, and Block (1958), pp. 23–47, for qualification. The important point, however, is that if we have a clear statement of a problem, brainstorming can be useful in considering a wide range of solutions, even though they may not seem appropriate at first glance. The rather unique solutions that are sometimes generated by this method require the participation of several individuals, all of whom thoroughly understand the problem.

influence on the lives of a work force, the acceptability of a solution may be of little concern in choosing an alternative, and only the technical quality of the solution need be assessed. In human situations, however, even the highest quality alternative may be a poor choice if no one involved finds it acceptable enough to be motivated to implement it. Some managers, because of their personalities or their experiences, may place entire emphasis on one dimension or the other, unaware of the important distinctions between the two. In choosing a solution, however, neither quality nor acceptability should be taken for granted. Both should be explicitly applied as criteria when assessing alternative solutions.

Criterion 1: Determining That a Solution Is of a Quality Satisfactory to Meet Organizational Goals

The solution ultimately chosen should be the best one available to solve the problem and meet organizational goals. That is, it should be the one which will most fully accomplish the desired short-run and long-run goals quickly, efficiently, and economically. It is this quality dimension of solution choice that most of the decision-making literature treats, and each functional area of business—marketing, finance, accounting, personnel, and so on—has developed its own body of knowledge about decision quality. The manager who must make decisions in any of these areas is, of course, expected to be technically qualified.

To facilitate the process of selecting the optimum course of action, the decision maker may use many types of decision tools. These tools, about which a great deal has been written, tend to stress techniques that are suitable for use with the rapidly developing computer technology. They include such varied techniques as decision theory, operations research, heuristic programming, linear programming, simulation, and game theory, all of which can offer insights into complicated multidimensional problems. They are designed to increase the manager's information, structure his choices, provide alternative courses of action, or provide a decision matrix that can assist him in weighting his choices.

In general, the usefulness of these specialized tools depends on the feasibility of quantifying important variables,[3] more likely in some types of situations than in others. Because at the present time the applicability of most quantitative tools to the problems of human relationships is at best indirect, they are of little day-to-day usefulness as methods of decision making on problems of organizational behavior, and therefore are not discussed here.[4] However, the criteria that

---

3. See Alexis and Wilson (1967), Chs. 4–6.
4. It is not the intent here to minimize in any way the contributions of quantitative techniques to decision making. The point, instead, is that a business manager is

a given here will assist the manager in deciding where and when such approaches can be useful.

Each manager will choose the tools most appropriate to his situation. Whatever tools he chooses, it is clear that his goal is to make the best decision possible—but quality alone does not necessarily make for the best decision.

Criterion 2: Determining That a Solution Is Acceptable

The second criterion for choosing a solution is that it be acceptable to those who are affected by it, and particularly by those who must implement it. When decisions are made relative to behavior, it is obvious that their acceptability is almost always a crucial factor. Of all the resources the businessman uses, the human resource is the only one that *cares* how it is used. A piece of steel does not care how it is processed; a dollar bill does not care how it is spent. Workers, on the other hand, may have passionate preferences; they cannot be manipulated in the same arbitrary manner as other resources. Thus the manager must attempt to understand motivations, and assess solutions in terms of the cooperation that can be elicited to implement them. Recognizing this, the decision maker is always aware that the best decision technically may not be workable or acceptable in a given situation.

In a sense, acceptability can be thought of as another dimension of quality, but the distinction aids the task of assessment in two ways. First, it helps the manager clarify the reasons for the strengths and weaknesses of his alternatives. Second, it reminds him that a good solution should allow for minimizing resistance and developing acceptance.

Observers' Reactions to Decisions

Although the criterion of acceptability should be considered primarily in relation to employees who are directly affected by the decision in question, a manager should also consider the reactions of those who merely observe the situation. Depending upon the nature of the situation, these observers may be inside or outside the firm; they may be other work groups or managers; they may be customers, suppliers, representatives of government agencies; or they may be stockholders. In any case, the reactions of such observers may be one of the overall consequences of a decision. In one experimental study, for example, observers of a role-playing situation, who were committed to a position on the subject under discussion, experienced as dramatic a change in attitude as did the participants (Elbing, 1967).

---

in day-by-day confrontation with problem situations in which his first responsibility is to understand the situation and define the nature of the problem; and at any stage of the process he may choose to quantify the information that is available to him. The important point is that he make a choice rather than automatically apply a particular technique.

If, therefore, the potential reaction of observers is important, this factor should be included in the assessment of a proposed solution. In choosing a solution, a manager is not merely solving a particular problem, he is setting the policy, precedent, and expectations for this type of problem in the eyes of observers. The handling of rioters by police, for example, affects not only the rioters and the police but the public's attitude on rioting (especially when they see the rioting on television). If a manager can identify and predict the attitudes and reactions of observers, he can avoid creating new problems in relationships that are important to the functions of his firm.

Employee Participation in Decision Making

One way of creating or increasing the acceptability of a solution is to allow the key persons involved in the problem situation to participate in choosing among the alternative solutions available. Employee participation in management decision making has been frequently discussed in the literature on management and has generated considerable pro-and-con comment (see Marrow, et al., 1967). To some writers, participation is *the* answer to most human difficulties in decision making. They argue that if an employee feels he is part of the process of making a decision, he will accept it more readily and be motivated to implement it more effectively. The imposition of an apparently arbitrary decision, it is claimed, may invite a passive or even a negative reaction (see McGregor, 1960, and Likert, 1961).

Other writers just as strongly oppose participation in decision making and stress its potential pitfalls. It must be recognized, they argue, that if the solutions chosen by employees turn out to be inadequate and are ultimately not used, more resistance will result than if the employees had not participated in the first place. In addition, they say, because a manager must forego some of his own prerogatives and managerial flexibility, further problems may appear, even in other situations. Finally, they argue that employee participation in decision making is a time-consuming, cumbersome, and costly process (see Jaques, 1951, and Sofer, 1961).

In considering the use of participation as a part of decision strategy, it is helpful to assess it in terms of the criteria of quality and acceptability. In a decision situation where the quality of the decision is considered to be paramount, participation by employees other than the specialists who determine this quality may be of questionable value. Its worth is particularly questionable if a decision's direct effect on the work group is minor and the factor of acceptability is therefore relatively unimportant. However, if all the alternatives are of equal or similar quality but employee response is crucial, participation may be a very useful method of winning acceptance.

Participation is not advisable when the manager has already

made a decision, or when the employee's feelings of personal or job security are at stake. Consider the reaction of the employee in the following instance to his superior's attempt to involve him in performance appraisal:

> Salary administration policy in my company requires an annual performance appraisal, tied directly to salary increases, which consists of a preprinted form with such questions as "What are this man's strengths?" and "What factors are most likely to hinder this man's future development?"
>
> The intent of this appraisal is to get the employee to improve his performance. However, I found that after each appraisal I was in a disturbed state of mind. Although my appraisals themselves were all above average, I found that each time my manager criticized my communication techniques I became defensive. I tried to refute each instance he cited of poor communication.
>
> Another criticism of his was that I did not pay sufficient attention to detail. Again, I defensively attempted to show him that his examples were less than one-tenth of one percent of my output. I finally stopped objecting and told him that I couldn't help getting defensive but did agree he had a point.
>
> I tried to analyze why I was so defensive and nonaccepting of criticism. The answer, I feel, was that the appraisal was tied directly to a salary increase. This meant a great deal to me, both financially and in showing that my work was appreciated.
>
> My manager later stated that he felt a little bad about the discussion we had but that he had to justify the budgeted raise already accorded to me.

In this situation the company's appraisal system, which was ostensibly designed to be participative, was actually used, at least in part, to justify an already existing salary decision. Rather than gaining the support of the employee, which might have been the result of a mutual search for areas of improvement, this use of "participation" produced a defensive employee who became skeptical of management's purposes.

A full assessment of participation for a specific decision process should include a predictive diagnosis of the capability of the particular group or individual to participate in the process. Such a prediction is more likely to be accurate and effective if it is based on an initial, systematic trial of the participative method. The potential rewards of the method make such a trial worth the effort. Potentially, participation can increase worker identification with organizational goals, motivate greater effort toward attaining those goals, and promote cooperation among the members of the participating group. It is a method of choosing a solution worth consideration whenever acceptability is crucial to implementation.

Criterion 3: Evaluating a Solution in Terms of Anticipated Responses to It

In a problem situation involving behavior, the ultimate goal of the decision maker is to create a specific change in the behavior that is at the root of the problem. If a solution is to be effective, it must produce that change. If it does not produce the desired behavioral change, the chosen alternative by definition was the wrong one.

Although the manager may to some extent be oriented to his own behavior (What shall *I* do?) or to the behavior of other managers who will attempt to solve the problem (What should *they* do?), it is the behavior he wishes to change that is of greatest importance. The critical questions, therefore, are, "How will they react?," and "*How* will the proposed solution bring about the desired behavior?"

In order to answer these questions, the decision maker must necessarily forecast behavior. In part, this forecast derives from specific information about the people and the situation in question; however, it also necessarily derives from his framework of assumptions about behavior in general. The more accurate the behavioral assumptions, the greater the probability that a decision will succeed as forecasted.

In the case of Oscar Larson, the importance of underlying behavioral assumptions is quite apparent. When the work force challenged the new pay rate based on Larson's study, management decided that Larson should explain the technical aspects of his time-and-motion study to the group, whereupon he gave the group a thorough explanation that clearly demonstrated the accuracy of his study. Management's—and apparently Larson's—behavioral assumptions apparently included the belief that the workers would accept the new pay rate on the basis of an understanding of the time-study process. Since the workers finally withdrew their objection to the new rate, management must have felt that its decision was effective and therefore that its assumptions about behavior in this situation were correct.

When the second rate change was also challenged, management chose the same course of action; it had worked before, why not again? Larson again explained the procedure and the workers again accepted the rate. But after the third rate change, the workers forcibly expelled Larson from the plant, which suggests that management's assumptions about behavior were inappropriate to the situation all along.

Additional information on the workers' frame of reference might have yielded several clues to the workers' emotional reaction to the situation—quite different from the "logical" assumptions made on the basis of management's frame of reference. Furthermore, a sounder general understanding of behavior would have made management aware that the basic human needs—more basic than the need for knowledge or information—are essentially emotional. In this case the workers had fears about job security, lowered income, or how hard they would be expected to work. When Larson's response to their challenge treated only the logical points of his time study, his explanation may have been perceived—within the workers' frame of reference—as really an attempt to justify a whole new pattern of lower pay rates. Sensitivity to the emotional factors that underlie behavior is essential to the sound forecasting of behavior necessary for choosing a good solution.

At the end of the Oscar Larson case, management is again faced with questions: What will it do in response to the treatment Larson received? Will it "get tough"? Will it ignore what happened? Will it discuss the problem with the union or with the workers? Whatever management decides to do, its reaction will reflect general assumptions about behavior as well as its understanding of the situation at hand. The accuracy of these assumptions and the corresponding level of understanding about the situation at hand will determine whether management can solve the problem, or whether it will merely treat a symptom, leaving the fundamental aspects of the problem unsolved.

While a sound knowledge and understanding of human behavior is important in all stages of the decision-making process, it is crucial in two steps: (1) the diagnosis, and (2) the selection of a solution which involves a forecast of behavior. Sound forecasting, like sound diagnosis, relies on concepts from the behavioral sciences. The models offered in Chapter 4 provide a framework that will help the manager prepare a realistic forecast. The individual behavior model is an aid in structuring information around one basic question which must be answered by a good forecast: How will the particular worker's frame of reference structure the proposed solution? The interpersonal behavior model aids the forecaster in structuring information around a second major question basic to good forecasting: How will the proposed solution affect and be affected by the existing interaction patterns? The group behavior model structures information around a third vital question: How will the proposed solution fit in with group norms, values, and attitudes?

One final note concerning the forecasting of behavior. The expected behavioral response to a solution must be compared with the existing solution goal of that problem situation. In order to assess a proposed solution, it is essential that the desired objective or goal be clear. To be clear, the goal—the desired equilibrium—should also be stated in specific behavioral terms, rather than in vague generalizations.

Criterion 4: Focusing on Present Solutions and Not Past Possibilities

In choosing a solution, it is important for a decision maker to distinguish between what should have been done in the past to have avoided a current problem and what can be done now to solve it. In some cases, these solutions will be the same. If, for example, a person finds that his automobile is out of gasoline, he realizes that he should have filled the tank, but filling the tank now will solve the problem. If a manager should have hired a replacement for a foreman who was promoted six weeks ago, hiring one now will fill the vacancy.

In most situations, however, what should have been done earlier and what should be done now are *not* the same. If the absent-minded auto owner failed to add oil to his car's engine, he may now have to overhaul or replace it. Failure on the part of the manager to hire a replacement for the foreman may have brought about a new set of social relationships and organizational expectations, creating new problems of wider scope. If management has failed to explain changes in a production process via regular communication channels and employees have responded with a wildcat strike, a standard communication may no longer be enough to put them back on the job. In the Oscar Larson case, it seems that Larson did not really answer the workers' objections initially, so that another speech by Larson could not be expected to solve the current problem.

There is a tendency to assume that, had we done something differently at an earlier time, the situation would be different now. This is, of course, in the realm of speculation; all we can really know about a situation is what did happen. To assume how matters might have developed had a different course of action been taken may only distract the decision maker from considering the existing effects of the course of action that was taken, and thereby distract him from dealing with the problem that currently has to be solved.

Although it is useful to search during the diagnostic stage of the decision process for the causes of the problem situations that face us, it is wasteful to dwell on lost opportunities during the solution-choice stage. Rather than attempt to solve a problem situation that has passed, the decision maker should assess proposed solutions in terms of the current problem.

Criterion 5: Considering the Risks of Each Alternative Solution

Not only should alternative solutions be examined in terms of their probability of success, they should also be examined in terms of associated risks. Implicit in any solution, of course, is the risk that it will fail, and analysis of this risk should be coincident with analysis of a solution's potential success. If the failure cost of a particular solution is great, it may not be feasible to try it. Risks can also be personal as well as organizational; that is, the choice of a solution may risk the reputation of the employees involved, as in the electrical industry price-fixing cases of 1961 (see Walton and Cleveland, 1964).

A top-level manager should be aware that when he places the members of his organization under great personal risk for failure, and defines failure in rigid terms, he may get "solutions" that are misleading. Consider the consequences of the decision made in the following instance, as reported by a middle manager:

At our shop, a foreman whose unit doesn't maintain an 80-percent production time/total time ratio is in trouble. If his group misses consistently, he loses his foreman's job. Therefore, foremen turn in false crane waiting time, machine down time, engineering time, and so on, all of which does not count against production time. By doing this, they can cover low productivity and get their 80 percent. No one is ever reprimanded for turning in too much waiting time—even though the written policy specifies that time should be reported accurately. The few "fanatics" who have played it straight and reported actual time lost their jobs.

On occasion this conflict of written and implicit policy backfires. One example of this occurred this month. A cracked $50,000 casting came through. Castings can be ground to remove surface defects, but if a casting has a deep crack, it must be scrapped. However, scrapping a casting this expensive can cause a major disruption in production. So the foreman said to the machinist, "Grind around the edge to remove that defect. If this one is scrapped the department will miss the schedule." The worker saw that the defect was too deep to correct by grinding, so he welded the area to disguise the crack. The crack was in a critical area and the welding was ineffective. The unit failed in testing, and a new casting had to be substituted, at great expense and loss of time. The worker thought he was doing what the foreman wanted. The foreman had communicated the message, "Get the casting processed at all costs."

At the end of the year all in-process inventory is subjected to a state tax. The superintendents have gotten the message, "Reduce inventory at all costs." The last week of December many extra railroad cars are ordered to ship parts and get them out of inventory. It is common practice to have parts finished, boxed, and painted while in the railroad yard. This practice makes control of inventory, finances, and shipments almost impossible.

At this company, top management had set a framework designed to insure the success of its solutions to production and inventory problems which, in actual practice, merely led to the concealment of problems and the creation of additional problems. The lower-level decision makers (managers, foremen, and workers) could not afford to consider any risks involved in solutions except the risks to their job security.

Criterion 6: Arranging Multiple Solutions in Proper Sequence

A common assumption of decision makers is that alternative solutions must be mutually exclusive and independent of one another and, therefore, that decisions must be limited to one alternative. In certain situations, however, various courses of action thought of as alternatives can be arranged in a hierarchical order and performed in sequence. Some of the alternatives—or steps in the decision sequence —may be so easy to implement, entail so little risk, and even provide substantial additional information, that they are worth trying before proceeding to other courses of action that may be more complicated, time consuming, or risky. It is useful, therefore, to determine whether alternatives can in some way be related to one another and placed in a sequence of steps.

In the Merdon State College case, Dean Langston is faced with a committee meeting which, in his best estimate, will reject his position on athletic scholarships by a 4 to 2 vote. He has four days in which to decide what he should do. The following possible courses of action were proposed by one group of students who discussed the case. He could:

1. Resign his job.
2. Seek the support of President Kirkman, who has remained outside the controversy.
3. Appeal to the student body for support.
4. Seek support among the other committee members.
5. Propose a modified scholarship program to the committee.
6. Discuss the problem with Salvio, the coach, to discover his position.
7. Ascertain the practice of other schools in the conference.
8. Accept the committee's decision.

At least seven different actions are available to Langston. On examination, it is obvious that they are not all mutually exclusive. They could be ordered and arranged to form a *critical path,* or a sequential strategy for solving his problem.

Step 1: First, he can inquire into the practices of other conference schools on the matter of athletic scholarships. This would result in his discovery that the existing pattern of athletic scholarships is either acceptable to him or it is not—a critical point. If it is acceptable, he can prepare a proposal that reflects the pattern of these programs and argue for a comparable Merdon program. If, on the other hand, the existing pattern is not acceptable to him, he can develop a proposal that is acceptable to him.

Step 2: He can talk to Salvio to discover the coach's ideas for the scholarship program—another critical point. Salvio's ideas and Langston's might be compatible. In this case, a majority of the board would probably vote for a proposal Langston could accept. If, however, Salvio desires a program that is unacceptable to Langston, or if he refuses to disclose his recommendation, Langston will at least have learned something about his opposition.

Step 3: He can discuss the alternatives with Kirkman and seek the president's support—a third critical point. If Kirkman supports Langston's position, he will do so actively or passively. If his support is active, pressure can be applied to other committee members. This is another critical point, and the proper steps can be worked out for this eventuality. If Kirkman's support is passive, alternative steps can be developed with the assurance that the president is at least behind Langston. On the other hand, if Kirkman refuses to take a position, as before, Langston could talk with the other committee members.

Step 4: Knowing the probable position of the student members of the committee, he could attempt to determine the positions of the other two voting members—another critical point. He can present his case to them and attempt to gain a commitment from them, or at least an insight into how they will vote. If they choose to vote with him, he may have a tie vote at the meeting which could delay the decision and give him more time. If, on the other hand, he cannot get assurance of their support, Langston would be faced with three final alternatives: (1) accepting the committee's decision, (2) continuing to seek support, or (3) resigning. Inasmuch as neither (1) nor (3) is necessary as yet, and depending upon the importance attached to the issue, Langston could take step 5.

Step 5: He could approach the student body for support. This alternative has long-term risks, but if Langston has strong convictions, he may wish to make this approach despite the risks. Again, he will face a critical juncture: either he will gain student support or he will not. If he does, this support can be channeled toward changing the vote of the student members of the committee. If he does not get student support, he is again faced with alternatives (1) and (3): accepting the committee's decision, or resigning. (This, of course, is the ultimate pair of alternatives for all decision makers; at one point or another they must accept a decision of others in the organization and live with it, or leave the organization.)

This case-example points up the fact that a decision maker need not consider all alternatives as being of equal value or as mutually exclusive. He can prepare a planned sequence of acts which includes alternative moves at various critical junctures. Such a "decision tree" is an aid in preparing creative strategies in advance for various eventualities. Furthermore, it uses several good solution ideas instead of risking success on one strategy.

One alternative has been left out so far: Langston could simply do nothing—which in effect would be to accept the decision of the committee. However, it is important to distinguish between *deciding* to do nothing, and failing to define or face a problem. Although both may have the same outcome, they do have considerably different meanings. A manager who performs the decision process, considers all alternatives, and then decides that the best alternative is to do nothing, has emotionally mastered the situation and has fulfilled his responsibility as a manager. If, however, he fails to decide because he did not define the problem or because he could not make up his mind what to do, he has not mastered the situation and he has not performed his responsibilities as a manager.

The implications of the distinction between deciding to do nothing and failing to decide can be very significant. A manager who is unskilled in the processes of observing disequilibria, diagnosing problem situations, stating problems, and assessing solutions will regularly fail to decide. Some of these failures will turn out well. Ultimately, however, his organization will be weakened by the absence of managerial decision making.

Summary

Many techniques are available to the decision maker for choosing a course of action as the solution of a problem. But no matter what resources he chooses to use, his solutions will be sounder if he assesses them in terms of certain criteria. Thus an important step in the decision-making process is choosing among alternative solutions. This choice is facilitated by testing each proposed solution against the following criteria:

1. A solution should be of a quality satisfactory to meet organizational goals.
2. A solution must be acceptable to those affected by it and to those who must implement it.
3. A solution should be evaluated in terms of the anticipated responses to it.
4. The choice of a solution should focus on present alternatives, not past possibilities.
5. The risks of each alternative solution should be considered.
6. Multiple solutions should be arranged in a proper sequence.

In Chapter 7 the process of implementing solutions in the realm of behavior is considered. Although the choice of a decision can hardly proceed without concern for its implementation, the two steps are separated in this book for purposes of discussion.

References

Alexis, Marcus, and Charles Z. Wilson. *Organizational Decision Making.* Prentice-Hall, 1967.

Elbing, Alvar O., Jr. "The Influence of Prior Attitudes on Role Playing Results." *Personnel Psychology,* Vol. 20, No. 3, Autumn 1967.

Jaques, Elliott. *The Changing Culture of the Factory.* Tavistock, 1951.

Likert, Rensis. *New Patterns of Management.* McGraw-Hill, 1961.

McGregor, Douglas. *The Human Side of Enterprise.* McGraw-Hill, 1960.

Marrow, Alfred J., David G. Bowers, and Stanley E. Seashore. *Management by Participation.* Harper & Row, 1967.

Osborn, Alexander. *Applied Imagination: Principles and Procedures of Creative Problem Solving,* 3rd ed. Scribners, 1963.

Sofer, Cyril. *The Organization from Within.* Quadrangle, 1961.

Taylor, Donald W. "Decision Making and Problem Solving." In *Handbook of Organizations,* ed. James G. March. Rand McNally, 1965.

——, Paul C. Berry, and Clifford H. Block. "Does Group Participation when Using Brainstorming Facilitate or Inhibit Creative Thinking?" *Administrative Science Quarterly,* Vol. 3, 1958.

Walton, Clarence C., and Frederick W. Cleveland, Jr. *Corporations on Trial: The Electric Cases.* Wadsworth, 1964.

The Case of Savemore Food Store 5116

The Savemore Corporation is a chain of 400 retail supermarkets located primarily in the northeastern section of the United States. Store 5116 employs over 50 persons, all of whom live within suburban Portage, New York, where the store is located.

From *Organizational Behavior: Cases and Readings,* by Austin Grimshaw and John W. Hennessey. Copyright © 1960 by McGraw-Hill, Inc. Used with the permission of McGraw-Hill Book Company and John W. Hennessey.

At the time of this case, the author, a college student, was employed for the summer as a checker and stockboy in store 5116.

Wally Shultz served as general manager of store 5116 for six years. Last April he was transferred to another store in the chain. At that time the employees were told by the district manager, Mr. Finnie, that Wally Shultz was being promoted to manage a larger store in another township.

Most of the employees seemed unhappy to lose their old manager. Nearly everyone agreed with the opinion that Shultz was a "good guy to work for." As examples of his desirability as a boss the employees told how Wally had frequently helped the arthritic Negro porter with his floor mopping, how he had shut the store five minutes early each night so that certain employees might catch their busses, of a Christmas party held each year for employees at his own expense, and his general willingness to pitch in. All employees had been on a first-name basis with the manager. About half of them had begun work with the Savemore Corporation when the Portage store was opened.

Wally Shultz was replaced by Clark Raymond. Raymond, about 25 years old, was a graduate of an ivy league college and had been with Savemore a little over one year. After completion of his six-month training program, he served as manager of one of the chain's smaller stores, before being advanced to store 5116. In introducing Raymond to the employees, Mr. Finnie stressed his rapid advancement and the profit increase that occurred while Raymond had charge of his last store.

I began my employment in store 5116 early in June. Mr. Raymond was the first person I met in the store, and he impressed me as being more intelligent and efficient than the managers I had worked for in previous summers at other stores. After a brief conversation concerning our respective colleges, he assigned me to a cash register, and I began my duties as a checker and bagger.

In the course of the next month I began to sense that relationships between Raymond and his employees were somewhat strained. This attitude was particularly evident among the older employees of the store, who had worked in store 5116 since its opening. As we all ate our sandwiches together in the cage (an area about 20 feet square in the cellar fenced in by chicken wire, to be used during coffee breaks and lunch hours), I began to question some of the older employees as to why they disliked Mr. Raymond. Laura Morgan, a fellow checker about 40 years of age and the mother of two grade-school boys, gave the most specific answers. Her complaints were:

1. Raymond had fired the arthritic Negro porter on the grounds that a porter who "can't mop is no good to the company."
2. Raymond had not employed new help to make up for normal attrition. Because of this, everybody's work load was much heavier than it ever had been before.

3. The new manager made everyone call him "mister. . . . He's unfriendly."
4. Raymond didn't pitch in. Wally Shultz had, according to Laura, helped people when they were behind in their work. She said that Shultz had helped her bag on rushed Friday nights when a long line waited at her checkout booth, but "Raymond wouldn't lift a finger if you were dying."
5. Employees were no longer let out early to catch busses. Because of the relative infrequency of this means of transportation, some employees now arrived home up to an hour later.
6. "Young Mr. Know-it-all with his fancy degree . . . takes all the fun out of this place."

Other employees had similar complaints. Gloria, another checker, claimed that "he sends the company nurse to your home every time you call in sick." Margo, a meat wrapper, remarked: "Everyone knows how he's having an affair with that new bookkeeper he hired to replace Carol when she quit." Pops Devery, the head checker, who had been with the chain for over ten years, was perhaps the most vehement of the group. He expressed his views in the following manner: "That new guy's a real louse . . . got a mean streak a mile long. Always trying to cut corners. First it's not enough help, then no overtime, and now, come Saturday mornings, we have to use boxes for the orders 'till the truck arrives.[1] If it wasn't just a year 'til retirement, I'd leave. Things just aren't what they used to be when Wally was around." The last statement was repeated in different forms by many of the other employees. Hearing all this praise of Wally, I was rather surprised when Mr. Finnie dropped the comment to me one morning that Wally had been demoted for inefficiency, and that no one at store 5116 had been told this. It was important that Mr. Shultz save face, Mr. Finnie told me.

A few days later, on Saturday of the busy weekend preceding the July 4 holiday, store 5116 again ran out of paper bags. However, the delivery truck did not arrive at ten o'clock, and by 10:30 the supply of cardboard cartons was also low. Mr. Raymond put in a hurried call to the warehouse. The men there did not know the whereabouts of the truck but promised to get an emergency supply of bags to us around noon. By eleven o'clock, there were no more containers of any type available, and Mr. Raymond reluctantly locked the doors to all further customers. The 20 checkers and packers remained in their respective booths, chatting among themselves. After a few minutes, Mr. Ray-

---

1. The truck from the company warehouse bringing merchandise for sale and store supplies normally arrived at ten o'clock on Saturday mornings. Frequently, the stock of large paper bags would be temporarily depleted. It was then necessary to pack orders in cardboard cartons until the truck was unloaded.

mond requested that they all retire to the cellar cage because he had a few words for them. As soon as the group was seated on the wooden benches in the chicken-wire enclosed area, Mr. Raymond began to speak, his back to the cellar stairs. In what appeared to be an angered tone, he began, "I'm out for myself first, Savemore second, the customer third, and you last. The inefficiency in this store has amazed me from the moment I arrived here. . . ."

At about this time I noticed Mr. Finnie, the district manager, standing at the head of the cellar stairs. It was not surprising to see him at this time because he usually made three or four unannounced visits to the store each week as part of his regular supervisory procedure. Mr. Raymond, his back turned, had not observed Finnie's entrance.

Mr. Raymond continued, "Contrary to what seems to be the opinion of many of you, the Savemore Corporation is not running a social club here. We're in business for just one thing . . . to make money. One way that we lose money is by closing the store on Saturday morning at eleven o'clock. Another way that we lose money is by using a 60-pound paper bag to do the job of a 20-pound bag. A 60-pound bag costs us over 2 cents apiece; a 20-pound bag costs less than a penny. So when you sell a couple of quarts of milk or a loaf of bread, don't use the big bags. Why do you think we have four different sizes anyway? There's no great intelligence or effort required to pick the right size. So do it. This store wouldn't be closed right now if you'd used your common sense. We started out this week with enough bags to last 'til Monday . . . and they would have lasted 'til Monday if you'd only used your brains. This kind of thing doesn't look good for the store, and it doesn't look good for me. Some of you have been bagging for over five years . . . you oughta be able to do it right by now. . . ." Mr. Raymond paused and then said, "I trust I've made myself clear on this point."

The cage was silent for a moment, and then Pops Devery, the head checker, spoke up: "Just one thing, Mis-tuh Raymond. Things were running pretty well before you came around. When Wally was here we never ran outa bags. The customers never complained about overloaded bags or the bottoms falling out before you got here. What're you gonna tell somebody when they ask for a couple extra bags to use in garbage cans? What're you gonna tell somebody when they want their groceries in a bag, an' not a box? You gonna tell them the manager's too damn cheap to give 'em bags? Is that what you're gonna tell 'em? No sir, things were never like this when Wally Shultz was around. We never had to apologize for a cheap manager who didn't order enough then. Whatta you got to say to that, Mis-tuh Raymond?"

Mr. Raymond, his tone more emphatic, began again. "I've got

just one thing to say to that, Mr. Devery, and that's this: store 5116 never did much better than break even when Shultz was in charge here. I've shown a profit better than the best he ever hit in six years every week since I've been here. You can check that fact in the book upstairs any time you want. If you don't like the way I'm running things around here, there's nobody begging you to stay. . . ."

At this point, Pops Devery interrupted and, looking up the stairs at the district manager, asked, "What about that, Mr. Finnie? You've been around here as long as I have. You told us how Wally got promoted 'cause he was such a good boss. Supposin' you tell this young feller here what a good manager is really like? How about that, Mr. Finnie?"

A rather surprised Mr. Raymond turned around to look up the stairs at Mr. Finnie. The manager of store 5116 and his checkers and packers waited for Mr. Finnie's answer.

Slade Company Case

Ralph Porter, production manager of the Slade Company, was concerned by reports of dishonesty among some employees in the plating department. From reliable sources he had learned that a few men were "punching" the time cards of a number of their workmates who had left early. Mr. Porter was shocked by this conspiracy and was determined to expose it and subject every participant to the severest penalties.

The Slade Company was a prosperous manufacturer of metal products designed for industrial application. Its manufacturing plant, located in central Michigan, employed nearly 500 workers who were engaged in producing a large variety of clamps, inserts, knobs, and similar items. Orders for these products were usually large and on a recurrent basis. The volume of orders fluctuated sharply from time to

This case, The Slade Company, EA-A 368, was prepared by John A. Seiler under the direction of Paul Lawrence of the Harvard University Graduate School of Business Administration as a basis for classroom discussion rather than to illustrate either effective or ineffective handling of administrative situations. Copyright © 1960 by the President and Fellows of Harvard College. Used by specific permission.

Figure 1 Slade Company Manufacturing Division Organization

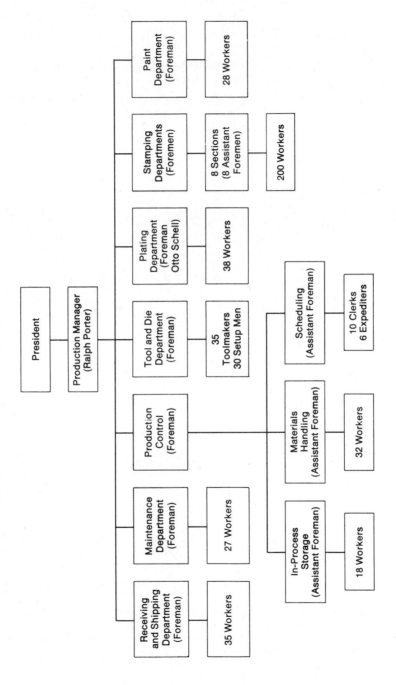

time in response to business conditions pertaining in the primary industries which Slade served. At the time of this case, sales volume had been consistently high for over a year. The bases upon which Slade secured orders, in the order of their importance, were quantity, delivery, and reasonable price.

The organization of manufacturing operations at the Slade plant is shown in Figure 1. The departments listed there are, from left to right, approximately in the order in which material flowed through the plant. The diemaking and setup operations required the greatest degree of skill, supplied by highly paid, long-service craftsmen. The

Figure 2   Slade Company Plating Room Layout

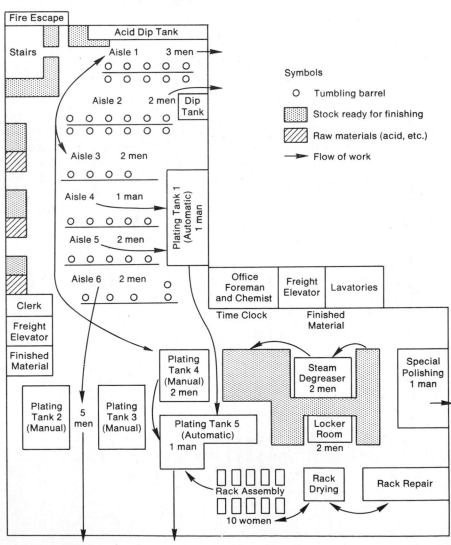

finishing departments, divided operationally and geographically between plating and painting, attracted less highly trained but relatively skilled workers, some of whom had been employed by Slade for many years. The remaining operations were largely unskilled in nature and were characterized by relatively low-pay and high-turnover personnel.

The plating room was the sole occupant of the top floor of the plant. Figure 2 shows the floor plan, the disposition of workers, and the flow of work throughout the department. Thirty-eight men and women worked in the department at jobs which fixed a plate or oxide to the metal parts or prepared parts for the application of paint at another location in the plant. The department's work occurred in response to a steady volume of orders communicated by production schedules which were revised daily. Table 1 outlines the activities of

Table 1   Outline of Plating Room Work Flow

Aisle 1	Worked closely with aisle 3 in preparation of parts by barrel tumbling and acid dipping for high-quality plating in tanks 4 and 5.[a] Also did a considerable quantity of highly specialized, high-quality acid-etching work not requiring further processing.	
Aisle 2	Tumbled items of regular quality and design in preparation for painting. Less frequently, did oxidation dipping work of regular quality, but sometimes of special design, not requiring further processing.	
Aisle 3	Worked closely with aisle 1 on high-quality tumbling work for tanks 4 and 5.	
Aisles 4 and 5	Produced regular tumbling work for tank 1.	
Aisle 6	Did high-quality tumbling work for special products plated in tanks 2 and 3.	
Tank 1	Worked on standard, automated plating of regular quality not further processed in plating room, and regular work further processed in tank 5.	
Tanks 2 and 3	Produced special, high-quality plating work not requiring further processing.	
Tank 4	Did special, high-quality plating work further plated in tank 5.	
Tank 5	Automated production of high- and regular-quality, special- and regular-design plated parts sent directly to shipping.	
Rack Assembly	Placed parts to be plated in tank 5 on racks.	
Rack Repair	Performed routine replacement and repair of racks used in tank 5.	
Polishing	Processed, by manual or semimanual methods, odd-lot special orders which were sent directly to shipping. Also, sorted and reclaimed parts rejected by inspectors in the shipping department.	
Degreasing	Took incoming raw stock, processed it through caustic solution, and placed clean stock in storage ready for processing elsewhere in the plating room.	

a) "High or regular quality:" the quality of finishes could broadly be distingushed by the thickness of plate and/or care in preparation. "Regular or special work:" the complexity of work depended on the routine or special character of design and finish specifications.

the various jobs, their interrelationships, and the type of work in which each specialized. Table 2 rates the various types of jobs in terms of the technical skill, physical effort, discomfort, and training time associated with their performance.

The activities which took place in the plating room were of three main types: (1) acid dipping, in which parts were etched by being placed in baskets which were manually immersed and agitated in an acid solution; (2) barrel tumbling, in which parts were roughened or smoothed by being loaded into machine-powered revolving drums containing abrasive, caustic, or corrosive solutions; and (3) plating, either manual, in which parts were loaded on racks and were immersed by hand through the plating sequence, or automatic, in which racks or baskets were manually loaded with parts which were then carried by a conveyor system through the plating sequence. Within these main divisions there were a number of variables, such as cycle times, chemical formulae, abrasive mixtures, and so forth, which distinguished particular jobs as they have been categorized in Table 1.

The work of the plating room was received in batch lots whose size averaged 1000 pieces. The clerk moved each batch, which was accompanied by a routing slip, to its first operation. From the accumulation of orders before him, each man was to organize his own

Table 2   Skill Indices by Job Group [a]

Jobs	Technical Skill Required	Physical Effort Required	Degree of Discomfort Involved	Degree of Training Required [b]
Aisle 1	1	1	1	1
Tanks 2–4	3	2	1	2
Aisles 2–6	5	1	1	5
Tank 5	1	5	7	2
Tank 1	8	5	5	7
Degreasing	9	3	7	10
Polishing	6	9	9	7
Rack assembly & repair	10	10	10	10

a) Rated on scales of 1 (the greatest) to 10 (the least) in each category.
b) The amount of experience required to assume complete responsibility for the job.

work schedule so as to make optimal use of equipment, materials, and time. Upon completion of an order, each man moved the lot to its next work position or to the finished material location near the freight elevator.

Working conditions in the plating room varied considerably. That part of the department containing the tumbling barrels and the plating machines was constantly awash, alternatively with cold water, steaming acid, or caustic soda. Men working in this part of the room wore knee boots, long rubber aprons and high-gauntleted rubber gloves. This uniform, consistent with the general atmosphere of the "wet" part of the room, was hot in the summer, cold in the winter. In contrast, the remainder of the room was dry, relatively odor-free, and provided reasonably stable temperature and humidity conditions for those who worked there.

The men and women employed in the plating room are listed in Table 3. This exhibit provides certain personal data on each department member, including a productivity-skill rating (based on subjective and objective appraisals of potential performance) as reported by the members of the department.

The pay scale implied by Table 3 was low for the central Michi-

Location	Name	Age	Marital Status	Company/Department Seniority (in years)	Hourly Pay	Education	Familial Relationships	Productivity Skill Rating (1–10)
Aisle 1	Sarto	30	m	13/13	$1.50	hs	Patrici (uncle) Facelli (cousin)	1
1	Facelli	26	m	8/8	1.30	hs	Patrici (uncle) Sarto (cousin)	2
1	Iambi	31	m	5/5	1.20	2 yrs hs		2
2	H. Schell	48	s	26/26	1.45	gs	O. Schell (brother)	8
2	Kirk	23	m	6 mos/6 mos	0.90	college		—
3	Pantaleoni	31	m	10/10	1.30	1 yr hs		2
3	Maletta	32	m	12/12	1.30	3 yrs hs		3
4	Pearson	22	s	4/4	1.15	gs	Father in tool and die department	1
5	Malone	44	m	22/8	1.25	gs		
5	Lacey	41	s	9/5	1.20	1 yr hs	Brother in paint department	7
6	Martin	30	s	7/7	1.25	hs		4
6	Mansch	41	m	6/2	1.10	gs		4
Tank 1	LaForte	38	m	14/6	1.25	hs		6
2,3	Parker	25	s	7/7	1.20	hs		4
2,3	Harding	27	s	8/8	1.20	hs		4
2,3	Flood	22	s	5/5	1.15	hs		5
2,3	Clark	29	m	8/8	1.20	hs		3
2,3	Bond	25	s	6/6	1.20	hs		4
4	Bonzani	27	m	9/9	1.25	hs		2
4	Bartolo	24	m	6/6	1.25	hs		3
5	Patrici	47	s	14/14	1.45	2 yrs college	Sarto (nephew) Facelli (nephew)	1
Rack Assembly	Ten women	30–40	9 m, 1 s	10/10 av	1.05	gs av	Six husbands in company	4 av
Rack Maintenance	Partridge	57	m	14/2	1.20	gs		7
Degreasing	Swan	62	m	3/3	1.10	gs		7
	Susi	45	s	1/1	1.05	hs		5
	Maher	41	m	4/4	1.05	gs		6
Polishing	Perkins	49	m	12/2	1.20	gs		4
Foreman	O. Schell	46	m	35/35	na	hs	H. Schell (brother)	3
Clerk	Pierce	32	m	10/4	1.15	hs		4

gan area. The average starting wage for factory work in the community was about $1.25. However, working hours for the plating room were long (from 60 hours to a possible and frequently available 76 hours per week). The first 60 hours (the normal five-day week) were paid for on straight-time rates. Saturday work was paid for at time and one half; Sunday pay was calculated on a double-time basis.

Philip Kirk, a worker in aisle 2, provided the data for this case. After he had been a member of the department for several months, Kirk noted that certain members of the department tended to seek each other out during free time on and off the job. He then observed that these informal associations were enduring, built upon common

Figure 3   Informal Groupings in the Slade Company Plating Room

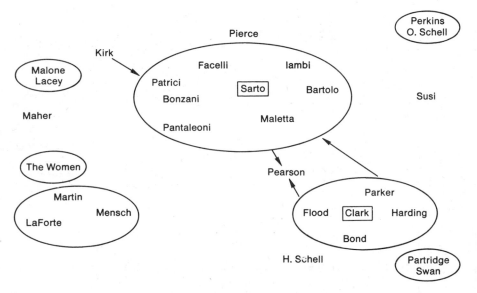

activities and shared ideas about what was and what was not legitimate behavior in the department. His estimate of the pattern of these associations is diagrammed in Figure 3. The boxes indicate those men who clearly demonstrated leadership behavior (most clearly personified the values shared by their groups, were most often sought for help and arbitration, and so forth). Although the two and three-man groupings had little informal contact outside their own boundaries, the five-man group did seek to join the largest group in extraplant social affairs. These affairs were relatively infrequent. Although not an active member of any group, Bob Pearson was regarded with affection by the two large groups.

The Sarto group, so named because Tony Sarto was its most respected member and the one who acted as arbiter between the other members, was the largest in the department. The group, except for

Louis Patrici, Al Bartolo, and Frank Bonzani (who spelled each other
during break periods), invariably ate lunch together on the fire escape
near aisle 1. On those Saturdays and Sundays when overtime work
was required, the Sarto group operated as a team, regardless of
weekday work assignments, to get overtime work completed as
quickly as possible. (Few department members not affiliated with
either the Sarto or the Clark group worked on weekends.) Off the job,
Sarto group members often joined in parties or weekend trips. Sarto's
summer camp was a frequent rendezvous.

Sarto's group was also the most cohesive one in the department
in terms of its organized punch-in and punch-out system. Since the
men were regularly scheduled to work from 7 a.m. to 7 p.m. week-
days, and since all supervision was removed at 5 p.m., it was possible
almost every day to finish a "day's work" by 5:30 and leave the plant.
What is more, if one man were to stay until 7 p.m., he could punch
the time cards of a number of men and help them gain free time
without pay loss. (This system operated on weekends also, at which
times members of supervision teams were present, if at all, only for
short periods.) In Sarto's group the duty of staying late rotated, so
that no man did so more than once a week. In addition, the group
members would punch a man in in the morning if he were unavoida-
bly delayed. However, such a practice never occurred without prior
notice from the man who expected to be late and never if the tardi-
ness was expected to last beyond 8 a.m., the start of the day for the
foreman.

Tony Sarto explained the logic behind the system to Kirk:

You know that our hourly pay rate is quite low, compared to
other companies. What makes this the best place to work is the
feeling of security you get. No one ever gets laid off in this
department. With all the hours in the week, all the company ever
has to do is shorten the work week when orders fall off. We have
to tighten our belts, but we can all get along. When things are
going well, as they are now, the company is only interested in
getting out the work. It doesn't help to get it out faster than it's
really needed—so we go home a little early whenever we can. Of
course, some guys abuse this sort of thing—like Herman—but
others work even harder, and it averages out.

Whenever an extra order has to be pushed through, naturally I work until 7:00. So do a lot of the others. I believe that if I
stay until my work is caught up and my equipment is in good
shape, that's all the company wants of me. They leave us alone
and expect us to produce—and we do.

When Kirk asked Tony if he would not rather work shorter
hours at higher pay in a union shop (Slade employees were not

organized), he just laughed and said, "It wouldn't come close to an even trade."

The members of Sarto's group were explicit about what constituted a fair day's work. Customarily, they cited Herman Schell, Kirk's work partner and the foreman's brother, as an example of what was not legitimate. Kirk received an informal orientation from Herman during his first days on the job. As Herman put it:

> I've worked at this job for a good many years, and I expect to stay here a good many more. You're just starting out, and you don't know which end is up yet. We spend a lot of time in here, and no matter how hard we work, the pile of work never goes down. There's always more to take its place. And I think you've found out by now that this isn't light work. You can wear yourself out fast if you're not smart. Look at Pearson up in aisle 4. There's a kid who's just going to burn himself out. He won't last long. If he thinks he's going to get somewhere working like that, he's nuts. They'll give him all the work he can take. It makes no difference to me, but he makes it tough on everybody else and does himself harm in the bargain.

Kirk reported further on his observations of the department:

> Tony and his group couldn't understand Herman. While Herman arrived late, Tony was always a half hour early. If there were a push to get out an extra amount of work, most everyone but Herman would work that much harder. Herman never worked overtime on weekends, while Tony's group and the men on the manual tanks almost always did. When a time study of the department was made, no one in the aisles slowed down, except Herman, with the possible exception, to a lesser degree, of Charlie Malone. I did hear that the men in the dry end of the room slowed down so much you could hardly see them move, but we had little to do with them, anyway. While the men I knew best seemed to find a rather full life in their work, Herman never really got involved. It's no wonder they couldn't understand each other.
>
> There was quite a different feeling about Bobby Pearson. Without the slightest doubt, Bob worked harder than anyone else in the room. Because of the tremendous variety of work produced, it was hard to make output comparisons, but I'm sure I wouldn't be far wrong in saying that Bob put out twice as much as Herman and 50 percent more than almost anyone else in the aisles. No one but Herman and a few oldtimers at the dry end ever criticized Bobby for his efforts. Tony and his group seemed

to feel a distant affection for Bob, but the only contact they or anyone else had with him consisted of brief greetings.

To the men in Tony's group the most severe penalty that could be inflicted on others was social exclusion. This they did to both Pearson and Herman. Pearson, however, was tolerated; Herman was not. Evidently, Herman felt his exclusion keenly, though he responded to it with derision and aggression. Herman kept up a steady stream of stories concerning his attempts and his failure to gain acceptance outside the company. He wrote popular music which was always rejected by publishers. He attempted to join several social and athletic clubs, mostly without success. His favorite pastime was surf fishing. He told me that surf casters were a friendly bunch and he enjoyed meeting new people whenever he went fishing. Nevertheless, he was particularly quick to explain that he preferred to keep his distance from the men in the department.

Tony's group emphasized more than just quantity in judging a man's work. Among them had grown a confidence that they could master and even improve upon any known finishing technique. Tony, himself, epitomized this skill. Before him, Tony's father had operated aisle 1 and had trained Tony to take his place. Tony, in his turn, was training his cousin, Pete. When a new finishing problem arose from a change in customer specifications, the foreman, the department chemist, and any of the men directly involved would come to Tony for help, and Tony would give it willingly. For example, when a part with a special plastic embossing was designed, Tony was the only one who could discover how to treat the metal without damaging the plastic. To a lesser degree, the other members of the group were also inventive about the problems which arose in their own sections.

Herman, for his part, talked incessantly about his feats in design and finish creations. As far as I could tell during the year I worked in the department, the objects of these stories were obsolete or of minor importance. What's more, I never saw any department member seek Herman's help.

Willingness to be of help was a trait Sarto's group prized. The most valued help of all was of a personal kind, though work help was also important. The members of Sarto's group were constantly lending and borrowing money, cars, clothing, and tools among themselves and, less frequently, with other members of the department. Their daily lunch bag procedure typified the "common property" feeling among them. Everyone's lunch was opened and added to a common pile, from which each member of the group chose his meal.

On the other hand, Herman refused to help others in any

way. He never left his aisle to aid those near him who were in the midst of a rush of work or a machine failure, though this was customary throughout most of the department. I can distinctly recall the picture of Herman leaning on the hot and cold water faucets which were located directly above each tumbling barrel. He would stand gazing into the tumbling pieces for hours. To the passing, casual visitor, he looked busy; and as he told me, that's just what he wanted. He, of course, expected me to act this same way, and it was this enforced boredom that I found virtually intolerable.

More than this, Herman took no responsibility for breaking in his assigned helpers as they first entered the department, or thereafter. He had had four helpers in the space of little more than a year. Each had asked for a transfer to another department, publicly citing the work as cause, privately blaming Herman. Tony was the one who taught me the ropes when I first entered the department.

The men who congregated around Harry Clark tended to talk like and copy the behavior of the Sarto group, though they never approached the degree of inventive skill or the amount of helping activities that Tony's group did. They sought outside social contact with the Sarto group; and several times a year the two groups went "on the town" together. Clark's group did maintain a high level of performance in the volume of work they turned out.

The remainder of the people in the department stayed pretty much to themselves or associated in pairs or triplets. None of these people was as inventive, as helpful, or as productive as Sarto's or Clark's groups, but most of them gave verbal support to the same values as those groups held.

The distinction between the two organized groups and the rest of the department was clearest in the punching-out routine. The women could not work past 3 p.m., so they were not involved. Malone and Lacey, Partridge and Swan, and Martin, LaForte, and Mensch arranged within their small groups for punch-outs, or they remained beyond 5:00 and slept or read when they finished their work. Perkins and Pierce went home when the foreman did. Herman Schell, Susi, and Maher had no punch-out organization to rely upon. Susi and Maher invariably stayed in the department until 7 p.m. Herman was reported to have established an arrangement with Partridge whereby the latter punched Herman out for a fee. Such a practice was unthinkable from the point of view of Sarto's group. It evidently did not occur often because Herman usually went to sleep behind piles of work when his brother left or, particularly during the fishing season, punched himself out early. He constantly railed against the dishonesty of other men in the department, yet urged me to punch him out on several "emergency occasions."

Just before I left the Slade Company to return to school after 14 months on the job, I had a casual conversation with Mr. Porter, the production manager, in which he asked me how I had enjoyed my experience with the organization. During the conversation, I learned that he knew of the punch-out system in the plating department. What's more, he told me, he was wondering if he ought to "blow the lid off the whole mess."

Providence City Bank Case

For a number of years prior to April 1953, Mr. Andover, vice president and manager of the loans and mortgages department of the Providence City Bank, had been somewhat dissatisfied with the job performance of Mr. Freemantle, the manager of the statistics and records division of Mr. Andover's department. Mr. Freemantle was an "oldtimer" of the department who had been employed by the bank for 38 years, having started work with the company as office boy when he was 18 years of age.

Mr. Andover had had an outstanding career with the bank. A college graduate with postgraduate training in business administration, Mr. Andover had been selected for special training and special assignments in different departments of the bank prior to his appointment, after 15 years' service, to his current position. Mr. Andover had the reputation among his associates for being a very capable man, with outstanding ability for planning and for solving technical problems, as well as for his skill in organizing people to get things done.

Mr. Andover knew that Mr. Freemantle had been passed over several times by previous managers of the department when they had

This case, Providence City Bank, EA-A 202R, was prepared by Harold Craig under the direction of John D. Glover of the Harvard University Graduate School of Business Administration as a basis for classroom discussion rather than to illustrate either effective or ineffective handling of administrative situations. Copyright © 1954 by the President and Fellows of Harvard College. Used by specific permission.

been considering the selection of divisional managers for promotion to positions on the staff of the department. Mr. Andover said to the case writer that this was some indication of Mr. Freemantle's performance on the job because the usual policy of the management of the bank was to count seniority and long service as an important element in the selection of men for promotion. Mr. Andover commented on his view of Mr. Freemantle as follows:

> Freemantle knows what I think of him, because I've personally passed him over two or three times when selecting men for promotion, and twice he's come to me complaining about promotions and his salary. In my opinion he's being paid more now than I'd ever pay him if he was working for me personally. I inherited him as a manager of the division. I would never have promoted him to that job myself, but he was manager there when I was appointed manager of this department. He's a bit of a bush lawyer, too. He thinks he knows everything. If he gets an opinion from our legal department, he often says that the counsel is wrong and decides to go another way. I believe he thinks it's quite a mistake that I happen to be the manager of this department. He also thinks that Mr. Ford should not be vice president and that he himself really should have the job. But he is not a good manager. He works hard, but he keeps everything to himself and doesn't know how to hand work out. If a letter comes to his desk, whether it has anything to do with him or not, he will answer it. He doesn't seem to have any discrimination or any sense in the way he does things.
>
> I just don't seem to be able to get him to understand at all. I'm not the only one that he resents. As a matter of fact, his attitude is that he's a better man than any of the other people who are superior to him. He is such an egotist that he thinks he can do my job better than I can. I like a man to be aggressive, providing he has something to back his aggressiveness up, but when he is just aggressive and stupid I don't like it.
>
> Here's an example of some of his work: I happen to have on my desk a report that he hands in every year (shown at end of case). I've told him two or three times that I didn't want all this figure work done on these reports. I happen to have this report here at the moment because someone asked me a question about our statistics and I dug out the report just to get a couple of figures from it. If the questions had related to one of the other divisions I probably would have telephoned the manager and said I wanted a couple of figures. As this question concerned Freemantle's area, I thought I'd get out this report because it was there. Take a look at this table. He's got here figures of mortgages for twenty-one years through to 1952. What does he think

I'm interested in the figures of the last twenty-one years for? If he thinks I'm interested in how many files or mortgages his division handled in 1932, he's got another think coming.

I wouldn't be bothered reading this report. I told him that, too, and I think that this report is a bit of an improvement on the one he gave me last year because, if I remember rightly, last year's report was even thicker than this one. I can't be bothered reading through all these statistics of what has happened in the last twenty-one years. I'm normally only interested in the last year, and what's more, I know that some of the figures he's got here are wrong. He hasn't even classified things correctly. It sometimes bothers me because it must cost quite a bit to collect all these figures, and I'm interested in who does all the work that is involved, because it just seems to me to be a waste of time. This report is no use to me because it isn't what I want. You would think that when you tell a man three times that you don't want this rubbish he wouldn't send it to you, but he just doesn't take any notice. I tell him I don't want the report, and it comes in to me just the same. He just doesn't take any notice of what anyone tells him.

You know, I just can't quite understand Freemantle. I'm the youngest executive in this department, and I have come in over the top of all of them, and I think I can say I've handled myself pretty well. It's been a little difficult at times, but I've handled myself so that I don't think there's any antagonism from any of the others except this fellow, Freemantle, and he has really been a thorn in my side. For example, we have a setup here with two assistant managers of the department. All personnel matters go to Geddes and questions of methods or procedures go to Day, but it took me a long time to get into Freemantle's thick head the fact that he was not to come directly to me on such matters. I found that for quite a while he would telephone me any time he wanted to, and I spent at least a year explaining that I didn't want him to.

I'll give you another example. We have a system of merit rating for clerks which we use for salary administration. This year we tried to keep the overall percentage increase of salaries in the department to 6 percent of the payroll. We decided that a reasonable rating spread for clerks would be 5 percent in the excellent class, 25 percent in the very good, 40 percent in the medium to fair, 25 percent in the fairly good, and 5 percent poor. Theoretically, if we gave a 12 percent increase to the excellent workers, 9 percent to the good workers, and 6 percent to the people who break even, leaving 3 percent for the fair and nothing for poor workers, this would work out at 6 percent across the board. Of course, in practice we push it together a bit, and we don't normally give the excellent ones quite 12 percent or give the poor ones nothing. Anyhow, this system was set up for considering increases of clerks.

At the same time of year we review the salaries of managers, and this year I decided to give Freemantle a 6 percent increase. I've always had to battle to give him any increase of any kind in the past, because nobody else on the salary committee seems to want to support me in giving him any increase. Anyhow, I decided to give him the 6 percent, and he rang me on the phone and said, "How did you rate me?" I said, "What do you mean, rate you?" "Well, you've given me a 6 percent increase. Now, if I'm excellent, I should get a 12 percent increase and I think I'm an excellent worker." The funny part was that this rating schedule was for rating clerks, not for managers, and what annoyed me was that he should have adopted this attitude and phoned me about it. I said, "I have not considered rating you at all; I have decided that a 6 percent increase would be appropriate for you." He said, "Well, I'm not satisfied; I think I'm excellent, and I want to go and see Mr. Ford" [the executive vice president]. At this stage I was mad. I told Freemantle that if he didn't want the 6 percent I would not give him any increase. You know, I don't often do a thing like that because I think it's pretty wrong to bully people and to take advantage of your position, and I don't like to speak to people like that, but I was a bit fed up. I knew that if he'd go and see Mr. Ford, Mr. Ford wouldn't give him anything, because he was inclined to disagree with my suggestion of 6 percent. As it was, I was treating Freemantle very well, and that's what made me mad.

The case writer was interested in Mr. Andover's remarks regarding Mr. Freemantle. A number of other people had commented on Mr. Freemantle at different times during the period the case writer was engaged in studying the company. For example, Mr. Day, the assistant manager of the department in charge of methods and procedures throughout the department, commented as follows:

There is only one divisional manager we have about whom I'm at all concerned. That is Freemantle. I think we've got certain responsibilities to Freemantle but I don't think we want to give him any more responsibility. I remember there was an occasion when we could have eliminated Freemantle's job by incorporating the work that's done in his division with work in other divisions. I remember that Mr. Ford said that we had a responsibility to the man because he had been a divisional manager for a number of years at that time, and we didn't quite know what to do with him if we didn't leave him in charge of the statistics and records division. If we put him on the staff, that would have meant a promotion and no one wanted to promote him, and if we eliminated his division, as was proposed at that time, we wouldn't know what job to give him. As Mr. Ford said, "The company has the responsibility to people who have served the company over a period of years." So we decided to leave his job as it was. It meant rearranging our other plans, because in some ways we felt that maintaining Freemantle's division would make for less efficient organization than incorporation of the work of that division with other divisions.

In April 1953, Mr. Andover had occasion to be particularly displeased with Mr. Freemantle on another matter. One day Mr. Andover heard that Mr. Freemantle had sent some statistics outside the loans and mortgages department. The first thing Mr. Andover heard of the statistics was a question which arose regarding the validity of the figures. Mr. Andover checked and found that the figures were incorrect; so he telephoned Mr. Freemantle and said:

Andover: What did you send out these figures on mortgages for? Those figures are wrong, and I don't want you sending out figures outside this department without my approval. I wouldn't mind so much if the figures were correct, but these figures are wrong.

Freemantle: They're not wrong, they're right. I checked them with the accounting department, and they say that they're right.

Andover: They're wrong and I'll prove it to you. You come up to my office and I'll show you.

When Mr. Freemantle came to Mr. Andover's office, Mr. Andover showed him where the figures were incorrect and told Mr. Freemantle to take them away to correct them and bring them back to him. Mr. Freemantle took the figures away. He soon came back, looking very annoyed. With tears welling in his eyes, Mr. Freemantle threw the file of figures on Mr. Andover's desk and said:

Freemantle: I don't know why I should have to put up with this sort of thing from a whippersnapper like you. After all the years that I've worked for this company and the $5000 they owe me for overtime work that I've never claimed for, here I have to put up with this sort of thing from a whippersnapper like you. I ought to punch you in the nose.

Freemantle's Statistical Report to Andover

Attached is a statement covering operations [1] of the Statistics and Records Division as of December 31, 1952.

Volumewise, the 1952 transactions did not vary much from those of the previous year. Many minor decreases occurred in differ-

---

1. The statement of operations consisted of 10 pages of detailed figures which supported the aggregate figures given in this memorandum.

ent phases of records in 1952, as may be noted from pages one and three; but most of the trends in the last quarter of 1952 were heading upward. One of the items which, sooner or later, will have a noticeable effect on the other phases of records work is the increasing number of forms received and processed. Against 3,897 forms received in 1951, 4,957 were received in 1952, an increase of 27.2 percent.

During the past 21 years 43,180 records of consumer credit applications and 2,356 agreements covering all other types of loans (45,536 in all) have been carried out in full.

Twelve clerks resigned in 1952 from our Filing Section and only three have been replaced. This situation has necessitated a rearrangement of our files. Prior to September 1952, there were 20 such file cabinets in use, maintained by 10 file clerks—two apiece. Now, mainly because of the drop in personnel, seven clerks maintain 21 cabinets, or three apiece.

This reduction in file clerks has hampered somewhat the smooth, speedy flow of prior-to-issue applications which are checked daily against our rejection file, now made up of 23 cabinets. At the end of 1951, there were 21 clerks trained on that file. Gradually, that number dwindled to 10, but there has been little delay in rushing through the work. In time, we hope to build up the unit again so that the applications received every week may be checked against this file with the greatest possible dispatch.

L. FREEMANTLE
Statistics and Records Division

Modern Decorators Case

Mr. George R. Neal, owner and operator of Modern Decorators, was born in 1902. His father was a cattle rancher and law enforcement officer. Mr. Neal was the oldest of five children and quite often reminisces about the hardships of his childhood. Mr. Neal feels that the hardships and strict discipline of his youth were excellent training for overcoming difficulties in his adult life. In 1920 Mr. Neal entered a large midwestern university on an athletic scholarship. He was an outstanding athlete for two years but withdrew in the middle of his junior year to marry a childhood sweetheart. Of his college education Mr. Neal today says, "The only darn thing I learned was how to put my elbow in somebody's eye without the referee seeing it."

After his withdrawal from college Mr. Neal returned to his home state and became an automobile salesman. In 1926, Mr. Neal, with his wife and two children, moved to the Pacific Coast where he became a salesman and later district manager for a large radio and record company. When the company eliminated all sales branches on the Pacific Coast in 1932, Mr. Neal returned to his home state and entered the real estate and insurance business, and after several years began building houses for sale. This business was only moderately successful but Mr. Neal remained in it until the latter part of 1939. In 1939 Mrs. Neal divorced her husband on the grounds of mental cruelty. Mrs. Neal was awarded full custody of both children.

In January, 1940, Mr. Neal entered the Navy as a chief warrant officer. He was assigned to a battleship and was aboard that ship when it was bombed at Pearl Harbor. Mr. Neal was retired from the Navy in December, 1943, with the rank of lieutenant commander. He was retired rather than placed in the reserve because at that time it appeared that injuries received at Pearl Harbor would seriously handicap him the rest of his life. However, within a year Mr. Neal regained his health, at which time he asked for and received a transfer to an inactive reserve status.

During his tour of duty with the Navy, Mr. Neal had decided to enter the paint-contracting business in his present location. He picked the location because of the postwar growth potential and the high percentage of fine homes in the area. He decided on paint contracting because from his previous experience he felt he could do well in the building trades, and he felt that of all the building trades, painting had the lowest percentage of good businessmen. Moreover, Mr. Neal painted watercolors as a hobby and thought his ability to work with colors would give him a real competitive advantage.

From 1944 to the spring of 1947 Mr. Neal maintained a crew of four to six men. Practically all of his work was redecorating in expensive homes. Mr. Neal spent at least 60 percent of his time on the job and closely supervised all operations. During this time he built a reputation as a good businessman and an excellent decorator. During this period Mr. Neal discovered that painters, as a class, had the reputation of being heavy drinkers. In order to minimize the effects of this reputation on his operations, Mr. Neal instituted a strict "no drinking on the job" rule. Whenever a man was hired it was carefully explained to him that the breaking of this rule would result in instant dismissal regardless of whether the man had drunk one beer with his lunch or had drunk a quart of whiskey while working. Mr. Neal was always careful to point out that he had no objection to drinking moderately while not on the job. He openly told the worker that there was always liquor in the Neal household. In his first three and one half years of operation, Mr. Neal had only one occasion to enforce this rule.

In the spring of 1947, Mr. Neal began work on two separate projects of new middle-class homes. The new contracts necessitated a greatly expanded crew and a new foreman. Mr. Neal decided to keep his present crew intact and leave them on the fairly steady flow of redecorating work. The men hired for the new work were hired partly on their ability to work fast, while with the old crew speed was seldom a factor. Mr. Neal hired 12 new men in April of 1947 and estimated that within two years he would be employing at least 50 men. Because of the large volume of business he anticipated, Mr. Neal knew he would be unable to spend much time on the job in the future. Therefore he was prepared to pay a foreman a relatively large salary and guarantee him year-round employment. Mr. Neal thought a good foreman should have the following qualifications:

1. Be able to get maximum output from workers without creating unrest.
2. Be able to lay out work.
3. Be able to spot bottlenecks before they occur.
4. Be able to accurately estimate material and labor needs.
5. Be able to mix colors quickly and accurately.

Until such a man could be found, Mr. Neal intended to set up his crew with one leadman to each five journeymen. The leadman would be a working supervisor who spent two-thirds of his time painting. The leadmen were to be paid $8 per week over union scale.

The company operated until March of 1948 without a foreman. At this time Mr. Neal was employing 40 men and expected the number to reach 65 by July. Mr. Neal was spending 75 to 80 hours a week on company business and felt that he could not keep up the pace. So, with some misgivings, Mr. Neal gave the foreman's job to Mr. Hansen. Mr. Hansen had been hired in 1944 and had been leadman on the redecorating crew for a year. Mr. Hansen was 59 years old and an excellent workman. On taking the job, Mr. Hansen said that he knew he couldn't handle the color mixing but was quite confident he could meet the other qualifications for foreman.

At the end of six months Mr. Neal found that labor costs, as a percentage of gross sales, had increased 4 percent. He thought this was mostly due to Hansen's methods of dealing with the men, which consisted of steadily warning that any slacker would be immediately fired. Mr. Neal did not approve of these methods but was unable to suggest any alternative method that Mr. Hansen would use. In December of 1948 Mr. Hansen asked if he could have back his old job as leadman on the redecorating crew. He said that his health was being ruined by the constant pressure to get work out of men who just wouldn't work. Since Mr. Hansen's old job on the redecorating crew had never been filled, Mr. Neal complied with the request.

The following week Mr. Neal advertised in local papers for a foreman. He received many replies, but only six which he felt warranted personal interviews. Of the six men interviewed he felt only one, Ralph Hawkins, showed promise of meeting his standards for a foreman.

Mr. Hawkins had a pleasant personality and talked intelligently on several subjects. He seemed to have an exceptional knowledge of paint contracting and the problems involved. From the interview and from later inquiries Mr. Neal received the following information on Mr. Hawkins's personal history:

1916–33: Born in 1916 to a very well-to-do family, Hawkins attended private schools until 1933, when his father's business went bankrupt.

1933–36: Apprenticed as a painter and began boxing as a hobby.

1936–39: Became a professional boxer and in 1939 was considered a leading challenger for the world's championship.

1939–43: In 1939 enlisted in the Canadian army. In 1942 he was seriously wounded. He was discharged in 1943 and was married shortly after his discharge. He was unable to continue his boxing career because of the serious leg wounds he had received.

1943–48: In late 1943, Mr. Hawkins moved to his present location and went to work as a painter in a defense plant. In five months Mr. Hawkins became foreman of the paint crew, a job he held until late 1945. In January of 1946 he entered the paint contracting business. He remained in this business until November of 1948.

In his interview, Mr. Hawkins said he went out of business mainly because he could not cope with the financial problems that arose. Mr. Hawkins gave Mr. Neal a list of 25 of his customers and six of his suppliers. Mr. Neal called all the suppliers and five of the customers, and every one gave Mr. Hawkins the highest recommendations.

Mr. Hawkins was hired at a salary of $450 per month with the promise of a $100 per month raise if operations were running smoothly at the end of six months. Mr. Hawkins was to be given full authority and responsibility for operations on the different jobs. His job would include hiring, and, when necessary, firing. Mr. Neal particularly stressed to Mr. Hawkins that he wanted to maintain good labor relations, both with the individual workers and with the union. Mr. Hawkins was in full agreement on this objective and also agreed with Mr. Neal's "no drinking" rule.

At the end of 12 weeks, Mr. Neal was more than satisfied with his new foreman. His percentage of labor cost had been substantially reduced and the crew seemed very pleased with the changes Mr. Hawkins had instituted. These changes were: work crew assignments were permanent; each man was issued a complete set of brushes, for which he was responsible; and job sheets were worked out so that every man could be told at the beginning of the day about what he was expected to do for the day. These daily assignments were not inflexible but acted as guides. Any man who consistently did more than his daily assignments was paid at a rate above union scale but Mr. Hawkins stressed to the leadmen that no man was to be "bawled out" for not making a daily assignment. If a man failed to make his assignment consistently, the leadman was to call in Mr. Hawkins, who talked to the man and usually transferred the man to another crew. Mr. Hawkins often stated that any man who was hired was capable of making any daily assignment. Mr. Hawkins felt that if a man fell short of his goal quite often it was the fault of either the leadman or Mr. Hawkins. Mr. Hawkins appeared to have the complete confidence of all the leadmen. As a result of this excellent record, Mr. Neal raised Mr. Hawkins's salary to $600 per month.

At this time Mr. Neal was able to devote almost full time to the administrative aspects of the business and, as a result, had contracts for about seven months in the future that would keep his present crew busy.

In the summer of 1949, the company was engaged in many different activities. About 45 of the men employed were working on new construction. This new construction consisted of three separate projects: two near the business address of the company and one very large project 25 miles away. Ten men were kept busy on a maintenance contract Mr. Neal had with an oil company. Ten men were engaged in redecorating a large apartment building, and six men were in the original redecorating crew. Because of the widespread activities, a great deal of Mr. Hawkins's time was taken up in traveling from job to job. Mr. Neal and Mr. Hawkins talked about this loss of operating efficiency and decided that Mr. Hawkins should pick and train a man to take care of all materials ordering and scheduling on the different jobs. In June, Hawkins selected Bob Martin, a young leadman, for this job.

The last week in July the company was starting work on a new project. Mr. Neal, Mr. Hawkins, and Mr. Martin had visited the project the previous week. Mr. Hawkins and Mr. Martin worked out a materials sheet, and Mr. Neal and Mr. Hawkins worked out the job sheets. On the Monday morning that work was to begin on the project, Mr. Neal had an appointment to go over blueprints on a new job and could not be at the new project. At 9:15 Mr. Neal was called out of the conference to answer a phone call. He was being called by Bob Martin and the following conversation took place.

Neal: Hello.

Martin: Hello, Mr. Neal? This is Bob Martin. I'm out on the new job and things are really messed up. Ralph is all fouled up some place and there are five crews wandering around here drawing pay.

Neal: What do you mean Ralph's fouled up? Where is he?

Martin: Oh, I don't know, but he isn't here.

Neal: Well, call the office and try to get Hansen out there. You and Hansen work it out and I'll be there at noon.

Mr. Neal arrived at the project at noon and found that Martin and Hansen had everyone busy. Mr. Neal then went to the office and called the Hawkins's home. Mrs. Hawkins answered the phone and said that Mr. Hawkins had been called out of town late the night before by his mother's sudden illness. Mrs. Hawkins said that her husband had left instructions to call Mr. Neal's home early Monday morning but that she had forgotten to make the call. Mr. Hawkins returned to work the following morning and confirmed his wife's story.

The following week a painter was fired for drinking on the job. Mr. Hawkins saw the man take a drink from a pint whiskey bottle and return the bottle to his brush box. Mr. Hawkins told the man to go to the office and pick up his check. Mr. Hawkins then called the office and explained the situation to Mr. Neal. When the discharged painter, Mr. Smith, arrived at the office, the following conversation took place between Mr. Neal and Mr. Smith.

Neal: Well, Smith, here's your check. I'm very sorry I have to let you go, but this rule was explained to you.

Smith: That's right, but here's something that hasn't been explained to me. How come I get canned for taking one drink when Hawkins can take off a whole day just to round out a three-day drunk?

Neal: I don't have any idea what you're talking about. If you mean that day Ralph missed last week, I'm sure you're wrong.

Smith: Well, I know a couple of guys who aren't so sure. They're sure he was out in Riverdale [a nearby small town] on a binge.

Neal: I would certainly be interested in hearing these two men tell me that in Ralph's presence. Would you care to give me their names?

Smith: "Oh, the hell with it—you wouldn't believe it anyway.

With the last remark, Mr. Smith picked up his check and left. Mr. Neal considered talking to Mr. Hawkins about the above conversation but decided against it.

Work progressed smoothly until the third week in September. During this week three projects were scheduled for completion and two more were to be started. This would call for overtime work on the part of Mr. Neal, Mr. Hawkins, and Mr. Martin. On Monday morning of this week Mrs. Hawkins called Mr. Neal and said her husband was ill, but would be at work on Tuesday if he was better. Mr. Hawkins did come to work on Tuesday and averaged 14 hours a day on the job for the rest of the week. On Friday evening of that week Mr. Neal attended the local chamber of commerce meeting, where the following conversation took place between Mr. Neal and Mr. Kenny, a local electrical contractor.

Kenny: Say, George, do you always give your boys Monday off?

Neal: What's the gag, Ken?

Kenny: No gag at all; I saw your foreman out in Riverdale Monday, so figured maybe you closed down for a day.

Neal: You saw Ralph in Riverdale? What was he doing?

Kenny: Well George, I don't want to put the guy on the spot but I guess you should know. He was in that place called the Royal Hotel. He was drunk as could be and all tangled up with one of those girls that hang around there.

Neal: You're sure it was Ralph?

Kenny: No doubt about it.

For the rest of the weekend Mr. Neal wondered whether or not he should confront Mr. Hawkins with the facts he now had. He decided against saying anything, however, mainly because of Hawkins's excellent record.

Three weeks later, on Saturday night, Mr. Neal saw Mr. Hawkins in a tavern near the theater Mr. Neal had just left. Mr. Hawkins was in the company of two of the leadmen. All three of them were obviously quite drunk.

The following Monday Mr. Neal called Mr. Hawkins into the office and the following conversation took place:

Neal: Ralph, you know that what you do off the job is your business, but just as a friend I'd like to say that getting drunk with your leadmen isn't a very smart move.

Hawkins: You're right of course. I really fouled up Saturday night; I guess that's what you mean, isn't it?

Neal: Yes, that is it. I'm not snooping, I just happened to see you.

Hawkins: Well I know you'd never stoop to spying on anyone. [Pause.] I guess I might as well tell you about that day I took off a few weeks ago. I wasn't sick, I was just full of whiskey. As a matter of fact that's what happened in July when I messed up on the opening of Clayton's project.

Neal: I'd heard that was the case, Ralph, but I'm certainly glad to hear you tell me yourself.

Hawkins: I don't know, George, maybe I just can't handle this job.

Neal: Of course you can handle this job. Ralph, I'll be frank with you. I don't think I could find a man to replace you if I looked for a year. You're worth a lot more than I'm paying you, but I intend to make that up at Christmas time.

Hawkins: That's sure nice to hear, George.

Neal: Well it's the truth. Look, Ralph, we'll just forget this other business. I know you're working harder than a man should. We'll work out a two-week vacation for you this winter and next year Martin will be able to take some of the load off you.

Hawkins: I'm sure glad we had this talk, George. I feel a lot better, and I can promise you I won't miss any more work unless I have to.

During the remaining fall months, work progressed smoothly. At Christmas time Mr. Hawkins was given two weeks' vacation and a substantial bonus.

During January and February Mr. Hawkins and Mr. Neal began training four of the most promising leadmen for project foremen. When the new construction began in the spring, the company employed 75 journeymen, who reported to ten leadmen. The ten leadmen reported to the four project foremen, who in turn reported to Mr. Hawkins. Mr. Martin worked with Mr. Hawkins on material needs and Mr. Neal seldom took an active part in the direction of actual operations. This organization had more supervisory personnel than most painting companies of the same size; however, the profit margin for this company was 5 percent below the industry average and Mr. Neal was usually able to underbid his competitors. Mr. Neal felt that a major share of his success was due to Mr. Hawkins's ability to organize the work properly and to see that it was carried out. Mr. Neal was particularly pleased with the fact that Mr. Hawkins was very well liked by all the men and had never been heard to raise his voice or lose his temper on the job.

By the late spring of 1950 the company employed 15 additional men. While the new project foremen were doing much of the work Mr. Hawkins had done the year before, he still had to put in 50 to 55 hours a week on the job. In June of 1950, Mr. Hawkins's salary was raised to $800 per month.

Beginning with the third Monday in July, Mr. Hawkins missed three consecutive Mondays at work. On each occasion his wife called the office and left word that Mr. Hawkins was sick. On the Tuesday following the third Monday Mr. Hawkins was absent, Mr. Neal called him into the office and the following conversation took place:

Neal: Ralph, I'd like to get one thing straight. If you've really been sick the past three Mondays, there's no need for us to talk about it, and I owe you an apology. If you haven't been sick, I think we'd better talk about what's to be done about the situation.

Hawkins: Well, I thought Irene called in and told you I was sick.

Neal: That's right, Ralph; if you want to stand on that I'll accept it. [Pause.]

Hawkins: Well, I guess there's no use kidding myself; you know as well as I do what happened to me. [Pause.] This is the best job I've ever had, and you're a great man to work for.

Neal: Now here's the way I feel about it, Ralph. I've told you before that I'd have a tough time replacing you, but if I never know when you're going to show up I might as well not have a foreman.

Hawkins: I guess I just get feeling sorry for myself. [Very long pause.]

Neal: I guess we all do sometimes. If you think you need more help on the job, we can arrange that.

Hawkins: Oh, I can handle that all right.

Neal: If you're having trouble someplace else, I'd be glad to help you.

Hawkins: No, it's just me; everything's o.k.

Neal: Well, how about it then, do you think you'll lose any more time?

Hawkins: No, I'm sure I won't.

Neal: I sure hope you don't, Ralph; I don't even like to think about the alternative.

In discussing this interview later, Mr. Neal said he ended it with the implied threat of discharge, hoping that this would stop Mr. Hawkins from drinking on weekends.

In the second week in October Mr. Hawkins missed Monday, Tuesday, and Wednesday. On Monday evening Mr. Hawkins called and said he had developed a light case of chickenpox. When Mr. Hawkins returned to work Thursday, he showed no signs of the disease. Mr. Neal was told later that week by a doctor that the skin eruptions caused by chickenpox *never* disappear in less than eight days.

The first week in December, Mr. Neal made an unscheduled trip to one of the projects to see the general contractor. The first man he met on the job was Mr. Hawkins, who was quite drunk. Mr. Neal told him to get in his car and he drove him home. No conversation took place during the ride. When Mr. Hawkins got out of the car at his home, Mr. Neal said, "If you're sober tomorrow I'd like to see you at ten o'clock in the office."

The following conversation took place the next morning in the office:

Neal: Well, that was pretty bad yesterday, Ralph. How in hell can we expect the men to stick to a rule the foreman breaks?

Hawkins: We can't.

Neal: My God, Ralph, can't you see what you're doing? You're drinking yourself out of a good job. Now we'll show a fine profit this year and the future looks great. With your bonus this year, your income will be well into five figures. Now you aren't stupid enough to throw that away for no good reason. What's behind these sprees, Ralph?

Hawkins: I don't know, George, I guess it's just me.

Neal: Well, that's hard to believe, Ralph. I don't think you're the type of man that lets a bottle of booze beat him. [Long pause.] Ralph, I'd like you to take the rest of the week off. Come in and see me Saturday and we'll decide then what's to be done.

Hawkins: Okay, George; you're really being swell about this.

Chapter Seven

Implementation

The final step in the decision process is implementation of the selected solution. In this chapter we discuss its importance as a unique decision step, and the major considerations or guidelines by which it may be continuously assessed. Finally, we discuss the concept of problem prevention (as contrasted with problem solving) as one aspect of effective decision making.

The Importance of Considering Implementation as a Separate Decision Step

In many technical decision situations it is not necessary to give special consideration to implementation; once a solution has been decided upon, implementation may be a simple and obvious matter of course. For example, if a decision has been made for new landscaping, air conditioning, or a new accounting system, a manager may implement the decision simply by having someone install it. However, in decision making related to behavioral problems, and indeed for most technical problems, implementation may be a crucial factor in decision effectiveness.

The *choice* of a solution may not be the end of a problem. It often happens that the more difficult and crucial step in the management process, at least in situations where people are involved, is *effecting* this solution. If, for example, we decide to change a malfunctioning work group by rearranging work assignments, or by changing

314

its work standards, or by hiring or fire a group member, the success of the decision may well hinge on the plan for implementation and how skillfully it is carried out. Even the success of a purely technical decision, such as installing new machinery or adjusting a lighting system,[1] may depend on the strategic psychological adjustments made during the process of implementation. In short, a decision is worthless unless it can be implemented in the organizational situation.

The ultimate test of the soundness of all decisions involving human factors is their realization in changed behavior. No solution is so astute or mathematically precise that it cannot be undermined by inept motivation of employee response. In all human situations, therefore, the question of what solution to choose must always be followed by another question, *How?* That is, by what *method* is the solution to be brought about? To omit this question from a concept of decision making is to divorce the decision process from the practical realities of the dynamic social system of the organization.

Some Basic Considerations for Sound Implementation

In its broadest sense, good implementation is good management. This chapter is not an attempt to catalog good management principles, but it does offer some basic guidelines to help avoid common pitfalls in planning and managing the implementation of a solution. (In keeping with the overall purpose of the book, these guidelines deal with the social or human aspects of implementation, rather than with the technical.)

The general guidelines offered here are factors which should be considered throughout the implementation process, until a solution is finally achieved. They apply to the assessment of implementation, whether assessment takes a few minutes while the manager is preparing for a meeting, or whether it involves elaborate procedures to achieve major organizational change over a period of years. These guidelines include considerations of (1) assessment of solution workability, (2) the specification of each step in motivating and activating behavior, (3) provision for feedback as an integral part of the implementation plan and procedure, (4) the planning and carrying out of leadership functions.

Assessment of Workability

Before hastily initiating implementation to get a problem out of the way, the manager should assess the chosen solution in terms of its potential workability. Not every "solution" can be implemented,

---

1. The lighting studies in Western Electric's Hawthorne plant are credited with arousing interest in human reactions to the implementation process; see Roethlisberger and Dickson (1947).

although if the solution has been properly chosen in the first place, workability has already been taken into consideration. (Specifically, if, as was discussed in Chapter 6, the solution was chosen on the basis of acceptability as well as quality, and if it was designed in terms of a realistic forecast of behavioral responses, there is a sound basis for proceeding with implementation plans.) However, if the manager did not participate in the solution choice, the question of workability should be explicitly raised before he attempts to go ahead. Better early confrontation on this point, than failure after a costly attempt.

The Slade Case is a clear example of a situation in which the workability of any proposed solution should be assessed before its implementation. If Porter, the production manager, makes a thorough diagnosis of the situation, he will be aware of the importance to the plating-room unit of the norms and values of the Sarto group. In addition, if he has some understanding of group processes in general, he will recognize that his ability to accomplish any change must take into account the Sarto group's key position in the plating room. In short, he will be well aware that the capacity of any solution to be implemented depends on its treatment of group norms. On the other hand, if Porter plunges into an implementation process without assessment of the workability of his plan, his impulse "to blow the lid off" the plating room is likely to backfire.

Motivating and Activating Each Change in Behavior

The implementation plan should specify how each step of behavioral change is to be motivated and activated. This point is first considered when a solution is chosen; in implementation, it takes the form of preparing plans. If these plans are to be realistic, they must *specify* in concrete terms how behavioral change is to be brought about.

The first step in implementation planning, whether implementation time is a matter of minutes or months, *must begin with the existing situation*. This point is stressed because of the strong tendency in decision making to assume that the people who are involved in a problem situation can, as it were, erase the past and start from scratch. In real situations, unfortunately, people do not behave that way. It is impossible for them to ignore their immediate social situation, to forget the past, and to transform relationships instantly.

In the Slade case, Porter must first face the existing conditions, certain norms of behavior exist, that an incentive sysem is implicit in what is happening, that the environmental conditions are what they are, and that he himself is furious. Merely deciding to "change things" will not suffice. Because any change will have to begin with the situation in the plating room, Porter has no choice but to base his thinking and remedial planning on that situation. It is useless to begin implementation by attempting to carry out a fantasy of the situation as it ought to be.

All implementation planning, therefore, should begin with explicit, detailed answers to these questions: Where are we now in relation to the problem? What is the situation in which we now find ourselves? How will the members of the work group react to the proposed changes? What will motivate and activate each desired behavioral change from this point to the desired goal?

No step in the implementation plan should assume abrupt changes in behavior. Rather, the steps should develop a strategy which clearly shows what motivates and activates behavior from point A to point B, from point B to point C, and so on, until the behavioral goal is reached. Finally, implementation plans should never assume changes in attitude or behavior for which a motivating force neither exists nor has been provided.

Provision for Feedback

Each step of an implementation plan should be performed on the basis of a continuing assessment of feedback or responses from the preceding step. The feedback from step A should be assessed before proceeding to step B, and so on. Thus every good plan has built-in feedback flexibility.

The importance of feedback is perhaps best illustrated by instances that reveal what can happen when feedback is ignored. A large electronics company decided to change the name of one of its subsidiaries to that of the parent company—shortly after it had replaced the subsidiary's popular general manager with a man from the home office. Although the replaced manager became a corporation director, the move was abrupt and unexplained. Announcement of the name change was equally abrupt. It was made in a full-page advertisement in a trade newspaper, which was the first indication of the name change for the employees of the subsidiary company.

Because the parent company did not provide for feedback on these changes, it was unaware of the fact that, for many employees, the old name carried status not associated with the parent-company name. In fact, some employees had chosen to work for the subsidiary rather than other divisions of the parent company at the time they were recruited, because they preferred to be identified with its respected name.

Feedback of employee reaction to the changes did not reach the parent company until a state of open conflict had developed between the new manager and the employees, cooperation and productivity had fallen to an all-time low, and several valued employees had quit their jobs. The employees' anger at the impersonal announcement of the name change and the sudden change of general managers had precipitated a series of resistant attitudes to all subsequent executive acts, which culminated in the crisis. Although more or less aware of an atmosphere of unrest, the new manager had uncritically appraised the feedback that had come to him and had continued "implementation" by merely issuing orders.

Resistance to what was perceived as a takeover increased to the point that the manager's ability to implement further organizational changes was critically impaired. Ultimately, the parent company had no alternative but to undertake another, costly replacement of the general manager and a much more elaborate problem-solving procedure than would have been necessary if provisions for feedback had been built into the original decision processes. The assumption that a decision to make a change is tantamount to its success is not viable where human behavior is concerned; in such instances, plans for feedback are a critical part of the overall implementation plan.

As feedback comes in, its relevance to each of the decision steps must be assessed (1) to determine changes in disequilibria, (2) to appraise the diagnosis in terms of new information, (3) to determine whether the problem requires redefinition or whether an entirely new problem may have arisen, (4) to monitor the effectiveness of the chosen solution, and (5) to monitor the effectiveness of the method of implementation.

It is in the process of assessing feedback that a decision maker becomes fully aware of the usefulness of having made explicit diagnoses, explicit problem statements, and explicit solution plans. If these steps have not been explicit, there is little clear basis for the assessment of feedback. The meaning of incoming information can be clear-cut only if its context has been structured in a clear-cut way.

As a manager continues to assess feedback, it is important that he recognize the point at which he faces a distinct new problem. New stimuli—even the particular "solution" being implemented—may create a new and different problem. If the new problem is recognized, the decision-making process begins anew, focusing on the new disequilibrium, a fresh diagnosis, a new problem statement, and so on.

One pitfall in decision making is the tendency to assess feedback in terms of a previously defined problem; that is, to define all new problems in terms of old problems. Managers should be aware of the probability that every implementation step may in some way alter a problem situation. It is therefore vital that the decision maker, as he assesses feedback, continually distinguish between his original definition of a problem and the existing problem situation.

Planning and Carrying Out Leadership Functions

While it may be feasible to take for granted the exercise of leadership in certain limited technical decisions—for example, with respect to using wood or brick in building a partition—in situations that involve behavioral problems, managerial leadership may largely determine the successful implementation of a decision. Such leadership functions include motivating, activating, coordinating, supervising, and selectively reinforcing employes' action. Active, participative leadership is particularly necessary when marked changes in attitudes or relationships among people are required. In such cases, "implementation" that consists merely of making announcements and issuing orders is likely to fail.

Part of a manager's effect on a situation derives not only from his leadership skills but from his very role as leader, which subordinates often view as "larger than life." In their eyes a manager is, in a very real sense, an "authority figure" or "father figure." Some company executives are seen as benevolent grandfathers, whom everyone tries to please; some as top sergeants, whom everyone tries to outwit; some as absentee, impersonal executives, the center of rumors and fears; and so on. Thus the leadership role can be a very important variable in the implementation of a plan—in either a negative or a positive sense. Each style of leadership influences the style of implementation.

One consequence of a manager's leadership style is the particular "tone" or emotional atmosphere it creates. A manager's style is created by his attitudes toward himself, his attitudes toward other people in the organization, and his attitudes toward the subject at issue. This cluster of attitudes tends to call forth reciprocal attitudes in those around him. Poor attitudes toward his own role, toward other people, or toward the problem under discussion can elicit poor attitudes in response.

For example, one executive was unconsciously secretive about the total picture of company operations when he was with his division managers. The managers developed the uneasy suspicion that something in the hidden picture of the company must be disadvantageous to them personally. Also, because they were insulted by the executives' lack of trust in them, they developed subtly competitive rather than cooperative attitudes toward him.

Another executive, who was genuinely interested in new ideas, unconsciously frowned at each new idea presented to him and immediately bombarded it with analytical, scrutinizing questions, responses that his subordinates interpreted as hostile. Gradually, as he came to recognize that no new ideas were being presented to him, he learned to give new ideas strong positive reinforcement before sub-jecting them to analysis, and to end discussions with further positive reinforcement. In the two foregoing instances the managerial "tone" affected employee behavior.

It is particularly important that the manager does not impute hostile or malicious motives to others in advance of valid feedback, and thereby elicit hostility. Imputing any attitude to others tends to elicit the very attitude imputed. For example, in a particular office, many beginning managers, because of their own insecurity in giving orders for the first time, imputed hostility to a secretary who was merely impersonal. She tended to give them hostility in return. On the other hand, secure managers, who did not impute hostility to her and therefore approached her openly and in good humor, received her ready cooperation.

To employees, the tone created by the manager's leadership style colors all his attempts at implementing decisions. However, a manag-er's tone cannot be transformed overnight in an attempt to manipu-late behavior. For example, a manager who habitually approaches his subordinates in an autocratic, impersonal manner will lack credibility if he suddenly begins to employ a folksy, personal manner in an attempt to maneuver a particular change. A "tone" conducive to effective leadership must of necessity be developed over time. Con-sider the following instance:

> The management of the general manufacturing division in my company has developed a reputation for being inconsiderate and generally not telling the truth. They are working hard to overcome this reputation, but it is very difficult. Any benefits or genuine interest shown by the company are suspected of involv-ing ulterior motives. Because of this, the stock purchase plan developed to provide employee security has had little success among hourly workers. The plan calls for matching company payments on stock purchase and is a definite benefit to the employee. However, participation in the manufacturing division is less than 5 percent. The hourly workers do not believe the company would give them something for nothing.

Because the tone of this organization created a "credibility gap," its attempts to implement a program actually designed to benefit work-ers were largely negated.

The importance of managerial tone in implementation is one more indication of the need for self-awareness on the part of the manager. It is hardly possible for a manager to develop a positive atmosphere or tone, which is an outgrowth of his attitudes, without first being aware of his attitudes. This is one of the reasons why management-development programs should include experiences that build self-awareness and skill in leadership functions, as well as inculcating knowledge from the behavioral and managerial sciences.

Preventive Decision Making

Preventive problem solving is best discussed in conjunction with implementation because it is when the manager attempts to implement solutions to difficult problems that he becomes most keenly aware of the importance of prevention. At that point, whatever he has or has not done to forestall problems directly affects the resources at his disposal. In other words, implementation is a test of preventive decision making.

Preventive decision making is the constructive process of building good relationships among members of the social system of an organization. This entails the creation of an atmosphere in which the work force can relieve its tensions, find answers to its questions, receive the emotional support it needs, and freely communicate about problems as they arise. The more that a work force is able to do these things, the greater the likelihood that a manager can avoid the problem situations that are the most difficult to solve.

In preventive decision making, a manager's efforts at building good relationships should include building positive support for himself. The building of such support has been aptly compared to building a bank account: a manager builds up "funds" in the management-employee relationship that he can draw upon when he needs them.[2] If, over time, his "deposits" to this relationship have accumulated a balance in his favor, he can expect cooperation in implementing quality decisions, which otherwise might be resisted. On the other hand, if he has not built up a leadership "bank account" within his organization, he has no capital on which to draw when he needs organizational support in implementing a difficult solution. Furthermore, if the relationship between a manager and his subordinates has been psychologically "overdrawn" for an extended period, an ordinary problem can precipitate a crisis.

An example of this "bank account" concept can be seen in the electronics company subsidiary case discussed earlier in this chapter. The former general manager of the subsidiary had built such reserves of good will that the employees anticipated problems and discussed them freely. When the parent company removed him and changed the name of the subsidiary, however, such a hostile environment began to build up around his replacement that the new manager found himself with no "bank account" in the organization; he was "overdrawn" before he started. Resistance to his directives reached

---

2. I am indebted to Professor Robert H. Guest for this concept.

the point that he was unable to implement effectively even the smallest organizational changes, and he had to be replaced.

A program of prevention not only facilitates implementation but every other step of decision making as well. When the relationships within an organization are positive and communication is good, it is relatively easy for the manager to identify a disequilibrium at an early stage, when it is most easily corrected. (It is deep-felt frustrations, which fester in a hostile environment, that are most difficult to uncover.) Diagnosis is also facilitated because the causes behind problems are more willingly exposed in a positive atmosphere. (In an environment that is perceived as hostile, on the other hand, workers are reluctant to reveal the underlying reasons for difficulties.) Therefore, because a better diagnosis is possible, a more complete and accurate definition of a problem is possible and, in turn, a more appropriate solution may be developed. Furthermore, managers have a greater choice of alternative solutions because they can count on a greater degree of cooperation from their work force.

Thus, although discussions of decision making generally presume that the process begins with a problem, it is a fitting culmination for our discussion to emphasize the fact that decision making need not—and should not—begin with problems and thus be restricted to "firefighting." There will be fewer fires to put out if decision making is conceived as a process of creating optimal organizational conditions rather than as a process of merely combatting problems as they erupt. Obviously, the best way of "solving" a problem is to prevent its occurrence. It is difficult, of course, to anticipate and avoid all problems. Nevertheless, the overall relationship that develops between a manager and his work groups will, to a large extent, determine the nature and number of problems that occur.

Summary

The final step in the decision-making process—the implementation of a chosen solution—is a step of significantly greater importance in the realm of problem solving related to behavior than in the technical realm. Man, as the vehicle through which decisions are implemented, reacts not only to the quality of the decision, but to the total sociotechnical environment associated with the decision. He cannot be manipulated in the same sense that other resources can be. Therefore, the manager's job is not limited to the exercise of knowledge and skill in choosing desirable solutions; it also includes the knowledge and skill required to transform those solutions into the dynamics of behavior in a particular organizational social system.

In the process of implementation, the manager will be aided by careful consideration of several guidelines appropriate to the process: (1) the assessment of solution workability; (2) the specification of each step in motivating and activating behavior; (3) provision for feedback as an integral part of implementation; and (4) the planning and carrying out of leadership functions.

The best groundwork for good implementation, however, is preventive decision making. Problems prevented are problems solved. The decision steps presented in this book can serve as a basic framework for an ongoing observation of an organization for the purpose of anticipating and preventing problem situations, and building the kind of organization in which the potential for human crisis is reduced.

A Final Note on Decision Making

Although we have reached the end of the model, in reality the decision-making process in large-scale organizations has no beginning and no end. The decision maker, because he must be constantly alert to clues of disequilibria in his organization, is always engaged in a process of diagnosis to determine whether or not he is faced with a problem. And once implemented, his solutions are constantly under scrutiny to determine their effectiveness. When approached systematically, this decision-feedback cycle can be developed over time to the point where the skilled decision maker has become so sensitive to the processes operating in his environment that he can truly engage in "preventive decision making." In this sense, then, decision making and managing are synonymous.

Breaking down this process into its various steps serves primarily to clarify the decision maker's stage in the process at a given time. Obviously, there is frequently not time during the active process of day-to-day decision making for a full examination of each situation in terms of all the criteria presented in this section. Nevertheless, when the manager becomes fully experienced in identifying where he is in the process, and hence what his next step is, decision-making time can be significantly reduced by the elimination of wasted effort.

Decision making, therefore, is an entire approach to management rather than simply one task. The effective decision maker is one who understands the structure of his environment, who approaches situations systematically, and who uses the best methods available to him in investigating and solving problems.

References

Argyris, Chris. *Interpersonal Competence and Organizational Effectiveness.* Irwin (Dorsey), 1962.

Berelson, Bernard, and Gary A. Steiner. *Human Behavior: An Inventory of Scientific Findings.* Harcourt, Brace and World, 1964.

Bennis, Warren G. *Changing Organizations.* McGraw-Hill, 1966.

Bradford, Leland P., Jack R. Gibb, and Kenneth D. Benne. *T-Group Theory and Laboratory Method.* Wiley, 1964.

Guest, Robert H. *Organizational Change: The Effect of Successful Leadership.* Irwin, 1962.

Krech, David, Richard S. Crutchfield, and Egerton L. Ballachey. *Individual in Society.* McGraw-Hill, 1962.

Roethlisberger, Fritz, and William Dickson. *Management and the Worker.* Harvard University Press, 1947.

West Yanga College of Engineering Case

The West Yanga College of Engineering is a national African college for students who intend to take up professional careers in surveying, drafting, or general engineering. It is a government-aided college that has a nonstatutory board of governors appointed by the Ministry of Education. The principal of the college is also secretary of the board, and acts as its executive between the meetings of the board. He is not restricted in matters of general administration. When it comes to taking disciplinary action against a teacher or student, however, his powers are limited. He can only suspend a student for a maximum of seven days. A teacher can be suspended only by the Ministry of Education on the recommendation of the entire board.

During the period 1965–69 the college had three principals: Mr. George Broderick (1965–67), Mr. Kenneth Rangor (1967–69), and Mr. Alan Watson (1969–).

George Broderick was an Englishman with a long record of engineering experience in Great Britain. He had been head of a department at the Kent College of Engineering for about two years before accepting a four-year assignment with the West Yanga government. His staff consisted of 24 lecturers: one American, two Canadians, three West Yangans, and 18 Englishmen.

One of the West Yangan faculty members was Kenneth Rangor. Rangor came from a very religious Catholic family of Indian descent, which had amassed great wealth through trade in a remote part of

---

This case was written under the supervision of Alvar O. Elbing. Names of people and places have been disguised.

West Yanga. He had attended the University of Calcutta, earning a Bachelor of Engineering degree, along with a Bachelor of Arts. In 1964 he had been awarded a scholarship to go to the United Kingdom to work for a certificate in engineering education. Upon his return to West Yanga in mid 1965, he was appointed lecturer in engineering. During the following two years, Broderick was confronted with a number of incidents involving Rangor.

During Rangor's first term at the college, there were student complaints about his teaching. It was reported that he merely read a textbook to the class, a practice the students felt was of little value to them. Broderick did not believe this story completely, however, since Rangor's educational background was sound and it was generally felt that he should be a competent teacher.

Toward the end of 1965 it was reported that Rangor was telling his classes that Broderick was a racist, that he was against Africans, and that he was there only for the interests of his fellow Englishmen. It was reported that Rangor urged the students to fight Broderick in order to have a West Yangan as principal. Such a change, it was argued, would mean a lot to people who had been independent of the British for such a short time. There was some unrest at this time among the students.

At about the same time, the head of the surveying department, John Harper, was thought to be interested in one of the girl students. One evening this girl left the dormitory after the curfew hour and went with one of the boy students to a nightclub, where they happened to meet Harper. This led to an unpleasant exchange between Harper and the boy. The following day the boy was expelled, but nothing happened to the girl.

Coincidentally, and for other reasons, the West Yangan members of the staff called for an extraordinary meeting of the entire faculty that same day. This was refused by the principal, who allowed them to have a departmental meeting instead. Since the three West Yangan teachers were all in John Harper's department, they explained to the principal that such a meeting would be useless. Broderick then agreed to chair the meeting, which all the members of the surveying department attended. During the discussion Rangor brought up the rumor of the department head's alleged interest in the girl as the reason for her friend's dismissal. He also pointed out that only the board of governors could dismiss a student, and he asked how a power denied to the principal of the college could be exercised by a mere department head. It then became clear that Broderick was unaware of the expulsion. He had thought it was a suspension and had endorsed it as such. He was now in a difficult position. A hot exchange took place between Harper and Broderick, concluding with Harper's shouting, "I know you Africans and stupid Indians are against us. You don't like us. Well, we hate you too!" In response, all the Africans walked out of the meeting. Rangor remained, however, and the meeting soon ended.

Within a week the story of this meeting was known to every student on the campus—but the events were somewhat altered. The story that went around was that the above-quoted insult was made by the principal. There was no doubt as to who had spread the misquotation. The Ministry of Education was told the correct story, however, and it gave Harper the option of taking a demotion or leaving the country. He chose the demotion, and resentment of Harper largely subsided.

The unrest that had begun to sweep the campus did not subside. Though there was little overt action, feelings were running high, and Rangor seemed to be involved with most of this unrest. Complaints about his teachings methods were no longer heard, although he continued to read from the textbook. At the end of his classes students were observed gathering around him to discuss various issues.

There was also unrest among the faculty. A rumor spread that Broderick was having secret meetings with the 18 Englishmen on the staff. This could not be confirmed, but Rangor capitalized on the rumor. He arranged a countermeeting of all the non-English staff to discuss the issue. After this meeting, a memorandum of complaint was prepared to be sent to the principal. For unknown reasons, the memorandum was never turned over to the principal, but the fact of the meeting came to Broderick's attention.

In October 1967 Broderick met with the students of one class to discuss the current unrest. In the middle of the meeting the students walked out. This so infuriated Broderick that he suspended the whole class for an indefinite period of time. The suspension was immediately reported to the Ministry of Education, which requested an explanation from Broderick for this drastic action. It also asked him why he had failed to consult with the ministry's board of governors and even to report the matter. In his rage, Broderick stated that he had not come to Africa to be bullied by "young idiots." He was subsequently called to the minister's office. During the discussion, reportedly hot on both sides, Broderick was quoted as saying that West Yanga was the worst country he had ever served. Because of this, he was considered a persona non grata, given a ticket to the United Kingdom, and told to leave "within a month's time."

Because of this hasty decision by the ministry, it was necessary to make a quick and immediate replacement. It did not want another Englishman in that office so soon after Mr. Broderick's insulting words. At the same time, there was no African at the college sufficiently experienced for the post. The only choice was Kenneth Rangor.

Rangor, thus appointed acting principal of the college, opened the first staff meeting by saying, "It is now time for West Yangans to rule themselves. We have suffered injustices and it will be my duty to rectify them. You must, therefore, know that I am a big man. I may be small in stature and colored, but I am the principal. You must respect me or else I'll send you back to Britain." This statement shocked not only the Englishmen on the staff but the Africans as well. In response, the 18 Englishmen, one African, and the American joined together to send a memorandum to the Ministry of Education rejecting the acting principal. The post of principal, however, was appointive and not elective, and the ministry sent a representative to the college who threatened to expel any rebelling lecturers. Thus the overt opposition to Rangor died down.

Late in January 1968, Rangor called in one of the students and demanded that he write a letter complaining about one of the African lecturers. The boy resisted and was threatened with expulsion. He was then forced to sign a letter, already written by Rangor, alleging that Mr. Kasubi, the African teacher, was regularly late to class and that he was a drunkard. (Mr. Kasubi, incidently, was a nondrinker.) The student reported the incident to his class. Kasubi confronted Rangor and asked why he had done this. Rangor told him merely that he had received a letter from a student and that it was confidential. Mr. Kasubi reported this to the ministry officials, but his story was not believed.

Prior to Kenneth Rangor's appointment as acting principal, an African teacher, Mr. James Bwarobi, had joined the drafting department. He had been appointed a student adviser. At that time, the students were expecting Mr. Rangor to make improvements in the things for which he had been criticizing Broderick, but he made only one concession: students could visit his office any time they liked. Apart from this, the rules were very stringent. The students were not satisfied with the "changes." It was also alleged that Rangor had special arrangements with the food suppliers, and the students thought they were being fed on rotten beans and decaying bread. When the students threatened to strike, Rangor put the blame for instigating the strike on Bwarobi, who tendered his resignation in response to this charge. But the resignation was refused.

Rangor then called a meeting of the entire staff and issued a warning that any member who instigated a student strike would be dealt with severely. This warning was followed by a similar one, published in a special bulletin to both students and faculty. Mr. Rangor also called a student assembly and gave a similar warning. What surprised the staff was Rangor's consistent insinuation that the teachers were the ones who were telling the students to go on strike. They wondered why he was telling this to the students. As a result of these and other incidents, Mr. Bwarobi resigned. Another African teacher threatened to resign if things did not change.

All of these stories were reported to the ministry. In February 1969 an advertisement appeared in the *London Economist* for a principal for the West Yanga College of Engineering. When this news reached West Yanga, Rangor became desperate. He called a board of governor's meeting and reported the matter of the London ad. He said that it would be very ungrateful and unpatriotic for the Ministry of Education to bring a foreigner to head the college once again. He also called on ministry officials and made the same accusations. However, in April of 1969 a Mr. Alan Watson came to West Yanga for two weeks as a specialist in engineering education and advisor to the West Yanga government. His special assignment was at the West Yanga College of Engineering, which was indication enough that he would be the next principal. He returned in June in that position.

Watson was 72 years old. Before World War II he had been a department head in a British college for one year. After the war he had been an inspector of engineering education for Her Majesty's government, until September 1968, when he resigned because of age. On his arrival in West Yanga he had an hour's meeting with each member of the staff. He talked of his long experience in administration but confessed he had never been a principal before. He said that he was interested only in the welfare of the country and its people and that his main ambition was to leave an African in his chair as principal when he left.

Rangor was offered a post as a head of drafting studies, but declined on the ground that he had been promised the post of vice principal. He was made a lecturer in engineering. Within only a few weeks, Watson was receiving reports that Rangor was telling the students that the principal was a retired veteran who was just waiting to be buried and that he did not think this was the type of man the country needed. Because Mr. Watson did not accept these rumors as true, he did nothing about them.

An early rule change that Watson put into effect made the administrative block out of bounds to all students unless they had permission from one of the lecturers. The students did not like this change, but they did not resist it and they obeyed the rule. Later, Rangor told his classes that the new principal did not want "to look at black faces" and that this was the reason the rule had been instituted. One of the students went to the principal and reported these comments. Although Watson said nothing, he called some of the staff members together to learn whether they had heard the same rumor. Almost all of them reported that Rangor had mentioned it to them. Watson decided that it was time to talk to Rangor. He called him into the office and spoke very sharply: "Mr. Rangor, you have been a failure as a principal and even as a mere teacher. Now I am giving you an ultimatum. You either stop this nonsense [of spreading false rumors] or else I will have you out. Now get out of my office."

Rangor left the office visibly shaken and remained quiet for a month or two. Then he reported to the students on his talk with the principal. He also wrote letters to the ministry and the board of governors complaining about mistreatment. The ministry offered him a job in the headquarters office, but he declined, saying that he would remain in the college until he became principal.

During the same week, letters began to appear in the local and national press about racial discrimination at the West Yanga College of Engineering. They accused the ministry of being incapable of investigating the issue and not taking necessary measures. They also alleged that the principal was too old and knew nothing of adminis- tration, that the West Yangan staff was being mistreated, and that the students were being suspended or dismissed without cause.

Watson was worried about these letters, but, as they were all anonymous, he did not know who wrote them. He suspected Rangor but he had no proof. He wasn't sure how he should handle the situation.

Crownbar Corporation Case

When Richard Haring was ordered into Crownbar Corporation head- quarters, as of January 2, for a year's training in the president's office, he was told that his next scheduled assignment would be as a division manager (see the notes at the end of this case). He was also told that he should regard his headquarters tour of duty primarily as an oppor- tunity to get on familiar terms with key members of the central staff and to absorb from them all that he could about functional areas in which his training and experience were deficient, particularly sales. Haring's prior service with Crownbar had been entirely in the manu-

From *Organizational Behavior: Cases and Readings,* by Austin Grimshaw and John W. Hennessey. Copyright © 1960 by McGraw-Hill, Inc. Used with the permission of McGraw-Hill Book Company and John W. Hennessey.

facturing end as an accountant, purchasing agent, and plant foreman and superintendent.

Just before Labor Day he was informed that he was to take over the Atlanta division on December 1. During the next few months he assembled all the information he could about Atlanta operations and its top personnel. One item in particular disturbed him. This concerned the plant manager, George Mumford. While visiting headquarters, Carl Long, the incumbent division manager at Atlanta, reported that Mumford was in personal financial difficulty and warned Haring that this was beginning to affect his business judgment. Mumford, he said, was 61 years old, had worked 40 years for Crownbar, including ten as plant superintendent at Atlanta, was within four years of retirement, and would accordingly have to be handled on a kid-glove basis. His performance over the years had been about average. He had been a competent though never an outstanding supervisor.

Long said Mumford was one of a top group of five department heads at Atlanta. He was the highest paid of the five and oldest in both division and company length of service, a sort of dean. Either he or the auditor, O'Day, was in charge when Long was away.

Long said that he had recently felt it necessary to call Mumford in and discuss the latter's personal financial worries. Mumford had indicated that they stemmed from years of living constantly just a little bit above his means. He blamed his wife for this. She came from a well-to-do family which in their early married years had helped them out quite a bit financially. She had never, Mumford said, faced up to the fact that his income was limited and spent money freely whether they had any or not.

Haring decided, upon arrival at Atlanta, to watch the Mumford situation closely but to do nothing about it for a while. In March, however, his hand was forced by a strong suggestion from the headquarters industrial-relations people that he had better get Mumford on the carpet. He called Mumford in and broached the matter.

Mumford said: "Things are tough at home, really tough. We owe money to everybody. I'm being dunned all the time and it's driving me nuts."

Haring replied: "Why don't you tell me the whole story, how far in the hole you are, how you got there and all. Maybe we can get together on it, arrange for a loan from the company to bail you out, pay off your creditors, and wipe the slate clean."

Mumford asked and was granted a few days to get all his overdue bills together. At a subsequent conference he produced a list of debts which totaled about $7000. He had no bank balance, no savings accounts, no assets convertible into cash, and was worse than flat broke. Included in his debts was a maximum loan from the Crownbar credit union, an employee-owned and operated organization. Haring knew from prior conversations with the division auditor, Michael O'Day, who was also the credit union treasurer and quite a gossip, that Mumford had put pressure unsuccessfully on two of his subordinates, who happened to be members of the credit committee, to lend him more than the maximum.

After reviewing the facts, Haring decided to recommend to the treasurer that a $7000 loan be made to Mumford, this to be repaid as a salary deduction over a three-year period. To save face for Mumford, he allowed the latter to present the request directly to headquarters himself. Haring sent along a covering letter in which he stated that his objective in supporting the loan application was to help out a loyal old employee and make his last years more productive. Mumford's work performance, he explained, had been adversely affected by financial worries, as had been his relationships with associates. On a number of recent occasions he had been absent from the plant, without prior notice or subsequent explanation.

Haring was aware that, although company loans were not uncommon to cover such emergencies as illness and house purchase on transfer, they were not ordinarily available to improvident employees. Nor did Crownbar normally make it a practice to check up on the finances of its executives and supervisors. He felt, however, that Mumford's might be considered a special case, because of the latter's long service.

The treasurer, after consultation with the plant personnel committee (headquarters),[1] approved Mumford's request, with the stipulation that Haring talk to Mumford and his wife about the necessity of their living within their income thereafter. Haring did so; and all three signed a memorandum in which it was agreed that Mumford would in the future handle the family finances and that he and his wife would live within the limits of his monthly salary check. Mumford also agreed orally to keep Haring posted on his financial condition, and above all not to go back into debt. The meeting proved most embarrassing to the three persons involved.

The treasurer stipulated also that Mumford's debts be paid directly by company checks made out to creditors, with Mumford endorsing the checks before mailing. This procedure was followed.

During the next year Haring talked to Mumford at least once a month about his finances. The latter answered each inquiry with a statement that he was now in fine shape, thanks to Haring, and very grateful for his helpful intervention. Haring accepted his words at face value, since he had no reason to believe otherwise. Mumford's performance had improved considerably; he was once again a firm

---

1. The five members comprising this committee were the general manager, the vice president of manufacturing, the general superintendent, the vice president of industrial relations, and the industrial relations manager.

and considerate boss, and he seemed to be thoroughly straightened around.

One day in April, in Haring's second year as Atlanta division manager, a representative from the general auditor's office came in unannounced, as was the customary practice, to check on division affairs. He had with him the Mumford loan file, with instructions to make a routine on-the-ground investigation.

The traveling auditor, together with Haring, approached two banks which handled Mumford's accounts and learned from their officers that Mumford had borrowed again at both banks. Two of three currently outstanding notes had been endorsed by Crownbar Atlanta division employees, one of whom reported directly to Mumford. This was a violation in spirit, at least, if not in fact of a company policy, published in the personnel manual, which stated that no employee could borrow from a subordinate.

Haring immediately called Mumford in, faced him with the evidence, told him that he had violated his signed agreement, and that he had periodically lied to Haring about his financial situation. Mumford admitted under questioning that he had borrowed about $2400, approximately the amount deducted from his pay to date to pay off the $7000 loan. He had, he said, lived just within his total salary, before loan repayment deduction, but above the agreed-upon standard. He made no attempt to justify or defend his action.

Under Crownbar policy, Haring had no authority to take disciplinary action against Mumford himself. Instead, two lines of action were open to him: He could stop short of punitive measures requiring headquarters approval; or he could report the complete facts to the headquarter's plant personnel committee, with his own recommendation for disciplinary action.

If he adopted the first alternative he would have to permit Mumford to continue as Atlanta Division plant superintendent. He would be limited, in effect, to giving Mumford a thorough dressing down and extracting another promise of good behavior. Mumford might possibly break down and resign under fire, but Haring thought the chances were much against such a result. Even if he did, headquarters would want to know the reasons for the resignation of a man so near retirement and might refuse to accept it. A further argument against this approach, in Haring's opinion, was the probability that a large number of people in the division already knew, over the grapevine, about the loan to Mumford and would soon know that Mumford had double-crossed him. To take no punitive action in such a situation, Haring decided, could not but undermine his authority. He therefore rejected the "do-nothing" approach.

Under the second alternative, he could recommend any of several actions. These included, in increasing order of severity:

1. Demotion in rank and salary, but retention in the Atlanta Division plant organization.
2. Demotion in rank and salary, and transfer to another division.
3. Retirement, with reduced pension to compensate for premature retirement.
4. Dismissal, with forfeiture of pension.

Haring chose to recommend (2) above. He hoped that this solution, if approved, might—by uprooting the Mumfords and getting them out of town, away from their many friends—help them live on a less expensive scale.

Haring's recommendation was sustained by the plant personnel committee (headquarters) by a 3 to 2 vote. The treasurer, who was consulted as a matter of courtesy and because about $4500 of the loan was still outstanding, also concurred in the committee's action. This was to transfer Mumford to a plant clerical position in another division, with a 10-percent reduction in salary. His salary in the new post would still be about double the going rate for the job.

Haring's boss, Mr. Hartline, the general manager, in reporting the committee decision to Haring, told him that he and two members from industrial relations had supported throughout the discussion Haring's position that permanent demotion and transfer was the best way out. The vice president of manufacturing, and the general superintendent, however, had considered Haring's proposed penalty as too severe. They had held out at first for keeping Mumford on as Atlanta Division plant superintendent. When they got no support from the other 3 members for this disposition of the case, they had argued for a compromise, with Mumford demoted but remaining as a supervisor in the Atlanta plant.

Notes on Crownbar Organization

Under the Crownbar plan of organization (see Figure 1), division managers were responsible on a line basis to the general manager, Mr. Hartline, who in turn reported to the operations vice president. The company also maintained a central staff, composed of people who were regarded as the best brains in the organization for the specific functions which they supervised. Their functional counterparts in the various divisions were expected to take full advantage of the experience of the senior men on central staff. Suggestions from central staff were generally regarded, as a matter of actual although not stated fact, as pretty much in the nature of commands. Division managers had line authority over all personnel within their divisions and their subordinates were required to keep them informed of all the significant developments in their respective functional areas which affected divisional operations. The division managers themselves

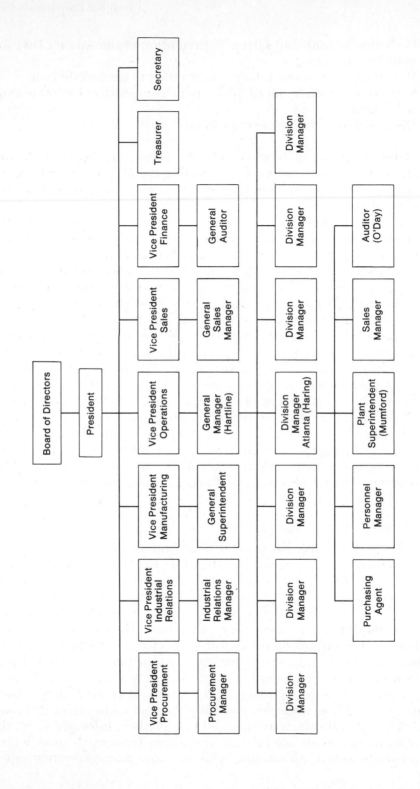

Figure 1 Crownbar Corporation Organization Chart

were also expected to work closely with the various members of central staff. Contacts might be made on problems, or central staff members might instead initiate contacts themselves whenever they felt it advisable. For all practical purposes, division managers had several functional bosses in addition to their line boss, Mr. Hartline.

The Worthington Bank Case

The Worthington Bank and Trust Company has extensive national and international operations. In total assets, it ranks among the top ten banking institutions in the nation. The Worthington maintains a system of approximately 100 branch banks in New York City, where its headquarters is located.

One afternoon in April 1964, Mrs. Juan Rodriguez, a woman of about 70, walked into Worthington's main-office branch in downtown Manhattan at about 1:30 p.m. She went to a teller's window, presented her passbook, and explained that she wanted to see her money and count it.

"I don't quite understand, Mrs. Rodriguez," the teller replied. "Do you wish to make a withdrawal, or are you referring to our tour service?"

"My book says I have one thousand and one hundred and seventy-two dollars, no?" said Mrs. Rodriguez.

"Yes, ma'am, your balance is eleven-seventy-two."

"Well, I only want to see it and count to see if it is all there," she calmly and politely answered.

The teller, taking into account her age and obvious foreign background, felt he understood her problem. Therefore, he tried to explain briefly to her how a bank works. He explained that her funds were pooled with those of others and that a bank uses such funds to help people who need capital. As the teller talked he began to realize from Mrs. Rodriguez's confused expression that she did not understand. She apparently was upset over the realization that her money

This case was prepared by John W. Hennessey. Names of people and places have been disguised. Used with the permission of John W. Hennessey.

was not tucked away in its own box somewhere in the vault. Her confusion seemed to turn to fear, and she was quite upset over the whereabouts of her money.

At this point, the head teller, who had heard part of the conversation and who was becoming concerned over the commotion, stepped into the teller's cage and politely introduced himself to Mrs. Rodriguez. He realized that she had become quite excited, so he very cordially invited her to come into his office and speak with him. Mrs. Rodriguez seemed somewhat placated by the intrusion of this "higher authority." She went quietly into the office of the head teller, Mr. Scott Weiss.

Mr. Weiss tried to assure Mrs. Rodriguez that "everything's all right now." Mr. Weiss quietly and patiently explained the problem to her.

"Yes, of course you're concerned over your savings, and you should be. That is precisely why we have good sound banks for people to keep their money in. You see, we at the bank keep your savings safe and sound for you. . . ." Mr. Weiss went on to explain how Mrs. Rodriguez's money was watched closely. He invited her to come in on any Tuesday and take a tour of the bank to see its "large vault" and its new machines which "ensure all depositors against any mistakes in the records of their savings."

Mrs. Rodriguez listened patiently and politely while Mr. Weiss explained the situation. When Mr. Weiss felt that she was sufficiently calmed, he smiled obligingly and asked her if everything was now all right.

"Yes, I understand fine," she answered, sounding satisfied with his explanation. "Now, if my money is all safe and there are no mistakes, it is all right that I can see it and count it, no?"

Mr. Weiss realized, to his dismay, that he had solved nothing. He tried to explain how her money was kept in a "common pool" with other people's savings and how other people, who had no savings, could borrow some of this money.

Immediately, Mrs. Rodriguez seemed to become nervous over this idea. She could not understand why her money was not kept separate. She did not want others using her savings. Now, she seemed convinced that she had better "see and count" her money to make sure it was all there. Mr. Weiss tried several new explanations; however, Mrs. Rodriguez insisted that she had the right to see her money.

Although reluctant to have Mrs. Rodriguez make a withdrawal of her funds, Mr. Weiss felt that this might be the only solution. Therefore, he decided to check on her balance himself and then let her make a withdrawal of the entire amount if she so desired. He rose and excused himself, explaining that he would be right back.

Mr. Weiss checked the Rodriguez account and the balance was all in order. However, one additional complication now arose. Mrs.

Rodriguez's account was, in fact, a joint account with her daughter. Mr. Weiss realized that he could not allow her to make a withdrawal without her daughter's signature. While Mr. Weiss was at first dismayed by this new complication, he decided that this could serve as his "out." Telling Mrs. Rodriguez that she needed her daughter's signature would be a way of getting rid of her temporarily, and then maybe her daughter would be able to explain the whole misunderstanding to her. With this "perfect solution" in his mind, Mr. Weiss returned to Mrs. Rodriguez.

He laid the bank's record of her account in front of her and explained how that proved that her money was all there and was accounted for. He said nothing more for the moment, hoping this would satisfy her. She agreed with this account perfectly; however, she still wanted to see her cash.

"Well, Mrs. Rodriguez, all I can suggest then is that you come down with your daughter and then the two of you can make a withdrawal of any or all of your money. This is your money in this account and any time you and your daughter wish to withdraw some or all of it, you may do so."

"My daughter is away. She cannot come here. She is away now. Why can I not have my money? It is my money, no? I put it in here to keep it safe, no? Now, if I want to make sure it is safe, I cannot. You show me papers and numbers and say my money is safe, but you do not let me see my money or have it. This I do not understand."

Mrs. Rodriguez's confusion was apparent. She was becoming increasingly upset. Mr. Weiss offered to give her a withdrawal slip to send to her daughter to sign. She could not understand this. It seemed as though nothing but the $1172 in cash would calm her. However, Mr. Weiss did not feel he could possibly present her with the money even to count it. If she got that far she might decide to take it with her.

Suddenly Mrs. Rodriguez rose and announced that she wanted to see Mr. Swanson, the president of the Worthington Bank, for he would certainly help her. Mr. Weiss, taken by surprise, did not know what to say. Mrs. Rodriguez had apparently seen Mr. Swanson's name in the papers and she felt that he could handle her problem. Mr. Weiss tried to explain that this would be impossible, that Mr. Swanson did not handle problems of this nature, and that he was not in anyway. He really did not know what to say. Mrs. Rodriguez quite firmly stated that she was going to see Mr. Swanson and that was final! She would wait until he returned if he were out, but she very firmly stated that she absolutely would not leave until she had spoken with Mr. Swanson and had made sure her money was safe.

By this time Mrs. Rodriguez had become quite agitated. She said that she would not be "fooled or cheated" just because she was "a foreigner." She stated further that if she could not see Mr. Swanson and check on her money, she would call the "police, the newspaper-men, and the pastor." At this point she walked into the lobby and there took a seat on a bench.

While Mr. Weiss stood somewhat dumbfounded by Mrs. Rodriguez's closing ultimatum, Mr. Theodore Hall, the assistant manager of the branch, went to Weiss's office. Mr. Hall knew nothing of the matter under discussion, but he had apparently seen that Mr. Weiss was having some difficulties. Mr. Weiss explained Mrs. Rodriguez's confusion and told Mr. Hall of her closing ultimatum. The two men discussed what had happened. Then Mr. Hall left with this parting remark:

"Well, Scott, you get these nuts from time to time. I'm sure you can straighten out the situation. Personally, I don't think 'Big Bob' [Mr. Swanson, the president] would have time to chat with her today," he added facetiously. "You sure can't give her any cash because it's probably her daughter's savings anyway. And whatever you do, don't get the damned newspaper guys in on this. Those tabloids would make some tear-jerking, 'wicked-big-business' story out of this, sure as hell!"

At this point, Mr. Weiss was confused as to what he should do.

Northeastern Electric Light and Power Corporation Case

Introduction

The material presented in this case study was gathered from the observations made by Bill Peterson during the summer of 1967. Peterson, a newly graduated engineer, had accepted summer employment with the Northeastern Electric Light and Power Corporation in order to earn money to finance a graduate education in personnel management.

Bill, along with another college student, Fred Greene, had been hired as an engineering aid for the company's land surveying department. This was one of the smallest departments in the company,

This case was written by Andrew P. Krueger, under the supervision of Alvar O. Elbing. Names of people and places have been disguised.

which was one of the largest utilities in the country. There were 14 people in this department: seven aids, three instrument operators, three crew chiefs, and a chief surveyor.

The duties of the crew chief were to plan the work assignments that were given to him by the chief surveyor every week. He was to make sure that the work was finished during the week, take care of the crew's expense account money, make out the daily time sheets, and generally oversee the three or four men on his crew.

The instrument man on each crew had one major function; this was operating and maintaining the surveyor's transit that each crew had. In addition, he was to take charge of the crew in the crew chief's absence and also to assist him in the preparation of charts, maps, and other engineering paperwork.

The aids were responsible for the upkeep of the truck supplies and were required to take turns driving to the sites of various company projects. They were also supposed to help the chief with surface measuring (done with steel and cloth measuring tapes) and to hold range poles and measuring rods for the instrument man. Other duties ranged from washing the trucks each week to sharpening the axes and brush hooks that were needed for cutting foliage in some areas.

The chief surveyor, Don Williams, was the overall boss of the three crews. A large part of his time was spent in the drafting room of the company, working with the foreman of the drafting department. Don and the drafting foreman passed information and drawings back and forth between the two departments. Williams was relatively new to the job, having previously been a licensed surveyor in Illinois until Northeastern hired him in May, 1967. At the beginning of the summer, according to the older employees in the department, he did not seem to know his job very well. Up until the end of June, Don Williams spent most of his time working with Mr. James, the company's chief engineer. Mr. James was in charge of the engineering section, of which the drafting and surveying departments were part. The chief engineer had his own office adjacent to the drafting room —located on the third floor of the large building, which also housed administrative offices and a garage for company vehicles—and he was rarely seen by any of the surveying crew. His orders and assignments were usually passed to Don, the drafting foreman, and two other foremen in different departments of the engineering section.

Organization of the Surveying Crews

The thirteen employees—other than Don—were organized into three crews. Each consisted of a crew chief, an instrument man, and two or three aids. One group had three aids and the other two groups had two aids. There was also a panel truck with a complete set of surveying equipment for each crew. The trucks had been specially outfitted with drawers, compartments, and a foldout desk. Thus in most cases, the three groups were completely independent of one another.

In practice, the personnel were switched between crews every week. There were several reasons for this. The aids, some of whom carried quite a bit of seniority, were changed almost every week. Those with seniority were entitled to have the first chance to work on the projects that were more than 40 miles away from the plant. These projects carried more pay than did the "in-town" jobs. The company paid $10.50 per day on "out-of-town work for board and lodging and only $1.50 per day on in-town work for lunch money. The instrument men were also changed, but with much less regularity than the aids. All three of them had equal seniority, but they possessed slightly different skills with the "gun," which made it desirable to have them working on certain projects. They were usually rotated between in-town and out-of-town very regularly, as were the crew chiefs, because of union rules regarding employees having equal seniority. Most of the time everyone—except Peterson and Greene, who were nonunion and had no seniority—was satisfied that he was getting his share of out-of-town work. Table 1 gives more explicit data on the personal background, seniority, and work status of the individual members of the surveying department.

Relations between the Employees

Table 1 shows that there was quite a difference in personal background among several of the men in the surveying department. Bill noticed, however, that these disparities actually made little difference in the status of each group member.

There was only one striking exception to this. That was Herb, the oldest aid. During the very first week that Bill was with the group, Herb had remarked privately: "This is a pretty good job. The work's not bad—most of the guys have a good time out here. But you got to watch out for guys like Pat. He'll go out of his way to make you look bad if you let him—he's always trying to cut somebody's throat. Some of the others will too, but not as much as Pat."

Pat, a crew chief and the union steward for the surveyors, was generally agreed by most to be a tough but fair boss. He had no great liking for Herb, though, as was evidenced by his constant complaining about Herb's "stupidity." At Pat's request, however, Herb was usually put on his crew because he was the most experienced of the aids. This made quite a difference to Pat, who had, on occasion, remeasured some of the younger aids' work because he did not trust them.

Pat was noted for getting the work done on schedule. On one occasion, Jim (an instrument man) had said: "If that damn Pat wasn't the steward, he'd probably work everyone to death. No matter

Table 1   Background Data of the Survey Crew Members

Name and Job	Age	Seniority (in years)	Education	Marital Status
Pat (chief)	50	21	gs	m
Doug (chief)	59	22	hs	m
Jack (chief)	48	20	hs	m
Jim ("gunman")	48	20	2 yrs hs	s
"Stick" ("gunman")	44	21	hs	m
Hank ("gunman")	48	18	hs	m
Fred (aid)	20	0	3 yrs college	s
Bill (aid)	21	0	college	s
Ralph (aid)	23	1	hs	m
Dave (aid)	23	1	hs	m
Alan (aid)	19	5 mos	1½ yrs college	m
Gerry (aid)	24	2	hs	m
Herb (aid)	42	20	gs	m

what else, he always gets his work done. They see that upstairs and they like it. That's why Pat gets most of the good jobs."

Jim, "Stick" (a contraction of his last name), and Hank were the instrument men. It was generally agreed that they did their jobs well and were good men to work with. Pat was the only one to criticize them, but he was the "complainer" in the group and the instrument men (many of whom had been here as long as Pat) paid little attention to him.

The remaining two crew chiefs were Doug and Jack, both of whom were amiable and easygoing and were highly regarded by the aids and instrument men. Neither of them was noted for being particularly industrious, however, and this was the reason Pat was usually put on the important projects. Don had quickly recognized this and had gone so far as to nickname Doug, the oldest member of the group, "the old speedball."

The remaining four aids were about the same age and had about the same experience. Ralph and Dave had been in military service together before coming to work for the company in 1966. They had gone to high school together, and now lived quite near each other. Alan had started to work for the company in February 1967, after dropping out of an engineering program in college halfway through his sophomore year. Gerry had come to the department from another one of the company's largest generating plants in the middle of May, just before Bill and Fred started their summer work. Thus there were three new men in the department—Bill, Fred, and Gerry.

Company Organization

The Northeastern Electric Light and Power Corporation, which served portions of three large states, was broken into nine divisions. There were three divisions per state: the eastern, western, and central divisions. Each division had its own survey crews that were responsible for, among other things, the layout of new and relocated transmission and distribution lines, the layout of natural-gas pipelines, and the site engineering of new substation facilities.

The area of the crews that Bill Peterson worked with was approximately 6000 square miles. It was frequently a long distance from the main plant to the projects that they were working on. Some jobs were within a mile or two of the plant, while others were as far as 170 miles away. When the employees had to travel more than 40 miles to their jobs, as mentioned above, the company paid extra for board and room if the job lasted more than one day. With this extra pay, the men were expected to stay near the job until it was finished.

Work started at 8 a.m. and was to progress until 5 p.m., with an hour out for lunch between 12 and 1 p.m. In actual practice, however, none of the crews ever operated this way. (The work behavior of the crews is discussed in the next section.)

During the summer months, the crews worked a six-day week. Rarely did anyone complain about this; but if somebody wanted a Saturday off, he only had to tell Don a few days in advance.

Activities of the Group

The work routine of the survey crews started at 8 a.m. on Monday. At this time, everyone checked the crew schedule to find out what crew he was to be with for the coming week. Since Don and Mr. James came in around 8:30, there was a little time for the crew chiefs to make out the time sheets and expense-account reports for the previous week. Usually the instrument men helped the chiefs with this work, while the aids were busy cleaning the trucks and restocking them with supplies. At 8:30 the crew chiefs would go up to Don's office to get the assignment sheets and be briefed on the week's projects. These briefings ran anywhere from one-half hour and sometimes as long as two hours.

As soon as the aids and instrument men were finished taking care of the trucks, tool sharpening, and resupplying, they usually went off to other parts of the garage to talk to friends in different departments. Monday morning was the only time that the members of the surveying department had to get together with others in different groups. Bill eventually became good friends with Pete, a young man who worked in the supply cage. Pete always gave Bill a good supply of pens, pencils, and paper, which Bill felt would come in handy during school the following fall. During this time, Fred, Ralph, and Dave could be found talking to Dave's uncle, who was a "hot wire" line foreman. His truck was always parked down at the far end of the garage. During this time, all the men in the department (except the crew chiefs) were spread out all over the plant. Consequently, each crew chief had to walk around and find his crew members when he was ready to leave.

After leaving the plant, the crews usually met at a prearranged place for coffee and to talk over the upcoming work. (Only if a crew had to travel a great distance for a one-day job did they fail to have coffee with the group.) Then each crew would go its own way to the job. After working until about 11:30, the crew would load the equipment back into the truck and go to lunch. Most of the chiefs knew all of the good places to eat, no matter where the crew was.

The lunch period lasted as long as the crew chief desired. Pat usually took about a half an hour; Jack about an hour or an hour and a quarter; Doug sometimes as much as two hours, depending on the job and the weather. After lunch, the crews would drive back to the job and work until between 3:30 and 5:00 or until they finished, depending on the crew chief.

Pat usually worked until at least 4:30; Doug and Jack were known to quit as early as 3:00 on days when they were doing out-of-town work. After work, the crews with Doug and Jack would almost always adjourn to a favorite bar and have a beer or two before starting for home. Occasionally, the two crews would meet, but this was not the usual case.

The trip home was another story. Everyone always went home at night, even if they had been working hundreds of miles away. This was easy enough to do because, on out-of-town jobs, one member of the crew always brought his car. The truck was left in a company-approved service station near the job. The individuals on each crew would take turns during the week driving to the service station in a car pool which met near the members' homes in the morning. The drawback to this was the fact that in order to get anything at all accomplished during the day, it was often necessary to meet as early as 5:30 in the morning. However, the company's $10.50 a day "handout" more than made up for this inconvenience. Except for the aid whose turn it was to drive, everyone usually slept on the way out to the job, so that no sleep was lost.

Because Don never came down to the garage until he left at 5:30 p.m., it was possible for the "in-town" crews to bring their trucks in as early as 4:00 and quietly leave in their own cars, which were parked in the company's parking lot on the side of the plant away from Don's window.

On two successive Wednesdays in the latter part of July, Bill Peterson made the following observations on the operation of two of the crews:

Jack's Crew ("Out")

7:15	Meet at car pool.
8:00	Finish having coffee; drive to the job.
9:30	Arrive at project site.
10:00	Set up equipment and start work.
11:30	Stop work, repack equipment, go to lunch.
1:15	Leave lunch, return to work.
1:45	Set up equipment and start work.
3:15	Pack up and leave work.
4:45	Arrive at service station.

Doug's Crew ("In")

8:00	Report to plant.
8:20	Leave plant (just in time to miss Don coming in).
8:50	Arrive at diner, have coffee, talk about day's work.
10:00	Leave diner, drive to work.
10:15	Arrive at project site.
10:30	Unpack equipment, begin work.
11:30	Pack up, go to lunch.
1:15	Leave lunch, return to work.
1:30	Unpack equipment, start work.
3:30	Stop work, pack up equipment.
3:45	Leave project site.
4:10	Arrive at plant, put truck away, leave for home.

Foreman's Reactions and Conclusion

It is obvious from the above schedules that the self-imposed work day of the crews was quiet different from the standards which the company had set up. According to Doug, however, it had always been that way, from the time that Clyde Daniels (Don's predecessor) was the chief surveyor. Jack's reaction to Bill's questions on the subject were the same.

"What's the difference?" Jack had said. "We always get our weekly assignments done. You've seen that on some Saturdays, when we're getting time and a half, that we don't have a damn thing to do after lunchtime." To be sure, this was true. The crews always had their weekly work completed by quitting time Saturday. Bill had observed, however, that some projects had to be redone by another crew right after the first crew had supposedly finished them. On one occasion a certain substation layout was done three times in three successive weeks by three different crews before the engineering section was satisfied with the work.

Around the middle of August, Don started to get out of the plant more often than he had when he first came to work for the company. On several occasions he personally visited the project sites where the crews were working. Most of the time he either visited Pat's crew, who put in a pretty full day, or else he dropped by after lunch when the other two crews were working as they were supposed to.

After a while Don began to visit every crew at least three times a week and started to find out how the different crew chiefs went about their work. Now he started to realize that perhaps they were not getting as much work to do as they were capable of doing. In the next few weeks, the weekly work assignments became longer. All assignments were completed, but the quality of the work took a drastic dip. The previously mentioned substation project was a prime example of the problem that Don now realized he was facing. Because of company policies and union contract clauses, it was almost impossible to lay off help that was not needed. There were three crews to watch, plus the fact that he had his own office work to do. The company also advised him that he should not consider laying off the two students because they were personnel the company was trying to attract for full-time employment after their studies were completed.

At the end of Bill's summer employment (the middle of September), the situation was still the same. At this time there had developed a considerable amount of animosity on the part of the workers towards Don. Part of this was due to the lectures on efficiency that the crew chiefs were constantly getting from him, and part of it was caused by the fact that the employees regarded Don's visits to the sites as "spy trips." At the end of the summer, Don Williams was faced with a very real problem.

A Dilemma for President Watkins

Harvey O. Watkins was installed as president of Poe College on November 20, 1965. Poe College is a private, nonsectarian four-year college located in Hamilton, Indiana. For its first ten years, Poe was a junior college offering associate degrees in various liberal arts subjects and in some technical and professional fields. In the summer of

This case was written by John W. Hennessey. Names of people and places have been disguised. Used with the permission of John W. Hennessey.

1965 the college achieved accreditation as a four-year institution after a lengthy campaign of fund raising to bring the faculty, the library, and other vital areas of the college's life up to the standards required for full collegiate status.

President Watkins was chosen to be the first leader of Poe College, after a six-month nationwide search for the right man. Prior to coming to Poe, Mr. Watkins had achieved a reputation as the successful president of a community junior college in Harrisburg, Pennsylvania. Mr. Watkins was born in 1929, educated at Lehigh University in Bethlehem, Pennsylvania, and at Columbia University Law School. He had practiced law in Philadelphia and spent one successful term as a state legislator in Pennsylvania before becoming president of Harrisburg Community College in 1961.

The board of trustees of Poe College consisted entirely of business and professional men from the greater urban area of Hamilton, Indiana, which comprised nearly an entire county with a population of some 125,000. President Watkins' early contacts with the board gave him considerable respect for the trustees' sincere interest in the progress of the institution and genuine wish to be helpful in the government of the college. Board members invited President Watkins to call on them freely for any help they could give and gave unstintingly of their time when requests came. None of the trustees had had any direct experience in educational administration; indeed, the only academic experience represented on the board came from the fact that all but one of the 12 board members had college degrees. The age of board members ranged from 45 to 70.

On the morning of May 2, 1966, President Watkins received a telephone call from Mr. William Lathrop, trustee of Poe College and president of the Hamilton Electrical Supply Company. The following conversation ensued:

Lathrop: Harvey, I'm really upset by what I saw in the student newspaper. We've got a real problem on our hands. You've seen the advertisement, haven't you?

Watkins: No, I haven't seen the morning paper, Bill, but it's right here in my chair. Wait a minute and I'll get it. [He gets the paper.] Now, what's the ad you refer to?

Lathrop: It jumps right out from page 3. It occupies a quarter of the page and hit me like a ton of bricks. Let me read it to you while you look at it.

The opportunity of a lifetime. Only $2.95 for a message which may change your life. Hear Dr. Timothy Leary give his most successful lecture on the meaning of modern existence revealed through experiences with LSD. Now available for the first time an LP phonograph record to bring Dr. Leary's message to the modern generation. Send your $2.95 to Vista Record Mart, 398 Broad Street, New York, New York.

Harvey, I couldn't have been more shocked, and I know you must feel the same way. What could ever have gone through the students' minds to let them accept an ad like that?

Watkins: Bill, I'm as surprised as you are to see this ad, and I will look into it right away.

Lathrop: I know you will, Harvey. I wanted to call because I know I will be seeing some of the other trustees at lunch today and this is bound to be a topic of conversation, as you can imagine. In fact if I can be helpful to you by mentioning at lunch what action you plan to take, I would be glad to do it. I suspect the sooner we deal with this situation the easier it will be to manage in the community.

Watkins: Thanks Bill; I appreciate your interest and your telephone call. Goodbye.

Mr. Watkins put the telephone receiver on its cradle and sat back in his chair with a sigh. Just two weeks ago he had commended the editors of the student paper for their courage in taking a stand on unpopular issues, and promised them his support for their freedom "to call the shots as you see them." He said he wanted the editors to have the freedom and responsibility to learn from their own mistakes.

But he was sobered and even chilled by the ad for the LSD lecture. This matter had legal as well as moral implications of a rather serious kind.

President Watkins recognized that he was facing a dilemma, but that is the name of the game for a college president! He knew he had to act quickly, and he decided to try to settle the whole matter that morning.

Part III

Behavioral Science Foundations
for Management: Readings

The voluminous literature on human behavior contains not only writing based on the various scientific disciplines concerned with such behavior but also much "undisciplined" writing—writing based primarily on common sense, intuition, and experience. Some of the literature contains useful insights; some of it contains misconceptions, prejudices, erroneous analogies, and wishful thinking. If this large body of material is to be of use to the serious student of human behavior, and to the decision maker, it must be examined critically in terms of the arguments, evidence, methods, and purpose of each author. Some literature, indeed, presents us with the findings of critical investigations, findings we can legitimately adopt for our own frame of reference. Other literature, however, may present only insightful hypotheses whose usefulness has yet to be demonstrated and therefore are not yet usable as bases for decision making.

Rather than take all such literature on its face value, the decision maker should attempt to understand the purpose, method, and conclusions of each investigation and develop a personally useful reservoir of findings that best pass the tests of his own critical inquiry. As he builds such a reservoir of knowledge about human behavior—knowledge on which to base his diagnoses and forecasts of behavioral response to his decisions—he should keep that reservoir open to examination and reinvestigation in light of alternative explanations of behavior that might better withstand his critical tests.

The manager's reservoir of behavioral knowledge, instead of being regarded as consisting of "truths" about human behavior (and therefore stagnant in content), should be thought of as including the best insights available at a given time, but always open to new ideas that have stronger supporting evidence.

The readings in this section are offered as a starting point for developing a personal reservoir of behavioral knowledge. The identification of each author's purpose, method, and conclusions is a useful step in the process of building such a reservoir.

This group of readings is divided into four sections, reflecting four levels of analysis. The first level treats the *individual*. The authors here discuss the "internal variables" that are important to the individual's frame of reference. These are the personal variables an individual brings with him to the organization, and might well be thought of as the residue of his lifetime experiences. These internal variables may change over time or they may resist change, depending on the role they play in the psychological structure of the individual. The behavioral manifestations of these variables, observable by those around him, can be thought of as the individual's "personality."

The internal variables—those forces that operate within the individual—do not develop magically or in a vacuum; they develop primarily from the interactions of the individual with the world around him. The authors in the second section treat the most basic form of such interaction, the *two-way interpersonal relationship*. On the job, the individual must interact with supervisors, subordinates, peers, vendors, salesmen, customers, and so on. Thus the frame of reference he brings to the organization is regularly juxtaposed with the frames of reference of other individuals whose behavior constitutes an important external variable for him, that is, an important influence on his behavior that originates outside himself. The readings in the second section build an understanding of the process and effects of interpersonal interaction and communication. They demonstrate that the behavior of others not only influences the behavior of the individual, they also can serve to change his frame of reference.

An even stronger influence on an individual's frame of reference —in fact the source of most of his norms and values—is his interaction and identification with *groups* in his organization. As individuals interact over time, groups may form, or an individual may begin to identify with existing groups. The tendency, with such identification, is to accept the group's norms and values as one's own. The readings in the third section treat this important organizational process both in terms of the individual's relationship to his "reference" groups and in terms of the relationship of those groups to other groups, that is, in terms of *intergroup* behavior. Although in most of these readings the group phenomenon is viewed from a scientific standpoint, the article by Mort Stern is a vivid description of the process of group identification from the standpoint of an individual whose behavior was dramatically changed by the influence of group norms.

The environment in which individuals develop their frames of reference, interact with others, and form identifications with groups is also a variable influencing behavior. This environment includes the organizational environment and the environment external to the organization. Understanding the nature of such organizational factors as leadership behavior, the level of technology, and the social conditions of the workplace contributes to an understanding of the overall behavior observed there. The fourth section offers several readings that constitute an introduction to the rather extensive literature on this broad *organizational level of analysis.*

Although the readings in Part III have been grouped by level of analysis, they are not mutually exclusive. Individuals in an organization reflect their environment, just as this environment is influenced by the individuals who constitute it. Two-way interaction influences group norms, and group norms influence two-person relationships. The purpose of distinguishing among these levels is to facilitate our understanding of the role each level plays in influencing behavior and the manner in which they affect one another.

In addition, the literature of each level reflects differing interests and different research tools. These variations are both a help and a problem for the decision maker. The problem lies in the fact that because most research on human behavior is done at only one level at a time, it fails to consider and/or clarify the influences of the other levels. The help to the decision maker lies in the fact that the results of research conducted at these different levels enrich his diagnostic resources and provide him with a broader and sounder basis on which to make decisions.

The readings in Part III, even though they merely scratch the surface of the available behavioral knowledge, have been carefully selected a present a sound, practical beginning for the study of human behavior in large-scale organizations.

The Individual

Alvar O. Elbing

Perception, Motivation, and Business Behavior

Traditional explanations of firm behavior have tended to be based on the premise that the primary if not the single motivation of the businessman is profit maximization. Implicit in this premise is the assumption that to achieve this goal, the profit maximizing individual rationally chooses the best of all possible courses of action, based on his omniscient analysis of all the available alternatives. Investigations in the social and behavioral sciences, however, have opened a number of roads of inquiry into human behavior which bring this assumption into question and which offer considerable insight into the issues which must be faced in building a generally applicable theory of firm behavior.

It is our purpose here to examine certain current concepts in theories of perception and motivation which offer insight into the processes of human behavior and which, therefore, must be considered in the building of any theory of firm behavior. There will be no attempt to develop a general theory of firm behavior based on these concepts nor to answer all of the many unanswered questions about firm behavior. Rather, our purpose will be to identify appropriate questions raised by current concepts of perception and motivation

From *Interdisciplinary Studies in Business Behavior*, Joseph W. McGuire, ed., South-Western Publishing Co., 1962. Reprinted by permission of the publisher.

which must be faced in any eventual construction of a general theory of firm behavior.

Traditional economic theory has considered the firm to be an abstract unit separate from the individuals who are a part of it. Actions of the firm have been explained in terms of rational goals of a business enterprise, e.g., maximization of profit; these goals were then assumed to be those of the individuals who made up the firm. Can we, however, consider an organization apart from the individuals who form that organization? E. Wight Bakke of Yale University suggests that we cannot. He states (1952, p. 7):

> When we observe an "organization" we are observing people organized, and when we observe "organizational activity" we are observing the behavior of people acting as agents of the organizations. When, therefore, we refer to an organization and its activities, we are referring to agents of the organization and their behavior. The substance of an organization is human behavior; the structure of an organization is defined simply as human behavior which is systematized and stabilized.

If we accept Bakke's assumption, then, that firm behavior is the composite of the behavior of individuals who make up the firm, it is appropriate that we examine the current concepts of individual perception and motivation as essential considerations in any theory of firm behavior.

Perception

What are some of the currently advanced key concepts of human perception that must be applied to behavior in a firm? The assumption that human beings simply perceive precisely "what is there" is no longer considered a safe assumption. It is no longer generally accepted that there is a necessary, obvious, and inevitable correlation between objective factors in the environment and human perception of them. According to Mason Haire (1956, p. 40):

> If we make a separation between the physical world outside of us, on the one hand, and the psychological environment, or the world that we see, on the other, we come to see that the order and organization is not in the physical stimulus but in the observer.

Psychologists today, in advancing the theory that there is no fixed correlation between data in the environment and perceived data, describe perception as a process. Any data perceived might be described appropriately as "processed data." The processing of data through perception operates in certain general ways. First, we know that persons tend to selectively perceive data in ways that enable them to cope most readily with it. On the visual level of perception, for example, we tend to take in primarily that visual data which enables us to judge distance quickly for the immediate purpose of reaching an object or taking a step down a stair or otherwise carrying out an immediate practical purpose. Thus we do not register all sense data on an equal basis; we tend to focus on those factors in the environment which enable us to make a ready adjustment. The individual, in fact, never perceives an entire situation, nor does he construct what he does see in the same way on different occasions.

Further, our perceptions tend to have fixity. If a certain perceptual framework for coping with a repeated problem has worked before, that perception tends to become fixed. We then tend to think of the perceptual judgments as existing in the reality "out there," rather than recognizing that we are merely using a portion of what is out there to pick up certain clues which will enable us to maintain stable behavior. If we accept these two concepts—that perceptions do not necessarily have direct correlation with "reality" and that perceptions, whether corresponding to reality or not, have fixity—we must call into question a basic assumption of traditional economic theory: that the businessman is able to perceive and take into account all factors objectively in making a business decision.

Organization of Perception

Another concept of perception is that individuals tend to perceive data as organized wholes. This perceiving of data as organized wholes is one of the ways we "process" data. We do not register data as an audiometer might record units of sound; rather, we tend to organize what we perceive automatically. Numerous illustrations of this human tendency have been provided through psychological experiments. As just one example, the following group of dots in parentheses (: :) is normally perceived as forming a square; i.e., as forming an organized whole. This organizing tendency obviously could affect firm behavior in numerous ways. A businessman in hiring employees may fail to "see" certain aspects of individuals under consideration because he may perceive each as an "organized whole" personality type. As Haire states, "in putting together items of information, we tend to make organized wholes which may distort the meaning of some of the parts which are included. This is particularly true when the items are aspects of a personality" (1956, p. 161).

It should be pointed out that this tendency to perceive things as organized wholes involves certain very important processes that affect the data perceived. (1) In perceiving things as organized wholes, we tend to leave out certain factors which spoil the neatness of our organization. For example, a businessman may be unable to notice certain data which indicate his product is becoming obsolete because such an observation would spoil the neatly organized picture he has of his firm. (2) In perceiving data in terms of an organized whole, we tend to add to the data to make our "organized wholes" more reasonable. For example, a sales manager, in preparing a market analysis that gives some sort of organized picture, may unconsciously add to the data, overemphasizing certain factors to make for a more organized report. (3) In perceiving data in terms of organized wholes, we tend to structure the data; i.e., to perceive it in some kind of intelligible pattern. An executive may see an authoritarian personnel manager as highly effective because he has always perceived authoritarian behavior as part of the role pattern of any managerial position. Or an executive may assume that his competitors will move in a certain direction on the assumption, or projection, that they will act as he would act if in their situation, a situation which he may see as an organized whole different from that "whole" which his competitor sees. It is apparent, then, that an individual constantly distorts data in a number of ways to fit in with the organizing tendency of his perception.

Another concept of perception is that an individual tends to perceive data in terms of his already existing picture of reality. Each person has his own unique frame of reference through which he perceives data, based on his own particular past experiences, biases, sets, attitudes, goals, etc. Herbert Simon expresses a variation of this "picture of reality" concept when he states that people are constantly engaged in mentally building organized "models" of the world. He states that people never see the real world as it "is," but continually perceive that "model" of the world which they themselves have built (1957, p. 199). They are engaged in a continuous process of perceiving miscellaneous data in terms of their model, again leaving out that which cannot fit within the framework of the model, adding to it in order to make the model complete, and structuring it to keep the pattern of the model safe from disturbances. The concept that there is a certain set of objective data which all executives or managers would perceive in the same way and from which any two of them would make the same decision with regard to maximizing profit would not stand up under current analysis with regard to perception theory.

Perception as Factual and Rational

Even the supposed "factuality" of certain data may be a relative matter. Research in the social sciences has suggested that we tend to perceive only those data as "factual" which society generally agrees upon as being "factual." It has been pointed out that the only way an individual can adjust to other human beings is by checking his own impressions and observations against others' opinions. Only when his perceptions are adjusted to correspond sufficiently with the perceptions of others can he relate to others and communicate with them at all. Thus, perceptions of everyone in a society or social group tend to conform to one another. Persons actually tend to perceive only those things which fit in with an agreed-upon picture of things. As a result of this conformance to socially accepted actuality, it may be difficult for a manager not only to raise as a problem something which he feels his superiors will not see as a problem, but it may be difficult for him even to perceive such a problem in the first place.

The two opposing processes—that of building our own unique perceptual framework from our own individual experiences, and that of trimming and supplementing our perceptual framework to conform with others' perceptions (others' opinions being part of our individual experience)—go on continuously. However, it should be clear that neither of these perceptual processes results necessarily in objective perception of data. When a part of a person's unique perceptual processes conforms to society, this does not mean it conforms to "reality."

Another factor affecting human perception in our culture is that persons want to perceive data as having a rational basis and want to give rational explanations for data. This concept suggests the possibility that the entire theory of firm behavior proposed by traditional economists may have been created in an effort to perceive firm behavior as having an objective, rational basis. Once such a rational theory is created, most people would be more willing to hold onto that rationality than to begin investigation again in a realm of nonrational flux.

Despite the fact that we may view the perceived data as rational, emotion and many other nonrational factors may strongly affect perception (see Wittreich, 1959, pp. 56–60). Karen Horney stresses particularly the distorting effect of anxiety upon perception. Horney has pointed out that states of anxiety or perceived threat cause the perceiving individual to narrow significantly his perceptual framework (Horney, 1937, Ch. 3). An anxious person, a person who perceives himself under threat, actually does not observe as much as he does when not threatened. Individuals in a firm who are operating more or less continually under threat will have correspondingly limited perceptual behavior. Surely this is a factor of importance in any theory which attempts to account for the behavior of firms when dealing with crucial problems under threatening conditions.

Persistence of Perceptual Framework

The great attachment man has for his perceptual framework can scarcely be overemphasized. He is highly reluctant to give up any of his perceptions, his organized wholes, his models which seem to work. If a frame of reference for perception allows the individual to operate without too much stress and without blocking him with too many problems, he will cling vigorously to that perceptual frame. One of man's strongest desires is for the security of an ordered environment. According to Haire, man "is reluctant to give up any organizations that seem to work, because of the danger that is involved in being lost in a disorganized environment" (*op. cit.*, p. 41). Man does not wish to upset areas of order except when forced to do so, even though such order may be only illusional. Since a man's own self-concept is involved in that perceptual frame, giving up his perceptual frame may mean giving up his sense of his own identity and meaningfulness. Thus, in many businesses, we observe that outmoded techniques continue to be retained longer than the concept of "maximization of profit" and other traditional concepts of firm behavior would suggest.

Motivation

In the search for a theory of firm behavior, it is also important to be aware of certain assumptions about human "motivation." It no longer appears possible to assume that executives and managers are simply embodiments of the motivation for profit maximization and that their behavior can be explained merely in terms of this single motive. In order to attempt to understand the behavior of businessmen, we must take into account other concepts of motivation.

It should be noted at the outset, however, that concepts of motivation cannot be separated from related concepts of perception. The separation of these two aspects of behavior for the purposes of this chapter should be considered as a method which, although useful in analysis, is somewhat unrealistic in that behavior is "seamless."

Definition of "Motive"

The idea of a "motive" is so common in lay conversation and thinking that it might be well to outline briefly the concept of motivation as it is used here. Motivation may be meaningfully discussed from two angles. First, it may be discussed in terms of its internal aspect, its reference to a state of inner dissatisfaction, a state of needs, wants, or desires, a state in which bodily energy is mobilized, a state of a drive which the organism is impelled to relieve. Secondly, motivation may be discussed from its outer aspect, as a sequence of behavior selectively directed in terms of a goal. Goal, then, refers to the outer directional aspect of behavior in a given situation. Thus, we may define motivation as characterized both by a state of drive and by the direction of behavior toward some goal selected in preference to other possible goals. Since all theories do not give equal emphasis to these two aspects of motivation, let us begin by considering the two approaches separately.

"Inner Motivation": Emphasis on the Individual

One widely accepted concept is that all persons are motivated by certain needs. Various lists of such needs have been advanced by a number of investigators, and though we find differences among the lists, they are generally similar. Perhaps most investigators would agree upon this basic list of needs: physiological needs (need for air, food, water, etc.), social needs (need to belong to a group and to have social relations with others), and ego or individual needs (need for approval, acceptance, mastery, etc.). There are certainly many longer lists which include such items as need for security, need for wider experience, need for a sense of meaningfulness, etc. Theodore Brammeld, however, considers a list of even three needs too long, since it implies that man is somehow composed of separate compartments. Brammeld points out that there is no sense of ego separate from the socially perceived ego; and therefore the self is a social self. Further, the physical components of the organism cannot be separated from the mental or psychological components. Brammeld therefore suggests that man has but one basic drive or motivating force: "social self-realization" (1956, p. 119).

The assumption that businessmen are motivated for maximization of profit is very different from the assumption that men have certain basic needs or drives seeking fulfillment. Maximization of profit certainly may serve in some ways several of these physiological, social, and ego needs, but it is evident that other channels as well present themselves as means for serving these drives in the atmosphere of the business organization. Some of the opportunities for serving man's needs may be in actual conflict with the firm's maximization of profit.

"Outer Motivation": Emphasis on the Situation

On the other end of the continuum there are those theorists who see motivation as having its roots primarily in the situation or in environment. Karl Mannheim, a representative of this view, states that "both motives and actions very often originate not from within but from the situation in which individuals find themselves" (1940, p. 249). Allport suggests that "situational variability has led many social scientists to the conviction that any search for a consistent personality with specifiable motives and traits is doomed to failure" (1956, p. 243). He goes on to quote William James to the effect that each situation has different motives: "A man has as many selves as there are distinct groups about whose opinion he cares" (p. 244). When considering the motives of businessmen, one must be aware of the influence of the business situation. At the same time, it is a dangerous generalization to assume that any two situations are ever the same or that any two individual businessmen will perceive any situation in exactly the same way, or even that one businessman will perceive the same situation the same way on two different occasions. Further, it may be readily seen that the business environment may provide many motives for the individual in addition to that of profit maximization. The businessman may be motivated by titles, large offices, or personal friendships as well as by his personal or family security. Such motives may have no direct connection with the goals of the firm.

Role Theory in Relation to Motivation

This emphasis on the situation borders on the concept of "role theory," which assumes that individuals take on certain motives as they assume different roles. A "role" is defined by Sargent as "a pattern or type of social behavior which seems situationally appropriate to the individual in terms of the demands and expectations of those in his group" (1950, p. 279). Role theory suggests that as the individual's position in the group changes, his motivations may also change. Mannheim, for example, posits that businessmen change their motives as they assume different roles on the way up the business ladder. "There is normally a graduated scale of motives by which men from different social classes are driven to work. . . . Whenever a man rises to a higher class . . . he switches over from one set of motives to another" (Mannheim, *op. cit.*, p. 316). It should be noted however that not all writers on role theory place this much emphasis on role as a motivating factor. The sociologist Nelson Foote, for example, states that "roles as such do not provide their own motives" (1951, p. 14). Mason Haire suggests that the "social definition" of a role is not specific enough to completely govern the behavior of an individual (*op. cit.*, p. 184). According to Herbert Simon: "Any particular concrete behavior is a resultant of a large number of premises, only some of which are prescribed by the role" (1959, p. 274). Although role theory does not appear to give a total explanation to individual motivation in a particular setting, it does suggest one additional source of motivation. If we can become aware of how individuals perceive their role at a particular time, we may be able to gain insight into behavior at that time.

Middle of the Continuum

A number of writers stress the importance of understanding both the "inner" individual and the "outer" situation in order to understand the motivation of the individual. George Kelly, while stating that a knowledge of the situation is essential to understanding psychological motives involved (1958, p. 63), indicates the reciprocal relationship between the two. Allport is another who gives both factors weight: "The perceiver himself may . . . be the principal source of variance; the situation in which the object-person acts may be the second source of variance; and the fixed traits and motives of the object-person may be only a minor factor" (*op. cit.*, p. 243).

Complexity and Multiplicity of Motivations

Traditional economists suggest a single business motivation, that of profit maximization. Recent psychological and sociological research, however, seems to indicate the interrelatedness of motives. Maslow, as a result of his investigations, concludes: "Most behavior is multimotivated. Within the sphere of motivational determinants, any behavior tends to be determined by several or all the basic needs simultaneously rather than by any one of them" (1954, p. 102). According to Allport, "It seems clear that the units we seek in personality and in motivation are relatively complex structures, not molecular" (*op. cit.*, p. 242). An attempt to explain business behavior based on a single overriding motive appears unrealistic in view of current research. A businessman's personal goals probably are not the same as those of the "organization," and, in fact, as Festinger points out, the satisfaction of either the goals of the business or of the individual may prohibit the satisfaction of the other's goals (1958, pp. 65–86). However, Festinger also suggests that in a situation in which the goals of the individual conflict with the goals of the firm, "there will be some tendency for the person to attempt to change one of them so that they do fit together, thus reducing or eliminating the dissonance" (p. 70). Yet it may be the organizational goals he attempts to change in favor of his own.

Aspiration Level

One aspect of motivation which has received some attention recently and which proponents feel offers considerable insight into understanding and predicting human behavior is the concept of "level of aspiration." J. D. Frank, an early writer on this concept, defines "level of aspiration" as "the level of future performance in a familiar task which an individual, knowing his level of past performance in that task, explicitly undertakes to reach" (1935, p. 119). Kurt Lewin found from his experiments that "success and failure influence deeply the emotional status of the person, his goals, and his social relations. . . . After success, a person generally sets himself a higher goal. After failure, his level of aspiration generally goes down" (1936, p. 926). Lewin states: "The stronger the success the greater will be the percentage of raising the level of aspiration, and the stronger the failure the greater the percent of lowering the level of aspiration" (1944, p. 338). Simon stresses the correspondence of the two from his findings, stating: "In the long run the level of aspiration and attainable maximum will be very close together" (*op. cit.*, p. 272).

Such findings suggest that if we know the level of aspiration of a particular businessman we could begin to predict his behavior in certain situations. For example, if the owner of a construction firm had aspirations of a future large job, such an individual might retain his employees in relation to such aspirations rather than let workers go when work is slack. In such a case, prediction of behavior in terms of aspiration levels might be considerably different from a prediction in terms of maximization of profit.

The concept of "aspiration level," however, is not without criticism. John Gardner suggests that there may be a "region" of aspiration or a "direction" of aspiration, but that a "level" does not appear to be a realistic term. He views the concept of a "level of aspiration" as an attempt to quantify something which is qualitative. He also suggests that there may be two or more aspiration levels operating in an individual at a particular time (1958, pp. 229–34). Katona questions the concept of individual "levels of aspirations" in that "aspirations are influenced by the performance of the members of the group to which one belongs" (1953, p. 316). Here again we are confronted with those internal-external factors of motivation discussed earlier. Nevertheless, the concept of "level of aspiration" with regard to motivation is a concept which must be faced by businessmen and economists in attempting to develop a general theory of firm behavior.

In summary, it may be said that modern psychological concepts of motivation do not support the traditional economic theory that firm behavior may be explained by the single motivation of maximization of profit. Human motivation is not single but complex, and even conflicting. Further, human motives based on a number of needs or drives may well be satisfied through the firm in ways other than through maximization of profit.

Comments and Conclusions

Having presented some general concepts in the theories of perception and motivation, we must point out that although the two subjects were separated for the purposes of analysis, they are inherently interrelated, and their contributions toward an understanding of firm behavior are of the same nature. There are, however, certain limitations to the usefulness of the concepts of perception and motivation.

Problems in Ascertaining Motivations and Perceptions

Probably the most serious limitations of these theories involve the difficulty of ascertaining perceptions and motivations. Two methods for determining perceptions and motivations are (1) to have the individual state what his motivations are and how he sees or perceives the world, or (2) to observe overt actions and draw assumptions from these actions.

A problem in the first method is that we are faced with the task of interpreting the individual's statement about his motivations. Even though he desired to communicate his perceptions and motivations accurately, we find that his word symbols for his subjective experiences may be difficult to interpret with assurance. The problem is further complicated because of the fact that an individual's verbal behavior is not necessarily indicative of his attitudes. Behavior which is visible to others may be "edited" so that it appears acceptable to others. A number of writers have asked businessmen what their motives are, yet the results may be no more valuable than the original concept of profit maximization (see Hickman and Kuhn, 1956, Ch. 2).

The second alternative for ascertaining perceptions and motivations—that of observing behavior—adds the problem of the projection of the motivations and perceptions of the observer on to the observed and the fact that the observations are recorded in the vocabulary of the observer rather than that of the observed. As noted above, the observer may influence the data with his own specific, individualized meaning.

Other Criticisms of Motivation and Perception Theory

Certain aspects of motivation theory have been criticized on several grounds other than the difficulty of ascertainment. Maslow has stated that "too many of the findings that have been made in animals have been proven to be true only for animals and not for human beings. There is no reason whatsoever why we should start with animals in order to study human motivation" (*op. cit.*, pp. 103–4). This criticism seems to suggest that much of the investigation about theories of motivation has been "zoo-morphic." Maslow also points out that many of the findings in motivation theory have come from the study of seriously disturbed people and that these generalizations may not hold true for individuals who appear to be able to cope with society, e.g., businessmen. Further, motivation theory has been criticized as being static, i.e., based on a premise of static properties in individuals. Finally, as has been suggested previously, motivation theory has been criticized as being highly prone to the dangers of projection. It has been suggested that possibly we can tell more about the person who attributes certain motives to another than we can about the person to whom the motives were attributed. Methods of investigating motivations must involve specific means of offsetting the dangers presented above.

Despite certain specific criticisms of motivation theory, however, it seems to be well established that human motivation is so complex that no single explanation of motivation, such as that of profit maximization, can be applied to all businessmen or to all business behavior. It may be difficult to accommodate ourselves to this conclusion, however, because it makes the building of a "tight" business model very difficult.

Conclusion

The problem of building a theory of firm behavior *today* can readily be seen to be highly complex. It is possible that, in a previous era, motivation of the individual in the firm could have been conceived in more singular terms than it is today. Indeed, Schumpeter points out that during the late nineteenth century a primary emphasis of the businessman appeared to be the acquisition of a large home, a large family, and a large estate to leave to his descendants (1950, pp. 156–63). Thus, perhaps it is possible that during the late nineteenth century the motivations of businessmen could be explained in more single terms, for example, by the motive of profit maximization, than they may be today. However, the problem of constructing a theory of firm behavior, in view of recent investigations into individual perception and behavior, can no longer be resolved by the simple positing of a single and rational profit motive.

Nevertheless, while the explanation of business motivation in terms of a single primary motivation of profit maximization appears to be an unwarranted oversimplification of business behavior, we cannot altogether reject the profit motive as an important factor in business behavior. As Katona stated: "There can be no doubt that in present-day American business thinking the function and role of profits is substantial." (1951, p. 194). What must be thrown open to question and further investigation is the extent to which actions of businessmen can be explained by the profit motive as well as by the many other motives that propel human behavior.

This article has presented some of the current investigations into motivation and perception which must be considered in constructing a new theory of firm behavior. It may be seen that perception and motivation theories do not in themselves provide a ready-made general theory of firm behavior applicable to all situations. It may be, in fact, that such an all-encompassing theory is not feasible. Katona suggests that "the proximate aim of scientific research is a body of empirically validatable generalizations and not a theory that is validated under any and all circumstances" (1953, p. 317). Yet, in the search for a variety of such generalizations capable of explaining behavior under given circumstances, motivation and perception theory will offer considerable insight into firm behavior.

References

Allport, Gordon W. "What Units Shall We Employ?" In *Assessment of Human Motives*, ed. Gardner Lindzey. Holt, Rinehart & Winston, 1958.

Bakke, E. Wight. *Organization and the Individual*. Yale University Labor and Management Center, 1952.

Brammeld, Theodore. *Toward a Reconstructed Philosophy of Education.* Dryden Press, 1956.

Festinger, Leon. "The Motivating Effect of Cognitive Dissonance." In *Assessment of Human Motives,* ed. Gardner Lindzey. Holt, Rinehart & Winston, 1958.

Foote, Nelson N. "Identification as the Basis for a Theory of Motivation." *American Sociological Review,* Vol. 16, No. 1, February 1951.

Frank, J. D. "Individual Differences in Certain Aspects of the Level of Aspiration." *American Journal of Psychology,* Vol. 45, 1935.

Gardner, John W. "The Use of the Term 'Level of Aspiration.'" In *Understanding Human Motivation,* eds. C. L. Stacey and M. F. Martino. Howard Allen, 1958.

Haire, Mason. *Psychology in Management.* McGraw-Hill, 1956.

Hickman, C. A., and M. H. Kuhn. *Individuals, Groups, and Economic Behavior.* Dryden Press, 1956.

Horney, Karen. *The Neurotic Personality of Our Time.* Norton, 1937.

Katona, George. "Rational Behavior and Economic Behavior." *Psychological Review,* July 1953.

———. *Psychological Analysis of Economic Behavior.* McGraw-Hill, 1951.

Kelly, George A. "Man's Construction of His Alternatives." In *Assessment of Human Motives,* ed. Gardner Lindzey. Holt, Rinehart & Winston, 1958.

Lewin, Kurt. "Psychology of Success and Failure." *Occupations,* Vol. 14, No. 9, June 1936.

Lewin, Kurt, Tamara Dembo, Leon Festinger, and Pauline Sears. "Level of Aspiration." In *Personality and the Behavior Disorders,* ed. J. McV. Hunt. Howard Allen, 1958 (2 vols.).

Mannheim, Karl. *Man and Society in an Age of Reconstruction.* Harcourt, Brace & World, 1940.

Maslow, A. H. *Motivation and Personality.* Harper, 1954.

Sargent, S. Stansfeld. *Social Psychology: An Integrative Interpretation.* Ronald Press, 1950.

Schumpeter, Joseph A. *Capitalism, Socialism, and Democracy,* 3rd ed. Harper & Row, 1950.

Simon, Herbert A. "Decision Making in Economics." *American Economic Review,* June 1959.

———. *Models of Man: Social and Rational.* Wiley, 1957.

Wittreich, Warren J. "Visual Perception and Personality." *Scientific American,* April 1959.

Abraham Maslow

A Theory of Human Motivation

Dynamics of the Basic Needs

The "Physiological" Needs

The needs that are usually taken as the starting point for motivation theory are the so-called physiological drives. Two recent lines of research make it necessary to revise our customary notions about these needs: first, the development of the concept of homeostasis, and, second, the finding that appetites (preferential choices among foods) are a fairly efficient indication of actual needs or lacks in the body.

Homeostasis refers to the body's automatic efforts to maintain a constant, normal state of the blood stream. Cannon (1932) has described this process for (1) the water content of the blood, (2) salt content, (3) sugar content, (4) protein content, (5) fat content, (6) calcium content, (7) oxygen content, (8) constant hydrogen-ion level (acid-base balance) and (9) constant temperature of the blood. Obviously this list can be extended to include other minerals, the hormones, vitamins, etc.

Young, in a recent article (1946, pp. 129–64), has summarized the work on appetite in its relation to body needs. If the body lacks some chemical, the individual will tend to develop a specific appetite or partial hunger for that food element.

Thus it seems impossible as well as useless to make any list of fundamental physiological needs for they can come to almost any number one might wish, depending on the degree of specificity of description. We cannot identify all physiological needs as homeostatic. That sexual desire, sleepiness, sheer activity, and maternal behavior in animals are homeostatic has not yet been demonstrated. Furthermore, this list would not include the various sensory pleasures (tastes, smells, tickling, stroking) which are probably physiological and which may become the goals of motivated behavior.

From Abraham Maslow, "A Theory of Motivation," *Psychological Review*, Vol. 50, 1943, pp. 370–396. Copyright © 1943 by the American Psychological Association, and reproduced by permission.

In a previous paper (Maslow, 1943, pp. 85–92) it has been pointed out that these physiological drives or needs are to be considered unusual rather than typical because they are isolable and because they are localizable somatically. That is to say, they are relatively independent of each other, of other motivations and of the organism as a whole, and, in many cases, it is possible to demonstrate a localized, underlying somatic base for the drive. This is true less generally than has been thought (exceptions are fatigue, sleepiness, maternal responses), but it is still true in the classic instances of hunger, sex, and thirst.

It should be pointed out again that any of the physiological needs and the consummatory behavior involved with them serve as channels for all sorts of other needs as well. The person who thinks he is hungry may actually be seeking more for comfort or dependence than for vitamins or proteins. Conversely, it is possible to satisfy the hunger need in part by other activities, such as drinking water or smoking cigarettes. In other words, these physiological needs are only relatively isolable.

Undoubtedly these physiological needs are the most prepotent of all needs. What this means specifically is that, in the human being who is missing everything in life in an extreme fashion, it is most likely that the major motivation would be the physiological needs rather than any others. A person who is lacking food, safety, love, and esteem would most probably hunger for food more strongly than for anything else.

If all the needs are unsatisfied, and the organism is then dominated by the physiological needs, all other needs may become simply non-existent or be pushed into the background. It is then fair to characterize the whole organism by saying simply that it is hungry, for consciousness is almost completely pre-empted by hunger. All capacities are put into the service of hunger-satisfaction, and the organization of these capacities is almost entirely determined by the one purpose of satisfying hunger. The receptors and effectors, the intelligence, memory, habits, all may now be defined simply as hunger-gratifying tools. Capacities that are not useful for this purpose lie dormant or are pushed into the background. The urge to write poetry, the desire to acquire an automobile, the interest in American history, the desire for a new pair of shoes are, in the extreme case, forgotten or become of secondary importance. For the man who is extremely and dangerously hungry, no other interests exist but food. He dreams food, he remembers food, he thinks about food, he emotes only about food, he perceives only food, and he wants only food. The more subtle determinants that ordinarily fuse with the physiological drives in organizing even feeding, drinking, or sexual behavior may now be so completely overwhelmed as to allow us to speak at this time (but *only* at this time) of pure hunger drive and behavior, with the one unqualified aim of relief.

Another peculiar characteristic of the human organism when it is dominated by a certain need is that the whole philosophy of the future tends also to change. For our chronically and extremely hungry man, utopia can be defined very simply as a place where there is plenty of food. He tends to think that, if only he is guaranteed food for the rest of his life, he will be perfectly happy and will never want anything more. Life itself tends to be defined in terms of eating. Anything else will be defined as unimportant. Freedom, love, community feeling, respect, philosophy, may all be waved aside as fripperies which are useless, since they fail to fill the stomach. Such a man may fairly be said to live by bread alone.

It cannot possibly be denied that such things are true, but their *generality* can be denied. Emergency conditions are, almost by definition, rare in the normally functioning peaceful society. That this truism can be forgotten is due mainly to two reasons. First, rats have few motivations other than physiological ones, and since so much of the research upon motivation has been made with these animals, it is easy to carry the rat-picture over to the human being. Second, it is too often not realized that culture itself is an adaptive tool, one of whose main functions is to make the physiological emergencies come less and less often. In most of the known societies, chronic extreme hunger of the emergency type is rare rather than common. In any case, this is still true in the United States. The average American citizen is experiencing appetite rather than hunger when he says, "I am hungry." He is apt to experience sheer life-and-death hunger only by accident and then only a few times through his entire life.

Obviously a good way to obscure the "higher" motivations, and to get a lopsided view of human capacities and human nature, is to make the organism extremely and chronically hungry or thirsty. Anyone who attempts to make an emergency picture into a typical one and who will measure all of man's goals and desires by his behavior during extreme physiological deprivation is certainly being blind to many things. It is quite true that man lives by bread alone—when there is no bread. But what happens to man's desires when there *is* plenty of bread and when his belly is chronically filled?

At once other (and "higher") needs emerge and these, rather than physiological hungers, dominate the organism. And when these in turn are satisfied, again new (and still "higher") needs emerge, and so on. This is what we mean by saying that the basic human needs are organized into a hierarchy of relative prepotency.

One main implication of this phrasing is that gratification becomes as important a concept as deprivation in motivation theory, for it releases the organism from the domination of a relatively more physiological need, permitting thereby the emergence of other, more social goals. The physiological needs, along with their partial goals, when chronically gratified cease to exist as active determinants or organizers of behavior. They now exist only in a potential fashion in the sense that they may emerge again to dominate the organism if they are thwarted. But a want that is satisfied is no longer a want. The organism is dominated and its behavior organized only by unsatisfied needs. If hunger is satisfied, it becomes unimportant in the current dynamics of the individual.

This statement is somewhat qualified by a hypothesis to be discussed more fully later, namely, that it is precisely those individuals in whom a certain need has always been satisfied who are best equipped to tolerate deprivation of that need in the future; furthermore, those who have been deprived in the past will react to current satisfactions differently from the one who has never been deprived.

The Safety Needs

If the physiological needs are relatively well gratified, there then emerges a new set of needs, which we may categorize roughly as the safety needs. All that has been said of the physiological needs is equally true, although in lesser degree, of these desires. The organism may equally well be wholly dominated by them. They may serve as the almost exclusive organizers of behavior, recruiting all the capacities of the organism in their service, and we may then fairly describe the whole organism as a safety-seeking mechanism. Again we may say of the receptors, the effectors, of the intellect and the other capacities that they are primarily safety-seeking tools. Again, as in the hungry man, we find that the dominating goal is a strong determinant not only of his current world-outlook and philosophy but also of his philosophy of the future. Practically everything looks less important than safety (even sometimes the physiological needs, which, being satisfied, are now underestimated). A man in this state, if it is extreme enough and chronic enough, may be characterized as living almost for safety alone.

Although in this paper we are interested primarily in the needs of the adult, we can approach an understanding of his safety needs perhaps more efficiently by observation of infants and children, in whom these needs are much more simple and obvious. One reason for the clearer appearance of the threat or danger reaction in infants is that they do not inhibit this reaction at all, whereas adults in our society have been taught to inhibit it at all costs. Thus even when adults do feel their safety to be threatened, we may not be able to see this on the surface. Infants will react in a total fashion, and as if they were endangered, if they are disturbed or dropped suddenly, startled by loud noises, flashing light, or other unusual sensory stimulation, by rough handling, by general loss of support in the mother's arms, or by inadequate support.[1]

In infants we can also see a much more direct reaction to bodily illnesses of various kinds. Sometimes these illnesses seem to be immediately and per se threatening and seem to make the child feel unsafe. For instance, vomiting, colic, or other sharp pains seem to make the child look at the whole world in a different way. At such a moment of pain, it may be postulated that, for the child, the appearance of the whole world suddenly changes from sunniness to darkness, so to speak, and becomes a place in which anything at all might happen, in which previously stable things have suddenly become unstable. Thus a child who because of some bad food is taken ill may, for a day or two, develop fear, nightmares, and a need for protection and reassurance never seen in him before his illness.

Another indication of the child's need for safety is his preference for some kind of undisrupted routine or rhythm. He seems to want a predictable, orderly world. For instance, injustice, unfairness, or inconsistency in the parents seems to make a child feel anxious and unsafe. This attitude may be not so much because of the injustice per se or any particular pains involved, but rather because this treatment threatens to make the world look unreliable or unsafe or unpredictable. Young children seem to thrive better under a system which has at least a skeletal outline of rigidity, in which there is a schedule of a kind, some sort of routine, something that can be counted upon, not only for the present, but also far into the future. Perhaps one could express this more accurately by saying that the child needs an organized world rather than an unorganized or unstructured one.

The central role of the parents and the normal family setup are indisputable. Quarreling, physical assault, separation, divorce, or death within the family may be particularly terrifying. Also parental outbursts of rage or threats of punishment directed to the child, calling him names, speaking to him harshly, shaking him, handling him roughly, or actual physical punishment sometimes elicit such total panic and terror in the child that we must assume more is involved than the physical pain alone. While it is true that in some children this terror may represent also a fear of loss of parental love, it can also occur in completely rejected children, who seem to cling to the hating parents more for sheer safety and protection than because of hope of love.

Confronting the average child with new, unfamiliar, strange, un-

---

1. As the child grows up, sheer knowledge and familiarity as well as better motor development make these "dangers" less and less dangerous and more and more manageable. Throughout life it may be said that one of the main conative functions of education is this neutralizing of apparent dangers through knowledge, e.g., I am not afraid of thunder because I know something about it.

manageable stimuli or situations will too frequently elicit the danger or terror reaction, as, for example, getting lost or even being separated from the parents for a short time, being confronted with new faces, new situations, or new tasks, the sight of strange, unfamiliar or uncontrollable objects, illness, or death. Particularly at such times, the child's frantic clinging to his parents is eloquent testimony to their role as protectors (quite apart from their roles as food-givers and love-givers).

From these and similar observations, we may generalize and say that the average child in our society usually prefers a safe, orderly, predictable, organized world which he can count on and in which unexpected, unmanageable, or other dangerous things do not happen and in which, in any case, he has all-powerful parents who protect and shield him from harm.

That these reactions may so easily be observed in children is in a way a proof of the fact that children in our society feel too unsafe (or, in a word, are badly brought up). Children who are reared in an unthreatening, loving family do *not* ordinarily react as we have described above (see Shirley, 1941, pp. 201–17). In such children the danger reactions are apt to come mostly to objects or situations that adults too would consider dangerous.[2]

The healthy, normal, fortunate adult in our culture is largely satisfied in his safety needs. The peaceful, smoothly running, "good" society ordinarily makes its members feel safe enough from wild animals, extremes of temperature, criminals, assault and murder, tyranny, etc. Therefore, in a very real sense, they no longer have any safety needs as active motivators. Just as a sated man no longer feels hungry, a safe man no longer feels endangered. If we wish to see these needs directly and clearly, we must turn to neurotic or near-neurotic individuals, and to the economic and social underdogs. In between these extremes, we can perceive the expressions of safety needs only in such phenomena as, for instance, the common preference for a job with tenure and protection, the desire for a savings account, and for insurance of various kinds (medical, dental, unemployment, disability, old age).

Other broader aspects of the attempt to seek safety and stability in the world are seen in the very common preference for familiar rather than unfamiliar things, or for the known rather than the

_____

2. A "test battery" for safety might be confronting the child with a small exploding firecracker or with a bewhiskered face, having the mother leave the room, putting him upon a high ladder, giving him a hypodermic injection, having a mouse crawl up to him, etc. Of course I cannot seriously recommend the deliberate use of such "tests," for they might very well harm the child being tested. But these and similar situations come up by the score in the child's ordinary day-to-day living and may be observed. There is no reason why these stimuli should not be used with, for example, young chimpanzees.

unknown. The tendency to have some religion or world-philosophy that organizes the universe and the men in it into some sort of satisfactorily coherent, meaningful whole is also in part motivated by safety-seeking. Here too we may list science and philosophy in general as partially motivated by the safety needs (we shall see later that there are also other motivations to scientific, philosophical, or religious endeavor).

Otherwise the need for safety is seen as an active and dominant mobilizer of the organism's resources only in emergencies, e.g., war, disease, natural catastrophes, crime waves, societal disorganization, neurosis, brain injury—chronically bad situations.

Some neurotic adults in our society are, in many ways, like the unsafe child in their desire for safety, although in the former it takes on a somewhat special appearance. They often react to unknown, psychological dangers in a world that is perceived to be hostile, overwhelming and threatening. Such a person behaves as if a great catastrophe were almost always impending, i.e., he is usually responding as if to an emergency. His safety needs often find specific expression in a search for a protector, or a stronger person on whom he may depend, or perhaps a *Führer*.

The neurotic individual may be described in a slightly different way, with some usefulness, as a grown-up person who retains his childish attitudes toward the world. That is to say, a neurotic adult may be said to behave "as if" he were actually afraid of a spanking or of his mother's disapproval or of being abandoned by his parents or of having his food taken away from him. It is as if his childish attitudes of fear and threat reaction to a dangerous world had gone underground and, untouched by the growing up and learning processes, were now ready to be called out by any stimulus that would make a child feel endangered and threatened.[3]

The neurosis in which the search for safety takes its clearest form is in the compulsive-obsessive neurosis. Compulsive-obsessives try frantically to order and stabilize the world so that no unmanageable, unexpected, or unfamiliar dangers will ever appear (see Maslow and Mittelmann, 1941). They hedge themselves about with all sorts of ceremonials, rules, and formulas so that every possible contingency may be provided for and so that no new contingencies may appear. They are much like the brain-injured cases, described by Goldstein (1939), who manage to maintain their equilibrium by avoiding everything unfamiliar and strange and by ordering their restricted world in such a neat, disciplined, orderly fashion that everything in the world can be counted upon. They try to arrange the

---

3. Not all neurotic individuals feel unsafe. Neurosis may have at its core a thwarting of the affection and esteem needs in a person who is generally safe.

world so that anything unexpected (dangers) cannot possibly occur. If, through no fault of their own, something unexpected does occur, they go into a panic reaction as if this unexpected occurrence constituted a grave danger. What we can see only as a none-too-strong preference in the healthy person, e.g., preference for the familiar, becomes a life-and-death necessity in abnormal cases.

The Love Needs

If both the physiological and the safety needs are fairly well gratified, then there will emerge the love and affection and belongingness needs, and the whole cycle already described will repeat itself with this new center. Now the person will feel keenly, as never before, the absence of friends or a sweetheart or a wife or children. He will hunger for affectionate relations with people in general, namely, for a place in his group, and he will strive with great intensity to achieve this goal. He will want to attain such a place more than anything else in the world and may even forget that once, when he was hungry, he sneered at love.

In our society the thwarting of these needs is the most commonly found core in cases of maladjustment and more severe psychopathology. Love and affection, as well as their possible expression in sexuality, are generally looked upon with ambivalence and are customarily hedged about with many restrictions and inhibitions. Practically all theorists of psychopathology have stressed thwarting of the love needs as basic in the picture of maladjustment. Many clinical studies have therefore been made of this need and we know more about it, perhaps, than any of the other needs except the physiological ones (see Maslow and Mittelmann, *op. cit.*).

One thing that must be stressed at this point is that love is not synonymous with sex. Sex may be studied as a purely physiological need. Ordinarily sexual behavior is multi-determined, that is to say, determined not only by sexual but also by other needs, chief among which are the love and affection needs. Also not to be overlooked is the fact that the love needs involve both giving *and* receiving love (see Maslow, 1942, pp. 331–44; and Plant, 1937, Ch. 5).

The Esteem Needs

All people in our society (with a few pathological exceptions) have a need or desire for a stable, firmly based (usually) high evaluation of themselves, for self-respect, or self-esteem, and for the esteem of others. By firmly based self-esteen, we mean that which is soundly based upon real capacity, achievement, and respect from others. These needs may be classified into two subsidiary sets. These are, first, the desire for strength, for achievement, for adequacy, for confidence in the face of the world, and for independence and freedom.[4] Second, we have what we may call the desire for reputation or prestige (defining it as respect or esteem from other people), recognition, attention, importance, or appreciation.[5] These needs have been relatively stressed by Alfred Adler and his followers, and have been relatively neglected by Freud and the psychoanalysts. More and more today, however, there is appearing widespread appreciation of their central importance.

Satisfaction of the self-esteem need leads to feelings of self-confidence, worth, strength, capability, and adequacy, of being useful and necessary in the world. But thwarting of these needs produces feelings of inferiority, of weakness, and of helplessness. These feelings in turn give rise to either basic discouragement or else compensatory or neurotic trends. An appreciation of the necessity of basic self-confidence and an understanding of how helpless people are without it can be easily gained from a study of severe traumatic neurosis (Kardiner, 1941).[6]

The Need for Self-Actualization

Even if all these needs are satisfied, we may still often (if not always) expect that a new discontent and restlessness will soon develop, unless the individual is doing what he is fitted for. A musician must make music, an artist must paint, a poet must write, if he is to be ultimately happy. What a man *can* be, he *must* be. This need we may call self-actualization.

This term, first coined by Kurt Goldstein, is being used in this paper in a much more specific and limited fashion. It refers to the desire for self-fulfilment, namely, to the tendency for one to become actualized in what one is potentially. This tendency might be phrased as the desire to become more and more what one is, to become everything that one is capable of becoming.

The specific form that these needs take will of course vary greatly from person to person. In one individual it may be expressed maternally, as the desire to be an ideal mother, in another athleti-

---

4. Whether or not this particular desire is universal we do not know. The crucial question, especially important today, is "Will men who are enslaved and dominated inevitably feel dissatisfied and rebellious?" We may assume on the basis of commonly known clinical data that a man who has known true freedom (not paid for by giving up safety and security but rather built on the basis of adequate safety and security) will not willingly or easily allow his freedom to be taken away from him. But we do not know that this is true for the person born into slavery. The events of the next decade should give us our answer. See the discussion of this problem in Fromm (1941), Ch. 5.

5. Perhaps the desire for prestige and respect from others is subsidiary to the desire for self-esteem or confidence in one's self. Observation of children seems to indicate that this is so, but clinical data give no clear support of such a conclusion.

6. For more extensive discussion of normal self-esteem, as well as for reports of various researches, see Maslow (1939), pp. 3–39.

cally, in still another aesthetically, in the painting of pictures, and in another inventively in the creation of new contrivances. It is not necessarily a creative urge, although in people who have any capabilities for creation it will take this form.

The clear emergence of these needs rests upon prior satisfaction of the physiological, safety, love and esteem needs. We shall call people who are satisfied in these needs basically satisfied people, and it is from these that we may expect the fullest (and healthiest) creativeness.[7] Since, in our society, basically satisfied people are the exception, we do not know much about self-actualization, either experimentally or clinically. It remains a challenging problem for research.

There are certain conditions which are immediate prerequisites for the basic need satisfactions. Danger to these is reacted to almost as if it were a direct danger to the basic needs themselves. Such conditions as freedom to speak, freedom to do what one wishes so long as no harm is done to others, freedom to express one's self, freedom to investigate and seek for information, freedom to defend one's self, justice, fairness, honesty, orderliness in the group are examples of such preconditions for basic need satisfactions. Thwarting of these freedoms will be reacted to with a threat or emergency response. These conditions are not ends in themselves but they are *almost* so, since they are so closely related to the basic needs, which are apparently the only ends in themselves. These conditions are defended because without them the basic satisfactions are quite impossible, or at least, very severely endangered.

If we remember that the cognitive capacities (perceptual, intellectual, learning) are a set of adjustive tools, which have, among other functions, that of satisfaction of our basic needs, then it is clear that any danger to them, any deprivation or blocking of their free use, must also be indirectly threatening to the basic needs themselves. Such a statement is a partial solution of the general problems of curiosity, the search for knowledge, truth, and wisdom, and the ever persistent urge to solve the cosmic mysteries.

We must therefore introduce another hypothesis and speak of degrees of closeness to the basic needs, for we have already pointed out that *any* conscious desires (partial goals) are more or less important as they are more or less close to the basic needs. The same

---

7. Clearly creative behavior, like painting, is like any other behavior in having multiple determinants. It may be seen in "innately creative" people whether they are satisfied or not, happy or unhappy, hungry or sated. Also, it is clear that creative activity may be compensatory, ameliorative, or purely economic. It is my impression (as yet unconfirmed) that it is possible to distinguish the artistic and intellectual products of basically satisfied people from those of basically unsatisfied people by inspection alone. In any case, here too we must distinguish, in a dynamic fashion, the overt behavior itself from its various motivations or purposes.

statement may be made for various behavior acts. An act is psychologically important if it contributes directly to satisfaction of basic needs. The less directly it so contributes, or the weaker this contribution is, the less important this act must be conceived to be from the point of view of dynamic psychology. A similar statement may be made for the various defense or coping mechanisms. Some are very directly related to the protection or attainment of the basic needs, others are only weakly and distantly related. Indeed, if we wished, we could speak of more basic and less basic defense mechanisms and then affirm that danger to the more basic defenses is more threatening than danger to less basic defenses (always remembering that this is so only because of their relationship to the basic needs).

So far, we have mentioned the cognitive needs only in passing. Acquiring knowledge and systematizing the universe have been considered as, in part, techniques for the achievement of basic safety in the world, or, for the intelligent man, expressions of self-actualization. Also freedom of inquiry and expression have been discussed as preconditions of satisfactions of the basic needs. True though these formulations may be, they do not constitute definitive answers to the question as to the motivation role of curiosity, learning, philosophizing, experimenting, etc. They are, at best, no more than partial answers.

This question is especially difficult because we know so little about the facts. Curiosity, exploration, desire for the facts, desire to know may certainly be observed easily enough. The fact that they often are pursued even at great cost to the individual's safety is an earnest of the partial character of our previous discussion. In addition, the writer must admit that, though he has sufficient clinical evidence to postulate the desire to know as a very strong drive in intelligent people, no data are available for unintelligent people. It may then be largely a function of relatively high intelligence. Rather tentatively, then, and largely in the hope of stimulating discussion and research, we shall postulate a basic desire to know, to be aware of reality, to get the facts, to satisfy curiosity, or as Wertheimer phrases it, to see rather than to be blind.

This postulation, however, is not enough. Even after we know, we are impelled to know more and more minutely and microscopically, on the one hand, and, on the other, more and more extensively in the direction of a world philosophy, religion, etc. The facts that we acquire, if they are isolated or atomistic, inevitably get theorized about, and either analyzed or organized or both. This process has been phrased by some as the search for "meaning." We shall then postulate a desire to understand, to systematize, to organize, to analyze, to look for relations and meanings.

Once these desires are accepted for discussion, we see that they too form themselves into a small hierarchy in which the desire to know is prepotent over the desire to understand. All the characteristics of a hierarchy of prepotency that we have described above seem to hold for this one as well.

We must guard ourselves against the too easy tendency to separate these desires from the basic needs we have discussed above, i.e., to make a sharp dichotomy between "cognitive" and "conative" needs. The desire to know and to understand are themselves conative, i.e., have a striving character, and are as much personality needs as the "basic needs" we have already discussed (Wertheimer, unpublished lectures).

Further Characteristics of the Basic Needs

The Degree of Fixity of the Hierarchy of Basic Needs

We have spoken so far as if this hierarchy were a fixed order but actually it is not nearly as rigid as we may have implied. It is true that most of the people with whom we have worked have seemed to have these basic needs in about the order that has been indicated. However, there have been a number of exceptions.

1. There are some people in whom, for instance, self-esteem seems to be more important than love. This most common reversal in the hierarchy is usually due to the development of the notion that the person who is most likely to be loved is a strong or powerful person, one who inspires respect or fear and who is self-confident or aggressive. Therefore, such people who lack love and seek it may try hard to put on a front of aggressive, confident behavior. But essentially they seek high self-esteem and its behavior expressions more as a means-to-an-end than for its own sake; they seek self-assertion for the sake of love rather than for self-esteem itself.

2. There are other, apparently innately creative people in whom the drive to creativeness seems to be more important than any other counterdeterminant. Their creativeness might appear as self-actualization released not by basic satisfaction but in spite of their lack of basic satisfaction.

3. In certain people the level of aspiration may be permanently deadened or lowered. That is to say, the less prepotent goals may simply be lost and may disappear forever, so that the person who has experienced life at a very low level, i.e., chronic unemployment, may continue to be satisfied for the rest of his life if only he can get enough food.

4. The so-called "psychopathic personality" is another example of permanent loss of the love needs. These are people who, according to the best data available (see Levy 1937, pp. 643–52), have been starved for love in the earliest months of their lives and have simply

lost forever the desire and the ability to give and to receive affection (as animals lose sucking or pecking reflexes that are not exercised soon enough after birth).

5. Another cause of reversal of the hierarchy is that when a need has been satisfied for a long time, this need may be underevaluated. People who have never experienced chronic hunger are apt to underestimate its effects and to look upon food as a rather unimportant thing. If they are dominated by a higher need, this higher need will seem to be the most important of all. It then becomes possible, and indeed does actually happen, that they may, for the sake of this higher need, put themselves into the position of being deprived in a more basic need. We may expect that after a long-time deprivation of the more basic need there will be a tendency to re-evaluate both needs so that the more prepotent need will actually become consciously prepotent for the individual who may have given it up very lightly. Thus, a man who has given up his job rather than lose his self-respect, and who then starves for six months or so, may be willing to take his job back even at the price of losing his self-respect.

6. Another partial explanation of *apparent* reversals is seen in the fact that we have been talking about the hierarchy of prepotency in terms of consciously felt wants or desires rather than of behavior. Looking at behavior itself may give us the wrong impression. What we have claimed is that the person will *want* the more basic of two needs when deprived in both. There is no necessary implication here that he will act upon his desires. Let us say again that there are many determinants of behavior other than needs and desires.

7. Perhaps more important than all these exceptions are the ones that involve ideals, high social standards, high values, and the like. With such values people become martyrs; they will give up everything for the sake of a particular ideal, or value. These people may be understood, at least in part, by reference to one basic concept (or hypothesis) which may be called "increased frustration-tolerance through early gratification." People who have been satisfied in their basic needs throughout their lives, particularly in their earlier years, seem to develop exceptional power to withstand present or future thwarting of these needs simply because they have strong, healthy character structure as a result of basic satisfaction. They are the "strong" people who can easily weather disagreement or opposition, who can swim against the stream of public opinion, and who can stand up for the truth at great personal cost. It is those who have loved and been well loved and who have had many deep friendships who can hold out against hatred, rejection or persecution.

I say all this in spite of the fact that there is a certain amount of sheer habituation which is also involved in any full discussion of frustration tolerance. For instance, it is likely that those persons who have been accustomed to relative starvation for a long time are partially enabled thereby to withstand food deprivation. What sort of balance must be made between these two tendencies, of habituation on the one hand, and of past satisfaction breeding present frustration tolerance on the other hand, remains to be worked out by further research. Meanwhile we may assume that they are both operative, side by side, since they do not contradict each other. In respect to this phenomenon of increased frustration tolerance, it seems probable that the most important gratifications come in the first two years of life. That is to say, people who have been made secure and strong in the earliest years tend to remain secure and strong thereafter in the face of whatever threatens.

Degrees of Relative Satisfaction

So far, our theoretical discussion may have given the impression that these five sets of needs are somehow in a stepwise, all-or-none relationship to one another. We have spoken in such terms as the following: "If one need is satisfied, then another emerges." This statement might give the false impression that a need must be satisfied 100 percent before the next need emerges. In actual fact, most members of our society who are normal are partially satisfied in all their basic needs and partially unsatisfied in all their basic needs at the same time. A more realistic description of the hierarchy would be in terms of decreasing percentages of satisfaction as we go up the hierarchy of prepotency. For instance, if I may assign arbitrary figures for the sake of illustration, it is as if the average citizen is satisfied perhaps 85 percent in his physiological needs, 70 percent in his safety needs, 50 percent in his love needs, 40 percent in his self-esteem needs, and 10 percent in his self-actualization needs.

As for the concept of emergence of a new need after satisfaction of the prepotent need, this emergence is not a sudden, saltatory phenomenon but rather a gradual emergence by slow degrees from nothingness. For instance, if prepotent need A is satisfied only 10 percent, then need B may not be visible at all. However, as this need A becomes satisfied 25 percent, need B may emerge 5 percent; as need A becomes satisfied 75 percent, need B may emerge 90 percent; and so on.

Unconscious Character of Needs

These needs are neither necessarily conscious nor unconscious. On the whole, however, in the average person, they are more often unconscious. It is not necessary at this point to overhaul the tremendous mass of evidence which indicates the crucial importance of unconscious motivation. It would by now be expected, on a priori grounds alone, that unconscious motivations would on the whole be rather more important than the conscious motivations. What we have called the basic needs are very often largely unconscious, although they may, with suitable techniques and with sophisticated people, become conscious.

The Role of Gratified Needs

It has been pointed out above several times that our higher needs usually emerge only when more prepotent needs have been gratified. Thus gratification has an important role in motivation theory. Apart from this, however, needs cease to play an active determining or organizing role as soon as they are gratified.

What this means, for example, is that a basically satisfied person no longer has the needs for esteem, love, safety, etc. The only sense in which he might be said to have them is in the almost metaphysical sense that a sated man has hunger or a filled bottle has emptiness. If we are interested in what *actually* motivates us and not in what has, will, or might motivate us, then a satisfied need is not a motivator. It must be considered, for all practical purposes, simply not to exist, to have disappeared. This point should be emphasized because it has been either overlooked or contradicted in every theory of motivation I know.[8] The perfectly healthy, normal, fortunate man has no sex needs or hunger needs, or needs for safety or for love or for prestige or for self-esteem, except in stray moments of quickly passing threat. If we were to say otherwise, we should also have to aver that every man had all the pathological reflexes (e.g., Babinski, etc.), because if his nervous system were damaged, these would appear.

It is such considerations as these that suggest the bold postulation that a man who is thwarted in any of his basic needs may fairly be envisaged simply as a sick man. This is a fair parallel to our designation as "sick" of the man who lacks vitamins or minerals. Who is to say that a lack of love is less important than a lack of vitamins? Since we know the pathogenic effects of love starvation, who is to say that we are invoking value-questions in an unscientific or illegitimate way, any more than the physician does who diagnoses and treats pellagra or scurvy? If I were permitted this usage, I should then say simply that a healthy man is primarily motivated by his needs to develop and actualize his fullest potentialities and capacities. If a man has any other basic needs in any active, chronic sense, then he is simply an unhealthy man. He is as surely sick as if he had suddenly developed a strong salt-hunger or calcium hunger.[9]

---

8. Note that acceptance of this theory necessitates basic revision of the Freudian theory.

9. If we were to use the "sick" in this way, we should then also have to face squarely the relations of man to his society. One clear implication of our definition would be that (1) since a man is to be called sick who is basically thwarted, and (2) since such basic thwarting is made possible ultimately only by forces outside the

If this statement seems unusual or paradoxical the reader may be assured that this is only one among many such paradoxes that will appear as we revise our ways of looking at man's deeper motivations. When we ask what man wants of life, we deal with his very essence.

Summary

1. There are at least five sets of goals which we may call basic needs. These are, briefly, physiological, safety, love, esteem, and self-actualization. In addition, we are motivated by the desire to achieve or maintain the various conditions upon which these basic satisfactions rest and by certain more intellectual desires.

2. These basic goals are related to one another, being arranged in a hierarchy of prepotency. This means that the most prepotent goal will monopolize consciousness and will tend of itself to organize the recruitment of the various capacities of the organism. The less prepotent needs are minimized, even forgotten or denied. But when a need is fairly well satisfied, the next prepotent ("higher") need emerges, in turn to dominate the conscious life and to serve as the center of organization of behavior, since gratified needs are not active motivators.

Thus man is a perpetually wanting animal. Ordinarily the satisfaction of these wants is not altogether mutually exclusive but only tends to be. The average member of our society is most often partially satisfied and partially unsatisfied in all of his wants. The hierarchy principle is usually empirically observed in terms of increasing percentages of non-satisfaction as we go up the hierarchy. Reversals of the average order of the hierarchy are sometimes observed. Also it has been observed that an individual may permanently lose the higher wants in the hierarchy under special conditions. There are not only ordinarily multiple motivations for usual behavior but, in addition, many determinants other than motives.

3. Any thwarting or possibility of thwarting these basic human goals, or danger to the defenses which protect them or to the conditions upon which they rest, is considered to be a psychological threat. With a few exceptions, all psychopathology may be partially traced to such threats. A basically thwarted man may actually be defined as a "sick" man.

4. It is such basic threats which bring about the general emergency reactions.

5. Certain other basic problems have not been dealt with because of limitations of space. Among these are (a) the problem of values in any definitive motivation theory, (b) the relation between

individual, then (3) sickness in the individual must come ultimately from a sickness in the society. The "good" or healthy society would then be defined as one that permitted man's highest purposes to emerge by satisfying all his prepotent basic needs.

appetites, desires, needs and what is "good" for the organism, (c) the etiology of the basic needs and their possible derivation in early childhood, (d) redefinition of motivational concepts, i.e., drive, desire, wish, need, goal, (e) implication of our theory for hedonistic theory, (f) the nature of the uncompleted act, of success and failure, and of aspiration-level, (g) the role of association, habit, and conditioning, (h) relation to the theory of interpersonal relations, (i) implications for psychotherapy, (j) implication for theory of society, (k) the theory of selfishness, (l) the relation between needs and cultural patterns, (m) the relation between this theory and Allport's theory of functional autonomy. These as well as certain other less important questions must be considered as motivation theory attempts to become definitive.

References

Cannon, W. B. *Wisdom of the Body.* Norton, 1932.

Fromm, Eric. *Escape from Freedom.* Holt, Rinehart & Winston, 1941.

Goldstein, K. *The Organism.* American Book Company, 1939.

Kardiner, K. *The Traumatic Neuroses of War.* Hoeber, 1941.

Levy, D. M. "Primary Affect Hunger." *American Journal of Psychiatry,* Vol. 94, 1937.

Maslow, A. H. "A Preface to Motivation Theory." *Psychosomatic Medicine,* Vol. 5, 1943.

————. "The Dynamics of Psychological Security-Insecurity." *Character and Personality,* Vol. 10, 1942.

————. "Dominance, Personality, and Social Behavior in Women." *Journal of Social Psychology,* Vol. 10, 1939.

————, and B. Mittelmann. *Principles of Abnormal Psychology.* Harper, 1941.

Plant, J. *Personality and the Cultural Pattern.* Commonwealth Fund, 1937.

Shirley, M. "Children's Adjustment to a Strange Situation." *Journal of Abnormal and Social Psychology,* Vol. 37, 1942.

Wertheimer, M. Unpublished lectures at the New School for Social Research, New York, N. Y.

Young, P. T. "The Experimental Analysis of Appetite." *Psychological Bulletin,* Vol. 38, 1941.

Mason Haire

The Problem of Learning
and The Law of Effect

We are constantly faced, in industry, with the problem of making changes in behavior. The job of management is very seldom to keep people doing exactly as they are doing. Usually we either want a group of people to start doing something that they aren't doing now, or to stop doing something that they are doing. Almost always, the big problems come in changing behavior. Since a large part of human activity is involved in the process of modifying behavior patterns and shaping them so that they will be more nearly goal oriented, it is important for us to look at the processes that occur and the principles that govern them, so that we may utilize these principles efficiently in producing changes.

Psychologists speak frequently of a principle of learning which is called "the Law of Effect." It means, simply, that behavior which seems to lead to reward tends to be repeated, while behavior which seems not to lead to reward or seems to lead to punishment tends not to be repeated. It is not a particularly complicated principle, but it is very important in shaping behavior. For some reason, we all seem to be able to keep it clearly in mind and to use it in practice when we are, for example, housebreaking a dog, but when we become involved in more complicated situations in human interactions we lose track of it. The principle is exactly the same in human behavior, and it is essential for us to see it clearly in the cases in which we want to modify behavior.

It is part of the superior's role in a hierarchical organization that he controls many, if not most, of the rewards that are available to subordinates. All people at work are looking for the satisfaction of many of their needs. We shall have to go into the kinds of needs that motivate people a little later on, but the fact remains that everyone is constantly striving for need satisfactions. It is part of the nature of the situation that, at work, the superior controls many of the means to need-satisfaction. By the proper use of his control of the means for need-satisfaction, he can provide or withhold rewards at appropriate times. When we remember the principle of the Law of Effect—that behavior which seems to be rewarded tends to be repeated, while that which seems not to lead to reward or seems to lead to punishment tends to be eliminated—it is clear that the superior has a great opportunity for shaping behavior. Indeed, whether he is conscious of it or not, the superior is bound to be constantly shaping the behavior of his subordinates by the way in which he utilizes the rewards that are at his disposal, and he will inevitably modify the behavior patterns of his work group thereby. For this reason, it is important to see as clearly as possible what is going on, so that the changes can be planned and chosen in advance, rather than simply accepted after the fact.

An example may make the point clear in its application to industrial practice. It is not at all uncommon to hear members of management describe a situation in which two applicants for a promotion are nearly equal in merit. The poorer one, however, let us say, has considerably more seniority. Although there is leeway in the contract for a promotion on the basis of merit, the man with the greater seniority is promoted, in order to avoid argument. It is also not at all uncommon to hear the same people say at another time, "Our biggest problem is that people don't try hard any more, the way they used to. They used to figure that if they worked hard they'd get ahead, but now they just figure that if they wait long enough they'll be promoted, so they sweat it out rather than trying to do a good job." The members of management, in these cases, are not entitled to express surprise or dissatisfaction at their subordinates' performance. The reason the subordinates produce the kind of behavior they do is because they have been trained to behave that way. They have been shown that rewards come for seniority and not for merit. According to the principle, the behavior that seems to lead to reward tends to be repeated, while the behavior that seems not to lead to reward tends to be dropped out. The way in which the reward is administered determines the behavior.

This does not mean that rewards for seniority are bad. Long service deserves compensations. However, in order to produce the kind of behavior we want, we should not let it become confused and with other kinds of reward that are properly designed to encourage other types of activity. Protection by virtue of seniority is a reward for certain kinds of behavior which we want to encourage, as well as an obligation to the senior worker. However, if we want to encourage quality in performance, in addition to simple long-term service, we should be careful that the rewards for the two do not overlap, and that they do not compete with each other. Clear-cut rewards must be retained for merit and must be clearly structured so that they are seen as such.

A similar situation develops in all kinds of small everyday administrations which do not seem, at first glance, to be rewards or punishments, but which operate that way just the same. We often hear it said, "The men in the work force don't ever give a thought to ways to do their jobs better." We think of this as a general characteristic of a group of people. But have we trained them to act this way, or have we, on the other hand, provided actual rewards in practice for just such thinking about the job? When someone approaches a foreman with a suggestion about something to do, does the foreman imply by his tone and manner, "Your job is to do the work—I'll do the planning"? This can be as effective a punishment, or at least lack of reward, as many more carefully planned acts, and these small everyday occurrences are the day-by-day administrations of reward and punishment by which the superior shapes the behavior of his subordinates. Underlying the process throughout, we have the principle of the Law of Effect: that behavior which seems not to lead to reward, or to lead to punishment, tends not to be repeated. As we go on to other problems and practices of dealing with people we shall see this principle coming into play repeatedly.

One often hears members of bank managements complain that their tellers are not sufficiently zealous in building good customer contact. They wish the teller would realize that the bank's continued success depends on the customer, and make him feel welcome and well treated. Too often, they say, when a depositor approaches the window, the teller gives the impression that he has been interrupted in an important job (if, indeed, the customer hasn't been made to wait while the teller finishes adding his column of figures) and that the customer will throw his figures out of balance by making a transaction. Why does this kind of thing happen? The members of management might well ask themselves whether they have trained the tellers to do just this and, if so, whether this is the way they should be trained. The teller has found all his rewards in the past for careful balancing of the books, and his punishments for failures in this line. He has probably never been rewarded or punished for his treatment of customers. Under these circumstances, an understanding of the Law of Effect will let us predict certainly what will happen. Those behaviors which seem to lead to reward (balancing the books) will tend to be repeated; those behaviors which seem not to lead to reward (dealing with the customers well) will tend to be eliminated. The bank will suffer. Because of the overriding nature of the problem of control within banks, they have often slipped inadvertently into a policy which they would never make explicit: balancing the books is the only important thing. From this implicit policy has flowed a daily training which has taught the teller how to behave: balance the books at all costs; anything which interrupts that task is a liability. There has never been a real decision to train the tellers this way, but the silent focusing on the problem of control has put it into the actions of every level of management, and because the subordinates are subject to the operation of the Law of Effect, it works as a training policy.

What could be done differently? No one would ask that management adopt a policy that it doesn't matter whether the books balance, as long as the customers are happy. As in the case of the example a little earlier concerning promotion on merit or seniority, both aspects of the teller's work are important. Rewards must be provided both for his balancing and for his customer contact, and they must be kept separate and distinct, so that it is possible to create a situation where both kinds of behavior tend to be repeated. In order to do this it is necessary to be clear and explicit about the aims of the business, about the things that need to be done, and about the rewards that are provided for doing these things. Otherwise we slip into the situation of inadvertently training out an essential pattern of behavior.

One further point should be made clear before we leave the Law of Effect. We must be careful to notice that it is stated that "behavior which *seems* to lead to reward tends to be repeated, and behavior which *seems* not to lead to reward or *seems* to lead to punishment tends not to be repeated." It is not always true that the behavior which in fact leads to reward, or which was the boss's reason for providing the reward, will be seen to be the path to reward by the subordinate. If the reward occurs too long after the behavior, it may be ineffective; if the connection between the behavior and the reward is difficult to see, it may be ineffective. Moreover, in many cases the subordinate may mistakenly assume that a reward came for a particular bit of behavior which was not at all what management intended to reward. We shall see in more detail later on how this problem of the subordinate's making sense of the world and organizing things in his own mind complicates the picture. Here we need simply to realize that the effective rewards are those that he has put with a particular bit of behavior. In addition to providing reward and punishment, management must accept the responsibility for seeing that the appropriate connection between behavior and reward is appreciated by the recipient of the reward.

There is some evidence, in the laboratory, that those behaviors which are followed by reward tend to be repeated whether or not the individual is aware of the connection. Learning is probably not as effective in this situation as it is when the connection is clear, but it is not impossible, either. This means that in many cases where it is difficult to maintain a close contact in the employee's mind between behavior and reward—where the situation is too complex, or the time too long, or the like—it is still possible to rely on the operation of the

Law of Effect. This kind of "silent" operation of the principle only points up the responsibility of management for the consistent provision of rewards in modifying behavior.

It would be well, at this point, to say another word about the operation of reward and punishment under the Law of Effect. We have so far spoken of them as if they operated equally, but in the opposite directions. This is not quite true. While it is true that those behaviors which seem to lead to punishment tend not to be repeated, it is also clear, in laboratory experiments, that the most important effect of punishment is to produce variability of behavior, so that it becomes possible for the superior to provide reward for the desired behavior and hence increase its likelihood of repetition. Often the response to the positive side of the Law of Effect seems to be, "It's very well to talk about rewarding the kind of behavior that you want repeated. What do you do when it occurs so seldom that you don't get any chance to reward it?" It is just here that the role of punishment is most effective. The consistent application of punishment in the face of undesirable behavior leads the person to try other kinds of behavior from his repertoire of responses, and this variability makes it possible to find and reward the desired behavior.

Kurt Lewin

The Psychology of Success and Failure

I

The great importance of success and failure is recognized by practically all psychological schools. Thorndike's law of effect,[1] as well as Adler's ideas, has close relation to this problem. Pedagogically, the importance of success is universally stressed.

From *Occupations*, Vol. 14, 1936, pp. 926–930. Reprinted by permission of the American Personnel and Guidance Association.
1. Law of effect: One learns quickly those reactions which are accompanied or followed by a satisfying state of affairs; one does not learn quickly those which result in an annoying state of affairs or learns not to make such reactions. See English (1934).

Indeed, success and failure influence deeply the emotional status of the person, his goals, and his social relations. From the point of view of guidance, one can emphasize the fact that these problems are important throughout the whole age range and are as basic for the very young child as for the adult.

In spite of the common recognition of these factors, our knowledge about the psychology of success and failure is meager. The law of effect may, for instance, suggest that a person who has succeeded in a special activity will have a tendency to repeat that activity. Indeed, children of two or three years tend to repeat activities again and again. Yet experiments show, at least for older persons, that a spontaneous repetition of a successful act is not very likely and that, if it does occur, the activity is generally distinctly changed. As a matter of fact, the tendency to go back spontaneously to a special activity is, as Ovseankina has shown, about ninety times as high if the activity is not completed as if it is successfully completed. This shows, at least, that the whole problem is much more complicated than one might expect.

II

The first question one should be able to answer is: Under what conditions will a person experience success or failure? The experiments of Hoppe point to some fundamental facts which one could have learned from everyday experience; namely, it is not possible to correlate the objective achievement on the one side with the feeling of success or failure on the other. The same achievement can result once in the feeling of great success, another time in the feeling of complete failure. This is true not only for different individuals, but even for the same individual. For instance, a person may throw a discus forty yards the first time. The second time he may reach fifty, and feel very successful. After short practice, he may reach sixty-five. If he then throws fifty yards again, he will experience a definite failure in spite of the fact that he got a thrill out of the same achievement but a short time before. This means that the experience of success and failure does not depend upon the achievement as such, but rather upon the relation between the achievement and the person's expectation. One can speak, in this respect, about the person's "level of aspiration," and can say that the experience and the degree of success and failure depend upon whether the achievement is above or below the momentary level of aspiration.[2]

One may ask whether a person always has a definite level of

2. The problems discussed here are treated more thoroughly in Lewin (1935). Here also may be found the references for the experimental work.

aspiration in respect to a certain task. The answer is no. If one, for instance, does something for the first time, one generally does not set himself a definite goal. It is interesting additional evidence of the relation between success and the level of aspiration that in such situations no strong failure is experienced. If one wishes to avoid or diminish the feeling of failure in the child, one often says to him: "Just try." In this way a definite level of aspiration is eliminated.

Not only is the level of aspiration fundamental for the experience of success and failure, but the level of aspiration itself is changed by success and failure. After success, a person generally sets himself a higher goal. After failure, his level of aspiration generally goes down. There are some exceptions to this general trend which one should notice. In the experiments of Hoppe, success led to a rise of the level of aspiration only in 69 percent, in 7 percent it remained the same; and in 24 percent the person stopped the activity entirely. After failure, the level of aspiration was never raised, but it was lowered in only 50 percent of the cases. In 21 percent it remained the same; in 2 percent the person consoled himself by the realization of previous successes; and in 27 percent the person ceased the activity entirely. This varying behavior is due partly to the fact that there are cases which are neither clear successes nor clear failures. On the whole, the person is more ready to raise the level of aspiration after success than to lower it after failure.

It is important to note that a person, instead of lowering his level of aspiration after failure, may stop entirely. There is a significant difference between individuals in this respect. Some persons are relatively easily influenced to lower their levels of aspiration, whereas others show a stiff backbone. The latter maintain their levels of aspiration in spite of failures and may prefer to leave the field entirely rather than to lower it. Lack of persistence sometimes has to be attributed to such an unwillingness to yield. On the other hand, there are cases of apparent persistence, in which a person sticks to an activity only at the price of constantly lowering his level of aspiration. This sort of persistency may be found in the hysteric type. In problems of guidance involving unusually high or low persistency, the possible reasons behind such behavior should be carefully examined, because the advisable measures should be different in accordance with the underlying psychological facts.

Surprisingly enough, a person may leave the field of activity not only after failure but after success, too. Such abandonment of the field after success occurs generally when this success follows a series of failures. One obviously does not like to quit a task after failure. One continues, eager to find a successful termination, and uses the first occasion to stop, out of fear that further repetitions may bring new failures.

III

One has to consider quite detailed facts in order to understand the forces which govern the level of aspiration.

The first point to mention is that any goal has a position within a set of goals. If a child is asked, "How much is three times four?" the answer, "Twelve," determines a definite circumscribed goal he has to reach. The answer will be either right or wrong. But if the child has to write an English composition or to translate a passage of French or to build a wooden boat, there is no such absolutely determined goal but, rather, a variety of possible achievements which may differ greatly in quality. Most tasks are of this nature. It is generally technically possible to order the different possible achievements of a task according to their degree of difficulty. This allows one to compare the achievement and the level of aspiration of different persons and to determine in a given case the effect of success and failure. The range of acceptable achievement has often a "natural maximum" and a "natural minimum." In Hoppe's experiment, for instance, the subject had to solve one of a group of puzzles, each different in difficulty. A subject who was not able to solve any one of the puzzles but who was able to return the stones to their proper places in the box would certainly not have reached the natural minimum of the task. On the other hand, it would be above the natural maximum to reach a solution of the most difficult puzzle within one second. Some tasks have no natural maximum. This holds, for instance, for many sport activities—there is always the possibility of jumping higher and running faster. The lack of this natural maximum within the goal structure of many sport activities has led to a biologically unsound race without end.

The individual usually is conscious of the variety of possible goals within the task. He conceives the single action in its significance for a larger field of actions. Besides the goals for the momentary act, he has some general goal in regard to this larger field. For instance, when a person in a competition throws a discus, his goal for a certain trial might be to throw at least fifty yards; his goal for the whole group of actions would be to win! There always exists besides the goal for the next act, or, as we may say, besides the immediate goal, an ideal goal. This ideal goal may be to become the best discus thrower of the college or even to become world champion.

Such a goal can possess any degree of reality or unreality. For the student who does well in the first weeks of his sporting activities, the ideal to become world champion may be only an occasional daydream without any significance. The ideal goal, to become the best player of the university, may have considerably more reality. In a vague way, a student entering college may dream about the possibility of becoming a leading surgeon, without even confessing this goal to himself. If he progresses in college, and does well in medical school, this ideal goal may become somewhat more real. According to Hoppe, success narrows the gap between the immediate goal and the ideal goal and brings the ideal goal from the level of unreality gradually down to the level of reality. Failure has the opposite effect: a previously real goal vanishes into the world of dreams. If the ideal goal should be reached (a case more frequent in experiments than in life), generally a new ideal goal arises.

IV

If it is true that the degree of success and failure depends upon the amount of difference between the immediate goal and the achievement, it should be possible to create a very strong feeling of success by making the task so easy that the achievement will be much better than the task demands. On the other hand, it should be possible to create a very strong feeling of failure by assigning a very difficult task. Experiments show that this is not true. If the task is above a certain degree of difficulty, no feeling of failure arises, and no feeling of success arises if the task is below a certain degree of difficulty. In other words, if one represents the possible degree of difficulty of a task on a scale, this scale is infinite in direction, both to greater ease and to greater difficulty. But an individual reacts with success and failure only to a small region within this scale. In fact, the tasks which an individual considers "very easy," "easy," "medium," "difficult," and "very difficult" circumscribe only a small region in the scale. Above and below this region lie a great many tasks which the individual calls "too easy" or "too difficult." The "too difficult" tasks are considered "objectively impossible," entirely out of the range of the individual's ability, and no feeling of failure is attached to such a task. Similarly, in the case of a "too easy" task, the achievement is taken so much for granted that no feeling of success is aroused. Contrary to the scale of possible difficulties, the scale of possible achievements is not infinite but has a definite upper limit for a given individual at a given time. Both success and failure occur only if the difficulty of the task lies close to the upper limit of achievement. In other words, the feeling of failure occurs only if there is a chance for success, and a feeling of success occurs only if there is a chance for failure. Behind success and failure, therefore, one can always find a conflict situation.

This conflict situation makes somewhat understandable the laws which govern the position and the change in the level of aspiration. These laws are probably among the most fundamental for all human behavior. They are quite complicated, and we are only beginning to understand them. If it were true that life is ruled by the tendency to get as much pleasure as possible, one might expect that everybody would keep his level of aspiration as low as possible, because in this case his performance would be always above his level of aspiration, and he would feel successful. As a matter of fact, there is a marked tendency to keep the level of aspiration down out of fear of failure. Yet there is at the same time a strong tendency to raise the level of aspiration as high as possible. The experiments of J. D. Frank (1935a, pp. 119–28, 1935b, pp. 285–93, and 1935c) show that both tendencies are of different strength in different individuals and that a third tendency may have to be distinguished, namely, the tendency to keep one's expectation about one's future performance as close as possible to reality. A cautious person usually starts with a relatively low level of aspiration and, after succeeding, he raises the level only by short steps. Other persons tend to maintain their levels of aspiration well above their achievements. The rigidity of the level of aspiration, i.e., the tendency to keep the level constant rather than to shift it, shows marked differences among individuals. Frank found that these differences are highly reliable and largely independent of the special nature of the task.

It is important to know whether success and failure change the level of aspiration only in the particular activity in question, or whether success and failure in one task influence the level of aspiration in another task too. This is important for problems of guidance, where the effects of achievement or failure in different fields of activity on each other are of great significance, as, for instance, in the realm of school motivation and of delinquency. Frank found a marked relationship between success and failure in one task and the level of aspiration in another, if the tasks concerned had sufficient psychological relations. Mr. Jacknat's experiments verified this result but showed that this influence is weak or negligible if past experience has rigidly fixed the level of aspiration within a task.

V

These studies point to a relation between the level of aspiration for a specific task and something that one may call self-esteem, which means the feeling of the person about his own status and general standards. All experiments indicate that this relation is very fundamental. There is, for instance, a marked tendency, in the case of failure, to blame an inadequate tool or an accident for the lack of achievement. To experience success or failure the person has to attribute the result of an action to himself in a very specific way. In case of inadequate performance, the person often tries to get rid of the feeling of failure by cutting the tie of belongingness between him and the result, and by rejecting his responsibility for the outcome. Also the tendency to raise the level of aspiration as high as possible seems to be closely related to the self-esteem, particularly to the feeling of the person about his status in the social group. The level of aspiration is determined first by the upper limit of the person's achievement—in other words, by his ability. A second fundamental factor is the level of achievement prevailing in the social group to which a person belongs—for instance, among his business friends, his comrades, his playmates. The social group can have a strong influence in keeping the level of aspiration either too high or too low for a person's ability. This is especially true for children. The expectation of his parents, or the standards of his group, may keep the level of aspiration for the less able child too high and lead to continuous failure and overtension, whereas the level of aspiration for the very able child may be kept too low. (This may be the reason for Wellman's finding that children with a relatively high IQ gain less in IQ in the nursery school than children with a relatively low IQ.)

Fajans has shown that success and failure influence greatly the degree of activeness among active and passive children. Chase found an increase in achievement following success. Fajans has further determined the degree to which praise has an effect similar to real success. The effects of being successful, and of being socially recognized or being loved, resemble each other closely. This relation is important for adults, and even more so in the case of adolescents and children.

References

English, H. B. A *Student's Dictionary of Psychological Terms*. Harper, 1934.

Frank, Jerome D. "Individual Difference in Certain Aspects of the Level of Aspiration." *American Journal of Psychology*, Vol. 47, January 1935a.

———. "Some Psychological Detriments of the Level of Aspiration." *AJP*, Vol. 47, April 1935b.

———. "The Influence of the Level of Performance in One Task on the Level of Performance in Another." *Journal of Experimental Psychology*, Vol. 18, No. 2, April 1935c.

Lewin, Kurt. A *Dynamic Theory of Personality*. McGraw-Hill, 1935.

Douglas M. McGregor

The Human Side of Enterprise

It has become trite to say that the most significant developments of the next quarter-century will take place not in the physical but in the social sciences, that industry—the economic organ of society—has the fundamental know-how to utilize physical science and technology for the material benefit of mankind, and that we must now learn how to utilize the social sciences to make our human organizations truly effective.

Many people agree in principle with such statements; but so far they represent a pious hope—and little else. Consider with me, if you will, something of what may be involved when we attempt to transform the hope into reality.

Problems and Opportunities Facing Management

Let me begin with an analogy. A quarter-century ago basic conceptions of the nature of matter and energy had changed profoundly from what they had been since Newton's time. The physical scientists were persuaded that under proper conditions new and hitherto unimagined sources of energy could be made available to mankind.

We know what has happened since then. First came the bomb. Then, during the past decade, have come many other attempts to exploit these scientific discoveries—some successful, some not.

The point of my analogy, however, is that the application of theory in this field is a slow and costly matter. We expect it always to be thus. No one is impatient with the scientist because he cannot tell industry how to build a simple, cheap, all-purpose source of atomic energy today. That it will take at least another decade and the investment of billions of dollars to achieve results which are economically competitive with present sources of power is understood and accepted.

It is transparently pretentious to suggest any *direct* similarity between the developments in the physical sciences leading to the

Reprinted from *Adventures in Thought and Action: Proceedings of the Fifth Anniversary Convocation of the School of Industrial Management*, M.I.T. Press, April 9, 1957.

harnessing of atomic energy and potential developments in the social sciences. Nevertheless, the analogy is not as absurd as it might appear to be at first glance.

To a lesser degree, and in a much more tentative fashion, we are in a position in the social sciences today like that of the physical sciences with respect to atomic energy in the thirties. We know that past conceptions of the nature of man are inadequate and in many ways incorrect. We are becoming quite certain that, under proper conditions, unimagined resources of creative human energy could become available within the organizational setting.

We cannot tell industrial management how to apply this new knowledge in simple, economic ways. We know it will require years of exploration, much costly development research, and a substantial amount of creative imagination on the part of management to discover how to apply this growing knowledge to the organization of human effort in industry.

May I ask that you keep this analogy in mind—overdrawn and pretentious though it may be—as a framework for what I have to say.

Management's Task: Conventional View

The conventional conception of management's task in harnessing human energy to organizational requirements can be stated broadly in terms of three propositions. In order to avoid the complications introduced by a label, I shall call this set of propositions "Theory X":

1. Management is responsible for organizing the elements of productive enterprise—money, materials, equipment, people—in the interest of economic ends.
2. With respect to people, this is a process of directing their efforts, motivating them, controlling their actions, modifying their behavior to fit the needs of the organization.
3. Without this active intervention by management, people would be passive—even resistant—to organizational needs. They must therefore be persuaded, rewarded, punished, controlled—their activities must be directed. This is management's task—in managing subordinate managers or workers. We often sum it up by saying that management consists of getting things done through other people.

Behind this conventional theory there are several additional beliefs—less explicit, but widespread:

4. The average man is by nature indolent—he works as little as possible.
5. He lacks ambition, dislikes responsibility, prefers to be led.

6. He is inherently self-centered, indifferent to organizational needs.
7. He is by nature resistant to change.
8. He is gullible, not very bright, the ready dupe of the charlatan and the demagogue.

The human side of economic enterprise today is fashioned from propositions and beliefs such as these. Conventional organization structures, managerial policies, practices, and programs reflect these assumptions.

In accomplishing its task—with these assumptions as guides—management has conceived of a range of possibilities between two extremes.

The Hard or the Soft Approach?

At one extreme, management can be "hard" or "strong." The methods for directing behavior involve coercion and threat (usually disguised), close supervision, tight controls over behavior. At the other extreme, management can be "soft" or "weak." The methods for directing behavior involve being permissive, satisfying people's demands, achieving harmony. Then they will be tractable, accept direction.

This range has been fairly completely explored during the past half-century, and management has learned some things from the exploration. There are difficulties in the "hard" approach. Force breeds counterforces: restriction of output, antagonism, militant unionism, subtle but effective sabotage of management objectives. This approach is especially difficult during times of full employment.

There are also difficulties in the "soft" approach. It leads frequently to the abdication of management—to harmony, perhaps, but to indifferent performance. People take advantage of the soft approach. They continually expect more, but they give less and less.

Currently, the popular theme is "firm but fair." This is an attempt to gain the advantages of both the hard and the soft approaches. It is reminiscent of Teddy Roosevelt's "speak softly and carry a big stick."

Is The Conventional View Correct?

The findings which are beginning to emerge from the social sciences challenge this whole set of beliefs about man and human nature and about the task of management. The evidence is far from conclusive, certainly, but it is suggestive. It comes from the laboratory, the clinic, the schoolroom, the home, and even to a limited extent from industry itself.

The social scientist does not deny that human behavior in industrial organization today is approximately what management perceives it to be. He has, in fact, observed it and studied it fairly extensively. But he is pretty sure that this behavior is *not* a consequence of man's inherent nature. It is a consequence, rather, of the nature of industrial organizations, of management philosophy, policy, and practice. The conventional approach of Theory X is based on mistaken notions of what is cause and what is effect.

"Well," you ask, "what then is the *true* nature of man? What evidence leads the social scientist to deny what is obvious?" And, if I am not mistaken, you are also thinking, "Tell me—simply, and without a lot of scientific verbiage—what you think you know that is so unusual. Give me—without a lot of intellectual claptrap and theoretical nonsense—some practical ideas which will enable me to improve the situation in my organization. And remember, I'm faced with increasing costs and narrowing profit margins. I want proof that such ideas won't result simply in new and costly human relations frills. I want practical results, and I want them now."

If these are your wishes, you are going to be disappointed. Such requests can no more be met by the social scientist today than could comparable ones with respect to atomic energy be met by the physicist fifteen years ago. I can, however, indicate a few of the reasons for asserting that conventional assumptions about the human side of enterprise are inadequate. And I can suggest—tentatively—some of the propositions that will comprise a more adequate theory of the management of people. The magnitude of the task that confronts us will then, I think, be apparent.

Man as a Wanting Animal

Perhaps the best way to indicate why the conventional approach of management is inadequate is to consider the subject of motivation. In discussing this subject I will draw heavily on the work of my colleague, Abraham Maslow of Brandeis University. His is the most fruitful approach I know. Naturally, what I have to say will be overgeneralized and will ignore important qualifications. In the time at our disposal, this is inevitable.

Physiological and Safety Needs

Man is a wanting animal—as soon as one of his needs is satisfied, another appears in its place. This process is unending. It continues from birth to death.

Man's needs are organized in a series of levels—a hierarchy of importance. At the lowest level, but pre-eminent in importance when they are thwarted, are his physiological needs. Man lives by bread alone, when there is no bread. Unless the circumstances are unusual, his needs for love, for status, for recognition are inoperative when his stomach has been empty for a while. But when he eats regularly and adequately, hunger ceases to be an important need. The sated man has hunger only in the sense that a full bottle has emptiness. The same is true of the other physiological needs of man—for rest, exercise, shelter, protection from the elements.

A satisfied need is not a motivator of behavior! This is a fact of profound significance. It is a fact which is regularly ignored in the conventional approach to the management of people. I shall return to it later. For the moment, one example will make my point. Consider your own need for air. Except as you are deprived of it, it has no appreciable motivating effect upon your behavior.

When the physiological needs are reasonably satisfied, needs at the next higher level begin to dominate man's behavior—to motivate him. These are called safety needs. They are needs for protection against danger, threat, deprivation. Some people mistakenly refer to these as needs for security. However, unless man is in a dependent relationship where he fears arbitrary deprivation, he does not demand security. The need is for the "fairest possible break." When he is confident of this, he is more than willing to take risks. But when he feels threatened or dependent, his greatest need is for guarantees, for protection, for security.

The fact needs little emphasis that since every industrial employee is in a dependent relationship, safety needs may assume considerable importance. Arbitrary management actions, behavior which arouses uncertainty with respect to continued employment or which reflects favoritism or discrimination, unpredictable administration of policy—these can be powerful motivators of the safety needs in the employment relationship *at every level* from worker to vice president.

Social Needs

When man's physiological needs are satisfied and he is no longer fearful about his physical welfare, his social needs become important motivators of his behavior—for belonging, for association, for acceptance by his fellows, for giving and receiving friendship and love.

Management knows today of the existence of these needs, but it often assumes quite wrongly that they represent a threat to the organization. Many studies have demonstrated that the tightly knit, cohesive work group may, under proper conditions, be far more effective than an equal number of separate individuals in achieving organizational goals.

Yet management, fearing group hostility to its own objectives, often goes to considerable lengths to control and direct human efforts in ways that are inimical to the natural "groupiness" of human beings. When man's social needs—and perhaps his safety needs, too—are thus thwarted, he behaves in ways which tend to defeat organizational objectives. He becomes resistant, antagonistic, unco-operative. But this behavior is a consequence, not a cause.

Ego Needs

Above the social needs—in the sense that they do not become motivators until lower needs are reasonably satisfied—are the needs of greatest significance to management and to man himself. They are the egoistic needs, and they are of two kinds:

1. Those needs that relate to one's self-esteem—needs for self-confidence, for independence, for achievement, for competence, for knowledge.
2. Those needs that relate to one's reputation—needs for status, for recognition, for appreciation, for the deserved respect of one's fellows.

Unlike the lower needs, these are rarely satisfied; man seeks indefinitely for more satisfaction of these needs once they have become important to him. But they do not appear in any significant way until physiological, safety, and social needs are all reasonably satisfied.

The typical industrial organization offers few opportunities for the satisfaction of these egoistic needs to people at lower levels in the hierarchy. The conventional methods of organizing work, particularly in mass production industries, give little heed to these aspects of human motivation. If the practices of scientific management were deliberately calculated to thwart these needs—which, of course, they are not—they could hardly accomplish this purpose better than they do.

Self-Fulfillment Needs

Finally—a capstone, as it were, on the hierarchy of man's needs —there are what we may call the needs for self-fulfillment. These are the needs for realizing one's own potentialities, for continued self-development, for being creative in the broadest sense of that term.

It is clear that the conditions of modern life give only limited opportunity for these relatively weak needs to obtain expression. The deprivation most people experience with respect to other lower-level needs diverts their energies into the struggle to satisfy *those* needs, and the needs for self-fulfillment remain dormant.

The Dynamics of Motivation

Now, briefly, a few general comments about motivation.

We recognize readily enough that a man suffering from a severe dietary deficiency is sick. The deprivation of physiological needs has behavioral consequences. The same is true—although less well recognized—of deprivation of higher-level needs. The man whose needs for safety, association, independence, or status are thwarted is sick just as surely as is he who has rickets. And his sickness will have behavioral consequences. We will be mistaken if we attribute his resultant passivity, his hostility, his refusal to accept responsibility to his inherent "human nature." These forms of behavior are *symptoms* of illness —of deprivation of his social and egoistic needs.

The man whose lower-level needs are satisfied is not motivated to satisfy those needs any longer. For practical purposes, they exist no longer. (Remember my point about your need for air.) Management often asks, "Why aren't people more productive? We pay good wages, provide good working conditions, have excellent fringe benefits and steady employment. Yet people do not seem to be willing to put forth more than minimum effort."

The fact that management has provided for these physiological and safety needs has shifted the motivational emphasis to the social and perhaps to the egoistic needs. Unless there are opportunities *at work* to satisfy these higher-level needs, people will be deprived; and their behavior will reflect this deprivation. Under such conditions, if management continues to focus its attention on physiological needs, its efforts are bound to be ineffective.

People *will* make insistent demands for more money under these conditions. It becomes more important than ever to buy the material goods and services which can provide limited satisfaction of the thwarted needs. Although money has only limited value in satisfying many higher-level needs, it can become the focus of interest if it is the *only* means available.

The Carrot and Stick Approach

The carrot and stick theory of motivation (like Newtonian physical theory) works reasonably well under certain circumstances. The *means* for satisfying man's physiological and (within limits) his safety needs can be provided or withheld by management. Employment itself is such a means, and so are wages, working conditions, and benefits. By these means the individual can be controlled so long as he is struggling for subsistence. Man lives for bread alone when there is no bread.

But the carrot and stick theory does not work at all once man has reached an adequate subsistence level and is motivated primarily by higher needs. Management cannot provide a man with self-respect, or with the respect of his fellows, or with the satisfaction of needs for self-fulfillment. It can create conditions such that he is encouraged and enabled to seek such satisfactions *for himself,* or it can thwart him by failing to create those conditions.

By this creation of conditions is not "control." It is not a good device for directing behavior. And so management finds itself in an odd position. The high standard of living created by our modern technological know-how provides quite adequately for the satisfaction of physiological and safety needs. The only significant exception is where management practices have not created confidence in a "fair break"—and thus where safety needs are thwarted. But by making possible the satisfaction of low-level needs, management has deprived itself of the ability to use as motivators the devices on which conventional theory has taught it to rely—rewards, promises, incentives, or threats and other coercive devices.

Neither Hard nor Soft

The philosophy of management by direction and control—*regardless of whether it is hard or soft*—is inadequate to motivate because the human needs on which this approach relies are today unimportant motivators of behavior. Direction and control are essentially unless in motivating people whose important needs are social and egoistic. Both the hard and the soft approach fail today because they are simply irrelevant to the situation.

People, deprived of opportunities to satisfy at work the needs which are now important to them, behave exactly as we might predict —with indolence, passivity, resistance to change, lack of responsibility, willingness to follow the demagogue, unreasonable demands for economic benefits. It would seem that we are caught in a web of our own weaving.

In summary, then, of these comments about motivation: Management by direction and control—whether implemented with the hard, the soft, or the firm but fair approach—fails under today's conditions to provide effective motivation of human effort toward organizational objectives. It fails because direction and control are useless methods of motivating people whose physiological and safety needs are reasonably satisfied and whose social, egoistic, and self-fulfillment needs are predominant.

A New Perspective

For these and many other reasons, we require a different theory of the task of managing people based on more adequate assumptions about human nature and human motivation. I am going to be so bold as to suggest the broad dimensions of such a theory. Call it "Theory Y," if you will.

1. Management is responsible for organizing the elements of productive enterprise—money, materials, equipment, people—in the interest of economic ends.
2. People are *not* by nature passive or resistant to organizational needs. They have become so as a result of experience in organizations.
3. The motivation, the potential for development, the capacity for

assuming responsibility, the readiness to direct behavior toward organizational goals are all present in people. Management does not put them there. It is a responsibility of management to make it possible for people to recognize and develop these human characteristics for themselves.

4. The essential task of management is to arrange organizational conditions and methods of operation so that people can achieve their own goals *best* by directing *their own* efforts toward organizational objectives.

This is a process primarily of creating opportunities, releasing potential, removing obstacles, encouraging growth, providing guidance. It is what Peter Drucker has called "management by objectives" in contrast to "management by control."

And I hasten to add that it does *not* involve the abdication of management, the absence of leadership, the lowering of standards, or the other characteristics usually associated with the "soft" approach under Theory X. Much to the contrary. It is no more possible to create an organization today which will be a fully effective application of this theory than it was to build an atomic power plant in 1945. There are many formidable obstacles to overcome.

Some Difficulties

The conditions imposed by conventional organization theory and by the approach of scientific management for the past half-century have tied men to limited jobs which do not utilize their capabilities, have discouraged the acceptance of responsibility, have encouraged passivity, have eliminated meaning from work. Man's habits, attitudes, expectations—his whole conception of membership in an industrial organization—have been conditioned by his experience under these circumstances. Changes in the direction of Theory Y will be slow, and it will require extensive modification of the attitudes of management and workers alike.

People today are accustomed to being directed, manipulated, controlled in industrial organizations and to finding satisfaction for their social, egoistic, and self-fulfilment needs away from the job. This is true of much of management as well as of workers. Genuine "industrial citizenship"—to borrow again in term from Drucker—is a remote and unrealistic idea, the meaning of which has not even been considered by most members of industrial organizations.

Another way of saying this is that Theory X places exclusive reliance upon external control of human behavior, while Theory Y relies heavily on self-control and self-direction. It is worth noting that this difference is the difference between treating people as children and treating them as mature adults. After generations of the former, we cannot expect to shift to the latter overnight.

Applications of the Theory

Before we are overwhelmed by the obstacles, let us remember that the application of theory is always slow. Progress is usually achieved in small steps.

Consider with me a few innovative ideas which are entirely consistent with Theory Y and which are today being applied with some success.

Decentralization and Delegation

These are ways of freeing people from the too-close control of conventional organization, giving them a degree of freedom to direct their own activities, to assume responsibility, and, importantly, to satisfy their egoistic needs. In this connection, the flat organization of Sears, Roebuck and Company provides an interesting example. It forces "management by objectives" since it enlarges the number of people reporting to a manager until he cannot direct and control them in the conventional manner.

Job Enlargement

This concept, pioneered by I.B.M. and Detroit Edison, is quite consistent with Theory Y. It encourages the acceptance of responsibility at the bottom of the organization; it provides opportunities for satisfying social and egoistic needs. In fact, the reorganization of work at the factory level offers one of the most challenging opportunities for innovation consistent with Theory Y. The studies at A. T. M. Wilson and his associates of British coal mining and Indian textile manufacture have added appreciably to our understanding of work organization. Moreover, the economic and psychological results achieved by this work have been substantial.

Participation and Consultative Management

Under proper conditions these results provide encouragement to people to direct their creative energies toward organizational objectives, give them some voice in decisions that affect them, provide significant opportunities for the satisfaction of social and egoistic needs. I need only mention the Scanlon Plan as the outstanding embodiment of these ideas in practice.

The not infrequent failure of such ideas as these to work as well as expected is often attributable to the fact that a management has "bought the idea" but applied it within the framework of Theory X and its assumptions.

Delegation is not an effective way of exercising management by control. Participation becomes a farce when it is applied as a sales gimmick or a device for kidding people into thinking they are important. Only the management that has confidence in human capacities and is itself directed toward organizational objectives rather than toward the preservation of personal power can grasp the implications of this emerging theory. Such management will find and apply successfully other innovative ideas as we move slowly toward the full implementation of a theory like Y.

Performance Appraisal

Before I stop, let me mention one other practical application of Theory Y which—while still highly tentative—may well have important consequences. This has to do with performance appraisal within the ranks of management. Even a cursory examination of conventional programs of performance appraisal will reveal how completely consistent they are with Theory X. In fact, most such programs tend to treat the individual as though he were a product under inspection on the assembly line.

Take the typical plan: substitute "product" for "subordinate being appraised," substitute "inspector" for "superior making the appraisal," substitute "rework" for "training or development," and, except for the attributes being judged, the human appraisal process will be virtually indistinguishable from the product inspection process.

A few companies—among them General Mills, Ansul Chemical, and General Electric—have been experimenting with approaches which involve the individual in setting "targets" or objectives *for himself* and in a *self*-evaluation of performance semi-annually or annually. Of course, the superior plays an important leadership role in this process—one, in fact, which demands substantially more competence than the conventional approach. The role is, however, considerably more congenial to many managers than the role of "judge" or "inspector" which is forced upon them by conventional performance. Above all, the individual is encouraged to take a greater responsibility for planning and appraising his own contribution to organizational objectives; and the accompanying effects on egoistic and self-fulfillment needs are substantial. This approach to performance appraisal represents one more innovative idea being explored by a few managements who are moving toward the implementation of Theory Y.

Conclusion

And now I am back where I began. I share the belief that we could realize substantial improvements in the effectiveness of industrial organizations during the next decade or two. Moreover, I believe the social sciences can contribute much to such developments. We are only beginning to grasp the implications of the growing body of knowledge in these fields. But if this conviction is to become a reality instead of a pious hope, we will need to view the process much as we view the process of releasing the energy of the atom for constructive human ends—as a slow, costly, sometimes discouraging approach toward a goal which would seem to many to be quite unrealistic.

The ingenuity and the perseverance of industrial management in the pursuit of economic ends have changed many scientific and technological dreams into commonplace realities. It is now becoming clear that the application of these same talents to the human side of enterprise will not only enhance substantially these materialistic achievements but will bring us one step closer to "the good society." Shall we get on with the job?

Kingsley Davis

Status and Related Concepts

Identity within the Situation

Essential in the interacting situation is the identity of each participant, for not everybody is supposed to expect the same thing. A husband expects sexual response from his wife, but not every man has the right to expect such a response from her. A president expects certain advice and help from his cabinet ministers, but nobody else may expect these things from them. A person therefore enters a social situation with an identity already established. His identity refers to his *position*, or *status*, within the social structure applicable to the given situation, and establishes his rights and obligations with reference to others holding positions within the same structure. His position and consequently his identity in the particular situation result from all the other positions he holds in other major social structures, especially in the other structures most closely related to the one he is acting in at the moment.

In the course of an individual's life very broad positions are first acquired. He begins with a general identity—such as that of class,

Reprinted with permission of The Macmillan Company from *Human Society* by Kingsley Davis. Copyright, 1948, 1949 by The Macmillan Company.

sex, and family—which will later govern his position in many particular situations. As he goes through life he acquires more specific
positions, and his actual behavior in the various situations to which
these positions apply serves to refine and modify the initially assigned
identity. Thus as time goes by he has for each new situation a more
complete and more unique identity. Such progressive refinement
gives a dynamic, developmental character to his positional history.
For instance, a male acquires certain broad rights and obligations
simply because of his quality of maleness, and these enter to some
degree into nearly every situation in which he participates. But his
subsequent personal history in day-to-day interaction contributes further to his social identity and differentiates him in many respects
from other males.

The normative system lays down the formal rights and obligations in connection with a position. Though it permits a certain
amount of legitimate variation within the limits imposed, it also lays
down rules to be followed in case the individual oversteps the limits.
A right is a legitimate expectation entertained by a person in one
position with respect to the behavior of a person in another position.
From the point of view of the other person this claim represents an
obligation. "Right" and "obligation," therefore, are simply different
definitions of the same relationship.

Although many norms are expressed independently of particular
positions and situations—like the simple exhortation to be honest—
they must, when applied in behavior, vary according to the status of
the actor and the situation he is in. Absolute honesty in the sense of
speaking the truth on all occasions is an impossible ideal; there are
many occasions when persons do not wish to hear the truth, particularly about themselves, and will penalize the person who tells it to
them. The same is true of other absolute or abstract norms. All
norms, no matter how expressed, are relative to the particular situation. Which norm applies in a given case depends upon the relations
between the statuses of the interacting persons.

The Organization of Statuses

Each person occupies many different statuses. We sometimes
speak of *the* status or *the* social position of a given individual, meaning the sum total of his specific statuses and roles, especially in so far
as they bear upon his general "social standing." More often, however,
we qualify our statement by giving at the same time the context to
which our statement applies. Thus we may say that Dr. Jones has a
high standing *in his profession,* or that Mrs. Jones is well known *as a
clubwoman.* In other words, we rate the person's behavior according
to the norms applying to a specific status. We implicitly recognize
that he has many statuses and that we are singling one out for
particular mention.

All the positions occupied by a single individual constitute, when taken together, an important element in his personality. Since each person has but so much time, energy, and ability, and since his activity must achieve results and satisfy needs, his system of statuses must be to some degree integrated. His personal efficiency, his mental stability and contentment depend to a large extent on the integration of his various social positions.

Similarly, the total system of positions in the entire society or group must be reasonably well integrated. Otherwise the society or group could not carry on its existence. Ordinarily the various statuses —occupational, familial, political, religious—are so bound together in terms of interlocking rights and obligations that their manifestation in behavior gets things accomplished and the collectivity is perpetuated. One of the things that is perpetuated, of course, is the system of positions itself. Basically the positions tend to remain the same; it is mainly the occupants of the positions who change.

Status and Office

For clarity, one should recognize that some social positions are, so to speak, in the folkways and mores whereas others are merely in the by-laws and rules of specific organizations. Some are generalized and known to everybody; others are limited and known only to a few. Perhaps it will aid understanding if we give a name to each half of this continuum, calling the one *status* and the other *office*. The term status would then designate a position in the general institutional system, recognized and supported by the entire society, spontaneously evolved rather than deliberately created, rooted in the folkways and mores. Office, on the other hand, would designate a position in a deliberately created organization, governed by specific and limited rules in a limited group, more generally achieved than ascribed. An example of a status in our society would be "skilled laborer"; of an office, "head carpenter of the Blank Construction Company." Another example of status would be "professor"; and of a corresponding office, "professor of government at the University of Arizona."

Station and Stratum

Since any single individual occupies not one but many statuses and offices, and since for his personal and social efficiency he must find some coherence in the several positions he fills, we could expect that in any society certain positions will tend to adhere together in different individuals. Such is actually the case, and so we may speak of a *station*, meaning by this term a cluster of statuses and offices that tend to be combined in one person as a locus and are publicly recognized as so combined in a great many cases. Whereas a single status or office defines one's position with reference to a limited sector of social interaction, a station embodies one's generalized status (the sum total of one's major positions) in the over-all social structure. A station is therefore a recurrent combination of statuses having a certain degree of fixity.

The name that is given to a particular station often comes from one of the major statuses constituting it. For instance, we sometimes speak of the "landowning class," by which we mean more than simply landownership. We mean a whole group of rights and privileges which happen to be associated with landowning but are not necessarily a part of it. A man may own no land and still be a member of the landowning class, because he has all the other positions that landowners in the given society generally have; and contrariwise a man may own land without being a member of the landowning class. Furthermore, the particular position that gives a name to the whole station may not itself be uniform; it may be really a name for a class of positions which are roughly similar and which tend to have the same associated positions. Thus doctor, lawyer, and professor are each different occupational positions, but are on about the same level of evaluation and accompanied by similar allied positions. A common name, "professionals," designating a station is therefore given the incumbents.

For a mass of persons in a given society who enjoy roughly the same station, we can use the word *stratum*. Any population is commonly divided into strata. In fact, specifying the strata is one of the most convenient and frequently used ways of giving a shorthand description of a social structure. Such a procedure implies the extensive of relative rank. Different stations are felt to be unequal in the public estimation and hence a hierarchy of strata is recognized. It is also known that individuals occupying the same station and hence failing in the same stratum tend to look at the world from the same point of view. They have like interests and common problems. Sometimes, though not always, they stick together, manifesting a solid front towards persons in other strata. We may speak of this collective front, when it occurs, as stratum solidarity.

Several types of stratified organization may be distinguished according to the kinds of positions constituting the station, the degree of stratum solidarity, the methods by which persons reach and leave the station, etc. The best-known types are the caste system at one extreme and the open class system at the other.

How Positions Are Filled: Ascription and Achievement

The process by which the statuses in a society are constantly being filled by the infiltration of new personnel to take the place of the old is sometimes called, by organic analogy, social metabolism. Such metabolism is fully as important to a society as digestion is to an organism. In both cases raw materials are being absorbed and made to furnish the energy that gives life to the whole structure. In the case of the organism it is food substances that are taken in, whereas in the case of society it is new individuals.

Faced with a constant stream of raw material in the form of new babies, which it must so process and so distribute that the variegated system of interlocking adult statuses will be filled and the business of group living accomplished, every society is caught on what Linton (1936, p. 115) regards as the horns of a dilemma. On the one hand, as we know, the formation of the individual's habits and attitudes begins at birth; consequently the earlier his training for specific statuses can begin, the more complete will be his eventual adjustment. For this reason there arises a tendency to ascribe the individual's status at birth and to begin fitting him at once for the duties that will subsequently be his. On the other hand, we know that no two individuals (not even identical twins) are inherently the same at birth. Their capacities differ from one to another and there is as yet no way of telling, short of subsequent experience, what their peculiar capacities are. For this reason there arises a tendency to postpone the determination of adult statuses until each individual has shown which statuses he is peculiarly fitted for.

Here, then, are two opposite possibilities—the ascription of status independently of individual qualities or the achievement of status according to individual accomplishment—each with societal advantages and disadvantages on its side. Every society is confronted with the necessity of making an unconscious but difficult choice between the two. It is possible to imagine one type of society in which status is exclusively ascribed and to deduce the qualities that such a society would have. In fact, there are some societies that go far in this direction. It is equally possible to imagine another type of society in which status is exclusively achieved and to deduce the qualities that it would have. But the truth is that no human society seizes either horn of the dilemma completely. Every known society makes some use of both principles. The question really boils down, then, to the degree of ascription and achievement in any given case, and also what types of statuses lend themselves to one or the other kind of recruitment.

Ascribed Status [1]

The fabrication of the infant for future positions must begin as soon as possible. Socialization is at best a long and tedious process, one that is never perfectly achieved. It pays to begin the training as soon as possible, when the child is in its most plastic stage.

Paradoxically, however, the fabrication of the child for future statuses cannot begin until he already has a status. This is due to the

---

1. Parts of this section are taken almost verbatim from Davis (1940).

fact that the work of socialization, if it is to be accomplished, must be assigned to particular persons whose responsibilities and rights with respect to the infant are clearly defined and who are motivated by various social mechanisms to perform the appropriate tasks. Such assignment, such arbitrary connection of the child with persons who already have a status in the social structure, immediately gives the infant membership in the society and a specific place in the system of statuses. The statuses he receives at this time, some temporary and some permanent, are clearly ascribed statuses because the infant has certainly not achieved them.

However blind and arbitrary the ascription of statuses may be from the point of view of innate capacity, it is nonetheless done according to a certain unconscious order—an order varying from one society to another and yet everywhere have an underlying uniformity. The rationale of the process can be seen by raising this question: What is there about the infant that a society *can* use as a basis for the arbitrary assignment of status? The newborn baby is so undifferentiated, so inscrutable as to its future capabilities, that one wonders what a society does or *can* seize upon as a basis for immediate status ascription. The answer is that there is little indeed to serve such a purpose. What little there is can be reduced to four categories, viz., sex, age, age relationship, and kinship. Let us discuss each of these.

Sex

The infant's sex is a definite, highly visible physiological fact which appears at birth and remains fixed for life. It provides a universally applicable dichotomy for dividing all individuals into two permanent classes, male and female. It also denotes on the part of each class a differential but complementary system of biological traits and processes which during a long period of the person's life will be associated with reproductive functions. The biological system, furthermore, is characterized by the peculiar primate reproductive physiology leading to continuous sexual interest and elaborate sexual conditioning and harboring a libidinous urge tremendously significant in human motivation. Sex difference is consequently a very convenient, not wholly fortuitous basis for the ascription of lifetime statuses. This is why in every society it is utilized not only for assigning definite statuses but also for giving monopolies on achieved statuses—which means in effect that many otherwise achieved positions are at the same time sex-ascribed.

Given this functional ascription on the basis of sex, it seems inevitable that an evaluative ascription should also be made, one sex receiving more prestige than the other. Social position, as we have seen, is seldom merely a matter of prescribed activities. It is usually also a matter of invidious judgment as well.

The great error in interpreting the ascription of status on the basis of sex (as in other cases of ascription) is to assume that the ascribed behavior springs from the biological qualities of the groups concerned. In many societies the male-female division of statuses is rationalized in terms of the alleged inherent traits of men and women. In Western culture, for instance, women were long pictured as naturally more stupid, delicate, emotional, intuitive, religious, and monogamous than men. This notion justified women's exclusion from higher education and better occupations, their disbarment from certain property rights, their submission to the double standard of morality, and their subordination to men generally.

The secret both of woman's physical weakness and of her usual assignment of status is her child-bearing function. Forced to carry the parasitic embryo in her body for an extended time and to nurse the helpless young for a period thereafter, she is limited as to what she can do. As in most mammalian species, her whole body is specialized to some extent for reproduction, whereas the male, with his greater strength but shorter life span, is specialized for fighting. It is not surprising, then, that the tasks usually associated with womanhood are those most compatible with reproduction. Keeping house, cooking, gardening, sewing, making pots, etc., all fit with bearing and rearing children. Hunting, fishing, fighting, herding cattle—particularly if they require long trips and great physical exertion—are not so compatible and tend to be allocated to men.

Age

Among the various bases for the ascription of status, age holds a peculiar place. Like sex, it is a definite, highly visible physiological fact apparent at birth. The baby's zero age does not distinguish him from other infants but it does separate him from older persons. Unlike sex, however, age is a steadily changing condition and therefore cannot give rise to permanent lifetime statuses. Each individual, if he lives, must eventually abandon any given category. The only way between given persons (e.g., between parent and child, elder brother and younger brother, senior member and junior member), in which case it is the time interval between the parties and not age itself that remains fixed. The feature of variability makes age totally impractical as a basis of caste and, in contrast to race or sex differentiation, minimizes the development of a characteristic personality for each rung in the scale.

Furthermore, except in terms of an age relationship, age is not a dichotomy but a continuum which can provide a basis for several rather than two general statuses. It is a continuum with infinitely small gradations, yet if too many distinctions are made within this continuum age loses its character of high visibility (small differences of chronological age being hard to detect) and its character of intrinsic social relevance (for only in terms of broad age grades can there be an intrinsic connection between the physical condition and the social condition associated with age). Hence there are usually only a few age statuses—fixed in the culture but not permanently for the person—through which, if he lives, every individual passes. These stages must usually be characterized by definite manifestations, such as those of infancy, childhood, puberty, maturity, and old age. No matter how broadly they are conceived, however, the grades overlap and the classification becomes arbitrary. Most age statuses that purport to be based on physiology are in reality dependent to an equal degree on social events and attitudes that have at best only a rough correlation with actual age.

All societies recognize age as a basis of status, but some of them emphasize it more than others. It is well known, for example, that in the old culture of China and Japan a great deal depended on the person's age, whereas in modern Western society much less depends on it.

Age status would be exhibited in its purest form if it were not limited by any other basis of status. As a matter of fact, however, it is always limited by sex status, since in all known cultures men and women of the same age are treated differently. It tends also to be limited by kinship status. In the Chinese and Japanese cases it was clearly tied to kinship, for the stress was upon filial piety and in particular upon the father-son relationship. In some primitive tribes, however, everybody of roughly the same age and sex is regarded as belonging to a certain organized social group, a phenomenon called *age-grading* by the social anthropologists.

Generally a society recognizes at least four age periods: infancy, childhood, maturity, and old age. Many societies have in addition two other peculiar age periods to which they attach importance—namely, the unborn and the dead. The unborn may be believed to be the spirits of departed ancestors. The primitive Australians, for example, thought these spirits dwelt in the clan's totemic water hole and that one entering the womb of a woman was later born as a member of the clan. The Hindus think of the unborn in a vague way as the spirits of persons or animals who lived in former incarnations. Sometimes unborn children are betrothed to other unborn children according to some pattern of arranging marriages.

Kinship

In addition to sex and age, another characteristic of the raw infant which can be utilized in giving him an initial status is kinship, his relation to his parents and siblings. The simplest form of ascription on this basis is the identification of the infant's status in the community with that of his parents. Even more than in the previous cases mentioned, such ascription is highly arbitrary. There is no necessary relation between the capacities of the parents and those of the offspring. Brilliant parents may have stupid children and vice versa. The socially ascribed identity between parent and child is therefore more complete than the genetics of inheritance would warrant. Consequently the universal tendency to ascribe status on the basis of this identity cannot be explained in terms of biological fact, as the apologists of class rigidity have sometimes attempted to do. It must be explained in terms of sociological principles, and the first of these is that it is socially convenient. The family appears as a universal social institution, and in it the child is closely associated with the parents and is initially socialized by them. In view of this close association and the fact that the parents are given responsibility for the child, it is a matter of pure economy to identify the child's status with them rather than with someone else. This is what was meant when it was said earlier that the rearing of the child requires that he be given a status at the very start; somebody must be made responsible for him and hence must be given a status with reference to him. The first responsibility, and hence the first status connection, accordingly rests with the parents.

The child may take the parents' status immediately, as in a caste system, or he may acquire it later but begin training for it at once (as in succession or inheritance). In the latter case we may speak of the process as "delayed ascription." Finally, the child may seek achieved positions that are different from those of the parents but with a competitive advantage or disadvantage provided by his parents (as in open-class occupational placement). This we may speak of as "fluid ascription," understanding that in this the element of achievement has reached a rather large proportion but has not entirely displaced the element of ascription. In any case, through identification with the parents the child becomes automatically related to the rest of the society and is trained accordingly. So important, indeed, is this *jus sanguinis* principle that a wide number of important statuses depended upon it. The ascription of citizenship, religious affiliation, and community membership, for instance, is in most cases a matter of identification with parents who are already citizens, communicants, and members. From an ethical point of view, the most controversial type of status transmitted from parent to child of that of class position. The child inevitably derives an advantage or disadvantage according to his parents' rank in the social scale, and in some societies his position is fixed for life.

The child at birth not only acquires some elements of the parents' status in the larger society but he acquires a position in the family itself. He acquires an individual status as son or daughter.

Since his parents are kin to other individuals, his relation to his parents defines his relation to these more distant kinsmen. Thus he is not only a son but also a grandson, a nephew, a brother, a cousin, etc. Human societies universally recognize rights and obligations in accordance with these kinship connections. In some cases, as in our own society, the extended kinship ties have dropped into the background but the immediate family ties remain socially important. Although there is great variation in the precise kinds of rights and obligations associated with kinship statuses, the fact of such association is universal.

Other Bases of Ascription

Sex, age, and kinship do not exhaust all the bases for the ascription of status. The newborn infant, for example, manifests the physical stigmata of his race. It is therefore possible to assign him a status on the basis of his racial traits and thus create in the society a system of racial castes. Since racial features are inherited, however, this basis of ascription is very similar to ascription on the basis of the parents' status. In fact, even when a racial basis is assumed, there is a tendency to assign the child's position on the basis of his parents' position. In the United States a child of "Negro" parentage tends to be defined as "Negro" regardless of the fact that he may be almost totally white in a physical sense. Some of the Southern states define as a Negro any person who has a drop of Negro blood in his veins. Such a definition is obviously more sociological than racial.

There are still other circumstances affecting the child's status. Illegitimacy, for example, prevents full identification with the parents. Plural birth in some societies give the children so born a peculiar status, occasionally resulting in death for them. The total number of children born in the family, the fact of adoption, the fact of the death of a parent, the occurrence of divorce—all these can affect the infant's status independently of his will. One can see that the so-called "accident of birth" is ubiquitous and extremely important in society.

The Achievement of Status

In any society, no matter how rigid, there is knowledge of individual accomplishment and individual failure. The give and take of everyday life, the intimate play of personalities in the interacting situation, provide a setting for the irrepressible expression of natural differences. People assess one another with shrewd and practiced eyes and give their private allegiance to those who are kindly, capable, talented, and original. The role and the role personality are never governed solely by the status and the status personality but are determined by individual differences of many kinds. It follows that esteem and prestige are not necessarily synonymous, that an ascribed status system is never able to hold all individuals in complete fixity. There are always men who are so cunning, so gifted, so energetic, and so drivingly ambitious that they become leaders despite every known obstacle. The history of all lands and all times is studded with their names, for they are the men who make history. They are the men who can use the institutional machinery, whatever its form, to control other people and can subtly change the system in order to give themselves a place in it.

Our present interest, however, lies not in the exceptional individual but in the institutional order itself. Though we know that personal accomplishment always plays a part in interaction, we still must ask to what extent the social system institutionalizes the recognition of achievement. To what extent does it provide for an orderly and legitimate change of status according to the individual's manifestation of talent and effort? If the social system encourages its members in this way, it will not drive the exceptional person into illicit channels but will make use of his capacities for common social ends. It will also make use of people who would not have the genius to overcome great obstacles but who, with encouragement, can put into effect very useful capacities that would otherwise be suppressed. Finally, by providing for an orderly change of status the social system can prevent the filling of high positions by incompetents who would become simply tools in the hands of sharp-witted but unscrupulous and irresponsible men.

It is not easy to say why some societies institutionalize achieved status and others do not, but it is possible to cite some interesting correlations between these factors and other societal traits. In primitive society an emphasis on achieved status apparently goes with warfare and dangerous occupations such as hunting, raiding, and deep-sea fishing. In civilized society a tendency toward commerce, an extreme division of labor, urban conditions of life, and rapid social changes seem to be correlated with an emphasis on achieved status. Whether such social characteristics are the result or the cause of the prominence of achieved status is virtually impossible and perhaps not important to decide; but the functional relations are easy to see. Commercial activity implies that economic behavior has won some independence from noneconomic controls; and since it deals with scarce commodities purely as means to greater gain, it offers the individual a prime opportunity to advance by the use of his native capacities. An extreme division of labor gives a competitive advantage to the person who is talented in his work; but it is possible to overemphasize this point, because a person trained from childhood to perform the duties of an ascribed status may develop a high skill despite a merely average talent. By concentrating a large population in a small territory and supporting itself by varied enterprises, the city enables individuals to be readily selected for particular positions according to their manifest achievements. Finally, rapid social change provides continually new statuses which, precisely because they are new, cannot be filled by ascription.

It is interesting to ask not only what kinds of societies emphasize achieved status but also what kinds of statuses are likely to be thrown open to achievement. Obviously one would expect that those statuses requiring the possession of unusual talent would be the first to be thrown open. All the education in the world will not make of a mediocre person a great violinist or a great mathematician, a great actor or a great writer, a great prize fighter or a great track star. Next, one would expect that those statuses depending on the informal and spontaneous approval of the populace would be predominantly achieved. For this reason the theatre and the sports arena, the rostrum and the printed page have long been avenues by which persons of humble birth could advance themselves socially. Finally, one would guess that those statuses requiring such long and costly education that private resources cannot supply it, and hence necessitating public provision of training, would be thrown open to achievement. The training of the doctor or lawyer in modern society cannot be accomplished within the family. It requires large schools with elaborate resources and professional faculties. Anyone who can get himself into these schools and show enough effort and ability to pass through them is in a fair way to becoming a doctor or a lawyer. The schools are therefore channels of vertical mobility.

The Relation of Ascribed to Achieved Status

Both ascription and achievement are found in every culture. Each, though opposite in principle, is complementary in function and therefore essential to society. In order that the infant be fabricated for specialized statuses, his socialization must start at the earliest possible moment. For this he must be initially placed in the social structure. Yet it is precisely at this point that least is known about him. The initial placement, therefore, despite its tremendous subsequent importance, is a matter of arbitrary social rule based on the few available external characteristics. Later the individual's achievements must also be recognized, and not long after birth each child's accomplishments, however, are already partial products of statuses ascribed at birth, so that differences of achievement can never be interpreted purely as differences of inherent capacity. Ascribed statuses, coming first in life, lay the framework within which the transmission of the cultural heritage is to take place. They determine the general goals (e.g., the adult statuses) toward which training shall aim and the initial persons who shall carry it out. When, accordingly, we know the child's sex, age, age relations, and the class, religion, region, community, and nation of his parents, we know fairly well what his socialization—indeed, his life—will be.

Ascribed statuses also give a feeling of security that purely achieved positions can never give. All of life cannot be thrown open to competition. One cannot feel that every person is a competitor for whatever status one holds. Above all, one cannot feel that there is no limit to the sheer manipulation of means, no rules and principles that are fixed beyond the power of the ambitious to change. Hence laborers, bureaucrats, and professionals each band together to lessen competition among themselves. Businesses enter collusive agreements to hold up prices. Producers advocate tariffs to protect themselves from foreign competition. The community frowns on easy divorce, on repeated changes of religious belief, on rapid change of citizenship, on outright and open opportunism in all things.

On the other hand, within the framework of authority and security laid down by the system of ascribed statuses there must necessarily be some achievement. The value of achieved status is not only that it places the right persons in the right place but that it stimulates effort. The duties connected with statuses are often onerous and exacting and cannot be accomplished without hard training. Without competition there would be an inevitable tendency to demand the rewards of the status without adequately fulfilling its duties. The lassitude of monopoly and the stimulation of competition are too well known to require documentation.

The usual condition in society, then, is that broad outlines of status are laid down by ascription while many specific statuses are open to achievement. Even an ascribed status requires, unless it is purely passive, some degree of training. A king who rules by divine right must nevertheless know something about the behavior required of a king. Even an achieved status is usually limited in one way or another by ascription. The usual mode of limitation of achieved status is through limitation of the number of competitors. In a sense, the presidency of the United States is an achieved office, since no one can get there without going through the competitive process of winning an election. But the Constitution forbids anyone to compete for this office who is not a native-born citizen, not thirty-five years of age or over, and not at least fourteen years a resident within the country. Furthermore, we know that there are certain customary limitations that are as effective as if they were written into the constitution. No woman, no Negro, no Oriental, no Jew has ever been president. It is conceivable that one of these might someday get the office, but it will be only by overcoming a great handicap. Thus [a large proportion] in the United States are effectively excluded from becoming president of the United States. Nearly always there are such limitations on achieved status, so that any concrete social position can generally be said to be partly ascribed, partly achieved. In this sense, ascription and achievement are abstractions, but they are nonetheless real.

References

Davis, Kingsley. "The Child and Social Structure." *Journal of Educational Psychology,* Vol. 14, 1940.

Linton R. *The Study of Man.* Appleton-Century-Crofts, 1936.

Rollo May

The Nature of Anxiety and Its Relation to Fear

It is agreed by the students of anxiety—Freud, Goldstein, Horney, to mention only three—that anxiety is a *diffuse* apprehension, and that the central difference between fear and anxiety is that fear is a reaction to a specific danger while anxiety is unspecific, "vague," "objectless." The special characteristics of anxiety are the feelings of *uncertainty* and *helplessness* in the face of the danger. The nature of anxiety can be understood when we ask *what* is threatened in the experience which produces anxiety. The threat is to something in the "core or essence" of the personality. *Anxiety is the apprehension cued off by a threat to some value which the individual holds essential to his existence as a personality.* The threat may be to physical or psychological life (death, or loss of freedom), or it may be to some other value which the individual identifies with his existence (patriotism, the love of another person, "success," etc.). This identification of a value with one's existence as a personality is vividly illustrated in the remark of Tom in his period of anxiety over whether he would be retained in his job or be forced to resort again to government relief: "If I couldn't support my family, I'd as soon jump off the end of the dock." This, put simply, is his way of saying that if he could not preserve the self-respecting position of being the responsible wage-earner, his whole life would have no meaning and he might as well not exist. The occasions of anxiety will vary with different people as widely as the values on which they depend vary, but what will always be true in anxiety is that the threat is to a value held by that particular individual to be essential to his existence and consequently to his security as a personality.

The terms "diffuse" and "vague" do not mean that anxiety is less intense in its painfulness than other affects. Indeed, other things being equal, anxiety is regularly more painful than fear. Nor do these terms refer merely to the generalized, "over-all" psychophysical quality of anxiety. Other emotions, like fear, anger, hostility, also permeate the whole organism. Rather, the diffuse and undifferentiated quality of anxiety refers to the *level* in the personality on which the threat is experienced. An individual experiences various fears on the basis of a security pattern he has developed; *but in anxiety it is this security pattern itself which is threatened.* However uncomfortable a fear may be, it is experienced as a threat which can be located spatially and to which an adjustment can, at least in theory, be made. The relation of the organism to a given object is what is important, and if that object can be removed, either by reassurance or appropriate flight, the apprehension disappears. But since anxiety attacks the foundation (core, essence) of the personality, the individual cannot "stand outside" the threat, cannot objectify it, and thereby is powerless to take steps to meet it. In common parlance, he feels caught, or if the anxiety is severe, overwhelmed; he is afraid but uncertain of what he fears. The fact that anxiety is a threat to the essential, rather than to the peripheral, security of the person has led some authors to describe it as a "cosmic" experience (Sullivan).

These considerations aid in understanding why anxiety appears as a subjective, objectless experience. When Kierkegaard emphasizes that anxiety refers to an inner state and Freud holds that in anxiety the object is "ignored," it is not meant (or *ought* not to be meant) that the danger situation which cues off the anxiety is unimportant. Nor does the term "objectless" refer simply to the fact that the danger causing the anxiety, in the case of neurotic anxiety, has been repressed into unconsciousness. Rather anxiety is objectless because it strikes at that basis of the psychological structure on which the perception of one's self as distinct from the world of objects occurs. Sullivan has remarked that the self-dynamism is developed in order to protect the individual from anxiety; the converse is as true, that mounting anxiety reduces self-awareness. In proportion to the increase in anxiety, the awareness of one's self as a subject related to objects in the external world is confused. Awareness of one's self is simply a correlate of awareness of objects in the external world. It is precisely this differentiation between subjectivity and objectivity which breaks down in proportion to the severity of the anxiety experienced. Hence the expression that anxiety "attacks from the rear," or from all sides at once. In anxiety the individual is proportionately less able to see himself in relation to stimuli and hence less abel to make adequate evaluation of the stimuli. In various languages the usual expressions, accurately enough, are "One *has* a fear" but "One *is* anxious." Thus in severe clinical cases anxiety is often experienced as a "dissolution of the self." *In fine,* the objectless nature of anxiety arises from the fact that *the security base itself of the individual is threatened, and since it is in terms of this security base that the individual has been able to experience himself as a self in relation to objects, the distinction between subject and object also breaks down.*

Since anxiety threatens the basis of selfhood, it is described on the philosophical level as the realization that one may cease to exist as a self. This is phrased by Tillich as the threat of "nonbeing." One is a being, a self, but there is at any moment the possibility of "not being." The normal anxiety associated in the minds of most people with death is one common form of this anxiety. But the dissolution of the self may consist not simply of physical death; it may consist also of the loss of psychological or spiritual meaning which is identified with one's existence as a self—i.e., *the threat of meaninglessness.* Hence Kierkegaard's statement that anxiety is the "fear of nothingness" means in this context the fear of becoming nothing. . . .

Normal anxiety is, like any anxiety, a reaction to threats to values the individual holds essential to his existence as a personality; but normal anxiety is that reaction which (1) is not disproportionate to the objective threat, (2) does not involve repression or other mechanisms of intrapsychic conflict, and, as a corollary to the second point, (3) does not require neurotic defense mechanisms for its management, but can be confronted constructively on the level of conscious awareness *or* can be relieved if the objective situation is altered. The undifferentiated and diffuse reactions of the very young infant to threats—such as falling or not being fed—fall in the category of normal anxiety, since they occur before the infant is mature enough for the intrapsychic processes of repression and conflict involved in neurotic anxiety and since, so far as we know, the threats may be experienced by the infant in its state of relative helplessness as objectively real dangers to its existence.

Normal anxiety continues throughout life in the form of what Freud termed "objective anxiety." The existence of normal anxiety in adults is frequently overlooked because the intensity of the experience is often so much less than that of neurotic anxiety; and, since one characteristic of normal anxiety is that it can be managed constructively, it does not show itself in "panic" or in other dramatic forms. But the *quantity* of reaction should not be confused with its *quality*. The intensity of the reaction is important as a distinction between neurotic and normal anxiety only when we are considering the question of whether the reaction is proportionate to the objective threat. Every individual experiences greater or lesser threats to his existence and to values he identifies with his existence in the course of his normal development as a human being. But he normally confronts these experiences constructively, uses them as "learning experiences" (in the broad and profound meaning of that term), and moves on in his development. . . .

Another common form of normal anxiety is that related to the fact that each human being develops as an individual in a social matrix, a world of other individuals. As seen most clearly in the development of the child, this growth as an individual in a context of social relationships involves a progressive breaking of dependent ties with parents, which in turn involves greater or lesser crises and clashes with parents. This source of anxiety has been discussed by Kierkegaard and Fromm. Otto Rank, likewise, has emphasized that normal anxiety inheres in all experiences of "separation" throughout the individual's life career. If these potentially anxiety-creating experiences are negotiated successfully, they lead not only to greater independence on the part of the child but to re-establishment of relations with parents and other persons on new levels. The anxiety in such cases should then be described as "normal" rather than "neurotic."

In the above examples of normal anxiety, it will be seen that in each case the anxiety is proportionate to an objective threat, does not involve repression or intrapsychic conflict, and can be met by constructive development and increasing employment of the person's own courage and powers rather than retrenchment into neurotic defense mechanisms. . . .

We speak of anxiety as "basic" not only in the sense that it is the general, original response to threat, but also because it is a response to threat on the basic level of the personality; i.e., it is a response to a threat to the "core" or "essence" of the personality rather than to a peripheral danger. Fears are the responses to threats before they get to this basic level. By reacting adequately to the various specific dangers which threaten him (i.e., by reacting adequately on the level of fears), the individual avoids having his essential values threatened, avoids being threatened at the "inner citadel" of his security system. If however he cannot cope with dangers in their specific forms, he will be threatened on the deeper level which we have called the "core" or "essence" of personality. Using a military analogy supplied by the Battle of France in the last war, battles on various segments of the front lines represent specific threats; so long as the battle can be fought out on the periphery, so long as the dangers can be warded off in the area of the outer fortifications, the vital areas are not threatened. But when the enemy breaks through into the capital of the country, when the inner lines of communication are broken and the battle is no longer localized; when, that is, the enemy attacks from all directions and the defending soldiers do not know which way to march or where to take a stand, we have the threat of being overwhelmed, with its corollaries, panic and frantic behavior. This latter is analogous to the threat to the basic values, the "inner citadel" of the personality; and *in individual psychological terms it is the threat responded to as anxiety.* Thus, figuratively speaking, we may describe fear as the armor against anxiety. The phrase "fear of fear," employed by President Franklin D. Roosevelt as well as by several other previous figures in history, refers to the apprehension that one will not be able to cope with dangers as they arise and will thereby be thrown into a catastrophic situation. "Fear of fear," thus, really means anxiety. . . .

The anxiety of a given individual is conditioned by the fact that he lives in a given culture at a particular point in the historical development of that culture. Though the majority of writers on anxiety would agree with this statement in some measure, there are wide divergencies in the literature with respect to the relative emphasis placed on culture and how culture is treated. In general, those who have viewed the problem of anxiety in terms of the expression of indigenous individual drives have tended to omit cultural factors (like the early Freud) or to treat culture negatively (like the later Freud). On the other hand, those who see personality development as occurring at every moment within a social matrix have emphasized that the problem of anxiety must always be viewed in the context of the interrelation of the individual with his culture (Horney, Sullivan, Fromm, etc.). It is fair to say that there has been in recent years a considerable trend in the latter direction, with an emergence only lately of an endeavor to trace the historical backgrounds of cultural patterns which underlie contemporaneous anxiety (Fromm, Kardiner).

The problem of anxiety and culture may be broken down into two phases. First, the *kinds* (forms, occasions) of anxiety experienced by a given individual are culturally conditioned in the respect that *the values or goals held by an individual to be essential to his existence as a personality are largely cultural products.* Second, the *quantities* of anxiety experienced by a given individual are conditioned by the degree of unity and stability in his culture. If the culture is relatively unified and stable, the individual will be able to orient himself (whether he is in accord with cultural mores or not) and his experiences of anxiety will be relatively less frequent and less intense.

If, as in the case of the contemporaneous period, the culture is in a state of disunity and traumatic change, the individual will not only reflect this disunity in his own psychological life, but also his orientation to his changing culture will be proportionately more difficult. Hence his anxiety will be more frequent and more intense.

Competitive Individual Success as an Example of a Cultural Value

There are many demonstrations of the fact that social prestige goals are dominant in our culture, and that these social prestige goals take the chief form of a high valuation of individual competitive success. If that value is threatened, conflict and anxiety ensue. It is generally agreed, for one example, that the high incidence of gastric ulcer among men in our times is related to the highly competitive nature of our culture, which takes the form of the stringent need of many men to appear independent and triumphant and to repress dependent needs. For another example, in the studies of children's fears it was found that as the child grew older fears related to competitive status increased. Jersild interprets this as a sign of the increasing impact of the culture upon the child. The adults reporting their childhood fears, moreover, gave a much larger incidence of fears related to competitive success and failure than the children, which Jersild interprets as a "reading back" into childhood of fears which have become important to them as adults. The literature indicates that the goal of individual competitive success is not only *a* dominant goal but probably *the* dominant goal in our culture from Wall Street at one extreme to Plainville at the other, and in varying forms from the Renaissance to the present day. This goal is by no means limited to economic activity, though in that realm it receives its clearest definition; it carries over into school and family, sex and love as well.

The goal of individual competitive success is accorded such crucial weight because it is identified with self-esteem and self-worth. It is to the modern man what salvation was to the citizen of the Middle Ages (Kardiner). Competitive success in our culture is not essentially a matter of achieving material security, nor is it in the realms of sex and love a matter of achieving an abundance of libidinal satisfactions. Rather, it is a means of gaining security, because it is accepted as a proof of one's power in one's own eyes and in the eyes of others. In this sense the economic valuation becomes the valuation of persons. Since success is competitive, it involves a striving to triumph over others, augmenting intrasocial hostility and interpersonal isolation. Since it is a value which is always relative to the success of others, it is insatiable. Failure in the struggle to achieve competitive success involves not only social contempt but, more important, self-contempt and feelings of worthlessness. The above observations indicate why, when this value is threatened, the individual in our culture generally experiences profound anxiety. Since success is the chief form of self-validation, feelings of anxiety generally lead to redoubled efforts to attain success. Hence, a vicious circle results: competitive striving→ intrasocial hostility→ interpersonal isolation→ anxiety→ increased competitive striving.

A goal like competitive individual success, in the stringent form it takes in modern society, is not an "immutable attribute" of human nature but *a cultural product which has its historical genesis and development.* . . .

There is wide agreement that in Western culture the present century is characterized by disunity and traumatic change. Hence the culture is marked by many inconsistencies and contradictions, which are reflected as contradictions in the psychological patterns of the individuals in the culture. For one example, in our culture the individual is taught that he can attain competitive success by hard work and initiative, whereas in actual fact his success is to a great extent determined by such suprapersonal forces as capital and the market. Since our culture is itself in contradiction, the values the individual members of the culture identify with their existence are bound to be frequently threatened, and widespread anxiety is the result.

It is the present writer's belief, based on his understanding of the evidence, that the trauma of our culture is not peripheral but involves *a threatening of the basic patterns on which the culture itself has depended for security.* On this assumption it can be understood why a relatively minor trauma—like a stock-market fluctuation—is experienced by many individuals as a catastrophic situation. It is not a peripheral threat, to be responded to as a fear, but a threat to values which the individuals in the culture hold essential to their existence as personalities. . . .

Methods of Dealing with Anxiety

Negative Methods

The negative methods of dealing with anxiety range all the way from simple behavior traits like shyness, through the gamut of neuroses and psychosomatic illnesses, to the extreme of psychosis and, in very severe conflict situations, death. The negative methods consist of allaying or avoiding the anxiety without solving the conflict which causes the anxiety; or, in other terms, evading the danger situation rather than resolving it.

The avoidance of anxiety is the purpose of many behavior traits which could be called relatively "normal" and are "neurotic" only in their compulsive forms. For example rigidity of thinking, which may be observed in religious or scientific dogmatism, is a way of armoring one's values so that they are protected from threat. Avoidance of anxiety is temporarily achieved, but at the price of the possibilities of discovering new truth, the exclusion of new learning, and the stunting of capacities to adapt to new situations. Kierkegaard adds that the belief in fate or necessity, like the belief in superstition, is a method of avoiding full responsibility for one's conflicts, thus circumventing anxiety but at the price of loss of creativity. When the values the individual needs to protect are especially vulnerable to threat (often because of their own inner contradictions) and the individual is relatively less able to adapt to new situations, rigidity of thinking and behavior may take the form of compulsion neurosis.

The many methods of relieving tension involved in conflict and anxiety vary from the normal function of laughter to alcoholism or compulsive sexual activity. Frantic activity of any sort—e.g., compulsive work—may serve to relieve the tension mobilized in the organism by anxiety. But frantic activity is generally neither productive nor directed toward solving the problem which causes the tension. The significant question is whether the activity pursued permits the release of tension without resolving the underlying conflict, in which case the activity tends to become compulsive, since the conflict remains. . . .

Constructive Methods

With respect to neurotic anxiety, it is agreed that the anxiety indicates the presence of a problem which needs to be solved. Neurotic anxiety can be treated constructively as a warning that something is amiss within the personality (and at the same time amiss in one's interpersonal relations). And the anxiety can be accepted as a challenge to clarify and resolve the underlying problem (Horney). Anxiety indicates that a conflict is ensuing, and so long as there is conflict a positive solution is within the realm of possibility. In this respect anxiety has been likened to the prognostic value of fever: it is a sign of struggle within the personality and an indication, speaking in psychopathological terms, that serious disintegration has not yet occurred (Yaskin). In regard to the method of solving the problem causing the anxiety, two processes are held in common by the various schools of psychotherapy: (1) *an expansion of awareness*—the individual sees what value (goal) is threatened, together with becoming aware of the conflicts between his goals and how this conflict developed; (2) *re-education*—the individual restructures his goals, makes a conscious choice of values, and proceeds toward the attainment of these values responsibly and realistically.

But whereas the use of neurotic anxiety as a challenge for problem-solving has been agreed upon, it has often been overlooked that *normal* anxiety also indicates possibility and may be used constructively. The tendency in our culture to regard fears and anxiety chiefly in a negative light, as results of unfortunate learning, is not only an oversimplification but tends by implication to remove the possibility of the constructive acceptance and use of the day-to-day anxiety experiences which cannot be called specifically neurotic. To be sure, neurotic anxiety *is* the result of unfortunate learning in the respect that the individual was forced to deal with threatening situations at a period—usually in early childhood—when he was incapable of coping directly or constructively with such experiences. In this respect, *neurotic anxiety is the result of the failure to cope with the previous anxiety situations in one's experiences.* But normal anxiety is not the result of unfortunate learning; it arises rather from a realistic appraisal of one's situation of danger. To the extent that a person can succeed in constructively meeting the normal day-to-day anxiety experiences as they arise, he avoids the repression and retrenchment which make for later neurotic anxiety.

In fine, the goal with regard to neurotic anxiety is the solving of the underlying problem and thus the overcoming of the anxiety. When we are thinking of neurotic anxiety, the oft-expressed criterion of mental health, "the ability to live without anxiety," is sound. But with regard to normal anxiety—the anxiety which arises from real threats, and which, as we have earlier pointed out, inheres in such aspects of human contingency as death, in the threat of isolation which accompanies the development of individuality, and so forth— the desideratum cannot be the complete absence of anxiety. . . .

Anxiety and the Development of the Self

The term "self" is used in two senses by writers on anxiety. In its broader meaning, self refers to the sum total of the individual's capacities (Goldstein). In its more limited sense, "self" refers to the capacity of the human organism to have conscious awareness of its activities and through this awareness to exercise a measure of freedom in directing these activities (Kierkegaard, Sullivan, Fromm). Anxiety is involved in the development of the self in both of these meanings of the term.

Goldstein holds that self-actualization—i.e., expression and creative use of the individual's capacities—can occur only as the individual confronts and moves through anxiety-creating experiences. The freedom of the healthy individual inheres in his capacity to avail himself of new possibilities in the meeting and overcoming of potential threats to his existence. By moving through anxiety-creating experiences one achieves self-realization, i.e., one enlarges the scope of his activity and at the same time increases his freedom. The capacity to bear anxiety is one measure of selfhood. This capacity is found least of all in the brain-injured patient, more in the child, and most of all in the creative adult.

Using the term "self" in its more limited sense, namely the function of awareness of one's activities, Sullivan has made a significant contribution. He holds that it is in anxiety experiences in the young child that the self comes into being. The infant in its early relations with its mother learns which activities will receive approbation and reward and which will receive disapproval and possible punishment. The latter activities arouse anxiety. The self-dynamism, as Sullivan terms it, develops as a process by which the anxiety-creating experiences are excluded from activity and awareness and the approved activities are incorporated into the child's awareness and behavior. In this sense, the self comes into being to preserve the individual's security, to protect him from anxiety. This view emphasizes the negative function of anxiety in the development of the self and illuminates the very common phenomenon that anxiety experiences which are dealt with unconstructively lead to a constriction of the self. Sullivan also indicates—pointing toward the constructive use of anxiety—that the areas in the personality marked by anxiety often become the areas of significant growth when, as in psychotherapy or favorable human relationships, the individual can deal with his anxiety constructively.

We turn now to the positive aspects of selfhood—freedom, enlarged self-awareness, responsibility. The emergence of individual freedom is very closely connected with anxiety; indeed, the possibility of freedom always arouses anxiety, and how the anxiety is met will determine whether the freedom is utilized or sacrificed by the individual (Kierkegaard, Fromm). The child's need progressively to break the primary ties of dependence on its parents always involves some anxiety (Fromm). In the healthy child this anxiety is overcome by new relatedness on the basis of a larger degree of self-direction and autonomy. But if independence from parents brings with it an insupportable degree of anxiety (as in the case of the child of hostile or excessively anxious parents), if the price in increased feelings of helplessness and isolation is too great, the child retreats into new forms of dependency and that particular possibility of enlarged selfhood is sacrificed. An enlarging of self-awareness occurs whenever one moves through new possibilities (Kierkegaard). Whereas the first anxiety of the infant is without content, a change occurs after the emergence of self-awareness. (Kierkegaard terms this emergence of self-awareness a "qualitative leap"; it is described in a different context in dynamic psychology as the emergence of the ego.) Now the child becomes aware that freedom involves responsibility—responsibility to "be one's self" as well as responsibility to others. The converse side of this responsibility is guilt feeling. To the extent that an individual seeks to avoid anxiety, responsibility, and guilt feeling by refusing to avail himself of his new possibilities, by refusing to move from the familiar to the unfamiliar, he sacrifices his freedom and constricts his autonomy and his self-awareness. Availing oneself of possibilities, confronting the anxiety, and accepting the responsibility and guilt feeling involved result in increased self-awareness and freedom and enlarged spheres of creativity. The more creative the individual, the more possibilities he has, the more he is confronted with anxiety and its concomitant responsibilty and guilt feeling (Kierkegaard, Goldstein). Increased self-awareness means increased selfhood (Sullivan); or, as Kierkegaard phrases it, "The more consciousness, the more self." *In fine, the positive aspects of selfhood develop as the individual confronts, moves through, and overcomes anxiety-creating experiences.*

References

Freud, Sigmund. *A General Introduction to Psychoanalysis.* Liveright, 1920.

———. *New Introductory Lectures in Psychoanalysis.* Norton, 1933.

———. *The Problem of Anxiety,* tr. H. A. Bunker. Norton, 1936.

———. *An Outline of Psychoanalysis.* Norton, 1949.

Fromm, Erich. "Selfishness and Self-Love." *Psychiatry,* Vol. 2, 1939.

———. *Escape From Freedom.* Holt, Rinehart & Winston, 1941.

———. *Man for Himself, An Inquiry into the Psychology of Ethics.* Holt, Rinehart & Winston, 1947.

Goldstein, Kurt. "A Further Comparison of the Moro Reflex and the Startle Pattern." *Journal of Psychology,* Vol. 6, 1938.

———. *The Organism, A Holistic Approach to Biology.* American Book, 1939.

———. *Human Nature in the Light of Psychopathology.* Harvard University Press, 1940.

Horney, Karen. *The Neurotic Personality of Our Time.* Norton, 1937.

———. *New Ways in Psychoanalysis.* Norton, 1939.

———. *Our Inner Conflicts, A Constructive Theory of Neurosis.* Norton, 1945.

Jersild, A. T. *Child Psychology,* rev. ed. Prentice-Hall, 1933.

———. "Methods of Overcoming Children's Fears." *Journal of Psychology,* Vol. 1, 1935.

Kardiner, Abram. *The Individual and His Society—The Psychodynamics of Primitive Social Organization.* Columbia University Press, 1939.

———. *The Psychological Frontiers of Society.* Columbia University Press, 1945.

Kierkegaard, Søren. *Sickness unto Death,* tr. W. Lowrie. Princeton University Press, 1941.

———. *The Concept of Dread,* tr. W. Lowrie. Princeton University Press, 1944.

Rank, Otto. *The Trauma of Birth*. Harcourt, Brace & World, 1929.

――――. *Will Therapy*, Knopf, 1936.

Sullivan, Harry S. *Conceptions of Modern Psychiatry*. W. A. White Psychiatric Foundation, 1947.

――――. "The Meaning of Anxiety in Psychiatry and Life." *Psychiatry*, Vol. 2, 1948.

――――. "The Theory of Anxiety and the Nature of Psychotherapy." *Psychiatry*, Vol. 12, 1949.

Yaskin, Joseph. "The Psychobiology of Anxiety, A Clinical Study." *Psychoanalysis Review*, Supp. to Vols. 23 & 24, 1937.

Edward Joseph Shoben, Jr.

Toward a Concept of the Normal Personality

Clinical practice and the behavioral sciences alike have typically focused on the pathological in their studies of personality and behavior dynamics. While much of crucial importance remains to be learned, there is an abundant empirical knowledge and an impressive body of theory concerning the deviant and the diseased, the anxious and the neurotic, the disturbed and the maladjusted. In contrast, there is little information and even less conceptual clarity about the nature of psychological normality. Indeed, there are even those (Darrah, 1939, pp. 730–39, and Hacker, 1945, pp. 47–64) who argue that there is no such thing as a normal man; there are only those who manage their inter-personal relationships in such a way that others are strongly motivated to avoid them, even by committing them to a mental hospital or a prison, as opposed to those who do not incite such degrees of social ostracism.

This argument has two characteristics. First, it appears to dispose of the problem by simply distributing people along a dimension of pathology. All men are a little queer, but some are much more so than others. Second, it has affinities with the two major ideas that

E. J. Shoben, "Toward a Concept of the Normal Personality," *American Psychologist*, Vol. 12, pp. 183–189. Reproduced by permission of the author and the American Psychological Association.

have been brought to bear on the question of what constitutes normal or abnormal behavior: the statistical conception of the usual or the average and the notion of cultural relativism. If pathology is conceived as the extent to which one is tolerated by one's fellows, then any individual can theoretically be described in terms of some index number that reflects the degree of acceptability accorded him. The resulting distribution would effectively amount to an ordering of people from the least to the most pathological. Similarly, if the positions on this continuum are thought of as functions of one's acceptance or avoidance by others, then they can only be defined by reference to some group. The implications here are twofold. First, the conception of pathology is necessarily relativistic, varying from group to group or culture to culture. Second, the degree of pathology is defined as the obverse of the degree of conformity to group norms. The more one's behavior conforms to the standards of the group, the less is he likely to be subject to social avoidance; whereas the more one's behavior deviates from the rules, the greater is the probability of ostracism to the point of institutional commitment.

Statistical and Relativistic Concepts of Normality

Yet the issues are fully clarified by these statistical or culturally relativistic ideas. Is it most fruitful to regard normality or integrative behavior as merely reflecting a minimal degree of pathology, or may there be a certain merit in considering the asset side of personality, the positive aspects of human development? This question becomes particularly relevant when one is concerned with the socialization process or with the goals and outcomes of psychotherapy or various rehabilitative efforts.

It seems most improbable that the family, the church, and the school, the main agents of socialization, exist for the minimizing of inevitable pathological traits in the developing members of the community. Rather, parents, priests, and educators are likely to insist that their function is that of facilitating some sort of positive growth, the progressive acquisition of those characteristics, including skills, knowledge, and attitudes, which permit more productive, contributory, and satisfying ways of life. Similarly, while psychotherapists may sometimes accept the limited goals of simply trying to inhibit pathological processes, there are certainly those (see Fromm, 1955, and May, 1953) who take the position that therapy is to be judged more in terms of how much it contributes to a patient's ability to achieve adult gratifications rather than its sheer efficiency in reducing symptoms or shoring up pathological defenses.

A general concern for such a point of view seems to be emerging in the field of public mental health (MHA subcommittee, 1955). Beginning with an emphasis on treatment, the concept of community mental health swung to a preventive phase with the main interest focused on identifying the antecedents of mental disease and on reducing morbidity rates by attacking their determinants. The vogue of eugenics was one illustrative feature of this stage. More recently, there has been a considerable dissatisfaction with the whole notion of interpreting psychological states in terms of disease analogues (see Marzolf, 1947, pp. 211–21; and Riese, 1953). Maladjustive behavior patterns, the neuroses, and—perhaps to a lesser extent—the psychoses may possibly be better understood as disordered, ineffective, and defensive styles of life than as forms of sickness. In consequence, there seems to be a growing tendency to conceive of the public mental health enterprise as emphasizing positive development with the prevention and treatment of pathology regarded as vital but secondary.

But in what does positive development consist? The statistical concept of the average is not very helpful. Tiegs and Katz (1941), for example, reported a study of college students who had been rated for fourteen different evidences of "nervousness." By and large, these traits were normally distributed, suggesting that those subjects rated low must be considered just as "abnormal" (unusual) as those rated high. This conception seems to provide a superficial quantitative model only at the expense of hopeless self-contradiction and violence to the ordinary categories of communication. Even in a case that at first blush seems to cause no difficulty, the problem remains. Criminal behavior, for example, is distributed in a J-shaped fashion with most cases concentrated at the point of zero offenses, ranging to a relatively few instances of many-time offenders. Few would argue that the usual behavior here is not also the most "positive." But one suspects that the sheer frequency of law-abiding behavior has little to do with its acknowledged integrative character. If conformity to social rules is generally considered more desirable than criminality, it is not because of its rate of occurrence but because of its consequences for both society and the individual.

Thus, a statistical emphasis on the usual as the criterion of positive adjustment or normality shades into a socially relativistic concept with an implied criterion of conformity. The terms "usual" or "most frequent" or "average" are meaningless without reference to some group, and this state of affairs poses two problems. First, conformity in itself, as history abundantly demonstrates, is a dubious guide to conduct. Innovation is as necessary to a culture's survival as are tradition and conservation, and conformity has frequently meant acquiescence in conditions undermining the maturity and positive development of human beings rather than their enhancement. On more personal levels, conformity sometimes seems related in some degree to personality processes that can quite properly be called pathological (see Adorno, 1950; and Riesman, 1950. Second, relativistic conceptions of normality pose serious questions as to the reference group against which any individual is to be assessed. Benedict (1934), for example, has made it quite clear that behavior which is considered abnormal in one culture is quite acceptable in others, that certain forms of abnormalities which occur in some societies are absent in others, and that conduct which is thought completely normal in one group may be regarded as intensely pathological in another. Such observations, while descriptively sound, can lead readily to two troublesome inferences. One is that the storm trooper must be considered as the prototype of integrative adjustment in Nazi culture, the members of the Politburo as best representing human normality Soviet style, and the cruelest adolescent in a delinquent gang as its most positively developed member. The other is that any evaluative judgment of cultures and societies must be regarded as inappropriate. Since normality is conceived only in terms of conformity to group standards, the group itself must be beyond appraisal. Thus, the suspicion and mistrust of Dobu (Fortune, 1932) the sense of resigned futility that permeates Alor (DuBois, 1944) and the regimentation that characterizes totalitarian nations can logically only be taken as norms in terms of which individual behavior may be interpreted, not as indications of abnormal tendencies in the cultures themselves.

Wegrocki (1939), in criticizing such relativistic notions, argues that it is not the form of behavior, the actual acts themselves, that defines its normal or pathological character. Rather, it is its function. What he calls the "quintessence of abnormality" lies in reactions which represent an escape from conflicts and problems rather than a facing of them. This formulation, implying that integrative adjustments are those which most directly confront conflicts and problems, seems essentially free of the difficulties inherent in statistical conceptions and the idea of cultural relativism. But it presents troubles of its own. For instance, what does it mean to "face" a problem or conflict? On what ground, other than the most arbitrarily moralistic one, can such confrontations be defended as more positive than escape? Finally, does this facing of one's problems have any relationship to the matter of conformity in the sense of helping to clarify decisions regarding the acceptance or rejection of group standards?

To deal with such questions requires coming to grips with certain problems of value. It is at this point that the behavioral sciences and ethics meet and merge, and it seems unlikely that any conception of normality can be developed apart from some general considerations that are fundamentally moral. Once the purely relativistic ideas of normality are swept away, it becomes difficult to avoid some concern for the issues of happiness and right conduct, i.e., conduct leading to the greatest degree of human satisfaction, that are the traditional province of the literary interpreter of human experience, the theologian, and the moral philosopher. A primary challenge here is that of providing a rational and naturalistic basis for a concept of integrative adjustment that is at once consistent with the stance and contributions of empirical science and in harmony with whatever wisdom mankind has accumulated through its history.

Symbolic and Social Aspects of Human Nature

One way to meet this challenge is by frankly postulating a basic principle of value. The fundamental contention advanced here is that behavior is "positive" or "integrative" to the extent that it reflects the unique attributes of the human animal. There are undoubtedly other ways of approaching a fruitful concept of normality. Nevertheless, this assertion is consistent with the implications of organic evolution, escapes the fallacy of the survival-of-the-fittest doctrine in its various forms, and permits a derivation of more specific criteria of positive adjustment from the distinctive characteristics of man. No discontinuity within the phylogenetic scale need be assumed. It seems clear, however, that man, while certainly an animal, can hardly be described as "nothing but" an animal; and his normality or integration seems much more likely to consist in the fulfillment of his unique potentialities than in the development of those he shares with infrahuman organisms.

Foremost among these uniquely human potentialities, as Cassirer (1944) and Langer (1942) make clear, is the enormous capacity for symbolization. What is most characteristic of men is their pervasive employment of *propositional* language. While other organisms, especially dogs (see Pavlov, 1927) and the higher apes (see Yerkes, 1943), react to symbols, their faculty for doing so indicates only an ability to respond to mediate or representative as well as direct stimuli. Man, on the other hand, uses symbols designatively, as a vehicle for recollecting past events, for dealing with things which are not physically present, and for projecting experience into the future. Goldstein (1940) makes the same point in his discussion of the "attitude toward the merely possible," the ability to deal with things that are only imagined or which are not part of an immediate, concrete situation. In patients whose speech has been impaired because of brain damage, this attitude toward the possible is disrupted. Thus, aphasics are typically unable to say such things as, "The snow is black" or "The moon shines in the daytime"; similarly, they are incapable of *pretending* to comb their hair or to take a drink of water although they can actually *perform* these acts. Such patients appear to have lost the uniquely human capacity for thinking *about* things as well as directly "thinking things."

It is his symbolic ability, then, that makes man the only creature who can "look before and after and pine for what is not." Propositional speech makes it possible for him to learn from not only his own personal experience but from that of other men in other times and places, to forecast the consequences of his own behavior, and to have ideals. These three symbol-given attributes—the aptitude for capitalizing on experience, including the experience of others over time, the capacity for foresight and the self-imposed control of behavior through the anticipation of its outcomes, and the ability to envision worlds closer than the present one to the heart's desire—constitute a basic set of distinctively human potentialities.

A second set of such potentialities seems related to the long period of helpless dependence that characterizes infancy and childhood. Made mandatory by the relative biological incompleteness of the human body, this phase of development is likely to be lengthened as cultures become more complex. Thus, in such simpler societies as the Samoan (see Mead, 1928), children can achieve a higher degree of independence at an earlier age than in the civilizations of the West, for example, where the necessity for learning complicated and specialized economic skills extends the period of dependence through adolescence and even into chronological young adulthood. The central point, however, is that unlike the young of any other species, human children in *all* cultural settings must spend a long time during which the gratification of their most basic needs is mediated by somebody else and is dependent on their relationship to somebody else.

This state of affairs exposes youngsters during their earliest and most formative stages of development to two fundamental conditions of human life. The first is that one's survival, contentment, and need fulfillment involve an inevitable element of reliance on other people. The second is that the relative autonomy, authority, and power that characterize the parent figures and others on whom one relies in childhood are always perceived to a greater or lesser extent in association with responsibility and a kind of altruism. That is, the enjoyment of adult privileges and status tends to occur in conjunction with the acceptance in some degree of the task of in some way mediating the need gratifications of others. Mowrer and Kluckhohn (1944) seem to be speaking of a similar pattern when they describe the socialization process as progressing from childhood *dependency* through *independence* to adult *dependability*.

Moreover, this reciprocal relationship between reliance and responsibility seems to obtain on adult levels as well as between children and parents, with the degree of reciprocity a partial function of the complexity of the culture. In simpler societies, a relatively small number of persons may assume primary responsibility for virtually all of the needs of the group in excess of its bare subsistence demands. Under civilized conditions, however, the specialization made necessary by technology and the pattern of urban living means that each adult is dependent on some other adult in some way and that, conversely, he is responsible in some fashion for the welfare of some other adult. The difference between the simpler and the more complex cultures, however, is only one of degree. The crucial point is that, throughout human society, men are in one way or another dependent on each other both in the familiar situation of parents and children and in the course of adult living. This pattern of interdependency gives to human life a social character to be found nowhere else in the animal kingdom. Even among the remarkable social insects, the patterns of symbiosis found there seem to be a result of a genetically determined division of labor rather than the fulfillment of a potentiality for the mutual sharing of responsibilities for each other.

It is in this notion of the fulfillment of distinctively human potentialities that a fruitful conception of positive adjustment may have its roots. From the symbolic and peculiarly social character of human life, it may be possible to derive a set of potential attributes the cultivation of which results in something different from the mere absence of pathology and which forms a standard against which to assess the degree of integration in individual persons. To accept this task is to attempt the construction of a normative or ideal model of a normal, positively developed, or integratively adjusted human being.

A Model of Integrative Adjustment

In the first place, it would seem that as the symbolic capacity that endows man with foresight develops in an individual, there is a concomitant increase in his ability to control his own behavior by anticipating its probable long-range consequences. The normal person is, first of all, one who has learned that in many situations his greatest satisfaction is gained by forgoing the immediate opportunities for comfort and pleasure in the interest of more remote rewards. He lives according to what Paul Elmer More, the Anglican theologian, calls "the law of costingness":

> The simple and tyrannical fact that, whether in the world physical, or in the world intellectual, or in the world spiritual, we can get nothing without paying an exacted price. The fool is he who ignores, and the villain is he who thinks he can outwit, the vigilance of the nemesis guarding this law of costingness . . . all [one's] progress is dependent on surrendering one interest or value for a higher interest or value (More, 1931, p. 158).

Mowrer and Ullman (1945, pp. 61–90) have made the same point in arguing, from the results of an ingenious experiment, that normality results in large part from the acquired ability to subject impulses to control through the symbolic cues one presents to oneself in the course of estimating the consequences of one's own behavior.

Through symbolization, the future outcomes of one's actions are drawn into the psychological present; the strength of more remote rewards or punishments is consequently increased; and a long-range inhibitory or facilitating effect on incipient conduct is thereby exercised.

This increase in self-control means a lessened need for control by external authority, and conformity consequently becomes a relatively unimportant issue. The integratively adjusted person either conforms to the standards of his group because their acceptance leads to the most rewarding long-range consequences for him, or he rebels against authority, whether of persons or of law or custom, on *considered* grounds. This considered form of revolt implies two things. The first is an honest conviction that rules or the ruler are somehow unjust and that the implementation of his own values is likely to lead to a more broadly satisfying state of affairs. Such an attack on authority is very different from revolts that occur out of sheer needs for self-assertion or desires for power or as expressions of displaced hostility. The main dimension of difference is that of honesty as opposed to deception. The normal person is relatively well aware of his motives in either conforming or rebelling. The pathological rebel, on the other hand, tends to deceive himself and others about his goals. His reasons for nonconformity amount to rationalizations, and his justifications are typically projections. This kind of self-defeating and socially disruptive deceptiveness is seen daily in clinical practice.

The second characteristic of nonconformity in the normal person is that it is undertaken with an essential acceptance of the possible consequences. Having considered the risks beforehand, he is inclined neither to whine nor to ask that his rebellious conduct be overlooked if he runs afoul of trouble. In keeping with the "law of costingness," he is willing to pay the price for behaving in accordance with his own idiosyncratic values. "We have the right to lead our own lives," John Erskine (1925) makes Helen of Troy say to her daughter Hermione, "but that right implies another—to suffer the consequences. . . . Do your best, and if it's a mistake, hide nothing and be glad to suffer for it. That's morality." A psychological paraphrase of this bit of belletristic wisdom is not inappropriate: The assumption of responsibility [1] for one's actions is one of the attributes of personal integration.

---

1. This conception of responsibility is by no means antideterministic. As Fingarette (1955, pp. 18–36) points out, one can *understand* his own or another's behavior, in the sense of accounting for it or rationally explaining it, by the retrospective process of examining the past. Responsibility, on the other hand, is neither retrospective in orientation nor explanatory in function. It is future-oriented and refers to the *act* of proclaiming oneself as answerable for one's own conduct and its consequences. Thus, "responsibility," in this context, is not a logical term, implying causation, but a behavioral and attitudinal one, descriptive of a class of human actions.

But if personal responsibility and self-control through foresight can be derived as aspects of integrative adjustment from man's symbolic capacity, a third characteristic of interpersonal responsibility can be deduced from his social nature. If interdependency is an essential part of human social life, then the normal person becomes one who can act dependably in relation to others and at the same time acknowledge his need for others. The roots of the former probably lie, as McClelland (1951) has pointed out, in the role perceptions which developing children form of parent figures and other agents of the socialization process. By conceiving of such people as at least in some degree the nurturant guides of others and through identification with them, the integratively adjusted individual "wants to be" himself trustworthy and altruistic in the sense of being dependable and acting out of a genuine concern for the welfare of others as he can best conceive it. Altruism in this context, therefore, means nothing sentimental. It certainly includes the making and enforcement of disciplinary rules and the imposition of behavioral limits, but only if these steps are motivated by an interest in helping others and express concern and affection rather than mere personal annoyance or the power conferred by a superior status.

Similarly, the acknowledgment of one's needs for others implies a learned capacity for forming and maintaining intimate interpersonal relationships. Erikson (1950) refers to this aspect of the normal personality as the attitude of "basic trust," and it is not far from what can be meaningfully styled in plain language as the ability to love. One suspects that the origins of this ability lie in the long experience during childhood of having need gratifications frequently associated with the presence of another person, typically a parent figure. By this association and the process of generalization, one comes to attach a positive affect to others. But as the youngster develops, he gradually learns that the need-mediating behavior of others is maintained only by his reciprocating, by his entering into a relationship of mutuality with others. If this kind of mutuality is not required of him, he is likely to perpetuate his dependency beyond the period his biological level of development and the complexity of his culture define as appropriate; whereas if he is required to demonstrate this mutuality too soon, he is likely to form the schema that interpersonal relationships are essentially matters of traded favors and that, instead of basic trust, the proper attitude is one of getting as much as possible while giving no more than necessary. The pursuit in research and thought of such hypotheses as these might shed a good deal of light on the determinants of friendship, marital happiness, and effective parenthood, the relational expressions of effective personal integration.

But there is still another interpersonal attitude relevant to a positive conception of adjustment that is somewhat different from that bound up with relationships of an intimate and personal kind. There is a sense in which each individual, even if he regards himself as unfortunate and unhappy, owes his essential humanity to the group which enabled him to survive his helpless infancy. As studies of feral children (see Singh and Zingg, 1942) have shown, even the humanly distinctive and enormously adaptive trait of propositional speech does not become usable without the stimulation and nurture of other people. A kind of obligation is therefore created for the person to be an asset rather than a burden to society. It is partly to the discharging of this obligation that Adler (1938) referred in developing his concept of social interest as a mark of normality. While the notion certainly implies the learning of local loyalties and personal affections, it also transcends the provincial limits of group and era. Because man's symbolic capacity enables him to benefit from the record of human history and to anticipate the future, and because his pattern of social interdependency, especially in civilized societies, reaches across the boundaries of political units and parochial affiliations, it seems reasonable to expect the positively developed person to behave in such a fashion as to contribute, according to his own particular lights, to the general welfare of humanity, to take as his frame of reference mankind at large as best he understands it rather than his own group or clan.

Ideologies are at issue here, but there need be neither embarrassment nor a lack of room for debate regarding the specifics of policy and values in the hypothesis that democratic attitudes are closely bound up with personality integration. After all, democracy in psychological terms implies only a concern about others, a valuing of persons above things, and a willingness to participate in mutually gratifying relationships with many categories of persons, including those of which one has only vicarious knowledge. Departures from democratic attitudes in this psychological sense mean a restriction on the potentiality for friendship and imply both a fear of others and a valuation of such things as power over people, thus endangering the interpersonal rewards that come from acting on the attitude of basic trust. Democratic social interest, then, means simply the most direct route to the fulfillment of a distinctively human capacity derived from man's symbolic character and the inevitability of his social life.

Finally, man's ability to assume an attitude toward the "merely possible" suggests that the normal person has ideals and standards that he tries to live up to even though they often exceed his grasp. For an integrative adjustment does not consist in the attainment of perfection but in a striving to act in accordance with the best principles of conduct that one can conceive. Operationally, this notion implies that there is an optimum discrepancy between one's self-concept and one's ego-ideal. Those for whom this discrepancy is too large (in favor, of course, of the ideal) are likely to condemn themselves to the frustration of never approximating their goals and to an almost perpetually low self-esteem. Those whose discrepancies are too low, on the other hand, are probably less than integratively adjusted, either because they are failing to fulfill their human capacity to envision themselves as they could be or because they are self-deceptively overestimating themselves.

This model of integrative adjustment as characterized by self-control, personal responsibility, social responsibility, democratic social interest, and ideals must be regarded only in the most tentative fashion. Nevertheless, it does seem to take into account some realistic considerations. It avoids the impossible conception of the normal person as one who is always happy, free from conflict, and without problems. Rather, it suggests that he may often fall short of his ideals; and because of ignorance, the limitations under which an individual lives in a complex world, or the strength of immediate pressures, he may sometimes behave in ways that prove to be short-sighted or self-defeating. Consequently, he knows something of the experience of guilt at times, and because he tries to be fully aware of the risks he takes, he can hardly be entirely free from fear and worry. On the other hand, a person who is congruent to the model is likely to be one who enjoys a relatively consistent and high degree of self-respect and who elicits a predominantly positive and warm reaction from others. Moreover, it is such a person who seems to learn wisdom rather than hostile bitterness or pathologically frightened withdrawal from whatever disappointments or suffering may be his lot. Guilt, for example, becomes a challenge to his honesty, especially with himself but also with others; and it signalizes for him the desirability of modifying his behavior, or greater effort to live up to his ideals, rather than the need to defend himself by such mechanisms as rationalization or projection. Finally, the model permits a wide variation in the actual behaviors in which normal people may engage and even makes allowance for a wide range of disagreements among them. Integrative adjustment does not consist in the individual's fitting a preconceived behavioral mold. It may well consist in the degree to which his efforts fulfill the symbolic and social potentialities that are distinctively human.

References

Adler, A. *Social Interest: A Challenge to Mankind.* Faber & Faber, 1938.

Adorno, T. W., Else Frankel-Brunswik, D. J. Levinson, and R. N. Sanford. *The Authoritarian Personality.* Harper, 1950.

Benedict, Ruth. "Anthropology and the Abnormal." *Journal of General Psychology,* Vol. 10, 1934.

Cassirer, E. *An Essay on Man.* Yale University Press, 1944.

Darrah, L. W. "The Difficulty of Being Normal." *Journal of Nervous Mental Disorders,* Vol. 90, 1939.

DuBois, Cora. *The People of Alor.* University of Minnesota Press, 1944.

Erikson, E. H. *Childhood and Society.* Norton, 1950.

Erskine, J. *The Private Life of Helen of Troy.* Bobbs-Merrill, 1925.

Fingarette, H. "Psychoanalytic Perspectives on Moral Guilt and Responsibility: A Re-Evaluation." *Philosophical and Phenomenological Research,* Vol. 16, 1955.

Fortune, R. F. *Sorcerers of Dobu.* Routledge, 1932.

Fromm, Eric. *The Sane Society.* Holt, Rinehart and Winston, 1955.

Goldstein, K. *Human Nature in the Light of Psychopathology.* Harvard University Press, 1940.

Hacker, H. F. "The Concept of Normality and Its Practical Significance." *American Journal of Orthopsychiatry,* Vol. 15, 1945.

Langer, Susanne K. *Philosophy in a New Key.* Harvard University Press, 1942.

Marzolf, S. S. "The Disease Concept in Psychology." *Psychological Review,* Vol. 54, 1947.

May, R. *Man's Search for Himself.* Norton, 1953.

McClelland, D. *Personality.* William Sloane Associates, 1951.

Mead, Margaret. *Coming of Age in Samoa.* Morrow, 1928.

More, P. E. *The Catholic Faith.* Princeton University Press, 1931.

Mowrer, O. H., and C. Kluckhohn. "A Dynamic Theory of Personality." In *Personality and the Behavior Disorders,* ed. J. M. Hunt. Ronald Press, 1944.

———, and A. D. Ullman. "Time as a Determinant in Integrative Learning." *Psychological Review,* Vol. 52, 1945.

Pavlov, I. P. *Conditioned Reflexes.* Oxford University Press, 1927.

Riese, W. *The Conception of Disease.* Philosophical Library, 1953.

Riesman, D. *The Lonely Crowd.* Yale University Press, 1950.

Singh, J. A. L., and R. M. Zingg. *Wolf-Children and Feral Man.* Harper, 1942.

Subcommittee on Evaluation of Mental Health Activities. *Evaluation in Mental Health.* Public Health Service, 1955.

Tiegs, E. W., and B. Katz. *Mental Hygiene in Education.* Ronald, 1941.

Wegrocki, H. J. "A Critique of Cultural and Statistical Concepts of Abnormality." *Journal of Abnormal & Social Psychology,* Vol. 34, 1939.

Yerkes, R. M. *Chimpanzees: A Laboratory Colony.* Yale University Press, 1943.

Interpersonal Relations

Chris Argyris

Interpersonal Barriers
to Decision Making

The actual behavior of top executives during decision-making meetings often does not jibe with their attitudes and prescriptions about effective executive action.

The gap that often exists between what executives say and how they behave helps create barriers to openness and trust, to the effective search for alternatives, to innovation, and to flexibility in the organization.

These barriers are more destructive in important decision-making meetings than in routine meetings, and they upset effective managers more than ineffective ones.

The barriers cannot be broken down simply by intellectual exercises. Rather, executives need feedback concerning their behavior and opportunities to develop self-awareness in action. To this end, certain kinds of questioning are valuable; playing back and analyzing tape recordings of meetings has proved to be a helpful step; and laboratory education programs are valuable.

These are a few of the major findings of a study of executive decision making in six representative companies. The findings have

From *Harvard Business Review*, March–April 1966. © 1966 by the President and Fellows of Harvard College; all rights reserved.

vital implications for management groups everywhere; for while some organizations are less subject to the weaknesses described than are others, *all* groups have them in some degree. In this article I shall discuss the findings in detail and examine the implications for executives up and down the line. (For information on the company sample and research methods used in the study, see "Nature of the Study" at the end of this article.)

Words versus Actions

According to top management, the effectiveness of decision-making activities depends on the degree of innovation, risk taking, flexibility, and trust in the executive system. (Risk taking is defined here as any act where the executive risks his self-esteem. This could be a moment, for example, when he goes against the group view; when he tells someone, especially the person with the highest power, something negative about his impact on the organization; or when he seeks to put millions of dollars in a new investment.)

Nearly 95 percent of the executives in our study emphasize that an organization is only as good as its top people. They constantly repeat the importance of their responsibility to help themselves and others to develop their abilities. Almost as often they report that the qualities just mentioned—motivation, risk taking, and so on—are key characteristics of any successful executive system. "People problems" head the list as the most difficult, perplexing, and crucial.

In short, the executives vote overwhelmingly for executive systems where the contributions of each executive can be maximized and where innovation, risk taking, flexibility, and trust reign supreme. Nevertheless, the *behavior* of these same executives tends to create decision-making processes that are *not* very effective. Their behavior can be fitted into two basic patterns:

Pattern A: Thoughtful, Rational, and Mildly Competitive

This is the behavior most frequently observed during the decision-making meetings. Executives following this pattern own up to their ideas in a style that emphasizes a serious concern for ideas. As they constantly battle for scarce resources and "sell" their views, their openness to others' ideas is relatively high, not because of a sincere interest in learning about the point of view of others, but so they can engage in a form of "oneupmanship"—that is, gain information about the others' points of view in order to politely discredit them.

Pattern B: Competitive First, Thoughtful and Rational Second

In this pattern, conformity to ideas replaces concern for ideas as the strongest norms. Also, antagonism to ideas is higher—in many cases higher than openness to ideas. The relatively high antagonism

Exhibit 1 Management Groups with Pattern A and Pattern B Characteristics

	Pattern A				Pattern B			
Total Number of Units Analyzed [a]	Group 1 198		Group 2 143		Group 3 201		Group 4 131	
Units Characterized by:	Number	Percent	Number	Percent	Number	Percent	Number	Percent
Owning up to Own Ideas	146	74	105	74	156	78	102	78
Concern for Others' Ideas	122	62	89	62	52	26	56	43
Conformity to Others' Ideas	54	27	38	26	87	43	62	47
Openness to Others' Ideas	46	23	34	24	31	15	25	19
Individuality	4	2	12	8	30	15	8	6
Antagonism to Others' Ideas	18	9	4	3	32	16	5	4
Unwillingness to Help Others Own up to Their Ideas	5	2	3	2	14	7	4	3

a) A unit is an instance of a manager speaking on a topic. If during the course of speaking he changes to a new topic, another unit is created.

scores usually indicate, in addition to high competitiveness, a high degree of conflict and pent-up feelings.

Exhibit 1 summarizes data for four illustrative groups of managers—two groups with pattern A characteristics and two with pattern B characteristics.

Practical Consequences

In both patterns executives are rarely observed: taking risks or experimenting with new ideas or feelings; helping others to own up, be open, and take risks; using a style of behavior that supports the norm of individuality and trust as well as mistrust; expressing feelings, positive or negative.

These results should not be interpreted as implying that the executives do not have feelings. We know from the interviews that many of the executives have strong feelings indeed. However, the overwhelming majority (84 percent) feel that it is a sign of immaturity to express feelings openly *during decision-making meetings*. Nor should the results be interpreted to mean that the executives do not enjoy risk taking. The data permit us to conclude only that few risk-taking actions were *observed* during the meetings. (Also, we have to keep in mind that the executives were always observed in groups; it may be that their behavior in groups varies significantly from their behavior as individuals.)

Before I attempt to give my views about the reasons for the discrepancy between executives' words and actions, I should like to point out that these results are not unique to business organizations. I have obtained similar behavior patterns from leaders in education, research, the ministry, trade unions, and government. Indeed, one of the fascinating questions for me is why so many different people in so many different kinds of organizations tend to manifest similar problems.

Why the Discrepancy?

The more I observe such problems in different organizations possessing different technologies and varying greatly in size, the more I become impressed with the importance of the role played by the values or assumptions top people hold on the nature of effective human relationships and the best ways to run an organization.

Basic Values

In the studies so far I have isolated three basic values that seem to be very important:

1. *The significant human relationships are the ones which have to do with achieving the organization's objective.* My studies of over 265 different types and sizes of meetings indicate that executives

almost always tend to focus their behavior on "getting the job done." In literally thousands of units of behavior, almost none are observed where the men spend some time in analyzing and maintaining their group's effectiveness. This is true even though in many meetings the group's effectiveness "bogged down" and the objectives were not being reached because of interpersonal factors. When the executives are interviewed and asked why they did not spend some time in examining the group operations or processes, they reply that they were there to get a job done. They add: "If the group isn't effective, it is up to the leader to get it back on the track by directing it."

2. *Cognitive rationality is to be emphasized; feelings and emotions are to be played down.* This value influences executives to see cognitive, intellectual discussions as "relevant," "good," "work," and so on. Emotional and interpersonal discussions tend to be viewed as "irrelevant," "immature," "not work," and so on.

As a result, when emotions and interpersonal variables become blocks to group effectiveness, all the executives report feeling that they should *not* deal with them. For example, in the event of an emotional disagreement, they would tell the members to "get back to facts" or "keep personalities out of this."

3. *Human relationships are most effectively influenced through unilateral direction, coercion, and control, as well as by rewards and penalties that sanction all three values.* This third value of direction and control is implicit in the chain of command and also in the elaborate managerial controls that have been developed within organizations.

Influence on Operations

The impact of these values can be considerable. For example, to the extent that individuals dedicate themselves to the value of intellectual rationality and "getting the job done," they will tend to be aware of and emphasize the intellectual aspects of issues in an organization and (consciously or unconsciously) to suppress the interpersonal and emotional aspects, especially those which do not seem relevant to achieving the task.

As the interpersonal and emotional aspects of behavior become suppressed, organizational norms that coerce individuals to hide their feelings or to disguise them and bring them up as technical, intellectual problems will tend to arise.

Under these conditions the individual may tend to find it very difficult to develop competence in dealing with feelings and interpersonal relationships. Also, in a world where the expression of feelings is not valued, individuals may build personal and organizational defenses to help them suppress their own feelings or inhibit others in such expression. Or they may refuse to consider ideas which, if exploded, could expose suppressed feelings.

Such a defensive reaction in an organization could eventually inhibit creativity and innovation during decision making. The participants might learn to limit themselves to those ideas and values that were not threatening. They might also decrease their openness to new ideas and values. And as the degree of openness decreased, the capacity to experiment would also decrease, and fear of taking risks would increase. This would reduce the *probability* of experimentation, thus decreasing openness to new ideas still further and constricting risk taking even more than formerly. We would thereby have a closed circuit which could become an important cause of loss of vitality in an organization.

Some Consequences

Aside from the impact of values on vitality, what are some other consequences of the executive behavior patterns earlier described on top-management decision making and on the effective functioning of the organization? For the sake of brevity, I shall include only examples of those consequences that were found to exist in one form or another in all organizations studied.

Restricted Commitment

One of the most frequent findings is that in major decisions that are introduced by the president, there tends to be less than open discussion of the issues, and the commitment of the officers tends to be less than complete (although they may assure the president to the contrary). For instance, consider what happened in one organization where a major administrative decision made during the period of the research was the establishment of several top-management committees to explore basic long-range problems:

As is customary with major decisions, the president discussed it in advance at a meeting of the executive committee. He began the meeting by circulating, as a basis for discussion, a draft of the announcement of the committees. Most of the members' discussion was concerned with raising questions about the wording of the proposal:

"Is the word 'action' too strong?"
"I recommend that we change 'steps can be taken' to 'recommendations can be made.' "
"We'd better change the word 'lead' to 'maintain.' "

As the discussion seemed to come to an end, one executive said he was worried that the announcement of the committees might be interpreted by the people below as an implication "that the executive committee believes the organization is in trouble. Let's get the idea in that all is well."

There was spontaneous agreement by all executives: "Hear, hear!"

A brief silence was broken by another executive who apparently was not satisfied with the concept of the committees. He raised a series of questions. The manner in which it was done was interesting. As he raised each issue, he kept assuring the president and the group that he was not against the concept. He just wanted to be certain that the executive committee was clear on what it was doing. For example, he assured them:

"I'm not clear. Just asking."
"I'm trying to get a better picture."
"I'm just trying to get clarification."
"Just so that we understand what the words mean."

The president nodded in agreement, but he seemed to become slightly impatient. He remarked that many of these problems would not arise if the members of these new committees took an overall company point of view. An executive commented (laughingly), "Oh, I'm for motherhood too!"

The proposal was tabled in order for the written statement to be revised and discussed further during the next meeting. It appeared that the proposal was the president's personal "baby," and the executive committee members would naturally go along with it. The most responsibility some felt was that they should raise questions so the president would be clear about *his* (not *their*) decision.

At the next meeting the decision-making process was the same as at the first. The president circulated copies of the revised proposal. During this session a smaller number of executives asked questions. Two pushed (with appropriate care) the notion that the duties of one of the committees were defined too broadly.

The president began to defend his proposal by citing an extremely long list of examples, indicating that in his mind "reasonable" people should find the duties clear. This comment and the long list of examples may have communicated to others a feeling that the president was becoming impatient. When he finished, there was a lengthy silence. The president then turned to one of the executives and asked directly, "Why are you worried about this?" The executive explained; then quickly added that as far as he could see the differences were not major ones and his point of view could be integrated with the president's by "changing some words."

The president agreed to the changes, looked up, and asked, "I take it now there is common agreement?" All executives replied "Yes" or nodded their heads affirmatively.

As I listened, I had begun to wonder about the commitment of the executive committee members to the idea. In subsequent interviews I asked each about his view of the proposal. Half felt that it was a good proposal. The other half had reservations ranging from moderate to serious. However, being loyal members, they would certainly do their best to make it work, they said.

Subordinate Gamesmanship

I can best illustrate the second consequence by citing from a study of the effectiveness of product planning and program review activities in another of the organizations studied:

It was company policy that peers at any given level should make the decisions. Whenever they could not agree or whenever a decision went beyond their authority, the problem was supposed to be sent to the next higher level. The buck passing stopped at the highest level. A meeting with the president became a great event. Beforehand a group would "dry run" its presentation until all were satisfied that they could present their view effectively.

Few difficulties were observed when the meeting was held to present a recommendation agreed to by all at the lower levels. The difficulties arose when "negative" information had to be fed upward. For example, a major error in the program, a major delay, or a major disagreement among the members was likely to cause such trouble.

The dynamics of these meetings was very interesting. In one case the problem to present was a major delay in a development project. In the dry run the subordinates planned to begin the session with information that "updated" the president. The information was usually presented in such a way that slowly and carefully the president was alerted to the fact that a major problem was about to be announced. One could hear such key phrases as:

"We are a bit later than expected."
"We're not on plan."
"We have had greater difficulties than expected."
"It is now clear that no one should have promised what we did."

These phrases were usually followed by some reassuring statement such as:

"However, we're on top of this."
"Things are really looking better now."
"Although we are late, we have advanced the state of the art."

"If you give us another three months, we are certain that we can solve this problem."

To the observer's eyes, it is difficult to see how the president could deny the request. Apparently he felt the same way because he granted it. However, he took nearly 20 minutes to say that this shocked him; he was wondering if everyone was *really* doing everything they could; this was a serious program; this was not the way he wanted to see things run; he was sure they would agree with him; and he wanted their assurances that this would be the final delay.

A careful listening to the tape after the meeting brought out the fact that no subordinate gave such assurances. They simply kept saying that they were doing their best; they had poured a lot into this; or they had the best technical know-how working on it.

Another interesting observation is that most subordinates in this company, especially in presentations to the president, tended to go along with certain unwritten rules:

1. Before you give any bad news, give good news. Especially emphasize the capacity of the department to work hard and to rebound from a failure.

2. Play down the impact of a failure by emphasizing how close you came to achieving the target or how soon the target can be reached. If neither seems reasonable, emphasize how difficult it is to define such targets, and point out that because the state of the art is so primitive, the original commitment was not a wise one.

3. In a meeting with the president it is unfair to take advantage of another department that is in trouble, even if it is a "natural enemy." The sporting thing to do is say something nice about the other department and offer to help it in any way possible. (The offer is usually not made in concrete form, nor does the department in difficulty respond with the famous phrase, "What do you have in mind?")

The subordinates also were in agreement that too much time was spent in long presentations in order to make the president happy. The president, however, confided to the researcher that he did not enjoy listening to long and, at times, dry presentations (especially when he had seen most of the key data anyway). However, he felt that it was important to go through this because it might give the subordinates a greater sense of commitment to the problem!

Lack of Awareness

One of our most common observations in company studies is that executives lack awareness of their own behavioral patterns as well as of the negative impact of their behavior on others. This is not to imply that they are completely unaware; each individual usually senses some aspects of a problem. However, we rarely find an individual or group of individuals who is aware of enough of the scope and depth of a problem so that the need for effective action can be fully understood.

For example, during the study of the decision-making processes of the president and the nine vice presidents of a firm with nearly 3000 employees, I concluded that the members unknowingly behaved in such a way as *not* to encourage risk taking, openness, expression of feelings, and cohesive, trusting relationships. But subsequent interviews with the ten top executives showed that they held a completely different point of view from mine. They admitted that negative feelings were not expressed, but said the reason was that "we trust each other and respect each other." According to six of the men, individuality was high and conformity low; where conformity was agreed to be high, the reason given was the necessity of agreeing with the man who is boss. According to eight of the men, "We help each other all the time." Issues loaded with conflict were not handled during meetings, it was reported, for these reasons:

> "We should not discuss emotional disagreements before the executive committee because when people are emotional, they are not rational."
> "We should not air our dirty linen in front of the people who may come in to make a presentation."
> "Why take up people's time with subjective debates?"
> "Most members are not acquainted with all the details. Under our system the person who presents the issues has really thought them through."
> "Pre-discussion of issues helps to prevent anyone from sandbagging the executive committee."
> "Rarely emotional; when it does happen, you can pardon it."

The executive committee climate or emotional tone was characterized by such words as: "Friendly." "Not critical of each other." "Not tense." "Frank and no tensions because we've known each other for years."

How was I to fit the executives' views with mine? I went back and listened to all the interviews again. As I analyzed the tapes, I began to realize that an interesting set of contradictions arose during many of the interviews. In the early stages of the interviews the executives tended to say things that they contradicted later; Exhibit 2 contains examples of contradictions repeated by six or more of the ten top executives.

What accounts for these contradictions? My explanation is that

Exhibit 2   Contradictory Statements

During One Part of The Interview an Executive said:	Yet Later in The Same Interview He Said:
The relationship among the executive committee members is "close," "friendly," and based on years of working together.	"I do not know how [my peers] feel about me. That's a tough question to answer."
"The strength of this company lies in its top people. They are a dedicated, friendly group. We never have the kinds of disagreements and fights that I hear others do."	"Yes, the more I think of it, the more I feel this is a major weakness of the company. Management is afraid to hold someone accountable, to say, 'You said you would do it. What happened?' "
"I have an open relationship with my superior."	"I have no direct idea how my superior evaluates my work and feels about me."
"The group discussions are warm, friendly, not critical."	"We trust each other not to upset one another."
"We say pretty much what we think."	"We are careful not to say anything that will antagonize anyone."
"We respect and have faith in each other."	"People do not knowingly upset each other, so they are careful in what they say."
"The executive committee tackles all issues."	"The executive committee tends to spend too much time talking about relatively unimportant issues."
"The executive committee makes decisions quickly and effectively."	"A big problem of the executive committee is that it takes forever and a day to make important decisions."
"The members trust each other."	"The members are careful not to say something that may make another member look bad. It may be misinterpreted."
"The executive committee makes the major policy decisions."	"On many major issues, decisions are really made outside the executive committee meetings. The executive committee convenes to approve a decision and have 'holy water' placed on it."

over time the executives had come to mirror, in their behavior, the values of their culture (e.g., be rational, nonemotional, diplomatically open, and so on). They had created a culture that reinforced their own leadership styles. If an executive wanted to behave differently, he probably ran the risk of being considered a deviant. In most of the cases the executives decided to forgo this risk, and they behaved like the majority. These men, in order to live with themselves, probably had to develop various defenses and blinders about their acquiescence to an executive culture that may not have been the one they personally preferred and valued.

Incidentally, in this group there were two men who had decided to take the other route. Both men were viewed by the others as "a bit rough at the edges" or "a little too aggressive."

To check the validity of some of the findings reported, we interviewed the top 25 executives below the executive committee. If our analysis was correct, we knew, then they should tend to report that the members of the executive committee were low in openness to uncomfortable information, risk taking, trust, and capacity to deal with conflicts openly, and high in conformity. The results were as predicted (see Exhibit 3).

Exhibit 3   How the Executive Committee Was Rated by 25 Executives below It

Characteristic Rated	Number of Managers Rating The Committee as:		
	Low	Moderate	High
"Openness" to "uncomfortable" information [a]	12	6	4
Risk Taking	20	4	1
Trust	14	9	2
Conformity	.0	2	23
Ability to deal with conflicts	19	6	0

a) Three executives gave a "don't know" response.

Blind Spots

Another result found in all organizations studied is the tendency for executives to be unaware of the negative feelings that their subordinates have about them. This finding is not startling in view of the fact that the executive problem-solving processes do not tend to reward the upward communication of information about interpersonal issues that is emotionally laden and risky to communicate. To illustrate:

In one organization, all but one of the top executive committee members reported that their relationships with their subordinates were "relatively good to excellent." When asked how they judged their relationships, most of the executives responded with such statements as: "They do everything that I ask for willingly," and "We talk together frequently and openly."

The picture from the middle management men who were the immediate subordinates was different. Apparently, top management was unaware that:

71 percent of the middle managers did not know where they stood with their superiors; they considered their relationships as ambiguous, and they were not aware of such important facts as how they were being evaluated.

65 percent of the middle managers did not know what qualities led to success in their organizations.

87 percent felt that conflicts were very seldom coped with; and that when they were, the attempts tended to be inadequate.

65 percent thought that the most important unsolved problem of the organization was that the top management was unable to help them overcome the intergroup rivalries, lack of cooperation, and poor

communications; 53 percent said that if they could alter one aspect of their superior's behavior, it would be to help him see the "dog eat dog" communication problems that existed in middle management.

59 percent evaluated top management effectiveness as not too good or about average; and 62 percent reported that the development of a cohesive management team was the second most important unsolved problem.

82 percent of the middle managers wished that the status of their function and job could be increased but doubted if they could communicate this openly to the top management.

Interestingly, in all the cases that I have observed where the president asked for a discussion of any problems that the top and middle management men present thought important, the problems mentioned above were never raised.

Rather, the most frequently mentioned problem (74 percent of the cases) was the overload problem. The executives and managers reported that they were overloaded and that the situation was getting worse. The president's usual reply was that he appreciated their predicament, but "That is life." The few times he asked if the men had any suggestions, he received such replies as "More help," "Fewer meetings," "Fewer reports," "Delay of schedules," and so on. As we will see, few of these suggestions made sense, since the men were asking either for increases in costs or for a decrease in the very controls that the top management used to administer the organization.

Distrust and Antagonism

Another result of the behavior patterns earlier described is that management tends to keep promotions semisecret and most of the actual reasons for executive changes completely secret. Here is an example from an organization whose board we studied in some detail over a period of two years:

The executives complained of three practices of the board about which the board members were apparently unaware: (1) the constant alteration of organizational positions and charts, and keeping the most up-to-date versions semiconfidential; (2) shifting top executives without adequate discussion with all executives involved and without clearly communicating the real reasons for the move; and (3) developing new departments with product goals that overlapped and competed with the goals of already existing departments.

The board members admitted these practices but tended not to see them as being incompatible with the interests of the organization. For example, to take the first complaint, they defended their practice with such statements as: "If you tell them everything, all they do is worry, and we get a flood of rumors"; "The changes do not *really* affect them"; and "It will only cut in on their busy schedule and interrupt their productivity."

The void of clear-cut information from the board was, however, filled in by the executives. Their explanations ranged from such statements as "They must be changing things because they are not happy with the way things are going" to "The unhappiness is so strong they do not tell us." Even the executives who profited from some of these moves reported some concern and bewilderment. For example, three reported instances where they had been promoted over some "old-timers." In all cases they were told to "soft-pedal the promotion aspect" until the old-timers were diplomatically informed. Unfortunately, it took months to inform the latter men, and in some cases it was never done.

There was another practice of the board that produced difficulties in the organization:

Department heads cited the board's increasing intervention into the detailed administration of a department when its profit picture looked shaky. This practice was, from these subordinates' view, in violation of the stated philosophy of decentralization.

When asked, board members tended to explain this practice by saying that it was done only when they had doubts about the department head's competence, and when it was always in the interests of efficiency. When they were alerted about a department that was not doing well, they believed that the best reaction was to tighten controls, "take a closer and more frequent look," and "make sure the department head is on top of things." They quickly added that they did not tell the man in question they were beginning to doubt his competence for fear of upsetting him. Thus, again we see how the values of de-emphasizing the expression of negative feelings and the emphasizing of controls influenced the board's behavior.

The department heads, on the other hand, reported different reactions. "Why are they bothered with details? Don't they trust me? If not, why don't they say so?" Such reactions tended to produce more conformity, antagonism, mistrust, and fear of experimenting.

Still another board practice was the "diplomatic" rejection of an executive's idea that was, in the eyes of the board, offbeat, a bit too wild, or not in keeping with the corporate mission. The reasons given by the board for not being open about the evaluation again reflected adherence to the pyramidal values. For example, a board member would say, "We do not want to embarrass them," or "If you really tell them, you might restrict creativity."

This practice tended to have precisely the impact that the superiors wished to *avoid*. The subordinates reacted by asking, "Why don't they give me an opportunity to really explain it?" or "What do they mean when they suggest that the 'timing is not right' or 'funds are not currently available'?"

Processes Damaged

It is significant that defensive activities like those described are rarely observed during group meetings dealing with minor or relatively routine decisions. These activities become most noticeable when the decision is an important one in terms of dollars or in terms of the impact on the various departments in the organization. *The forces toward ineffectiveness operate most strongly during the important decision-making meetings.* The group and organizational defenses operate most frequently when they can do the most harm to decision-making effectiveness.

Another interesting finding is that the more effective and more committed executives tend to be upset about these facts, whereas the less effective, less committed people tend simply to lament them. They also tend to take on an "I told them so" attitude—one of resignation and noninvolvement in correcting the situation. In short, it is the better executives who are negatively affected.

What Can Be Done?

What can the executive do to change this situation?

I wish that I could answer this question as fully as I should like to. Unfortunately, I cannot. Nevertheless, there are some suggestions I can make.

Blind Alleys

First, let me state what I believe will *not* work.

Learning about these problems by listening to lectures, reading about them, or exploring them through cases is not adequate; an article or book can pose some issues and get thinking started, but—in this area, at least—it cannot change behavior. Thus, in one study with 60 top executives:

Lectures were given and cases discussed on this subject for nearly a week. A test at the end of the week showed that the executives rated the lecturers very high, liked the cases, and accepted the diagnoses. Yet when they attempted to apply their new-found knowledge outside the learning situation, most were unable to do so. The major problem was that they had not learned how to make these new ideas come to life in their behavior.

As one executive stated, pointing to his head: "I know up here what I should do, but when it comes to a real meeting, I behave in the same old way. It sure is frustrating." (See Argyris, 1965a, p. 255.)

Learning about these problems through a detailed diagnosis of executives' behavior is also not enough. For example:

I studied a top-management group for nearly four months through interviews and tape recordings of their decision-making meetings. Eventually, I fed back the analysis. The executives agreed with the diagnosis as well as with the statement by one executive that he found it depressing. Another executive, however, said he now felt that he had a clearer and more coherent picture of some of the causes of their problems, and he was going to change his behavior. I predicted that he would probably find that he would be unable to change his behavior—and even if he did change, his subordinates, peers, and superiors might resist dealing with him in the new way.

The executive asked, "How can you be so sure that we can't change?" I responded that I knew of no case where managers were able successfully to alter their behavior, their group dynamics, and so forth by simply realizing intellectually that such a change was necessary. The key to success was for them to be able to show these new strategies in their behavior. To my knowledge, behavior of this type, groups with these dynamics, and organizational cultures endowed with these characteristics were very difficult to change. What kind of thin-skinned individuals would they be, and how brittle would their groups and their organizations be if they could be altered that easily?

Three of the executives decided that they were going to prove the prediction to be incorrect. They took my report and studied it carefully. In one case the executive asked his subordinates to do the same. Then they tried to alter their behavior. According to their own accounts, they were unable to do so. The only changes they reported were (1) a softening of the selling activities, (2) a reduction of their aggressive persuasion, and (3) a genuine increase in their asking for the subordinates' views.

My subsequent observations and interviews uncovered the fact that the first two changes were mistrusted by the subordinates, who had by now adapted to the old behavior of their superiors. They tended to play it carefully and to be guarded. This hesitation aggravated the executives, who felt that their subordinates were not responding to their new behavior with the enthusiasm that they (the superiors) had expected.

However, *the executives did not deal with this issue openly*. They kept working at trying to be rational, patient, and rewarding. The more irritated they became and the more they showed this irritation in their behavior, the more the subordinates felt that the superiors' "new" behavior was a gimmick.

Eventually, the process of influencing subordinates slowed down so much that the senior men returned to their more controlling styles. The irony was that in most cases the top executives interpreted the subordinates' behavior as proof that they needed to be needled and pushed, while the subordinates interpreted the top managers' behavior as proof that they did not trust their assistants and would never change.

The reason I doubt that these approaches will probide anything but temporary cures is that they do not go far enough. If changes are going to be made in the behavior of an executive, if trust is to be developed, if risk taking is to flourish, he must be placed in a different situation. He should be helped to (*a*) expose his leadership style so that he and others can take a look at its true impact; (*b*) deepen his awareness of himself and the dynamics of effective leadership; and (*c*) strive for these goals under conditions where he is in control of the amount, pace, and depth of learning.

These conditions for learning are difficult to achieve. Ideally, they require the help of a professional consultant. Also, it would be important to get away from the organization—its interruptions, pressures, and daily administrative tensions.

Value of Questions

The executive can strive to be aware that he is probably programmed with a set of values which cause him to behave in ways that are not always helpful to others and which his subordinates will not discuss frankly even when they believe he is not being helpful. He can also strive to find time to uncover, through careful questioning, his impact on others. Once in a while a session that is focused on the "How am I doing?" question can enlighten the executive and make his colleagues more flexible in dealing with him.

One simple question I have heard several presidents ask their vice presidents with success is: "Tell me what, if anything, I do that tends to prevent (or help) your being the kind of vice president you wish to be?" These presidents are careful to ask these questions during a time when they seem natural (e.g., performance review sessions), or they work hard ahead of time to create a climate so that such a discussion will not take the subordinate by surprise.

Some presidents feel uncomfortable in raising these questions, and others point out that the vice presidents are also uncomfortable. I can see how both would have such feelings. A chief executive officer may feel that he is showing weakness by asking his subordinates about his impact. The subordinate may or may not feel this way, but he may sense that his chief does, and that is enough to make him uncomfortable.

Yet in two companies I have studied where such questions were asked, superiors and subordinates soon learned that authority which gained strength by a lack of openness was weak and brittle, whereas authority resting on open feedback from below was truly strong and viable.

Working with the Group

Another step that an executive can take is to vow not to accept group ineffectiveness as part of life. Often I have heard people say, "Groups are no damned good; strong leadership is what is necessary." I agree that many groups are ineffective. I doubt, however, if either of the two leadership patterns described earlier will help the situation. As we have seen, both patterns tend to make the executive group increasingly less effective.

If my data are valid, the search process in executive decision making has become so complicated that group participation is essential. No one man seems to be able to have all the knowledge necessary to make an effective decision. If individual contributions are necessary in group meetings, it is important that a climate be created that does not discourage innovation, risk taking, and honest leveling between managers in their conversations with one another. The value of a group is to maximize individual contributions.

Interestingly, the chief executive officers in these studies are rarely observed making policy decisions in the classic sense, viz., critical selections from several alternatives and determination of future directions to be taken. This does not mean that they shy away from taking responsibility. Quite the contrary. Many report that they enjoy making decisions by themselves. Their big frustration comes from realizing that most of the major decisions they face are extremely complex and require the coordinated, honest inputs of many different executives. They are impatient at the slowness of meetings, the increasingly quantitative nature of the inputs, and, in many cases, their ignorance of what the staff groups did to the decision inputs long before they received them.

The more management deals with complexity by the use of computers and quantitative approaches, the more it will be forced to work with inputs of many different people, and the more important will be the group dynamics of decision-making meetings. If anyone doubts this, let him observe the dry runs subordinates go through to get a presentation ready for the top. He will observe, I believe, that many data are included and excluded by subordinates on the basis of what they believe those at the top can hear.

In short, *one of the main tasks of the chief executive is to build and maintain an effective decision-making network.* I doubt that he has much choice *except* to spend time in exploring how well his group functions.

Such explorations could occur during the regular workday. For example, in one organization the president began by periodically asking members of his top group, immediately after a decision was made, to think back during the meeting and describe when they felt that the group was not being as effective as they wished. How could these conditions be altered?

As trust and openness increased, the members began to level with each other as to when they were inhibited, irritated, suppressed, confused, and withholding information. The president tried to be as encouraging as he could, and he especially rewarded people who truly leveled. Soon the executives began to think of mechanisms they could build into their group functioning so they would be alerted to these group problems and correct them early. As one man said, "We have not eliminated all our problems, but we are building a competence in our group to deal with them effectively if and when they arise."

Utilizing Feedback

Another useful exercise is for the superior and his group members to tape-record a decision-making meeting, especially one which is expected to be difficult. At a later date, the group members can gather and listen to the tape. I believe it is safe to say that simply listening to the tape is an education in itself. If one can draw from skilled company or outside help, then useful analyses can be made of group or individual behavior.

Recently, I experimented with this procedure with an "inside" board of directors of a company. The directors met once a month and listened to tape recordings of their monthly board meetings. With my help they analyzed their behavior, trying to find how they could improve their individual and group effectiveness. Listening to tapes became a very involving experience for them. They spent nearly four hours in the first meeting discussing less than ten minutes of the tape.

'Binds' Created. One of the major gains of these sessions was that the board members became aware of the "binds" they were creating for each other and of the impact they each had on the group's functioning. Thus Executive A was frequently heard antagonizing Executive B by saying something that B perceived as "needling." For example, A might seem to be questioning B's competence. "Look here," he would say, "anyone who can do simple arithmetic should realize that. . . ."

Executive B responded by fighting. B's way of fighting back was to utilize his extremely high capacity to verbalize and intellectualize. B's favorite tactic was to show A where he missed five important points and where his logic was faulty.

Executive A became increasingly upset as the "barrage of logic" found its mark. He tended to counteract by (*a*) remaining silent but manifesting a sense of being flustered and becoming red-faced; and/ or (*b*) insisting that his logic *was* sound even though he did not express it in "highfalutin' language" as did B.

Executive B pushed harder (presumably to make A admit he was wrong) by continuing his "barrage of logic" or implying that A could not see his errors because he was upset.

Executive A would respond to this by insisting that he was not upset. "The point you are making is so simple, why, anyone can see it. Why should I be upset?"

Executive B responded by pushing harder and doing more intellectualizing. When Executive A eventually reached his breaking point, he too began to shout and fight.

At this point, Executives C, D, and E could be observed withdrawing, until A and B wore each other out.

Progress Achieved. As a result of the meetings, the executives reported in interviews, board members experienced fewer binds, less hostility, less frustration, and did more constructive work. One member wondered if the group had lost some of its "zip," but the others disagreed. Here is an excerpt from the transcript of one discussion on this point:

Executive A: My feeling is, as I have said, that we have just opened this thing up, and I for one feel that we have benefited a great deal from it. I think I have improved; maybe I am merely reflecting the fact that you [Executive B] have improved. But at least I think there has been improvement in our relationship. I also see signs of not as good a relationship in other places as there might be.

I think on the whole we are much better off today than we were a year ago. I think there is a whole lot less friction today than there was a year ago, but there's still enough of it.

Now we have a much clearer organization setup; if we were to sit down here and name the people, we would probably all name exactly the same people. I don't think there is much question about who should be included and who should not be included; we've got a pretty clean organization.

Executive B: You're talking now about asking the consultant about going on with this week's session?

Executive A: It would be very nice to have the consultant if he can do it; then we should see how we can do it without him, but it'd be better with him.

Executive B: But that's the step, as I understand it, that should be taken at this stage. Is that right?

Executive A: Well, I would certainly favor doing something; I don't know what. I'm not making a specific recommendation; I just don't like to let go of it.

Executive C: What do you think?

Executive D: I'm not as optimistic as A. I wonder if anybody here agrees with me that maybe we haven't made as much progress as we think. I've personally enjoyed these experiences, and I'd like to see them continued.

Executive A: Would you like to venture to say why I think we have made progress and why I might be fooled?

Executive D: Well, I think maybe you are in the worst position to evaluate progress because if the worst possible thing that can happen is for people to no longer fight and struggle, but to say, "Yes, sir," you might call that progress. That might be the worst thing that could happen, and I sort of sense some degree of resignation—I don't think it's progress. I don't know. I might be all alone in this. What do you think?

Executive C: On one level it is progress. Whether it is institutional progress and whether it produces commensurate institutional benefits is a debatable question. It may in fact do so. I think it's very clear that there is in our meetings and in individual contact less heat, less overt friction, petulance, tension, than certainly was consistently the case. Do you agree?

Executive D: Yes, I think so.

Executive C: It has made us a great deal more aware of the extent and nature of the friction and clearly has made all of us intent on fighting less. There's some benefit to it; but there are some drawbacks.

Executive A: Well, if you and D are right, I would say for that reason we need more of the program.

Laboratory Training

Another possibility is for the executive to attend a program designed to help increase competence in this area, such as laboratory education and its various offshoots ("T-groups," the "managerial grid," "conflict management labs," and so on).[1] These learning experiences are available at various university and National Training Laboratory executive programs. They can also be tailor-made for the individual organization.

I believe outside programs offer the better way of becoming acquainted with this type of learning. Bear in mind, though, that since typically only one or two executives attend from the same

1. For detailed discussions of such variations, see Argyris (1964), p. 60; Blake, *et al.* (1964), p. 135; and Schein and Bennis (1965).

organization, the biggest payoff is for the individual. The inside program provides greater possibilities for payoff to the organization.

At the same time, however, it should also be kept in mind that in-house programs *can* be dangerous to the organization. I would recommend that a thorough study be made ahead of time to ascertain whether or not a laboratory educational experience would be helpful to company executives individually and to the organization.

Open Discussion

I have never observed a group whose members wanted it to decay. I have never studied a group or an organization that was decaying where there were not some members who were aware that decay was occurring. Accordingly, one key to group and organizational effectiveness is to get this knowledge out into the open and to discuss it thoroughly. The human "motors" of the group and the organization have to be checked periodically, just as does the motor of an automobile. Without proper maintenance, all will fail.

Nature of the Study

The six companies studied include: (1) an electronics firm with 40,000 employees, (2) a manufacturer and marketer of a new innovative product with 4000 employees, (3) a large research and development company with 3000 employees, (4) a small research and development organization with 150 employees, (5) a consulting-research firm with 400 employees, and (6) a producer of heavy equipment with 4,000 employees.

The main focus of the investigation reported here was on the behavior of 165 top executives in these companies. The executives were board members, executive committee members, upper-level managers, and (in a few cases) middle-level managers.

Approximately 265 decision-making meetings were studied and nearly 10,000 units of behavior analyzed. The topics of the meetings ranged widely, covering investment decisions, new products, manufacturing problems, marketing strategies, new pricing policies, administrative changes, and personnel issues. An observer took notes during all but ten of the meetings; for research purposes, these ten meetings were analyzed "blind" from tapes (i.e., without ever meeting the executives). All other meetings were taped also, but analyzed at a later time.

The major device for analyzing the tapes was a new system of categories for scoring decision-making meetings.[2] Briefly, the executives' behavior was scored according to how often they: owned up to

---

2. For a detailed discussion of the system of categories and other aspects of methodology, see Argyris (1965b).

and accepted responsibility for their ideas or feelings; opened up to receive others' ideas or feelings; experimented and took risks with ideas or feelings; helped others to own up, be open, and take risks; did not own up; were not open; did not take risks; and did not help others in any of these activities.

A second scoring system was developed to produce a quantitative index of the *norms* of the executive culture. There were both positive and negative norms. The positive norms were:

1. *Individuality,* especially rewarding behavior that focused on and valued the uniqueness of each individual's ideas and feelings.
2. *Concern* for others' ideas and feelings.
3. *Trust* in others' ideas and feelings.

The negative norms were:

1. *Conformity* to others' ideas and feelings.
2. *Antagonism* toward these ideas and feelings.
3. *Mistrust* of these ideas and feelings.

In addition to our observations of the men at work, at least one semistructured interview was conducted with each executive. All of these interviews were likewise taped, and the typewritten protocols served as the basis for further analysis.

References

Argyris, Chris. "Explorations in Interpersonal Competence, II." *Applied Behavioral Science,* Vol. 1, No. 3, 1965a.

———. *Organization and Innovation.* Irwin, 1965b.

———. "T-Groups for Organizational Effectiveness." *Harvard Business Review,* March–April 1964.

Blake, R. R., J. S. Mouton, L. B. Barnes, and L. E. Greiner. "Breakthrough in Organization Development." *Harvard Business Review,* November–December 1964.

Schein, Edgar, and Warren Bennis. *Organizational Change through Laboratory Methods.* Wiley, 1965.

Abraham Zaleznik

Managerial Behavior and Interpersonal Competence

The questions of what, if anything, is competent interpersonal behavior and how such competence relates to the functioning of managers have been of long-standing concern to practicing managers, researchers, and educators. The strength of this concern is attested to by the ubiquity of human relations training within and outside of universities. A central objective of these training efforts is to modify behavior, usually interpersonal, according to some set of norms that relate to organizational effectiveness or improved individual and group performance.

The purpose of this paper is to raise for inquiry the adequacy of existing notions of what interpersonal competence is, how it relates to the manager's job, and the best means for helping managers achieve this competence. By stating my purpose as *inquiry* rather than *advocacy* I mean to cast doubt on ideas that have been too readily accepted as firm conclusions rather than departures for exploration.

Classes of Executive Functions

Homeostatic Functions

Involvement in interpersonal processes is one dimension along which the managerial career is generally distinguished from other professional careers. This characteristic results from the interpersonal complexities of the organizational milieu. Organizations are viewed as systems of relationships, bound together by purposes, ideologies, and expectations that set the organization off from its environment and that also serve to differentiate the many parts of the system. A manager, according to Barnard, operates in two spheres simultaneously. He performs a set of functions that relate directly to the technical aspects of his job, such as deciding on a brand name for a new product, or preparing a capital expenditures budget for the

Reprinted by permission of the author and *Behavioral Science,* 9(2), 1964, 156–166.

firm. Barnard calls these functions nonexecutive, and they can be expected to vary in content from job to job and organization to organization (Barnard, 1958). Another set of functions that Barnard calls the executive functions of the manager deal with the organization as a co-operative system in which interpersonal phenomena are a significant aspect. To quote Barnard:

> It is important to observe, however, that not all work done by persons who occupy executive positions is in connection with the executive functions, the co-ordination of activities of others. Some of the work of such persons, though *organization* work, is not executive. For example, if the president of a corporation goes out personally to sell products of his company or engages in some of the production work, these are not executive services. If the president of a university gives lectures to a class of students, this is not executive work. If the head of a government department spends time on complaints or disputes about services rendered by the department, this is not necessarily executive work. Executive work is not that *of* the organization, but the specialized work of *maintaining* the organization in operation (p. 125).

Earlier, Barnard states:

> *Organization results from the modification of the action of the individual through control of or influence upon* . . . [(1) purposes, desires, impulses of the moment, and (2) the alternatives external to the individual recognized by him as available]. Deliberate conscious and specialized control of them is the executive function (p. 17).

The juxtaposition of these two quotations serves to raise one fundamental issue in considering the nature of interpersonal competence as an aspect of the executive role. Barnard stresses as the core of the executive function the problems arising from personal and interpersonal attributes of organizations as systems of cooperation. With his emphasis on executive work as the specialized work of *"maintaining* the organization," he implicitly points to interpersonal behavior of the executive that is directed toward assuring the internal stability of the organization. This function may properly be related to the homeostatic processes discussed by Cannon, whose concept of an organism suggest that certain automatic devices must operate within the system to maintain a steady state in the face of changing conditions in the environment (Cannon, 1915 and 1945).

Following this line of thought, one's attention is then directed toward an understanding of the interpersonal processes that are associated with *maintenance* of this organization. These processes we shall refer to as the interpersonal behavior directed toward the *homeostatic* functions of the executive.

Mediative Functions

The second part of the quotation from Barnard cited earlier produces a note different from maintenance. "Organization results from the modification of the action of the individual through control and influence." This statement suggests that the executive function proceeds through a kind of intervention, not directed necessarily toward maintaining a steady state, but directed instead toward altering behavior and attitudes with conscious intent. The way behavior is to be altered presumably is determined by the organization's problems of mutual adaptation with its environment. We can conceive of the environment as establishing pressure on the organization, requiring some internal change. The executive function, then, is to influence individuals and groups within the organization to modify behavior and attitudes so that some different adaptation to the environment is established.

This second set of executive functions we shall call *mediative,* since it is concerned with internal change in response to environmental press. Now presumably mediative functions imply certain kinds of interpersonal processes that may or may not be different from the homeostatic. We shall return to this issue because, as it should be clear, we are attempting to analyze the different interpersonal processes with which managerial behavior is concerned, and to re-examine competence in terms of the *multiple* functions of the executive rather than a single function that dictates a rather limited kind of interpersonal activity.

There is still a third kind of executive function that is not too clearly delineated by Barnard or other students of organizations. If we were to seek for a set of continua along which to describe the executive functions, particularly those implying different modes of interpersonal behavior, one such continuum clearly implied in the discussion so far is the passive-active.

The homeostatic function is positioned toward the passive end of the scale, since it views the organization as a system tending toward a steady state. The way the steady state is maintained presumably depends on an interpersonal process where the executive intervenes least. He uses instead the existing forces within the system to permit the modest alterations necessary to return to the steady state. The problem is comparable to the healing process in medicine which adopts a conservative point of view concerning the role of the physician. This view was stated well by Cannon and is worth quoting:

The fathers of medicine made use of the expression, "the healing force of nature." . . . It indicates, of course, recognition of the fact that processes of repair after injury, and restoration of health after disease go on quite independent of any treatment which a physician may give (Cannon, 1932).

Earlier, Cannon stated:

The ability of living beings to maintain their own constancy has long impressed biologists. The idea that disease is cured by natural processes . . . an idea which was held by Hippocrates (460–377 B.C.), implies the existence of agencies which are ready to operate correctively when the normal state of the organism is upset (*ibid.*, pp. 20–21).

If only by analogy, we can visualize the homeostatic functions as requiring very modest activity on the part of the executive to set in motion forces already existing within the organization to re-establish the steady state.

While space does not permit detailed illustrations, it would be worthwhile to note the types of situations that involve homeostatic processes in organizations. A good instance would be one where an internal disruption, such as vying for informal leadership, takes place in the otherwise co-operative relations among a group of employees. Such a disruption can occur at any level in the organization and requires the introduction of a corrective procedure. This procedure often consists of listening to the complaints of involved persons and helping them to assess reality. Such executive behavior is homeostatic in character and calls for a relatively passive response.

The mediative functions are more active in character than the homeostatic functions. The primary differences arises from the source of the stimulus. Mediative processes occur under the impact of environmental press. A set of forces in the environment creates the need for internal adaptation. As indicated above, the homeostatic functions become necessary where internal disruptions act as stimuli.

Mediative functions require a more active mode of behavior, since they tap into functions that only managers can perform. Because of their location in the organization, managers stand closer to the environmental processes than do other employees, and the higher the manager's status, the more he becomes concerned with issues arising outside the boundaries of the firm.

In response to environmental press, the manager activates change. He formulates goals, and communicates them within the internal network of the organization. When we compare the mediative with the homeostatic functions, the mode of interpersonal behavior tends to be more aggressive and less permissive in the former. Nevertheless, the aggressive mode has certain limits in mediative functions. When it is possible, for example, to separate goals and objectives from means and procedures, managers may seek to limit aggressive responses to the formulation and communication of goals while withdrawing in favor of informal processes for establishing means and procedures. Something of this pattern occurs under conditions of decentralization in an organization.

Proactive Functions

We are now ready to examine the third class of executive functions underlying the various modes of interpersonal behavior. It would be grossly inadequate to leave executive behavior restricted to the homeostatic and mediative functions. Ordinary observation shows a type of executive function that actively seeks out environmental possibilities. Instead of being reactive to environmental press, the behavior is proactive and in a sense induces change in the environment to conform to the creative use of resources available within the organization. We need not dwell too long on establishing the significance of proaction. The automobile, for example, did not emerge from environmental press, but rather from innovative behaviors of certain individuals who used a new level of scientific and technological sophistication. Let us for purposes of discussion call the third set of executive functions the proactive, although innovative would do just as well.

All too little is known about the psychology of proactive behavior, and this area of our understanding is at the frontier of knowledge. But what we do know suggests a conversion and release of aggressive energy directed toward altering the environment. It is anything but conservative, and typically becomes the type of managerial behavior that in its interpersonal frame tends to induce resistance, counter-aggression, and in some cases outright hostility. We should note also how sharply the proactive set differs from the more conservative homeostatic and mediative sets. In terms of the primacy of goals, the homeostatic function stresses maintaining the stability of the system as the fundamental goal, sometimes to the point where it becomes a substitute for activity in the environment. Proaction, on the other hand, disrupts internal relations in the service of changing the environment.

To recapitulate, we have implicit in the delineation of three sets of executive functions, homeostatic, mediative, and proactive, a series of dimensions that relate to modes of interpersonal behavior, cognition, and problem solving. These dimensions include the passive-active, conservative-innovative, inward-oriented/outward-oriented (in relation to the environment), a narrow-wide effective scope of thought and relationships, a short-range/long-range span of thought (Lazarsfeld and Thielens, 1958, pp. 262–65).

It should be quite evident from this discussion of executive functions that the differences in modes of behavior implied in each of the three types of functions is significantly different. Just how these differences become manifest in organizations and with what consequences requires far more research than has been done to date. But enough is available to underscore the basic differences. It should also begin to be clear that any consideration of interpersonal competence has to center on just what executive functions the competence is directed toward. I shall return to this issue later in the paper. In the meantime, I should like to shift the course of this discussion from the functions implied in an analysis of organizational requisites to the nature of personality development and character structure as these are pertinent for an understanding of the inner determinants of interpersonal behavior.

Personality Development and Interpersonal Behavior

The psychoanalytic study of personality and character provides, in my view, potentially the fullest and most challenging statement of the conditions in human development that determine the way executives pattern their role within the framework of the three types of functions discussed above.

The three sets of executive functions provide the nucleus of a description of an individual's adaptive mode. In establishing a career and in developing an organized way of working, the individual manifests the state of his ego organization. Reflected in this organization are the pecipitates of the identifications with objects important in the individual's personal history. Successively, the mother, father, teachers, and later authority figures provide the building blocks out of which a unique ego may emerge. Coupled with the identifications, the ego also contains the residues of competences that the individual has cultivated, learned, and expressed in the course of his life history. These competences reflect his constitutional endowment and the way it enters into transactions with the environment. Did the individual activate talents, cultivate them, and express them in ways that resulted in rewards from his environment? If so, these successive experiences of producing and being rewarded help form a core sense of self-esteem and a basic knowledge about the talents one has and those one does not have. This sense of self-esteem yields a tendency to seek situations and experiences where one can make the greatest use of himself. I have preferred in other contexts to call this tendency "leading from strength" rather than weakness. It is paradoxical, yet borne out by observation, to note that the tendency to lead from strength is a developmental gain that assures continued growth. The reverse, leading from weakness, reflects a developmental failure where a stage in the person's history resulted in unsolved problems of significant proportions. The learning process failed, and in an effort to master the unsolved problems the individual seeks in his current reality to repeat the experiences of the past, but usually with the same negative outcome (Freud, 1922).

A third relevant aspect of the ego organization is the nature of the individual's defenses and the energy available for work and human relationships. Psychic energy, its biological derivations and the process by which it becomes converted into action, remains a mystery in psychology. Psychoanalytic theory assumes that a basic energy reservoir exists undifferentiated as an aspect of biological endowment (Freud, 1927). In the course of development, primitive drive energy becomes free of intrapsychic conflict, is neutralized, and then is available to the ego for goal-directed activity and expressivity (Hartmann, 1958). A certain portion of the available energy becomes engaged in defensive processes to control anxiety that arises from dangers of intrapsychic conflicts (A. Freud, 1937). The ego defenses are a normal and necessary part of ego development, but when a disproportionate share of available energy is utilized in defending against anxiety, then presumably less is available for utilization in need satisfaction and work. Under these conditions, the individual functions with relatively severe constriction of the ego, and has difficulty in career development as well as in human relationships.

The state of the ego as reflected in identity, self-esteem, and energy utilization is genetically determined. The genetic hypothesis in psychoanalytic theory views development as a function of a biologically determined timetable in which sexual development proceeds according to a pattern of shifting zones of excitation. Interacting with the changing zones or centers of instinctual excitation are the changing relevances of object relationships and the demands of society (Erickson, 1959, pp. 18–19; and Freud, 1949). Each stage in development helps establish the conditions under which the successive life stages are experienced.

Now one of the most common sources of confusion in the minds of many people concerning Freud's theory of human development is the belief that Freud viewed development as effectively concluded and sealed off by the time the individual experiences the oedipal-phallic stage of development and enters the latency period (approximately age six). This erroneous belief probably exists because emphasis is in fact given to the three stages of infancy as major precursors of later development. Freud did not, however, suggest that developmental processes in later life stages are irrelevant. Rather, he established the crucial role of the formative years, and part of the unfinished business in developmental theory is to establish the connections among all the stages of the life cycle, including the career years.

Predispositional Sets

In considering the issues of interpersonal competence in the managerial role, we are faced immediately with problems of under- standing development in the career years, as these relate both to earlier and later stages in the life cycle. By the time an individual joins an organization to embark on a managerial career, he has established internal sets that frame how he seeks to engage his environment. The sets represent essentially the direction of emotional energy outward, or the individual's energy cathexes. The objects to- ward which the cathexes are directcd are of two main kinds: persons and ideas. In one internal set the individual may direct his emotional energy toward the tasks—technically, we speak of his cathecting the idea aspects of work. The personal and interpersonal aspects of work are not cathected to the same degree and may even, in fact, be defended against (Moment and Zaleznik, 1963).

A second internal set consists of a strong orientation toward persons—the cathexis is directed toward human relationships. Tasks may assume relatively little significance in the individual's inner need and value structure, and in fact the cognitive-technical aspects of work may be defended against. To indicate how these two predisposi- tional sets relate to stimuli in the environment, let us examine a data specimen from my current research.

A population of professional personnel completed a series of imaginative stories written in response to ambiguous pictures, part of the series in Murray's Thematic Apperception Test (Murray, *et al.*, 1938). Two of the pictures showed a single individual. Each of the two pictures was otherwise unpopulated. A simple analysis of the story content designed to measure the extent to which respondents populate their stories with persons showed a sharp division between two groups among our respondents: those whose manifest career goal is along a technical route, and those whose goal is along a managerial route. As you might expect, the managerial subgroup wrote stories involving interpersonal situations while those in a technical career route had few persons in the story plots. We would assume that the extent to which an individual's fantasy world incorporates other per- sons reflects his outward orientation toward other individuals.

A third predispositional set represents a fusion of cathexes. In this case, the individual, in his inner world, weighs both persons and ideas as important to him and blends them in his concerns with situations in the real world.

A fourth set exists which is real enough, but which for purposes of this paper had best be excluded from consideration. This set can be characterized as conflicted or ambivalent, in the sense that the cathexes are shifting and subject to immediate internal resistances and conflicts.

The three main predispositional sets we have presented in our discussion of individual development (cathexis of persons, ideas, and a fusion of persons and ideas) represent the center of outward concern of the ego. These concerns are a product of the ego processes discussed earlier (identification, self-esteem, and energy utilization) and emerge through the various precareer stages of the life cycle. We have some evidence suggesting how the ego processes are related to the formation of the predispositional sets and it would be useful to cite some of this evidence, although it must be viewed as highly tentative at this stage (Moment and Zaleznik, 1963).

Ego Processes and Predispositional Sets

In terms of identifications and identify formation, the person-oriented individual tends to have been influenced far more by the feminine figures in his life than by the masculine. His dominant identification trend is passive-feminine. Just how this trend occurs is subject to alternate explanations, ranging from excessive maternal dominance with relatively passive male influences in his development, to traumatic experiences in the infancy stages of development.

The identification patterns for the fusion types represent the results of parents who tended to minimize role differentiation. Both parents were capable of and showed affection and nurturance while exercising influence and dominance. In the case of the idea set, parental role differentiation appeared sharply drawn along classical lines. The mother appeared affectionate and nurturant, while the father appeared distant, cold, but also influential in the course of development. The distant father should not be confused with the laissez-faire father. The idea suggests a strong identification with a cold father who himself probably cathected ideas against persons in the career setting.

In terms of self-esteem, the idea set appears to have a strong sense of competence and self-worth, although it may manifest itself later in life than in the case of the fusion set. In our culture, the idea man comes into his own relatively late simply because the earlier stages of latency and adolescence are rooted in interpersonal settings. The idea man tends to show a history of individual work, while his counterparts in the fusion sets excel in sports and group activity, but not necessarily to the exclusion of good school work. The self-esteem of the fusion types revolves around a sense of being with others in co-operative activity. Our data do not permit many statements regarding the self-esteem issues of the person-oriented set. While appearing congenial in interpersonal settings and valued as friends, they are less valued for leadership functions. We should also note the fact that a male who is strongly person-oriented may not fare too well in our culture, largely because his activity may be incongruent with the types of performances that receive the more tangible rewards. Furthermore, a male whose dominant identifications are passive-feminine may be subject to self-doubting and reduced self-esteem.

Self-esteem is built in part through intimate experience with the cycle of productivity and reward. An individual acts and produces; he is evaluated and rewarded. This simple two-step cycle is important for building competence and self-esteem. We should not ignore the significance of environmental opportunities in this cycle because it is here that we see the effects of relative deprivations associated with membership in the lower social classes. Individuals with backgrounds in lower socioeconomic classes generally have less environmental opportunity and consequently less direct experience with a productivity-reward cycle that is free of anxiety.

With the introduction of the concept of anxiety, let us examine briefly the energy-utilization process in ego development as it relates to the three predispositional sets under consideration. We suggested earlier that energy available for work, interpersonal or otherwise, is derived from the sources of instinctual energy that is neutralized and freed of internal conflict. Available energy is also a function of the defensive requirements of the ego in its efforts to ward off anxiety. No individual can be free of anxiety and a system of defenses. Nevertheless, an excessive proportion of energy for defensive purposes results in a constriction of the ego (Freud, 1959, Vol. 5).

We can speculate, based on various kinds of evidence, on the defenses characteristic of the person, fusion, and idea predispositional sets. The person set defends against conflict and aggression. The conscious attitudes are generally altruistic as against egoistic, with strong identification with the underdog. The idea set supports aggression but defends against feelings, particularly the more tender and ambiguous feelings frequently encountered in human interaction. The fusion set may in the net have less need for strong defenses than the other two types, but the system of defenses would be mobilized to assume responsibility and to internalize conflict, both of which are highly socialized mechanisms. Responsibility and internalization are defensive insofar as they counter instinctual wishes of a potentially regressive character. When these defenses become excessive, one observes in such individuals marked feelings of guilt and depression (Moment and Zaleznik, 1963, Ch. 8). This defensive aspect of responsibility is even more significant if it becomes tied to fear of loss of love and approval.

This brief and somewhat oversimplified discussion of ego processes in the predispositional sets will serve as a foundation for our later consideration of the development of interpersonal competence through educational procedure. Before we can consider this issue more directly, we have one further piece of work ahead of us.

We have indicated so far the existence of at least three classes of executive functions that are organizational requisites—the homeostatic, the mediative, and the proactive. These functions define the shifting emphasis of managerial behavior from concern with internal processes (homeostatic) to concern with changing the environment (proactive). On the side of the individual who assumes a managerial role, we have examined the developmental issues that affect the condition of the ego as it presents itself in the work career. Here, our intent was to differentiate three predispositional sets that determine the particular way the individual builds his career on the one hand, but *that* is, on the other hand, determined by the individual's history and experience. We called these predispositional sets person-oriented, fusion-oriented, and idea-oriented.

The questions we shall pose at this juncture are as follow: What are the interrelations between the executive functions and predispositional sets? Although we may need to speculate, can we foresee how the various predispositional sets will interact with the executive functions?

Interrelations Between Functions and Sets

Our approach to these questions follows from arranging the two variables in the form of a matrix, as presented in figure 1.

The matrix in figure 1 permits us to ask several questions: (1) Would there be a tendency for an individual with a dominant set of one kind to select for specialization one of the three executive functions? (2) What types of interpersonal modalities are represented by the specializations implicit in each cell? (3) From the point of view

Figure 1   The Interaction of Executive Functions and Predispositional Sets

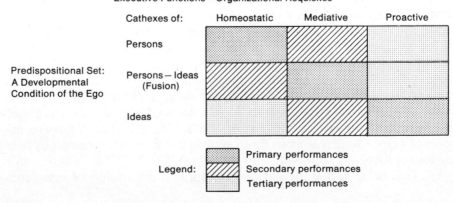

of organizational effectiveness, does optimal managerial behavior imply the capacity for flexibility in interpersonal modalities, or is there a requirement that the functions be performed within a constellation of executive roles that exemplify mutuality and complementarity? (4) From the point of view of individual development through the career years, should emphasis be placed on flexibility in both functions performed and consequent modifications of the underlying predispositional sets? (5) Or does individual development proceed more fruitfully by optimization of performance within an existing predispositional set?

We can only speculate on the answers to these questions, since these serve to indicate new avenues for investigation, rather than as issues that can be decided on the basis of existing evidence.

It would seem that the predispositional sets are conducive for performance within specialized functions. This idea is expressed by the shadings within each cell. While every individual can probably shift interpersonal modes to conform to the various functional requisites, each set would appear to be selectively oriented toward a particular function. The person-oriented individual would perform most easily in the range of interpersonal behaviors associated with the homeostatic functions. We would assume that such an individual would, relatively speaking, avoid proactive functions. Under conditions where proaction was thrust upon him and avoidance became difficult, the defensive apparatus of the individual would be under stress.

The idea-oriented individual, on the other hand, would perform most easily in the proactive functions, utilizing aggression and dominance as major components of his interpersonal style. Presumably, the homeostatic functions are not well understood by a proactive individual and may be strongly avoided. To continue our speculations, organizational effectiveness would seem to require as a prerequisite some mix in the performance of executive functions to assure both the securing of purpose and the maintenance of the internal capacities of the organization. Parsons and Bales express this most clearly in their view of a social system. The achievement of a purpose, or work, requires the release of energy, the engagement in aggressive-competitive activity directed toward solving problems. This activity results in a buildup of tension that, beyond a certain level, must be discharged to assure the continuity of the system. Tension-release processes are closely related to the homeostatic functions discussed earlier. Activity in a social system, then, proceeds in cycles of tension buildup and tension release. Following this broad hypothesis, the absence of relevant executive functions can result in the reduction of organizational effectiveness (Parsons and Bales, 1955).

There are two main competing views presented for understanding the structure and dynamics of executive performances. As a result of experimental work with small groups in problem-solving activity, Bales and his associates present the view that the effectiveness of a social system depends on a distribution of functions to appropriate specialists (Bales, 1953, pp. 111–61; and Hare, *et al.*, 1955, pp. 498–515). The task specialist exercises leadership through task performances; the social specialist exercises leadership through his efforts to restore the equilibrium in the system by emotional expressivity and tension release. This view sees leadership as occurring in a bipartite distribution of executive functions.

The bipartite model is prototypical insofar as it represents the condition in the nuclear family where the maternal figure is equivalent to the social specialist and the paternal figure to the task specialist. This model may well be oversimplified, yet it presents an excellent point of departure for the exploration and analysis of performances in social systems.

The alternate view, implied in a paper by Benne and Sheats (1948, pp. 41–49), views organizational effectiveness as the result of flexible performances by individuals who are capable of responding according to the demands of the situation. Benne and Sheats, like Bales, start with the assumption that functional requirements of a social system are of two kinds: task and maintenance. But, rather than establishing joint leadership according to the bipartite principle of specialization, they develop the view that both organizational effectiveness and individual development are enhanced under conditions of distributive leadership, where the social system is of a kind that permits all members to become flexible in their interpersonal performances and to meet the changing situational requirements.

This view is most closely associated with the group dynamics movement but is also an accepted premise of most workers in the human relations field, whether or not they are students of Kurt Lewin and his followers (Argyris, 1962, Bradford, *et al.*, 1953, and Roethlisberger, 1954). These two positions lend themselves to many significant comparisons, including the values implicit in each, their scientific validity, implications for a theory of interpersonal behavior in organizations, and implications for management education and development. It is to this last comparison that we shall now devote attention.

Education and Development

Role Specialization

Depending on which of the two views one adopts, the implications for managerial training and development differ. The theory of role specialization would not necessarily attempt to establish one ideal of role flexibility. It would view performances of the individual as an aspect of his ego development and character structure that is itself genetically determined. The dynamics of developmental experience become the main sources for understanding the type of functions an individual will assume in his managerial role. To a certain extent most individuals do perform within a range of the behavioral spectrum—extreme specialization occurs under conditions of severe restrictions in personal development. To broaden further the range of behavior may in and of itself require marked alterations in personality structure that are not feasible within the limits of educational processes, and are not necessarily desirable. Role specialization, then, is viewed as a condition *within which* education seeks to improve interpersonal performance. To attempt to achieve competence otherwise ignores the constraints of developmental history and may involve ill-advised direct attempts at shifting the defensive and adaptive balance the individual has achieved.

A further position in role specialization views alterations in interpersonal performances as guided by the individual's stage in the life cycle. The young man embarking on a managerial career will most likely be sensitive to social processes because of his own needs for security and membership. In his early thirties, a shift can begin in his performances where he stresses, relatively speaking, ideas and technical functions rather than social processes. Other shifts can also occur during other periods in his career development.

The alterations in performance are contained within the individual's dominant cathexes, but reflect individual concerns and situational pressures that are specific to particular phases of development. One would therefore conclude that a single overriding objective of increased flexibility in functions performed would be difficult to achieve, if not irrelevant for certain stages in the career period of the life cycle.

Role Flexibility

The second view, that of role flexibility as a normative principle in training for interpersonal competence, assumes in the first place that situational constraints are strategic in determining managerial performance. The kind of social system in which one performs will establish through the structure of behavioral norms permissible limits on behavior. By altering the norms, one achieves increased flexibility, especially as this is supported by appropriate training methods and experiences.

Educational procedures following this second set of assumptions seek to establish an ideal type of social system based on broad philosophical foundations of democracy and the scientific method (Bennis, 1962, pp. 1–27). With this ideal culture, individual growth, which includes flexible performances and distributive leadership, flourishes.

The proponents of this second view, while placing the strategic variable for interpersonal competence within the social system, tend to ignore the developmental determinants of individual behavior. Their view is in keeping with a liberal tradition of social reform, but the object of the reform is the organization rather than the individual. How organizations or societies can change apart from individual change is still an open question.

One further distinction between the individualistic-organizational frames of reference is important for our purposes, although it has been implied in the previous discussion. An individualistic frame of reference seeks to avoid the highly charged and abstract philosophical constraints characteristic of the organizational reform groups. Broad normative premises becomes molds to which individuals have to adapt and in this sense are inconsistent with a philosophy of education for individual growth.

Conclusions

Professional education for a managerial career rightfully concerns itself with issues of competence in the management of human affairs. It is here that the behavioral sciences may make a lasting contribution to business. A danger exists, however, when certain normative premises are accepted without critical scrutiny. One such set of premises seeks to establish criteria of interpersonal competence within a tradition of organizational and cultural reform, ignoring the significance of what has been learned of human development.

It is fallacious to describe the managerial role and interpersonal behavior underlying it in terms of one set of ideals, especially a set of ideals that are attributes of a culture. There are many different types of managerial role performances that present different configurations of interpersonal behaviors. The validity of a performance can be understood in terms of its relation to ego development, not in its degree of conformity to cultural ideologies. One set of behaviors that conforms to cultural norms may exist at the expense of a tenuous internal balance in ego functioning. Another set of behaviors may violate tenets of good human relations practice, but represent a developmental continuity that builds successively upon new ego strengths. This latter position, I believe, contains the greatest degree of validity and, in the final analysis, may result in a highly moral individual.

References

Argyris, C. *Interpersonal Competence and Organization Effectiveness.* Irwin, 1962.

Bales, R. F. "The Equilibrium Problem in Small Groups." In *Working Papers in the Theory of Action,* ed. T. Parsons, R. F. Bales, and E. A. Shils. The Free Press, 1953.

Barnard, C. *The Functions of the Executive*. Harvard University Press, 1958.

Benne, K. D., and P. Sheats. "Functional Roles of Group Members." *Journal of Social Issues*, Vol. 4, No. 2, 1948.

Bennis, W. G. "Toward a 'Truly' Scientific Management: The Concept of Organization Health." *Industrial Management Review*, Vol. 4, 1962.

Bradford, L. P., *et al. Explorations in Human Relations Training*. National Training Laboratory in Group Development (Washington, D. C.), 1953.

Cannon, W. B. *The Way of an Investigator*. Norton, 1945.

———. *The Wisdom of the Body*. Norton, 1932.

———. *Bodily Changes in Pain, Hunger, Fear and Rage*. Appleton-Century-Crofts, 1915.

Erikson, E. H. "Identity and the Life Cycle." *Psychology Issues*, Vol. 1, 1959.

Freud, A. *The Ego and Mechanisms of Defense*. Hogarth, 1937.

Freud, S. *Collected Papers*. Vol 5: *Analysis Terminable and Interminable*. Basic Books, 1959.

———. *Three Essays on the Theory of Sexuality*. Imago, 1949.

———. *The Ego and the Id*. Hogarth, 1927.

———. *Beyond the Pleasure Principle*. International Psychoanalytical Press, 1922.

Hare, A. P., E. F. Borgatta, and R. F. Bales, eds. *Small Groups: Studies in Social Interaction*. Appleton-Century-Crofts, 1955.

Hartmann, H. *Ego Psychology and the Problem of Adaptation*. International Universities Press, 1958.

Lazarsfeld, P. F., and W. Thielens. *The Academic Mind*. Free Press, 1958.

Moment, D., A. Zaleznik. *Role Development and Interpersonal Competence*. Harvard University Graduate School of Business Administration, Division of Research, 1963.

Murray, H., *et al. Explorations in Personality*. Oxford University Press, 1938.

Parsons, T., and R. F. Bales. *Family Socialization and Interaction Process*. The Free Press, 1955.

Roethlisberger, F. J., *et al. Training for Human Relations*. Harvard University Graduate School of Business Administration, Division of Research, 1954.

Warren G. Bennis

Interpersonal Communication

The human being is distinguished from lower forms of animals by his ability to communicate and to develop systems of communication about communication. Mathematics is perhaps the most elegant and unambiguous form of symbols about communication. Unfortunately, there are many aspects of communication that are not easily rendered in formal symbols—particularly those matters dealing with interpersonal relations. We have only the crudest of tools and the vaguest of concepts to communicate to each other about the human conditions. The ambiguity and complexity of human behavior probably explains to some extent one of the reasons why the science of human behavior is the youngest offspring of the physical and natural sciences. The very object of study, the human being, is also the individual conducting the study; which is another way of explaining the difficulty of interpreting group behavior.

The purpose of this presentation is to offer some notions about communication, most particularly *listening* and *talking;* notions that might be helpful in formulating a wide range of communication behavior. I will focus especially on communications between two persons, independent of any organization setting, status, or personality factors. The decision to focus on only two people was made primarily because the complexities of looking at group communication confound the analysis to be presented. It is hoped, however, that the analysis of the two-person relationship can be generalized to more complicated settings.

Communication—Verbal and Nonverbal

Communication plays a large part in our total personality make-up. It is communication that "presents our self" to others; it is communication that we use to negotiate and exchange interpersonally; it is communication that we utilize to expose our innermost feelings and that provides the data by which inferences about our innermost feelings are made. Figure 1 presents an oversimplified way of viewing communication as the mediator between our personality and the outside world of reality.

Now, not all our communication is verbal; in fact, at times the most persuasive and important part of our communication apparatus is nonverbal; a gesture, dress, accent, manner of speech, posture, even our home furnishings, cars, and so on. While I said earlier that communication is what saves us from being savages, the communication tangles, which also characterize humans, seem at times to make us savages. What are some of these blocks and barriers toward greater understanding between people?

**Figure 1   Communication as Media-
tor   Between   Personality
and Reality**

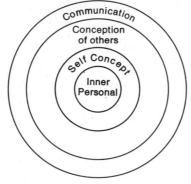

Selective Inattention

One of the problems in communication is that we very often communicate to others elements that we do not intend to, and that in fact may be at some variance with what we intended to communicate. This element of communication is directly related to the "not-self" and contains aspects of ourselves that have not been entirely integrated with our self-concept. The trouble is they are transmitted with ease to the listener. Sometimes these hidden elements are communicated in surprising ways. The best example that comes to mind is a woman who denied herself any gratification of her own impulses. She abhorred marriage and refused to have anything to do with men. At the same time she was "victimized" by a facial habit, a tic, which seemed to offset her puritanical notions quite directly. Every so often, and quite involuntarily she would wink with her right eye. To the listener, her unequivocal and stern values would be contradicted by the flirtatious wink. Examples, more subtle, of this kind could be multiplied. The point is that A communicates to B certain aspects of A's personality which are blocked off from A for whatever reasons but which are communicated to B. This "selective inattention" on the part of A creates what I will call an "arc of distortion" between A and his listener B.

Figure 2 illustrates this. In this diagram we see that A is really communicating at least two things to B, the intended as well as that which is selectively unattended to by A. This puts B in quite a bind as to how he should respond. Usually, as adults, we attempt to discover at which level the talker would like us to communicate, and then reciprocate at A's expected level.

The "arc of distortion" may be further confounded by B's "selective inattention." It may well be that B "hears" A saying something which A not only did not intend, but which he in fact *did not* communicate. The following example, while an extreme and pathological

Figure 2   Arc of Distortion

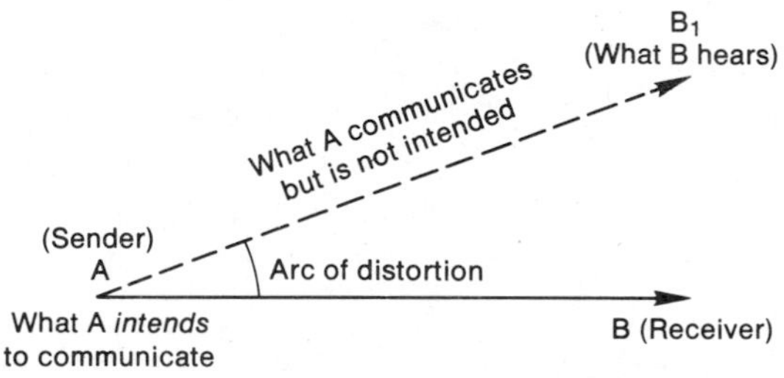

one, best illustrates this. The paranoic typically complains that others are rejecting him and persecuting him; he tends only to hear hostility and aggression, whether or not it is present.

One realistic way to reduce the "arcs of distortion," on the part both of the listener and of the talker, is to have an opportunity to check what the other is saying by feeding back to A what you, B, think he was saying, perhaps checking with other group members, and then to see how closely this matches A's intentions.

Multiple Meanings

The richness of language is tied up with the range of meanings attributed to a given symbol. Thus one word, like "dig," may mean excavating earth, understanding jazz music at the "gut level," probing, and probably other things. Our sentence structure and phraseology further muddy the meaning. One can start by a compliment and end up with a whiplash criticism. Stephen Potter's *Gamesmanship* is filled with examples such as these. "My, George, you're looking well today," somehow implying that this is rather an unusual event for poor George.

Double meanings in everyday language provide an expression for our basic "ambivalence" toward other human beings. Thus, the mother who is sick and tired of her 10-year-old-child, but who cannot directly tolerate negative feelings toward him, may ask her child if he would like to go to camp this summer. On the one hand the child is delighted with the idea of enriching his experience with a "sleep-away camp"; on the other hand, he may also wonder if his mother does not want to get rid of him for a while. Sometimes these interpersonal communications are implicit in the content of the discussion: Grandfather talks incessantly about the lack of energy and initiative of modern youth in order to impress others with the fact that he is a successful self-made man. Grandmother talks incessantly about sickness, calamity, and death, to remind others that the time may be short to repay her for the sacrifices she has made for her children. Grandmother never says, "You should feel guilty and devoted to me." She may only be quoting from the obituary column of the evening paper. Grandfather's remark may be concerned with the 40-hour work week.

Principle of Training

The meanings of our communication—as they are interpreted by the listener—often have a narrow and restricted range. Without our necessarily being aware of it, we tend in many situations to train others to respond to us in ways that we find comfortable to us; ways that help maintain our self-image. That is, we typically "train" others to respond to us in definite ways. This training is an involuntary reflex action that tends to pull from the other the behavior we want. Thus the passive, meek, and dependent subordinate typically finds himself in a situation where he is working for a dominant and aggressive boss. This seems to satisfy both subordinate and supervisor; they have found each other compatible because they have successfully trained each other to reciprocate their behavior with preferred behavior.

So often the trainer does not realize he is training at all. I have talked to many individuals who desire very much to change their interpersonal situations. The passive and meek person mentioned above may resent finding himself continually in a subordinate position; he finds that he is not fulfilling all his needs in this situation. He complains bitterly that he always finds himself working for the same kind of boss. What he does not realize is that he evokes and *directly pulls* from other people in his working situation dominant behavior toward him because he transmits to the others cues which can only be responded to by "taking care of him." What I am trying to communicate here is that there is a degree of self-determination in the way the other relates to you; that we often elicit from others behavior which is at extreme variance with what we basically want, that by becoming aware of this training behavior—or by increasing our repertory of communication reflexes—a new set of interpersonal relations can develop.

Reality Testing

One path to better understanding of others is through some mechanism for testing the communication. "Feedback" is introduced as one mechanism for communicating about communication. Ways have to be developed to increase the range of valid communication by developing methods whereby individuals can develop ways of communicating about their communication.

Jack R. Gibb

Defensive Communication

One way to understand communication is to view it as a people process rather than as a language process. If one is to make fundamental improvement in communication, he must make changes in interpersonal relationships. One possible type of alteration—and the one with which this paper is concerned—is that of reducing the degree of defensiveness.

Definition and Significance

"Defensive behavior" is behavior which occurs when an individual perceives threat or anticipates threat in the group. The person who behaves defensively, even though he also gives some attention to the common task, devotes an appreciable portion of his energy to defending himself. Besides talking about the topic, he thinks about how he appears to others, how he may be seen more favorably, how he may win, dominate, impress, or escape punishment, and/or how he may avoid or mitigate a perceived or an anticipated attack.

Such inner feelings and outward acts tend to create similarly defensive postures in others; and, if unchecked, the ensuing circular response becomes increasingly destructive. Defensive behavior, in short, engenders defensive listening, and this in turn produces pos-

From the *Journal of Communication*, Vol. 11(3), September 1961, pp. 141–148. Reprinted by permission of the author and the *Journal of Communication*.

tural, facial, and verbal cues which raise the defense level of the original communicator.

Defensive arousal prevents the listener from concentrating upon the message. Not only do defensive communicators send off multiple value, motive, and affect cues, but also defensive recipients distort what they receive. As a person becomes more and more defensive, he becomes less and less able to perceive accurately the motives, the values, and the emotions of the sender. The writer's analyses of tape recorded discussions revealed that increases in defensive behavior were correlated positively with losses in efficiency in communication (Gibb, 1961, pp. 61–81). Specifically, distortions became greater when defensive states existed in the groups.

The converse also is true. The more "supportive" or defense reductive the climate the less the receiver reads into the communication distorted loadings which arise from projections of his own anxieties, motives, and concerns. As defenses are reduced, the receivers become better able to concentrate upon the structure, the content, and the cognitive meanings of the message.

Categories of Defensive and Supportive Communication

In working over an eight-year period with recordings of discussions occurring in varied settings, the writer developed the six pairs of defensive and supportive categories presented in Table 1. Behavior

Table 1   Categories of Behavior Characteristic of Supportive and Defensive Climates in Small Goups

Defensive Climates	Supportive Climates
1. Evaluation	1. Description
2. Control	2. Problem orientation
3. Strategy	3. Spontaneity
4. Neutrality	4. Empathy
5. Superiority	5. Equality
6. Certainty	6. Provisionalism

which a listener perceives as possessing any of the characteristics listed in the left-hand column arouses defensiveness, whereas that which he interprets as having any of the qualities designated as supportive reduces defensive feelings. The degree to which these reactions occur depends upon the personal level of defensiveness and upon the general climate in the group at the time (Gibb, 1960, pp. 115–35).

Evaluation and Description

Speech or other behavior which appears evaluative increases defensiveness. If by expression, manner of speech, tone of voice, or verbal content the sender seems to be evaluating or judging the listener, then the receiver goes on guard. Of course, other factors may inhibit the reaction. If the listener thinks that the speaker regards him as an equal and is being open and spontaneous, for example, the evaluativeness in a message will be neutralized and perhaps not even perceived. This same principle applies equally to the other five categories of potentially defense-producing climates. The six sets are interactive.

Because our attitudes toward other persons are frequently, and often necessarily, evaluative, expressions which the defensive person will regard as non-judgmental are hard to frame. Even the simplest question usually conveys the answer that the sender wishes or implies the response that would fit into his value system. A mother, for example, immediately following an earth tremor that shook the house, sought for her small son with the question: "Bobby, where are you?" The timid and plaintive "Mommy, I didn't do it" indicated how Bobby's chronic mild defensiveness predisposed him to react with a projection of his own guilt and in the context of his chronic assumption that questions are full of accusation.

Anyone who has attempted to train professionals to use information-seeking speech with neutral affect appreciates how difficult it is to teach a person to say even the simple "Who did that?" without being seen as accusing. Speech is so frequently judgmental that there is a reality base for the defensive interpretations which are so common.

When insecure, group members are particularly likely to place blame, to see others as fitting into categories of good or bad, to make moral judgments of their colleagues, and to question the value, motive, and affect loadings of the speech which they hear. Since value loadings imply a judgment of others, a belief that the standards of the speaker differ from his own causes the listener to become defensive.

Descriptive speech, in contrast to that which is evaluative, tends to arouse a minimum of uneasiness. Speech acts which the listener perceives as genuine requests for information or as material with neutral loadings is descriptive. Specifically, presentations of feelings, events, perceptions, or processes which do not ask or imply that the receiver change behavior or attitude are minimally defense-producing. The difficulty in avoiding overtone is illustrated by the problems of news reporters in writing stories about unions, Communists, Negroes, and religious activities without tipping off the "party" line of the newspaper. One can often tell from the opening words in a news article which side the newspaper's editorial policy favors.

Control and Problem Orientation

Speech which is used to control the listener evokes resistance. In most of our social intercourse someone is trying to do something to someone else—to change an attitude, to influence behavior, or to restrict the field of activity. The degree to which attempts to control produce defensiveness depends upon the openness of the effort, for a suspicion that hidden motives exist heightens resistance. For this reason attempts of non-directive therapists and progressive educators to refrain from imposing a set of values, a point of view, or a problem solution upon the receivers meet with many barriers. Since the norm is control, non-controllers must earn the perceptions that their efforts have no hidden motives. A bombardment of persuasive "messages" in the fields of politics, education, special causes, advertising, religion, medicine, industrial relations, and guidance has bred cynical and paranoidal responses in listeners.

Implicit in all attempts to alter another person is the assumption by the change agent that the person to be altered is inadequate. That the speaker secretly views the listener as ignorant, unable to make his own decisions, uninformed, immature, unwise, or possessed of wrong or inadequate attitudes is a subconscious perception which gives the latter a valid base for defensive reactions.

Methods of control are many and varied. Legalistic insistence on detail, restrictive regulations and policies, conformity norms, and all laws are among the methods. Gestures, facial expressions, other forms of non-verbal communication, and even such simple acts as holding a door open in a particular manner, are means of imposing one's will upon another and hence are potential sources of resistance.

Problem orientation, on the other hand, is the antithesis of persuasion. When the sender communicates a desire to collaborate in defining a mutual problem and in seeking its solution, he tends to create the same problem orientation in the listener; and, of greater importance, he implies that he has no predetermined solution, attitude, or method to impose. Such behavior is permissive in that it allows the receiver to set his own goals, make his own decisions, and evaluate his own progress—or to share with the sender in doing so. The exact methods of attaining permissiveness are not known, but they must involve a constellation of cues, and they certainly go beyond mere verbal assurances that the communicator has no hidden desires to exercise control.

Strategy and Spontaneity

When the sender is perceived as engaged in a stratagem involving ambiguous and multiple motivations, the receiver becomes defensive. No one wishes to be a guinea pig, a role player, or an impressed actor, and no one likes to be the victim of some hidden motivation. That which is concealed, also, may appear larger than it really is, with the degree of defensiveness of the listener determining the perceived size of the suppressed element. The intense reaction of the reading audience to the material in the *Hidden Persuaders* indicates the prevalence of defensive reactions to multiple motivations behind strategy. Group members who are seen as "taking a role," as feigning emotion, as toying with their colleagues, as withholding information, or as having special sources of data are especially resented. One participant once complained that another was "using a listening technique" on him!

A large part of the adverse reaction to much of the so-called human relations training is a feeling against what are perceived as gimmicks and tricks to fool or to "involve" people, to make a person think he is making his own decision, or to make the listener feel that the sender is genuinely interested in him as a person. Particularly violent reactions occur when it appears that someone is trying to make a stratagem appear spontaneous. One person has reported a boss who incurred resentment by habitually using the gimmick of "spontaneously" looking at his watch and saying, "My gosh, look at the time—I must run to an appointment." The belief was that the boss would create less irritation by honestly asking to be excused.

Similarly, the deliberate assumption of guilelessness and natural simplicity is especially resented. Monitoring the tapes of feedback and evaluation sessions in training groups indicates the surprising extent to which members perceive the strategies of their colleagues. This perceptual clarity may be quite shocking to the strategist, who usually feels that he has cleverly hidden the motivational aura around the gimmick.

This aversion to deceit may account for one's resistance to politicians who are suspected of behind-the-scenes planning to get his vote; to psychologists whose listening apparently is motivated by more than the manifest or content-level interest in his behavior; or to the sophisticated, smooth, or clever person whose "oneupmanship" is marked with guile. In training groups the role-flexible person frequently is resented because his changes in behavior are perceived as strategic maneuvers.

Conversely, behavior which appears to be spontaneous and free of deception is defensive reductive. If the communicator is seen as having a clean id, as having uncomplicated motivations, as being straightforward and honest, and as behaving spontaneously in response to the situation, he is likely to arouse minimal defense.

Neutrality and Empathy

When neutrality in speech appears to the listener to indicate a lack of concern for his welfare, he becomes defensive. Group members usually desire to be perceived as valued persons, as individuals of special worth, and as objects of concern and affection. The clinical, detached, person-is-an-object-of-study attitude on the part of many psychologist–trainers is resented by group members. Speech with low affect that communicates little warmth or caring is in such contrast with the affect-laden speech in social situations that it sometimes communicates rejection.

Communication that conveys empathy for the feelings and respect for the worth of the listener, however, is particularly supportive and defense reductive. Reassurance results when a message indicates that the speaker identifies himself with the listener's problems, shares his feelings, and accepts his emotional reactions at face value. Abortive efforts to deny the legitimacy of the receiver's emotions by assuring the receiver that he need not feel bad, that he should not feel rejected, or that he is overly anxious, though often intended as support-giving, may impress the listener as lack of acceptance. The combination of understanding and empathizing with the other person's emotions with no accompanying effort to change him apparently is supportive at a high level.

The importance of gestural behavioral cues in communicating empathy should be mentioned. Apparently spontaneous facial and bodily evidences of concern are often interpreted as especially valid evidence of deep-level acceptance.

Superiority and Equality

When a person communicates to another that he feels superior in position, power, wealth, intellectual ability, physical characteristics, or other ways, he arouses defensiveness. Here, as with the other sources of disturbance, whatever arouses feelings of inadequacy causes the listener to center upon the affect loading of the statement rather than upon the cognitive elements. The receiver then reacts by not hearing the message, by forgetting it, by competing with the sender, or by becoming jealous of him.

The person who is perceived as feeling superior communicates that he is not willing to enter into a shared problem-solving relationship, that he probably does not desire feedback, that he does not require help, and/or that he will be likely to try to reduce the power, the status, or the worth of the receiver.

Many ways exist for creating the atmosphere that the sender feels himself equal to the listener. Defenses are reduced when one perceives the sender as being willing to enter into participative planning with mutual trust and respect. Differences in talent, ability, worth, appearance, status, and power often exist, but the low-defense communicator seems to attach little importance to these distinctions.

Certainty and Provisionalism

The effects of dogmatism in producing defensiveness are well known. Those who seem to know the answers, to require no additional data, and to regard themselves as teachers rather than as co-workers tend to put others on guard. Moreover, in the writer's experiment, listeners often perceived manifest expressions of certainty as connoting inward feelings of inferiority. They saw the dogmatic individual as needing to be right, as wanting to win an argument rather than solve a problem, and as seeing his ideas as truths to be defended. This kind of behavior often was associated with acts which others regarded as attempts to exercise control. People who were right seemed to have low tolerance for members who were "wrong"—i.e., who did not agree with the sender.

One reduces the defensiveness of the listener when he communicates that he is willing to experiment with his own behavior, attitudes, and ideas. The person who appears to be taking provisional attitudes, to be investigating issues rather than taking sides on them, to be problem solving rather than debating, and to be willing to experiment and explore tends to communicate that the listener may have some control over the shared quest or the investigation of the ideas. If a person is genuinely searching for information and data, he does not resent help or company along the way.

Conclusion

The implications of the above material for the parent, the teacher, the manager, the administrator, or the therapist are fairly obvious. Arousing defensiveness interferes with communication and thus makes it difficult—and sometimes impossible—for anyone to convey ideas clearly and to move effectively toward the solution of therapeutic, educational, or managerial problems.

References

Gibb, Jack R. "Defense Level and Influence in Small Groups." In *Leadership and Interpersonal Behavior,* eds. L. Petrullo and B. M. Bass. Holt, Rinehart & Winston, 1961.

————. "Sociophysiological Processes of Work Instruction." In *The Dynamics of Instructional Groups,* ed. N. B. Henry (59th yearbook of the National Society for the Study of Education, part 2, 1960).

Carl Rogers and Fritz Roethlisberger

Barriers and Gateways to Communication

Communication among human beings has always been a problem. But it is only fairly recently that management and management advisers have become so concerned about it and the way it works or does not work in industry. Now, as the result of endless discussion, speculation, and plans of action, a whole cloud of catchwords and catchthoughts has sprung up and surrounded it.

It is hoped that the following two descriptions of barriers and gateways to communication may help to bring the problem down to earth and show what it means in terms of simple fundamentals. First Carl R. Rogers analyzes it from the standpoint of human behavior generally (part I); then F. J. Roethlisberger illustrates it in an industrial context (part II).

I

It may seem curious that a person like myself, whose whole professional effort is devoted to psychotherapy, should be interested in problems of communication. What relationship is there between obstacles to communication and providing therapeutic help to individuals with emotional maladjustments?

Actually, the relationship is very close indeed. The whole task of psychotherapy is the task of dealing with a failure in communication. The emotionally maladjusted person, the "neurotic," is in difficulty, first, because communication within himself has broken down and, secondly, because—as a result of this—his communication with others has been damaged. To put it another way, the "neurotic" individual parts of himself which have been termed unconscious, or repressed, or denied to awareness, become blocked off so that they no longer communicate themselves to the conscious or managing part of himself. As long as this is true, there are distortions in the way he

Reprinted by permission of the publishers from Fritz J. Roethlisberger *Man-In-Organization*, Cambridge, Mass.: The Belknap Press of Harvard University Press, Copyright, 1968, by the President and Fellows of Harvard College.

communicates himself to others, and so he suffers both within himself and in his interpersonal relations.

The task of psychotherapy is to help the person achieve, through a special relationship with a therapist, good communication within himself. Once this is achieved, he can communicate more freely and more effectively with others. We may say then that psychotherapy is good communication, within and between men. We may also turn that statement around and it will still be true. Good communication, free communication, within or between men, is always therapeutic.

It is, then, from a background of experience with communication in counseling and psychotherapy that I want to present two ideas: (1) I wish to state what I believe is one of the major factors in blocking or impeding communication, and then (2) I wish to present what in our experience has proved to be a very important way of improving or facilitating communication.

Barrier: The Tendency to Evaluate

I should like to propose, as a hypothesis for consideration, that the major barrier to mutual interpersonal communication is our very natural tendency to judge, to evaluate, to approve (or disapprove) the statement of the other person or the other group. Let me illustrate my meaning with some very simple examples. Suppose someone, commenting on this discussion, makes the statement, "I didn't like what that man said." What will you respond? Almost invariably your reply will be either approval or disapproval of the attitude expressed. Either you respond, "I didn't either; I thought it was terrible," or else you tend to reply, "Oh, I thought it was really good." In other words, your primary reaction is to evaluate it from your point of view, your own frame of reference.

Or take another example. Suppose I say with some feeling, "I think the Republicans are behaving in ways that show a lot of good sound sense these days." What is the response that arises in your mind? The overwhelming likelihood is that it will be evaluative. In other words, you will find yourself agreeing or disagreeing, or making some judgment about me such as "He must be conservative," or "He seems solid in his thinking." Or let us take an illustration from the international scene. Russia says vehemently, "The treaty with Japan is a war plot on the part of the United States." We rise as one person to say, "That's a lie!"

This last illustration brings in another element connected with my hypothesis. Although the tendency to make evaluations is common in almost all interchange of language, it is very much heightened in those situations where feelings and emotions are deeply involved. So the stronger our feelings, the more likely it is that there will be no mutual element in the communication. There will be just two ideas, two feelings, two judgments, missing each other in psychological space.

I am sure you recognize this from your own experience. When you have not been emotionally involved yourself and have listened to a heated discussion, you often go away thinking, "Well, they actually weren't talking about the same thing." And they were not. Each was making a judgment, an evaluation, from his own frame of reference. There was really nothing which could be called communication in any genuine sense. This tendency to react to any emotionally meaningful statement by forming an evaluation of it from our point of view is, I repeat, the major barrier to interpersonal communication.

Gateway: Listening with Understanding

Is there any way of solving this problem, of avoiding this barrier? I feel that we are making exciting progress toward this goal, and I should like to present it as simply as I can. Real communication occurs, and this evaluative tendency is avoided, when we listen with understanding. What does that mean? It means to see the expressed idea and attitude from the other person's point of view, to sense how it feels to him, to achieve his frame of reference in regard to the thing he is talking about.

Stated so brief, this may sound absurdly simple, but it is not. It is an approach which we have found extremely potent in the field of psychotherapy. It is the most effective agent we know for altering the basic personality structure of an individual and for improving his relationships and his communications with others. If I can listen to what he can tell me, if I can understand how it seems to him, if I can see its personal meaning for him, if I can sense the emotional flavor which it has for him, then I will be releasing potent forces of change in him.

Again, if I can really understand how he hates his father, or hates the company, or hates Communists—if I can catch the flavor of his fear of insanity, or his fear of atom bombs, or of Russia—it will be of the greatest help to him in altering those hatreds and fears and in establishing realistic and harmonious relationships with the very people and situations toward which he has felt hatred and fear. We know from our research that such emphatic understanding—understanding with a person, not about him—is such an effective approach that it can bring about major changes in personality.

Some of you may be feeling that you listen well to people and yet you have never seen such results. The chances are great indeed that your listening has not been of the type I have described. Fortunately, I can suggest a little laboratory experiment which you can try to test the quality of your understanding. The next time you get into an argument with your wife, or your friend, or with a small group of friends, just stop the discussion for a moment and, for an experiment, institute this rule: "Each person can speak up for himself only after he has first restated the ideas and feelings of the previous speaker accurately and to that speaker's satisfaction."

You see what this would mean. It would simply mean that before presenting your own point of view, it would be necessary for you to achieve the other speaker's frame of reference—to understand his thoughts and feelings so well that you could summarize them for him. Sounds simple, doesn't it? But if you try it, you will discover that it is one of the most difficult things you have ever tried to do. However, once you have been able to see the other's point of view, your own comments will have to be drastically revised. You will also find the emotion going out of the discussion, the differences being reduced, and those differences which remain being of a rational and understandable sort.

Can you imagine what this kind of an approach would mean if it were projected into larger areas? What would happen to a labor-management dispute if it were conducted in such a way that labor, without necessarily agreeing, could accurately state management's point of view in a way that management could accept; and management, without approving labor's stand, could state labor's case in a way that labor agreed was accurate? It would mean that real communication was established, and one could practically guarantee that some reasonable solution would be reached.

If, then, this way of approach is an effective avenue to good communication and good relationships, as I am quite sure you will agree if you try the experiment I have mentioned, why is it not more widely tried and used? I will try to list the difficulties which keep it from being utilized.

Need for Courage

In the first place it takes courage, a quality which is not too widespread. I am indebted to Dr. S. I. Hayakawa, the semanticist, for pointing out that to carry on psychotherapy in this fashion is to take a very real risk, and that courage is required. If you really understand another person in this way, if you are willing to enter his private world and see the way life appears to him, without any attempt to make evaluative judgments, you run the risk of being changed yourself. You might see it his way; you might find yourself influenced in your attitudes or your personality.

This risk of being changed is one of the most frightening prospects many of us can face. If I enter, as fully as I am able, into the private world of a neurotic or psychotic individual, isn't there a risk that I might become lost in that world? Most of us are afraid to take that risk. Or if we were listening to a Russian Communist, or Senator

Joe McCarthy, how many of us would dare to see the world from each of their points of view? The great majority of us could not listen; we would find ourselves compelled to evaluate, because listening would seem too dangerous. So the first requirement is courage, and we do not always have it.

Heightened Emotions

But there is a second obstacle. It is just when emotions are strongest that it is most difficult to achieve the frame of reference of the other person or group. Yet it is then that the attitude is most needed if communication is to be established. We have not found this to be an insuperable obstacle in our experience in psychotherapy. A third party, who is able to lay aside his own feelings and evaluations, can assist greatly by listening with understanding to each person or group and clarifying the views and attitudes each holds.

We have found this effective in small groups in which contradictory or antagonistic attitudes exist. When the parties to a dispute realize that they are being understood, that someone sees how the situation seems to them, the statements grow less exaggerated and less defensive, and it is no longer necessary to maintain the attitude, "I am 100 percent right and you are 100 percent wrong." The influence of such an understanding catalyst in the group permits the members to come closer and closer to the objective truth involved in the relationship. In this way mutual communication is established, and some type of agreement becomes much more possible.

So we may say that though heightened emotions make it much more difficult to understand with an opponent, our experience makes it clear that a neutral, understanding, catalyst type of leader or therapist can overcome this obstacle in a small group.

Size of Group

That last phrase, however, suggests another obstacle to utilizing the approach I have described. Thus far all our experience has been with small face-to-face groups—groups exhibiting industrial tensions, religious tensions, racial tensions, and therapy groups in which many personal tensions are present. In these small groups our experience, confirmed by a limited amount of research, shows that this basic approach leads to improved communication, to greater acceptance of others and by others, and to attitudes which are most positive and more problem-solving in nature. There is a decrease in defensiveness, in exaggerated statements, in evaluative and critical behavior.

But these findings are from small groups. What about trying to achieve understanding between larger groups that are geographically remote, or between face-to-face groups that are not speaking for themselves but simply as representative of others, like the delegates at Kaesong? Frankly, we do not know the answers to these questions. I believe the situation might be put this way: As social scientists we have a tentative test-tube solution of the problem of breakdown in communication. But to confirm the validity of this test-tube solution and to adapt it to the enormous problems of communication breakdown between classes, groups, and nations would involve additional funds, much more research, and creative thinking of a high order.

Yet with our present limited knowledge, we can see some steps which might be taken, even in large groups, to increase the amount of listening with, and decrease the amount of evaluation about. To be imaginative for a moment, let us suppose that a therapeutically oriented international group went to the Russian leaders and said, "We want to achieve a genuine understanding of your views and, even more important, of your attitudes and feelings toward the United States. We will summarize and resummarize these views and feelings if necessary, until you agree that our description represents the situation as it seems to you."

Then suppose they did the same thing with the leaders in our own country. If they then gave the widest possible distribution to these views, with the feelings clearly described but not expressed in name-calling, might not the effect be very great? It would not guarantee the type of understanding I have been describing, but it would make it much more possible. We can understand the feelings of a person who hates us much more readily when his attitudes are accurately described to us by a neutral third party than we can when he is shaking his fist at us.

Faith in Social Sciences

But even to describe such a first step is to suggest another obstacle to this approach of understanding. Our civilization does not yet have enough faith in the social sciences to utilize their findings. The opposite is true of the physical sciences. During the war, when a test-tube solution was found to the problem of synthetic rubber, millions of dollars and an army of talent were turned loose on the problem of using that finding. If synthetic rubber could be made in milligrams, it could and would be made in the thousands of tons. And it was. But in the social science realm, if a way is found of facilitating communications and mutual understanding in small groups, there is no guarantee that the finding will be utilized. It may be a generation or more before the money and the brains will be turned loose to exploit that finding.

Summary

In closing, I should like to summarize this small-scale solution to the problem of barriers in communication, and to point out certain of its characteristics.

I have said that our research and experience to date would make it appear that breakdown in communication, and the evaluative tendency which is the major barrier to communication, can be avoided. The solution is provided by creating a situation in which each of the different parties comes to understand the other from the *other's* point of view. This has been achieved, in practice, even when feelings run high, by the influence of a person who is willing to understand each point of view emphatically, and who thus acts as a catalyst to precipitate further understanding.

This procedure has important characteristics. It can be initiated by one party, without waiting for the other to be ready. It can even be initiated by a neutral third person, provided he can gain a minimum of cooperation from one of the parties.

This procedure can deal with the insincerities, the defensive exaggerations, the lies, the "false fronts" which characterize almost every failure in communications. These defensive distortions drop away with astonishing speed as people find that the only intent is to understand, not to judge.

This approach leads steadily and rapidly toward the discovery of the truth, toward a realistic appraisal of the objective barriers to communication. The dropping of some defensiveness by one party leads to further dropping of defensiveness by the other party, and truth is thus approached.

This procedure gradually achieves mutual communication. Mutual communication tends to be pointed toward solving a problem rather than toward attacking a person or group. It leads to a situation in which I see how the problem appears to you as well as to me, and you see how it appears to me as well as to you. Thus accurately and realistically defined, the problem is almost certain to yield to intelligent attack; or if it is in part insoluble, it will be comfortably accepted as such.

This then appears to be a test-tube solution to the breakdown of communication as it occurs in small groups. Can we take this small-scale answer, investigate it further, refine it, develop it, and apply it to the tragic and well-nigh fatal failures of communication which threaten the very existence of our modern world? It seems to me that this is a possibility and a challenge which we should explore.

II

In thinking about the many barriers to personal communication, particularly those that are due to differences of background, experience, and motivation, it seems to me extraordinary that any two persons can ever understand each other. Such reflections provoke the question of how communication is possible when people do not see and assume the same things and share the same values.

On this question there are two schools of thought. One school assumes that communication between A and B, for example, has failed when B does not accept what A has to say as being fact, true, or valid; and that the goal of communication is to get B to agree with A's opinions, ideas, facts, or information.

The position of the other school of thought is quite different. It assumes that communication has failed when B does not feel free to express his feelings to A because B fears they will not be accepted by A. Communication is facilitated when, on the part of A or B or both, there is a willingness to express and accept differences.

As these are quite divergent conceptions, let us explore them further with an example. Bill, an employee, is talking with his boss in the boss's office. The boss says, "I think, Bill, that this is the best way to do your job." Bill says, "Oh yeah!" According to the first school of thought, this reply would be a sign of poor communication. Bill does not understand the best way of doing his work. To improve communication, therefore, it is up to the boss to explain to Bill why his way is the best.

From the point of view of the second school of thought, Bill's reply is a sign neither of good nor of bad communication. Bill's response is indeterminate. But the boss has an opportunity to find out what Bill means if he so desires. Let us assume that this is what he chooses to do, i.e., to find out what Bill means. So the boss tries to get Bill to talk more about his job while he (the boss) listens.

For purposes of simplification, I shall call the boss representing the first school of thought "Smith" and the boss representing the second school of thought "Jones." In the presence of the so-called same stimulus each behaves differently. Smith chooses to explain; Jones chooses to listen. In my experience Jones's response works better than Smith's. It works better because Jones is making a more proper evaluation of what is taking place between him and Bill than Smith is. Let us test this hypothesis by continuing with our example.

What Smith Assumes, Sees, and Feels

Smith assumes that he understands what Bill means when Bill says, "Oh yeah!" so there is no need to find out. Smith is sure that Bill does not understand why this is the best way to do his job, so Smith has to tell him. In this process let us assume Smith is logical, lucid, and clear. He presents his facts and evidence well. But, alas, Bill remains unconvinced. What does Smith do? Operating under the assumption that what is taking place between him and Bill is something essentially logical, Smith can draw only one of two conclusions: either (1) he has not been clear enough, or (2) Bill is too damned stupid to understand. So he either has to "spell out" his case in words of fewer and fewer syllables or give up. Smith is reluctant to do the latter, so he continues to explain. What happens?

If Bill still does not accept Smith's explanation of why this is the best way for him to do his job, a pattern of interacting feelings is produced of which Smith is often unaware. The more Smith cannot get Bill to understand him, the more frustrated Smith becomes and the more Bill becomes a threat to his logical capacity. Since Smith sees himself as a fairly reasonable and logical chap, this is a difficult feeling to accept. It is much easier for him to perceive Bill as uncooperative or stupid. This perception, however, will affect what Smith says and does. Under these pressures Bill comes to be evaluated more and more in terms of Smith's values. By this process Smith tends to treat Bill's values as unimportant. He tends to deny Bill's uniqueness and difference. He treats Bill as if he had little capacity for self-direction.

Let us be clear. Smith does not see that he is doing these things. When he is feverishly scratching hieroglyphics on the back of an envelope, trying to explain to Bill why this is the best way to do his job, Smith is trying to be helpful. He is a man of goodwill, and he wants to set Bill straight. This is the way Smith sees himself and his behavior. But it is for this very reason that Bill's "Oh yeah!" is getting under Smith's skin.

"How dumb can a guy be?" is Smith's attitude, and unfortunately Bill will hear that more than Smith's good intentions. Bill will feel misunderstood. He will not see Smith as a man of goodwill trying to be helpful. Rather he will perceive him as a threat to his self-esteem and personal integrity. Against this threat Bill will feel the need to defend himself at all cost. Not being so logically articulate as Smith, Bill expresses this need, again, by saying, "Oh yeah!"

What Jones Assumes, Sees, and Feels

Let us leave this sad scene between Smith and Bill, which I fear is going to terminate by Bill's either leaving in a huff or being kicked out of Smith's office. Let us turn for a moment to Jones and see what he is assuming, seeing, hearing, feeling, doing, and saying when he interacts with Bill.

Jones, it will be remembered, does not assume that he knows what Bill means when he says, "Oh yeah!" so he has to find out. Moreover, he assumes that when Bill said this, he had not exhausted his vocabulary or his feelings. Bill may not necessarily mean one thing; he may mean several different things. So Jones decides to listen.

In this process Jones is not under any illusion that what will take place will be eventually logical. Rather he is assuming that what will take place will be primarily an interaction of feelings. Therefore, he cannot ignore the feelings of Bill, the effect of Bill's feelings on him, or the effect of his feelings on Bill. In other words, he cannot ignore his relationship to Bill; he cannot assume that it will make no difference to what Bill will hear or accept.

Therefore, Jones will be paying strict attention to all of the things Smith has ignored. He will be addressing himself to Bill's feelings, his own feelings, and the interacions between them.

Jones will therefore realize that he has ruffled Bill's feelings with his comment, "I think, Bill, this is the best way to do your job." So instead of trying to get Bill to understand him he decides to try to understand Bill. He does this by encouraging Bill to speak. Instead of telling Bill how he should feel or think, he asks Bill such questions as, "Is this what you feel?" "Is this what you see?" "Is this what you assume?" Instead of ignoring Bill's evaluations as irrelevant, not valid, or inconsequential, or false, he tries to understand Bill's reality as he feels it, perceives it, and assumes it to be. As Bill begins to open up, Jones's curiosity is piqued by this process.

"Bill isn't so dumb; he's quite an interesting guy" becomes Jones's attitude. And that is what Bill hears. Therefore Bill feels understood and accepted as a person. He becomes less defensive. He is in a better frame of mind to explore and re-examine his own perceptions, feelings, and assumptions. In this process he perceives Jones as a source of help. Bill feels free to express his differences. He feels that Jones has some respect for his capacity for self-direction. These positive feelings toward Jones make Bill more inclined to say, "Well, Jones, I don't quite agree with you that this is the best way to do my job, but I'll tell you what I'll do. I'll try to do it that way for a few days, and then I'll tell you what I think."

Conclusion

I grant that my two orientations do not work themselves out in practice in quite so simple or neat a fashion as I have been able to work them out on paper. There are many other ways in which Bill could have responded to Smith in the first place. He might even have said, "O.K., boss, I agree that your way of doing my job is better." But Smith still would not have known how Bill felt when he made this statement or whether Bill was actually going to do his job differently. Likewise, Bill could have responded to Jones in a way different from my example. In spite of Jones's attitude, Bill might still be reluctant to express himself freely to his boss.

The purpose of my examples has not been to demonstrate the right or wrong way of communicating. My purpose has been simply to provide something concrete to point to when I make the following generalizations:

1. Smith represents to me a very common pattern of misunder-

standing. The misunderstanding does not arise because Smith is not clear enough in expressing himself. It arises because of Smith's misevaluation of what is taking place when two people are talking together.

2. Smith's misevaluation of the process of personal communication consists of certain very common assumptions, e.g. (*a*) that what is taking place is something essentially logical, (*b*) that words in themselves, apart from the people involved, mean something, and (*c*) that the purpose of the interaction is to get Bill to see things from Smith's point of view.

3. Because of these assumptions, a chain reaction of perceptions and negative feelings is engendered which blocks communication. By ignoring Bill's feelings and by rationalizing his own, Smith ignores his relationship to Bill as one of the most important determinants of the communication. As a result, Bill hears Smith's attitude more clearly than the logical content of Smith's words. Bill feels that his individual uniqueness is being denied. His personal integrity being at stake, he becomes defensive and belligerent. As a result, Smith feels frustrated. He perceives Bill as Stupid. So he says and does things which only provoke more defensiveness on the part of Bill.

4. In the case of Jones, I have tried to show what might possibly happen if we made a different evaluation of what is taking place when two people are talking together. Jones makes a different set of assumptions. He assumes (*a*) that what is taking place between him and Bill is an interaction of sentiments; (*b*) that Bill—not his words in themselves—means something; (*c*) that the object of the interaction is to give Bill an opportunity to express his differences freely.

5. Because of these assumptions, a psychological chain reaction of reinforcing feelings and perceptions is set up which facilitates communication between Bill and Smith. When Jones addresses himself to Bill's feelings and perceptions from Bill's point of view, Bill feels understood and accepted as a person; he feels free to express his differences. Bill sees Jones as a source of help; Jones sees Bill as an interesting person. Bill in turn becomes more cooperative.

6. If I have identified correctly these very common patterns of personal communication, then some interesting hypotheses can be stated:

a) Jones's method works better than Smith's, not because of any magic but because Jones has a better map than Smith of the process of personal communication.

b) The practice of Jones's method, however, is not merely an intellectual exercise. It depends on Jones's capacity and willingness to see and accept points of view different from his own, and to practice this orientation in a face-to-face relationship. This practice involves an emotional as well as an intellectual achievement. It depends in part on Jones's awareness of himself, in part on the practice of a skill.

c) Although our colleges and universities try to get students to intellectually appreciate points of view different from their own, very little is done to help them to implement this general intellectual appreciation in a simple face-to-face relationship—at the level of a skill. Most educational institutions train their students to be logical, lucid, and clear. Very little is done to help them to listen more skillfully. As a result, our educated world contains too many Smiths and too few Joneses.

d) The biggest block to personal communication is man's inability to listen intelligently, understandingly, and skillfully to another person. This deficiency in the modern world is widespread and appalling. In our universities, as well as elsewhere, too little is being done about it.

7. In conclusion, let me apologize for acting toward you the way Smith did. But who am I to violate a long-standing academic tradition!

Alvar O. Elbing

A Model for Viewing Decision Making in Interaction Situations from an Historical Perspective

Much of the theoretical analysis of the business community being done by business scholars is currently focused on decision makers, on the nature of decision, and on the decision-making process—especially on the complex process of decision making in interaction situations. Historically, however, it appears that the primary focus has

From *University of Washington Business Review*, June 1961, published by the Graduate School of Business Administration, University of Washington.

been on only two of these factors—decision makers and the nature of decisions—with little evaluation of the decision process, except for the general assumption of its rationality. Yet, as Susanne K. Langer indicates, "It is the mode of handling problems, rather than what they are about that assigns them to an age" (1942, p. 15). Although the problems involved in understanding the decision process in historical retrospect are numerous, such an analysis would offer considerable insight concerning both decisions and decision makers.

Robert Lindner, a well-known psychiatrist, has suggested that a psychological history of man is needed, for "history as it is ordinarily written takes little account of man's nature. It tends to ignore the instincts which energize his activities, the motives which power events, the strivings which make a current that bears people and races along the river of time. Generally, history is written from a point of view external to man" (1952, p. 146).

Certainly if such a chronicle of man's nature were available, the decision-making processes of history would be laid before us. In its absence, however, the historical decision-making process is still open to speculative analysis.

Purpose

The purpose of this article is to provide an approach to the historical analysis of interaction decision-making situations by proposing a broad framework or model within which the decision-making process can be viewed historically or recorded for the benefit of future generations. The model is designed to clarify the relationships among the numerous interacting factors and to indicate their position in the historical continuum. Recognizing that every past decision-making situation is historical, this analytical tool should be as valuable in considering current decision-making situations as it is in considering the decision-making situations of bygone years.

The focus in this article is on decisions which are made in interaction situations, in contrast to those which judiciously can be made unilaterally. The interaction decisions are those made in situations where two or more parties are negotiating, bargaining, or competing on an interpersonal or intergroup basis, and where, for the various parties, the decisions usually are not mutually exclusive events. In such situations, the decision of one party cannot be made independent of considering the decisions of the other party or parties. Certainly, all decisions involve a degree of interaction, but those of person-to-person interaction more clearly reflect the varying power relationships of the period. It is in these interaction decision situations that the decision-making process reveals the tone of the historical period, because the historical changes in mores concerning role relationships between parties, e.g., employer-employee, have been quite significant.

What Is a Model?

In attempting to understand a decision-making situation, it is evident immediately that many variables must be considered. There are many factors which influence the decision makers, the situation, and the process of decision making, of which the analyst must be constantly aware if he is to understand the particular decision-making process. In order to focus on as many of these variables as possible, a model of the decision-making process can be a useful frame of reference for analysis.

Aid to Analysis

Although a decision-making model is stated in symbolic terms, its use is not inherently different from the use of a physical model or mock-up in the design of an airplane or automobile. In such a case, a small-scale physical replica is generally prepared before production of the actual item. By incorporating many of the features of the finished product in the physical model, the design can be analyzed and observed under conditions similar to those which would be encountered by the full-sized finished product. Yet the analysis can be performed at considerably less than the cost of attempting to work out the problems directly in the concrete situation without previous analysis. Thus, if a person views a decision-making situation through the framework of a model, it may aid him in keeping in mind the many variables influencing the situation so that the analysis will be more complete, yet be less costly in time and effort.

Model Limitations

It should be kept in mind that, just as a physical model cannot encompass all of the features of the full-scale item, the decision-making model can never include all of the variables influencing a given situation. It can, however, enable the analyst to focus his attention on the important variables and give him a framework in which to make his analysis. The model presented here is just such a symbolic representation of the "real" situation and attempts to aid the observer in focusing on the significant variables in the interaction decision-making process.

Criteria for the Construction of a Model

In constructing a model, certain necessary criteria are set up which ought to be met if the model is to be useful in interrelating numerous variables in a meaningful way.

The Period under Consideration

The model should convey the period under consideration in relation to other historical vantage points, as well as in terms of the insights of the period of the observer. As Susanne K. Langer points out in *Philosophy in a New Key*, a historical period should be viewed in terms of the questions which were important to the period and in terms of the approaches to the questions—not just in terms of the answers to the questions. Our first criterion, then, is that the decision-making process, or the questions which were raised while making the decision, be couched in terms of the historical era rather than merely in terms of the criteria of today—that the situation be viewed in terms of the "setting" of the period rather than solely in terms of the categorizations of events made meaningful by subsequent events.

The Vantage Points of the Parties

The second criterion is that the framework convey the separate vantage points of the two parties in the interaction situation. This would necessitate attempting to separate the views or perceptions of the various parties from the situation itself. The ways in which each party perceives or anticipates the situation will differ, and these different perceptions become part of the situation. George Kelly describes this in his paper, "Man's Construction of His Alternatives":

> If we want to know why man does what he does, then the terms of our whys should extend themselves in time rather than in space; they should be events rather than things; they should be mileposts rather than destinations. . . .
>
> We can say it this way: *A person's processes are psychologically channelized by the ways in which he anticipates events* (1958, p. 56).

Thus, the mental sets resulting from anticipations, which guide the processes of the interacting parties, should be included in the model.

Factors Not Observable by Participants

The model of interaction decision-making situations must also include factors which play a part in that situation, but which are not seen by either of the individual participants through their frames of references. Environmental factors play a part in every interaction decision situation, and though the participants are aware of some of these factors, others can be perceived only from a broader vantage point, either chronologically or geographically. Others we can assume to exist, though they may not yet be recognizable from any known vantage point; the model should show such undiscovered frontiers of data in the interaction decision situation as well.

In light of these general criteria, let us look at the constructed model within which interaction decision-making situations may be viewed historically.

Model

Figure 1 is a paradigmatic representation of an interaction decision situation. The problem is represented by the square, *ABCD*. The

Figure 1   A Model for Viewing Decision Making in Interaction Situations from an Historical Perspective

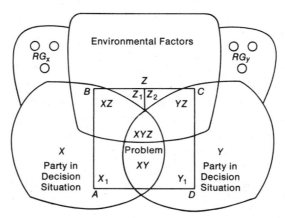

xz	Alternatives perceived by *X* and acceptable in the existing environment	z_1 Socially acceptable alternatives not perceived by the parties in the situation
yz	Alternatives perceived by *Y* and acceptable in the existing environment	z_2 Alternatives not perceivable at that time
xy	Alternatives perceived by both *X* and *Y* but *not* acceptable in the environment	*xyz* Alternatives perceived by both parties and acceptable in the environment
$x_1 y_1$	Alternatives perceived by one party but *not* acceptable in the environment	RG_x Reference groups for party *X* RG_y Reference groups for party *Y*

parties in the situation, *X* and *Y*, are represented by two large areas which are not concentric, but which overlap somewhat in the area of the problem. Thus, the area *X* is the total psychological make-up of one individual, his frame of reference, or what the German's would call his *Weltanschauung*. Area *Y* stands for the other party's frame of reference and how it differs in regard to the interaction decision-making process. The restriction of each individual's perceptual processes is shown by the fact that each one's perception of the problem, *ABCD*, differs and that their frames of reference overlap in only part of the problem area.

Individual Perception

The problem, labeled *ABCD*, is partially covered by the various individual perceptions, but as this model indicates, there may be more than one explicit problem as such. Here the model raises the question: When X and Y perceive the problem area differently, can we successfully refer to "the" problem as extending beyond their perceptions? It was found to be useful to include a hypothetical area of the problem, beyond the perceptions of the individuals involved, because this visual representation allows the observer to keep in mind the limitations of human perception and its selective effects.

At this point the model appears to have satisfied the first and second criteria, in that it points to the problem as perceived by the individuals, and focuses on their views, or on their questions, concerning the problem.

Environmental Factors

A third factor, besides X and Y, which enters all interaction decision relationships is what we can consider the environmental forces, labeled Z in the model. This general, rather inclusive area is meant to represent all the social, political, and economic conditions existing at the time of the situation being analyzed, which determine the boundaries of possible decision alternatives. It is intended to include the concept of socially acceptable behavior, since this concept influences the ability of the parties to perceive the alternatives in the decision situation. How the individuals perceive this environment determines, to a considerable degree, how they are able to view their particular problem situation.

Social Factors

This area of the model, representing social factors, is considered in two parts, which are represented by z_1 and z_2. One part, z_1, is perceivable by the participants, though each individual's awareness of these conditions may not be the same as another's, since the same information is not available to all, and, also, the structural effect of each individual's frame of reference differs. Although the environmental factors may be considered apart from the decision-making situation, their perception by the parties determines the degree to which they are brought into the decision situation.

Historical Retrospect

The other part of area Z, part z_2, is the section unavailable to the parties in the decision situation. These are factors which are influencing the situation, but which become understandable only from a different point of historical time, location, or psychological vantage. Sometimes it is only in historical retrospect that we are aware of some of these factors and the influence they had on the particular situation. In some instances they amounted to alternatives of which the parties were unaware, but which were potentially acceptable solutions. This section of the model appears to satisfy the third criterion.

Reference Groups

At this point, while discussing the influence of the environmental factors, it is important to point out that they influence not only the problem situation and the manner in which it can be perceived but also influence the individual's entire personality. This influence is shown in the model as operating through groups of which the individuals are members, or through groups to which the individuals refer. In the diagram, this influence is represented by RG_x and RG_y, which reflect the reference group identifications of the individuals and their influence on the decision-making situation.

Norms and Values

The findings of social psychology suggest that individual attitudes and resulting behavior reflect the norms and values of groups to which the individuals refer.[1] The norms and values of these reference groups, therefore, amount to one additional influence upon an individual's view of the decision-making situation. In any particular situation an individual will tend to react in terms of the reference group which he perceives as most relevant to that situation. Although a number of groups' norms may be appropriate, his behavior will reflect the influence of the one group which dominates him under the particular situation. We see here, then, a two-way action: (1) the individual perceives and reacts to a situation in terms of the norms of the most relevant reference group, while (2) his reference groups determine how he can perceive the situation.

The influence of reference groups is shown as a connection between the environment in which the groups exist and the individuals whose behavior reflects group norms. It should be noticed that all of the circles do not extend from the environment (Z) because groups to which individuals refer may not all be "real" groups. An individual may respond to what he perceives to be the norms of a group which is merely conceptual, not having a referent in the real world.[2]

Implications of the Model

Having defined the various influences in the interaction decision-making situation, let us consider the manner in which the two parties, X and Y, overlap in the area of the problem. The decisions in

---

1. For a more detailed discussion of reference groups, see Sherif and Sherif (1956), p. 175, or Newcomb (1950), Ch. 7.
2. For more information on conceptual groups, see Sherif and Sherif (*op. cit.*), Ch. 18.

such an interaction situation are contingent upon the individual's perceptions of the alternatives available to them. The model shows the various categories into which these alternatives fall. This breakdown, however, does not suggest that the individual rationally views all of the alternative courses of action before choosing one. We do see, however, that no decision is considered an alternative unless it is perceived as being one, and that some alternatives are so readily perceivable that they tend to be chosen over less perceivable ones.

Viewing the model, then, we see that party X in the decision situation perceives the possible solutions to the problem as including the alternatives which would fall into section x_1, xy, xz, and xyz. Party Y perceives the possible solutions to the problem as including alternatives y_1, xy, yz, and xyz. At the same time, the environment limits the possible solutions to the alternatives in sections z_1, xz, yz, and xyz. (As noted above, alternatives z_2 are not perceivable under the conditions of the period.) Suggesting that the environment or the "external conditions" do not include all of what are perceived as alternatives is not meant to minimize the importance of sections x_1, y_1, and xy. If, as suggested above, individuals perceive these to be alternatives, then truly they are a part of the problem for the individual.

According to this model, party X in the decision situation perceives the alternatives x_1 as being pertinent to the problem, while they are not observed as such by Y, nor were they socially acceptable alternatives at that time (Z). Alternatives xz are perceived by party X and are socially acceptable, but are not perceived as acceptable alternatives by party Y. Alternatives xy are jointly perceived by X and Y, but are not socially acceptable or functional, or are not environmentally possible. Therefore, unless the parties are powerful enough to change or ignore society, these are not alternatives. Alternatives xyz are viewed as acceptable by both parties and are environmentally possible. Viewing the situation from the standpoint of party Y, the corresponding analysis would hold. The alternatives z_1 are socially functional alternatives, not perceived as such by either party. They are, in effect, alternatives which would be functional in the existing environment, but which are not perceived as such by the parties.

In the negotiation for a solution to a particular problem, therefore, alternatives xyz are the alternatives acceptable to the parties in the existing social framework. This assumes, of course, that the parties are of comparable power in the relationship, which is not always the case. Should one party—for example, Y—be able to exert more socially acceptable power, the solution may come from alternatives yz, alternatives not perceived as acceptable by party X, but forced upon him.

Illustrative Application of the Model

Although the major function of this model has been to serve as an aid in conceptualizing the decision-making process in interaction situations from an historical perspective, it may also be useful to consider briefly a hypothetical situation, in terms of the model, as an example of the approach one might take in analyzing such a process.

It should be kept in mind, however, that the primary value of such a model is that of an analytical tool to assist in focusing on significant factors in an interaction relationship. It should also be remembered that the model is not intended to serve as a rigid structure into which various factors can be placed and a solution automatically found. Being cognizant of the dangers of oversimplification, then, let us consider an employer-employee relationship in the early history of this country as an example of how the model might aid a person in his analysis of that relationship.

Background of Problem

It is known that during the early 19th century wages were relatively low in manufacturing and that, as a consequence, the frontier opportunities appeared attractive to many industrial workers —especially to many of the recent immigrants. On the basis of this fact, we can immediately see two broad possibilities for the workers: (1) to stay in industrial employment under some set of desirable or undesirable conditions, or (2) to move to the frontier where uncertainty, yet potential or opportunity, existed. (Other alternatives such as returning to Europe were available also, but for simplicity only these two will be considered in this example.) Looking at this situation in terms of the model, then, we can attempt to reconstruct the problem as perceived by the two parties.

What Was the Problem?

As seen by the worker, the problem appears to have been something like "How can I receive an income large enough to support my family, and yet retain the freedom which I came to this country to obtain?" At the same time, the employer possibly saw the problem as "How can I pay a wage adequate to maintain a work force, yet retain profits large enough to compensate me for my risks and position, protect myself against hard times, and keep the worker in his proper place in society?" It is immediately apparent that if the problem is thus differently perceived by the two parties, probably the alternative solutions for the two parties also were perceived differently.

Perhaps, therefore, the chief value of the application of this model is that it focuses attention on the problem as it was perceived differently by the two parties, rather than misleading us into thinking that both parties defined the crisis situation in the same terms. The emphasis on a single or absolute definition of the problem fails to consider all of the aspects of the perceived situation which are influencing the parties in the situation. In this example, then, what factors might influence the two parties' views of the problem?

The Employee

In the early 19th century, the employee was in an environment which had real and perceived boundaries for him in terms of religious codes, legal restraints, his societal position, and the free-enterprise economic philosophy, etc., to mention just a few. These factors influenced the alternative solutions available to him, and at the same time his perception of these factors influenced his ability to deal with the alternatives.

A part of this environment for the individual consisted of a number of groups whose norms strongly influenced his behavior. He was, for example, a member of two families, both his wife and children, and his parents, whom he left in Europe; he was a member of a community, a church, an ethnic group, and a work force, as well as a "member" of the United States. The norms of those groups which were most important to him under particular conditions strongly influenced his behavior in those situations. Therefore, not only was his behavior a function of the larger environmental context, it was channeled by these group identifications.

The Employer

The same factors held true, in general, for the employer, but of course the pressures and influences were different from those operating on the employee. Some of the broad environmental forces were similar for both the employee and the employer, but the employer's different perceptions of these forces and his group identifications directed his willingness and ability to utilize the alternatives. Other factors in the environment were *actually* different, and these differences also influenced the availability of mutually acceptable alternatives.

Alternatives

Considering our problem area as being that of the acceptability of wages in early industrial America, it is possible that a crisis or decision situation could have arisen when an employee asked for an increase in his wages. Utilizing the model as a framework for viewing the various alternatives, this process can be analyzed in terms of the differing acceptability of the various alternative solutions for the parties. (To simplify the discussion, the number of specific alternatives within the two broad alternatives stated above will be limited to eleven. However, these alternatives are only examples and are not an exhaustive list.)

Wage or benefit increase. The alternatives shown in Table 1 include three possible increases in wages—slight, moderate, or substantial; the maintenance of the status quo; and a reduction in wages. Also included are three possible increases in worker benefits which could include such things as housing furnished by the employer; the use of the employer's land on which to grow food; or other methods of increasing the employee's standard of living. The final alternatives are for the worker to leave the job for another job, to leave the job for the frontier, or to band together with other workers into a union or other form of collective action.

Table 1   The Categorization of Alternative Solutions to a Hypothetical Problem Concerning a Wage Increase

Alternative	Acceptability to Parties				Category of Acceptability			Retrospect
	x_1	y_1	z_1	xz	yz	xy	xyz	z_2
Increase wages slightly	U	A	A		✓			A
Increase wages moderately	A	U	A	✓				A
Increase wages substantially	U	U	U					A
No change in wages	U	A	A		✓			A
Lower wages	U	A	U[a]					U[a]
Nonmonetary benefits:								
Small	U	A	A		✓			A
Moderate	A	U	A	✓				A
Substantial	U	U	U[b]					A
Leave job for new job	U	A	A		✓			A
Leave job for the frontier	A	A	A				✓	A
Band together (unions)	A	U	U					A

A Acceptable; U Unacceptable
(See figure 1 for meaning of x_1, y_1, etc.)
a) Unacceptable if wages are already at a near starvation level.
b) Total support of the individual by the employer probably would not have been compatible with the economic system.

Acceptability. From the model, it can be seen that, depending upon the availability of new workers, a slight wage increase might be acceptable to the employer (y_1), and there may be no environmental restrictions (z_1), so that the alternative would fall into category *yz*. At the same time, if the increase was not perceived by the employee as large enough to make a difference, and if the employer was not powerful enough to force the employee to accept this alternative, it would not be a mutually acceptable solution to the problem. On the other hand, a moderate increase might be acceptable to the employee (x_1) and there also might be no environmental restrictions (z_1), so that the alternative would fall into category xz. But if not acceptable to the employer, it also would not solve the problem. A large wage increase might have appeared entirely improper at the time, from the standpoint of all parties, because even the employee may not have considered this appropriate under the existing religious, political, or economic philosophy. In restrospect (z_2), however, we can see that perhaps greater purchasing power at certain times, and under certain conditions, would have been beneficial for all parties. This alternative may not have been perceived as acceptable in the environment of the time, however.

Each of the alternative solutions could similarly be analyzed as suggested in Table 1, in which, for example, it is suggested that the employee leaving for the frontier may have been an acceptable solution from the standpoint of all parties concerned. In this example, in fact, it may have been the *only* acceptable solution from the parties' standpoints (xyz). If other alternatives had also fallen into the xyz category, e.g., if there had been an overlap between the employer's and the employee's perception of an acceptable wage, then some other factors would have entered in to influence the ultimate decision.

Although the example was set in an early historical context, the same analytical process could be used on the same type of problem situation in more recent times. Certainly the perception of the problem of wage adjustments, as well as the alternative solutions available, would differ from those of 150 years ago. But the process of analysis would not be significantly different.

More than Two People

Although this model was constructed to diagrammatically relate two parties in a decision situation, a similar representation could be made for a larger group, such as a committee. It takes but a little imagination to envision the rapidly increasing complexity of such situations.

Conclusion

This model contributes to the establishment of an historically relative vantage point for viewing interaction decision-making processes in that it differentiates individual frames of reference from any absolute conception of the problem. Any problem stated in absolute fashion has no historical context. However, as soon as we indicate individual frames of reference as structuring and limiting the problem, the factor of historical relativity enters into the concept. The frame of reference of any individual in any historical period is bound to be circumscribed by that historical period. His frame of reference can extend no further than the concepts, assumptions, norms, methods, etc., available in his own day. By clearly differentiating the individual frame of reference from the theoretical problem and from the totality of environmental data, we are indicating historical limitations on perceptions available to him.

The model is also useful in helping us to view the process historically in that the data included in the model may be developed indefinitely through historical time, i.e., we may continue to add, restructure, reanalyze, and resynthesize environmental data as long as new data, methods, or theories are discovered. Yet historical relativity continues to be maintained since the individual's frame of reference indicated in the model remains circumscribed by his historical period.

References

Kelly, George A. "Man's Construction of His Alternatives." In *Assessment of Human Motives,* ed. Gardner Lindzey. Holt, Rinehart & Winston, 1958.

Langer, Susanne K. *Philosophy in a New Key.* Harvard University Press, 1942.

Lindner, Robert. *Prescription for Rebellion.* Holt, Rinehart & Winston, 1952.

Group and Intergroup Behavior

Muzafer Sherif

Group Formation

Groups are composed of individuals. But when and how does a collection of individuals become a group? The phrase "group formation" suggests that something is formed. The task here is to trace the appearance of essential properties, or characteristics, which distinguish a human group.

Both for theory and research, it is instructive to adopt the strategy of tracing the formation of informal groups, rather than those instituted formally through blueprints handed down by outside authority (such as a committee or board). Despite the limitation in considering groups formed through the interaction of the membership, the implications are broad. Many social institutions and formal organizations (including governments) had informal beginnings if one goes into their histories. Informal groups are found almost invariably within stable formal structures, such as industrial, commercial, political, educational, religious, military, and recreational organizations. Finally, informal groups possess the minimum of the essential characteristics of any organized association, whether large or small.

Reprinted with permission of the publisher from the *International Encyclopedia of the Social Sciences*, David L. Sills, ed., Vol. 6, pages 276–283. Copyright © 1968 by Crowell Collier and Macmillan, Inc.

Background

The properties characterizing the formation of a group were treated by the 19th-century social philosophers for various reasons and with varying emphasis, each using illustrative examples known to him. But the topic was doomed to controversy until data were collected through scientific methods.

In the 1920s, Robert E. Park of the University of Chicago inspired and directed a series of investigations on human groups and their relationships to their settings (for example, Thrasher, 1927, Landesco, 1929, Shaw, 1929, Zorbaugh, 1929). Initiated to deal with the dire problem of homeless and antisocial children, the work of the Soviet educator Makarenko included concrete data on the formation of group properties, which he gradually came to regard as crucial conditions for the effectiveness of his educational efforts (Makarenko, 1955, Bowen, 1962).

In the thirties, under the impetus of Elton Mayo of the Harvard Business School, studies in Western Electric's Hawthorne plant revealed the rise of groups and their impact upon the behavior of workers who had been placed together in observation rooms initially for the purpose of studying the effects of varying illumination and rest periods (Roethlisberger and Dickson, 1939). J. L. Moreno (1934) and his co-workers began the systematic sociometric mapping of friendship choices among girls in reformatory cottages and children in classrooms. Using the methods of laboratory psychology, Sherif (1939) tested sociological theories on the formation of social norms in situations of ambiguity and instability, demonstrating their subsequent retention as personal standards when individuals were alone. Lewin and his students (1939) initiated experiments varying the manner of adult supervisors of children's clubs. Meanwhile, the failures of "personality" or "intelligence" tests for selecting military leaders led the military in several countries to sponsor studies of what came to be called "leaderless groups" (Gibb, 1954, OSS, 1948).

Defining the Properties of What Is Formed

The definition presented here includes only the minimum properties found essential through extensive surveys of empirical and theoretical literature on groups of all kinds (Sherif, 1948, Sherif and Cantril, 1947, Sherif and Sherif, 1956).

Definition

A group is a social unit consisting of a number of individuals who stand in status and role relationships to one another, stabilized in some degree at a given time, and who possess a set of values or norms regulating their behavior, at least in matters of consequence to the group.

By this definition, the "groupness" of a group is a matter of degree. A collection of persons forms into a group proportional to (a) the degree of the stability of its organization (consisting of roles and status relations) and (b) the degree to which its particular set of norms for behavior are shared and binding for the participants. The undefined terms in the definition (role, status, norms) will be specified through research operations with conceptual relationship to the process of group formation.

It should be noted that this definition includes the properties covered in many modern works, while excluding others. Similar specifications are found in Bales (1949); Blau and Scott (1962), Bonner (1959), Cartwright and Zander (1960), Golembiewski (1962), and Hare (1962). The following characteristics, included by some investigators, were omitted here for the following reasons:

Interaction and *communication* are not distinctive to group formation but are essential to any kind of human association of consequence. *Shared sentiments, attitudes* and *behavior patterns* of group members are implied in the normative property; in fact the extent of sharing is one of the research measures for the degree of group formation at a given time. Many properties of existing groups (for example, *morale, solidarity* or *cohesiveness, loyalty* of members) are dependent upon the conditions of group formation, especially the degree of stability attained.

The properties essential in group formation will aid the reader in evaluating the large body of experimental research on small groups conducted both in the United States and in Europe since World War II. In summarizing this literature, Golembiewski (1962, p. 47) found that the great majority consisted of unknown persons in the laboratory briefly exposed to tasks or instructions creating temporary interdependence among individuals in their performance. Very few studies have allowed a sufficient time span for group properties to form.

Generality of Group Formation

Beneath the organized forms and routines of societies, the formation and disintegration of groups occurs in all walks of life, frequently with important consequences. Informal group formation is well documented within industrial, military, school, prison, and neighborhood settings (see Hare, 1962, Sherif and Sherif, 1956). In studying the Near North Side of Chicago, Zorbaugh (1929, p. 192) reported group formations in neighborhoods of all socioeconomic ranks with "an enormously important role in the lives of their members": exclusive clubs in the fashionable "Gold Coast," intimate groups of "nonconformists" in artists' studios, mutual benefit societies in foreign colonies, "gangs" in slum areas, cults and sects in the rooming house district.

The extensive documentation on the generality of group formation also shows the striking dependence of the process on other groups, on the material and ideational features and facilities of the environment. The process of group formation is not insulated by the bounds of the membership. The formation which results is not a closed system. The circumstances bringing individuals together initially, their motives in continuing to interact, the particular organization and norms that develop, and the degree of their stability are inevitably dependent upon the environmental circumstances and their stability or change. Included in the environmental circumstances are other groups whose activities and aims impinge favorably or unfavorably upon those of the group in formation.

Four Essentials in the Process of Group Formation

Starting with the initial conditions for interaction among individuals, the essentials of group formation can now be traced. The encounter with another person is the most elementary social situation. Even the mere presence of other persons has consequential effects on behavior and task performance. From the time when individuals are merely together to the time when the properties of a group begin to appear, we see that the consequential effects on behavior begin to assume regularities. As time goes on, these regularities reflect patterns which are the organizational and normative properties of the group. Accordingly, the essentials in the process of group formation are the following:

1. A motivational base conducive to repeated interaction.
2. Formation of an organization (structure), consisting of roles and statuses.
3. Formation of rules, traditions, values or norms.
4. Differential effects of the group properties on the attitude and behavior of participants over time.

Motivational Base

Any human motive, frustration, problem or desired goal which an individual cannot handle effectively alone is conducive to his interaction with others who are seen in the same plight. The prerequisite for group formation is that persons with motives conducive to initial interaction have the opportunity over time to recognize the concerns they share, or reciprocate, and to attempt to deal with them in concert.

The common motive faced in initial stages of interaction may be one or several of those found in any society, for example, hunger, sexual desire, desire for recognition or power in some respect, fear or anxiety in the face of threat. They may be culturally defined, for example, desire for material possessions, prestige through particular activities, or pursuit of political goals. Here only a few points can be considered.

The common problem, motive, or goal conducive to repeated interactions is necessarily dependent on environmental circumstances, both in its occurrence and in attempts to deal with it. Whatever its nature, the motivational base for group formation invariably affects the activities and tasks engaged in by members, and the kinds of personal qualities which become prized by them. When a set of norms forms, those most binding are typically related to the motives or problems which initially brought the persons together. One reason why many controversies over problems of conformity-nonconformity are inconclusive is that many theorists pay scant attention to the relationship between the particular norms of a group and the initial motivational base underlying them.

However, to the degree that group formation achieves a degree of stability over time, new sources of motivation and new goals are generated among the members. They may even take precedence over those bringing the members together. Thus, the hungry person may refrain from eating until he can share with his starving fellows; the politician may spurn an advantageous political bargain out of loyalty to his supporters; the member of a group struggling for equal opportunity and freedom from fear may undergo great deprivation and bodily injury to secure recognition of his group.

Formation of Organization or Structure

Over a period of time as individuals interact in activities related to the common problems which brought them together, their behavior and their expectations for each other's behavior assume regularities from which a pattern can be constructed. Here we shall define certain features of these regularities which appear to be crucial in any group formation. Heavy reliance will be placed upon findings from three experiments on group formation and relations between groups, each lasting several weeks (summarized in Sherif and Sherif, 1956, chs. 6 and 9, and in Sherif, 1966), and from more recent studies of naturally formed groups (Sherif and Sherif, 1964). The experiments started in each case with unacquainted persons divided into collections of ten to twelve as similar as possible in composition. All of these studies were conducted under naturalistic conditions, and data were collected without the constant awareness by the individuals that they were being investigated.

The development of organization has been defined in terms of role and status relationships among a number of individuals. *Role* denotes reciprocities in the treatments and expectations of individuals, each for the others. Unlike well-defined occupational or sex roles, definite prescriptions for behavior are lacking when unacquainted persons first meet. Reciprocities among them must be built on the basis of performance in the activities engaged in, the reactions of others to the person, and his reactions to them. The typical finding at early stages of interaction is that individual contributions to task performance differ from one activity to the next (OSS, 1948, Gibb, 1954). Thus, observers rating behavior in the different situations find that the degree of participation and prominence of the individuals differs from one task to the next, according to the individual differences in skills, abilities, temperament, or physical resources and tools, relative to the activities in question.

The single, most salient feature of group formation is that, over time, the various member roles become differentiated, not merely with regard to task performance or personal qualities, but according to the evaluation of the roles by the members. Members are accorded differing degrees of prestige and respect by their fellows. The member roles acquire differences in the relative *power* of individuals to initiate and control activities important to them all.

A member's position (rank) in a developing power structure is his *status* in the group, defined in terms of the relative effectiveness of his actions in initiating activities, making or approving decisions affecting the group, coordinating interaction, and invoking correctives for deviation.

Power, defined as effective initiative, is not identical with influence, in the limited sense that Person A affects the actions of Person B. Influence of this kind may occur with little or no relation to the effectiveness of Person A's actions in the group. Power is implemented with sanctions, while influence is not.

Status (rank in power) is not identical with popularity or the degree to which the person is liked. In fact, status and popularity may be poorly correlated (see Hare, 1962, p. 115; Sherif and Sherif, 1964, ch. 6). Nor should status be confused with the use of force or aggression. As Whyte (1943) showed, even in a street corner group whose members valued masculine toughness, the best potential fighter was not necessarily highest in status. Status was rooted in "mutual obligations" incurred among them over time and the reliability with which a member lived up to his obligations.

Since it is defined as effective initiative, status in a group is necessarily hierarchical. The highest status represents the leadership role. Especially in societies or situations where social equality is emphasized, the operational leader, defined by observation of his effectiveness over time, may not be designated openly as "leader" by the members.

Figure 1   Gradations of Organization Structure

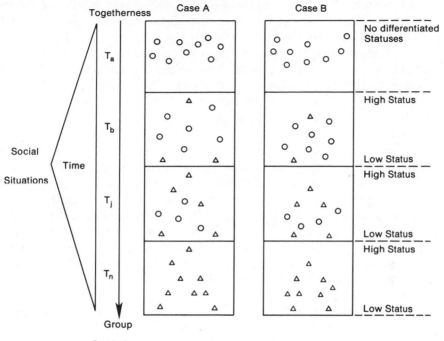

Symbols:
O   Individual whose status is not yet stabilized
△   Individual whose status is stabilized

Figure 1 is a diagram of the stabilization of statuses, based on experimental findings for six groups. At the top (*time a*) the individuals in two collections have first encountered one another. The circles represent the individuals and indicate that, at this time, independent observers do not agree from one situation to the next on regularities in the relationships among them. Instead, their ratings of effective initiative are different in various activities.

Just below, at *time b,* the observers' ratings begin to agree (from one activity to the next and from one day to the next) that the highest and lowest positions (represented by triangles) are stabilized. Both in the experiments and in real-life groups, the leader position typically stabilizes earlier than other high positions. This does not imply that group formation consists of the "search for a leader." On the contrary, leadership is subject to change. As Hofstatter correctly pointed out (1957, esp. p. 24), tracing group organization over time is necessary to clear up many glib formulae propagated without sufficient evidence.

At *time j* in the figure, observers are able to agree on the positions most members occupy, except in the middle of the diagram. Again, this is a typical finding. In part, it reflects attempts by those in the middle to improve their standing or to align themselves with those higher in status. At *time n* in the diagram, the status relationships are stabilized, all observers agreeing on the status structure which is also revealed in a member's perceptions of it.

The diagram is intended to be representative. The different patterns of status in the two groups are intended to suggest that there is no predetermined form to the "steepness" or "flatness" of the hierarchy. Group formation represents an ideal occasion to study factors affecting the organization of groups, but little research has been done on this problem.

The rate of stabilization varies. In the experiments, the groups stabilized within about a week of continuous living together. Other investigators have reported the discernible beginnings of group structure among individuals meeting in the same location in similar activities within three to five meetings of a few hours' duration (Merei, 1949; Blake, Shepard, and Mouton, 1964). Environmental events are equally as important as internal events in affecting the speed of stabilization. The stability of the pattern is sensitive to the introduction of new members, to changes in location and facilities, and to outside threat or emergency.

In particular, the stabilization of group structure is never independent of the relationships with other groups. Prolonged competition between groups for mutually incompatible goals is particularly effective in quickly stabilizing a structure. Important intergroup confrontations, especially those resulting in defeat or humiliation, produce changes in the internal organization of a group (Sherif, 1966).

The leader of a group is, though most powerful, still a member subject to loss of status. When the group structure is stabilized in some degree for the time being, no person within it is free to ignore its regulation. It defines for its members the bounds of "we" or the in-group, as compared to others who are not members. If sufficiently stabilized, the group can continue after a leader's departure with little disruption (see Toki, 1935). This persistence of a group structure and the effects of the group even on the leader are clearer in terms of the normative property of group formation.

Formation of Group Norms

As a group structure takes shape, members come to prefer certain ways of going about their important activities. They may adopt a group name. They set up standards for the ways members should and should not behave among themselves and with outsiders. The term "norm" is a general term to refer to such products of interaction producing regularities in attitude and behavior among members.

Unlike the norm on an examination, a group norm does not, necessarily, refer to the average of individual behaviors. It designates what is expected as proper, as moral, or even as ideal. Yet a group norm seldom denotes a single action as the only way to behave. A range for individual variations is permissible in any group. A norm denotes the range of behaviors which members come to deem as socially desirable and acceptable (latitude of acceptance) and a range of behaviors condemned as objectionable (latitude of rejection).

A norm is defined, therefore, as an evaluative scale (a measuring rod), defining for individual members a latitude of acceptance and a latitude of rejection, to regulate their behavior in matters of consequence to the group (Sherif, Sherif, and Nebergall, 1965). Not all social behavior is regulated by clear-cut norms, particularly when groups are in formation.

How can a group norm be detected? There are at least three objective ways:

1. By observing similarities and regularities in the behaviors (words and deeds) which are found among one set of persons but not another set in a similar situation.
2. By observing correctives (sanctions) for certain behaviors and praise or reward for others. Reactions to deviations are among the best evidence of the bounds of acceptable behavior. These may range from disapproval and frown correctives to threats and actual punishment.
3. By noting the increasing similarity or convergence over time in the behaviors of individuals who initially behaved differently. For example, the entrance of a new member into a group provides an opportunity to detect the existence of its norms.

When groups are in the process of formation, as in the experiments, one of the best indicators of the tability is the degree of consensus among members on the correctness of their norms, and the degree to which the latitude of acceptance is binding without direct social pressure or threat of sanctions. Stabilization of the set of norms is indicated when members privately regulate their own behavior within the latitude of acceptance. The person's own conception of how he should behave and how others should act comes to fall within bounds defined by the norms. Especially when the individual has had a part in creating the norms as a group member, they become aspects of his self-concept relative to others. He experiences personal guilt or shame if he violates them.

The personal acceptance of group norms during group formation accounts in large measure for the tenacity of tradition once established. Merei (1949) demonstrated this tenacity by permitting play groups to develop procedures and rules, then introducing a new child who was older and had evidenced leadership skills in other situations.

Sherif and Sherif (1964) present evidence that the stringency of norms and resistance to their change varies according to the importance of the norm for the group. Violations in major activities, in dealings with outsiders, exposure of group secrets, or otherwise jeopardizing the maintenance of the group were unerringly responded to by strong sanctions, such as expulsion, threat, or physical punishment. Even leaders whose actions exposed the group or its members to humiliation, embarrassment, or danger were chastised.

In less important activities, the range of tolerance for individual differences was much wider, particularly for the leader and higher-status members. In matters of daily routine or amusement strictly within the group, leaders were free to innovate and sometimes engaged in behavior which would not have been tolerated from lesser members. In these fairly stable groups, the great bulk of conforming behavior occurred without direct social pressure or threat of sanctions, particularly behavior by members of moderate or high status.

Differential Effects of Group Formation on Member Attitude and Behavior

The formation of a group structure and norms has consequences for the attitude and behavior of individuals within its fold. These consequences may be referred to as the differential effects of group formation.

Any social situation provides a context for behavior which differs from a solitary situation. The context includes other people present, the activities and tasks undertaken, the physical site and its facilities, and the person's relationship to all of these. Experiments have repeatedly shown the differential effects of different aspects of the social context on behavior, compared to behavior alone.

The formation of a role system and norms during interaction among persons, over time, brings about alterations in the relative contribution of the task, activity, setting, and individual reactions. When the persons without stabilized reciprocities are at first simply *together*, their personal characteristics and skills relative to the tasks and those of other people are important determinants of behavior (Gibb, 1954; Hare, 1962). As the process of group formation starts taking shape, the developing organizational and normative schemes become more and more binding for members. As a result, over time, characteristics of the task, and the location—in short, immediate situational factors—recede in relative importance and behavior increasingly reflects the person's role in the group, the roles of others, and the emerging norms.

The group formation experiments (Sherif and Sherif, 1956, chs.

6 and 9) traced the development of a "we-feeling," such that socio-metric friendship choices became almost exclusively concentrated within the group, even though initial choices before group formation had been given predominantly to persons placed (deliberately) in another group. In one experiment, it was shown that estimates made by members of each other's performance became significantly related to the member's status, the relationship being closer when the structure was more stable. Performance by high-status members was over-estimated, that of low status persons was minimized.

In another experiment, the groups formed separately, then competed for a series of mutually exclusive goals. As predicted, norms developed in each group justifying hostility to the other group. The performance by members of the other group in a novel task was estimated to be significantly lower than performance by members of the in-group, revealing the prejudicial norm in the judgments of individual members (Sherif, *et al.*, 1961).

Proportional to the significance of a particular group in a person's life, the impact of his membership in determining his attitude and behavior increases. As the group formation stabilizes, his sense of identity becomes tied to being a member of that group, proportional to its scope and importance in his daily living. For this reason, the socialization of the person is incompletely described only by reference to his acquisition of formal prescriptions from family, school, and other official institutions. From early childhood through adolescence, groups formed among age-mates exert compelling impact upon the person's conceptions of what is desirable for him, what is acceptable in others, and what is right and wrong (Campbell, 1964; Sherif and Sherif, 1964). In other words, they become aspects of his own conscience.

Recognition of the consequences for self-concepts and attitudes of participants has led to attempts in various countries to utilize group formation for corrective and therapeutic purposes. The varied outcomes reveal both the gaps in knowledge of group formation and the lack of familiarity on the part of many practitioners with the knowledge available (Rosenbaum and Berger, 1963, esp. pp. 1–32).

The emphasis earlier in this article on the motivational base of group formation and on the importance of environmental alternatives suggests fruitful lines of inquiry. The significance of the motivational base was revealed in a study of group formation among "emotionally disturbed young adolescents of poor prognosis" by Rafferty (1962, p. 263). They interacted in a wide range of activities rather freely for five hours daily, five days a week for nine months. They lacked motivation toward the institution's aim of changing their behavior, and their personal disturbances hindered any kind of stable interpersonal relationship. However, they did unite with incipient group formation in activities reflecting a motivation genuine to them: defiance of the hospital staff in forbidden activities.

This instructive finding raises the issue of predicting or controlling the character of the structure and norms during group formation. Here, the importance of the environmental setting and the behavioral alternatives it encourages or permits becomes evident. In the group experiments referred to frequently here, solidary groups were formed, devoted to constructive activities, simply by placing unacquainted persons in situations of high appeal to them, with facilities and conditions so arranged that coordination of activity was the only way to secure individual satisfaction. Subsequently, conflict and hostility between the groups were produced; then came their reduction through cooperative efforts of the groups, entirely by varying the facilities available, other persons present, and other conditions external to both groups. Future research on group formation and its applied implications might profitably focus on the effects of varying the environmental alternatives and facilities available to groups, including those established by the presence of other groups and persons, upon the character of organization and norms which develop.

Conclusions

Whenever individuals with similar concerns, similar motives, similar frustrations, similar personal concerns for acceptance, for recognition, for stabilizing their perception of themselves encounter one another;

Whenever these goal-directed concerns are not effectively dealt with through the established channels of custom and law and the routine of prevailing arrangements of social organization—then individuals thus caught in the same boat tend to interact among themselves.

Repeated interaction in some common striving is conducive to differentiation of roles or functions to be performed towards the common end. And differentiation of roles and functions among the participating individuals, *over a time span,* is the pattern or formation which can be designated as *the group.* Every such human formation creates its own set of rules or norms to stabilize the regulation of behavior and attitude of members within its bounds.

In a natural group, as in any other group, the rules or norms that count, that have salience in the eyes of the members, are the ones that pertain to the existence and perpetuation of the group and the spheres of activity which are related to the common motivational concerns, that were initially conducive to repeated interaction among the individuals in question.

The main properties of the group thus formed are an organization (structure) of roles and statuses and a set of rules or standards (norms) for their activities toward the common ends. The "organization" (which need not be formally recognized) and the set of norms (which need not be formally written in blueprints) define their sense of "we-ness" cherished within the group and upheld by members in their dealings with outsiders.

In time, the standards or norms shared in the feeling of "we-ness" become personally binding for individual members. The members who are worthy and true make their judgments, justify or condemn events within the sphere related to their "we-ness" in terms of their sense of identification within the group. Proportional to the importance of the group in the lives of members, the person's self-picture, his sense of personal accountability, his loyalty, and the "dos" and "don'ts" of the group become parts of his conscience. Hence, group formation has broad implications in regulating individual attitude and behavior with and without external sanctions and controls.

References

Bales, R. F. *Interaation Process Analysis: A Method for the Study of Small Groups.* Addison-Wesley, 1949.

Blake, R. R., H. Shepard, and Jane S. Mouton. *Managing Intergroup Relations in Industry.* Gulf Publishing Co., 1964.

Blau, P. M., and W. R. Scott. *Formal Organizations: A Comparative Approach.* Chandler, 1962.

Bonner, H. *Group Dynamics: Principles and Applications.* Ronald Press, 1959.

Bowen, J. *Soviet Education: Anton Makarenko and the Years of Experiment.* University of Wisconsin Press, 1962.

Campbell, J. D. "Peer Relations in Childhood." In *Review of Child Development Resumé.* Russell Sage Foundation, 1964, Vol. 1.

Cartwright, D., and A. Zander, eds. *Group Dynamics: Research and Theory,* 2nd ed. Harper & Row, 1960.

Gibb, C. A. "Leadership." In *Handbook of Social Psychology* (Vol. 2), ed. Gardner Lindzey. Addison-Wesley, 1954.

Golembiewski, R. T. *The Small Group: An Analysis of Research Concepts and Operations.* Rand McNally, 1962.

Hare, A. P. *Handbook of Small Group Research.* The Free Press, 1962.

Hofstätter, P. R. *Gruppendynamik: Kritik der Massenspsychologie.* Rowolt, 1957.

Landesco, J. "Organized Crime in Chicago." In *Illinois Crime Survey.* Illinois Association for Criminal Justice, 1929.

Lewin, K., R. Lippitt, and R. K. White. "Patterns of Aggressive Behavior in Experimentally Created 'Social Climates.'" *Journal of Social Psychology,* Vol. 10, 1939.

Makarenko, A. S. *The Road to Life: An Epic of Education* (3 vols.). Foreign Languages Publishing House, 1955.

Merei, F. "Group Leadership and Institutionalism." *Human Relations,* Vol. 2, 1949.

Moreno, J. L. *Who Shall Survive?* Nervous and Mental Disease Publishing Co., 1934.

OSS (Office of Strategic Services) Assessment Staff. *The Assessment of Men.* Holt, Rinehardt and Winston, 1948.

Rafferty, F. T. "Development of a Social Structure in Treatment Institutions." *Journal of Nervous and Mental Disease,* Vol. 134, 1962.

Roethlisberger, F. J., and W. J. Dickson. *Management and the Worker.* Harvard University Press, 1939.

Rosenbaum. M., and M. Berger, eds. *Group Psychotherapy and Group Function.* Basic Books, 1963.

Shaw, C. R. *Delinquency Areas.* University of Chicago Press, 1929.

Sherif, Carolyn W., Muzafer Sherif, and R. E. Nebergall. *Attitude and Attitude Change.* Saunders, 1965.

Sherif, Muzafer. *Friend and Foe in Common Predicament.* Houghton Mifflin, 1966.

———. *An Outline of Social Psychology.* Harper & Row, 1948.

———. *The Psychology of Social Norms.* Harper & Row, 1936.

———, and H. Cantril. *The Psychology of Ego-Involvements.* Wiley, 1947.

———, O. J. Harvey, B. J. White, W. R. Hood, and Carolyn Sherif. *Intergroup Conflict and Cooperation.* Institute of Group Relations, 1961.

———, and Carolyn W. Sherif. *Reference Groups: Exploration into Conformity and Deviation of Adolescents.* Harper & Row, 1964.

———. *Outline of Social Psychology,* rev. ed. Harper & Row, 1956.

Thrasher, F. M. *The Gang.* University of Chicago Press, 1927.

Toki, K. "The Leader-Follower Structure in the School Class." *Japanese Journal of Psychology,* Vol. 10, 1935. English summary in E. L. Hartley and Ruth E. Hartley, *Fundamentals of Social Psychology,* Knopf, 1952.

Whyte, W. F. *Street Corner Society,* 2nd ed. University of Chicago Press, 1955.

Zorbaugh, H. W. *The Gold Coast and the Slum.* University of Chicago Press, 1929.

Herbert Thelen
and Watson Dickerman

The Growth of Groups

Varied social mechanisms differ in the explicitness of their policies of operation. In an association which operates according to a constitution, by-laws, and parliamentary procedure, policies of operation are comparatively explicit. In an informal group, such as a club or discussion group, policies of operation are much less explicit. Members do have concepts, frequently at a stereotypic level, about policies of operation—how the leader is to be chosen, how decisions are to be made, how status among the members is to be determined. But these concepts differ considerably from member to member, and often conflicts, which reduce the group's productivity, result. These conflicts are the more difficult to reconcile because the members of the group do not realize that they are the direct result of the varying concepts which the members hold about the group's operational policies. Or, if they realize this, they assume that each one's concepts about these policies are within his area of freedom of belicf and, thus, nobody's business but his own.

Groups in Action

What are these stereotypes about the operation of groups and how are they related to the stages by which a group grows in productivity? Groups which were in operation for three weeks at the 1948 session of the National Training Laboratory on Group Development serve to illustrate stereotypes at various stages of group growth. We shall try to describe both the phases in the development of these groups and the stereotypes about policies of operation which accompanied these phases. Our data are the sound recordings of the discussions of the eight groups at different stages in their development and the daily written records of the observer in each group.

In the light of what happened in these eight groups at the NTL, a group may perhaps be seen as going through four phases as it grows

From *Educational Leadership*, 6(5): 309–16; February 1949. Reprinted with permission of the Association for Supervision and Curriculum Development and Herbert Thelen and Watson Dickerman. Copyright © 1949 by the Association for Supervision and Curriculum Development.

in ability to operate efficiently. *In the first phase various members of the group quickly attempt to establish their customary places in the leadership hierarchy.* In effect, this may be thought of as an attempt to establish the "peck order" of the group. *The second phase consists of a period of frustration and conflict brought about by the leader's steadfast rejection of the concept of peck order and the authoritarian atmosphere in which the concept of peck order is rooted. The third phase sees the development of cohesiveness among the members of the group, accompanied by a certain amount of complacency and smugness.* It seems to be characterized by a determination to achieve and maintain harmony at all costs. Insofar as this effort is successful, it results in an atmosphere of deceptive "sweetness and light," which, nevertheless, is sufficiently permissive to enable the members to assess their own positions, modes of interaction, and attitudes in the group. This phase is unstable because it is unrealistic, and it gives way to a fourth phase. *In the fourth phase the members retain the group-centeredness and sensitivities which characterized the third phase, but they develop also a sense of purpose and urgency which make the group potentially an effective social instrument.*

We turn now to an effort to identify some of the stereotypes about policies of operation which seem to characterize these four phases of the growth of our groups.

Phase I: Individually Centered

Every group needs a strong, expert leader.

Good group membership consists of active, oral participation; those who do not talk are not good group members.

The group is wasting its time unless it is absorbing information or doing something active—listening to lectures, receiving bibliographies, making long lists on the blackboard, role playing, working in subcommittees, passing resolutions.

The group cannot become cohesive or efficient until each member has certain "necessary" information about the other members—occupation, title, job responsibilities, age, education, family, hobbies.

The group's observer makes his assessment of the group's process by using his intuition. He gives the members interesting information about themselves.

Any expression of feeling, particularly of aggression or hostility, is bad. It upsets the group and should be squelched.

The chief function of the leader is to manipulate the group toward the goals which he knows are appropriate for it because of his competence and authority.

Each member sees the other members primarily as individuals rather than as parts of a group. Each must be dealt with individually through the kinds of appeals which are persuasive for him.

Phase II: Frustration and Conflict among Stereotypes

The stereotypic conflicts which characterize this phase are perceived quite differently by the members of the group at the beginning of the phase and at its end. At the beginning the leader is seen as a frustrating figure because he has refused to fit the stereotypes which characterized Phase I. This results in the direction of a good deal of hostility against him, which may be expressed quite overtly. By the end of Phase II, this and other stereotypic conflicts are seen as simply the verbalization of the ambivalences of members of the group. In other words, they are seen as representing unsolved problems which plague all of us but which we manage to repress if our group has a strong leader who is willing to act as such. These conflicts seem to the writers to pose some of the most fundamental problems that individuals have to solve before they can become secure as members of a group. Typical stereotypic conflicts which characterize Phase II follow:

We must have a leader who is strong to the point of being dominating and autocratic *versus* We must have a leader who is permissive to the point of being laissez faire.

Our troubles of operation would disappear if only the leader would tell us the theory of group dynamics *versus* Our troubles can disappear only when we have acquired skill in formulating a theory about and assessing the operations of our group.

Democratic group process requires a strong leader who is subject to criticism and recall by the group at any time *versus* Democratic group process requires a chairman whose primary job is to conciliate interpersonal conflicts among the active members of the group.

Efforts to assess our own group processes are an invasion of the sacredness of individual personalities *versus* Assessment of group process is a sounder starting point for intelligent group action than is attention to motivations and attitudes of individual members of the group.

Our basic problem is that members do not take enough initiative and responsibility *versus* Members who exhibit initiative and willingness to assume responsibility are competing with the leader.

A decision by majority vote is binding on all members of the group *versus* No individual should be coerced into going along with what he thinks is wrong.

Leadership is a role vested in a single competent member of the group *versus* Leadership is a complex function which should be distributed among all members of a group.

The first problem, which runs through most of these conflicts, appears to be the notion that the answer must be either A or B. Such thinking is most fruitless when neither A nor B is satisfactory. Members of a group must learn to ask, "Under what conditions is this policy wise?" rather than, "What policy is wise under all conditions?" The latter alternative is, of course, a legitimate question. But its answer would require appraisal of each of the alternative policies, followed by identification of the essential criteria for answering the first question. The answer to the second would probably be: Any policy is wise if it satisfies this list of criteria; and the list of criteria would then have to be given.

It seems likely that the members of a group must reorient their ideas about how knowledge should be formulated. The notion that a set of generalizations about psychological phenomena can be given is less tenable than the notion that the legitimate content of psychological knowledge is only description and rationale for a set of procedures by which appropriate policy can be determined in a given situation. We are asserting, in effect, that content knowledge in the area of group dynamics consists, not of generalizations about psychological phenomena per se, but of generalizations about how to proceed in determining right conduct. Generalizations of the first kind enter into generalizations of the second kind only insofar as they help us to speculate about whether or not a suggested method of procedure will have the consequences required by the criteria.

A second major problem which a group faces, in the light of the conflicts which have been described, is how to ask the right kind of questions—those which will lead to fruitful answers.

For example, an important question is: What is the relationship between an individual's rights and his duties to society? An unfruitful way to get at this relationship is to ask: What are the rights of individuals? The question might better be phrased: What are the characteristics of individual participation which most facilitate those types of interaction through which both the individual and his society can develop in desirable directions? The change in wording makes a *sine qua non* of neither the inalienable rights of individuals nor the demands of society. Instead, it focuses attention on the kinds of individual action which can contribute most both to his own individual growth and to a healthy society.

A third problem is partly one of insight of the group's goal and the steps necessary to reach it, and partly one of skill in communicating such insight to one another. Many of the conflicts arose because members of the group felt forced to take untenable positions—for example, on the nature of good leadership or the characteristics of democratic group process. When one has taken an untenable position, he is vulnerable to attack and is likely to become defensive because even he can see that his position is weak.

Each member, by the development of insight about goals and skill in his communication, could have contributed by his responses to the sequential solution of the problems the group was trying to solve rather than fritter away the group's time and strength on inconsequential flank skirmishes. For example, it may be that these destructive side battles could have been avoided if the members had seen the group's goal in terms of a series of subgoals, each of which was to be reached through group action. One such subgoal might be the existence of enough permissiveness so that members could alleviate their anxieties rather than project them into stereotypic conflicts. Another might be orientation in the methodology of action research so that members would acquire more know-how about solving problems. Another might be the acquisition of skill in making group decisions. Surmounting each of these subgoals would carry the group forward progressively toward the final goal instead of encouraging endless and fruitless stereotypic conflicts.

Phase III: Attempted Consolidation of Group Harmony

During this phase, the group's major purpose appears to be to avoid conflict of the sort that was so debilitating during the second period. This requires the development of skill in playing supportive roles, conciliating roles, integrating roles. It also requires the members to become more responsive to subtle cues and to take more responsibility for indicating agreement or disagreement with tentative notions, rather than flat rejections or acceptances of proposed solutions. Perhaps the major pitfall to be avoided at this point is that of glossing over significant differences for the sake of apparent harmony.

During the third period, then, we find the following stereotypes dominant:

The goal of the group is cohesiveness, not productivity.

Group-centered behavior is essentially a kind of polite behavior which avoids upsetting the group. Each individual must curb his impulses in such a way that conflict does not become open.

The leader is essentially a laissez faire chairman.

Planning or steering committees should be used to make concrete proposals for the group's consideration.

A person who is silent must be brought into the discussion so we can tell if he is unhappy.

Our most important goal is satisfaction for each individual in the group. We must work at this objectively and with considerable self-assessment. The self-assessment, however, must not reveal apparent individual weaknesses but rather the difficulties of a normal individual who is struggling with difficult problems.

Our leader may be seen as a fairly worthy person to have brought us to this pleasant position but, nevertheless, we will divide the job of chairmanship among ourselves.

During this third phase there is a marked increase in the sense of individual responsibility for satisfying group needs. One might see the preceding period of frustration as one in which every individual became highly involved emotionally in the group's process; in it, it is no longer possible to sit back to judge or to be amused. On the other hand, the desire to avoid further bitterness and conflict acts as a strong disciplining influence and stimulates the development of skill which the members did not previously possess—those skills which allow a person to participate and yet avoid conflict. The former leader is now reinstated, not as a leader but as a resource person; and the group discussion shows fairly clearly that it is rejecting the concept of leadership as a personal role in favor of the concept of leadership as one aspect of good group membership—a function which is shared by all.

In a very real sense, the test of whether the preceding experiences of the members of the group have resulted in understanding may well be whether they move out of this stage in which "we all love each other with qualifications" but in which, also, significant skills are developing, to a later stage in which the group becomes a social instrument geared for action, directed outward toward improvement of its environment rather than inward toward the adjustment of members to the present environment. Until this moving on to a later stage takes place, it is as if the group were operating with some elements of fantasy, primarily in regard to its own goals. This fantasy is perilously close to the institutionalization of complacency on the one hand and to fear of ideational and other conflicts associated with solving action problems on the other.

It is probable that the only way in which this socially reinforced complacency can be broken down is through each individual's objective self-assessment. This will enable him to realize that if this period is too prolonged it will become an obstacle to any further growth on his part. It is necessary, then, for skills to be developed in a new functional area—skills which will enable each individual to realize his own needs for action in the group as distinguished from skills required for the individual to realize his needs for position and security. Along with this, at the conceptual level, must come the understanding that security is not a sufficient goal in itself but is the necessary condition for effective action.

Phase IV: Individual Self-Assessment, Flexibility of Group Processes, and Emphasis upon Productivity in Problem Solving

We present the apparent stereotypes of this fourth phase with somewhat less confidence than those of the other phases because most of our groups did not go on into the social action stage. They did not actually tackle problems of adjusting their own environment. One had the feeling that the Laboratory ended with the groups in the middle of a phase, with things yet to happen. It is quite possible, also, that even if there had been time for this fourth phase to completely develop, other still more mature phases may lie beyond it. There are, however, a number of impressions that most of the observers seemed to concur inn which suggest directions such as those described in the preceding paragraph and which require the development of skills beyond those required in the third phase.

The two most obvious characteristics of this fourth phase are the attainment by the members of much greater objectivity with regard to individual roles in the group, and the attainment of much greater ease in making decisions and much more flexibility in controlling group processes. For a third characteristic of the fourth phase, namely, participation as a group in problem-solving activities designed to change or modify the social scene through direct impact on it rather than merely through the changed attitudes and skills of individuals, we have less evidence than expectation. But there is some reason to believe that readiness for this kind of activity is developing.

Another difficulty encountered in trying to describe the stereotypes which govern this fourth phase is that stereotypic thinking was much less frequent, and in many of the group members there was a definite feeling of revulsion whenever anyone attempted to produce a capsule evaluation as to whether the chairman was behaving in a "democratic" manner or not. It is as if the conceptualization had been driven down into a much deeper level, whose complexity made verbalization difficult. Permissiveness had developed at the level of individual thinking; that is, individuals arc now frcc to thcorizc about these processes in their own way.

It is the introduction of this element which takes the method of control out of the laissez-faire area in which there is considerable permissiveness of specific behaviors but very little permissiveness of conceptualization and thinking about behaviors. It is because of the deeper, more personalized conceptualizations that frustration and impasse due to conflict can be avoided in a climate having this second sort of permissiveness.

The stereotypes that we can identify, then, in the fourth phase, should probably be thought of not as verbalizations whose relation to operation is vague and conflicting in the minds of members, but rather as principles of operation which have developed inductively and more or less consciously as by-products of the individual's attempt to meet his own needs in the group. Among these notions are:

Each individual has a personality of his own which is different from that of other group members and is not to be judged as either good or bad.

The nature of this personality determines the efficiency and ease with which individuals will be able to play different roles in the group.

If a member of a group is to grow in ability to participate in the group, other members must help him by demonstrating their expectation that he will grow and their approval of his growing ability to formulate perceptions about group process.

This, in turn, means that all individual perceptions and differences among them have to be treated as realities. It also means that we cannot assume that any one individual's perceptions are the "right" ones.

Contributions of each individual must be assumed to be relevant to the problem under consideration. It is up to the group to find out what the relevance is. Only thus can the goal directions of each individual be continually woven into the goal direction of the group as a whole.

Although the deeper meanings of each individual's contribution cannot be taken for granted, enough rapport has developed that the members know about what to expect from each individual. It is only when these expectations are violated by the introduction of novel and threatening elements into the situation that a serious problem arises.

The question "What is our purpose at this point? What is the problem we are trying to solve?" is recognized as one of the most helpful questions that can be asked instead of one of the most obstructing questions which should, at all costs, be avoided and resented.

In a sense, every member is expected to play all roles at appropriate times. The question of which roles should be formally structured by the group and assigned to particular individuals and for what periods of time remains unanswered. The members seem to feel that the answer lies in analysis of what roles are needed by the group for the solution of the problems at hand and of the interests and needs of individuals for playing these roles.

The place of ethics, as a source of guidance for the group, lies in making the formulation of criteria for success in particular situations easier. It does not, in itself, provide the policies for running the group.

A Hypothesis Proposed

The identification of the four phases of group growth which have been discussed amounts to stating a hypothesis about the course of group growth:

Beginning with individual needs for finding security and activity in a social environment, we proceed, first, to emotional involvement of the individuals with each other, and, second, to the development of a group as a rather limited universe of interaction among individuals and as the source of individual security. We then find that security of position in the group loses its significance except that as the group attempts to solve problems it structures its activities in such a way that each individual can play a role which may be described as successful or not in terms of whether the group successfully solved the problem it had set itself.

It is not our contention that these four phases develop in sequential order. We have attempted to identify some of the stereotypes which seem to us to represent the perceptions of the members of these groups at different stages in the development into groups. We do not claim that this particular course of development of stereotypes about policies of operation would be found in all groups under all conditions. We do feel that identification of the members' stereotypes about policies of operation would help many groups in their growth as individually satisfying social milieus and as effective social action instruments.

Dorwin Cartwright

Achieving Change in People: Some Applications of Group Dynamics Theory

I

We hear all around us today the assertion that the problems of the twentieth century are problems of human relations. The survival of civilization, it is said, will depend upon man's ability to create social inventions capable of harnessing, for society's constructive use, the vast physical energies now at man's disposal. Or, to put the matter more simply, we must learn how to change the way in which people behave toward one another. In broad outline, the specifications for a good society are clear, but a serious technical problem remains: How can we change people so that they neither restrict the freedom nor limit the potentialities for growth of others; so that they accept and

From *Human Relations*, Vol. 4, No. 4, 1951, pp. 318–392. Reprinted by permission of Plenum Publishing Company Limited, London.

respect people of different religion, nationality, color, or political opinion; so that nations can exist in a world without war, and so that the fruits of our technological advances can bring economic well-being and freedom from disease to all the people of the world? Although few people would disagree with these objectives when stated abstractly, when we become more specific, differences of opinion quickly arise. How is change to be produced? Who is to do it? Who is to be changed? These questions permit no ready answers.

Before we consider in detail these questions of social technology, let us clear away some semantic obstacles. The word "change" produces emotional reactions. It is not a neutral word. To many people it is threatening. It conjures up visions of a revolutionary, a dissatisfied idealist, a trouble-maker, a malcontent. Nicer words referring to the process of changing people are education, training, orientation, guidance, indoctrination, therapy. We are more ready to have others "educate" us than to have them "change" us. We, ourselves, feel less guilty in "training" others than in "changing" them. Why this emotional response? What makes the two kinds of words have such different meanings? I believe that a large part of the difference lies in the fact that the safer words (like education or therapy) carry the implicit assurance that the only changes produced will be good ones, acceptable within a currently held value system. The cold, unmodified word "change," on the contrary, promises no respect for values; it might even tamper with values themselves. Perhaps for this very reason it will foster straight thinking if we use the word "change" and thus force ourselves to struggle directly and self-consciously with the problems of value that are involved. Words like education, training, or therapy, by the very fact that they are not so disturbing, may close our eyes to the fact that they too inevitably involve values.

Another advantage of using the word "change" rather than other related words is that it does not restrict our thinking to a limited set of aspects of people that are legitimate targets of change. Anyone familiar with the history of education knows that there has been endless controversy over what it is about people that "education" properly attempts to modify. Some educators have viewed education simply as imparting knowledge, others mainly as providing skills for doing things, still others as producing healthy "attitudes," and some have aspired to instill a way of life. Of if we choose to use a word like "therapy," we can hardly claim that we refer to a more clearly defined realm of change. Furthermore, one can become inextricably entangled in distinctions and vested interests by attempting to distinguish sharply between, let us say, the domain of education and that of therapy. If we are to try to take a broader view and to develop some basic principles that promise to apply to all types of modifications in people, we had better use a word like "change" to keep our thinking general enough.

The proposal that social technology may be employed to solve the problems of society suggests that social science may be applied in ways not different from those used in the physical sciences. Does social science, in fact, have any practically useful knowledge which may be brought to bear significantly on society's most urgent problems? What scientifically based principles are there for guiding programs of social change: In this paper we shall restrict our considerations to certain parts of a relatively new branch of social science known as "group dynamics." We shall examine some of the implications for social action which stem from research in this field of scientific investigation.

What is "group dynamics"? Perhaps it will be most useful to start by looking at the derivation of the word "dynamics." It comes from a Greek word meaning force. In careful usage of the phrase, "group dynamics" refers to the forces operating in groups. The investigation of group dynamics, then, consists of a study of these forces: what gives rise to them, what conditions modify them, what consequences they have, etc. The practical application of group dynamics (or the technology of group dynamics) consists of the utilization of knowledge about these forces for the achievement of some purpose. In keeping with this definition, then, it is clear that group dynamics, as a realm of investigation, is not particularly novel, nor is it the exclusive property of any person or institution. It goes back at least to the outstanding work of men like Simmel, Freud, and Colley.

Although interest in groups has a long and respectable history, the past fifteen years have witnessed a new flowering of activity in this field. Today, research centers in several countries are carrying out substantial programs of research designed to reveal the nature of groups and of their functioning. The phrase "group dynamics" has come into common usage during this time and intense efforts have been devoted to the development of the field, both as a branch of social science and as a form of social technology.

In this development the name of Kurt Lewin has been outstanding. As a consequence of his work in the field of individual psychology and from his analysis of the nature of the pressing problems of the contemporary world, Lewin became convinced of society's urgent need for a *scientific approach;* to the understanding of the dynamics of groups. In 1945 he established the Research Center for Group Dynamics to meet this need. Since that date the Center has been devoting its efforts to improving our scientific understanding of groups through laboratory experimentation, field studies, and the use of techniques of action research. It has also attempted in various ways to help get the findings of social science more widely used by social management. Much of what I have to say in this paper is drawn from the experiences of this Center in its brief existence of a little more than five years (Cartwright, 1950).

II

For various reasons we have found that much of our work has been devoted to an attempt to gain a better understanding of the ways in which people change their behavior or resist efforts by others to have them do so. Whether we set for ourselves the practical goal of improving behavior or whether we take on the intellectual task of understanding why people do what they do, we have to investigate processes of communication, influence, social pressure—in short, problems of change.

In this work we have encountered great frustration. The problems have been most difficult to solve. Looking back over our experience, I have become convinced that no small part of the trouble has resulted from an irresistible tendency to conceive of our problems in terms of the individual. We live in an individualistic culture. We value the individual highly, and rightly so. But I am inclined to believe that our political and social concern for the individual has narrowed our thinking as social scientists so much that we have not been able to state our research problems properly. Perhaps we have taken the individual as the unit of observation and study when some larger unit would have been more appropriate. Let us look at a few examples.

Consider first some matters having to do with the mental health of an individual. We can all agree, I believe, that an important mark of a healthy personality is that the individual's self-esteem has not been undermined. But on what does self-esteem depend? From research on this problem we have discovered that, among other things, repeated experiences of failure or traumatic failures on matters of central importance serve to undermine one's self-esteem. We also know that whether a person experiences success or failure as a result of some undertaking depends upon the level of aspiration which he has set for himself. Now, if we try to discover how the level of aspiration gets set, we are immediately involved in the person's relationships to groups. The groups to which he belongs set standards for his behavior which he must accept if he is to remain in the group. If his capacities do not allow him to reach these standards, he experiences failure, he withdraws or is rejected by the group and his self-esteem suffers a shock.

Suppose, then, that we accept a task of therapy, of rebuilding his self-esteem. It would appear plausible from our analysis of the problem that we should attempt to work with variables of the same sort that produced the difficulty, that is to work with him either in the groups to which he now belongs or to introduce him into new groups which are selected for the purpose and to work upon his relationships to groups as such. From the point of view of preventive mental health, we might even attempt to train the groups in our communities —classes in schools, work groups in business, families, unions, religious and cultural groups—to make use of practices better designed to protect the self-esteem of their members.

Consider a second example. A teacher finds that in her class she has a number of trouble-makers, full of aggression. She wants to know why these children are so aggressive and what can be done about it. A foreman in a factory has the same kind of problem with some of his workers. He wants the same kind of help. The solution most tempting to both the teacher and the foreman often is to transfer the worst trouble-makers to someone else, or if facilities are available, to refer them for counselling. But is the problem really of such a nature that it can be solved by removing the trouble-maker from the situation or by working on his individual motivations and emotional life? What leads does research give us? The evidence indicates, of course, that there are many causes of aggressiveness in people, but one aspect of the problem has become increasingly clear in recent years. If we observe carefully the amount of aggressive behavior and the number of trouble-makers to be found in a large collection of groups, we find that these characteristics can vary tremendously from group to group even when the different groups are composed essentially of the same kinds of people. In the now classic experiments of Lewin, Lippitt, and White (1939) on the effects of different styles of leadership, it was found that the same group of children displayed markedly different levels of aggressive behavior when under different styles of leadership. Moreover, when individual children were transferred from one group to another, their levels of aggressiveness shifted to conform to the atmosphere of the new group. Efforts to account for one child's aggressiveness under one style of leadership merely in terms of his personality traits could hardly succeed under these conditions. This is not to say that a person's behavior is entirely to be accounted for by the atmosphere and structure of the immediate group, but it is remarkable to what an extent a strong, cohesive group can control aspects of a member's behavior traditionally thought to be expressive of enduring personality traits. Recognition of this fact rephrases the problem of how to change such behavior. It directs us to a study of the sources of the influence of the group on its members.

Let us take an example from a different field. What can we learn from efforts to change people by mass media and mass persuasion? In those rare instances when educators, propagandists, advertisers, and others who want to influence large numbers of people, have bothered to make an objective evauation of the enduring changes produced by their efforts, they have been able to demonstrate only the most negligible effects (Cartwright, 1949). The inefficiency of attempts to influence the public by mass media would be scandalous if there were agreement that it was important or even desirable to have such influences strongly exerted. In fact, it is no exaggeration to say that all of the research and experience of generations has not improved the efficiency of lectures or other means of mass influence to any noticeable degree. Something must be wrong with our theories of learning, motivation, and social psychology.

Within very recent years some research data have been accumulating which may give us a clue to the solution of our problem. In one series of experiments directed by Lewin (1951, pp. 229–236), it was found that a method of group decision, in which the group as a whole made a decision to have its members change their behavior, was from two to ten times as effective in producing actual change as was a lecture presenting exhortation to change. We have yet to learn precisely what produces these differences of effectiveness, but it is clear that by introducing group forces into the situation a whole new level of influence has been achieved.

The experience has been essentially the same when people have attempted to increase the productivity of individuals in work settings. Traditional conceptions of how to increase the output of workers have stressed the individual: select the right man for the job; simplify the job for him; train him in the skills required; motivate him by economic incentives; make it clear to whom he reports; keep the lines of authority and responsibility simple and straight. But even when all these conditions are fully met we are finding that productivity is far below full potential. There is even good reason to conclude that this individualistic conception of the determinants of productivity actually fosters negative consequences. The individual, now isolated and subjected to the demands of the organization through the commands of his boss, finds that he must create with his fellow employees informal groups, not shown on any table of organization, in order to protect himself from arbitrary control of his life, from the boredom produced by the endless repetition of mechanically sanitary and routine operations, and from the impoverishment of his emotional and social life brought about by the frustration of his basic needs for social interaction, participation, and acceptance in a stable group. Recent experiments have demonstrated clearly that the productivity of work groups can be greatly increased by methods of work organization and supervision which give more responsibility to work groups, which allow for fuller participation in important decisions, and which make stable groups the firm basis for support of the individual's social needs (Coch and French, 1948). I am convinced that future research will also demonstrate that people working under such conditions become more mature and creative individuals in their homes, in community life, and as citizens.

As a final example, let us examine the experience of efforts to train people in workshops, institutes, and special training courses. Such efforts are common in various areas of social welfare, intergroup relations, political affairs, industry, and adult education generally. It is an unfortunate fact that objective evaluation of the effects of such training efforts has only rarely been undertaken, but there is evidence for those who will look that the actual change in behavior produced is most disappointing. A workshop not infrequently develops keen interest among the participants, high morale and enthusiasm, and a firm resolve on the part of many to apply all the wonderful insights back home. But what happens back home? The trainee discovers that his colleagues don't share his enthusiasm. He learns that the task of changing others' expectations and ways of doing things is discouragingly difficult. He senses, perhaps not very clearly, that it would make all the difference in the world if only there were a few other people sharing his enthusiasm and insights with whom he could plan activities, evaluate consequences of efforts, and from whom he could gain emotional and motivational support. The approach to training which conceives of its task as being merely that of changing the individual probably produces frustration, demoralization, and disillusionment in as large a measure as it accomplishes more positive results.

A few years ago the Research Center for Group Dynamics undertook to shed light on this problem by investigating the operation of a workshop for training leaders in intercultural relations. In a project, directed by Lippitt (1949), we set out to compare systematically the different effects of the workshop upon trainees who came as isolated individuals in contrast to those who came as teams. Since one of the problems in the field of intercultural relations is that of getting people of good will to be more active in community efforts to improve intergroup relations, one goal of the training workshop was to increase the activity of the trainees in such community affairs. We found that before the workshop there was no difference in the activity level of the people who were to be trained as isolates and of those who were to be trained as teams. Six months after the workshop, however, those who had been trained as isolates were only slightly more active than before the workshop whereas those who had been members of strong training teams were now much more active. We do not have clear evidence on the point, but we would be quite certain that the maintenance of heightened activity over a long period of time would also be much better for members of teams. For the isolates the effect of the workshop had the characteristic of a "shot in the arm" while for the team member it produced a more enduring change because the team provided continuous support and reinforcement for its members.

III

What conclusions may we draw from these examples? What principles of achieving change in people can we see emerging? To begin with the most general proposition, we may state that the behavior, attitudes, beliefs, and values of the individual are all firmly grounded in the groups to which he belongs. How aggressive or cooperative a person is, how much self-respect and self-confidence he has, how energetic and productive his work is, what he aspires to, what he believes to be true and good, whom he loves or hates, and what beliefs and prejudices he holds—all these characteristics are highly determined by the individual's group memberships. In a real sense, they are properties of groups and of the relationships between people. Whether they change or resist change will, therefore, be greatly influenced by the nature of these groups. Attempts to change them must be concerned with the dynamics of groups.

In examining more specifically how groups enter into the process of change, we find it useful to view groups in at least three different ways. In the first view, the group is seen as a source of influence over its members. Efforts to change behavior can be supported or blocked by pressures on members stemming from the group. To make constructive use of these pressures the group must be used *as a medium of change*. In the second view, the group itself becomes the *target of change*. To change the behavior of individuals it may be necessary to change the standards of the group, its style of leadership, its emotional atmosphere, or its stratification into cliques and hierarchies. Even though the goal may be to change the behavior of *individuals*, the target of change becomes the group. In the third view, it is recognized that many changes of behavior can be brought about only by the organized efforts of groups *as agents of change*. A committee to combat intolerance, a labor union, an employers association, a citizens group to increase the pay of teachers—any action group will be more or less effective depending upon the way it is organized, the satisfactions it provides to its members, the degree to which its goals are clear, and a host of other properties of the group.

An adequate social technology of change, then, requires at the very least a scientific understanding of groups viewed in each of these ways. We shall consider here only the first two aspects of the problem: the group as a medium of change and as a target of change.

The Group as a Medium of Change

Principle No. 1. If the group is to be used effectively as a medium of change, those people who are to be changed and those who are to exert influence for change must have a strong sense of belonging to the same group.

Kurt Lewin (1948) described this principle well: "The normal gap between teacher and student, doctor and patient, social worker and public, can . . . be a real obstacle to acceptance of the advocated conduct" (p. 67). In other words, in spite of whatever status differences there might be between them, the teacher and the student have to feel as members of one group in matters involving their sense of values. The chances for re-education seem to be increased whenever a strong we-feeling is created. Recent experiments by Preston and Heintz (1949) have demonstrated greater changes of opinions among members of discussion groups operating with participatory leadership than among those with supervisory leadership. The implications of this principle for classroom teaching are far-reaching. The same may be said of supervision in the factory, army, or hospital.

Principle No. 2. The more attractive the group is to its members the greater is the influence that the group can exert on its members.

This principle has been extensively documented by Festinger and his co-workers (1950). They have been able to show in a variety of settings that in more cohesive groups there is a greater readiness of members to attempt to influence others, a greater readiness to be influenced by others, and stronger pressures toward conformity when conformity is a relevant matter for the group. Important for the practitioner wanting to make use of this principle is, of course, the question of how to increase the attractiveness of groups. This is a question with many answers. Suffice it to say that a group is more attractive the more it satisfies the needs of its members. We have been able to demonstrate experimentally an increase in group cohesiveness by increasing the liking of members for each other as persons, by increasing the perceived importance of the group goal, and by increasing the prestige of the group among other groups. Experienced group workers could add many other ways to this list.

Principle No. 3. In attempts to change attitudes, values, or behavior, the more relevant they are to the basis of attraction to the group, the greater will be the influence that the group can exert upon them.

I believe this principle gives a clue to some otherwise puzzling phenomena. How does it happen that a group, like a labor union, seems to be able to exert such strong discipline over its members in some matters (let us say in dealings with management), while it seems unable to exert nearly the same influence in other matters (let us say in political action)? If we examine why it is that members are attracted to the group, I believe we will find that a particular reason for belonging seems more related to some of the group's activities than to others. If a man joins a union mainly to keep his job and to improve his working conditions, he may be largely uninfluenced by the union's attempt to modify his attitudes toward national and international affairs. Groups differ tremendously in the range of matters that are relevant to them and hence over which they have influence. Much of the inefficiency of adult education could be reduced if more attention were paid to the need that influence attempts be appropriate to the groups in which they are made.

Principle No. 4. The greater the prestige of a group member in the eyes of the other members, the greater the influence he can exert.

Polansky, Lippitt, and Redl (1950) have demonstrated this principle with great care and methodological ingenuity in a series of studies in children's summer camps. From a practical point of view it must be emphasized that the things giving prestige to a member may not be those characteristics most prized by the official management of the group. The most prestige-carrying member of a Sunday School class may not possess the characteristics most similar to the minister of the church. The teacher's pet may be a poor source of influence within a class. This principle is the basis for the common observation that the official leader and the actual leader of a group are often not the same individual.

Principle No. 5. Efforts to change individuals or subparts of a group which, if successful, would have the result of making them deviate from the norms of the group will encounter strong resistance.

During the past few years a great deal of evidence has been accumulated showing the tremendous pressures which groups can exert upon members to conform to the group's norms. The price of deviation in most groups is rejection or even expulsion. If the member really wants to belong and be accepted, he cannot withstand this type of pressure. It is for this reason that efforts to change people by taking them from the group and giving them special training so often have disappointing results. This principle also accounts for the finding that people thus trained sometimes display increased tension, aggressiveness toward the group, or a tendency to form cults or cliques with others who have shared their training.

These five principles concerning the group as a medium of change would appear to have readiest application to groups created for the purpose of producing changes in people. They provide certain specifications for building effective training or therapy groups. They also point, however, to a difficulty in producing change in people in that they show how resistant an individual is to changing in any way contrary to group pressures and expectations. In order to achieve many kinds of changes in people, therefore, it is necessary to deal with the group as a target of change.

The Group as a Target of Change

Principle No. 6. Strong pressure for changes in the group can be established by creating a shared perception by members of the need for change, thus making the source of pressure for change lie within the group.

Marrow and French (1945) report a dramatic case-study which illustrates this principle quite well. A manufacturing concern had a policy against hiring women over thirty because it was believed that they were slower, more difficult to train, and more likely to be absent. The staff psychologist was able to present to management evidence that this belief was clearly unwarranted at least within their own company. The psychologist's facts, however, were rejected and ignored as a basis for action because they violated accepted beliefs. It was claimed that they went against the direct experience of the foremen. Then the psychologist hit upon a plan for achieving change which differed drastically from the usual one of argument, persuasion, and pressure. He proposed that management conduct in its own analysis of the situation. With his help management collected all the facts which they believed were relevant to the problem. When the results were in they were now their own facts rather than those of some "outside" expert. Policy was immediately changed without further resistance. The important point here is that facts are not enough. The facts must be the accepted property of the group if they are to become an effective basis for change. There seems to be all the difference in the world in changes actually carried out between those cases in which a consulting firm is hired to do a study and present a report and those in which technical experts are asked to collaborate with the group in doing its own study.

Principle No. 7. Information relating to the need for change, plans for change, and consequences of change must be shared by all relevant people in the group.

Another way of stating this principle is to say that change of a group ordinarily requires the opening of communication channels. Newcomb (1947) has shown how one of the first consequences of mistrust and hostility is the avoidance of communicating openly and freely about the things producing the tension. If you look closely at a pathological group (that is, one that has trouble making decisions or effecting coordinated efforts of its members), you will certainly find strong restraints in that group against communicating vital information among its members. Until these restraints are removed there can be little hope for any real and lasting changes in the group's functioning. In passing it should be pointed out that the removal of barriers to communication will ordinarily be accompanied by a sudden increase in the communication of hostility. The group may appear to be falling apart, and it will certainly be a painful experience to many of the members. This pain and the fear that things are getting out of hand often stop the process of change once begun.

Principle No. 8. Changes in one part of a group produce strain in other related parts which can be reduced only by eliminating the change or by bringing about readjustments in the related parts.

It is a common practice to undertake improvements in group functioning by providing training programs for certain classes of people in the organization. A training program for foremen, for nurses, for teachers, or for group workers is established. If the content of the training is relevant for organizational change, it must of necessity deal with the relationships these people have with other subgroups. If nurses in a hospital change their behavior significantly, it will affect their relations both with the patients and with the doctors. It is unrealistic to assume that both these groups will remain indifferent to any significant changes in this respect. In hierarchical structures this process is most clear. Lippitt has proposed on the basis of research and experience that in such organizations attempts at change should always involve three levels, one being the major target of change and the other two being the one above and the one below.

IV

These eight principles represent a few of the basic propositions emerging from research in group dynamics. Since research is constantly going on and since it is the very nature of research to revise and reformulate our conceptions, we may be sure that these principles will have to be modified and improved as time goes by. In the meantime they may serve as guides in our endeavors to develop a scientifically based technology of social management.

In social technology, just as in physical technology, invention plays a crucial role. In both fields progress consists of the creation of new mechanisms for the accomplishment of certain goals. In both fields inventions arise in response to practical needs and are to be evaluated by how effectively they satisfy these needs. The relation of invention to scientific development is indirect but important. Inventions cannot proceed too far ahead of basic scientific development, nor should they be allowed to fall to far behind. They will be more effective the more they make good use of known principles of science, and they often make new developments in science possible. On the other hand, they are in no sense logical derivations from scientific principles.

I have taken this brief excursion into the theory of invention in order to make a final point. To many people "group dynamics" is known only for the social inventions which have developed in recent years in work with groups. Group dynamics is often thought of as certain techniques to be used with groups. Role playing, buzz groups, process observers, post-meeting reaction sheets, and feedback of group observations are devices popularly associated with the phrase "group dynamics." I trust that I have been able to show that group dynamics is more than a collection of gadgets. It certainly aspires to be a science as well as a technology.

This is not to underplay the importance of these inventions nor of the function of inventing. As inventions they are all mechanisms designed to help accomplish important goals. How effective they are will depend upon how skillfully they are used and how appropriate they are to the purposes to which they are put. Careful evaluative research must be the ultimate judge of their usefulness in comparison with alternative inventions. I believe that the principles enumerated in this paper indicate some of the specifications that social inventions in this field must meet.

References

Cartwright, D. "Some Principles of Mass Persuasion: Selected Findings of Research on the Sale of United States War Bonds." *Human Relations*, Vol. 2, No. 3, 1949.

——. *The Research Center for Group Dynamics: A Report of Five Years' Activities and a View of Future Needs.* Institute for Social Research, 1950.

Coch, L., and J. R. P. French, Jr. "Overcoming Resistance to Change." *Human Relations*, Vol. 1, No. 4, 1948.

Festinger, L., *et al. Theory and Experiment in Social Communication:* Collected papers. Institute for Social Research, 1950.

Lewin, K. *Resolving Social Conflicts.* Harper & Row, 1948.

——. *Field Theory in Social Science.* New York: Harper & Row, 1951.

——, R. Lippitt, and R. K. White. "Patterns of Aggressive Behavior in Experimentally Created 'Social Climates'." *Journal of Social Psychology*, Vol. 10, 1939.

Lippitt, R. *Training in Community Relations.* Harper & Row, 1949.

Marrow, A. J., and J. R. P. French, Jr. "Changing a Stereotype in Industry." *Journal of Social Issues*, Vol. 1, No. 3, 1945.

Newcomb, T. M. "Autistic Hostility and Social Reality." *Human Relations*, Vol. 1, No. 1, 1947.

Polansky, N., R. Lippitt, and F. Redl. "An Investigation of Behavioral Contagion in Groups." *Human Relations*, Vol. 3, No. 4, 1950.

Preston, M. G., and R. K. Heintz. "Effects of Participatory vs. Supervisory Leadership on Group Judgment." *Journal of Abnormal and Social Psychology*, Vol. 44, 1949.

Josephine Klein

Changing Ideas
in Theory and Practice

Ideas confine a man to certain social groups and social groups confine a man to certain ideas. Many ideas are more easily changed by aiming at a group than by aiming at an individual. The unfreezing of ideas is the normal consequence of entering a new group; it is achieved through contact with new facts and new values. A skilled discussion leader can create conditions favorable to the unfreezing of old ideas and commitment to new ones. This skill is a practical application of knowledge of the normal decision-making process. The techniques available for changing ideas can also be used in committee; the chairman normally plays the part of skilled discussion leader, but many components of his role can be taken over by other members.

The conditions which produce an efficient and happy discussion group need not be left to chance. [Here we are] concerned with an examination of the techniques which the members have at their disposal to secure good conditions. Normally, of course, the main responsibility for this rests on the discussion leader or the chairman. But it has already been shown that it is more important that the necessary functions should be performed than that they should be performed by the officially appointed member. The use of these techniques is therefore open to anyone.

First, however, it may be fruitful to look again at the origin of the ideas exchanged in discussion, and in particular to stress their social nature.

If a man has a more or less integrated personality, he will have more or less consistent ideas. Some of these will go very deep, arising out of, as well as shaping, his most fundamental views of life. This tends to be true for facts as well as for more personal preferences and values.

From *Working With Groups*, by Josephine Klein, Hutchinson University Library, 1961, pp. 119–132. Reprinted by permission of Hutchinson Publishing Group Ltd., London.

Most of these ideas will not have been acquired by a deliberate effort of the intelligence: a man does not usually examine and sift ideas, finally giving allegiance only to those that are truest and most elevating. The ideas that form his working capital depend to a great extent on the social groups of which he is a member. In so far as ideas are shared by those with whom one is in frequent contact, they will remain unexamined and unverified. The social consensus supports them: there is no encouragement to question them. They may indeed be supported by factual evidence, but emotionally they are retained because in the group they are regarded as obvious and proper: they constitute social reality.

In addition, people who have interests in common seek each other out to talk shop. This is not only because they are useful to each other in adding to the other's stock of facts. They get on well together because they share the same values—both ideas about what pursuits are worth while and ideas that are formed and strengthened by the disciplines required to pursue these interests successfully. Consider the facts, values, and views likely to be current in a family keen on bird-watching or Bach, in a local dramatic society or tennis club, among amateur botanists or jazz enthusiasts. Members of such groups share the same kinds of knowledge and, to some extent, the same kinds of ignorance as well.

Just as shared ideas create or cement groups, so unshared ideas serve to isolate and divide. Just as we tend to seek out and like those who share our ideas, so we tend to avoid and be a little bored by those who disagree with us, who will not understand us, or whose stock of facts or values seems strange to us. We tend to feel on these occasions that the others are wrong, not merely different, and though we cannot put a finger on the argument that would convince them, we feel sure that there is such an argument somewhere. Just as group membership serves to confirm ideas when members happen to share them, so members will regard with doubt and suspicion anyone who does not share their ideas; they will feel that he is not "one of us" if he does not see what is so self-evident to them. Unfamiliar ideas may be ignored, may not even be heard, or may provoke hostility.

The result is that ideas are difficult to alter. A man under pressure to change his ideas may be deterred by the fear of appearing odd to his friends. The advantages of changing ideas through group action rather than by changing isolated individuals are therefore clear. The individual, embedded in his group, will lose his standing in the group if he changes and they do not. If he values his group he will be anxious not to find himself in conflict, and it will be relatively more difficult to persuade him to change. Conversely, if all the members of the group can be persuaded together, the new attitude will be supported by the same social forces that had supported the previous attitude.

According to Lewin, changes of attitude in the group, as else-vhere, move through three phases: (1) An "unfreezing" of previous attitudes, (2) A change in attitude, and (3) a "freezing" of the new attitude.

Unfreezing

Before any change is possible the inadequacy of present behavior must be recognized. This is the "unfreezing" process. In interaction, this may start quite informally, when one member makes a suggestion for action which seems quite obvious to him, only to find that others are unwilling to agree. The ground on which they disagree informs him of further considerations which he has to take into account, if he still wants the group to take the action he advocates. Or he may find, on entering a new group, that the grounds on which other members make decisions are quite different from those he habitually considers. In the first case he finds that he has not (or they have not) taken all the facts into account: it may be the wrong time of year, or the place may be too far away, or the necessary resources may not be available. In other words his (or their) information may be at fault. In the second case he finds that other people have preferences different from his own, and that some considerations, say kindliness, may count more for him than for them, whereas they would rather be efficient than kind. In other words, they do not share all his values. In such a case, even when he ultimately still maintains his own ranking of preferences intact, there is a period of uncertainty during which he recognizes that the decision he advocates is not the obvious and inevitable one for all.

There are, however, also many personal habits of thought and expression which have no factual or moral significance in themselves and which yet make it difficult for the group to arrive at the best possible course of action (or inaction) in the circumstances. According to Maier, who has done a good deal of work on the training of discussion leaders, we tend to be handicapped in our thinking by being frozen in a habit of thought which has ceased to be efficient. "If we are to influence or aid the thinking of others, this can more readily be achieved by recognizing and influencing the direction their thinking is taking. "Such recognition and influence, which is a kind of "unfreezing," takes place naturally in a group at any time, just because nobody thinks along exactly the same lines as everyone else. On the other hand, there are ways in which the group handicaps good thinking. The most important of these handicaps is that some people, who are not necessarily less intelligent, are more diffident in putting forward their own views; also, their ability may be underestimated in a particular group so that their opinions are not listened to with the same respect or attention as are those of other more highly esteemed, but not necessarily more intelligent, members of the group.

For both these reasons it is important that someone in the group, normally the discussion leader or chairman, plays a facilitating role, particularly when it is desired to introduce a change of outlook into a rather inward-looking group with settled views. This presents the outside expert with formidable problems. And yet such cases are more frequent than one might think. Besides the professional social scientist who accepts an assignment to smooth over or introduce a change, there are others who are technical experts in their field— Members of Parliament, engineers, youth club leaders, the clergy— who may advocate a policy which they believe to be a good one on grounds connected with their own expertise and yet find themselves in difficulties because of their lack of social skills.

Maier has written out a set of instructions for the expert who finds himself working with an unskilled group. They are reproduced in italics below, with a commentary to bring out their implications more fully and to show their relevance to the argument pursued in this book.

1. Do not present the group with a problem but instead determine from the group whether they have a problem. If the expert attempts to change opinions or behavior, he must start from where the people concerned stand. They may have another problem which is so urgent to them that they hardly have attention to spare for what he is saying, and which may wrongly color the problem he desires to present to them. It may also be noted that by this means the expert, who is often more articulate and more definite in his views than the rest of the committee, may be prevented from confusing the issue by imposing his own values on the others. Tolerance of what seems irrelevant in the early stages may avoid a lot of irrelevant discussion when the group finally gets down to brass tacks.

2. Make a list of all suggestions so that all types of considerations are included. No one knows beforehand which information and which values will be felt to be essential. When the time for proposals comes, it is very hard to remember everything that has been contributed. A list serves as a kind of collective memory and keeps the attention of a member on all the points that have been made, not merely on those that had an immediate appeal for him. A blackboard is ideal for this purpose, because then people can see what has gone before, and this may stimulate them to think further. If there is no blackboard, a competent secretary, who may be the expert himself, to write down all the suggestions and repeat them at intervals, is essential.

3. Recognize all suggestions and protect individuals from the criticism of other group members by interpreting all remarks in a favorable light. This must be done to preserve good feeling in the group and to avoid any impression of favoritism. A really skilled leader has a chance here, in the process of repeating and interpreting members' contributions, to disentangle the fact element from the value element. It is fruitful, although not always possible, to keep several lists: one of relevant facts and one of relevant values. Explicit proposals should be separately recorded and discussion of them postponed until it is felt that information-exchange is complete.

4. *Good suggestions may be kept in the discussion by asking 'How would that work out?' etc.* In this way a man has the chance of explaining in more detail; and the more valuable ideas are given proper prominence.

5. *Do not hasten the solution by capitalizing on the first good lead or in any other way reflect your preferences.* The expert must never forget that there may be a better solution than the one he has in mind. He must be patient in accumulating all information that may conceivably be relevant to a solution of the problem. Even what he considers to be irrelevant may, for reasons he has not explored, be felt by the members to be closely connected with the problem.

6. *When the list is fairly complete, probing questions may be asked, e.g., 'How can we change things so as to combine some of these features?' etc.* This is the stage of proposal and agreement. It is at this point that the "co-ordinator" is required. This stage should not be too quickly reached. When it comes, all members must be encouraged to participate. They must be involved in the decision-making process if they are to feel that the solution is their own.

This whole sequence is part of the "unfreezing" process. Not only is knowledge of fact submitted openly to all concerned for criticism and correction, but a loosening-up of old habits of thought is also encouraged. The members are stimulated into looking at the problem in the round and they themselves are often astonished to find that they are abandoning trains of thought they have long taken for granted. Of course, this momentary effect will not last, another habit will soon be built up, but at this moment the opportunity presents itself to make a change.

Freezing

It is to be hoped that by these techniques someone will finally make a proposal for action and that the group will come to agreement. To what can disagreement be due? Either to the fact that some members need further information before they can be persuaded, in which case the group moves back to the unfreezing exchange of information, or else to the fact that the deviant individuals estimate the information in the light of values and preferences not shared by the group. Ultimately, nothing can be done about this latter problem —*de gustibus non est disputandum*—but it may be said in passing that only a very strong personality can stand out against group pressures, and one may ask oneself whether the deviant does not belong to some other group which has more influence on him and through which one would have to work if one sought to reach him.

If, however, agreement is reached, the information that went into that agreement will now keep the decision at once stable and flexible, knowledge of fact and value consensus contributing to the same end. The members know exactly what considerations led to the decision and are therefore capable of adjusting in an informed way to minor changes in circumstance—hence the decision will be flexible. The members would have to be strongly impressed by a new item of information before they changed again—therefore the decision will be stable. Further, stability may be maintained because in any group in which members see each other from day to day there is a constant check on whether the new plan is still being followed. It is difficult to be a backslider in such circumstances.

The line of argument pursued here derives from a very large number of studies on attitude changes and decision making in small groups. Coch and French used the technique for introducing changes in methods of work and payment in a sewing-machine factory, Levine and Butler in teaching foremen to assess their workers' performance correctly, Lewin in persuading American housewives in wartime to use "offal" meats like liver, sweetbreads, and kidneys, Jaques to increase efficiency at high management level and improve inter-level understanding at a London engineering works.

The technique works, and it has from the beginning been taken for granted that the explanation of its efficacy lies in a combination of intellectual factors and emotional group pressures. Because the members of the group *participate* in the deliberations that lead up to the change and because they *participate* in encouraging and exhorting each other to maintain the new situation, it has been thought that the discussion method is responsible for these effects, which the straightforward lecture or announcement had failed to bring about. But recently Bennett has queried the too facile conclusions that have been drawn at times from the studies mentioned above. Her starting point is the following argument: "The investigators found that a group of housewives who participated in a discussion and made a public decision by raising their hands, and were then told that there would be a follow-up study to check on what they did, were more likely to serve non-preferred meat than another group who listened to a lecture without making a decision and without being told to expect a follow-up study."

She therefore set up an experiment in which it was possible to distinguish not only between the effects of a lecture versus those of a group discussion, but also between subjects who were induced to come to a definite decision (*either* after discussion *or* after a lecture) and subjects who were not asked to make such a decision (again either after a lecture or after discussion). In this study the action desired was that students should volunteer to be guinea pigs in a psychological experiment that was to be held later in the week, and it was on this that the students had to make a decision. Bennett found that there was less difference in response between the groups who discussed and those who were lectured to, than between groups who were asked to decide then and there and those who were not. She concludes that *it is a deliberate commitment to a course of action, rather than the fact of discussion, that "freezes" the new attitude.*

Clearly Bennett's study was timely and her contribution to our knowledge of group changes very valuable. But it is important to realize, for fear of undervaluing what has been said on the subject of "unfreezing," that generally no very deep-seated attitudes or settled habits are involved in being a guinea pig. For Bennett's subjects, therefore, clarification of issues, insight into problems, and trying out new ways of behavior are very much less important than in the studies made by Lewin, Jaques, or Coch and French. Knowledge of fact, as such, matters less here than does the outlook of the group.

For "freezing" an attitude, therefore, conscious decision and commitment are of great importance and may need to be encouraged (as the popular evangelist knows) even in those groups where discussion has helped in "unfreezing" a previous attitude; the conscious decision sets the seal on a new way of behavior.

In the Committee

It is amusing and instructive to apply the ideas born in the laboratory to the practical working of a committee. By applying the technical terms with which we have been working to a subject of which everyone has some knowledge, the consistency of the theoretical framework can be tested. The good practitioner, with an untrained but intuitive insight into social process, will recognize that the theory makes sense, in so far as it is any good. Indeed, having read thus far he may have begun to realize that "the end of all our striving is to arrive where we started, and know the place for the first time." In so far as the theory is not good, now is the time for its weaknesses to be tested, and this also is a matter for satisfaction. A good wrong theory is one which allows others to put a finger on its faults.

To recapitulate: a good decision is one arrived at after the fullest possible exchange of information and values, and is one to which all members agree. This ensures that all the available facts are taken into consideration and that the morale of the group remains high. A number of functions have to be performed to this end, and techniques are available to achieve it. Responsibility rests on all members of the group, and not on the leader only. Indeed, provided that the necessary functions are carried out, it is a minor matter whether they are carried out by a specially appointed official or not.

The process of steering a proposal through a committee must now be discussed in the light of these considerations. Then attention will be directed more specifically to the normal chairman's functions.

Mr. Jones gives notice at some committee meeting, perhaps under "any other business," that he has been giving some thought to, say, the question of co-opting new members on to the committee and that he hopes to circulate his ideas on the subject to the present members, in the expectation that the matter can be discussed at length on some future occasion. This notifies the others that they will be receiving some communication from him before long, and that his proposal will not be made on a sudden impulse; it will give them time to consider their own ideas on the subject.

After this, he will, if possible, discuss his ideas with the chairman and secretary of his committee, who will be putting the proposal on the agenda for the next meeting. The chairman and secretary are likely to be important and experienced committee members. Good relations in the group demand that they should be consulted early in the proceedings. There may be others in the organization, superior or subordinate, to whom this also applies. It is moreover useful to Mr. Jones, for they may be aware of factual aspects of the matter which may not have occurred to him and a discussion will help him to avoid pitfalls he had not envisaged. Co-option to a committee may seem a small matter, but if it changes the balance of power within that committee, a number of people have to be reassured or consulted. It should be said, in passing, that sound ethics and considerations of courtesy require that discussions at this stage be purely at the level of clarification and fact finding; they are not occasions for canvassing support or for persuasion. Before Jones writes his report he will naturally wish to talk to everyone who can help him to present as co-ordinated and informed a proposal as is possible in the circumstances. It may well be that he has left out some views which others consider important and with which he would not wish to be suddenly confronted at the next committee meeting, where they may easily sway the balance from *pro* to *con*. Difficulties are more easily, and less emotionally, ironed out at this period than at any other. It is even possible that as a result of his informal discussions he will see that his proposal is premature, mistaken, or for some other reason unlikely to gain a majority, in which case he may save his efforts and dignity and withdraw his motion. Nothing harms a current proposal more than the fact that the proposer has had a large number of previous proposals defeated after long arguments. He comes to be regarded as "not an opinion leader."

He therefore sets himself to secure on paper the fullest possible exchange of information and views. His memorandum takes the form of a brief analysis of the present situation, at the end of which he states his proposal. In the next paragraph he lists the advantages and disadvantages of the present position. Then he will show how his proposals will obviate the present disadvantages and procure further advantages. Some difficulties may remain or may even be created by the proposed change. It is wise to state these explicitly, not only so that the fullest information will be provided, but also because it makes it easier in the committee meeting if he is able to show that he understands the objections to his proposal and still feels it worth while to continue. It often seems difficult at a meeting to convince one's opponents that one sees the full force of their objections—to anticipate them on paper saves time later on. It will be noted that after stating his views Mr. Jones has to reformulate them in terms of explicit, concrete proposals.

The memorandum is circulated to the committee and other interested parties. . . . Some other member of the committee may feel sufficiently concerned to circulate his reply, on points where he disagrees. There may indeed be a veritable paperchase. If no reaction is forthcoming, Mr. Jones himself may get in touch with some of his fellow members and ask them for their reactions. The additional information gained in these ways may profoundly affect the proposal that he finally lays before the committee. He has made sure that the committee is as fully informed as lies in his power.

In the committee's discussion of the proposal, much depends on the chairman. A good chairman is the greatest single asset a committee can possess. Unfortunately, not every chairman is ideal. (This is, of course, an additional reason for discussing a proposal with him at length, so that he is at least sure of what is involved. On occasion this may turn almost into a "briefing meeting," in which Mr. Jones makes clear what he wishes to bring out in the discussion and what issue he considers to be less relevant or less pressing.)

Although chairmen may be weak, self-opinionated or stupid, some committees are more handicapped by this than they need be. They tend to use the chairman as a scapegoat for their own lack of skills. It is possible for committee members to take over, in an informal way, some of the chairman's functions, if he is in some respects inadequate. For instance, any member can propose that the motion be now put, and thus attempt to bring the discussion to an end. Or a member may clarify the issue by asking for further information: "What exactly is it that we are called upon to decide, or have decided, and who is to take action on this decision?" (The secretary will often do this in the normal course of his duties.) Or a member may ask that the discussion be continued at the next meeting because no agreement seems possible at present. This enables the committee to move on to the next item. A committee member may even take over the protective role of the chairman for the sake of good feeling in the group. This is patently not the best way of running a committee, but it is better than letting the whole procedure slide for lack of a *de facto* chairman.

A good chairman ensures that everyone contributes to the discussion. His main function is that of facilitator, though he exercises control by discouraging irrelevancies. Some committee members are notoriously slower than others in grasping points; they will be resentful and unco-operative if they feel, at the time or later, that decisions are being made over their heads or in too great a hurry. It is important, therefore, to see that they are following the arguments and have time to digest and consider what is being said. Sometimes the chairman will speak for a little while without adding materially to the argument, "padding" in order to allow such members to catch up, or he will allow some other member to do so. The previous circulation of memoranda is also of great help in overcoming this handicap. A chairman should also keep a constant watch for members who have something to contribute but are diffident about breaking into the discussion. He may occasionally call on such members quite explicitly and ask them to give their views. In some ways he will be behaving like the expert faced with a lay group described earlier in this chapter.

The chairman also keeps order. Speakers often move away from the main point without realizing it and listeners are beguiled into discussing points which do not bear on the decisions to be made. Although some care has necessarily to be taken not to seem overbearing, and some intelligence has to be applied before one can identify with certainty that the point under discussion is in fact irrelevant (and also with due regard to the uses of "padding"), a moment arrives when it is the chairman's duty to suggest that the point now being discussed might be more usefully brought up again under "any other business." To bring discussion back to the right lines, it is helpful to sum up the (relevant) arguments up to the present moment.

References

Allport, G. W. "Catharsis and the Reduction of Prejudice." *Journal of Social Issues*, Vol. 1, 1945.

Bennett, E. B. "Discussion, Decision, Commitment and Consensus in Group Decision." *Human Relations*, Vol. 8, 1955.

Cartwright, D. "Achieving Change in People." *Human Relations*, Vol. 4, 1951.

Coch, L., and J. R. P. French. "Overcoming Resistance to Change." *Human Relations*, Vol. 1, 1948.

Fox, W. M. "Group Reactions to Two Types of Conference Leadership." *Human Relations*, Vol. 10, 1957.

Guetzkow, H., and J. Gyr. "An Analysis of Conflict in Decision-making Groups." *Human Relations*, Vol. 7, 1954.

Jaques, E. "Interpretative Group Discussion as a Method of Facilitating Social Change." *Human Relations*, Vol. 1, 1947.

————. *The Changing Culture of a Factory*, 1951.

Levine, J., and J. Butler. "Lecture versus Group Discussion in Changing Behavior." In *Group Dynamics: Research and Theory*, ed. D. Cartwright and A. Zander. Harper & Row, 1953.

Lewin, K. *Resolving Social Conflicts*. Harper & Row, 1948.

Likert, R. "Behavioral Research: A Guide for Effective Action." In *Some Applications of Behavioral Research*, ed. R. Likert and S. P. Hayes. UNESCO, 1956.

Lippitt, R. *Training in Community Relations*. Harper & Row, 1949.

Maier, N. R. F. "An Experimental Test of the Effect of Training on Discussion Leadership." *Human Relations*, Vol. 6, 1953.

————. "The Quality of Group Discussion as Influenced by a Discussion Leader." *Human Relations*, Vol. 3, 1950.

————, and A. R. Solem. "The Contribution of a Discussion Leader to the Quality of Group Thinking: The Effective Use of Minority Opinions." In *Group Dynamics: Research and Theory*, ed. D. Cartwright and A. Zander, Harper & Row, 1953.

Miller, N. E. "Learnable Drives and Rewards." In *Handbook of Experimental Psychology*, ed. S. S. Stevens. Wiley, 1951.

Seashore, S. "Administrative Leadership and Organizational Effectiveness" and "The Training of Leaders for Effective Human Relations." In *Some Applications of Behavioral Research*, ed. R. Likert and S. P. Hayes. UNESCO, 1956.

Thelen, H. A. *Dynamics of Groups at Work*. University of Chicago Press, 1954.

Ziller, R. C. "Scales of Judgment: A Determinant of the Accuracy of Group Decision." *Human Relations*, Vol. 8, 1955.

Leland P. Bradford, Dorothy Stock
and Murray Horwitz

How to Diagnose Group Problems

A group has two things in common with a machine or with any organism anywhere: (1) it has something to do; (2) it must be kept in running order to do it. These twin functions require continual attention. Groups show their concern for the first—their specific jobs, goals, activities—by establishing procedures, rules of order, expected leadership responsibilities. But sometimes the rules a group sets up for itself fail to take into account its maintenance needs. When this happens the group finds itself bogging down.

The importance of the maintenance function is immediately recognized in other situations. Airliners require the services of maintenance crews as well as navigators. An automobile, a sewing machine, a typewriter, or a whistling peanut wagon that has no care paid to its upkeep soon begins to break down.

We can't, of course, carry the analogy too far. Among the important ways in which groups differ from machines, consider this: a new machine has its peak of efficiency at the beginning of its life. A new group, on the other hand, is likely to be more inept and less efficient at the beginning than it is later. If it is healthy, a group grows and changes, becoming more cohesive, more productive, more capable of helping its individual members in specific ways. The problem of maintenance, therefore, is inseparable from the process of growth.

This [article] will analyze the causes and symptoms of some common problems that interfere with group growth and productivity, and describe some methods of diagnosis.

Group Problems

Three of the most common group problems are: conflict or fight; apathy and non-participation; inadequate decision making.

Fight

We don't necessarily mean a heavyweight bout. Fight here means disagreement, argumentation, the nasty crack, the tense atmosphere, conflict.

From *Adult Leadership*, December 1953, pp. 12–19. Reprinted by permission of American Education Association.

Some ways in which fight can be expressed are: members are impatient with each other; ideas are attacked before they are completely expressed; members take sides and refuse to compromise; members disagree on plans or suggestions; comments and suggestions are made with a great deal of vehemence; members attack each other on a personal level in subtle ways; members insist that the group doesn't have the know-how or experience to get anywhere; members feel the group can't get ahead because it is too large or too small; members disagree with the leader's suggestions; members accuse each other of not understanding the real point; members hear distorted fragments of other members' contributions.

The following are several possible reasons for such fight behavior:

1. The group has been given an impossible job and members are frustrated because they feel unable to meet the demands made of them. This frequently happens when the group is a committee of a larger organization. Perhaps the committee has a job which is impossible because it doesn't have enough members. Or perhaps the job is impossible because it is ambiguous—the task for the committee has not been clearly defined by the larger group. (Under these circumstances the committee has no way of knowing to what extent alternative plans are appropriate or will be acceptable to the larger group.) For whatever reason, an impossible task can easily produce frustration and tension among the members of a group, and this may be expressed in bickering and attack.

2. The main concern of members is to find status in the group. Although the group is ostensibly working on some task, the task is being used by the members as a means of jockeying for power, establishing alignments and cliques, or trying to suppress certain individuals or cliques. Under such circumstances certain members may oppose each other stubbornly on some issue for reasons which have nothing to do with the issue. Or there may be a lot of attack on a personal level which is intended to deflate and reduce the prestige of another member. This kind of power struggle may involve the leader. If it does, the attack will include him, perhaps in the form of refusing to understand or to follow his suggestions (if members can show that the leader is not a good leader, then he should be deposed).

3. Members are loyal to outside groups of conflicting interests. This can happen when the members of a committee are each representing some outside organization. They have an interest in getting a job done within the committee but they also have a loyalty to their own organization. This situation creates conflicts within each individual so that he doesn't know whether he should behave as a member of this committee or as a member of another group. His behavior may be inconsistent and rigid and his inner confusion may burst out as irritation or stubbornness. His loyalty to his own organization may make him feel that he has to protect its interests carefully, keep the others from pulling something over on him, be careful not to give more than he gets. This may lead to a refusal to cooperate, expressions of passive resistance, etc.

4. *Members feel involved and are working hard on a problem.* Members may frequently express impatience, irritation, or disagreement because they have a real stake in the issue being discussed. They fight for a certain plan because it is important to them—and this fight may take the form of real irritation with others because they can't "see" or won't go along with a suggestion which—to the member —is obviously the best one. As long as there is a clearly understood goal and continuing movement on a problem, this kind of fight contributes to good problem solving.

These are not intended to be *all* the possible reasons for fight behavior, but they are some, and they are quite different from each other. The obvious question arises: How can a member or leader tell which diagnosis is appropriate to a specific situation? If the fourth situation obtains, then fight is operating in the service of work and should not worry a group. If fight is interfering with getting things done on the work task, as it is in the other three situations, then it is important to know which description fits the group so that the underlying causes can be attacked.

The solution to this diagnostic problem lies in the need to understand the context in which the symptoms has occurred. That is, one cannot understand fight, or any other symptom, by looking at the symptom only. It is necessary to broaden one's view and look at the syndrome—all the other things which are going on in the group at the same time.

Let's re-examine our four descriptions of symptoms, this time in terms of possible diagnoses.

If every suggestion made seems impossible for practical reasons; if some members feel the committee is too small; if everyone seems to feel pushed for time; if members are impatient with each other; if members insist the group doesn't have the know-how or experience to get anywhere; if each member has a different idea of what the committee is supposed to do; if whenever a suggestion is made, at least one member feels it won't satisfy the larger organization:

Then the group may have been given an impossible job and members are frustrated because they feel unable to meet the demands made of them, or the task is not clear or is disturbing.

If ideas are attacked before they are completely expressed; if members take sides and refuse to compromise; if there is no movement toward a solution of the problem; if the group keeps getting stuck on inconsequential points; if members attack each other on a

personal level in subtle ways; if there are subtle attacks on the
leadership; if there is no concern with finding a goal or sticking to the
point; if there is much clique formation:

Then the main concern of members may be in finding status in
the group. The main interest is not in the problem. The problem is
merely being used as a vehicle for expressing interpersonal concerns.

If the goal is stated in very general, non-operational terms; if
members take sides and refuse to compromise; if each member is
pushing his own plan; if suggestions don't build on previous suggestions, each member seeming to start again from the beginning; if
members disagree on plans or suggestions; if members don't listen to
each other, each waiting for a chance to say something:

Then each member is probably operating from a unique, unshared point of view, perhaps because the members are loyal to
different outside groups with conflicting interests.

If there is a goal which members understand and agree on; if
most comments are relevant to the problems; if members frequently
disagree with each other over suggestions; if comments and suggestions are made with a great deal of vehemence; if there are occasional
expressions of warmth; if members are frequently impatient with
each other; if there is general movement toward some solution of the
problem:

Then, probably, members feel involved and are working hard on
a problem. The fight being expressed is constructive rather than
destructive in character and reflects real interest on the part of
members.

Apathy

An apathetic membership is a frequent ailment of groups.
Groups may suffer in different degrees from this disease. In some
cases members may show complete indifference to the group task,
and give evidences of marked boredom. In others, apathy may take
the form of a lack of genuine enthusiasm for the job, a failure to
mobilize much energy, lack of persistence, or satisfaction with poor
work.

Some ways in which apathy may be expressed are: frequent
yawns; people dozing off; members lose the point of the discussion;
low level of participation; conversation drags; members come late;
are frequently absent; slouching and restlessness; overquick decisions; failure to follow through on decisions; ready suggestions for
adjournment; failure to consider necessary arrangements for the next
meeting; reluctance to assume any further responsibility.

A commonly held idea is that people require inspirational leadership in order to maintain a high level of interest and morale and to
overcome apathy. An outgrowth of this belief is the prescription of pep

talks which, unfortunately, have only momentary effects, if any, and which become less and less effective the more often they are used. To overcome or prevent apathy, we must treat the causes rather than the symptoms.

Here are some of the common reasons for apathy:

1. *The problem upon which the group is working does not seem important to the members, or it may seem less important than some other problem on which they would prefer to be working.* The problem may be important to someone. Perhaps to some outside part, perhaps to the total organization of which the group is a part, perhaps to the group leader, or even to a minority of the members. But it fails to arouse positive feelings or "involvement" on the part of the apathetic members.

Sometimes problems will be considered because of tradition. Again, members may find it difficult to express themselves freely enough to call for reconsideration of an unsatisfactory group goal. Sometimes, in organizational settings, problems are assigned, and the members haven't enough information to judge why the problem is important, except that "somebody upstairs" thinks it is. Again, the problem may be important to the leader or to some dominant member, and the group is coerced by these individuals into working on the problem as if it were really its own. In all of these cases the members will feel that they have had no part in initiating the problem, but that it has been imposed upon them. The basic feature of such imposed, "meaningless" tasks is that they are not related to the present needs of the members.

2. *The problem may seem important to members, but there are reasons which lead them to avoid attempting to solve the problem.* If members both desire to achieve the goal and fear attempting to achieve it, they are placed in a situation of conflict which may lead to tension, fatigue, apathy. Where subordinates feel they will be punished for mistakes, they will avoid taking action, hoping to shift responsibility to someone higher up the line of organizational authority. Similar fears, and similar desires to avoid working on particular problems, may stem from hostile feelings to other individuals, or to subgroups within the group. Sometimes the group atmosphere is such that members avoid exposing themselves to attack or ridicule, and feel insecure, self-conscious or embarrassed about presenting their ideas.

3. *The group may have inadequate procedures for solving the problem.* Inadequacies in procedure arise from many sources. There may be lack of knowledge about the steps which are necessary to reach the goal. There may be poor communication among members within the group, based on a failure to develop mutual understanding. There may be a poor coordination of effort so that contributions to the

discussion are made in a disorganized, haphazard way, with a failure of one contribution to build upon previous ones. Members may not have the habit of collecting facts against which to test decisions, so that decisions turn out to be unrealistic and unrealizable.

4. *Members may feel powerless about influencing final decisions.* Although none of the apathy-producing conditions described above exist, it is possible that any decisions they arrive at are "meaningless." If the decisions will have no practical effects, the activity of problem solving becomes only an academic exercise. Examples of this may be found in committees within an organization which are assigned some job, where members feel that their recommendations will get lost somewhere up the line. Or perhaps they may feel that the top personnel in the organization are pretending to be "democratic," and are only making a show of getting participation, but will in all likelihood ignore their suggestions. In such cases groups tend to operate ritualistically, going through the required motions, without involvement.

The same effect may occur if within the group there is a domineering leader, who is recognized by other members as making all the decisions. Again, it is pointless for the members to invest their emotional energy in attempting to create solutions to the problem. Apathy may also arise because individual members are passed by while a smoothly functioning subgroup forces quick decisions, not giving the slower members opportunity to make decisions. Status differences within the group will frequently have the same effect. People with lower status may find it difficult to get an opportunity to be heard by other members, with the result that they come to feel that their contributions will have little effect upon the outcome.

5. *A prolonged and deep fight between a few members has dominated the group. Frequently two or three dominant and talkative members of a group will compete with each other or with the leader so much that every activity in the group is overshadowed by the conflict. Less dominant members who feel inadequate to help solve the conflict become apathetic and withdraw from participation.*

In considering these five types of causes for apathy, it seems clear we have to direct our attention to underlying conditions, rather than symptoms. Measures which are taken, directed at the symptom itself—pep talks, for example, may be completely off the mark. It should also be borne in mind that while a single explanation may largely account for the apathetic behavior, this is not necessarily the case. Any of the suggested reasons may apply, in any combination, and in varying degrees. To determine whether a given reason applies to a particular group situation, it is sometimes helpful to look for the set of symptoms, the syndrome—which may be associated with each cause. Not all the symptoms under each set need be present to indicate that the disease is of a given type, but if several can be observed, it is probably a good bet that the particular diagnosis applies.

If questions may be raised about what's really our job, what do *they* want us to do; if members fail to follow through on decisions; if there is no expectation that members will contribute responsibly, and confused, irrelevant statements are allowed to go by without question; if members wonder about the reason for working on this problem; if suggestions are made that we work on something else; if the attitude is expressed that we should just decide on anything, the decision doesn't really matter; if members seem to be waiting for a respectable amount of time to pass before referring the decision to the leader, or to a committee; if members are inattentive, seem to get lost and not to have heard parts of the preceding discussion; if suggestions frequently "plop," are not taken up and built on by others; if no one will volunteer for additional work:

Then the group goal may seem unimportant to the members.

If there are long delays in getting started, much irrelevant preliminary conversation; if the group shows embarrassment or reluctance in discussing the problem at hand; if members emphasize the consequences of making wrong decisions, imagine dire consequences which have little reference to ascertainable facts; if members make suggestions apologetically, are over-tentative, and hedge their contributions with many "ifs" and "buts"; if proposed solutions are frequently attacked as unrealistic; if suggestions are made that someone else ought to make the decision—the leader, an outside expert, or some qualified person outside the group; if members insist that we haven't enough information or ability to make a decision, and appear to demand an unrealistically high level of competence; if the group has a standard of cautiousness in action; if numerous alternative proposals are suggested, with the group apparently unable to select among them:

Then members probably fear working toward the group goal.

If no one is able to suggest the first step in getting started toward the goal; members seem to be unable to stay on a given point, and each person seems to start on a new tack; if members appear to talk past, to misunderstand each other, and the same points are made over and over; if the group appears to be unable to develop adequate summaries, or restatements of points of agreement; if there is little evaluation of the possible consequences of decisions reached, and little attention is given to fact finding or use of special resources; if members continually shift into related, but off-target tasks; if complaints are made that the group's job is an impossible one; if subgroups continually form around the table, with private discussions held off to the side; if there is no follow-through on decisions or disagreement in the group about what the decisions really were; if complaints are made that you can't decide things in a group anyway, and the leader or somebody else should do the job:

Then the group may have inadequate problem-solving procedures.

If the view is expressed that someone else with more power in the organization should be present in the meeting, that it is difficult to communicate with him at a distance; if unrealistic decisions are made, and there is an absence of sense of responsibility for evaluating consequences of decisions; if the position is taken that the decision doesn't really matter because the leader or someone outside the group isn't really going to listen to what we say; if there is a tendency to ignore reaching consensus among members, the important thing being to get the leader to understand and listen; if the discussion is oriented toward power relations, either within the group, jockeying to win over the leader, or outside the group, with interest directed toward questions about who really counts in the organization; if doubts are voiced about whether we're just wasting our efforts in working on this program; if members leave the meeting feeling they had good ideas which they didn't seem to be able to get across:

Then members feel powerless about influencing final decisions.

If two or three members dominate all discussion, but never agree; if conflict between strong members comes out no matter what is discussed; if dominant members occasionally appeal to others for support, but otherwise control conversation; if decisions are made by only two or three members:

Then a conflict among a few members is creating apathy in the others.

Inadequate Decision Making

Getting satisfactory decisions made is often a major struggle in the group. . . . Here is a list of common symptoms of inefficient decision making.

If the group swings between making too rapid decisions and having difficulty in deciding anything; if the group almost makes the decision but at the last minute retreats; if group members call for definition and redefinition of minute points; if the discussion wanders into abstractions:

Then there has been a premature calling for a decision, or the decision is too difficult, or the group is low in cohesiveness and lacks faith in itself.

If the group has lack of clarity as to what the decision is; if there is disagreement as to where consensus is; if a decision is apparently made but challenged at the end; if group members refuse responsibility; if there is continued effort to leave decision making to a leader, subgroup or outside source:

Then the decision area may be threatening to the group, either because of unclear consequences, fear of reactions of other groups, or fear of failure for the individuals.

Improving Group Efficiency

Today guided missiles have a feedback mechanism built into them that continuously collects information about the position of the target in relation to the flight of the missile. When the collected information indicates a shift of the target or a discrepancy in the arc of flight of the missile, the feedback mechanism corrects the flight of the missile.

Most houses with central heating today have a small feedback mechanism, called a thermostat. When the information collected by it indicates the temperature is below a certain point, the mechanism signals the furnace to turn itself on. When information is collected by the thermostat indicates that the temperature is too high, it signals the furnace to stop.

Groups need to build in feedback mechanisms to help in their own steering. Such a process of feedback calls for collecting information on the discrepancy between what the group wants to do (its target) and what it is doing (reaching its target) so that it can make corrections in its direction.

Diagnosis and Feedback

Human beings, and therefore groups, not only need continuous self-correction in direction but also (and here they differ from machines) need to learn or grow or improve. Collecting adequate data and using this information to make decisions about doing things differently is one of the major ways of learning.

There are three basic parts to the process of changing group behavior: collecting information; reporting the information to the group; making diagnoses and decisions for change.

Who Should Diagnose?

If a member of a group strives to improve his own behavior in the group so that he can make more useful contributions, he will need to make his own personal observations and diagnoses about the group and about his behavior in it. Each member has this individual responsibility.

If the group as a whole is to make decisions about changing its procedures or processes, then the entire group must assume responsibility for collaborative diagnoses of its difficulties and its effective-

ness. If the leader takes over this function, he continues to direct and dominate the group—leading them like sheep. If only the leader analyzes group difficulties and acts upon them, only he learns. Similar problems arise if diagnosis is left to any group member; he may too readily use this job to steer the group in the direction he desires.

Each member and the leader may guide and encourage the group toward diagnosis, but the responsibility for self-steering and the opportunities to learn and to grow must remain with the group if it is to improve its operational effectiveness.

Collecting Information

While analysis and evaluation of information and decision about what to do should be carried out by the total group, the collecting of information may be delegated. A number of patterns of delegation are possible.

1. The leader, serving also as observer, can report to the group certain pertinent observations he has made about problems and difficulties of group operation. However, although the leader may have more experience with groups, to add the function of observer to his leadership responsibilities complicates his job and also tends to create greater dependency upon him.

But when the group is unfamiliar with the process of observation, the leader may play an informal observer role for a few meetings, gradually getting other group members to assume this function.

2. The group may appoint one of its members, perhaps on a rotating basis, to serve as group observer, with the task of noting the manner in which the group works. While a group loses a member as far as work on its task is concerned, it can gain in the growth and improvement of the group.

Frequently there is a leader-team made up of a discussion leader and observer. The leader and observer work together in behalf of the group, one helping to guide the group and making procedural suggestions, the other watching how it works.

When a leader-team is formed, it makes possible team planning for each meeting. Between meetings the leader-observer team can look back at the past meeting from two vantage points, and look forward to the next meeting.

3. A third method calls for all group members to be as sensitive as they can, while participating actively, to the particular problems the group faces. Although in mature groups members may raise a question about group procedures or maintenance at any time as a normal contribution to the discussion, in new groups the leader may start a discussion looking at how the group has worked and what its problems are. This may occur at some time during the discussion,

when the group has bogged down, or during the last fifteen minutes to half an hour as an evaluation of the entire meeting.

What Information to Collect?

Because of the many group problems and the many causes of these problems, there is a wide range of information that a group may need at different points in time. General questions such as these may help it get started:

1. What is our goal? Are we "on" or "off the beam"?
2. Where are we in our discussion? At the point of analyzing the problem? Suggesting solutions? Testing ideas?
3. How fast are we moving? Are we bogged down?
4. Are we using the best methods of work?
5. Are all of us working or just a few?
6. Are we making any improvement in our ability to work together?

In any observation of a group, more can be seen than can possibly be used for steering, corrective, or growth purposes. The following questions may help guide an observer in collecting data about a group.

1. What basic problems does the group seem to have for which information is needed?
2. What is the most important or pertinent information? What information will lead the group into stray paths?
3. What is the essential minimum of material the group needs?

Methods of Observation

Just as there are many areas of information about group behavior, so there are many possible guides and scales for observation. Frequently groups develop such scales to fit their particular needs. Three techniques of observation are given, each useful for collecting a different kind of information.

Who Talks to Whom?

The number of lines made by the observer on [Form 1] indicates the number of statements made in a fifteen-minute period—20. Four of these were made to the group as a whole, and so the arrows go only to the middle of the circle. Those with arrows at each end of a line show that the statement made by one person to another was responded to by the recipient.

We see that one person, Harold, had more statements directed toward him than did anyone else and that he responded or partici-

Form 1

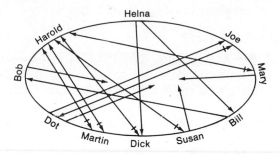

Form 2

Member No.	1	2	3	4	5	6	7	8	9	10
1. Encourages										
2. Agrees, accepts										
3. Arbitrates										
4. Proposes action										
5. Asks suggestion										
6. Gives opinion										
7. Asks opinion										
8. Gives information										
9. Seeks information										
10. Poses problem										
11. Defines position										
12. Asks position										
13. Routine direction										
14. Depreciates self										
15. Autocratic manner										
16. Disagrees										
17. Self-assertion										
18. Active aggression										
19. Passive aggression										
20. Out-of-field										

(Based upon observation categories discussed in *Interaction Process Analysis*, by Robert F. Bales. Addison-Wesley, 1950.)

pated more than anyone else. The short lines drawn at the head of one of the pair of arrows indicate who initiated the remark. Harold, the leader, in other words, had remarks directed at him calling for response from four other people.

Who Makes What Kinds of Contribution?

[Form 2] makes possible the quick rating not only of who talked, but the type of contribution. Individuals in the group are given numbers which are listed at the top of the columns. At the end of a time period it is possible to note the frequency and type of participation by each member.

What Happened in the Group?

[Form 3] can be used as a checklist by an observer to sum up his observations, or it can be filled out by all group members to start an evaluation discussion. Forms 1 and 2 can be used only by a full-time observer.

Form 3

1. What was the general atmosphere in the group?
   Formal————   Informal————
   Competitive————   Cooperative————
   Hostile————   Supportive————
   Inhibited————   Permissive————
   Comments:_____

2. Quantity and quality of work accomplished?
   Accomplishment: High_____ Low_____
   Quality of Production: High_____ Low_____
   Goals: Clear————   Vague————
   Methods: Clear————   Vague————
               Flexible————   Inflexible————
   Comments:_____

3. Leader behavior?
   Attentive to group needs————
   Supported others————
   Concerned only with topic————   Took sides————
   Dominated group————   Helped group————
   Comments:_____

4. Participation?
   Most people talked————   Only few talked————
   Members involved————   Members apathetic————
   Group united————   Group divided————
   Comments:_____

Reporting Information to The Group

The second step is feeding back pertinent information to the entire group. Whether the information is collected and reported by the leader or by the observer, it is very easy to hurt the group rather than help it. The following cautions are particularly pertinent in reporting to the group.

1. Be sensitive to what information the group is ready to use—what will be most helpful to the group now, rather than what was the most interesting point observed.
2. Don't avalanche the group with information. If too much information is given it can't be used. Select only two or three observations which will stimulate thinking and discussion. Let the group ask for more information as they need it.
3. Don't praise the group too much. Learning doesn't take place by being told only when we are on the beam. Mentioning accomplishments is desirable as it helps difficulties get honestly faced.
4. Don't punish or preach or judge. The observer can't play the role of God. He says, "It was interesting that participation was less widespread today than yesterday." He doesn't say, "Some of you dominated the discussion today."
5. It is easier to discuss role behavior than people's behavior. "What role did the group need filled at that time?" rather than "That behavior is bad."
6. Go light on personality clashes. It is usually better to discuss what helped and what hindered the whole group.

Evaluating Information and Deciding about Change

The third stage is diagnosis from the information reported and the consideration of what the group and its members will do differently in the future. Usually this has a number of steps.

1. The members assess the observations, relate them to their experiences, test to see if they agree with the report.
2. The group examines the reasons. What caused a thing to happen? Could we have recognized it earlier?
3. The group moves to a decision of what to do. What can be done in future similar circumstances? What can individual members do earlier to help? What methods or procedures should be changed? What new directions sought?

This stage is the crucial one if the group is to benefit from its feedback activities. Unless the members are able to gain new insights into the functioning of the group, and are able to find new ways of behaving, the group will not improve its processes and continue in its growth and development.

It is very easy for the time of the discussion to be consumed by the first two steps in this procedure. The leader, as well as the members, needs to be sensitive to this danger and encourage the group to move into the third step of decision. Although the decisions which are made may be quite simple, agreement on future action sets up common expectations for the next meeting and gives a point to the evaluation.

References

Benne, Kenneth, and Bozidar Muntyan. *Human Relations in Curriculum Change.* Dryden Press, 1951. Brings together representative samples from recent literature on the improvement of group operation.

Cartwright, Dorwin, and Alvin Zander (eds.). *Group Dynamics: Research and Theory.* Harper & Row, 1953. A collection of basic research reports.

Strauss, Bert, and Frances Strauss. *New Ways to Better Meetings.* Viking, 1951. A popular presentation of concepts and methods of group operation.

Daniel Katz
and Robert L. Kahn

The Taking
of Organizational Roles

Frame of reference is everything. Macro- and micro-economics appear to the noneconomist as minor subdivisions of a generally homogeneous field. To the dwellers within each of those specialized areas, however, the differences are cosmic and irreconcilable. Psychologists and sociologists also have been guilty of stringing a certain amount of barbed wire along the boundary between their disciplines, each sometimes insisting that there is something slightly suspect if not superfluous about the level of explanation which the other has chosen for his own. On top of this ideological fence sits the social psychologist, striving to look as comfortable as the metaphor will allow. All too often he eases his pain by avoiding the synthesis of sociological and psychological levels of discourse which should be the hallmark of his trade.

To the extent that choice of concepts can contribute to so complex a synthesis, the concept of role is singularly promising. It is at

From Daniel Katz and Robert L. Kahn, *The Social Psychology of Organizations,* John Wiley & Sons, Inc., 1966, pp. 171–198. Reprinted by permission of the publisher once the building block of social systems and the summation of the requirements with which the system confronts the individual member. Indeed, it has been touted for a generation as the example of a concept uniquely fitted to social-psychological investigation and theory.

Linton (1936) was perhaps the first to give the notion of role a central place in any of the social sciences; Newcomb (1950) brought it from anthropology into social psychology and made it the key concept in his theoretical approach. Parsons (1951) and Merton (1957) consider it essential to understanding social action and social structure. In spite of these and other advocates, however, the role concept has been viewed with justifiable disenchantment by writers who combed the literature seeking in vain the research fulfillment of that conceptual promise (Neiman and Hughes, 1951).

. . . [Here we] link the organizational and individual levels by making explicit the social-psychological processes by which organizational roles are defined and role behavior is evoked in the ongoing organization. More specifically, we will review briefly the implications of viewing the organization as a system of roles. We will consider role-sending as a continuing cyclical process by means of which each person is socialized into his organizational role, informed about the acceptability of his role behavior, and corrected as necessary. We will examine some of the properties of the organization which determine the nature of specific roles. Finally we will consider the extent to which the process of role-taking is modified by enduring properties of personality and of interpersonal relations.

The Organization as a System of Roles

In defining human organizations as open systems of roles, we emphasize two cardinal facts: the *contrived nature* of human organizations, and the unique properties of a *structure consisting of acts or events* rather than unchanging physical components.[1] There are, of course, many ramifications of these facts. It follows, for example, that human organizations attain constancy and stability in terms of the relationships among their units, rather than in terms of the units themselves. Indeed, one of the chief strengths of formal organization is its constancy under conditions of persistent turnover of personnel. It follows also that, since the units of organization are not linked physically, they must be linked psychologically. Since the organization consists of the patterned and motivated acts of human beings, it will continue to exist only so long as the attitudes, beliefs, perceptions, habits, and expectations of human beings evoke the required motivation and behavior. In short, each behavioral element in the

---

1. The exposition of role and related concepts draws heavily on Chapter 2 of Kahn, *et al.* (1964).

pattern is to a large extent caused and secured by the others. These facts in turn imply that human organizations are characterized by a paradoxical combination of durability and fragility. They remain intact only so long as the intangible psychological cement holds, and yet their intactness and longevity is independent of the life-span of any and all organizational members. There is a variability and flexibility to these social contrivances which free them from the biological cycle of birth, growth, and death.

The emphasis on interdependent acts as the substance of organization is reminiscent of symbiotic relationships. . . . Formal organizations, however, involve no symbiosis in the strict sense of that term; it is not instinct and immediate biological gratification which motivates role behavior in organizations. Rather, it is a process of learning the expectations of others, accepting them, and fulfilling them—primarily for the extrinsic rewards of membership, although many other motives enter into the taking of organizational roles. There is intrinsic satisfaction in the skillful and successful meshing of our own efforts with those of others, in meeting their expectations as they meet ours, especially if the process affords the expression of valued abilities or the acquisition of new ones.

When we observe an organization in motion, its systemic nature is immediately visible. We have only to look beyond the buildings and grounds, and the individuals present, to see that what is literally organized are acts—people acting on materials, acting on machines, but above all interacting with each other. In any organization we can locate each individual in the total set of ongoing relationships and behaviors comprised by the organization. The key concept for doing this is *office*, by which is meant a particular point in organizational space; space in turn is defined in terms of a structure of interrelated offices and the pattern of activities associated with them. Office is essentially a relational concept, defining each position in terms of its relationship to others and to the system as a whole. Associated with each office is a set of *activities* or expected behaviors. These activities constitute the *role* to be performed, at least approximately, by any person who occupies that office.

Each office in an organization is directly related to certain others, less directly to still others, and only remotely related to some offices in the organization. The closeness of such relationships is defined by the work flow and technology of the organization, and by the lines of authority (managerial subsystem).

Consider the office of press foreman in a factory manufacturing external trim parts for automobiles. The offices most directly related to that of the press foreman might include the general foreman of the trim department and the superintendent of sheet-metal operations. From these offices emanate the work assignments to the office of press foreman, and to these offices he turns for approval of work done. Also directly related to the office of press foreman might be that of the stock foreman, whose section provides sheet-metal blanks for the presses, the inspector who must pass or reject the completed stampings, the shipping foreman whose section receives and packages the stampings, and, let us say, 14 press operators whose work the press foreman directs. Imagine the organization spread out like a vast fishnet, in which each knot represents an office and each string a functional relationship between offices. If we pick up the net by seizing any office, the offices to which it is directly attached are immediately seen. Thus the office of press foreman is directly attached to 19 others—general foreman, superintendent, stock foreman, inspector, shipping foreman, and 14 press operators. These 19 offices make up the *role set* (Merton, 1957) for the office of press foreman.

Similarly, each member of an organization is directly associated with a relatively small number of others, usually the occupants of offices adjacent to his in the work-flow structure or in the hierarchy of authority. They constitute his role set and typically include his immediate supervisor (and perhaps his supervisor's immediate superior), his subordinates, and certain members of his own or other departments with whom he must work closely. These offices are defined into his role set by virtue of the work-flow, technology, and authority structure of the organization.

Definition of Role Behavior

Generically, role behavior refers to the recurring actions of an individual, appropriately interrelated with the repetitive activities of others so as to yield a predictable outcome. The set of interdependent behaviors comprise a social system or subsystem, a stable collective pattern in which people play their parts.

When we abstract some of the essential persisting features from the specific acts comprising role behavior we speak of roles. For example, we can speak of the role of the quarterback on a football team in general terms of play selection without specifying the particular signals he barks to his teammates or the specific plays with which they respond. This general description applies to roles both within and outside formal organizations. The various members of the family interact in consistent ways in assuming their roles as father, mother, son, daughter, husband, and wife. In formal organizations many of the functionally specific behaviors comprising the system are specified in written and coded presentations. Moreover, in formal organizations the roles people play are more a function of the social setting than of their own personality characteristics. The basic criterion, then, for studying role behavior is to identify the relevant social system or subsystem and locate the recurring events which fit together in converting some input into an output. This can be done by ascertaining the role expectations of a given set of related offices, since such expectations are one of the main elements in maintaining the role system and inducing the required role behavior.

The Process of Role Sending

All members of a person's role set depend upon his performance in some fashion; they are rewarded by it, judged in terms of it, or require it in order to perform their own tasks. Because they have a stake in his performance they develop beliefs and attitudes about what he should and should not do as part of his role. The prescriptions and proscriptions held by members of a role set are designated *role expectations;* in the aggregate they help to define his role, the behaviors which are expected of him. The role expectations held for a certain person by a member of his role set will reflect that member's conception of the person's office and of his abilities. The content of these expectations may include preferences with respect to specific acts and personal characteristics or styles; they may deal with what the person should do, what kind of person he should be, what he should think or believe, and how he should relate to others. Role expectations are by no means restricted to the job description as it might be given by the head of the organization or prepared by some specialist in personnel, although these individuals are likely to be influential members of the role sets of many persons in the organization.

The mention of influence raises additional issues of definition and theory. Role expectations for any given office and its occupant exist in the minds of members of his role set and represent standards in terms of which they evaluate his performance. The expectations do not remain in the minds of members of the role set, however. They tend to be communicated in many ways; sometimes as direct instructions, as when a supervisor describes to a subordinate the requirements of his job; sometimes less directly, as when a colleague expresses admiration or disappointment in some behavior. The crucial point (for our theoretical view) is that the activities which define a role are maintained through the expectations of members of the role set, and that these expectations are communicated or "sent" to the focal person.[2] In referring to role expectations as sent, we are following the formulation of Rommetveit (1954). He refers to members of a role set as role senders, and to their communicated expectations as the *sent role*.

The numerous acts which make up the process of role sending

2. The term *focal person* will be used to refer to any individual whose role or office is under consideration.

are not merely informational. They are attempts at influence, directed at the focal person and intended to bring about conformity to the expectations of the senders. Some of these influence attempts (for example, those from superiors) may be directed toward the accomplishment of formally specified responsibilities and objectives of office. Others (perhaps from peers or subordinates) may be directed toward making life easier or more pleasant for the senders themselves, in ways which contravene official requirements.

Thus each individual in an organization acts in relation to and in response to the expectations of the members of his role set, not because those expectations constitute some mentalistic field of forces but because they are expressed in explicit behavioral ways. The expression need not be continuous; human memory can be long, and adults in our society have already graduated from a lengthy period of training and socialization in organizational role taking. They have learned a quality and technique of role readiness which lets them anticipate many of the role expectations of others with few cues. But let a person stop performing within the range of organizational acceptability, and there will immediately become visible the membership of his role set and the expectations which they hold for him.

As a communicative and influential process, acts of role sending can be characterized in terms of any of the dimensions appropriate to the measurement of communication and influence. Some of the more important ones proposed by Gross, Mason, and McEachern (1958) include sign (prescriptive or proscriptive), magnitude (strength of the influence attempt), specificity (extent to which the expected behaviors are made concrete and detailed), intensity (extent to which the focal person is allowed freedom of choice in complying or refusing compliance), and range of conditions under which compliance is intended. . . . Our interest in the role-sending process centers upon magnitude or strength of the influence attempt. We are interested also in the psychological basis of influence on which different acts of role-sending depend. Every attempt at influence implies consequences for compliance or noncompliance. In organizations, as we have seen, these commonly take the form of sanctions—gratifications or deprivations which a role sender might arrange for the focal person, depending on his having conformed to the sender's expectation or not. The concept of legitimacy, and its acceptance by organizational members, makes the actual use of such sanctions infrequent. Members obey because the source and substance of the command are legitimate. The availability and visibility of sanctions are important, however, whether or not they are used or even threatened. The strengthening of role sending with the possibility of sanctions is the major basis for gaining compliance with the requirements of formal organization.

The mention of sanctions as necessary to the functioning of formal organizations has become unfashionable, and the word has acquired an unpleasant ring. Yet both the problem and necessity of coercive power in government and in other organizational contexts have been often explored and acknowledged. Such exploration has seldom been carried deeper or carried out with greater effort and anguish than in the formative years of our federal government. With the inadequacies of the confederation still visible, Webster spoke of "the powers of Congress which are perhaps nearly sufficient to answer the needs of our union, were there any method of enforcing their resolutions. . . . A law without a penalty is *mere advice;* a magistrate without the power of punishment is a cypher . . ." (Hockett, 1939).

The Received Role

To understand the response of any member of an organization to the complex pattern of role sending addressed specifically to him, we must regard the organization from the vantage point of his office. When we do so, we see that the members of his role set and the influential pressures which they direct to him are part of his objective environment. To consider his compliance with or deviation from his sent role, however, takes us immediately beyond the objective organization and environment. Each individual responds to the organization in terms of his perceptions of it, which may differ in various ways from the actual organization. In the immediate sense, the individual responds not to the objective organization in his objective social environment but to that representation of it which is in his psychological environment.

The objective organization and the psychological organization of a person may or may not be congruent, depending on his ability and opportunity to perceive organizational reality. Thus for each person in an organization there is not only a sent role, consisting of the influential and communicative acts of the members of his role set, there is also a *received role,* consisting of his perceptions and cognitions of what was sent. How closely the received role corresponds to the sent role is an empirical question for each focal person and set of role senders, and will depend upon properties of the senders, the focal person, the substantive content of the sent expectations, the clarity of the communication, and the like.

It is the sent role by means of which the organization communicates to each of its members the do's and don'ts associated with his office. It is the received role, however, which is the immediate influence on his behavior and the immediate source of his motivation for role performance. Each sent expectation can be regarded as arousing in the focal person a motivational force of some magnitude and direction. This is not to say that these motivational role forces are identical in magnitude and direction with the sent influence attempts that evoked them. When sent-role expectaions are seen by the focal person as illegitimate or coercive, they may arouse strong resistance forces which lead to outcomes different from or even opposite to the expected behavior. It is such processes, repeated for many persons over long periods of time, that produce the persistent component of unintended effects in organizational behavior. Pressures to increase production sometimes result in slowdowns. Moreover, every person is subject to a variety of psychological forces in addition to those stimulated by pressures from his role set in the work situation. Role sendings are thus only a partial determinant of his behavior on the job.

Additional and important sources of influence in role taking are the objective, impersonal properties of the situation itself. In some situations the taking of roles may be aided by the nature of the task and the previous experience of the individual with respect to similar tasks. The soldier in combat seeks cover when under fire not so much because of the expectations of members of his role set as because of the demands of the situation. The man on the assembly line tightens the belt on the passing car both because he has been told that it is his job and because the structuring of his work situation is a constant reminder of what he is supposed to do. People can be conditioned to play their roles by cues other than those of the communicated expectations from other system members. Nevertheless, in most organizations, role behavior is largely dependent upon role sending.

In addition to the motivational forces aroused by sent expectations and other cues, there are important internal sources of motivation for role performance. For example, there is the intrinsic satisfaction derived from the content of the role. The concert pianist has many motives which lead him to give performances; one of them is probably the intrinsic psychological return from exercising a hard-won and valued skill.[3] But there is, in addition to intrinsic satisfaction in expressing valued abilities, another kind of "own force" important in the motivation of role behavior. In a sense each person is a "self sender," that is, a role sender to himself. He too has a conception of his office and a set of attitudes and beliefs about what he should and should not do while in that position. He has some awareness of what behaviors will fulfill his responsibilities, lead to the accomplishment of organizational objectives, or further his own interest. He may even have had a major part in determining the formal responsibilities of his office, especially if he occupies a line or staff position well up in the hierarchy.

Moreover, some of the persisting motives of the individual are

---

3. The patterns of motivation for role behavior, together with the organizational conditions which evoke them and the organizational outcomes which they produce, [are] discussed in Chapter 12, Katz and Kahn (1966).

likely to include the sector of organizational behavior. Through a long process of socialization and formal training within the organization and in the larger culture of which it and he are parts, he has acquired a set of values and expectations about his own behavior and abilities, about the nature of human organizations and the conditions for membership in them. As Miller and Dollard (1962), Dai (1955), and others have observed, the person has an occupational self-identity and is motivated to behave in ways which affirm and enhance the valued attributes of that identity. He comes to the job in a state of what we refer to as role-readiness, a state which includes the acceptance of legitimate authority and compliance with its requests, a compliance which for many people extends to acts which they do not understand and which may violate many of their own values. Milgram's recent work (1963, 1964), reporting that two-thirds of the adult subjects in an experiment obeyed an instruction to administer what they believed to be electrical shocks of several hundred volts to groaning and protesting victims, only highlights the phenomenon of compliance in role behavior.

Multiple Roles and Multiple Activities

An organization is a complex arrangement of many collective cycles of behavior, some of which intersect, others of which are tangential to one another, while still others are connected only indirectly. In other words, the organization is made up of many subsystems. The common treatment of *role* and *office* tends to oversimplify this complexity by neglecting the fact that one office can be located in a number of such role subsystems and that one individual can be involved in many organizational subsystems.

Let us examine more closely the meaning and implications of these assertions. The basic unit of organizational life is the *molar unit of behavior*, the behavioral cycle. This is what we mean by *an activity:* a recurring behavior sequence which has organizational relevance, is held in the form of role expectations by some members of the role set, and which affords some sense of closure on completion. For example, taking four bolts out of a barrel and using them to fasten the left rear fender of an automobile to the body is an activity on the assembly line.

A role consists of one or more recurrent activities out of a total pattern of interdependent activities which in combination produce the organizational output. Role, unless otherwise qualified, will refer to a set of such activities within a single subsystem of the organization and within a single office.

An office is a point (location) in organizational space defined by one or more roles (and thereby one or more activities) intended for performance by a single individual. It locates the individual in relation to his fellows with respect to the job to be done and the giving and taking of orders.

The simplest organizational arrangement occurs when one activity defines role and office. Thus, the job of assembly-line operator No. 23 might consist of the one activity described in the previous example, bolting on the left rear fender. That activity defines the role, and the office is merely the point in organizational space associated with that role and activity.

The situation can become more complex in any of several ways:

Multiple activities may be defined into a single role.
Multiple roles may be defined into a single office.
Multiple offices may be held by a single person.

We have suggested that the simplest organizational arrangement occurs when one activity defines role and office. In fact, a general trend in organizations is to move toward such simplification and to fractionate many jobs into their component activities. That, however, is only part of the total story; the more such role specialization develops at one level, the greater is the need for coordination at a higher level. Thus, the very organization which follows the simplified arrangement of one activity, one role, and one office for its assembly line workers must adopt a more complex plan for higher offices, multiplying their activities and roles. The many specialized subsystems must be interrelated and hence offices created in which these various substructures intersect. In fine, the less the coordinative demand within roles, the greater will be the demand for some means of coordination between roles. That means is usually the creation of a new coordinative office.

The inclusion of multiple activities in a single role and multiple roles in a single office is increasingly evident as we move up the hierarchy in most large organizations. The office of first-line supervisor typically involves two roles; the supervisor is a member of two subsystems—the managerial structure and his own immediate task force. Members of middle management may be involved in relations with the various productive, procurement, and marketing subsystems. Top management has an even greater range of roles today.

Recognition of the many roles assumed by a single person is sometimes expressed by his holding more than one office. The Dean of a graduate school may also be University Vice President for Research. The Secretary of the Communist Party may also be the Premier of the Soviet Union. It is interesting that we generally look upon the holding of multiple offices in an organization as indicating something amiss: a seizure of power, as when a dictator picks up for himself the portfolios of several cabinet ministers; a lack of appropriate manpower; or an inadequacy in the formal organizational plan. There is less tendency, however, to be critical of the same basic process of multiplying the roles played by a single person when all of them are tied to a single office. The essential dilemma is that there is no escape from the coordinative needs resulting from specialized subsystems and fractionated jobs.

It is interesting to speculate on the organizational implications of role definition and office definition within the terms stipulated above. We would offer the following predictions:

1. The more activities contained within a role, the more likely it is to be varied and satisfying, the more likely it is to involve coordination among the activities it comprises, and the less immediate will be the necessity for coordination with other roles and offices.

For example, in a television factory in which each worker (role) builds a complete TV set, there is much coordination of activities within the role but little needed between roles. In a television factory in which the assembly-line system is used, with each worker soldering only a single part or part-cluster into the chassis, there is virtually no intrarole coordination of activities but great need for coordination between roles. If any role is not performed, no workable product is completed. The relationships between roles are multiplicative, not additive.

2. The more interrole coordination an organization requires, the more the achievement of coordination is assigned to offices high in the organizational structure.

The problem of information overload is charactcristically built into the top echelons of large organizations with many specialized subsystems. The offices at the upper levels are typically associated with several subsystems and include several roles; the incumbents are subject to information input from all the subsystems in which they have a role, and the likelihood of overload becomes correspondingly great.

3. The more coordinative demands concentrated in a given office, the more the incumbent seeks a generalized, programmed solution—as in the precise, split-second timing of jobs and subassemblies into the final assembly line. Such a programmed solution is sought because it can be set up to hold for a considerable period of time, thus relieving the incumbent of the continuing press of certain types of decisions. Moreover, it affords similar relief to persons who occupy related offices, by presenting them with a set of predictable behaviors to which they can adjust.

4. The greater the programming of interjob coordination, the greater will be the use of organizational authority and sanctions to prevent any failure of role performance.

All this reminds us again of the costs of "efficiency." The gains of

Taylorism may be real, but they must be computed in a way which includes Taylor's salary. In short, coordination is not free, and reducing the worker role to subhuman specifications has efficiency limits as well as limits suggested by other values. It often involves relocating coordinative costs rather than eliminating them.

The Role Episode

Our description of role sending and role receiving has been based on four concepts: *role expectations,* which are evaluative standards applied to the behavior of any person who occupies a given organizational office or position; *sent role,* which consists of communications stemming from role expectations and sent by members of the role set as attempts to influence the focal person; *received role,* which is the focal person's perception of the role sendings addressed to him, including those he "sends" to himself; and *role behavior,* which is the response of the focal person to the complex of information and influence he has received.

These four concepts can be thought of as constituting a sequence or role episode. The first two, role expectations and sent role, have to do with the motivations, cognitions, and behavior of the members of the role set; the latter two, received role and role behavior, have to do with the cognitions, motivations, and behavior of the focal person. A model of the role episode is presented in Figure 1.

Figure 1   A Model of the Role Episode

Role senders		Focal person	
Expectations	Sent role	Received role	Role behavior
Perception of focal person's behavior; evaluation	Information; attempts at influence	Perception of role, and perception of role sending	Compliance; resistance; "side effects"
I	II	III	IV

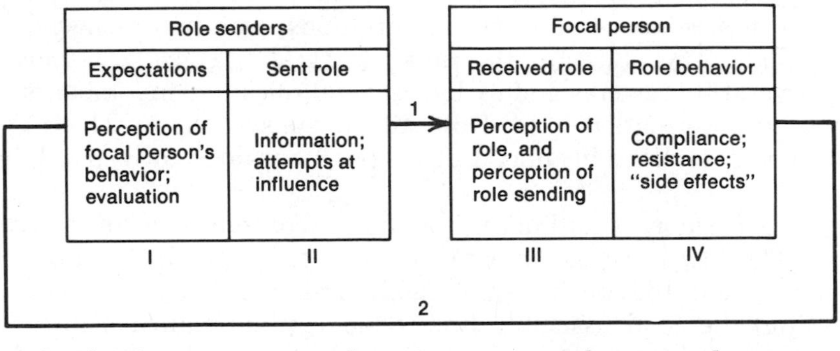

As the figure suggests, there is symmetry between the two complementary phases of the role episode—the cognitions and behavior of role senders on the one hand, and the cognitions and behavior of the focal person on the other. There is also a kind of orderliness to the model viewed in another way; boxes I and III represent processes of perception, cognition, and motivation—processes internal to the person, the role sender in box I, and the focal person in box III. Boxes II and IV represent behaviors—acts undertaken in expression of cognitive and motivational processes. These acts are viewed as role sending when they are the behaviors of members of a role set under our observation, and as role behavior when they are the acts of a focal person (that is, any office occupant whom we have singled out for study).

The designation of an office or person as *focal* is, of course, a matter of convenience; it serves merely to identify our terms of reference for viewing some part of an ongoing organization. A complete study of an organization would require that each office in it be successively treated as focal, its role set identified, the role expectations and sent role measured, and the received role and role behavior similarly described. Every person in an organization receives role sending from one or more others, and in most organizations each person is also a role sender for one or more others.

The ongoing life of a large organization involves many continuous cycles of sending, receiving, responding, evaluating, and sending again by persons in many overlapping role sets. In Figure 1, arrow 1 represents the process of role sending, and arrow 2 represents the process of which the role sender (a) estimates the degree of compliance which he has apparently induced on the part of the focal person and (b) prepares to initiate another cycle.

Arrow 2 is thus a feedback loop; the degree to which a person's behavior conforms to the expectations held for him at one point in time will affect the state of those expectations at the next moment. If his response is essentially a hostile counterattack, his role senders are apt to think of him and behave toward him in ways quite different than if he were submissively compliant. If he complies partially under pressure, they may increase the pressure; if he is obviously overcome with tension and anxiety, they may "lay off." In sum, the role episode is abstracted from a process which is cyclic and ongoing: the response of the focal person to role sending feeds back to each sender in ways that alter or reinforce his expectations and subsequent role sending. The current role sendings of each member of the set depend on his evaluations of the response to his last sendings, and thus a new episode begins.

Even this brief description of the process of role sending and role receiving indicates that the model presented in Figure 1 is in many respects oversimplified. Three of these are of particular importance:

1. The notion of a role episode—neatly fulfilling the Aristotelian aesthetic requirements of beginning, middle, and end—is an abstraction. It is merely a convenient way of representing what we believe to be a complex ongoing process involving all the members of an organization. The convenience consists of assuming role expectations as a starting point, and presenting them as if the process of interaction were a sequence of discrete episodes.

2. A further simplification is the treatment of role expectations

as if there were only a single role sender and he were completely consistent in his expectations, or as if there were consensus among role senders. In fact such consistency and consensus is not attained, and some degree of role conflict is characteristic of human organizations.

3. The third oversimplification inherent in the concept of the role episode is its abstraction from the larger context of organizational events. Every act of role sending and role receiving is in part determined by the context within which it occurs.

Of these three limitations, the first requires no further discussion; the second and third we will consider at greater length.

Role Conflict

To assert that some degree of role conflict is characteristic of human organizations does not imply violence as a way of organizational life. We define *role conflict* as the simultaneous occurrence of two (or more) role sendings such that compliance with one would make more difficult compliance with the other. In the extreme case, compliance with one expectation as sent would exclude completely the possibility of compliance with the other; the two expectations are mutually contradictory. For example, a person's superior may make it clear to him that he is expected to hold his subordinates strictly to company rules. At the same time, his subordinates may indicate in various ways that they would like loose, relaxed supervision, and that they will make things difficult if they are pushed too hard. Here the pressures from above and below are incompatible, since a style of supervision which satisfies one set of expectations violates the other set. Such cases are so common that a whole literature has been created on the problem of the first-line supervisor as "the man in the middle," the "master and victim of double-talk."

Several types of role conflict can be identified. One might be termed *intrasender:* the expectations from a single member of a role set may be incompatible, as for example when a supervisor orders a subordinate to acquire material which is unavailable through normal channels and at the same time warns him against violating those channels. A second type of role conflict we can call *intersender:* expectations sent from one sender are in conflict with those from one or more other senders. The earlier example of the foreman urged by his superior to supervise more closely and by his subordinates to allow them greater freedom fits the category of intersender conflict.

If we look beyond the organization, another type of role conflict becomes apparent—conflict between roles. Such *interrole* conflict occurs whenever the sent expectations for one role are in conflict with those for another role played by the same person. Demands from role senders on the job for overtime or take-home work may conflict with pressures from one's wife to give undivided attention to family affairs during evening hours. The conflict arises between the role of the focal person as worker and his role as husband and father.

All three of these types of conflict—intrasender, intersender, and interrole—are conflicts in the content of the role as sent; they exist as conflicts in the objective environment of the focal person. They give rise, of course, to psychological conflicts of some kind and degree within the focal person. Other types of conflict, however, are generated directly by a combination of externally sent role expectations and internal forces or role expectations which the focal person requires of himself. This fourth type of conflict, which we may call *person-role* conflict occurs when role requirements violate the needs, values, or capacities of the focal person. Pressures on an executive to conclude a profitable agreement in restraint of trade, for example, might be opposed by his personal code of ethics. In other cases of person-role conflict the person's needs and values may lead to behavior which is unacceptable to members of his role set; for example, an ambitious young man may be called up short by his associates for stepping on their toes in his haste to advance in the organization.

From these four basic types of conflict other complex forms of conflict sometimes develop. A very prevalent form of conflict in industrial organizations, for example, is role overload. Overload is typically encountered as a kind of intersender conflict in which the sent expectations of various members of the role set are legitimate and are not logically incompatible. The focal person, however, finds that he cannot complete all of the tasks urged on him by various people within the stipulated time limits and requirements of quality. He is likely to experience overload as a conflict of priorities or as a conflict between quality and quantity. He must decide which pressures to comply with and which to hold off. If it is impossible to deny any of the pressures, he may be taxed beyond the limit of his abilities. Thus overload involves a kind of person-role conflict, and is perhaps best regarded as a complex-emergent type combining aspects of conflict between role senders and conflict between senders and focal person.

The major issue with respect to role conflict, however, is not the typology which one chooses or constructs; it is the prevalence of role conflict as a fact. In a nationwide study of male wage and salary workers, Kahn and his colleagues (1964) found nearly half to be working under conditions of noticeable conflict. Forty-eight percent reported that from time to time they were caught between two sets of people who wanted different things from them, and 15 percent reported this to be a frequent and serious problem. Thirty-nine percent reported being bothered by their inability to satisfy the conflicting demands of their various role senders. The hierarchical and depersonalized nature of large-scale organization is also reflected in these data: 88 percent of all role conflicts reportedly involve pressures from above, and in 57 percent of these cases the spontaneous description of the source of these pressures was given in such impersonal terms as "the company" or "management."

The Context of Role-Taking

The last of the oversimplifications to which we pointed in our model of the role episode was its abstraction from the context in which it occurs. That context can be thought of as consisting of all the enduring properties, the more or less stable characteristics, of the situation within which a role episode takes place. Some of these will be properties of the organization itself; some will be traits of the persons involved in the process of role sending and role receiving; some will be properties of the interpersonal relationships which already exist between the actors in the role episode.

These three additional classes of variables—organizational, personality, and interpersonal—can be conveniently represented in an enlargement and extension of Figure 1. That figure presented a causal sequence: role expectations (I) lead to role-sending (II), which leads to received role (III), which leads to behavior in response to the role as received (IV). That figure and the sequence it represents also forms the core of Figure 2.

The circles in Figure 2 represent not the momentary events of the role episode, but enduring states of the organization, the person, and the interpersonal relations between focal person and role send-

Figure 2   A Theoretical Model of the Factors Involved in Taking Organizational Roles

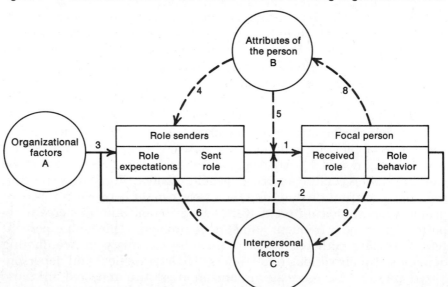

ers. Such enduring properties are for the most part abstractions and generalizations based upon recurrent events and behaviors. For example, characterizing a relationship as supportive means simply that the parties to the relationship have behaved in a supportive manner toward one another on a sufficient number of occasions so that we feel justified in inferring supportiveness as a quality of the relationship. Such repetitions and patterns of events provide the basis and context within each new occurrence can best be understood.

To a considerable extent the role expectations held by the members of a role set—the prescriptions and proscriptions associated with a particular office—are determined by the broader organizational context. The technology of the organization, the structure of its subsystems, its formal policies, and its rewards and penalties dictate in large degree the content of a given office. What the occupant of that office is supposed to do, with and for whom, is given by these and other properties of the organization itself. Although human beings are doing the "supposing" and rewarding, the structural properties of organization are sufficiently stable so that they can be treated as independent of the particular persons in the role set. For such properties as size, number of echelons, and rate of growth, the justifiable abstraction of organizational properties from individual behavior is even more obvious.

The organizational circle (A) in Figure 2 represents a set of variables. Some of them characterize the organization as a whole; others describe some part of it. Arrow 3 asserts a causal relationship between certain organizational variables and the role expectations held about and sent to a particular position. For example, there is an almost linear relationship between organizational size and the amount of reported role conflict and tension in the organization (Kahn, *et al.*, 1964).

Enduring attributes of the person (circle B) refer to all those variables which describe the propensity of an individual to behave in certain ways—his motives and values, his defense preferences, his sensitivities and fears. Such factors affect the role episode in several ways. First, some traits of the person tend to evoke or facilitate certain evaluations and behaviors from his role senders (arrow 4). Second, the same sent role can be experienced differently by different people; that is, personality factors act as conditioning variables in the relationship between the role as sent and the role as received and responded to. Finally, we propose as a hypothesis that role behavior has effects on personality (arrow 8). This is simply the hypothesis that we become what we do, and in a sense we un-become what we do not do. The man who is required to play a subservient role, for example, cannot do so over an extended time without consequent changes in personality. Most abilities atrophy if unexercised.

As Figure 2 indicates, interpersonal relations (circle C) fulfill functions parallel to those already described for attributes of the person. The expectations held for and sent to a focal person depend to some degree on the quality of interpersonal relations between him and the members of his role set (arrow 6). He will also interpret differently the role sendings he receives, depending on his interpersonal relations with the senders (arrow 7). Praise and blame have one set of meanings when they come from a trusted source, and another when they stem from untrusted sources. Finally, the behavior of the focal person feeds back to and has effects on his interpersonal relations with members of his role set (arrow 9). If he suddenly and persistently refuses to comply in any respect with their role sendings, for example, we would predict not only an immediate change in their evaluation of his role behavior (arrow 2), but an enduring change in their liking for him (arrow 9).

The research evidence for this model of role taking in organizations is substantial in quantity but irregular in quality and in relevance. That distinctive attitudes, values, and points of view are characteristically associated with different roles has been a part of human experience and folk wisdom for time beyond recollection, and within the past 20 years this fact has been well documented.

Stouffer and his colleagues (1949) reported sharp differences between officers and enlisted men in their attitudes toward the army, with officer opinions consistently more favorable. Jacobson's findings (1951) showed similar differences among workers, foremen, and stewards in their attitudes toward the company and the union. Research on the differential perceptions of supervisors and subordinates shows consistently that role or position in the organization is related to perceptions no less than to attitudes and values. Mann's findings (Likert, 1961) that 76 percent of the foremen in a utility report that they "always or almost always get their subordinates' ideas in the solution of job problems" but that only 16 percent of the workers report being so consulted, is typical of such research.

Most such findings lend themselves to either of two interpretations or perhaps to a combination of both. One can argue that the role shapes the attitudes and perceptions of the individual, or that the individual is selected for his psychological goodness-of-fit to the role requirements. Lieberman (1956) has contributed the most definitive evidence for the former interpretation. He was able to measure the perceptions and attitudes of employees in two appliance plants three times during a period of three years: once when all were rank-and-file workers, a year later when 23 had become foremen and 35 had been elected stewards, and two years later still when about half of the new foremen and stewards had reverted to nonsupervisory jobs and half had continued in their new roles.

In their rank-and-file days, there were no significant differences between future foremen and future stewards, although both groups were more ambitious, more critical, and less unquestioningly loyal to the company than were the workers destined to become neither foremen nor stewards. On becoming foremen, Lieberman's subjects tended to report more favorably about the company as a place to work, to be more favorable in their perceptions of top management, and to endorse the principle of incentive pay. Those men who became union stewards became, according to their responses, more favorable toward unions in general, toward the top officers of their own union, and toward the principle of seniority rather than ability as a basis for wage payments. Those foremen and stewards who subsequently returned to the worker role tended also to revert to the perceptions and attitudes of workers; those who remained as foremen and stewards showed more sharply as time passed the kinds of differences described above. Mean differences between future foremen and future stewards on the numerous scales used were less than one percentage point at the time when all subjects were workers; 48 percent between the foremen and stewards after one year in role, and 62 percent after three years in role.

Even these data, however, leave unsupported many of the linkages stipulated in the model. Lieberman's data argue strongly for a causal relationship between the office an individual occupies in an organization (foreman, steward) and his expressed attitudes on job-relevant matters. Whether the characteristic changes in attitude are brought about because of the causal sequence of different role expectations, the sending of these expectations as attempts at influence, the receiving of such communications, and the subsequent response to them remains untested by Lieberman's research. The formulation of such a process with respect to the sending of norms was first proposed by Rommetveit (1954), but he was concerned with the religious attitudes and sex roles of Norwegian adolescents rather than the work situation and the organizational context. Other research, however, can be interpreted as supporting many of the hypotheses specified by the model. Let us consider some of this research, in the order suggested by the numbered arrows in Figure 2.

The Relationship between Role Expectations and Response (Arrow 1)

Sarbin and Williams (1953) conducted a laboratory experiment which demonstrated something of the expertise which people acquire in receiving and understanding communications from role senders. The subjects of the experiment listened to 38 sentences, each conveying some role expectation; their task was to determine the age, sex, and role of the sender, the intended receiver, and the action or role behavior which was being requested. Performance of the experimental subjects was so accurate that the resulting distributions showed the typical J-curve of conforming behavior.

Gross, Mason, and McEachern (1958), in their excellent study of school boards and school superintendents, demonstrated a number of significant relationships between the expectations and sending to members of a role set, on the one hand, and the perceptions and responses of the target or focal person on the other. Role sending from the school board to the superintendent was associated with high job satisfaction on the part of the superintendent when the expectations of the board were consistent with his professional standards, and with low job satisfaction when they were not.

Kahn and his colleagues (1964), in their studies of role conflict and ambiguity, found that objective role conflict (measured by the statements of role senders that they wished for specific changes in the focal person's role behavior) was related to low job satisfaction, low confidence in the organization, and a high degree of job-related tension. The effects of role ambiguity (defined as lack of information regarding supervisory evaluation of one's work, about opportunities for advancement, scope of responsibility, and expectations of role senders) were in general comparable to those of role conflict. Persons subjected to conditions of ambiguity on the job tended to be low in job satisfaction, low in self-confidence, high in tension and in a sense of futility.

Gross and his colleagues (1958) also found that role conflict around such issues as hiring, promotion, teacher salaries, and budgetary matters was associated with low job satisfaction on the part of the superintendent. Getzels and Guba (1954) had previously demonstrated a relationship between role conflict and reduced teaching effectiveness in nine air force training schools.

The Feedback Effect of Role Behavior on the Expectations of Role Senders (Arrow 2)

This effect, which is stipulated in the model, has yet to be appropriately tested. The required research would be longitudinal in design, in order to answer the question of whether the performance of the focal person in successive cycles of role sending and response leads to modifications of the expectations of role senders. Some suggestive findings are available, however. Jackson and his colleagues (1951) found that workers tended to express anti-union attitudes when their stewards failed to involve them in decision making. Jacobson interpreted this to be the result of the workers' discovery that their initial expectations were unfulfilled, but the data permit other interpretations as well. Kahn and his colleagues (1964) found that role senders expressed fewer intentions to bring about change on the part of focal persons who were high in rigidity, presumably because the intractable performance of the focal person had led to a reduction of expectations on the part of his role senders.

Organizational Factors as Determinants of Role Expectations (Arrow 3)

This category of findings reminds us that role expectations and the process of role sending do not arise as spontaneous and idiosyncratic expressions on the part of role senders nor as simple responses to some previous behavior of the focal person to whom the expectations were sent. Such factors serve only to mediate the major determinants of role sending, which are to be found in the systemic properties of the organization as a whole, the subsystem in which the role senders are located, and the particular position occupied by each.

Gross, Mason, and McEachern (1958) found that organizational size was a determinant of the pattern of role expectations. Lack of consensus was more frequent in large school systems, and to some extent in communities which utilized complex organizational forms of decision making rather than the open town meeting. Moreover, members of large school boards were less accepting of any deviation from established lines of authority.

Getzels and Guba (1954) had found earlier that, among the nine air force schools included in their study, strict adherence to military procedure as an organizational norm was associated with lesser role conflict. This finding they interpreted as a problem in normative congruence between system and supersystem, asserting that those schools which maintained strict military procedure were consistent with the norms of the air force and the military establishment as a whole, while those schools which deviated from such procedure created problems of conflict for their staff, who were necessarily members of both the school and the larger military organization.

Kahn and his colleagues (1964) identified five dimensions of normative expectations which appeared to be characteristic of organizations as systems rather than of individual persons or roles. These included the extent to which one is expected to obey rules and follow orders, the extent to which supervisors are expected to show personal interest in and nurture their subordinates, the closeness or generality with which supervision is to be accomplished, the extent to which all relationships are conducted according to general (universalistic) standards, and the extent to which organization members are expected to strive strenuously for achievement and advancement.

Evidence is ample that expectations are shaped by position in organization, as well as by such organization-wide factors. According to the study of Jacobson and his colleagues (1951), almost 70 percent of the workers held the expectation that the steward should be active in representing the interests of his men rather than waiting until some grievance was presented to him. Only 30 percent of the foremen took this view of the steward's role, even though the foremen closely resembled the workers in demographic characteristics and had typically been workers in the same plant before their promotion to foreman.

In the studies of role conflict and ambiguity cited above (Kahn, et al., 1964) the location of positions within the organization was found to be related to the degree of objective conflict to which the occupant of the position was subjected. In general, positions contained deep within the organizational structure were relatively conflict-free; positions located near the skin or boundary of the organization were likely to be conflict-ridden. Thus jobs involving labor negotiations, purchasing, selling, or otherwise representing the organization to the public were subjected to greater stress. Living near an intraorganization boundary—for example, serving as liaison between two or more departments—revealed many of the same effects but to a lesser degree.

The objective content of the role activities seems also to be related to the pattern of expectations and to the amount of conflict among them. Roles which demand innovative problem solving are characterized by objective conflict and subjective tension. The occupants of such roles appear to become engaged in conflict primarily with the organizational old guard—men of greater age and power who want to maintain the status quo. Among the major role conflicts of such innovative jobs is the conflict of priority between the nonroutine activities which are at the core of the creative job, and the routine activities of administration or paper work.

Finally, the same research discovered consistent relationships between hierarchical position and the prevalence of conflicting role expectations. The often heard assertion that the lowest levels of supervision are subjected to the greatest conflict is not borne out; rather there is a curvilinear relationship in which the maximum of conflict occurs at the upper middle levels of management. Supervisory responsibility, both direct and indirect, is associated with conflict among role senders with respect to the appropriate style and requirements of the role.

The significant principle reflected by all these specific data is that characteristics of the organization as a whole, of its subsystems, and of the location of particular positions act to determine the expectations which role senders will hold and communicate to the occupant of a particular job. The holding and sending of such expectation is personal and direct; their content is nevertheless shaped by systemic factors.

Personality Factors as Determinants
of Role Expectations (Arrow 4)

The influence of personality on role sending is one of those undeniable facts of organizational life which nevertheless awaits measurement and documentation. Anyone who has worked under a number of different bosses has become a student of such personality differences; anyone who has supervised a number of subordinates has discovered how differently they respond to uniform tasks and supervisory behavior. Gross and his colleagues (1958) measured the homogeneity of members of role sets on certain demographic and personality attributes and found some tendency for the degree of such homogeneity to be related to their consensus on expectations for the school superintendent. The combined correlation of political-economic conservatism, religious preference, and motivation to represent some constituent group was 0.54 with the measure of consensus in role expectations.

Kahn and his coauthors (1964) report similar findings in the industrial context. They found that people who were flexible rather than rigid were subjected to greater pressures to change by their role senders. The behavior of role senders toward extremely rigid focal persons seemed to reflect a judgment of futility and acceptance and the abandonment of continuing attempts to influence behavior in the direction of ideal performance. Role expectations and role sending were also related to the achievement orientation of the focal person. The greater the achievement orientation, especially when such orientation took on a cast of neurotic striving, the more likely were role senders to apply increased pressures to change the style of the focal person.

Personality Factors as Mediators between
Role Expectations and Response (Arrow 5)

During the past 15 years, the empirical evidence for the mediating influence of enduring properties of the person (demographic, experiential, and personality) has been steadily accumulating. Although such factors are still too often omitted from organizational studies, thus increasing the unexplained variance in organizational behavior, their effects have been reported by dozens of research workers. Stouffer and Toby (1951), in an experiment based on Stouffer's earlier work (1949), found that the chosen behaviors indicated by their experimental subjects in hypothetical situations of role conflict tended to express the predisposition of subjects with respect to the norms of universalism or particularism. Jacobson and his colleagues in the same year (1951) found that the conflict experience of foremen was higher among those who had previously served as stewards, presumably because they had internalized the values of the earlier role.

Sarbin and various colleagues (Sarbin and Rosenberg, 1955; Sarbin and Hardyck, 1952; Albrecht and Sarbin, 1952; Sarbin and Stephenson, 1952) engaged in a series of laboratory experiments showing that the ability of individuals to respond appropriately to role expectations was a function of various personality attributes. The ability to perceive accurately demands of a role was related to a measure of neuroticism based on self-description. Role-taking ability was also related, apparently via the capacity to empathize, to such dimensions as equalitarianism-authoritarianism, and flexibility-rigidity. Extreme inability to take roles was manifested by schizophrenics and psychopaths, a finding consistent with Gough's (1948) earlier theory of psychopathy. He proposed that the characteristic problem of the psychopath is inability to empathize, that is to respond in the focal role *as if* he understood and felt the forces to which the role senders were subjected. Such an interpretation of psychopathy was given some support by Baker's (1954) small comparative study of psychopathic and nonpsychopathic prisoners. Questioning these subjects in terms which others used in appraising and describing them, Baker found that the psychopaths had significantly greater difficulty recognizing in themselves the ascribed traits.

Gross, Mason, and McEachern (1958) found that the effects of role conflict on job satisfaction and expressions of worry among school superintendents were consistently mediated by the characteristic anxiety level of the individual. They also utilized personality variables in attempting to predict the conflict-resolving behavior of the superintendents in four hypothetical situations, involving hiring and promotion, time allocation, salary recommendations for teachers, and budget recommendations. The personality predictor was based on a categorization of the superintendents as moralists, moral-expedients, or expedients—according to their predisposition to emphasize legitimacy or sanctions in response to a series of test items.

Kahn and his coauthors (1964) found that several personality dimensions mediate significantly the degree to which a given intensity of objective conflict is experienced as strain by the focal person. These personality dimensions include emotional sensitivity, introversion-extroversion, flexibility-rigidity, and the need for career achievement.

> For example, the effects of objective role conflict on interpersonal bonds and on tension are more pronounced for introverts. The introverts develop social relations which, while sometimes congenial and trusting, are easily undermined by conditions of

stress. The preference of such people for autonomy becomes manifest primarily when social contacts are stressful, that is, when others are exerting strong pressures and thereby creating conflict for them. In similar fashion, emotional sensitivity mediates the relationship between objective conflict and tension, with emotionally sensitive persons showing substantially higher tension scores for any given degree of objective conflict. An individual who is strongly achievement-oriented exhibits a high degree of personal involvement with his job, and the adverse effects of role conflict are more pronounced for him than for those who are less involved (p. 384).

Personality as Affected by Role Behavior (Arrow 8)

It is usual for psychologists to treat the characteristics of adult personality as relatively fixed, having been formed during earlier years of life and by earlier experiences. Our approach to personality is more dynamic than that; we believe the personality is essentially the product of social interaction, and that the process of personality formation continues throughout life. More specifically, the model of role taking which we are proposing treats personality variables in three ways: as a determinant of the role expectations of others, as mediating factors between sent role and the ways in which it is experienced and responded to, and as factors which are affected by experience and behavior in organizational roles. It is the last of these three views of personality to which we now turn.

The empirical evidence for the effects of role experience and behavior on personality is thin, perhaps because it has not been often sought. The truth of the folk saying that "you become what you do" has yet to be put to systematic test. However, Cameron and Magaret (1951) reported that the absence of role-taking skills seemed to contribute to the development of paranoid symptoms. Gough and Peterson (1952) found that the number of roles played by an individual was related to his ability to be self-critical, and that deficiencies in role performance led to an increasing inability to see oneself in objective terms and to identify with the views of others. In an extended experiment involving the manipulation of the level of decision making in a large clerical operation, Tannenbaum (1957) showed that both the autonomous and the hierarchical conditions produced significant changes in personality. The personality changes were in the direction of increasing congruence between role and person.

Earlier accounts of the effects of role on personality were unsupported by quantitative data, and were concentrated primarily on the dysfunctional effects of bureaucratic requirements. Veblen's discussion of "trained incapacity," Dewey's description of "occupational psychosis," and Warnotte's reference to "professional deformation" are perhaps the major examples of this line of argument. Merton (1957) builds on them in his own exposition of bureaucratic structure and personality, and concludes with a plea for "studies of religious, educational, military, economic, and political bureaucracies dealing with the interdependence of social organization and personality formation. . . ." The conclusion remains appropriate today.

The Significance of Interpersonal Relations in Role-Taking (Arrows 6, 7, and 9)

In theory, enduring properties of the interpersonal relationship between a focal person and members of his role set enter into the process of role sending and response in ways analogous to enduring properties of the person. That is to say, we expect that the interpersonal relations between focal person and role senders will help to determine their role expectations, will intervene between sent role and received role, and will in turn be affected by the role behavior of the focal person. Some evidence for all three of these effects is available from the research on role conflict already cited (Kahn, *et al.*, 1964):

> The sources of pressure and conflict for a person can be expressed rather fully in terms of his interpersonal relations with these pressure sources (arrow 6). The greatest pressure is directed to a person from other people who are in the same department as he is, who are his superiors in the hierarchy, and who are sufficiently dependent on his performance to care about his adequacy without being so completely dependent as to be inhibited in making their demands known. The people who are least likely to apply such pressures are a person's peers and role senders outside his own department.
>
> The kinds of influence techniques which people are prepared to apply, as well as the degree of pressure they exert, vary with their formal relationship to the potential target of their pressures. To a considerable degree the actual power structure of organizations follows the lines of formal authority. Legitimate power, rewards, and coercive power over an organizational member are largely in the hands of his direct organizational superiors. Although a supervisor has coercive power available to him as a basis for influencing his subordinates, he is likely to refrain from using it where it might impede the performance of these subordinates and perhaps reflect upon the supervisor himself. On the other hand, the techniques used by subordinates to apply coercive power are precisely those which threaten the efficiency of the organization. They include the withholding of aid and information.

The deleterious effects of role conflict are most severe where the network of an individual's organizational relations binds him closely to members of his role set (arrow 7). When a person must deal with others who are highly dependent on him, who have high power over him, and who exert high pressure on him, his response is typically one of apathy and withdrawal—psychological if not behavioral. Under such circumstances the experience of role conflict is intense and job satisfaction correspondingly low. Emotionally, the focal person experiences a sense of futility, and he attempts a hopeless withdrawal from his coworkers. Likewise, the costs of role conflict upon the focal person are most dear where there is a generally high level of communication between the focal person and his role senders.

Since close ties to role senders with regard to functional dependence, power, and communication intensify the effects of an existing conflict, an obvious means of coping with conflict is to sever ties with one's role senders. Symptomatic of this pattern of withdrawal in the face of conflict is the tendency of an individual experiencing role conflict to reduce the amount of communication with his role senders, to derogate bonds with these senders (arrow 9). Although this pattern of coping with stress is common, its logic is questionable. Withdrawal may be successful in alleviating the effects of stress for a time; in the longer run it is likely to prove self-defeating. Withdrawal may not only leave the initial conflict unresolved, but may in addition set off a chain reaction of derivative conflicts (pp. 382–383).

Summary

The concept of role is proposed as the major means for linking the individual and organizational levels of research and theory; it is at once the building block of social systems and the summation of the requirements with which such systems confront their members as individuals. Each person in an organization is linked to some set of other members by virtue of the functional requirements of the system which are heavily implemented through the expectations those members have of him; he is the focal person for that set. An organization can be viewed as consisting of a number of such sets, one for each person in the organization.

The process by which the expectations of members of a role set are linked to the behavior of the focal person for that set is described in terms of role episodes. The role episode in turn consists of a sequence of events involving members of a role set and the focal person. The sequence begins with the role expectations held by members of the set for the focal person; these are activities which they require of him in order to perform their own roles or to maintain their own satisfactions. The next step in the role episode is the sending of these expectations from the members of the set to the focal person, the communication of role requirements in terms intended to influence his behavior.

With the communication of role expectations from role set to focal person, the first half of the role episode is completed. The second half has to do with the perceptions and behavior of the focal person. He receives, with greater or lesser distortion, the role expectations sent to him. It is the received role which is the immediate source of influence and motivation of his behavior (insofar as it is influenced by members of his role set). Finally, the focal person acts; he behaves in role, showing some combination of compliance and noncompliance with the expectations of his role set. They observe and evaluate his behavior in relation to their expectations and needs, and thus the cycle moves into another episode.

Several complications are considered in connection with the treatment of organizational role in these terms. One role may involve many activities; multiple roles may be incorporated in a single office, that is, intended for performance by a single individual. Moreover, one person may hold a number of offices. Each of these elaborations adds its own complications to the simple situation in which a single recurrent activity comprises a role, which in turn comprises an office occupied by a person without additional organizational commitments.

Three oversimplifications of the role episode are considered: the fact that organizational life is continuous rather than made up of discrete episodes, the fact that members of a role set are often in disagreement among themselves with respect to what the focal person should do, and the fact that the role episode occurs within and is shaped by a matrix of organizational influences. Four basic categories of role conflict are considered: incompatible expectations held by a given member of a role set (intrasender conflict); incompatible expectations held by two or more members (intersender conflict); incompatibilities between two or more roles held by the same focal person (interrole conflict); and incompatibilities between the requirements of a role and the needs or values of the person holding it (person-role conflict).

References

Albrecht, R., and T. R. Sarbin. "Contributions to Role-Taking Theory: Annoyability as a Function of the Self." Unpub. ms., 1952.

Baker, B. "Accuracy of Social Perceptions of Psychopathic and Non-Psychopathic Prison Inmates." Unpub. ms., 1954.

Cameron, N., and A. Margaret. *Behavior Pathology.* Houghton Mifflin, 1951.

Dai, B. "A Socio-Psychiatric Approach to Personality Organization." In *Mental Health and Mental Disorder,* ed. A. Rose. Norton, 1955.

Getzels, J. W., and E. G. Guba. "Role, Role Conflict and Effectiveness: An Empirical Study." *American Sociological Review,* Vol. 19, 1954.

Gough, H. G. "A Sociological Theory of Psychotherapy." *American Journal of Sociology,* Vol. 53, 1948.

———, and D. R. Peterson. "The Identification and Measurement of Predispositional Factors in Crime and Delinquency." *Journal of Consulting Psychology,* Vol. 16, 1952.

Gross, N., W. Mason, and A. W. McEachern. *Explorations in Role Analysis: Studies of the School Superintendency Role.* Wiley, 1958.

Hockett, H. C. *The Constitutional History of the United States.* Macmillan, 1939.

Jacobson, E. "Foremen-Steward Participation Practices and Work Attitudes in a Unionized Factory." Unpub. PhD diss., University of Michigan, 1951.

———, W. W. Charters, Jr., and S. Lieberman. "The Use of the Role Concept in the Study of Complex Organization." *Journal of Social Issues,* Vol. 7, 1951.

Kahn, R. L., D. M. Wolfe, R. P. Quinn, J. D. Snoek, and R. A. Rosenthal. *Organizational Stress: Studies in Role Conflict and Ambiguity.* Wiley, 1964.

Katz, D., and R. L. Kahn. *The Social Psychology of Organizations.* Wiley, 1966.

Lieberman, S. "The Effects of Changes in Roles on the Attitudes of Role Occupants." *Human Relations,* Vol. 9, 1956.

Likert, R. *New Patterns of Management.* McGraw-Hill, 1961.

Linton, R. *The Study of Man.* Appleton-Century-Crofts, 1936.

Merton, R. K. *Social Theory and Social Structure,* rev. ed. The Free Press, 1957.

Milgram, S. "Behavioral Study of Obedience." *Journal of Abnormal & Social Psychology,* Vol. 67, 1963.

———. "Group Pressure and Action Against a Person." *Journal of Abnormal & Social Psychology,* Vol. 69, 1964.

Miller, N. E., and J. Dollard. *Social Learning and Imitation.* Yale University Press, 1962.

Neiman, L. J., and J. W. Hughes. "The Problems of the Concept of Role—A Re-Survey of the Literature." *Social Forces,* Vol. 30, 1951.

Newcomb, T. M. *Social Psychology.* Holt, Rinehart and Winston, 1950.

Parsons, T. *The Social System.* The Free Press, 1951.

Rommetveit, R. *Social Norms and Roles.* University of Minnesota Press, 1954.

Sarbin, T. R., and C. Hardyck. "Contributions to Role-Taking Theory: Role Perception on the Basis of Postural Clues." Unpub. ms., 1952.

———, and B. G. Rosenberg. "Contributions to Role-Taking Theory. IV. A Method for a Qualitative Analysis of the Self." *Journal of Social Psychology,* Vol. 42, 1955.

Sarbin, T. R., and R. W. Stephenson. "Contributions to Role-Taking Theory: Authoritarian Attitudes and Role-Taking Skill." Unpub. ms., 1952.

————, and J. D. Williams. "Contributions to Role-Taking Theory. V. Role Perception on the Basis of Limited Auditory Stimuli." Unpub. ms., 1953.

Stouffer, S. A., et al. The American Soldier. Princeton University Press, 1949.

————, and J. Toby. "Role Conflict and Personality." American Journal of Sociology, Vol. 56, 1951.

Tannenbaum, A. S. "Personality Change as a Result of an Experimental Change of Environmental Conditions." Journal of Abnormal & Social Psychology, Vol. 55, 1957.

Edgar H. Schein

Organizational Socialization and the Profession of Management

Introduction

I can define my topic of concern best by reviewing very briefly the kinds of issues upon which I have focused my research over the last several years. In one way or another I have been trying to understand what happens to an individual when he enters and accepts membership in an organization. My interest was originally kindled by studies of the civilian and military prisoners of the Communists during the Korean War. I thought I could discern parallels between the kind of indoctrination to which these prisoners were subjected and some of the indoctrination which goes on in American corporations when college and business school graduates first go to work for them. My research efforts came to be devoted to learning what sorts of attitudes and values students had when they left school, and what happened to these attitudes and values in the first few years of work. To this end I followed several panels of graduates of the Sloan School into their early career.

From Industrial Management Review, Winter 1968, pp. 1–16. Reprinted by permission.

When these studies were well under way, it suddenly became quite apparent to me that if I wanted to study the impact of an organization on the attitudes and values of its members, I might as well start closer to home. We have a school through which we put some 200 men per year—undergraduates, regular master's students, Sloan fellows, and senior executives. Studies of our own students and faculty revealed that not only did the student groups differ from each other in various attitude areas, but that they also differed from the faculty.

For example, if one takes a scale built up of items which deal with the relations of government and business, one finds that the senior executives in our program are consistently against any form of government intervention, the Sloans are not as extreme, the master's students are roughly in the middle, and the faculty are in favor of such intervention. A similar line-up of attitudes can be found with respect to labor-management relations, and with respect to cynicism about how one gets ahead in industry. In case you did not guess, the senior executives are least cynical and the faculty are most cynical.

We also found that student attitudes change in many areas during school, and that they change away from business attitudes toward the faculty position. However, a recent study of Sloan fellows, conducted after their graduation, indicated that most of the changes toward the faculty had reversed themselves to a considerable degree within one year, a finding which is not unfamiliar to us in studies of training programs of all sorts.

The different positions of different groups at different stages of their managerial career and the observed changes during school clearly indicate that attitudes and values change several times during the managerial career. It is the process which brings about these changes which I would like to focus on today—a process which the sociologists would call "occupational socialization," but which I would prefer to call "organizational socialization" in order to keep our focus clearly on the setting in which the process occurs.

Organizational socialization is the process of "learning the ropes," the process of being indoctrinated and trained, the process of being taught what is important in an organization or some subunit thereof. This process occurs in school. It occurs again, and perhaps most dramatically, when the graduate enters an organization on his first job. It occurs again when he switches within the organization from one department to another, or from one rank level to another. It occurs all over again if he leaves one organization and enters another. And it occurs again when he goes back to school, and again when he returns to the organization after school.

Indeed, the process is so ubiquitous and we go through it so often during our total career that it is all too easy to overlook it. Yet it is a process which can make or break a career, and which can make or break organizational systems of manpower planning. The speed and effectiveness of socialization determine employee loyalty, commitment, productivity, and turnover. The basic stability and effectiveness of organizations therefore depends upon their ability to socialize new members.

Let us see whether we can bring the process of socialization to life by describing how it occurs. I hope to show you the power of this process, particularly as it occurs within industrial organizations. Having done this, I would like to explore a major dilemma which I see at the interface between organizations and graduate management schools. Schools socialize their students toward a concept of a profession, organizations socialize their new members to be effective members. Do the two processes of socialization supplement each other or conflict? If they conflict, what can we do about it in organizations and in the schools?

Some Basic Elements of Organizational Socialization

The term socialization has a fairly clear meaning in sociology, but it has been a difficult one to assimilate in the behavioral sciences and in management. To many of my colleagues it implies unnecessary jargon, and to many of my business acquaintances it implies the teaching of socialism—a kiss of death for the concept right there. Yet the concept is most useful because it focuses clearly on the interaction between a stable social system and the new members who enter it. The concept refers to the process by which a new member learns the value system, the norms, and the required behavior patterns of the society, organization, or group which he is entering. It does not include all learning. It includes only the learning of those values, norms, and behavior patterns which, from the organization's point of view or group's point of view, it is necessary for any new member to learn. This learning is defined as the price of membership.

What are such values, norms, and behavior patterns all about? Usually they involve:

1. The basic *goals* of the organization.
2. The preferred *means* by which these goals should be attained.
3. The basic *responsibilities* of the member in the role which is being granted to him by the organization.
4. The *behavior patterns* which are required for effective performance in the role.
5. A set of rules or principles which pertain to the *maintenance of the identity and integrity* of the organization.

The new member must learn not to drive Chevrolets if he is working for Ford, not to criticize the organization in public, not to wear the wrong kind of clothes or be seen in the wrong kinds of places. If the organization is a school, beyond learning the content of what is taught, the student must accept the value of education, he must try to learn without cheating, he must accept the authority of the faculty and behave appropriately to the student role. He must not be rude in the classroom or openly disrespectful to the professor.

By what processes does the novice learn the required values and norms? The answer to this question depends in part upon the degree of prior socialization. If the novice has correctly anticipated the norms of the organization he is joining, the socialization process merely involves a reaffirmation of these norms through various communication channels, the personal example of key people in the organization, and direct instructions from supervisors, trainers, and informal coaches.

If, however, the novice comes to the organization with values and behavior patterns which are in varying degrees out of line with those expected by the organization, then the socialization process first involves a destructive or unfreezing phase. This phase serves the function of detaching the person from his former values, of proving to him that his present self is worthless from the point of view of the organization and that he must redefine himself in terms of the new roles which he is to be granted.

The extremes of this process can be seen in initiation rites or novitiates for religious orders. When the novice enters his training period, his old self is symbolically destroyed by loss of clothing, name, often his hair, titles and other self-defining equipment. These are replaced with uniforms, new names and titles, and other self-defining equipment consonant with the new role he is being trained for.

It may be comforting to think of activities like this as being characteristic only of primitive tribes or total institutions like military basic training camps, academies, and religious orders. But even a little examination of areas closer to home will reveal the same processes both in our graduate schools and in the business organizations to which our graduates go.

Perhaps the commonest version of the process in school is the imposition of a tight schedule, of an impossibly heavy reading program, and of the assignment of problems which are likely to be too difficult for the student to solve. Whether these techniques are deliberate or not, they serve effectively to remind the student that he is not as smart or capable as he may have thought he was, and, therefore, that there are still things to be learned. As our Sloan fellows tell us every year, the first summer in the program pretty well destroys many aspects of their self-image. Homework in statistics appears to enjoy a unique status comparable to having one's head shaved and clothes burned.

Studies of medical schools and our own observations of the Sloan program suggest that the work overload on students leads to the development of a peer culture, a kind of banding together of the students as a defense against the threatening faculty and as a problem-solving device to develop norms of what and how to study. If the group solutions which are developed support the organizational norms, the peer group becomes an effective instrument of socialization. However, from the school's point of view, there is the risk that peer group norms will set up counter-socializing forces and sow the seeds of sabotage, rebellion, or revolution. The positive gains of a supportive peer group generally make it worthwhile to run the risks of rebellion, however, which usually motivates the organization to encourage or actually to facilitate peer group formation.

Many of our Sloan-fellow alumni tell us that one of the most powerful features of the Sloan program is the fact that a group of some 40 men share the same fate of being put through a very tough educational regimen. The peer group ties formed during the year have proven to be one of the most durable end-results of the educational program and, of course, are one of the key supports to maintaining some of the values and attitudes learned in school. The power of this kind of socializing force can be appreciated best by pondering a further statement which many alumni have made. They stated that prior to the program they identified themselves primarily with their company. Following the program they identified themselves primarily with the other Sloan fellows, and such identification has lasted, as far as we can tell, for the rest of their career.

Let me next illustrate the industrial counterpart of these processes. Many of my panel members, when interviewed about the first six months in their new jobs, told stories of what we finally labeled as "upending experiences." Upending experiences are deliberately planned or accidentally created circumstances which dramatically and unequivocally upset or disconfirm some of the major assumptions which the new man holds about himself, his company, or his job.

One class of such experiences is to receive assignments which are so easy or so trivial that they carry the clear message that the new man is not worthy of being given anything important to do. Another class of such experiences is at the other extreme—assignments which are so difficult that failure is a certainty, thus proving unequivocally to the new man that he may not be as smart as he thought he was. Giving work which is clearly for practice only, asking for reports which are then unread or not acted upon, protracted periods of training during which the person observes others work, all have the same upending effect.

The most vivid example came from an engineering company

where a supervisor had a conscious and deliberate strategy for dealing with what he considered to be unwarranted arrogance on the part of engineers whom they hired. He asked each new man to examine and diagnose a particular complex circuit, which happened to violate a number of textbook principles but actually worked very well. The new man would usually announce with confidence, even after an invitation to double-check, that the circuit could not possibly work. At this point the manager would demonstrate the circuit, tell the new man that they had been selling it for several years without customer complaint, and demand that the new man figure out why it did work. None of the men so far tested were able to do it, but all of them were thoroughly chastened and came to the manager anxious to learn where their knowledge was inadequate and needed supplementing. According to this manager, it was much easier from this point on to establish a good give-and-take relationship with his new man.

It should be noted that the success of such socializing techniques depends upon two factors which are not always under the control of the organization. The first factor is the initial motivation of the entrant to join the organization. If his motivation is high, as in the case of a fraternity pledge, he will tolerate all kinds of uncomfortable socialization experiences, even to the extremes of "hell week." If his motivation for membership is low, he may well decide to leave the organization rather than tolerate uncomfortable initiation rites. If he leaves, the socialization process has obviously failed.

The second factor is the degree to which the organization can hold the new member captive during the period of socialization. His motivation is obviously one element here, but one finds organizations using other forces as well. In the case of basic training there are legal forces to make him remain. In the case of many schools one must pay one's tuition in advance, in other words, invest one's self materially so that leaving the system becomes expensive. In the case of religious orders one must make strong initial psychological commitments in the form of vows and the severing of relationships outside the religious order. The situation is defined as one in which one will lose face or be humiliated if one leaves the organization.

In the case of business organizations the pressures are more subtle but nevertheless identifiable. New members are encouraged to get financially committed by joining pension plans, stock option plans, and/or house purchasing plans which would mean material loss if the person decided to leave. Even more subtle is the reminder by the boss that it takes a year or so to learn any new business; therefore, if you leave, you will have to start all over again. Why not suffer it out with the hope that things will look more rosy once the initiation period is over?

Several of my panel members told me at the end of one year at

work that they were quite dissatisfied, but were not sure they should
leave because they had invested a year of learning in that company.
Usually their boss encouraged them to think about staying. Whether
or not such pressures will work depends, of course, on the labor
market and other factors not under the control of the organization.

Let me summarize. Organizations socialize their new members
by creating a series of events which serve the function of undoing old
values so that the person will be prepared to learn the new values.
This process of undoing or unfreezing is often unpleasant and therefore requires either strong motivation to endure it or strong organizational forces to make the person endure it. The formation of a peer
group of novices is often a solution to the problem of defense against
the powerful organization, and, at the same time, can strongly enhance the socialization process if peer group norms support organizational norms.

Let us look next at the positive side of the socialization process.
Given some readiness to learn, how does the novice acquire his new
learning? The answer is that he acquires it from multiple sources—
the official literature of the organization; the example set by key
models in the organization; the instructions given to him directly by
his trainer, coach, or boss; the example of peers who have been in the
organization longer and thus serve as big brothers; the rewards and
punishments which result from his own efforts at problem solving
and experimenting with new values and new behavior.

The instructions and guidelines given by senior members of the
organization are probably one of the most potent positive sources. I
can illustrate this point best by recalling several incidents from my
own socialization into the Sloan School back in 1956. I came here
from a research job at the invitation of Doug McGregor. I had no
prior teaching experience or knowledge of organizational or managerial matters. Contrary to my expectations, I was told by Doug that
knowledge of organizational psychology and management was not
important, but that some interest in learning about these matters
was.

The first socializing incident occurred in an initial interview
with Elting Morison, who was then on our faculty. He said in a
completely blunt manner that if I knew what I wanted to do and
could go ahead on my own, the Sloan School would be a great place to
be. If I wasn't sure and would look to others for guidance, not to
bother to come.

The second incident occurred in a conversation with our then
dean, Penn Brooks, a few weeks before the opening of the semester.
We were discussing what and how I might teach. Penn said to me
that he basically wanted each of his faculty members to find his own
approach to management education. I could do whatever I wanted—

so long as I did not imitate our sister school up the river. Case discussion leaders need not apply, was the clear message.

The third incident (you see I was a slow learner) occurred a few days later when I was planning my subject in social psychology for our master's students. I was quite nervous about it and unsure of how to decide what to include in the subject. I went to Doug and innocently asked him to lend me outlines of previous versions of the subject, which had been taught by Alex Bavelas, or at least to give me some advice on what to include and exclude. Doug was very nice and very patient, but also quite firm in his refusal to give me either outlines or advice. He thought there was really no need to rely on history, and expressed confidence that I could probably make up my own mind. I suffered that term but learned a good deal about the value system of the Sloan School, as well as how to organize a subject. I was, in fact, so well socialized by these early experiences that nowadays no one can get me to coordinate anything with anybody else.

Similar kinds of lessons can be learned during the course of training programs, in orientation sessions, and through company literature. But the more subtle kinds of values which the organization holds, which indeed may not even be well understood by the senior people, are often communicated through peers operating as helpful big brothers. They can communicate the subtleties of how the boss wants things done, how higher management feels about things, the kinds of things which are considered heroic in the organization, the kinds of things which are taboo.

Of course, sometimes the values of the immediate group into which a new person is hired are partially out of line with the value system of the organization as a whole. If this is the case, the new person will learn the immediate group's values much more quickly than those of the total organization, often to the chagrin of the higher levels of management. This is best exemplified at the level of hourly workers where fellow employees will have much more socializing power than the boss.

An interesting managerial example of this conflict was provided by one recent graduate who was hired into a group whose purpose was to develop cost reduction systems for a large manufacturing operation. His colleagues on the job, however, showed him how to pad his expense account whenever they traveled together. The end result of this kind of conflict was to accept neither the cost reduction values of the company nor the cost inflation values of the peer group. The man left the company in disgust to start up some businesses of his own.

One of the important functions of organizational socialization is to build commitment and loyalty to the organization. How is this accomplished? One mechanism is to invest much effort and time in the new member and thereby build up expectations of being repaid by loyalty, hard work, and rapid learning. Another mechanism is to get the new member to make a series of small behavioral commitments which can only be justified by him through the acceptance and incorporation of company values. He then becomes his own agent of socialization. Both mechanisms involve the subtle manipulation of guilt.

To illustrate the first mechanism, one of our graduates went to a public relations firm which made it clear to him that he had sufficient knowledge and skill to advance, but that his values and attitudes would have to be evaluated for a couple of years before he would be fully accepted. During the first several months he was frequently invited to join high ranking members of the organization at their luncheon meetings in order to learn more about how they thought about things. He was so flattered by the amount of time they spent on him that he worked extra hard to learn their values and became highly committed to the organization. He said that he would have felt guilty at the thought of not learning or of leaving the company. Sending people to expensive training programs, giving them extra perquisites, indeed the whole philosophy of paternalism, is built on the assumption that if you invest in the employee he will repay the company with loyalty and hard work. He would feel guilty if he did not.

The second mechanism, that of getting behavioral commitments, was most beautifully illustrated in Communist techniques of coercive persuasion. The Communists made tremendous efforts to elicit a public confession from a prisoner. One of the key functions of such a public confession, even if the prisoner knew he was making a false confession, was that it committed him publicly. Once he made this commitment, he found himself under strong internal and external pressure to justify why he had confessed. For many people it proved easier to justify the confession by coming to believe in their own crimes than to have to face the fact that they were too weak to withstand the captor's pressure.

In organizations, a similar effect can be achieved by promoting a rebellious person into a position of responsibility. The same values which the new member may have criticized and jeered at from his position at the bottom of the hierarchy suddenly look different when he has subordinates of his own whose commitment he must obtain.

Many of my panel members had very strong moral and ethical standards when they first went to work, and these stood up quite well during their first year at work, even in the face of less ethical practices by their peers and superiors. But they reported with considerable shock that some of the practices they had condemned in their bosses were quickly adopted by them once they had themselves been promoted and faced the pressures of the new position. As one man put it very poignantly—"My ethical standards changed so gradually over the first five years of work that I hardly noticed it, but it was a great shock to suddenly realize what my feelings had been five years ago and how much they had changed."

Another version of obtaining commitment is to gain the new member's acceptance of very general ideals, like "One must work for the good of the company," or "One must meet the competition." Whenever any counter-organizational behavior occurs, one can then point out that the ideal is being violated. The engineer who does not come to work on time is reminded that his behavior indicates lack of concern for the good of the company. The employee who wears the wrong kind of clothes, lives in the wrong neighborhood, or associates with the wrong people can be reminded that he is hurting the company image.

One of my panel members on a product research assignment discovered that an additive which was approved by the Food and Drug Administration might in fact be harmful to consumers. He was strongly encouraged to forget about it. His boss told him that it was the F.D.A.'s problem. If the company worried about things like that it might force prices up and thus make it tough to meet the competition.

Many of the upending experiences which new members of organizations endure are justified to them by the unarguable ideal that they should learn how the company really works before expecting a position of real responsibility. Once the new man accepts this ideal it serves to justify all kinds of training and quantities of menial work which others who have been around longer are unwilling to do themselves. This practice is known as "learning the business from the ground up," or "I had to do it when I first joined the company, now it's someone else's turn." There are clear elements of hazing involved not too different from those associated with fraternity initiations and other rites of passage.

The final mechanism to be noted in a socialization process is the transition to full-fledged member. The purpose of such transitional events is to help the new member incorporate his new values, attitudes, and norms into his identity so that they become part of him, not merely something to which he pays lip service. Initiation rites which involve severe tests of the novice serve to prove to him that he is capable of fulfilling the new role—that he now is a man, no longer merely a boy.

Organizations usually signal this transition by giving the new man some important responsibility or a position of power which, if mishandled or misused, could genuinely hurt the organization. With this transition often come titles, symbols of status, extra rights or prerogatives, sharing of confidential information or other things which in one way or another indicate that the new member has earned the trust of the organization. Although such events may not always be visible to the outside observer, they are felt strongly by the new member. He knows when he has finally "been accepted," and feels it when he becomes "identified with the company."

So much for examples of the process of socialization. Let us now look at some of the dilemmas and conflicts which arise within it.

Failures of Socialization: Nonconformity and Overconformity

Most organizations attach differing amounts of importance to different norms and values. Some are *pivotal*. Any member of a business organization who does not believe in the value of getting a job done will not survive long. Other pivotal values in most business organizations might be belief in a reasonable profit, belief in the free enterprise system and competition, belief in a hierarchy of authority as a good way to get things done, and so on.

Other values or norms are what may be called *relevant*. These are norms which it is not absolutely necessary to accept as the price of membership, but which are considered desirable and good to accept. Many of these norms pertain to standards of dress and decorum, not being publicly disloyal to the company, living in the right neighborhood and belonging to the right political party and clubs. In some organizations some of these norms may be pivotal. Organizations vary in this regard. You all know the stereotype of IBM as a company that requires the wearing of white shirts and hats. In some parts of IBM such values are indeed pivotal; in other parts they are only relevant, and in some parts they are quite peripheral. The point is that not all norms to which the new member is exposed are equally important for the organization.

The socialization process operates across the whole range of norms, but the amount of reward and punishment for compliance or noncompliance will vary with the importance of the norm. This variation allows the new member some degrees of freedom in terms of how far to conform and allows the organization some degrees of freedom in how much conformity to demand. The new man can accept none of the values, he can accept only the pivotal values, but carefully remain independent on all those areas not seen as pivotal, or he can accept the whole range of values and norms. He can tune in so completely on what he sees to be the way others are handling themselves that he becomes a carbon copy and sometimes a caricature of them.

These basic responses to socialization can be labeled as follows:

Type 1: Rebellion—rejection of all values and norms.
Type 2: Creative individualism—acceptance only of pivotal values and norms; rejection of all others.
Type 3: Conformity—acceptance of all values and norms.

Most analyses of conformity deal only with the type 1 and 3 cases, failing to note that both can be viewed as socialization failures. The rebellious individual either is expelled from the organization or turns his energies toward defeating its goals. The conforming individual curbs his creativity and thereby moves the organization toward a sterile form of bureaucracy. The trick for most organizations is to create the type 2 response—acceptance of pivotal values and norms, but rejection of all others, a response which I would like to call "creative individualism."

To remain creatively individualistic in an organization is particularly difficult because of the constant resocialization pressures which come with promotion or lateral transfer. Every time the employee learns part of the value system of the particular group to which he is assigned, he may be laying the groundwork for conflict when he is transferred. The engineer has difficulty accepting the values of the sales department, the staff man has difficulty accepting the high pressure ways of the production department, and the line manager has difficulties accepting the service and helping ethic of a staff group. With each transfer, the forces are great toward either conforming or rebelling. It is difficult to keep focused on what is pivotal and retain one's basic individualism.

Professional Socialization and Organizational Socialization

The issue of how to maintain individualism in the face of organizational socialization pressures brings us to the final and most problematical area of concern. In the traditional professions, like medicine, law, and teaching, individualism is supported by a set of professional attitudes which serve to immunize the person against some of the forces of the organization. The questions now to be considered are (1) Is management a profession? (2) If so, do professional attitudes develop in managers? and (3) If so, do these support or conflict with organizational norms and values?

Professionalism can be defined by a number of characteristics:

1. Professional decisions are made by means of general principles, theories, or propositions which are independent of the particular case under consideration. For management this would mean that there are certain principles of how to handle people, money, information, etc., independent of any particular company. The fact that we can and do teach general subjects in these areas would support management's claim to being a profession.

2. Professional decisions imply knowledge in a specific area in which the person is expert, not a generalized body of wisdom. The professional is an expert only in his profession, not an expert at everything. He has no license to be a "wise man." Does management fit by this criterion? I will let you decide.

3. The professional's relations with his clients are objective and independent of particular sentiments about them. The doctor or lawyer makes his decisions independently of his liking or disliking his patients or clients. On this criterion we have a real difficulty since, in the first place, it is very difficult to specify an appropriate single client for a manger, and, in the second place, it is not at all clear that decisions can or should be made independently of sentiments. What is objectively best for the stockholder may conflict with what is best for the enterprise, which, in turn may conflict with what is best for the customer.

4. A professional achieves his status by accomplishment, not by inherent qualities such as birth order, his relationship to people in power, his race, religion, or color. Industry is increasingly moving toward an acceptance of this principle for managerial selection, but in practice the process of organizational socialization may undermine it by rewarding the conformist and rejecting the individualist whose professional orientation may make him look disloyal to the organization.

5. A professional's decisions are assumed to be on behalf of the client and to be independent of self-interest. Clearly this principle is at best equivocal in manager-customer relations, though again one senses that industry is moving closer to accepting the idea.

6. The professional typically relates to a voluntary association of fellow professionals, and accepts only the authority of these colleagues as a sanction on his own behavior. The manager is least like the professional in this regard, in that he is expected to accept a principle of hierarchical authority. The dilemma is best illustrated by the previous example which I gave of our Sloan-fellow alumni who, after the program, related themselves more to other Sloans than to their company hierarchy. By this criterion they had become truly professionalized.

7. A professional has sometimes been called someone who knows better what is good for his client than the client. The professional's expertness puts the client into a very vulnerable position. This vulnerability has necessitated the development of strong professional codes and ethics which serve to protect the client. Such codes are enforced through the colleague peer group. One sees relatively few attempts to develop codes of ethics for managers or systems of enforcement.

On several bases, then, management is a profession, but on several others it is clearly not yet a profession.

This long description of what is a profession was motivated by the need to make a very crucial point. I believe that management education, particularly in a graduate school like the Sloan School, is increasingly attempting to train professionals, and in this process is socializing the students to a set of professional values which are, in fact, in severe and direct conflict with typical organizational values.

For example, I see us teaching general principles in the behavioral sciences, economics, and quantitative methods. Our applied subjects, like marketing, operations management, and finance, are also taught as bodies of knowledge governed by general principles which are applicable to a wide variety of situations. Our students are given very broad concepts which apply to the corporation as a whole, and are taught to see the relationship between the corporation, the community, and the society. They are taught to value the long-range health and survival of economic institutions, not the short-range profit of a particular company. They come to appreciate the necessary interrelationships between government, labor, and management rather than to define these as mutually warring camps. They are taught to look at organizations from the perspective of high ranking management, to solve the basic problems of the enterprise rather than the day-to-day practical problems of staff or line management. Finally, they are taught an ethic of pure rationality and emotional neutrality—analyze the problem and make the decisions independently of feelings about people, the product, the company, or the community. All of these are essentially professional values.

Organizations value many of the same things, in principle. But what is valued in principle by the higher ranking and senior people in the organization often is neither supported by their own behavior, nor even valued lower down in the organization. In fact, the value system which the graduates encounter on their first job is in many respects diametrically opposed to the professional values taught in school. The graduate is immediately expected to develop loyalty and concern for a particular company with all of its particular idiosyncrasies. He is expected to recognize the limitation of his general knowledge and to develop the sort of *ad hoc* wisdom which the school has taught him to avoid. He is expected to look to his boss for evaluation rather than to some group of colleagues outside the company.

Whereas the professional training tells him that knowledge is power, the graduate now must learn that knowledge by itself is nothing. It is the ability to "sell" knowledge to other people which is power. Only by being able to sell an application of knowledge to a highly specific, local situation can the graduate obtain respect for what he knows. Where his education has taught the graduate principles of how to manage others and to take the corporate point of view, his organizational socialization tries to teach him how to be a good subordinate, how to be influenced, and how to sell ideas from a position of low power.

On the one hand, the organization via its recruiters and senior people tells the graduate that it is counting on him to bring fresh points of view and new techniques to bear on its problems. On the other hand, the man's first boss and peers try to socialize him into their traditional mold.

A man is hired to introduce linear programming into a production department, but once he is there he is told to lay off because if he succeeds he will make the old supervisors and engineers look bad. Another man is hired for his financial analysis skills but is not permitted access to data worth analyzing because the company does not trust him to keep them confidential. A third man is hired into a large group responsible for developing cost reduction programs in a large defense industry, and is told to ignore the fact that the group is overstaffed, inefficient, and willing to pad its expense accounts. A fourth man, hired for his energy and capability, put it this way as an explanation of why he quit to go into private consulting: "They were quite pleased with work that required only two hours per day; I wasn't."

In my panel of 1962 graduates, 73 percent have already left their first job and many are on their third or fourth. In the class of 1963, the percentage is 67, and in the class of 1964, the percentage is 50. Apparently, most of our graduates are unwilling to be socialized into organizations whose values are incompatible with the ones we teach. Yet these organizations are precisely the ones who may need creative individualists most.

What seems to happen in the early stages of the managerial career is either a kind of postponement of professional socialization while organizational socialization takes precedence, or a rebelling by the graduate against organizational socialization. The young man who submits must first learn to be a good apprentice, a good staff man, a good junior analyst, and perhaps a good low level administrator. He must prove his loyalty to the company by accepting this career path with good graces, before he is trusted enough to be given a position of power. If he has not lost his education by then, he can begin to apply some general principles when he achieves such a position of power.

The businessman wants the school to provide both the professional education and the humility which would make organizational socialization smoother. He is not aware that teaching management concepts of the future precludes justifying the practices of today. Some professional schools clearly do set out to train for the needs of the profession as it is designed today. The Sloan School appears to me to reject this concept. Instead we have a faculty which is looking at the professional manager of five, ten, or twenty years from now, and are training our graduates in management techniques which we believe are coming in the future.

Symptomatic of this approach is the fact that in many of our subjects we are highly critical of the management practices of today, and highly committed to re-educating those managers like Sloan fellows and senior executives who come back to study at M.I.T. We get across in a dozen different ways the belief that most organizations of today are obsolete, conscrvative, "constipated," and ignorant of their own problems. Furthermore, I believe that this point of view is what society and the business community demands of a good professional school.

It would be no solution to abandon our own vision of the manager of the future, and I doubt that those of you in the audience from business and industry would really want us to do this. What you probably want is to have your cake and eat it too—you want us to teach our students the management concepts of tomorrow, and you want us to teach them how to put these concepts into deep freeze while they learn the business of today. Then, when they have proven themselves worthy of advancement and have achieved a position of some influence, they should magically resurrect their education and put it to work.

Unfortunately, socialization processes are usually too powerful to permit that solution. If you succeed in socializing your young graduates to your organizations, you will probably also succeed in proving to them that their education was pretty worthless and might as well be put on a permanent rather than temporary shelf. We have research evidence that many well educated graduates do learn to be complacent and to play the organizational game. It is not at all clear whether they later ever resurrect their educational arsenal.

What Is to Be Done about This Situation?

I think we need to accept, at the outset, the reality of organizational socialization phenomena. As my colleague, Leo Moore, so aptly put it, organizations like to put their fingerprints on people, and they have every right to do so. By the same token, graduate schools of business have a right and an obligation to pursue professional socialization to the best of their ability. We must find a way to ameliorate the conflicts at the interface, without, however, concluding that either schools or organizations are to blame and should stop what they are doing.

What the Schools Can Do

The schools, our school in particular, can do several concrete things which would help the situation. First, we can insert into our total curriculum more apprenticeship experience which would bring the realities of organizational life home to the student earlier. But such apprenticeship experiences will not become educational unless we combine them with a second idea, that of providing a practicum on how to change organizations. Such a practicum should draw on each of the course specialties and should be specifically designed to teach a student how to translate his professional knowledge into viable action programs at whatever level of the organization he is working.

Ten years ago we would not have known how to do this. Today there is no excuse for not doing it. Whether the field is operations research, sophisticated quantitative marketing, industrial dynamics, organizational psychology of whatever, we must give our students experience in trying to implement their new ideas, and we must teach them how to make the implementation effective. In effect, we must teach our students to become change agents, whatever their disciplinary specialty turns out to be. We must teach them how to influence their organizations from low positions of power without sacrificing their professional values in the process. We must teach them how to remain creative individualists in the face of strong organizational socialization pressures.

Combined with these two things, we need to do a third thing. We need to become more involved in the student's efforts at career planning and we need to coordinate our activities more closely with the company recruiters and the university placement officers. At the present I suspect that most of our faculty is quite indifferent to the student's struggles to find the right kind of a job. I suspect that this indifference leaves the door wide open to faulty selection on the part of the student, which can only lead, in the end, to an undermining of the education into which we pour so much effort. We need to work harder to insure that our graduates get jobs in which they can further the values and methods we inculcate.

What the Companies Can Do

Companies can do at least two things. First, they can make a genuine effort to become aware of and understand their own organizational socialization practices. I fear very few higher level executives know what is going on at the bottom of their organization, where all the high priced talent they call for is actually employed. At the same time, I suspect that it is their own value system which ultimately determines the socialization activities which occur throughout all segments of the organization. Greater awareness and understanding of these practices should make possible more rational choices as to which practices to encourage and which to de-emphasize. The focus should be on pivotal values only, not on peripheral or irrelevant ones.

Second, companies must come to appreciate the delicate problems which exist both for the graduate and for his first boss in the early years of the career when socialization pressures are at the maximum. If more companies appreciated the nature of this dilemma they would recognize the necessity of giving some training to the men who will be the first bosses of the graduates.

I have argued for such training for many years, but still find that most company effort goes into training the graduate rather than his boss. Yet it is the boss who really has the power to create the climate which will lead to rebellion, conformity, or creative individualism. If the companies care whether their newly hired use one or the other of these adaptation strategies, they had better start looking at the behavior of the first boss and training him for what the company wants and hopes for. Too many bosses concentrate on teaching too many peripheral values and thus undermine the possibilities for creative individualism and organization improvement.

Conclusion

The essence of management is to understand the forces acting in a situation and to gain control over them. It is high time that some of our managerial knowledge and skill be focused on those forces in the organizational environment which derive from the fact that organizations are social systems who do socialize their new members. If we do not learn to analyze and control the forces of organizational socialization, we are abdicating one of our primary managerial responsibilities. Let us not shrink from a little bit of social engineering and management in this most important area of the human side of the enterprise.

References

Blau, P. M., and R. W. Scott. *Formal Organizations.* Chandler, 1962.

Goffman, E. *Asylums.* Doubleday-Anchor, 1961.

Schein, E. H. "The Wall of Misunderstanding on the First Job." *Journal of College Placement,* February–March 1967.

———. "Attitude Change during Management Education." *Administrative Science Quarterly,* Vol. 11, 1967.

———. "The Problem of Moral Education for the Business Manager." *Industrial Management Review,* Vol. 8, 1966.

Schein, E. H. *Organizational Psychology.* Prentice-Hall, 1965.

———. "Training in Industry: Education or Indoctrination." *Industrial Medicine and Surgery,* Vol. 33, 1964.

———. "How to Break In the College Graduate." *Harvard Business Review,* Vol. 42, 1964.

———. "Forces Which Undermine Management Development." *California Management Review,* Vol. 5, Summer 1963.

———. "Management Development as a Process of Influence." *Industrial Management Review,* Vol. 2, 1961.

———, Inge Schneier, and C. H. Barker. *Coercive Persuasion.* Norton, 1961.

As told to Mort Stern

Ex-Policeman Tells
What Makes a "Bad Cop"

What makes a policeman go sour? I can tell you. I was a Denver policeman until not so long ago. Then I quit so I could hold my head up.

Don't get me wrong. I'm not trying to shift the burden of responsibility for the burglaries, break-ins, safe jobs and that sort of thing. That is bad, very bad. But I will leave it to the big shots and the newspapers and the courts to say and do what needs to be said and done about that.

My concern is about the individual officer, the ordinary, hard-working, basically honest but awfully hard-pressed guy who is really suffering now.

Young fellows don't put on those blue uniforms to be crooks. There are a lot of reasons, but for most of the guys it adds up to the fact they thought it was an honorable, decent way of making a living.

Somewhere along the line a guy's disillusioned. Along the way the pressures mount up. Somewhere along the way he may decide to

---

From The *Denver Post,* November 4, 1961. Reprinted by permission.

quit fighting them and make the conscious decisions to try to "beat" society instead.

But long before he gets to that point, almost as soon as he dons the uniform in fact, he is taking the first little steps down the road that does, for some, eventually lead to the penitentiary.

Let me back up a little. I want to talk about how you get to be a policeman, because this is where the trouble really starts.

Almost any able-bodied man can become a policeman in Denver. If he is within the age brackets, if he is a high school graduate, if he has no criminal record, he is a cinch.

There isn't much to getting through the screening, and some bad ones do get through. There are the usual examinations and question-naires. Then there is the interview. A few command officers ask questions. There is a representative of civil service and a psychiatrist present.

They ask the predictable questions and just about everybody gives the predictable answers: "Why do you want to become a police-man?" "I've always wanted to be a policeman. I want to help people." Five or ten minutes and it is over.

Five or ten minutes to spot the sadist, the psychopath—or the guy with an eye for an easy buck. I guess they weed some out. Some others they get at the Police Academy. But some get through.

Along with those few bad ones, there are more good ones, and a lot of average, ordinary human beings who have this in common: They want to be policemen.

The job has (or had) some glamor for the young man who likes authority, who finds appeal in making a career of public service, who is extroverted or aggressive.

Before you knock those qualities, remember two things. First, they are the same qualities we admire in a business executive. Sec-ond, if it weren't for men with these qualities, you wouldn't have any police protection.

The Police Academy is point No. 2 in my bill of particulars. It is a fine thing, in a way. You meet the cream of the Police Department. Your expectations soar. You know you are going to make the grade and be a good officer. But how well are you really prepared?

There are six weeks at the academy—four weeks in my time. Six hectic weeks in which to learn all about the criminal laws you have sworn to enforce, to assimilate the rules of evidence, methods of arbitration, use of firearms, mob and riot control, first aid (including, if you please, some basic obstetrics), public relations and so on.

There is an intangible something else that is not on the formal agenda. You begin to learn that this is a fraternity into which you are not automatically accepted by your fellows. You have to earn your way in; you have to establish that you are "all right."

And even this early there is a slight sour note. You knew, of course, that you had to provide your own uniforms, your own hat, shoes, shirts, pistol and bullets out of your $393 a month.

You knew the city would generously provide you with the cloth for two pair of trousers and a uniform blouse.

What you didn't know was that you don't just choose a tailor shop for price and get the job done.

You are sent to a place by the Police Department to get the tailoring done. You pay the price even though the work may be ill-fitting. It seems a little odd to you that it is always the same establishment. But it is a small point and you have other things on your mind.

So the rookie, full of pride and high spirit, his head full of partly learned information, is turned over to a more experienced man for breaking in. He is on "probation" for six months.

The rookie knows he is being watched by all the older hands around him. He is eager to be accepted. He accepts advice gratefully.

Then he gets little signs that he has been making a good impression. It may happen like this: The older man stops at a bar, comes out with some packages of cigarets. He does this several times. He explains that this is part of the job, getting cigarets free from proprietors to resell, and that as a part of the rookie's training it is his turn to "make the butts."

So he goes into a skid-road bar and stands uncomfortably at the end waiting for the bartender to acknowledge his presence and disdainfully toss him two packages of butts.

The feeling of pride slips away and a hint of shame takes hold. But he tells himself this is unusual, that he will say nothing that will upset his probation standing. In six months, after he gets his commission, he will be the upright officer he meant to be.

One thing leads to another for the rookies. After six months they have become conditioned to accept free meals, a few packages of cigarets, turkeys at Thanksgiving and liquor at Christmas from the respectable people in their district.

The rule book forbids all this. But it isn't enforced. It is winked at at all levels.

So the rookies say to themselves that this is O.K., that this is a far cry from stealing and they still can be good policemen. Besides, they are becoming accepted as "good guys" by their fellow officers.

This becomes more and more important as the young policeman begins to sense a hostility toward him in the community. This is fostered to a degree by some of the saltier old hands in the department. But the public plays its part.

Americans are funny. They have a resentment for authority. And the policeman is authority in person. The respectable person may soon forget that a policeman found his lost youngster in the past, but he remembers that a policeman gave him a traffic ticket.

The negative aspect of the job builds up. The majority of the people he comes in contact with during his working hours are thieves, con men, narcotics addicts and out-and-out nuts.

Off the job his associations narrow. Part of the time when he isn't working, he is sleeping. His waking, off-duty hours are such as to make him not much of a neighbor. And then he wants to spend as much time as he can with his family.

Sometimes, when he tries to mix with his neighbors, he senses a kind of strain. When he is introduced to someone, it is not likely to be, "This is John Jones, my friend," or "my neighbor"; it is more likely to be, "This is John Jones. He's a policeman."

And the other fellow, he takes it up, too. He is likely to tell you that he has always supported pay increases for policemen, that he likes policemen as a whole, but that there are just a few guys in uniform he hates.

No wonder the officer begins to think of himself as a member of the smallest minority group in the community. The idea gradually sinks into him that the only people who understand him, that he can be close to, are his fellow officers.

It is in this kind of atmosphere that you can find the young policeman trying to make the grade in the fraternity. But that is not the whole story.

A policeman lives with tensions, and with fears.

Part of the tensions come from the incredible monotony. He is cooped up with another man, day after day, doing routine things over and over. The excitement that most people think of as the constant occupation of policemen is so infrequent as to come as a relief.

Part of the tensions come from the manifold fears. I don't mean that these men are cowards. This is no place for cowards. But they are human beings. And fears work on all human beings.

Paramount is the physical fear that he will get hurt to the point where he can't go on working, or the fear that he will be killed. The fear for his family.

There is the fear that he will make a wrong decision in a crucial moment, a life-and-death decision. A man has been in a fight. Should he call the paddy wagon or the ambulance? A man aims a pistol at him. Should he try to talk to him, or shoot him?

But the biggest fear he has is that he will show fear to some of his fellow officers. This is the reason he will rush heedlessly in on a cornered burglar or armed maniac if a couple of officers are present —something he wouldn't do if he were alone. He is tormented by his fears and he doesn't dare show them. He knows he has to present a cool, calm front to the public.

As a group, policemen have a very high rate of ulcers, heart attacks, suicides and divorces. These things torment him, too. Divorce is a big problem to policemen. A man can't be a policeman for eight hours and then just turn it off and go home and be a loving father and husband—particularly if he just has had somebody die in the back of his police car.

So once again, the pressure is on him to belong, to be accepted and welcomed into the only group that knows what is going on inside him.

If the influences aren't right, he can be hooked.

So he is at the stage where he wants to be one of the guys. And then this kind of thing may happen. One night his car is sent to check in a "Code 26"—a silent burglar alarm.

The officer and his partner go in to investigate. The burglar is gone. They call the proprietor. He comes down to look things over. And maybe he says, "Boys, this is covered by insurance, so why don't you take a jacket for your wife, or a pair of shoes?" And maybe he does, maybe just because his partner does, and he says to himself, "What the hell, who has been hurt?"

Or maybe the proprietor didn't come down. But after they get back in the car his partner pulls out four $10 bills and hands him two. "Burglar got careless," says the partner.

The young officer who isn't involved soon learns that this kind of thing goes on. He even may find himself checking on a burglary call, say to a drugstore, and see some officers there eyeing him peculiarly.

Maybe at this point the young officer feels the pressure to belong so strongly that he reaches over and picks up something, cigars perhaps. Then he is "in," and the others can do what they wish.

Mind you, not all officers will do this. Somewhere along the line all of them have to make a decision, and it is at that point where the stuff they are made of shows through. But the past experience of the handouts, the official indifference to them, and the pressures and tensions of the job don't make the decision any easier.

And neither he nor the department has had any advance warning, such as might come from thorough psychiatric screening, as to what his decision will be.

Some men may go this far and no farther. They might rationalize that they have not done anything that isn't really accepted by smart people in society.

This is no doubt where the hard-core guy, the one who is a thief already, steps in. A policeman is a trained observer and he is smart in back-alley psychology. This is especially true of the hard-core guy and he has been watching the young fellows come along.

When he and his cronies in a burglary ring spot a guy who may have what it takes to be one of them, they may approach him and try him out as a lookout. From then on it is just short steps to the actual participation in and planning of crimes.

Bear in mind that by this stage we have left all but a few policemen behind. But all of them figure in the story at one stage or another. And what has happened to a few could happen to others. I suppose that is the main point I am trying to make.

Muzafer Sherif

Intergroup Relations and Leadership

This introductory statement to problems of intergroup relations and leadership will start by pointing them out—the safest step we can take, at the start, in approaching the study of complex human problems. Then, a little brush clearing will be done to prepare the ground for an adequate conception of intergroup relations. The implications of this conception for interdisciplinary research strategies conducive to generalizations pertinent to the actualities of various areas of the social scene will be mentioned. Leadership, delegation, representation, bargaining, decision making, and policy making will be viewed as part processes within the framework of group functioning. The statement will close with application of the foregoing formulations to assessment of effective steps in the reduction of prevailing intergroup conflicts.

Importance of Intergroup Relations in Human Affairs Today

Obviously, intergroup relations refer to states of friendship or hostility, cooperation or competition, alliance or enmity, peace or war between two or more groups and their respective members. Such states between groups have always been important and fateful in human affairs. History books have been written chiefly as records of them.

From *Intergroup Relations and Leadership*, edited by Muzafer Sherif. John Wiley & Sons, Inc., 1962. Reprinted by permission of the publisher.

But today, we hear repeatedly from policy makers and analysts of current affairs that the very fate of human beings depends on the state of relations between groups and blocks of nations. The impact of these relations is reflected even in the way our family expenditures are budgeted and our personal goals are regulated relative to the uncertainties of the future.

Groups and nations are no longer closed systems. The internal affairs of groups and nations, the rise or fall of leaders are demonstrably affected by the impact of their intergroup relations. This is being strikingly demonstrated in a study of the recent presidential election we have completed on the West Coast and in the Southwest. Guided by the hypothesis that various campaign issues (such as foreign-relations issues, the peace issue, farm, labor, and civil rights issues) would have different weights for voters, we arranged for our samples to rank these issues in order of their importance. The data indicate that peace and foreign relations rank higher than other issues.

Demarcation of the Problem Area
of Intergroup Relations

Since we have noted the importance of intergroup relations, we can turn to the demarcation of the problem. What states of friendship or hostility, what kind of positive or negative functional relations between human beings, are characteristic of intergroup relations? This is not an idle question. Many technically excellent studies have fallen short in dealing with the problem because they were not initially designed on the basis of an adequate characterization of intergroup relations.

Not every friendly or unfriendly act toward others is a case of intergroup relations. We have to differentiate those actions which can properly be called intergroup behavior.

Let us start by specifying the main concepts involved. This specification must begin with an adequate conception of the key term "group" itself. We define a group as a social unit (1) which consists of a number of individuals who, at a given time, stand in more or less definite interdependent status or role relationships with one another, and (2) which explicitly or implicitly possesses a set of values or norms of its own regulating behavior of individual members, at least in matters of consequence to the group. Shared attitudes, shared sentiments, shared aspirations and goals are related to and implicit in the common values or norms of the group. For group norms are expected, and even ideal modes of behavior, defining for members the limits or latitude of acceptable behavior. Thus defined, a norm is not *necessarily* a statistical average of behaviors in a group. The expected or ideal modes of behavior defined by norms relate to motives and goals that members share in common, or concern the existence and perpetuation of the group itself, along with the reciprocal expectations that regulate the functioning of the organizational pattern.

The term "intergroup relations" refers to relations between two or more groups and their respective members. Whenever individuals belonging to one group interact, collectively or individually, with another group or its members in terms of their group identification, we have an instance of intergroup behavior.

The appropriate frame of reference for studying intergroup behavior is the functional relations between two or more groups, which may be positive or negative. The functional relationship between groups whose members perceive them as *in-groups* has properties of its own. These properties are generated during interaction between particular groups. Intergroup situations are not voids.

Though not independent of the relationships within the groups in question, *the characteristics of functional relations between groups cannot be deduced or extrapolated solely from the properties of relations prevailing among members within the group itself.* Prevailing modes of behavior within groups, in the way of cooperativeness and solidarity, or competitiveness and rivalry, among members need not be the prevalent modes of behavior in their relations with other groups. Hostility towards out-groups may, at times, be proportional to the degree of solidarity within the group. Democracy at home need not imply democratic attitudes toward out-groups.

Some Blind Alleys in Intergroup Conceptions

. . . There is good reason to believe that some persons growing up under unfortunate life circumstances may become more intense in their prejudices and hostilities. But such cases are not the crux of the problem of intergroup relations. At best, they can explain the intensity of behavior in a given dimension. On the whole, established stereotypes of out-groups are not the doings of a few frantic or frustrated individuals.

When there is conflict between two groups, such as a strike or a war, it is usually the more responsible, the more talented, the more exemplary members of the group who are in control. Activities in conflict are conducted by individuals who can withstand the strains imposed by the conflict. When members of a group correctly or incorrectly perceive threat, unjust treatment, or invasion of their rights by another group, opinion in their group is consolidated, slogans are formulated, and decisions are made for effective measures —but not usually by a few neurotic or deviate individuals. Those recognized as the most responsible take the lead. Deviate personalities or frustrated members ordinarily exhibit their intense reactions within the latitudes for acceptable behavior established in their respective settings, which may include hostility toward other groups as well as sacrifice for one's own.

If intergroup behavior were first and foremost a matter of deviate behavior, it would not be the issue of vital consequence that it is today. I repeat: *Intergroup behavior is not primarily a problem of deviate behavior.* It is primarily a problem of participation by individual members within the social distance scale of their group in more stable times, and in the developing trends in relations between their group and others in periods of flux and change, such as that characteristic of our own times.

On the basis of UNESCO studies in India, Gardner Murphy (1953) concluded in his book, *In the Minds of Men,* that to be a "good" Hindu or a "good" Muslim implied believing all the nasty qualities and practices attributed by one's own group to the adversary. The "good" members, who usually constitute the overwhelming majority, remain deaf and dumb to favorable or correct information disseminated concerning their adversary. On the whole, occasions for further conflicts arise by making social contacts and opening the avenues for communication.

It has been argued that aggressive behavior directed against other groups is a result of pent-up aggressive impulses accumulated by group members owing to their individual frustrations. If this be so, how can we explain the fact that acts of violence against other groups do not necessarily occur where the probability of individual frustrations is greatest?

Otto Klineberg . . . asked penetrating questions in this regard in his survey of *Tensions Affecting International Understanding* (1950). He noted that white Brazilians are, on the whole, much more frustrated economically than white Americans, that economic standards in Brazil are much lower, that Brazilians, too, endure the fluctuations of the business cycle. He asked why, then, were there no lynchings of Brazilian Negroes? "This fact," Klineberg stated, "makes it clearly inadequate to explain aggression against the Negro, or in more general terms, hostility against other groups (which may take the form of war in extreme cases) entirely in terms of the aggressive impulses developed within the individual as a result of his frustrations" (p. 198).

Klineberg continued this line of questioning: "Why, if war is due to these factors within the individual, are the majority of individuals opposed to war? Why must they be made to fight? Why must every country, in seeking to build its army, have recourse to conscription?" (p. 199).

Modern warfare is conflict between modern states with definite organizations and value systems. As the English psychologist, Pear, noted in *Psychological Factors of Peace and War* (1950), a solely psychological theory of war "fails to distinguish between the aggressiveness of the warmakers, which can be very real indeed . . . and the attitudes of the general population" (p. 40).

L. F. Richardson (1950) compiled statistics on the number of wars engaged in by major world powers from 1850 to 1941. Britain heads the list with twenty wars—more than the Japanese (with nine), the Germans (with eight), or the United States (with seven). We often hear explanations of Germany's warlike tendencies on the basis of the authoritarian character of the German family and educational training and the resulting frustration to the individual German. Do these statistics indicate that the British people are more frustrated than the Germans? In this connection, it seems reasonable to ask a question which historians and other social scientists can help us answer: "Doesn't having an empire with far-flung interests to be protected and expanded have anything to do with this frequency of war?"

Today we are told that it would be extremely difficult for the United States to remain aloof from a major conflict in any part of the world, since it is one of the two major powers. Does the democratic or authoritarian upbringing of individual Americans in Iowa or Maine or Arizona have anything to do with the likelihood of the United States being involved or not being involved in a war?

Level of Interaction in Intergroup Behavior

Such considerations lead to conclusions concerning the effects of motivational components, that is, of aspirations, frustrations, aggressive impulses, at different levels of interaction—individual, group, and intergroup interaction.

We cannot legitimately extrapolate from the effects of the individual's motivational urges and frustrations to group situations, as if a group situation were a void and the interaction processes and reciprocities within it were a play of shadows. Similarly, compelling material conditions (technology, socioeconomic forces) influence human relations as affected by the existing organizational structure and the system of beliefs or norms. Oscar Lewis has demonstrated this in a striking way in his book, *Five Families* (1959), which has in its subtitle the phrase "the culture of poverty." . . .

We cannot extrapolate from the properties of individuals to the characteristics of group situations. It is equally erroneous to extrapolate from the properties of relations within a group to explain relations between groups, as though the area of interaction between groups consisted of a vacuum, or even of the cozy atmosphere of a conference room. The character of relations and norms that prevail within groups does influence their relations with other groups, but intergroup relations are potently determined by the process of interaction between the groups. The give-and-take between groups may be full of conflict or in a state of flow. And it is this area of conflict, in the case of negative relations, or of flow, in the cases of cooperation or alliance, which may produce consequential reverberations within the groups themselves (Sherif and Sherif, 1953).

What determines the positive or negative nature of interaction between groups? In large part, it is determined by the reciprocal interests of the groups involved and the degree of their significance to the groups in question. The issues at stake must be interests of considerable concern to the groups, if they are to play a part in intergroup relations. A matter of concern may relate to values or goals shared by group members. It may be a real or imagined threat to the safety of the group as a whole, an economic interest, a political advantage, a military consideration, prestige, or a number of others. Once a particular issue comes to the foreground as the dominant influence in intergroup relations, it may become the *limiting factor*, the main anchorage in the interaction process between them.

Empirical Generalizations

The foregoing approach to in-group and intergroup relations was formulated on the basis of extensive surveys of pertinent theoretical works and empirical research. Empirical field studies are full of pregnant leads for experimentalists in formulating valid and testable hypotheses. A series of hypotheses was derived concerning formation and functioning of in-group structure or organization (that is, status or leader-follower behavior and ensuing member attitudes), concerning conditions conducive to positive and negative intergroup attitudes, and concerning measures for the reduction of intergroup conflict (Sherif and Sherif, 1956; Sherif, *et al.*, 1961).

In order to study the effects of aspirations, deprivations, frustrations, and other goal-directed components within an appropriate level of interaction, as the first step in our research, autonomous in-groups were formed experimentally. Then these groups, whose natural history was ascertained step by step, were brought into functional contact under reciprocally competitive and frustrating conditions. Finally, study of reduction of intergroup conflict was undertaken. Our large-scale experiments were carried out in 1949, 1953, and 1954. In 1954 the research was sufficiently advanced to tackle the difficult task of reducing intergroup conflict.

As a background to points raised later in this introductory statement, only the generalizations pertinent to the major hypotheses will be stated here in brief.

Generalizations concerning group formation:

1. A definite group organization (structure) manifested in differentiated status positions is produced when a number of individuals

(even without previously established interpersonal relations) interact with one another under conditions (*a*) which embody goals with appeal value to the individuals, and (*b*) which require interdependent activities for their attainment.

2. The structure or organization is reflected in a consistent pattern of communication among group members. The higher the status of a group member, the greater the frequency of suggestions concerning group activities addressed or relayed to him.

3. Concomitant with the formation of a group organization, group norms emerge and are stabilized, regulating the members' behaviors within specifiable *latitudes of acceptable behavior*, in practices and activities commonly engaged in.

Generalizations concerning negative intergroup relations and the rise of prejudice and stereotypes of the out-group:

1. When groups engage in reciprocally competitive and frustrating activities, such that the victory or gain of a desired goal by one group results in the defeat or loss for the other group, unfavorable stereotypes come into use in relation to the out-group and its members. In time, these unfavorable stereotypes are standardized in a group, placing the out-group at a prejudicial distance (proportional to the degree of negative relations between them.

2. Concomitant with the rise of mutually prejudicial attitudes between groups, self-glorifying or self-justifying attitudes toward the in-group are strengthened. The performance of the out-group is deprecated and the moves of the out-group and its members are perceived in a suspicious light.

Note that in the research on which these generalizations are based the members of the groups were meticulously selected to be socially well-adjusted and academically successful individuals from established families. They were not from broken homes or families with undue behavior problems. Therefore, it would be decidedly off the mark to explain their behavior in intergroup relations on the basis of severe frustrations or instabilities during their prior life histories.

Now, generalizations concerning reduction of intergroup conflict:

1. *Contact* between groups in close proximity in activities which are individually enjoyed by the members of each group does not produce a decrease in the existing state of intergroup hostility. In fact, such occasions of intergroup proximity may be utilized for further exchanges of invectives across group lines and for attribution of the blame for the existing state of affairs to the out-group.

2. The next generalization concerns the measure that proved effective in this research: introduction of superordinate goals. *Superordinate goals* are defined as goals which are compelling for all and cannot be ignored, but which cannot be achieved by the efforts and

resources of one group alone. They require the coordinated efforts and resources of the groups involved. The generalization in this regard is: When groups in a state of friction come into contact under conditions embodying superordinate goals, they tend to cooperate toward the common goal.

But reduction of intergroup conflict is not a one-shot affair. The next generalization brings in the *time* dimension.

3. It was necessary to introduce various superordinate goals over a time span to sustain cooperation and, along with it, to decrease friction and weaken unfavorable stereotypes. Examples of superordinate goals used in our 1954 experiment were a crisis due to shortage of one of the basic necessities of daily living, breakdown of the available transportation that affected everyone, and opportunities for greatly desired activities.

4. The last generalization to be mentioned from these experiments concerns the impact of the state of intergroup relations on in-group relations and organization. It was found that functional relations between groups which are of consequence to the groups in question bring about changes in the pattern of relations within the groups involved. Illustrative of this generalization are the following: When defeat followed defeat for one group in the 1949 experiment, the leader of that group, even though daring, became demoralized. Operational leadership was undertaken by another group member, who, out of friendship for the leader, had not taken the reins earlier, even though he could easily have done so. In the 1954 experiment the leadership changed hands when the peace-time leader could not live up to the requirements of conflict to be in the front lines leading his group in engagements with the adversary.

This finding illustrates the inadequacy of extrapolations from practices and trends within groups to the explanation of intergroup relations and practices. Practices and trends within groups are themselves affected by relations with other groups. The practical implication is that in-group democracy, friendship, and solidarity need not be extended to cooperativeness, friendship, and solidarity with out-groups.

The generalizations just presented may warrant the following summary of the rise of favorable and unfavorable attitudes toward the in-group and toward out-groups:

In the process of interaction among members, the group is endowed with qualities which tend to be favorable, and may be self-justifying and even self-glorifying. Individual members, in their strivings to get along well in their interpersonal relations, to be accepted or rewarded, tend to develop qualities or traits, put at a premium in their reference groups through the example of other members they look up to, through verbal dictums and through a set of sanctions applied to cases of deviation from the prevailing acceptable modes of behavior.

Out-groups and their respective members are attributed favorable or unfavorable traits depending on the positive or negative nature of functional relations between the groups in question. Are the groups or a combination of groups competing with each other to excel in prestige, toward economic ends, political ends, territorial ends, so that the gain of one party is necessarily the loss of the other? Does the victory of one party mean the sure defeat of the other? Does possession by one party mean deprivation or humiliation for the other? Or are the attainments of such ends by one party compatible with the ends of the other? These possibilities are illustrative of the situations conducive to positive or negative functional relations between groups. Experiments indicate that negative functional relations between groups give rise to hostile attitudes and unfavorable stereotypes toward the out-group irrespective of the objective qualities of the individuals involved. For example, if the enemy kills fifty of us he is labeled "fanatic" and "cruel," but the in-group member is cited as "brave" or "heroic" for killing the enemy.

Hence, upholding the conception that one's reference group maintains about an out-group is not essentially a problem of a deviate or highly frustrated individual. It is a problem of participation by in-group members in evaluative processes and activities directed toward the out-group on the part of "good" members, who ordinarily constitute the majority of membership so long as group solidarity and morale are sustained.

It is in states of transition, rapid change, or acculturation that cases of nonconformity and lack of consensus increase in frequency. At such times, development of schisms and factions within social units becomes accelerated. For adequate formulations about such periods of transition and the rise of factions, we need a great deal of information from anthropological field observations. . . .

Once hostile attitudes and unfavorable stereotypes are stabilized toward another group and its members, they become a part of the cultural repertory of the group, coloring the light in which the out-group is seen and outlasting the actual intergroup relations in which they originally developed. . . .

Problems of Research and Validity

The formulations presented so far have been based primarily on surveys of theory and factual evidence concerning relatively small social units and experiments on small groups of young people. . . .

To insure that generalizations from small group research have relevance for actual groups, small and large, it is necessary to raise the much neglected problem of *validity* of experimental findings. The validity of research findings should be a major concern of interdisciplinary efforts, provided that members of each discipline have learned enough about intergroup relations that we can talk with one another, rather than at each other across the particular brand and jargon of our respective disciplines.

The problem of validity includes the question of the relative adequacy of experimental and empirical findings for understanding and predicting problems of leader-follower relations, friendship, and hostility among groups, reduction of conflict and unfavorable stereotypes in actual settings of political, economic, and social life.

Doubts and negation of the validity of small group research have been stated by authors dealing with hard "facts of life"—for example, by David Truman in his chapter in *Research Frontiers in Politics and Government* (1955), following in the footsteps of V. O. Key. They are raised by the Columbia anthropologist, Conrad Arensberg (1951), in his discussion of small group research and large organizations, and by the sociologist, Arnold Rose (1954), in his comments on intergroup experiments.

On the other hand, it is contended by confirmed experimentalists that experimentation lends itself to greater generality of results—to generalizations applicable in a wider variety of situations. I propose that neither party to this discussion presents an adequate picture. In their revised *Group Dynamics,* Cartwright and Zander (1960) illustrate the wide generality of experimental findings with studies on norm formation utilizing the autokinetic effect. If these experiments have generality, I think it comes from the fact that they were preceded by extensive surveys of the phenomena in question and the conditions in which they occurred. They were not undertaken for the mere sake of testing hypotheses derived by analogy from physical models, which may or may not be valid models for actualities of social happenings in the problem area.

The validity of both experimental and empirical findings is bounded by the special conditions under which the study is conducted. This limitation applies to field research just as much as to experimental research. In reporting experiments, the usual practice has been to specify only those variables actually manipulated by the experimenter. On the whole, such meticulous concern has not been shown in specifying variables or conditions which are not intentionally manipulated but which, nevertheless, enter into determining the results. The practice of plunging into hypothesis testing because certain techniques have become fashionable at the time and without sufficient grounding in the background and actualities of the problem area invites justified criticism of experimentation. The price of such practices is reports of contradictory generalizations, each of which might be true, but only for the particular conditions of the study, which are unspecified and may be unrepresentative. No wonder, then, that even the relatively brief history of experimental social psychology is in part the graveyard of artifacts lacking in validity from the point of view of problems purportedly claimed to be studied.

For example, if we are intent on proving that leadership quality is specific to situations, we can do so by choosing subjects who are not, at the start, acquainted with one another and setting them to a variety of motivationally neutral tasks called "problem solving" situations. On the other hand, if we are set to prove the generality of leadership quality, we can define experimental conditions conducive to showing it; namely, by having members of a group with established reciprocities face genuine problem situations, such as tasks which have been of real concern to them day in and day out.

This does not mean that experimentation is necessarily invalid and fruitless. On the contrary, experimentation is the "crowning touch in analysis" when we can attain that level of analysis without mutilating the very problem we intend to study. The contradictory results of leadership studies fall into a meaningful pattern if evaluated in the light of the conditions of the studies—namely, the presence or absence of established relationships and expectations among individuals and the motivational relevance of the problem situations faced. The point could be illustrated further with the topics of the relative achievement in individual versus group performance, the relative efficiency of decision making in small and relatively larger groups, and other measures of decision making in role playing and conference situations.

The remedy, in my opinion, is not concentration on experimental work or on field work to the exclusion of the other, but constant evaluation of the *formulation* of the problems of intergroup relations and constant evaluation of the *conditions* in which they are studied in the light of persistent problems and persistent findings encountered in labor-management relations, in existing and emerging factions in societies in the throes of transition, in events ensuing under the magic spell of nationalism, and between nations encountering the sometimes grim problems of internationalism.

Needed Perspective for Study of Intergroup Relations

In order to evaluate properly the conditions bounding particular intergroup relations in various areas (political, cultural, ethnic, etc.), one of the greatest needs is placing them in proper perspective. Operationally, this amounts to explicit recognition and assessment of part processes relative to the total system of relationships. This oft-repeated dictum not infrequently remains only lip service. Its urgency is compelling as soon as one tries to coordinate generalizations concerning large social units with those concerning small units which operate within them. Robert Dubin has dealt with such problems in terms of "linkages" within a large system, for example, in his chapter in the book edited by Haire: *Modern Organization Theory* (1959). . . .

In seeking perspective on special areas of intergroup relations through consideration of the systems of which they are parts, we immediately encounter the *power* dimension, which has been one of the most neglected aspects of small group research. We share the conception of those writers who characterize *social power* in terms of the *initiation or suppression of activity in others in requested or expected directions, with means and instrumentalities to apply sanctions when there is noncompliance.* Thus defined, the problem of power becomes integral to the study of any organizational framework, small or large, formally or informally organized. The initiation of activities in others without the possibility of sanction may be usefully designated by another term, such as *influence.*

The differentiated statuses which define any organization from an operational point of view are positions in a power dimension, whatever else they may be. As such, every group is a power group, even though means and instrumentalities of sanctions do differ in formal and informal organizations. For this reason, exploration of leader-follower relations within groups and in intergroup relations is fanciful without bringing the power aspect prominently into the picture. . . .

Leadership, Policy Making, and Representation as Group Functions

Within groups, small or large, formal or informal, the focus of power resides in the leadership and other high status members. But the leadership status itself is within a group, and not outside of it, as Cecil Gibb (1954) maintained in the most comprehensive survey of leadership studies to date. The leader himself is not immune from sanctions if he deviates too far from the bounds of acceptable behavior prevailing in the group. Leaders, delegates, and representatives of the groups must remain a part of the power structure of the group if their actions are to be effective. The significance of the power structure for assessing the behavior of individuals in such positions is immediately seen when their actions deviate widely from the expectations of the membership. The newspaper accounts of the business leader who has arrangements with a supplier, of the union leader who makes a deal with company representatives to his own advantage, of the prime minister who appears to succumb to the inducements of the enemy, tell us what happens in such cases.

Delegation and representation of authority are integral aspects of group functioning, especially in relations with other groups. Studies by Ralph Stogdill and his associates show that, within a large organization, subordinate members expect superiors to delegate authority and regard those who delegate more freely as better leaders. Yet Stogdill, in his recent book, *Individual Behavior and Group Achievement* (1959), observes that there are limiting situations "where a high degree of co-ordination is required," and delegation may result in "confusion and mis-directed effort" (p. 189).

Thus, in critical situations, leaders tend to take over the reins. If representatives in a collective bargaining situation are not making effective headway, the top leaders may, for the first time, get *directly* into these procedures. Similarly, a critical international situation temporarily reduces the authority of representatives on international councils, and at such times top leadership may step to the front line of negotiations.

In dealings between groups, the problem of power is mainfested in different ways. Within a large organization or within a society, relations between groups are ordinarily subject to sanctions by the still larger organization. However, in a "casually patterned" society, to use the sociologist Lynd's characterization, the relations between some of the constituent organizations may not be regulated by sanctions applicable to all parties within the all-embracing organization. These areas of intergroup relations—in what Bierstedt (1957) has called the "unorganized interstices" of society—are in the foreground of major social problems in this country today.

In the relations between nations, the extent of regulation by commonly accepted sanctions is still smaller. Thus, power is not infrequently manifested in the form of force and threat of force. It is in such contexts that relationships between groups become vital to the survival of the groups in question. It is in such contexts that the problems of reduction of intergroup conflict, hostility, and its by-products become the urgent problems of our time.

Superordinate Goals in Reduction of Conflicts

In concluding, I venture to state some of the things that we have learned about the reduction of intergroup conflict. It is true that lines of *communication*, that is, *contact*, between groups must be opened before prevailing conflicts can be reduced. But if contact between groups takes place without superordinate goals—that is, goals which are *urgent* and *compelling* for *all* groups involved, under the circumstances—the communication channels and the contacts serve as mediums for further accusations and recriminations. The discussion becomes bogged down in direct and indirect reference to the vicious circle of "Who's to blame?"

When contact situations involve superordinate goals, communication is utilized in the direction of reducing conflict in order to attain the common goals.

In regard to dissemination of *information*, favorable information about a disliked out-group tends to be ignored, rejected, or reinterpreted to fit prevailing stereotypes. But when groups are pulling together toward superordinate goals, true and favorable information about the out-group is seen in a new light, and the probability of information being effective is enormously enhanced.

When groups cooperate toward superordinate goals, *leaders* are in a position to take bolder steps toward bringing about understanding and harmonious relations. When groups are directed toward goals which are mutually incompatible, genuine moves by a leader to reduce intergroup conflict may be seen by the membership of his own group as out-of-step and ill-advised. He may be subjected to severe criticism and even loss of faith. When compelling superordinate goals become articulated, the leader can make moves to further cooperative efforts, he can more freely delegate authority, and representation processes can proceed more effectively. The decisions reached are more likely to receive support from other group members.

In short, various measures suggested for the reduction of intergroup conflict, such as dissemination of information, increasing social contacts, and conferences of leaders and representatives, acquire new significance and new effectiveness when they become part and parcel of interaction processes between groups oriented toward superordinate goals which have real and compelling value for all groups concerned.

Over a period of time, the interaction of groups toward superordinate goals which have genuine and compelling value for all groups concerned should assume organizational forms. If the tasks of building such organizations seem formidable, they are no more formidable, I think, than those which a modern war might impose. And surely there can be no doubt that man's potentialities can be realized better in the course of such efforts than in preoccupation with assigning blame for the state of affairs, in pursuits of old fears, old hostilities, and old conflicts, with their awesome possibilities in this present world.

Concentrated efforts of all parties toward superordinate goals, rather than preoccupation with assessment of blame and clearing away all existing grudges, have a psychological implication as well. In the process of such efforts, man will be creating new organizations, new values, and thereby transforming himself. Just as the properties of part of a pattern are colored by the overall system of which it is part, the old grudges and stereotypes will acquire a different significance in the context of joint efforts toward common goals and their by-products. This is the plea made so eloquently by Gardner Murphy in his book *Human Potentialities* (1958), of which the Yale physicist, Henry Margenau, wrote: "Here a psychologist of vision casts knowledge of man's present abilities into temporal perspective and portrays the forms which human development may take."

References

Arensberg, C. H. "Behavior and Organization: Industrial Studies." In *Social Psychology at the Crossroads,* ed. J. H. Rohrer and M. Sherif. Harper & Row, 1951.

Bierstedt, R. "An Analysis of Social Power." In *Sociological Theory: A Book of Readings,* ed. L. A. Coser and B. Rosenberg. Macmillan, 1957.

Cartwright, D., and A. Zander. *Group Dynamics: Research and Theory,* 2nd ed. Harper & Row, 1960.

Dubin, R. "Stability in Human Organization." In *Modern Organization Theory,* ed. M. Haire. Wiley, 1959.

Gibb, C. A. "Leadership." In *Handbook of Social Psychology* (Vol. 2), ed. G. Lindzey. Addison-Wesley, 1954.

Klineberg, O. *Tensions Affecting International Understanding.* Social Science Research Council Bulletin 62, 1950.

Lewis, O. *Five Families: Mexican Case Studies in the Culture of Poverty.* Basic Books, 1959.

Murphy, G. *Human Potentialities.* Basic Books, 1958.

————. *In the Minds of Men.* Basic Books, 1953.

Pear, T. H., ed. *Psychological Factors of Peace and War.* Philosophical Library, 1950.

Richardson, L. F. "Statistics of Deadly Quarrels." In *Psychological Factors of Peace and War,* ed. T. H. Pear. Philosophical Library, 1950.

Rose, A. M. *Theory and Method in the Social Sciences.* University of Minnesota Press, 1954.

Sherif, M., O. J. Harvey, B. J. White, W. R. Hood, and Carolyn W. Sherif. *Intergroup Conflict and Cooperation: The Robbers' Cave Experiment.* University of Oklahoma Book Exchange, 1961.

Sherif, M., and Carolyn W. Sherif. *Groups in Harmony and Tension.* Harper, 1953.

————. *Outline of Social Psychology,* rev. ed. Harper & Row, 1956.

Stogdill, R. M. *Individual Behavior and Group Achievement.* Oxford University Press, 1959.

Truman, D. B. "The Impact on Political Science of the Revolution in the Behavioral Sciences." In *Research Frontiers in Politics and Government.* Brookings Institution, 1955.

Robert K. Merton

The Self-Fulfilling Prophecy

In a series of works seldom consulted outside the academic fraternity, W. I. Thomas, the dean of American sociologists, set forth a theorem basic to the social sciences: "If men define situations as real, they are real in their consequences." Were the Thomas theorem and its implications more widely known, more men would understand more of the workings of our society. Though it lacks the sweep and precision of a Newtonian theorem, it possesses the same gift of relevance, being instructively applicable to many, if indeed not most, social processes.

The Thomas Theorem

"If men define situations as real, they are real in their consequences," wrote Professor Thomas. The suspicion that he was driving at a crucial point becomes all the more insistent when we note that essentially the same theorem had been repeatedly set forth by disciplined and observant minds long before Thomas.

When we find such otherwise discrepant minds as the redoubtable Bishop Bossuet in his passionate seventeenth-century defense of Catholic orthodoxy, the ironic Mandeville in his eighteenth-century allegory honeycombed with observations on the paradoxes of human society, the irascible genius Marx in his revision of Hegel's theory of historical change, the seminal Freud in works which have perhaps gone further than any others of his day toward modifying man's outlook on man, and the erudite, dogmatic, and occasionally sound Yale professor, William Graham Sumner, who lives on as the Karl Marx of the middle classes—when we find this mixed company (and I select from a longer if less distinguished list) agreeing on the truth and the pertinence of what is substantially the Thomas theorem, we may conclude that perhaps it is worth our attention as well.

To what, then, are Thomas and Bossuet, Mandeville, Marx, Freud and Sumner directing our attention?

The first part of the theorem provides an unceasing reminder that men respond not only to the objective features of a situation, but also, and at times primarily, to the meaning this situation has for them. And once they have assigned some meaning to the situation, their consequent behavior and some of the consequences of that behavior are determined by the ascribed meaning. But this is still rather abstract, and abstractions have a way of becoming unintelligible if they are not occasionally tied to concrete data. What is a case in point?

A Sociological Parable

It is the year 1932. The Last National Bank is a flourishing institution. A large part of its resources is liquid without being watered. Cartwright Millingville has ample reason to be proud of the banking institution over which he presides. Until Black Wednesday. As he enters his bank, he notices that business is unusually brisk. A little odd that, since the men at the A.M.O.K. steel plant and the K.O.M.A. mattress factory are not usually paid until Saturday. Yet here are two dozen men, obviously from the factories, queued up in front of the tellers' cages. As he turns into his private office, the president muses rather compassionately: "Hope they haven't been laid off in midweek. They should be in the shop at this hour."

But speculations of this sort have never made for a thriving bank, and Millingville turns to the pile of documents upon his desk. His precise signature is affixed to fewer than a score of papers when he is disturbed by the absence of something familiar and the intrusion of something alien. The low, discreet hum of bank business has given way to a strange and annoying stridency of many voices. A situation has been defined as real. And that is the beginning of what ends as Black Wednesday—the last Wednesday, it might be noted, of the Last National Bank.

Cartwright Millingville had never heard of the Thomas theorem. But he had no difficulty in recognizing its workings. He knew that, despite the comparative liquidity of the bank's assets, a rumor of insolvency, once believed by enough depositors, would result in the insolvency of the bank. And by the close of Black Wednesday—and Blacker Thursday—when the long lines of anxious depositors, each frantically seeking to salvage his own, grew to longer lines of even more anxious depositors, it turned out that he was right.

The stable financial structure of the bank had depended upon one set of definitions of the situation: belief in the validity of the interlocking system of economic promises men live by. Once depositors had defined the situation otherwise, once they questioned the possibility of having these promises fulfilled, the consequences of this unreal definition were real enough.

A familiar type case this, and one doesn't need the Thomas theorem to understand how it happened—not, at least, if one is old enough to have voted for Franklin Roosevelt in 1932. But with the aid of the theorem the tragic history of Millingville's bank can perhaps be converted into a sociological parable which may help us understand not only what happened to hundreds of banks in the 1930s but also what happens to the relations between Negro and white, between Protestant and Catholic and Jew in these days.

The parable tells us that public definitions of a situation (prophecies or predictions) become an integral part of the situation and thus affect subsequent developments. This is peculiar to human affairs. It is not found in the world of nature, untouched by human hands. Predictions of the return of Halley's comet do not influence its orbit. But the rumored insolvency of Millingville's bank did affect the actual outcome. The prophecy of collapse led to its own fulfillment.

So common is the pattern of the self-fulfilling prophecy that each of us has his favored specimen. Consider the case of the examination neurosis. Convinced that he is destined to fail, the anxious student devotes more time to worry than to study and then turns in a poor examination. The initially fallacious anxiety is transformed into an entirely justified fear. Or it is believed that war between two nations is inevitable. Actuated by this conviction, representatives of the two nations become progressively alienated, apprehensively countering each "offensive" move of the other with a "defensive" move of their own. Stockpiles of armaments, raw materials, and armed men grow larger and eventually the anticipation of war helps create the actuality.

The self-fulfilling prophecy is, in the beginning, a *false* definition of the situation evoking a new behavior which makes the originally false conception come *true*. The specious validity of the self-fulfilling prophecy perpetuates a reign of error. For the prophet will cite the actual course of events as proof that he was right from the very beginning. (Yet we know that Millingville's bank was solvent, that it would have survived for many years had not the misleading rumor *created* the very conditions of its own fulfillment.) Such are the perversities of social logic.

It is the self-fulfilling prophecy which goes far toward explaining the dynamics of ethnic and racial conflict in the America of today. That this is the case, at least for relations between Negroes and whites, may be gathered from the fifteen hundred pages which make up Gunnar Myrdal's *An American Dilemma*. That the self-fulfilling prophecy may have even more general bearing upon the relations between ethnic groups than Myrdal has indicated is the thesis of the considerably briefer discussion that follows.[1]

---

1. Counterpart of the self-fulfilling prophecy is the "suicidal prophecy," which so alters human behavior from what would have been its course had the prophecy not been made that it *fails* to be borne out. The prophecy destroys itself. This important type is not considered here. For examples of both types of social prophecy, see MacIver (1948); for a general statement, see Merton (1936).

Social Beliefs and Social Reality

As a result of their failure to comprehend the operation of the self-fulfilling prophecy, many Americans of good will (sometimes reluctantly) retain enduring ethnic and racial prejudices. They experience these beliefs, not as prejudices, not as prejudgments, but as irresistible products of their own observation. "The facts of the case" permit them no other conclusion.

Thus our fair-minded white citizen strongly supports a policy of excluding Negroes from his labor union. His views are, of course, based not upon prejudice, but upon the cold hard facts. And the facts seem clear enough. Negroes, "lately from the nonindustrial South, are undisciplined in traditions of trade unionism and the art of collective bargaining." The Negro is a strikebreaker. The Negro, with his "low standard of living," rushes in to take jobs at less than prevailing wages. The Negro is, in short, "a traitor to the working class," and should manifestly be excluded from union organizations. So run the facts of the case as seen by our tolerant but hard-headed union member, innocent of any understanding of the self-fulfilling prophecy as a basic process of society.

Our unionist fails to see, of course, that he and his kind have produced the very "facts" which he observes. For by defining the situation as one in which Negroes are held to be incorrigibly at odds with principles of unionism and by excluding Negroes from unions, he invited a series of consequences which indeed made it difficult if not impossible for many Negroes to avoid the role of scab. Out of work after World War I, and kept out of unions, thousands of Negroes could not resist strikebound employers who held a door invitingly open upon a world of jobs from which they were otherwise excluded.

History creates its own test of the theory of self-fulfilling prophecies. That Negroes were strikebreakers because they were excluded from unions (and from a wide range of jobs) rather than excluded because they were strikebreakers can be seen from the virtual disappearance of Negroes as scabs in industries where they have gained admission to unions in the last decades.

The application of the Thomas theorem also suggests how the tragic, often vicious, circle of self-fulfilling prophecies can be broken. The initial definition of the situation which has set the circle in motion must be abandoned. Only when the original assumption is questioned and a new definition of the situation introduced does the consequent flow of events give the lie to the assumption. Only then does the belief no longer father the reality.

But to question these deep-rooted definitions of the situation is no simple act of the will. The will, or for that matter, good will, cannot be turned on and off like a faucet. Social intelligence and good will are themselves *products* of distinct social forces. They are not brought into being by mass propaganda and mass education, in the usual sense of these terms, so dear to the sociological panaceans. In the social realm, no more than in the psychological realm, do false ideas quietly vanish when confronted with the truth. One does not expect a paranoiac to abandon his hard-won distortions and delusions upon being informed that they are altogether groundless. If psychic ills could be cured merely by the dissemination of truth, the psychiatrists of this country would be suffering from technological unemployment rather than from overwork. Nor will a continuing "educational campaign" itself destroy racial prejudice and discrimination.

This is not a particularly popular position. The appeal to education as a cure-all for the most varied social problems is rooted deep in the mores of America. Yet it is nonetheless illusory for all that. For how would this program of racial education proceed? Who is to do the educating? The teachers in our communities? But, in some measure like many other Americans, the teachers share the same prejudices they are being urged to combat. And when they don't, aren't they being asked to serve as conscientious martyrs in the cause of educational utopianism? How long the tenure of an elementary school teacher in Alabama or Mississippi or Georgia who attempted meticulously to disabuse his young pupils of the racial beliefs they acquired at home? Education may serve as an operational adjunct but not as the chief basis for any but excruciatingly slow change in the prevailing patterns of race relations.

To understand further why educational campaigns cannot be counted on to eliminate prevailing ethnic hostilities, we must examine the operation of in-groups and out-groups in our society. Ethnic out-groups, to adopt Sumner's useful bit of sociological jargon, consist of all those who are believed to differ significantly from "ourselves" in terms of nationality, race, or religion. Counterpart of the ethnic out-group is of course the ethnic in-group, constituted by those who "belong." There is nothing fixed or eternal about the lines separating the in-group from out-groups. As situations change, the lines of separation change. For a large number of white Americans, Joe Louis is a member of an out-group—when the situation is defined in racial terms. On another occasion, when Louis defeated the nazified Schmeling, many of these same white Americans acclaimed him as a member of the (national) in-group. National loyalty took precedence over racial separatism. These abrupt shifts in group boundaries sometimes prove embarrassing. Thus, when Negro-Americans ran away with the honors in the Olympic games held in Berlin, the Nazis, pointing to the second-class citizenship assigned Negroes in various regions of this country, denied that the United States had really won the games, since the Negro athletes were by our own admission "not full-fledged" Americans. And what could Bilbo or Rankin say to that?

Under the benevolent guidance of the dominant in-group, ethnic out-groups are continuously subjected to a lively process of prejudice which, I think, goes far toward vitiating mass education and mass propaganda for ethnic tolerance. This is the process whereby "in-group virtues become out-group vices," to paraphrase a remark by the sociologist Donald Young. Or, more colloquially and perhaps more instructively, it may be called the "damned-if-you-do and damned-if-you-don't" process in ethnic and racial relations.

In-Group Virtues and Out-Group Vices

To discover that ethnic out-groups are damned if they do embrace the values of white Protestant society and damned if they don't, we have first to turn to one of the in-group culture heroes, examine the qualities with which he is endowed by biographers and popular belief, and thus distill the qualities of mind and action and character which are generally regarded as altogether admirable.

Periodic public opinion polls are not needed to justify the selection of Abe Lincoln as the culture hero who most fully embodies the cardinal American virtues. As the Lynds point out in *Middletown,* the people of that typical small city allow George Washington alone to join Lincoln as the greatest of Americans. He is claimed as their very own by almost as many well-to-do Republicans as by less well-to-do Democrats.[2]

Even the inevitable schoolboy knows that Lincoln was thrifty, hard-working, eager for knowledge, ambitious, devoted to the rights of the average man, and eminently successful in climbing the ladder of opportunity from the lowermost rung of laborer to the respectable heights of merchant and lawyer. (We need follow his dizzying ascent no further.)

---

2. On Lincoln as culture hero, see the perceptive essay, "Getting Right with Lincoln," by David Donald in *Lincoln Reconsidered* (1956), pp. 3–18.

Though Lincoln nominally remains, of course, the symbolic leader of the Republicans, this may be just another paradox of political history of the same kind which Lincoln noted in his day with regard to Jefferson and the Democrats.

"Remembering, too, that the Jefferson party was formed upon its supposed superior devotion to the personal rights of men, holding the rights of property to be secondary only, and greatly inferior, and assuming that the so-called Democrats of to-day are the Jefferson, and their opponents the anti-Jefferson, party, it will be equally interesting to note how completely the two have changed hands as to the principle upon which they were originally supposed to be divided. The Democrats of to-day hold the liberty of one man to be absolutely nothing, when in conflict with another man's right of property; Republicans, on the contrary, are for both the man and the dollar, but in case of conflict the man before the dollar.

"I remember being once much amused at seeing two partially intoxicated men engaged in a fight with their great-coats on, which fight, after a long and rather harmless contest, ended in each having fought himself out of his own coat and into that of the other. If the two leading parties of this day are really identical with the two in the days of Jefferson and Adams, they have performed the same feat as the two drunken men." (Abraham Lincoln, in a letter to H. L. Pierce and others, April 6, 1859, in *Complete Works of Abraham Lincoln,* eds. Nicolay and Hay, 1894, Vol. 5, 125–26.)

If one did not know that these attributes and achievements are numbered high among the values of middle-class America, one would soon discover it by glancing through the Lynds' account of "the Middletown spirit." For there we find the image of the Great Emancipator fully reflected in the values in which Middletown believes. And since these are their values, it is not surprising to find the Middletowns of America condemning and disparaging those individuals and groups who fail, presumably, to exhibit these virtues. If it appears to the white in-group that Negroes are *not* educated in the same measure as themselves, that they have an "unduly" high proportion of unskilled workers and an "unduly" low proportion of successful business and professional men, that they are thriftless, and so on through the catalogue of middle-class virtue and sin, it is not difficult to understand the charge that the Negro is "inferior" to the white.

Sensitized to the workings of the self-fulfilling prophecy, we should be prepared to find that the anti-Negro charges which are not patently false are only speciously true. The allegations are true in the Pickwickian sense that we have found self-fulfilling prophecies in general to be true. Thus, if the dominant in-group believes that Negroes are inferior, and sees to it that funds for education are not "wasted on these incompetents" and then proclaims as final evidence of this inferiority that Negroes have proportionately "only" one-fifth as many college graduates as whites, one can scarcely be amazed by this transparent bit of social legerdemain. Having seen the rabbit carefully though not too adroitly placed in the hat, we can only look askance at the triumphant air with which it is finally produced. (In fact, it is a little embarrassing to note that a larger proportion of Negro than of white high school graduates have gone on to college; apparently, the Negroes who are hardy enough to scale the high walls of discrimination represent an even more highly selected group than the run-of-the-high-school white population.)

So, too, when the gentleman from Mississippi (a state which spends five times as much on the average white pupil as on the average Negro pupil) proclaims the essential inferiority of the Negro by pointing to the per capita ratio of physicians among Negroes as less than one-fourth that of whites, we are impressed more by his scrambled logic than by his profound prejudices. So plain is the mechanism of the self-fulfilling prophecy in these instances that only those forever devoted to the victory of sentiment over fact can take these specious evidences seriously. Yet the spurious evidence often creates a genuine belief. Self-hypnosis through one's own propaganda is a not infrequent phase of the self-fulfilling prophecy.

So much for out-groups being damned if they don't (apparently) manifest in-group virtues. It is a tasteless bit of ethnocentrism, seasoned with self-interest. But what of the second phase of this process?

Can one seriously mean that out-groups are also damned if they *do* possess these virtues? One can.

Through a faultlessly bisymmetrical prejudice, ethnic and racial out-groups get it coming and going. The systematic condemnation of the out-grouper continues largely *irrespective of what he does.* More: through a freakish exercise of capricious judicial logic, the victim is punished for the crime. Superficial appearances notwithstanding, prejudice and discrimination aimed at the out-group are not a result of what the out-group does, but are rooted deep in the structure of our society and the social psychology of its members.

To understand how this happens, we must examine the moral alchemy through which the in-group readily transmutes virtue into vice and vice into virtue, as the occasion may demand. Our studies will proceed by the case method.

We begin with the engagingly simple formula of moral alchemy: the same behavior must be differently evaluated according to the person who exhibits it. For example, the proficient alchemist will at once know that the word "firm" is properly declined as follows:

> I am firm,
> Thou art obstinate,
> He is pigheaded.

There are some, unversed in the skills of this science, who will tell you that one and the same term should be applied to all three instances of identical behavior. Such unalchemical nonsense should simply be ignored.

With this experiment in mind, we are prepared to observe how the very same behavior undergoes a complete change of evaluation in its transition from the in-group Abe Lincoln to the out-group Abe Cohen or Abe Kurokawa. We proceed systematically. Did Lincoln work far into the night? This testifies that he was industrious, resolute, perseverant, and eager to realize his capacities to the full. Do the out-group Jews or Japanese keep these same hours? This only bears witness to their sweatshop mentality, their ruthless undercutting of American standards, their unfair competitive practices. Is the in-group hero frugal, thrifty, and sparing? Then the out-group villain is stingy, miserly, and penny-pinching. All honor is due the in-group Abe for his having been smart, shrewd, and intelligent, and, by the same token, all contempt is owing the out-group Abes for their being sharp, cunning, crafty, and too clever by far. Did the indomitable Lincoln refuse to remain content with a life of work with the hands? Did he prefer to make use of his brain? Then, all praise for his plucky climb up the shaky ladder of opportunity. But, of course, the eschewing of manual work for brain work among the merchants and lawyers of the out-group deserves nothing but censure for a parasitic way of life. Was Abe Lincoln eager to learn the accumulated wisdom of the ages by unending study? The trouble with the Jew is that he's a greasy grind, with his head always in a book, while decent people are going to a show or a ball game. Was the resolute Lincoln unwilling to limit his standards to those of his provincial community? That is what we should expect of a man of vision. And if the out-groupers criticize the vulnerable areas in our society, then send 'em back where they came from. Did Lincoln, rising high above his origins, never forget the rights of the common man and applaud the right of workers to strike? This testifies only that, like all real Americans, this greatest of Americans was deathlessly devoted to the cause of freedom. But, as you examine the statistics on strikes, remember that these un-American practices are the result of out-groupers pursuing their evil agitation among otherwise contented workers.

Once stated, the classical formula of moral alchemy is clear enough. Through the adroit use of these rich vocabularies of encomium and opprobrium, the in-group readily transmutes its own virtues into others' vices. But why do so many in-groupers qualify as moral alchemists? Why are so many in the dominant in-group so fully devoted to this continuing experiment in moral transmutation?

An explanation may be found by putting ourselves at some distance from this country and following the anthropologist Malinowski to the Trobriand Islands. For there we find an instructively similar pattern. Among the Trobrianders, to a degree which Americans, despite Hollywood and the confession magazines, have apparently not yet approximated, success with women confers honor and prestige on a man. Sexual prowess is a positive value, a moral virtue. But if a rank-and-file Trobriander has "too much" sexual success, if he achieves "too many" triumphs of the heart, an achievement which should of course be limited to the elite, the chiefs or men of power, then this glorious record becomes a scandal and an abomination. The chiefs are quick *to resent any personal achievement not warranted by social position*. The moral virtues remain virtues only so long as they are jealously confined to the proper in-group. The right activity by the wrong people becomes a thing of contempt, not of honor. For clearly, only in this way, by holding these virtues exclusively to themselves, can the men of power retain their distinction, their prestige, and their power. No wiser procedure could be devised to hold intact a system of social stratification and social power.

The Trobrianders could teach us more. For it seems clear that the chiefs have not calculatingly devised this program of entrenchment. Their behavior is spontaneous, unthinking, and immediate. Their resentment of "too much" ambition or "too much" success in the ordinary Trobriander is not contrived, it is genuine. It just happens that this prompt emotional response to the "misplaced" manifestation of in-group virtues also serves the useful expedient of reinforcing the chiefs' special claims to the good things of Trobriand life. Nothing could be more remote from the truth and more distorted a reading of the facts than to assume that this conversion of in-group virtues into out-group vices is part of a calculated, deliberate plot of Trobriand chiefs to keep Trobriand commoners in their place. It is merely that the chiefs have been indoctrinated with an appreciation of the proper order of things, and see it as their heavy burden to enforce the mediocrity of others.

Nor, in quick revulsion from the culpabilities of the moral alchemists, need we succumb to the equivalent error of simply upending the moral status of the in-group and the out-groups. It is not that Jews and Negroes are one and all angelic while Gentiles and whites are one and all fiendish. It is not that individual virtue will now be found exclusively on the wrong side of the ethnic-racial tracks and individual viciousness on the right side. It is conceivable even that there are as many corrupt and vicious men and women among Negroes and Jews as among Gentile whites. It is only that the ugly fence which encloses the in-group happens to exclude the people who make up the out-groups from being treated with the decency ordinarily accorded human beings.

Social Functions and Dysfunctions

We have only to look at the consequences of this peculiar moral alchemy to see that there is no paradox at all in damning out-groupers when they do and when they don't exhibit in-group virtues. Condemnation on these two scores performs one and the same social function. Seeming opposites coalesce. When Negroes are tagged as incorrigibly inferior because they (apparently) don't manifest these virtues, this confirms the natural rightness of their being assigned an inferior status in society. And when Jews or Japanese are tagged as having too many of the in-group values, it becomes plain that they must be securely controlled by the high walls of discrimination. In both cases, the special status assigned the several out-groups can be seen to be eminently reasonable.

Yet this distinctly reasonable arrangement persists in having most unreasonable consequences, both logical and social. Consider only a few of these.

In some contexts, the limitations enforced upon the out-group—say, rationing the number of Jews permitted to enter colleges and professional schools—logically imply a fear of the alleged superiority of the out-group. Were it otherwise, no discrimination need be practiced. The unyielding, impersonal forces of academic competition would soon trim down the number of Jewish (or Japanese or Negro) students to an "appropriate" size.

This implied belief in the superiority of the out-group seems premature. There is simply not enough scientific evidence to demonstrate Jewish or Japanese or Negro superiority. The effort of the in-group discriminator to supplant the myth of Aryan superiority with the myth of non-Aryan superiority is condemned to failure by science. Moreover, such myths are ill-advised. Eventually, life in a world of myth must collide with fact in the world of reality. As a matter of simple self-interest and social therapy, therefore, it might be wise for the in-group to abandon the myth and cling to the reality.

The pattern of being damned-if-you-do and damned-if-you-don't has further consequences—among the out-groups themselves. The response to alleged deficiencies is as clear as it is predictable. If one is repeatedly told that one is inferior, that one lacks any positive accomplishments, it is all too human to seize upon every bit of evidence to the contrary. The in-group definitions force upon the allegedly inferior out-group a defensive tendency to magnify and exalt "race accomplishments." As the distinguished Negro sociologist, Franklin Frazier, has noted, the Negro newspapers are "intensely race conscious and exhibit considerable pride in the achievements of the Negro, most of which are meagre performances as measured by broader standards." Self-glorification, found in some measure among all groups, becomes a frequent counter-response to persistent belittlement from without.

It is the damnation of out-groups for excessive achievement, however, which gives rise to truly bizarre behavior. For after a time and often as a matter of self-defense, these out-groups become persuaded that their virtues really are vices. And this provides the final episode in a tragi-comedy of inverted values.

Let us try to follow the plot through its intricate maze of self-contradictions. Respectful admiration for the arduous climb from office boy to president is rooted deep in American culture. This long and strenuous ascent carries with it a two-fold testimonial: it testifies that careers are abundantly open to genuine talent in American society and it testifies to the worth of the man who has distinguished himself by his heroic rise. It would be invidious to choose among the many stalwart figures who have fought their way up, against all odds, until they have reached the pinnacle, there to sit at the head of the long conference table in the longer conference room of The Board. Taken at random, the saga of Frederick H. Ecker, chairman of the board of one of the largest privately managed corporations in the world, the Metropolitan Life Insurance Company, will suffice as the prototype. From a menial and poorly paid job, he rose to a position of eminence. Appropriately enough, an unceasing flow of honors has come to this man of large power and large achievement. It so happens, though it is a matter personal to this eminent man of finance, that Mr. Ecker is a Presbyterian. Yet at last report, no elder of the Presbyterian church has risen publicly to announce that Mr. Ecker's successful career should not be taken too seriously, that, after all, relatively few Presbyterians have risen from rags to riches and that Presbyterians do not actually "control" the world of finance—or life insurance, or investment houses. Rather, one would suppose, Presbyterian elders join with other Americans imbued with middle-class standards of success to felicitate the eminently successful Mr. Ecker and to acclaim other sons of the faith who have risen to almost equal heights. Secure in their in-group status, they point the finger of pride rather than the finger of dismay at individual success.

Prompted by the practice of moral alchemy, noteworthy achievements by out-groupers elicit other responses. Patently, if achievement is a vice, the achievements must be disclaimed—or at least, discounted. Under these conditions, what is an occasion for Presbyterian pride must become an occasion for Jewish dismay. If the Jew is condemned for his educational or professional or scientific or economic success, then, understandably enough, many Jews will come to feel that these accomplishments must be minimized in simple self-defense. Thus is the circle of paradox closed by out-groupers busily engaged in assuring the powerful in-group that they have not, in fact, been guilty of inordinate contributions to science, the professions, the arts, the government, and the economy.

In a society which ordinarily looks upon wealth as a warrant of ability, an out-group is compelled by the inverted attitudes of the dominant in-group to deny that many men of wealth are among its members. "Among the 200 largest non-banking corporations . . . only ten have a Jew as president or chairman of the board." Is this an observation of an anti-Semite, intent on proving the incapacity and inferiority of Jews who have done so little "to build the corporations which have built America?" No; it is a retort of the Anti-Defamation League of B'nai B'rith to anti-Semitic propaganda.

In a society where, as a recent survey by the National Opinion Research Center has shown, the profession of medicine ranks higher in social prestige than any other of ninety occupations (save that of United States Supreme Court Justice), we find some Jewish spokesmen maneuverd by the attacking in-group into the fantastic position of announcing their "deep concern" over the number of Jews in medical practice, which is "disproportionate to the number of Jews in other occupations." In a nation suffering from a notorious undersupply of physicians, the Jewish doctor becomes a deplorable occasion for deep concern, rather than receiving applause for his hard-won acquisition of knowledge and skills and for his social utility. Only when the New York Yankees publicly announce deep concern over their numerous World Series titles, so disproportionate to the number of triumphs achieved by other major league teams, will this self-abnegation seem part of the normal order of things.

In a culture which consistently judges the professionals higher in social value than even the most skilled hewers of wood and drawers of water, the out-group finds itself in the anomalous position of pointing with defensive relief to the large number of Jewish painters and paper hangers, plasterers and electricians, plumbers and sheet-metal workers.

But the ultimate reversal of values is yet to be noted. Each succeeding census finds more and more Americans in the city and its suburbs. Americans have traveled the road to urbanization until fewer than one-fifth of the nation's population live on farms. Plainly, it is high time for the Methodist and the Catholic, the Baptist and the Episcopalian to recognize the iniquity of this trek of their coreligionists to the city. For, as is well known, one of the central accusations leveled against the Jew is his heinous tendency to live in cities. Jewish leaders, therefore, find themselves in the incredible position of defensively urging their people to move into the very farm areas being hastily vacated by city-bound hordes of Christians. Perhaps this is not altogether necessary. As the Jewish crime of urbanism becomes ever more popular among the in-group, it may be reshaped into transcendent virtue. But, admittedly, one can't be certain. For in this daft confusion of inverted values, it soon becomes impossible to determine when virtue is sin and sin is moral perfection.

Amid this confusion, one fact remains unambiguous. The Jews, like other peoples, have made distinguished contributions to world culture. Consider only an abbreviated catalogue. In the field of creative literature (and with acknowledgment of large variations in the calibre of achievement), Jewish authors include Heine, Karl Kraus, Börne, Hofmannsthal, Schnitzler, Kafka. In the realm of musical composition, there are Meyerbeer, Felix Mendelssohn, Offenbach, Mahler, and Schönberg. Among the musical virtuosi, consider only Rosenthal, Schnabel, Godowsky, Pachmann, Kreisler, Hubermann, Milstein, Elman, Heifetz, Joachim, and Menuhin. And among scientists of a stature sufficient to merit the Nobel Prize, examine the familiar list which includes Beranyi, Mayerhof, Ehrlich, Michelson, Lippmann, Haber, Willstätter, and Einstein. Or in the esoteric and imaginative universe of mathematical invention, take note only of Kronecker, the creator of the modern theory of numbers; Hermann Minkowski,[3] who supplied the mathematical foundations of the special theory of relativity; or Jacobi, with his basic work in the theory of elliptical functions. And so, through each special province of cultural achievement, we are supplied with a list of pre-eminent men and women who happened to be Jews.

---

3. Obviously, the forename must be explicitly mentioned here, else Hermann Minkowski, the mathematician, may be confused with Eugen Minkowski, who contributed so notably to our knowledge of schizophrenia, or with Oskar Minkowski, discoverer of pancreatic diabetes.

And who is thus busily engaged in singing the praises of the Jews? Who has so assiduously compiled the list of many hundreds of distinguished Jews who contributed so notably to science, literature and the arts—a list from which these few cases were excerpted? A philo-Semite, eager to demonstrate that his people have contributed their due share to world culture? No, by now we should know better than that. The complete list will be found in the thirty-sixth edition of the anti-Semitic handbook by the racist Fritsch. In accord with the alchemical formula for transmuting in-group virtues into out-group vices, he presents this as a roll call of sinister spirits who have usurped the accomplishments properly owing the Aryan in-group.

Once we comprehend the predominant role of the in-group in defining the situation, the further paradox of the seemingly opposed behavior of the Negro out-group and the Jewish out-group falls away. The behavior of both minority groups is in response to the majority-group allegations.

If the Negroes are accused of inferiority, and their alleged failure to contribute to world culture is cited in support of this accusation, the human urge for self-respect and a concern for security often leads them *defensively* to magnify each and every achievement by members of the race. If Jews are accused of excessive achievements and excessive ambitions, and lists of pre-eminent Jews are compiled in support of this accusation, then the urge for security leads them *defensively* to minimize the actual achievements of members of the group. Apparently opposed types of behavior have the same psychological and social functions. Self-assertion and self-effacement become the devices for seeking to cope with condemnation for alleged group deficiency and condemnation for alleged group excesses, respectively. And with a fine sense of moral superiority, the secure in-group looks on these curious performances by the out-groups with mingled derision and contempt.

Enacted Institutional Change

Will this desolate tragi-comedy run on and on, marked only by minor changes in the cast? Not necessarily.

Were moral scruples and a sense of decency the only bases for bringing the play to an end, one would indeed expect it to continue an indefinitely long run. In and of themselves, moral sentiments are not much more effective in curing social ills than in curing physical ills. Moral sentiments no doubt help to motivate efforts for change, but they are no substitute for hard-headed instrumentalities for achieving the objective, as the thickly populated graveyard of soft-headed utopias bears witness.

There are ample indications that a deliberate and planned halt can be put to the workings of the self-fulfilling prophecy and the vicious circle in society. The sequel to our sociological parable of the

Last National Bank provides one clue to the way in which this can be achieved. During the fabulous 1920s, when Coolidge undoubtedly caused a Republican era of lush prosperity, an average of 635 banks a year quietly suspended operations. And during the four years immediately before and after the Crash, when Hoover undoubtedly did not cause a Republican era of sluggish depression, this zoomed to the more spectacular average of 2276 bank suspensions annually. But, interestingly enough, in the 12 years following the establishment of the Federal Deposit Insurance Corporation and the enactment of other banking legislation while Roosevelt presided over Democratic depression and revival, recession and boom, bank suspensions dropped to a niggardly average of 28 a year. Perhaps money panics have not been institutionally exorcized by legislation. Nevertheless, millions of depositors no longer have occasion to give way to panic-motivated runs on banks simply because deliberate institutional change has removed the grounds for panic. Occasions for racial hostility are no more inborn psychological constants than are occasions for panic. Despite the teachings of amateur psychologists, blind panic and racial aggression are not rooted in human nature. These patterns of human behavior are largely a product of the modifiable structure of society.

For a further clue, return to our instance of widespread hostility of white unionists toward the Negro strikebreakers brought into industry by employers after the close of the very first World War. Once the initial definition of Negroes as not deserving of union membership had largely broken down, the Negro, with a wider range of work opportunities, no longer found it necessary to enter industry through the doors held open by strike-bound employers. Again, appropriate institutional change broke through the tragic circle of the self-fulfilling prophecy. Deliberate social change gave the lie to the firm conviction that "it just ain't in the nature of the nigra" to join co-operatively with his white fellows in trade unions.

A final instance is drawn from a study of a biracial housing project. Located in Pittsburgh, this community of Hilltown is made up of 50 percent Negro families and 50 percent white. It is not a 20th century utopia. There is some interpersonal friction here as elsewhere. But in a community made up of equal numbers of the two races, fewer than a fifth of the whites and less than a third of the Negroes report that this friction occurs between members of *different* races. By their own testimony, it is very largely confined to disagreements *within* each racial group. Yet only one in every twenty-five whites initially *expected* relations between the races in this community to run smoothly, whereas five times as many expected serious trouble, the remainder anticipating a tolerable, if not altogether pleasant, situation. So much for expectations. Upon reviewing their actual experience, three of every four of the most apprehensive whites subsequently found that the "races get along fairly well," after all. This is not the place to report the findings of this study in detail, but, substantially, these demonstrate anew that under *appropriate institutional and administrative conditions*, the experience of interracial amity can supplant the fear of interracial conflict.

These changes, and others of the same kind, do not occur automatically. *The self-fulfilling prophecy, whereby fears are translated into reality, operates only in the absence of deliberate institutional controls.* And it is only with the rejection of social fatalism implied in the notion of unchangeable human nature that the tragic circle of fear, social disaster, and reinforced fear can be broken.

Ethnic prejudices do die—but slowly. They can be helped over the threshold of oblivion, not by insisting that it is unreasonable and unworthy of them to survive, but by cutting off the sustenance now provided them by certain institutions of our society.

If we find ourselves doubting man's capacity to control man and his society, if we persist in our tendency to find in the patterns of the past the chart of the future, it is perhaps time to take up anew the wisdom of Tocqueville's century-old remark: "I am tempted to believe that what we call necessary institutions are often no more than institutions to which we have grown accustomed, and that in matters of social constitution the field of possibilities is much more extensive than men living in their various societies are ready to imagine."

Nor can widespread, even typical, failures in planning human relations between ethnic groups be cited as evidence for pessimism. In the world laboratory of the sociologist, as in the more secluded laboratories of the physicist and chemist, it is the successful experiment which is decisive and not the thousand-and-one failures which preceded it. More is learned from the single success than from the multiple failures. A single success proves it can be done. Thereafter, it is necessary only to learn what made it work. This, at least, is what I take to be the sociological sense of those revealing words of Thomas Love Peacock: "Whatever is, is possible."

References

David, Donald. *Lincoln Reconsidered.* Knopf, 1956.

Lincoln, Abraham. *Complete Works of Abraham Lincoln,* ed. John C. Nicolay and John Hay, 1894.

MacIver, R. M. *The More Perfect Union.* Macmillan, 1948.

Merton, R. K. "The Unanticipated Consequences of Purposive Social Action." *American Sociological Review,* Vol. 1, 1936.

Organizations and Leadership

Chris Argyris

Organizational Leadership

In my early studies of leadership, I believed that organizational leadership was not much different, on a conceptual level, from other types of leadership and was interested in arriving at generalizations about leadership in any situation. For example, although I conducted a study of the leadership pattern of a particular plant manager within an industrial organization, I paid little attention to the organization. As carefully as I could (and as much as the situation permitted) I studied (*a*) the impact of the plant manager upon his subordinates, (*b*) the subordinates' adaptation to the leader, and (*c*) their adaptation to each other (Argyris, 1953a). The results of this field study confirmed the results of such experimental studies as those of Lewin (1948) and Lippitt and White (1957); namely, that an autocratic leader's impact leads the subordinates to become dependent, submissive, and leader-centered, to be in competition against one another, which at times results in interpersonal rivalry and hostility, to be productive when the leader is present, and to lose a high degree of productiveness when the leader departs.

During the feedback stage of this study, the "subjects" agreed that many of the conclusions such as those listed above mirrored reality as they perceived and experienced it. However, after further discussions it became painfully clear that such phenomena as the managerial controls (for example, budgets, production bogeys), performance ratings, and the formal policies and practices tended to have basically similar impact upon the subordinates as that attributed to the autocratic leadership of their superior. After repeated discussions with the subordinates it became uncomfortably clear that it was impossible for them to separate the impact of the leader from the impact of the organization's controls and formal policies. Many of the subordinates even spent long hours trying to help construct questionnaires and other research instruments which would effectively control the other relevant variables except the leadership pattern. But, as one man remarked, formal policies and managerial controls were, for him, so integrated with the leadership pattern that when he tried to focus *only* on the boss's leadership pattern, "it just didn't make sense."

Let it be clear that the research team had no difficulty in differentiating between the leadership pattern and formal policies and managerial controls. Consequently, it was hoped that some research instruments could be created that would permit the subjects to make the same differentiations. At one point, the indications were that we were succeeding. It seemed as if accurate instruments had been constructed that truly measured the impact of the leadership pattern alone. However, after careful analysis leading to an agonizing reappraisal, it became evident, and was confirmed later by the subjects, that the data did not represent how the subjects truly felt as much as how they knew we wanted them to feel. As one man put it, "After getting to know you so well and watching you struggle to study leadership, what the hell, I tried to give you as much information about leadership in this plant as possible. But now that you pin me down, sure, some of the same answers hold for the budgets and the company policies."

Leadership Theory as a Special Case of Organizational Theory

After a number of similar failures, I concluded that reality *for the subjects* being studied in an *organizational setting* was a pattern of variables (leadership, managerial controls, and so on) so inextricably interrelated that it was impossible for the subjects to separate them and still speak of reality.

The next step was to conduct a research project in an organization where such variables as controls and formal policies and practices and technology were similar in two units (departments) while the leadership pattern was different. Such an organization was found and a study begun. Shortly, it became obvious that even in such a controlled situation the variables were so interrelated that they critically influenced each other. Thus, in the two departments the same controls and policies were *not* the same for the subjects. The differences in leadership pattern within each department made the same budgets and policies different in the eyes of the subjects.

The more I studied human behavior in an organizational context, the greater became my frustration at the difficulty in controlling variables. Unlike the experimental situations, variables relatively independent of one another seemed nonexistent. As I learned later, it is the very nature of organization not to have independent variables. *An organization is a pattern of variables and dissecting the pattern, even analytically, is no longer a study of the organization.* I was, therefore, forced to conclude that organizational leadership must be studied not with the major emphasis on leadership, but on the organization.

Leadership theory became a special case of organizational theory. *How does one study leadership through organization?* One important clue related to studying organization (and eventually organizational leadership) came from some early clinical-field-theoretical leadership studies by McGregor and Knickerbocker. They proposed that leadership is a set of functions required by all groups and that a leader in a group free to choose its leadership will tend to be that person who is viewed by the group members as best capable of fulfilling their needs. They also hypothesized that the person selected to lead must be a leader if he accepts the group's "call" (McGregor, Knickerbocker, Haire, and Bavelas, 1948).

If this logic is valid, then why would not organizational leadership represent those functions that are necessary for an organization to fulfill its needs? This immediately raises the question, What are the needs of an organization? In order to ascertain these needs we need to know first the properties of organization.

There are a number of ways one can go about defining the properties of organization. One is to develop the properties by conducting empirical research. Another way, and the one I chose, is to define what one believes to be the nature of organization by reviewing the available literature.

The task of reviewing the literature in organizational behavior and developing a theoretical framework was completed. A summary outline of the main propositions which will serve here as the guide for discussion follows. (For greater detail see Argyris, 1957.)

Organization Viewed as Strategy

Personality research suggests that the personality of an individual represents his best attempts to integrate himself internally and with the environment in which he is embedded. It represents his strategy for living. May not the same be hypothesized for an organization? The makeup of an organization becomes simply its strategy to achieve its objectives. These are postulated to be achieving its goals (intended consequences), maintaining itself internally, and adapting to its external environment.

Who chooses the strategy that the organization will follow? At the outset, those signing the legal charter to create the organization have much to say as to how it shall be organized. They plan an organizational structure which they assume represents the best strategy for the organization. Because of historical reasons too complex to discuss here, the basic characteristics of the structure are usually defined by generalizations from economics, scientific management, public administration, and traditional formal organization theory. This strategy is crystallized, "photographed," and represented as a typical organizational chart.

Let us look more closely at the nature of the phenomena depicted by the organizational chart.

The Intended Rationality of Formal Organization

The first requirement (or the first characteristic of the strategy) is for the organization to be rational and to make rational demands upon employees. Thus the initial or formal structure represents the intended rational strategy of the organization. Urwick (1953), one of the pioneers in formal organizational theory, describes the property of intended rationality eloquently. He insists that the creation of a formal organization requires a logical approach. Although he admits that "nine times out of ten it is impossible to start with a clean sheet," the organizer should sit down and in a "cold-blooded, detached spirit . . . draw an ideal structure." The task of the organizer, therefore, is to create a logically ordered world where, as Fayol suggests, there is a "proper order" and a "place for everything (everyone)" (Koontz and O'Donnell, 1955).

The possibility that the formal organization can be altered by personalities, as found by Arensberg and McGregor (1942) and Stodgill and Koehler (1952), is not denied by formal organizational experts. Urwick, for example, states that the planner must take into account the human element. But he perceives these adjustments as "temporary deviations from the pattern in order to deal with idiosyncrasy of personality." If possible, these deviations should be minimized by careful prior planning.

Some Basic Principles of Formal Organization [1]

Along with the emphasis upon rationality is the emphasis on specialization of tasks, power, and conformity to and loyalty for company objectives. These emphases are embodied in four principles —more accurately, assumptions—of scientific management theories represented by the work of men like Urwick (1944), Mooney (1947),

---

1. For a more detailed discussion see Argyris (1957), Ch. 3.

Holden, *et al.* (1951), Fayol (1949), Dennison (1931), Brown (1947), Gulick (1927), White (1939), Gauss (1936), Stene (1940), Hopf (1935), and Taylor (1948). Anyone wishing to understand the nature of present formal organization should become well acquainted with the work of these men.

Briefly these principles may be stated as follows:

Task (Work) Specialization

If concentrating effort on a limited field of endeavor increases the quality and quantity of output, organizational and administrative efficiency is increased by specialization of tasks assigned to the participants of the organization.

Chain of Command

The principle of task specialization creates a plurality of parts, each performing a highly specialized task. However, a plurality of parts busily performing their particular objective does not form an organization. A pattern of parts must be formed so that the interrelationship among parts creates the organization. Following the logic of specialization, the planners create a new function—leadership—whose primary responsibility is the control, direction, and coordination of the interrelationships of parts and to make certain that each part performs its objectives adequately. Thus the assumption is made that administrative and organizational efficiency is increased by arranging the parts in a determinate hierarchy of authority where the part on top can direct and control the part on the bottom.

If the parts being considered are individuals, then they must be motivated to accept direction, control, and coordination of their behavior. The leader is therefore assigned formal power to hire, discharge, reward, and penalize the individuals in order that their behavior be molded toward the organization's objectives.

Unity of Direction

If the tasks of every person in a unit are specialized, the objective or purpose of the unit must be specialized. The principle of unity of direction states that administrative and organizational efficiency increases if each unity has a single activity (or homogeneous set of activities) that is planned and directed by the leader.

Span of Control [2]

The principle of control states that administration efficiency is increased by limiting the span of control of a leader to no more than five or six subordinates whose work interlocks.

---

2. First defined by Graicunas (1927).

The Impact of The Formal Organization upon The Individual [3]

The impact of the principles above is to place employees in work situations where (1) they are provided minimal control over their workaday world, (2) they are expected to be passive, dependent, and subordinate, (3) they are expected to have a short-time perspective, (4) they are induced to perfect and value the frequent use of a few skin-surface, shallow abilities, and (5) they are expected to produce under conditions leading to psychological failure.

All these characteristics can be shown to be incongruent to the ones *healthy* human beings in our culture are postulated to desire. They are much more congruent with the needs of infants in our culture. In effect, therefore, organizations adapt an initial strategy where they are willing to pay high wages and provide adequate seniority if mature adults will, for eight hours a day, behave in a less than mature manner.

The findings up to this point about the nature of organization in terms of propositions, are:

Proposition 1

There is a lack of congruency between the needs of healthy individuals and the demands of the formal organization.

If one uses the traditional formal principles of organization (that is, traditional chain of command or task specialization) to create a social organization, and if one uses, as input, agents who tend toward a mature state of psychological development (they are predisposed toward relative independence, activeness, use of their important abilities, control over their immediate work world),[4] then a disturbance is created because the needs of healthy individuals (listed above) are not congruent with the requirements of formal organization, which tends to require the agents to work in situations where they are dependent, passive, and use few and unimportant abilities.

Corollary 1. The disturbance will vary in proportion to the degree of incongruency between the needs of the individuals and the requirements of the formal organization.

An administrator, therefore, is always faced with an inherent tendency toward continual disturbance.

Drawing on the existing knowledge of the human personality, a second proposition can be stated.

---

3. For a detailed discussion of these principles plus their impact upon the individual see Argyris (1957).
4. A model for understanding healthy personality is presented in *ibid.*, ch. 2.

Proposition 2

The resultants of this disturbance are frustration, failure, short-time perspective, and conflict.

If the participants in the organization desire a healthy, more mature self-actualization, they will tend to experience:

1. Frustration, because their self-expression will be blocked (Barker, Dembo, and Lewin, 1941; Dollard, 1939).
2. Failure, because they will not be permitted to define their own goals in relation to central needs or the paths to these goals (Lewin, et al., 1944; Lippitt and Bradford, 1945).
3. Short-time perspective, because they have no control over the clarity and stability of their future (Lewin, 1948).
4. Conflict, because, as healthy agents, they will dislike frustration, failure, and short-time perspective, which is characteristic of the present job. However, if they leave they may not find a new job easily and even if a new job is found, it may not be different (Newcomb, 1950).

Based upon analysis of the nature of formal organization, one may state a third proposition.

Proposition 3

Under certain conditions the degree of frustration, failure, short-time perspective, and conflict will tend to increase.

The resultants of the disturbance in the organization will tend to increase (in degree):

1. As individual agents increase in degree of maturity.
2. As the degree of dependence, subordination, passivity increases. This in turn tends to occur (*a*) as one goes down the chain of command; (*b*) as directive leadership increases; (*c*) as management controls are increased; (*d*) as human relations programs are undertaken but improperly implemented.
3. As the jobs become more specialized.
4. As the exactness with which the traditional formal principles are used increases.

Proposition 4

The nature of the formal principles of organization cause the subordinates, at any given level, to experience competition, rivalry, intersubordinate hostility and to develop a focus toward the parts rather than the whole.

1. Because of the degree of dependence or subordination of the

subordinates toward the leader, and because the number of positions above any given level always tend to decrease, the subordinates aspiring to perform effectively and to advance will tend to find themselves in competition with and receiving hostility from each other.[5]

2. Because, according to formal principles, subordinates are directed toward and rewarded for performing their own task well, subordinates tend to develop an orientation toward their own particular part rather than toward the whole.

3. This part-orientation increases the need for the leader to coordinate activity among the parts in order to maintain the whole. This need for the leader, in turn, increases subordinates' degree of dependence or subordination, creating a circular process whose impact maintains or increases the degree of dependence and subordination plus the rivalry and competition for the leader's favor.

Proposition 5

Employees react to the formal organization by creating informal activities.

Continuing from proposition 2, it can be shown that under conflict, frustration, failure, and short-time perspective, employees will tend to maintain self-integration by creating specific adaptive (informal) behavior,[6] such as:

1. Leaving the organization.
2. Climbing the organizational ladder.
3. Manifesting defense reactions (day dreaming, aggression, ambivalence, regression, projection).
4. Becoming apathetic and disinterested toward the organization, its make-up and goals. This leads to such phenomena as (*a*) employees reduce the number and potency of the needs they expect to fulfill while at work; (*b*) employees goldbrick, set rates, restrict quotas, make errors, cheat, slow down.
5. Creating informal groups to sanction defense reactions, apathy, disinterest, and lack of self-involvement.
6. Forming informal groups.
7. Evolving group norms that perpetuate the behavior outline in 3, 4, 5, and 6 above.
8. Evolving a psychological set that human or nonmaterial factors are becoming increasingly unimportant while material factors become increasingly important.
9. Acculturating the youth to accept the norms discussed in 7 and 8.

---

5. These problems may not arise for the subordinate who decides to become apathetic or disinterested.

6. Adaptive activities numbered one to nine become major categories under which much empirical research can be included.

Comparing the informal organization, we may state:

Proposition 6

Employee adaptive behavior maintains individual self-integration and simultaneously impedes integration with the formal organization.

Proposition 7

Adaptive behavior of employees has a cumulative effect, feeds back into the formal organization, and further entrenches itself.

1. Adaptive reactions reinforce each other so that they not only have their individual impact on the system, but they also have a cumulative impact. Their total impact increases the degree of dependence and submissiveness, and also increases the resulting turnover, apathy, disinterest. Thus a feedback process exists where the adaptive mechanisms become self-maintaining.

2. The continual existence of these adaptive mechanisms tends to make them norms or codes which, in turn, act to maintain adaptive behavior and to make it the proper behavior for the system.

3. If the above is valid, then employees who may desire to behave differently from the norms will tend to feel deviant, different, not part of the work community (for example, rate busters).

The individual and cumulative impact of defense mechanisms is to influence the output-input ratio in such a way that greater input (energy, money, machines) will be required to maintain a constant output.

Proposition 8

Certain management reactions tend to increase the antagonisms underlying adaptive behavior.

1. Those managements that base their judgment on the logics of formal organization will tend to dislike the employee. It follows, therefore, that these managements should tend to take those "corrective" actions that are congruent with the logics of formal organization. These actions tend to be: (*a*) increasing the degree of directive leadership; (*b*) increasing the degree of management controls; (*c*) increasing the number of pseudo-human relations programs.

The first two modes of reaction tend to compound, reinforce, and maintain the basic disturbance outlined in proposition 1. It follows, therefore, that the behavior included in propositions 4, 6, and 7 will also be reinforced. (This is the behavior management desires to change in the first place.) The third mode of reaction tends to increase the distance and mistrust between employee and management because it does not jibe with the realities of the system within which the employee works.

One must conclude that the management behavior described in

proposition 8 primarily acts to influence the output-input ratio so that a much greater input is required to obtain the same constant output, or that a disproportionately higher input will be necessary for a given increment of increased output.

A word about the propositions outlined above: it is possible for a physical scientist to make such predictions as: If one passes electricity through wire, heat will result. However, he cannot predict a priori *how much* heat will result. The amount of heat can be predicted only by ascertaining the values of such variables as the length and type of wire, the capacity of the battery, the milieu in which the experiment is conducted.

The propositions presented above are on a similar level of generalization. They make such predictions as that the dependence and submissiveness that people will experience will tend to be caused by formal organization, directive leadership, and managerial controls— to list three major variables. They predict that dependence and submissiveness will frustrate people and place them in conflict *if* people aspire toward the mature ends of the continua listed above. They predict, further, that people will tend to react by creating informal activities (apathy, indifference, goldbricking, rate setting). Nothing is said, however, about *how much* dependence, submissiveness, conflict, frustration, apathy, and indifference is caused. This is a matter of empirical research. The value of theoretical propositions is that they guide the researcher in his choice of relevant variables and the probable relationships among these variables.

For example, one can predict that conflict and frustration will tend to be high when the formal organizational structure, the directive leadership, and the controls require (*a*) "maturity-directed" people to be directed toward infancy [7] and (*b*) "infancy-directed" people to be directed toward maturity. One can predict, therefore, that absenteeism, turnover, and apathy will be as high when "mature" people are frustrated by being required to be immature as when "immature" people are frustrated by being required to be mature. Furthermore, one can predict that the conflict, frustration, and so on will tend to be minimal when (*c*) "infancy-directed" employees are required to behave immaturely, and (*d*) when "maturity-directed" employees are required to behave maturely.[8]

The predictions above assume that the *amount* of impact of the

---

7. The "amount" of conflict, frustration, etc., must be empirically ascertained by measuring the "maturity-directiveness" of employees and the degree to which the organization requires that they be "infancy-directed."

8. Case (*a*) was chosen to be illustrated in *Personality and Organization* because most of the research literature that the writer is aware of supports the view. This does *not* imply that *all* organizations can be so categorized. Organizations will differ and the same organization may differ at different periods of time. In *Personality and Organization,* job enlargement and role enlargement are cited as two activities that work against the trend predicted above.

formal organization structure, leadership, and managerial controls is the same. This may not be the case in actual practice. One might find that the directive leadership, in a given organization, causes more dependence than do the formal organizational structure or the controls. In another organization, the controls may be the major cause of dependence. In short, in the actual world many different combinations are possible. The predictions above also assume that the *direction* of impact for all three variabels is the same. Thus, the theory hypothesizes that if the formal structure is defined according to such principles as unity of command or task specialization and if the leadership is directive, and if the controls are defined as they are in scientific management, then employees will tend to experience dependence and submissiveness.[9] Thus the theory hypothesized a priori that these three variables (as defined in the theory) will always lead toward dependence, submissiveness, and so on.[10]

Recapitulation

The main points that I have tried to communicate so far are:

1. It may not be possible to study leadership phenomena in an organizational setting without studying the nature of the organization. An organization is a patterning of variables, one of which is leadership. Consequently, to study organizational leadership without relating it to the other variables is futile.

2. Broadly defined, leadership within the organization will function to fulfill the organization's demands in its attempt to achieve its objectives, maintain itself internally, and adapt to the sociocultural milieu in which it is embedded. It follows that to understand the basic functions of organizational leadership we need to understand the nature of organization.

3. Organizations are grand strategies individuals create to achieve objectives that require the effort of many. For historical reasons, most social organizations follow a particular initial or formal strategy whose roots may be found in military theory, industrial economics, scientific management, or public administration.

4. The strategy derived from these roots leads to a pyramid-shaped formal organization defined by such principles as chain of command, unity of direction, span of control, and task specialization. If this formal strategy works as intended, then the analysis could end

9. Readers and especially practitioners should be reminded that the model purports to understand all organizations who use, at the outset, a pyramidal structure and people. Thus, for example, churches, families, schools, and scout troops tend to coerce dependency long before people become employees of industrial organizations.

10. Again, the problem of ascertaining *how much* dependence or submissiveness is an empirical one that requires research. Also, the impact or effect of dependence submissiveness upon the individuals and in turn upon the organization cannot be predicted without knowing the needs of the individuals. If they desire to be dependent, the effect will be different than if they desire to be independent.

here. Unfortunately, the formal organizational strategy hits some snags, the primary one being the individual human being.

5. Mutual adaptations take place where the organization modifies the individual's personality and the individual, through informal activities, modifies the formal organization. These modifications become part of the organization.

6. A total organization therefore is more than the formal organization. Conceptualizing it as a behavioral system, we may conclude that an organization is a composite of four different but interrelated subsystems resulting in the following kinds of behavior: (a) the behavior that results from the formal organizational demands; (b) the behavior that results from the demands of informal activities; (c) the behavior that results from each individual's attempt to fulfill his idiosyncratic needs; (d) the behavior that is a resultant of the unique patterning for each organization of the preceding three levels.

The Need for a New Theory of Organization

These four levels of behavior, as just described, do not exist in real life as separate categories. They are highly interrelated and inseparable.

It now becomes clear that organizational leadership must concern itself with all levels of behavior and not simply with the needs of formal organization. To be sure, most administrators (industrial, governmental, etc.) view the leader as being the guardian of formal activities. According to our analysis, however, informal activities and idiosyncratic activities are not only an integral part of the organization, but they assist the organization to achieve its formal objectives (Argyris, 1957, pp. 229–232).

Viewing the formal and informal as inextricably interrelated points up the difficult position of the organizational leader. For example, if he follows the logic of formal organization, he would not reward employee apathy, indifference, rate setting, and goldbricking. Yet these behaviors may be necessary if employees are to maintain mental stability. He could overcome some of these "undesirable" states by becoming a more directive leader and by tightening managerial controls. This may well increase production but it will also increase the dependence and submissiveness of employees, which in turn will increase employee apathy, indifference, and so on (Likert, 1958), the very "states" he wants to overcome. Moreover, if directive leadership becomes the rewarded and accepted leadership pattern— and this *is* the most prevalent in industry today (McMurry, 1952, p. 47)—it will tend to inhibit the development of management. The directive, aggressive, upwardly mobile executive tends to have little patience, and even less capability, to develop a cohesive executive *peer* group (Argyris, 1955).

How is the organizational leader to function effectively if he is responsible for administering an organization whose formal and informal subsystems require acts that may run the gamut from being congruent to interfering to being completely incompatible with one another? [11] Which demands shall receive priority? For example, should he, for the sake of the formal goals, emphasize dependent, submissive subordination? What informal activities are in the interests of formal organization? Are apathy, indifference, goldbricking, rate setting acceptable? Are absenteeism, turnover, grievances, and conflict necessarily unhealthy? If some conflict is healthy, how much should be permitted and under what conditions? How much idiosyncratic behavior is helpful to the total organization? If there is fear of the organization man (Whyte, 1956), the opposite extreme of organizational chaos may be even more deadly.

These questions cannot be answered by traditional formal theories of organization because they do not sufficiently take into account the needs of healthy human beings. The informal system or human relations theories of organization are also inadequate because they have little to say about the importance of the achievement of formal goals.

In short, the formal and informal subsystems, although part of the total organization, actually emphasize different values. The differences may be illustrated in the model shown. This model represents a series of dimensions, each of which is a continuum. On one end is the subsystem whose focus is on individual needs (informal); on the other, the subsystem whose focus is on attainment of the formal objective.

A theory of organization is required which will provide a framework broad enough to include formal and informal behavior as part of a larger, more inclusive system. The theory should stipulate the objectives and the internal structure of the organization as well as the relationships it would have with the environment in which it is embedded.[12]

Such a complete theory is not only unavailable, it requires much research that at this time is not even possible to envision. Has any reader tried to create (even on paper) an organization that fundamentally changes the basic concepts of power, control, and task specialization it may use? Nevertheless a first step must be taken, even if it is to be tentative and requires early revision. Some point of departure is needed. What should it be?

One possible *first step* in the development of a more inclusive

---

11. The problems that arise when subsystems of the whole require antagonistic behavior. See Barker, Wright, and Gonick (1946).

12. The relationships between the organization and the environment are represented by strategies not even considered in this paper. However, they must be taken into account if the final theory is to be truly comprehensive.

Formal Organization	Informal Organization
1*a*. At the outset interpersonal relations are *prescribed,* and they reflect the *organization's* idea of the most effective structure within which to achieve the *organization's goals.*	1*a*. At the outset interpersonal relations *arise* from members' interaction and reflect the *need of members* to interact with each other in order to fulfill their needs.
1*b*. The *leadership* role is assigned to the person the *organization* feels can best perform *organizationally* defined duties.	1*b*. The leadership role is delegated to the individual the *members* believe will best fulfill their needs.
2*a*. The formal behavior in organization manifested by an individual is "caused" by the individual's acceptance of *organizationally* defined reward and penalty (sanctions).	2*a*. All behavior of individual members in the group is caused by the attempts of individual members to *fulfill their needs.*
2*b*. The dependency of members upon the leader is *accepted* by members because of the existing organizational sanctions.	2*b*. *Dependency* of members upon the leader is created and accepted by members because they believe it will fulfill their *needs.*

theory is to define a series of dimensions "external to" or "independent of" the formal and informal activities. They could be used to ascertain quantitatively the present "mix" of these activities and serve as a basis for the selection of the "proper mix" desired for the organization. To put this another way, formal and informal activities are strategies. Each is a strategy designed to organize human effort in such a way as to maximize certain values. Formal activities based on scientific management strive to maximize the formal objectives of the organization. Informal activities based on human relations focus on the actualization of the individuals. *Neither activity (alone or combined) is adequate because it cannot specify the proper mix that is required of both.* A new strategy needs to be developed for this purpose.

How is this new and more inclusive strategy to be evolved? Neither of the strategies above is based upon knowledge about the *nature* (properties) of organization. Would it not be possible to develop a more basic strategy by deriving it from what is presently known about the properties of organization? Instead of relating our strategy to the nature of human personality, why not relate it to the nature of organization *per se*? Could not a set of criteria be inferred from the existing literature of organization that can provide the conceptual tools to select the "proper mix" of formal and informal organizational strategies?

Such an approach assumes that we know the properties of organization. Clearly, complete knowledge about the properties of organization does not exist. However, there is an increasing number of scholars in many different fields dedicated toward understanding organization. Part of the impetus stems from a group of scholars interested in unity of knowledge. They believe that the concept of organization may provide the conceptual link among the many levels of analysis that exist today. Another impetus stems from an increasing number of physical scientists (chemist, physicists, and especially biologists) who are beginning to view "organization" as the basis of life—if not life itself.

The writer decided to attempt to develop from readings such as those listed below a first approximation definition of the nature of the organization.[13] The hypothesis was that if some properties of organization could be defined, even if they were very tentative, they might form the basis for defining dimensions of the new, more inclusive organizational framework being sought.

A search of the literature revealed that some ideas about the nature of organization keep recurring in the writings of people representing many diverse disciplines. The writer kept an inventory of these basic propositions, which eventually formed the basis for a conceptual definition of the nature of organization. Some examples of propositions that the writer found useful were: An organization is characterized by an arrangement of parts that form a unity or whole which feeds back to help maintain the parts (Wiener, 1950). A part of an organization is actually an "organic" part in that it exists by virtue of its position in the pattern that is the whole (Kluckhohn, 1955). The whole, in turn, may be differentiated from the parts along two dimensions. First, the whole has a different boundary than any given part (or subset of parts) (Herbst, 1957; Simon, 1952). Second, the functional unity of the whole displays properties only revealed in the actual process of full operation of the whole (Kurtz, 1956).

These propositions have led the writer to form a tentative conceptual definition of organization. An organization is (1) a plurality of parts (2) co-existing and interrelated in such a manner that (3)

---

13. Gerard (1958), Redfield (1942), Feibleman (1954), Nadel (1951), Boulding (1956), Klein (1953), Szasz (1955), Bertalanffy (1952 and 1956), Sinnott (1950), Schneirla (1951), Goldstein (1939), Margenau (1950), Allport (1955), Mace (1953), Sinnott (1952), Cameron (1950).

the parts exist because of their interrelatedness, and (4) simultaneously these parts achieve specific objectives and (5) while accomplishing 3 and 4 adapt to the external environment, thereby (6) maintaining the interrelated state of the parts.

We may now hypothesize that the present "mix" of formal and informal activities of a given organization may be understood and quantified by using a model that incorporates as dimensions the properties implied in the definition above. The properties are: (1) The organization is a pattern of parts. (2) The parts maintain the whole through their interrelatedness. No one part (or subset of parts) controls or dominates the whole. (3) The parts change their interrelationships to cope with, and adapt to, new stimuli threatening the organization. (4) The whole is able to control the environment up to the point that is necessary for maintenance of itself.

The next question that arises is how to use these dimensions. In attempting to answer this question, an assumption is made that each of these dimensions does not represent a clear-cut state of affairs. For example, considering the dimension of control (4) we are not implying that one should view it as "no control" versus "control" over the environment. The real world, it is assumed, is not organized in such a "black or white" manner. It is assumed that if the dimensions are to represent the empirical world accurately, each should be stated in terms of degrees (more or less control). In other words, the dimensions that are being evolved will be used to measure the *degree* to which an organization has control over its internal make-up, the environment, and other factors.

Each represents a process of minimum to maximum degree of expression. (Minimum and maximum are theoretically rather than empirically definable points.) A process is defined as a sequence of behavior leading to an intended consequence. Each process is assumed to be reversible.

It may seem that an implicit value judgment in the theoretical viewpoint being proposed is that it is "good" to maximize dimensions such as the organization's control over its internal make-up and its environment. If such a dimension could be considered independent of the others, then such a value judgment would indeed be made. However, the position taken here is that organization exists when *all* the properties exist *simultaneously*. It follows, therefore, that *all* the properties ought to be maximized simultaneously. An examination of these properties, however, will show that by their very nature they are not all maximizable at the same time. For example, control over the environment could be maximized if one part (or subset of parts) dominates the whole. If this occurs, then the dimension of "the whole being created through the patterning of the parts" is greatly inhibited.

The hypothesis *is* made that every organization should find that *state of optimization* where *all* the dimensions are obtaining maximum possible expression (that is, each dimension is *optimized* in relation to the other dimensions). It is the hypothesis of the writer that no one state of optimization will be "best" for all conditions. Rather, there may be different states of optimization, depending upon the conditions being considered at a given time.

The value of the model being proposed lies in its providing the participants of any organization with a systematic methodology by which to determine the degree of expression of each dimension at a given time and to consider the probable outcomes of other states of optimization. By "probable outcomes" one means simply the effect of a change in any one (or more) dimension(s) on the remaining dimensions. It is assumed that there are not any other relevant outputs for an organization. This suggests another value of the model, namely, that it alerts its user to the number of dimensions (and their interrelationships) to be taken into account in considering what is the "proper mix" of the human, formal organizational, and environmental activities in the organization.

A Tentative Model for Understanding the Organizational Mix

By using the four basic properties of organization listed above, the following model for understanding the mix may be offered for consideration (see table 1). Four of these dimensions are simply

Table 1   Dimensions for Understanding the Organizational Mix

1. Awareness of self as plurality of parts	Awareness of wholeness
2. Domination of whole by one part or a subset of parts	Maintenance of whole by interrelationships of parts
3. Inability to influence internal make-up	Influencing internal make-up as desired by participants (parts)
4. Few and limited abilities in problem solving	Many and deeper abilities in problem solving
5. Dependent upon and controlled by environment	Controlling own environment and being master of own fate
6. Short-time perspective	Longer time perspective
7. Achieving its objectives	Achieving objectives so that is can continue to achieve its objectives

direct copies of the four dimensions discussed above. The other three are inferred from the first four. They are listed as separate dimensions in order to evolve a more differentiated model with greater potential in the empirical world.

1. Awareness Dimension

From an awareness of itself as a plurality of parts to an increasing awareness of itself as a pattern of parts (that is, an awareness of the nature of its internal wholeness).

The first dimension is for the organization to become aware of what it is (its wholeness). Obvious as this dimension may be, few organizations take it seriously. Many managers, in fact, find it easier to treat the organization as if it were a series of discrete parts.[14] They continually make decisions about one department, fully expecting it not to affect the total organization. The fundamental philosophy of managerial controls compounds this practice. Budgets, for example, split an organization into a plurality of discrete parts. The unity, if it is to exist, is to be found in the office of the top official. Such a situation leads to very few people in the organization being aware of, and feeling responsibility for, the pattern (the whole organization). Moreover, if top management performs its coordination function well, it can be shown that this will tend to inhibit the expression of the next dimension, which will be discussed below (Argyris, 1953b).

Being aware of the uniqueness of the organization is also important because it provides a manageable (conceptual) picture for participants, enabling them to identify with the organization. At the same time, the uniqueness of the organization (its organizational charter), to quote Bakke, is valuable for communicating to the outside world the "personality" of the organization (Bakke, 1954). Such knowledge can significantly influence the type of person attracted to the organization as an employee. It also influences customers (individuals or other organizations) to decide if they wish to conduct business with the organization.

2. Control Dimension

From domination of the whole by any part or subset of parts to the maintenance of the whole by the interrelationships of all the parts.

This dimension focuses on the extent to which the organization is controlled or dominated by a particular part. The traditional domination, of course, is that of management over employees. However, this is by no means the only example. In some organizations "sales," in others manufacturing or research and development, dominate.

The reader may be interested to learn of a pioneering experiment being conducted in a plant where the traditional concepts of power are being seriously questioned. In this organization any individual is given organizational power as a function of what the individual contributes to decision making. If he is capable of providing much help for a particular decision, the concomitant organizational power will be given to him. The amount of organizational power an individual (or department) is given varies from decision to decision depending upon the role he (or it) plays in that decision.

---

14. For example, see the work of E. W. Bakke, Ernest Dale, Robert Dubin, Mason Haire, Douglas McGregor, William Newman, and William F. Whyte.

In this experiment thought is now being given to changing the financial rewards system along similar lines. In the traditional scheme, organizational power is fixed and static. Mr. A is assigned a particular responsibility and given a particular scope of authority. Mr. A's wages tend to correlate with the authority and responsibility assigned to him. In the example cited above, the organization is conceived as a series of problem-solving processes, some very simple and some highly complex. Following the first and third dimension, as many parts are included in a decision as is necessary. A given individual, Mr. A, receives organizational power as a function of his contributions to a particular decision. Similarly, his wages might also be computed as a function of his contribution in that decision-making process.

3. The Internal Influence Dimension

From an inability to influence its internal make-up to influencing the internal make-up as the participants deem desirable.

If we assume that internal adjustments and modifications will be necessary if the internal equilibrium is to be maintained, then it follows that the organization should be able to change itself as it desires. Considering the dimensions of awareness and control, one would also say that as the number of parts that are capable of instituting, participating, and completing changes increases, the organization's effectiveness along this dimension (3) also increases.

One may also hypothesize that any organizational activity the participants desire to change but cannot is a sign of the participants' being controlled by the organization's defenses. Organizational activity that continues against the desires and is beyond the control of the participants is a sign of compulsive activity. It may also be hypothesized that as the participants increase their control over the organizational activity, they will also tend to increase their feelings of success, and subsequently feelings of self-worth. These feelings of success, it may be further hypothesized, will tend to lead to organizations developing a "climate" of success.

4. The Problem-solving Dimension

From a few and limited abilities in problem solving to many and deeper abilities. Deeper abilities are those that lead to an analysis of problems in their full complexity and wholeness. Limited abilities are those that lead to analysis of partial aspects of the problem (oversimplification).

In this dimension the properties of "wholeness" and the participation of all the relevant parts to a particular decision-making process are imputed to the problem-solving process per se. Not only must an organization become aware of its wholeness, but it must strive to become aware of the wholeness of the problems that it faces. The more an organization is aware of, or willing to become aware of, its problems, the greater are its chances of solving these problems. Those problems and activities that are kept from conscious awareness and discussion tend to be more rigid, compulsive, and uncontrollable. The more the discussion of these problems and activities is suppressed or inhibited, the greater the rigidity and uncontrollability of these activities.[15]

Modern organizations have tended to try to maximize this dimension by delegating the more complex decision analysis or decision making to high-level staff or line groups. Although such groups could theoretically maximize the expression of this dimension, to the extent that they succeed they will tend to inhibit the achievement of the dimensions awareness, control, and internal influence. This paradox emphasizes that problem solving per se is a crucial catalyst with which to achieve the expression of the other dimension or organizational health. To use an example, it may be that an organization can facilitate its influence over the environment (dimension 5) if an expert operations research team finds ways of solving complex marketing problems that traditionally take much time and much effort of many people throughout the entire organization. It can, however, also inhibit the dimensions of control and internal influence because (1) fewer people become aware of the wholeness of the organization, and (2) a few people dominate the decision making, thereby emphasizing a power structure where power resides in the few.

5. The External Influence Dimension

From being highly dependent upon and controlled by the environment to controlling the environment to the extent that the organization becomes master of its own fate (relative independence).

An organization must be capable of modifying or adapting to the environment so that it can maintain itself. If the organization exists in competition with others, then it must find appropriate strategies in order to survive. Research and development and marketing and finance tend to play crucial roles in this dimension. So much has been given this dimension by administrators in the past that further discussion seems unnecessary.

6. The Time Perspective Dimension

From a short-time perspective where the present largely determines the organization's behavior to a longer-time perspective where the behavior is increasingly affected by considerations including the past and future.

---

15. For a stimulating discussion of awareness and therapy see Collier (1956 and 1957).

An organization that wishes not to be dominated by its environment and that wishes to develop deeper problem-solving abilities characteristically may plan ahead to foresee as much of the future as possible. The longer the perspective the greater the opportunity to discover new analyses and to make the necessary internal changes in order to adapt to the external environment.

7. The Organizational Objective Dimension

From achieving its objectives to achieving them in such a way that the organization will be permitted to continue to achieve them.

This dimension is inferred from the fact that the organization exists in an environment where legal, economic, and ethical demands may be made of it. An organization that does not take into account the demands of the cultural milieu within which it is embedded may well find that it is jeopardizing its existence. For example, years ago, when many managements operated without thinking of the cultural milieu, laws were passed regulating their behavior. In short, the organization can be facilitated or inhibited by the socioeconomic-political matrix in which it is embedded.

The dimensions above provide only the barest and most tentative outline for measuring the impact of the organizational formal and informal activities mix. They are not offered as definitive but as suggestive of possible fruitful directions. Clearly, much research needs to be done to learn if the proposed concept is meaningful and empirically fruitful. Research is needed especially to specify the interrelationships among dimensions. Some dimensions (for example, awareness and control) seem to be congruent. Some are congruent at certain points along the continua but become antagonistic at other points. Thus internal influence may increase its degree of congruency with awareness and control as the number of participants involved increases. It may decrease its degree of congruency as the opposite trend occurs.

Along with the study of the interrelationships among dimensions, much research is needed to determine the resultants of a given pattern of dimensions. An organization may wish to know what the "outputs" would be for different combinations or patterns of expression of these dimensions. What would the difference be, for example, if one decreased the expression of awareness, control, and internal influence and increased the expression of problem solving, external influence, and time perspective? One might increase the tolerance that the organization has toward stress, but also decrease its profit making and increase the dominance of certain parts over others. The different outputs would have to be defined for all possible patterning of the dimensions.

One final word about use of the model. In the discussion above, such phrases are used as "the organization needs," "the organization must," and "the organization strives." The question arises to what does "the organization" refer? Do we imply that there is a unity, independent of the parts? How is the position of "the organization" along each dimension ascertained?

No attempt is being made here to return to the old concepts of "group mind" or "organization mind." In actuality, the organization is composed of a number of interdependent subunits (top management, informal groups). For certain problems the organization's position on a given dimension may be a composite score of the three levels of management and employees (the degree of awareness of the whole may increase as one goes up the line). For other problems the organizations position might be a composite of top management and the remainder of the participants (the top management may dominate everyone). In short, the actual empirical referrants for the concept of "the organization" on any given dimension will be made explicit in each study. The point being made is that we are not attempting to reify the concept of organization.

Some Implications of The Model
for Understanding Present Leadership Literature

It is very difficult to discuss the implications of a concept which itself has not been clearly defined. Nevertheless, there are a few implications that seem probable and may perhaps provide some idea of the usefulness of the concept.

It is interesting to note that there is nothing in the model that implies a particular leadership style (democratic or autocratic, or laissez-faire, or employee-centered, or collaborative leadership style) is best. It is the writer's hypothesis that the type of leadership that will be most effective will depend upon the specific dimensions one decides to emphasize.

Evidence to support this hypothesis is obtained by comparing some of the existing leadership research with the dimensions above. For example, it may be that when a leader attempts to increase the expression of dimensions control and problem solving, he may find it unnecessary to be understanding but necessary to be judgmental and critical (Fiedler, 1957). Similarly, could not dimensions control and problem solving be achieved without maintaining maximum friendly atmosphere (Torrance, 1955; Cattell, 1951, Martin, Darley, and Gross, 1952)? Is it possible that Case's (1954) and Davison's (1954) findings that an effective leader may go against public opinion could be related to the organization's attempt to decrease the environment's control over its destiny? Cannot Halpin's (1954) and Hemphill's (1955) findings that both consideration and initiating structure are important dimensions be inferred from the model? In short, the model may well provide a conceptual bridge to integrate many presently seemingly discrete and, at times, antagonistic findings that have been emerging from leadership research.

May not the model also shed light on the old problem of leadership trait theory versus the situational theory? Stogdill (1948), Gouldner (1950), Krech and Crutchfield (1948), Gibb (1947), Jennings (1943), and many others criticize the trait theory of leadership, but when faced with the task of providing a conclusion they suggest that leadership behavior depends primarily upon the situation and not upon any inherent leadership traits—although some traits may be common to all leaders. Carter typifies this middle-of-the-road conclusion when he states, "As a general statement, it would appear that leadership is neither completely general nor completely specific to the situation" (Carter, 1953).

If one focuses on a total organization, one immediately notes that organizations tend to evolve a particular culture or character. This culture tends to define what is appropriate leadership. As organizational norms coerce conformity to particular types of leadership patterns, individuals soon learn how they should behave as leaders within these organizations (Argyris, 1958). Thus the nature of the organization's culture defines the accepted leadership behaviors, which are then internalized by the "successful" leaders. As soon as one accepts the possibility of a feedback from the environment "into" individuals, then the trait versus situational argument becomes fruitless.

If the organization coerces leadership toward a narrow band of behaviors, then a homogeneous list of appropriate leadership behaviors will evolve. Assuming organizational leaders follow the dictates of the organization, then they make the appropriate behavior part of themselves (perhaps through unconscious processes, such as identification and suppression). Under these conditions leadership traits will tend to make sense. If, on the other hand, an organization coerces a variety of leadership behaviors and rewards nonconformity, then the trait theory will not tend to be particularly applicable.

Some Implications of the Model
for Organizational Effectiveness Measures

For many years the armed forces and certain large organizations have been conducting research to measure the effectiveness of a unit. The logic is that if organizational effectiveness can be understood, then the tasks of organizational leadership would become evident. In these studies *formal organizational strategy* is used to obtain dimensions of effectiveness. Thus if absentee rates, grievances, turnover, work stoppages are low and production is high, the organization is assumed to be healthy (Merrehue and Katzell, 1955).

The difficulty with this approach is shown in recent research conducted by the writer. A plant was studied that was evaluated as "excellent" and "the best in the system" by the top corporate staff and by the top local management of the plant. Moreover, the employees themselves reported high positive attitudes toward the company. They liked it and remained very loyal to it. As a result, grievances, turnover, and absenteeism were so low that no central records were kept either at the plant level or the corporate headquarters. Production was high. By the typical indices this plant was highly effective.

However, after careful investigation it is now apparent that, along with the above indices of effectiveness, one also finds a very high degree of (*a*) emphasis on money and security by employees, (*b*) high *non*involvement in the company's financial and organizational problems, (*c*) high desire *not* to interact with management or employees, and (*d*) high degree of alienation (Argyris, 1959). These results can be made intelligible by showing that this organization's "mix" includes only a few of the dimensions defined above.

A second limitation of the majority of "organizational effectiveness" studies is that they focus on *end products*, such as loyalty, morale, turnover, grievance rates, and so on. There are two basic problems that arise from this approach. First, such end products as these are *symptoms* of the *internal* system. They may, but they may *not,* be accurate signs of the internal state of the organism.

In the field of medicine some symptoms (for instance, the absence of cancer) turn out to be quite inaccurate under more careful diagnosis. Thus if end products are regarded as symptoms, they may not necessarily represent a true picture of the internal state of the organization. Moreover, since organizations exist in an ever changing milieu no one set of symptoms can remain valid for a lengthy period of time. One way medicine attempts to increase the predictive validity of its symptoms is to pick those symptoms that are derived from research knowledge about the *mechanisms* of illness. This should provide a hint for organizational research.

It may be more useful to focus on the *processes* (mechanisms) by which effectiveness or noneffectiveness is created rather than on end results. The defined dimensions are hypothesized to be valid processes and can serve as the basis for such studies.

Some Implications of the Model
for Organizational Leadership [16]

What implications are to be inferred from the model for the functions of an organizational leader?

First, an effective organizational leader is aware that the formal

---

16. These dimensions are presumably valid for any kind of activity within the organization. Economic, technological, and human activities should presumably strive

organization is designed with a much simpler concept of organizational effectiveness in mind. High profits and high human loyalty to the formal organization are the primary components of the traditional theories of organization. In the model above, profits have their place. For example, an organization cannot, in our culture, produce without a profit and at the same time minimize its dependence upon the environment (5) and guarantee continued production (7). But there may be much more to effectiveness than profits. The dimensions control, internal influence, and problem solving do not deal directly with profits. On the other hand, the informal or human relations theories are also incomplete and an overemphasis on them could lead to other difficulties. Consequently, the organizational leader must find ways to optimize (not maximize) the degree to which individuals obtain self-expression and, simultaneously, formal organization achieves a profit.

As was mentioned before, the reason that optimization is desirable is that the organizational leader is faced with some dimensions whose maximization may lead to the minimization of another dimension.

The organizational leader functions to help departments and divisions become aware of their organizationally determined defenses and rigidities. Once awareness is obtained, the next step is to control these defenses and rigidities. Control over the organization's defenses can lead, if the participants wish, to their modification.

These examples illustrate some questions that can be raised when the model presented here is used and is adequate enough to show the theoretical and practical possibilities in studying organizational leadership by focusing on the total organization.

References

Allport, F. H. *Theories of Perception and the Concept of Structure*. Wiley, 1955.

Arensberg, C. M., and D. McGregor. "Determination of Morale in an Industrial Company." *Applied Anthropology*, Vol. 1, 1942.

Argyris, C. "The Individual and Organization: An Empirical Test." *Administrative Science Quarterly*, Vol. 4, 1959.

———. "Some Problems in Conceptualizing Organizational Climate." *Administrative Science Quarterly*, Vol. 2, 1958.

———. *Personality and Organization*. Harper & Row, 1957.

———. "Top Management Dilemma." *Personnel*, Vol. 32, No. 2, 1955.

———. *Executive Leadership*. Harper & Row, 1953a.

---

to maximize the organization's position along each of the continua above. In the case of leadership activities within the economic and technological aspects of the organization, little can be said by this author. I can only hope that some economists and engineers might find these dimensions useful and develop operational measures for each.

————. "Human Problems with Budgets." *Harvard Business Review*, Vol. 31, 1953b.

Bakke, E. W. *The Fusion Process*. Yale Labor and Management Center, 1954.

Barker, R. G., T. Dembo, and K. Lewin. *Frustration and Regression*. University of Iowa Press, 1941.

Barker, R. G., B. A. Wright, and M. R. Gonick. "Adjustment to Physical Handicap and Illness: A Survey of the Social Psychology of Physique and Disability." *Social Science Research Council*, Vol. 55, 1946.

Bertalanffy, L. V. *Problems of Life*. Wiley, 1952.

————. "Problems of General System Theory." *Human Biology*, Vol. 23, 1951.

————, and A. Rapoport, eds. *General Systems*, (Vol. 1). Society for the Advancement of General Systems Theory, 1956.

Boulding, K. *The Image*. University of Michigan Press, 1956.

Brown, A. *Organization of Industry*. Prentice-Hall, 1947.

Cameron, E. *General Psychotherapy*. Grune and Stratton, 1950.

Carter, L. F. "Leadership in Small Group Behavior." In *Group Relations at the Crossroads*, ed. M. Sherif and M. O. Wilson. Harper & Row, 1953.

Case, L. M. *French Opinion on War and Diplomacy during the Second Empire*. University of Pennsylvania Press, 1954.

Cattell, R. B. "New Concepts for Measuring Leadership in Terms of Group Syntality." *Human Relations*, Vol. 4 (1951).

Collier, R. M. "Consciousness as a Regulatory Field: A Theory of Psychotherapy." *Journal of Abnormal Social Psychology*, Vol. 55, (1957).

————. "Consciousness as a Regulatory Field: A Theory of Psychopathology." *Psychological Review*, Vol. 63 (1956).

Davison, W. P. *Preliminary Finds Reported in a Paper Identified as "P-851."* Rand Corp.

Dennison, H. S. *Organization Engineering*. McGraw-Hill, 1931.

Dollard, J., *et al. Frustration and Aggression*. Yale University Press, 1939.

Fayol, H. *General and Industrial Management*. Pitman, 1949.

Feibleman, J. K. "Theory of Integrative Levels." *British Journal of Philosophical Science*, Vols. 5 and 17, 1954.

Fiedler, F. C. "Nonfraternization between Leaders and Followers and Its Effects on Group Productivity and Psychological Adjustment." Paper presented at the Symposium on Preventive and Social Psychiatry, Walter Reed Army Institute of Research, April 1957.

Gauss, J. M., L. D. White, and M. E. Demack, eds. *The Frontiers of Public Administration*. University of Chicago Press, 1936.

Gerard, R. W., ed. "Concepts in Biology." *Behavioral Science*, Vol. 3, No. 2, 1958.

Gibb, C. A. "The Principles and Traits of Leadership." *Journal of Abnormal Social Psychology*, Vol. 3, 1947.

Goldstein, K. The Organism. American Book, 1939.

Goldstein, K. *The Organism*. American Book, 1939.

Gouldner, A. *Studies in Leadership*. Harper & Row, 1950.

Graicunas, V. A. "Relationship in Organization." In *Papers on the Science of Administration*, eds. L. Gulick and L. Urwick. Institute of Public Administration, 1927.

Halpin, A. W. "The Leadership Behavior and Combat Performance of Airplane Commanders." *Journal of Abnormal and Social Psychology*, Vol. 49, 1954.

Hemphill, J. K. "Leadership Behavior Associated with the Administrative Reputation of College Departments." *Journal of Educational Psychology*, Vol. 46, No. 2, 1955.

Herbst, P. G. "Situation Dynamics and the Theory of Behavior System." *Behavioral Science*, Vol. 3, 1957.

Holden, P. E., S. Fish, and H. L. Smith. *Top Management Organization and Control*. McGraw-Hill, 1951.

Hopf, H. A. *Management and the Optimum*. Hopf Institute of Management, 1935.

Jennings, H. H. *Leadership and Isolation*. Longmans, 1943.

Klein, M. J. "Order, Organization, and Entropy." *British Journal of Philosophical Science*, Vol. 4, 1953.

Kluckhohn, A. "Anthropology." In *What Is Science?* ed. J. C. Newman. Simon & Schuster, 1955.

Koontz, H., and C. O'Donnell. *Principles of Management*. McGraw-Hill, 1955.

Krech, D., and R. S. Crutchfield. *Theory and Problems of Social Psychology*. McGraw-Hill, 1948.

Kurtz, P. W. "Human Nature, Homeostasis, and Value." *Philosophical and Phenomenological Research*, Vol. 17, 1956.

Lewin, K. "Time Perspective and Morale." In *Resolving Social Conflicts*, ed. G. W. Lewin. Harper & Row, 1948.

————, et al. "Level of Aspiration." In *Personality and the Behavior Disorders*, ed. J. McV. Hunt. Ronald Press, 1944.

Likert, R. "Measuring Organizational Performance." *Harvard Business Review*, Vol. 36, 1958.

Lippitt, R., and L. Bradford. "Employee Success in Work Groups." *Personnel Administration*, Vol. 5, 1945.

Lippitt, R., and R. K. White. "An Experimental Study of Leadership and Group Life." In *Readings in Social Psychology*, ed. T. M. Newcomb and E. L. Hartley. Holt, Rinehart and Winston, 1957.

Mace, A. "Homeostasis, Needs, and Values." *British Journal of Psychology*, Vol. 20, Pt. 3, 1953.

McGregor, D., I. Knickerbocker, M. Haire, and A. Bavelas. "The Consultant Role and Organizational Leadership." *Journal of Social Issues*, Vol. 4, 1948.

McMurray, R. N. "Manhunt for Top Executives." *Harvard Business Review,* Vol. 32, No. 1, 1952.

Margenau, H. *The Nature of Physical Reality.* McGraw-Hill, 1950.

Martin, W. E., J. G. Darley, and N. Gross. "Studies in Group Behavior, II." *Educational Psychological Measurement,* Vol. 12, 1952.

Merrehue, W. V., and R. A. Katzell. "ERI—Yardstick of Employee Relations." *Harvard Business Review,* 1955.

Mooney, J. D. *The Principles of Organization.* Harper & Row, 1947.

Morley, R. *Bio Politics.* Dent.

Nadel, S. F. *The Foundations of Social Anthropology.* Cohen and West, 1951.

Newcomb, T. M. *Social Psychology.* Holt, Rinehart and Winston, 1950.

Redfield, R., ed. *Levels of Integration in Biological and Social Systems.* Jacques Cattel Press, 1942.

Schneirla T. C. "The 'Levels' Concept in the Study of Social Organization in Animals." In *Social Psychology at the Crossroads,* ed. J. H. Rohrer. Harper & Row, 1951.

Simon, H. A. "Comments on the Theory of Organization." *American Political Science Review,* Vol. 46, 1952.

Sinnott, E. W. "The Biology of Purpose." *American Journal of Ortho-Psychiatry,* Vol. 22, 1952.

————. *Cell and Psyche: The Biology of Purpose.* University of North Carolina Press, 1950.

Stene, E. D. "An Approach to a Science of Administration." *American Political Science Review,* Vol. 34, 1940.

Stogdill, R. M. "Personal Factors Associated with Leadership: A Survey of the Literature." *Journal of Psychology,* Vol. 25, 1948.

————, and K. Koehler. *Measures of Leadership Structure and Organization Change.* Ohio State University Personal Research Board, 1952.

Szasz, T. A. "Entropy, Organization, and the Problems of the Economy of Human Relationships." *International Journal of Psychoanalysis,* Vol. 36, 1955.

Taylor, F. W. *Scientific Management.* Harper & Row, 1948.

Torrance, E. P. "Perception of Group Functions as a Predictor of Group Performance." *Journal of Sociological Psychology,* Vol. 24, 1955.

Urwick, I. *The Elements of Administration.* Harper & Row, 1953.

White, L. D. *Introduction to the Study of Public Administration.* Macmillan, 1939.

Whyte, W. H. *Organization Man.* Simon & Schuster, 1956.

Wiener, N. *The Human Use of Human Beings.* Houghton Mifflin, 1950.

Warren G. Bennis

New Patterns of Leadership for Tomorrow's Organizations

Two years ago, I forecast that in the next 25 to 50 years we would participate in the end of bureaucracy as we know it and in the rise of new social systems better suited to the twentieth-century demands of industrialization (see *Technology Review* [April 1966], pp. 36 ff.). This forecast was based on the evolutionary principle that every age develops an organizational form appropriate to its genius and that the prevailing form today—the pyramidal, centralized, functionally specialized, impersonal mechanism known as *bureaucracy*—is out of joint with contemporary realities.

This breakdown of a venerable form of organization so appropriate to nineteenth-century conditions is caused, I argued, by a number of factors, but chiefly the following four:

1. Rapid and unexpected change.
2. Growth in size where the volume of an organization's traditional product is not enough to sustain growth.
3. Complexity of modern technology, where integration between activities and persons of very diverse, highly specialized competence is required.
4. The psychological threat springing from a change in managerial values toward more humanistic, democratic practices.

Organizations of the future, I predicted, would have some unique characteristics. The key word will be "temporary." There will be adaptive, rapidly changing *temporary systems*. Organization charts will consist of project groups rather than stratified functional groups, which now is the case. Adaptive problem-solving, temporary systems of diverse specialists, linked together by co-ordinating executives in organic flux—this is the organizational form that will gradually replace bureaucracy.

Ironically, the bold future I was predicting two years ago is now a mundane reality; it can be observed today where the most interesting and advanced practices exist. We live in a time and place where rapid social and technological change is endemic, and so perhaps it should not be too surprising that a distant future can invade overnight, so to speak—certainly before the forecast is fully comprehended.

New Styles and Tasks of Leadership

The question of the leadership of these new-style organizations was left unanswered in the original article. Are there any guidelines transferable to their management from present managerial practices? Do the behavioral sciences provide any suggestions for leaders of the future? How can these complex, ever-changing, free-form, kaleidoscopic patterns be co-ordinated? There can be no definitive answers to these questions until the future emerges in a more or less unambiguous way. But we clearly need to attempt an evaluation of the leadership requirements for organizations of the future, for without the effort we shall inevitably back into the future instead of managing it effectively.

Developing Rewarding Human Systems

The general direction of these organizational changes—toward more service and professional organizations, toward more educated, younger, and mobile employees, toward more diverse, complex, science-based systems, toward a more turbulent and uncertain environment—forces us to consider new styles of leadership. Leading the enterprise of the future will become a significant social process, requiring as much interpersonal competence as substantive competence, if not more.

One convenient focus for a discussion of leadership is to summarize the main problems confronting modern organizations and to understand the kinds of tasks and strategies linked to the solution of these problems. These are summarized in Table 1, which also shows some possible executive steps.

A simple way to understand the problem of integration is to compute the ratio between what an individual gives and what he receives in his day-to-day transactions. In organizational terms, we can ask: Are the *contributions* to the organization about equivalent to the *inducements* received? There is nothing startling or new about this formulation. What is interesting is that organizations frequently do not know what is truly rewarding. This is particularly true in the case of the professionals and highly trained workers who will dominate the organizations of the future, with whom conventional policies

and practices regarding incentives—never particularly sensitive—
tend to be inappropriate.

Most organizations regard economic rewards as the primary
incentive to peak performance. These are not unimportant to the
professional, but—provided economic rewards are equitable—other
incentives become far more potent. Professionals tend to seek such
rewards as full utilization of their talent and training; professional
status (not necessarily within the organization, but externally with
respect to their profession); and opportunities for development and
further learning. The "good place to work" resembles a super-graduate
school, alive with dialogue and senior colleagues, where the employee

Table 1   Main Tasks and Strategies of Leadership in Contemporary Organizations

Problem	Tasks of the Leader
Integration The problem of integrating individual needs and organizational goals	Developing rewarding human systems
Social Influence The problem of distributing power	Developing executive "constellations"
Collaboration The problem of producing mechanisms for the control of conflict	Building a collaborative climate
Adaptation The problem of responding to a turbulent, uncertain environment	Identification with the adaptive process
Identity The problem of clarity, commitment, and consensus to organizational goals	Developing supra-organizational goals
Revitalization The problem of growth and decay	Organizational "self-renewal"

Modern organizations are confronted with a series of circumstances and problems which have
no true counterparts in corporate history, and these needs require new strategies and impose new
tasks upon modern corporate leadership. This chart attempts to list the new problems, and their consequences, in grossly oversimplified form.

will work not only to satisfy organizational demands but, perhaps
primarily, to fulfill self-imposed demands of his profession.

How (or even *if*) these needs can be deliberately controlled by
the leadership is not at all clear. Company-sponsored courses, T-
groups, and other so-called adult education courses may contribute.
The idea that education has a terminal point is clearly old-fashioned.
A "drop-out" may soon be redefined to mean anyone who has not
returned to school.

However the problem of professional and personal growth is
resolved, it is clear that many of the older forms of incentives will
have to be reconstituted. Even more profound will be the blurring of

the boundaries between work and play, between affiliative and achievement drives which nineteenth-century necessities and mores have unsuccessfully attempted to compartmentalize.

Developing Executive Collaboration

It is quaint to think that one man, no matter how omniscient and omnipotent, can comprehend, to say nothing of control, the diversity and complexity of the modern organization. Followers and leaders who think this is possible are entrapped in a false dream, a child's fantasy of absolute power and absolute dependence. As a result, there has been a tendency to move away (tacitly) from a "presidential" form of power to a "cabinet" or team concept. Such a system of an "executive constellation" by no means implies an abdication of responsibility by the chief executive. It is a way of multiplying executive power through a realistic allocation of effort. Despite all the problems inherent in the executive constellation concept—the difficulties of building an effective team, of achieving compatibility, etc. —it is hard to see other valid solutions to the constraints of magnitude and sheer overload of the leader's role.

Not unrelated to the problem of developing an effective executive constellation is another key task of the leader—building a collaborative climate. An effective collaborative climate is easier to experience and harder to achieve than a formal description, but most students of group behavior would agree that it should include the following ingredients: flexible and adaptive structure; utilization of members' talents; clear and agreed-upon goals; norms of openness, trust, and co-operation; interdependence; high intrinsic rewards; and transactional controls—i.e., members of the unit should have a high degree of autonomy and a high degree of participation in making key decisions.

Developing this group "synergy" is difficult. Lack of experience and strong cultural biases against group efforts worsen the problem. Groups, like other highly complicated organisms, need interaction, trust, communication, and commitment, and these ingredients require a period of gestation. But expensive and time-consuming as it is, building synergetic and collaborative cultures will become essential. Modern problems, too complex and diversified for one man or one discipline, require a blending of skills and perspectives, and only effective problem-solving units will be able to master them.

Identification with the Adaptive Process

Man's accommodation to change is generally painful, but characteristically and ironically he continues to seek out new inventions which disorder his serenity and undermine his competence. One striking index of the rapidity of modern change—for me, the most dramatic single index—is the shrinking interval between the time of a discovery and its commercial application. The transistor was discovered in 1948; by 1960 over 50 percent of *all* electronic equipment utilized transistors in place of conventional vacuum tubes.

The increasing tempo of discovery and its application make modern organizations acutely dependent on their success in responding flexibly and appropriately to new information. How can the leadership create an atmosphere of continuity and stability in this environment of chance? Whitehead put the problem well when he said: "The art of society consists first in the maintenance of the symbolic code, and secondly, in the fearlessness of revision. . . . Those societies which cannot combine reverence to their symbols with freedom of revision must ultimately decay."

There is no easy solution to the tension between stability and change. We are not yet an emotionally adaptive society, though a remarkable aspect of our generation is its commitment to change in thought and action. Executive leadership must take some responsibility in creating a climate that provides the security to identify with the adaptive process without fear of losing status and its psychological companion, a lowered self-esteem. Creating an environment that increases a tolerance for ambiguity and where one can make a virtue out of contingency, in contrast to an environment which induces hesitancy and its reckless counterpart, expedience, is one of the most challenging tasks for the new leadership.

Supra-Organizational Goals and Commitments

The new organizations we speak of, with their bands of "pseudo-species" coping within a turbulent environment, are particularly allergic to problems of identity. Professional and regional orientations lead frequently to fragmentation, intergroup conflicts and power plays, and rigid compartmentalization devoid of any unifying sense of purpose or mission.

The university is a wondrous place for the development of advanced battle techniques between groups which far overshadow their business counterparts in subterfuge and sabotage. Quite often a university becomes a loose collection of competing departments, schools, institutes, committees, centers, and programs, largely noncommunicating because of the multiplicity of specialist jargons and interests and held together, as Robert Hutchins once said, chiefly by a central heating system. Having heard variations of this theme over the years, a number of faculty and administrators at one large university, who thought they could "wear the over-all university hat," formed what later came to be known as "the HATS group." They came from many departments and hierarchical levels, represented a rough microcosm of the entire university, and have become a prototype through the important role they have played in influencing university policy.

There are a number of functions that leadership can perform in addition to encouraging HATS groups. It can identify and support those individuals who can serve as articulating points between various groups and departments. There are many individuals who have a bi-cultural facility, a capacity for psychological and intellectual affinity with different languages and cultures, who can provide articulation between seemingly inimical interests, who can break down the pseudo-species, transcend vested interests, regional ties, and professional biases. Leadership can seek out and encourage these people. It can work at the interfaces of the pseudo-species, setting up new programs in the interstitial areas, in order to create more intergroup articulations. This is precisely what Mary Parker Follett had in mind when she discussed leadership in terms of an ability to bring about a "creative synthesis" between differing codes of conduct. Chester Barnard in his classic *Functions of the Executive* recognized this, and he also recognized the cost in personal energy of this kind of synthesis. He wrote: "It seems to me that the struggle to maintain cooperation among men should as surely destroy some men morally as battle destroys some physically."

Revitalization: Controlling Destiny

The issue of revitalization—the organization's taking conscious responsibility for its own evolution—confronts the leader with the penultimate challenge: growth or decay. His urgent problem is to develop a climate of inquiry and enough psychological and employment security for continual reassessment and renewal. The organizational culture must encourage individuals to participate in social evolution against unknown, uncertain, and implacable forces and to collect valid data and act on limited information without fear of losing control.

The three-step "action-research" model of data-generation, feedback, and action-planning sounds deceptively simple. In fact, it is difficult. Quite often the important data cannot be collected by the leader. Even when the data are known, there are many organizational short circuits and "dithering devices" which distort and prevent the data from reaching the right places at the right time. And even when data-generation and feedback are satisfactorily completed, organizational inhibitions may not lead to implementation. But some progressive organizations are setting up organizational development departments that attempt to reduce the "implementation gap" between information, new ideas, and action. These departments become the center for the entire strategic side of the organization, including not only long-run planning but plans for gaining participation and commitment to the plans. This last step is the most crucial for the guarantee of successful implementation.

New Concepts for Leadership

In addition to substantive competence and comprehension of both social and technical systems, the new leader will have to possess interpersonal skills, not the least of which is the ability to defer his own immediate desires and gratifications in order to cultivate the talents of others. Just as salesmen are admonished that "you gotta know the territory," so too the manager must be at home in the "social territory," the complex and dynamic interaction of individuals, roles, groups, and organizational and cultural systems.

Leadership is as much craft as science. Analytical methods, drawn primarily from social psychology and sociology, suffice for business leaders to understand the scientific aspects of their profession, but the main instrument or "tool" for the leader-as-a-craftsman is *himself* and how creatively he can use his own personality. Leaders, like physicians, are "iatrogenic"—that is, capable of spreading as well as curing disease. Unless the leader understands his actions and their effects on others, he may be a "carrier" rather than a solver of problems. Thus he must be willing and able to set up reliable mechanisms of feedback so that he can conceptualize the "social territory" of which he is an important part—and at the same time realize how he influences it.

Another aspect of the "social territory" that has key significance for leadership is the idea of *system*. At least two decades of research have been making this point unsuccessfully. Research has shown that productivity can be modified by group norms, that training effects deteriorate if the training is not compatible with the goals of the social system, that group cohesiveness is a powerful motivator, that intergroup conflict is a major problem facing organizations, that individuals take many of their cues and derive a good deal of their satisfaction from their primary work group, that identification with the small work group turns out to be the only stable predictor of productivity, and so on.

This evidence is often cited and rarely acted upon. It seems that individuals, living amidst complex and subtle organizational conditions, tend to oversimplify and distort complex realities so that "people" rather than conditions embody the problem. This tendency toward personalization can be observed in many situations. We can see it in distorted polarizations such as the "good guy" leader and his "hatchet man" assistant. It is easier to blame heroes and villains than the system. For if the problems are embroidered into the fabric of the system, complex as it is, the system can be changed. But it is hard to change people.

"Other-Directed" Leadership

One famous typology in the social sciences was introduced by David Riesman in his book *The Lonely Crowd.* He asserted that contemporary man is more "other-directed" than his father—or certainly than his grandfather, who would have been characterized as "inner-directed." These character types refer essentially to the ways individuals are influenced and the forces which shape their perspectives. "Other-directed" man takes his cues from his peer group rather than from his parents; in other words, he takes his relationships more seriously than he does his relatives. His ideology, values, and norms are transmitted to him and accepted by the particular social group with which he associates. He is a "pleaser," co-operative and accommodating. "Inner-directed" man, to extend an exaggeration, responds to some internal gyroscope, typically internalized parental pressures. He responds not to any social grouping but to some inner cues, shadowed reflections of his parents' dictates. "Inner-directed" man is rigid, unyielding, and acts on principles. Studies conducted in industrial settings have consistently shown that organizations tend to reward the aggressive, forceful, decisive "inner-directed" leader rather than the co-operative, adaptable, "other-directed" leader. Now a new study of the leadership in service-oriented organizations by E. E. Lawlor and L. W. Porter shows that "other-directed" leaders tend to be more highly rewarded in this setting than "inner-directed" leaders. In the service-oriented growth industries of education, health, welfare, government, and professional organizations, the prime requisites of a leader are interpersonal competence and "other-directedness."

An Agricultural Model of Leadership

I have not found the right word or phrase that accurately portrays the concept of future leadership I have in mind. The most appropriate metaphor I have found to characterize adaptive leadership is an "agricultural" model: the leader's job is to build a climate where growth and development are culturally induced, conditions where people and ideas and resources can be seeded, cultivated, and integrated to optimum effectiveness and growth. Roy Ash, an astute industrialist who is chairman of Litton Industries, remarked recently: "If the larger corporations, classically viewed as efficient machines rather than hothouses for fomenting innovation, can become both of these at once, industrial competition will have taken on new dimensions." I think Ash captures exactly the shift in metaphor I am getting at, from a mechanical model to an organic one.

Up until very recent times, the metaphor most commonly used to describe power and leadership in organizations derived from Helmholtz's laws of mechanics, and the language reflects this derivation:

social engineering, equilibrium, friction, and resistance are typical of the words we use. The vocabulary for adaptive organizations requires an organic metaphor, a description of *process*—not of structural arrangements. This description must include such terms as open, dynamic systems, developmental, organic, and adaptive.

The key aspect of the process insofar as leadership is concerned is the ability of the leader to develop a collaborative relationship with his subordinates. This is not to say that the leader should be a "good guy" or seek popularity, but it does mean that he will have to learn to negotiate and collaborate with his associates. Because the leader cannot know everything, his subordinates will have the information and competences that the leader needs; his access to this information will depend entirely on his ability to collaborate with his employees and colleagues. While Marx argued that power accrues to the man with property, we argue that power accrues to the man who can gather and control information wisely. The psychological "contract," if we may use that term, between leader and led is more satisfying and almost always more productive if the relationship is based on collaboration. Studies of scientists and engineers, for example, show that no unilateral conditions, where scientists decide for themselves or where the director decides for them, ever matched the quality of work under a collaborative relationship where research and development decisions were reached through a collaborative process.

Toward a New Leadership Style

All of these strategic and practical considerations lead to a totally new concept of leadership, the pivotal aspect of which is that the leader depends less on substantive knowledge about a particular topic than on the understanding and possession of skills summarized under the agricultural model.

The role of the leader has become infinitely more complex, for he is now at the center of a highly variegated set of pressures and roles. He presides over a complex establishment; his job is to co-ordinate, transact, motivate, and integrate. Simply, he must have the knowledge and competence to produce environments where the most able people can realize their talents, co-ordinate their efforts, remain committed to organizational goals, and integrate their efforts in a manner that no one of them working alone could surpass. Perhaps the most difficult aspect of this style of leadership is to transact (and confront) those recalcitrant parts of the system that are retarded, stunted, or afraid to grow. This will require enormous energy, saintly patience, and a sophisticated optimism in growth (or a high tolerance for disenchantment).

This new concept of leadership embraces five important sets of competences:

1. Knowledge of large, complex systems, their dynamics and their "tribal customs."

2. Practical theories of intervening and guiding these systems, theories that encompass methods for seeding, nurturing, and integrating individuals and groups.

3. Interpersonal competence. This includes at least three components: (*a*) the sensitivity to understand the effects of one's own behavior on others and how one's own personality shapes his particular leadership style and value system; (*b*) a capacity to develop adequate methods for valid feedback; and (*c*) managing conflict. (There was a time when I believed that consensus was a valid operating procedure. I no longer think this is realistic given the scale and diversity of organizations. In fact, I've come to think that the quest for consensus, except in pre-literate face-to-face cultures where it may be feasible, is a misplaced nostalgia for a folk society as chimerical, incidentally, as the American adolescent search for "identity.")

4. A set of values and competences which enables one to know when to confront and attack, if necessary, and when to support and provide the psychological safety so necessary for growth.

5. An ability to develop and use all types of information systems, including high-speed electronic computers. The job of the leader will be to collect, organize, and transmit information.

The role of leadership described here is clearly more demanding and formidable than any historical precedent, including both king and pope. Let us hope that this new role of leadership is not only more potent but also more gratifying.

Jack R. Gibb

Is Help Helpful?

People in the service professions often see themselves as primarily engaged in the job of helping others. Helping becomes both the personal style of life and a core activity that gives meaning and

From *Forum*, February 1964, pp. 25–27. Reprinted by permission of the author and *Forum*.

purpose to the life of the professional. The youth worker, the camp director, the counselor, the consultant, the therapist, the teacher, the lawyer—each is a helper.

Helping is a central social process. The den mother, the committee chairman, the parent, the personal friend, the board member, the dance sponsor—each is a helper.

Help, however, is not always helpful. The recipient of the proffered help may not see it as useful. The offering may not lead to greater satisfaction or to better performance. Even less often does the helping process meet a more rigorous criterion—leading to continued growth on the part of the participants.

To begin with, a person may have varied motivations for offering help. He may wish to improve performance of a subordinate, reduce his own guilt, obtain gratitude, make someone happy, or give meaning to his own life. He may wish to demonstrate his superior skill or knowledge, induce indebtedness, control others, establish dependency, punish others, or simply meet a job prescription. These conscious or partially conscious motivations are so intermingled in any act of help that it is impossible for either the helper or the recipient to sort them out.

Depending upon his own needs and upon the way he sees the motives of the helper, the recipient will have varied reactions. He may feel gratitude, resentment, or admiration. He may feel helpless and dependent, or jealous of the helper who has the strength or resources to be in the helper role. He may feel indebted, or pressured to conform to the perceived demands or beliefs of the helper.

We have all noticed that in certain cases the recipient of the help becomes more helpless and dependent, less able to make his own decisions or initiate his own actions, less self-sufficient, more apathetic and passive, less willing to take risks, more concerned about propriety and conformity, and less creative and venturesome. We have also seen circumstances in which, following help, recipients become more creative, less dependent upon the helper, more willing to make risk decisions, more highly motivated to tackle tough problems, less concerned about conformity, and more effective at working independently or interdependently. Help may or may not lead to personal growth and organizational health.

Under certain conditions both the giver and the receiver grow and develop. In general, people tend to grow when there is reciprocal dependence—*inter*dependence, joint determination of goals, real communication in depth, and reciprocal trust. To the degree that these conditions are absent, people fail to grow.

From the standpoint of the organization, help must meet two criteria: the job or program must be done more effectively, and the individual members must grow and develop. These two criteria tend to merge. The program and the organization are effective only as the participants grow. The same conditions lead to personal growth. Table 1 presents a theory of the helping relationship. Seven parallel sets of orientations are presented. One set of conditions maximize help and a parallel set of conditions minimize help.

Table 1   The Helping Relationship

Orientations that help	Orientations that hinder
1. Reciprocal trust (confidence, warmth, acceptance)	1. Distrust (fear, punitiveness, defensiveness)
2. Cooperative learning (inquiry, exploration, quest)	2. Teaching (training, advice giving, indoctrinating)
3. Mutual growth (becoming, actualizing, fulfilling)	3. Evaluating (fixing, correcting, providing a remedy)
4. Reciprocal openness (spontaneity, candor, honesty)	4. Strategy (planning, maneuvering, gamesmanship)
5. Shared problem solving (defining, producing alternatives, testing)	5. Modeling (demonstrating, information giving, guiding)
6. Autonomy (freedom, interdependence, equality)	6. Coaching (molding, steering, controlling)
7. Experimentation (play, innovation, provisional try)	7. Patterning (standard, static, fixed)

Reciprocal Trust

People accept help from those they trust. When the relationship is one of acceptance and trust, offers of help are appreciated, listened to, seen as potentially helpful, and often acted upon. The receiver accepts help from one whose perceived motives are congenial to him. He tends to reject offers from people whose offering is seen as a guise for attempts to control, punish, correct, or gain power. Help is most helpful when given in an atmosphere in which people have *reciprocal* feelings of confidence, warmth, and acceptance. When one feels that his worth *as a person* is valued, he is able to place himself in psychological readiness to receive aid.

Distrust

When people fear and distrust each other, even well-intended help is resisted, resented, or seen as unhelpful. Offers of help are sometimes given in service of motivations that are unacceptable to the receiver. That is, one offers help in order to place the other person in a dependent position, elicit expressions of gratitude, assert one's superiority, or punish him. In distrust, the recipient's guard is up. He is likely to project his distrusts into the helper and to resist or resent the help.

One often gives help to camouflage or assuage his desire to

change another person—change his character, habits, or misconceptions. The desire to change another person is essentially hostile. At a deep level, one who genuinely accepts another person does not wish to change him. A person who is accepted is allowed *to be,* become, determine his own goals and follow them at his own pace. The person who genuinely wishes to help offers the help that *the recipient wishes.* Genuine help is not foisted upon the receiver. Neither the punisher nor the child really believes that the punishment is given "for the good of the child."

Punishment or censure may be given with a conscious desire to help, but usually is accompanied by a deep component of retaliation, or by a desire to hurt, control, or assert superiority. The giver often speaks of his act as "helpful" in order to rationalize to himself and to the receiver acts that are done for other motivations.

Cooperative Learning

People are helpful to each other when they are engaged in a cooperative quest for learning. The learning atmosphere is one of joint inquiry and exploration. Needs for help and impulses to give help arise out of the demands of the common cooperative task. Help is thus reciprocal. The helper and helpee roles are interchangeable. Each participant has the *intent* to learn and feels he can learn from the partners and from the common task. The boss and the subordinate, the teacher and the student, the professional worker and the youth—all are most helpful when each member of the pair sees the relationship as a quest with potential learning for each. An effective project team is guided by the task and not by the teacher. It is motivated by the shared potential for learning.

Teaching

When one participant in a project sets out to teach, train, advise, persuade, or indoctrinate the other members, or is *seen* as wanting to do so, the learning of each member is reduced. People cannot be taught. People must learn. People cannot be trained. They grow and develop. The most deeply helpful relationship is one of common inquiry and quest, a relationship between co-learners and co-managers in which each is equally dependent upon the other for significant help and in which each sees and accepts this relationship.

Mutual Growth

The most permanent and significant help occurs in a relationship in which both members are continually growing, becoming, and seeking fulfillment. Each member participates in a mutual assessment of progress, accepts this reality of growth, and participates in a way that will maximize the growth of both participants. In a fundamental sense, one can only help himself. The helper can only participate with another in an effort to create a climate in which growth can occur.

Evaluating

Growth is often hindered when one member of the helping team sets out to appraise or remedy the defects in the other member. Help is most effective when it is seen as a force moving toward growth rather than as an effort to remove gaps, remedy defects, or bring another person up to a standard criterion. The limits of growth of any person are extremely diffiicult to foresee or to assess. The potential for growth is consistently underestimated by both participants in the helping relationship.

Reciprocal Openness

One of the essential conditions for effective human learning is the opportunity for feedback or knowledge of progress. Feedback is essential in acquiring skills, knowledge, and attitudes. In the areas where professional help is most commonly sought or given, the essential progress in learning and growth is blocked most often by the failure to obtain adequate data on people's feelings and perceptions of each other. In order to do effective work one must know how others feel and how they see things. In the usual situations in which professional helpers find themselves, there are many pressures which camouflage or distort the relevant data necessary for efficient work and best learning. Many factors reduce the availability of the relevant data: differential status, differential perceived power, and fears that one can hurt or be hurt.

Strategy

When some part of the helping process is closed or unavailable to all participants, people are likely to become anxious, resentful, or resistant. Neither participant in the helping process can "use" the other for his own needs. The helping process is most effective when one plans *with* another, not *for* another. One is not helped when he is maneuvered into some action which he does not understand. Gamesmanship and gimmicks are antithetical to the helping process.

Shared Problem Solving

The productive helping relationship focuses upon the problem to be solved. Problem solving involves a joint determination of the problem, continual redefinition of the problem as successive insights are gained, joint focus upon possible alternative solutions, joint exploration of the data, and continual reality testing of the alternatives. The expertness and resources of each person are shared. The aspect of the behavior about which help is given is seen as a *shared problem*—not as a defect to be remedied or as something to be solved by the helper as consultant.

Modeling

A common image of the helping relationship is one where the helper offers a model for the advisee to follow. The expert gives a demonstration of how the recipient may solve his problems. The problem is defined by the expert. Diagnosis is made by the expert. The expert is challenged to offer additional alternatives to the solution of the problem and perhaps even to test the solutions. The process is uni-directional. The limitations of modeling are many. Dependency is increased. The pupil seldom gets better than the model. The worker tries to conform to the image of the supervisor. Growth is limited.

Autonomy

The ideal relationship for helping is an interdependent one in which each person sees the other as both helper and recipient in an exchange among equals. It is essential that each participant preserve his freedom and maintain his autonomous responsibility for guiding himself toward his own learnings, growth, and problem solving. The helper must work himself out of the helping job. The supervisor, youth worker, and counselor must become decreasingly necessary to the people being helped. Psychological weaning, however painful to both helper and recipient, must continue if help is to be truly helpful.

Coaching

The coach molds, steers, or controls the behavior of the recipient, much as a tennis coach or physical education director molds the behavior of the athlete or skill-directed recipient of help. This is another uni-directional process in which the coach is assumed to have special diagnostic and observational powers which he applies in a skilled way to the behavior of the recipient, who puts himself in the hands of the coach. The recipient of help is encouraged to maintain respectful dependency upon the coach, to not challenge his authority or expertness, to put implicit trust in his abilities and powers, and to receive from the coach motivational or inspirational guidance. Both coach and pupil suffer under this pattern. Each *may* gain in skill. Neither grows *as a person*.

Experimentation

Tentativeness and innovative experimentation are characteristic of the most productive helping relationship. There is a sense of play, excitement, and fun in the common exploratory quest for new solutions to continually changing problems. The helping process is viewed as a series of provisional trials. Each participant joins in the game and adds to the general excitement. Errors can be made—and are perhaps expected. Help is a search. Finding creative solutions to newly defined problems is a game—full of zest and intrinsic drives that keep the game going.

Patterning

Help is limited when the process is seen as an attempt on the part of one person to help another meet a prescribed standard, come up to a criterion, or reach a goal specified in advance. Helping is a creative synthesis of growth and a continual search for new forms.

Help is not always helpful—but *it can be*. Both the helper and the recipient can grow and learn when help is given in a relationship of trust, joint inquiry, openness, and interdependence. Growth-centered helping processes lead to healthy groups and effective organizations.

James V. Clark

A Healthy Organization

What constitutes a "good" organization remains a matter of much debate. In this paper, I shall spell out my own current concept of organizational health and illustrate it by describing an organization I call healthy.

I consider an organization to be healthy if its members observe certain unstated but quite uniform codes of behavior which they accept as normal things to do, provided these codes produce behavior which allows all levels of the organization to meet two basic but diverse requirements—maintenance of the status quo, and growth.

Since man is a social being and business a group activity, the healthy organization must afford groups as well as individuals chances to fulfill their tendencies and capacities for equilibrium and

© 1962 by The Regents of the University of California. Reprinted from *California Management Review*, Summer 1962, pp. 16–30, by permission of The Regents, and the author.

growth. It must do this for the individual, for small groups, for intergroup relationships, and for the total organization.

It goes without saying that each and all of these tendencies and capacities can never be completely and simultaneously maximized. That's not in the nature of things (see Lawrence, 1958, ch. 10). But on balance and over time the healthy organization is one in which its component parts—the group and individual—somehow manage to achieve an optional resolution of their tendencies toward equilibrium (maintenance, homeostasis, status quo, or call it what you will) and their capacities for growth (elaboration, complication, differentiation, negative entropy, or what not).

Before we go into particulars about the healthy organization, as I have just defined it, we must lay some groundwork. Let us, therefore, take a quick look at some of the different aspects of human behavior and some of the divergent ways in which these aspects have been studied. Then I shall illustrate these different aspects with common examples from business and everyday life. We will need, also, to examine what I mean by a norm which governs social behavior. After we have done all this, I will return to the subject of a healthy organization and try to show one in action.

Aspects of Behavioral Systems

For some time behavioral scientists have described individuals, small groups, intergroup complexes, total organizations and societies as systems, that is, "wholes," composed of interrelated, interdependent parts. Investigators have tended to concentrate on what could be called the "reactive" side of a system, which means behavior which is analogous to a balloon returning to its original state after a finger has been inserted and withdrawn from its side.

More or less, these various investigators have played on some variation of Freud's "pleasure principle," that the primordial or initial principle of life is to reduce tension. Tension is said to be regarded as pain and absence of tension as pleasure. Individuals, small groups, and bureaucracies have all been seen, in this light, as equilibrium-seeking, homeostatic, reacting, defensive, "closed" systems.

Recently, however, interest in so-called "open-ended" systems has intensified. Students regarding systems in such a light stress what might be called the "proactive" side of systems, that behavior which is forward-pushing, growing, striving, learning, becoming. Such writers emphasize what are often called the "transactional" aspects of behavior—that as a system matures it enters into a more and more complex set of give-and-take relations with its environment, what Gordon Allport has described as "extensive transactional commerce" (see Allport, 1960). Growth for a behavioral system, then, involves a greater complexity of relations with its environment; hence "open-ended" is an appropriate term.

While those who emphasize the "reactive" side of behavior often deny the "proactive" side, and vice versa, many careful observers maintain that any system requires both aspects. A human being grows, but it also has a capacity to restore itself to health after an invasion of germs or injuries. A small group tends to perpetuate itself, but it also elaborates a complicated structure of power, interaction, beliefs, communication, and so on.

To me, any piece of organizational behavior tends to exhibit both aspects—reaction and proaction, maintenance and growth, even if one capacity is present only by virtue of its frustration. Hence, I will try to show that a healthy organization must somehow take account of both these tendencies. I have discussed briefly the attachment different students have had to these different tendencies so the reader may be on guard against any such parochial leanings in himself (see Clark).

Levels of Behavioral Systems

In addition to studying one or the other of these tendencies, investigators of behavior in formal organizations have often tended to concentrate on only one or two levels of investigation. This has usually been out of necessity, for one can't study everything. Nevertheless, the impression has sometimes been created that organizational well-being is arrived at only through satisfying individual needs, or small group needs, or by developing intergroup harmony, or by dealing rationally with only the formal organizational structure, or in some other partial manner.

As Koontz has illustrated (1961, pp. 174–188), the "management theory jungle" is peopled with schools of investigators which often center on aspects of administration and organizational behavior as if these aspects were the totality. It seems to me, however, that the different levels of organizational behavior are all in operation at any one time, and, in some sense, must all be taken into consideration. I cannot visualize a successful formal organization as one which attends only to individual needs for growth, or to small groups' needs for perpetuity, continuation, and elaboration, or to the total firm's needs for accomplishing its purpose to the exclusion of all else.

In summary, it can be said that, notwithstanding the historical preferences of different investigators, behavioral systems in formal organization can be seen on the different levels of individual, small group, intergroup and total organization, and exhibit both reactive and proactive tendencies and capacities at each level.

Behavioral Systems Illustrated

The different aspects and levels of organizational behavior are represented in figure 1. In it I show a dotted line weaving back and forth between the two aspects of each different level, because it is

Figure 1   Organizational Behavior

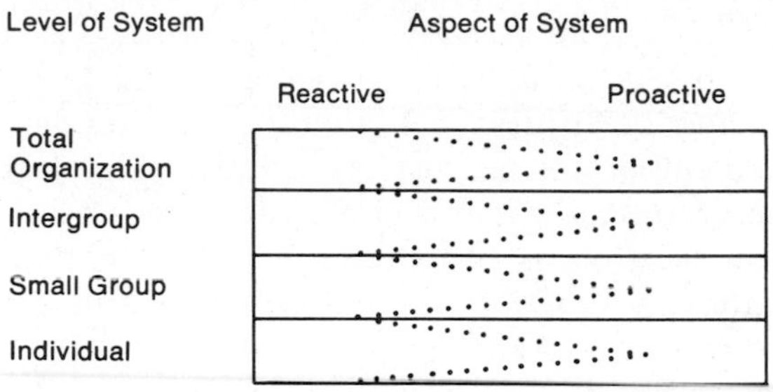

Level of System   Aspect of System

                          Reactive   Proactive

Total
Organization

Intergroup

Small Group

Individual

almost always impossible to identify an instance of purely reactive or purely proactive behavior. As we shall show in succeeding paragraphs, what is apparently proactive behavior often has a hidden reactive meaning. I don't wish to claim or imply here, therefore, that a researcher or an administrator in an organization can categorically state what *the* meaning of a piece of behavior is. In fact that's my point; one can't. Any piece of behavior always has a variety of meanings, and my thesis is that any organization, to be healthy, must recognize that variety.

To make these points clearer, I shall illustrate aspects of behavior that fit into the different boxes. Hidden meanings will not be alluded to in most instances since psychology and sociology have made us all generally familiar with them. I will, however, discuss such problems in relation to some of the boxes on our diagram, for these are places where we are not so accustomed to look for hidden meanings as we may be in individual behavior. Each of the areas in figure 1 will be illustrated one at a time.

Individual Behavior

Instances of reactive behavior on the individual level are familiar to all of us. Typical examples are the student who defends his belief that he is an intelligent person by denigrating his professor's capacity to communicate, the professor who avoids examining his own capacity to teach by bemoaning the decline in student motivation over the past generation, the mother who maintains her self-concept as a loving person by decrying her inconsiderate children, etc. Such individuals are fending off new information which, if allowed to penetrate, would call for too radical a reorganization of the way in which they see themselves.

Proactive behavior on the part of an individual covers the whole range of human behavior designed to reorganize something in the self-world relationship. The ten-year-old boy struggling night and day to build something, the mother testing new ways of behaving with her children, the researcher trying to discover a new uniformity, the contemplative searching for a deeper understanding of man, nature, or God, the industrial worker designing a new tool bit for his lathe— all these show evidence of growthful, proactive behavior.

Of course, as any sensitive participant in human affairs knows, what looks like proactive behavior often turns out, on closer analysis, to have a strong reactive component, but such are the challenges and pitfalls confronted by those who choose to develop a science of human behavior—they simply cannot avoid the study of meaning. We will encounter this problem when I illustrate behavior at the total organizational level.

Small Group Behavior

On the level of the small group, an instance of reactive behavior is seen in the strengthening of shared beliefs and codes which occurs in a group when an outsider attempts to change it. Such behavior has been seen when industrial work groups face a methods man who has new ideas about how they should be organized, or when a branch plant management team receives new directions or a reorganization plan from headquarters, or when a group of high ranking military officers is visited by a critical congressman.

Outside of organizations, such behavior is encountered, for example, when an insensitive Easterner wears a suit and tie to a Los Angeles poolside party, or indeed when any representative of one culture encounters a group from another, and so on. Any group finds it difficult to assimilate such deviant people and behaviors and has an almost instantaneous reaction designed to restore its equilibrium roughly to where it was. At least the group members strive to establish equilibrium.

Proaction on the group level is seen in certain aspects of the behavior of a group of smelter workers recently observed by the author. One night this group sweated for an hour over 2000° molten metal to pull out a tool bit which would have left a trace impurity in the metal and for which they could not possible have been held accountable nor received any credit for correcting (Lawrence, *et al.*, 1961, pp. 126–127). This behavior was not called for either by their formal job requirements (technically, they were supposed to work alone) or their group norms to help one another with their work assignments, but represented a new pattern of behavior and beliefs not seen earlier in the structure of the group.

Something similar occurred in a freezing room group Louis B. Barnes and I studied in 1957 (Barnes and Clark, 1957). This group of five or six workers in an ice cream plant spent nearly a year meeting at each other's homes to design and eventually execute a whole new methods handling system in their department. Their work went on unknown to management for months and involved new behavior patterns in the group and new effects on the group environment.

Such developmental behavior was also seen by Trist and his colleagues among longwall method coal workers in Britain when they were offered the chance to organize their own socio-technological relationship (Trist, Murray, Higgin, and Pollock, 1959). Similar development was charted by Barnes (1960) in an engineering group which was given comparatively high freedom to influence its own job structure.

Of course, groups, like other behavioral systems, will always tend to increase the differentiation of their parts through time. The rich rubric of social interaction which develops around betting, eating, coffee drinking, joking, and gaming rituals among so many white- and blue-collar work groups in American organizations illustrates this. So one cannot say that group development always helps achieve management goals. In fact, it is only when certain specific variables are present that such activity will tend to become conscious and result in a group increasing its transactions with its environment (Clark, 1960/61, pp. 199–208; see also Barnes, 1960).

Intergroup Behavior

Reactive behavior on the intergroup level is seen when two groups increase their internal solidarity by facing each other, the "us" versus "them" pattern. An individual member of one of these groups feels good to the extent he feels more securely identified with his group as it is different from the other group. As an example, when a senator says to a large gathering of fearful and angry people in Los Angeles, as he did, "Make no mistake about it, the Communists are black and all black. There are no greys among them," he is behaving in such a way as to facilitate the clear-cut identification of one group against another. The bewildered and frightened people in his audience feel that they *are* something, and that something is "us" versus "them." Much of what is called "bickering" between different departments of an organization—the classic disputes between sales and production, for example—can be viewed as serving this same function.

Professor Robert Blake of the University of Texas has illustrated reactive intergroup behavior dramatically in his laboratory simulations of intergroup conflict. Among other things, he has shown conclusively that groups in problem-solving competition situations inevitably pick their own solution as rationally superior to others, even in the absence of any rational criteria for making the judgment. Such phenomena are also encountered at the United Nations or around any labor-management negotiation table.

Proactive behavior between groups occurs when members break through their group boundaries and set up give-and-take relations between their group and another. Thus new patterns of behavior and beliefs emerge which change the relation between the groups. This was seen in R. L. Katz and J. A. Seiler's study (1962) of the management organization in a 500-man firm, when individuals clearly emerged as linkers between groups. Of course, as expected, these linkers were almost never the people with the formal authority for relating the activities of the two groups. They emerged as the system matured, and they helped hold the total system together by relating its clearly differentiated subparts; and thus we are brought to the total organization.

Total Organizational Behavior

At the level of the total organization, great complexity enters the picture. Reactive behavior of a certain kind is easy to identify. For instance, the famous old Boston restaurant, Durgin Park, will not serve its renowned Indian pudding without ice cream, regardless of any customer's pleas to the contrary. The representatives of this organization feel rewarded when they perpetuate its age-old traditions, even in the face of customer derision, irritation, or withdrawal. The belief system of the organization thus reinforces itself against change from the outside.

The problem of analysis becomes complicated here, however, because much of what superficially looks like proactive behavior has a strong reactive component. That is, members of many organizations sense acceptance from their peers if they *talk* in terms of changing things through the use of stronger authority, firmer plans, clearer organization, an active anti-union program, or what not. On the face of it, one can't tell whether such talk serves primarily the function of reestablishing cherished belief around which the organization is held together, or of describing actual proactive behavior.

Such questions often require careful research to answer. So much talk about "inner directedness," for example, or "rugged individualism" takes on a different cast when one realizes the extent to which certain individuals get social satisfaction from others by conforming to certain accepted codes. That is, an individual often gains membership in a management group or club to the extent he professes to value rugged individualism.

Here are some instances of behavior which have had the function of reestablishing and underscoring shared beliefs and values held by the powerful figures in an organization, but which were ostensibly proactive.

The Case of the Too-Productive Crew

In one electronics company recently investigated by Melvin Steckler at Harvard (Lawrence, *et al.*, 1961, pp. 266–302), a small group of production girls was found to be contributing about 120 percent toward the profit of the firm. Because of an explicit action experiment by their foreman, these girls—most of whom had little formal education in general and none at all in electronics—were solving production and design problems which university professors and members of the company's engineering department couldn't cope with. Also, productivity was constantly increasing in the group, some 300 percent in two years, and they were not on an incentive system.

As might be expected, these girls had considerable freedom in their jobs. They designed and operated their own testing equipment; their maintenance man made and supervised their expense and supplies budget, which constantly showed a lower and lower percentage in relation to volume; they moved around a lot, traded jobs, and so forth.

After this had been going on for over a year, higher-ups could stand it no longer, and instituted proceedings to break up the activity. The foreman was promoted away from the group, a new engineer was imported from Europe to "straighten up the confusion in the department," etc. What an engineering executive said to the researcher shortly before these proceedings were launched is instructive. As we listen to him talk, we are hearing strong reactive sentiments, sentiment so strong they even overlook making money—another variable sometimes seen as rewarding by organizational members. Said the engineer:

> Dollarwise they're doing a pretty good job in here, as far as it goes, but they've got one overriding weakness in the way they are presently set up. Do you realize the girls do all their own testing in here? The same girls that make the tubes test them. It just isn't logical. Human nature isn't that way. You can't trust the same people who make something to also test it. It's not healthy.
>   . . . We've got plans in the works for taking on this place and really making it over. And when we do we'll see to it that the testing operations are carried on in a separate department. We'll really whip this operation into shape. . . . I'd like to make this a model showplace for the company. Right now its the worst in the company.
>   This place has never been under engineering control. That's the trouble with it. . . . Most of the product design changes that have been made have been developed and put into practice by the production people themselves. That's not good. . . . They design their own products; they alter and maintain their own production equipment and processes; and they are free to go off in all different directions at once. The first thing we would do if we could get hold of this room would be to put every operation under close engineering surveillance.

This engineer sounds proactive, but it is clear that the main underlying meaning of his behavior is to push back into shape a disequilibrium about which he feels deeply upset. Moreover, it is possible this disequilibrium is felt by him in many ways: as a threat to his knowledge and status, as a threat to the position of the engineering group in the company, as a violation of the status system in the company as a whole, and as a violation of the Western European culture's assumption about authority as appropriately flowing from "up" toward "down" through the vehicles of role incumbents (Miller, 1955, pp. 271–289).

The Case of the Speeding Assembly Line

Something similar was observed by Alex Bavelas in a toy factory on a paint line conveyor (Whyte, *et al.*, 1955, Ch. 10). There, a group of girls were allowed to control the speed of the conveyor on which they were working. They sped it up when they felt like working, and they slowed it down when they didn't. Productivity and earnings soared, and soared higher by far than that which the engineers had believed to be normal output.

Consequently, the engineers took the control of the line's speed away from the workers and restored it to a steady, predictable pace. The girls, apparently, had established an equilibrium of their own, for they all quit in protest. So did their foreman. As with the engineer in the electronics company, the belief of the management group that control of a technological process ought to move from the top down was reinforced, again to the exclusion of other beliefs, such as the goodness of high productivity.

These are instances of one of the most commonly encountered findings of organizational research. Time and time again, management groups in business and elsewhere enforce procedures designed to keep behavior in line with beliefs about what "ought to be" under the guise that they are usefully effecting task accomplishment. In the instances above, for example, actual task efficiency was sacrificed for order and congruence with management beliefs.

In summary, it is no accident that the conditions under which groups achieve high job involvement, high productivity, high creativity, high satisfaction, low absenteeism and low turnover are among the best-known findings in organizational behavior research and are perhaps those most ignored by managements. Of course this shouldn't surprise us, since the need of any behavioral system—individual, group, organizational, or what not—to maintain itself through time is almost always stronger than mere new knowledge. Anyone knows this who has tried to change another's mind through what he believes is logic.

Having underscored in this way the extreme difficulty of assessing the meaning of behavior from the point of view of the total organization, we must realize that classifying behavior as proactive is just as difficult as pegging reactive tendencies.

However, consciously conceived and executed expansion is certainly an instance. Reorganization which introduces new differentiation into the system is another. Other examples can be seen in the increasing variety of special interests of the modern, large corporations. They are relating themselves to their community and wider cultural contexts in an array of ways hardly considered a few decades ago.

Art exhibits, gifts to colleges, community relations programs, educational aids and the like are all examples of the variety of transactions being sought and achieved by corporations. It is true that most of these activities are spoken of as having an economic base in good public relations, but the fact that the environment puts such pressures on growing organizations may indicate that the wider social context expects such increasing transactions from a growing subunit. Be that as it may, many activities of these kinds have only the vaguest connection to the often allegedly superordinate goal of profit. Indeed, as Robert N. Anthony has pointed out (1960, pp. 126–134), most corporations today have ceased maximizing profit, and have done so because of their other transactional relations with the wider society.

What Is a Norm?

Having thus illustrated the different aspects of organizational behavior, let us now examine what is meant by a norm.

What is meant by a norm is a belief which a group of people act as if they hold, so that, if any person exhibits behavior which differs from the norm, the group will act to make the deviant person conform. By way of illustration, we might cite the situation of the Easterner who shows up at a Los Angeles swimming pool party dressed in a suit and tie. An elaboration of this event is instructive. Shortly after the Easterner's arrival the native members of this poolside group, both female and male, began to interact quite heavily with the deviant new member, making jokes about Easterners, expressing desires to someday see the new member in a sport shirt, making overtures of affection and welcome toward the new member, and even presenting him with the local costume, a sport shirt hastily borrowed from the oldest son of the host. The natives said that they wished to make the new member more comfortable this way.

The Easterner, remaining insensitive to the social meaning of the offering—to produce cohesion in the group—refused it, saying he was already comfortable, which was physically true. Thereafter, interaction dropped off sharply with the new member, an outcome predicted by S. Schacter's research on deviation (1951, pp. 190–207). (Subsequent research, by the way, indicates that in the future the Easterner and his mate are considering clothing themselves in native garments.)

The illustration chosen is perhaps trivial, but groups cannot exist without norms; human beings require affiliation for life, just as they require oxygen and water, and norm-breaking can be a serious thing. Anyone who doubts it might, to continue the illustration just cited, try going to an Eastern cocktail party dressed comfortably in a sport shirt.

One Healthy Organization

With this brief description of a norm and its function of maintaining a group, let us turn to some behavior in the Marshall Company, an organization studied by a group of field investigators from Harvard (Lawrence, *et al.*, 1961, pp. 634–692). It is one which illustrates my definition of a healthy organization, where members share norms such that they explicitly recognize the validity of the aspects of behavior in each of the areas shown in figure 1. They also work to resolve the inevitable conflicts that arise between these different aspects.

As I state the Marshall Company norms and then illustrate them with behavior, we shall see the extent to which the different aspects of behavioral systems seen in our diagram are legitimatized by the norms we encounter.

The norms surrounding training, development, promotion and transfer in the Marshall Company were most interesting. Members of the organization behaved as if they believed that "training occurs on the job and occurs when an individual asks questions and otherwise demonstrates a desire to know more about his work. Anyone in a superior position, including higher ranking production crew personnel, should give subordinates a chance to express their views on tasks and problems and allow them to help in areas of interest to them. A subordinate is not required to take initiative and to be eager to learn, though. It is acceptable in the Marshall Company for someone to stay on his present job until he decides he wants to retire."

A number of events were recorded by the field researchers which indicated the existence of such norms. For example, researchers observed the superintendent of the power machines both training and being trained as he went about his business. Once, a new and very complicated paper machine was starting up, a process which took several hours. During this time, the superintendent's superior, the production manager, stood in the background and watched, along with a crowd of workers from other parts of the plant, as well as several men who had come in on an off day to observe. During the start-up period, the superintendent said to the researcher: "He [the production manager] doesn't often say much to me when I'm starting up a machine. Later on, he will tell me things he thought might have been improved—even some of the little things. But now, he won't bother me."

The next day the men attempted to run paper through the machine. The superintendent observed a crew member—the "second hand"—climb up on the machine and try several times to thread new, wet paper into the press rolls. This was a difficult procedure and all gathered to watch. The man tried and failed a half dozen times, after which the superintendent placed his hand on the crewman's leg. The "second hand" immediately got down and the "first hand," who had been watching from a position near his own job, came over and climbed up. On his second try, he was successful. However, the paper started several times, but each time it broke within a few minutes. Once the superintendent himself fed the paper into the driers. Concerning the event with the "second hand," the superintendent said, "He's o.k. He just got a little nervous."

A few days after the machine had been operating, the researchers talked with a young foreman who was having a great deal of trouble with one part of the machine, although production was moving along steadily. The foreman could not solve the problem, and was often observed sitting by himself, staring at the floor. At one point he said, "I wish we had the old machinery back."

The researchers knew that the young foreman's progress in the company was well known to the production superintendent, who felt he had "brought him along" to be foreman. When the researcher, some days later, asked the superintendent about this particular technical problem, he learned that the superintendent had solved the problem mentally but hadn't yet told the young foreman about it. Grinning broadly, the superintendent said, "He's got enough to think about now, and there's no use trying to look too far ahead."

Why Training Really Worked

There were other instances of training practices among the men on the machines. For example, researchers observed a "second hand" on one of the paper machines helping a "third hand" temporarily perform the "second hand's" work. When asked about this, the "second hand" talked about how crewmen advanced at Marshall, saying:

> You really just learn by doing. You master your own job, and then you watch the next fellow working, and do as much as you can. . . . A good man will keep you busy answering his questions; and when he does that, you bring him along. Of course,

you've gotta keep learning so you know more than the other guys. . . . There's one fellow, he's no good. He came over from the other side [of the river dividing our plant here] during the war and worked up to be second hand. Now, guys are coming back from the service who know more than he does. Men under him are better than he is, but he gives orders and pretends to know more than anyone else. No one likes him.

In terms of my thesis, what are some of the significances of these various events? First of all, the ways in which individuals grow and learn are not violated by the norms that exist among the members of the Marshall Company. Men are rewarded by learning new tasks, but they are not pushed into such new behavior, except when the organization's proaction requires it, as it would in the case of the necessity for a faster or better machine, for example. Moreover, a man can choose not to learn any new tasks at all, and he will not be punished for it, so long as he doesn't prevent others from satisfying their proactive needs. Thus an individual's needs for reactive behavior are legitimate in the Marshall Company system.

Notice, too, that the behavior which must surround an individual's proaction becomes the content for group norms in the Marshall Company. That is, behavior which does not support individual proaction is reacted against by the group. These were the instances of deviation observed in our examples: the crew member reporting the social ostracism of the man who gives orders to and doesn't help the people under him, for example, or the superintendent's punishing the young foreman by withholding help and assistance, because the foreman had given up on the problem and not asked for help.

The company-wide codes support requesting and giving help after an individual has tried on his own. Notice that such codes foster reciprocity between groups (superior-subordinate groups, for example), thus encouraging intergroup proactive behavior, and also are functional at the level of the total organization, which needs both to have problems solved and to have problem solvers developed.

There is another manner in which these codes make legitimate the different aspects of organizational behavior. Notice that an individual must always ask for help, which places him in a subordinate position socially. But one of the basic aspects of elementary social behavior which holds groups together is the exchange of regard for help. At Marshall, the codes demand that not only should one ask for help from others whose knowledge is greater, but also one must give help to those who ask for it. Thus, this kind of social reciprocity, so vital to the continuation of social groups (as such authors as Alvin Gouldner [1960, pp. 161–178] and George C. Homans [1961, Chs. 3

and 4] have pointed out) is institutionalized in such a way as to meet both the proactive and reactive needs of individuals, groups, and the total organization. A truly remarkable social invention.

Work Groups Cooperate

There are other instances of such multidimensionally useful behavior in Marshall, and all of them are not built around training. For example, the researchers noticed how any emergency was met by everyone in the area with the relevant skills jumping in to help. As those familiar with paper making know, the machines are rarely stopped. If a break occurs, a mountain of waste forms almost immediately.

The norm here was stated when a researcher said to a crew member, "I'm interested in the way you fellows jump to the breaks. . . . The first fellow on the spot goes ahead." "Oh, sure, you have to," the crew member replied. "The thing is, you all have to work together. You can't just do your own job, you have to pull with the crew."

Here we see an instance of a group norm which is clearly useful to the group because technological failure is so obviously the responsibility of a given crew at a given time. The Marshall Company technology is such that social relationships are congruent with an identifiable task and form the basis for what E. L. Trist has called an effective "socio-technical system" (see Trist, 1960).

Although we cannot examine this extremely important point further here, there is evidence to suggest that when an organization designs a given technological task in such a way as to require an effective, separate social group for its performance, then the group responds by maintaining a high level of contribution to the organizational tasks (see Rice, 1953, and Miller, 1959, pp. 243–272; see also Trist, *et al.*, 1959). For example, at Marshall, the crews rarely used a fancy resting room facility the company had built since it would take them away from their constant surveillance of their machines. Also, recall how several members of the crews came in on a holiday to watch the start up of the new machine.

Departments Work Together

Although we could continue examining instances of Marshall Company norms and behavior for some time, we shall conclude with one more type. As is well known, the typical company is plagued with conflicts between groups within it. The way the Marshall Company social practices deal with this is extremely interesting. First of all, a person develops his own area of competence in the company. No organization chart exists. The real organization of the company is an ongoing creation of the members themselves.

People know who in the company is the person in charge of a

given interest, for example, the quality of special coated papers, or the purchase of pulp, or customer relations with the printing industry. People grow into these positions as their interests, and their developing competence allow, and no two "generations" of management personnel define these positions in quite the same way. That is, a person takes on a bundle of tasks in which he has interest and demonstrates competence.

There are several such people who interact frequently with the paper-making crews, and the norm of the organization is "When there are no conflicts between values or points of view, then an individual can contact a paper crew directly." No foreman, therefore, is offended when the quality control man lets his presence be known by his familiar red circle around some item on the "spec sheet" which is posted near a machine during any particular run. He knows that a visit has been made and that one or more of his men has likely been spoken to.

When there are interest conflicts in the company, the code is something like this: "Each of us has our special interest in one or another phase of our operation. We all know and respect the legitimacy of these special interests. We cannot force others to relinquish their interests to solve our problems. We must discuss and resolve conflicts with our peers."

An instance of this norm in operation occurred during the research when a machine was making paper too thick for a book-publishing customer's specifications. Since paper was scarce, the customer was reluctantly continuing to accept it, but some people at the plant were worried. Two executives—both concerned with aspects of quality—were discussing the problem. They first discussed running the paper on other machines, which could produce it correctly, but discovered that it would create almost insoluble problems for the scheduling office. They then thought of slowing the machine down, but rejected that since it would cut into the bonus of the production people and also because the tonnage for the month for the whole plant was a little behind projections. Next they considered changing the kind of pulp, but rejected that because other customers had already been promised paper requiring that sort of pulp. A decision was reached to let the situation alone for the time being—it was the lesser of several evils.

Notice the extent to which participants in this conversation considered the different legitimate interests in the organization. Is worker morale more important than total customer satisfaction? Is one customer's satisfaction more important than another's? Is better paper on one run worth slowing down production and consequent delivery of other orders, as would happen if machines were changed? These interests are all legitimate, of course, and somehow must be dealt with in any decision. Notice how this particular form of institutionally supported decision making explicitly dealt with intergroup reciprocity, as the two executives discussed the consequences for the different groups of each possible decision.

Is It Good Business?

Because the Marshall Company sounds so unusual, it may well be asked whether such an organization of people also meets the reactive needs of the organization to make money and satisfy stockholders as well as the proactive needs of the organization to change and advance. Concerning the first of these questions, the Marshall Company, some 14 years after the investigation discussed here, had a production growth rate 33 percent higher than the industry, a sales growth rate 30 percent higher, and a net profit to sales ratio 30 percent above the industry average. Return on invested capital compared even more favorably with the rest of the industry. And market value of common stock was up 900 percent a share. Concerning the second question, Marshall was regarded by the foremost supplier of instruments and electronic control devices for paper making as "one of the most progressive firms in the paper industry."

Summary

Thus we can see that the Marshall Company has norms which make legitimate the behavior of its members addressed toward the satisfaction of needs at all levels of affiliation—individual, group, intergroup and total organizational, and not simply needs for proaction, but maintaining, equilibrium-seeking, reactive needs as well.

Although space does not permit us to illustrate this further, it can be seen that I would not call any organization healthy which denied the legitimacy of any of these needs; which denied, for example, the needs of individuals to grow at their own pace, or the needs of small group social systems to develop and maintain themselves around tasks. I say around tasks, for without this important sociotechnical qualification, such social systems could develop no transactions with their environment, and they would develop only the internal differentiations seen so much in industrial research: betting, restriction of output, gaming, joking, excessive coffee breaks, etc.

Moreover, any organization which was set up only to meet the needs of individuals to grow, or to participate, or to be creative, or what not, and which did not consider the needs of people to form into groups, or of the total organization to engage in satisfactory transactions with outside groups such as stockholders or customers, cannot be considered healthy.

So many scientifically or humanistically oriented critics of large organizations make an unfortunate mistake in regard to this last point which hinders the progress they so earnestly seek. Such critics make the double observation that (1) an organization is different from other social groupings in that it has a formal purpose, and in that its members seek to guide their own behavior rationally to accomplish that purpose, and (2) that many organizations plan without knowledge of the needs of their various components. As a result, the critics maintain, we see the much-deplored stunted creativity of individuals, the alienation or senseless social behavior of group members, inefficient intergroup competition, and so forth.

But these are not necessary outcomes of planful activity. As Gilbert David (1955) and Paul R. Lawrence (1958, Ch. 10) have pointed out, there is nothing humanistically wrong with planning per se. It is planning without awareness of the individual, small group, and intergroup reactive and proactive needs that is scientifically and humanistically wrong, to say nothing of inefficient.

As I hope I have been able to demonstrate, one achieves the values of neither humanism nor efficiency if one maintains either value exclusively. It is my personal opinion that our capacity to understand and produce organizational health will develop only to the extent that we bring to it some kind of a multidimensional approach. Whether or not the present conception of the multidimensionality which is in the world appears fruitful is not important. What is important is that organizational investigators, management theorists, and administrators adopt some point of view large enough to include the other points of view which exist in any situation and which inevitably conflict with each other.

References

Allport, Gordon. "The Open System in Personality Theory." In *Personality and Social Encounter*. Beacon Press, 1960.

Anthony, Robert N. "The Trouble with Profit Maximization." *Harvard Business Review*, Vol. 38, No. 6, November–December 1960.

Barnes, Louis B. *Organizational Systems and Engineering Groups: A Comparative Study of Two Technical Systems in Industry*. Harvard Business School Division of Research, 1960.

———, and James V. Clark. "Lakeview Diary." Harvard University (unpublished case study), 1957.

Clark, James V. "Motivation in Work Groups: A Tentative View." *Human Organization*, Vol. 19, No. 4, Winter 1960/61.

———. "Businessmen vs. Behavioral Scientists: The Dynamics of Misunderstanding." Unpublished paper.

David, Gilbert. "Your Organization . . . in Sickness and in Health." *Leader's Digest* (Adult Education Association), No. 2, 1955.

Gouldner, Alvin. "The Norm of Reciprocity: A Preliminary Statement." *American Sociological Review*, Vol. 25, No. 2, April 1960.

Homans, George C. *Social Behavior: Its Elementary Forms.* Harcourt, Brace & World, 1961.

Katz, R. L., and J. A. Seiler. *Management Behavior: The Physiology of Organization.* Harvard Business School Division of Research, 1962.

Koontz, Harold. "The Management Theory Jungle." *Journal of the Academy of Management,* Vol. 4, No. 3, December 1961.

Lawrence, P. R. *The Changing of Organizational Behavior Patterns: A Case Study of Decentralization.* Harvard Business School Division of Research, 1958.

————, et al. *Organizational Behavior and Administration: Cases, Concepts, and Research Findings.* Irwin, 1961.

Miller, Eric J. "Technology, Territory, and Time." *Human Relations,* Vol. 12, No. 3, 1959.

Miller, Walter H. "Two Concepts of Authority." *American Anthropologist,* Vol. 42, No. 2, April 1955. Condensed and reprinted in P. R. Lawrence, *et al.,* 1961.

Rice, A. K. "Productivity and Social Organization in an Indian Weaving Shed." *Human Relations,* Vol. 6, No. 4, 1953.

Schacter, S. "Deviations, Rejection, and Communication." *Journal of Social and Abnormal Psychology,* Vol. 46, 1951.

Trist, E. L. "Socio-Technical Systems." Tavistock Institute of Human Relations Doc. 572, 1960.

————, G. Murray, G. W. Higgin, and A. B. Pollock. "Work Organization at the Coal Face." Tavistock Institute of Human Relations Doc. 506, 1959.

Whyte, William F., *et al. Money and Motivation.* Harper & Row, 1955.

Mason Haire

Organizations

In the last few years there has been a great increase—both in the United States and all over the world—in the number of firms that have new departments called something like Department of Organization Planning. This development is part of the growing recognition of the fact that the integration and effective direction of large groups of people have become primary tasks of management. The rise of these new departments also leads us to focus on a group of very simple questions intimately connected with the problem of organization in a company.

One of the simplest of these is surely, *"How do you tell a good organization plan when you see one?"* Presumably these departments spend their time preparing several alternative plans and then pick the best one. The interesting question is how to pick the best one. What things are we trying to maximize and what characteristics of the organization will do it? Beyond this, we might wonder how much it is going to cost us—in a variety of ways—to build one organization scheme rather than another. These thoughts lead us to wonder what it is we're trying to accomplish with the organization plan, anyway, and lead us to the second simple question, *"What are the objectives of the organization plan?"* Finally, as we raise this question, we're bound to wonder what things we have to work with in making organizations of different shapes to accomplish these objectives, and we're led to the third question, *"What is organized in an organization?"* These are three very basic questions that ought to be answered by anyone—at any level of management—who thinks about how to organize and manage his group, whether it is a whole company, a section, or a work gang.

The Objective of an Organization

A small group where almost everyone knows what everyone else is doing doesn't need much organization. It's when it becomes larger and more complex that the real need for an organization plan is felt. Then it seems essential to recapture some of the *unity* that was lost when the group enlarged and broke apart into smaller units. At the same time, it seems necessary to put some *order* back into the system. When everyone knew what everyone else was doing, lack of order wasn't so noticeable. As the group grows larger, however, it seems necessary to specify functions a little more precisely so that the whole plan will fit together neatly. Finally, it seems necessary to have some *information and control* so that management will have a system for keeping track of what each of the parts is doing. These three things —unity, order, and information and control—seem to be the major objectives of what might be called "classical" organization theory, and they seem to be the major tests for recognizing a good organization plan. "Does it give a good orderly pattern of the whole job to be done with the appropriate information and control to direct it?"

We've left something out, however, and it's something the organization planners often leave out. In addition to the order, unity, and control of the job to be done, we want the *group* to be unified. We want the integration, initiative, innovation, and cooperation of all the people in the organization. This is surely one of the things we want to organize in an organization. Very often, in the past, we seem to have brought order and unity into the job at the expense of the unity and initiative in the people who are doing the job. This becomes more and more expensive as time goes on. One of the things we need to remember when we ask, "What is organized . . . ?" is that we want to organize a group doing a job and not just the job. Because a good deal of organization thinking in the past has come from industrial engineers and accountants, the focus has tended to be on the work rather than the people.

A much simpler answer is often given to the question, "What are the objectives of the organization plan?" Often one says, simply, "The best plan is the one that makes the most profits." The simplicity of this is often deceptive, however. It depends on which things we choose to measure—and, importantly, which things we choose not to measure. We usually focus on those things which are easy to measure —budget and production data—and neglect those which are harder to measure—notably the human variables, the degree of integration in the group, the degree of initiative, the extent to which the company's objectives are widely shared throughout the group, and the like. These are valuable assets of the company. If the profits—in budget and production terms—are obtained at the expense of liquidating these assets, they are as unreal as profits obtained by failure to maintain plant and equipment or by the dissipation of any other capital resource.

If a manager takes over a plant, he can show a profit by not replacing raw-material stocks and by cutting down on the maintenance crew and expense. But he will surely be held accountable for these things and his profitable operation discounted as a result. On the other hand, he may take over a plant with a good spirit in the employees, a closely knit group, and a real awareness of the company's objectives. After a few years of profitable operation (in simple terms), he may leave a plant with hostilities and resentments in the work groups, with the employees split into factions or banded together against the company, and with little motivation to produce. He is not held accountable for this resource in the same way that he was for the physical assets. The change in the employees is ascribed to "the spirit of the times," "an act of God," or "outside agitators," and the manager gets sympathy for having had such a hard time. But surely the maintenance of these human assets is part of his responsibility, and one of the primary objectives of the organization plan must be to create human assets, encourage them, and keep track of them. No organization plan that sacrifices initiative in the interest of control can be wholly accomplishing its objectives. No simple measure of profitability that omits the cost to the reservoir of human assets can be a wholly adequate guide to management practice. High among the objectives of the organization is profitable operation in the long run. On the other hand, *the thing that is organized is the group doing the job.* To obtain order and control at the expense of the initiative of this group is not accomplishing the objective. One of the ways to recognize a good organization plan is to see the degree to which it orders and unifies the job and at the same time integrates the group and maintains its productive drive. Both areas must be provided for by the organization plan, and, for the plan to be an effective tool to help the manager get his job done, he must be given measures that indicate how well he's doing in each.

The Changing Spirit of The Times: The Concept of Authority

A business cannot operate in a vacuum, independent of the society in which it is imbedded. Business, as a social institution, is part of the society, and its policies and practices must reflect the values of the society. Questions like "How hard should a man work?" "How much of himself can we expect a man to invest in his job?" "What kind of punishments can a company use to direct behavior?" —the answers to all these and many other similar questions cannot be found entirely *within* the firm. They depend on the values of society and on how the people are willing to think of themselves. If a company's views on these issues are out of harmony with society's, it may find itself at a competitive disadvantage. Another company, whose philosophy fits better with the society's values and the employees' views of themselves, taps reserves of energy that are simply not available otherwise. In competitive terms, then, a sensitivity to company policy and societal values is essential. In broader terms, for all of business, it is even more pressing. The very freedom to manage depends on the harmony between managerial and societal values. If business drifts far out of line, its very freedom to manage its own affairs is at stake. What sort of values are these and how do they fit in with the problem of organization?

Winds of change are sweeping the world. They are modifying all our major social institutions—the state, the church, the educational system, the family. Colonialism is disappearing; new independent nations are growing. Wider and wider groups of citizens are being enfranchised to vote, and their standards of living and education are rising. Through all these changes the broad sweep of history seems clearly to be a progressive change in the role and value accorded to the individual—the Common Man. Business—a major social institution—has largely resisted this change and is organized in terms of concepts of man that were acceptable to man himself 50 years ago.

To see some of these changes, let us ask ourselves, simply, "Why do people do what they're told in a business?" We usually worry more about why they don't do what they're told, but reversing the question will lead us into some of the problems of the changing concept of authority. In general, the answer to the question is that this is part of the implicit contract when a man takes a job. He contributes his skills and effort; the boss contributes the plant and equipment and the pay. The boss owns the plant—or at least represents the owners. When he says "Do it!" there is an implicit "or else"—and that "or else" is "Do it or get off my property!" (or, more recently, "the property I manage for the owner"). We are used to thinking of authority in an industrial organization as being in this way ultimately based in the rights of ownership. The authority to direct with respect to the use of property is one of the rights of property. The authority of the manager comes ultimately from the owner, vested, through the medium of the board of directors, in the president of the company and passed on down by him for day-to-day operation.

This view of the ultimate source of authority is intimately connected with general societal views regarding property rights which have set so many of our moral and legal positions as to what's right and wrong. We've had this particular pattern of thinking for so long that it seems eternal and inevitable. However, this hasn't always been true, and this particular belief seems to be undergoing radical change right now with tremendous implications for business organization.

The primary importance of property rights as a source of authority in business probably began about the time of the Industrial Revolution. Before that, the ultimate source of authority was the state. After the Roman conquests, businesses operated in the conquered territories as concessions. Managers set prices, wages, working conditions, and the like. But they did this with authority granted to them by the state, and it was the state that had to be satisfied with their operation. In return, the state guaranteed (and sometimes delivered) an orderly, safe world in which to do business. Since, in this period, protection was the main requisite, the state, which provided it, was the ultimate source of authority. It isn't necessary to go all the way back to the Roman Empire to see this happening. The British East India Company was a clear example of such a commercial operation depending on the state for protection and power. In extreme cases "gunboat diplomacy"—a show of force making it possible to do business safely—persisted into the twentieth century.

In general, however, except for colonial operations, the need for protection diminished as an orderly society was established. Both in business and in society in general, authority shifted from a coercive authority based on strength to a kind of formal authority working through explicit and implicit contracts resulting from the acceptance of a more ordered society. At about this time, in business, a new force appeared. In the Industrial Revolution, with the growth of machinery and production processes, capital was required to found and pay for the new plants. Taking the state's protection and an ordered society for granted, in the period when capital formation was the most pressing problem, the owner became the source of authority. The "rights of property" became important moral and societal values, and the authority of the manager stemmed ultimately from ownership.

This situation is no longer as true as it once was. In business the *source* of authority is shifting from ownership to the process of management itself. Recently we hear more about "the law of the situation" and the "imperatives of the logic of management." The necessity for a given action seems to flow more and more from the fact that it is the appropriate thing to do. The reason for doing it is grounded in the appropriateness of the action itself, and the authority of the manager, when he says, "Do it," comes less from the fact that he represents the owner than from the fact that the subordinate sees (or has faith) that it is the appropriate thing to do. In this way the force behind the manager's authority becomes grounded in the demands of the job and in the process of management itself.

A group of particular developments have been part of this change, and they have so modified the corporation as a social institution that they are worth looking at in a little detail. The rise of ownership as a source of authority was associated with the problems of capital formation itself. Two progressive changes have been especially important in separating the owner and manager and in diminishing the role of ownership as a source of authority. One of them is the widespread ownership of common stock. As the owners of a company become numbered in the thousands and hundreds of thousands, the "owner" becomes an impersonal, unidentifiable thing. Many company presidents would agree privately—though for obvious reasons it wouldn't be a good thing to say publicly—that the stockholders and the board of directors have nothing to do with day-to-day management. The relationship becomes a simple financial one. Management manages as it sees fit and tries to pay enough dividend to keep the stocholders quiet. Without making it explicit, we are moving to a position in which ownership as such carries with it no right to a voice in management. This separation of the owner and manager, with the focus on the manager's managing, is part of the change that led the source of authority to be grounded in the process of management itself.

The second financial development associated with this separation of owner and manager has been the tendency—since the end of World War II—to finance expansion and product diversification out of retained earnings. The manager no longer goes to the "owner" for new money. Even capital changes are proposed by management in solving management problems and are financed out of the fruits of past management. The owner is largely left out of the decision and is paid off in appreciation of his equity. This internal solution of the problem of capital growth moves further toward placing the source of authority in the process of management. It has another important effect that amounts, in many ways, to a really revolutionary change in the corporation as a social institution. The corporation is cut off from the traditional community check on its practices. In simple, classical, free-enterprise economics, the community can give or with-hold approval of corporate growth and product change. As the pro-posers of change go to the money markets, the community can veto the development by withholding funds. The tendency to finance out of retained earnings cuts the corporation off from the community, and thereby it becomes much more of an autonomous social institution. It forces management to develop a broad social responsibility, as part of management philosophy, and both the breadth and the autonomy put more weight inside the corporation on the process of managing.

One other—nonfinancial—development contributes to the proc-ess: the rise of the professional manager. One of the meanings of "professional" in this sense is that the manager feels himself to be a member of a broad horizontal group of managers of many companies rather than the narrow vertical group represented by the company itself. He tends to manage in ways that he thinks other managers would approve of—part of the development of feeling that he belongs to a professional group—rather than focusing entirely on the owner's approval. He feels that his management skills are not restricted to the one company. They are not narrowly related to the particular product or process but, since the process of management extends across companies, are general to the operation of a business. The source of authority is further split off from the owner and more closely tied to management itself.

Finally, in the years immediately after World War II, most companies operated in a tight labor market. Employees came to feel that they could get another job just as good around the corner. In this situation the force of the direction, "Do it or else," was greatly dimin-ished when the "or else" meant "get off the property." As this form of authority diminished, managers had to find other ways to enlist cooperation and direct behavior. They tended to find it in the logic of the production process, in what was clearly "good management." The "Do it" became more often "Do it because it is clear (or you can trust me) that it is the thing that has to be done."

All these things work in the same direction. They cut the source of authority off from ownership and move it further inside the com-pany to the process of management. This internalization of the source of authority is a continuation of the long historical process. When authority was grounded in the state, it rose from something wholly apart from business. As ownership became important, it moved closer, and the grounding in management takes it further inside. It seems likely that we are still in a process of evolutionary change in this development. The ultimate source of authority is moving further and further inside the company to the point where it is grounded in the work groups—at all levels of the organization. It becomes a kind of "consent of the governed." The authority that leads to compliance with the "do it" directive moves to the willingness of the groups themselves. It depends on the integration of the group, the degree to which the objectives of the company are widely shared, and the mutual confidence and trust within all the groups in the organization.

As this happens, as the source of authority moves inside to the work group, a very different situation develops. As McGregor puts it, the ultimate management control becomes self-control—widely spread throughout all the members of the organization. This self-control depends on their commitment to the organization, and the commitment, in turn, depends on their integration into it. The primary problem of the manager—and one of the first requisites of the organization—becomes that of securing and maintaining this integration and commitment upon which effective functioning depends. This development carries with it many specific requirements for the organization, and we shall go into them a little later. First, it is necessary to see a little more of the change in the social context of the corporation and the changing demands that are put on the organization. We leave this first line of change at the point where we see the source of authority in an organization being progressively internalized until it finally arises from all the work groups in the company.

The Changing Spirit of The Times: The Concept of Man

It is impossible to frame a plan of organization without making some assumptions about the nature of man. We have suggested that classical organization theories tended to organize the work rather than the work group. Even so, since people do the work, it was necessary to make some assumptions about people to suggest how the work they do could and should be organized. One great difficulty is that these assumptions about people are almost entirely implicit. We very seldom bring them out where we can examine them. The result is that we operate with a powerful theory about the nature of man. without ever evaluating whether it is an adequate theory. It is, of course, important to be aware of and to evaluate the ideas on which our policies are based. In this case it is particularly so since the concept of man which is acceptable to society—to man himself—is in the process of change. As standards of living and education rise, job security increases, political freedom and economic independence grow, man's view of himself changes. A theory of organization built on an unacceptable view of man will be much less than maximally effective. It can seriously handicap a firm (or a country) in competition with another organized on principles that the members can readily accept.

Let us look a little at the traditional pattern of organization and see what we can infer from it about the implicit ideas concerning the nature of man on which it is based. Most organization plans have been built on a model that comes from a combination of accounting and industrial engineering. They break the total job down rationally into separate boxes—job descriptions—which are hung on a kind of family tree. Neatness and control are maximized. The job-description boxes are clear and explicit to provide an overview, and they don't overlap; thus there will be a minimum of conflict in the system. A certain amount of authority is put into each box and a certain amount of responsibility is expected out to balance it. Great attention is paid to the detection and control of error. Information systems are built—primarily using budget and production data—to provide a constant check on error and an immediate opportunity to correct it. The parts of the organization exist because one part can't do all the work. Each additional box, consequently, represents a kind of "extra pair of hands" to help get the job done. Usually the job is described so that as little more as possible is demanded of the individual than the extra pair of hands. The people who fill these boxes are assumed to be relatively homogeneous and relatively stable. If we can simplify the job so that anyone can do it, it's easier to hire new people. Once we fill a box, the ideal is to have the man stay there; moving will only upset the system. The traditional organization is essentially centralized and its integration depends chiefly on the authority and control of the central mechanism.

Here, in very brief—and slightly caricatured—terms are some of the main characteristics of a traditional organizational plan. Taking these for a start, what kind of man must they have been designed to utilize? Several things stand out. First, the system is designed to use a man who is essentially lazy—one for whom inactivity is the goal. To deal with this, a careful pattern of incentive, prods, and measures of activity is provided. All of them are external to the person. As little as possible is left to his own initiative and self-starting. The system also assumes that he is shortsighted—not only won't he do anything unless he has to; he won't see that it ought to be done. Consequently, supervision tends to tell him exactly what to do. Self-direction is minimized as well as self-starting. Because they're somewhat narrowly focused on self-interest, rewards, job descriptions, and information are all as immediate and as closely related to the person as possible. He is apt to make mistakes; an error control system is essential. His judgment is poor; judgmental decisions are kept to a minimum.

Here, a little overdrawn—but not very much—are the characteristics of people which can be inferred from the main dimensions of traditional organizations. These aspects of the system wouldn't be put in if we didn't believe people had these characteristics. The policies and practices of the organization are built as safeguards against the assumed qualities of the people who make up the pool from which we draw employees. They are lazy, selfish, shortsighted, liable to error, and are poor decision makers. If we are to use them, we must build a system that allows for these qualities and protects the company against them.

In describing these characteristics, we have said "they" are like this. By "they" we mean, of course, "other people than myself." We tend to see other people as having these characteristics but not ourselves. This is a specific phenomenon of the problem of perceptual organization mentioned in earlier chapters. Our organization of the world may be very different from theirs. Yet as organization planners we often build an organization based on our perceptions and force "them" to work in it. A study done at the University of Michigan illustrates this problem within a company (see Table 1). Workers were asked to rate how important various things were to them on the job. Then their foremen were asked to make the same rating they thought the men would do for themselves. In this way we can see the men's self-perception and the foreman's perception of them. Next the foremen were asked to rate the same items for themselves. Now we can see how their perceptions of themselves differed from their perception of their subordinates. Finally, the general foremen were asked to make the rating the way they thought their foremen had done it and then to do it for themselves.

The three sets of ratings of these things for themselves—by the workers, foremen, and general foremen—were very much the same pattern. On the other hand, in each case the superior's estimation of how his subordinates felt about things was widely different from the subordinate's own. The two groups of superiors tended to see the same things in their subordinates (but not in themselves). In general, socially good traits—interest in the job, willingness to work hard, getting along with others, etc.—were seen as important to one's self but not to the other. If these people were to plan an organization, a quite different system would have to be built to take care of "the others" than of one's self. The difficulty is that who "the others" are depends on where you ask the question. The organization question is usually asked at a medium-high staff level. "The others" tend to be mainly the hourly paid workers and lower levels of management. They are seen as fairly pedestrain people with rather ignoble motives and serious flaws in judgment and initiative. Consequently an organization plan is built to take care of them; a very different plan would be built to take care of "people like me."

Much of this difference in the superior's perception of himself and his subordinates comes from an earlier era. At a time when there was a big difference in the educational level, standard of living, and social situation of managers and workers—and even between top (owner) managers and lower levels of management—this view was more useful. When a man was more nearly born into a class and level of work, his initiative to do more was less. When he went to work with very much less education than his boss, his ability to use broad information and see general company objectives was much more limited. When his job security and standard of living were such that his constant primary worry was narrowly focused on self-interest, his breadth of vision was less. None of these things is as true today. The error involved in seeing "the others" as essentially different from "people like me" gets bigger and bigger. As these changes in society change the way people are willing to see themselves, several things happen to organizations based on outmoded assumptions about the nature of people. In the first place, the organization fails to take advantage of the initiative, innovation, and commitment that is available and doesn't utilize the productive force the company has. In the second place, "the others," sensitive to a discriminatory demeaning estimation of themselves, develop a positive resentment of the system and the people who framed it. Finally, organizations tend to create men in their own image. If we treat men as if they are lazy, selfish, and shortsighted, they tend to behave that way. Short-term goals, narrow objectives and information, restrictive job descriptions all tend to produce the kind of behavior the practices are based on. The theory becomes self-validating, and the possibility of seeing more creative contributions to the company becomes less and less.

What would we do differently in an organization based on another concept of man? Suppose we assume that "the other" is essentially like me. In general terms, we would build an organization that used not just terms, we would build an organization that used not just the extra pair of hands, but the initiative, innovation, and judgment of the individual. It would maximize participation. . . . It would create an atmosphere where there is a freedom to make mistakes. While maintaining the necessary safeguards against error, it would permit the individual to try things, to learn, and to take risks. Such a system would assume man to be highly modifiable, and the growth and development of the members of the organization would be one of its major objectives. The integration in a structure of this type

Table 1 What Subordinates Want in a Job Compared with Their Superiors' Estimates

	As men	As foremen		As general foremen	
	Rated the variables for themselves	Estimated men would rate the variables	Rated the variables for themselves	Estimated foremen would rate the variables	Rated the variables for themselves
Economic variables:					
Steady work and steady wages	61%	79%	62%	86%	52%
High wages	28	61	17	58	11
Pensions and other old-age-security benefits	13	17	12	29	15
Not having to work too hard	13	30	4	25	2
Human-satisfaction variables:					
Getting along well with the people I work with	36%	17%	39%	22%	43%
Getting along well with my supervisor	28	14	28	15	24
Good chance to turn out good-quality work	16	11	18	13	27
Good chance to do interesting work	22	12	38	14	43
Other variables:					
Good chance for promotion	25%	23%	42%	24%	47%
Good physical working conditions	21	19	18	4	11
Number of cases	2,499	196	196	45	45

Source: "Human Relations on the Shop Floor" by Robert L. Kahn. *Human Relations and Modern Management*, ed. E. M. Hugh-Jones. 1958. North-Holland Publishing Company, Amsterdam.

would come from a feeling of membership, mutual confidence and trust, shared objectives, commitment, and one group of job skills necessary to operate it. The organization would be, in its essential character, decentralized. Before we go on to deal with specific aspects of such an organization, we should notice that the assumptions about the nature of man underlying it fit much better with the big societal change in the role of the individual and the individual's view of himself.

An Organization Structure Based on The Human Group

What would the organization be like? The older form was based on a model that grew out of accounting and industrial engineering. It organized jobs and money. A newer form would aim to organize people doing jobs and would be built on the model of the group. Likert has described it well in his book *New Patterns of Management*. The illustrative organization chart which appears in Figure 1 is taken

Figure 1   **The Overlapping Group Form of Organization. Work groups vary in size as circumstances require, although they are shown here as consisting of three persons (Rensis Likert, *New Patterns of Management*, McGraw-Hill, 1961).**

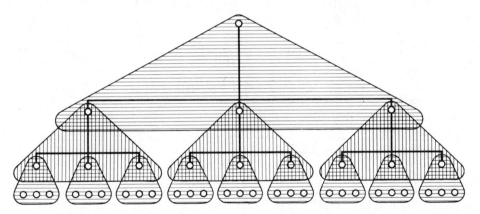

from him. In its basic structure it looks very much like the conventional family-tree type of chart. The important difference is the groups that link the levels throughout the organization. These are the "work groups" of which we have spoken. They are groups not only at the level of the hourly paid worker but at all levels through the structure. They are what tie the organization together.

In practice, this structure has some real implications. One set of them appears in the job of the superior at every level of the hierarchy. His first responsibility is to make sure that a group does, in fact, exist, following the diagrams illustrated on the chart. His second responsibility is to make sure that he is a member of the group. It very often happens that a man's subordinates form a closely knit group, part of whose defining character is that the boss isn't a member of it. This kind of development tends to create a series of autonomous little cliques not integrated into the company's objectives, whose group structure lends strength only to factionalism or to counter company policies. If there is no group, we have a series of individuals without integration. If there is a group and the superior isn't a member, we get factionalism and organized resistance. Consequently the superior's first two jobs are to see that a group exists and that he is a member of it.

The third job—and one of the defining characteristics of the superior at all levels—is to see that he is a member of the group above him—the group in which he is a subordinate. It also often happens that strong, almost impenetrable, horizontal layers develop in the company. This occurs when the superior creates a group below him and belongs to it but not to the one above him. He often does this by saying, essentially, "I know it's a silly rule, but *they* say we have to do it." This technique of joining the group below by fostering or approving a common rejection of the group above is seductive and attractive. On the other hand, it makes the organization of the whole structure completely impossible. The horizontal layering makes communication difficult and impedes any sharing of objectives between levels. This creation of an impersonal "they" to blame for things we don't like is also often supported by higher levels. In the absence of good vertical integration, higher levels tend to take the position, "They don't understand what we're trying to do." Thus each group is equipped with a comfortably inclusive "we" to belong to and an impersonal unconnected "they" on whom the blame can be shifted. This layering of the structure is probably the commonest fault in organizations. It occurs when the supervisor has not assured himself of his three basic functions: creating a group, being sure he's a member, and being a member of the group above. Each of them is important, of course. Together they make up what Likert has called the "linking-pin" function of the supervisor's job—being simultaneously a member of the groups above and below him.

Notice that a large part of the job of each member of the organization has already been specified without saying anything about what he is supposed to do in terms of product or process. It is in this sense that the organization is designed to organize people so that they can do a job, rather than to organize a job that has been rationalized and fragmented into bits in job-description boxes. Once this first group-structure step in the organization is assured, the job content and managerial practices fit naturally, as we shall see later. Unless the group is built, however, the job itself is not a very effective medium for integration.

The task of building this group structure is by no means easy. The company may need to stand ready to provide specialized training to help accomplish it. Everyone in the organization, as has been pointed out before, needs not only job skills to do the work, but group skills to make the organization work. In this latter area particularly we may need some special help. We probably need to provide some training in group leadership and in group membership. Most companies are used to leadership training but not to membership training. We used to think that leadership was a quality that was born in the person. Now we realize that we can and must develop it where it is needed. Similarly, most of us feel that we know how to be group members. Haven't we been members of a variety of groups all our lives? However, the task of being a good group member is not easy and cannot be taken for granted. It is possible to train people to become sensitive to the role they habitually take in groups—the silent-summer-up-later, the "let's define our terms" obstructionist, the you-go-your-way-I'll-go-mine isolate, and a host of others. It is also useful to see the action of specific behaviors on such things as group-building processes, objective setting, morale raising, and the like. Considerable help can be provided in these areas of group building and group membership. In addition, the company, to implement a good organization plan, must support it with training.

Beyond these tasks, the group leader has some other responsibilities that begin to come closer to the actual work of the company. First, he has built the group, and it is partly from this integration that the commitment comes. However, the commitment must be to goals and activities as well as just to the group. Now the "linking-pin" function becomes important in action. Between the two levels the leader carries the information and objectives until he can assure himself that he has widely shared objectives in the group below him and that they fit into the objectives he shares as a member of the group above him. As a leader of a group he takes part in setting objectives, making plans, and considering possibilities. As a member of the higher group he reports these goals and capabilities there. Here, too, he takes part in setting objectives—realistically, now that he represents the agreed capabilities and goals of his subordinates. He shares this information with the higher group and also information which the leader has brought—in a similar process—from still higher groups. Finally, he reports all this back to his own group to share the information there and, if necessary, reset their objectives. The new objectives will have been suggested above in the light of known expressions from the lower group and the modifications will be accepted only to the extent that they fit the group's own knowledge of its capabilities, the information it has, and its own objectives. This ability of the lower group to influence the upper group's decisions and policy making is an essential and will be discussed further in the next section.

The leader performs this "linking-pin" function of going back and forth between groups, carrying information both ways, and resetting objectives at both levels a dozen times a week or a day. With all this to do—build a group, belong to another, run back and forth between the two of them—one is tempted to say, "But when is he ever going to get his job done?" The answer to that is clear: This *is* his job. In discussing leadership, we pointed out that the superior is in a superior position because he is responsible for more work than one man can do. That's why he has subordinates to help him get it done. His job is not to do the work but to create a situation such that they will help him to get it done. This is a good description when we are discussing the individual's leadership role. When we turn to the organization problem and the task of fitting each leader and his group into the complex whole, it is just this "linking-pin" function that *is* his job. This is what creates the fabric of organization. This is what is organized—not the job. The structure is provided in this way to carry job content and information about the work up and down. The organization is in the group, not the job. The organization of the group makes the job possible.

The Human Group Model: Expanding Influence

In discussing the "linking-pin" function, we spoke of the fact that the lower groups influence the objective setting and policy making of higher groups. It is time to go into that in a little detail now. The point is clearly related to one we brought up earlier—the changing concept of authority and the tendency for the ultimate source of authority to be grounded in the work group. It is just this kind of work group that was meant and the operation of the authority depends on an extremely important principle: *The amount of influence a superior has with his subordinates depends on the degree to which they can influence him.* Put differently, it means you can't have any influence down unless you can influence up. The influence—or authority —comes from the mutual confidence and trust of the group, their shared information and objectives, and their integration and commitment. This comes because the subordinates *did* have the information and took part in setting the objectives, because they *are* a group and the leader is a member. He has confidence in them, as group members, to take part in setting and carrying out objectives. They have confidence in him—in his role as member of the higher group—to carry up the information about their capabilities and willingnesses and goals and to fit them into the objectives set at that level. Unless he can do this—and unless he can take part in and influence decisions at that level—he can't operate effectively at the lower level. He loses his ability to influence his subordinates if he can't influence his superiors. In that case he would have to fall back on coercive authority and the threat of dismissal, and the initiative of the group and the strength of the organization would be lost. The key to the successful operation of the organization is exactly in the linking-pin. It must be a two-way channel for influence as well as for information.

One somewhat startling and important phenomenon develops out of this kind of authority. There is reason to believe, from recent studies, that the total amount of authority in the system is capable of being expanded. The amount of influence is not a finite pie, to be divided up into appropriate slices, but can be increased. Conferred authority—the kind that is bestowed upon a job in the traditional organization—is necessarily limited in the total amount. The other kind of authority—of which we have been speaking—is accorded to the leader by the group. They can give more or less of it, and he can make much more authority than can ever be given to him by the centralized head. This has important implications for organization structure and practice. One of them is to allay the fears of the person who is afraid that giving his subordinates a participative voice in decision making and objective setting amounts to an abdication of his job. On the contrary, it becomes clear that giving the subordinates more opportunity to influence the superior actually *increases* the degree to which he can influence them. Not only do you have no influence down if your subordinates have no influence up, but, in general, the more they can influence you, the more you can influence them.

This has another important aspect for the size of the growing organization. One of the sticking points in growth is always the decentralization of authority. When we think in terms of a traditional concept, with conferred authority flowing from a centralized head, there is a real limit on expansion. When the authority stems from ownership and is vested in the chief executive officer through the medium of the board, it is a finite amount. The big boss is given the authority to manage. As he gives out subsidiary concessions to manage parts of the company lower down, he breaks off a piece of his original authority and confers it on the decentralized responsible man. At the same time, in such a system, he must retain enough of his original authority to keep a kind of majority voting control. In a sense, he has to keep 51 percent of the total authority. As the job is further decentralized, similar small chunks of authority are broken off and passed down, always keeping an overriding amount of authority at each higher level. Eventually, a real limit to possible expansion occurs when the amount that must be retained is so great and the amount that can be passed down is so small that further decentralization is impossible. The limit to growth comes from the finite initial authority, the necessity of keeping working control, and the idea of conferred authority. On the other hand, if the authority arises from the work group and is capable of expansion, the limits to growth disappear or recede into the far distance.

This description slightly restates the limitation on growth suggested by the economic theory of the firm. There, usually, the suggestion is that diminishing returns occur with growth because—owing to the triangular shape of the organization—there is only one man at the top of the company. He is a finite commodity in the company, but because the industry may have a large number of similar competing companies, their chief executives may be a virtually infinite commodity. Consequently, a single firm will feel the pinch of overloading the top officer while all the other, smaller firms spread the load among their many heads. Thus the diminishing return from increased size comes from the finite scope at the top of any one firm. Usually this finite commodity at the top is described as the decision-making capacity of the chief executive officer. When this is fully occupied, further growth leads to diminishing returns. But surely he can delegate decision making to subordinates as long as he retains an integrated organization with shared objectives and information. If his influence can be expanded to embrace the larger system, the point of diminishing returns with growth can be pushed further and further ahead.

One more point arising from this expanding authority seems worth a moment's notice. The basic idea is that if one gives up some of his formal authority by allowing subordinates to influence him, his total influence is not diminished thereby but actually increased. The same thing seems likely to be true in relations between groups. If one group joins a group or groups and gives up some of its independent authority to make decisions, it is not necessarily impoverished by the process. Its influence may, similarly, be increased. Nations which avoid multinational organizations in the interest of preserving sovereignty seem to be hoarding the same kind of finite conferred authority at the expense of an increasing authority accorded by the group. Companies that insist on "going it alone" seem to represent another expression of the same view of a unilateral authority that comes from concentrating on what you have rather than the kind that arises from the consent of the governed. The ramifications of this kind of view of the organization and its processes are remarkably broad.

Specific Differences in The Two Views
of Organization Authority and Responsibility

In more specific terms, what kind of things would happen differently in such an organization? A good many. First, the changed view of authority immediately comes in contact with one of the most frequently repeated old wives' tales in organization theory: the idea that authority should be commensurate with responsibility. A whole group of problems seems to arise on this issue. First, the statement requires a special, outmoded view of both authority and responsibility. Second, there seems no reason to insist on the equivalence of authority and responsibility. Third, it seems virtually impossible to maintain the equivalence in practice. Fourth, it seems an unnecessary hangover from the accounting tradition in organization theory. Finally, it comes into sharp conflict with some other sacred cows in organization jargon. Let us look at each of these points.

The statement that authority should be kept commensurate with responsibility (or vice versa) is almost always found in textbooks on management and organization. *Why* it should be so is not explained. It seems to be one of those myths that is repeated so often that it is unquestioningly accepted without inquiring about the reason. In no other sphere of one's life is authority commensurate with responsibility. Why should it be so in business? The citizen's responsibility far exceeds any authority he has. So does the neighbor's, the church member's—almost every group to which we belong. Perhaps clearest of all is the parent's case. His authority seems to be least just when his responsibility is most. Why, in this one special case, should the two be so carefully balanced? The argument seems to be that it is not right for a man to be responsible for something over which he has no authority. But it is just here that the special meaning of the two terms seems to arise.

If by "responsibility" one means that a man is completely answerable for the success or failure of an operation—that he will be blamed if it does not accomplish the objective—then, to protect himself, he must limit the responsibility he accepts to those things over which he has a direct and immediate control. But this narrow sense of responsibility cannot be the kind of thing we hope every member of the organization will feel. Surely we want him to feel a responsibility for broad objectives and general goals of the organization. We want him to feel responsible for creativity and innovation and things that were never described in his job. We want him to feel responsible for doing all he can to accomplish the objectives—not to feel that he can safely accept responsibility only for those things that can surely be done. Narrow responsibility shows up often in practice (and at great expense) when someone says, "I did what I was told; if it wasn't the right thing, it's not my fault." "That's his job; the reason I didn't do it is because I'm not supposed to." These attitudes cost companies immense (and unaccounted) sums in things not done or not done right because they're "not my responsibility." This meaning of the term "responsibility" is a long way from the feeling of general commitment to the organization which is a major goal. The narrow definition is part of a long tradition of evading responsibility by circumscribing responsibility that stretches from Pontius Pilate washing his hands of Christ's sentence because it was taken out of his jurisdiction to the generals who explained away war crimes by saying they only did what they were told. We can't afford narrow responsibility in a company or in a society.

A special meaning is necessary for "authority," too. Only formal conferred authority can be graded and defined in these measured units. The authority that arises from the group may be increased tremendously by leadership practices. Much more influence is available in the service of discharging responsibilities as one uses the personal authority that arises from his membership in the group and from their shared objectives. Just as the narrow definition of responsibility worked against organizational goals, the narrow definition of authority unnecessarily commits the organization to a specific and less than ideal concept of authority.

Beyond the limitations in authority and responsibility that the balance principle gets us into, there is the problem of how to do it. How do you make authority equal to responsibility? If he has more responsibility he should have more authority. How much more? In what kind of units should the authority be measured to tell us how much more authority should be given? These questions seem impossible to answer. Suppose a salesman has a given territory and, initially, presumably an authority commensurate to this responsibility. Better transporation and better communication make it possible to handle a bigger territory. He has more responsibility, so he should have more authority. But how much more? Well, first we need to know how much more he is responsible for. How do we measure it? The geographical size of his territory? The dollar volume he gets or the dollar volume he could get? The number of customers or the potential number of customers or the amount of competition he has to face? It seems very difficult to compute the quantitative increase in responsibility in order to fix the appropriate amount of authority that must be added.

The authority is easier to handle, at least on the surface. We are used to the idea of commitment authority. Such a level has the authority to commit so and so much money without prior review at a higher level. Now if we want to double authority we have at least a convenient scale for measuring amounts. We just double the number of dollars he can commit. However, this authority to spend is, we hope, a very small part of the authority he uses in doing his job. The rest is left untouched. Moreover, every experienced manager knows how to go beyond the intended authority by repeated commitments. On both sides of the equation the calculus seems virtually impossible.

The idea of the balance in the first place seems to have come from accounting practice, from the desire for a neat, orderly system, and from a desire to keep most of the drives in the system external to the individual. If we can give him authority and responsibility, we retain control at the top and we know at any moment how much there is anywhere. If he can expand (and contract) his feeling of responsibility depending on managerial practices, it is much less neat and arouses much more anxiety. Now the top manager is responsible not only for running the company, but for the very feeling of responsibility that his subordinates have. Similarly with authority: if the subordinate manager can increase his personal authority be the way he handles his work group, we need a quite new measure to know how the system's functioning. It is no longer the neat circumscribed structure we drew on paper. The accountants had set up a nice double-entry bookkeeping system that doesn't work any more. They drew authority from the top and put it into the subordinate's job. They expected responsibility from him in return and they credited it to the general company account. If the subordinate increases the authority and responsibility he has, it's as bad as printing more money; the books will never balance. This kind of input-output accounting model may be a good way to keep track of cash flow, but it's a poor system for regulating the operation of a human group where the variables are drives and commitments rather than dollars and cents. These are properly psychological variables and as such they arise from within the individual; they are not put in from outside in nicely measured amounts. The task of the organization plan is to create a situation that will nourish and expand these drives, not to circumscribe them unnecessarily and unrealistically.

Finally, if we persist in maintaining the commensurate character of authority and responsibility, we must eventually deal with that other hoary old institution in organization mythology: the separation of staff and line. In its frequency of repetition in textbooks, it is probably second only to authority and responsibility. It is constantly repeated that the staff's function is to provide advice and support to the line. It persuades on the basis of its expertness in its specialized function. It has no authority to put its point of view into practice. The authority belongs to the line—the "line authority." If we put these two notions together we reach a strange conclusion. If the staff has no authority and we maintain a balance between authority and responsibility, surely it follows that the staff has no responsibility! But no organization plan ever envisaged this. We just keep the two concepts simultaneously by maintaining them in logic-tight compartments while we think about the organization.

Again, the problem seems to be in what we mean by "authority" and "responsibility." The staff's persuasiveness arose from its expert understanding of its specialized function and its ability to point out that if we want a certain goal we must take certain actions to reach it.

The line, on the other hand, had the "do it or else" authority. But the staff's persuasiveness arising out of expert knowledge sounds more and more like the line manager's "law of the situation." The line manager progressively gives up the "or else" and his persuasiveness arises from the process of managing itself—from the fact that what he asks people to do is seen or believed to be the appropriate thing to do. The two kinds of influence come closer and closer together. Staff and line "authority" become indistinguishable. It's probably time to stop trying to distinguish them. Certainly in practice one company has differed from another so much in what it considered staff function that the distinction served very little useful purpose. Very little seems to be lost by giving up the distinction between the two. If we eliminate it, along with the idea of commensurate authority and responsibility, we can leave the expensive circumscribed responsibility and the narrow conferred authority and go on to a more fruitful concept of broad commitment and expanding influence grounded in the participation of the work group.

Information and Managerial Control

When Field Marshal (then General) Montgomery took over command of the Eighth Army in the desert in World War II, he postponed a major battle that had been fully planned. All the logistical and tactical preparations were complete. Montgomery postponed it long enough to talk himself with all the officers about the battle plans and to have them talk with all the men. He said, "If every unit commander knows what is wanted, them all will fight more intelligently and cohesion will be gained. . . . Every single soldier must know, before he goes into battle, how the little battle he is going to fight fits into the bigger picture and how the success of *his* fighting will influence the battle as a whole. The whole army then goes into battle knowing what is wanted and how it is to be achieved." The ideal expressed in this is one most people would agree with, and most companies would piously second it. The important thing is that Montgomery recognized its importance sufficiently to postpone the battle to build this integration. Like many personnel practices, the commander before him probably agreed with the principle but neglected the practice. Later, when Montgomery was made Commander of Allied Ground Forces in preparation for D-day, he insisted, similarly, that he must talk to all the officers and they to all the men. It was protested that this involved some six and a half million men. Montgomery realized that the large number only made the shared objective more important. He insisted on, and accomplished, the tremendous task of visiting every unit and talking to all officers. Many companies could profitably learn from this example. The investment—and even risk—involved in sharing information and objectives may be considerable. The return, in terms of cohesion, integration, and commitment, makes it essential. It is, unfortunately, easy to omit the step and then blame the rest of the organization for not having the company's interest at heart.

The newer organization structure would suggest a quite different routing of much information. Typically, today, budget and production data are generated by the action of groups at the middle and lower levels of the company. This information then goes immediately to the top to a centralized control. Here it is used almost entirely as a check on error and as a punitive weapon to chastise groups which have fallen below the mark. The first thing the group which produced the information knows about the results of its activity is when a superior descends, brandishing a summary, and complaining about the lack of performance. Budget and production data are not made available to help people solve their problems but to strengthen the centralized top control and to act as a prod and error control. In using the linking-pin structure, such information would appropriately go to the group which produced it. They could discuss why it was what it was, restate their objectives and modify their practices, and the leader, in his linking function, would carry it up. In this way the information would be used to guarantee shared objectives and solve problems rather than to centralize management control and provide a punitive weapon. Of course, while the major part of the information was being fed back into the system at the level which produced it, a certain amount would be siphoned off and fed to centralized levels for long-term planning of capital investment, production plans, marketing strategy, and the like. These are the functions appropriate to these levels, which need the information to perform them. It is injurious to the organization, however, when the information is centralized to strengthen managerial control.

The development of electronic data-processing equipment sharpens this question for organization structure. We have been reaching a point where sheer size has forced the decentralized dissemination of information. Now the speed of modern information systems offers a sharp alternative. Will they be used further to centralize information and management control, or will the same qualities of speed be utilized to provide the outlying parts of the organization with more information faster? The two possibilities face many companies clearly just now. One of them can be used to build and strengthen the organization. The other is designed to perpetuate an outmoded managerial technique. . . .

The Growth of Organizations

Growth is a problem in most companies. With it comes the question, What happens to the organization as the company grows? Can it simply grow proportionately, or are there special organizational problems in organizational growth? If the organization grows all over at the same rate, it means that the shape of the structure remains the same. Changes in shape are a function of the relative size of the parts. If a company doubles in size by having two men in every place where one man stood before, it grows without changing shape. If some of the parts grow faster than others, the shape changes. The question is, Which type of growth is appropriate, and, if the latter, which parts grow faster?

Very few things can become larger effectively and stay the same shape. In general, with physical objects, as a thing gets bigger, if it stays the same shape it grows weaker. A bridge of a perfect shape won't work if it is made much bigger and kept the same shape. More and more of its strength goes into the job of holding itself up and less and less is available for its function as a bridge. A plank 10 feet long, 1 foot wide, and 1 inch thick will just about lie flat supported at both ends. One 100 feet long, 10 feet wide, and 10 inches thick would bend or break in the middle. To support its increased size, some of its dimensions must grow faster than others—its shape has to change. The same thing is probably true of companies.

The British biologist D'Arcy Thompson gives a nice example in living organisms in the story of Jack the Giant Killer. In the illustrations the giant is shown as looking like a man but ten times as big. Thompson points out that, in this case, Jack had nothing to fear. If the giant were ten times the size of a man, his weight would be a thousand times as great, since he increased in all dimensions. But a cross section of his bones, increasing in only two dimensions, would only be a hundred times as big. Consequently he would put ten times as much load on his bones at his size as a normal man would. Since human bones, in general, won't support ten times as much weight as they normally do, if the giant stood up, his legs would break. Jack was perfectly safe, protected by the fact that an increase in size without a change in shape is insupportable. The same thing is probably true of companies. How does it work out?

One more phenomenon from physical growth helps us to know what to look for in changes in shape as companies grow. In general, when objects change shape with increased size they become stronger at the point where the force tending to destroy the object is strongest. A shelf built out from the wall has a shelf bracket that is thickest right at the wall and tapers off further out; if a shelf breaks, the likeliest joint is right at the wall. The graceful bowstring arch on small bridges is not built that way for purely aesthetic reasons. It is strongest where the force tending to destroy the bridge is strongest. In general, the shape of the support for physical objects that have grown is a perfect diagram of the forces tending to destroy it. Similarly in a company. As the size changes, the shape must change. Some parts must grow faster than others. Those parts must grow fastest which resist the forces tending to destroy the organizations which are threatened by increasing size. We have already spoken of the tendency for organizations to fly apart because they are made of collections of individuals. To combat this with increased size we generally see a rapid growth of functions associated with organization building and communication. Also, needs for specialized skills develop as a result of size—labor relations, accounting, marketing, and the like—and these grow faster. In the early stages of growth the staff functions grow faster than the line and become a larger and larger proportion of the whole until their percentage of the total usually levels off and remains relatively constant for the rest of the life of the company. These things are not exactly the same from company to company, but a measure of this sort and the view of the problem that lies behind it can help us see, in a particular organization, where the forces threatening the organization are greatest.

As an organization grows it almost inevitably faces the problem of decentralization. Today in most large firms it is fashionable to praise the virtues of decentralization. The word, however, doesn't always have the same meaning. For this reason, what seems like failure to one man may be success to another. The difference usually becomes apparent at an early stage in the process. When decentralization begins, we soon face the question, "Does decentralization include the autonomy, at lower levels, to run a centralized show?" It certainly often happens that an executive pushes authority and responsibility down to a subordinate who gathers more and more of them to himself to operate a tighter and tighter organization below himself. This isn't necessarily wrong, but it may disturb the superior who initiated the process, depending on what his original goal was. He now wonders, Can he pull back the autonomy and order the subordinate to push decentralization down further? Or will this centralized intervention to further decentralization destroy the decentralization?

Some firms aim at decentralization fairly simply as a response to size. The front office chooses to act as a kind of financial holding company, giving subordinate managers virtually complete autonomy and holding them responsible for little more than a profitable operation of their sector. Other firms want decentralization to provide initiative through a greater sense of participation, commitment, an acceptance of system-wide responsibility, and a feeling of shared objectives. Between these two there is a wide difference. In the second case, the tendency for autonomy to stop at the level immediately below the decision to decentralize is indeed a failure. The two types of decentralization must be approached differently. Decentralization in response to size can be accomplished by centralized order—"Effective at 0800 tomorrow we will be decentralized." The other kind requires a long and careful process. Executives must be retrained or created to handle it. Systems of reward must be rethought or overhauled. Traditional controls (budget and production) must be relinquished and information provided at lower levels. The new philosophy of management must be widely, slowly, and carefully shared throughout the organization. The two processes are so different that it is a pity they share the same name. Certainly the goals and processes of one will be a shock to an executive who thought in terms of the other.

A final problem that the question of decentralization brings up is the cost of the organization itself. If we shift a little from the decentralization of authority to the decentralization of decision making, the organizational cost becomes clear. Most decentralized firms retain a good deal of the business decision in the central office. For example, geographically dispersed managers may be restricted in independent authority for purchasing, accepting orders, setting prices, and the like. Otherwise two managers, acting in ignorance of each other, might compete with one another, overload the firm's production capacity, overcommit cash, or fail to take advantage of geographical differences in the market among either producers or consumers. For these reasons, to take advantage of the center's overview of both situations, the final decision tends to be retained at the home office. Under some circumstances, however, these factors—the probability of price variations, the profitability of contracting to purchase or produce—are stable enough so that decision rules can be set up telling the centralized subordinates how to operate in certain circumstances. To the extent that this is possible, it focuses attention on the alternative—maintaining a centralized decision-making operation. Now we have to ask, "What is the organization cost of the centralized style?" The cost of the organization may be more than the advantage gained from the single overview. For example, in a large retail operation, branch managers have relatively local price problems, what one manager does has little influence on another's action, and the probability of straining the company in money or production is low. In this situation a great deal of decentralization of decision making is possible, as in the classic Sears Roebuck case. Other cases may have much more interdependence of managers' actions, highly correlated prices across areas, and a tight supply of centralized production. In this case centralized structures would be worth a good deal. But we should begin to count the organizational cost to choose realistically between the cases where it is worth much or little. In general, this organization cost is one that we haven't measured. In addition to specifying clearly the objectives of the organization and measuring its effectiveness, it is time to begin to assess its cost.

Summary

1. The world is changing. With it go changes in the pressures that are put on business for organization. To survive as a social institution, business must be responsive and adaptive to the changing pressures.

2. We need to answer more clearly the questions: What are the objectives of an organization? How do you tell a good organization plan when you see one? What is organized in an organization?

3. The traditional organization theory is based on a model which grew out of accounting and industrial engineering. Developments in research and theory in the social sciences make it possible to frame an alternative based on the model of the human group.

4. In a group-based model we move toward a point where the source of authority is in the group itself. The ultimate control is self-control. This depends on commitment, which in turn depends on integration. Under these circumstances there is reason to believe that the total amount of influence or authority in the system can be expanded.

5. We have traditionally measured the things that are easy to measure. These are primarily budget and production data. A firm's philosophy and a manager's practices flow from measurements. Measurements define jobs more than job descriptions do. Social science technology now makes available measures related to attitudes, group strength, initiative, and commitment. To build an adaptive organization these data are essential.

6. As an organization grows its shape has to change. The parts that grow fastest should be those that maximally resist forces tending to destroy the organization as it grows.

7. Decentralization raises the question of organization cost. At what expense do we maintain centralized organization? At what return? Finally, to understand a particular decentralization the goals of different types must be understood.

Robert H. Guest

Technology and Change:
The Meaning of Work

Technological innovation has been and will continue to be one of the most profound forces for change in Western society. Its effect is manifest today through the entire spectrum of human experience. Technology has revolutionized agriculture, industry, medicine, and education in a remarkably short space of time. The products of technology and their uses easily become matters of common knowledge. The secondary effects of technology on social institutions and on human interchange are also recognized, even if not fully understood until after they have become part of the total fabric of life.

Time and space have been shortened by the harnessing of the air waves and by the extraordinary developments in propulsion, but technology has also broadened social horizons and changed the core family and traditional kinship relations. Technology has measurably altered the size and function of urban living. Innovations in science and technology have not only enhanced the treatment of the sick but have substantially increased the span of life itself. And technology has now also made possible the total destruction of all life.

The crucial issue is not whether technology will continue to change at an accelerated pace; it will. Rather, the fundamental question is whether society can create the social and political institutions needed to cope with technology's all-pervading effects.

This essay has a modest purpose. While viewing some of the large effects of technology somewhat impressionistically, it focuses on one aspect of the subject which has been neglected as an area of inquiry: man's direct relationship to the machine. How is modern technology changing the nature of work? What *meaning* does work have, other than the paycheck, for the hundreds of thousands who spend such a large part of their adult lives in direct contact with machines? Why shouldn't the hours a man spends at work be considered as important to him and to society as the products and services which are consumed outside the work place?

Technology has given America its high standard of living, or, more properly, its high level of consumption. But in a deeper sense the fulfillment of needs takes place not in leisure hours alone but at work as well. The notion that work is a means to other ends is deeply ingrained in the American ethos. There has also been a pervasive assumption that the benefits from the products of technology far outweigh the discontents that have been generated among those who produce the goods which they and the rest of society enjoy. But these assumptions conflict with another set of values related to man's "psychological health." We place a high premium on the notion of the "whole man." A psychologically healthy person is one who feels he has some control over his environment, and this control comes when he can utilize the full range of his capabilities.

The point has been made many times that the industrial revolution led to a fragmentation of work (see Blauner, 1964). This fragmentation created a condition of alienation which was psychologically unhealthy for the worker. Alienation exists when a person feels powerless to control his immediate environment, when he can see little relationship between his immediate job and the purpose of the larger organization of which he is a part, when he feels isolated or remote from the larger society, and when work is only a means to some end outside of the work place—notably, his wages and what they provide him beyond the factory gates.

At least one observer has held that men were not alienated from work during the earlier *craft* period of technology. Alienation set in with increased mechanization of the work process. One of the central conclusions of this essay is that in today's most advanced sectors of technology there is the potential for a decrease in work alienation and an emancipation that may lead to a fuller life at the work place. But if modern technology is leading to greater utilization of man's capacities, it is at the moment more the result of accident than of design, and a deliberate effort will have to be made to exploit the potential advantages. Work continues to be based on certain rational and mechanical principles that pay scant attention to fundamental human needs. To understand this we need to begin with a brief historical overview of technical innovations, with special attention to the concept of work rationalization introduced at the turn of the twentieth century. We can then analyze the actual work environments created by modern technology and emphasize the opportunity and challenge we have to make work more meaningful.

The Stages of Technology

A cursory knowledge of industrial history makes certain facts clear. The early days of industrialism saw many men, women, and children working under deplorable conditions. For those who worked in shops and factories there were few rewards: wages were low; hours of work were long; there was little security to employment. Many were driven to work out of sheer hunger and there were very few safeguards against hazardous conditions. Workers were regarded as so many "hands" whose only job was to keep machines running in return for modest wages.

The picture of the first hundred years of the industrial revolution is not all black, however. Many workers were still craftsmen in the true sense of the word: they had direct identification with the product. Craft skills were built up after years of apprenticeship, and control of both quantity and quality was vested wholly in the craftsman's hand. Production was not machine-paced.

The craftsmen were part of a stage of technological development that was soon overtaken, however. In American production, technology may be characterized by four stages of development.[1] The *craft* period falls in an early stage of low mechanization and hand tools. The introduction of steam power and mechanical devices for processing goods ushered in what might be described as the *machine* period. This phase dominated nineteenth-century technology and much of early twentieth-century industrial production. But the twentieth century also saw the introduction of *assembly-line* technology and, more recently, automatic continuous-flow processes, made possible by what is now known as *continuous-flow* technology, including the application of computers to the work process.

These four stages represent a kind of evolution through which many industries have passed. Many industries originally started as a craft type, moved into a machine technology, expanded to the use of assembly lines, and later became automated. Shoe manufacturing and glass making began as simple craft trades and today have reached an advanced stage of mechanization. In some industries, such as printing, many of the work tasks continue to be carried out as craft functions. Other industries, such as automobile manufacturing, had very short periods of craft technology. They quickly moved into a more advanced stage. The stages may also overlap. Indeed, the elements of all four types of technology may be found in virtually all modern industrial enterprises.

These four stages or types of mechanization have distinguishing characteristics which help to explain the intrinsic nature of human work. They determine the degree of freedom and control men exercise over the immediate work environment. They call for different ranges of mental and physical skills required to perform tasks and hence different ranges of opportunity for achieving what was described earlier as psychological health. The type of technology deter-

---

1. These technological stages are similar to Blauner's.

mines the size, structure, and function of work groups, hence the social relationships. The division of labor required to carry out industrial tasks varies considerably with the type of technology. As will be seen later, the most extreme subdivision of labor is usually associated with the assembly-line type of technology. Also, as one views the four types of technology as they evolved historically, one can see that in the last half-century there has come about a systematic rationalization of work to the point where most work behavior is determined by carefully spelled-out rules and procedures, based on work measurement, which have tended to limit further the worker's controls over the immediate work environment. One of the questions this essay raises is whether the application of logic and scientific management to the design of work has fulfilled both the requirements for productive efficiency and the needs for self-fulfillment by the individual. And, as indicated, our special concern will be with the last two phases of technological progress, assembly-line technology and continuous-process technology, both of which are common to industrial work at the present time.

The period of craft technology extends back into medieval times. In America it was the primary type of technology at the time of the settlement of the colonies and lasted into the early 1800s. Most of the materials (iron, copper, and wood) were "worked" by hand and with simple tools. Power, whether for transportation or for tilling the soil, relied largely on the muscle power of animals. Water-wheel power was also employed for such tasks as wheat grinding and in the early days of textile manufacturing.

The shift from craft technology to machine technology came with the invention of the reciprocating steam engine, which led to the mass production of spun yarn. It also created a new institution in the society, the *factory*. This came about primarily because central power required the concentration of manpower as well as machines in a central location. The former "putting-out" system was no longer feasible.

The rise of machine technology leading to the concentration of work in the larger factory organization was accelerated to some extent by an act of national policy in 1790, namely the Patent Act. Impressed by new developments in the grist mill industry, the significance of the steamboat, and other new inventions both at home and abroad, President Washington and members of Congress sought to encourage the development of new inventions through patent protection. Hamilton, in his *Report on Manufactures* a year later, recognized the economic benefits to the country by the increased production resulting from new inventions. The demand for greater production, Hamilton saw, would make for the employment of large numbers of workers.

Hamilton also recognized that the new technology would require new skills. Such skills were not readily available in the young America of the time. Both Hamilton and Jefferson, in one of their rare agreements, committed the nation to encouraging the immigration of skilled workers from abroad. America found it easier to "import" inventors and skilled craftsmen than it did the inventions themselves. In England, for example, Parliament had prohibited the exportation of inventions such as the power loom and the spinning jenny. But many inventors and craftsmen in England saw great opportunity for utilizing their skills in America. By the turn of the century, not only was American industry expanding by duplicating inventions from abroad but Americans, under the protection of the Patent Act, were also demonstrating a high level of creativity on their own part.

As the new inventions proliferated and factories were built, staffed by dozens and later hundreds of workers, the character of work itself underwent a basic change. Like the machine and the machine tool, workers became "instruments" of production. The home-spun era, although it predominated in rural America, was phasing out during the first half of the nineteenth century. America was becoming a market economy. The factory organization was superseding the family as the basic work group even though the larger proportion of citizens was engaged in agriculture.

Adam Smith had been remarkably perceptive in seeing the implications of the centralization of production. He saw that the factory system would involve a division of labor determined by the imperatives of the machine. By the end of the first quarter of the nineteenth century, Andrew Ure defined the factory system quite simply by calling it "the combined operations of many work people, adult and young, attending with assiduous skill a system of productive machines continuously impelled by a central power" (1835).

The degree of mechanization, which in turn determined the nature of the direct man-machine relationship, varied widely in the early period of industrial growth. In the textile industry there had already evolved a high degree of job specialization. In other types of manufacturing, such as glass making, tanning, and iron production, the individual worker had to apply a variety of skills. He was more responsible for what may be described as the total product. It was the introduction of the basic machine tool, the machine lathe, that brought on changes having far-reaching effects on the organization of work at the factory level. The machine tool made it possible to turn out interchangeable parts. No longer were individual parts hand made. They could be standardized and turned out in large quantity. Eli Whitney, in his contract to produce muskets for the U. S. army, is given credit for having applied the concept of standardization to the mass production of firearms.

By the end of the first quarter of the nineteenth century, westward expansion was well under way and with it began a proliferation of small shops, many of which later burgeoned into large industries. Iron production on a modest scale sprang up in the Pittsburgh area and along the banks of the Ohio. Pottery plants were built in western Virginia. By 1811 Wheeling had four iron foundries and four woolen and cotton mills, as well as a steam-engine plant. With the opening up of the canals and later the railroads, workers moved into Indiana, Illinois, Missouri, and other Midwestern states.

In the big cities other new industries were springing up, making possible such "modern" innovations as central heating, gas lighting, running water, and other consumer conveniences. Even before the mid-century London Exhibition, British observers were impressed by the many American technological innovations. Virgil Maxey was able to say in 1839, "The ingenious Americans with their new machines are rapidly gaining control over the power of the elements and are making fire, air, earth, and water their ministering servants" (Oliver, 1956, p. 112).

Although the new inventions in America were rapidly leading to a market economy with a broad industrial base, the era of large-scale mass production (except in textiles) had not yet begun. America had yet to become an export nation. To the British and to the Europeans it seems to have been taken for granted that the Old World would continue to be the major exporter of both the ideas and the hardware of the new technology. This condition began to change in the 1840s and the late 1850s. Not only were Americans beginning to copy British locomotives, but these products could be produced in large quantity at low cost. By mid-century, American locomotives were being sold in England itself. American engineers were hired by Czar Nicholas I to aid in the construction of the Moscow–St. Petersburg railroad. Friedrich List, the "father of the German railway system," developed his basic plans from his contacts with American experts. France, Austria-Hungary, and other nations were making greater use of American railroad technology.

American technology received its first dramatic exposure abroad with the London Exhibition of 1851. More than five major awards were given to American designs, the most outstanding being McCormick's reaper, labeled at first as the "ugly duckling." The successful tests of the reaper at the exhibition won the unanimous praise of the judges. As Charles T. Rodgers put it in 1852, the McCormick reaper "mowed down British prejudice and opened the way for bringing our countrymen and their contributions before the public in a proper light" (ibid., p. 255). The London Exhibition also revealed the remarkable technological developments in rubber technology, vehicles of many types, firearms, machine tools, and various scientific measuring devices and compasses. To crown the American triumphs, the schooner *America* won the international yacht race at Cowes.

Continued westward expansion, a large population increase amplified by immigration from abroad, and foreign investment stimulated by technological progress—these forces brought America to the verge of its great mass-production period. The Civil War gave it added impetus. As in later wars, the military requirements in the Civil War led to a "spin-off" of a number of inventions adapted for civilian use. Telegraphy and photography appeared for the first time on a large scale. The iron-clad ship was born. Basic industries that were formerly limited to isolated and small-scale operations grew in size and complexity. Steel making saw the introduction of large concentrations of manpower in the Bessemers, open hearths, rolling mills, and the fabricating component industries.

Subtle but important changes were also taking place in the man-machine relationship at the immediate job level. The need for craft skills continued on certain types of jobs, but the bulk of the work was performed with unskilled and semi-skilled labor. The technical processes were determining the character of the jobs, the pace at which men worked, and the degree of control workers could exercise. The blue-collar worker worked on a fraction of the product. Jobs were broken down into small segments. Industrial organizations were becoming complex bureaucracies. Administrative staffs were added. The maintenance of the total work processes required an increase in clerical staffs and auxiliary groups. The worker who formerly had a direct relationship to owner-managers lost what may be described as the social "connective tissue" to the larger organization.

The rise of vertically integrated mass-production industries laid the groundwork for the assembly-line type of industrial operation. The classic example of such technology was the introduction of the assembly line by Henry Ford. The concept of progressive work flow along a moving sequence of operations was not new. The meat processing industry had adopted conveyor belt and continuous trolley mechanisms a quarter of a century earlier. Indeed, one can find examples of mass assembly as far back as the fourteenth century. The Venetians, for instance, were able to build, outfit, and provision vessels ready to sail at a rate of more than thirteen per day. But it was not until the twentieth century that assembly-line principles were adopted on a mass scale employing large numbers of the total working population.

For our purposes, the most important development of assembly-line technology was not in machines and hardware alone but in the application of scientific measurement to human work itself, first introduced by the "father" of scientific management, Frederick W. Taylor. What Taylor did in applying systematic measurement to human work is, in many respects, as significant as Ford's introduction of the automobile assembly line. Taylor, and later Gantt and Gilbreth, came to realize that it was not enough to apply scientific reasoning in the design of the machine and factory layouts. There were gross inefficiencies in the human component of the man-machine system.

In essence, Taylor's method for rationalizing work was through job analysis and time study. A job could be considered as the sum of many individual operations performed by both men and machines. Job analysis distinguishes what is essential to the completion of a task and what is waste motion. Once the individual operations are identified it becomes possible to time the components using a stop watch. The times can be added together, thus permitting a re-analysis and a re-combination of all elements in the most efficient manner.

The system permits a high degree of control. Standardized procedures can be instituted to minimize errors. Movements of machines and muscles can be synchronized according to predetermined metric units of time. The operator is relieved of the necessity to make individual judgments.

The rationale for the Taylor system of analysis and measurement was not new. It was a synthesis of ideas that had been applied formerly to machine processes themselves. It had its philosophical origins in eighteenth-century rationalism and nineteenth-century Benthamite utilitarianism. Yet as applied to human effort, it was a cultural innovation of considerable importance in its own right. It created a system of human manipulation and control not only for workers but for vast numbers of people at all levels of our complex production organizations.

The Worker on the Assembly Line

The principal criticism of Taylor and of the work rationalization concept is that they ignored the workers' feelings and motivations. Taylor himself vigorously denied this. The basis for his denial was that men would respond favorably to the obvious logic of its benefits. The worker would certainly appreciate the elimination of wasteful and unproductive motions. He would be glad to have tasks simplified without having to make complicated decisions. He would welcome guidance as to the "best way" of performing the task. He would be given the right tools to do the job. Machines would be kept in proper adjustment. The worker would be paid fairly for his effort. Indeed, wage incentives could be established on a piece-work basis so that extra compensation could be given for extra effort. He, like any normal human being, would respond to man's natural desire to benefit himself economically.

Frederick Taylor could never quite comprehend why the application of his theory of work measurement brought about such a strong reaction in those plants where the new scheme was tried out. The first major installation was made in 1908 at the U. S. army arsenal at Watertown, Massachusetts. It caused something more than just a strike. It brought on a congressional investigation resulting in legislation barring the use of work measurement systems in all government production facilities (Aitken, 1960). The law stayed on the books for thirty-five years. Unions became aware of a new threat. While continuing to fight for the usual economic and security benefits, a few unions took up the new challenge against the slide rule and stop watch. But most unions at the time were structured along craft lines; the large mass of industrial workers was not yet organized.

In the larger industries the Taylor movement gained strong support in management. An entirely new profession of time-study experts and industrial engineers came into being. Time and motion became the passwords of industrial efficiency.

By the mid-1930s the scientific management revolution was in full bloom. This was also the time of the rise of the industrial union as we know it today. The industrial union continued many of the basic traditional union functions: bargaining for wages, establishing grievance procedures, setting up agreements with respect to seniority, hours, and other general conditions of employment. From the beginning, the industrial unions clashed head on with problems of work standards and wage incentives—problems whose origins could be traced in part to the Taylor movement of work rationalization.

Assembly-line technology continues to play an important part in the total production system even though automated, continuous-flow technology is gaining rapidly. It is also from the assembly-line experience that one can find clues about the way to tap the potential benefits of the more advanced technology in terms of enriching the working hours. To do this, it is well to consider precisely how the worker views the world of the assembly line. A case that offers deep insights is that of the auto assembly worker on the "final line." "The extraordinary ingenuity that has gone into the construction of automobile assembly lines, their perfected synchronization, the 'all but human' or 'more than human' character of the machines, the miracle of a car rolling off the conveyor each minute under its own power— all this has caught and held the world's imagination for a quarter of a century. On the other hand, the extreme subdivision of labor (the man who puts a nut on a bolt is the symbol) conjoined with the 'endlessly moving belt' has made the [automobile] assembly line the classic symbol of the subjection of man to the machine in our industrial age" (Walker and Guest, 1952).

Utilizing the two basic principles of standardization and interchangeability, Henry Ford was able to work out and apply three additional "principles" of progressive manufacture in pioneering the automobile assembly line:

1. The orderly progression of the product through the shop in a series of planned operations so arranged that the right part always arrives at the right place at the right time.
2. The mechanical delivery of these parts to the operators, and the mechanical delivery of the product from the operators, as it is assembled.
3. A breakdown of operations into their simple constituent motions.

These principles are purely mechanical. Extended to the human component of the total work flow system, they mean the following for the worker: mechanically controlled work pace; repetition of simple motions; minimum skill requirements; pre-determined operating procedures; small fraction of the total product is worked on; superficial mental attention.

How does the man on the line react? Here is one worker's response.[2] It is typical of hundreds which this observer and others have heard in the course of their research. The worker is J. D., a graduate of a public vocational training school, thirty-six years old, married, with two children. He makes good wages and is buying his own home. He is being interviewed at home.

> Some years back I heard that they were hiring people for the assembly plant. Must have been thousands of fellows lined up for the job. The word got around that they were paying real good money. It was a big outfit, too. No fly-by-night affair.
> Figured I'd get any job and then, with a little electrician experience I had in vocational school, I could work my way up to a good job. And the idea of making automobiles sounded like something. Lucky for me, I got a job and was made a spot welder on the front cowling. There wasn't much to the job itself. Picked it up in about a week. I tried to get into the Maintenance Department as an electrician, but there was no opening, so I went back to the line—we call it the iron horse. They made me a welder again, and that's what I have been doing ever since.

The worker then went on to describe his job:

> My job is to weld the cowl to the metal underbody. I take a jig off the bench, put it in place and weld the parts together. The jig is all made up and the welds are made in set places along the

---

2. Parts of this interview are reprinted from *Personnel* (May 1955), with permission of the American Management Association.

metal. Exactly twenty-five spots. The line runs according to schedule. Takes me one minute and fifty-two seconds for each job. I walk along the line as it moves. Then I snap the jig off, walk back down the line, throw it on the bench, grab another just in time to start on the next car. The cars differ, but it's practically the same thing. Finish one—then have another one staring me in the face.

I don't like to work on the line—no man likes to work on a moving line. You can't beat the machine. Sure, maybe I can keep it up for an hour, but it's rugged doing it eight hours a day, every day in the week all year long.

During each day I get a chance for a breather ten minutes in the morning, then a half-hour for lunch, then a few minutes in the afternoon. When I'm working there is not much chance to get a breather. Sometimes the line breaks down. When it does we all yell "Whoopee!" As long as the line keeps moving I've got to keep up with it. On a few jobs I know some fellows can work like hell up the line, then coast. Most jobs you can't do that. If I get ahead maybe ten seconds, the next model has more welds to it, so it takes ten seconds extra. You hardly break even. You're always behind. When you get too far behind, you get in a hole— that's what we call it. All hell breaks loose. I get in the next guy's way. The foreman gets sore and they have to rush in a relief man to bail you out.

It's easy for them time-study fellows to come down there with a stop watch and figure out just how much a man can do in a minute and fifty-two seconds. There are some things they can see and record with their stop watch. But they can't clock how a man feels from one day to the next. Those guys ought to work on the line for a few weeks and maybe they'll feel some things that they never pick up on the stop watch.

I like a job where you feel like you're accomplishing something and doing it right. When everything's laid out for you and the parts are all alike, there's not much you feel you accomplish. The big thing is that steady push of the conveyor—a gigantic machine which I can't control.

You know, it's hard to feel that you are doing a good quality job. There is that constant push at high speed. You may improve after you've done a thing over and over again, but you never reach a point where you can stand back and say, "Boy, I done that one good. That's one car that got built right." If I could do my best I'd get some satisfaction out of working, but I can't do as good work as I know I can do.

My job is all engineered out. The jigs and fixtures are all designed and set out according to specifications. There are a lot of little things you could tell them but they never ask you. You go by the bible. They have a suggestion system, but the fellows don't use it too much because they're scared that a new way to do it may do one of your buddies out of a job.

There's only three guys close by—me and my partner and a couple of fellows up the line a bit. I talk to my partner quite a lot. We gripe about the job 90 percent of the time. You don't have time for any real conversation. The guys get along okay—you know the old saying, "Misery loves company."

My foreman's an all right guy. I see him once in a while outside, and he's 100 percent. But in the shop he can't be. If I was a foreman nobody would like me either. As a foreman he has to push you all the time to get production out so that somebody above won't push him. But the average guy on the line has no one to push—you can't fight the line. The line pushes you. We sometimes kid about it and say we don't need no foreman. That line is the foreman. Some joke.

The worker then discussed the general working conditions in the plant—the lighting, ventilation, safety conditions, cafeteria facilities, and the plant hospital. He thought these conditions were all good, but then added:

But you know it's a funny thing. These things are all good, but they don't make the job good. It's what you spend most of the time doing that counts.

My chances for promotion aren't so hot. You see, almost everybody makes the same rate. The jobs have been made so simple that there is not much room to move up from one skill to another. In other places where the jobs aren't broken down this way, the average fellow has something to look forward to. He can go from one stop to another right up the ladder. Here it's possible to make foreman. But none of the guys on the line think there's much chance to go higher than that. To manage a complicated machine like that, you need a college degree. They bring in smart college boys and train them for the better jobs.

Interviewer: "What does you wife think about your job?"

At this point his wife spoke up: "I often wish he'd get another job. He comes home at night, plops down in a chair and just sits for about fifteen minutes. I don't know much about what he does at the plant, but it does something to him. Of course, I shouldn't complain. He gets good pay. We've been able to buy a refrigerator and a TV set —a lot of things we couldn't have had otherwise. But sometimes I wonder whether these are more important to us than having Joe get all nervous and tensed up. He snaps at the kids and snaps at me—but he doesn't mean it."

The worker was then asked if he had considered working elsewhere:

> I'll tell you honest. I'm scared to leave. I'm afraid to take the gamble on the outside. I'm not staying because I want to. You see, I'm getting good pay. We live according to the pay I get. It would be tough to change the way we live. With the cost of living what it is, it's too much of a gamble. Then there's another thing. I got good seniority. I take another job and I start from scratch. Comes a depression or something and I'm the first to get knocked off. Also, they got a pension plan. I'm thirty-seven and I'd lose that. Course the joker in that pension plan is that most guys out there chasing the line probably won't live till they're sixty-five. Sorta trapped—you get what I mean?

The subject of the worker's relationship to his union came up in the course of the interview:

> The union has helped somewhat. Before they organized, it was pretty brutal. The bosses played favorites—they kept jacking up the speed of the line every time after they had a breakdown. But the union can't do much about the schedule and the way a job is set up. Management is responsible for that.
>
> We'd had a walk-out last year. They called it an unauthorized strike. Somebody got bounced because he wouldn't keep up his job on the line. The union lost the case because it should have gone through the grievance procedure. The company was dead right to insist that the union file a grievance.
>
> But it was one of those things it's hard to explain. When word got around that the guy was bounced—we all sort of looked at each other, dropped our tools, and walked. Somehow that guy was every one of us. The tension on the line had been building up for a long time. We had to blow our top—so we did. We were wrong—the union knew it and so did the company. We stayed out a few hours and back we came. We all felt better, like we got something off our chests.
>
> Some of these strikes you read about may be over wages. Or they may be unions trying to play politics. But I sometimes think that the thing that will drive a man to lose all that pay is deeper than wages. Maybe other guys feel like we did the day we walked out.

Toward the end of the interview, the worker spoke of the company he worked for:

> They are doing what they can—like the hospital, the safety, the pay, and all like that. And the people who run the plant, I guess, are pretty good guys themselves. But sometimes I think that the company doesn't think much of the individual. If they did they wouldn't have a production line like that one. You're just a number to them. They number the stock and they number you. There's a different feeling in this kind of a plant. It's like a kid who goes up to a grown man and starts talking to him. There doesn't seem to be a friendly feeling. Here a man is just so much horsepower. You're just a cog in the wheel.

Notice, first, that this worker's dissatisfaction was not due primarily to the things that are usually considered important to a job. This man's pay was good. His job was secure. He worked for a sound company. He had substantial seniority. He had a pension, hospitalization and disability benefits when he became sick, and a good boss; at least he did not hold the kind of job he had against his boss. Working conditions, heating, lighting, cafeteria facilities, and safety conditions were as good if not better than the average found in industrial plants. Yet J. D. despised his job.

The simple fact is that the impact of "sound" engineering principles, when translated into human experience, had a profound effect on his view of the meaning of work. In this interview we find most of the elements of *alienation* referred to earlier. Both the technical setup and the application of work rationalization principles made this man feel hardly more than an extension of the machine. The sense of anonymity implicit in much of what he said can be traced back to some of the basic characteristics of his immediate job.

The conveyor belt determined the *pace* at which he worked. He had no control over his work rhythm.

Because the task was broken down into simple motions, the job was highly *repetitive*.

Simple repetitive motions meant that there was little need to call upon a variety of *skills*.

The tools and the work procedures were pre-determined. And when techniques changed, it was the engineer—not the worker—who controlled the change.

He worked on *a fraction of the product*, which meant that he never felt a sense of the "whole."

Some attention was required—too much to allow him to day-dream or carry on any sustained conversation with others—but not enough to allow him to become absorbed in the work itself.

The technical setup determined the character of his work relationships. This man identified himself with the partner who worked with him on the opposite side of the line, but beyond that he displayed almost no identification with a work group as such. Men on the line work as an aggregate of individuals, each man performing his operation more or less independently of the others. The lack of an intimate group awareness appeared to reinforce the same sense of anonymity fostered by the conveyor-paced, repetitive character of the job itself.

The worker's comments about promotion and job aspirations are also pertinent. He saw little hope for advancement because most of the production jobs paid about the same. By applying principles of work rationalization, the industrial engineer, in the best interests of efficiency, had simplified the tasks so that differences in skill from one job to the next were all but eliminated. It was difficult for the average worker to move vertically through a series of distinct steps in promotion.

This case is only one of over four hundred actual work careers that have been studied. Only a few had experienced any substantial change in job classification during a period of from twelve to fifteen years. Collectively, all the workers had improved their overall economic status; individually, few had experienced much change in their relative job status. The net effect of this condition was to increase the *de*-personalization of the job.

The case of an automobile assembly-line worker is in many respects an extreme case in the application of the principles of work rationalization. There are many types and conditions of work in which the degree of dissatisfaction is not expressed as strongly as it was in this case. Nevertheless, there is little evidence that work in highly repetitive, conveyor-paced jobs is looked upon as a meaningful end in itself.

The Coming of Automation

Although the basic characteristics of assembly-line technology pervade many segments of industrial production, there are significant changes in technology which may lead to a new "emancipation" for the worker. Popularly known as automation, the new technology, like assembly-line technology, is based on the principle of continuous flow. What is new is that mechanical and electronic devices have been substituted for human organs of decision and effort.

Automatic continuous-flow technology came of age in the petroleum refining and industrial chemical industries. Later the same principles were applied in basic steel production and even to the machining and fabricating of metals. Materials are fed into and pass through a sequence of operations, each of which is programmed and controlled with a minimum of direct human intervention. In more advanced types of operations linked to computers, the equipment has "built-in" self-correcting devices which not only signal the need for mechanical adjustments but actually set in motion the mechanisms to make such adjustments. For many years the automatic continuous-flow principle was adaptable only to the large-scale production of identical or near-identical products. In small-lot production, human skills were required to "re-set the job" for runs of different items. Today it is possible to program equipment automatically for short runs of products with different specifications for each run.

The immediate and pressing problem of the new technology is not usually seen in terms of its effects on the meaning of work. Rather, it is related to the broad problem of displacement of men by machines. This is not only important as a matter of national employment policy; it also has an effect on those currently employed who see accelerated technical changes being made all around them. Uppermost in their minds is the question, "Am I the one to go next?" This question has a marked effect on how men look at work itself.

Technological displacement has been a fact of industrial life since the start of the industrial revolution. History is strewn with examples of attempts to arrest the installation of labor-saving devices. Riots by the Luddites to destroy new machinery in the early nineteenth century stemmed from the same fears of displacement reflected in the crippling strikes—or threat of strikes—in the 1960s in railroads, airlines, construction trades, the atomic production industry, and in disputes at missile launching sites.

Whole industries have experienced growth in productive capacity despite a sharply declining relative rate of employment. Automobile production increased 50 percent from 1947 to 1960 while employment fell 2.9 percent (Blum, 1964, p. 13). In five years prior to 1960, employment in the telephone industry dropped 5.5 percent, or 33,000 jobs, while business increased by 25 percent. In a similar period, employment among production and related workers in the electrical machine industry was down 80,000 jobs—but productivity rose by 20 percent. Similar trends can be seen in many industries, especially those rapidly adopting more advanced forms of mechanization. In spite of an overall increase in industrial employment from 58 million in 1949 to 68 million in 1963, the part of the work force without jobs increased to between 5 and 6 percent in 1963. By the first quarter of 1965 the unemployment rate had declined to 5 percent, but the absolute numbers of unemployed had increased.

Even the expansion of the service, communications, and transportation industries has not had a substantial effect on the unemployment picture. There is the additional problem of population growth, with an estimated 26 million young men and women expected to enter the labor force during the 1960s (*ibid.*, p. 15). In spite of efforts to expand markets, many consumer industries are approaching a saturation point. How many more television sets or automobiles can be sold? Even with the opening up of new markets for different products, the ratio of employees to units produced will continue to decline. Thus with little appreciable increase in total production there will continue to be a constant decrease in needed manpower.

It is also becoming quite clear which segments of the potential work force are hardest hit by the new automated technology. In 1963 the unemployment rate among teen-agers was 15 percent (*TTR*, p. 8). The rate for Negro teen-agers had been twice that of whites. In depressed areas the general unemployment rate runs as high as 50 percent.

Business, labor, and public authorities are now highly aware of displacement problems associated with the new technology. There is growing realization that the economic and technological system does not have enough inherent "automatic" devices of adjustment and accommodation. Solutions will come only through deliberate and planned programs promoted by business, promoted through collective bargaining, or promoted at the highest levels of government as a matter of national policy.

Thomas J. Watson, Jr., president of IBM, a major manufacturer of automated equipment, has warned that adjustment to technological change cannot be left solely to the individual to work out his own problems (Blum, 1964, p. 15). He pleads for vast improvements in education and training, for relocation allowances, early retirement systems, a shorter work week, and fiscal reforms on a national scale. Unions have been especially outspoken in their demands to protect jobs or to negotiate agreements to cushion the effects of automation. They are asking for training programs to help displaced workers to be relocated. They are asking for the shorter work week, increased severance pay, guaranteed wages, longer vacations, and early retirement programs.

The President's Advisory Committee on Labor-Management Policy in 1962 put forward major policy recommendations. Legislation has since been adopted in the Accelerated Public Works Act, job retraining statutes, the anti-poverty bill, expanded social security, and many other programs. All are clearly directed at the central issue of machine displacement.

Many critics maintain that public and private programs now in effect or being considered merely scratch the surface of the problem. They call for a massive program of education, even suggesting the training of an additional 100,000 teachers a year over the present rate. They call for a public works program to create 200,000 jobs per year in the construction of dams, water and air pollution-control facilities, community recreation facilities, public buildings, and so forth. Public and private housing construction should be increased, they say, to the rate of between 700,000 and 1,000,000 units per year. Urban renewal programs need to be stepped up, with basic support coming from federal funds. The list of suggestions is almost without limit.

Such proposals might go far in reducing the unemployment dislocations caused by technological change. But to adopt them on such a massive scale would require American society to accept an entircly new set of assumptions with respect to the role of government. It seems unlikely that, barring a major depression, Americans are willing to place such power in the hands of government at present, notwithstanding the powerful thrusts made under the Johnson administration.

There is also an international dimension to the problem. Failure to solve the problem of machine displacement, whether through public or private efforts, will have serious consequences beyond our borders. Nations eager to adopt American technology will be increasingly concerned with its social consequences. If America fails to come up with effective plans for coping with machine displacement, we have only added more fuel to the fires of today's frustrating anti-Americanism. It would be a sign that democracy is unable to meet the problems of modernization.

The big issue of displacement of men by machines is only one side of the dilemma, however. What about the question of automation in microcosm—the direct man-machine relationship among the large number of the working population who are not displaced? Is the new technology providing man with the opportunity for greater enrichment while at work, or is it leading into new eras of work alienation?

In a technical sense, we have begun to acquire basic information about the characteristics of various types of automated technology. Unfortunately, data on the psychological and social effects are scarce and inconclusive. Most observers agree that the drudgery of the assembly-line technology is eliminated in the automated continuous-flow type of operation. Physical effort is no longer tied to machine pacing. General working conditions are considerably improved. At this point agreement ends. Some experts claim that work on automated jobs is merely a new extension of the work rationalization movement leading to a new kind of alienation. The argument here is that automated jobs for those directly linked to the production process do not call for a broadening of technical or intellectual skills. Limits of action are highly circumscribed by standard rules of procedure that allow for little deviation. Human control over the flow process is minimized because of "built-in" automatic feedback and self-correcting devices that eliminate the need for human judgment. Decision skills, it is said, can be programmed into computers, which in turn are linked to the machinery. In short, the operator is reduced to the role of gauge-watcher and dial-setter.

On the basis of a limited number of interviews and observations in a dozen different types of highly automated operations, this writer would agree with some of the above speculations. In certain chemical operations, when experienced workers make the transition to almost fully automatic jobs, they complain that some of their former skills have been discarded. They imply resentment over the fact that engineers and specialists make the more important mechanical and electrical adjustments when serious problems arise. Interestingly enough, in a large pharmaceutical company it was discovered that many operators with no formal technical background could be trained to develop some highly sophisticated technical skills. The workers' reactions were enthusiastic.

In a newly automated seamless tube rolling mill in the steel industry, we found a similar pattern: resentment at the loss of some former skills, concern about reliance on engineers, and a certain degree of boredom at having to monitor gauges instead of the product itself. A similar pattern was observed among many workers at one of the most highly automated precision machining operations in the country.

On balance, however, most observations support the thesis that there is the potential, at least, for more work enrichment and less alienation from the job in many sectors of the new technology. Extrapolating from what is now known, we can make some tentative predictions. The worker will no longer be responsible for a small fractionated segment of the work process. He will be a "supervisor" of a more complex series of integrated operations. Unlike the man on the assembly line, he will have more freedom of movement. His pace of work will not be determined by the conveyor. Elimination of manual work in a prescribed job cycle will reduce the degree of repetitiveness. There may be relatively long periods of time with virtually nothing to do followed by periods of total involvement when the machinery runs into difficulties.

The worker will, moreover, have to be trained in a variety of maintenance and repair skills requiring technical judgments. The new technology may bring about a higher scientific orientation toward the total tasks. Improvements in the processes will mean periods of new training during employment. The integration of several presently separate operations will link the operator more closely with other operators, thus generating a sense of collective responsibility. In automated operations there is also a trend toward smaller plants, and these plants are being located outside the large urban concentrations. This could have favorable consequences leading to greater social identification with the work organization and the community.

Work measurement using standard motion and time techniques will be obsolete. This change could alter the entire concept of monetary payments for work performed. Piece-work incentive plans, a persistent source of industrial unrest, will not be feasible in the automated continuous-flow type of operation. Even the age-old system of wage payment by the hour will become obsolete. Increased pressure by unions for a guaranteed annual wage is not simply a new bargaining device. It has a technological rationale. The new "equipment supervisor," as distinguished from the "factory hand," will not directly control given units of output. The metric hour for units produced will continue to be important for measuring machine output, but it is meaningless with respect to the "productivity" of the individual worker. In short, what an operator does to manage his part of a complex system will be hardly different from what managers and engineers are paid to do *by salary* in running their parts of the system.

Much of what has been said about the nature of work in the new technology is speculative. At best all one can do is to project possible consequences based on general trends. Just as government and private industry are collecting quantities of data on problems of unemployment because of technological displacement, so we need more detailed information about the nature of work itself on the new horizons of technology.

Collecting more information is not the only task. As stated earlier, what man does in his working life is just as important to him and to society as the goods and services he consumes in his leisure hours. This is a value accepted by the scientist, engineer, educator, manager, artist, politician, and many others who are not linked directly to the machine. Workers hold these same values, but too often technological constraints preclude their fulfillment. Does it have to be this way? This is the central question. Does technology have to be considered as a "given," meaning that humans as individuals, or as members of larger groups, must struggle to find *after-the-fact* ways to adapt? We think not. We believe that the same ingenuity and effort that has gone into the creation of our machines can be used to enrich the lives of those who operate them.

Applying the needed ingenuity is not an easy task. Old assumptions must be re-examined in light of new knowledge about human behavior. The function of work should be considered not solely in terms of immediate and measurable productive efficiency. The needs and potentials of humans *as humans* should be made a central consideration. The two are not necessarily antithetical. There is encouraging evidence strongly suggesting how technical requirements can be met at the same time that a broad spectrum of human needs and aspirations is fulfilled.

Some years ago a department of a large American company began experimenting with a new idea which came to be known as *job enlargement* (see Guest, 1964, p. 3). Dissatisfied with the application of scientific management principles in the design of tasks, the officials of the organization and a number of employees consulted on new ways of performing the required work. The workers convinced their superiors that instead of routinizing and fractionating work they would find it more challenging to work on a variety of tasks involving the production of a major component of the product. Management agreed—with reservations—and the experiment went forward. To management's astonishment, not only was the rate of production maintained but the quality of work was vastly improved. Even more astonishing was the ingenuity of the workers in devising better ways of setting up the operations. They also made suggestions about the design of the product—suggestions which even design engineers had not thought of.

The experiment was observed by a group of social scientists who publicized it in an obscure academic publication (see Walker and Richardson, 1947). In time, a number of other experiments were conducted in other organizations. Although the proliferation of the job enlargement concept never took on the form of a great national "movement," it did shatter many assumptions held so strongly by the practitioners of scientific management. It gave encouragement to those who believed that human beings, even those with limited intelligence and education, were capable of being creative at work.

Job enlargement as a concept has been limited to fractionated tasks characterized by the assembly-line technology. It has not been deliberately considered in more automated operations, possibly because automated machine supervision, as noted above, does make use of an enlarged set of skills and capabilities. But again, this may be more the result of chance rather than of design. In most operations men are still viewed essentially as instruments performing work which the machine is not capable of doing itself.

The radical suggestion being made here is that we look first at the human needs and give men the fullest possible opportunity to express these needs in the work environment. This calls for something more than simply making jobs interesting. It involves a different relationship of workers to the whole system of organization. It calls for greater involvement in organizational as well as technical decisions by workers. It means a change in deeply held assumptions about competition between jobs at the work place. It calls for the elimination of many of the bureaucratic restraints and controls which those in positions of authority have felt are absolutely essential. It demands that the needs of higher level self-fulfillment must be met as well as the more basic security needs.

Finally, it should be recognized that as the level of education rises in our society there is a concomitant rise in expectations among the millions of youths seeking useful employment. On one hand, the new technology demands this higher level of education and training for those who will become the scientists, engineers, and managers. But for the great majority, more education could compound the frustrations of youth if, in their working lives, only limited use is made of their learning and of the full range of their human capacities. Surely, as the most technologically advanced society in the world, this is a challenge to which we can respond. It may mean a thoroughgoing shift in the motivations and bases of American industry. But it is obvious that these are already changing. Our task is to control change for the fuller life—at work and at leisure—that we can provide for all men.

References

Aitken, Hugh G. J. *Taylorism at Watertown Arsenal: Scientific Management in Action, 1908–1915.* Harvard University Press, 1960.

Blauner, Robert. *Alienation and Freedom: The Factory Worker and His Industry.* University of Chicago Press, 1964.

Blum, Albert A. "America's Reactions to Technological Change and Automation: A Comparative View." *Management of Personnel Quarterly,* Vol. 3, No. 3, Fall 1964.

Guest, Robert H. "Better Utilization of Skills through Job Design." *Management of Personnel Quarterly,* Vol. 3, No. 3, Fall 1964.

Oliver, John W. *History of American Technology.* 1956.

The Triple Revolution. Ad Hoc Committee on the Triple Revolution, 1964.

Ure, Andrew. *The Philosophy of Manufactures.* London, 1835. Quoted in John W. Oliver, *History of American Technology.* 1956.

Walker, Charles R., and Robert H. Guest. *The Man on the Assembly Line.* Harvard University Press, 1952.

——, and Frederick L. W. Richardson. *Human Relations in an Expanding Company.* Yale University Press, 1947.

Edgar H. Schein

Organizational Effectiveness

Early theories of organization were content to talk of "profit maximization," "providing an efficient service," "high productivity," and "good
employee morale" as sufficient criteria of effectiveness. What has
undermined these as viable criteria has been (1) the discovery that
seemingly rational organizations behave ineffectively if the sole criterion is profit or providing a good service, and (2) the discovery that
organizations fulfill multiple functions and have multiple goals, some
of which may be in conflict with each other. For example, if we think
of organizations like universities, teaching hospitals, or prisons, we
can immediately name several functions or goals, all of which are
primary and essential. The university must teach and, at the same
time, must create valid knowledge through research; the teaching
hospital must take care of and cure patients, and must provide learning opportunities for interns and residents; the prison must keep
criminals out of circulation, and must provide opportunities for reha-
bilitation. Is the effectiveness of the organization to be judged by its
performance on one function, on both separately, or on some integration of the several functions?

One attempted resolution to these dilemmas has been to define
effectiveness in terms of systems-level criteria. Acknowledging that
every system has multiple functions and that it exists within an
environment which provides unpredictable inputs, a system's effectiveness can be defined as its capacity to survive, adapt, maintain
itself, and grow, regardless of the particular functions it fulfills. A
number of students of organization, such as Argyris, Trist, Rice, and
Bennis, have argued explicitly for this type of conception. Perhaps the
clearest statement of effectiveness criteria in these terms has been
given by Bennis (1962, p. 273). He introduces these ideas in reference to the traditional approaches of measuring output and satisfaction at a given point in time:

> If we view organizations as adaptive, problem-solving, organic
> structures, then inferences about effectiveness have to be made,

Edgar H. Schein, *Organizational Psychology* © 1965. Reprinted by permission
of Prentice-Hall, Inc.

not from static measures of output, though these may be helpful, but on the basis of the processes through which the organization approaches problems. In other words, no single measurement of organizational efficiency or satisfaction—no single time slice of organizational performance—can provide valid indicators of organizational health.

Instead, Bennis proposes the following three criteria of health, criteria which, interestingly, closely mirror recent formulations about mental health proposed by Jahoda (1958):

1. *Adaptability*—the ability to solve problems and to react with flexibility to changing environmental demands.

2. *A sense of identity*—knowledge and insight on the part of the organization of what it is, what its goals are, and what it is to do. Pertinent questions are: To what extent are goals understood and shared widely by members of the organization, and to what extent is self-perception on the part of organization members in line with perceptions of the organization by others?

3. *Capacity to test reality*—the ability to search out, accurately perceive, and correctly interpret the real properties of the environment, particularly those which have relevance for the functioning of the organization.

A fourth criterion which is often mentioned, one which in effect underlies the others, is a state of "integration" among the subparts of the total organization, such that the parts are not working at cross-purposes. For Argyris, for example, this criterion is central, and he devotes most of his research and theorizing to finding those conditions which will permit an integration of individual needs and organizational goals (Argyris, 1964). What he regards as unhealthy or ineffective are restrictions on output, destructive competition, and apathy among employees in order to fulfill personal needs at the expense of organizational goals.

McGregor has argued in a similar vein for the integration of personal and organizational goals (McGregor, 1960). According to his theory, if management develops practices built on a more valid set of assumptions about man, it will produce this integration and hence greater effectiveness. Finally, Blake and Mouton (1964) argue for the integration of concern for production and concern for people. Organizational effectiveness, according to Blake and Mouton is achieved when management succeeds in being both production- and people-centered. To support this theory, they have developed training programs which explicitly attempt to develop this managerial style. In summary, a systems-level criterion of organizational effectiveness must be a *multiple* criterion involving adaptability, sense of identity, capacity to test reality, and internal integration.

To the extent that effectiveness is a *multiple* criterion, we must be careful to avoid the trap of concluding that it depends on merely one thing. Thus, it would be a mistake to assume that if one selected the right people and trained them to do the job, effectiveness would be insured. It would be equally erroneous to assume that the establishment of a mutually satisfactory psychological contract with employees, or the reduction of intergroup competition, or leadership training, any of these alone, would guarantee effectiveness. Rather, the systems conception leads us to a different way of thinking about the problem: Viewed as a total system, how does an organization cope with its environment? How does it obtain information and process it validly? What mechanisms exist for translating information, particularly about alterations in the environment, into changed operations? Are the internal operations flexible enough to cope with changes?

Maintaining Effectiveness through an Adaptive-Coping Cycle

The sequence of activities or processes which begin with some change in the internal or external environment and end with a more adaptive dynamic equilibrium for dealing with the change is the organization's *adaptive-coping cycle*. If we identify the various stages or processes of this cycle, we will also be able to identify the points where organizations typically may fail to cope adequately and where, therefore, consultants and researchers have been able in a variety of ways to help increase organizational effectiveness.

The stages of the adaptive-coping cycle are sixfold, as follows:

1. Sensing a change in the internal or external environment.
2. Importing the relevant information about the change into those parts of the organization which can act upon it.
3. Changing production or conversion processes inside the organization according to the information obtained.
4. Stabilizing internal changes while reducing or managing undesired by-products (undesired changes in related systems which have resulted from the desired changes).
5. Exporting new products, services, and so on which are more in line with the originally perceived changes in the environment.
6. Obtaining feedback on the success of the change through further sensing of the state of the external environment and the degree of integration of the internal environment.

Let us illustrate this process with two simple examples. Suppose a manufacturing concern producing electronic equipment learns that the space program is going to increase the demand for this equipment a great deal (stage 1). The information about this change in demand must be imported into the organization in the sense of being taken seriously by those members who are in a position to do something about it. It is not sufficient for the market research department to have the information if it cannot convince the general management (stage 2). If management becomes convinced, it must change its production processes to enable the company to produce more of the equipment (stage 3). These changes must be accomplished without producing other undesirable internal changes (for example, a strike in response to unreasonable demands for increased production), and they must be stabilized (stage 4). The increased production must be marketed and sold (stage 5). And, finally, sales figures and future-demand figures must then be analyzed to determine whether the organizational change has been "successful" in terms of increased marketability, and the internal environment must be assessed to determine whether unanticipated costs in the form of lowered morale or intergroup competition have been minimized (stage 6).

For a different example, let us take a college fraternity as the organization. The fraternity leadership might sense in the college administration a shift in policy toward shutting down fraternities unless scholastic standards increase (stage 1). Stage 2 would then be to get the membership to recognize the real danger to the survival of the fraternity. Stage 3 might be a program of changing norms by reducing emphasis on social activities and increasing emphasis on scholastic activities, without (stage 4) producing undesired changes, such as total loss of prestige among other fraternities. In connection with these stages, the fraternity leaders might also recognize the necessity of convincing *other* fraternities on the campus to develop similar programs in their own houses, because of the likelihood that university policy would respond only to changes in the whole fraternity system. Stage 5 would be the actual improvement in grades, test performance, and classroom behavior, while stage 6 would be a matter of checking with the administration about whether the fraternity's standing was improving, whether policy would again change, and what fraternity member attitudes now were.

Both examples cited start with some changes in the external environment. The coping cycle is no different, however, if the first step is the recognition that something is not right in the *internal* environment. Thus, an organization may sense that employee morale is too low, or that several departments are destructively competing with one another, or that a technologically sound process is not being used correctly in production, or that management attitudes and practices are failing to elicit adequate motivation and loyalty among the employees. Once the information of some change or problem is sensed by some part of the organization, it must then be imported and lead to changes in the manner described if organizational effectiveness is to be increased.

Problems and Pitfalls in the Adaptive-Coping Cycle

One advantage of considering the adaptive-coping cycle as a series of stages lies in its helping to identify areas of difficulty in maintaining and improving effectiveness in response to a changing environment. Certain problems and pitfalls characteristically are associated with each stage.

1. *Failure to sense changes in the environment or incorrectly sensing what is happening.* There are innumerable cases of organizations which have failed to survive because they did not sense either a decline in the demand for their product or an important internal problem. Many businesses can adjust to new conditions provided the organization can sense when the time is ripe to develop new products, or services, or procedures. If the organization has multiple functions, as does a university, it becomes especially important to accurately sense changing attitudes about education, the role of the university in the community, the feelings of alumni about contributions, the reputation it enjoys within the academic community, the morale of its faculty, and so on. Consulting and applied research specialities, like market research, consumer psychology, and public opinion polling, have developed partly in response to organizational needs for more accurate sensing of internal and external environmental changes.

2. *Failure to get the relevant information to those parts of the organization which can act upon it or use it.* One of the commonest problems of present-day large-scale organizations is that staff units within them obtain information which they are unable to impart to line management. For example, many personnel departments have become convinced that the management process would be more effective if line management would adopt different assumptions about the nature of man. . . . One could say that the personnel departments have correctly sensed a change in the state of research knowledge concerning the management process. But unless this knowledge can be imparted in a meaningful way to line managers, one cannot say that the information has really been imported into the system. This example illustrates another difficulty. To change assumptions about the nature of man involves a change of attitudes, self-images, and working procedures. Such a change will typically be strongly resisted because of its threatening nature. Any change implies that the former way of functioning has been erroneous. To get the information imported, therefore, might involve a major and lengthy program of influencing attitudes, self-images, and working procedures.

Often a research department or other unit of an organization comes upon information which argues for changes in technology, production methods, and the like, yet is unable to convince key management to consider the information seriously. Difficulties in introducing automatic data processing equipment into various organizational departments often stem from a refusal of management to pay attention to information on how the equipment would really work because the implied change is too threatening to established ways of working, attitudes, and basic assumptions.

These difficulties of importing information into the relevant system have led to the use of external consultants or researchers as information transmitters. A staff group which already correctly senses a problem may find itself hiring a consultant to re-identify the problem and import it to other parts of the system. The consultant uses his prestige to help import the information into those parts of the system that have the power to do something about it.

3. *Failure to influence the conversion or production system to make the necessary changes.* Effecting internal changes in an organization requires more than the recognition that such changes are necessary. Organization planners or top managers often naïvely assume that simply announcing the need for a change and giving orders that the change should be made will produce the desired outcome. In practice, however, resistance to change is one of the most ubiquitous organizational phenomena. Whether it be an increase in production which is desired, or adaptation to a new technology, or a new method of doing the work, it is generally found that those workers and managers who are directly affected will resist the change or sabotage it if it is forced upon them. . . .

Probably the major reason for resistance to change is that the conversion or production parts of any organization are themselves systems—they generate ways of working, stable interpersonal relationships, common norms and values, and techniques of coping and surviving in their own environment. In other words, the subsystems of an organization operate by the same coping principles as the whole organization. In order to change, therefore, the subsystem must sense a change in management policy, be able to import this information into itself, manage its own change, stabilize it, export better results in terms of the desires of management, and obtain feedback on how it is doing. The line manager desiring the change can, from this point of view, accomplish more by viewing his own role as that of helping the system to change or cope, rather than giving orders or issuing directives. There is some evidence that one of the best ways of giving this help is to involve the system concerned in the decision making about *how* to produce the necessary changes. The more the system which must change participates in decisions about how to manage the change, the less likely it is to resist the change and the more stable the change is likely to be (Lewin, 1958, and Coch and French, 1948, pp. 512–32).

4. *Failure to consider the impact of changes on other systems*

and failure to achieve stable change. There are some classic cases where attitudes changed during a program of training in human relations but reverted completely following a return to the job. Cases can also be cited where changes in administrative procedure in one department were so threatening to another department that they had to be abandoned to preserve the overall morale of the organization (Bavelas and Strauss, 1962). Because the various parts of an organization tend to be linked, a proposed change in one part must be carefully assessed in terms of its likely impact on other parts. Wherever possible, the linkage between systems should be used to positive advantage, in the sense that certain desired changes, if started in one part of the system, will tend to spread by themselves to other parts of the system.

A good example of this process would be in the changing of assumptions and attitudes toward people. If the top management of the organization can be helped to alter attitudes, then because of their strategic linkage to all parts of the organization, their resultant behavior change would automatically act as a force on all of their subordinates toward similar changes. The same change in attitudes in the middle or near the bottom of the hierarchy may fail to spread, or even to maintain itself, because of inadequate upward and lateral linkages to other systems.

5. *Failure to export the new product, service, or information.* Once changes have been made within the organization, there remains the problem of exporting the new results. In the case of business concerns, this is a problem of sales and marketing. In the case of other organizations, such as the fraternity cited above, it may be a problem of communicating as rapidly as possible to the relevant environmental systems the changes which have occurred. It does little good for the fraternity to change its norms of scholastic achievement if the time before grades improve is so long that the administration has already decided to close the fraternities.

If the organization wants to export information, the problem is one of advertising. But because advertising involves gaining a competitive advantage over another organization, forces that distort information are generated. Here, as in the above cases, one role the consultant has played has been to export *reliable* information about changes in the system. Thus, a neutral faculty member may be appointed jointly by the administration and the fraternity to evaluate changes in members' attitudes. Similarly, we send "political observers" to countries requesting foreign aid to evaluate the validity of their claims that they are changing toward democratic forms of government; government agencies send representatives to industrial firms that claim to have developed the capacity to provide a weapons system or some other product efficiently and cheaply. In all these cases, what is involved is accurate export of information about changes in the system which may not be immediately visible in such indexes as higher production rates or new products and services.

6. *Failure to obtain feedback on the success of the change.* The problems here are essentially the same as the problems of sensing changes in the environment in the first place. We need only add that many organizations have explicitly created systems to assess the impact of changes and thus to provide themselves the necessary feedback information. In the case of internal changes, there may be a research group in the employee relations department whose prime job is to survey employees periodically to determine how they are reacting to changes in management policy; political organizations will run polls immediately after a change in political platform to determine the public's reaction; production control units will assess whether a new process is producing the desired increase in efficiency; and so on.

In summary, for each stage in the adaptive-coping cycle one can identify characteristic pitfalls and problems. The important point is that the maintenance and increase of organizational effectiveness depend on successful coping, which means that *all* of the stages must be successfully negotiated. It does little good to have the best market research department in the world if the organization is unable to influence its own production systems; nor does it help to have a highly flexible production or conversion operation which cannot sense or digest information about environmental changes.

Organizational Conditions for Effective Coping

We began this [essay] with some general criteria of organizational effectiveness or health. We then specified the coping processes which appear to be necessary in a rapidly changing environment for such effectiveness or health to be maintained or increased. In this final section, I would like to outline what internal organizational conditions appear to be necessary for effective coping to occur. To some extent the argument becomes circular here, in that some health must be present for health to maintain itself or increase. The organizational conditions I will identify will, therefore, somewhat resemble the ultimate criteria of health cited by Bennis.

1. Successful coping requires the ability to take in and communicate information reliably and validly.
2. Successful coping requires internal flexibility and creativity to make the changes which are demanded by the information obtained.
3. Successful coping requires integration and commitment to the goals of the organization, from which comes the willingness to change.

4. Successful coping requires an internal climate of support and freedom from threat, since being threatened undermines good communication, reduces flexibility, and stimulates self-protection rather than concern for the total system.

These four conditions are not easy to achieve in a complex system such as a large organization, but some guidelines for their achievement can be outlined. . . .

1. If we look first at the *recruitment, selection, induction, and training of human resources,* [we can ask the following questions]. Are many of the methods currently being used for the selection, testing, and training of employees likely to produce an image in the minds of employees that the organization is relatively indifferent to their personal needs and capacities? And is it possible, therefore, that employees learn early in their career to withhold involvement, to make their performance routine, and to respond to demands for changes by feeling threatened and anxious rather than helpful and committed?

If the organization is genuinely concerned about building long-range effectiveness, must it not develop a system for hiring employees which makes them feel wanted, secure, meaningfully engaged in their job, and positively committed to organizational goals, and must it not develop training and management development programs which stimulate genuine psychological growth in order to insure the flexibility and creativity that may be required at some future time? It would appear that one of the best guarantees of ability to cope with an unpredictable environment would be to develop everyone to a maximum degree, even at the expense of short-run efficiency.

2. Turning next to the *utilization of employees and the psychological contract,* it would appear evident that if the organization expects its members to be committed, flexible, and in good communication with one another for the sake of overall organizational effectiveness, it is in effect asking them to be *morally* involved in the enterprise, to be committed to organizational goals and to value these. And if it expects them to be involved to this degree, the organization must for its part provide rewards and conditions consistent with such involvement. It cannot merely pay more money to obtain commitment, creativity, and flexibility; there must be the possibility of obtaining noneconomic rewards, such as autonomy, genuine responsibility, opportunities for challenge and for psychological growth.

Probably the most important thing the organization can do in this regard is to develop assumptions about people which fit reality. This, in turn, implies some willingness to find out what each man is like and what he truly wants. By making broad generalizations about people, the organization not only runs the risk of being wrong about the empirical realities, but, perhaps worse, it insults its employees by assuming they are all basically alike. If managerial assumptions begin to be exposed and tested, not only will this change provide a basis for learning what the facts are, but also the willingness to test assumptions will communicate a degree of concern for people which will reduce their feeling of being threatened or demeaned. As assumptions become increasingly realistic, management practices will begin to build the kind of climate which is needed for reliable and valid communication, creative effort, flexibility, and commitment.

3. Next, let us look at the *problem of groups and intergroup relations*. There is little question that groups are an integral part of any organization and that the basic choice is not whether to have them but, rather, how to create conditions under which group forces work toward organizational goals rather than counter to them. The first part of an answer is to be found in points 1 and 2 above, for the evidence seems quite clear that if employees feel threatened, demeaned, and unappreciated they will form together into *anti*-management groups. To prevent such groups from forming, therefore, requires management practices which are less threatening to the individual and more likely to enable him to integrate his own needs with organizational goals.

A second part of the answer lies in training for effective group membership and leadership. Though most of us have had much experience in groups, it is unlikely that we have had the opportunity to focus clearly on those factors which make groups more or less effective. If members of the organization come to understand better how groups work, they are less likely to form groups which are bound to fail. If groups are formed which can achieve some degree of psychological success, and if this success is perceived to be in part the result of good management, the group forces are more likely to be turned toward organizational goals. The point is, however, that it takes more than good intentions to make an effective group. It requires knowledge and training in how groups work.

When we turn to problems of intergroup competition, the answer seems clear that competition between the units or groups of a single organization or system must in the long run reduce effectiveness because competition leads to faulty communication, to greater pressures for conformity and hence less flexibility, and to commitment to subgroup rather than organizational goals. The dilemma is that competition also produces very high levels of motivation and productivity. As many case examples have shown, however, when organizationl units are stimulated into competition, the short-run gains of increased production are greatly outweighed by the long-run losses of reduced internal communication and flexibility. What organizations must develop is programs which obtain motivation and commitment in an integrative manner, which keep communication channels between subparts open, and which maintain the focus on total, organizational performance rather than individual, subgroup performance.

4. Finally, let us look at a variable which has been implicit throughout, but has not been explicitly treated—the variable of *leadership*. Much has been written on leadership, and it is beyond the scope of this discussion to review even cursorily the mass of research findings and theoretical positions which have been published. Two points are worth noting, however.

First, leadership is a *function* in the organization, rather than the trait of an individual. It is *distributed among the members of a group or organization,* and is not automatically vested in the chairman or the person with the formal authority. Good leadership and good membership therefore blend into each other in an effective organization. It is just as much the task of a member to help the group reach its goals as it is the task of the formal leader.

Second, leadership has a unique obligation to manage the relationships between a system and its environment, particularly in reference to the key functions of setting goals for the organization and defining the values or norms in terms of which the organization must basically develop a sense of identity (Selznick, 1951). This function must be fulfilled by those members who are in contact with the organization-environment boundary and who have the power to set policy for organization. This leadership function, which usually falls to the top executives of organizations, is critical. If the organization does not have clear goals and cannot develop a sense of identity, there is nothing to be committed to and nothing to communicate. At the same time, no organization need have its goals and identity *imposed* by its top executives. There is no reason why the organization cannot develop its goals and identity collaboratively and participatively, engaging every member down to the lowest echelons. What the top executives must do is to insure that goals are somehow set, but they may choose a variety of ways of allowing this to occur.

Conclusion

I have tried to argue for an approach to organizational effectiveness which hinges upon good communication, flexibility, creativity, and genuine psychological commitment. These conditions are to be obtained by (1) recruitment, selection, and training practices which stimulate rather than demean people; (2) more realistic psychological relationships based on a more realistic psychological contract; (3) more effective group action; and (4) better leadership in the sense of goal setting and value definition. The argument is not based on the assumption that this would be nice for people or make them feel better. Rather, the argument is that systems *work better* if their parts are in good communication with each other, are committed, and are creative and flexible.

References

Argyris, C. *Integrating the Individual and the Organization.* Wiley, 1964.

Bavelas, A., and G. Strauss. "Group Dynamics and Intergroup Relations." In *The Planning of Change,* ed. W. Bennis, K. Benne, and R. Chin. Holt, Rinehart and Winston, 1962.

Bennis, W. G. "Toward a 'Truly' Scientific Management: The Concept of Organizational Health." *General Systems Yearbook,* Vol. 7, 1962.

Blake, R. R., and Jane S. Mouton. *The Managerial Grid.* Gulf Publishing Co., 1964.

Coch, L., and J. R. P. French. "Overcoming Resistance to Change." *Human Relations,* Vol. 1, 1948.

Jahoda, M. *Current Concepts of Positive Mental Health.* Basic Books, 1958.

Lewin, K. "Group Decision and Social Change." In *Readings in Social Psychology,* ed. E. Maccoby, T. Newcomb, and E. Hartley. Holt, Rinehart and Winston, 1958.

McGregor, D. *The Human Side of Enterprise.* McGraw-Hill, 1960.

Selznick, P. *Leadership in Administration.* Harper & Row, 1957.

Part IV

Value Dimensions
of the Decision Process

Chapter Eight

The Value Issue of Business

Perhaps more than at any time in its economic history, the United States is faced with what can be called "the value issue of business." Questions are regularly raised in the public forum concerning business and its relationship to problems such as unemployment, racial discrimination, social conformity, automobile safety, air and water pollution, and collusion. The very raising of these questions, however, brings with it some explicit or implicit theoretical concept of the nature of the relationship between man's values and his economic activity. To understand the value issue of business, it is necessary to understand what concepts the businessman brings to these problems.

Economics as a Value System

The basic concepts which are commonly accepted today of the relationship between economic activity and values are a direct outgrowth of a formulation laid down by Adam Smith some 200 years ago. "Capitalism," "free enterprise," or, as it is commonly labeled, "the classical economic model," is the basic philosophical rationale to which most businessmen turn when faced with social value questions. To understand the businessman's approach to "the value issue," we need to understand the relationship between the classical economic rationale and social value questions.

This chapter was prepared with Carol J. Elbing. It is a summary of some of the major arguments which are fully developed in Elbing and Elbing (1967).

From its inception, the classical economic model has combined a "scientific" theory—a descriptive-predictive theory about the exchange of economic units—and an ethical theory—a theory of social values. Moreover, from its inception, it has offered both its scientific and social value theories not only as theories of how economic activity and social values *ought* to be worked out, but as theories of how they *will*, more or less automatically, be worked out. The model presents the economic marketplace as a self-regulating device, at both the scientific and ethical levels.

Briefly, the important assumptions of this economic model are that the production of goods and services in the pursuit of self-interest are automatically regulated by the interactions of the marketplace. Those items which are "best," "most wanted," "least expensive," and so on will prevail, driving the others from the market. The ultimate result of such competition is the economic good of the nation. This is the mechanism behind the descriptive-predictive aspect of the economic model. The workings of this system have been the subject of continuing discussion among economists and, indeed, is a topic basic to their discipline. It is to this rationale that the businessman tends to turn when confronted with questions about the relationship of his actions to social values.

Confusion about the two aspects of the economic model—the scientific and the ethical—underlies many of the difficulties facing businessmen as they attempt to deal with the value issue of business. Social value problems are frequently taken for granted, on the assumption that they are worked out automatically in the economic exchange of goods and services. How does the economic model stand as a social value rationale as well as a descriptive-predictive model?

Economics as "Moral"

One rationale for dealing with the relationship between economic activity and social values is the notion that greater social good is directly concomitant with greater economic good. As Charles Wilson, former Secretary of Defense, is so often quoted as having said, "What is good for business is good for the country." The implicit social value theory here is that the value issue of business is dealt with automatically by the marketplace, in the same manner by which it works out the problems of economic exchange. This rationale thus posits economics as a moral system.

The difficulty with this argument is that, of course, the marketplace does not arbitrate all values optimally in the same sense that it optimally arbitrates the exchange of goods. The marketplace is neither democratic, objective, scientific, or rational. Furthermore, it cannot be assumed that the marketplace even touches on all social value problems: many important business value issues are not affected by marketplace exchange. The quality of life in an organization, for example, is one value issue of business not directly arbitrated by the marketplace. The effects of multinational firms on the cultures of the world is another. Thus, whatever the usefulness of the marketplace as an optimum economic regulator, it is no guaranteed device for the automatic working out of social value problems. The assumption does not stand up to critical analysis that any economic system insures moral or social values by its very nature, so that value issues need not be of active and direct concern.

Thus, even if we could substantiate that the greatest profit to business brought about the greatest national wealth and the greatest *economic* well-being to the greatest number of individuals, the value issue is not thereby disposed. It is not justifiable to treat the entire value issue of business only by pointing to some standard of economic well-being. Although the economic model is a useful explanation of the exchange of economic units, it must be concluded that it is inadequate if taken as a social or moral value rationale for business. The surface of the value issue is barely scratched by application of the rationale of the nonobjective and nonrepresentative marketplace arbitrating the production of goods and services, or by reference to a broad general index of national economic level of activity.

Economics as "Amoral"

One way of attempting to dispose of the logical difficulties of the economic model as a social value rationale is to disengage it from all claims to its being a moral philosophy, and define it as amoral, having no reference to value issues. It is advised by some that the economic model should claim only technical or scientific utility and be judged in such terms only. Far from purporting to deal with behavior, values, or with the general relationship of economic activity to values, the economic model, conceived as amoral, claims to deal solely with economic man, economic events, and economic ends, and to take as given the relationship of economic activity to social values. The economist Frank Knight (1965), for example, has said: "The science (of economics) abstracts from *error* much as mechanics does from friction. . . . Analysis must begin with individual economic conduct, hence, with the man isolated from society. . . ."

Economic data of all kinds are thus declared to be separate from any value connotations. Whenever "man" is referred to in such a model, it is not social man or moral man or the total man, but an abstract "economic" man, who is presumed, for the purposes of economic discussion, to operate rationally in terms of purely economic factors. Similarly, in terms of this amoral model, economic activity is abstracted from the complex of human and social moral actions and viewed narrowly as a purely economic or technical pursuit. The implicit claim is merely that, *given* the economic system, the model serves a descriptive-predictive function.

It is commonly assumed that such a model of economic activity, claiming only technical or scientific utility and asking to be judged in such terms only, is entirely value free. But however much an amoral model of economic activity may be desired, such a model is as fraught with value assumptions as a broad social philosophy. At first it may seem that such an amoral model has narrowed itself to a strictly scientific theory, has avoided entanglements with value issues, and has placed value questions in a realm separate from economics and business, presumably to be dealt with by other disciplines. In actuality, it has not accomplished those feats at all. Inherent in such a model is the assumption that economic actions lead to consequences which are, if not positively good, at least socially or morally harmless. Thus, far from being value-free, the model fosters an assumption about the relationship between economic activities and values—the assumption that the two can, with impunity, be considered in isolation.

This value assumption is the most undermining of the value issue of business. While it is conceivable that we might generally isolate, with social and moral impunity, a concept of mechanics from a concept of friction, it is not conceivable that we could generally isolate economics from social value issues. Economic action does not in fact exist separately from social or moral action, any more than mechanical action exists separately from friction. Economic value is always a social value, always interacting with other values in the arena of human action, and strongly affected by and affecting other social values. Obviously it is legitimate to declare—in any field—that for certain technical problems it is useful to artifically set aside social value considerations as given. In a value context, however, any attempt to isolate economic and social considerations is not realistic.

The Shortcomings of Economics as a Value System

The economic model blocks active work on vital business value issues in that it fosters a groundless optimism. In the moral version of the model, the marketplace is imagined to be an automatic device for working out not only economic but social value questions and for insuring not only material but social progress. In the amoral model, the abstraction of social value issues from economic considerations fosters another sort of optimism, the optimism that somehow economic processes are of such nature that they can go on revolutionizing society without disrupting human values.

Both the moral and amoral economic models foster the attitude that the value issue of business is of merely peripheral concern. When business processes are broadly considered as automatically worked out in the marketplace or as inherently morally justifiable or legitimately amoral, value problems are seen as a mere side issue. Once social value is conceived as a side issue, an oversimplified formula may seem adequate to the magnitude of the social value problem. Values and business can then be discussed in terms of easy platitudes, or the entire issue can be reduced to a strictly legal matter, or it can be set aside as a matter for personal conscience.

Business as a Social System

The fundamental reason why the value issue cannot be satisfactorily formulated within a purely economic model is that the business institution is not merely an economic-technical system. It is a social system as well. Indeed, economic activity *is* social activity. Every business act, whether or not it has direct economic connotations and ramifications, is a social act in that it is a social response to other human beings. Even purely "technical" and "economic" acts have their social dimension. Business produces not only economic consequences—goods and services, profit and wealth (and the social ramifications of these economic consequences)—it also produces a great variety of important social consequences. Its moral nature derives from that fact. The value issue of business derives from the pervasive social (hence moral) nature of business, and cannot be extrapolated merely from its abstracted economic functions. Thus the full scope of the value issue of business can be understood and formulated adequately only when it is viewed within a social framework which includes all the social effects of business action.

Business and the Individual

Because the firm is a social system, its effect on the individual goes well beyond economics, influencing the individual's sense of self and his functioning in the firm, family, and community. When the firm is recognized as a social system as well as a technical-economic system, the values of individuals are seen as growing, in part, out of social interaction within that system. The firm is thus recognized as a basic *source* of individual values as well as an arena for their enactment, affecting the individual's own evaluation of himself, his value outlook toward his world, and in turn, the sort of influence he will have on the values of that world.

Business and Other Groups

The relationships among various business groups—managers, workers, unions, stockholders, consumers, government agencies, schools of business, and so on—generate intergroup attitudes, social trends, and values far beyond those of merely economic import. Norms, goals, and values are formed within groups and solidified through intergroup action. Group action thus results not only in economic change but change in the social groups themselves. When business is viewed solely as an economic system in terms of the traditional economic model, it appears logical that its only responsibility is toward one group, its capital investors. However, when the various groups within the business institution are also recognized as claimants, all intergroup action, being social action, is seen to involve *reciprocal* social responsibility.

Business and Society in the United States

The influence of business on society as a whole in the United States extends so far beyond merely economic considerations that the United States is often characterized as a distinctly business culture. The relationship between business and society is not primarily economic, nor is it primarily determined by the marketplace. When business is recognized as a vast social system, it is also recognized that a vast array of its social transactions, little affected by the marketplace, are as primary a function of business as its economic transactions. The social value implications of this cultural climate go far beyond what can be formulated in terms of the classical economic framework. The climate of this vast network of social transactions is a significant aspect of the characteristically American culture.

Business and Foreign Societies

The relationship of business to foreign societies must also be viewed within a social framework. American business in foreign countries influences not only the economic life of the world, but the entire social-political climate of a precarious international scene. Foreign trade today is often justified—as it was in the eighteenth century —in terms of national wealth and power, with the added boon of economic development for other nations. Now, as then, economic progress is equated with social progress. Yet the relationship between social values and economic forces should not be assumed *a priori*, but should be subjected to broad social analysis, in keeping with the fact that business abroad does have critical social impact beyond its economic impact. Only by examining within a social framework our business relationships with other countries can we begin to assess how economic values relate to other crucial social values.

In summary, any attempt to deal with the *value* issue of business on any level—at the level of the individual, of groups, of domestic society, or at the level of the broad international scene—must begin by placing business in a social framework, rather than in the traditional economic framework. Whatever the utility may be of viewing the social relationships of business in narrowly economic terms for specified technical purposes, the traditional economic framework is useless for the purpose of formulating values. It merely distorts and reduces the value issue. The relationship between economic and other social values in society requires broad social analysis, rather than mere economic analysis, in keeping with the broad social influence of business.

A New Social Value Theory for Business

We have concluded that the value issue of business is distorted and reduced when formulated in terms of the economic model. Let us now state explicitly the fundamentals of a *new social value theory* to replace the social value theory of the economic model. All of the foregoing discussion, of course, has been an implicit reformulation of theory, but a concise statement of basic principles is now possible on the basis of the foregoing discussion, and may serve as a useful reference point.

The first principle of a social value theory based on a recognition of business as a social system is that the moral nature of business inheres in all of its social acts, and is therefore pervasive. The social value rationale of the economic model is a claim that the moral nature of business inheres in its production of economic goods, services, and national wealth (and in directly resulting social goods). A value rationale derived from a social model is a recognition that the moral nature of business inheres in all of its social, not merely economic, acts and effects. The social influence of business is seen to be truly extensive when it is recognized that every act—even every "economic" act of business—is a social act. When it is recognized that every social act implies moral value, it can be seen that the value issue of business is pervasive.

The second principle of the theory is that business-social transactions at all levels are value arbitrations. The social value rationale of the economic model assumes the marketplace to be the arbiter of social values, but it has been demonstrated that the marketplace does not and cannot achieve such a role. It is clear that the social values of business are, in fact, worked out by all of the social actions and transaction of the entire business system, not merely those of the marketplace. All choices and acts regarding production, finance, advertising, marketing—all relationships with workers, stockholders, buyers, sellers, consumers, government—work out the value issue, not merely marketplace choices and acts.

The third principle of the theory is that because the social effects of business go beyond the economic, economic measures cannot be used as indexes for other social values. The social value rationale of the economic model makes the implicit claim that it is feasible to measure the social value of business in economic terms, and to take for granted all other social values as parallel; and it makes only economic factors explicit while all other social factors are implicit or taken as given. A value theory based on a social model recognizes that, in order to assess the social effects of business, it is essential to measure them explicitly.

The fourth principle of the theory is that the social value issue is as important as the economic issue of business. The social value rationale of the economic model assumes business to be an economic-technical system and the social value issue to be peripheral. A value rationale based on a social model recognizes that business inescapably functions as a social system, and that social value issues cannot be subordinated. Recognized as a social system with pervasive social and moral influence, business cannot be written off as amoral, nor can economic considerations be said to be the main issue of business and social and moral value concerns as side issues. While it is perfectly true that the economic profitability of the firm is essential to its ability to function at all, it is just as true that its overall "social" profitability is what justifies its existence in the first place.

Conclusions

Two hundred years after the first Industrial Revolution, business has become a continual revolutionizing force in U. S. society and in those societies with whom the U. S. does business. The danger is that so long as the rationale of the economic model is the working social value theory, economic value will continue to be the driving revolutionary force, and technological means will determine social ends. If we are interested in social values, we are concerned that the growth and development of society and of the individuals within it be commensurate with technological revolution and business advance. Business being a social system, a social value framework which includes criteria from all of the social sciences, not just economics, must be used to assess the social growth of business.

If we are concerned with the value issue of business, we are concerned that it be an active field of direct inquiry, and we are also concerned that the best methods available be used in the pursuit of such inquiry. Once freed from the assumptions of the economic model, which attempts to guarantee that values will be worked out automatically, the value issue of business is seen as a matter *requiring* investigation. Yet the concept of objective systematic investigation, of "method," in the value realm is not a commonly accepted one.

There has been skepticism about the actual feasibility of "method" in the value realm. Certainly if by "method" we mean such popular concepts of method as those of the physical sciences, technology, mathematics, or computer programming, it may well be that the concept of method for social value inquiry is inappropriate. However, if by "method" we mean the most critical procedures available pertinent to the question of concern, the concept of method is not only appropriate but essential to value inquiry.

Some method is bound to be used in every inevitable encounter with the value issue of business. Insofar as our moral aspirations are high, our standards for methods of pursuing them must also be high. Certainly, business being a social system, methods from all of the social sciences, not just economics, must be used to deal with business value questions. They are essential if the value issue of business is to become an active field of study commensurate with its significance. If our most rigorous critical methods are merely harnessed to technological means and to the market, they will assuredly run away with ultimate ends.

Not only must interest in the social value issue of business be translated into direct critical inquiry, it must be translated into the very practical process of decision making. Values inhere in every stage of that process, so that the question is not whether we deal with value issues in decision making, but whether we deal with them by design or default. Viewed in a social framework, however, it is clear that the inherent value issue in decision making is by no means vital only to the business manager. It is through the decision making of all citizens that social values are made concrete in a business society.

References

Elbing, Alvar O. Jr., and Carol J. Elbing. *The Value Issue of Business.* McGraw-Hill, 1967.

England, George W. "Personal Value Systems of American Managers." *Academy of Management Journal,* March 1967.

Freedman, Robert. "The Challenge of Business Ethics." *Atlanta Economic Review,* May 1962.

Galbraith, John K. *The Affluent Society.* Houghton Mifflin, 1958.

Heilbroner, Robert. "The Future of Capitalism." *Commentary,* April 1966.

Knight, Frank H. "Understanding Society through Economics." *American Behavioral Scientist,* September 1965.

Leighton, Dorothea, *et. al. The Character of Danger.* Basic Books, 1963.

Parsons, Talcott, and Edward A. Shils, eds. *Toward a General Theory of Action.* Harvard University Press, 1951.

Schein, Edgar H. "Organizational Socialization and the Profession of Management." *Industrial Management Review,* Winter 1968.

Whyte, William F. Jr. *The Organization Man.* Doubleday, 1956.

Readings on the Value Issue

The value issue of business, in general, is concerned with the basic theoretical rationale underlying organized activities. In Chapter 8 the discussion focuses on the rationale derived from traditional economics. However, any consideration of the value issue must include the concept of business as a social system as well as a technical and economic system, and, therefore, it must examine the social as well as the narrowly economic consequences of business. The value problem is the same in every field. Government is not just a political system; it is also a social organization with social consequences. Hospitals are social as well as medical organizations. Schools, churches, societies, all are social organizations as well as organizations concerned with a specialized "technical" purpose. In each case the value issue involves not only the consequences of technical action but also the consequences of social action.

The purpose of the readings in this section is to explore this issue further. Erich Fromm examines the relationship of the marketplace and personality; Dorothy Lee considers the influence of one organization, her children's school, on creativity; Dero Saunders pursues the discontent of the executive in the large organization; and Jacques Ellul discusses the effect of technological change on mankind. John Ward examines the historical meaning of individualism, and Carl Rogers contemplates the value consequences of manipulating human behavior. Robert Hutchins, in a satirical piece, pointedly raises value issues that are at stake in the modern world.

The value issue is not resolved nor even thoroughly debated by the presentations in this section, but they do pose some of the most vital value questions inherent in the social transactions of business. A decision maker who pursues these broad value issues as they relate to the consequences of his decisions cannot be accused of hiding behind *ceteris paribus* or of ignoring the value consequences of his decisions.

Erich Fromm

Personality and the Marketplace

The marketing orientation developed as a dominant one only in the modern era. In order to understand its nature one must consider the economic function of the market in modern society as being not only analogous to this character orientation but as the basis and the main condition for its development in modern man.

Barter is one of the oldest economic mechanisms. The traditional local market, however, is essentially different from the market as it has developed in modern capitalism. Bartering on a local market offered an opportunity to meet for the purpose of exchanging commodities. Producers and customers became acquainted; they were relatively small groups; the demand was more or less known; so the producer could produce for this specific demand.

The modern market [1] is no longer a meeting place but a mechanism characterized by abstract and impersonal demand. One produces for this market, not for a known circle of customers; its verdict is based on laws of supply and demand; and it determines whether the commodity can be sold and at what price. No matter what the *use value* of a pair of shoes may be, for instance, if the supply is greater than the demand, some shoes will be sentenced to economic death; they might as well not have been produced at all. The market day is the "day of judgment" as far as the *exchange value* of commodities is concerned.

The reader may object that this description of the market is oversimplified. The producer does try to judge the demand in advance, and under monopoly conditions even obtains a certain degree of control over it. Nevertheless, the regulatory function of the market has been, and still is, predominant enough to have a profound influence on the character formation of the urban middle class and, through the latter's social and cultural influence, on the whole population. The market concept of value, the emphasis on exchange value

1. For a study of the history and function of the modern market, see Polanyi (1944).

rather than on use value, has led to a similar concept of value with regard to people and particularly to oneself. The character orientation which is rooted in the experience of oneself as a commodity and of one's value as exchange value I call the marketing orientation.

In our time the marketing orientation has been growing rapidly, together with the development of a new market that is a phenomenon of the last decades—the "personality market." Clerks and salesmen, business executives and doctors, lawyers and artists all appear on this market. It is true that their legal status and economic positions are different: some are independent, charging for their services; others are employed, receiving salaries. But all are dependent for their material success on a personal acceptance by those who need their services or who employ them.

The principle of evaluation is the same on both the personality and the commodity market: on the one, personalities are offered for sale; on the other, commodities. Value in both cases is their exchange value, for which use value is a necessary but not a sufficient condition. It is true, our economic system could not function if people were not skilled in the particular work they have to perform and were gifted only with a pleasant personality. Even the best bedside manner and the most beautifully equipped office on Park Avenue would not make a New York doctor successful if he did not have a minimum of medical knowledge and skill. Even the most winning personality would not prevent a secretary from losing her job unless she could type reasonably fast. However, if we ask what the respective weight of skill and personality as a condition for success is, we find that only in exceptional cases is success predominantly the result of skill and of certain other human qualities like honesty, decency, and integrity. Although the proportion between skill and human qualities on the one hand and "personality" on the other hand as prerequisites for sucecss varies, the "personality factor" always plays a decisive role. Success depends largely on how well a person sells himself on the market, how well he gets his personality across, how nice a "package" he is; whether he is "cheerful," "sound," "aggressive," "reliable," "ambitious"; furthermore, what his family background is, what clubs he belongs to, and whether he knows the right people. The type of personality required depends to some degree on the special field in which a person works. A stockbroker, a salesman, a secretary, a railroad executive, a college professor, or a hotel manager must each offer different kinds of personality that, regardless of their differences, must fulfill one condition: to be in demand.

The fact that in order to have success it is not sufficient to have the skill and equipment for performing a given task but that one must be able to "put across" one's personality in competition with many others shapes the attitude toward oneself. If it were enough for the purpose of making a living to rely on what one knows and what one can do, ones self-esteem would be in proportion to one's capacities, that is, to one's use value; but since success depends largely on how one sells one's personality, one experiences oneself as a commodity, or rather simultaneously as the seller and the commodity to be sold. A person is not concerned with his life and happiness, but with becoming salable. This feeling might be compared to that of a commodity, of handbags on a counter, for instance, could they feel and think. Each handbag would try to make itself as "attractive" as possible in order to attract customers and to look as expensive as possible in order to obtain a higher price than its rivals. The handbag sold for the highest price would feel elated, since that would mean it was the most "valuable" one; the one which was not sold would feel sad and convinced of its own worthlessness. This fate might befall a bag which, though excellent in appearance and usefulness, had the bad luck to be out of date because of a change in fashion.

Like the handbag, one has to be in fashion on the personality market, and in order to be in fashion one has to know what kind of personality is most in demand. This knowledge is transmitted in a general way throughout the whole process of education, from kindergarten to college, and implemented by the family. The knowledge acquired at this early stage is not sufficient, however; it emphasizes only certain general qualities like adaptability, ambition, and sensitivity to the changing expectations of other people. The more specific picture of the models for success one gets elsewhere. The pictorial magazines, newspapers, and newsreels show the pictures and life stories of the successful in many variations. Pictorial advertising has a similar function. The successful executive who is pictured in a tailor's advertisement is the image of how one should look and be, if one is to draw down the "big money" on the contemporary personality market.

The most important means of transmitting the desired personality pattern to the average man is the motion picture. The young girl tries to emulate the facial expression, coiffure, gestures of a high-priced star as the most promising way to success. The young man tries to look and be like the model he sees on the screen. While the average citizen has little contact with the life of the most successful people, his relationship with the motion-picture stars is different. It is true that he has no real contact with them either, but he can see them on the screen again and again, can write them and receive their autographed pictures. In contrast to the time when the actor was socially despised but was nevertheless the transmitter of the works of great poets to his audience, our motion-picture stars have no great works or ideas to transmit, but their function is to serve as the link an average person has with the world of the "great." Even if he can not hope to become as successful as they are, he can try to emulate them;

they are his saints, and because of their success they embody the norms for living.

Since modern man experiences himself both as the seller and as the commodity to be sold on the market, his self-esteem depends on conditions beyond his control. If he is "successful," he is valuable; if he is not, he is worthless. The degree of insecurity which results from this orientation can hardly be overestimated. If one feels that one's own value is not constituted primarily by the human qualities one possesses, but by one's success on a competitive market with ever-changing conditions, one's self-esteem is bound to be shaky and in constant need of confirmation by others. Hence one is driven to strive relentlessly for success, and any setback is a severe threat to one's self-esteem; helplessness, insecurity, and inferiority feelings are the result. If the vicissitudes of the market are the judges of one's value, the sense of dignity and pride is destroyed.

But the problem is not only that of self-evaluation and self-esteem but of one's experience of oneself as an independent entity, of one's *identity with oneself*. As we shall see later, the mature and productive individual derives his feeling of identity from the experience of himself as the agent who is one with his powers; this feeling of self can be briefly expressed as meaning "*I am what I do.*" In the marketing orientation man encounters his own powers as commodities alienated from him. He is not one with them but they are masked from him because what matters is not his self-realization in the process of using them but his success in the process of selling them. Both his powers and what they create become estranged, something different from himself, something for others to judge and to use; thus his feeling of identity becomes as shaky as his self-esteem; it is constituted by the sum total of roles one can play: "*I am as you desire me.*"

Ibsen has expressed this state of selfhood in Peer Gynt: Peer Gynt tries to discover his self and he finds that he is like an onion—one layer after the other can be peeled off and there is no core to be found. Since man cannot live doubting his identity, he must, in the marketing orientation, find the conviction of identity not in reference to himself and his powers but in the opinion of others about him. His prestige, status, success, the fact that he is known to others as being a certain person are a substitute for the genuine feeling of identity. This situation makes him utterly dependent on the way others look at him and forces him to keep up the role in which he once had become successful. If I and my powers are separated from each other, then, indeed, is my self constituted by the price I fetch.

The way one experiences others is not different from the way one experiences oneself. Others are experienced as commodities like oneself; they too do not present *themselves* but their salable part. The difference between people is reduced to a merely quantitative difference of being *more or less* successful, attractive, hence valuable. This process is not different from what happens to commodities on the market. A painting and a pair of shoes can both be expressed in, and reduced to, their exchange value, their price; so many pairs of shoes are "equal" to one painting. In the same way the difference between people is reduced to a common element, their price on the market. Their individuality, that which is peculiar and unique in them, is valueless and, in fact, a ballast. The meaning which the word *peculiar* has assumed is quite expressive of this attitude. Instead of denoting the greatest achievement of man—that of having developed his individuality—it has become almost synonymous with *queer*. The word *equality* has also changed its meaning. The idea that all men are created equal implied that all men have the same fundamental right to be considered as ends in themselves and not as means. Today, equality has become equivalent to *interchangeability*, and is the very negation of individuality. Equality, instead of being the condition for the development of each man's peculiarity, means the extinction of individuality, the "selflessness" characteristic of the marketing orientation. Equality was conjunctive with difference, but it has become synonymous with "in-difference," and, indeed, indifference is what characterizes modern man's relationship to himself and to others.

These conditions necessarily color all human relationships. When the individual self is neglected, the relationships between people must of necessity become superficial, because not they themselves but interchangeable commodities are related. People are not able and cannot afford to be concerned with that which is unique and "peculiar" in each other. However, the market creates a kind of comradeship of its own. Everybody is involved in the same battle of competition, shares the same striving for success; all meet under the same conditions of the market (or at least believe they do). Everyone knows how the others feel because each is in the same boat: alone, afraid to fail, eager to please; no quarter is given or expected in this battle.

The superficial character of human relationships leads many to hope that they can find depth and intensity of feeling in individual love. But love for one person and love for one's neighbor are indivisible; in any given culture, love relationships are only a more intense expression of the relatedness to man prevalent in that culture. Hence it is an illusion to expect that the loneliness of man, rooted in the marketing orientation, can be cured by individual love.

Thinking as well as feeling is determined by the marketing orientation. Thinking assumes the function of grasping things quickly so as to be able to manipulate them successfully. Furthered by widespread and efficient education, this leads to a high degree of intelligence, but not of reason. For manipulative purposes, all that is necessary to know is the surface features of things, the superficial. The truth, to be uncovered by penetrating to the essence of phenomena, becomes an obsolete concept—truth not only in the pre-scientific sence of "absolute" truth, dogmatically maintained without reference to empirical data, but also in the sense of truth attained by man's reason applied to his observations and open to revisions. Most intelligence tests are attuned to this kind of thinking; they measure not so much the capacity for reason and understanding as the capacity for quick mental adaptation to a given situation; "mental adjustment tests" would be the adequate name for them (see Schachtel, 1937, pp. 597–624). For this kind of thinking the application of the categories of comparison and of quantitative measurement—rather than a thorough analysis of a given phenomenon and its quality—is essential. All problems are equally "interesting" and there is little sense of the respective differences in their importance. Knowledge itself becomes a commodity. Here, too, man is alienated from his own power; thinking and knowing are experienced as a tool to produce results. Knowledge of man himself, psychology, which in the great tradition of Western thought was held to be the condition for virtue, for right living, for happiness, has degenerated into an instrument to be used for better manipulation of others and oneself, in market research, in political propaganda, in advertising, and so on.

Evidently this type of thinking has a profound effect on our educational system. From grade school to graduate school, the aim of learning is to gather as much information as possible that is mainly useful for the purposes of the market. Students are supposed to learn so many things that they have hardly time and energy left to *think*. Not the interest in the subjects taught or in knowledge and insight as such, but the enhanced exchange value knowledge gives, is the main incentive for wanting more and better education. We find today a tremendous enthusiasm for knowledge and education, but at the same time a skeptical or contemptuous attitude toward the allegedly impractical and useless thinking which is concerned "only" with the truth and which has no exchange value on the market.

Although I have presented the marketing orientation as one of the nonproductive orientations, it is in many ways so different that it belongs in a category of its own. The receptive, exploitative, and hoarding orientations have one thing in common: each is one form of human relatedness which, if dominant in a person, is specific of him and characterizes him. . . . The marketing orientation, however, does not develop something which is potentially in the person (unless we make the absurd assertion that "nothing" is also part of the human equipment); its very nature is that no specific and permanent kind of relatedness is developed, but that the very changeability of attitudes is the only permanent quality of such orientation. In this orientation, those qualities are developed which can best be sold. Not one particular attitude is predominant, but the emptiness which can be filled most quickly with the desired quality. This quality, however, ceases to be one in the proper sense of the word; it is only a role, the pretense of a quality, to be readily exchanged if another one is more desirable. Thus, for instance, respectability is sometimes desirable. The salesmen in certain branches of business ought to impress the public with those qualities of reliability, soberness, and respectability which were genuine in many a businessman of the nineteenth century. Now one looks for a man who instills confidence because he *looks* as if he had these qualities; what this man sells on the personality market is his ability to look the part; what kind of person is behind that role does not matter and is nobody's concern. He himself is not interested in his honesty, but in what it gets for him on the market. The premise of the marketing orientation is emptiness, the lack of any specific quality which could not be subject to change, since any persistent trait of character might conflict some day with the requirements of the market. Some roles would not fit in with the peculiarities of the person; therefore we must do away with them—not with the roles but with the peculiarities. The marketing personality must be free, free of all individuality.

The character orientations which have been described so far are by no means as separate from one another as it may appear from this sketch. The receptive orientation, for instance, may be dominant in a person but it is usually blended with any or all of the other orientations. While I shall discuss the various blendings later on, I want to stress at this point that all orientations are part of the human equipment, and the dominance of any specific orientation depends to a large extent on the peculiarity of the culture in which the individual lives. Although a more detailed analysis of the relationship between the various orientations and social patterns must be reserved for a study which deals primarily with problems of social psychology, I should like to suggest here a tentative hypothesis as to the social conditions making for the dominance of any of the four nonproductive types. It should be noted that the significance of the study of the correlation between character orientation and social structure lies not only in the fact that it helps us understand some of the most significant causes for the formation of character, but also in the fact that specific orientations—inasmuch as they are common to most members of a culture or social class—represent powerful emotional forces the operation of which we must know in order to understand the functioning of society. In view of the current emphasis on the impact of culture on personality, I should like to state that the relationship between society and the individual is not to be understood simply in the sense that cultural patterns and social institutions "influence" the individual. The interaction goes much deeper; the whole personality of the average individual is molded by the way people relate to each other, and it is determined by the socioeconomic and political structure of society to such an extent that, in principle, one can infer from the analysis of one individual the totality of the social structure in which he lives.

The receptive orientation is often to be found in societies in which the right of one group to exploit another is firmly established. Since the exploited group has no power to change, or any idea of changing, its situation, it will tend to look up to its masters as to its providers, as to those from whom one receives everything life can give. No matter how little the slave receives, he feels that by his own effort he could have acquired even less, since the structure of his society impresses him with the fact that he is unable to organize it and to rely on his own activity and reason. As far as contemporary American culture is concerned, it seems at first glance that the receptive attitude is entirely absent. Our whole culture, its ideas, and its practice discourage the receptive orientation and emphasize that each one has to look out, and be responsible, for himself and that he has to use his own initiative if he wants to "get anywhere." However, while the receptive orientation is discouraged, it is by no means absent. The need to conform and to please, which has been discussed in the foregoing pages, leads to the feeling of helplessness, which is the root of subtle receptiveness in modern man. It appears particulary in the attitude toward the "expert" and public opinion. People expect that in every field there is an expert who can tell them how things are and how they ought to be done, and that all they ought to do is listen to him and swallow his ideas. There are experts for science, experts for happiness, and writers become experts in the art of living by the very fact that they are authors of best sellers. This subtle but rather general receptiveness assumes somewhat grotesque forms in modern "folklore," fostered particularly by advertising. While everyone knows that realistically the "get-rich-quick" schemes do not work, there is a widespread daydream of the effortless life. It is partly expressed in connection with the use of gadgets; the car which needs no shifting, the fountain pen which saves the trouble of removing the cap are only random examples of this phantasy. It is particularly prevalent in those schemes which deal with happiness. A very characteristic quotation is the following: "This book," the author says, "tells you how to be twice the man or woman you ever were before—happy, well, brimming with energy, confident, capable and free of care. You are required to follow no laborious mental or physical program; it is much simpler than that. . . . As laid down here the route to that promised profit may appear strange, for few of us can imagine *getting without striving.* . . . Yet that is so, as you will see" (Falvey, 1946).

The exploitative character, with its motto "I take what I need," goes back to piratical and feudal ancestors and goes forward from there to the robber barons of the nineteenth century who exploited the natural resources of the continent. The "pariah" and "adventure" capitalists, to use Max Weber's terms, roaming the earth for profit, are men of this stamp, men whose aim was to buy cheap and sell dear and who ruthlessly pursued power and wealth. The free market, as it operated in the eighteenth and nineteenth centuries under competitive conditions, nurtured this type. Our own age has seen a revival of naked exploitativeness in the authoritarian systems which attempted to exploit the natural and human resources, not so much of their own country but of any other country they were powerful enough to invade. They proclaimed the right of might and rationalized it by pointing to the law of nature which makes the stronger survive; love and decency were signs of weakness; thinking was the occupation of cowards and degenerates.

The hoarding orientation existed side by side with the exploitative orientation in the eighteenth and nineteenth centuries. The hoarding type was conservative, less interested in ruthless acquisition than in methodical economic pursuits, based on sound principles and on the preservation of what had been acquired. To him property was a symbol of his self and its protection a supreme value. This orientation gave him a great deal of security; his possession of property and family, protected as they were by the relatively stable conditions of the nineteenth century, constituted a safe and manageable world. Puritan ethics, with the emphasis on work and success as evidence of goodness, supported the feeling of security and tended to give life meaning and a religious sense of fulfillment. This combination of a stable world, stable possessions, and a stable ethic gave the members of the middle class a feeling of belonging, self-confidence, and pride.

The marketing orientation does not come out of the eighteenth or nineteenth centuries; it is definitely a modern product. It is only recently that the package, the label, the brand name have become important, in people as well as in commodities. The gospel of working loses weight and the gospel of selling becomes paramount. In feudal times, social mobility was exceedingly limited and one could not use one's personality to get ahead. In the days of the competitive market, social mobility was relatively great, especially in the United States; if one "delivered the goods" one could get ahead. Today, the opportunities for the lone individual who can make a fortune all by himself are, in comparison with the previous period, greatly diminished. He who wants to "get ahead" has to fit into large organizations, and his ability to play the expected role is one of his main assets.

The depersonalization, the emptiness, the meaninglessness of life, the automatization of the individual result in a growing dissatisfaction and in a need to search for a more adequate way of living and for norms which could guide man to this end. . . .

References

Falvey, Hal. *Ten Seconds That Will Change Your Life.* Wilcox & Follett, 1946.

Polanyi, K. *The Great Transformation.* Holt, Rinehart and Winston, 1945.

Schachtel, Ernest. "Zum Begriff und zur Diagnosis der Persönlichkeit in 'Personality Tests'" [On the Concept and Diagnosis of Personality Tests]. *Zeitschrift für Sozialforschung,* No. 6, 1937.

Dorothy Lee

Personal Significance
and Group Structure

I have written this paper in response to a request to present a dilemma in my family life, and describe the compromise through which I solved it. But when I began speaking of such a situation in my family, I realized that it was not a dilemma but rather what I would call a problematic situation. When I looked at it, I saw that there was one way that I simply could not go, and another way that was the only way I could go. It was not a question of weighing alternatives, and certainly not one of making a compromise. When I pursued it to its basic issues, I found that I had to choose between personal growth and autonomy for my children on the one hand, the submersion of the self in the group on the other; and to me the choice was clear.

A factor in the situation which confronted me came from my own personal history. I am of Greek origin. I came to this country as a foreign student, eventually married an American, and I am now bringing up four children in this country with full rights to the heritage of its culture. I am constantly aware of the fact that the only upbringing I have experienced immediately is Greek, whereas I am bringing up four American citizens who must feel American, think

American, and relate themselves in an American way, not a Greek way.

My husband and I raised our children according to principles which we shared. One of these was that the self should never be conceived as an isolate, nor as the focus of the universe, but rather that it should be defined as a social self. We valued society. We believed that only through society could the self grow, be enriched, find strength. We strongly believed in what MacIver calls "community"—in the *Gemeinschaft*. However, we became increasingly aware of the fact that our children were individuals, that they liked to make their own choices and decisions. They did not like to conform to the standards of a group, and in fact they did not enjoy groups. They did not seek out gangs of children of their own age. They did not classify according to age; they liked "people," and referred to other children as "people." They enjoyed groups only when these were based on individual friendships binding person to person. They preferred to choose one or two friends, and to develop a deep and growing relationship.

The one group which they completely enjoyed, in which they were completely involved, was the family. But it was not a group to them; it just happened to them; it was not a group they went out to join, but one that just grew. They had taken no steps to create such a group. Within the family they did not seem to seek individual independent behavior or choice which went counter to the ends of the family. But when it came to joining organizations such as the Scouts, they all turned away. And this reluctance to see meaning in organized groups with a group purpose seemed completely un-American.

I did not worry about this while my husband, who came from generations of Americans, was with me to carry the burden of making the children into good Americans. But when I was left to bring up the children alone, I felt the need to go against the family-centered upbringing of my Greek culture, so as to "socialize" my children in the American way. I was afraid that, falling between two stools, my children would grow into isolated individuals, cut off from all social nourishment. And I believed in society, as a person and as an anthropologist. Among the primitive societies I had studied, I found people who were rich in human quality, poised, strong, true, unique, people who grew from birth until death. These were people who had social selves, who lived in societies where individual ends and social ends coincided.

While I was considering this problem, I was offered an opportunity to move to a Middle West city where there was much concern over group development and group participation; where group awareness and participation were being implemented at all levels in the schools. This transfer seemed to offer the solution I was looking for. We moved. The children were unhappy at school, but I tried to help them to acquiesce to the new system, to understand its principles, to adjust to a group-centered environment. But, since my working hours coincided with school hours, I had no direct experience of what went on until the parents' open night before Thanksgiving.

I went first of all to my son's room, the seventh grade. The teacher showed me a mural, covering all the walls, depicting the life of the ancient Egyptians. It was a group project, and the teacher pointed out the part for which my son was responsible. The painting depicted a war scene: some pinkish, sleek, placid, fat, lifeless horses. These were nothing like the horses I had seen my son draw at previous times—skinny, elongated beasts, full of straining movement and savage life. I protested that these lifeless horses could not be my son's doing. The teacher explained that my son had not been allowed to paint his own unique horses; they were too different. Since this was a group project, uniformity was essential, so the children had all copied illustrations from a history textbook. As I turned away, appalled and only half-convinced, I spotted the tiny figure of a bird, of no known genus, scraggy, leering, menacing, and I knew that my son's uniqueness had not been entirely mowed down in the drive for uniformity; it had burst through, however irrelevantly and illicitly. It reminded me of the mushrooms which push up a cement pavement, cracking and disrupting its even surface. I was happy to see it.

Disturbed at this interpretation of the concept of the group, I went to the classroom of my daughter who was in the fourth grade. The teacher pointed to a frieze of Pilgrims and Indians in profile that ran around the wall of the room, and obviously waited for my admiring response. All the Pilgrims were alike, all the Indians alike without deviation; alike in size and shape and color. I did not know what I was expected to admire, and finally asked whether the children had pasted up the frieze. The teacher explained that they not only had pasted it, they had actually made it, as a group project. "It was hard to make all the heads alike," she said. "When the children first painted the pictures they all looked different, so we had to throw them away. And then I made an Indian profile and a Pilgrim profile; I wrote directions for coloring each part, and the children traced them and cut out their own. And now they make *one* frieze."

I had another daughter in the tenth grade in high school; and soon after this sad night, her grade decided to have a bake sale to help raise money for a trip to Washington in their senior year. This did seem like good group participation. The trip was to be a truly cooperative venture, since all the students in the class were working toward it, though not all would manage to go eventually. This time each student was asked to bring a cake or cookies for the sale.

My daughter Mary took the bake sale seriously, and was using it as a learning opportunity. She stayed up late making four batches of cookies for which I contributed the ingredients. She found out the cost of the ingredients, and priced the cookies, adding an appropriate amount for her skilled labor. When she took them to school, she discovered that this was not what had been expected of her. Half the children had asked their mothers to bake for them, and most of the rest had bought baked goods at the corner bakery. Mary's cookies were priced below the cost of the raw materials, as were all the other goods, to make sure that they would sell; yet the students were congratulated on raising all this money for their trip through their own exertions.

Mary, concerned over what seemed hypocrisy, decided that the work of the students in selling the cookies would represent their involvement, their share in the raising of funds. But when the time came for the sale, the homeroom teacher was there to sell. The teenagers could not be trusted to make change. True, they were studying geometry, but they might make a mistake in subtraction; and besides they might yield to temptation. The group could not expose itself to the fallibility of its members; it could not take a chance on the integrity or the ability of its constituent members. In the interest of ensuring good results for the group project, all the strivings of the individual self had to be suppressed, while the homeroom teacher handled the project.

This is what I found in my children's schools. Was this the end of my search for true group experience? Was this the meaning of the self in society? I saw here not nourishment and enrichment, but impoverishment and diminution of the self. The group here demanded the sacrifice of the very generative force of the self, the vitality, the vagary, the spontaneity. It was superimposed upon the self as an external standard, and could be sustained only through a Procrustean conformity. In these schools the children were not people, not individual persons with integrity peculiar to each. Their being did not call forth respect. What was demanded of them was to form a class based on undeviating similarity; and to achieve this, the striving of the self had to be throttled. Only through destruction of the self could the group thrive.

I was not convinced that this was necessary to the creation of a group. In my study of other people, I had come across societies where the group was far more permeating in the life of the individual, yet where even the private thoughts and feelings of individuals affected the group. I had studied the Hopi, where, within a strong group structure, each person had unique significance; where the people were spontaneous, vital, free, strong. So I went back to a consideration of the Hopi, to find out what there was about their culture which made it possible for an individual to maintain uniqueness and significance within the group structure.

Whatever I say here about the Hopi refers to them as they have been until recently. Change has been going on, and particularly since the past war, when many Hopi went out, either with the armed forces, or to factories, and became more and more exposed to our ways of arranging things, to our way of life. If I use what seems to be the present tense, I use it in its reference to the timeless: to what they call the Hopi way—the good, the right path; not necessarily to how they live, but to the good life. Only when I give specific examples do I speak of individual Hopi, of the actual events of time and space. At this time, there are only two villages where the traditional Hopi way is maintained.

The Hopi are Pueblo Indians, living in Arizona. They reckon descent through the mother, and houses belong to the women of the lineage, where their husbands come to join them. In the older villages, the closely related women—sisters, mothers and daughters, aunts and cousins—with their families, occupy one or more adjacent households, where the work of living goes on cooperatively. The men herd, farm, hunt, collect fuel, perhaps spin and weave; the women cooperate in preparing food for the group, caring for young children and for the house, hauling water, making pottery and baskets. And when I say men and women, I include boys and girls, who from an early age have the right to work alongside the adults, doing work important to the welfare of the group.

The group, starting from the unit of the immediate family of birth, but expanding through systematic introduction into wider areas until it includes eventually the entire universe, is the focus to which the behavior and feeling and entire being of an individual is oriented. Much, if not all, of what a person thinks and does has a reference to the group. For example, if I go visiting a new mother in my society, I shall probably smile with the joy of seeing her again, with congratulations for her new baby. The Hopi visitor will smile also, but here the smile has a significance beyond this, as the happiness it expresses helps the baby to thrive and the new mother to recover her strength; and, conversely, a face expressing worry would bring harm at this time.

A person enters the unit by birth, and all of an individual's behavior is geared to this social unit which he has joined through no choice of his own. His loyalties are to this group; they are not person-to-person loyalties. And parents have been known deliberately to try to shift a child's affection from concentration upon one family member to diffusion among the group. The area of an individual's work, of responsible participation, is therefore not one he has chosen, but is given also, as it is coextensive with the group. Every individual, young and old, is charged with responsibility for the welfare of the social unit; and this they apparently accept voluntarily, considering it good.

Richard Brandt, a philosopher making a study of Hopi ethics, found that his informants considered that one of the main things which make a man ashamed was that of not having any children alive. This "shows sin"; that is, it shows that a man's behavior, his thoughts, his willing, his emotions were not social enough to keep his children alive. People were expected to be ashamed of not helping in cooperative undertakings, not giving, not participating in ceremonials for the welfare of the unit—in this last case, the entire universe. No, said the informants, a man need not be ashamed of being poor, or of being dumb, so long as he was good to others. Brandt made arrangements to see informants in absolute secrecy, to protect them against possible criticism; but even so, he found that the informant might not be ready to talk until he had made sure that no harm would come to the group from his disclosures.

Related to this is the Hopi reluctance to stand out, to be singled out from the group. Teachers in Hopi schools have reported discomfort and even tears as a reaction to praise in public. It appears that what is in fact disturbing is the comparative evaluation that results in singling out and praising. Hopi do not compare their achievements, nor the importance of their work, and "a highly skilled stone-cutter is perfectly content to accept the same wages as an unskilled day laborer." Children cannot be persuaded to compete in school, in classwork or in playing games. One school reported that the children learned to play basketball easily, and delighted in the game; but they could not be taught to keep score. They played by the hour, without knowing who was winning. Without emphasis on the score, the structure of the game, with everyone doing his utmost within his established role, is in a simplified way similar to the kind of structure we find in the Hopi group.

As I have indicated earlier, it is not only the physical act, or overt behavior, which is effective, according to the Hopi view. Thought and will and intent are at least as effective; so that it is not enough for the individual to act peacefully; he must also feel nonaggressive, think harmonious thoughts, and be imbued with a singleness of purpose. It is his duty to be happy for the sake of the group, and a mind in conflict and full of anxiety brings disruption, ill-being, to the social unit, and, at a time of prayer and ceremonial, to the entire universe.

Brandt found that one of the personal traits highly valued was that of being "happy in his heart." One informant told him, "This is like a flower or a cornfield: when in bloom it beautifies the whole earth. . . . It is a kind of gratitude. . . . When you go into the fields you should sing to the corn." Another informant praised a man who, even when upset, made "himself happy while talking" with others. Superficially, this is similar to valued behavior in our own society, too; but with the Hopi it is an aspect of working for the group.

Human society is a part of a larger structured whole, so an individual cooperates with even more than the members of this human group. Every aspect of nature, plants and rocks and animals, colors and cardinal directions and numbers and sex distinctions, the dead and the living, all have a cooperative share in the maintenance of the universal order. Eventually, the effort of each individual, human or not, goes into this huge whole. And here, too, it is every aspect of a person which counts. The entire being of the Hop individual affects the balance of nature; and as each individual develops his inner potential, as he enhances his participation, so does the entire universe become invigorated. Not his behavior alone, not his achievement, but his entire unique being is significant.

Much of the time and energy of the Hopi goes into working at ceremonials. These are highly organized and form part of an established ceremonial cycle. Each ceremoney "belongs to" a secret society, usually a men's society, and only members of this society have the privilege and the responsibility of carrying out the ceremony. Each main ceremony involves an exceedingly complex order of detailed acts; preparatory rites, acts of purification, gathering of materials, preparation of masks and sand paintings and medicine water, composition of new songs, rehearsal of dances. The women prepare food to be exchanged reciprocally. The ceremonials themselves last nine or seventeen days. Though only one secret society is charged with the responsibility of a specific ceremony, the entire group of "spectators" —all the villagers and visitors from other pueblos who come to the public performances—eventually participate, through keeping a "good heart," through their wholehearted involvement in what they watch, through laughing at the burlesque and pranks afforded by the clowns.

Each main ceremony has reference to a phase of the agricultural cycle, helping the universal order to become actual. There is an established course for the sun, for example, within the cosmic order; but the winter solstice ceremony is necessary to actualize this order into the here and now, so that the sun can actually follow the prescribed course, and so turn northward. The growing of the corn also has its established order; the stages of growth are given in the order of nature; but the corn cannot move through them, from germination to fruition, without the cooperative effort of man, who must transform, by means of his ceremonials, potentiality into actuality. So, in the end, when a field of corn is ready to harvest, it is a result of the cooperative effort of every member of the group, in addition to the man who has dug and hoed and planted and weeded.

Though each ceremonial has specific reference within the agricultural cycle, each main ceremony also has reference to the whole of life, to the entire cosmic system. The aim is the well-being of the universal whole, not of the individual. If the individual profits by the ceremonial, it is because he is an integral part of this whole which has become invigorated. The individual maintains harmony with the universe for the sake of the universal order, and only derivatively for his own sake. Eventually, through the maintenance of this harmony, the human group thrives, the sun moves along its established course from solstice to solstice, the thunderclouds gather and release their rain, the corn sprouts and roots and fills and ripens.

In all this, the individual is working along given lines, for given ends, for a group which he did not create of his own choice. This seems the denial of all freedom and initiative.

In addition, the geographic location of the Hopi seems to make for determinism, and an absence of individual freedom. They live and practice agriculture in country where it would seem at first glance to be impossible to depend on the land for a living. The rain may not come at all, or may fall in torrents and wash away the crops; high winds may blow away the seed. The growing cycle of corn, the main crop, is almost coincidental with the growing season, which is cut short at both ends by killing frosts. As Laura Thompson says: "The arid north Arizona plateau posed unyielding imperatives which had to be met habitually and unerringly if the tribe were to survive and reproduce itself." This means that the environment imposes rigid limits to behavior and choice. How can man have personal freedom to will, to act, to be, in these circumstances when the very environment dictates behavior, and where there is so little margin for human fallibility? Where can there be room for personal initiative? Who can be proud of bringing his stand of corn to fruition when even the laughter of a child has gone to grow it? How can there be motivation for work, when the responsibility and the results and the work itself are all shared, to a greater or less extent? Does not this mean that personal effort is lost in the undifferentiated immensity, that the individual is submerged and lost in the group and in the universal whole?

The genius of his culture has made it possible for the Hopi to find spontaneity, significance and freedom, motivation and personal integrity within this structured universe, within the given society, and the difficult environment. It is true that there is probably no joy of independent achievement, but this does not mean that there is no motivation, no personal initiative.

Certainly, there is no such thing as individualism, in our sense of the term. There is no private enterprise; there is avoidance of outstandingness. There is no undertaking which an individual initiates and brings to a conclusion alone, with the pride of success. When a farmer is harvesting a "successful" corn crop, who has "succeeded"? Throughout the year, the members of his pueblo, in different organizations, have performed an established series of ceremonies to bring about this harvest. The children have played organized ball games for days with the children from another pueblo, and thus helped the corn to grow. Men have refrained from intercourse with their wives and sweethearts, eaglets have been captured at considerable risk, women and children have laughed heartily at the antics of ceremonial clowns, priests have gone into retirement and meditation, and much more has been done and wished and thought, to bring about this good harvest. The farmer's achievement in all this may be seen as insignificant; yet it may also be seen as superbly significant.

For the immensity of effort is not undifferentiated; the individual effort is not like a grain of sand, lost in the universal whole. Every individual within the system has his unique role,[1] and each role is different and indispensable. The structured whole of the universe, or of the human group, contains a precise position for each and every member. No one is expendable. In Laura Thompson's words, "Every individual in the group, male and female, young or old, has his proper place and role in the organization of the community . . . with duties and rights commensurate with their age and status." And, in the universal whole, every part of nature has its unique and indispensable role. Man supplies the moving principle in this order through his ability to will, and through his ceremonials.

So each individual person, through the uniqueness of his role and the indispensability of his own specific effort, has great significance. Group effort and community of ends does not mean totalitarianism and the loss of individual uniqueness. In fact, the group can prosper only to the extent that this uniqueness is fully actualized. Only in so far as each member of each *kiva* carries out his own unique responsibility, fulfills his role in putting on and performing the ceremony which is the responsibility of this particular ceremonial association, will the ceremony help the corn to move into the next stage of growth. In this, each individual member has an indispensable and precise function.

The clarity of role, the preciseness of structure and of place in the structure, is such that the individual knows what is open to him to do; and, as it is apparently satisfying to work in terms of the social unit, the individual can and does work autonomously within his role. O'Kane writes, "A Hopi household is a self-directing group, the members of which seem to achieve automatic coordination of their activities. No one tells the others what they should do, or when, or how. No one exercises authority. The various members seem to fall naturally into a pattern in which the abilities of the individual and the needs of the household are satisfactorily served."

---

1. By "role" I mean a specific place in the structural whole, which carries with it a responsible, non-interchangeable function.

Thus an individual can decide to what extent he will fill the responsibility which is his privilege. For example, O'Kane tells how three fellow clansmen decided to get turtles to supply themselves with shell for the leg rattles used in ceremonial dancing. This was done at their own initiative, but within an established framework—that is, the rattles were to be attached to a specified part of the leg, they were to be of specified shell, worn at specified times in specified roles, and so forth. The individual decision brought more shell rattles, or newer rattles to the *kivas* involved; it enriched the group. The decision involved much arduous work, including a return journey of some six hundred miles. Each of the three contributed of what he had to offer —one his car, another gas, the third his knowledge and skill. There was no attempt at uniformity, nor at equalization; there was no suppression of individuality; rather, through the variety of individual contribution, the whole could be achieved.

The individual is free to choose ways in which to actualize his responsibility; as, for example, when three children, whose grandmother was dying in their home, asked to stay after school because they were afraid that they could not avoid anxious thoughts if they went back to the pueblo. The projective tests reported by Thompson and Joseph show that for Hopi children responsible group participation is often named a happy experience.

It is clear that the welfare of the group and of the entire universe enventually depends on the individual; yet the individual is neither tethered, nor monitored, nor shackled, nor coerced, to insure his safe carrying out of his responsibilities. When Brandt was asking questions involving ethical principles, he found that there was no adherence to group morals as categorical. "It is up to him to decide what is right or wrong," the individual stated repeatedly, and the desirability of consent was stressed: "I don't believe in forcing anybody to do anything. . . . If he gives his consent, it is all right."

It is evident, then, that a tremendous respect and trust is accorded to the individual since no provision is made for a man's failure, neglect, error. The entire group and the entire universe is vulnerable, exposed to the fallibility of the individual. Even a child, allowing himself to have anxious thoughts, can bring ill to the pueblo. This means a great responsibility, and can be seen as a frightening and overwhelming burden. Yet, instead of blocking the individual with its immensity, this responsibility seems to function as a motivating factor, affording a channel for spontaneity. Instead of cutting off the protruding variations, the idiosyncrasies of the individual; instead of submerging the self within a uniform mass, the group encourages individual quality, and enriches itself through it. The significant place given to each person and the full trust accorded to each means that the group thrives only through the full exercise of the individual self.

This is what I had missed in the school situation of my children; I had missed significance and respect for unique being. There was no trust in the potentiality of each child, of *this* child. The homeroom protected itself against its members; it would not take a chance on the honesty or mathematical ability or industry of its members. The person had no individual worth; and, in fact, effort was directed toward making the members of the group interchangeable, until the artistic expression of one could not be distinguished from that of another. There was no appreciation of difference; it was treated as disruptive and threatening to group welfare; and, being cast into the outer darkness, it did, in fact, disrupt. If my son had drawn the Egyptian war scene in his own peculiar lines, he would have had no occasion to introduce his minute discordant bird in the corner. Some growth of the self did occur, because of its tremendous impetus; but it met with discouragement. I found here that the group existed at the expense of the individual; and this was totalitarianism.

At this point my problem was clear and I solved it. What did I do? I decided that I needed a school where the group was conceived accordingly to democratic principles; where the individual was given a significant place within the structured group; where the group was considered to prosper only through the optimum growth of each and every member—not through the stunting of any one; where uniqueness was valued; where individual and group could grow and thrive only together. I found such a school and moved to that town, fifty miles away. I solved my problem. My children are growing up in true American democracy.

References

Brandt, Richard B. *Hopi Ethics: A Theoretical Analysis.* University of Chicago Press, 1954.

O'Kane, Walter Collins. *The Hopis: Portrait of a Desert People.* University of Oklahoma Press, 1953.

Simmons, Leo W. *Sun Chief.* Yale University Press, 1942.

Stephen, Alexander M. *Hopi Journal,* ed. E. C. Parsons. Columbia University Press, 1936.

Thompson, Laura. *Culture in Crisis: A Study of the Hopi Indians.* Harper, 1950.

———, and Alice Joseph. *The Hopi Way.* University of Chicago Press, 1944.

Dero A. Saunders

Executive Discontent

A manufacturing company with half a dozen plants is faced with the prospect of naming a new production vice president. The logical candidates are the managers of its three largest plants. All three men are able, all three are in their late forties, all are bucking for the job, and all realize that this is their best and may possibly be their last chance to break into the top-management circle.

Two men, no matter how able, are not going to make it. It was not unexpected: all three knew—had long known—that only one could be chosen. Very rarely will the losers crack up—they will master their feelings, put on a cheerful face. But, underneath, they cannot escape a feeling of entrapment. The alternatives have suddenly narrowed: though the losers are still ambitious and relatively young, they are old enough, and deeply enough committed to their own company, so that a switch to a new one seems fraught with hazard. That second career, long so comforting to speculate about, they see as the illusion it always was. For many there is the personal disillusionment of realizing that they have used up twenty years of their working lives in pursuit of goals that may never be reached, and there is no starting over. Now there is the chill prospect that the final stretch—which seemed so remote when they were young—is indeed just ahead. Moreover, this withering of the career goals on which they have lavished so much energy usually coincides with certain pervasive and unsettling changes in the middle-rank executive's personal life; and it is an iron law of human psychology that emotional energy thwarted at one outlet must find another.

Some such experience faces most forty-to-fifty-year-old executives in medium-sized to large U. S. corporations today. (Family enterprises are different.) The vigorous expansion of the U. S. economy does not obliterate the fact that there are many more middle-rank executives than can possibly be promoted into top management. It is quite possible that the discontents of the middle-rank executive stem as much from personal as from business circumstances. But the

Reprinted from the October 1956 issue of *Fortune* magazine by special permission. © 1956 by Time, Inc.

focus of his discontent is the gulf in his career between aspiration and reality—between his belief in his right and duty to get ahead (which helped make him an executive in the first place) and the abrupt narrowing that occurs near the top of the executive pyramid.

The discontents of thwarted aspiration hardly constitute a new problem—indeed, it can be argued that it should be much less a one in these prosperous days than ever before. Yet, curiously, there have probably never been so many people preoccupied with the problem. And many of the most preoccupied are people who have not yet experienced a defeat—young men who will make up the next generation of managers. The question they raise in this: Is executive discontent an inevitable by-product of a competitive economy?

The younger men swear it won't happen to them. They have reflected on the perils of amibition, and have concluded that the concentration on work and achievement shown by today's senior executives is downright maladjustment. "Well-roundedness," the younger men hold, is the antidote, and in two ways they think they will achieve it. First, they have deliberately tempered their business ambitions, the better to lead the full life with wife, home, and family. Second, they hope to modify the business environment.

With the blessing of many personnel men and business school people, these younger men expect to replace the economic free-for-all with an orderly system of team play. While they will not crave success, they intend to achieve success (modified style) in a new way, based on the science of management. In the never-ending expansion of the economy, the corporate management teams which guide that expansion will rise in orderly progression toward the top, with the team members reaping steadily greater rewards as they are carried upward. Individually, goes the line of thought, few will reach pre-eminence, but it won't much matter. Success will be institutionalized; it will depend upon team rather than individual effort; and it will be semiautomatic, paralleling the long-range growth of the economy. The rat race, in short, must go.

Will this approach serve to protect the rising management generation from their fathers' disillusionments? It all depends on the true sources of executive discontent—and whether they are deeper than a mere craving for promotion.

Realists, Optimists, and Pessimists

The differences between generations are crucial. U. S. executives today tend to divide into three fairly distinct generations, differing not merely in age but in outlook, values, and motivation. These are (1) the pre-crash generation, (2) the depression-war generation, and (3) the postwar generation. While the lines are not rigid, most executives fall in one or another of the three, according to the time of their last college and first work years.

The bulk of U. S. top management today is made up of members of the pre-crash generation, now in their fifties and up, who left school for their first jobs well before the 1929 crash. Most of them came of age in a period of roaring prosperity, which many thought would last forever. Then they experienced the long slide into depression, followed by slow and painful recovery, war, and then boom again.

This succession of experiences has left them, above all, realists. Even at the nadir of the depression they could foresee the possibility of a future boom, having known one in their own past; today, on the other hand, they well recall the decade of the 1930s. All together, this breadth of background has made them a remarkable group, about the best possible one to which a boom might be entrusted.

At the other end of the executive scale is the postwar generation, as yet largely in junior executive positions, made up of men whose entire college and working lives began after the end of World War II. Some years back *Fortune* commented ("The Class of '49" [June 1949]) on the emergence from its chrysalis stage of this new generation, whose members seemed to be modest, to say the least, in economic ambition, resolute in their determination to let someone else do the business adventuring and entrepreneuring, anxious to rest upon the bosom of a large corporation, and quite content to fare as their employer fared. .. . .

Sandwiched between these two groups is today's middle management, composed predominantly of a generation whose members were molded by the common experiences of depression and war. Basically they are of the same temper as the previous generation. They, too, are impelled by the traditional drives to achievement, and they remember well enough to be just a bit wary of the boom. Like their elders, many of them can anticipate with a kind of grim pleasure the shock hard times would bring for their carefree younger contemporaries.

An Executive Menopause?

. . . What preoccupies him . . . is a growing sense of entrapment; for he can easily calculate the number of top jobs that are likely to open up in his own company while he is still of promotable age, and moving to another company can suddenly begin to seem both difficult and dangerous. In short, he begins to see the likely end of the road, though he may not yet have arrived there. "Despite all the emphasis on executive development," observed a psychiatric consultant to a large Eastern company, "a guy over forty-five has a hell of a time getting a job; and even at forty-five he doesn't have the freedom to move any more. At forty-five you're caught in a cultural trap."

Two other factors tend to reinforce the executive's discontent at his entrapment. Many of today's middle-aged executives played exciting roles, whether in or out of uniform, during World War II; thus their present confinement is often silhouetted against a blackdrop of glamorous wartime recollections. And especially chafing to the middle-rank executive of forty or forty-five is the fact that *his* boss is taking his own sweet time about retiring. "When a man gets to be fifty-five or sixty," says one consultant on executive retirement, "he explains, 'I meant to retire at fifty-five, but I've changed my mind. I've got standing here, I'm looked up to, and I'm recognized as a member of the team. I don't want to lose that.' His forty-five-year-old subordinate sees him letting down, lacking the drive and the technical equipment, and his reaction is 'What's wrong with that guy? He's got money, he could go fishing or do anything he likes. Why doesn't he leave?' "

At the same time so many middle-aged executives are being forced to pare down their ambitions, they may also be undergoing an even more fundamental change in outlook. Professor William E. Henry of the University of Chicago's Committee on Human Development, drawing upon recent studies of a large number of executives in different age brackets, suggests that a change occurs in something as basic as the attitude toward the outside world. Whereas the young (say, thirty to thirty-five) executive looks upon the external environment as a thing to be manipulated or adjusted to, for the middle-aged executive "the outer world begins to take on a kind of life of its own and to be seen as greatly more complex and full of unknowns"—at times even malign in influence.[1]

Since the nature of the outer world itself presumably does not change as a man grows older, the executive's changed attitude toward it must reflect a slow inner erosion of those qualities of vigor, self-confidence, and decisiveness that executives are expected, both by the world and by themselves, to possess. For all its scholastic trappings, there is bright menace in Professor Henry's statement of the problem: "This sense of the perpetually unattained is an integral part of the executive personality and is part of its dilemma. It means that there is always some place to go, but no defined point at which to stop. The executive is 'self-propelled' and needs to keep moving always and to see another goal ever ahead, which also suggests that cessation of mobility and of struggling for new achievements will be

---

1. M.I.T.'s School of Industrial Management has observed interesting differences between the Sloan Fellows, young executives usually under thirty-five, and the Senior Executive Group, of forty-five- to fifty-year-olds. "The Sloan Fellows just know that they are going up and will get there," said one M.I.T. faculty member. "The senior executives wonder whether their efforts are worth making. Their questioning isn't questioning of the system—though they got the full shock of the depression—but rather of a moral, ethical, philosophical kind: their concern is how it all fits together."

accompanied by an inversion of this constant energy. The person whose mobility is blocked, either by his own limitations or by those of the social system, finds this energy diverted into other channels. Psychosomatic symptoms, the enlargement of interpersonal dissatisfactions, and the development of rationalized compulsive- and/or paranoid-type defenses may reflect the redirection of this potent energy demand."

In these middle years, the executive may be suffering a loss of purpose in his private life. Industrial consultant Dr. Melvin Thorner, of the University of Pennsylvania Graduate School of Medicine, put it this way to a recent meeting of utility executives at Columbia University's Arden House: "In the forties or early fifties, many an executive has just about realized many of his youthful goals. His house is owned, his insurance paid up, his children married, and his income nearly adequate. (Absolute adequacy of income is one goal that is apparently seldom reached by anyone.) This gradual dissolution of goals may be very disturbing, and this disturbed emotional state may have marked effects upon his capacity for adequate decisiveness."

There is, of course, another side to the coin. When an executive has achieved such goals as the education of his children, paid-up insurance, a mortgage-free house, he is that much less subject to money worries; that much freer to entertain other goals—such as civic work or a neglected hobby. This new phase of his life he may find quite as satisfying as the previous one, and sometimes more so.

Indeed a number of middle-aged, middle-rank executives achieve such a satisfactory home and community life that promotion can become a threat. "One of the commonest problems that we see among executives," says Dr. William C. Menninger of Topeka's Menninger Foundation, "are the poor fellows who have run the shop out in Squedunk for twenty-five years where they have deep roots and their kids belong to the Scout troop, and they are pillars in the local church and in the Chamber of Commerce, who then are promoted to be one of those dime-a-dozen V.P. in the metropolitan area."

The Frustrated Ones

One psychiatrist who has counseled both executives and corporations says that he finds the most characteristic example of middle-management discontent in a situation something like this: At forty-five, a man is an assistant plant manager for a large manufacturing concern whose technology is in rapid change. The road up looks extremely precarious—though whether because of his own limitations, or simply because there are too many men of the wrong ages above him, is of no concern. At the same time that his children begin to leave home, the company is hiring a new wave of engineers whose newer technical training gives them some advantage over the assistant plant manager. "Thus his children," concludes the psychiatrist, "are unconsciously seen as 'deserting' him at home—only to return and 'attack' him as newly hired engineers."

The psychiatrist claims that the outcome can be very bad indeed. If such an executive is at all insecure, he says, he is in danger of grave personal conflict. He cannot express his discontent toward his bosses, for this would threaten his job as well as choke off his chances for future promotion; and his superiors, after the first couple of young engineers quit in a huff, will not allow him to take it out overtly on his subordinates. So he turns his rages upon himself. In his personal life, he may become estranged from his wife and set about philandering; suffer obvious emotional upset or breakdown; or become a prey to psychosomatic illness (one large firm's medical director estimated that over half of the complaints executives bring to him "have no physical basis"). On the job, he may become the crabbed builder of a tiny power empire; sabotage his superiors behind a mask of acquiescence; or, very commonly, engage in pointless competition with younger subordinates, often by devising goals and setting work standards whose unconscious purpose is to prove that he is a better man than they. . . .

There is one cause of executive discontent that is perhaps too obvious and uncomplicated for the psychiatrists to spend much time on. That is the simple fact that people get tired of doing the same thing for years and years. The middle-aged, middle-rank executive may have been with his company twenty-five years; he's had promotions and changes of scene within the company, but that one company is still a pretty small corner of a big and interesting world. Hence that beguiling daydream, the second career.

The second career is not merely a move to a salaried job in another company, for that would usually mean a continuation of much the same kind of thing the executive did before. The executive who begins pondering a second career is sometimes remembering a much earlier dream—the favorite college course that almost led to a different choice of job. Often, of course, he's thinking of a little business of his own.

The man indulging in these reveries is by no means a failure; much more frequently he is quite successful—and therein lies part of his restlessness. First, like most people who are very good at one thing, he does indeed possess aptitudes, however latent, for quite different kinds of work. For another thing, his success may pall just a little bit more than he ever thought it would. In these days of super-prosperity, his big paycheck does not seem the achievement it would have been in more difficult times. More and more he begins to wonder if his work is enough *fun*. Before he gets much older, he thinks, he will get around to that second career. But he won't. *Fortune* interviewed a cross section of executives, corporations, and management consultants, and found scarcely any clear-cut cases of executives turning to entirely new careers in business or the professions.[2]

When he thinks it over, apparently, the executive comes to the conclusion that he has made much too large an investment in his present work. It is not merely the company ties and the entrapment of pension- and retirement-fund plans—many executives do shift from one company to another. What may be the main factor is the executive's realization that he will be abandoning much of the capital his present skills represent, and he is enough of a realist to know that the difficulty of mastering a new job—and the risks—is a little too great. Still, it has been a solace, and once in a while he can pause to think what a hell of a job he could have done if it hadn't been for all those other things.

---

2. In defining "second careers," *Fortune* included only businessmen between forty and sixty; under forty is still a period of youthful job changing, over-sixty shifts get mixed up with impending retirement.

Jacques Ellul

A Look at the Future

It is vanity to pretend [that the monolithic technical world that is coming to be] can be checked or guided. Indeed, the human race is beginning confusedly to understand at last that it is living in a new and unfamiliar universe. The new order was meant to be a buffer between man and nature. Unfortunately, it has evolved autonomously in such a way that man has lost all contact with his natural framework and has to do only with the organized technical intermediary which sustains relations both with the world of life and with the world of brute matter. Enclosed within his artificial creation, man finds that there is "no exit"; that he cannot pierce the shell of technol-

---

ogy to find again the ancient milieu to which he was adapted for hundreds of thousands of years.

The new milieu has its own specific laws which are not the laws of organic or inorganic matter. Man is still ignorant of these laws. It nevertheless begins to appear with crushing finality that a new necessity is taking over from the old. It is easy to boast of victory over ancient oppression, but what if victory has been gained at the price of an even greater subjection to the forces of the artificial necessity of the technical society which has come to dominate our lives?

In our cities there is no more day or night or heat or cold. But there is overpopulation, thraldom to press and television, total absence of purpose. All men are constrained by means external to them to ends equally external. The further the technical mechanism develops which allows us to escape natural necessity, the more we are subjected to artificial technical necessities. (I have analyzed human victory over hunger in this vein.) The artificial necessity of technique is not less harsh and implacable for being much less obviously menacing than natural necessity. When the Communists claim that they place the development of the technical society in a historical framework that automatically leads to freedom through the medium of the dialectical process; when Humanists such as Bergson, or Catholics such as Mounier, assert that man must regain control over the technical "means" by an additional quantity of soul, all of them alike show both their ignorance of the technical phenomenon and an impenitent idealism that unfortunately bears no relation to truth or reality.

Alongside these parades of mere verbalisms, there has been a real effort, on the part of the technicians themselves, to control the future of technical evolution. The principle here is the old one we have so often encountered: "A technical problem demands a technical solution." At present, there are two kinds of new techniques which the technicians propose as solutions.

The first solution hinges on the creation of new technical instruments able to mediate between man and his new technical milieu. Robert Jungk, for example, in connection with the fact that man is not completely adaptable to the demands of the technical age, writes that "it is impossible to create interstellar man out of the existing prime matter; auxiliary technical instruments and apparatus must compensate for his insufficiencies." The best and most striking example of such subsidiary instruments is furnished by the complex of so-called "thinking machines," which certainly belong to a very different category of techniques than those that have been applied up to now. But the whole ensemble of means designed to permit human mastery of what were means and have now become milieu are techniques of the second degree, and nothing more. Pierre de Latil, in his

La Pensée artificielle, gives an excellent characterization of some of
these machines of the second degree:

> In the machine, the notion of finality makes its appearance, a
> notion sometimes attributed in living beings to some intelligence
> inherent in the species, innate to life itself. Finality is artificially
> built into the machine and regulates it, and effect requiring that
> some factor be modified or reinforced so that the effect itself
> does not disturb the equilibrium. . . . Errors are corrected with-
> out human analysis, or knowledge, without even being sus-
> pected. The error itself corrects the error. A deviation from the
> prescribed track itself enables the automatic pilot to rectify the
> deviation. . . . For the machine, as for animals, error is fruitful;
> it conditions the correct path.

The second solution revolves about the effort to discover (or
rediscovery) a new end for human society in the technical age. The
aims of technology, which were clear enough a century and a half
ago, have gradually disappeared from view. Humanity seems to have
forgotten the wherefore of all its travail, as though its goals had been
translated into an abstraction or had become implicit; or as though its
ends rested in an unforeseeable future of undetermined date, as in
the case of Communist society. Everything today seems to happen as
though ends disappear, as a result of the magnitude of the very
means at our disposal.

Comprehending that the proliferation of means brings about the
disappearance of the ends, we have become preoccupied with redis-
covering a purpose or a goal. Some optimists of good will assert that
they have rediscovered a humanism to which the technical movement
is subordinated. The orientation of this humanism may be Communist or non-Communist, but it hardly makes any difference. In both
cases it is merely a pious hope with no chance whatsoever of influencing technical evolution. The further we advance, the more the purpose of our techniques fades out of sight. Even things which not long
ago seemed to be immediate objectives—rising living standards, hygiene, comfort—no longer seem to have that character, possibly because man finds the endless adaptation to new circumstances disagreeable. In many cases, indeed, a higher technique obliges him to
sacrifice comfort and hygienic amenities to the evolving technology
which possesses a monopoly of the instruments necessary to satisfy
them. Extreme examples are furnished by the scientists isolated at
Los Alamos in the middle of the desert because of the danger of their
experiments; or by the would-be astronauts who are forced to live in
the discomfort of experimental camps in the manner so graphically
described by Jungk.

But the optimistic technician is not a man to lose heart. If ends and goals are required, he will find them in a finality which can be imposed on technical evolution precisely because this finality can be technically established and calculated. It seems clear that there must be some common measure between the means and the ends subordinated to it. The required solution, then, must be a technical inquiry into ends, and this alone can bring about a systematization of ends and means. The problem becomes that of analyzing individual and social requirements technically, of establishing, numerically and mechanistically, the constancy of human needs. It follows that a complete knowledge of ends is requisite for mastery of means. But, as Jacques Aventur has demonstrated, such knowledge can only be technical knowledge. Alas, the panacea of merely theoretical humanism is as vain as any other.[1]

"Man, in his biological reality, must remain the sole possible reference point for classifying needs," writes Aventur. Aventur's dictum must be extended to include man's psychology and sociology, since these have also been reduced to mathematical calculation. Technology cannot put up with intuitions and "literature." It must necessarily don mathematical vestments. Everything in human life that does not lend itself to mathematical treatment must be excluded —because it is not a possible end for technique—and left to the sphere of dreams.

Who is too blind to see that a profound mutation is being advocated here? A new dismembering and a complete reconstitution of the human being so that he can at last become the objective (and also the total object) of techniques. If we exclude all but the mathematical element, he is indeed a fit end for the means he has constructed. He is also completely despoiled of everything that traditionally constituted his essence. Man becomes a pure appearance, a kaleidoscope of external shapes, an abstraction in a milieu that is frighteningly concrete —an abstraction armed with all the sovereign signs of Jupiter the Thunderer.

A Look at the Year 2000

In 1960 the weekly *l'Express* of Paris published a series of extracts from texts by American and Russian scientists concerning society in the year 2000. As long as such visions were purely a literary concern of science-fiction writers and sensational journalists, it was

---

1. It must be clear that the ends sought cannot be determined by moral science. The dubiousness of ethical judgments, and the differences between systems, make moral science unfit for establishing these ends. But, above all, its subjectivity is a fatal blemish. It depends essentially on the refinement of the individual moral conscience. An average morality is ceaselessly confronted with excessive demands with which it cannot comply. Technical modalities cannot tolerate subjectivity.

possible to smile at them.[2] Now we have like works from Nobel Prize winners, members of the Academy of Sciences of Moscow, and other scientific notables whose qualifications are beyond dispute. The visions of these gentlemen put science fiction in the shade. By the year 2000, voyages to the moon will be commonplace; so will inhabited artificial satellites. All food will be completely synthetic. The world's population will have increased fourfold but will have been stabilized. Sea water and ordinary rocks will yield all the necessary metals. Disease, as well as famine, will have been eliminated; and there will be universal hygienic inspection and control. The problems of energy production will have been completely resolved. Serious scientists, it must be repeated, are the source of these predictions, which hitherto were found only in philosophic utopias.

The most remarkable predictions concern the transformation of educational methods and the problem of human reproduction. Knowledge will be accumulated in "electronic banks" and transmitted directly to the human nervous system by means of coded electronic messages. There will no longer be any need for reading or learning mountains of useless information; everything will be received and registered according to the needs of the moment. There will be no need of attention or effort. What is needed will pass directly from the machine to the brain without going through consciousness.

In the domain of genetics, natural reproduction will be forbidden. A stable population will be necessary, and it will consist of the highest human types. Artificial insemination will be employed. This, according to Muller, will "permit the introduction into a carrier uterus of an ovum fertilized *in vitro*, ovum and sperm . . . having been taken from persons representing the masculine ideal and the feminine ideal, respectively. The reproductive cells in question will preferably be those of persons dead long enough that a true perspective of their lives and works, free of all personal prejudice, can be seen. Such cells will be taken from cell banks and will represent the most precious genetic heritage of humanity . . . The method will have to be applied universally. If the people of a single country were to apply it intelligently and intensively . . . they would quickly attain a practically invincible level of superiority." Here is a future Huxley never dreamed of.

Perhaps, instead of marveling or being shocked, we ought to reflect a little. A question no one ever asks when confronted with the scientific wonders of the future concerns the interim period. Consider, for example, the problems of automation, which will become

---

2. Some excellent works, such as Robert Jungk's *Le Futur a déjà commencé*, were included in this classification.

acute in a very short time. How, socially, politically, morally, and humanly, shall we contrive to get there? How are the prodigious economic problems, for example, of unemployment, to be solved? And, in Muller's more distant utopia, how shall we force humanity to refrain from begetting children naturally? How shall we force them to submit to constant and rigorous hygienic controls? How shall man be persuaded to accept a radical transformation of his traditional modes of nutrition? How and where shall we relocate a billion and a half persons who today make their livings from agriculture and who, in the promised ultrarapid conversion of the next forty years, will become completely useless as cultivators of the soil? How shall we distribute such numbers of people equably over the surface of the earth, particularly if the promised fourfold increase in population materializes? How will we handle the control and occupation of outer space in order to provide a stable *modus vivendi*? How shall national boundaries be made to disappear? (One of the last two would be a necessity.) There are many other "hows," but they are conveniently left unformulated. When we reflect on the serious although relatively minor problems that were provoked by the industrial exploitation of coal and electricity, when we reflect that after a hundred and fifty years these problems are still not satisfactorily resolved, we are entitled to ask whether there are any solutions to the infinitely more complex "hows" of the next forty years. In fact, there is one and only one means to their solution, a world-wide totalitarian dictatorship which will allow technique its full scope and at the same time resolve the concomitant difficulties. It is not difficult to understand why the scientists and worshippers of technology prefer not to dwell on this solution, but rather to leap nimbly across the dull and uninteresting intermediary period and land squarely in the golden age. We might indeed ask ourselves if we will succeed in getting through the transition period of all, or if the blood and the suffering required are not perhaps too high a price to pay for this golden age.

If we take a hard, unromantic look at the golden age itself, we are struck with the incredible naïveté of these scientists. They say, for example, that they will be able to shape and reshape at will human emotions, desires, and thoughts and arrive scientifically at certain efficient, pre-established collective decisions. They claim they will be in a position to develop certain collective desires, to constitute certain homogeneous social units out of aggregates of individuals, to forbid men to raise their children, and even to persuade them to renounce having any. At the same time, they speak of assuring the triumph of freedom and of the necessity of avoiding dictatorship at any price.[3] They seem incapable of grasping the contradiction involved, or of

_____

3. The material here and below is cited from actual texts.

understanding that what they are proposing, even after the intermediary period, is in fact the harshest of dictatorships. In comparison, Hitler's was a trifling affair. That it is to be a dictatorship of test tubes rather than of hobnailed boots will not make it any less a dictatorship.

When our savants characterize their golden age in any but scientific terms, they emit a quantity of down-at-the-heel platitudes that would gladden the heart of the pettiest politician. Let's take a few samples. "To render human nature nobler, more beautiful, and more harmonious." What on earth can this mean? What criteria, what content, do they propose? Not many, I fear, would be able to reply. "To assure the triumph of peace, liberty, and reason." Fine words with no substance behind them. "To eliminate cultural lag." What culture? And would the culture they have in mind be able to subsist in this harsh social organization? "To conquer outer space." For what purpose? The conquest of space seems to be an end in itself, which dispenses with any need for reflection.

We are forced to conclude that our scientists are incapable of any but the emptiest platitudes when they stray from their specialities. It makes one think back on the collection of mediocrities accumulated by Einstein when he spoke of God, the state, peace, and the meaning of life. It is clear that Einstein, extraordinary mathematical genius that he was, was no Pascal; he knew nothing of political or human reality, or, in fact, anything at all outside his mathematical reach. The banality of Einstein's remarks in matters outside his specialty is as astonishing as his genius within it. It seems as though the specialized application of all one's faculties in a particular area inhibits the consideration of things in general. Even J. Robert Oppenheimer, who seems receptive to a general culture, is not outside this judgment. His political and social declarations, for example, scarcely go beyond the level of those of the man in the street. And the opinions of the scientists quoted by *l'Express* are not even on the level of Einstein or Oppenheimer. Their pomposities, in fact, do not rise to the level of the average. They are vague generalities inherited from the nineteenth century, and the fact that they represent the furthest limits of thought of our scientific worthies must be symptomatic of arrested development or of a mental block. Particularly disquieting is the gap between the enormous power they wield and their critical ability, which must be estimated as nil. To wield power well entails a certain faculty of criticism, discrimination, judgment, and option. It is impossible to have confidence in men who apparently lack these faculties. Yet it is apparently our fate to be facing a "golden age" in the power of sorcerers who are totally blind to the meaning of the human adventure. When they speak of preserving the seed of outstanding men, whom, pray, do they mean to be the judges? It is clear, alas, that they propose to sit in judgment themselves. It is hardly likely that they will deem a Rimbaud or a Nietszche worthy of posterity. When they announce that they will conserve the genetic mutations which appear to them most favorable, and that they propose to modify the very germ cells in order to produce such and such traits; and when we consider the mediocrity of the scientists themselves outside the confines of their specialties, we can only shudder at the thought of what they will esteem most "favorable."

None of our wise men ever pose the question of the end of all their marvels. The "wherefore" is resolutely passed by. The response which would occur to our contemporaries is: for the sake of happiness. Unfortunately, there is no longer any question of that. One of our best-known specialists in diseases of the nervous system writes: "We will be able to modify man's emotions, desires and thoughts, as we have already done in a rudimentary way with tranquillizers." It will be possible, says our specialist, to produce a conviction or an impression of happiness without any real basis for it. Our man of the golden age, therefore, will be capable of "happiness" amid the worst privations. Why, then, promise us extraordinary comforts, hygiene, knowledge, and nourishment if, by simply manipulating our nervous systems, we can be happy without them? The last meager motive we could possibly ascribe to the technical adventure thus vanishes into thin air through the very existence of technique itself.

But what good is it to pose questions of motives? of why? All that must be the work of some miserable intellectual who balks at technical progress. The attitude of the scientists, at any rate, is clear. Technique exists because it is technique. The golden age will be because it will be. Any other answer is superfluous.

John William Ward

The Ideal of Individualism
and the Reality of Organization

The purpose of this essay is to trace the history of the ideal of individualism in American culture and then to use that history in order to understand better the deep concern for the place of the individual in contemporary American society. Our society, like all modern industrial societies, is characterized by economic and social interdependence, specialization of activity, and largescale organization—social phenomena that pose troublesome problems for traditional American attitudes toward the relation of the individual to society. One way of coming to grips with our predicament is to see how we came to it in the first place.

"The profit of studying history," George Santayana once said, "lies in something else than in a dead knowledge of what happens to have happened" (Santayana, 1918, pp. 52–53). Yet no good historian —and the adjective will quickly exclude those who may disagree— would suggest that history will give us ready and pat answers to problems in the present. What history can do is enlarge our experience of the events that have entered into the shaping of the present in which we live and move and, thus, make us more aware, itself a virtue, and perhaps through awareness better able to act. Since my final purpose is to bring an excursion into the past to bear upon the present, perhaps it will serve that purpose to begin in the present.

There is an embarrassment of riches when one looks for a contemporary text from which to begin. One thinks of the fortieth anniversary issue of *Time* magazine (May 10, 1963), "The Individual in America," with its cover story on Lincoln, "the greatest, the classic, the archetypical individual in the American imagination," who knew about the organization man because "in a sense he was one himself, and a good one" (p. 20). But I have chosen as my text an article from *Fortune* magazine for two reasons: it is shorter and therefore more adaptable to my needs; but more important, it comes from a maga-

Abridged from *The Business Establishment,* Earl F. Cheit, editor, John Wiley & Sons, Inc., 1964, pp. 37–49 and 70–76. Reprinted by permission of the publisher and John William Ward.

zine that addresses itself specifically to the leaders of American business.

Some years ago—in 1951 to be precise—in the political stalemate following the end of the Second World War, the editors of *Fortune* looked about and discovered half the world on their right hand and half on their left. There seemed to be no ground to stand on between "fascist totalitarianism," the world of the right, and "paternal state socialism," the world of the left. So *Fortune* decided to establish one. In a world made cold by the winds of change, America, in its fat and warm contentment, seemed to offer too visible a target. Although what the editors of *Fortune* were after was what they themselves called a "middle of the road" solution, they packaged it handsomely under the brand name of "the permanent revolution."

The irony cuts deeper than that. The "third force" that the world needed to combat fascism and socialism was that old American tradition, "individualism." The editors faced the cliché without flinching:

> Americans are fond of saying that the state exists for the individual, not the individual for the state. Despite its truistic character, this aphorism has enormous meaning. A proletarian approach, which subordinates the individual to the group or class, represents for the American, not an advance but a reaction. . . . If a really dynamic third force is to be created . . . the principle of individualism must constitute its foundation.[1]

But the dynamic principle of a conservative revolution based on the ideal of individualism had some awkward facts to face. The editors went on to say:

> In our time, individualism has clashed with the whole industrial development, mass production and the division of labor. The key to industrialization is not independence but interdependence; no individual is self-sufficient; each is involved with others in complicated relationships. Dominating all this is the modern corporation, an organization of vast powers, which exacts of its managers purely impersonal decisions. It is little wonder that men have turned to the state to protect themselves in such a world.

The world of the state was, of course, the world of fascism or socialism. Yet, if America was to maintain its conservative, permanent revolution, it had to remain true to what the editors of *Fortune* took to be the basic proposition of American society—private, individual responsibility. To turn to the state would only further compromise

---

1. *Fortune* (February 1951), p. 176. The articles in this issue of *Fortune* are gathered in Davenport (1951).

the integrity of the industrial American, dependent on his fellows but lonely in a world of impersonal decisions. *"The solution is to be found,"* discovered the editors, so delighted that they put their discovery in italics, *"The solution is to be found not through a growth in government, but through a growth in the stature of the individual."*

The dialectic begins to pick up speed here, and one has to watch closely.

> The concept that appears to be emerging, as the answer of the modern individual to this challenge, is the concept of the *team*. It is an old concept but it is being put to new uses. As a member of a team an individual can find full opportunity for self-expression and still retain a dynamic relationship to other individuals . . . the concept of the team has the power to challenge the individual to seek his self-expression, not along purely egoistic channels. . . . A community—big or little—is created, and through it the individual finds a higher expression of himself.

If one stops as one reads that the individual is to realize himself as part of a team, if one stops to wonder what happened to that reactionary proletarian danger of immersing the individual in a group, one will see the same thing happened to it that happened to that independent individual. The group has become community; interdependence has become team play; complicated relationships have become dynamic relationships. "Community," "team," "dynamic"; these are all plus words. We respond to them positively and happily, perhaps even mindlessly. Unless we watch the verbal magic, we will not notice that the individualism put in the hat at the beginning is not the individualism that pops out at the end.

The traditional American individual, once wrapped warmly in the pleasant connotations of self-reliance and independence, reappears as that well-known fellow, the other-directed individual, trying to find out who he truly is by relating himself to others in his society.

Now, the semanticist will find a certain perverse delight in all of this, but the historian will find a text. What the editors of *Fortune* did was to run over a century of American history through a single article. The projector works so fast that we tend to see only the blurred confusion. However, rather than blame the operator we might better be thankful for seeing what we may well have been missing in the slow-motion version of history.

At the beginning when Americans spoke of individualism, they meant the kind of independence the editors of *Fortune* point to in their beginning. Individualism meant the primacy of the individual person, the denial of social restraint, freedom from involvement with others. After an awkward transition in which they tried to make this ideal apply to conditions that made it increasingly anachronistic, Americans have begun to shift the connotations of the word in precisely the fashion that the editors of *Fortune* do when they draw to their conclusion. Individualism comes to mean participation in society. One achieves a higher expression of one's self through the organization of society. The early version, that is, *freedom from society*, was essentially negative; the modern version, that is, *freedom to cooperate* in society, is essentially positive.[2]

What Americans have been doing for more than a century is gradually changing their system of values under the protection of big, umbrella words like "individualism." The word stays the same; it provides comfort against the rude weather of change. But the meaning moves, and we come out from under the umbrella in a different climate altogether.

The History of Individualism as a Concept

The concept, individualism, appeared first in France as *"individualisme,"* after the French Revolution. Prior to the Revolution the French word for individual, *individu*, was used to describe someone who did not belong to any of the corporate bodies that constituted society, someone who had no social identity (see Palmer, 1948). After the Revolution when all corporate bodies had been abolished, the word *individualisme*, used by conservatives, liberals, and socialists alike, first appeared to describe the evil and anti-social impulses of self-interest. This is also Edmund Burke's charge against the French Revolution—that the political philosophy of the Revolution with its celebration of abstract rights would lead to the point where, in his words, "the commonwealth itself would, in a few generations, crumble away, be disconnected into the dust and powder of individuality, and at length dispersed to all the winds of heaven" (Burke, 1955, p. 109).

In Europe, then, individualism meant the atomization of society, a threat to the common good, the suffocating dust of equality. Notice, however, that Burke uses the word "individuality," not "individualism," and for a good and simple reason. The word was not yet available to him; it had not yet come into the English language. According to the *Oxford English Dictionary*, "individualism" made its appearance in English in 1835 with the translation of Tocqueville's justly famous *Democracy in America*. The *Oxford English Dictionary* happens to be wrong in its particulars but still generally right. It has the date of the translation of Tocqueville wrong; it should be 1840.

---

2. There is the danger of evoking emotional connotations in using words like "positive" and "negative" as descriptive terms, but the same danger goes with any other air of descriptive terms that I have been able to think of. I settled on these two, because they are also used by Isaiah Berlin (1958), and in the hope that the echo might remind us that our problem far transcends the dimensions of American history.

Also, there are a few other uses of the word in English prior to the translation of Tocqueville, but the *Oxford English Dictionary* is right in the sense that "individualism" came into the English language in response to the need for a word to describe the social philosophy of America in the 1830's, the period of Jacksonian democracy. So, since the attribution is correct in the terms that count, let us begin with Tocqueville, because he clearly sets forth the original meaning of the word.[3]

Tocqueville and the Novelty of Individualism

In describing the attitude that developed because of the conditions of social equality in America, Tocqueville found himself at a loss for a word to name the social philosophy of Americans. So he introduced a new one.[4] "*Individualism*," he wrote, emphasizing the word, "is a novel expression, to which a novel idea has given birth" (Tocqueville, 1948, p. 98). Tocqueville's English translator, Henry Reeve, felt the same sense of something new. When he translated the word from the French, he simply dropped the French "e" from its end, rendered it as "individualism," and put a note at the bottom of his page: "I adopt the expression of the original," he explained, "however strange it may sound to the English ear . . . because I know of no English word exactly equivalent to the expression."

What Tocqueville wanted to describe by using his new word was a social philosophy that he had discovered in America concerning the relation of the individual to society. His need for a new word is the

---

3. Tocqueville published the *Democracy* in two parts, each part appearing in two volumes, in 1835 and 1840. Both parts were immediately translated into English, appearing in London also in 1835 and 1840, by Henry Reeve, public official and author who was later to become editor of the *Edinburgh Review*. The *Oxford English Dictionary* dates Reeve's translation of Tocqueville's use of "individualism" as 1835, but the usage occurred in Tocqueville's chapter, "Of Individualism in Democratic Countries," in the second part of 1840. The editor may have been misled because the first part appeared in two volumes, or he may simply have taken the earliest date of the title, *Democracy in America*, to arrive at the date 1835. The error kept him from noting the appearance of the word in English before Reeve used it. In 1839, T. G. Bradford in Boston, translating the third edition of Michael Chevalier's *Lettres sur l'Amérique du Nord* (1838), uses "individualism" without any sign that he is self-conscious about employing a neologism. (See Chevalier, 1961, pp. 104, 356, 391.) Chevalier uses the word in the same sense Tocqueville was to use it: "Under the influence of Protestantism and republicanism, social progress had been achieved by pushing the process of division to its extreme, that is, individualism; for Protestantism, republicanism, and individualism are all one. Individuals have cut themselves off from each other; each has isolated his personality in order to protect it" (p. 356).

"Individualism" also appeared in an unsigned article in the *United States Magazine and Democratic Review*, VI (1839), pp. 208–209. Here again, the American writer is unembarrassed by the word, which suggests that a further hunt would uncover previous uses of it; more importantly, he, unlike his European contemporaries, uses the word in an honorific sense. But that is to anticipate my text.

4. More precisely, he seems to have thought that he was using a new word. In France, the concept of individualism was relatively new, but it had been in the political vocabulary at least 16 years before Tocqueville wrote. However, all—whether extreme reactionaries like Bonald or Maistre, liberals like Tocqueville, or Saint-Simonian socialists like Chevalier—used the word to mean the disintegration of society. (See Swart, 1962, pp. 77–90.)

best measure we have of his sense that the future, which he thought was embodied in America, meant a radical departure from the past of Europe. But Tocqueville was not happy with the texture of the world that he saw unfolding before his eyes. What in Europe seemed odious —the notion that the individual was superior to society—was in America "a mature and calm feeling." Tocqueville was at pains to discriminate the social philosophy of individualism from sheer egoism, sheer selfishness, but he thought that Americans, in developing a social philosophy that detached the individual from his fellow men, might come to as mean a failure as if they had acted from mere thoughtless selfishness. "Selfishness," he wrote, "originates in blind instinct; individualism proceeds from erroneous judgement more than from depraved feelings; it originates as much in deficiencies of mind as in perversity of heart." The judgment is the typical European critique: Americans mean well, but they lack mind. With all the good heart in the world, Americans, thought Tocqueville, were organizing society around a notion of the individual person, which would in the long run destroy all social virtue and end in social disaster.

Yet, Tocqueville recognized that in Jacksonian America individualism was an ideal of behavior, not simply an antisocial impulse. In attributing to much power to an idea, Tocqueville was no Platonist. As much as any modern sociologist he knew that social conditions have their characteristic intellectual counterparts. In his analysis, individualism was the idea, social equality was the condition. The tendency of the American to look to himself alone was, thought Tocqueville, a function of his environment. However, as a member of the *petite noblesse* of French society Tocqueville could not face the logical consequences of social equality and individualism without considerable apprehension. His image of the good society was formed by the notion of a social hierarchy, a chain of being in which each member of the community belonged to a clearly defined place in the hierarchical order of things. "Aristocracy," he said, "had made a chain of all the members of the community, from the peasant to the king; democracy breaks that chain and severs every link of it" (Tocqueville, 1948, p. 99).[5] It was this shattering separation of man from man, the rupture of all social relationships and social obligations, that defined individualism for Tocqueville:

> As social conditions become more equal, the number of persons increases who, although they are neither rich nor powerful enough to exercise any great influence over their fellows, have nevertheless acquired or retained sufficient education and fortune to satisfy their own wants. They owe nothing to any man,

---

5. For the rich tradition out of which Tocqueville spoke, see Lovejoy (1936).

they expect nothing from any man, they acquire the habit of
always considering themselves as standing alone, and they are
apt to imagine that their whole destiny is in their own hands.
Thus not only does democracy make every man forget his ancestors, but it hides his descendants and separates his contemporaries from him; it throws him back forever upon himself alone and
threatens in the end to confine him entirely within the solitude
of his own heart (*ibid.*, p. 98).[6]

The Democratic Hero: The Autonomous Individual

There is much one might say of Tocqueville's bleak adumbration
of the myth of the self-made man, but for present purposes I would
like to make one simple point about it. Tocqueville deplored the
consequences of individualism, but from his context it is apparent
that Americans did not. What Europeans feared, Americans celebrated. What was for Tocqueville a danger, was for the American
democrat an intoxicating ideal. Whereas, to make society possible at
all, Tocqueville sought countervailing tendencies against individualism, so American a spokesman as Ralph Waldo Emerson wrote in his
journals in 1840, the same year in which Tocqueville published: "In
all my lectures, I have taught one doctrine, namely, the infinitude of
the private man" (Whicher, 1957, p. 139).

A considerable body of assumptions lies behind so bold an assertion, but in insisting on the individual as the ultimate reality in
society Emerson was a characteristic spokesman for his time. In the
early nineteenth century, Americans did not like the state any more
than the editors of *Fortune* do today. "The less government we have
the better" was the rallying cry of Jeffersonians and Jacksonians
alike. "The antidote," said Emerson, in almost the precise words that
Fortune was to use more than a century later, "is the influence of
private character, the growth of the individual." Emerson went on, in
a long series of remarkable negatives, to strip this full-grown individual of every conceivable extrinsic support:

The appearance of character makes the State unnecessary. The
wise man is the State. He needs no army, fort, or navy—he loves
men too well; no bribe, or feast, or palace, to draw friends to
him; no vantage ground, no favorable circumstances. He needs
no library, for he has not done thinking; no church, for he is a
prophet; no statute-book, for he has the law-giver; no money, for

6. By "democracy" Tocqueville generally meant, as he clearly does in the passage
here, the equality of social conditions. Reeve did Tocqueville a mild disservice by
translating *démocratie* directly into our word; Tocqueville even considered calling the
second part of 1840, *Egalité en Amérique* to make his sense clearer, but he was not
above confusing the sense of "democracy" in his own usage. (See Pierson, 1938, pp.
747, 748 n.)

he is value; no road, for he is at home where he is; no experience, for the life of the creator shoots through him. . . . He has
no personal friends (*ibid.*, pp. 249–250).

The figure of this grandly isolated man, nakedly alone, without
any helpful circumstance, without the accumulated knowledge and
the traditions of the past, homeless, gladly bereft of friends, is a
chilling ideal—unless, that is, one can share the assumption that
makes it possible. Emerson and most Americans of his time could
embrace this figure because of the calm belief that there was an order
that existed apart from society, a natural order, which ultimately
validated the rejection of the artificial order of society and the state.
As Emerson put it elsewhere, "you take the way from man, not to
man" (*ibid.*, p. 158). This centrifugal thrust was kept from spinning
madly away by a deep trust in a natural order, which guaranteed
social unity. So society emerges miraculously as the sum of all the
individual rejections of society.

I have said that in this kind of assertion Emerson was a characteristically American thinker; he was. One can see the same attitude
of thought, the same conception of the relation of the individual to
society, in Jacksonian political thought, in economic thought, in revi-
valistic and evangelical Protestantism, in literature, and in the popular ideals of American society in Emerson's time—the America that
we sometimes tend to forget was the object of Tocqueville's analysis.[7]
The mood rises to a climax by the end of the nineteenth century in
the historical interpretation of the meaning of American history in
the hands of Frederick Jackson Turner and his followers in the
frontier interpretation of our history, the notion that the meaning of
American life lies in the movement out of society, away from others,
to a new beginning.[8]

The Unforeseen Consequence of Individualism

What happened to that heroic individual, standing alone, independent of others, the editors of *Fortune* put quite well: "The key to
industrialization is not independence, but interdependence." From
where we stand, looking backward, it surely seems ironic that an ideal
of independence and simple harmony should have been formulated
by a society on the verge of complexity and conflict, the society of

---

7. See Ward (1960), pp. 380–392, for a slightly fuller description of this general
pattern; see also the short concluding chapter of Ward (1955) for the way in which
popular ideals of the time centered optimistically on the energetic and self-reliant
individual.

8. See Smith (1950), especially the third section, The Garden of the World; it
concludes with an analysis of the way in which Turner's frontier hypothesis is the
culmination of a long cultural tradition in American thought, which "conferred on
him the authority of one who speaks from the distilled experience of his people"
(p. 251).

industrial America. Actually, the unintended consequence of the ideal of uninhibited individual action, of this negative theory of the state, of the denial of the reality of society, was to accelerate the powerful energies of an acquisitive capitalism and to lead finally to where we now stand.[9] Richard Hofstadter has observed that "the same forces in American life that had made Jacksonian equalitarianism possible and had given to the equalitarian theme in the agrarian romance its most compelling appeal had also unleashed in the nation an entrepreneurial zeal probably without precedent in history" (Hofstadter, 1955, p. 40).

The processes of machine industry and technology, which characterize the modern world, have made organization, the rationalization of activity, specialization, and social interdependence utterly necessary. The first response of Americans to the world that they had made was to try to keep the social benefits made possible through the economies of large-scale organization and, at the same time, to invoke and maintain an ideal of individualism, which organization and its logical consequences were rendering obsolete. Whatever the consequences (we can see them easily, because we have experienced them), Jacksonian America drew its emotional energy from the belief and assumption that there existed a simple, natural order, which would emerge spontaneously and unbidden if each individual went his own separate way.

It was, of course, the very fluidity and openness of Jacksonian society that provided a material basis for the heady optimism of this ultimately anarchic ideal of individualism. For an historian looking back on early America, the social circumstances bulk large; they may properly be primary in his assessment of the age. But for those living in the age, there was also an ideal, a moral basis for their optimism, a "cosmic optimism" built on a belief in a cosmic natural order, which undergirded and validated the ideal of the free and autonomous individual.

The original ideal of individualism in Jacksonian America was a secular jeremiad, an exhortation to begin over again, sloughing off the complexities of society by returning to a natural state of grace. Somewhat ironically, it was the material expansiveness of the society that made it possible to entertain such an ideal, to believe in the possibility of constantly beginning anew, of turning away from society to create one's own future. More ironically, it was the same

9. A problem that still puzzles historians of the Jacksonian period is whether the age wished somehow to recapture the simplicity of Jefferson's pastoral politics or to seize the main chance and exploit the opportunities of a rapidly growing society. Perhaps, being human, Americans of the time entertained both emotions, however incompatible. We can say without attempting to solve the puzzle that the ideal of the free and independent person, unencumbered by social restraint, could logically serve either goal. For a review of the historical literature of the period, see Ward (1962).

material expansiveness, itself accelerated by the lack of social restraint implicit in the ideal, that finally destroyed the ideal itself.
There were two "natures" in American society: the normative Nature
of the Jeffersonians, the Jacksonians, and the Transcendentalists;
and a physical nature of coal, iron, and oil—the raw materials of the
vast industrial and technological society in which we now live. The
unforeseen consequence of the Jacksonian program was, as I have
already said, to liberate the energies of industrial capitalism and,
thus, to accelerate the creation of our modern complex world. . . .

The Problem of Individualism and Organization

. . . I began by saying that I intended to bring this long historical excursion to bear upon a present problem. The problem is familiar
enough. From all sides we hear that the American is an organization
man lost in the lonely crowd of mass society, that the American has
ceased to be a self-reliant individual, and that this is all somehow a
betrayal of the American way of life. In the popular version, about the
longest perspective brought to bear on this faceless man in a gray
flannel suit is the accusation that progressive education started the
problem by preaching something called "adjustment." But the problem is much older than that, and a long historical process has gone
into its making. If you accept my account of the historical process,
then there are three logical ways one might attack the relationship of
the ideal of individualism to the reality of organization in modern
America.

The first would be to restrict the word "individualism" to the
early nineteenth century, to insist that the word has significance only
in a discussion of the historical context that gave rise to it. The
simplicity of this solution has a certain appeal, but one would be
sanguine indeed to think that he could legislate out of existence a
word with such massive emotional associations. It ignores the very
terms of the problem—that is, that it *is* a problem, that American
culture has a deep affective stake in the historical connotations of the
concept of individualism and will not lightly surrender it on the
grounds of being responsible to some intellectual demand for historical accuracy and logical consistency. Yet, it is a solution that some
intellectual historians might accept.[10]

The second answer would be to decide upon reflection that the

---

10. The suggestion is not just a possibility. Curiously, historians who stand at
opposite poles in their view of history have come to just such a conclusion. Arthur
O. Lovejoy has taught students of ideas to use large abstractions in the plural and
never in the singular, but Lovejoy's goal is to achieve analytical precision in the definition of the meaning of ideas. See, for example, Lovejoy (1948a, 6). Lovejoy treats
ideas largely in terms of their rational and internal dynamics. Writing from a position
quite the opposite, Charles A. Beard (1931), at the time largely under the influence of
Karl Mannheim and the sociology of knowledge, said of the idea of individualism in
1931: "The task before us, then, is not to furbish up an old slogan, but to get rid of
it" (p. 22).

real meaning of the word *should be* the collective sense, that the individual realizes himself by committing himself to some worthy enterprise larger than himself, that the older ideal of autonomy was simply an egoistic mistake, a mistake made possible by the peculiar and special circumstances of a passing moment in our national history. Despite its identification with the positive hero of the authoritarian mind, this version of individualism is a concept not totally alien to American culture, as we have already seen. If it were totally alien to our culture, there would be no problem. In the context of the necessary organization of our economic and social life, Americans have begun to develop a native definition of the individual as a member of the group. At its most innocuous level, this means simply that the individual should be able to get along with others, to adjust to the demands of living and working with others. At its most serious, it means a submersion of the individual in the group. The individual is defined by his function; one's role in the organization becomes one's real self. The rest is mere appendage. The will of God embodied in a church; the law of history embodied in a party; the good of society embodied in a corporation; or even the good of society, the national interest itself—these are not strange and unusual creeds in our time. Yet, they are creeds that are difficult for Americans to accept, even when they act in terms of them, because of the very past out of which American society has come. Again, this second solution may be acceptable to some, but not, I think, to Americans generally.

There is a third answer to the problem, which, in turn, has so many problems in it that it may not be an answer in any responsible sense of the word. It is a political answer, not in the narrow sense of the government but rather in the wider sense of the structuring of all the institutions affecting our daily lives. But to suggest it requires first a comment on the history that I have just recounted.

The paradoxical thing about the ideal of individualism in Jacksonian America, which celebrated the individual to the point of denying the reality of society, is that it was, in its very rejection of social forces, itself a social ideal. That is, only a particular kind of society could have generated an ideal that denied society. It took an outsider, a foreign observer like Tocqueville, to see that the heroically self-reliant American was possible only because of a widely shared consensus on matters that counted. The general will, which Rousseau had to hypothesize in order to make society possible at all, was in America the general experience under conditions of approximate social equality. In similar fashion, the violent swing to an opposite ideal still calling itself individualism but with radically different connotations; an ideal that makes the individual a part of society; an ideal that at its furthest reaches attributes reality to society and makes the individual simply a shadow of its will—this too is the product of our history.

All this is simply to say that the historian can describe two different systems of values both going under the name "individualism" that verge toward opposites—one toward the isolated person, the other toward society—and be descriptively correct in saying that at different moments in our history Americans have moved toward one and then the other. But the critical historian must then say that to put the question in terms of one *or* the other, of the individual *versus* society, is a false question. To put the matter in its baldest terms, to be a human being at all is a social achievement; the human animal is simply animal without society. At the same time, society, conceived as something apart from the human beings who compose it, is simply an abstraction—a convenient one so long as we remember it, a monstrous one if we forget it. Such resounding platitudes, however, leave us nowhere but in that comfortable American position, the middle of the road, unless one asks what follows. On the one hand we can ask what kind of individuals we want, and on the other what kind of organizations we want.

The first of this linked pair of questions admits no answer. To describe attributes that say that one is an individual only if one possesses particular qualities is to violate the very integrity of the individual person. Here we are at the emotional heart of the problem that troubles contemporary America—the notion that you can properly make no demands on the individual that are not his demands too. To do otherwise is to bully the actual, empirical individual, with the added insult that you are doing it to get him to be what he really wants to be, what his ideal self demands if only his ignorant actual self would recognize it. To construct a social definition of the nature of the individual and impose it on actual individuals would result, ironically, in a uniformity that tolerated no individual differences.

At this point criticism is driven back to history once again. It is true that the notion of consent—the idea that the individual must first accept emotionally and intellectually what power demands before power is legitimate—is itself an historical ideal; that is, it is relative. It has no universal, transcendental sanction behind it. It is the achievement of a particular history, a particular culture. There are cultures, not only in the past but also in the present, that would find such an ideal exotic or incomprehensible. However, it is an ideal that has informed American culture throughout its history. It is what we mean when we say that America is democratic. A democratic society is one in which those in positions of power, public or private, are responsible for their decisions to those whom their decisions affect. That definition forces us, then, to ask how the organizations of our modern, complex society might be made responsible to the individual and serve the ends of a democratic society.

An actual example is the best way to proceed. In the 1930s, when the United Auto Workers were locked in a fierce struggle with the management and owners of the automobile industry, the union was powerful because the worker identified himself with the union. As one might expect, the literature of the union movement in its militant phase provides an excellent source of illustration for what we have called the positive version of individualism. The worker, by a disciplined and dedicated commitment to the union, to the group of which he was a part, realized his own interest—not simply his immediate self-interest, but more importantly his own identification, his sense of who he was and where he was in a society fashioned somewhat closer to his desires. But having achieved recognition and having won his battle with management, the worker discovered that the union was itself no organic unitary thing; he discovered opponents in his own leadership. He did not have to read Michels on the "iron law of oligarchy" to discover that the leaders of any organization develop interests that conflict with the interests of the constituent members. The ideal of the union allowed for no such discrepancy, no such internal conflict, just as the ideal of positive individualism assumes a congruence between the ends of the group and the self-realization of the individual member. But conflict arose.

At this point, the leadership of the UAW performed an act of considerable political intelligence. They built into their organizational structure a Public Review Board, an impartial agency with the power of final adjudication to which the membership could appeal some decisions made by the leadership (Steiber, et al., 1960). By this action, the UAW has tried to bring its organizational structure into line with the theory of democracy that holds that leaders must be responsible to the individuals whom their decisions affect. Unless that theory is to remain empty rhetoric, there must be some means by which those affected can protest and, furthermore, they must feel free to exercise those means. The UAW Review Board is one attempt to create the means; such institutional safeguards allow the individual to participate in group action without surrendering himself entirely to a point of reference lying entirely outside his own self. Obviously, a staggering number of problems still remain, but some such feature must be present in the structure of the organization before other problems can be faced at all, and some such feature is the only means of guaranteeing to the individual some importance in the bureaucratic style of life that we call the organization.

What this comes down to is the need for a certain kind of organization. Our choice is not between organization and something else. It is a choice between organizations that serve our needs and ideals and organizations that do not. One of the humanly disturbing features of the modern world is that the individual, drawn tighter and tighter into a network of functional relations with a greater and greater number of other individuals, feels an increasing depersonalization, the sense of emotional distance that accompanies actual physical dependence. To borrow a word from biology, our relations are increasingly symbiotic. The classic example of such a relation is the embryo in the womb, dependent directly on the mother for nourishment. Today, we depend on an untold number of others to do their work, so our life may go on. These kinds of social relationships are not only necessary; they must exist (as they do) at some level of unawareness much as the functioning and organization of the nervous system in our body. But, to pursue the analogy, the social skills of specialization and organization must serve some larger end than simply intake and output. If Americans insist that society exists to serve the individual, not the individual to serve society, then we must show more imagination with the organization of our organizations in order to bring them at least within hailing distance of our professed ideals. As one looks about, one can fairly say that there is almost no evidence of such imagination at work in our society. We see, instead, cynicism masking itself in praise of the individual. Thus, *Time* magazine (May 10, 1963) in its issue on The Individual in America says: "Like all freedoms, this freedom of choice is also a burden, and that is one reason why there is so much 'conformity.' . . . To expect every individual to take in all of life through a thinking man's filter—to have his own independent, personal convictions about politics, ethics, culture—is to ask the impossible. It is, in fact, to ask for a mass elite" (p. 24).

It is. In all its outrageous innocence, this is what America has asked for from the beginning—sufficient individual character to control the realities of society. It may be impossible, but it will surely be impossible if we decide so beforehand.

References

Beard, Charles A. "The Myth of Rugged Individualism." *Harper's*, Vol. 164, 1931.

Berlin, Isaiah. *Two Concepts of Liberty.* Oxford, England: Clarendon Press, 1958.

Burke, Edmund. *Reflections on the Revolution in France*, ed. Thomas H. D. Mahoney. Bobbs-Merrill, 1955.

Chevalier, Michael. *Society, Manners, and Politics in the United States: Letters on North America*, tr. and ed. John W. Ward. Doubleday-Anchor, 1961.

Davenport, Russell. *USA: The Permanent Revolution.* Prentice-Hall, 1951.

Hofstadter, Richard. *The Age of Reform: From Bryan to F. D. R.* Knopf, 1955.

Lovejoy, Arthur O. *The Great Chain of Being.* Harvard University Press, 1936.

———. " 'Nature' as Aesthetic Norm." In *Essays in the History of Ideas.* Johns Hopkins Press, 1948a.

———. "On the Discrimination of Romanticisms." *Ibid.*, 1948b.

Palmer, Robert R. "Man and Citizen: Applications of Individualism in the French Revolution." In *Essays in Political Theory*, ed. Milton R. Konvitz and Arthur E. Murphy. Cornell University Press, 1948.

Pierson, George W. *Tocqueville and Beaumont in America*. Oxford University Press, 1938.

Santayana, George. "Reason in Science." In *The Life of Reason, or The Phases of Human Progress*, Vol. 5. Scribner's, 1918.

Smith, Henry Nash. *Virgin Land: The American West as Symbol and Myth*. Harvard University Press, 1950.

Steiber, Jack, Walter E. Oberer, and Michael Harrington. *Democracy and Public Review: An Analysis of the UAW Public Review Board*. Center for the Study of Democratic Institutions, 1960.

Swart, Koenraad W. "'Individualism' in the Mid-Nineteenth Century (1826–1860)." *Journal of the History of Ideas*, Vol. 23, 1962.

de Tocqueville, Alexis. *Democracy in America*, Part II, ed. Phillips Bradley. Knopf, 1948.

Ward, John W. *Andrew Jackson: Symbol for an Age*. Oxford University Press, 1955.

———. "Individualism Today." *Yale Review*, Vol. 49, Spring 1960.

———. "The Age of the Common Man." In *The Reconstruction of American History*, ed. John Higham. Harper & Row, 1962.

Whicher, Stephen E., ed. *Selections from Ralph Waldo Emerson*. Houghton Mifflin, 1957.

Carl Rogers

The Place of the Individual in the New World of the Behavioral Sciences

Elsewhere I have endeavored to point out, in a very sketchy manner, the advances of the behavioral sciences in their ability to predict and control behavior. I have tried to suggest the new world into which we will be advancing at an ever more headlong pace. Here I want to consider the question of how we—as individuals, as groups, as a culture—will live in, will respond to, will adapt to this brave new world. What stance will we take in the face of these new developments?

I am going to describe two answers which have been given to this question, and then I wish to suggest some considerations which may lead to a third answer.

Deny and Ignore

One attitude which we can take is to deny that these scientific advances are taking place, and simply take the view that there can be no study of human behavior which is truly scientific. We can hold that the human animal cannot possibly take an objective attitude toward himself, and that therefore no real science of behavior can exist. We can say that man is always a free agent, in some sense that makes scientific study of his behavior impossible. Not long ago, at a conference on the social sciences, curiously enough, I heard a well-known economist take just this view. And one of this country's most noted theologians writes, "In any event, no scientific investigation of past behavior can become the basis of predictions of future behavior" (Niebuhr, 1955, p. 47).

The attitude of the general public is somewhat similar. Without necessarily denying the possibility of a behavioral science, the man in the street simply ignores the developments which are taking place. To be sure, he becomes excited for a time when he hears it said that the Communists have attempted to change the soldiers they have captured by means of "brainwashing." He may show a mild reaction of annoyance to the revelations of a book such as Whyte's *Organization Man* (1956), which shows how heavily, and in what manipulative fashion, the findings of the behavioral sciences are used by modern industrial corporations. But by and large he sees nothing in all this to be concerned about, any more than he did in the first theoretical statements that the atom could be split.

We may, if we wish, join him in ignoring the problem. We may go further, like the older intellectuals I have cited, and, looking at the behavioral sciences, may declare that "there ain't no such animal." But since these reactions do not seem particularly intelligent, I shall leave them to describe a much more sophisticated and much more prevalent point of view.

The Formulation of Human Life in Terms of Science

Among behavioral scientists, it seems to be largely taken for granted that the findings of such science will be used in the prediction and control of human behavior. Yet most psychologists and other scientists have given little thought to what this would mean. An exception to this general tendency is Dr. B. F. Skinner of Harvard, who has been quite explicit in urging psychologists to use the powers of control which they have in the interest of creating a better world. In an attempt to show what he means, Dr. Skinner wrote a book some years ago, entitled *Walden Two* (1948), in which he gives a fictional account of what he regards as a utopian community in which the learnings of the behavioral sciences are fully utilized in all aspects of life—marriage, child rearing, ethical conduct, work, play, and artistic endeavor. (I shall quote from his writings several times.)

There are also some writers of fiction who have seen the significance of the coming influence of the behavioral sciences. Aldous Huxley, in his *Brave New World* (1946), has given a horrifying picture of saccharine happiness in a scientifically managed world, against which man eventually revolts. George Orwell, in *1984* (1953), has drawn a picture of the world, created by dictatorial power, in which the behavioral sciences are used as instruments of absolute control of individuals so that not behavior alone but even thought is controlled.

The writers of science fiction have also played a role in visualizing for us some of the possible developments in a world where behavior and personality are as much the subject of science as chemical compounds or electrical impulses.

I should like to try to present, as well as I can, a simplified picture of the cultural pattern which emerges if we endeavor to shape human life in terms of the behavioral sciences.

There is first of all the recognition, almost the assumption, that scientific knowledge is the power to manipulate. Dr. Skinner says (1955/56, pp. 56–57):

> We must accept the fact that some kind of control of human affairs is inevitable. We cannot use good sense in human affairs unless someone engages in the design and construction of environmental conditions which affect the behavior of men. Environmental changes have always been the condition for the improvement of cultural patterns, and we can hardly use the more effective methods of science without making changes on a grander scale. . . . Science has turned up dangerous processes and materials before. To use the facts and techniques of a science of man to the fullest extent without making some monstrous mistake will be difficult and obviously perilous. It is no time for self-deception, emotional indulgence, or the assumption of attitudes which are no longer useful.

The next assumption is that such power to control is to be used. Skinner sees it as being used benevolently, though he recognized the danger of its being misused. Huxley sees it as being used with benevolent intent, but actually creating a nightmare. Orwell describes the results if such power is used malignantly, to enhance the degree of regulation exercised by a dictatorial government.

Steps in the Process

Let us look at some of the elements which are involved in the concept of the control of human behavior as mediated by the behavioral sciences. What would be the steps in the process by which a society might organize itself so as to formulate human life in terms of the science of man?

First would come the selection of goals. In a paper of his, Dr. Skinner suggests that one possible goal to be assigned to the behavioral technology is this: "Let man be happy, informed, skillful, well-behaved, and productive" (1955/56, p. 47). In his *Walden Two*, where he can use the guise of fiction to express his views, he becomes more expansive. His hero says:

> "Well, what do you say to the design of personalities? Would that interest you? The control of temperament? Give me the specifications, and I'll give you the man! What do you say to the control of motivation, building the interests which will make men most productive and most successful? Does that seem to you fantastic? Yet some of the techniques are available, and more can be worked out experimentally. Think of the possibilities! . . . Let us control the lives of our children and see what we can make of them" (p. 243).

What Skinner is essentially saying here is that the current knowledge in the behavioral sciences, plus that which the future will bring, will enable us to specify, to a degree which today would seem incredible, the kind of behavioral and personality results which we wish to achieve. This is obviously both an opportunity and a very heavy burden.

The second element in this process would be one which is familiar to every scientist who has worked in the field of applied science. Given the purpose, the goal, we proceed by the method of science—by controlled experimentation—to discover the means to these ends. If, for example, our present knowledge of the conditions which cause men to be productive is limited, further investigation and experimentation would surely lead us to new knowledge in this field. And still further work will provide us with the knowledge of even more effective means. The method of science is self-correcting in thus arriving at increasingly effective ways of achieving the purpose we have selected.

The third element in the control of human behavior through the behavioral sciences involves the question of power. As the conditions or methods are discovered by which to achieve our goal, some person or group obtains the power to establish those conditions or use those methods. There has been too little recognition of the problem involved in this. To hope that the power being made available by the behavioral sciences will be exercised by the scientists, or by a benevolent group, seems to me a hope little supported by either recent or distant history. It seems far more likely that behavioral scientists, holding their present attitudes, will be in the position of the German rocket scientists specializing in guided missiles. First, they worked devotedly for Hitler to destroy Russia and the United States. Now, depending on who captured them, they work devotedly for Russia in the interest of destroying the United States, or devotedly for the United States in the interest of destroying Russia. If behavioral scientists are concerned solely with advancing their science, it seems most probable that they will serve the purposes of whatever individual or group has the power.

But this is, in a sense, a digression. The main point of this view is that some person or group will have and use the power to put into effect the methods which have been discovered for achieving the desired goal.

The fourth step in this process whereby a society might formulate its life in terms of the behavioral sciences is the exposure of individuals to the methods and conditions mentioned. As individuals are exposed to the prescribed conditions, this leads, with a high degree of probability, to the behavior which has been desired. Men then become productive, if that has been the goal, or submissive, or whatever it has been decided to make them.

To give something of the flavor of this aspect of the process as seen by one of its advocates, let me again quote the hero of *Walden Two:*

> Now that we *know* how positive reinforcement works, and why negative doesn't [he says, commenting on the method he is advocating], we can be more deliberate, and hence more successful, in our cultural design. We can achieve a sort of control under which the controlled, though they are following a code much more scrupulously than was ever the case under the old system, nevertheless *feel free.* They are doing what they want to do, not what they are forced to do. That's the source of the tremendous power of positive reinforcement—there's no restraint and no revolt. By a careful design, we control not the final behavior, but the *inclination* to behave—the motives, the desires, the wishes. The curious thing is that in that case *the question of freedom never arises* (p. 218).

The Picture and Its Implications

Let me see if I can sum up very briefly the picture of the impact of the behavioral sciences upon the individual and upon society as this impact is explicitly seen by Dr. Skinner, and implied in the attitudes and work of many, perhaps most, behavioral scientists. Behavioral science is clearly moving forward; its increasing power for control will be held by some one or some group; such an individual or group will surely choose the purposes or goals to be achieved; and most of us will then be increasingly controlled by means so subtle we will not even be aware of them as controls. Thus, whether a council of wise psychologists (if this is not a contradiction in terms) or a Stalin or a Big Brother has the power, and whether the goal is happiness, or productivity, or resolution of the Oedipus complex, or submission, or love of Big Brother, we will inevitably find ourselves moving toward the chosen goal, and probably thinking that we ourselves desire it. Thus if this line of reasoning is correct, it appears that some form of completely controlled society—a *Walden Two* or a *1984*—is coming. The fact that it would surely arrive piecemeal, rather than all at once, does not greatly change the fundamental issues. Man and his behavior would become a planned product of a scientific society.

You may well ask, "But what about individual freedom? What about the democratic concepts of the rights of the individual?" Here, too, Dr. Skinner is quite specific. He says quite bluntly:

> The hypothesis that man is not free is essential to the application of scientific method to the study of human behavior. The free inner man who is held responsible for the behavior of the external biological organism is only a pre-scientific substitute for the kinds of causes which are discovered in the course of a scientific analysis. All these alternative causes lie *outside* the individual (1953, p. 447).

In another source, he explains this at somewhat more length:

> As the use of science increases, we are forced to accept the theoretical structure with which science represents its facts. The difficulty is that this structure is clearly at odds with the traditional democratic conception of man. Every discovery of an event which has a part in shaping a man's behavior seems to leave so much the less to be credited to the man himself; and as such explanations become more and more comprehensive, the contribution which may be claimed by the individual himself appears to approach zero. Man's vaunted creative powers, his original accomplishments in art, science and morals, his capac-

ity to choose and our right to hold him responsible for the consequences of his choice—none of these is conspicuous in this new self-portrait. Man, we once believed, was free to express himself in art, music and literature, to inquire into nature, to seek salvation in his own way. He could initiate action and make spontaneous and capricious changes of course. Under the most extreme duress, some sort of choice remained to him. He could resist any effort to control him, though it might cost him his life. But science insists that action is initiated by forces impinging upon the individual, and that caprice is only another name for behavior for which we have not yet found a cause (1955/56, p. 52–53).

The democratic philosophy of human nature and of government is seen by Skinner as having served a useful purpose at one time. "In rallying men against tyranny it was necessary that the individual be strengthened, that he be taught that he had rights and could govern himself. To give the common man a new conception of his worth, his dignity, and his power to save himself, both here and hereafter, was often the only resource of the revolutionist" (*ibid.*, p. 53). He regards this philosophy as being now out of date, and indeed an obstacle "if it prevents us from applying to human affairs the science of man" (*ibid.*, p. 54).

A Personal Reaction

I have endeavored, up to this point, to give an objective picture of some of the developments in the behavioral sciences, and an objective picture of the kind of society which might emerge out of these developments. I do, however, have strong personal reactions to the kind of world I have been describing, a world which Skinner explicitly (and many other scientists implicitly) expect and hope for in the future. To me this kind of world would destroy the human person as I have come to know him in the deepest moments of psychotherapy. In such moments I am in relationship with a person who is spontaneous, who is responsibly free, that is, aware of his freedom to choose who he will be, and aware also of the consequences of his choice. To believe, as Skinner holds, that all this is an illusion, and that spontaneity, freedom, responsibility, and choice have no real existence, would be impossible for me.

I feel that to the limit of my ability I have played my part in advancing the behavioral sciences, but if the result of my efforts and those of others is that man becomes a robot, created and controlled by a science of his own making, then I am very unhappy indeed. If the good life of the future consists in so conditioning individuals through the control of their environment, and through the control of the rewards they receive, that they will be inexorably productive, well behaved, happy, or whatever, then I want none of it. To me this is a pseudo form of the good life which includes everything save that which makes it good.

And so, I ask myself, is there any flaw in the logic of this development? Is there any alternative view to what the behavioral sciences might mean to the individual and to society? It seems to me that I perceive such a flaw, and that I can conceive of an alternative view. These I would like to set before you.

Ends and Values in Relation to Science

It seems to me that the view I have presented rests upon a faulty perception of the relationship of goals and values to the enterprise of science. The significance of the *purpose* of a scientific undertaking is, I believe, grossly underestimated. I would like to state a two-pronged thesis which in my estimation deserves consideration. Then I will elaborate the meaning of these two points.

1. In any scientific endeavor—whether "pure" or applied science—there is a prior personal subjective choice of the purpose or value which that scientific work is perceived as serving.
2. This subjective value choice which brings the scientific endeavor into being must always lie outside that endeavor, and can never become a part of the science involved in that endeavor.

Let me illustrate the first point from Dr. Skinner's writings. When he suggests that the task for the behavioral sciences is to make man "productive," "well-behaved," etc., it is obvious that he is making a choice. He might have chosen to make men submissive, dependent, and gregarious, for example. Yet, by his own statement in another context—man's "capacity to choose," his freedom to select his course and to initiate action—these powers do not exist in the scientific picture of man. Here is, I believe, the deep-seated contradiction, or paradox. Let me spell it out as clearly as I can.

Science, to be sure, rests on the assumption that behavior is caused—that a specified event is followed by a consequent event. Hence all is determined, nothing is free, choice is impossible. But we must recall that science itself, and each specific scientific endeavor, each change of course in a scientific research, each interpretation of the meaning of a scientific finding, and each decision as to how the finding shall be applied, rests upon a personal, subjective choice. Thus science in general exists in the same paradoxical situation as does Dr. Skinner. A personal, subjective choice made by man sets in motion the operations of science, which in time poclaims that there can be no such thing as a personal subjective choice. I shall make some comments about this continuing paradox at a later point.

I stressed the fact that each of these choices, initiating or furthering the scientific venture, is a value choice. The scientist investigates this rather than that because he feels the first investigation has more value for him. He chooses one method for his study rather than another because he values it more highly. He interprets his findings in one way rather than another because he believes the first way is closer to the truth, or more valid—in other words, that it is closer to a criterion which he values. Now these value choices are never a part of the scientific venture itself. The value choices connected with a particular scientific enterprise always and necessarily lie outside that enterprise.

I wish to make it clear that I am not saying that values cannot be included as a subject of science. It is not true that science deals only with certain classes of "facts" and that these classes do not include values. It is a bit more complex than that, as a simple illustration or two may make clear.

If I value knowledge of the "three Rs" as a goal of education, the methods of science can give me increasingly accurate information as to how this goal may be achieved. If I value problem-solving ability as a goal of education, the scientific method can give me the same kind of help.

Now if I wish to determine whether problem-solving ability is "better" than knowledge of the three Rs, then scientific method can also study those two values, but *only*—and this is very important—*only* in terms of some other value which I have subjectively chosen. I may value college success. Then I can determine whether problem-solving ability or knowledge of the three Rs is most closely associated with that value. I may value personal integration or vocational success or responsible citizenship. I can determine whether problem-solving ability or knowledge of the three Rs is "better" for achieving any one of these values. But the value or purpose which gives meaning to a particular scientific endeavor must always lie outside that endeavor.

What I have been saying seems equally true of applied and pure science. In pure science the usual prior subjective value choice is the discovery of truth. But this is a subjective choice, and science can never say whether it is the best choice, save in the light of some other value. Geneticists in Russia, for example, had to make a subjective choice of whether it was better to pursue truth or to discover facts which upheld a governmental dogma. Which choice is "better"? We could make a scientific investigation of those alternatives, but only in the light of some other subjectively chosen value. If, for example, we value the survival of a culture, then we could begin to investigate with the methods of science the question whether pursuit of truth or support of governmental dogma is most closely associated with cultural survival.

My point, then, is that any scientific endeavor, pure or applied, is carried on in the pursuit of a purpose or value which is subjectively chosen by persons. It is important that this choice be made explicit, since the particular value which is being sought can never be tested or evaluated, confirmed or denied, by the scientific endeavor to which it gives birth and meaning. The initial purpose or value always and necessarily lies outside the scope of the scientific effort which it sets in motion.

Among other things, this means that if we choose some particular goal or series of goals for human beings, and then set out on a large scale to control human behavior to the end of achieving those goals, we are locked in the rigidity of our initial choice, because such a scientific endeavor can never transcend itself to select new goals. Only subjective human persons can do that. Thus if we choose as our goal the state of happiness for human beings (a goal deservedly ridiculed by Aldous Huxley in *Brave New World*), and if we involved all of society in a successful scientific program by which people became happy, we would be locked in a colossal rigidity in which no one would be free to question this goal, because our scientific operations could not transcend themselves to question their guiding purposes. And, without laboring this point, I would remark that colossal rigidity, whether in dinosaurs or dictatorships, has a very poor record of evolutionary survival.

If, however, a part of our scheme is to set free some "planners" who do not have to be happy, who are not controlled, and who are therefore free to choose other values, this has several meanings. It means that the purpose we have chosen as our goal is not a sufficient and satisfying one for human beings, but must be supplemented. It also means that if it is necessary to set up an elite group which is free, then this shows all too clearly that the great majority are only the slaves—no matter by what high-sounding name we call them—of those who select the goals.

Perhaps, however, the thought is that a continuing scientific endeavor will evolve its own goals, that the initial findings will alter the directions, and subsequent findings will alter them still further, and that the science somehow develops its own purpose. This seems to be a view implicitly held by many scientists. It is surely a reasonable description, but it overlooks one element in this continuing development, which is that subjective, personal choice enters in at every point at which the direction changes. The findings of a science, the results of an experiment, do not and never can tell us what scientific purpose to pursue next. Even in the purest science, the scientist must

decide what the findings mean, and must subjectively choose what next step will be most profitable in the pursuit of his purpose. And if we are speaking of the application of scientific knowledge, then it is distressingly clear that the increasing scientific knowledge of the structure of the atom carries with it no necessary choice as to the purpose to which this knowledge will be put. This is a subjective, personal choice which must be made by many individuals.

Thus I return to the proposition with which I began this section —and which I now repeat in different words. Science has its meaning as the objective pursuit of a purpose which has been subjectively chosen by a person or persons. This purpose or value can never be investigated by the particular scientific experiment or investigation to which it has given birth and meaning. Consequently, any discussion of the control of human beings by the behavioral sciences must first and most deeply concern itself with the subjectively chosen purposes which such an application of science is intended to implement.

An Alternative Set of Values

If the line of reasoning I have been presenting is valid, then it opens new doors to us. If we frankly face the fact that science takes off from a subjectively chosen set of values, then we are free to select the values we wish to pursue. We are not limited to such stultifying goals as producing a controlled state of happiness, productivity, and the like. I would like to suggest a radically different alternative.

Suppose we start with a set of ends, values, purposes, quite different from the type of goals we have been considering. Suppose we do this quite openly, setting them forth as a possible value choice to be accepted or rejected. Suppose we select a set of values which focuses on fluid elements of process, rather than static attributes. We might then value:

1. Man as a process of becoming, as a process of achieving worth and dignity through the development of his potentialities.
2. The individual human being as a self-actualizing process, moving on to more challenging and enriching experiences.
3. The process by which the individual creatively adapts to an ever new and changing world.
4. The process by which knowledge transcends itself; for example, the theory of relativity transcended Newtonian physics, and will itself be transcended in some future day by a new perception.

If we select values such as these, we turn to our science and technology of behavior with a very different set of questions. We will want to know such things as these:

1. Can science aid us in the discovery of new modes of richly rewarding living? More meaningful and satisfying modes of interpersonal relationships?
2. Can science inform us as to how the human race can become a
   more intelligent participant in its own evolution—its physical,
   psychological, and social evolution?
3. Can science inform us as to ways of releasing the creative capacity
   of individuals, which seem so necessary if we are to survive in this
   fantastically expanding atomic age? Dr. Oppenheimer has pointed
   out (1956) that knowledge, which used to double in millennia or
   centuries, now doubles in a generation or a decade. It appears that
   we will need to discover the utmost in the release of creativity if
   we are to be able to adapt effectively.
4. In short, can science discover the methods by which man can most
   readily become a continually developing and self-transcending
   process, in his behavior, his thinking, his knowledge? Can science
   predict and release an essentially "unpredictable" freedom?

It is one of the virtues of science as a method that it is as able to
advance and implement goals and purposes of this sort as it is to
serve static values, such as states of being well informed, happy,
obedient. Indeed, we have some evidence of this.

A Small Example

I will perhaps be forgiven if I document some of the possibilities
along this line by turning to psychotherapy, the field I know best.

Psychotherapy, as Meerloo (1955, pp. 353–60) and others have
pointed out, can be one of the most subtle tools for the control of one
person by another. The therapist can subtly mold individuals in imitation of himself. He can cause an individual to become a submissive
and conforming being. When certain therapeutic principles are used
in extreme fashion, we call it brainwashing—an instance of the
disintegration of the personality and a reformulation of the person
along lines desired by the controlling individual. So the principles of
therapy can be used as a most effective means of external control of
human personality and behavior. Can psychotherapy be anything
else?

I find the developments in client-centered psychotherapy (Rogers, 1951) an exciting hint of what a behavioral science can do in
achieving the kinds of values I have stated. Quite aside from being a
somewhat new orientation in psychotherapy, this development has
important implications regarding the relation of a behavioral science
to the control of human behavior. Let me describe our experience as it
relates to the issues of the present discussion.

In client-centered therapy, we are deeply engaged in the predic-

tion and influencing of behavior. As therapists, we institute certain attitudinal conditions, and the client has relatively little voice in the establishment of these conditions. To put it very briefly, we have found that the therapist is most effective if he is (a) genuine, integrated, transparently real in the relationship; (b) acceptant of the client as a separate, different person, and acceptant of each fluctuating aspect of the client as it comes to expression; and (c) sensitively empathic in his understanding, or seeing the world through the client's eyes. Our research permits us to predict that if these attitudinal conditions are instituted or established, certain behavioral consequences will ensue. Putting it this way sounds as if we are again back in the familiar groove of being able to predict behavior, and hence able to control it. But it is precisely here that we find a sharp difference.

The conditions we have chosen to establish predict such behavioral consequences as these: the client will become more self-directing, less rigid, more open to the evidence of his senses, better organized and integrated, more similar to the ideal which he has chosen for himself. In other words, by external control we have established conditions which we predict will be followed by internal control by the individual, in pursuit of internally chosen goals. We have set the conditions which predict various classes of behavior—self-directing behaviors, sensitivity to realities within and without, flexible adaptiveness—which are by their very nature *unpredictable* in their specifics. The conditions we have established predict behavior which is essentially "free." Our recent research (Rogers and Dymond, 1954), indicates that our predictions are to a significant degree corroborated, and our commitment to the scientific method causes us to believe that more effective means of achieving these goals may be realized.

Research exists in other fields—industry, education, group dynamics—which seems to support our own findings. I believe it may be conservatively stated that scientific progress has been made in identifying those conditions in an interpersonal relationship which, if they exist in B, are followed in A by greater maturity in behavior, less dependence upon others, an increase in expressiveness as a person, an increase in variability, flexibility and effectiveness of adaptation, an increase in self-responsibility and self-direction. And quite in contrast to the concern expressed by some, we do not find that the creatively adaptive behavior which results from such self-directed variability of expression is too chaotic or too fluid. Rather, the individual who is open to his experience, and self-directing, is harmonious, not chaotic, and ingenious rather than random as he orders his responses imaginatively toward the achievement of his own purposes. His creative actions are no more a chaotic accident than was Einstein's development of the theory of relativity.

Thus we find ourselves in fundamental agreement with John Dewey's statement: "Science has made its way by releasing, not by suppressing, the elements of variation, of invention and innovation, of novel creation in individuals" (in Ratner, 1939, p. 359). We have come to believe that progress in personal life and in group living is made in the same way, by releasing variation, freedom, creativity.

A Possible Concept of the Control of Human Behavior

It is quite clear that the point of view I am expressing is in sharp contrast to the usual conception of the relationship of the behavioral sciences to the control of human behavior, previously mentioned. In order to make this contrast even more blunt, I will state this possibility in a form parallel to the steps which I described before:

1. It is possible for us to choose to value man as a self-actualizing process of becoming; to value creativity, and the process by which knowledge becomes self-transcending.
2. We can proceed, by the methods of science, to discover the conditions which necessarily precede these processes, and, through continuing experimentation, to discover better means of achieving these purposes.
3. It is possible for individuals or groups to set these conditions, with a minimum of power or control. According to present knowledge, the only authority necessary is the authority to establish certain qualities of interpersonal relationship.
4. Present knowledge suggests that, exposed to these conditions, individuals become more self-responsible, make progress in self-actualization, become more flexible, more unique and varied, more creatively adaptive.
5. Thus such an initial choice would inaugurate the beginnings of a social system or subsystem in which values, knowledge, adaptive skills, and even the concept of science would be continually changing and self-transcending. The emphasis would be upon man as a process of becoming.

I believe it is clear that such a view as I have been describing does not lead to any definable Utopia. It would be impossible to predict its final outcome. It involves a step-by-step development, based upon a continuing subjective choice of purposes, which are implemented by the behavioral sciences. It is in the direction of the "open society," as that term has been defined by Popper (1945), where individuals carry responsibility for personal decisions. It is at the opposite pole from his concept of the closed society, of which *Walden Two* would be an example.

I trust it is also evident that the whole emphasis is upon process, not upon end states of being. I am suggesting that it is by choosing to value certain qualitative elements of the process of becoming that we can find a pathway toward the open society.

The Choice

It is my hope that I have helped to clarify the range of choice which will lie before us and our children in regard to the behavioral sciences. We can choose to use our growing knowledge to enslave people in ways never dreamed of before, depersonalizing them, controlling them by means so carefully selected that they will perhaps never be aware of their loss of personhood. We can choose to utilize our scientific knowledge to make men necessarily happy, well behaved, and productive, as Dr. Skinner suggests. We can, if we wish, choose to make men submissive, conforming, docile. Or, at the other end of the spectrum of choice, we can choose to use the behavioral sciences in ways which will free, not control; which will bring about constructive variability, not conformity; which will develop creativity, not contentment; which will facilitate each person in his self-directed process of becoming; which will aid individuals, groups, and even the concept of science to become self-transcending in freshly adaptive ways of meeting life and its problems. The choice is up to us, and because the human race is what it is, we are likely to stumble about, making at times some nearly disastrous value choices, and at other times highly constructive ones.

If we choose to utilize our scientific knowledge to free men, then it will demand that we live openly and frankly with the great paradox of the behavioral sciences. We will recognize that behavior, when examined scientifically, is surely best understood as determined by prior causation. This is the great fact of science. But responsible personal choice, which is the most essential element in being a person, which is the core experience in psychotherapy, which exists prior to any scientific endeavor, is an equally prominent fact in our lives. We will have to live with the realization that to deny the reality of the experience of responsible personal choice is as stultifying, as closed minded, as to deny the possibility of a behavioral science. That these two important elements of our experience appear to be in contradiction has perhaps the same significance as the contradiction between the wave theory and the corpuscular theory of light, both of which can be shown to be true, even though incompatible. We cannot profitably deny our subjective life, any more than we can deny the objective description of that life.

In conclusion, then, it is my contention that science cannot come into being without a personal choice of the values we wish to achieve. And the values we choose to implement will forever lie outside the science which implements them; the goals we select, the purposes we wish to follow, must always be outside the science which achieves them. To me this has the encouraging meaning that the human person, with his capacity of subjective choice, can and will always exist separate from and prior to any of his scientific undertakings. Unless, as individuals and groups, we choose to relinquish our capacity of subjective choice, we will always remain free persons, not simply pawns of a self-created behavioral science.

References

Huxley, Aldous. *Brave New World.* Harper & Row, 1946.

Meerloo, J. A. M. "Medication into Submission: The Danger of Therapeutic Coercion." *Journal of Nervous and Mental Disorders,* Vol. 122, 1955.

Niebuhr, Reinhold. *The Self and the Dramas of History.* Scribner, 1955.

Oppenheimer, J. Robert. "Science and our Times." *Roosevelt University Occasional Papers,* Vol. 2, 1956.

Orwell, George. *1984.* Harcourt, Brace & World, 1948.

Popper, K. R. *The Open Society and Its Enemies.* Routledge and Kegan Paul, 1945.

Ratner, J., ed. *Intelligence in the Modern World: John Dewey's Philosophy.* 1939.

Rogers, C. R. *Client-centered Therapy.* Houghton Mifflin, 1951.

————, and Rosalind Dymond, ed. *Psychotherapy and Personality Change.* University of Chicago Press, 1954.

Skinner, B. F. "Freedom and the Control of Men." *American Scholar,* Vol. 25, Winter 1955/56.

————. *Science and Human Behavior.* Macmillan, 1953.

————. *Walden Two.* Macmillan, 1948.

Whyte, William H., Jr. *The Organization Man.* Simon & Schuster, 1956.

Robert Hutchins and Joseph P. Lyford

Living without Guilt

Lyford: It is a great pleasure to be able to discuss the work of a newly discovered philosopher, lamentably now dead, with the one man who is thoroughly acquainted with his works and who knew him personally. The philosopher, whose theories promise to have a far-reaching impact on modern thought, is Dr. Alexander Zuckerkandl. Dr. Zuckerkandl was an Austrian, who spent his entire life in obscurity. Dr. Zuckerkandl's discoverer, his interpreter, in a sense his Boswell, is Robert M. Hutchins, former President and Chancellor of the University of Chicago and now President of the Center for the Study of Democratic Institutions.

Mr. Hutchins, perhaps you could tell us a little bit about Alexander Zuckerkandl the man and how you met him, and then we could talk about his main philosophical lines of thought.

Hutchins: I should be glad to do that. It was in a small café in Baden-Baden many years ago that I first encountered my late friend. He was, I think, the greatest diagnostician of our age, but I must admit that few, if any, of the indicia of genius appeared in his face or figure. The only feature that distinguished him from the other habitués of the café or saloon was a small goatee that he wore in honor of his former teacher Sigmund Freud. He had once gone so far as to cut himself deliberately while shaving so that he might have the same scar on his chin that Freud refers to in his great work, *The Interpretation of Dreams.* I sat down beside him because it was the only seat that was vacant. He welcomed me to his table with a bow and spoke to me in a language which was at that time unintelligible. I don't know whether you would like to have me tell you about his language now, or whether you want to get into that later.

Lyford: Any time you wish.

Hutchins: The reason that what he said to me was unintelligible was that he was speaking to me in the dialect of his native village, the village of Adl in Austria. Adl has 397 people according to the census of 1960, generally called Adlescents.

From *The Center Diary,* a publication of the Center for the Study of Democratic Institutions. Reprinted by permission.

Why did Dr. Zuckerkandl habitually resort to this dialect? Because his philosophy requires the elimination of all sensation. He recognizes, of course, that this is not practically possible at all times, but this is the ideal towards which we strive, the elimination of all sensation. And what, he would say, what is it that lays a person, even the most devout Zuckerkandlite, open to the most violent and varied sensations, sensations of the most disturbing kind, over which he has no control? Communication, of course. Zuckerkandlism demands that communication be reduced to a minimum. This effort is immensely facilitated by the selection of a medium of communication through which communication is made almost impossible. Since there are only 397 people in the world who could speak Adlian, the chance that Dr. Zuckerkandl would be interrupted by communication in this language was rather slight.

One reason why we may guess that Zuckerkandlism is the philosophy of the future is that it reflects the deepest sentiments of mankind, as we can see by the insistence on the maintenance or revival of parochial languages in places as widely scattered as Ireland and India, Texas and Brooklyn, South Africa and Wales, and by the popularity of President Eisenhower's extemporaneous utterances, which were clearly designed to prevent communication in every way that is possible. For example, when President Eisenhower, during his term of office, was asked about the great crisis in school integration in the South, he replied by saying, "However, when the Federal court gets into the thing, you have got a judicial thing, or I mean a legal thing, that I have gone as far as I know the answer." A thing like that is a typical Zuckerkandlite masterpiece, designed instantly to cut off communication.

Dr. Zuckerkandl was fond of quoting a celebrated passage from the works of F. S. C. Northrop, the author of *The Meeting of East and West*. He always felt that Dr. Northrop was a Zuckerkandlite. In this passage Dr. Northrop says: "This error arises from the restrictedly positivistic conception of human knowledge, restraining it solely to the realm of the immediately apprehended, denying any component in the nature of things of which the immediately apprehended is the epistemic correlate or the sign, and tending to reject all postulationally designated, indirectly verified, theoretically known factors which mathematical and logical methods alone can determine in a trustworthy manner."

To resume my narrative, it turned out later what Dr. Zuckerkandl was saying when I met him was, "How do you do?" or "Sit down," or something like that. Until I discovered the cause of his taciturnity, I suspected he was following the maxim of his favorite poet: "*Das Beste, was du wissen kannst, darfst du den Buben doch nicht sagen.*" Or, "Don't tell the boobs all you know." I was already under his spell.

I have to admit that at first glance his exterior was not very prepossessing, and his personality was colorless. If you had seen him in a crowd, you would have said, if you had noticed him at all, that he was an undertaker's assistant. But he had a profound attraction for me. The reason was the harmony that he personified. He was the embodiment of his own philosophy. He lived as he thought, and he thought as he lived. In the old phrase, he practiced what he preached.

Lyford: Splendid. Were you able to get through to the dominant motive in his philosophy, the dominant theme? From the papers you have shown me, I deduce that the main point of his philosophy was simply that the aim of life is to get through it with as little sensation as possible.

Hutchins: I think that is substantially true, yes. I'll have to explain how this all came about. I was at that time President of the University of Chicago, I had nothing to do, and so when Doctor Zuckerkandl invited me to go to Adl with him, I went, and for a time I stayed with him in his tiny house on the Adlpät. I gradually mastered the dialect, and he turned over to me the papers that he had assembled. I was so impressed by them that I undertook to translate them. I have never been able to get the leisure to finish the translation, and consequently these documents have not yet appeared, as I hope they will some time.

I think this is the way to put it: If you were going to sum up the importance of Dr. Zuckerkandl, you would have to say that all other philosophers who have built systems have failed, and they have failed for one simple reason. That reason is that they wanted to change mankind. The teachings, or in Adlian the *Schwarmereien,* of Zuckerkandl proceed from quite a different and a far sounder premise. They supply mankind with the reasons for doing what it is doing already. They do not, for example, like Milton's doctrine, "justify the ways of God to man." They justify the ways of man to God.

Now, the question is, how could this little man single-handed break the chains that have bound us, absorb what all the other great thinkers have taught us, and pass beyond them into the clear, calm, pure air of Zuckerkandlism? I do not know. The ways of genius are inscrutable. But this I do know: He had read everything—Plato and the pre-Socratics, Aristotle and Aquinas, William James and John Dewey, Vico and Pareto. He had also read Dale Carnegie, Fulton J. Sheen, Rabbi Lehman, Norman Vincent Peale, and Smiley Blanton.

These great American thinkers, incidentally, had come to him in a curious way. Their books, together with two or three copies of *Life, Look,* and the *Ladies Home Journal,* had reached him in a CARE package, marked plainly on the outside, "POUR MANGER STELLEN SIE BITTE UND SOFORT IN FRIGIDAIRE BUON APPETITO." The only food in the box, in short, was of the spiritual kind. Whether the packer had decided to get rid of some waste paper and keep the food for himself, or whether he felt that the unknown recipient would profit more by reading than by eating the products of our country, we shall never know. We may be thankful to this anonymous working man, however, for the materials that he sent Dr. Zuckerkandl provided the stimulus that drove him from the easy chair to his desk. If *they* could do it, Zuckerkandl said, so can I.

Now, if you start at the right place, as Dr. Zuckerkandl did, and you have the right attitude, you are bound to come out with the right result. That is where Dr. Zuckerkandl comes out. His central position, as you have indicated, is that the object of life is to get through it. Of course, it is not adequate simply to get through it. The aim is to get through it without pain. This is where Zuckerkandl made his great discovery, which is that all sensations are painful. Freud said, "All pain is sensation." His genius did not carry him to the insight of Zuckerkandl: "All sensation is pain." Emerson's inkling of this insight peeps out through the cloak of metaphor: "If we walk in the woods, we must feed mosquitoes."

The ancient distinction between pleasure and pain is invalid. Lawrence of Arabia reports that the Arabs gave themselves pain for pleasure. This shows how ridiculous the distinction is. And since there is no distinction between pain and pleasure, they are both equally bad. Zuckerkandl tries to get us into the frame of mind that Mark Twain found in the serene confidence of the Christian with four aces in his hand. Or you remember the story Zuckerkandl was fond of repeating, first told by Freud, Zuckerkandl's teacher. A man said to his wife, "If one of us dies, I shall move to Paris." This is the state of mind that was recommended by Zuckerkandl.

Lyford: That is called composure.

Hutchins: Yes. It's what he called the Disentangled Life. Dr. Zuckerkandl would have liked the Shakers if he had known them. They used to say:

Leave the flurry
to the masses;
Take your time
and shine your glasses.

Now, if what you have to do is to get rid of sensation—pleasure and pain being an invalid distinction—the question is, how do you do it? Zuckerkandl, you will observe, has already had one great insight, namely, that there is no difference between pleasure and pain. They are both equally bad. The second great insight is that you get rid of pleasure and pain through habit. Ouspensky, for example, tells how through practice he came to perform quite significant acts like buying cigarettes, calling on his friends, having discussions with his printer, and walking about town. At the conclusion of one rather long period of this kind, he said, on coming to, "Suddenly I remembered that I had forgotten to remember myself." This is the aim of Zuckerkandlism.

You remember Flaubert's definition of habit: *"Habitude est une seconde nature. Les habitudes de collège sont de mauvaises habitudes. Avec de l'habitude on peut jouer du violon comme Paganini."* Or, as one might say: "Habit is second nature. College habits are bad. With of the habit one is able to play of the violin like little pagans."

Lyford: There is one thing that bothers me. You say that Dr. Zuckerkandl was a pupil of Freud, yet Dr. Zuckerkandl seems to have devoted his life to reversing the Freudian idea. Freud tried to make us conscious of our unconscious, and Dr. Zuckerkandl tries to make us unconscious of our conscious.

Hutchins: That is exactly correct. It is true that Zuckerkandl was a pupil of Freud. But he didn't stop with Freud. He went beyond Freud and showed the enormous gaps in Freud's education, in his psychology, and in his philosophy. In fact, Dr. Zuckerkandl declared flatly, and of course correctly, that he had "brought together the tentative [the Adlian word is *halbgekocht*] ideas and emotions of our time and transmuted them in the crucible [*Kammerpot* in Adlian] of my own mind into a reasoned, coherent, practical philosophy for Modern Man."

As you say, Dr. Zuckerkandl points out that Freud had it just backwards. The aim is not to become conscious of our unconscious but to become unconscious of our conscious. He shows too that Professor Suzuki, the interpreter of Zen, has made the same mistake in suggesting that the aim of spiritual life is to become conscious of the unconscious. Dr. Zuckerkandl felt that the Buddha hinted at the answer, which he called Nirvana. But he was all mixed up in what our great teacher calls *"Karma, Kali, und kindlishkomisch Klappentrappen,"* and so could not hope to make any impression on white people.

Now, we achieve this state of mind, if we can achieve it at all, through habit. Habit may be exemplified by the case of the child who learns to tie its shoelace. You may be young enough to remember how difficult it was to perform this feat of engineering. Today, of course, you don't notice it. And if I were to ask you which trouser leg you got into first this morning you would be unable to tell me, because you perform these acts habitually. Hence you perform them unconsciously. These acts may be taken as types of Zuckerkandlite habituation, rendering us unconscious of our conscious. This, you will observe, is the total drift, force, and tendency of our whole psychological apparatus.

How can you habituate yourself to things that are unpleasant, so that you don't notice them? Clearly it would be injudicious for a Zuckerkandlite to experience unpleasantness in order to become habituated to it. At this point Zuckerkandl has his third great insight, which is the theory of vicarious experience. One of his works, entitled, I am sorry to say, in a somewhat popular tone, is *Let All Your Experiences Be Vicarious*. Clearly, if you can have these experiences vicariously, you will be habituated to them without having the sensations of them. The formula is that whereas our own sensations are debilitating, the sensations of others, particularly their misfortunes, are invigorating, and even exhilarating. If evidence were needed, it could be found in the long lives and cheerful dispositions of those who, like the Justices of the Supreme Court of the United States, spend their time exclusively in contemplating, sometimes in causing, the misfortunes of others, and, while doing so, occupy positions of assured superiority and guaranteed income. This was also the relation of mankind to the Greek gods, who were immortal and who, according to common gossip, had a very good time. It must be said, therefore, that the Greeks had the same insight that Zuckerkandl had, but, unlike him, they did not have the courage to set it forth in plain English or Greek or Adlian. They felt compelled to shroud their vision in semitransparent veils of an allegorized mythology.

The theory of vicarious experience leads directly to another of Dr. Zuckerkandl's contributions, which is called the theory of the mass arts. The object of the mass arts, Dr. Zuckerkandl shows, is to provide us with brutalizing, horrendous, dreadful, horrible, painful experiences without causing in us any of the sensations that we would have if we had these experiences ourselves. Take Aristotle's doctrine of *catharsis,* which has annoyed people for two thousand years, not merely because of the distressing connotations of the word, but because of the obscurity of the idea. What Aristotle groped for Zuckerkandl found.

Lyford: Are you talking about TV?

Hutchins: Well, that is one thing that Dr. Zuckerkandl may have had in mind. The great American psychologist Angelo Patri once stated that "youngsters need television for their morale as much as they need fresh air and sunshine for their health." Television and the other mass arts enable us to ignore pity, fear, shame, all these very distressing emotions that would arise if we had these sensations ourselves. Habituation being the answer, you must find a way to achieve this habit without suffering the pain or the sensation. The theory of vicarious experience, the theory of the mass arts, provides the answer to this problem.

In the light of Zuckerkandlism, we are able to say that such artists as Mickey Spillane and the authors of comic books are rendering a vital public service. They are training our youth to lives of vicarious experience. This is why we can only applaud the way in which professional sports are conducted by the institutions of higher learning in this country. They limit athletics to a few paid hands who take the rap for the alumni and students, and so our colleges and universities are performing a truly educational function: they are habituating our people to lives of vicarious experience. All tendencies of this sort must receive the applause of right-thinking men.

Lyford: I am trying to cast around to see if we have groups of people in our country who are perhaps unconscious Zuckerkandlites. It seems to me that the only good Zuckerkandlite is an unconscious Zuckerkandlite.

Hutchins: Some of Zuckerkandl's most interesting observations were conducted on a visit that he paid to this country before I met him. He said, "Our experience shows that we grow accustomed to bad smells, distressing sights, unpleasant people, poor relations, the dentist, famine in India, traffic accidents, political speeches, puns, and other disagreeable phenomena to the point where we do not notice them. The first day's work in a glue factory is horrible. Numerous studies of glue makers, however, show that within a few days the aroma of the factory becomes as satisfying to them as Chanel No. 5 or roasting coffee is to other people. This is known as olfactory or, more technically, glufactory fatigue."

During his visit to the United States Dr. Zuckerkandl studied the race of commuters with a view to confirming or disproving his theories. It was a kind of test case. He also had resort to the works of Professor Maximilian von der Vogelweide, who made a very elaborate study of commuters. The professor was financed by a breakfast food company, and he began his inquiries by asking commuters what they had had for breakfast. In the first year of commuting, 37 percent of all commuters everywhere arriving at the office remember what they had for breakfast. Only 18 percent remember in the second year, and in the third year only 1.3 percent remember they had any breakfast at all. Of course there was no way of telling whether 98.7 percent of this last group *did* have any breakfast because their wives couldn't remember either, since they were both habituated to this process.

Lyford: Was this any help to the breakfast food company? It must have been surprising and disappointing.

Hutchins: I'm sorry to say that it was, yes. However, Dr. Zuckerkandl seems to have gathered ample statistics about commuters, whom he regarded as typifying the life of the future. As he said, "You see how happy these people are. They are a favored race. And why is it that they are? Why, because from one morning to the next they are as free from sensation as you can become." He said, "Take this business of getting on the New Haven train in the morning and reading the *New York Times* all the way to New York. This is the equivalent of the wall-gazing recommended by Zen Buddhism."

Lyford: If I remember, didn't Dr. Zuckerkandl have some discussion on college presidents?

Hutchins: Yes, in particular a remark that he attributes to Frank Moore Colby, a great American, who said: "It is the rule among college presidents that the mental disturbance following any of their remarks shall be almost as imperceptible as if the remarks had not been made. A line that is not only calm itself, but the cause of calm in others, that is the true college presidential ideal, and as a rule it is realized especially on public occasions."

I think this true. One can say that of all the people in this country the university presidents are probably closer to the Zuckerkandlite ideal than most of our fellow citizens. They are consciously closer, since their object is to communicate as little sensation, as little disturbance, to their audiences as they possibly can.

I think we ought to say that a great insight Dr. Zuckerkandl had is his insight into the whole problem of Original Sin. He is the only man I know who has observed that Original Sin is the sin of what the Greeks used to call *hubris*. It is the sin of excessive curiosity. It is clear that our remote ancestors, Adam and Eve, suffered from this sin of excessive curiosity, or *hubris*, and that they should have stayed where they were. The original move they made was the Original Sin. It is from this lack of self-control on the part of our prime progenitors that all our troubles have followed. Professor Rameses MacIntosh of the University of Aberdeen studied this problem, too, in his work, *Whose Ooze?* but of course nothing like as systematically and as well as Dr. Zuckerkandl.

Take the Freudian doctrine that we all want to return to the womb. This is again a confirmation of the proposition that what we want is to be unconscious because when we were in the womb we *were* unconscious. The pictures in the anatomy books do not disclose anything particularly attractive about this location. Why, then, should we want to return there? Dr. Zuckerkandl says, rightly, that it is because we look back upon our nine months' vacation there as the least unhappy period of our lives. Dr. Zuckerkandl would have dismissed as inaccurate, as well as vulgar, Cyril Connolly's remark that we are all our lives seeking a womb with a view. A womb, yes; a view, no.

I think that one of the other great insights Dr. Zuckerkandl had is his insight that nothing that has not been proved in the laboratory can be true. The great thing about Zuckerkandlism is that it is a scientific philosophy. And I think we all recognize today that unless something is scientific, it is not only not true, it isn't even worth thinking about. So, I am happy to say that Dr. Zuckerkandl has established his philosophy on a scientific basis.

You can see how this must be so. William James, by monkeying around with the striped muscles, established that habit was a matter of muscular action. He could dissect these muscles in the laboratory and tell you how much of the habit you had got just by looking at the stripes in your muscles. Dr. Zuckerkandl goes on from this scientific basis, and *his* whole examination of our behavior is thoroughly scientific.

It is true that there have been various attempts to establish morality on a scientific basis. One of them was made by Professor Sorokin of the Harvard Institute of Altruism. He made a study of the lives of over 3,000 saints honored by the Protestant, Catholic, and Eastern Orthodox churches, and it showed that they lived an average of sixty-one years, which is much longer than their fellow men, in spite of the fact that 27 percent of them had been martyred very young, many of them at a tender age. The trouble with this is that Professor Random Sample of the Harvard School of Business examined the mortality records of 3,000 gangsters and showed that they lived an average of sixty-two years, as against the saints' sixty-one, in spite of the fact that 28 percent of them had been martyred very young, many of them at a tender age.

Lyford: I think we do have to congratulate Professor Sorokin for trying, even though he was unable to prove his point.

Hutchins: Yes, we can congratulate him for trying, but we certainly, at the same time, would have to deplore the extravagant claims he made on the basis of this statistical examination. All that he showed was that the saints were tough. He showed that they were the juvenile delinquents of their generation, just as the gangsters of Professor Sample were in theirs.

As I have said, there is nothing more scientific than the basis of Dr. Zuckerkandl's philosophy, because there is nothing more scientific than habit. Here, of course, the pioneer work was done by Pavlov. He rang a bell when he gave his dogs their food. Then he rang a bell and gave them none. They salivated and went through the other physiological changes associated with eating even though there was nothing on their plates. An inquiry seemed to show, as it did in the case of the commuters when they were asked about their breakfasts, that Pavlov's dogs didn't know whether they had had any breakfast or not.

Francis Galton carried the work still further and applied it to human beings instead of dogs and to mystical objects instead of food. He got into the habit of pretending that a nonsense rhyme was a prayer and that a cartoon from *Punch* was an icon. He found himself much elevated when he thought of the rhyme and gazed at the cartoon. His heart was filled with reverence and his mind with faith. Which shows that with habit you can do anything.

For example, John B. Watson founded behaviorism on this solid truth. He followed the insight of Aristotle, Pavlov, and Galton, that man is an animal much like a dog, and he concluded that, since dogs were creatures of habit, men were, too. When he was challenged with the dubious proposition that men think and dogs do not, Watson proved that thinking is merely sublaryngeal speech. Men have the habit, in short, of talking to themselves. He was just about to prove that dogs have the same habit when he went into the advertising business, where he got so rich he didn't have to do any more work.

We see, then, that the only knowledge is scientific knowledge, and habit is about the most scientific thing there is. Scientific knowledge is the only knowledge that is knowledge of *fact;* it is not based on thought. That's the important thing to remember about scientific knowledge: It is not based on thought, it is based on experiment and empirical observation. Lord Rutherford, one of the greatest scientists who ever lived, admirably stated the modern position. He said to Samuel Alexander, the distinguished British philosopher, "When you think of all the years that you have been thinking about these things, Alexander, what does it all add up to? Hot air, nothing but hot air." The logical positivists have shown beyond the shadow of a doubt that no proposition has any meaning unless it can be operationally verified. For example, Lord Rutherford could have operationally verified the truth of his statement that Alexander's philosophy was hot air by measuring the changes in the temperature of the room while Alexander was speaking. On the other hand, propositions like "Life has a purpose," or "Let us now be up and doing," or "The aim of the state is the common good," and so on are absolutely meaningless because they are absolutely unverifiable in the laboratory. Therefore, we may have confidence in science. Confidence means peace of mind. In order to be free from worry, all you have to do is to make sure that your way of life is scientifically grounded.

Freud's example of the scientific method is the story of the Scottish king who had an infallible way of detecting witches. He would set them to simmer over a slow fire. He would then taste the broth and as he did so he would say, "This one was a witch, this one was not a witch," and so on. If we assume, as we must, in view of the source of this anecdote, that the king in question had through experiment and observation perfected his taste so that it would function without the possibility of error, we must agree that his knowledge was based on fact, that he could make his diagnoses with confidence, and that his science brought peace of mind to him, his kingdom, and all his subjects. Such peace of mind comes through a commitment to the attainment of the unconscious life through habit. And such peace of mind comes with a minimum of effort. It is unnecessary to think in order to enter upon it. Mere repetitions of acts and impressions will form the habits that will do the work. It is unnecessary to think in order to justify such peace of mind. It is scientific.

Lyford: Wouldn't Calvin Coolidge have qualified as somebody who was . . .

Hutchins: Yes, I think so. In fact, he raises another aspect of Zuckerkandl's philosophy that is very important. The original proposition is, you remember, that the object of life is to get through it, to get through it without pain. This means getting through it without pleasure, it means getting through it without sensation. Now, as a result of this basic theoretical position, Zuckerkandlites have a basic *practical* position. The basic practical, social position is: Do not get involved! The one thing a Zuckerkandlite will never do if he can avoid it is to get involved, because this produces a whole flood of sensations over which he has no control.

Coolidge was an approximate Zuckerkandlite as evidenced by this: After he retired from politics a lady in Washington asked him if he was the Mr. Coolidge who was President of the United States, and he replied, "Was I?" showing that he was not going to get involved, either before, during, or after. Nobody was going to get him into an argument about the Coolidge era or about American politics or about anything else. The historians tell us that the reason Coolidge was elected, and the reason he was so popular during his tenure, was that he symbolized the desires and aspirations of the American people.

Lyford: I was told that Dr. Zuckerkandl, in his study in Adl, possessed a small statue of William McKinley. Was this just a historical accident?

Hutchins: I think that Dr. Zuckerkandl selected his bric-à-brac with a view to the exemplification of his philosophy.

Now, I must tell you what I regard really as the greatest of all the Zuckerkandl insights after the original insight. It follows from the original insight, and yet it is easy to see how it could have been overlooked. It shows the remorseless rationality of Dr. Zuckerkandl's researches. If all sensations are painful, and if it is extremely difficult, even with vicarious experience and the application of the mass arts, to eliminate sensation, and if the only purpose of life is to get through it, why should we go on?

The Romans, who were, as you know, an uncivilized and primitive race, had the idea that if things didn't go well all you did was fall on your sword or whatever it was you had around that was sharp enough to put an end to your life. So Dr. Zuckerkandl has to face the problem of suicide. He also has to face the problem of drugs. If sensation is as bad as it is, why shouldn't you dope yourself to the point where you don't have any?

Granted that his theoretical position is that the object of life is to get through it without sensation, granted his empirical observation that this is what people actually want to do, then why is it that resort to suicide and drugs, resort to liquor, resort to yoga, is not legitimate or proper in the Zuckerkandlite view or empirically observable as a desideratum on the part of mankind? Obviously, there are painless ways of committing suicide, there are certainly painless ways of taking drugs and alcohol. Yoga is a rather vulgar exercise; one wouldn't care to go around in public very much reversing the peristalsis of one's intestines, but, still, it is something that one could do if one wanted to eliminate sensation.

Lyford: Aldous Huxley said that he could do it if he really tried.

Hutchins: Yes. Aldous Huxley said, at least, that he had a friend who could do it. But as for me, as for Dr. Zuckerkandl, we wouldn't want friends of that kind. Dr. Zuckerkandl is very clear on this. He describes these antics as *"Orientalischenflimmenflammen."*

The point is, Dr. Zuckerkandl asks why. Why do you not commit suicide, why do you not dope yourself, why don't you stay drunk, why don't you reverse the peristalsis of your intestines whenever you feel like it? There is no explanation except the one that Dr. Zuckerkandl offers. The answer is that you do not do these things because of what people would say.

The reason you do not commit suicide is not that it would be painful to you but that it would be regarded as a social error. There is nothing bad about anything, Dr. Zuckerkandl said, except that it is a social error. And there is nothing good about anything except that it is socially correct. Goodness and badness are formed by the society in which you live. And, therefore, if you want to commit suicide, you must find a society in which suicide is regarded as proper.

Professor von der Vogelweide's study of commuters, which we talked about earlier, showed that 89 percent of all commuters everywhere wanted to commit suicide during some part of every day. They were about evenly divided between those who wished to shoot themselves as they reached the office and those who wished to hang themselves when they reached home. Ninety-one percent, when asked why they didn't do one or the other, responded that it was "not the thing to do." Six and a half percent said they were "superstitious," and the remainder were undecided.

Lyford: I would like to get back to what seems to me a rather bitter relationship between Sigmund Freud and Dr. Zuckerkandl. Dr. Zuckerkandl, I believe, once said that Freud was the scientific equivalent of another nuisance, George Bernard Shaw. Were these men enemies at the latter part of their lives?

Hutchins: I don't believe that Dr. Zuckerkandl and Dr. Freud were enemies. It was merely that, as he went on in his own researches, Dr. Zuckerkandl came to see the weakness of Freud's position. He could only believe that Freud had made some of his statements because of a desire to annoy. The whole principle of the superego, which Dr. Zuckerkandl used to say was nothing but the doctrine of Original Sin dressed up in costumes from *Die Fledermaus,* is clearly fallacious, since it requires the inheritance for countless generations of habits that are obviously not transmittable. Since we all go back to Adam and Eve, if Adam and Eve were afflicted either by Original Sin or by the superego, then we, their descendants, all ought to have an equal measure of the superego or of Original Sin, or of the feeling of guilt accompanying these two items. Actually, of course, as Freud himself points out, conscience is very unevenly distributed through the human race. And this would seem to be enough to refute the proposition that it is possible by racial inheritance to acquire either Original Sin or the superego. So Dr. Zuckerkandl concluded that Freud's object was to annoy people. This may be stated more charitably as saying that Freud's object was to arouse people or to get them to think about things, which from Dr. Zuckerkandl's point of view is just as bad.

Dr. Zuckerkandl's view of Shaw was, of course, the same. If you believe that what we should do is to get through life without sensation, that we should lead as close to a vegetable existence as is humanly possible, then the spectacle of a man bouncing around in a long red beard, cracking jokes, and trying to get you excited to do something about a lot of things from woman suffrage to Fabian socialism is very repulsive. And it was so to Dr. Zuckerkandl.

Lyford: What about people like Mao or Bertrand Russell? Wouldn't there be difficulties to be overcome in the kind of world that Dr. Zuckerkandl wished to attain?

Hutchins: Oh, there is no doubt that as long as there are these irrational people in the world there is going to be trouble in the world. It is this trouble that Dr. Zuckerkandl wishes to avoid, or, if it comes, he wishes us to be as untouched by it as possible. After all, the theory of vicarious experience should enable us to get used to poverty, illiteracy, illness, disease, want. If enough of us can acquire imperviousness to these phenomena, Mao and other people like him would never have a chance.

Lyford: It seems to me that what Dr. Zuckerkandl has done has been to introduce anaesthesia into Stoicism. Whereas the Stoic once bore all things without flinching, now he can bear all things without feeling.

Hutchins: But the Stoic was a fool. The Stoic was pre-scientific. What Dr. Zuckerkandl does is to afford you the scientific basis of achieving a result that the Stoic achieved, or sought to achieve, through sheer ignorance and superstition. Above all, Dr. Zuckerkandl removes guilt. He proves to us that there is no purpose to life. All earlier philosophers committed two colossal, fundamental errors. One was the assumption that there is a purpose in life over and above getting through it. Their efforts to find this purpose failed. No one has described this failure more tersely than Shakespeare: "All the yarn she spun in Ulysses' absence did but fill Ithaca full of moths." Nevertheless, purpose remained the theme of all primitive thinkers. What was worse, they kept telling us that if we didn't try to accomplish it we were not doing our duty, as Kant said, or we were damned sinners, as everybody else said. In either case, we were guilty. But Dr. Zuckerkandl proves that since there is no purpose, you cannot fail to achieve it. Since there is no purpose, and since you cannot fail, have not failed, and are not failing, you are not guilty. Since you are not guilty, you should not have, must not have, any feelings of guilt. Without feelings of guilt, you will have no feelings of inferiority. Without feelings of inferiority, you will not fall a prey to ambition, antagonism, war, lust, or insanity. But this is only half the story. The other error of earlier thinkers was the error of omission. It may be said of them as it was said of Lo, a great American: "Lo, the poor Indian, whose untutored mind clothes him in front but leaves him bare behind." They pull the apron of purpose around to cover their nakedness only to leave their rear exposed to sensations of the most painful kind.

Lyford: There is an inconsistency here. I don't know whether you share Dr. Zuckerkandl's viewpoint on all of these matters, but Dr. Zuckerkandl apparently was fond of quoting somebody named Bill Nye, who was supposedly a nineteenth-century philosopher.

Hutchins: A great American thinker of the nineteenth century, yes.

Lyford: He quotes him as saying, "I arise from bed the first thing in the morning, not because I am dissatisfied with it, but because I cannot carry it with me during the day." Now, if this reflects Zuckerkandlism and perhaps your own view, I shall have to ask about an occasion when you are alleged to have said that whenever you feel the need of exercise you lie down until the feeling goes away. Is this a correct attribution?

Hutchins: No, this is incorrect. I agree with the statement, and I wish I had make it, but I wasn't clever enough to make it. J. P. McEvoy interviewed me, and in the story that he wrote he said, "Mr. Hutchins agrees with the unsung hero who said that when he felt the urge to exercise he lay down until it passed away." The unsung hero, of course, was McEvoy. He immediately dropped out of the story, and now in all anthologies of humor and so on I am credited with this remark, for which I am very grateful. But one has to recognize the limitations on this principle. I have suffered from them a great deal. In fact, as a loyal follower of Dr. Zuckerkandl, one of my most serious difficulties has been verging on a social error in this connection.

The reason that Bill Nye got up was not merely that he couldn't carry his bed with him during the day. It was that it would have been a social error for him to lie in bed all day. And so it has been frequently suggested to me that it is a social and financial error for me not to exercise when I feel the urge to do so. It has been pointed out to me that I might have been a great financial success if I had played golf. I would have a great many more friends than I have today.

This is the line that every Zuckerkandlite has to try to draw—the line between having no sensations and committing no social errors. Because a social error can result in very serious consequences in this society.

Lyford: You are an early riser, and this seems to be the sort of thing that Dr. Zuckerkandl approved of.

Hutchins: On the contrary, Dr. Zuckerkandl classifies early rising as among the absurd devices that people who feel guilty employ as methods of atonement. In this connection he quotes Flaubert, who said, "Early rising: proof of morality. If one goes to bed at four o'clock in the morning and gets up at eight, one is a parasite [*paresseux*], but if one goes to bed at nine in the evening in order to go out the next morning at five, one is active."

However, Dr. Zuckerkandl's main point is to get into the habit of doing whatever you are going to do so you won't care. The reason that I get up early in the morning is that my father was a Presbyterian minister who got us all up at six o'clock so that we could have full morning prayers every day. Since I am habituated to early rising, I don't notice it. I don't complain about it. It might be very painful for me to have to stay in bed longer. The point is that, whatever you do, do it habitually and you will gradually become unconscious of it as I am unconscious of early rising.

Lyford: I have been fishing about for an example of national Zuckerkandlism or at least a sample of public behavior that might indicate this insensitivity. What about the dropping of the atomic bombs on Hiroshima and Nagasaki? I remember reading in a newspaper editorial that the American people have never allowed themselves to think about the real implications of this act. Would this be an example?

Hutchins: Oh yes, oh yes, a fine example. You take all the phenomena of the last twenty-five years where we have seen brutalization on the largest scale in history. How is this done? It is done by habituation. Part of it vicarious, part of it direct. After you have exterminated one population, the extermination of another population is easier. After you have watched that extermination, it is easier to watch the extermination of still another population, so that you eventually get to the position where you don't even see that anybody is being exterminated. You go along, just as the great majority of the Germans did during the Nazi period. You hear things, but then you get used to hearing them and finally you don't hear them any more. This is straight Zuckerkandlism.

Lyford: When I visited Dachau several years ago, I was surprised that even though the concentration camp was located right on the outskirts of this little community, apparently nobody in the town had ever known that there was some kind of peculiar institution there. Wasn't there a drunken soldier or somebody who tended the ovens who got a day off and said something to his girl about what was going on? Didn't anybody find out?

Hutchins: They were all Zuckerkandlites.

Index

Acceptability in solution choice, 512–513

Activities: informal, 665; in group model, 196; role, 583

Adaptability as leadership strategy, 688–690, 768

Adaptive-coping cycle, 769–774

Adjustment, integrative, 435–439

Administrators: training of, 58–64, 87–88; understanding the behavioral sciences, 109–123

Alienation, 746, 758

Allee, W. C., 99–100

Altruism, 437

Ambiguity, tolerance for, 690

Antagonism, 463

Anxiety: culture and, 422; dealing with (constructive methods of, 525–426; negative methods of, 424–425); definition of, 418–19; neurotic, 426; normal, 420–422; objectless, 419–420; relation to fear, 418–129; and self-awareness, 419–420, 426–428

Apathy in groups, 564–568

Aspiration, level of. See Level of aspiration

Assembly line, 752–759

Assumptions: about human behavior, 189, 278; in decision making, 155–156

Attitudes: freezing of, 554–556; influence of group norms on, 524–426; of managers, 319; unfreezing of, 552–554

Attraction, 78

Authority: changing concept of, 721–725; conferred, 734; in Hopi culture, 808; in interpersonal relationships, 852; and responsibility, 736–739; shift in source of, 723

Automation, 759–766, 821–822

Autonomy, 700

Awareness, organizational, 674–675

Barnard, Chester, 464–465, 691

Becoming, 48, 849

Behavior: adaptive, 666–667; assumptions about, 278; caused, 846–847; control of, 852–853; creative, 375; creatively adaptive, 849; defensive, 484–485; examining our, 133–134; forecast of, 277; group model of, 193–199; individual, 704–705; individual model of, 189–191; inner-directed, 693, 707; intergroup, 706–707; interpersonal, 441–463 (model of, 191–193; and personality, 469–474); law of effect, 383–388; managerial, 464–479; motivating change in, 316–317; other-directed, 693; rational (assumptions about, 191; rules for, 51–52); reactive, 704–707; role, 583 (see also Role, organizational); small-group, 705–706; standards of method in study of, 4; and stimulus, 190–191; total organizational, 707–710; transactional, 702

Behavioral models, 189–202

Behavioral science, 105–106, 702; and administrators, 109–123; definition of, 10–11; critical methods in, 9; deny and ignore, 840; and the individual, 839–854; and values, 432–433

Blame vs. cause in diagnosis, 157–159

Brainstorming, 272

Brown, J. A. C., 101

Bureaucracy, out of date, 686

Business: and domestic society, 786; and foreign society, 786–787; and the individual, 785; and other groups, 785–786; as a social system, 785–787; social-value theory of, 787–788; value issue of, 781–789

Case method, 19, 58–64, 649; incident-process, 62; laboratory, 63; role playing, 62–63; written cases, 61–62

Cause: multiple causality in diagnosis, 159–160; vs. blame in diagnosis, 157–159

Center for study of democratic institutions, 855

Certainty, continuum of, 156
Chain of command, 662
Chairmen, 558–559
Chance, definition of, 39
Change: achieving, in people, 537–549; deliberate social, 655–657; emotional reactions to, 538; in environment, 771; feedback on, 774; group as medium for, 544–547; group as target of, 544, 547–548; impact of, on other systems, 772–773; motivating, in behavior, 316–317; resistance to, 772; and stability, 690; and technology, 745–766; technological and social, 745; unfreezing and freezing for, 552–556
Change agents, groups as, 544
Changing ideas in theory and practice, 550–560
Choice, 47; and the behavioral sciences, 853; and science, 846
Choice making role of manager, 18
Climate: collaborative, in organizations, 689, 693. See also Tone, organizational
Coaching, 700
Collaboration, executive, 689
Collins, Orvis, 153
Commitment, restricted in decision making, 446–448
Committees, 556–559
Communication: barriers and gateways to, 491–502; control of, 486–487; defensive, 484–491; empathy in, 488–489; and evaluation, 485–486, 492–493; interpersonal, 480–484; listening, 493–496; non-verbal, 480–481; between peoples, 43; and perception, 501; selective, 480–482; strategy in, 487–488; superiority, 489; as training objective, 66–67; verbal, 480–481
Conant, James, "On Understanding Science," 40
Conflict: control of, 688; group problem, 561–564; intergroup, 690; reduction of, role of superordinate goals in, 639–641; role, 588–590
Conformity, 463
Control: of information, 739–740; managerial, 739–740; organizational, 675–676 (and leadership, 659); power to, 841–843
Cooperation and survival, 99–100
Cost, organizational, 743
Courage in communication, 494–495
Creative behavior, 375

Creative synthesis, 691
Critical method, 5–9; and the behavioral sciences, 9; and decision making, 9; and mathematical terminology, 7–8; specifications for, 6–7
Critical path, 281–283
Culture: and anxiety, 422; Hopi Indian, 803–807

Darwin, Charles, 93
Data: perceived, 128; vs. information, 128
Decentralization, 403, 734, 742–743
Decision making, 4; approach to management, 323; barriers to, 441–463; blind spots in, 452–453; critical method in, 9; definition of, 11–13; distrust and antagonism in, 453–455; environmental factors in, 507; feedback in, 459–461; frame of reference in, 131; freezing and unfreezing of attitudes in, 552–556; gamesmanship in, 448–449; good, 556–557; group, 542; historical perspective on, 502–514; and human decisions, 16–17; inadequate, in groups, 569; in interaction situations, 502–514; lack of awareness in, 449–452; network, 458–459; in new situations, 14–16; organizational, 677; perception in, 506–507; preventive, 321–322; rational, 49–57; and reference groups, 508; search process in, 458; social factors in, 507; solution choice acceptability in, 512–513; as systematic discipline, 13–14; and technical decisions, 16–17; value of questions in, 457; values in, 444–446; in working with groups, 458–459
Decision-making process, 12–13; as anticipated response to solution, 277–279; behavioral models in, 189–202; in diagnosis, 12–13, 151–162; and disequilibrium, 12–13, 127–137; feedback provisions in, 317–318; and implementation, 13, 314–324; leadership function in implementation, 319–321; and ordering solution alternatives, 281–283; participation in, 275–277; and present vs. past solutions, 279; and the problem statement, 12–13, 235–248; risks in solutions, 279–281; roadblocks in, 134–136; and solution choice, 13, 271–284

Decision process. *See* Decision-making process
Decision situations, technical, 272–273
Decision tree, 283
Democratic society, 836
Determinism, 46; cultural, 102–103; and free will, 46–47; scientific viewpoint on, 46
Diagnosis as decision-making stage, 12–13, 60; assumptions in, 155–156; behavioral models in, 189–202; and cause vs. blame, 157–159; cost of search in, 201; criteria for, 151–162; feedback in, 318; forecast of behavior in, 278; of group problems, 561–575; implicit, 152; importance of, 151–152; inferences in, 155–156; and language and events, 152–154; and multiple causality, 159–160; as part of problem statement, 237; precision of information in, 154–156; speculations in, 155–156; time as factor in, 200–201; who should do?, 569–570; working, 160–161
Discontent, executive, 811–817
Disequilibrium in an organizational situation, 12–13, 127–137, 158
Distrust, 697–698
Drucker, Peter, 402

Economics as a value system, 781–785; "amoral," 783–784; ethical, 782; "moral," 782–783; scientific, 782; shortcomings of, 784–785
Effectiveness: adaptive-coping cycle of, 769–774; organizational, 767–778; systems level criteria for, 767–769
Efficiency and Humanism, 717
Ego needs, 470; processes, 472–474
Empathy, 73–89, 191; and accuracy, 74–77; and attraction, 78; and communication, 488–489; errors in, 82–84; and familiarity, 79–80; and generalization, 79; and identification, 78; and personality, 81–82
Employee appraisal, 276
Environment: control of, 673; of individual, 104–105; in group model, 196
Esteem needs, 373
Ethics and the behavioral sciences, 432–433. *See also* Values
Evaluation, 134, 699, as barrier to communication, 492–493; referent vs. evaluator in, 136

Executive functions: homeostatic, 466–467; and influence, 465–466; mediative, 466–468; proactive, 468–469
Existentialism, 46
Experience: learned, 14, 134, 243; learning from, 14, 134, 243, 434; new vs. old, 134; and understanding others, 73; vicarious, 860
Experimentation, 700; controlled, 36–37; 842; laboratory, 24–25, 42; researcher and his data in, 37–38; validity of findings in, 635–636
External variables, 192

Facts, 156; vs. opinions, 154
Failure, 423–424. *See also* Success and failure
Familiarity, 79–80
Fear: definition of, 418; relationship of, to anxiety, 418–429; vs. love, 92
Feedback, 459–461, 549, 569; failure to obtain, 774; provisions for, in implementation, 317–318, 320; as reality testing, 484; of role behavior, 594–595; special steps in, 573–574
Feelings: and communication, 498–502; of group members, 70; identification and acceptance of, 131–132; and self awareness, 132–133; separated from situation, 133
Follett, Mary Parker, 691
Forecast of behavior, 277
Formal organization, 661–663; and the individual, 663–669
Frame of reference, 130–131, 190–191, 356–357, 575; as conceptual scheme, 44; in decision making, 131; external variables and, 130, 192; and intergroup relations, 629; internal variables of, 130, 191–192; of scientists, 46
Free will, 840; and determinism, 46–47
Freedom, 45–49
Freezing of attitudes, 554–556
Freud, Sigmund, 94–95, 101, 103, 419–420, 422, 470, 702, 855, 858–867
Fromm, Erich, 102–103
Frustration, 439, 664–667
Future, a look at the, 817–824

Gamesmanship, subordinate, 448–449
Generalization, 79
Goals, 819–820; and the behavioral sciences, 842–843; executive, 815; group, 567; multiple, 767; organizational, 273–274, 688 (as

standards in problem identification, 239); national, as standards in problem indentification, 239; single, 135; and success and failure, 390–392; superordinate, 634, 639–641; supra-organizational, 690–691. *See also* Needs; Organizational objectives; Organizational socialization
Group: decision making, 542; definition of, 194–195, 516–517, 628–629; peer, 608; as psychological concept, 195; reference, 197. *See also* Groups; Group formation
Group behavior model, 193–199
Group dynamics, 476; achieving change in people, 537–549
Group formation: consolidation of group harmony, 533–534; differential effects in, 524–526; and frustration and conflict among stereotypes, 531–533; generalizations about, 632–633; individually centered, 530–531; and motivation, 518–519; and norms, 522–524; and organization, 519–522; phases in, 529–537; and productivity in problem solving, 534–536
Group goals, 567
Group problems, diagnosis of, 561–575; apathy, 564–568; conflict, 561–564; inadequate decision making, 569
Group processes, 316
Group properties, 517
Group relations, 776–777
Groups: behavior of, 705–706; and business, 785–786; characteristics of, 194; diagnosis of problems in, 561–575; formation of, 515–528; growth of, 529–537; increasing efficiency in, 569; and the individual, 800–810; influence model of, 733–735; informal, 515; in-groups and out-groups, 634–635, 646–655; as links in organization, 730–733; maintenance functions in, 561; as medium of change, 544–547; methods of observation, 571–573; as not closed systems, 628; norms of, 710–711; norms of policemen, 622–627; obligations to, 438; and organizations, 721; and organizational structure, 730–733; size for communication, 495–496; and social system, 194; source of ideas, 551; synergy, 689; target of change, 544, 547–548; task

functions, 561; training in, 65–72; work of Homans in, 195–196; work of Sherifs in, 194–195; working with, 458–459. *See also* Intergroup relations; Group; Group formation
Group structure and personal significance, 800–810
Group theory, history of, 516
Growth: mutual, 698–699; organizational, 688, 734–735, 740–743
Guilt, living without, 855–870

Hawthorne experiments, 37
Health, organizational, 701–718
Help, is it helpful?, 695–701
Hierarchy of standards: problems are relative, 244
Homans, George, 195
Hopi Indians, 803–807
Horney, Karen, 103–104, 357
Human behavior: knowledge about, 16–17; literature on, 350
Human decisions and technical decisions, 16–17
Human problems and technological development, 17
Human relations and nature of man, 90–109
Human resources, training of, 775
Humanism and efficiency, 717

Identification, 78; of feelings, 131–132
Identity, sense of, 768
Implementation as decision-making stage, 13, 314–324; assessment of workability, 315–316; feedback provisions in, 317–318; leadership function, 319–321; motivating change in behavior, 316–317; preventive decision making, 321–322
Implementation gap, 691
Incentive systems, obsolete, 764
Incident process, 62
Individual: behavior of, 704–705; behavioral sciences on, 839–854; and business, 785; as commodity, 793; and competitive success, 423–424; in an environment, 104–105; and formal organization, 663–669; frame of reference, 190–191; related to organization through roles, 575–576, 601; value of, 540; values grounded in groups, 544
Individual behavior model, 189–191
Individualism, 707; consequences of, 832–834; group and individual, 837; history of, 828–834; and Hopi

culture, 807–809; and organization, 825–839; Tocqueville on, 829–831; two systems of values, 835–836

Individuality, 463, 795; and market orientation, 797

Inferences, 155–156, 190

Influence, 465–466, 579; organizational, 733–735; social, 688; system, 772

Information: evaluation of, 574–575; gathering of in-groups, 570–571; imparting, to user, 771; precision of, in diagnosis, 154–156; vs. data, 128

In-groups: and out-groups, 634–635, 646–655; virtues of, 647–651

Instinct, social, 98–99

Integration, organizational, 688, 768

Interaction situations and decision making, 502–514

Interactions in group model, 196

Intergroup action and business, 786

Intergroup behavior, 706–707; among nations, 630–631; definition of, 629; level of interaction, 631; not deviant behavior, 630

Intergroup conflict, generalizations about reductions in, 633–634

Intergroup relations, 198, 776–777; generalizations about out-groups, 633; and leadership, 627–614, 638–639; need perspective for study, 637–638

Internal variables, 191–192

Interpersonal behavior: and communication, 480–484; and decision making, 441–463; and managerial competence, 464–479; model of, 191–193; and personality, 469–474; and role-taking, 476–478; 600–601

Interpersonal competence, 687, 695

Interviewing, "self directive," 44

Invisible hand, 93–94

Job enlargement, 403, 765

Judgments, verifying, 155–156. See also Value judgments

Kluckhohn, Clyde, 134, 158–159

Laboratory experimentation, 24–25

Laboratory training, 84–85, 461–462

Langer, Susanne K., 503, 505

Language: assumptions, 155–156; and events in diagnosis, 152–154; inferences, 155–156; and perception, 153; and personality, 433–435; speculations, 155–156; words and actions, 442–444

Latitude of acceptance and rejection, 523

Law of effect, 383–388

Leadership, 319–321; adaptive-coping cycle, 769–774; agricultural model, 693–694; function in the organization, 777; iatrogenic, 692; and intergroup relations, 627–641, 638–639; is help helpful?, 695–701; linking pin function, 731–733; new patterns of, 686–695; organizational, 658–685; and organizational controls, 659; and organizational effectiveness, 777; organizational tone, 319–320; other-directed, 693; participative, 319; psychological contract, 694; and superordinate goals, 639–641; trait vs. situational theory, 680

Leadership functions, 660

Leadership theory and organizational theory, 659–660

Learning: cooperative, 698; and law of effect, 383–388; problem of, 383–387

Legitimacy of organizational roles, 580

Level of aspiration, 361–362, 377, 388–392, 540; and self-esteem, 392–393

Lewin, Kurt, 539, 545, 552

Likert, Rensis, 730

Line and staff, 738–739

Listening, gateway to communication, 493–496

Logic, 49–50

Love needs, 373

Machiavelli, 92

Man: as evaluating animal, 134; nature of (see Nature of man)

Management: conventional view, 395–396; and decision making, 323; executive discontent, 811–817; "hard" approach, 396; as building a bank account, 321; and motivation, 383–387; and oganizational socialization, 604–622; and ownership, 723–724; as a profession, 615–617, 724; rational, 56–57; as a science, 56–57; scientific, 752–753; source of authority, 721–725; systems concepts in, 112–123; techniques of, 403–404

Management by objectives, 402

Management science, 51–52; objections to, 53–55

Manager: role of, 18; style, 319.

See also Administrators; Decision making

Managerial behavior and interpersonal competence, 464–479

Marketplace, 782–783; orientation, 791–800; and personality, 791–800

Maslow, Abraham, 105, 191, 397

Maslow's need theory, 366–382, 397–399

Mathematics: and critical method, 7; and social sciences, 28

Mayo, Elton, 104–105

McGregor, Douglas, 90, 106, 610

Meaning: search for, 376. *See also* Thomas theorem

Mental health, 540–541

Method: case, 19, 58–64; critical, 5–10; noncritical, 8–9; scientific, 5, 26, 844–845 (self awareness and, 36–45); standards of, 4–5; in value study, 788–789

Mistrust, 403

Minnesota Multiphasic Personality Inventory (MMPI) and empathic accuracy, 77

Models: action-research, 691; behavioral, 189–202 (group, 193–199; individual, 189–191; interpersonal, 191–193); criteria for construction, 504–506; definition, 504; decision-making (historical, 506–510; historical application, 510–513); economic, 782–783; group influence, 733–735; in helping relationship, 700; leadership, 658–685; of leadership, agricultural, 693–694; linking pin, 730–733; usefulness, 199–200

Moral alchemy, 649–651, 653

Morality, law of costingness, 436

Morals, social basis of, 35

Motivation, 358–362; in behavioral change, 316–317; carrot-and-stick, 400–401; dynamics of, 399–401; and group formation, 518–519; inner, 359; to join organization, 609; and leadership, 694; Maslow's theory of, 366–382, 397–399; outer, 359–360; role of gratified need in, 380, 398; and role theory, 360; by sent roles, 582

Motives, 25, 824; definition, 358–359; to help, 696; imputing to others, 320; perception of, 485

Motivating, 319

Multiple causality, 159–160

National Training Laboratories (NTL), 63, 461, 529

Nature as rationality, 55–56

Nature of man, 90–109; cares how he is used, 274; changing concept of, 725–730; as evaluating animal, 158; optimistic view, 98–106; pessimistic view, 91–97; social aspects, 433–435; symbolic aspects, 433–435

Needs, 359; ego, 470; esteem, 373; fixity in, 377; gratified, 380, 398; to help, 696; hierarchy of, 191, 368–369, 377–379, 397–399 (reversal, 378); of individuals, 663–669; love, 373; for others, 437; physiological, 366–369, 397–398; relative satisfaction of, 379; safety, 369–373, 397–398; self-actualization, 374–377, 426–428; self-fulfillment, 399; social, 398–399; and values, 378–379

Neurosis, 491; and anxiety, 421; and safety needs, 372

Nonconformity, failure of organizational socialization, 614–615

Noncritical method, 8–9

Normal personality, 429–440

Normality, concepts of, 430–433

Norms, 406, 508, 522–524; definition of, 710–711; as evaluative scale, 523; examples, of, 710–716; group, 196–198 (standards in problem definition, 238); and group formation, 522–524

Objectives, organizational, 678–679, 732

Observation, 60, 133–134, 549; Bales approach, 572–573; method of, 571–573; participant, 65–72; relevant, 38–39; skill in, 39–40

Observer, affected by decision, 274–275

Office, 577, 583

Openness, reciprocal, 699

Opinions: stated as facts, 154; vs. facts, 154

Optimists, 812–813

Organizational effectiveness, 680–681; and leadership, 777; psychological contract, 775

Organizational leadership, 658–685

Organizational mix: awareness dimension, 674–675; control dimension, 675–676; external influence dimension, 677; internal influence dimension, 676; organizational objective dimension, 678–679; problem solving dimension, 676–677; time perspective dimension, 677–678

Organizational objectives. *See* Goals

Organizational socialization: failures, 614–615; and management, 604–622; manipulation of guilt, 612; membership, 613–614; unlearn old values, 610; and values, 611

Organizational theory: and leadership theory, 659–660; need for new, 669–674

Organizations, 718–744; concept of authority in, 721–725; contributions and inducement, 687; effectiveness, 767–778; formal, 661–663; formal vs. informal, 671; and group formation, 519–522; growth of, 740–743; healthy, 701–718; imagination in, 838; and individualism, 825–839; levels of, 703; maintaining, 465; multinational, 735; new patterns of leadership, 686–695; objectives of, 719–721; process orientation, 694; roles in, 575–604; sick, 119–120; as social, 790; temporary systems, 686; tone, 319–320; traditional, 726–727; viewed as strategy, 660–661, 671; what are good?, 701, 719; what kinds?, 837–838

Out-groups: and in-groups, 634–635, 646–655; vices, 647–651

Participation, 60, 319, 403–404; in decision making, 275–277; observant, 65–72

Patterning, 701

Perception, 353–358, 506–507, 849; and communication, 501; in decision making, 506–507; of disequilibrium, 127–137; errors in, 82–84; and language, 153; organization of, 355–356; process of, 130–131; and rationality, 356–357; selective, 355; of subordinates, 728

Performance appraisal, 404

Personal significance, and group structure, 800–810

Personality, 660; affected by role behavior, 599–600; and anxiety, 418; and empathy, 81–82; integrated, 550; and interpersonal behavior, 469–474; and language, 433–435; and the marketplace, 791–800; normal, 429–440; and role expectations, 597–599; standard in problem identification, 238

Pessimists, 812–813

Physiological needs, 366–369, 397–398

Planning for solution implementation, 316–317

Pleasure principle, 702

Preventive decision making, 321–322

Principles of organization, evaluation of, 663–669

Problem definition, 12–13

Problem orientation, 487

Problem solving, 847; ability, 847; organizational, 676–677; shared, 699–700. See also Decision making

Problem statement, 235–248; appears absolute, 241; criteria for, 236; explicit, 236–237; long and short run, 245–246; not a dilemma, 246–247; not implied solution, 243–244; significance of, 235; in specific behavioral terms, 241–243; standards violated, 237–241; whose problem, 244–245; and working diagnosis, 237–238

Problems: confusion with symptoms, 135–136; dealing with at face value, 135; organizational, 245; personal, 245; "unsolvable," 136

Process, 852–853; organizational, 694

Professional, 724

Professionalism, defined, 615–617

Professionals, rewards for, 688

Profitability, social, 788

Profit maximization, 353–354, 364

Property rights, as source of authority, 722

Protestant ethic, 97

Psychoanalytic study of personality, 469–470

Psychological point of view, errors in, 83

Psychological structuring, 130–131

Psychotherapy, 491–492; client-centered, 850–851

Quantification of variables, 273

Questions, value of, in decision making, 457

Rationality and perception, 356–357

Reactions, anxiety, quantity and quality, 421

Realists, 812–813

Reality, definition and consequences of, 642

Reality testing, 768

Reason, 49–51, 98–99

Reasoning and thinking, 50–51

Reference groups, 508, 635

Research Center for Group Dynamics, 539, 543

Response, automatic, 136

Responsibility: and authority, 736–739; for one's actions, 436–437

Revitalization, organizational, 691–692

Reward and punishment. *See* Law of effect

Rewards, organizational, 713

Risk: of being changed, 494–495; in decision making, 442; in solution choice, 279–281

Roadblocks to decision making, 134–136

Role: administrative, 59; conflict, 588–590; episode, 586; flexibility, 477–478; history of thought, 576; leader, 319; leadership, 671; organizational, 575–604, 835; receipt of, 581; relationships, 517, 520; sending, 579–581; of scientist, 32; specialization, 476–477; trainers, 67–72

Role behavior: definition of, 578–579; and personality, 599–600

Role expectations, 579; organizational factors influencing, 595–596; and personality, 597–599; and response, 593–594

Role playing, 62–63, 86–87, 274, 549

Role-taking, 590–593; and interpersonal relations, 600–601

Role theory, 360

Roles, multiple, 31–32, 583–586

Safety needs, 369–373, 397–398

Science, 23; and knowledge, 34; progress of, 39; social and behavioral, 111–112; and social problems, 23–36; and values, 846–849

Scientific method, 5; man not free, 844–845; and self awareness, 36–45

Search: cost of, 201; process in decision making, 458

Security, personal, 423

Self, and anxiety, 426–428

Self-actualization, 374–377, 849, 852

Self-awareness, 441; and anxiety, 419–420; and feelings, 132–133; lack of, 449–452; in leadership, 321; and scientific method, 36–45; and unstructured stimuli, 130–134

Self-control, 436–437, 725

Self-esteem, 472–473, 794; and level of aspiration, 392–393; and risk taking, 442

Self-fulfilling prophecy, 642–657

Self-fulfillment needs, 399

Sensitivity training, 84–85. *See also* T-group training

Sentiments in group model, 196

Sets, internal, 471–472

Sex and aggression, 94–95

Sherif, Muzafer and Carolyn, 194

Sick organizations, 119–120

Skinner, B. F., 841, 844

Sloan School of Industrial Management, 604–605, 608, 610–611, 617, 619, 814

Smith, Adam, 93–94

Social beliefs: and social reality, 645–647. *See also* Thomas theorem

Social change, deliberate, 655–657; technology of, 538–539, 544–545, 548

Social distance scale, 630

Social needs, 398–399

Social problems, 23; and science, 23–36

Social reality and social beliefs, 645–647

Social responsibility, 435–439

Social sciences: faith in, 496; future status, 29; and mathematics, 28; present status, 27–28

Social self-realization, 359

Social system, 194–195; task and maintenance functions, 476

Social territory, 692

Social-value theory for business, 787–788

Socialization, 606–614; professional, 615–619

Society: business and, 786; business and foreign, 786–787; democratic, 836; moral basis of, 35

Solution choice as decision-making stage, 271–284; acceptability, 272–273, 274–277, 512–513; anticipated response, 277–279; doing nothing, 283; feedback, 318; following statement of problem, 236; forecast of behavior, 277; ordering alternatives, 281–283; participation in, 275–277; present vs. past, 279; quality, 272–274 (based on diagnosis, 152); risks, 279–281. *See also* Implementation

Solution-orientation bias in problem statement, 243–244

Solution strategy, 13

Solutions: from professional disciplines, 134–135; use of available, 134–135; to wrong problems, 127

Span of control, 662

Specialization, 662

Speculations, 155–156

Spencer, Herbert, 93

Staff and line, 738–739

Standards, hierarchy of, 238–239

Status, 405–418; achieved, 414–416; ascribed, 409–414 (age, 411–412; kinship, 412–414; sex, 410–411); family, 804; group members, 562, 564; office, 407; organization of, 406–408; relationship of ascribed

to achieved, 416–418; relationships, 517, 520–521; station, 407–408
Stereotypes, 152
Stimuli: individual model, 190; structured, 128–129; unstructured, 128, 129–130
Strategy, 699; leadership, 688; organization viewed as, 660–661, 671
Subordinate gamesmanship, 448–449
Subsystems, 117
Success: and anxiety, 423–424; and failure, 387–393 (and level of aspiration, 388–392)
Sullivan, H. S., 101–102, 419, 427
Superordinate goals, 634, 639–641
Survival of the fittest, 93, 433
Symbols, 690; in communication, 480
Symptoms confused with problem, 135–136
Systems, 112–123; behavioral, 115–123, 702–704; characteristics of, 115–117; defining effectiveness of, 767–769; dynamic, 112–113; group (model, 196; not closed, 628); impact of other systems, 772–773; influence, 772; information, 695; interpersonal, 118; levels of, 117–121; multi-group, 118; organizational, 407; of organizational roles, 584; personal, 117–118; rewarding human, 687–689; social, 117, 692 (business as, 785–787); temporary, 686

T-group training, 65–72, 84–85, 461–462, 688
Taylor, Frederick, 96–97, 751–753
Teaching, 698
Technical decisions, 314–315; and human decisions, 16–17
Technological change, 17
Technological development and human problems, 17
Technology: assembly-line, 752–759; automation, 759–766; and change, 745–766; and the future, 817–824; history of, 746–752; stages of, 746–752
Theory X, 90, 395–396
Theory Y, 90, 401–404
Thinking, 795–796; and reasoning, 50–51
Thomas theorem, 642–645
Time: as factor in diagnosis, 200–201; perspective in organizations, 677–678
Tocqueville, Alexis de, 829–831
Tone, organizational, 319–320. See also Climate

Training, 464, 712; action vs. diagnostic, 60–61; case method, 58–64; and change, 538; in communication, 483–484; communication as objective, 66–67; laboratory, 461–462; and organizational socialization, 611; sensitivity, 84–85; T-group, 65–72, 84–85, 461–462, 688; trainer's role, 67–72
Trust, 463; reciprocal, 697

Uncertainty, interpersonal, 69–70
Unfreezing of attitudes, 552–554
Unity of direction, 662
Unstructured stimuli, 128, 129–130; and self-awareness, 130–134

Validity in experimental findings, 635–636
Value: choice, 847; exchange, 792–793; of individual, 540; success as, 423–424
Value issue of business, 781–789
Value judgments: fixing blame in diagnosis, 157–159; relative, 136
Values, 508; alternatives, 849–850; anxiety as threat to, 418; and behavioral sciences, 432–433; in business, 781–789; conflicting standards, 239–240; confusion about, 31; in decision making, 444–446; democratic, 438; executive discontent, 811–817; the future, 817–824; grounded in groups, 544; and group structure, 800–810; individual, as standard in problem identification, 238–239; in leadership, 695; living without guilt, 855–870; market, 792–793; and needs, 378–379; organizational, 721; personality and the marketplace, 791–800; and science, 30–31, 846–849; social, 782, 785; social theory for business, 787–788; as standards in problem statement, 237–241; ultimate human, as standards in problem identification, 239. See also Organizational socialization; Self-fulfilling prophecy

Walden Two, 841–843
Weber, Max, 97
Work, meaning of, 745–766
Workers: on assembly line, 752–759; and automation, 759–766

Zuckerkandl, Alexander, 855–870